David Buchanan

Leicester Business School, De Montfort University

Andrzej Huczynski

Department of Business and Management, University of Glasgow

Organiz... ...tory Text

fifth edition

FT Prentice Hall
FINANCIAL TIMES

An imprint of Pearson Education

Harlow, England • London • New York • Boston • San Francisco • Toronto • Sydney • Singapore • Hong Kong
Tokyo • Seoul • Taipei • New Delhi • Cape Town • Madrid • Mexico City • Amsterdam • Munich • Paris • Milan

Pearson Education Limited
Edinburgh Gate
Harlow
Essex CM20 2JE
England

and Associated Companies throughout the world

Visit us on the World Wide Web at:
www.pearsoned.co.uk

First published by Prentice Hall International (UK) Ltd, 1985
Second edition by Prentice Hall International (UK) Ltd, 1991
Third edition by Prentice Hall Europe, 1997
Fourth edition by Pearson Education Ltd 2001
Fifth edition 2004

ISBN 0 273 68222 9

British Library Cataloguing-in-Publication Data
A catalogue record for this book is available from the British Library

Library of Congress Cataloging-in-Publication Data
Buchanan, David A.
    Organizational behaviour : an introductory text / David Buchanan and Andrzej
Huczynski.-- 5th ed.
        p. cm.
    Huczynski's name appears first on the previous edition.
    Includes bibliographical references and index.
    ISBN 0-273-68222-9 (paper)
    1. Organizational behaviour. I. Huczynski, Andrzej. II. Title

    HD58.7.H83 2004
    302.3'5--dc22

2003058233

10 9 8 7 6 5 4 3 2 1
09 08 07 06 05 04

Typeset in 9½/12p Stone Serif by 3
Printed and bound by Mateu-Cromo, Artes Graficas, Spain
The publisher's policy is to use paper manufactured from sustainable forests.

From Dave
To Lesley, Andrew and Mairi

From Andrzej
To Janet, Sophie, Gregory and Tom

Outline contents

Full contents

Guided tour

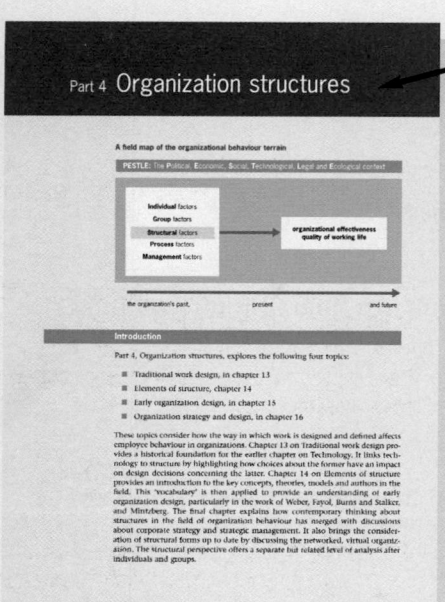

Parts: the book is divided into six parts, each with a 'part map' and full introduction. This makes the structure more transparent and makes it easier for the student to navigate.

Invitation to see: within each part section you will now find an exciting new feature called 'Invitation to see'. This feature explores how work and organizations are represented in photography and briefs students on how to analyze and 'decode' such images.

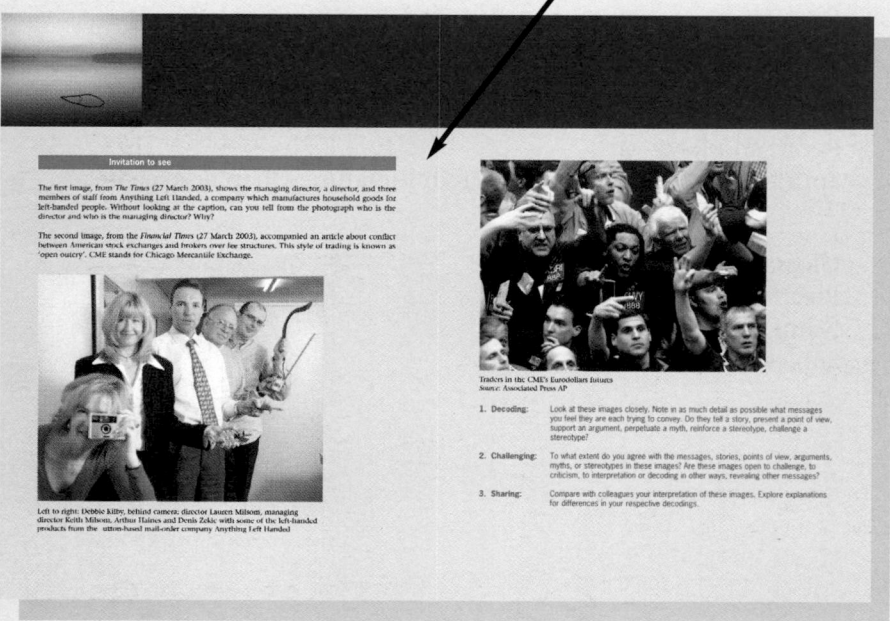

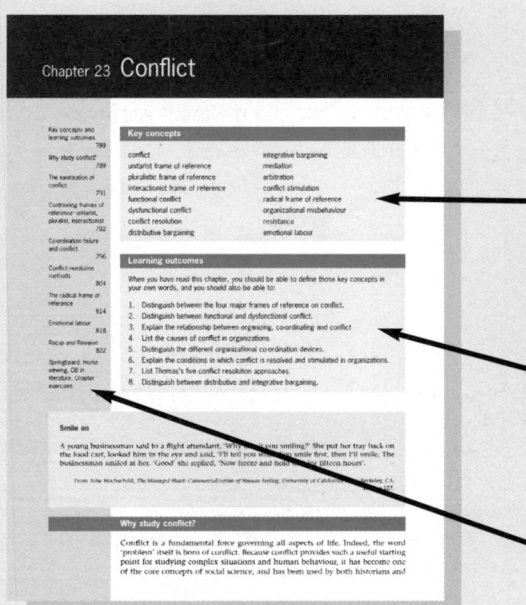

Key concepts: each chapter opens with a list of the main concepts defined, explained and illustrated in the chapter.

Learning outcomes to be achieved are stated at the beginning of every chapter. A recap section is provided at the end of each chapter, which summarizes the chapter content and can be used for reminder and revision.

Chapter contents are listed at the start of each chapter to enable easy navigation of the chapter.

Application and **illustration** of concepts, theories and frameworks are discussed throughout the text. These are clearly distinguishable from the text in colourful boxes and include recent management applications, international examples, examples of classic research and speculation about the future.

Definitions provide a summary of the key concepts introduced at the start of the chapter. The term is also highlighted within the text.

Portraits of the leading scholars who have contributed to our understanding of the subject.

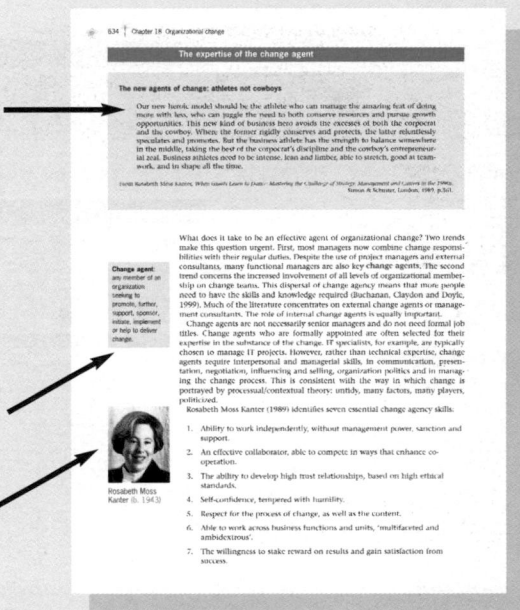

Cartoons, photos, tables, and **diagrams** feature throughout the text to make it all the more digestible, engaging and readable.

Stop and Criticize: readers are frequently invited to stop and think through contradictory and controversial points and arguments. Students are encouraged to apply ideas and analysis to their own experience and to challenge their own assumptions.

Recap and **Revision** provide a summary of the chapter content in relation to the learning outcomes and offer a series of typical essay questions which can either be used for personal study or as tutorial revision aids.

Springboard: a short annotated guide to further and more advanced reading.

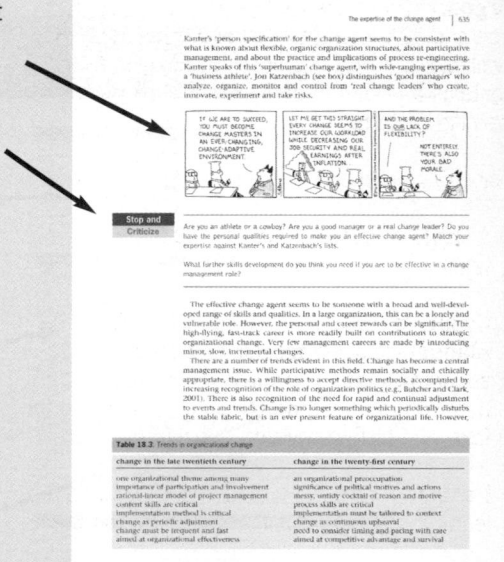

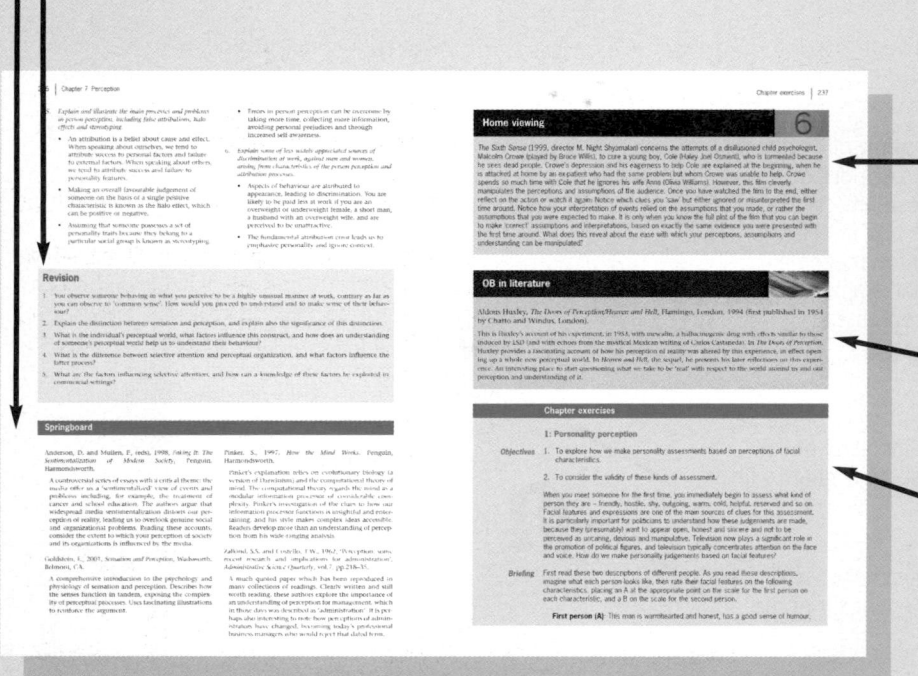

Home viewing identifies films, or television programmes which illustrate the wider relevance and application of the issues and ideas introduced in the chapter.

OB in literature: a novel or other source of creative writing is suggested to provide further illustration of concepts and themes from the chapter.

Chapter exercises: at the end of every chapter there are two exercises, one of which is designed for large classes and the other for smaller tutorial and seminar settings.

Organizational Behaviour is supported by a free and fully interactive **Companion Website**, available at www.booksites.net/buchuc, that contains a wealth of additional teaching and learning material.

For the Lecturer

- A range of password-protected extra teaching resources.

- Complete, downloadable **Instructor's Manual** including teaching ideas to accompany the new 'Invitation to see' feature, debriefings for all the chapter exercises in the text, and further revision questions.

- **Lecture ideas** – a total of 72 suggested lectures, based around chapters of the book.

- **Powerpoint slides** that can be downloaded and used as OHTs.

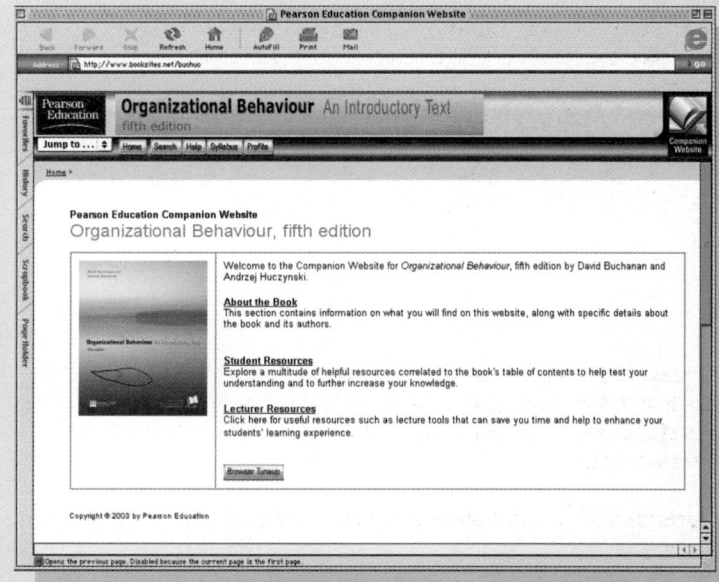

For the Student

- **Study material** designed to help you improve your results.

- **Learning objectives** for each chapter.

- Extensive multiple choice, fill-in-the-blank, true/false, and matching **questions** all with feedback on incorrect answers, to help develop your subject knowledge and improve your understanding.

- An online **glossary** to explain key concepts.

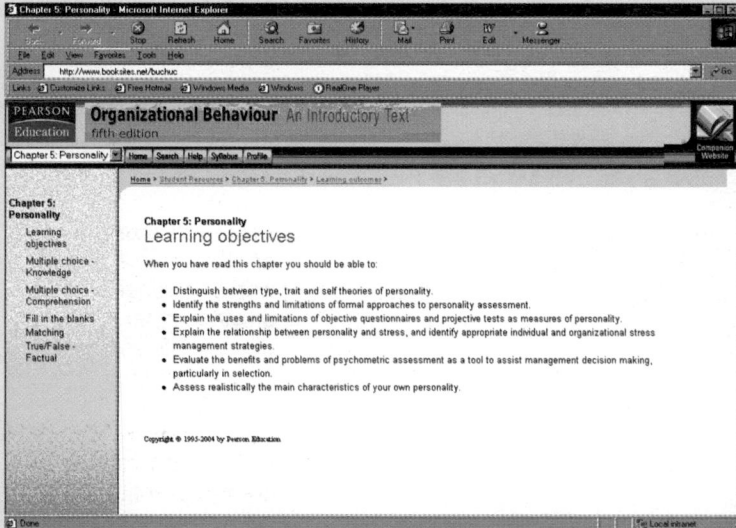

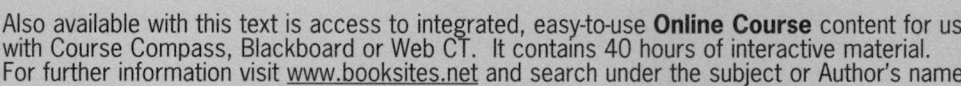

Also available with this text is access to integrated, easy-to-use **Online Course** content for use with Course Compass, Blackboard or Web CT. It contains 40 hours of interactive material. For further information visit www.booksites.net and search under the subject or Author's name.

Text aims and target readership

This book has four main aims:

1 To provide an **introduction** to the study of human behaviour in organizations for students with little or no social science background. The text can be used as a comprehensive introduction to the field and as a starting point for advanced study. We aim to stimulate wider interest in organizational behaviour and an enthusiasm for more knowledge.

2 To enable readers to translate organizational behaviour theories, concepts and techniques into **practice**, to work more effectively with the organizations which they are likely to encounter. If one is going to work for, work with, develop, subvert, or resist organizations, then one needs to know how and why they exist and function as they do.

3 To stimulate **debate** by encouraging a challenging, questioning, critical perspective. The 'correct' answers to organizational questions and solutions to problems can rarely be based on evidence and reason alone. Decisions and actions rely also on values, judgements and ideology. Our subject matter and its practical consequences, however 'rigorous' the research and 'authoritative' the source, are not beyond challenge.

4 To make the subject matter of social science applied to organizations **interesting and intelligible** to students from different educational and disciplinary backgrounds. Readers from other disciplines are often suspicious of what the social sciences can offer.

This book's target readership includes those who are new to the social sciences in general, and to the study of organizational behaviour in particular. This is a core subject on business and management studies degree and diploma programmes, undergraduate and postgraduate. In addition, accountants, lawyers, doctors, nurses, engineers, teachers, architects, computing scientists, bankers, hoteliers and surveyors, who often have no background in social science subjects, are also likely to find themselves studying organizational behaviour as a core element in their professional examination schemes.

This text is written from a *multidisciplinary social science perspective*. Our understanding of organizations derives from a number of disciplines. Other texts in this field adopt a managerial, psychological, or sociological perspective. However, our readers are not all going to be managers, psychologists or sociologists, and many readers beyond these occupations require, and can benefit from, an understanding of organizational behaviour.

Individual *chapters are self-contained*. The understanding of one chapter does not rely on a prior reading of others, although in practice these topics are interrelated. Ideas and theories build systematically, from the organizational context, to individual psychology, through social psychology, to organizational sociology, politics, and finally management topics. Each chapter introduces theoretical background and practical applications. Many issues are controversial, and each chapter aims to clarify competing views. The aim is not, however, to identify 'correct answers' or 'best practices', which are often simplistic and misleading. The intention behind presenting tensions and contradictions is to raise further questions, to trigger discussion and debate, and to stimulate challenge and critical thinking.

The book has a *flexible design*, appropriate for a two-semester programme or a three-term course. Although this is an introductory text, a significant proportion of the material is more advanced, and 'springboard' sections in each chapter offer guidance to further reading. The text may therefore be useful on second- and third-level courses. The subject matter overlaps with other topics, such as human resource management, and instructors and students are likely to find this text relevant to other modules. The material does not have to be covered in the sequence in which it is presented. This gives instructors the choice of which material to cover, in what sequence, and with what additional learning support.

The text incorporates material from a *variety of cultural settings*. Social science theories can be culture bound, as laws, norms and traditions vary from country to country, sub-culture to sub-culture. It is important to stimulate awareness of the range of social and cultural factors that influence behaviour in organizations. While admitting a British bias in the authorship, we – along with many colleagues – find ourselves typically working with multicultural student groups. It is increasingly important for students, and organization members, to understand and work effectively with cultural differences (see, for example, Adler, 2002).

Research summaries and *Stop and Criticize* exercises provide opportunities to explore controversial and comparative issues. One way of bringing into relief the ways in which we behave in organizations is to compare our practice with that of others. Comparative studies have a long tradition in the social sciences. Each year, most of the readers of this book engage in comparative study, in airlines, railways, buses, hotels, restaurants and hospitals, simply through exposure to different organizational settings.

The text uses a range of other features to help and also to challenge readers:

- Each chapter is introduced by a list of the *Key concepts* to be covered and the *Learning outcomes* to be achieved.

- Those key concepts can all be found in the *Glossary* at the end of the text.

- Readers are regularly invited to *Stop and criticize*, to think through contradictory and controversial points and arguments, to apply ideas and arguments to their own experience, to challenge their own assumptions.

- *Applications* of concepts, theories and frameworks are discussed throughout, sometimes in boxed illustrations from practical organizational experience.

- Each chapter has *Recap* and *Revision* sections which first summarize the chapter content in relation to the learning outcomes, and then offer a series of typical essay questions which can be used either for personal study or as tutorial revision aids.

- Each chapter has a *Home viewing* section which identifies a film (or films), and in some instances a television programme, which illustrates the issues and concepts in the chapter in a graphic and entertaining manner.

- Each chapter has an *OB in literature* section which indicates illustrations of the concepts and other material covered in the text in novels and other creative writing.

- Each chapter offers a *Springboard* section – a short, annotated guide to further and more advanced sources.

- At the end of each chapter are two *Chapter exercises*. One of these is designed for use with large classes and the other for small group tutorial and seminar settings.

■ Each part is prefaced with an *Invitation to see*, a selection of photographs showing how work and organizations are visually portrayed. Visual images are rarely neutral, and readers are invited to 'decode' these images for the range of obvious and more subtle meanings which they promote.

■ In addition, we have tried to make the book interesting and approachable by using novel, varied and unusual material where appropriate. Examples, cartoons, illustrations, exercises and cases are used to change the pace, rhythm and appearance of the text, to make it more digestible, more engaging, more readable.

The style and content of this book thus reflect the *participative teaching and learning* strategies now widely applied across the business and management studies curriculum. This implies a limited use of conventional lecture, and extensive use of a range of individual and group case and exercise work. Most instructors will, therefore, not teach *to* this text, but teach *from* it, using it to introduce key ideas and theories as a platform for discussion, exercise, casework and further advanced study.

Challenge and debate

We have used a number of text features to encourage *an active and questioning approach* to the subject. We want to challenge readers by inviting them to confront real, practical and theoretical problems and issues for themselves. Readers are invited regularly to stop reading and to consider controversial points, individually or in group discussion. We want to alert readers to the significance of organizational behaviour in everyday life. The study of organizational behaviour should not be confined to the lecture theatre and library. Eating a pizza in a restaurant, joining a queue at a cinema, returning a faulty product to a store, purchasing a train ticket, arguing with a colleague at work, taking a holiday job in a factory, reading a novel – are all experiences that can be related to the material in this book.

A further aim of this text is to strike a balance between three characteristics:

Introductory: the text provides a comprehensive grounding in the subject, and its scope, concerns, research traditions, language and applications.

Practical: the content explores the practical organizational applications and consequences of theoretical perspectives, research findings and management techniques.

Challenging: the treatment encourages readers to question and debate rather than to accept as 'authoritative' received ideas, and to subject concepts, theories and their applications to challenge.

Some organizational behaviour texts offer a *managerial perspective*, and give readers little encouragement to challenge the material or to consider other lines of reasoning and practice. Some texts offer a *critical perspective*, encouraging debate but without offering practical options. This text aims to strike a balance between these extremes.

There are at least five grounds for developing a critical, questioning approach.

1: Is the employment contract based on free choice?
The employment contract apparently relies on 'freedom of choice'. You choose

whether to take the job, and the organization chooses whether to hire you or not. However, employers are rarely dependent on individual employees, but can pick and choose from the labour market. For an employee, the 'free choice' may be between work and unemployment. The employment contract is an unequal one, and trade unions have not always been a solution to this power imbalance. Some commentators regard the employment contract in a capitalist economy as exploitative. One implication is that management techniques for improving employment conditions and the quality of working life can be seen as cynical, cosmetic attempts to conceal the exploitative nature of the employment relationship.

2: Is organizational hierarchy inevitable?

Organizational hierarchy appears to be 'normal'. It seems that managers have superior ability, better information, and well-developed powers of judgement, which is why they make the big decisions. Hierarchy, however, relies on power inequality, and creates patterns of domination (by the powerful elite) and subordination (of the powerless). One trend during the 1990s was 'delayering', reducing the number of levels in the management hierarchy, producing 'flat' organization structures. However, even delayered organizations have hierarchies which perpetuate power inequalities and exclude large numbers of employees from positions of influence over management decisions. Why do organizations not employ the same democratic structures as the wider democratic society of which they are a part? This argument has implications for organization structure.

3: Is the state a neutral arbiter between employer and employee?

The state, that is government, appears to be a neutral arbiter between competing interests in a pluralist society. Legislation upholds socially beneficial aims such as the maintenance of order and the deterrence of crime. This 'neutrality', however, is a fiction. Legislation strengthens rather than challenges the *status quo*, particularly with respect to the rights of trade unions and individuals to challenge management decisions in the workplace. The state typically acts for, and not against, established interests and power bases. In Part 1, we explore how the external environment of the organization, including political, economic, social, technological, legislative and ecological factors affect organization structures. Different perspectives on conflict – unitary, pluralist and radical – are explored in chapter 23.

4: Is the technical language of organization and management neutral?

Are we 'in control' of our thoughts, feelings, values and beliefs? Yes. We are presented with arguments and facts, we balance the evidence, we make up our minds. However, the language in which we receive information is not neutral. Take the statement, 'do a good job, and you will be promoted'. Sounds reasonable? This assumes that 'a better worker is a better person'; you are deviant if you are not 'a good worker'. Better, then, to prove your worth by being a committed employee. From a management perspective, this is an effective way of obtaining compliance from a potentially awkward workforce. The 'better worker' does not complain about conditions. The technical language of management (teamwork, flexibility, empowerment, discretion, appraisal, job enrichment) sounds appealing and liberating. However, these methods can be seen as covert tools of manipulation and exploitation. Reflecting what is called the 'linguistic turn' in postmodern social theory, language is not a tool for describing reality, but a way of promoting specific versions of that reality to further the interests of particular individuals and groups. In other words, management language does things, it makes things happen (Holman and Thorpe, 2003).

5: How 'new' are 'new' theories and techniques?

Management theorists generate a constant stream of new ideas and techniques. Managers tend to be fashion conscious, and are always interested in the latest thinking, which can create competitive advantage. Students (and textbook authors) also need to keep up with this flood of innovation. Armed with a knowledge of the history of the subject, however, one can often see in 'new' thinking and methods aspects of familiar, 'old' ideas. What appears to be new is less often a 'paradigm shift' in thinking, and more often a 'packaging shift'. Is the technique of 'job sculpting', invented in the late 1990s, really 'new' or just a reworking of 'job enrichment' from the 1960s? Is the 'McDonaldization' of work a contemporary trend or the continuing expression of early-twentieth-century management thinking? Is the currently fashionable concept of emotional intelligence a startling development of relevance to management in the twenty-first century or simply a restatement of ideas from the 1940s about personal and interpersonal awareness and sensitivity?

These five distinct issues are linked by the common desire to challenge and to debate ideas which appear to be plausible, familiar, sensible, inevitable, traditional, orthodox, novel and which may thus be accepted unquestioningly. Instead, we should question the notions that:

The contract between employer and employee is a fair one entered into freely.
Hierarchy is a natural model of organization, inevitable and beneficial.
The state plays a neutral role as arbiter in employment relations.
The technical language of organization and management is neutral.
What is advertised as new is always new.

We can thus argue that each of these statements may be false. A perspective that encourages debate, challenge and criticism involves asking the following kinds of question, when presented with a theory, an argument, evidence, or with a recommendation for action:

- Does this make sense, do I understand it, or is it confused and confusing?

- Is the supporting evidence compelling, or is it weak?

- Does a claim to 'novelty' survive comparison with previous thinking?

- Is the argument logical and coherent, or are there gaps and flaws?

- What biases and prejudices are revealed in this line of argument?

- Is a claim to 'neutrality' realistic, or does it conceal a hidden agenda?

- Are the arguments and judgements based convincingly on the evidence?

- Whose interests are served by this argument, and whose are damaged?

- Is the language of this argument designed to make it more appealing?

Where appropriate, chapters explore competing perspectives on the subject matter, from commentators who base their approaches on different assumptions and values. This approach is reinforced in the *Stop and Criticize* sections, and in the exercises at the end of each chapter. For a fuller treatment of a critical approach to understanding and researching organizational behaviour, see Mats Alvesson and Stanley Deetz (1999). For a highly regarded text written from a critical stance, see Paul Thompson and David McHugh (2002).

Home viewing

In a challenge to orthodox thinking, John Hassard and Ruth Holliday (1998) unkindly observe that textbooks like this offer a *sanitized* picture of organizational behaviour. Stephen Ackroyd and Paul Thompson (1999) similarly argue that orthodox texts overlook much evident *mis*behaviour – 'soldiering', sabotage, pilfering, practical jokes. Gibson Burrell (1998, p. 52) is uncompromising in his view of what contemporary organization theory neglects: 'there is little mention of sex, yet organizations are redolent with it; little mention of violence, yet organizations are stinking with it; little mention of pain, yet organizations rely upon it; little mention of the will to power, yet organizations would not exist without it'.

Hassard and Holliday note that film (and television), in contrast, 'plays out sex, violence, emotion, power struggle, the personal consequences of success and failure, and *dis*organization upon its stage'. The Media Institute, an American organization, studied the portrayal of organizations in 200 episodes of 50 television programmes. Its analysis (Overell, 2002) showed that with fictional businesses portrayed on television:

- only 3 per cent engage in socially or economically productive activity;

- 45 per cent of management behaviours are portrayed as illegal;

- 55 per cent of company bosses commit illegal acts, such as fraud and murder.

Is this view sensationalized or realistic? To what extent do film and television reinforce or challenge popular stereotypes of work, authority, power, status and organization structure?

Nelson Phillips (1995) argues that the use of narrative fiction, in film and other media such as novels, short stories, plays, songs and poems, is a way of strengthening the connection between organizational behaviour as an academic discipline and the subjective experience of organizational membership. The advertising for some films suggests that stereotypes are challenged: *Philadelphia* for its portrayal of AIDS; *Disclosure* for the portrayal of female rape and sexual harassment at work. Hassard and Holliday (1998) argue, however, that the media reinforce conservative values, reflecting social realities, albeit in a stylized manner, rather than presenting fundamental challenges. Read their text and you will never again watch police and hospital television dramas without boring your companions with critical commentary on the traditional portrayal of hierarchy, group dynamics, sex role stereotyping, power relations, the role of authority figures, and dysfunctional bureaucratic rules.

We aim to avoid the sanitization trap with *Home viewing* ideas for each chapter, identifying films that illustrate the concepts, theories and applications explored in the text. Further suggestions can be found in the work of Joseph Champoux (1999, 2001a, 2001b), and readers will identify other sources from the constant stream of new film releases.

OB in literature

Most of the topics and themes within the subject boundary of organizational behaviour are also addressed in powerful, insightful and entertaining ways in literature. To reinforce the aim of stimulating challenge and debate, considering and exploring ideas from unusual perspectives, each chapter identifies a relevant novel or other literature source.

Management courses based on novels have a long history. Novels can be deliberately written as didactic devices, illustrating points about, for example, quality management, as in *The Goal* (Goldratt and Cox, 1993) or employee exploitation as in *Human Resources* (Kemske, 1996). Fiction, however, can also be used for instructional purposes. The allegorical novel *Watership Down* (Adams, 1973) provides a basis for discussing the management roles identified by Henry Mintzberg (1973). Other sources include Thompson and McGivern (1996), Czarniawska-Joerges and de Monthoux (1994), Grottola (1994), Puffer (1991), and Knights and Willmott (1999). Barbara Czarniawska (1998, 1999) describes organization theory as a 'literary genre', observing that narratives which unfold in the typical sequence, 'and then, and then', imply causality and are therefore rich in theoretical insight.

Our literature selection has two limitations. First, it is inevitably idiosyncratic. Second, attention is often focused on a specific aspect of the work cited, which rarely does justice to an author's wider purpose. We hope that you will follow up these recommendations, and that you will analyze your own wider reading in these terms.

The postmodern justification: beyond home entertainment

Films and novels offer fresh and entertaining perspectives on organizational behaviour. However, there are other reasons why narrative fiction deserves our attention. Researchers, and film makers and writers, appear to have different purposes and use different methods and media. Researchers are concerned with scientific observation and the objective discovery of truth, resulting in peer-refereed journal papers. Film makers and novelists are concerned with creativity and entertainment, resulting in visually stimulating celluloid images and absorbing narratives in books. Do these groups have anything in common?

The screen writer or novelist has to create an entertaining fiction – a narrative – and then decide how best to present it to their audience. This involves choosing, within the broad conventions of novels and films, what will be revealed to the audience and what concealed, what will be shown or described in detail, and the sequence in which action is presented. This must also be a new story which the audience has not already seen or read.

The researcher has to create an interesting academic paper – a narrative – and then decide how best to present it to their audience. This involves choosing, within the broad conventions of academic journals, what will be revealed to the readers and what concealed, what will be shown or described in detail, and the sequence in which information is presented. This must also present new research findings with which readers are not already familiar.

Film makers, novelists and academic researchers are, of course, constrained by the conventions of their respective media. Creative and inventive as well as entertaining, the *James Bond* movies produced initially by Albert (Cubby) Broccoli follow a familiar formula. However ground-breaking in content, academic papers also follow a set of writing guidelines. Paradoxically, it is these constraints which turn both the writing of research papers and narrative fiction into creative acts. Authors must constantly make conscious choices so that their work will be meaningful, acceptable and credible within these limits.

Surely the work of the social scientist is different in being concerned with offering a faithful representation of social and organizational life? Well, film makers and novelists are also concerned with remaining faithful to individual experience, with presenting realistic accounts of the social world, and with the plausibility of their characters and narratives. Even in science fiction, a genre which deliberately departs from 'reality', if the setting, plot and characters are not plausible, then the film or novel is likely to be a critical failure.

The postmodern perspective, explored in chapter 2, makes two observations relevant here:

1. *All texts are social constructions*, as authors are influenced by the language, interests, norms and expectations of the wider society. Even 'alternative' writers, seeking to challenge and shock, have to define their position, however radical, in relation to whatever passes for 'the established view' at the time they are writing.

2. *There is no one 'correct' interpretation* of what an author has created. Different readers, from different backgrounds and perspectives, have different interpretations. Postmodernism argues that all interpretations of a piece of work are 'correct', and that an author's intentions should not be given any special privilege.

Research papers are generally regarded as having relatively high scientific value and low entertainment value. The opposing claim, that narrative fiction has low scientific value, does not hold true if we accept a postmodern account of the similarities between these domains. Films and novels may be seen as frivolous and entertaining examples of the ideas presented in a text such as this. However, a systematic analysis and interpretation of film can lead to quite different conclusions. An example demonstrates the possibilities.

Joel Foreman and Tojo Thatchenkery (1996) analyze the film *Rising Sun* (1993, director Philip Kaufman). *Rising Sun* concerns the murder of Cheryl, an American blonde, in the boardroom of the Nakamoto Corporation, a Japanese transplant in Los Angeles, during negotiations to acquire Microcon, an American defence company. John Connor (played by Sean Connery) and Web Smith (Wesley Snipes) are the detectives on the case. This thriller can be viewed from a number of different perspectives.

First, it can be seen as a study of a Japanese transplant in an alien culture, with the consequent clash of organizational behaviour styles. This culture clash is symbolized in the incongruous opening sequences. Portraying the (male) Japanese acquisition of American companies, technologies and women, the story also plays on American fears of Japanese business domination.

Second, it can be viewed as instruction in cross-cultural communication. Connor has to teach his partner how to do business with the Japanese. This involves explaining social norms and rituals, preserving 'face', conversation style, and interpersonal relationships.

Third, it can be viewed as a study of organizational power politics, demonstrated in the symbolic use of architecture, the exploitation of friendships, the use of surveillance technology, the significance of golfing relationships, and the links to national politics through the manipulation and blackmail of Senator John Morton (Ray Wise).

Fourth, it can be seen as a metaphor for the postmodern view of ambiguity, uncertainty, lack of 'closure' and the negotiable nature of reality. This is revealed in the relationship between Eddie Sakamura (Cary-Hiroyuki Tagawa) and his girlfriend Cheryl Austin (Tatjana Patitz); it looks like it, but did he murder her? This is also suggested in the closing scene with Web Smith and Jingo Asakuma (Tia Carrere) who reveals that she is (or was?) Connor's partner; she encourages him, but does Web get the girl? At the end, the plot returns to the opening theme of culture clash, between Japanese and American (in the relationship between Japanese Eddie and American Cheryl) and between Afro-American Web and Japanese Jingo. Does the lack of closure in this narrative leave you feeling uncomfortable?

Invitation to see

We live in a world saturated with visual imagery, from newspapers, magazines, street advertising, television, and the internet. We are also presented with a range of other visual information: the appearance and dress of the people we meet; the design, layout, colours and decoration of their workplaces; the architecture of the buildings in which they work; the technology in use. Despite its volume, richness and complexity, we tend to take most of this visual information for granted, as part of the 'background tapestry' in organizational and everyday life. While we may smile or grimace at the occasional photograph, we rarely pause for long to dissect, analyze, interpret and debate the content of these visual images.

Why should we pay attention to these transient images? We see them once and rarely feel the need to refer back to them again. Street advertisements and internet banners are displayed for brief periods before being updated. The photographs in magazines and newspapers are just illustrations, usually put into context and explained with a brief caption. It is the accompanying main text that matters. The images in television and street advertising are clearly contrived to attract our attention, and they cannot mislead us in that respect.

The problem is that visual images are rarely, if ever, neutral. They are not 'just' illustrations. They usually tell a story, present a point of view, support an argument, perpetuate a myth, reinforce a stereotype, challenge a stereotype. Images carry messages, which are sometimes obvious, sometimes subtle, sometimes clear, sometimes confusing. Visual imagery is thus a potentially valuable source of information, of data, which we often overlook. Visual research methods have been widely used in specialized areas in sociology and anthropology for many years (Bateson and Mead, 1942; Collier and Collier, 1986). There has been a recent growth of interest in the potential of visual methods in social science more generally, and in organizational behaviour (Prosser, 1998; Emmison and Smith, 2000; Buchanan, 2001).

We would like to encourage you to adopt a more critical perspective on visual information concerning organizational behaviour. To do this, we have introduced, at the beginning of each Part of the book, a short section titled *Invitation to see*. Visual information constitutes data in the same way that interviews and survey questionnaires provide data about organizational behaviour. *Invitation to see* displays one or more photographs showing a range of different aspects of work and organizations, and which invite interpretation.

The aims of *Invitation to see* are to:

■ demonstrate the value of visual data in offering insights into human and organizational behaviour;

■ introduce and develop the concept of interpreting or 'decoding' visual images;

■ encourage you to look at the organizational world, and the actors who populate it, in an entirely different way.

Photographs can be seen, read, interpreted or decoded in three main ways.

1: Reality captured

Images can be seen as captured fragments of reality, frozen in time, indisputably accurate renditions of scenes and actors. This was the way in which photography was regarded when it was first invented. The conclusion which many commentators drew from this was that 'art is dead'. The artist could never hope to capture reality as accurately as a photograph, so why bother? This perspective is reflected in the saying 'the camera doesn't lie'.

2: Reality fabricated

Photographs can instead be regarded as social and technological constructs, which reveal as much about the photographer as they do about the image. The photographer selects the scene, a camera, a lens (if it is that type of camera), and film. Film and camera type determine several properties of the image, such as sharpness, contrast, grain, and depth of field. More critically, the photographer selects the angle and framing of a shot, determining what is included and what is excluded, and also selects the moment to open the shutter and capture the image. Viewers thus see only what the photographer wants them to see. What is outside the frame, and the sequence of events before and after the shutter was fired, remain invisible. This perspective implies that 'the camera lies for the photographer'.

3: Multiple realities

The way in which an image is interpreted by viewers, independent of the photographer's intent, is also significant. For the cover of this book, we chose 'branch in the lake', an open landscape scene with no people, birds or animals. We wanted an image that had no direct association with organizations, factories, office buildings, managers, teams, aggressive animals, shoals of fish, or any other typical organizational metaphors.

There is a key question concerning whose interpretation of an image is correct, that of the photographer or that of the viewer? Both points of view are equally valid, and are of equal interest. As discussed in chapter 2, the idea that texts can have many valid interpretations also applies to visual images. The viewer does not have to know the photographer's intent, although that can often be inferred from the image and its caption. Photographers cannot predict the interpretations which viewers will place on their work, but it is those interpretations that condition the viewer's response, and not the photographer's intent.

With *Invitation to see*, therefore, three types of question are significant:

1. What did the photographer intend this image to convey? What message is it attempting to send? Does it tell a story, present a point of view, support an argument, perpetuate a myth, reinforce a stereotype, challenge a stereotype? What are you being invited to see here?

2. What does this image convey to you? How do you interpret this? What do you think this means? Do you agree with what is being said here? Is the message inaccurate or misleading, perhaps insulting in some respect? Does this image carry meanings which the photographer may not have intended?

3. How do others interpret this image? Do they decode it in different ways? Do they see other messages and points of view? How can differences of interpretation of the same image be explained?

This photograph appeared in *The Times* newspaper on Saturday 22 March 2003, illustrating an article explaining the car company Honda's decision to raise the retirement age for its employees in Britain from 60 to 62, to help meet the increasing cost of retirement pensions.

New vehicle: in a radical move to make good a £40 million hole in its pension fund Honda wants staff to work until 62
Source: Calyx

Here is one decoding of this image:

> The photographer (Richard Wintle) has presumably been sent to this car plant in Swindon, England, to take this shot to illustrate the article. This displays a small part of the story of car manufacturing, looking down a section of straight assembly track with three vehicles visible. The factory appears to be clean, spacious and well lit, with bright fluorescent lights in the high ceiling showing off the gleaming paintwork on a new vehicle which appears to be close to completion. The four or five assembly workers all appear to be male; this is man's work (although Volvo has used female assemblers for many years). The men are wearing white protective overalls and gloves, and two of them are wearing baseball caps. The door alignment equipment to the side of the track looks sophisticated; this is a complex job.

What else does this image reveal?

> The signs hanging from the ceiling are prohibition signs ('don't do that!'). Are the white overalls and gloves worn to protect the assemblers, or to protect the product? As the vehicle is nearing final assembly, product protection takes priority. The overalls make it difficult to distinguish between the men on the assembly track, and the baseball caps could be an attempt to regain individual identity. Why was the photograph taken in this part of the plant? Other stages in the assembly process are not so clean, and do not happen in such a well-lit setting. A 'dark satanic mill' photograph might damage the 'hi-tech' image of the company. If the people in this photograph were managers, they would almost certainly be looking towards the camera and smiling, perhaps with a hand (no glove) on the car, proud of their product. The people in this

shot are almost certainly not managers but assembly workers who have not been asked to stop work for a photograph. The figure in the foreground appears to be struggling awkwardly with his left hand, in the confined door space, to align the rear passenger door which his right hand is holding.

It is therefore possible to 'read' into this image indications of the 'tyranny of the assembly line', which we will encounter in chapter 3 in an exploration of 'mass production characteristics'. While the physical working conditions appear to be good, the constraints on aspects of employee behaviour and movement are also evident. It is perhaps also symbolic that the photographer did not ask those assemblers to stop working and to stand beside the car for the photograph, rather than to continue working. Did plant management suggest that the photograph be taken here? Did management request that work continued during shooting?

It is perhaps possible to read too much into such an image: the closing comments in the previous paragraph are speculative. The next question is, how do you read this image? What story does it suggest to you? What are you being invited to see here? With each image, or group of images, accompanying the six Part introductions in the rest of the text, you will therefore find the following questions:

Invitation to see: briefing

1. Decoding: Look at this image closely. Note in as much detail as possible what messages you feel the image is trying to convey. Does it tell a story, present a point of view, support an argument, perpetuate a myth, reinforce a stereotype, challenge a stereotype?

2. Challenging: To what extent do you agree with the message, story, point of view, argument, myth, or stereotype in this image? Is this image open to challenge, to criticism, to interpretation or decoding in other ways, revealing other messages?

3. Sharing: Compare with colleagues your interpretation of this image. Explore explanations for any differences in your respective decodings.

Acknowledgements

A large number of friends, colleagues and students have contributed their ideas, criticisms and advice to the development of this text. Our special thanks in this regard is therefore extended to Antti Ainamo, Minwir Al Shammari, Carol Boyd, Alan and Sue Bryman, Lesley Buchanan, Patrick Dawson, Moira Fischbacher, Stuart Hay, Janet Huczynska, Patricia Moriarty, Denise Picton, John Purcell, Neville Stanton, Marjolein van Offenbeek, Peter Prowse, Andrew Taylor, Willem de Villiers, and Richard Whittington. While this work has benefited immeasurably from their criticism, ideas and suggestions, the gaps and flaws remain the sole responsibility of the authors.

We would like to thank all those lecturers who reviewed the fourth edition of the text and who made numerous useful comments. Many of their comments and suggestions have been incorporated into this revision and we are very grateful for their ideas and advice. We would also like to thank those members of the Pearson development, design and production team who have contributed to this edition including: Nicola Chilvers, David Cox, Kay Holman, Adam Renvoize, Andrew Taylor, Amanda Thompson and Janey Webb.

Publisher's acknowledgements

We are grateful to the following for permission to reproduce copyright material:

Table 2.3 from Measuring and managing for environmental turbulence: the Ansoff Associates approach in *The Portable Conference on Change Management* edited by Alexander Watson Hiam, pub HRD Press, Inc., reprinted by permission of The Estate of H. Igor Ansoff (Ansoff, I. 1997); Chapter 3, p.80, Table from Ringing true in *People Management*, Vol.6, No.2, 20 January 2000, reprinted by permission of Alastair Hatchett (Hatchett, A. 2000); Chapter 3, p.95, Table adapted from Work systems, quality of working life and attitudes of workers: an empirical study towards the effects of team and non-teamwork in *New Technology, Work and Employment*, Vol.16, No.3, Blackwell Publishing Ltd (Steijn, B. 2001); Figure 4.3 from *The Learning Company: A Strategy for Sustainable Development, 2nd Edition*, McGraw-Hill International (UK) Limited (Pedler, M., Burgoyne, J. and Boydell, T. 1997); Figure 5.5 from Personality and personnel selection in *Trends in Organizational Behaviour* edited by C. L. Cooper and D. M. Rousseau, John Wiley & Sons Ltd (Robertson, I. T. 1994); Chapter 6, p.180, Table from *Focus*, May 1999, www.focusmag.co.uk, reprinted by permission of Origin Publishing; Chapter 6, p.192, Figure from *Gesture in Naples and Gesture in Classical Antiquity* translated by Adam Kenton, pub Indiana University Press, reprinted by permission of the Syndics of Cambridge University Library (de Jorio, A. 2001); Chapter 6, p.196, Table from When 'no' means 'yes' in *Marketing*, October, reproduced by permission of the copyright owner, Haymarket Business Publications Limited (Kiely, M. 1993); Chapter 7, p.228, Figure after Investigating pupils' images of mathematicians in *Educational Studies in Mathematics*, 43(1), reprinted by permission of Susan H. Picker (Picker, S. H. and Berry, J. 2000); Figure 8.4 from A new strategy for job enrichment in *California Management Review*, Vol.17, No.4, reprinted by permission of The Regents of the University of California (Hackman, J. R., Oldham, G., Janson, R. and Purdy, K. 1975); Table 9.1 from *Effective Behavior in Organizations, 6th Edition*, pub Irwin, reprinted by permission of The McGraw-Hill Companies (Cohen, A. R., Fink, S. L., Gadon, H. and Willits, R. D. 1995); Table 9.2 from Firing up the front line in *Harvard Business Review*, May–June, Harvard Business School Publishing Corporation (Katzenbach, J. R. and Santamaria, J. A. 1999); Figures 9.3 (right) and 10.4 from *Behavior in Organizations, 6th Edition*, pub Prentice-Hall, Inc., reprinted by permission of Pearson Education, Inc. (Greenberg, J. and Baron, R. A. 1997); Figure 9.6 from *New Patterns of Management*, The McGraw-Hill Companies (Likert, R. 1961); Figure 9.9 from *A Primer on Organizational Behavior*, John Wiley & Sons, Inc. (Bowditch, J. L. and Buono, A. F. 2001); Chapter 10, p.323, graphic by Linda Eckstein, text by Andrew E. Sewer from The Hellish Angels' Devilish Business in *Fortune*, 30 November 1992, © 1992 Time, Inc. All rights reserved, reprinted by permission of *Fortune* magazine; Table 10.2 based on Functional roles of group members in *Journal of Social Issues*, Vol.4, Blackwell Publishing Ltd (Benne, K. and Sheats, P. 1948); Figure 10.3 from Communication networks fourteen years later in *Group Processes* edited by L. Berkowitz, pub Academic Press, reprinted by permission of Elsevier (Shaw, M. E. 1978); Figure 10.7 from *The Coming Shape of Organization*, pub Butterworth-Heinemann, reprinted by permission of Belbin Associates (Belbin, R. M. 1996); Figures 11.2 and 11.4 from *Managing Behavior in Organizations, 2nd Edition*, pub Prentice-Hall, Inc., reprinted by permission of Pearson Education, Inc. (Greenberg, J. 1999); Figure 11.3 from *Social Psychology, 9th Edition*, Allyn and Bacon (Baron, R. A. and Byrne, D. 2000); Tables 11.3 and 22.7 from *A Diagnostic Approach to Organizational Behavior, 4th Edition*, reprinted by permission of Prentice-Hall, Inc. (Gordon, J. R. 1993); Figure 11.6 from *Social Psychology, 2nd Edition*, pub Macmillan, reproduced with permission of Palgrave Macmillan (Malim, T. and Birch, A. 1997); Chapter 11, p.373 and p.374, Figures from Effects of group pressure upon the modification and distortion of judgements in *Groups, Leadership and Men* edited by H. Guetzkow, Carnegie Press (Asch, S. E. 1951); Table 12.1 adapted from Work teams in *American Psychologist*, Vol.45, No.2, February, American Psychological Association (Sundstrom, E., De Meuse, K. and Futrell, D. 1990); Figure 12.3 from Work teams in *American Psychologist*, Vol.45, No.2, February, American Psychological Association (Sundstrom, E., De Meuse, K. and Futrell, D. 1990); Table 12.4 from The art of building a car: the Swedish experience re-examined in *New Technology, Work and Employment*, Vol.6, No.2, Blackwell Publishing Ltd (Hammarstrom, O. and Lansbury, R. D. 1991); Chapter 12, p.414, Table from Communities of practice: the organizational frontier in *Harvard Business Review*, January–February, Harvard Business School Publishing Corporation (Wenger, E.C. and Snyder, W.M. 2000); Chapter 12, p.416, Figure from Measuring group work: findings and lessons from a European survey in *New Technology, Work and Employment*, Vol.16, No.2, Blackwell Publishing Ltd (Benders, J., Huijgem, F. and Pekruhl, U. 2001); Chapter 13, p.437, Figure Midvale Steel Company, Free Library of Philadelphia, Map Collection; Figure 13.2 from *The Realities of Work, 2nd Edition*, pub Palgrave, reproduced with permission of Palgrave Macmillan (Noon, M. and Blyton, P. 2002); Chapter 14, p.464, advertisement, Ward Executive Ltd; Chapter 14, p.470, Table from *Bosses in British Business*, pub Routledge and Kegan Paul, reprinted by permission of Thomson Publishing Services (Jervis, F. R. 1974); Table 14.2 adapted from *Organizational Behavior: Concepts and Applications*, reprinted by permission of Prentice-Hall, Inc. (Gray, J. L. and Starke, F. A. 1977); Figure 14.5 from *Organizational Theory, 3rd Edition*, reprinted by permission of Prentice-Hall, Inc. (Robbins, S. P. 1990); Chapter 14, p.483 and p.484 from Organigraphs: drawing how companies really work in *Harvard Business Review*, September–October, Harvard Business School Publishing Corporation (Mintzberg, H.J. and van der Heyden, L. 1999); Chapter 15, p.508, typographic layout of article global village: a weekly posting from cyberspace from *The Times* 7.10.00, NI Syndication; Figure 15.2 from *Creative Organization Theory*, reprinted by permission of Sage Publications, Inc. (Morgan, G. 1989); Figure 15.3 from *Management and Technology*, Crown copyright material is reproduced under Class Licence Number C01W0000039 with the permission of the Controller of HMSO and the Queen's Printer for Scotland (Woodward, J. 1958); Table 15.5 from Evolution and revolution as organizations grow in *Harvard Business Review*, Vol.76, No.3, Harvard Business School Publishing Corporation (Grainer, L.E. 1998); Chapter 15, p.532, Figure from Washington's mega-merger in *The Economist*, reprinted by permission of The Economist Newspaper Limited, London, 23.11.02; Figure 16.1 from *Organizational Behavior,1st Edition*, reprinted by permission of South-Western, a division of Thomson Learning (Daft, R. L. 2001); Table 16.1 from *Contemporary Strategy Analysis, 4th Edition*, Blackwell Publishing Ltd (Grant, R. M. 2002); Chapter 16, p.546, Figure from *Organising and Managing Work*, pub Financial Times/Prentice Hall, reprinted by permission of Pearson Education Ltd (Watson, T. J. 2002); Table 16.3 based on Chaos, non-linear systems and day-to-day management in *European Management Journal*, Vol.14, No.1, Elsevier (Glass, N. 1996); Table 16.4 developed by Moira Fischbacher; Table 16.5 from Networks and inter-organizational relations in *Management: A Critical Text*, by L. Fulop and S. Linstead, pub Macmillan Business, reproduced with permission of Palgrave Macmillan (Buttery, E., Fulop, L. and Buttery, A. 1999); Table 16.6 from Corporate strategy in the digital age in *Strategy+Business*, Issue 15, 2nd Quarter, Booz Allen Hamilton, www.strategy-business.com (Callahan, C. V. and Pasternack, B. A. 1999); Chapter 16, p.563, Figure from Spontaneous organization in *Directions: The Ashridge Journal*, Ashridge web document:/directions/2000-1/04, Ashridge (Brown, M. and Beech, D. 2000); Chapter 16, p.566, Figure from *Human Resource Management: A Strategic Introduction, 2nd Edition*, Blackwell Publishing Ltd (Mabey, C., Salaman, G. and Storey, J. 1998); Figure 17.1 from *Leadership Dilemmas, Grid Solutions*, pub Gulf Publishing Company, reprinted by permission of Grid International, Inc. (Blake, E. E. and McCanse, A. A. 1991); Table 17.3 from *Planning and Managing Change,* (P769), Block 4, Open University Business School, reprinted by permission of Derek S. Pugh (Pugh, D. S. 1986); Chapter 18, p.635, Table adapted from *Real Change Leaders: How You Can Create Growth and High Performance at Your Company*, Nicholas Brealey Publishing (Katzenbach, J. and The Real Change Team 1997); Figure 19.1 from *Organizational Culture and Leadership*, John Wiley & Sons, Inc. (Schein, E. H. 1985); Table 19.1 from Corporate culture: Definition, diagnosis and change in *International Review of Industrial and Organizational Psychology, Vol. 8, Chapter 7* edited by C. L. Cooper and I. T. Robertson, John Wiley & Sons Ltd (Furnham, A. and Gunter, B. 1993); Table 19.2 from *Cultures in Organizations: Three Perspectives*, Oxford University Press, Inc. (Martin, J. 1992); Table 19.3 from Cultural acumen for the global manager: lessons from the Project GLOBE in *Organizational Dynamics*, Vol.29, No.4, Elsevier (Javidan, M. and House, R. J. 2001); Figure 19.4 from The paradox of 'corporate culture': Reconciling ourselves to socialization in *California Management Review*, Vol.27, No.2, reprinted by permission of The Regents of the University of California (Pascale, R. T. 1985); Figure 19.5 from Corporate culture; the last frontier of control? in *Journal of Management Studies*, Vol.23, No.3, Blackwell Publishing Ltd (Ray, C. A. 1986); Figure 19.6 from Living with a superpower in *The Economist*, reprinted by permission of The Economist Newspaper Limited, London, 4.1.03; Figure 20.2 from Industrial relations and human resource management in *Human Resource Management: A Critical Text, 2nd Edition* edited by J. Storey, pub Thomson Learning, reprinted by permission of Thomson Publishing Services (Guest, D. 2001); Figure 20.4 from *Strategic Human Resource Management*, John Wiley & Sons, Inc. (Fombrun, C. J., Tichy, N. and Devanna, M. A. 1984); Table 20.4 from Personnel management: paradigms, practice and prospects in

Personnel Management in Britain edited by Keith Sisson, Blackwell Publishing Ltd (Sisson, K. 1994); Figure 20.5 from *Managing Human Assets*, pub The Free Press, copyright held by Michael Beer and Bert Spector, reprinted by permission of Michael Beer and Bert Spector (Beer, M., Spector, B., Lawrence, P.R., Quinn Mills, D. and Walton, R.E. 1984); Figure 20.6 from Human resource management: an agenda for the 1990s in *International Journal of Human Resource Management*, Vol.1, No.1, Taylor & Francis Ltd, http://www.tandf.co.uk/journals (Hendry, C. and Pettigrew, A.M. 1990); Tables 20.6 and 20.7 republished with permission of Academy of Management, from Linking competitive strategies with human resource management practices by Randall S. Schuler and Susan E. Jackson in *Academy of Management Executive*, Vol.9, No.3, 1987; permission conveyed through Copyright Clearance Center, Inc.; Figure 20.7 adapted from *Understanding the People and Performance Link: Unlocking the black box*, Chartered Institute of Personnel and Development (Purcell, J., Kinnie, N., Hutchinson, S., Rayton, B. and Swart, J. 2003); Table 20.8 from *European Human Resource Management in Transition*, pub Prentice Hall, reprinted by permission of Pearson Education Ltd (Sparrow, P. and Hiltrop, J.-M. 1994); Figure 21.2 from How to choose a leadership pattern in *Harvard Business Review*, Vol.37, March–April, reprinted in *Harvard Business Review*, May–June 1973, Harvard Business School Publishing Corporation (Tannenbaum, R. and Schmidt, W. H. 1958); Figure 22.2 and Table 22.3 from *Leadership and Decision-Making*, University of Pittsburgh Press (Vroom, V. H. and Yetton, P.W. 1973); Chapter 22, p.777, Table from What you don't know about making decisions in *Harvard Business Review*, September, Harvard Business School Publishing Corporation (Garvin, D.A. and Roberto, M.A. 2001); Table 23.1 adapted from Can marketing and manufacturing coexist? in *Harvard Business Review*, 55, September–October, Harvard Business School Publishing Corporation (Shapiro, B.S. 1977); Table 23.3 adapted from *Managing Through Organization*, pub Routledge, reprinted by permission of Thomson Publishing Services (Hales, C. 1993); Figure 23.4 from Support for a two-dimensional model of conflict behaviour in *Organizational Behaviour and Human Performance*, Vol.16, Elsevier (Ruble, T.H. and Thomas, K. 1976); Tables 23.4 and 23.6 from *Developing Management Skills for Europe*, pub Financial Times/Prentice Hall, reprinted by permission of Pearson Education Ltd (Whetton, D., Cameron, K. and Woods, M. 2000); Figure 23.5 from *Organizational Misbehaviour*, reprinted by permission of Sage Publications Ltd (Ackroyd, S. and Thompson, P. 1999); Table 23.5 republished with permission of Academy of Management, from Towards multidimensional values in teaching: The example of conflict behaviours by Kenneth W. Thomas in *Academy of Management Review*, July 1997; permission conveyed through Copyright Clearance Center, Inc.; Table 23.7 from *Joining Together: Group Theory and Group Skills*, Allyn and Bacon (Johnson, D. W. and Johnson, F. P. 1975); Figure 24.1 from *Power in Organizations*, reprinted by permission of HarperCollins Publishers, Inc. (Pfeffer, J. 1981); Tables 24.3, 24.4 and 24.9 from *Power, Politics and Organizational Change*, reprinted by permission of Sage Publications Ltd (Buchanan, D. and Badham, R. 1999); Chapter 24, p.849, Table based on Personality and Charisma in the US Presidency: A Psychological Theory of Leader Effectiveness in *Administrative Science Quarterly*, Vol.36, No.3, September, reprinted by permission of Administrative Science Quarterly, Cornell University (House, R.J., Spangler, W.D. and Wyocke, J. 1991).

We are grateful to the following for permission to reproduce cartoons:

Pages 24, 54 and 607, Calvin and Hobbes, © Watterson. Reprinted with permission of Universal Press Syndicate. All rights reserved; Pages 78, 109, 151, 265, 337, 402, 557, 636, 661, 699, 763 and 819, Dilbert, © copyright United Feature Syndicate, Inc. Reproduced by permission; Pages 116, 191 and 538, Alex by Peattie and Taylor, reprinted by permission of Alex office; Page 232, Herman, © Jim Unger. Distributed by United Media. Reproduced by permission; Pages 250 and 285, © Mike Shapiro, reprinted by permission of Mike Shapiro; Page 370, © The New Yorker Collection 1976 Lee Lorenz from cartoonbank.com. All rights reserved; Page 433, © 2003 Mick Stevens from cartoonbank.com. All rights reserved; Page 472, Moulson © Telegraph Group Ltd 2000, reprinted by permission of Telegraph Group Ltd; Page 473, Austin. Copyright Pressdram Ltd 2002. Reproduced by permission; Page 505, © The New Yorker Collection 1986 Dean Vietor from cartoonbank.com. All rights reserved; Page 509, © The New Yorker Collection 1986 Leo Cullum from cartoonbank.com. All rights reserved; Page 589 Farcus® is reprinted with permission from LaughingStock Licensing Inc., Ottawa, Canada. All rights reserved; Page 594, © The New Yorker Collection 1987 J.B. Handelsman from cartoonbank.com. All rights reserved; Page 674, © 2002 P.C. Vey. Originally appeared in *Harvard Business Review*. Used by permission. The Cartoon Bank; Page 740, published in *Harvard Business Review*, June 2001, reprinted by permission of Dave Carpenter; Page 755, reprinted with special permission of King Features Syndicate; Page 799, Cathy, © Cathy Guisewite. Reprinted with permission of Universal Press Syndicate. All rights reserved; Page 833, reprinted by permission of Tony Husband; Page 849, © The New Yorker Collection 1977 Dana Fradon from cartoonbank.com. All rights reserved.

We are grateful to the following for permission to reproduce photographs:

Page xxxi Calyx; Pages 4 (top) and 301 Baker Library, Harvard Business School; Page 4 (bottom) © Keith Hill, courtesy of Derek S. Pugh; Page 32 © The Guardian; Pages 33 and 280 North News and Pictures Ltd; Page 48 courtesy of Merrelyn Emery; Page 49 courtesy of The Tavistock Institute; Page 90 (top) courtesy of Eric Miller; Page 90 (bottom) courtesy of Mrs J. Evans; Pages 104 and 425 Associated Press Ltd; Page 105 Newspix, Nationwide News Pty Ltd; Pages 114, 145 (bottom), 165 (top), 220, 227 (top), 230, 253, 342 (left), 375 and 587 Archives of the History of American Psychology – The University of Akron; Page 117 courtesy of the Library of Congress; Page 120 courtesy of Fred Luthans; Page 122 courtesy of Albert Bandura; Page 128 courtesy of Chris Argyris; Page 145 (top) and 849 Mary Evans Picture Library; Page 149 courtesy of Hans Jürgen Eysenck; Page 161 Charles Horton Cooley, Bentley Historical Library, University of Michigan; Page 163 courtesy of Carl Rogers Memorial Library; Page 165 (bottom) courtesy of David C. McClelland; Page 194 photograph by Colin McDougall; Page 227 (bottom) photograph by Fabian Bachrach/Camera Press Ltd, London; Page 241 photo courtesy MIT Museum; Page 245 courtesy of Brandeis University; Page 247 courtesy of Clayton Paul Alderfer; Page 254 courtesy of Victor Vroom; Page 255 (top) courtesy of Lyman W. Porter; Page 255 (bottom) courtesy of Edward E. Lawler; Page 257 courtesy of Edwin A. Locke; Page 260 courtesy of Frederick Herzberg; Page 281 www.shoutpictures.com; Page 290, Figures 9.1, 9.2, 9.3 and 9.4 property of AT&T Archives. Reprinted with permission of AT&T; Pages 296, 342 (right) and 731 courtesy of University of Michigan; Page 304 courtesy of Bruce W. Truckman; Page 332 courtesy of the Harvard University Archives; Page 337 courtesy of R. Meredith Belbin; Page 365 courtesy of the University of Oklahoma; Page 373 courtesy of Mrs F. Asch; Page 395 Armstrong Healthcare Ltd; Page 407 © Tom Wagner/CORBIS SABA; Page 424 The Times/John Cassidy reprinted by permission of NI Syndication; Page 429 Frederick Winslow Taylor Collection, S. C. Williams Library, Stevens Institute of Technology, Hoboken, NJ, USA; Pages 431 and 432 Bethlehem Steel Corporation; Page 435 © Underwood & Underwood/CORBIS; Page 437 (top) Smithsonian Institution, National Museum of American History; Page 437 (bottom) Special Collections, Stevens Institute of Technology, Library; Pages 438 and 440 Ford Motor Company; Page 442 popperfoto.com; Page 443 The Detroit Institute of Arts; Page 480 Royal Bank of Scotland/Peter Bentley; Pages 486 and 487 Philip G. Zimbardo, Stanford University; Page 490 courtesy of Henry Mintzberg; Page 504 copyright Leif Geiges, Staufen, reproduced by permission of Verena Gieges, Staufen; Page 510 Ancient Art and Architecture Collection Ltd; Page 514 Cason Hall & Co.; Page 521 © NI Syndication, London; Page 523 Archives Service Center, University of Pittsburgh; Page 524 courtesy of Charles Perrow; Page 527 courtesy of George McDonald Stalker; Pages 528 and 634 Harvard Business School; Page 541 (bottom) courtesy of Charles C. Snow; Pages 546 and 852 courtesy of Jeffrey Pfeffer; Page 574 Chris Bourchier; Page 575 Sinopix Photo Agency; Page 578 courtesy of Warren G. Bennis; Pages 588 and 644 courtesy of Edgar Schein; Page 591 Grid International, Inc; Page 612 © Katz, Katz Pictures; Page 643 (bottom) courtesy of Terrance Deal; Page 663 courtesy of Geert Hofstede; Page 688 (top) courtesy of Randall S. Schuler; Page 688 (bottom) courtesy of Susan E. Jackson; Page 700 Personnel Today; Page 703 Mousetrap Media Ltd; Page 712 Reuters News Picture Service; Page 713 The Daily Telegraph; Page 721 courtesy of The Ohio State University; Page 734 courtesy of Fred Fiedler; Page 736 (bottom) courtesy of Kenneth Blanchard; Page 736 (top) courtesy of Paul Hersey; Page 761 (top) courtesy of Carnegie Mellon University; Page 761 (middle) courtesy of James G. March; Page 767™ & © Boeing. Used under licence; Page 772 Yale Pictorial Records and Collections, Manuscripts and Archives, Yale University Library; Page 804 courtesy of Kenneth Thomas; Page 818 courtesy of Arlie Russell Hoschschild.

Anglian Water for an extract from their 2003 Vision and Values Statement; BBC Worldwide Limited for an extract from 'Letting Go' by Nick Clarke published in *20 Steps to Better Management* © Nicholson McBride 1996; the authors David Butcher and Penny Harvey (Cranfield School of Management) and People Management for the questionnaire 'Be Upstanding' published in *People Management*, Vol. 5, no 13; the author Tony Clarry and People Management for an extract adapted from 'Premium Bonding' published in *People Management*, Vol. 5 no 17; Curtis Brown Group Limited, London on behalf of Edmund Hillary for an extract from *Noting Ventured, Nothing Win* by E. Hillary © E Hillary 1975; Professor Jack Denfeld Wood, IMD, Lausanne, Switzerland, for the activity illustrating the generation of alternate hypotheses along different behavioural levels of analysis; The Economist for extracts from 'Jury Science' published in *The Economist* 8 July 1989 © The Economist Newspaper Limited, London 1989, 'Negotiating by Email' published in *The Economist* 8 April 2000 © The Economist Newspaper Limited, London 2000, and 'Military Revolutions' published in *The Economist* 20 July 2002 © The Economist Newspaper Limited, London 2002; Elsevier for an extract from *Studies in Machiavellianism* by Richard Christie and Florence Geiss, 1970; HarperCollins Publishers Limited and the author's agent for extracts from *21 Dog Years: Doing Time at Amazon.com* by Mike Daisey © Mike Daisey 2002; Harvard Business Review for an extract adapted from 'What Effective General Managers Really Do' by John P. Kotter published in *Harvard Business Review*, Vol. 77 no 2, 1999; Houghton Mifflin Company for an extract from *Practicing Management* edited by Ricky W. Griffin and Thomas C. Head, 1987; McGraw Hill for an extract from *Experiencing Social Psychology: Readings and Projects* by A. Pines and C. Malash, 1979; New Scientist for an extract from 'Boozing with the Boss' published in *New Scientist* 26 January 2002; Origin Publishing Limited for an extract from 'Irresistible Science of the Super-Sellers' by Gillian Drummond published in *Focus* in November 1994, www.focusmag.co.uk; Pearson Education Inc. for extracts from *Organizational Behaviour in New Zealand* by G. Elkin and K. Inkson, and 'Decision Types' published in *Experiencing Management* by Marshall Sashkin and William C. Morris, 1987; Personnel Today for extracts from 'Blurred Boundaries' by Paul Simpson published in *Personnel*

Today 16 November 1999 © Personnel Today, and 'Back on Song' by Jane Lewis published in *Personnel Today* 19 November 2002 © Personnel Today; Sage Publications for extracts from 'The Autonomy of Teams in the Car Industry – A Cross National Comparison' by Thomas Murakami published in *Work, Employment and Society*, Vol. 11 no 4, 1997, *Power, Politics and Organizational Change: Winning the Turf Game* by D. Buchanan and R. Badham, 1999, and *Introduction to Counselling Skills* by Richard Nelson-Jones, 2000; Sage Publications Inc. for an extract from *Working Across Cultures: Applications and Exercises* by Martin J. Gannon, 2001; and the author Ralph Windle for his poem 'The Job Description' from *The Bottom Line by Bertie Ramsbottom*, reprinted in *The Poetry of Business Life* edited by Ralph Windle published by Berrett-Koehler USA 1994, dis. Amazon.com.

We are grateful to the Financial Times Limited for permission to reprint the following material:

A speedier route from order to camcorder, © *Financial Times*, 12 February 2003; DirecTV is about changing one whole model of News Corp's output in the US, © *Financial Times*, 12 February 2003.

In some instances we have been unable to trace the owners of copyright material and we would appreciate any information that would enable us to do so.

Chapter 1 Prologue

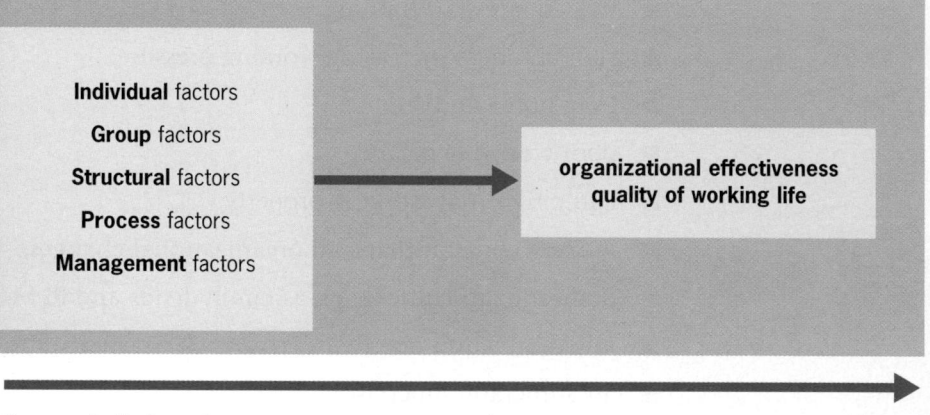

A field map of the organizational behaviour terrain

Key concepts

organizational behaviour	behaviour
organization	behaviourism
controlled performance	positivism
organizational dilemma	action
organizational effectiveness	cognitive psychology
balanced scorecard	phenomenology
operational definition	social construction of reality

Learning outcomes

When you have read this chapter, you should be able to define those key concepts in your own words, and you should also be able to:

1. Explain the importance of an understanding of organizational behaviour.
2. Explain and illustrate the central dilemma of organizational design.
3. Understand the need for explanations of behaviour in organizations that take account of relationships between factors at different levels of analysis.
4. Identify the features that differentiate the natural and social sciences, and the implications of this differentiation.

What is organizational behaviour?

Consider the last time you had a 'bad experience' in, say, a shop, a restaurant or a hotel. The person you dealt with was abrupt and unpleasant, and you left feeling angry, never to return.

What is the explanation? We could blame the 'wicked personality' of that shop assistant, waiter or receptionist, but there are other possibilities. Your bad experience could be due to:

- inadequate staff training;

- staff absences increasing working pressure;

- long hours and fatigue;

- poor work–life balance;

- equipment not working properly;

- anxiety about anticipated organizational changes;

- domestic difficulties such as family feuds and ill health;

- low motivation due to low pay;

- an autocratic supervisor;

- a dispute with colleagues created an uncomfortable working atmosphere;

- and you came in at the wrong moment.

Your treatment could be explained by a range of individual, group, organizational and contextual factors arising in the workplace and beyond. The customer walks away from all this. As a member of that organization, these are the issues that you have to deal with.

Organizational behaviour is now recognized as a significant field of investigation in its own right, drawing from across the social sciences. Is this a dry, theoretical subject divorced from day-to-day practical concerns? No. Your 'bad experience' suggests that an understanding of organizational behaviour has many practical applications.

Organizational behaviour: the study of the structure, functioning and performance of organizations, and the behaviour of groups and individuals within them.

Derek Pugh's (1971, p. 9) influential definition of the field of **organizational behaviour** is shown in the margin. The definition of a field of study identifies its scope, and the themes, questions, issues and problems that it seeks to address and to explain. This is a controversial matter as different commentators have different ideas about the appropriate scope of the field. This controversy is reflected in the range of titles to be found in the literature: organization theory, industrial sociology, organizational psychology, organizational analysis, organization studies. Organization theory and industrial sociology tend to concentrate on macro-level studies of groups and organizations. Organizational psychology tends to focus on micro-level studies of individual behaviour. Organizational analysis tends to adopt a practical rather than a theoretical perspective, although analysis is, of course, dependent on theory. Organization studies is a term which is increasingly used to reflect a significant widening of the range of issues and perspectives that this field embraces (Clegg, Hardy and Nord, 1996).

Pugh's (1971) definition covers macro-organizational and micro-individual concerns. Despite what other commentators suggest (Rollinson and Broadfield, 2002), the scope of organizational behaviour has traditionally been specified in broad terms. The subject has more recently been defined in this inclusive sense as:

the interdisciplinary body of knowledge and field of research, concerned with how formal organizations, behaviour of people within organizations, and salient features of their context and environment, evolve and take shape, why all these things happen the way they do, and what purposes they serve. (Sorge and Warner, 1997, p. xii)

Organizational behaviour enjoys a controversial relationship with management practice. Our text is not alone in considering practical applications of theory, and most American and some British texts (e.g., Mullins, 2002) adopt a managerialist perspective. However, this focus on management is regarded by some commentators as inappropriate, for at least four reasons, concerning power inequalities, the subject agenda, multiple stakeholders and fashion victims.

Power inequalities: Management is an elite occupational group, with access to information and resources beyond those available to mere employees. Organizations typically display inequalities of power and reward. Why should a field of study support exclusively the affluent powerful? Organizational behaviour used in this way becomes a 'servant of power'. A managerialist perspective on organizational behaviour encourages a non-critical approach to management practice.

Subject agenda: A managerialist perspective focuses on a narrow range of issues of perceived importance to managers, concerning management control and organizational performance. This pushes a range of other topics off the agenda, such as theoretical analyses that have limited practical application, topics significant to particular individuals and groups, and arguments critical of the managerial role. These topics can, however, be important to the wider community.

Multiple stakeholders: Management is only one social group with a stake in the behaviour of organizations and their members. An understanding of this subject is of value to employees, groups subjected to discrimination on a range of criteria, trade unionists, customers, suppliers, investors, and also to the wider community. Organizational behaviour is a subject of broad social and economic significance.

Fashion victims: Management is prone to pursue the latest in thinking and technique, in the interests of improving personal and organizational performance. A managerialist perspective on organizational behaviour, however, encourages a focus on current fashion trends. Some fashions survive while others quickly fade. As some fads turn out to be old ideas freshly packaged, it is important to consider these developments in the context of the history of the subject, to reach an informed assessment.

This text adopts the 'multiple-stakeholders-broad-agenda' view of organizational behaviour, developing an eclectic social science perspective and avoiding a managerialist stance. This does not mean that practical applications are ignored. However, readers are encouraged to take a critical perspective on research, theory and applications, rather than simply to accept a managerialist or a social scientific point of view.

Management is an elite group?

A salary survey carried out by the magazine *Management Today* in 2001 revealed the following international comparisons for average annual senior executive pay (sterling):

America	£993,000	France	£382,000
Britain	£509,000	Sweden	£311,000
Australia	£457,000	Germany	£298,000
Japan	£385,000		

In contrast, the average annual wage of a manufacturing worker is:

America	£31,000	France	£24,500
Germany	£26,000	Britain	£20,000

These averages obscure some extremely high salaries. The chief executive of Vodaphone had an annual income in 2001, including bonuses and share options, of approximately UK£13 million. In 2002, according to Walt Disney's annual report (January 2003), two executives, Michael Eisner and Bob Iger, between them got more than US$24 million in pay and bonuses.

Based on Mike Ingram, 'Pay survey highlights growth of inequality', *World Socialist Web Site*, July 2001 (www.wsws.org).

Fritz Jules
Roethlisberger
(1898–1974)

Derek S. Pugh
(b. 1930)

Jack Wood (1995) notes that the term 'organizational behaviour' was first used by Fritz Roethlisberger in the late 1950s, because it suggested a wider scope than human relations. The term 'behavioural sciences' was first used to describe a Ford Foundation research programme at Harvard in 1950, and in 1957 the Human Relations Group at Harvard (previously the Mayo Group) became the Organizational Behaviour Group. Organizational behaviour was recognized as a subject at Harvard in 1962, with Roethlisberger as the first area head (Roethlisberger, 1977). The first British appointments to chairs in organizational behaviour went to Professor Derek Pugh at London Business School in England in 1970 and to Professor David Weir at Glasgow University Business School in Scotland in 1974.

Organizations, of course, do not 'behave'. Only people can be said to behave. The term 'organizational behaviour' is a linguistic shorthand which refers to the activities and interactions of people in organizational settings such as hospitals, workshops, banks and police stations. Organizations pervade our physical, social, cultural, political and economic environment, offering jobs, providing goods and services, presenting us with substantial portions of our built environment, and sometimes contributing to the fabric of whole communities. However, we tend to take organizations for granted precisely because they affect everything that we do. Such familiarity can lead to an underestimation of their impact.

The study of organizations is multidisciplinary, drawing from psychology, social psychology, sociology, economics and political science, and to a lesser extent from history, geography and anthropology. The study of organizational behaviour has become a distinct discipline, with its own research traditions, academic journals and international networks. This is an area where the contributions of the different social and behavioural sciences can be integrated. The extent of that integration, however, is weak. 'Multidisciplinary' means drawing from a number of different subjects. 'Interdisciplinary' implies that different subjects collaborate. Full interdisciplinary collaboration is rare.

Organizational behaviour – a coherent subject area?

Management textbooks frequently state as fact that organizational behaviour is an inter-disciplinary field. It is not. It is in no way inter-disciplinary; multi-disciplinary perhaps, but not inter-disciplinary. OB is not a coherent field. It is a general area that encompasses thinking and research from numerous disciplines. It draws its material from psychology, sociology, anthropology, economics, the arts and humanities, law and medicine. Organizational behaviour is in reality a hodgepodge of various subjects; a collection of loosely related or even unrelated streams of scholarly and not-so-scholarly research. It is neither a discipline, nor is it a business function. And that makes it an anomalous area of management study.

From Jack Wood, 'Mastering management: organizational behaviour', *Financial Times*, supplement, 3 November 1995, p. 3.

Organization: a social arrangement for achieving controlled performance in pursuit of collective goals.

Stop and Criticize

At various points in this book, we will confront the issue of how terms are to be defined. This problem arises in various contexts, concerning, for example, what we mean by apparently straightforward terms like 'personality', or 'group', or 'conflict'. We must first address the problem of what we mean by the term **organization**.

Why should the term 'organization' be difficult to define? Consider the following list. Which of these you would call an organization, and which not, identifying the reasons for your decision in each case?

- A chemicals processing company
- The Jamieson family next door
- Leicester General Hospital
- A local street corner gang
- Clan Buchanan
- The local squash club
- A babysitting circle
- A famine relief charity
- The Azande tribe
- A primary school

Why are you uncomfortable about calling some of the items on this list 'organizations'? Perhaps you considered size as a factor? Or the provision of goods and services for sale? Or the existence of paid employment? If we define the term too widely, it can become meaningless.

The definition of organization in the margin should help to explain why you perhaps found it awkward to describe a street corner gang as an organization, but not a hospital, a company or a club. What about families, tribes, clans and babysitting circles? Let us examine this definition more closely.

Social arrangements

To say that organizations are social arrangements is simply to observe that they are groups of people who interact with each other as a consequence of their membership. However, all of the items on our list are social arrangements. This alone is not a distinctive feature.

Collective goals

Common membership of an organization implies shared objectives. Organizations are more likely to exist where individuals acting alone cannot achieve goals that are considered worthwhile pursuing. Once again, all of the items on our list are social arrangements for the pursuit of collective goals, so this is not a distinctive feature either.

Controlled performance

Organizations are concerned with performance in the pursuit of goals. The performance of an organization as a whole determines its survival. The performance of a department determines the amount of resources allocated to it. The performance of individuals determines pay and promotion prospects. Not any level of performance will do, however. We live in a world in which the resources available to us are not sufficient to meet all of our desires. We have to make the most efficient use of those scarce resources. Levels of performance, of individuals, departments and organizations, are therefore tied to standards which determine what counts as inadequate, satisfactory or good.

It is necessary to control performance, to ensure that it is either good enough, or that something is being done to improve it. An organization's members thus have to perform these control functions as well as the operating tasks required to fulfil the collective purpose of the organization. The need for controlled performance leads to a deliberate and ordered allocation of functions, or division of labour, between organizational members.

Admission to membership of organizations is controlled, usually with reference to standards of performance: will the person be able to do the job? The price of failure to perform to standard is usually loss of membership. The need for controlled performance leads to the establishment of authority relationships. The controls only work where members comply with the orders of those responsible for performing the control functions.

To what extent are the Jamieson family, the Azande tribe or the street gang preoccupied with determining and monitoring performance standards and correcting deviations? To what extent does their existence depend on their ability to meet predetermined targets? To what extent do they allocate control functions to their members, programme their activities and control their relationships with other members? The way in which you answer these questions may explain your readiness or reluctance to describe them as organizations.

It is the *preoccupation with performance* and the *need for control* which distinguish organizations from other social arrangements.

Stop and Criticize

In what ways could the Jamieson family be concerned with performance and control?

How is membership of a street gang determined? What do you have to do to become a member? What behaviours lead to exclusion from gang membership?

Are organizations different from other social arrangement in degree only, and not different in kind? Are all social groupings not concerned with setting, monitoring and correcting standards of behaviour and performance (defined in different ways)?

The way in which one defines a phenomenon determines ways of looking at and studying it. The study of organizational behaviour is characterized by the view that organizations should be studied from a range of different perspectives. In other words, it is pointless to dispute which is the 'correct' definition. The American management guru, Peter Drucker, presents another angle of view, arguing that organizations are like symphony orchestras. Information technology, he argues, reduces the need for manual and clerical skills, and increases demand for 'knowledge workers'. Like musicians, Drucker sees knowledge workers exploring outlets for their creative talent, seeking interesting challenges, enjoying the stimulation of working with other specialists. There are implications in this perspective for individual careers, organization structures and management styles (Golzen, 1989).

One author who has popularized the 'multiple perspectives' view of organizations is the Canadian academic Gareth Morgan. In *Images of Organizations* (1997), he offers eight metaphors which invite us to see organizations through a series of different lenses, as:

- machines;

- biological organisms;

- human brains;

- cultures or sub-cultures;

- political systems;

- psychic prisons;

- systems of change and transformation;

- instruments of domination.

Morgan presents these contrasting metaphors as ways of thinking about organizations, as approaches to the 'diagnostic reading' and 'critical evaluation' of organizational phenomena. The 'organization as machine' metaphor suggests an analysis of its component elements and their interaction. The 'psychic prison' metaphor, in contrast, implies an analysis of how the organization constrains and shapes the thinking and intellectual growth of its members. He suggests how, by using these different metaphors to understand their complex characteristics, it becomes possible to identify novel ways in which to design and manage organizations.

It is necessary, therefore, to view critically our definition of the concept of organization. There is value in adopting other perspectives and ways of seeing.

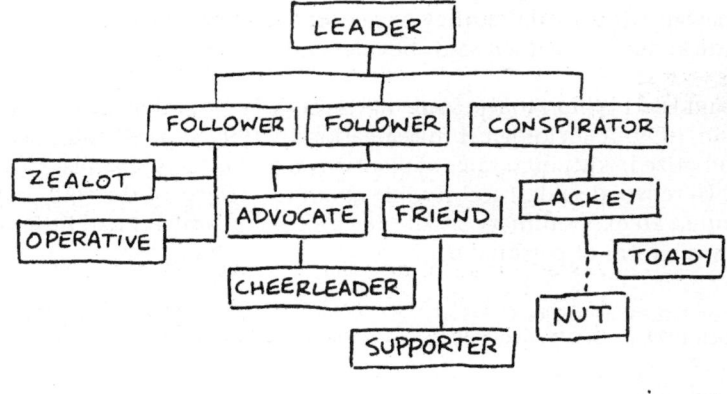

Redrawn from 'Organization chart' by Mark Litzler, *Harvard Business Review*, January 2003.

Why study organizational behaviour?

If we eventually destroy this planet, the cause will not lie with technology or weaponry. We will have destroyed it with ineffective organizations. The ultimate limitation on human aspirations lies not in intellect or in technology, but in our ability to work together. The cause of most major disasters (Bhopal, Chernobyl, Three Mile Island, Challenger Shuttle) can be traced to organizational factors as well as (if not contributing to) technical problems.

If we destroy this planet

Why did Joseph Hazelwood, in 1999, agree to spend five summers collecting rubbish in Alaska? On 24 March 1989, the tanker *Exxon Valdez* hit a reef in Prince William Sound, leaking 11 million gallons of crude oil into the sea off Alaska. This was the worst environmental disaster in American history, fouling 1,300 miles of coastline and damaging 23 species of local wildlife. The owners and crew of the vessel attracted global condemnation. First reports of the disaster blamed the Captain, Joseph Hazelwood: the *New York Times* headline read, 'Skipper Was Drunk'. He was harassed by journalists, received death threats, was fired by Exxon and was charged with criminal damage. *Time* magazine, however, argued that the evidence revealed a 'wider web of accountability', including organizational factors (which also contributed to the slow pace of the clean-up operation):

1. There was no clear evidence to confirm that Hazelwood was drunk when the ship ran aground. Although he had a history of alcohol abuse, crewmates said he was sober.

2. Although Exxon officially banned alcohol from its ships, it supplied low alcohol beer to tanker crewmen. Hazelwood claimed to have drunk two bottles before 9.00 pm on the eve of the accident, which took place while he was asleep at 12.10 am.

3. After the accident, Hazelwood adjusted the engines to keep the vessel stable against the reef, avoiding further spill and maybe saving lives; the coastguard praised his action.

4. Exxon had cut the *Valdez* crew sharply, arguing that new technology made this possible, leaving fewer sailors working longer hours; fatigue may have contributed to the disaster.

5. The Second Mate, who should have been piloting the vessel, was exhausted and asleep. The 'pilotage endorsement' of the Third Mate, who had control of the vessel in the Sound, was disputed.

6. The acting Helmsman had been promoted to Able Seaman one year earlier from his job as Room Steward and waiter in the gallery.

7. The coastguards failed to monitor the *Valdez* after it veered to avoid ice. They blamed this lapse on the weather, poor equipment and the 'change of shift preoccupations of a watchman'. The coastguards argued that they were not required to track ships as far as the reef which the *Valdez* struck; but the seamen said they depended on the coastguards.

Exxon paid US$1 billion to the State of Alaska in 1991, and made compensation payments to 82 Eyak Indians in 1999. A sociological investigation in 1999 showed that local people remained depressed and traumatized, with high rates of alcoholism and other social ills, and were still catching deformed salmon. Hazelwood said: 'I feel terrible about the effects of the spill, but I'm just an ordinary fellow caught up in an extraordinary situation – a situation which I had little control over.' His rubbish collection was a form of personal penance.

Based on Richard Behar, 'Joe's bad trip', *Time*, 24 July 1989, pp. 54–9; 'The Exxon Valdez: stains that remain', *The Economist*, 20 March 1999, p. 63; Giles Whittell, 'Exxon challenges payout a decade after Valdez spill', *The Times*, 25 March 1999, p. 20.

Groups can achieve much more than individuals acting alone. Humans, like many other creatures on this planet, are social animals. We achieve psychological satisfaction and material gain from organized activity. Organizations, in their recruitment and other publicity materials, like you to think that they are 'one big happy family' working towards the same ends. Everyone is a team player, shooting towards the same goals. Organizations, of course, do not have goals. People have goals. Collectively, the members of an organization may be making biscuits, curing patients or educating students, but individual members also pursue a variety of personal goals. Senior managers may decide on objectives and attempt to get others to agree with them by calling them an 'organizational mission' or 'corporate strategy', but they are still the goals of the people who determined them in the first place.

Organizations can mean different things to those who use them and who work in them, because they are significant personal and social sources of:

Organizational dilemma: the question of how to reconcile potential inconsistency between individual needs and aspirations on the one hand and the collective purpose of the organization on the other.

- money and physical resource;

- meaning, relevance, purpose;

- order and stability;

- security, support, protection;

- status, prestige, self-esteem, self-confidence;

- power, authority, control.

The goals pursued by individual members of an organization can be quite different from the collective purpose of their organized activity. This creates a central practical and theoretical **organizational dilemma** in the design and study of organizations.

Forces of light, forces of darkness

From the beginning, the forces of light and the forces of darkness have polarized the field of organizational analysis, and the struggle has been protracted and inconclusive. The forces of darkness have been represented by the mechanical school of organizational theory – those who treat the organization as machine. This school characterizes organizations in terms of such things as: centralized authority, clear lines of authority, specialization and expertise, marked division of labour, rules and regulations, and clear separation of staff and line.

The forces of light, which by mid-20th century came to be characterized as the human relations school, emphasizes people rather than machines, accommodations rather than machine-like precision, and draws its inspiration from biological systems rather than engineering systems. It has emphasized such things as: delegation of authority, employee autonomy, trust and openness, concerns with the 'whole person', and interpersonal dynamics.

From Charles Perrow, 'The short and glorious history of organizational theory', *Organizational Dynamics*, Summer, 1973.

Organizations are social arrangements in which people strive to achieve control over resources in order to produce goods and services efficiently. However, organizations are also political systems in which some individuals exert control over others. Power to define the collective purposes or goals of organizations is not evenly distributed. One of the main mechanisms of organizational control is hierarchy of authority. It is widely accepted (often with reluctance) that managers have the right to make the decisions while lower-level employees are obliged to comply, or leave.

A concern with performance leads to rules and procedures, and to jobs that are simple and monotonous. These features simplify the tasks of planning, organizing and co-ordinating the efforts of large numbers of people. This efficiency drive, however, conflicts with the desire for freedom of expression, autonomy, creativity and self-development. It is difficult to design organizations that are efficient in using resources and also in developing human potential. Many of the 'human' problems of organizations arise from conflicts between individual needs and the constraints imposed in the interests of collective purpose. Attempts to control and co-ordinate human behaviour are thus often self-defeating.

That is a pessimistic view. Organizations are social arrangements, designed by people who can also change them. Organizations can be repressive and stifling, but they can also be designed to provide opportunities for self-fulfilment and individual expression. The point is, the human consequences depend on how organizations are designed and run.

Happy cows give more milk

Clarence H. Eckles, in his book *Dairy Cattle and Milk Production* (Macmillan, New York, 1956, pp. 332–3), identifies a number of methods for maximizing milk production:

1. Cows become accustomed to a regular routine; disturbing this routine disturbs them and causes a decrease in milk production.

2. Attendants should come into close contact with the cows, and it is important that the best of relations exist between the cows and keepers.

3. The cows should not be afraid of the attendants.

4. Cows should never be hurried.

5. Chasing cows with dogs or driving them on the run should never be allowed.

6. In the barn, attendants must work quietly; loud shouting or quick movements upset cows and cause them to restrict production.

Based on Jerry L. Gray and Frederick A. Starke, *Organizational Behaviour: Concepts and Applications*, Merrill Publishing, Columbus, OH (third edition), 1984, p. 14.

A field map of the organizational behaviour terrain

How can human behaviour in organizational settings be explained? To answer this question, we will develop a model of organizational behaviour to provide a guide to the content of the text. In other words, we will construct a 'field map' of the organizational behaviour terrain. A text has to cover individual topics one at a time. In practice, these discrete topics overlap. These interrelationships can be seen more clearly when we attempt to explain actual events.

Figure 1.1 shows an outline of our field map. Organizations do not operate in a vacuum, but are influenced in various ways by their wider *context*, represented by the outer box on the map. One approach to understanding those influences is through 'PESTLE analysis', which explores the **P**olitical, **E**conomic, **S**ocial, **T**echnological, **L**egal and **E**cological forces impinging on the organization and its members. These are explored in chapters 2 and 3.

The map shows that we want to explain two sets of factors, *organizational effectiveness* and *quality of working life*, represented by the right-hand box. There are five sets of factors which potentially provide those explanations. These concern *individual*, *group*, *structural*, *process* and *management* factors, which are explored in Parts 2 to 6, and which are represented by the left-hand box. Finally, we cannot consider organizations as static entities. Organizations and their members have plans for the future which influence actions today. Past events shape current perceptions and actions, and it is necessary to explain behaviours with reference to their *location in time*, represented by the arrow at the bottom of the map.

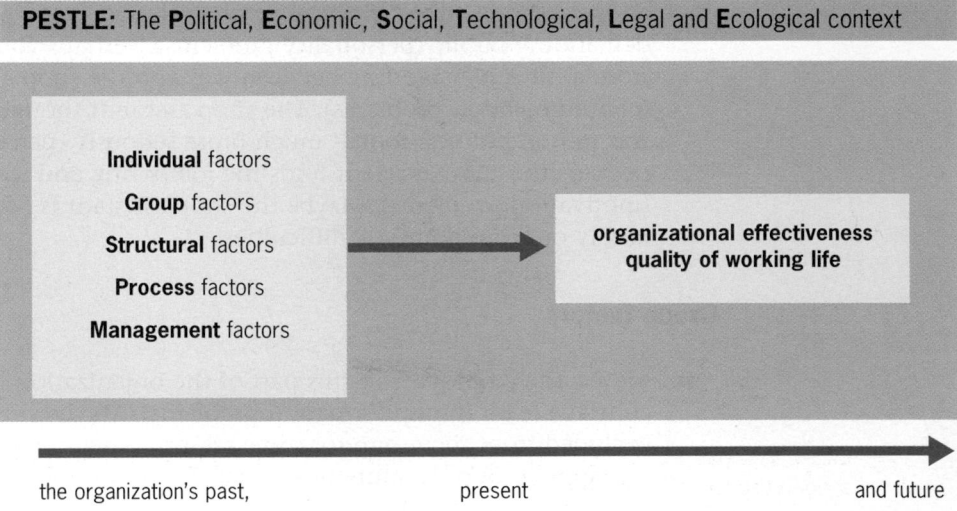

Figure 1.1: A field map of the organizational behaviour terrain

The atmosphere just isn't the same any more, and the place is losing customers. Staff in the bar or restaurant that you frequent are less helpful and friendly than they used to be. The quality of service that you receive has declined sharply. Why?

Use the field map in figure 1.1 as a source of possible explanations for this deterioration in performance. Can you blame context factors, new technology, particular individuals, aspects of teamworking, organization structure, recent changes to the culture, human resource management practices, or management style? Maybe the cause of the problem lies with a combination of factors?

Let us return to the 'bad experience' you had earlier in the chapter. We now have a framework with which to develop explanations. Your treatment is a key dimension of organizational effectiveness – quality of customer service. Let us assume we are dealing with a shop assistant. The map allows us to suggest the following *possible* explanations.

Context factors

■ Maybe the store is facing competition, sales have collapsed, the store is closing next month, and the loyal shop assistant is bitter about being made redundant (economic problems). Perhaps closure is threatened because the local population is declining, thus reducing sales (social problems). Perhaps the government faces European Union pressure for a new 'safe food tax' on retail outlets, making the cost structure of this store unviable (political problems). Maybe new 'point of sale' equipment has made staff anxious about their poor understanding of computer systems (technology problems).

Individual factors

■ Maybe the shop assistant is not coping with the demands of the job because training has not been provided (learning problems). Maybe this assistant is not suited to the kind of work that involves interaction with a demanding public (personality problems). Perhaps your treatment resulted from a misunderstanding between you and the shop assistant (communication problems). The shop assistant thought your complaint was minor, but you took it much more seriously (perception problems). Or perhaps the shop assistant finds the job boring and lacks challenge (motivation problems). Maybe the shop assistant is having personal, family or other domestic difficulties.

Group factors

■ Maybe the employees in this part of the organization have not formed a cohesive team (group formation problems). Maybe this shop assistant is excluded from the group for some reason (a newcomer, perhaps) and is unhappy (group structure problems). The informal norm for dealing with awkward customers like you is to be awkward in return, and this assistant is just 'playing by the rules' (group process problems). The organization may have introduced a new team approach without thinking through the training, supervision and pay issues (teamworking problems).

Structural factors

■ Perhaps the organization structure is slow and bureaucratic, and the shop assistant is anxiously waiting for a long-standing issue to be resolved. Maybe there is concern about the way in which work is allocated. Perhaps the unit manager is unable to deal with problems without referring them to a regional manager, who doesn't understand local issues. Maybe the supervisor has too many responsibilities and is too distant from the shop assistants, or perhaps a 'working supervisor' gets in the way. Perhaps the organization structure was suitable when the store opened ten years ago, but not for today's pace of business change and more demanding customers (structural problems).

Process factors

■ Perhaps the shop assistant is suffering from 'initiative fatigue' from the many changes introduced in recent years (change problems). Maybe communication problems and conflict with another unit have not been resolved (organization development problems). Perhaps the shop assistant is antagonistic towards many of this organization's taken-for-granted norms, processes and ways of working (organization culture problems). Maybe the shop assistant feels let down by the reward, training, promotion and career development systems (human resource management problems).

Management factors

■ Maybe the shop assistant is annoyed at the autocratic behaviour of the unit manager (leadership style problems). Perhaps the shop assistant feels that management has made decisions without consulting employees who have useful information and ideas (management decision-making problems). Maybe management has inadvertently created conflict between members of staff, and is not actively taking steps to address it (conflict problems). Perhaps managers and other staff have been playing 'power games' which have damaged the shop assistant in some way (politics problems).

This rehearsal of *possible* causes for your bad experience demonstrates a number of features of explanations of organizational behaviour.

First, it is always tempting to assume that the individual (our shop assistant) is to blame. However, it should be clear that this assumption will often be false. We need to look beyond such simple explanations and consider factors at different levels of analysis: individual, group, organization, management, the wider context.

Second, it is also tempting to look for single or main causes of organizational behaviour. However, it should also be clear that behaviour is influenced by a wide range of factors which in combination contribute to organizational effectiveness and the experience of work.

Third, while it is comparatively easy, and also helpful, to distinguish these factors and deal with them individually for the purposes of explanation and analysis, in practice they are interrelated. For example, in a crisis, or in a period of high uncertainty, some individuals may have a preference for a more directive style of management, particularly if that means fast and decisive action to restore order and predictability. So in this setting, we need to consider relationships between context factors, individual factors and management factors. These relationships are not shown in figure 1.1 (because they would make it look untidy).

Fourth, while this looks like a simple 'cause and effect' diagram, in practice the arrow between the two inside boxes also runs the other way. On the one hand, we might regard those individual, group, structural, process and managerial factors as **independent variables**, and organizational effectiveness and quality of working life as **dependent variables**. But the reverse can also be the case. For example, it is reasonable to assume that high organizational effectiveness will have an impact on individual motivation, on group cohesiveness and performance, on organization structure and culture, and perhaps on management style. This and the previous point emphasize the need for systemic thinking: we need to be aware of the interrelationships between these sets of factors.

It is necessary to give further consideration to the two factors we wish to explain: organizational effectiveness and quality of working life. The term **organizational effectiveness** is controversial because an organization's many stakeholders have different definitions of what counts as 'effectiveness'. A *stakeholder* (see glossary) is anyone with an interest, or stake, in the actions of the organization and its members. We thus have to consider internal and external stakeholders.

Independent variable: the factor which is manipulated by the researcher to discover what effect this has on another factor or variable.

Dependent variable: the factor whose behaviour is to be explained in terms of how it depends on some other factor.

Organizational effectiveness: a multidimensional concept defined differently by different stakeholders, using a range of quantitative and qualitative measures.

Stop and Criticize

Consider the institution in which you are currently studying. List the various internal and external stakeholders. Identify how you think each stakeholder would define 'organizational effectiveness' for this institution. Why the differences?

For commercial organizations, one obvious definition of effectiveness is 'profit'. But this is problematic for at least two reasons. First, timescale has to be considered, as actions to improve short-term profits may damage long-term profitability. Second, some organizations forgo profit, at least in the short to medium term, in the interests of gaining market share, which contributes to corporate survival, growth and stability of operations and employment. Shareholders want a return on investment, customers want quality products or services at reasonable prices, managers want high-flying careers, most employees want decent pay, good working conditions, development and promotion opportunities and job security.

Environmental groups want organizations to conserve buildings and woodland, reduce toxic emissions, traffic and noise levels, and so on. Organizational effectiveness is a slippery concept, and it has been difficult to demonstrate clearly the links between organization and management practice on the one hand, and performance measures on the other.

The term 'organizational effectiveness' thus appears on our map as 'shorthand' for a range of possible measures at different levels of analysis – individual, group, organizational and social. There is no common agreed definition of this term.

One increasingly popular approach to this dilemma concerns the development of a **balanced scorecard** approach. This involves deciding on a range of quantitative and qualitative measures of the organization's performance as a basis for evaluating management decisions and organizational effectiveness. The utility company Anglian Water, for example, uses a balanced scorecard to guide executive board decisions and to evaluate organizational performance on four sets of criteria: shareholder value, internal efficiencies, employee development and environmental concerns.

The phrase *quality of working life* carries similar difficulties, as we each have different needs and expectations from work. An additional difficulty with this concept is that it is intimately related both to organizational effectiveness and also to most of the other factors on the left-hand side of our map. It is difficult to talk about quality of working life without considering motivation, teamwork, organizational design, organization development and change, human resource policies and practices, and management style.

What kind of model of organizational behaviour is this? The 'outputs' are difficult to separate from the 'inputs'. We began by suggesting that this could be read as a 'cause and effect' analysis. Manipulate the factors on the left of the model, to change the values of organizational effectiveness and quality of working life on the right. That is an oversimplification. This is *one* way to view the terrain of organizational behaviour, but the 'simplifying assumptions' may cause us to overlook the interrelationships between the factors that we have separated out.

We need to be very cautious about using this model as a straightforward guide to 'cause and effect' in organizational behaviour. We would like to invite you instead to consider using this model as a guide to the text as a whole, as an 'organizing device', to locate each of the discrete chapters and parts in the wider context. We hope that this model will also serve as a reminder of the need for systemic thinking and analysis, recognizing the overlap and interrelationships between these factors.

> **Balanced scorecard**: an approach to organizational effectiveness that uses a range of quantitative and qualitative measures to assess organizational performance.

Natural and social sciences

Our field map of organizational behaviour highlights aspects of the debate surrounding the equivalence of natural and social sciences. There are two competing views on this issue. The *positivist* view claims that, as part of the natural world, human behaviour should be studied using methods comparable with those used to study the natural world.

Stop and Criticize

We know that metals and gases expand when heated. This observation can be demonstrated and proven, repeatedly and reliably, by experiment.

Consider human behaviour in a busy night club. Why can our behaviour in such a setting not be studied using the same observational and experimental methods used to study what happens when metals are heated?

The interpretative or *phenomenological* view claims that we are *self-interpreting* beings; in other words, we attach meanings to what we do. The implication is that we cannot be studied using techniques that apply to natural objects and events. Chemical substances and rare metals, for example, do not attach meaning to their behaviour. They do not give interviews or fill in questionnaires. This division into competing camps obscures the fact that there are a number of different shades of positivism, a variety of interpretative postures, leading to a range of organizational research approaches, a full examination of which is beyond the scope of our discussion (see Burrell and Morgan, 1979; Deetz, 1996).

Is it possible to submit people to any kind of study that can be called 'scientific'? One major stumbling block seems to be that, when we know that we are being studied, we react by altering our behaviour – to appear more competent, more enthusiastic, more diligent, or just to help the researcher. As a result of these 'reactive effects', what the researcher observes and measures can be artificial, a false reflection of our 'true' selves and our behaviour (Bryman, 1988, 1989, 2001). Avoiding these reactive effects can be a methodological headache. Studying people without their knowledge is one solution, but this raises ethical problems. It seems that the standards of investigation used in natural science cannot easily be transferred to the study of people. For these reasons, some social scientists deny that they are scientists in the sense that biologists, physicists and astronomers are scientists.

The contribution of social sciences to human knowledge is often regarded with scepticism and suspicion. It is a relatively simple matter to demonstrate the practical application of natural scientific endeavour. We can put people on the moon, deliver music, news and films to your computer down a phone line, send photographs using mobile telephones, genetically engineer disease-resistant crops, perform surgery using minimally invasive or 'keyhole' techniques, and so on. Natural science has also given us technologies with which we can do enormous damage, to each other and to the planet. Textbooks in electrical engineering, naval architecture, quantum mechanics and vascular surgery tell the reader how the world works, how to make things, and how to fix them. Students from these disciplines often find psychology and sociology texts disappointing because they do not offer such clear practical guidance. Social science texts often raise more questions than they answer, and instead draw attention to debates, conflicts, ambiguities and paradoxes which are then left unresolved. Science gives us *material technology* – personal transport, skyscrapers, antibiotics, DVD players and so on – but social science has not given us a convincing *social engineering*, of the kind which, for example, would reduce car theft and eliminate football hooliganism.

Are we, and our organizations, beyond the reach of scientific study? Surely not. We would like to encourage you to assess this issue for yourself. However, we would like to address the prejudice that can lead to a dismissal of anything that 'soft' social science may try to offer. We wish to encourage instead a critical approach to the social science enterprise in general, and to organizational research in particular, and to base that critical stance on an understanding of the issues that face all students of human behaviour.

The natural sciences – physics; astronomy, chemistry, biology, genetics – seem to be able to rely on direct observation, on consistent causal relationships between variables through time and space, on experimental methods to test hypotheses, and on mathematical reasoning. The study of human behaviour seems to founder on all of these issues. We cannot directly observe what is happening inside people's heads, different cultures and sub-cultures around the planet think and act differently, subjecting people to experimental methods is artificial and potentially unethical, and many aspects of behaviour cannot be readily quantified. The goals of science include description, explanation, prediction and control of events. These four goals represent increasing levels of sophistication. Table 1.1 summarizes the problems.

Table 1.1: Scientific goals and social science problems

Goals of science	Practical implications	Social science problems
description	measurement	invisible and ambiguous variables people change over time
explanation	identify the time order of events establish causal links between variables	timing of events not always clear cannot always see interactions
prediction	generalizing from one setting to another	uniqueness, complexity and lack of comparability between social settings
control	manipulation	ethical and legal constraints

These 'problems' only become serious if we expect social science to conform to natural science practice. However, if the study of people is a different kind of enterprise, then we need different procedures to advance our understanding, and different criteria will apply in evaluating success. Social science can thus be viewed as a different kind of science from the natural sciences. Social scientist are themselves divided on this issue.

Stop and Criticize

Your instructor claims that the high turnover of supermarket checkout staff can be explained by the routine, repetitive and boring nature of the work.

How would you examine this claim using a positivist research approach? How would you examine this claim differently using a phenomenological approach?

Some social scientists argue that there is 'unity of method' in the study of natural and human phenomena. In other words, we should all use the same research perspective and techniques. The theoretical basis of this argument lies in the claim that human behaviour is governed by universal laws of the same kind that govern the behaviour of natural phenomena. These laws may just be complex and difficult to discern, and our social sciences may be relatively young.

One implication of the 'unity of method' perspective is a concern with refining social science methodology. Great care is taken to define terms precisely, to measure and quantify, to conduct carefully designed experiments in which subjects are allocated at random to control and experimental groups (known in medical research as randomized control trials), and to avoid or minimize the reactive effects generated by a researcher's presence. In what is known as the 'double blind' randomized control trial, neither the experimenters nor the subjects are initially aware of who has been allocated to which control and experimental groups. Social scientists, and organizational researchers, may just have to work harder on these issues, although it is difficult to imagine many organizations giving researchers the freedom randomly to allocate employees and to subject them for study to, say, different forms of work design, payment system or management style. A second implication of this perspective is a concern with producing a social technology that can be used to predict and control human behaviour as effectively as we use material technologies to manipulate the natural order.

You discover that one of your instructors has a novel way of enhancing student performance on her module. She always gives students poor grades for their first assignment, regardless of their level of performance. This, she argues, stimulates higher levels of student performance in subsequent assignments.

This is an example of 'social engineering'. To what extent is this ethical?

Other social scientists argue that social and natural sciences are fundamentally different, and that the study of people cannot become more scientific by simply following more closely the procedures of quantum physicists and laboratory chemists. This distinction can be explored with respect to the four goals of description, explanation, prediction and control.

Description

There are three methods by which social scientists produce descriptions of the phenomena they study. These are observation, asking questions and studying documents. These methods can be applied in various different ways. The people studied may or may not know that they are research subjects. Questions can be asked in person by the researcher or through a self-report questionnaire. Documents of interest can include diaries, letters, company reports, committee minutes or published work. Physicists and chemists, for example, use only observation, albeit under specially designed and controlled conditions. Metals and chemicals, for example, do not respond to interrogation, and do not publish autobiographies in the style that has become popular among senior organization executives.

Observation is useful in organizational research too. The researcher can listen to and watch informal discussion in a cafeteria, join a selection interview, or follow participants through a training programme. However, in settings like these, it is often not possible to produce reliable measurements of terms that can be defined unambiguously. Suppose you want to measure aggression – a social phenomenon – at student dances through observation. How are you going to do this? A few

Jury science: a step towards social engineering?

To win a court case in America, litigants may soon need good behavioural scientists as well as good lawyers. Some companies are using them to help their lawyers distinguish friendly from unfriendly jurors and to assess how arguments in court are being received by the jury. University professors who are already boosting their earnings by providing such help occasionally must now reckon with Litigation Sciences, a firm based in California with 90 psychologists, sociologists, psychometrists and other professionals.

Its chairman, Dr Donald Vinson, holds a doctorate in marketing and sociology from the University of Colorado. He first got into the litigation business when, as an academic at the University of Southern California, his brains were picked by IBM in a $100 million anti-trust suit brought against it by California Computer Products. He recruited surrogate jurors who were as similar as possible to the real ones. Without disclosing which side had hired them, he asked his shadow jury to sit in court each day and quizzed them on their reaction to the arguments they had heard. His findings were passed on each night to IBM's lawyers to help them refine their strategy. IBM won the case.

From 'Jury science', *The Economist*, 8 July 1993, p. 86.

moments' thought should suggest that it is going to be difficult to decide *what counts* as 'aggressive' behaviour. Can you count as 'aggressive' the joking and friendly physical contact between people who know each other reasonably well? For research purposes, we must use terms like this precisely, and consistently, but this is not a straightforward matter.

The method that we use to decide *what counts* is known as an **operational definition** of the term in which we are interested.

Your operational definition of aggression could include raised and angry voices, physical contact, inflicting pain and damage to property. You could count each event that you observe where at least one factor is evident. You could use this operational definition to construct a simple 'aggressiveness scale', with events where all four factors are evident rated as 'more aggressive'. Compare this with an operational definition of 'job satisfaction'. In practice, this can be measured by

Operational definition: the method used to measure the incidence of a variable in practice.

For research purposes, we must use terms precisely and consistently

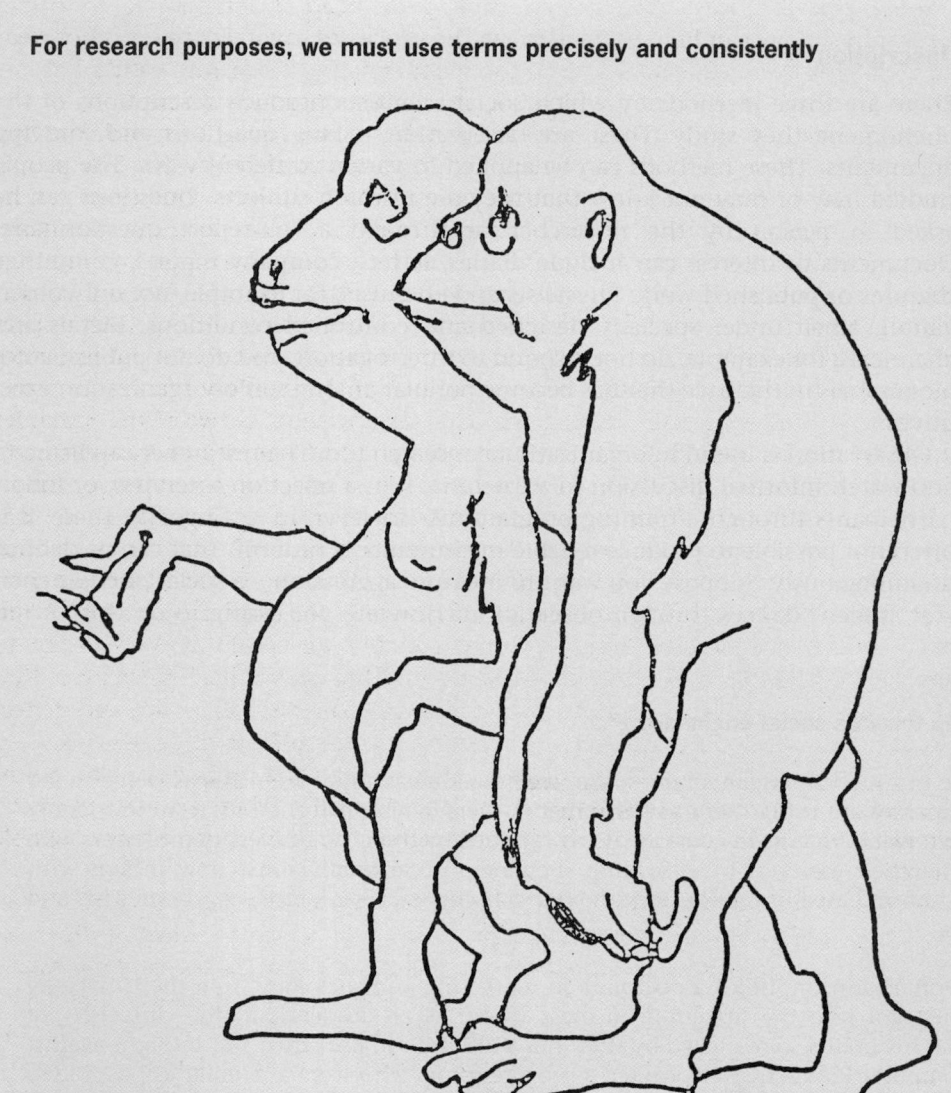

' . . . and then he raises the issue of, "how many angels can dance on the head of a pin?", and I say, "you haven't operationalized the question sufficiently – are you talking about classical ballet, jazz, the two-step, country swing . . ."'

asking a single question, 'how satisfied are you with your job?, seeking answers on a five-point rating scale from very satisfied, through neutral, to very dissatisfied. However, we may feel that job satisfaction is affected by a range of factors such as management style, financial rewards, development opportunities, promotion chances, flexible working hours, and so on. Our operational definition could thus be a lengthy questionnaire with items relating to each of those factors.

We can overcome our inability to observe interesting factors. Consider the process of learning (chapter 4). As you read through this book, we would like to think that you are indeed learning something about organizational behaviour. However, if we could open your head as you read, we would have difficulty finding anything that could be meaningfully described as 'the learning process' (although neurophysiology is making significant breakthroughs in understanding memory). This is a convenient label for an invisible (or at least, invisible to a social scientist) activity whose existence we can assume or infer.

Some changes must take place inside your head if learning is to occur. Neurophysiology can help to track down the processes involved, but it is not clear how an improved understanding of the biochemistry of learning would help us to design better organizational learning and job training programmes.

The procedures for studying learning by inference are straightforward. We can, for instance, examine your knowledge of organizational behaviour before you read this book, and repeat the examination afterwards. If the second set of results is better than the first, then we can confidently infer that learning has taken place. Your ability to perform a particular task has changed, and we can use that change to help us identify the factors that caused it. We can proceed in this manner to study the effects of varying inputs to the learning process, with respect to the characteristics of the teachers, learners, abilities, and the time and resources devoted to the process. We can study variations in the delivery process, in terms of methods and materials. In this way the relationships between the variables involved can be identified. Our understanding of the learning process can thus develop systematically, and from this knowledge we can suggest improvements.

Observation as a research method has many uses. Our understanding of what managers do, for example, is based largely on this method, but it has obvious limitations. What can we say about someone's motives merely by observing their behaviour? We could follow somebody – our target – around for a day or two, and make guesses about their motives. But eventually we would probably want to engage them in conversation and ask some probing questions. The answers that we get are now our research data. The validity of those data, as an accurate reflection of the 'truth' of the situation, is questionable for at least three reasons.

First, our target may lie. People who are planning a bank robbery, or who resent the intrusion of a researcher, may give misleading replies. There are ways in which we can check the accuracy of what people tell us, but this is not always possible or convenient.

Second, our target may not know. The mental processes related to our motives typically operate without conscious effort. Few of us make the effort to dig these processes out from our subconscious to examine them. Most of us struggle through life without the self-critical reflection that answers questions like, 'why am I here?', and 'what am I doing?' The researcher gets the answers of which the person is aware, or which seem to be appropriate, rational or 'correct' in the circumstances. The answers we get to some of our questions could be convenient inventions of the moment.

Third, our target may tell us what they think we want to hear. People rarely lie to researchers. They create problems by being helpful. It is easier to give a simple answer than to relate a complex history of intrigue, heartbreak and family strife. The socially acceptable answer is better than no answer at all. People may tell researchers about their attitudes to, say, a controversial item of government legislation although they have never studied the details. A research interview is a peculiar form of social interaction. The participants are usually strangers who quickly engage in a one-way exchange of (sometimes sensitive) information. The interview thus typically unfolds according to what the participants believe to be the unwritten social rules that guide such interactions. The researcher is expected to be curious, in control of the conversation, objective, friendly, non-threatening, and to respect confidentiality. The interviewee is expected to be open, honest and co-operative, and is allowed to be mildly curious about the researcher's aims. Both parties thus want to appear competent and ethical, criteria which can be shown to influence both the questioning strategies that researchers use and the answers that respondents provide. This does *not* mean that the answers we get are wrong; rather, we need to be aware of the social context in which information is collected.

Explanation

It is often possible to infer that one event has caused another even when the variables are not observable. If your organizational behaviour test score is higher after reading this book than before, and if you have not been studying other materials, then we can infer that reading this book has caused your score to improve. The timing of events is not always easy to establish. Causes must happen before the effects they are said to explain. You are debating with someone who believes that women have a higher tolerance for repetitive work than men. Try arguing that the causal arrow points in the opposite direction. Some women may learn to expect that the work available to them (in secretarial, clerical, retail, hotel, catering and manufacturing) will be boring and repetitive. In other words, the very notion of 'women's work' predates, or causes, the development of female 'acceptance'.

The rules or laws that govern human behaviour seem to be different from those that govern the behaviour of natural phenomena. The ways in which we understand causality in social affairs thus has to be different.

Consider, for instance, the meteorological law which states that 'clouds mean rain'. This law holds around our planet. A cloud cannot break that law, deliberately or by accident. The cloud does not have to be told, either as a youngster or when it approaches hills, about the business of raining. Compare this situation with the social law which states that 'red means stop'. A society can choose to change this law, to one which says that blue means stop, because some people are red–green colour blind (and thus cause hideous accidents). The human driver can get it wrong in two ways, by deliberately jumping the red light (in the early hours of a Sunday morning with no police in sight), or through lack of concentration and passing the red light accidentally. Clouds cannot vote to change the laws governing their behaviour, nor can they mischievously break these laws, or get them wrong by accident.

This has profound implications for social scientific research and understanding. The social scientist clearly cannot expect to discover laws that govern human behaviour consistently across time and place. Behaviour towards people over 40 years of age, as potential employees, changed markedly in the late 1990s, compared with what has come to be known as an 'ageist' attitude common in the 1980s and early 1990s (to judge from the wording of job advertisements and the job-seeking experiences of those over 40). The employment of children is illegal in most of the planet's northern hemisphere, but remains commonplace and acceptable for social and economic reasons in some developing countries.

We do not come into existence with pre-programmed behavioural guides, although it appears that we are programmed with the capabilities to learn certain behaviours, such as language (Pinker, 2002). We have to learn the rules that apply in our particular society at a given time. There are strikingly different cultural rules concerning relatively trivial matters, such as how close people should stand to each other in different kinds of social setting. We have (mostly unwritten) rules about how and when to shake hands and for how long the shake should last, about the styles of dress and address appropriate to different social occasions and sexes, about relationships between superior and subordinate, between men and women, between elderly and young. Even across the closely related cultures of Europe or of the Pacific Rim, there are striking differences in social rules, both between and within countries.

Social scientists concerned with explaining social and organizational behaviour have to start with the self-interpretations of their subjects. It is not enough to know *how* people do what they do; we also need to know *why*. People behave in accordance with their own theories and understanding of how the world works. These theories are not rigorously formulated or systematically tested. However, we share this understanding with other members of our society, and we are able to act competently without being objective and scientific about what we do. We know what behaviour is appropriate in particular settings, and what is not acceptable. We take our theories of how the world works for granted. We take our knowledge of how society, and its organizations, functions as common sense.

In addition, we live in a social and organizational world in which 'reality' means different things to different people. We live, therefore, in a world of multiple realities. The natural scientist does not have to confront this complication. Our individual views of reality depend on our unique social positions, and are influenced in particular by our organizational positions. As customers who have done nothing obviously wrong, we have probably all met the unhelpful bus driver, the disgruntled waiter or the angry store manager whose emotional responses to us seem to have been triggered at least in part by a recent work experience.

Social science uses common words in unusual and special ways. This is not unique. The medical profession also uses jargon. Your indigestion is dyspepsia to the doctor. This way of using language helps to ensure precision and consistency in our thinking. The problem is that the 'technical' terms are often words that we use regularly in everyday conversation, and this can lead to confusion if we are not careful. A critical reading of the literature is necessary to identify and overcome these jargon problems.

It will be helpful to define some relatively common words more precisely.

Behaviour: the term given to the things that people do that can be directly observed.

Some **behaviour** is observable. We see you walk, hear you talk, smell your perfume or aftershave, touch your hair and taste your cooking. There is a school of thought called **behaviourism** which argues that psychology should be confined to phenomena that can be directly observed, and rejects the study of mental states which can only be the subject of speculation.

Behaviourism: a psychological perspective which focuses on the study of observable behaviour.

Behaviourism thus argues that that it is pointless to explain behaviour in terms of unobservable factors, such as needs, drives, thought processes, attitudes or motives. The behaviourist stance has much in common with the *positivist* approach to social science. We cannot in this text address the range of perspectives and philosophical positions which claim the label of **positivism**. However, a brief definition is helpful.

Positivism: a social scientific perspective which assumes that the properties of the social world can be studied using objective methods.

Positivism believes that societies and organizations possesses objective realities that exist independently of anyone's attitudes towards or interpretations of them. The behaviourist and positivist perspectives strike many commentators as incomplete and restrictive. In particular, behaviourism does not seem to fit comfortably with our self-understanding; we do have motives and attitudes, do we not? We seem to have thought processes and internally stored images of the world around us. These processes and images are certainly part of our daily, personal, conscious experience. As they appear to influence our behaviour, do they not deserve to be recognized as valuable objects of study, with the same research status as observable behaviour?

Action: the term given to the things that people do, along with the reasons that they have for doing them.

Cognitive psychology: a perspective which accepts as legitimate the study of internal mental states and processes, even though they are not directly observable.

Phenomenology: a social scientific perspective which assumes that the social world has no external, objective, observable truth, and that reality is socially constructed.

Social construction of reality: a perspective which argues that our surroundings have no ultimate truth, and are determined by our experiences and interpretations.

Various schools of thought have developed in response to the criticisms of behaviourism and positivism, in psychology, and across the social sciences. In psychology and sociology, a research tradition has been established around the notion that, as people are self-interpreting, it makes sense to subject those self-interpretations to investigation, through the study of what is often now called **action**.

Action is thus also defined as *meaningful behaviour*, prompting us to ask the question 'why?' as well as 'what?' and 'how?'. The perspective that developed in response to behaviourism is known as **cognitive psychology**.

Cognitive psychology has much in common with the **phenomenological** approach to social scientific study mentioned earlier. Once again, we cannot address the range of perspectives and philosophical positions to which this broad term now apples (including, for example, hermeneutics, ethnomethodology, symbolic interactionism, semiotics, interpretative sociology; see Denzin and Lincoln, 2000), but a brief definition is helpful.

For phenomenology, the social science task is not to gather facts and measurements, but to study patterns of meanings and interpretations, to discover how experience is understood. The claim that 'reality is socially constructed' (Berger and Luckmann, 1966) is not a straightforward one to grasp on first reading, and an illustration may help.

We asked you earlier to consider how to measure the incidence of aggression at student functions, by devising an *operational definition* of the term. If we now say that 'the reality of aggression at student functions is **socially constructed**', what do we mean? Suppose you observe one male student shout at and punch another male student on the upper arm. The second student responds by shouting back and pushing the first student away. A table is shaken, drinks are spilled, glasses are broken. This has all the trademarks of an aggressive encounter. However, on speaking to the parties involved, you find that they describe their behaviour in terms of friendship, fun and play. The other members of their group agree with this definition of the situation which they too have observed. The socially defined version of events, for actors and for observers, does not concern aggression at all, but strengthens an existing relationship. The researcher who only observes is in danger of reaching inaccurate conclusions. From this perspective, your operational definition is arbitrary. What matters is how those involved in this setting interpret their own and each other's actions.

We therefore construct and reconstruct a version of reality for ourselves in interaction with others. Positivism and phenomenology are now represented by many varying shades of opinion within and between these two extreme views. The point which we want to establish here is that there are different standpoints from which people and organizations can be studied. There are, therefore, different approaches to producing explanations for human behaviour in social and organizational settings. While phenomenology and related interpretative perspectives have become more influential, much published organizational research is still rooted in a positivist tradition. Even the relationship between these perspectives is controversial. Some commentators argue that these views are irreconcilable, while some researchers claim to draw from both perspectives in their work.

Stop and Criticize

Hospital managers are concerned that some patients with medical emergencies wait too long in the casualty department before they are diagnosed and treated.

The positivist wants to observe and record emergency patient numbers, waiting and treatment times, staffing levels, bed numbers and the availability of other resources.

The phenomenologist wants to talk to the doctors, nurses and ambulance crews, to find out how they feel about working here and where they believe the problems lie.

Which approach is more likely to result in practical solutions to the waiting times problem, and why?

Prediction

Social science can often explain events without being able to make precise predictions (table 1.2). Social science predictions are often probabilistic, rather than determinate. We may be able to predict the rate of suicide in a given society, or the incidence of stress-related disorders in an occupational group. However, we can rarely predict whether specific individuals will try to kill themselves, or suffer sleep and eating disorders. This limitation in our predictive ability is not necessarily critical. We are often more interested in the behaviour of groups than individuals, and more interested in tendencies than in individual predictions.

There is a more fundamental problem. Researchers often communicate their findings to those who have been studied. Suppose you have never given much thought to the ultimate reality of human nature. One day, you read about an American psychologist, Abraham Maslow, who claims that we have a fundamental need for 'self-actualization', to develop our capabilities to their full potential. If this sounds like a good idea to you, and you act accordingly, then what he has said has become true, in your case. His claim has fulfilled itself. This may be because he has given you a new perspective on human existence, or because he has given you a label to explain some aspect of your existing intellectual makeup.

Some predictions are thus self-fulfilling. The act of saying something will happen can either make that happen or increase the likelihood of it happening. Equally, some predictions are intentionally self-defeating. Many of the disastrous predictions from economists, about exchange and interest rate movements, for example, are designed to trigger action to prevent those prophecies from coming true. In an organizational setting, one could predict that a particular management style will lead to the resignation of a number of valuable employees, in the hope that this will lead to a change in management style.

Table 1.2: We can explain – but we cannot predict

we can explain staff turnover in a supermarket in terms of the repetitive and boring nature of the work	but we cannot predict which members of staff will leave, or when they will choose to do so
we can explain how different management styles encourage greater or lower levels of employee commitment and performance	but we cannot predict which managers will achieve the highest levels of commitment and performance in a given setting
we can explain the factors that contribute to group cohesiveness in an organization	but we cannot predict the level of cohesion and performance of particular groups
we can explain why some types of organization structure are more adaptable in the face of external change than others	but we cannot predict the performance improvements that will follow an organizational structure change

Organizational research can point to the options, and demonstrate how those options can be evaluated. The researcher is often in a position to claim, say, that if a payment and appraisal system is designed in a particular way, the employee response is likely to be negative, and that an alternative approach would lead to more favourable outcomes. The prediction is thus made in the expectation that other options will be explored. The kinds of prediction that natural science makes cannot have such an effect on the phenomena studied.

Control

Social science findings induce social change; organizational research findings similarly induce change. The natural scientist does not study the natural order of things in order to be critical of that order, or to encourage that order to change and improve itself. It does not make much sense to argue whether nature could be better organized. It is hardly appropriate to evaluate, as good or bad, the observation that a gas expands when heated, or the number of components in a strand of DNA. Social scientists, on the other hand, are generally motivated by a desire to change society, or aspects of it, and its organizations. An understanding of how things currently work, and the strengths and weaknesses of current arrangements, is essential for that purpose. Such understanding, therefore, is not necessarily a useful end in itself. Social science can be deliberately critical of the social and organizational order that it uncovers, because that order is only one of many that we are capable of constructing.

An agenda directed at inducing social and organizational change is not the same as controlling or manipulating human behaviour, which many people would regard as unethical. As already indicated, we do not have a social technology, comparable to material technology, that enables us to manipulate other people anyway. Perhaps we should be grateful for this. However, table 1.3 identifies interventions, explained in following chapters, designed to control various aspects of employee behaviour.

Calvin and Hobbes

It is important to recognize that our judgements and our recommendations are based not only on evidence, but also on values. Social science has been criticized as 'ideology in disguise'. However, if one studies organizations in order to change and improve them, then that criticism is inescapable. Suppose we study repetitive clerical work in an insurance company, or unskilled packing work in biscuit-making. The people doing these jobs are bored and unhappy, and our research identifies work redesign options. Managers claim that their work system is a cost-effective way of producing the goods and services their customers want. The tension between these positions cannot be resolved with reference only to empirical evidence.

Table 1.4 summarizes the two contrasting perspectives from which human behaviour in general and organizational behaviour in particular can be studied.

Table 1.3: Interventions which attempt to control organizational behaviour

Organizational intervention	Attempts to control
staff training and development programmes (chapter 4)	employee knowledge and skills
psychometric assessments (chapter 5)	the types of people employed
employee communications (chapter 6)	employee understanding of and compliance with management-inspired goals
job redesign (chapter 8)	employee motivation, commitment and performance
teambuilding (part 3)	levels of team cohesion and performance
reorganization – structure change (part 4)	ability of the organization to respond to external turbulence
organizational change and development (chapters 17 and 18)	speed of change and reduction of conflict and resistance
organization culture change (chapter 19)	values, attitudes, beliefs and goals shared by management and employees

We must now revisit our field map of the organizational behaviour terrain, and reinforce the caution raised earlier concerning its status and use.

Seen from a *positivist* perspective, that model prompts the search for causal links: this organization structure will improve adaptability, that approach to job design will enhance motivation, quality of working life and performance. The positivist is looking for method, for technique, for specific and codified universal solutions to organizational problems.

Seen from a *phenomenological* perspective, the model prompts a range of other questions: how do we define and understand the term 'organization', and what does effectiveness mean to different stakeholder groups? What kind of work experiences are different individuals looking for, and how do they respond to their experience, and why? The phenomenologist seeks to trigger organizational change by stimulating self-critical awareness.

This field map or model, therefore, does not in any straightforward sense lay out causal links across the organizational behaviour terrain. It is simply one way of displaying a complex terrain quickly and simply. As indicated earlier, we hope that it serves as a reminder of the need for systemic thinking and analysis, and also as a reminder that there is no one 'correct' way to view this subject matter.

Table 1.4: Positivism versus phenomenology

	Perspective	
	Positivism or behaviourist	**Phenomenology or cognitive**
Description	studies observable behaviour	studies internal mental states, meanings and interpretations
Explanation	seeks fixed universal laws governing behaviour	focuses on individuals' understanding and interpretation of the world to explain behaviour
Prediction	based on knowledge of consistent relationships between variables	based on shared understanding and awareness of multiple social and organizational realities
Control	aims to shape behaviour by manipulating external variables	aims at social and organizational change through stimulating critical awareness

Recap

1. *Explain the significance of an understanding of organizational behaviour.*

   - Organizations influence almost every aspect of our daily lives in a multitude of ways.

   - If we eventually destroy this planet, the cause will not lie with technology or weaponry. We will have destroyed it with ineffective organizations.

2. *Explain and illustrate the central dilemma of organizational design.*

   - The organizational dilemma concerns how to reconcile the inconsistency between individual needs and aspirations, and the collective purpose of the organization.

3. *Understand the need for explanations of behaviour in organizations that take account of relationships between factors at different levels of analysis.*

   - The study of organizational behaviour is multidisciplinary, drawing in particular from psychology, social psychology, sociology, economics and political science.

   - Organizational behaviour involves a multi-level study of the external environment, and internal structure, functioning and performance of organizations, and the behaviour of groups and individuals.

   - Organizational effectiveness and quality of working life are explained by a combination of contextual, individual, group, structural, process and managerial factors.

   - In considering explanations of organizational behaviour, systemic thinking is required, avoiding explanations based on single causes and considering a range of interrelated factors at different levels of analysis.

4. *Identify the features that differentiate the natural and social sciences, and the implications of this differentiation.*

   - A positivist perspective assumes 'unity of method' with the natural sciences and attempts to use the same research methods and criteria.

   - It is difficult to apply conventional scientific research methods to people, mainly because of the 'reactive effects' which come into play when people know they are being studied.

   - A phenomenological or interpretative perspective assumes that, as human being are self-defining creatures who attach meanings to their behaviour, the social science enterprise is fundamentally different from natural science.

   - The phenomenological or interpretative perspective believes that reality is not 'out there' but is socially constructed.

   - An interpretative approach means abandoning scientific neutrality in the interests of seeking to stimulate social and organizational change through a combination of critical feedback and stimulating self-awareness.

Revision

1. How is organizational behaviour defined, what does the subject cover, and what is its practical relevance?

2. What are the advantages and disadvantages of a managerialist perspective on organizational behaviour?

3. If organizations are an everyday feature of our lives, why then is the concept of organization so difficult to define?

4. Describe an example of organizational *mis*behaviour, where you as customer were treated badly. Explore systematically the possible explanations for your treatment. What does this reveal about the nature of explanations of organizational behaviour?

5. What, for the study of organizational behaviour, are the theoretical and practical distinctions between positivism and phenomenology?

Springboard

Adler, N., 2002, *International Dimensions of Organizational Behaviour*, Thomson Learning, London (fourth edition).

Globalization, managing cultural diversity, and the cross-cultural transfer of organizational behaviour and management theory and practice are among the main themes explored in this highly regarded text. Considers a range of cultures: Asia, Africa, Eastern and Western Europe, North and South America, the Middle East.

Bryman, A., 2001, *Social Research Methods*, Oxford University Press, Oxford.

Offers a comprehensive and well-informed treatment of social science research methods. Also clearly explains methodological and epistemological debates. Alan and his colleague Emma Bell are working on a tailored edition of *Business Research Methods* which will be published in 2003.

Clegg, S., Hardy, C. and Nord, W.R., 1996, *Handbook of Organization Studies*, Sage Publications, London.

An award-winning collection of essays displaying the breadth of empirical concern and theoretical perspective now characterizing the field of organization studies. A challenging text (also available in paperback part-works) but a difficult read.

Denzin, N.K. and Lincoln, Y.S. (eds), 2000, *Handbook of Qualitative Research*, Sage Publications, Thousand Oaks, CA (second edition).

Benchmark text on qualitative research methods which explains the diversity of views and positions within the phenomenological or interpretative perspective.

Harrison, M.I., 1994, *Diagnosing Organizations: Methods, Models and Processes*, Sage Publications, Thousand Oaks, CA.

A more focused treatment of organization research methods, demonstrating the similarities between research methods and management consulting techniques.

Palmer, I. and Hardy, C., 2000, *Thinking About Management: Implications of Organizational Debates for Practice*, Sage Publications, London.

Excellent counter to those who prefer 'the correct answer' and 'the one best way'. Explores clearly the relevance of contemporary debates in organization theory in an engaging style which is not typical of similar critical writing on management.

Thomas, A.B., 2002, *Controversies in Management: Issues, Debates, Answers*, Routledge, London (second edition).

Written from a managerial perspective, this established text explores a series of contemporary debates about the nature of work, management and organizations, considering the practical as well as theoretical implications. Challenging and entertaining, it presents complex issues in a clear and accessible style.

Home viewing

Any Given Sunday (1999, director Oliver Stone) starring Al Pacino as the American football team coach Tony D'Amato graphically illustrates the influence of a range of management and organizational factors on team success. Emphasis is placed on the aggressive business and marketing approach adopted by the club's president and co-owner, played by Cameron Diaz. The role of the football players in the team's performance appears to be secondary. This is a useful complement to exercise 2 for this chapter, *This sporting life*.

Chicken Run (2000, directors Peter Lord and Nick Park) is an animated comedy about a bunch of chickens seeking fulfilment and self-actualization. The goal of the chickens' organization is to maximize egg production. The goal of management, The Old Rooster, is to be seen as an effective leader. The chickens just want to leave. They devote their energy to finding escape routes, while sharing laid eggs to protect the poor performers, and making sure that things look serene and normal to prevent management interference with the 'real' work. This is, therefore, an entertaining illustration of the organizational dilemma.

OB in literature

Franz Kafka, 1926/1957, *The Castle*, trans. Willa and Edwin Muir, Penguin, Harmondsworth (first published 1926 as *Das Schloss*, Wolff, Munich).

How is the organizational dilemma, in which the individual confronts a large, rigid, impersonal organization, illustrated in this novel? Here we see the individual's sense of autonomy and responsibility confronted with anonymous, impersonal and elusive organizational power. How well does this classic novel represent the relationships between employees and large bureaucratic organizations today?

Chapter exercises

1: Self-test

Objectives
1. To consider the nature of social science thinking and explanations.

2. To expose the limitations of common-sense explanations of human behaviour.

Briefing
We are all experts on human behaviour, or at least we like to think we are. There must be some truth in this belief, given the rich base of experiences from which we can draw. However, this thinking leads to the claim that psychology, social psychology and sociology, the subjects that underpin organizational behaviour, are merely common sense wrapped in jargon. It is therefore important to confront this perception.

Your task is to indicate whether each of the following 20 statements is either true or false by writing a T or an F at the side. (Your instructor may ask you to consider only ten of these, given time constraints.) In some cases you may want to answer, 'it depends'. However, you are asked to take a stand and indicate whether you feel that, on the whole, in most circumstances, for most practical purposes, the statement is true or false.

Compare your responses with at least two other people. Share your thinking, and establish why you have disagreed. If time allows, share your reasoning on items where you were particularly unhappy about making a clear commitment.

Twenty statements test

1. Men are naturally better than women when it comes to decisive managerial decision-making.

2. People who are satisfied in their work are more productive than those who are not.

3. Resistance to new technology increases with age.

4. Alcohol in small amounts is a stimulant.

5. You can always 'read' a person's emotional state by watching their facial expressions closely.

6. The more challenging the goals you face, the more you are likely to accomplish.

7. Selection interviews, handled correctly, are the best way to assess candidates' suitability for a job.

8. When asked to rank features of their work in order of personal importance, the vast majority of people put pay at the top.

9. Punishment is an effective way of eliminating undesirable behaviour.

10. When you have to work for several hours, it is better to take a small number of long rest periods than a larger number of short breaks.

11. When people share their thinking in groups, they come up with more original ideas than individuals working alone.

12. Most people, if they are honest with themselves, can tell you what their motives are.

13. Most people have a natural resistance to organizational change.

14. Conflict in an organization is always disruptive and should be avoided at all costs.

15. Some people are born leaders, as can be seen in their behaviour.

16. A reliable personality test is a good predictor of job performance.

17. People learn new tasks better when they are only told about their successes and their mistakes are overlooked.

18. It is not possible for individual managers to change their style because this reflects an innate aspect of personality.

19. Organizations always become ineffective when people do not have clear job descriptions that set out their responsibilities and define their place in the structure.

20. Extraverts make better salespersons.

2: This sporting life

Objectives
1. To illustrate the use of the field map of organizational behaviour as a diagnostic tool for understanding the factors contributing to organizational effectiveness.

2. To demonstrate the importance of systemic thinking, as opposed to looking for single causes, in developing explanations of organizational effectiveness.

Briefing
Why do some organizations succeed, while others fail? Why is an organization successful one year, and less successful the next? These simple questions can have complex answers. To understand more fully the factors contributing to organizational success, and to appreciate the complex nature of the relationships between these factors, it is instructive to analyze an organization with which you are familiar. For the purposes of this analysis, it does not matter which organization you choose. If you are working in a group, then it should be an organization with which most or all members of your group or syndicate are familiar.

However, we recommend that you choose a club from your favourite female or male team sport. Many sports clubs are commercial enterprises run in much the same way as any other profit-making business, generating revenue from ticket sales, advertising, sponsorship, television rights and 'cross-selling' of club merchandise such as clothing. Second, and more important for the purposes of this analysis, the success of a club is usually attributed to the players' skill. Is this the only factor to consider?

The tools for analyzing the organization's external environment are explained in chapter 2, so we will overlook this dimension for now. Your task is to identify, using the following table, the respective contributions, positive and negative, of individual, group, structural, process and management factors to club performance. If you are very familiar with the organization concerned, name names, point the finger, identify individuals where possible and appropriate.

Factors affecting sports success

Factors	Examples	Positive and negative contributions
Individual factors	players' skills and abilities; personalities and egos; interpersonal communications; achievement motivation; perception of club status	
Group factors	group cohesion; status and leadership structure in the team; team behavioural norms; do the players like each other?	
Structural factors	club ownership; flexible structure, or rigid bureaucratic approach; composition of the main board; financial health	
Process factors	plans for organization development; substance of organizational changes; how changes are implemented; the culture of the club; recruitment, retention, motivation and reward policies for players	
Management factors	leadership styles of team captain, coach and club chairman; power holders on the board; decision-making style; internal politics and conflicts	

When you have completed this analysis, consider in consultation with colleagues the following questions:

1. How do these factors interact with and reinforce each other in contributing to and explaining organizational effectiveness?

2. Given the range of factors that can influence organizational effectiveness, how important are the players? Given their contribution following this analysis, to what extent do they deserve the high fees that leading clubs often pay?

This analysis should demonstrate that there are many interrelated factors contributing to the success or failure of a sports club whether in football, netball, basketball or hockey. The skill of an individual player is clearly important, but this is only one consideration among many, and the skills which players demonstrate on the pitch are themselves affected by other factors.

Part 1 The organizational context

A field map of the organizational behaviour terrain

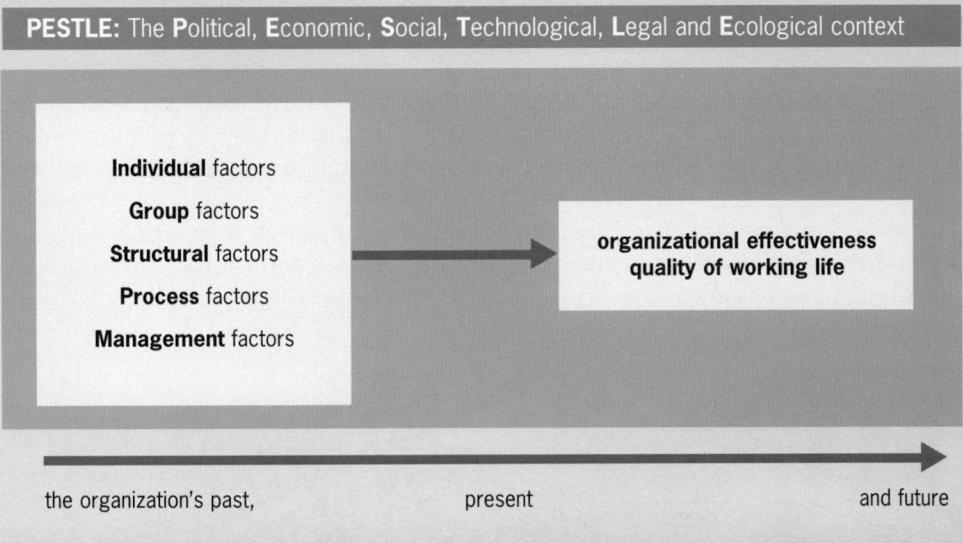

PESTLE: The **P**olitical, **E**conomic, **S**ocial, **T**echnological, **L**egal and **E**cological context

Individual factors
Group factors
Structural factors
Process factors
Management factors

**organizational effectiveness
quality of working life**

the organization's past,   present   and future

Introduction

Part 1, The organizational context, explores two topics:

- The relationships between internal organization structures and external environmental factors, in chapter 2.

- The influence of technology on jobs and organizations, in chapter 3.

The subject matter of organizational behaviour spans a number of levels of analysis – individual, group, organization and the wider environment, or context. Part 1 deals primarily with context. Technology can be regarded as one dimension of that context, but its implications are now so fundamental and widespread that it requires attention in its own right.

One of the recurring themes in this text concerns the design of jobs, and the organization and experience of work. The organization of work is subject to a number of shaping or influencing factors, operating at different levels of analysis. We explain how the experience and organization of work is influenced by:

- *contextual* factors, in chapter 2;

- *technological* factors, in chapter 3;

- *psychological* factors, in chapter 8;

- *social psychological* factors, in chapter 12;

- *historical* factors, in chapter 13;

- *human resource management* practices, in chapter 20.

Invitation to see

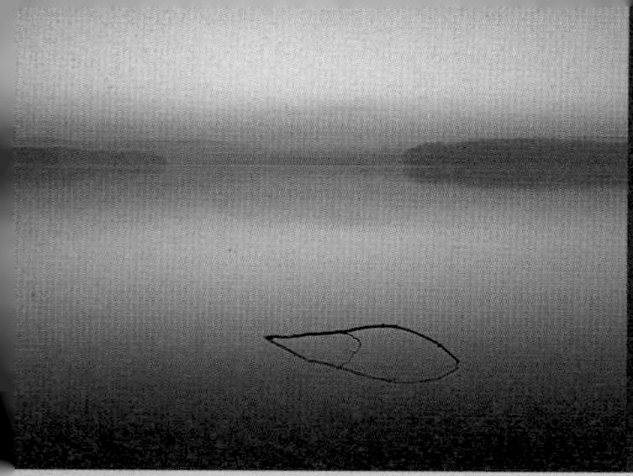

The first of these two images, from the *The Economist* (5 July 2003), was used to illustrate an article titled 'Time's up for ageism'. The article explores the costs and benefits of keeping 'oldies' in work, in the context of discussion concerning the introduction of a ban on forced retirement in the UK at a particular age.

The second image, from *The Times* (20 March 2003), illustrated an article describing the threat of strike action following an announcement by BT, a British telecommunications company, that it planned to outsource work to call centres in India. The photograph shows a call centre in Britain.

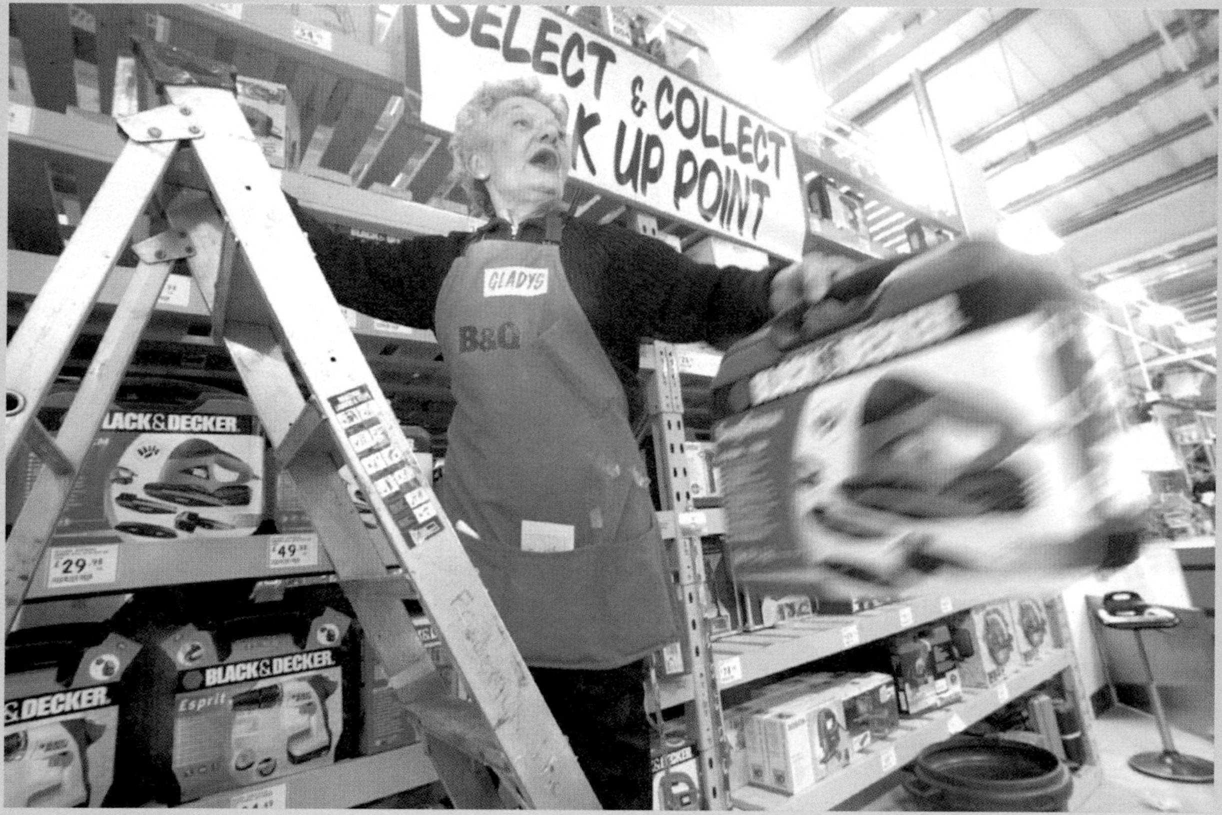

Glad to be Gladys
Source: © The Guardian/Frank Baron

Your call: the main staff union is threatening industrial action if BT presses ahead with plans for two new call centres in India
Source: North News and Pictures

1. Decoding: Look at these images closely. Note in as much detail as possible what messages you feel they are each trying to convey. Do they tell a story, present a point of view, support an argument, perpetuate a myth, reinforce a stereotype, challenge a stereotype?

2. Challenging: To what extent do you agree with the messages, stories, points of view, arguments, myths or stereotypes in these images? Are these images open to challenge, to criticism, to interpretation or decoding in other ways, revealing other messages?

3. Sharing: Compare with colleagues your interpretation of these images. Explore explanations for differences in your respective decodings.

Chapter 2 The world outside

Key concepts

environment	scenario planning	post-modern organization
environmental scanning	environmental uncertainty	postmodernism
globalization	environmental complexity	deconstruction
consolidation	environmental dynamism	
PESTLE analysis	environmental determinism	

Learning outcomes

When you have read this chapter, you should be able to define those key concepts in
your own words, and you should also be able to:

1. Understand the mutual interdependence between the organization and its
environment.
2. Appreciate the strengths and limitations of PESTLE analysis of organizational
environments.
3. Explain the main contemporary organizational responses to environmental
turbulence.
4. Describe the main features of the 'post-modern' organization.
5. Understand the main characteristics of a postmodern perspective on organizational
behaviour, and the creative and critical dimensions of this approach.

Why study the world outside?

Environment the
issues, trends and
events outside the
boundaries of the
organization which
influence internal
decisions and
behaviours.

An organization, in order to function and to survive, has to interact constantly
with the world outside, with its **environment**. Organizations do not operate in
a vacuum. The operations of any organization – corner grocery, local high
school, multinational motor car manufacturer – can be described in terms of its
'import-transformation-export' processes. The car plant imports from its environment a range of resources such as materials, component parts and manufacturing
equipment, storage facilities, staff to run the factory, and energy to provide heating and lighting and run the machinery. The car plant then transforms these
resources into vehicles, which are exported to a dealer network for sale to the
public. The organization is involved in a constant series of exchanges with suppliers, customers, regulatory agencies, and other stakeholders such as share
owners and trade unions.

The environment for a motor car plant in the early twenty-first century is complex. There is global overcapacity in car manufacturing. The industry consolidation of the late 1990s, in which smaller manufacturers (Saab, Rover,
Rolls-Royce, Jaguar, Volvo) were bought by larger companies (General Motors,
BMW, Ford), continues. Cost competition encourages manufacturers to locate
plants in low-wage countries (Hungary, Brazil, Romania), generating job loss and

resentment in traditional car manufacturing countries (Britain, America). In Japan, *gaiatsu*, or foreign pressure, justified major restructuring in Toyota, Honda and Nissan in the late 1990s. To reduce lead times and supply-chain costs, motor manufacturers are increasingly bypassing dealers and selling direct to customers through the internet.

Cost competition has also encouraged the application of 'lean manufacturing' methods, based on Japanese experience, with consequences for working practices and the quality of working life. There is continuing concern over the environmental pollution generated by internal combustion engines which burn petrol and diesel fuel, encouraging product innovation to reduce toxic emissions and to develop 'cleaner' engines. The volume of traffic in many cities around the world is driving governments to consider a range of road pricing, congestion charging, and car and petrol taxation measures to encourage more use of public transport, potentially reducing the demand for cars. These are just some of the factors in the external environment of a car plant, forcing constant internal adjustments to ways of thinking about the business of making cars, the organization's strategy, a host of management decisions, and the organization structure, working practices and design of jobs.

Stop and Criticize

What other factors, trends or developments in the external environment of a car plant have not been mentioned? How will these affect the company's behaviour?

What are the main factors in the external environment of a small grocery shop? What aspects of the behaviour of this business can you explain with reference to its external environment?

The argument of this chapter is illustrated in figure 2.1: 'the world out there' influences 'the world in here'.

Social science texts often annoy readers from other disciplines by first introducing a model, explaining it in detail, then revealing that it is wrong. As this is the strategy adopted in this chapter, an explanation is appropriate.

There are three reasons for using this 'build it up then knock it down' approach.

1. We have to start somewhere, so let us begin simple and work up to complex.

2. If we construct an argument using straightforward assumptions, then introduce more complex and realistic assumptions, the thinking behind the model and its interrelationships can be exposed more clearly.

3. It is important to consider models like figure 2.1 as singular perspectives, as 'one point of view', not necessarily beyond dispute. One of the other arguments of this chapter concerns the advantages of viewing organizations from many different standpoints. The search for 'the one best way' or 'the correct answer' is illusory.

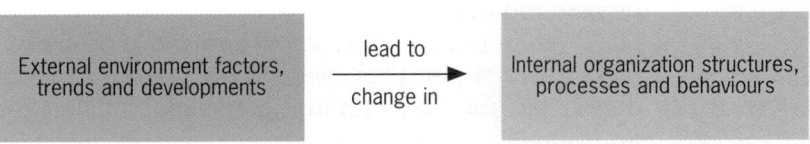

Figure 2.1: The external environment–internal organization link

An understanding of the dynamics of the environment is critical to organizational effectiveness, irrespective of organization size or sector. An organization which is 'out of fit' with its environment (still making stage-coaches now that railways have been invented) has to change, or go out of business. As the complexity and pace of environmental change seem to have increased, organizations that are able to adapt quickly to new pressures and opportunities are likely to be more effective than those which are slower to respond. A central concern for organizational behaviour, therefore, has been the search for 'fit' between the internal characteristics of the organization and features of the external environment.

Analyzing the organizational environment

Identifying current and future factors 'out there' which could impact on the organization usually generates a long list. For our grocery store, this is likely to include, for example, the price of bananas at large supermarkets on the one hand, and the preferences, values and shopping habits of an ageing population on the other. The first problem is to identify all of those factors. The next difficulty, however, is to predict their impact. Will elderly shoppers maintain the habits of their youth, with a weekly shop by car at an impersonal supermarket, or will they prefer convenient and friendly local service at higher prices?

The methods used to analyze the external environment of the organization are known as **environmental scanning** techniques.

Environmental scanning: a term for a number of techniques for identifying and predicting the potential impact of external trends and developments on the internal functioning of an organization.

Environmental scanning involves collecting relevant information from a range of sources: government statistics, newspapers and magazines, internet sites, specialist research and consulting agencies, demographic analysis, and market research and focus groups. Scanning can also be conducted at different levels of detail, from the broad and general to the highly specific. It appears that there are three major trends affecting just about all organizations. These are globalization, information technology, and social and demographic trends.

Globalization

Businesses in Europe and North America have been threatened, since the 1970s, from competition in the Pacific Rim region of the world, particularly from Japan, Taiwan, Korea and Hong Kong. These countries were able to produce cars, motorbikes and a range of consumer electronic and entertainment products with higher quality and lower prices, using shorter production times and new operating processes. European and American businesses in response have become significantly more cost- and quality-conscious, with an increased focus on continuous improvement and customer service. During the late 1990s, the economies of the Pacific Rim suffered through a combination of currency exchange rate collapses, banking system crises and cumbersome organization structures, but their earlier successes have made a lasting impression on European and American management practice.

The term given to these trends and developments (Giddens, 1990, p. 64) is **globalization**.

Globalization: the intensification of worldwide social and business relationships which link distant localities in such a way that local happenings are shaped by distant events, and vice versa.

Globalization involves what has come to be called 'the death of distance' (Cairncross, 1995, 2001), meaning that geographical separation, of countries and of individuals, has become insignificant. Globalization means that the fate of a Third World village, dependent on export sales revenues from a single crop, can be determined by price movements in exchanges in New York or Frankfurt. Globalization means that the actions of a financial markets trader in Singapore can cause the collapse of a London bank. Globalization means that decisions taken in Tokyo can influence employment in the English Midlands, where Toyota has a car plant – at the time of writing. Globalization means that a dispute between Brussels and Washington over trade regulations can close knitwear factories in the Borders region of Scotland.

Global communication, and the exchange of information and ideas, is now instantaneous, through a range of media including land-wired telephones, mobile telephones and satellite links, and the computer-based internet and email. Such instant communication permits the creation of *virtual organizations* whose members are scattered in different locations rather than working in the same building. Globalization has also been assisted by the development of free trade through national and international deregulation, which has made it easier to move goods and money around the planet, and to relocate production facilities (for goods and services) in regions where labour and other costs are relatively low. For some commentators, this means that the role of the single nation-state in economic affairs is reduced, and we see the increasing importance of supra-national bodies such as the European Union (EU), the Commonwealth of Independent States (CIS), the Council of the Baltic Sea States (CBSS), the Association of South East Asian Nations (ASEAN), the Organization for Economic Co-operation and Development (OECD) and the North American Free Trade Association (NAFTA). Global access to advanced technology and weaponry also now means that local conflicts quickly attract global attention.

A world of outsourcing

The jobs of skilled workers in Europe, America and Britain are being lost as companies 'outsource' operations to developing countries. This has been described as 'globalization's next wave – one of the biggest trends shaping the world economy'. Since the 1970s, outsourcing has been common in manufacturing. Now, with the internet and high-speed data exchange, knowledge work, which does not depend on location, is affected too: computer software development, home loans and insurance claims processing, company auditing, interpretation of medical test results such as CT scans, chip design for new-generation mobile phones, pharmaceutical research, architectural design. Countries benefiting include:

China	Coastal cities host call centres for Japanese and South Korean companies. Electronics companies such as General Electric, Philips and Microsoft have product development centres in China.
Philippines	Nine IT parks are linked with a fibre-optic network, where over 8,000 foreign companies have been attracted by large numbers of English-speaking accountants, software writers, architects and graphic artists.
Mexico	American car and electronics companies have moved their manufacturing operations across the border into Mexico, which is 'close to home' and has increased local demand for engineers.
Costa Rica	With low telecommunication costs and a well-educated workforce, the capital city San José has call centres catering for Spanish-speaking consumers in Europe and America. The consultancy firm Accenture has IT support and bookkeeping operations here.
South Africa	South Africa has call centres catering mainly for European companies. Well-educated speakers of French, German and English move across Africa to work here. Other call centres are opening in Mauritius.
Eastern Europe	Unemployed German- and English-speaking workers have attracted Indian and American IT service providers who have offices in Hungary, Poland and the Czech Republic. German multinational companies have IT workshops in Romania and Bulgaria.

| **Russia** | Russia has large numbers of science, mathematics and IT graduates with Masters degrees and doctorates. Boeing, Nortel, Intel and Motorola have research and development centres there. Local companies specialize in exporting complex software engineering project services. |
| **India** | Indian companies such as Tata, Infosys and Wipro have become world leaders in IT services, chip design, call centres and business back-office work, generating significant export revenue and attracting American IT service firms to locate in India. |

Based on Pete Engardio, Aaron Bernstein and Manjeet Kripalani, 'The new global job shift', *Business Week*, 3 February 2003, pp. 36–48.

Consider your own experience of globalization. This is probably reflected in holiday plans, overseas job opportunities, the clothes that you wear and the food and drink that you consume, and the way in which you use the internet, phones and media technology. You are thus likely to have a range of direct and indirect encounters with other cultures on a daily basis, and this experience in turn is likely to change our understanding of the world. However, it is important to remember that many people around the planet do not have access to the goods

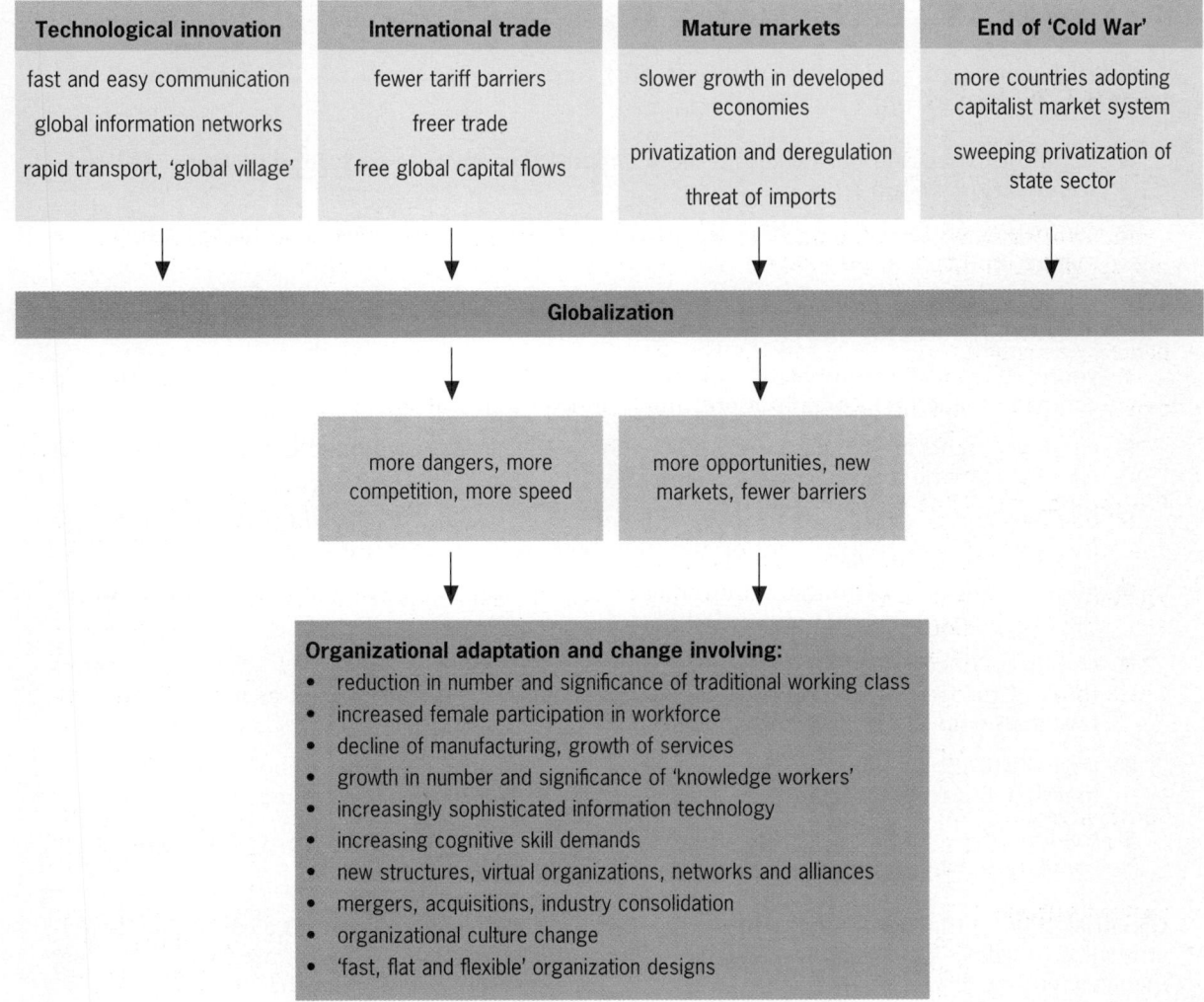

Figure 2.2: Globalization and organizational change

and technologies that constitute the experience of globalization for affluent individuals in developed economies. Globalization is an uneven economic and political process from which many are excluded. Many societies and groups reject the dislocation and disorientation of globalization, and object in particular to the spread of American culture, signified most clearly by its brand labels. For example, in December 2002, a bomb exploded in a McDonald's restaurant in Indonesia, killing three people and injuring eleven others.

We appear, however, to have entered an age of 'disorganized capitalism', complex and rapidly changing, in which the boundaries of large organizations in particular have become blurred, and in which the nature of work itself is in a constant state of flux. Figure 2.2, based on the work of John Kotter (1995b), summarizes this argument. The arrows running down the figure set out a causal chain, from the technological, economic and geopolitical trends at the top of the figure, to the organizational changes at the bottom. Kotter argues that organizational changes in the direction of becoming faster, flatter and more flexible, are determined by external environmental pressures which are driving globalization, introducing new threats and problems, and opening up organizational and market opportunities. Organizational change thus seems to be *inevitable*. The message is 'adapt to survive'.

The new order

Leonard Greenhalgh argues that the twenty-first century represents 'a new era for business'. The challenges in this new order include:

- significant domestic businesses are now rare; large companies have supply chains that transcend national boundaries

- companies no longer have homogeneous workforces and customers, and must find ways to manage and benefit from diversity

- the value of many products (e.g., computers) actually lie in the services which they provide (e.g., word processing and electronic mail)

- young technically competent employees are attracted to small entrepreneurial start-up companies, and other organizations find it difficult to recruit them

- employee rights are increasingly protected by both legislation and public opinion, which can take the extreme form of consumer boycotts

- quality standards that used to apply to luxury goods are now expected in all goods and services – and quality is dependent on the contributions of the lowest-level employees

- business and the environment movement were once separate, but companies must now consider their environmental responsibilities

- employees once valued for their skills are today valued for their knowledge; knowledge workers think of themselves not as subordinates requiring close supervision, but as independent professionals who can work autonomously

- large institutional investors used to avoid interfering in the organizations in which they invested, but today exert influence over issues such as performance and management pay

- the lone free-standing organization is being overtaken by extended networks of collaborating companies, which compete with other value-chain partnerships

Greenhalgh notes that the 'anthem' of many American low-skilled employees is a country-and-western ballad called, 'Take this job and shove it'. That attitude, he argues, is a response to inappropriate management behaviours, which have to change. Top-down decision-making has to be replaced by decentralization. Empowerment has to replace the concept of close monitoring and supervision of 'the cogs in the machine', or 'micromanagement'. Teamwork is more effective than individual performance. The role of management is to support and facilitate, not to direct and control. Managing relationships, internal and external, is as important as controlling operations. Customers and clients, not senior management, are the main drivers behind decisions. In organizations that have delayered, re-engineered, restructured and right-sized, middle management jobs are less secure and can have reduced status, power and upward mobility. Promotion now means accepting greater responsibility, not moving to a larger office with a prestige job title and special car parking space.

Based on Leonard Greenhalgh, 'Managers face up to the new era', *Financial Times*, Mastering People Management supplement, 11 October 2001.

Organizations traditionally have been regarded as independent entities, self-reliant and competing with each other. That perspective is no longer accurate. The traditional Japanese *keiretsu*, for example, are collections of companies which hold shares in each other, have interlocking boards of directors and are able to engage easily in joint ventures. The most widely known *keiretsu* is probably Mitsubishi. The Korean *chaebol* operate in a broadly similar manner, but are more centralized, and are often based on groups of managers who share a common background, such as family, educational institution or geographic region.

These kinds of intra-organizational arrangement and interdependency are not confined to the Pacific Rim. McDonald's, Disney and Coca-Cola, for example, have a joint global marketing alliance. At Animal World, a Disney theme park in Orlando, Florida, staff in the McDonald's restaurant wear uniforms depicting Disney characters, while an oversized bottle in the middle of the restaurant serves coke. Coca-Cola has been the sole soft drinks supplier at Disney theme parks since 1955. When Disney released the film *Armageddon* in 1998, McDonald's sold cinema tickets and 'Astromeals' to promote it (*The Economist*, 1998b).

Outlining ambitious plans to build a global empire, Burt and Larsen (2003) picture the complex ownership structure of Rupert Murdoch's News Corporation as shown in Figure 2.3.

Consolidation: the process through which company ownership in a sector becomes concentrated in a smaller number of much larger and sometimes global enterprises.

This industry structure reflects the process of **consolidation**, which several sectors have experienced since the 1990s. It has been predicted, for example, that the motor car industry will consolidate further during the first decade of the twenty-first century, leaving only six independent manufacturers, two in North America, two in Europe and two in Japan. The global entertainment sector is consolidated into around half a dozen major international organizations. The same process has also taken place globally in hotel and restaurant businesses. The next time you visit a city centre, identify how many of the restaurants ('quality' and 'fast food') you pass are independently owned, and how many are part of national (or international) restaurant chains. National and global consolidation has affected the catering sector too.

Information technology

New technology is probably the most visible and tangible aspect of contemporary environmental change. Applications of computing are now pervasive, affecting most aspects of social and organizational life, from entertainment to manufacturing methods, to the provision of many services, to modes of education. Developments in computing and communication have also led to an apparent increase in the number of 'knowledge workers' (a controversial term) whose value as employees depends more on what they know than on what they can do. Knowledge work, such as computer software design and 'back office' business

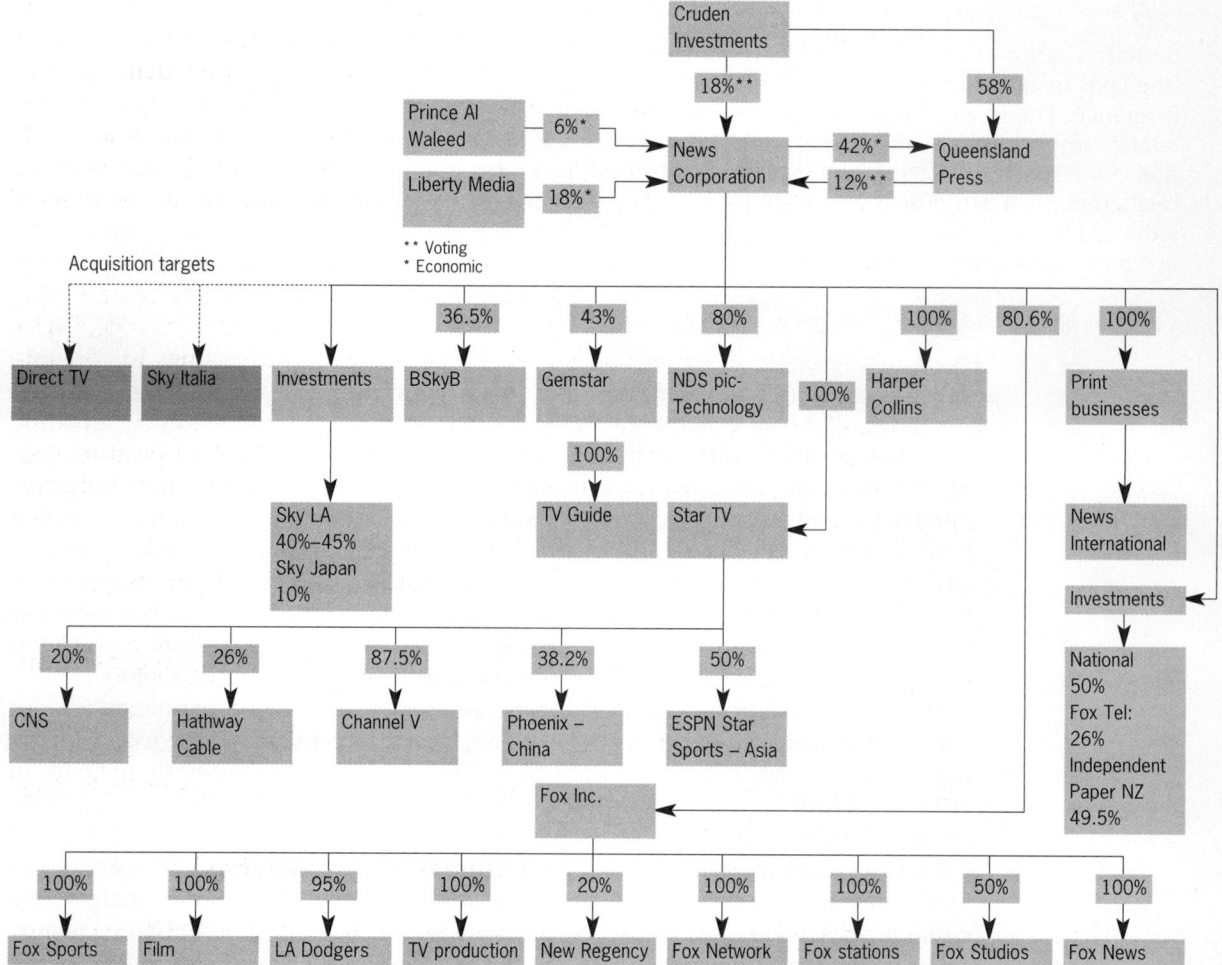

Figure 2.3: News Corporation's ownership structure
From *Financial Times*, Wednesday, February 12, 2003.

support operations, does not depend on location, and such activities are increasingly carried out in low-wage countries (such as India and China) rather than in Europe or America.

The preoccupation with computing can overlook technological developments in other fields, such as in new materials, for example, and in healthcare where the pace of development of new drugs, treatment regimes and equipment seems to be almost as rapid as in computing. The relationships between technology and organizational behaviour, and particularly information technology, will be explored in chapter 3.

Social and demographic trends

There are several demographic trends relevant to organizational behaviour. The workforce in Western industrialized economies is *ageing*. In other words, the proportion of the population who have retired from employment is growing relative to the proportion of the population still in work. Organizations that discriminate against older employees (which in some cases means over 30 or over 40 years of age) may find it difficult to recruit. An ageing population may have different needs as consumers, opening up new markets for organizations smart enough to identify and meet those needs, and also putting pressure on healthcare services.

A range of factors, including wars and improvements in transport and communication, have contributed to migration and a dispersion of the global workforce. This now means a higher ethnic, cultural and religious mix within a given workforce, putting a premium on the ability of the organization to manage that diversity of values, needs and preferences. Another demographic trend concerns what has been called the development of the 'hourglass economy', split between educated and skilled knowledge workers on the one hand, and poorly educated, untrained and poorly paid manual and clerical workers on the other. Other developments include the increasing proportion of women in the workforce.

Lifestyles and values are changing, affecting the formation and composition of households, patterns of living and consumption, trends in leisure and education, and preferences in working patterns. Social values also change. High levels of ecological concern, which are expressed in punitive fines for organizations which create toxic waste and in a wide range of public protests (over the building of new roads and airports, for example), were relatively uncommon before the 1980s. Working patterns throughout the European Union (EU) have the following characteristics (Department of Trade and Industry, 1999, p. 3):

- by 1996, 17 per cent of EU workers were part-time, from 4 per cent in Greece to 40 per cent in the Netherlands;

- around one-sixth of EU workers regularly do shift work, from 6 per cent in Portugal to 25 per cent in Sweden;

- one in seven workers in the EU works at night, regularly or occasionally;

- one in eight workers work from home, regularly or occasionally, including one in four in Britain;

- one in four workers in the EU sometimes work on Sundays.

The typical 40-hour working week, from Monday to Friday, is therefore becoming less common. This has implications for how and when we buy and use a whole range of goods and services, whose providers have to change their practices in turn. The internet now provides 24-hour shopping for many goods and services. To compete, conventional outlets may need to provide similar levels of service. There appears also to be a growing 'home management' industry, servicing in particular the needs of dual-income families where both partners work extended hours. Companies in this sector clean the house, tidy the garden, do the shopping, collect your car for servicing, and will even buy appropriate birthday presents.

Returning to figure 2.1, globalization, information technology and social demographic trends in combination make multiple demands, now and into the future, on the way organizations are structured and managed. The implications of these environmental trends can be felt at different levels, from long-term competitive

Stop and Criticize

In what three ways do your values differ from the values of your parents?

In what three ways do you expect your lifestyle to differ from that of your parents?

In what three ways do you expect that your experience of work will differ from that of your parents?

In what ways will your values and expectations as an employee make life easier or more difficult for the organizations that are likely to employ you?

PESTLE analysis: identifying the Political, Economic, Social, Technological, Legal and Ecological factors affecting an organization.

strategy, through organization structure changes, to the provision of special facilities for particular ethnic or religious groups.

One popular and more detailed approach to environmental scanning is **PESTLE analysis**, which offers a method for reducing the complexity of the task by providing a simple structure.

Some commentators prefer to use the PEST acronym, rolling legal and ecological issues into the political category. Other commentators prefer PETS or STEPS, which sound more 'friendly' and positive. Figure 2.4 places the organization at the centre of a typical range of external trends and pressures based on the PESTLE headings. The detail under each of the six main headings is illustrative, and not comprehensive.

The best way to approach environmental scanning is to do an analysis yourself. This will almost certainly reveal that the neat categories in the model overlap in a rather untidy way in practice. Many legislative changes are politically motivated. Ecological concerns reflect changing social values and preferences. Some technological developments (electric cars) are encouraged by

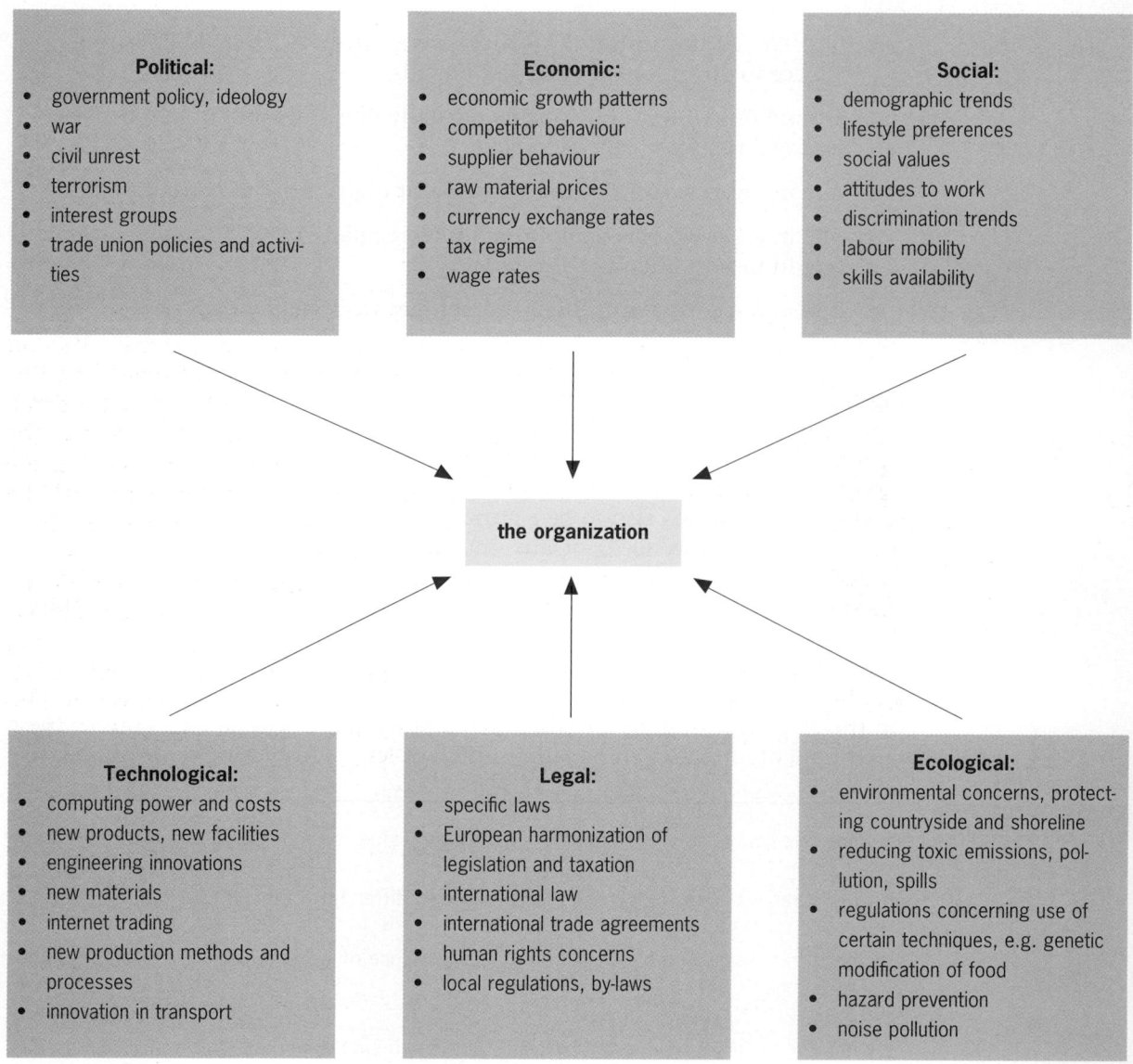

Figure 2.4: PESTLE factors affecting the organization

economic and ecological issues (the price and pollution of petrol). However, the point of the analysis is to identify the external environmental factors, their interrelationships and their impact. It is less important to get them into the 'correct' boxes.

Choose an interesting organization with which you are familiar: corner grocery, supermarket, university or college, the place you worked last summer.

Make a list of all the political, economic, social, technological, legislative and ecological factors and trends that you can think of affecting that organization.

Identify from this analysis the practical advice which you would feed back to the management of your chosen organization.

When you are finished, how would you rate the *value* of this exercise to the organization? Is this of practical significance, or was it just a theoretical exercise?

This analysis usually identifies a number of similar issues.

First, it is difficult to escape from the argument that the organization must pay attention to these PESTLE trends and developments in the external environment. The organization which ignores or fails to respond to those external factors will quickly run into difficulties. As indicated earlier, the implications of this analysis can affect all levels of the organization's functioning, including its strategy, structure, management style and working practices.

Second, the list of external factors, even under these neat headings, can quickly become long and intimidating. The range of factors 'out there' is extremely wide. Identifying which are most significant, and predicting their impact, can be difficult.

Third, a full understanding of those external factors can involve the collection and analysis of a substantial amount of information of different types, and this takes time. How about analyzing demographic trends in south-central Scotland, for example, or pan-European regulations affecting the food and drink industry, or forthcoming information technology software innovations, or collating the results of consumer surveys on lifestyle changes and consumption patterns? The time spent on these kinds of analysis has to be balanced against the need for a rapid response to the trends and developments being considered.

Environmental complexity makes prediction hazardous. We can predict demographic trends with some accuracy, with respect to mortality, and gender and age profiles. We can predict economic trends with some confidence in the short to medium term (up to three or five years), but not beyond. Trends in social values and lifestyles, in politics, in technological innovation or in the impact of new technology, cannot be predicted with much confidence (an observation which does not stop journalists and others from making the attempt). In other words, environmental scanning analysis requires a lot of informed guesswork and judgement.

The PESTLE environmental scanning approach thus has two strengths and four weaknesses:

The *strengths* are:

1. The analysis encourages consideration of the range of external factors affecting internal organizational arrangements.

2. The analysis is a convenient framework for ordering a complex and bewildering set of factors.

The *weaknesses* are:

1. Analysis of an organization's external environment can generate an infinite list of factors, not all of which may be significant. Striking a balance between identifying *all* relevant factors and *the* factors which are particularly important can be difficult.

2. It is difficult to anticipate 'defining events' such as wars, terrorist attacks, new discoveries, economic collapse or major political upheavals which shift country boundaries or radically change government policies.

3. This analysis, if it is to be complete, can involve the time-consuming and expensive collection of very substantial amounts of data, some of which may be readily available and some of which may have to be researched. This can quickly become a major undertaking for the staff involved.

4. The time spent in information gathering and subsequent analysis may inhibit a rapid and effective response to the very trends and developments being analysed.

Scenario planning: the imaginative development of one or more likely pictures of the dimensions and characteristics of the future for an organization.

Environmental analysis using PESTLE is often used for the purpose of **scenario planning**, a technique developed by the oil company Royal Dutch/Shell in the 1970s, and therefore also known as the 'Shell method'.

Scenario planning is based on environmental scanning and creative thinking, with an attempt to identify the most probable future scenario as a basis for planning and action. In the field of corporate strategy, scenario planning is used to explore 'best case, worst case' possibilities, and to encourage 'out-of-the-box' and creative 'blue skies' thinking. A typical scenario planning exercise for a small local grocery store is outlined in table 2.1.

Table 2.1: The grocer's scenarios

Scenario	Main characteristics
1: Revival	Transport gridlock, increased cost of car ownership, ageing population, impersonal hypermarkets; local convenience and traditional 'face-to-face' service become increasingly popular.
2: Decline	Price wars between superstores reduce prices and improve in-store atmosphere as stores add services to retain customer loyalty; small local stores survive but with decreasing profits.
3: Obliteration	Online banking and internet shopping combined with rapid delivery make traditional shopping redundant; large stores become warehousing and distribution centres.

Which of these scenarios is the most probable? The answer has fundamental implications for anyone planning to give up their day job and invest their life savings in a grocery store. Even if one believes that scenarios two and three are the most likely outcomes, there may still be innovations which the store owner could consider introducing to retain customers. It is instructive to consider what those innovations might be, in staffing, for example, or in organization design, service provision, relationships with customers, technology-based purchasing, and so on. This is not merely a theoretical exercise. Scenario planning can have a profound impact on organization strategy and planning, on management decision-making, and on triggering creative responses to environmental trends.

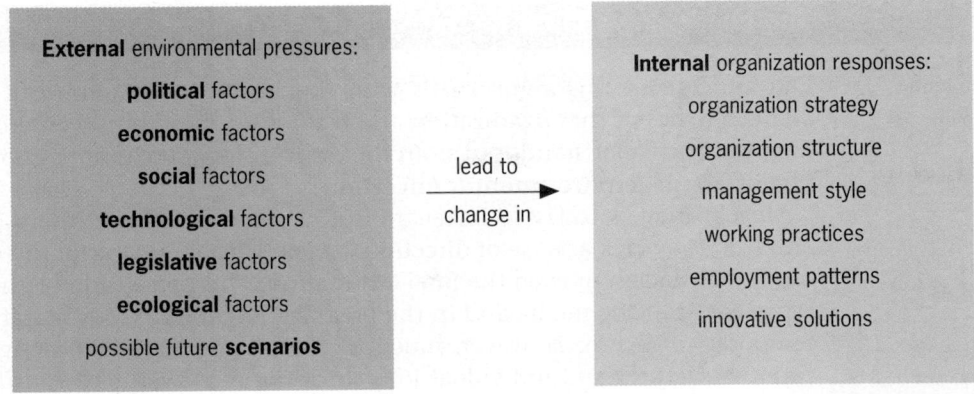

Figure 2.5: The external environment–internal organization link detailed

We have explored environmental scanning for two reasons, practical and theoretical. This is a useful predictive action planning tool, particularly when allied with scenario planning as a guide to creative organizational decision-making. This is also a useful theoretical framework which exposes the range of external environmental influences on internal organizational behaviour, and also highlights the relationships between those external factors. Environmental scanning has become a field in its own right, with its own texts, tools and techniques. A fuller treatment of these and related issues can be found in the corporate strategy literature (Johnson and Scholes, 2002).

We are now in a position to update the model introduced at the beginning of the chapter. Figure 2.5 shows the links between external environmental pressures and internal organizational responses in more detail.

This model relies on a number of basic assumptions:

■ It assumes that all the relevant data can be identified, collected and analyzed.

■ It assumes that the analysis will lead to accurate forecasts of current and future trends, and to the construction of realistic future scenarios.

■ It assumes that the analysis will be consistent, and not pull the organization in different directions at the same time.

■ It assumes that the kinds of internal organizational response indicated by the analysis can be implemented.

■ It assumes that practical recommendations for internal organizational change can be implemented quickly.

In practice, therefore, this kind of analysis has to be used with care. Environmental scanning and scenario planning can be more useful when carried out relatively quickly, relying on a combination of information, informed guesswork and judgement, rather than being driven by an insistence on fully comprehensive and verifiably accurate data. The results of a comprehensive analysis may be available too late to be of practical use to the organization.

The continuing search for 'fit'

Environmental uncertainty: the degree of unpredictable turbulence and change in the external political, economic, social, technological, legal and ecological context in which an organization operates; the more the dimensions of the external context are interrelated, the higher the environmental uncertainty.

Our concern in this argument is with the search for 'fit' between the internal characteristics of the organization and features of the external environment. One factor in particular stands out from the environmental scanning exercise for most organizations: **environmental uncertainty**.

Most managers today feel that the speed of events around them is increasing, and that they lack a sense of direction, a view of the way ahead, the nature of the terrain, obstacles, or even the final destination. This perception of change is often represented in the media and in the organizational behaviour literature as a contemporary concern. However, much of the research into the design of organization structures and individual jobs since the mid-twentieth century has been, and continues to be, concerned with appropriate organizational responses to turbulent, rapidly changing and unpredictable environments.

One of the first systematic attempts to explore the implications of environmental uncertainty is in the work of Fred Emery and Eric Trist (1965). They developed a typology describing four broad kinds of organizational environment, from 'placid' at one extreme to 'turbulent' at the other. They also identified the kinds of organizational arrangements suitable for those different environmental circumstances. Their approach is summarized in table 2.2.

Table 2.2: The Emery–Trist typology of organizational environments

Environment type	Characteristics	Organizational response
1: Placid, randomized	The simplest environment. Little uncertainty, stable, few changes.	Successful organizations have hierarchical, bureaucratic structures with standardized work processes.
2: Placid, clustered	Moderate uncertainty and a large number of variables to consider, somewhat predictable.	Planning becomes important, but some decentralization can be effective.
3: Disturbed, reactive	Increased levels of uncertainty and change, unstable environment confusing and difficult to predict.	Requires flexible, adaptable, decentralized structures to deal with change.
4: Turbulent field	Highly complex, rapidly changing environment, high interdependence between organizations and society, greatly increased uncertainty.	Requires very fluid organization structures, and flexible managers and staff at other levels.

Fred Edmund Emery (1925–97)

There are three main dimensions to this argument.

First, a hierarchical, bureaucratic organization can be effective when the external environment is relatively stable. Bureaucracy has had a bad press. Emery and Trist suggest that there are circumstances in which the rigid, hierarchical bureaucracy can be effective.

Second, the greater the degree of environmental turbulence, the higher the degree of internal flexibility required to deal with the unpredictability, the uncertainty and the consequent organizational change.

Third, Emery and Trist argue that, for most organizations, environments tend to become increasingly turbulent over time. It is interesting to note that, in the title of their paper, Emery and Trist (1965) refer to the 'causal texture' of the organizational environment. They felt that internal arrangements could be explained, at least in part, by external environmental factors.

Eric Landsdowne
Trist (1909–93)

Environmental complexity: the range of external factors relevant to the activities of the organization; the more factors, the higher the complexity.

Environmental dynamism: the pace of change in relevant factors external to the organization; the greater the pace of change, the more dynamic the environment.

Robert Duncan (1972, 1973, 1974, 1979) defined uncertainty as the lack of adequate information to reach an unambiguous decision, and argued that environmental uncertainty has two dimensions. One of these dimensions concerns degree of **simplicity** or **complexity**, and the other concerns the degree of **stability** or **dynamism**:

simple–complex   the number of different issues faced, the number of different factors to consider, the number of things to worry about

stable–dynamic   the extent to which those issues are changing or stable, and if they are subject to slow movement or to abrupt shifts

External factors can include customers, suppliers, regulatory agencies, competitors and partners in joint ventures. Duncan argued that the 'stable–dynamic' dimension is much more significant in determining environmental uncertainty. This is because complexity, which just means an awful lot of variables to consider, is easier to manage than dynamism, which means you don't know what is going to happen next most of the time. Plotting these two dimensions against each other, Duncan produced the typology of organizational environments shown in figure 2.6. This typology is usually applied at the level of the organization. However, it can also be used to understand the environments of business units or departments. Duncan's typology and argument are similar to that of Emery and Trist – different environments require different organizational responses.

However, there is a major difference between these positions. Duncan argues that an organization's location in this typology is dependent on *management perception*, and not on an objective observer's classification. In other words, if you don't perceive that your environment is turbulent, then you will probably not respond to it as such. As our perception can change, so the location of an organization's environment on this typology is unstable.

This is quite different from arguing that external environments determine internal structures and processes. Duncan's observation, that management decisions are based on *perceptions* of the external environment, is thus fundamental. Human perception is selective, with some factors given prominence and

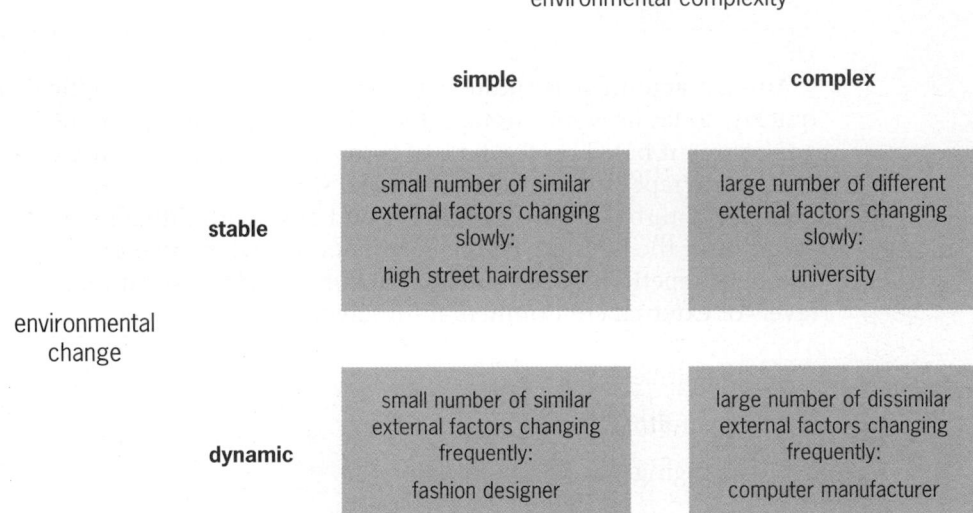

Figure 2.6: Duncan's typology of organizational environments

others filtered out. The same environment may thus be perceived differently by different managers and organizations, even in the same sector. It is management perceptions which affect decisions about organization strategy, structures and processes. In the language of Karl Weick (1979), managers *enact* rather than react to the external environment.

We thus have one perspective which claims that reality, the environment, is 'out there' waiting to be observed, studied, analyzed, understood and reacted to in an appropriate manner. The second perspective claims that, on the contrary, 'the environment' is only what we perceive, understand and interpret it to be, and which therefore is enacted. This distinction between believing that 'the truth is out there', on the one hand, and believing that 'the truth is what we interpret it to be', on the other hand, will be explored later in this chapter. This second perspective reflects the *social construction of reality* argument discussed in chapter 1. It is also a dimension of *postmodern thinking* to which we will turn shortly.

The work of Emery, Trist and Duncan dates from the 1960s and 1970s. What is the relevance of their analysis today? We can answer this question by examining the more recent work of Igor Ansoff (1997). Duncan's (1972) model is *descriptive*. In contrast, and like the model of Emery and Trist (1965), Ansoff's approach is *prescriptive*, offering advice.

Stop and Criticize

Can you apply Duncan's typology in practice? Where on this model would you position the following organizations?

- Oxfam charity organization
- The Leicester Royal Infirmary NHS Trust
- Burger King fast food chain
- Aldi discount food retailer
- A Scotch whisky distillery in a remote Highland glen
- Herz car rental company
- Marriot International hotels
- Oscar de la Renta perfume manufacturers
- BMW motor car company

In Duncan's typology, which type of environment, stable/simple or dynamic/complex, would you prefer to work in, and why? Share your choice with a colleague. You will have to consider this question every time you seek employment.

Ansoff's argument is summarized in table 2.3. This is a difficult table to read quickly, so let us work through it step by step. Ansoff first identifies five types of environment based on the type of turbulence or change being experienced, running from 'repetitive' at one extreme to 'surprising' at the other. This is similar to the 'placid–turbulent' scale of Emery and Trist, with different labels. The first two columns of the table have to be read *vertically*, taking you up and down this scale through 'repetitive', 'expanding', 'changing' and 'discontinuous' to 'surprising' levels of external environmental turbulence:

1. repetitive
2. expanding
3. changing
4. discontinuous
5. surprising

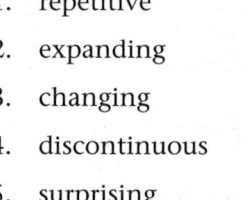

Now turn to level 1, the repetitive environment, and read the table *across* the row. Ansoff argues that we can identify the most appropriate organization strategy and management attitude for that environment. In a stable environment, strategy should be based on precedent. What made the organization successful in the past will continue to work in the future. Also in a stable environment, the appropriate management attitude is to seek stability. Innovation and change could ruin the business. In other words:

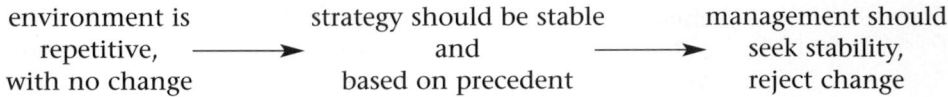

environment is repetitive, with no change ⟶ strategy should be stable and based on precedent ⟶ management should seek stability, reject change

Table 2.3: Turbulence, strategy and attitude – Ansoff's typology of environments

	Environmental change	Organization strategy	Management attitude
1	**Repetitive** little or no change	**Stable** based on precedent	**Stability seeking** rejects change
2	**Expanding** slow incremental change	**Reactive** incremental change based on experience	**Efficiency driven** adapts to change
3	**Changing** fast incremental change	**Anticipatory** incremental change based on extrapolation	**Market driven** seeks familiar change
4	**Discontinuous** discontinuous but predictable change	**Entrepreneurial** discontinuous new strategies based on observed opportunities	**Environment driven** seeks new but related change
5	**Surprising** discontinuous and unpredictable change	**Creative** discontinuous new and creative strategies	**Environment creating** seeks novel change

From I. Ansoff, 'Measuring and managing for environmental turbulence: the Ansoff Associates approach', in Alexander Watson Hiam (ed.), *The Portable Conference on Change Management*, HRSD Press Inc., 1997, pp. 67–83. Reprinted by permission of the Estate of H. Igor Ansoff.

Now jump down to level 5, to the surprising, discontinuous and unpredictable environment, and once again read across the row. As you might expect, the recommended organization strategy is creative, basing strategies not on what the organization has done in the past, but on new and creative approaches. What worked in the past cannot work in the future. The management attitude to surprising change has to be novelty-seeking, helping to shape, influence and create the environment in fresh ways. A failure to innovate by holding on to past precedents will in this context ruin the business. In other words:

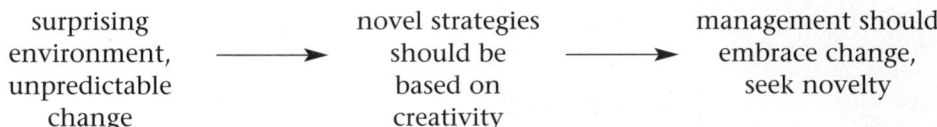

surprising environment, unpredictable change ⟶ novel strategies should be based on creativity ⟶ management should embrace change, seek novelty

Now read the other three intervening rows, again working *across* the table in each case, noting the strategy and management implications for each of the other levels of environmental change. Once that argument and the practical implications are clear, try reading the organization strategy column *vertically*. This can be read as an organization strategy scale, running from stability (precedent-driven) at one extreme to creativity (novelty-driven) at the other. The final column works in the same way. This offers a management attitude scale, from stability (rejecting change) at one extreme to creativity (embracing novelty) at the other.

In another departure from the typologies we have considered so far, Ansoff distinguishes between what he calls *extrapolative* and *discontinuous* environmental change, identified by the line on table 2.3 separating levels 3 and 4. Where environmental change is extrapolative, the future can be predicted, more or less, following (i.e., extrapolating from) current trends. When change is discontinuous, on the other hand, the ability to predict is much less clear. Ansoff (1997) claims that 80 per cent of managers say their organizations have level 4 or 5 environments.

Ansoff makes a number of cruel observations about managers who have been effective and successful in organizations with extrapolative environments. He claims that they are likely to lack the skills, knowledge, experience and attitudes required to deal with a discontinuous environment. Success in a discontinuous environment requires entrepreneurial vision, creativity, innovation and anticipation of change. He comments bluntly that 'Managers incapable of developing an entrepreneurial mindset must be replaced' (Ansoff, 1997, p. 76).

| **Stop and Criticize** | Does your educational institution face an extrapolative or a discontinuous change? |

Does your educational institution face an extrapolative or a discontinuous change?

To what extent is the institution's strategy and management attitude appropriate to that level of change, according to Ansoff's model?

Apply this analysis to yourself. What level of environmental change are you personally subject to, and how does this influence your behaviour?

We are now in a position to update yet again the model illustrated earlier in figures 2.1 and 2.4. The result is shown in figure 2.7. This can now be presented as a 'stimulus–response' model, in which the stimulus of external change prompts organizational responses. The main argument of this model is that the scale, dynamism and complexity of environmental stimuli encourage the development of a new approach to organization, a new flexible and adaptive, environmentally responsive organizational 'paradigm'. This is sometimes referred to as the *post-modern organization*, a concept explored in the following section.

We promised earlier that, having built a basic model, we would knock it down. This is an appropriate point at which to point out four of the flaws in the reasoning behind figure 2.7.

The first problem concerns the **environmental determinism** of this model. Duncan's argument about the role of perceptions is a powerful challenge to this perspective.

Environmental determinism: a perspective which claims that internal organizational responses are wholly or mainly shaped, influenced or determined by external environmental factors.

We know that internal organizational arrangements reflect the influence of a range of factors: the dynamics of the senior management team, their approach to decision-making, senior and middle management whims and preferences, plant-level trade union policy, employee suggestions, past experience. And we also know that, whatever the environmental reality 'out there', what really matters is how the environment is understood and interpreted 'in here'. This means that the environmental 'stimulus' is just one stimulus among many, and that this stimulus is not always guaranteed either a response or the obvious expected response.

The second problem concerns the assumptions which the model makes about organizational boundaries. The argument is that the distinction between what is

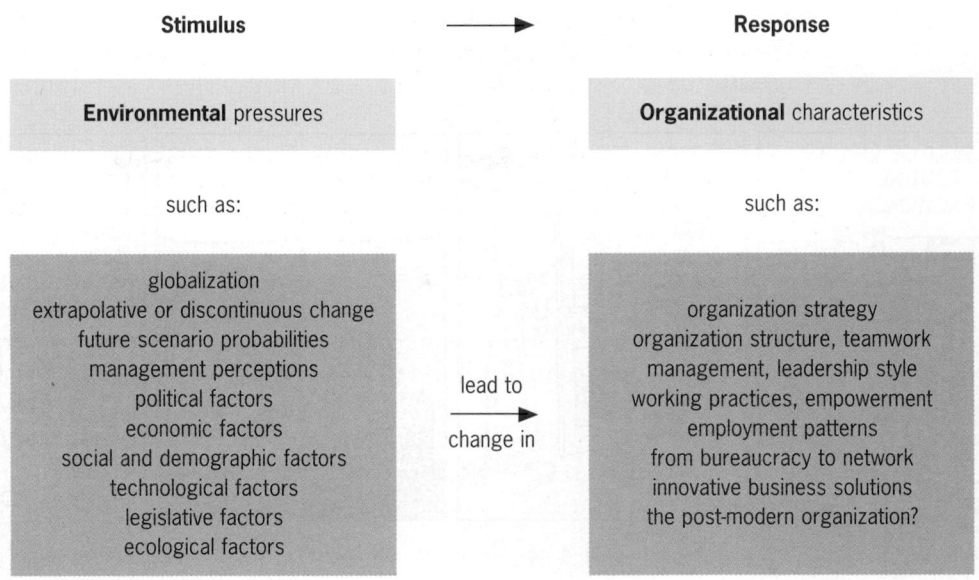

Figure 2.7: The search for environment–organization 'fit'

'out there', in the environment, and what is 'in here', in the organization, is clear. That is not the case. The organization is involved in a constant process of exchange with the environment, importing staff and resources, exporting goods and services. Employees are members of the wider society, whose values and preferences are thus 'inside' the organization. Many organizations have partnership arrangements with suppliers, who are linked by computer to generate orders for low stock items. Many organizations, such as some building societies and roadside assistance organizations for motorists, regard their customers as 'members' who can vote on changes to company rules and receive free copies of their company magazine. Partnership arrangements now commonly occur between competitors, who find it profitable to share the costs, for example, of developing new materials, new processes and sometimes new products. The boundaries between organizations, on the one hand, and between the organization and its environment, on the other, have become blurred.

The third problem is one of interpretation. We are considering 'environment' and 'organization' as separate domains. However, an organization chooses and influences its environment. The organization's environment is a matter of strategic choice (Child, 1997). For example, the grocery store on the corner changes its environment (its customers, its suppliers, its competitors) when the owner decides to stop selling fruit and vegetables and starts hiring out domestic repair and garden maintenance equipment instead. In other words, the external environment of the organization is *enacted*: the organization creates and to some extent even becomes its own environment, rather than being 'given' or 'presented with' that environment. The domains of external environment and internal organization overlap and are much less distinct than the language of our model presumes.

The final problem concerns continuity. The model presents a picture of 'all change', and of rapid and radical change. However, we know that is not the case. Looking back over the past century, we can identify many continuities, environmental and organizational. The relationship between environment and organization is not exclusively about change. Many of today's well-known companies even predate the twentieth century. The German Weihenstephan Brewery was founded in 1040, the Swedish company Stora in 1288, Oxford University Press in 1478, Beretta in 1530, Lloyd's in 1688, Sumitomo in 1690, Sotheby's in 1744, and Guinness in 1759.

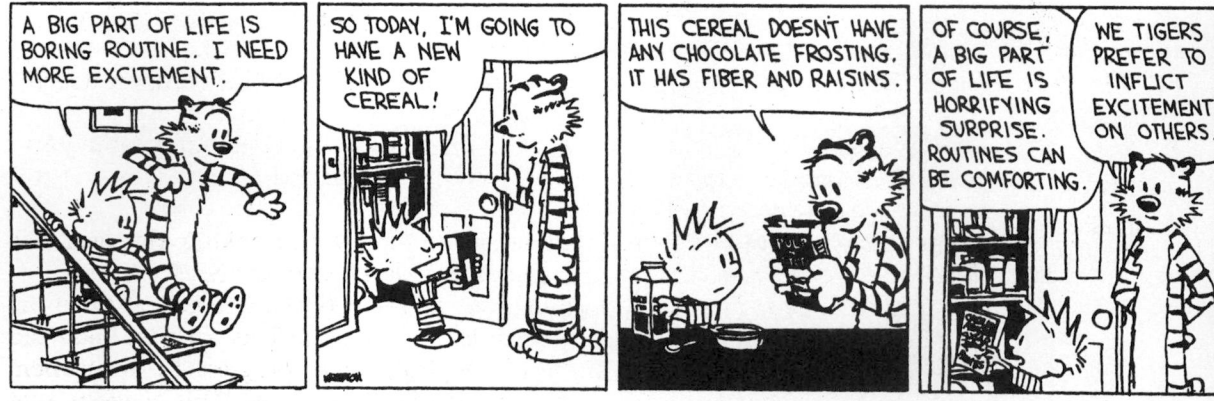

Source: CALVIN AND HOBBES © Watterson. Reprinted with permission of UNIVERSAL PRESS SYNDICATE. All rights reserved.

The post-modern organization

Is there any substance in the claim that an increasingly turbulent external environment has encouraged the development of a new organizational paradigm? Does it make sense to talk about the idealized concept of the **post-modern organization**?

It is fashionable to chart the development of organizational forms since the industrial revolution in the eighteenth century, as in table 2.4 (based on Narayanan and Rath, 1993).

Table 2.4: From classical to modern to post-modern organization form

'Classical' organization 1800–1970 *industrial age*	'Modern' organization 1970–1990 *technological age*	'Post-modern' organization 1900– *information age*
organization as machine	organization as open system	organization as flexible tool
rigid, hierarchical	decentralized	action matters, not design
focus on internal process	focus on human relations	lean, efficient, innovative
mass production	customization	time to market
routine, repetitive work	teamworking	entrepreneurial units
full-time employees	flexible working patterns	networks, sub-contractors
direct supervision	local problem-solving	rules don't matter
emphasized control, predictability	emphasized quality, customer service	emphasizes change, flux, quick decisions
find the one best way	contingency approach	response-oriented
avoid uncertainty	manage uncertainty	exploit uncertainty

Stewart Clegg (1990, p. 181) describes the post-modern organization in these terms:

Where the modernist organization was rigid, post-modern organization is flexible. Where modernist consumption was premised on mass forms, post-

post-modern organization: a networked, information-rich, delayered, downsized, boundary-less, high-commitment organization employing highly skilled, well-paid, autonomous knowledge workers.

modernist consumption is premised on niches. Where modernist organization was premised on technological determinism, post-modernist organization is premised on technological choices made possible through de-dedicated micro-electronic equipment. Where modernist organization and jobs were highly differentiated, demarcated and de-skilled, post-modernist organization and jobs are highly de-differentiated, de-demarcated and multiskilled. Employment relations as a fundamental relation of organization upon which has been constructed a whole discourse of the determinism of size as a contingency variable increasingly give way to more complex and fragmentary relational forms, such as subcontracting and networking.

Table 2.4 sets out one typical representation of current thinking. However, like our earlier model of environment–organization links, this one is also 'wrong'. For a start, those dates are arbitrary, giving only a very approximate indication of the timing of possible transitions in organization design. This kind of 'bad old days–good new days' picture suggests a logical, linear progression from 'then' until 'now', driven by external environmental imperatives. This suggests that rigid bureaucracy, macho managers and simple, boring jobs are all in the past, replaced by flexible organizations with participative, supportive managers and interesting, multiskilled, empowered jobs.

The evidence is mixed. A report produced by the British Department for Education and Employment in 1997 offers some support for the post-modern organization form. Employment in traditional manufacturing industry has declined, as employment in services has increased. This study found increasing skill levels across the workforce, and a movement away from traditional manufacturing methods and towards multiskilled, empowered teamworking. However, there is no evidence with respect to how widespread these organizational changes are.

Gallie et al. (1998), in their national survey of employment trends, found that the general response to technological change and competition in Britain had indeed involved job enrichment and devolved decision-making. But manual workers had experienced more intense supervision and work pacing. Managerial and professional grades, on the other hand, appear to have enjoyed more discretion, but are commonly subject to performance management systems based on target-setting, appraisal and merit pay. The authors note that 'this survey's picture is one of extensive and expanding control systems'. The evidence for empowerment and job enrichment thus has to be set against the evidence for tighter management controls.

Stop and Criticize

McDonald's restaurants has one of the world's most widely recognized corporate logos – the big yellow 'M' that sits above each of its outlets. McDonald's is a successful business, with restaurants in most towns and cities around the world.

Go visit a McDonald's restaurant. Observe closely as many of the staff as you can see, preparing food, serving customers, clearing tables, supervising the restaurant.

Which organizational model – classical, modern or post-modern – does McDonald's use, based on your observations?

How many organizations in your experience still display 'classical' features?

The single premise behind this apparent trend is that flexibility enhances organizational effectiveness and quality of working life. Is the post-modern form being forced on organizations as an inevitable consequence of environmental pressure? Will we see the pervasive spread of networked, information-rich, delay-ered, downsized, lean, boundary-less, high-commitment organizations with highly skilled, well-paid, autonomous knowledge workers? As the final section of this chapter demonstrates, it is possible to interpret this post-modern trend in pre-cisely the *opposite* direction, seeing stability, exploitation and domination where others see change, flexibility and empowerment.

Organization and labour market trends in Britain

- Primary and manufacturing sectors are expected to see further reductions in numbers employed, but future changes are likely to be smaller and more gradual than in the past. Between 1990 and 1996, employment declined in traditional manufacturing and expanded in the service sector. Employment grew in real estate, renting and business activities, education (11 per cent), health and social work (30 per cent), and other community services (18 per cent). Employment in mining and quarrying fell by 54 per cent, by 44 per cent in electricity, gas and water supply, by 15 per cent in manufacturing, and by 15 per cent in construction. These changes in the balance of employment between manufacturing and services are expected to continue.

- New jobs are likely to arise in skill-intensive, knowledge-based occupations. Competitive press-ures place a premium on communication skills, self-motivation, problem-solving and flexi-bility. The 1996 Skill Needs In Britain Survey found that the skills most lacking included management skills, communication, computer literacy and personal skills. Around one in six members of the workforce have literacy or numeracy problems.

- The general skills content – level and range – of most jobs is increasing, due to new businesses and production systems, often based on new technology and emphasizing increased quality and customer care. The 1996 Skill Needs Survey found that 74 per cent of employers thought the need for skills in the average employee was increasing. Demand for manual workers is expected to continue to fall, in favour of non-manual occupations requiring high levels of qualification.

- The labour force is expected to increase by 1.6 million by 2006, and women will make up 1.3 million of this increase (total employment in 1997 was around 26 million). Women now form the majority (52 per cent) of employees in non-manual occupations. Despite office computeri-zation, the role of the secretary – a female-dominated occupation – is increasingly important in flatter organization structures, with increased responsibility and autonomy and with higher-level technical and social skills.

- Ethnic minorities in Britain make up 6 per cent of the population, and are over-represented in lower-paid jobs and under-represented in higher-paid managerial positions.

- Under intense global competitive pressure, firms increasingly seek to concentrate on more cus-tomized products with shorter production runs, abandoning traditional production lines in favour of small, multiskilled manufacturing teams which have discretion in the organization of their own work. The life-cycle of products, production and administrative systems is short-ening, placing a premium on flexibility and on the ability to change.

Based on *A Plan for Objective 4 in Great Britain, 1998–1999*, Department for Education and Employment, November 1997.

Postmodernism: fresh perspectives on organizational behaviour

One of the factors which environmental scanning overlooks concerns changes in ways of thinking about social life in general, and organizations in particular. These changes lie within the domain of philosophy and epistemology. Chapter 1 explored the distinction between two broad epistemological perspectives within the social sciences. One of these is *positivism*, which relies on the natural science methods of testing hypotheses logically by deduction. The other has a range of labels, such as *phenomenology* and *social constructivism*. These perspectives are based on the premise that, as human beings are self-interpreting creatures who attach meaning to their behaviour, their study has to focus on those meanings and interpretations. This involves the use of a range of qualitative, ethnographic, inductive research methods quite different from the hypothetico-deductive methods of natural science.

One development not mentioned in chapter 1 concerns the influence of **post-modernism** in contemporary thought. Postmodernism represents a fundamental challenge to the ways in which we think about organizations, and about organizational behaviour. This is a potentially confusing issue, and one which is awkward to define and summarize clearly and briefly.

Postmodernism is a point of view which rejects the positivistic approach that underlies modern science (natural and social) as a way of developing our understanding of the world. The concept of postmodernism has two connotations. One concerns a period in time. The period in which organizations develop the characteristics described in the previous section can be described as the post-modern period, although putting a precise date to the end of the 'modern' and the beginning of the 'post-modern' is problematic. The second use of the term concerns ways of thinking about and of theorizing society and organizations. Following Karen Legge (1995) among others, the hyphenated term 'post-modern' is used in the former sense, and the unhyphenated term 'postmodern' is used in the latter sense:

post-modern a period in time, following the 'modern', a type of organization design appropriate for contemporary environmental conditions

postmodern a philosophy, an epistemological perspective, a way of looking at, of thinking about, of developing theories, of criticizing organizations

Postmodernism represents a challenge to contemporary (or 'modern') science by rejecting the taken-for-granted notions of rationality, order, clarity, truth, realism and the idea of intellectual progress. Postmodernism draws attention instead to disorder, to contradictory interpretations, to ambiguity. Modernism is concerned with the development of appropriate methods and procedures for establishing 'the truth'. Postmodernism, however, uses the method of **deconstruction** to reveal the strategies that are used to represent 'truth claims'. This means exposing, for example, how an author establishes credibility, how language is used to disarm challenge to an argument, how data are selected and interpreted to support particular conclusions and proposals. Postmodernism is thus concerned with the use of language to support particular versions of 'the truth', by concealing uncertainties and by suppressing opposite meanings and contradictory viewpoints.

The easiest way to understand this complex issue is to deconstruct a specific argument or 'truth claim'. The argument which we will deconstruct is this:

Contemporary organizations and their employees must respond to increasing environmental turbulence by becoming more flexible and adaptive.

1: What are the assumptions underlying this argument?
These assumptions seem to be:

- the external environment is now more turbulent than ever before;

- organizations can change their internal arrangements more or less easily;

Postmodernism: a mode of thinking which focuses on the way in which language is used symbolically and selectively to construct versions of 'truth' and 'reality' to serve the interests of particular social groupings.

Deconstruction: the process of (1) identifying the assumptions underpinning arguments about 'reality', (2) challenging those assumptions, and (3) asking whose interests are served by representing 'the truth' in that way.

- flexibility and adaptability lead to employee empowerment which is desirable;

- adaptation means organizational survival and job protection;

- failure to adapt will lead to organizational collapse and job loss;

- this is a natural, logical progress, replacing outdated 'classical' organizational forms.

2: How can we challenge these assumptions?

The counter-arguments look like this:

- today's environment is just as turbulent as it was at the beginning of the twentieth century – we only think that the pace of change is accelerating (Ogburn, 1922; Mintzberg, 1994);

- major changes to organization structure and culture are stressful and slow and can take years to deliver benefits;

- flexible, adaptable organization structures create uncertainty, instability and a lack of order which many people find uncomfortable and stressful;

- many organizations that have embarked on major restructuring have run into severe difficulties, sometimes with technology, but mainly with the human side of change;

- there are many highly successful organizations which have not adopted the characteristics of the 'post-modern organization' – McDonald's is one example;

- there is nothing 'progressive' about organizational arrangements which create pressure, stress and threat for many people.

When we set out to challenge and reject the original assumptions, it appears to be possible to produce an alternative set of counter-claims. If the assumptions that lie behind the original argument are shaky, what does this tell us about the argument itself?

3: Whose interests are served by representing 'the truth' in this manner?

Major changes to organization structures invariably generate resistance and conflict, which can be reduced if those affected by change agree with it and accept it. What arguments persuade people that 'change is inevitable and good'? Well, arguments that are based on impersonal, overwhelming and inevitable external pressures can be compelling. The argument that says, 'we have to change because of an external threat' is likely to be more acceptable than 'we have to change because I think it's a jolly good idea'. An appeal to environmental issues appears as more objective, convincing, powerful, imperative.

In other words, it looks as though *management* interests are served by representing 'the truth' in this way. Why? Because if this appeal to 'inevitable external pressures' is indeed compelling, then consent to management plans for change will be more readily forthcoming. This way of representing 'reality', therefore, is a way of ensuring compliance.

The deconstruction of our original 'truth claim' offers us a completely different perspective. What status does our argument about organizational responses to environmental pressures have now? The answer lies in a deeper consideration of 'whose interests are served'. We are now forced to consider what is *not* changing, given that we have rejected the assumptions behind the original argument. What is *not* changing includes:

- the ownership structure of the capitalist enterprise;
- the hierarchical nature of management–employee, superior–subordinate relationships;
- management–employee power inequalities;
- management–employee reward inequalities;
- differentials in physical working conditions;
- inequalities of development and career and opportunity.

Behind all this talk about organizational change thus lies considerable continuity. An argument which says 'adapt or die' is exposed as a potential fraud, as many features of work and organization are not changing. Here is an argument which, on the surface, is about 'radical change', but the argument is actually being used to perpetuate basic characteristics of organization structure and managerial prerogative. The nature of the management role, the employment relationship, and the ownership and control structures of capitalist organizations remain unscathed. A postmodern perspective, by deconstructing this argument or 'truth claim', leads to a conclusion *precisely the opposite of the original argument*. This may seem to be a 'negative' outcome, particularly as postmodernism denies *any* firm or valid conclusions or truths. Postmodernism has indeed been attacked for its critical perspective, for its denial and rejection of 'modern' thinking, for its abstraction, scepticism and nihilism.

However, a postmodern perspective can be used positively and creatively. By challenging assumptions, unconsidered alternatives are exposed. We can return to our alternative assumptions and to the organizational features that are untouched, to trigger a debate about how to change those features. In the original argument or 'truth claim', those organizational features were not on the agenda for discussion. Now, they are.

Truth and language games

We commonly think of language as a neutral tool for communicating 'the facts'. From a postmodern point of view, however, language creates and imposes meaning. As our deconstruction example demonstrates, language is used for constructing versions of reality. The implication of this argument is that meaning is 'unstable'; it depends on how you 'read' or interpret it. Postmodernism thus shifts attention away from the author of a text and concentrates instead on the reader, in the following way:

modernism asks   What does this text mean? What is the author really trying to say? What is the correct interpretation?

postmodernism asks   How do different readers interpret this text? What does it mean to them? One interpretation is as valid as another.

This means that our understanding of 'the truth' is always going to be fragmented, selective, biased and illusory. By injecting this sense of insecurity and indeterminacy into our thinking, postmodernism invites us to be sceptical and challenging when faced with arguments and claims which seek to tell us 'this is what it is *really* like, this is how it *really* is'.

Following the phenomenological, interpretative views introduced in chapter 1, postmodernism observes that 'the truth' is socially constructed. In other words, the claim that 'the truth is out there' is false. What we understand by 'reality' is actually a representation manufactured – manipulated – by the careful use of language and media image. Our contemporary understanding of, for example, war and famine is almost exclusively based on television imagery. Is that a problem? One aim of postmodern thinking is to make the commonplace problematic. While modern thinking will pursue 'the truth of the matter' and how to reach that understanding, the postmodern perspective is always asking, 'whose point of view is supported, whose interests are being served, by portraying issues and events in this way?'

Postmodernism thus removes our sense of certainty and order, by removing fixed reference points, by demonstrating that what we thought was 'solid' or 'fixed' or 'real' is a socially constructed product. We are instead invited to see transience, fragmentation, ephemera.

You are what you consume

The focus on meaning, and how it is constructed, applies not just to language, but also to the use of symbolism. Capitalism, it appears, is concerned less with the production of goods and services, and more with the production of signs, symbols and images. When we buy a product, we are invited to buy the image attributed to that product by advertising. The power of film and television images is such that it has become difficult to distinguish between what is representation and what is 'real'.

One of the central themes in postmodernist analysis concerns the notion of 'hypereality', when the image takes over and becomes perceived as more real, as more substantial, than the portrayal of reality. In many respects, what we assume to be 'the real world' appears mundane when compared to the hypereal world presented by the media. Form and substance merge; form *is* substance. The skills of the 'spin doctor', making sure that the message is articulated in the most acceptable, palatable, appealing way, become key political attributes.

This means that our sense of personal identity is also manufactured by the images that we consume. In the past, when someone asked 'who are you?', we might answer with the name of our employing organization, or the title of our job. In other words, our sense of identity is defined by our role in relation to production (of goods or services). But from a postmodern perspective, we are defined not by our role in production but by our patterns of consumption. We consume images – we are invited by advertising to consume images – rather than the actual 'use value' of goods and services.

| **Stop and Criticize** | Apply the argument that 'you are what you consume' to yourself. Consider the clothes, shoes, aftershave or perfume, and accessories that you wear, paying particular attention to the manufacturer's label or logo (which may be on display). How do these items reflect your identity, your self-image, the impression that you want to give to other people?

Consider the appearance of your friends and colleagues. How is their identity defined by their clothing – by the consumption of particular items for display to others? |

Positivism is dead

Modernism relies on scientific and technological rationality – what in chapter 1 was identified as the positivist perspective. The modern project of natural science is to discover fundamental truths, universal laws. We take the notion of scientific and technological progress for granted. Modern organizations, in turn, rely on bureaucratic rationality which seeks to establish organizational order through hierarchy, collective goals and controlled performance. This is reflected in the constant management pursuit of 'best practice'. This chapter has also presented an argument suggesting that there has been a rational development of organizational forms, from classical, to modern, to post-modern.

Postmodernism rejects the notion that 'the truth is out there' waiting to be discovered by rational, scientific, investigative or experimental procedures. There are no 'absolutes'. Understanding depends on the attribution of meaning. This is tied into earlier comments about language games. Postmodernism, as a way of thinking and theorizing, is therefore characterized by multiple perspectives. There is no single integrated perspective or theory.

The search for 'the truth', for 'the one best way' or for 'the single most appropriate perspective' is itself a target of postmodern attack. Postmodernism argues instead for accepting a diversity of perspective, rejecting the notion that we should be dominated by single points of view. This also means rejecting what is called 'the progress myth', that scientific knowledge accumulates in a rational manner through time. On the contrary, the postmodern perspective demonstrates how those in power use 'progress' as a rationale for maintaining vested interests in the *status quo*, in maintaining their privileged positions.

The postmodern perspective demonstrates the limitations of the organizational behaviour field map from chapter 1. We can 'read' that map as a causal model, showing how organizational effectiveness and quality of working life are shaped and determined by a set of identifiable factors. If only we knew more about those factors and how they interact, we could 'engineer' better performance and improve quality of working life. But that is only one way to 'read' and interpret the model.

Stop and Criticize

Consider the field map of the organizational behaviour terrain in chapter 1.

What are the assumptions underpinning that model?

Can those assumptions be challenged, rejected, restated?

Whose interests are served by presenting the field map in that way?

What is the wider value of the postmodern perspective to a practical understanding of organizational behaviour? Mary Jo Hatch (1997, p. 45) argues that:

> Predictions are that the future will find us occupying smaller, more decentralized, informal, and flexible organizations that will be predominantly service- or information-oriented and will use automated production strategies and computer-based technology. As a result of these changes, we will experience organizations as more eclectic, participative, and loosely coupled than ever before; with the implication that members of organizations will confront more paradox, contradiction and ambiguity. These themes resonate with the philosophy of postmodernism suggesting that a postmodernist perspective will help us to adapt to changes already taking place, ironically, as a result of continuing applications of modernist science and technology.

Hatch asks how we should best prepare ourselves for a postmodern future and, in summary, offers the following advice:

- learn to take nothing for granted;
- deconstruct all claims to truth by exploring the assumptions behind them;

- keep asking, whose point of view is benefited by this way of looking at things;

- focus on how language is used to construct reality and identity;

- focus on what is not said, on what is hidden by conventional expressions;

- avoid 'one right answer';

- dispute the categories into which we place people;

- forget the belief that everybody should think the same way that you do;

- be reflexive – challenge your own assumptions;

- maintain a critical distance between your idea of self, on the one hand, and socially and culturally defined ways of seeing the world, on the other;

- bring your own socially constructed understanding under conscious control and challenge;

- imagine alternatives to our 'taken-for-granted' understanding of organizational life;

- consider change 'as a form of thrill', 'as a state to be sought out as invigorating', as a welcome experience.

Postmodernism is thus a challenging perspective, offering positive and creative insights into personal identity, social relationships, and the structures and processes of organizations. This chapter has considered the effect of external environmental pressures on internal organizational arrangements. On the one hand, we can see organizational change as a predictable response to neutral, impersonal external forces. On the other hand, we can see organizational change as a vehicle for sustaining dominant social and organizational power positions, for maintaining management prerogatives and control. Resistance to control is disarmed by arguments about overwhelming external pressures which can be used to support the view that 'there is no choice' but to organize in this way. The postmodern perspective thus offers valuable fresh insights into ways of understanding organization and management.

Recap

1. *Understand the mutual interdependence between the organization and its environment.*

   - In order to survive, organizations have to adapt their internal structures, processes and behaviours to enable them to cope with complexity and the pace of external change.

   - External pressures on organizations come from the globalization of business, developments in information technology, and social and demographic trends.

2. *Appreciate the strengths and limitations of PESTLE analysis of organizational environments.*

   - PESTLE analysis for environmental scanning provides a coherent and comprehensive framework for the analysis of a diverse and complex range of factors.

   - PESTLE analysis generates vast amounts of information, creating a time-consuming analysis problem, and making predictions from this analysis difficult.

3. *Explain the main contemporary organizational responses to environmental turbulence.*

   - Emery, Trist and Ansoff argue that bureaucratic organizations are effective in stable environments, but that fluid structures are more effective in 'turbulent' environments.

   - Duncan and Weick argue that what counts is the management perception of environmental uncertainty; perception determines the management response.

4. *Describe the main features of the 'post-modern' organization.*

  - The 'classical' bureaucratic organization is being replaced by the 'post-modern' organization which is flexible and responsive and ignores hierarchy and rules. However, there are successful organizations which use traditional organizational designs.

5. *Understand the main characteristics of a postmodern perspective on organizational behaviour, and the creative and critical dimensions of this approach.*

  - Postmodernism does not regard language as a neutral tool for communicating 'facts', but as a way of creating and imposing meaning. As meaning depends on the interpretation of readers, meaning becomes unstable, transient and fragmentary.

  - Postmodernism uses deconstruction to explore the assumptions behind claims to 'the truth', exposing whose interests are served by expressing 'the truth' in that manner.

  - When deconstructed, the claim that 'organizations must adapt to survive' seems to rely on questionable assumptions, which disguise the fact that many key features of organization structure and management control do not change at all.

  - Postmodernism rejects attempts to find universal laws or truths, and encourages multiple and competing perspectives.

  - Postmodernism encourages creativity by showing how we can be liberated from the trap of conventional assumptions and the domination of particular viewpoints.

Revision

1. What is 'postmodernism', and how can this perspective be of value to an understanding of organizational behaviour?

2. Explain the 'environment–organization fit' argument. What are the main assumptions behind this argument?

3. How can organizational environments be classified, and what are the implications of such categorization for organization structures, strategies and managers?

4. What is environmental scanning? Illustrate your explanation with an appropriate example, and assess the strengths and limitations of this technique.

5. Explain the technique of deconstruction, and apply this approach to the argument that 'organizations must become more adaptable and flexible to survive'.

Springboard

Appignanesi, R. and Garratt, C., 1995, *Postmodernism for Beginners*, Icon Books, Cambridge.

Difficult read but with an informative introduction to the concept, made interesting with cartoons and drawings. Insightful on the postmodern perspective on the use of language and on the way in which contemporary film mixes image and reality.

Burrell, G., 1998, *Pandemonium: Towards a Retro-Theory of Organization*, Sage Publications, London.

Demonstrates how to write in a postmodern style, without using a modern, linear, rational approach. Don't expect to find a rational argument systematically developed here, however. The style is revealing, but not an easy book to read or to understand.

Dunphy, D., Benn, S. and Griffiths, A., 2002, *Organizational Change for Corporate Sustainability*, Routledge, London.

Explores the fashionable topic of organizational 'greening', arguing that 'third-wave corporations' must take more seriously their wider environmental and ecological responsibilities in the interests of sustainable global development.

Garten, J., 2002, *The Politics of Fortune: A New Agenda for Business Leaders*, Harvard University Press, Cambridge, MA.

Argues that organizations in the twenty-first century find themselves in 'a new era' as the expansion of international trade has slowed down, an anti-globalization movement has developed, terrorism has heightened geopolitical tension, corporate scandals at Enron and WorldCom tarnished the reputation of corporate governance, share prices have fallen sharply, and many internet businesses – dotcoms – have failed spectacularly.

Hardy, C. and Palmer, I., 1999, 'Pedagogical practice and postmodernist ideas', *Journal of Management Education*, vol. 23, no. 4, pp. 377–95.

An excellent and clear introduction to postmodern thinking, its relevance to and impact on organization and management, with innovative teaching ideas.

Hatch, M.J., 1997, *Organization Theory: Modern, Symbolic and Postmodern Perspectives*, Oxford University Press, Oxford.

An unconventional but clearly written and informative introduction to organizational behaviour, exploring issues from modernist (positivist), social constructivist and postmodern perspectives, demonstrating the contrasts in these three thinking styles.

Johnson, G. and Scholes, K., 2002, *Exploring Corporate Strategy*, Financial Times/Prentice Hall, Harlow.

Many of the issues explored in this chapter – environ-

mental scanning, PESTLE analysis, scenario planning, organizational 'fit' – are also part of the subject matter of the discipline of corporate strategy. This is one of the leading strategy texts.

Sennett, R., 1998, *The Corrosion of Character: The Personal Consequences of Work in the New Capitalism*, W.W. Norton, New York.

A highly readable essay on the experience of work in the flexible post-modern organization and the impact of change and insecurity on personal identity. It attacks the myths surrounding flexible multiskilled teamwork; not as much fun as it sounds.

Home viewing

The Matrix, and *The Matrix Reloaded* (1999 and 2003, directors Andy and Larry Wachowski) are based on the assumption that what we think of as 'reality' is actually a façade. The computer hacker Neo (played by Keanu Reeves) discovers that human perception is artificially controlled by 'The Matrix' and that the world in which we think we live is manipulated by advanced artificial intelligence. Humans exist in an elaborate computer simulation, living in pods to provide energy to fuel The Matrix. Only when Neo is exposed to this alternative reality by the rebels Morpheus (Laurence Fishburne) and Trinity (Carrie Ann Moss) does he decide to fight back. How else do these films illustrate the postmodern argument that reality is what we perceive reality to be?

eXistenZ (1999, director David Cronenberg), portrays a future society addicted to computer games. Allegra Geller (played by Jennifer Jason Leigh) has developed an organic virtual reality game which plugs into the nervous system through a 'port' at the base of the spine. This allows players to experience the game as hyper-real. Allegra is threatened by 'reality terrorists', anti-game fanatics who pursue her into her own game, where she is accompanied by Ted Pikul (Jude Law). Note how the lines between reality and fantasy, between 'real' identities and game personae intermingle, finally leaving characters and viewers uncertain about where the game stops and reality begins. What is image, which is reality?

OB in literature

Ian Banks, *The Business*, Little, Brown and Co., London, 1999.

Kate Telman is a technology specialist working for The Business, an organization with global reach: a Swiss headquarters, a ranch in America, a castle in Yorkshire, and a desire to buy a Himalayan principality to obtain a seat at the United Nations. A tale of organizational politics and world domination, is this what working life in the global corporation has become?

Michael Crichton, *Rising Sun*, Century Arrow, London, 1992.

Which elements of globalization affecting business practice are exposed in this murder story? This is the book of the film analyzed briefly in the section 'Text aims and target readership', page xxiv.

Chapter exercises

1: Social responsibility

Objectives
1. To explore the environmental pressure on organizations to be socially responsible.

2. To expose the tensions between the goals of social responsibility and profitability.

Briefing This chapter argues that organizations must be responsive to their environment. For example, organizations are expected to act in ways that demonstrate social responsibility with respect to the communities in which they operate, the physical environment, and the people whom they employ. However, social responsibility can be costly and conflict with commercial goals. As a manager, how would you resolve these tensions?

This questionnaire is designed to help you explore your perceptions of the conflict between social responsibility and business performance. You are a senior manager with a major commercial organization. How would you respond to the following items? Tick the appropriate box on the scale on the right. Share your answers with colleagues and identify the reasons for any differences in your opinions.

Your instructor will then reveal how managers in Britain answered this questionnaire in 1999.

Social responsibility survey

	strongly agree	agree	neutral	disagree	strongly disagree
1. the primary goal of any business should be to remain profitable over the long term in order to produce returns for shareholders	❑	❑	❑	❑	❑
2. the only social responsibility of business is wealth creation	❑	❑	❑	❑	❑
3. the social responsibility of business extends no further than behaving ethically in the pursuit of its business goal	❑	❑	❑	❑	❑
4. part of doing good business is taking responsibility for the impact of your activities on the natural environment	❑	❑	❑	❑	❑
5. business decision makers have a responsibility to take into account the impact of decisions on the communities in which they operate	❑	❑	❑	❑	❑
6. directors of a business should set an example as responsible and involved members of their communities	❑	❑	❑	❑	❑
7. since employment cannot be guaranteed, a socially responsible organization should support the employability of its staff through appropriate development	❑	❑	❑	❑	❑

Social responsibility survey (continued)

	strongly agree	agree	neutral	disagree	strongly disagree
8. organizations have a responsibility not only to conduct their affairs but also to develop their members as 'good citizens of society'	❑	❑	❑	❑	❑
9. in today's environment, businesses have to be seen to be socially responsible in order to remain competitive	❑	❑	❑	❑	❑
10. organizations can differentiate themselves in the marketplace by demonstrating social responsibility in the way they do business	❑	❑	❑	❑	❑
11. social responsibility needs to be balanced with pursuing economic interests	❑	❑	❑	❑	❑
12. business should seek to act in the interests of the wider society	❑	❑	❑	❑	❑
13. managers should see themselves as 'custodians of wealth', not only for shareholders but also for society as a whole	❑	❑	❑	❑	❑

This exercise is based on David Butcher and Penny Harvey, 'Be upstanding', *People Management*, vol. 5, no. 13, 1999, pp. 37–42.

2: The full impact of the environment

Choose an organization with which you are familiar. This could be an organization which you use as a consumer: supermarket, cinema, CD and video chain store, bar, restaurant, garage. Or this could be an organization which is currently in the news for some reason (probably concerned with the need to respond to environmental change). You are going to conduct an environmental scan for this organization. In other words, you are going to identify the issues, events, factors, development and trends, now and into the foreseeable future, which may have an impact, direct or indirect, on how this organization operates. You are also going to work this analysis through to a set of recommendations concerning organizational change. In other words, what are the practical implications of your analysis?

(a) Determine where on the Ansoff turbulence scale this organization is now operating:

1. repetitive

2. expanding

3. changing

4. discontinuous

5. surprising

(b) Use this template to record your analysis, taking turbulence level into account when framing your recommendations:

PESTLE factor	Trends and developments
Political	
Economic	
Social	
Technological	
Legal	
Ecological	

(c) Use your analysis to construct three possible future scenarios for this organization, identifying in each case the organization and management implications, and also identifying which scenario you think is the most probable, and why.

Scenario	Organization and management implications and recommendations
1:	
2:	
3:	

Chapter 3 Technology

Key concepts

material technology	job rotation
social technology	job enlargement
replacement mechanisms	autonomous work group
compensatory mechanisms	system
human-centred manufacturing	open system
the death of distance	socio-technical system
technological determinism	organizational choice
characteristics of mass production	lean production

Learning outcomes

When you have read this chapter, you should be able to define those key concepts in your own words, and you should also be able to:

1. Explain different uses of the term 'technology'.
2. Explain why predictions about technology and unemployment are often exaggerated.
3. Explain how new technology is changing the nature of work for some people, through teleworking, call centres and increased surveillance.
4. Demonstrate how the consequences of technological innovation for skill requirements depend on the organization of work and not simply on technical capabilities.
5. Define the characteristics of mass production and identify approaches to overcome them.
6. Apply the socio-technical system perspective to organizational analysis and design.
7. Contrast the Scandinavian and Japanese models of team-based work organization.

Why study technology?

Technological innovation is one of the defining features of industrialized societies. In this chapter we will focus on computing, telecommunications and other information technologies that are changing the nature of work and organizations. These innovations affect:

how we communicate with each other	email, mobile phone, video telephone, video conferencing, digital video and still cameras
how we buy goods and services	smart cash cards, e-commerce, internet access to news, information services, films and music
how we spend our leisure time	DVD, web surfing, interactive gaming, chat rooms, e-books, digital radio and television

Technology is a paradoxical topic. While 'state-of-the-art' computing technologies promise improvements in personal and corporate performance, analyses consistently conclude that these productivity gains are not being achieved. While new technology can liberate and empower, it can also be used to increase workload and stress, and tighten management control. Many 'high-profile', strategic information technology projects have been disasters; examples in Britain include the failed computerization of the London Stock Exchange, the London Ambulance Service, the Passport Office, the National Insurance system, and the Common User Data System at the Ministry of Defence. As one commentator has noted, the 'the bigger the project, the bigger the disaster' (Dearlove, 2000). The problems seem to lie not just with the technology, but also with organizational issues.

Technology clearly influences the organization of work and the design of jobs. In the popular media, technological change is often accused of causing unemployment, deskilling and the dehumanization of work. We would like to show that the influence of technology in organizational settings is more complex than some media accounts suggest, and also that new technology has benefits as well as disadvantages, depending on how it is used. The argument of the chapter is set out in the following sequence.

First, we will show that the impact of technological innovation on employment is indeterminate. New technology creates new jobs while making 'old' jobs redundant, and has an overall skills upgrading effect while deskilling some tasks.

Second, we will consider three specific ways in which new technology is changing the nature of work, through teleworking, call centres and employee surveillance, exploring in each case the benefits and disadvantages of these developments.

Third, we will examine the argument that the motives of management in implementing new technology explain the organizational consequences of change. Technology may have material benefits, but technology is also used to support social and political aims, affecting the status and power of particular groups.

Finally, we consider classic research into technology implications, showing that these are not 'new' concerns, and that findings from earlier studies are relevant today. This applies in particular to socio-technical systems thinking. We also explore the controversial debate concerning the relative merits of Swedish and Japanese approaches to the organization of work in motor car assembly, leading to the development of 'lean' and 'build to order' manufacturing systems.

When are you getting your implant?

Researchers at Reading University in England have been asked by a group of international companies to develop a microchip implant for workers to monitor their timekeeping and location. Professor Kevin Warwick says that 'For a business the potential is obvious. You can tell when people clock into work and when they leave the building. You would know at all times exactly where they were and who they were with. It is pushing at the limits of what society will accept but it is not such a big deal. Many employees already carry swipecards. I think this is just a step on from that.' The telecommunications company AT&T already uses smart cards and smart badges which relay signals back to a central computer to track staff movements around buildings so that their telephone calls can 'follow' them.

Based on Stephan Bevan, 'Companies seek chip implants to control staff', *The Sunday Times*, 9 May 1999, p. 1.7.

Why technology predictions are often false

We need to be clear what we mean by the term 'technology'. Langdon Winner demonstrates how our use of the term changed as concern for 'technological implications' grew. The term was used in the eighteenth and nineteenth centuries simply to refer to machines, tools, factories, industry, craft and engineering. However, the term 'is now widely used in ordinary and academic speech to talk about an unbelievably diverse collection of phenomena – tools, instruments, machines, organizations, methods, techniques, systems, and the totality of all these things in our experience' (Winner, 1977, p. 8).

Stop and Criticize

Which particular technologies shape your day-to-day experience?

Consider how you expect your life experiences to be different from those of your parents; what part does technology play in creating those differences?

How has this confusion arisen? Rapid developments in technology leave the language behind. The word 'technology' is simply a convenient umbrella term. Ambiguity in the language reflects the pace of innovation and the concern over technology and its consequences – individual, organizational and social. Winner also argues that this simplification of the language leads us to oversimplify and polarize the issues and arguments. Technology is either a good thing or a bad thing; you are either for it or against it.

The British sociologist Alan Fox (1974) distinguishes between **material technology** and **social technology**. Social technology includes job definitions, payment systems, authority relationships, communications, control systems, disciplinary codes and 'all the many other rules and decision-making procedures which seek to govern what work is done, how it is done, and the relationships that prevail between those doing it' (Fox, 1974, p. 1).

Considerable research effort has been devoted to identifying the effects of technology on organizations, jobs and society at large. Technology has often been regarded as the *independent variable* (see glossary), the factor whose effects are to be studied. Economic growth, employment levels, organization structures, skill requirements and quality of working life become *dependent variables* (see glossary), variables that are expected to be affected by technology. This relationship is illustrated in figure 3.1.

However, as we have seen, some definitions of technology go beyond the equipment itself and overlap with the dependent variables. Organization structures and the design of jobs can be considered as 'social technologies'. This makes it difficult to establish cause and effect.

Material technology: the tools, machinery and equipment that can be seen, touched and heard.

Social technology: the methods which order the behaviour and relationships of people in systematic, purposive ways through structures of co-ordination, control, motivation and reward.

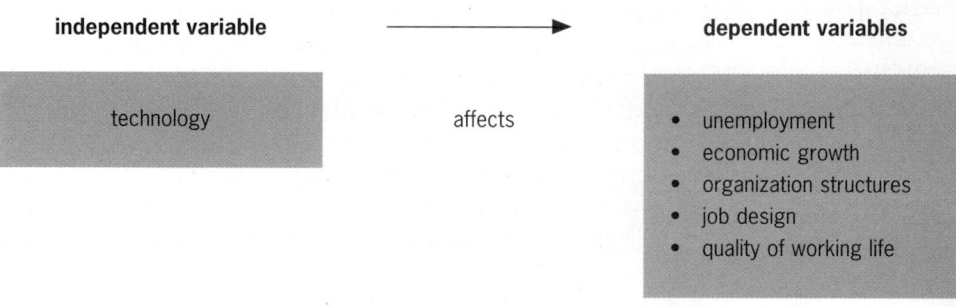

Figure 3.1: Technology as an independent variable

Advances in technology, and developments in computing and information technology in particular, continue to attract widespread media predictions of doom. Does the evidence support these predictions?

Which of the following typical media representations of the impact of technology do you agree with, and with which do you disagree?

■ Robots will replace people in manufacturing; the 'unstaffed factory' is a reality.
■ Office automation does away with clerical and administrative work; the 'paperless office' is here to stay.
■ Nobody needs to work in an office any more because we can all work from our networked computers at home; the 'virtual organization' is here to stay.
■ Where people are still required, work will be simple, routine, dehumanized.
■ The days of craft skill and worker autonomy are gone.

Compare your views with those of colleagues. Have the media got it wrong, or not?

These predictions are all correct, as some jobs have been eliminated by machinery, some work has been dehumanized by technological change, much paperwork has been declared redundant, some people work from a computer terminal at home, and some traditional crafts have disappeared.

In chapter 2, the concept of *environmental determinism* was challenged. In this chapter, the arguments behind *technological determinism* are given a similar critical examination. Let us first explore the argument that new technology causes unemployment.

Replacement mechanisms: processes through which intelligent machines are used to substitute for people in work organizations, leading to unemployment.

Technology, particularly in the form of computing and information technology, can increase organizational productivity through what are known as **replacement mechanisms**, resulting in unemployment.

Claims about the unemployment consequences of technology rely on the assumption that, as machines do more, people do less. Job opportunities are reduced by replacement mechanisms. These fears date from the early nineteenth century, when Luddites destroyed the mechanical looms that were stealing their jobs. Why has subsequent technological change not made the problem worse? Why is technological unemployment *not* chronic?

Compensatory mechanisms: processes that delay or deflect replacement effects, and which can lead to the creation of new products and services, new organizations and new jobs through technological innovation.

Technological development is consistent with employment growth. Unemployment levels are not higher today than in earlier decades, and there is little proof of a technology-led fall in job opportunities. The overall effects of technological developments also depend on a number of **compensatory mechanisms.**

There are six main compensatory mechanisms:

1: New products and services mean job creation
Technological innovation has given us mobile phones with built-in digital cameras, e-books, digital video disks, multimedia computers, the internet and email, cybercafés, electronic engine management systems in cars, video-conferencing, compact discs and their players, smart bankcards, personal organizers, portable text scanners, and so on. These developments create consumer demand, which leads to more investment in factories, offices and other infrastructure, thus creating jobs in manufacturing, distribution, sales and maintenance.

2: Lower costs increase demand
Technical innovation should improve productivity (same output, fewer resources) of existing operations. The consequent cost reduction leads to lower prices, and

hence to increased demand. This also means that consumers have more money to spend on other goods and services, increasing demand and job creation elsewhere.

3: Time lags can delay the implications

It takes time to build new technology into existing systems and into new products and services. Technical and organizational problems need to be overcome. This takes time and other resources. Organizations rarely adopt innovations as soon as they become available, and it is expensive to replace existing facilities quickly. Significant investments in factories and offices cannot be written off overnight. Despite the common complaint about the rapid pace of change, technological and organizational changes are often relatively slow.

4: Hedging risk can delay the implications

Most organizations turn to experimental and untested technologies slowly at first. The 'learning curve' with a new technology can be expensive, time consuming and painful. One way to carry these risks is to introduce technological innovation gradually and cautiously.

5: Expectations of demand

An organization usually embarks on expensive innovations, with disruptive changes, only when the market for its goods and services is likely to expand. In that case, the organization has to retain, if not expand, the existing workforce. Organizations which expect demand for their output to fall or remain stable are unlikely to invest heavily in change, other than to reverse those expectations.

6: Technical limitations

New technologies do not always live up to the claims of those who sell them. They may, in fact, not be able to do everything that the 'old' technology was capable of doing. Existing jobs, skills and equipment may be found working alongside new devices for some time. It is still common to find traditional landlines in households where family members have their own mobile phones. Conventional machine tools are still used in factories equipped with computer-controlled flexible manufacturing systems. The old technology, combined with 'old' human skills, can often perform tasks more easily, faster and more effectively.

It is therefore unrealistic to assume that new technology will increase unemployment. It is equally plausible to argue that technological innovation will create as many jobs as it eliminates, and could create more. In other words, the effects of technology on employment are indeterminate, depending on the complex interrelationship between replacement and compensatory mechanisms, and their respective timing.

If technology does not create unemployment, then surely the jobs that remain will be deskilled, at best, and dehumanized at worst? The evidence suggests that 'technological implications' are not as one-dimensional as they are often portrayed. Technology can deskill, in some contexts, but it can also increase the demands on human skill and understanding.

Research has confirmed the view expressed by Louis Davis and James Taylor (1975, 1976) that technological innovation opens up new opportunities for work organization and increases the demands on cognitive and social skills. Shoshana Zuboff (1988, pp. 75–6) concludes, from studies of automated process control applications:

> As information technology restructures the work situation, it abstracts
> thought from action. Absorption, immediacy, and organic responsiveness are

superseded by distance, coolness, and remoteness. Such distance brings an opportunity for reflection. There was little doubt in these workers' minds that the logic of their jobs had been fundamentally altered. As another worker from Tiger Creek summed it up, 'Sitting in this room and just thinking has become part of my job. It's the technology that lets me do these things.'

The thinking this operator refers to is of a different quality from the thinking that attended the display of action-centred skills. It combines abstraction, explicit inference, and procedural reasoning. Taken together, these elements make possible a new set of competencies that I call *intellective skills*. As long as the new technology signals only deskilling – the diminished importance of action-centred skills – there will be little probability of developing critical judgement at the data interface. To rekindle such judgement, though on a new, more abstract footing, a reskilling process is required. Mastery in a computer-mediated environment depends on developing intellective skills.

Zuboff's conclusion about the importance of 'intellective' or problem-solving skills is supported by a considerable body of evidence. Many studies of manufacturing technology suggest that sophisticated, flexible, expensive equipment needs sophisticated, flexible, expensive people to operate it effectively. Recent research shows that while computerization has reduced the labour content of industrial processes, it has triggered a trend away from low-wage blue-collar work towards higher-paid occupations (Bresnahan, 1999).

Richard Walton and Gerald Susman (1987) argue that advanced technology increases:

- interdependencies between organizational functions;

- skill requirements and dependence on skilled people;

- capital investment per employee;

- the speed, scope and costs of mistakes;

- sensitivity of performance to changes in skill and attitudes.

Walton and Susman argue that the appropriate organizational response to these trends involves the development of a skilled, flexible workforce with a flat management structure.

Too complex for mere mortals to comprehend

Instead of manning the bridge with helmet and heavy binoculars, the skipper of a $1 billion Aegis class cruiser exercises command from the hi-tech CIC, or Combat Information Center, a windowless room linked to the outside world through glowing computer and radar screens. Never before has a warship's captain had access to so much instant and accurate information. Even so, the skipper and his crew are not immune to confusion – the 'fog of war'. A horrified world learned precisely that in July [1988], when the *US Vincennes* shot down an Iranian airliner, killing 290 civilians.

The tragedy marked the first time an Aegis cruiser had fired its missiles in combat. And it should rekindle efforts to tame the complexity of weapons systems – especially with programs such as Star Wars looming. Ever since the Aegis was designed in the late 1970s, critics have worried that its systems are too complex for mere mortals to comprehend. In its recently released investigative report, the Navy touched on the issue of breakdowns between man and machine. But the inquiry team found that the highly sophisticated computer and radar systems aboard the *Vincennes* had performed flawlessly.

➤

The real lesson of the *Vincennes* is that electronic systems can produce far too much data for human beings to digest in the heat and strain of battle. Engineers who design such systems often forget this. . . . A review board did recommend some changes in Aegis. One culprit: a hard-to-read computer display that doesn't show an aircraft's altitude beside its radar track. Investigators called for a redesigned screen and better training. . . .

The loss of 290 innocent lives is too high a price for working out a new weapon system's bugs.

From Dave Griffiths, 'When man can't keep up with the machines of war', *Business Week*, 12 September 1988, p. 28.

Effective 'people policies' according to Walton and Susman include:

- job enrichment;

- multiskilling;

- teamwork;

- 'pay for knowledge' reward systems;

- reconsideration of the organizational level at which decisions are taken;

- attention to selection and training, and to management development.

Human-centred manufacturing: the design of production technologies in a way that complements human skills and abilities, rather than distances or replaces them.

These considerations have led to the development of **human-centred manufacturing**.

Human-centred manufacturing faces problems (McLoughlin and Clark, 1994). One concerns persuading organizations preoccupied with reducing costs to adopt such systems. A second concerns the problems of involving users in system design, given the complexity of the technology and the location and membership of technical and academic research teams.

Changing the nature of work (1): teleworking

Death of distance: geographical separation no longer determines the costs or difficulties of global, corporate and person-to-person communication.

One consequence of developments in computing and telecommunications concerns the **death of distance**. Personal and corporate communications with any location on the far side of the planet, using email, mobile telephony, video conferencing and old-fashioned facsimile transmission, are now inexpensive and virtually instantaneous.

There are three main types of teleworker (Daniels, Lamond and Standen, 2000):

home-based   works from home, technologically self-sufficient, may not come into the office at all, or makes only periodic visits

nomadic   works 'on the road', from their car, travelling to customers or clients, with portable computer and mobile phone

remote   works in a conveniently located satellite office, telecentre or telecottage remote from main office

There are also part-time teleworkers who work at home one or two days a week and in the main office for the rest of the time. Teleworkers are spared the daily trek to the office, but some have to turn part of their house into a workspace in return. The pace of change makes it difficult to give accurate figures about the number of people affected. One estimate says that there are over 2 million tele-workers in Britain, and 13 million worldwide (Stredwick and Ellis, 1998). This development has more relevance to service sector organizations and to office-based technical, administrative, clerical, financial, scientific and secretarial work. Manufacturing and other tasks that are tied to fixed locations are not so readily affected.

Stop and Criticize

Your employer gives you a computer with a modem and a fax machine and asks you to work at home. What are the advantages and disadvantages for the organization? For you? On the basis of this analysis, will you comply or resist?

Where in the world?

The death of distance will mean that any activity that relies on a screen or a telephone can be carried out anywhere in the world. Services as diverse as designing an engine, monitoring a security camera, selling insurance or running a secretarial paging service will become as easily exportable as car parts or refrigerators. India has built a flourishing computer software industry around Bangalore. Its exports more than doubled between 1990 and 1993, to US$270m. India is now attracting back-office work from airlines such as Swissair and British Airways. Some of Hong Kong's paging services are manned from China. In Perth, in Western Australia, EMS control systems monitors the air-conditioning, lighting, lifts and security in office blocks in Singapore, Malaysia, Sri Lanka, Indonesia and Taiwan. Telecom Ireland has been trying to build itself up as the main call centre for Europe, hand-ling toll-free 0800 calls from all over the continent. Last April, it launched an intercontinental serv-ice to allow companies to link their European and American call centres and to take advantage of the time differences between them.

From Frances Cairncross, 'The death of distance: a survey of telecommunications', *The Economist*, 30 September 1995, special supplement, p. 39.

Teleworking is not new. References first appeared in the 1970s. This has become a more attractive option with the availability of low-cost, high-specification com-puters which can be connected easily to the internet, electronic mail and corpor-ate databases. Self-employed teleworkers are known as 'elancers'. The popularity of teleworking, therefore, is technology-driven, but there is no 'one best way' to accomplish teleworking. The typical home-based teleworker needs the following:

- computer;
- modem;
- scanner;
- software;
- printer;
- dedicated second phone line;
- answerphone;
- fax machine;
- special office furniture;
- space in house for all this equipment.

The British telecommunications company BT estimates that it can cost £17,000 (at 1998 prices) to equip a teleworker. The employer may also have to pay for telephone bills, stationery, equipment insurance, technical support, and domestic rent and heating.

The time colonist

Kristin Hansen is a time colonist. She gets up at 6 am in a suburb of Tokyo. After a quick breakfast, she takes the train into the financial district where she has an office in a building owned by a major Japanese bank. Ms Hansen doesn't work for the Japanese bank. She is senior vice president of a Danish trading firm with collateral relations to the bank. Her job is to watch over the flow of investments of her company as they move around the world in an endless cycle of cash transfers between Copenhagen, Karachi, Tokyo, San Francisco, Chicago, New York, London and Copenhagen again. She also manages a limited number of major trades on a personal basis. Many traders work with short-term investments. Hansen watches over long-term trading positions: she may hold some of her investments for as long as half an hour. As a senior vice president, however, Hansen's most important task is making an occasional urgent decision when her colleagues in Copenhagen and New York are asleep.

Hansen's business is located in time, rather than in space. Money moves around the world at the speed of light. The markets operate twenty-four hours a day. A second here or a minute there may represent immense gains or losses – millions of dollars, millions of kroner, billions of yen.

When evening comes, Hansen stops at a Tokyo restaurant for a meal. Then she returns home to her suburban apartment. She logs on to her computer to check a few last details of market action for the day. Then she makes a phone call to her boyfriend, a chef in Paris who has just finished the day's shopping for his restaurant. Finally, she settles into a chair with a glass of wine and a stack of books to work on her doctorate. This weekend, she'll be at school in Scandinavia. At any rate, her mind will. Her body will be in Tokyo, while she interacts with students from Finland, Sweden, Denmark, England and Germany. Half of them are in Scandinavia. A few are in other countries. Some of them live in time colonies, as she does.

From Ken Friedman, 'Cities in the information age: a Scandinavian perspective', in M. Igbaria and M. Tan (eds), *The Virtual Workplace*, Idea Publishing, Hershey, PA, 1998, pp. 144–76.

An IRS survey (1996) identified five main and five subsidiary reasons for introducing teleworking from the organization's perspective:

Five main reasons

1. In response to requests from employees (the most common reason cited).
2. To reduce costs.
3. To cope with maternity.
4. To help reduce office overcrowding.
5. Following relocation of office, where some staff were unable to move.

Five subsidiary reasons

1. To cope with illness or disability.
2. Fits the kind of work that we do.
3. Because staff live some distance from the office.
4. Allows more undisturbed working time.
5. Database connections are faster out of main working hours.

Teleworking around Europe

Country	Number of teleworkers	% of workforce
Finland	355,000	16.8
Sweden	5,944,000	15.2
Netherlands	1,044,000	14.5
Britain	2,027,000	7.6
Germany	2,132,000	6.0
Ireland	61,000	4.4
Italy	720,000	3.6
France	635,000	2.9
Spain	357,000	2.8

Estimated European total teleworkers in 1999: 9 million

From Ursula Huws, 'Wired in the country', *People Management*, vol. 5, no. 23, 25 November 1999, pp. 46–7.

The personal and corporate advantages are many. Teleworkers need less expensive office space. There is no office 'chit chat' and other distractions. Reduced commuting means lower travel expenses and fewer frustrations, and more effective use of employee time. Many organizations report increased efficiency, productivity, work turnaround, accuracy, speed of response and morale. With jobs where location is not important, an organization can use people whom it might not otherwise employ. For the teleworker, there is no supervisor constantly checking, there is freedom to arrange the working day, you become your own boss.

There are, however, a number of disadvantages, such as:

■ the set-up costs can be high;

■ staff are not able to share equipment and other facilities;

■ lack of social interaction and sharing of ideas;

■ no team spirit;

■ staff lose touch with the organization culture;

■ staff can be unaware of organizational goals;

■ management cannot easily monitor and control activity;

■ no access to office records and facilities;

■ some customers expect to contact a 'conventional' office.

To what extent do the technologies contributing to teleworking *determine* the consequences for individual telecommuters and for the organizations which employ them? Clearly these technologies make some kinds of new working arrangement possible. The consequences therefore depend only in part on the technology, and primarily on how we decide to apply and use the technology in a given organizational context.

Telecommuting: a virtual disaster story

The claims about the changing nature of work are clearly exaggerated. Huge numbers of workers were mobile long before cellphones came along; on the other hand, some of the ties that tether people to their desks are much stronger than telephone wires. Five years ago TBWA Chiat/Day, an advertising agency, led the charge into the 'virtual workplace' when its offices in Venice, California, proved too small for a fast-expanding workforce. The company gave everyone a mobile phone, a laptop and a locker, and told them to come into the office only when they needed to. The experiment proved a disaster: workers complained of isolation and lack of creative interaction. Last year the company traded virtual communication for the real thing, moving into large offices where everybody had their own desk, along with plenty of open spaces for informal meetings. TBWA Chiat/Day is only one of a huge number of companies to discover that people need to 'share the same air' as well as to 'share the airwaves'.

From Adrian Wooldridge, 'The world in your pocket: a survey of telecommunications', *The Economist*, 9 October 1999, pp. 33–4.

Source: © copyright United Feature Syndicate, Inc. Reproduced by permission.

Changing the nature of work (2): call centres

A call centre is a facility for handling telephone enquiries from customers and clients. They are now common in financial services such as banks, building societies and insurance companies. First Direct, a bank, has a call centre in England employing 3,000 people; the Sky Television Subscriber Centre in Scotland employs 2,000 people (Stredwick and Ellis, 1998). In 1999, Air France opened a multilingual call centre in London, with 200 staff advising customers in English, French, German, Spanish, Catalan and Italian. Some 'multi-client' centres handle enquiries for several different organizations, making special skill and knowledge demands on operators as well as creating challenges for centre management (Carroll et al., 2002). By 2002, it was estimated that there were 6,000 call centres in Britain, employing 500,000 people, just under 2 per cent of the working population (Wyke, 2002), with half of all European call centre business being conducted in Britain (IPD, 1998). The average number of employees in a call centre is around 50, with some employing thousands.

Glasgow versus Delhi

European companies may be able to reduce costs by locating their call centres in India.

Average call centre employee in Britain	Average call centre employee in India
lives in London, Glasgow or South Wales	lives in Delhi
works 7 hours a day with a one-hour lunch break	works 8 hours a day, over three shifts starting at 5.00 am, 11.30 am or 8.30 pm
annual pay UK£10–13,000	annual pay UK£2,500
one-third of workforce are university graduates	almost all call centre employees are university graduates
numbers employed: 510,000	numbers employed: 100,000 by 2008

Based on Laura Peek, Sam Coates and Cathering Philp, 'Unions accuse BT of exporting call centre work', *The Times*, 8 March 2003, p. 5.

There are two main types of call centre – help desks and interactive processing centres:

help desk provides information, technical advice, flight and train times

interactive processing provides a service, sells a product, handles telephone transactions, no paperwork

Like teleworking, the development of call centres is technology-driven. The person answering your call sits at a computer screen with access to the organization's database. Customer information is brought on to the screen, transactions can be processed, questions can be answered. This is beneficial from the customer's point of view. From the employee's perspective, however, there are advantages and drawbacks.

Most call centre employees are multiskilled. In a traditional insurance company, one department handles enquiries and new business, while a separate department handles claims. The customer who telephones with a question or a problem speaks first to a receptionist who then has to transfer the call to the appropriate member of staff, who may in turn have to transfer the call again if the question or problem is complex or if the customer has more than one question. Call centre staff, in contrast, are often trained to deal with a range of customer requests, questions and problems. This requires a much broader base of knowledge and skill, and can also involve considerable discretion in helping to resolve customers' difficulties.

Call centres have three main organizational advantages:

1. Location is not important, and call centres can operate in parts of the country where property and wage costs are low, and staff are easier to recruit.

2. Call centre staff can deal with many more customers over the telephone than field staff in branch offices or mobile sales staff contacting customers directly.

3. Call centre employees can be closely monitored by the automated call distribution system which passes incoming calls to centre staff without the need for a conventional switchboard. Pay can be linked to the number of calls handled.

Factors affecting staff turnover in call centres

Factor	% of call centres citing as important
Intensity of the call centre environment	42
Competition for staff from other centres	40
Pay	34
Competitive local labour market	22
Working conditions	20
Other	30

From Alastair Hatchett, 'Ringing true', *People Management*, vol. 6, no. 2, 20 January 2000, pp. 40–1. Reprinted by permission of Alastair Hatchett.

The multiskilled call centre employee may be subjected to tight management control and working conditions in some call centres can be unpleasant. When the British Trades Union Congress opened a telephone complaints hotline in February 2001, 'big brother-style monitoring' was the main employee complaint against call centres. Over 700 call centre operators used the hotline, and more than half claimed that they were monitored when they went to the toilet. Other complaints concerned inadequate breaks, poor wages, stress and lack of flexibility over working hours. Stredwick and Ellis (1998, p. 166) point out:

There are call centres which resemble the industrial sweatshops of the past, involving very cramped conditions for staff who work on their computers throughout their shift under very tightly controlled conditions. Those on specialized sales areas even have a script written for them so that it is easy to believe that their individuality is being negated. In many ways this is identical to the assembly lines created by Ford engineers from the theories of Frederick Taylor and parodied by Charlie Chaplin in the film *Modern Times*.

Call centres thus tend to have high levels of absenteeism and staff turnover. Research suggests, however, that many centres have tried to shed their 'sweatshop' image by offering competitive pay, job security and trade union recognition. Some provide staff with swimming pools, saunas and subsidized restaurants. Conditions in some centres remain poor, and one study identified a condition called 'repetitive brain injury' which leaves sufferers unable to speak after working in a high-pressure call centre (Incomes Data Services, 1999).

Too young, too male, too intuitive?

Malcolm Higgs has been trying to find out what kind of people work best in a call centre environment, where payroll represents over 65 per cent of the running costs.

Working with Egg, Morgan Stanley and the British Department of Work and Pensions, he surveyed 286 call centre employees to identify links between personal qualities and performance. The most important factors contributing to performance were:

- conscientiousness;
- resilience;
- motivation;
- sensitivity.

Higgs found that women, on average, had higher levels of conscientiousness and sensitivity than men. He also found that older call centre workers had better customer service skills than their younger colleagues, particularly in building relationships. Higgs controversially recommends that call centres should target mature women in their recruitment procedures.

Why did the call centre employees who rated highly on intuitiveness tend to display lower performance? Many call centres rely on telephone scripts and standard operating procedures to maintain quality and consistency of response to customers. People who are highly intuitive, Higgs argues, find this kind of work environment restrictive and frustrating.

Based on Malcolm Higgs, 'Good call', *People Management*, vol. 9, no. 2, 23 January 2003, pp. 48–9.

As with teleworking, we can conclude that, while the development of call centres is technology-driven, it is not the technology alone that determines the quality of working life and performance of employees. Those consequences are influenced mainly by the way in which call centre jobs are organized and managed. The layout of facilities, the degree of variety and autonomy, the opportunities for job rotation, and the nature of supervision are all matters of managerial choice that are not determined by the technology.

Changing the nature of work (3): employee surveillance

A survey of 900 large companies in 1997 by the American Management Association found that two-thirds admitted to some form of electronic surveillance of their workers (*The Economist*, 1999b, p. 105). Computer usage is relatively easy to monitor where machines are connected to a central server. For example, the internet sites which employees explore can be logged, so that staff making 'recreational use' of this facility can be disciplined. Email traffic can be intercepted. Telephone conversations can be recorded, 'for training purposes', and the numbers and duration of calls can also be logged so that staff workloads can be compared. Some organizations use closed-circuit television cameras to monitor employee behaviour without their knowledge (Clarke, 1999).

There appears to be little legal protection against such uses of technology, and legislation differs from country to country. Protection is particularly weak if employees agree to be monitored as part of their employment conditions. If such consent is withheld, of course, then applicants may find that they are not offered a job. Human rights legislation in Europe may generate case law concerning breaches of, for example, the right to privacy, and government agencies and professional bodies have produced codes of conduct advising employers on 'best practice'. These are not definitive, and are mostly in the form of discussion documents at the time of writing. It will be necessary to monitor trends and developments in this area. One of the chapter exercises provides an opportunity to explore these issues from employee and managerial perspectives.

Determinism or choice?

Different technologies make different demands on those who work with them. The technology of an organization thus appears to determine the nature of work. When we compare a hospital with a call centre, or a retail store with a coal mine, it seems reasonable to argue that the organization's technology determines the kinds of task that need to be done; the nature of jobs; the organization of work and the grouping of jobs; the hierarchy through which work is planned, co-ordinated and controlled; the knowledge and skills required to perform the work; the values and attitudes of employees.

Does technology determine these factors? Can we predict the shape of an organization, and the nature and content of jobs, from a knowledge of technology? As we have seen, while new technologies enable some new kinds of working arrangement, they do not uniquely determine the organizational outcomes. The argument that technology does have predictable consequences for work and organizations is known as **technological determinism**.

Technological determinism: the argument that technology can explain the nature of jobs, work groupings, hierarchy, skills, values and attitudes in organizational settings.

The determinist position assumes that work has to be organized to meet the requirements of the technology. Different technologies have different 'technological imperatives'. Turner and Lawrence (1965), for example, explained the background to their work on manufacturing jobs in the following terms: '[T]his research started with the concept that every industrial job contained certain technologically determined task attributes which would influence the workers' response. By "task attributes" we meant such characteristics of the job as the amount of variety, autonomy, responsibility, and interaction with others built into the design.'

It is now widely accepted that technological determinism is an oversimplified perspective. Technology suggests and enables; technology does not merely determine. There are at least three broad areas of choice in the new technology implementation process.

First, there are choices in the design of tools, machinery, equipment and systems. One area of choice concerns the extent to which control is built into the machine or left to human intervention and discretion. There are many instances of automatic controls being removed from aircraft cockpits, ships' bridges and railway engine cabs following the discovery that pilots and drivers lose touch with the reality of their tasks, when surrounded by sophisticated controls which function without their understanding or help.

Second, there are choices in the goals that technology is used to achieve. David Preece (1995) demonstrates that competitive pressure for innovation is overriding. The need to reduce costs, improve quality and customer service, and improve management information can be critical. However, managers also promote innovation for personal and political reasons, to enhance power over resources and influence over decisions, to enhance status and prestige, and to exert closer surveillance and control over employees.

Third, there are choices in the way work is organized around technology. As explored later, car assembly work can be designed in a number of different ways, and it is not clear which of these approaches may be 'correct' or 'best'.

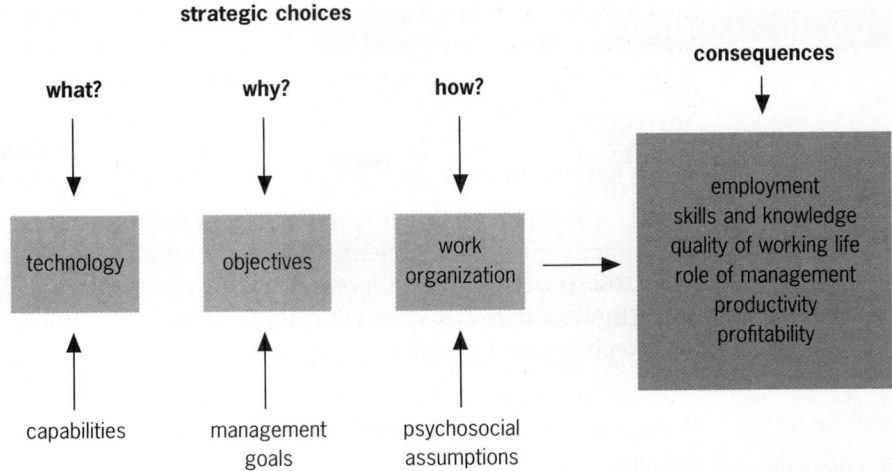

Figure 3.2: Technological indeterminism

These choices rely on the assumptions we make about human capabilities and organizational characteristics. They rely less on the capabilities of items of equipment. These are called 'psychosocial assumptions' because they relate to beliefs about individuals and groups. To consider the 'impact' of a technology, therefore, is to consider the wrong question. Technological innovations trigger a decision-making and negotiation process which is driven by the perceptions and goals of those involved. The choices that form in that process determine the 'impact'. Technology has a limited effect on work independent of the purposes of those who would use it and the responses of those who have to work with it.

Figure 3.2 summarizes this argument claiming that the consequences of technological change depend on the interaction of technical capabilities, objectives and how work is organized.

Is this argument oversimplified? Surely technology must have *some* independent influence on the nature of work and organizations? Two commentators who have challenged the 'organizational choice' argument, Ian McLoughlin and Jon Clark (1994; McLouglin, 1999), claim that rejection of technological determinism 'results in the technology baby being thrown out with the determinist bathwater'. Instead, they argue that new computing and information technologies *do* create imperatives. These include:

- a reduction or elimination of the number of tasks that require manual skills;

- the creation of complex tasks that require interpretative and problem-solving skills;

- the ability to combine knowledge of new with old technology;

- a relationship between technology and user that relies on informed intervention based on an understanding of system interdependencies.

In other words, 'action-centred' abilities become less important and cognitive skills become more valued. This is not to deny the significance of organizational choice or the role of social shaping and negotiation in affecting the outcomes for work experience that accompany particular technological innovations. Technology appears to have 'enabling' properties: the technology of motor car production enables task fragmentation and rigid supervisory control, but it also enables multiskilled, autonomous teamwork.

The politics of technology

Commentators as far back as the 1940s claimed that technological change increased task specialization, took skill and identity from work, and increased discipline in the workplace. This pessimistic viewpoint resurfaced in Harry Braverman's (1974) influential work which triggered a 'labour process debate' which still generates controversy today. Braverman's argument is that advances in technology give management progressive opportunities to reduce skill and discretion and to tighten surveillance and control over workers. It is important to draw a distinction here between what technology can achieve and what management uses technology to achieve. Braverman's argument concerns the latter.

Humanization or intensification?

The problem as it presents itself to those managing industry, trade and finance is very different from the problem as it appears in the academic or journalistic worlds. Management is habituated to carrying on labour processes in a setting of social antagonism and, in fact, has never known it to be otherwise. Corporate managers have neither the hope nor the expectation of altering this situation by a single stroke: rather, they are concerned to ameliorate it only when it interferes with the orderly functioning of their plants, offices, warehouses and stores.

For corporate management this is a problem in costs and controls, not in the 'humanization of work'. It compels their attention because it manifests itself in absenteeism, turnover and productivity levels that do not conform to their calculations and expectations. The solutions they will accept are only those which provide improvements in their labour costs and in their competitive positions domestically and in the world market.

From Harry Braverman, *Labour and Monopoly Capital: The Degradation of Work in the Twentieth Century,* Monthly Review Press, New York, 1974, p. 36.

This argument identifies technology as a political tool which managers use to maintain their position of relative power, and to manipulate employees and the conditions in which they work. This is an important observation because the technology of manufacturing and office work is usually discussed as politically neutral. However, if management can increase task specialization and reduce the level of skill required in a job, lower wages can be offered and the organization's dependence on those employees is reduced. If management can increase the discipline in work, improve surveillance and gain tighter control of employees, this can lead to reduced discretion and to work intensification.

Managers can manipulate employees by appealing to a technological determinist argument: 'we have no choice but to do it this way because of the technology'. Technological determinism can be used to justify and to protect from challenge unpopular decisions; those who argue clearly don't understand the technology. Improved control can lead to lower costs and, in turn, to higher profits, and also maintains the status and power of management. Some 'technology implications' can thus be seen instead as the result of management strategies to improve employee control through forms of work organization. The consequences of technology change are not the inescapable outcomes of the rigid demands of machinery.

Chapter 13 will explore *scientific management*, developed at the start of the twentieth century and still applied today. Scientific management offers a rationale for task fragmentation and simplification, and for tighter control. The typi-

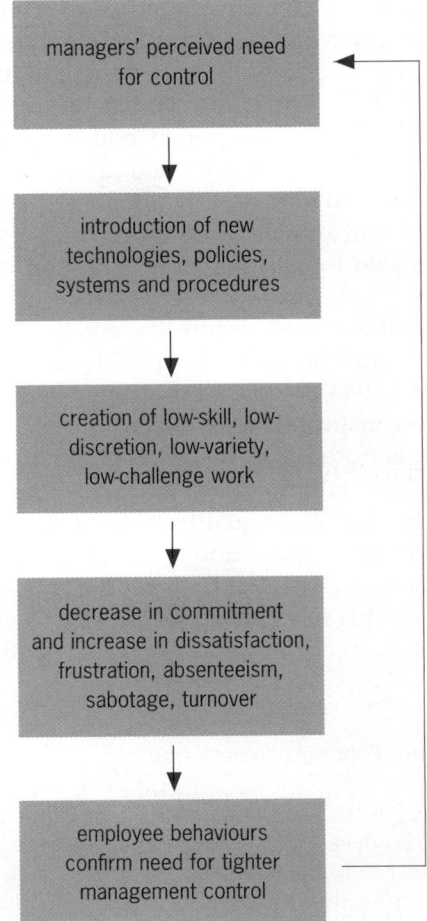

Figure 3.3: The vicious circle of control

Characteristics of mass production: these include the mechanical pacing of work, no choice of tools or methods, repetitiveness, minute subdivision of product, minimum skill requirements and surface mental attention.

cally antagonistic human response to simple repetitive work can confirm the management view that tight control of employees is necessary to maintain discipline and to produce goods and services effectively. Scientific management can become self-perpetuating through the 'vicious circle of control' (Clegg and Dunkerley, 1980), illustrated in figure 3.3.

This vicious circle can only be broken by a change in management perceptions, starting with higher trust in, and higher discretion for, employees. Braverman and his followers argue that such a change is unlikely in a capitalist economy. Technological determinism is replaced in this perspective with an inevitable and pessimistic economic and political logic, or rather, yet another form of gloomy determinism.

Classic studies on work and technology

One of the first studies of the relationship between technology and the nature of work was reported by Charles Walker and Robert Guest in *The Man on the Assembly Line* (1952). They argued, in determinist mode, that some production technologies prevent the formation of work groups and frustrate the social needs of employees. Their survey of 180 American automobile assembly workers identified six **characteristics of mass production** work.

Job rotation: a work design method in which employees are switched from task to task at regular intervals.

Job enlargement: a work design method in which tasks are recombined to widen the scope of a job.

The jobs of the car workers were scored on these characteristics. Despite being content with pay and conditions, employees in jobs with a high 'mass production score' disliked their work and had a higher rate of absenteeism than those in low-scoring jobs. These and similar findings prompted some managers to recognize that scientific management had taken task specialization too far. Morris Viteles (1950) argued that the combination of mechanization with scientific management created routine, repetitive tasks. Monotony and boredom reduced work rate, output and morale, and led to high levels of absenteeism and complaints. The 1950s solutions to boredom and monotony were **job rotation** and **job enlargement**.

The aim was to restore variety in work. The first account of job enlargement came from Charles Walker (1950), at the Endicott plant of the American company IBM. In 1944 the jobs of machine operators were enlarged to include machine set-up and inspection of finished product, jobs previously done by other workers. There is nothing in the technology of machining to prevent operators performing these additional tasks. The benefits from this simple change included improved product quality and a reduction in losses from scrap, less idle time for men and machines, and a 95 per cent reduction in set-up and inspection costs.

Although these methods reduce monotony and boredom and increase variety, they do this in a superficial way. However, job rotation and enlargement are still in use.

Job enlargement: the Linn Products experience

Linn Products was founded in 1973, near Glasgow, Scotland, manufacturing high-quality hi-fi equipment, including amplifiers, record decks, compact disc players and speakers. The company was nominated in 1990 by the British Institute of Management as one of the country's most advanced manufacturers. Linn first used a traditional assembly line, but as the business grew, problems arose over productivity, and delivery promises to customers were broken too often. The company's founder and managing director, Ivor Tiefenbrun, explains how they changed their methods, following a late night brainstorming session:

The next day I asked one of our assembly girls to go and get all the parts required to build a record player, build it and bring it into my office. Somewhat mystified, she did just that and returned about 17 minutes later. It took 27 minutes of labour to build the same item on our production line.

So we re-organized our factory. We eliminated 47 different main and buffer storage areas, went to a single store and a single-stage build where one responsible person builds the product from start to finish. To do this, we invested to create surplus capacity, so that we could pursue our objective of real-time manufacturing: to make what our customers want when they want it. Within six weeks we had made remarkable progress and three months later we were despatching the product the day the customer ordered it.

We now employ our home-grown principles of single-stage build and real-time manufacturing throughout our organization. This approach requires a higher skill level but is the route to a superior quality build. The actual output per employee on any specific product is irrelevant compared to the gain through improved labour flexibility.

The single-stage build method gives one person responsibility and control. Within the envelope of total time allocated to any particular task the individual has the freedom to take the time necessary over tasks which are difficult and to perform simpler tasks rapidly. No single component failure, instrument or plant failure or the non-appearance of any individual will necessarily have any impact on our ability to satisfy our customers' requirements. Pressure is removed from the manufacturing process and the person who builds, tests and packs his own product can take pride in his own workmanship and spot the connection between what he does, the way that product works and customer satisfaction.

Each employee on a conventional assembly line has to work at the same pace as the others, so that the whole line operates in a 'balanced' manner. Single-stage build, or job enlargement, overcomes this problem, and offers more meaningful and varied work at the same time.

From Ivor Tiefenbrun, 'Manufacturing in the future', *RSA Journal*, July 1993, p. 552.

Work with mass production characteristics can cause stress and illness, as well as boredom and monotony. Arthur Kornhauser's (1965) study of car assembly workers in Detroit showed that low-grade factory work could lead to job dissatisfaction and poor mental health. The workers he studied had a long list of grievances, including:

low pay	simplicity of job operations
job insecurity	repetitiveness and boredom
poor working conditions	lack of control over the work
low status	non-use of abilities
restricted promotion opportunities	feelings of futility
the style of the supervisors	

Workers in jobs with these characteristics had lower mental health, which meant that they:

were anxious and tense	were less satisfied with life
had negative self-concepts	were socially withdrawn
were hostile to others	suffered from isolation and despair

Kornhauser argued that work with mass production characteristics produces this pattern of psychological reactions. A later study showed that the most stressful jobs were those which combined high workload with low discretion (Karasek, 1979). Typical examples included assembly workers, garment stitchers, goods and materials handlers, nursing aides and orderlies, and telephone operators. The main symptoms were exhaustion and depression, including nervousness, anxiety and sleeping difficulties.

Stop and Criticize

What other jobs can you identify that combine a high workload with low discretion?

Do employees in those jobs display symptoms of fatigue or depression?

What advice could you give management to reduce workload and increase discretion in those jobs?

Swedish car makers were among the first to show that mass production characteristics can be avoided by creative work design. Saab-Scania began experimenting in 1970, when 40 workers in the chassis shop of a new truck factory were divided into production groups (Norstedt and Aguren, 1973). Group members were responsible for deciding how they would rotate between tasks, and also absorbed maintenance and quality control functions. These changes eventually affected about 600 manual workers, with the following results:

- productivity increased and product quality improved;

- unplanned stoppages of production were significantly reduced;

- costs were reduced to 5 per cent below budget;

- labour turnover was cut from 70 to 20 per cent;

- absenteeism was not affected;

- co-operation between management and workforce improved.

Technology and alienation

One classic study of the impact of technology on work was carried out by Robert Blauner, who analyzed working conditions in the early 1960s in:

printing, dominated by craft work

cotton spinning, dominated by machine minding

car manufacture, dominated by mass production

chemicals manufacture, dominated by process production

Blauner identified four components of alienation, concerning feelings of:

1. *Powerlessness*: loss of control over conditions of work, work processes, pace and methods.
2. *Meaninglessness*: loss of significance of work activities.
3. *Isolation*: loss of sense of community membership.
4. *Self-estrangement*: loss of personal identity, of a sense of work as a central life interest.

Printing workers set their own pace, were free from management pressure, chose their own techniques and methods, had powerful unions, practised a complex skill, had good social contacts at work, had high status, identified closely with their work and were not alienated.

Textile workers performed simple, rapid and repetitive operations over which they had little control, worked under strict supervision and had little social contact. Alienation, however, was low. Blauner argued that this was because textile workers lived in close rural communities whose values and way of life overcame feelings of alienation arising at work.

Car assembly workers had little control over work methods, saw little meaning in the tasks they performed, were socially isolated and developed no meaningful skills.

Chemicals processing workers operated prosperous, technically advanced plants where manual work had been automated. They controlled their own work pace, and had freedom of movement, social contact and teamwork. They developed an understanding of the chemical reactions which they monitored, and also developed a sense of belonging, achievement and responsibility. In addition, they had close contact with educated, modern management.

Blauner concluded that advanced technology would eliminate alienation.

Based on Robert Blauner, *Alienation and Freedom: The Factory Worker and His Job*, University of Chicago Press, Chicago, 1964.

Saab's best-known experiment was at its engine factory at Södertälje. Here an oblong conveyor loop moved engine blocks to seven assembly groups, each with three members (Thomas, 1974). Each group had its own U-shaped guide track in the floor, to the side of the main conveyor. Engine blocks were taken from the main track, assembled by the group and then returned to the conveyor. The engines arrived with their cylinder heads, and the groups handled the fitting of carburettors, distributors, spark plugs, camshafts and other components.

Each assembly group decided for themselves how the work was allocated. The guide track for each group was not mechanically driven. The group simply had half an hour to build each engine, and the group decided how that time would be spent. Individual jobs on the conventional assembly track had cycle times of less than two minutes. In 1974, Saab-Scania estimated that they saved around 65,000 Swedish kroner a year on recruitment and training costs alone with this approach. This form of work organization is known as the **autonomous work group** (or self-regulating or self-managing group or team).

Autonomous teams often make their own decisions about how tasks and responsibilities will be allocated, shared and rotated. This is similar to the *high performance work systems* discussed in chapter 8 and was the approach used by Sweden's other car maker, Volvo. Volvo's plant at Kalmar pioneered the concept of 'dock assembly', in which teams completed whole stages of the car assembly in static bays to one side of the moving assembly track.

> **Autonomous work group**: a team of workers allocated to a significant segment of the workflow, with discretion concerning how their work will be carried out.

Socio-technical systems analysis and design

Swedish managers did not invent the autonomous work group. The idea came from the work of British researchers at the Tavistock Institute of Human Relations in London. The Tavistock group developed the concept of the organization as a **system**.

The term 'system' can be applied to a range of phenomena: solar system, nervous system, traffic management system, telecommunications system, waste disposal system. Any system is defined by its boundaries, which in turn depend on what one wants to study, and why. In an organizational context, we may wish to analyze a performance management system, a product distribution system, a raw materials purchasing system or a production system.

The human organism and the organization share one important property. They are each dependent on their ability to conduct an exchange with their environments. We breathe air, consume food and drink, and absorb sensory information. We convert these imports into energy and actions, disposing of waste products and expending energy in chosen behaviours. The organization, like the human body, is also an **open system**.

Open systems import resources, such as people, materials, equipment, information and money. They transform those inputs, in organizations, through producing services and goods. They then export those products back into the environment, as goods and satisfied customers. This treatment of organizational behaviour in terms of living organisms is known as the organic analogy (Rice, 1958, 1963; Miller and Rice, 1967).

Another property of open systems is their ability to reach a particular outcome from a variety of starting points and routes. The autonomous work group at Saab, for example, could assemble an engine in many different ways but with the same end results. A chemical reaction, on the other hand, is a closed system in which the end result depends on the concentrations and quantities of the items used to begin with. This property is known as equifinality, and it has an interesting consequence for organizational design. Equifinality suggests that it is not necessary to

> **System**: something that functions by virtue of the interdependence of its component parts.

> **Open system**: a system that interacts, in a purposive way, with its external environment in order to survive.

- close co-operation between product and process development;
- computer-controlled ordering system;
- production capacity of final assembly is one car every 68 seconds.

Based on *NedCar in Perspective*, Netherlands Car BV, September 1996.

Organizational choice: the argument that work design is not determined by technology, that the technical system does not determine the social system.

The Tavistock researchers responsible for developing the socio-technical systems approach also introduced the concept of **organizational choice**.

Eric Trist and K.W. Bamforth developed the concept of the socio-technical system in their study of the social and psychological impact of longwall coal-mining methods in the 1940s (Trist and Bamforth, 1951; Bamforth had been a miner himself). Table 3.1 summarizes the developments in technology, work organization and job characteristics which they studied.

Their research, between 1955 and 1958 (Trist, Higgin, Murray and Pollock, 1963), contrasted the advantages of the traditional 'composite autonomous mining' method of single place working with the problems of highly mechanized coal getting. During their study, however, they found that some pits had developed a form of 'shortwall' working, with methods similar to those of composite single place working.

One case, called 'The Manley Innovation' after the name of the pit, describes how miners themselves developed a teamwork approach to shortwall mining in response to underground conditions which made it dangerous to support and work long coal faces. When management tried to restore conventional longwall working, to reduce costs, the men resisted and negotiated an agreement to continue with their approach. This was based on composite, multiskilled, self-selecting groups, collectively responsible for the whole coal-getting cycle on any one shift. This contrasted sharply with conventional longwall working, in which each shift was restricted to one stage of the coal-getting cycle, and each miner was limited to one fragmented task, with limited opportunity for the development of other underground skills. The Manley groups had no supervisors, but elected 'team captains' to liaise with pit management. They were paid on a common paynote, as all members were regarded as making equivalent contributions. The groups each comprised over forty miners, who arranged their own work allocations, to develop and maintain their underground skills.

Table 3.1: From single place to composite longwall coal mining

Technology	Work organization	Job characteristics
1: hand and pneumatic picks	single place	composite autonomous miner
2: mechanized coal cutters and belt conveyors	conventional cutting longwall	task fragmentation, mechanization, mass production features
3: electric coal cutters and belt conveyors	composite longwall	composite autonomous, self-regulating teams

The whole atmosphere on a composite longwall was different

The astonishing change in the physical appearance of the workplace, which would be the first thing to impress itself on a visitor, has come to be recognized as almost a hallmark of a composite group ... although the men were not responsible for equipment in the gates, they would use their lunch break to check and, if necessary, do repairs to the mothergate belt which leads to the face, anticipating and preventing possible disturbances of their work. No man was ever out of a job. If he finished hewing or pulling before others he would join and help them, or go on to some other job which was to follow. If work was stopped owing to breakdowns in the transport system on which the group was dependent for its supply of tubs, the men would go on to do maintenance work.

From p. G. Herbst, *Autonomous Group Functioning*, Tavistock, London, 1962, p. 6.

This research led to two main conclusions.

1. Work in groups is more likely to provide meaningful work, develop responsibility and satisfy human needs than work that is allocated to separately supervised individuals.

2. Work can be organized in this way regardless of the technology in use. Social system design is not uniquely determined by technical system characteristics and demands.

The work organization introduced when mechanical coal-getting methods replaced traditional techniques was not determined by the new technology. In other words, technical change is consistent with *organizational choice*, or with what John Bessant (1983) calls 'design space'.

Stop and Criticize

Coal mining is hardly 'typical' manufacturing work. To what extent can the concept of organizational choice be applied to other kinds of work and organization?

Socio-technical systems thinking remains influential, particularly in the Netherlands and Sweden. Under the influence of Swedish Ulbo de Sitter and Dutch colleagues (1994; de Sitter, den Hertog and Dankbaar, 1997), a more elaborate socio-technical system design methodology has been developed (Benders, Doorewaard and Poutsma, 2000):

1. An analysis of the environment to establish the main organizational design criteria, such as market objectives, but also quality of working life and labour relations.

2. An analysis of the product flow pattern.

3. Design of the production structure, first approximate and then in detail, based on semi-autonomous production units operated by 'whole task groups'.

4. Design of the control structure, allocating control tasks to the lowest possible level, which can be an individual workstation or an autonomous group.

5. The creation of 'operational groups' which combine support and line functions (such as maintenance and quality control) and which assist a number of whole task groups.

Contemporary examples of autonomous teamworking are explored in chapter 12.

Team versus lean: competing socio-technical paradigms

Until the early 1990s, the pioneering team-based plants of the Swedish car manufacturers Saab and Volvo were popular 'management tourist' attractions. Volvo's president, Pehr Gyllenhammar, explained his company's approach to making cars and organizing people in his book, *People at Work* (1977). The team-based approach remained popular in America into the 1990s, one study suggesting that over half of American manufacturing companies had scrapped their assembly lines in favour of 'cellular manufacturing' methods (*The Economist*, 1994a).

Volvo built a new assembly plant at Uddevalla, on Sweden's west coast, in the late 1980s. Autonomous teams of eight to ten car builders were responsible for final assembly, on a static assembly dock, not on a paced assembly line. The plant had a central materials store from which parts and sub-assemblies were delivered to teams by automatically guided vehicles. Each team was responsible for its own recruitment, training, maintenance, tooling and task planning. Without supervisors, teams elected spokespersons who handled planning, assigned work, led discussions, dealt with problems and communicated with management.

In 1990 Saab sold its motor car business to General Motors, and in 1991 closed its team-based plant at Malmo. In 1993, Volvo closed its plants at Kalmar and Uddevalla, and concentrated production at its traditionally organized factory at Torslanda, outside Gothenburg. The Uddevalla plant was subsequently reopened to manufacture special vehicles. In January 1999, Volvo Car Corporation was sold to Ford Motor Company. As the Swedish car manufacturers were selling and closing their facilities, Japanese car companies such as Toyota, Honda and Nissan were opening new plants in Europe and America based on traditional assembly-line methods, with publicity and success.

These developments helped to tarnish the image of team-based manufacturing. What went wrong? One explanation comes from the work of James Womack, Dan Jones and Daniel Roos. In their book, *The Machine That Changed The World* (1990), they compare the productivity of car manufacturers around the world and explain the wide variations in terms of production methods. One of their measures was the number of hours of direct labour used to build, paint and finally assemble a car. The main differences in 1989, between the best and the worst companies, on this measure of labour assembly hours, were as follows:

	Best	Worst
Japan	13.2	25.9
North America	18.6	30.7
Europe	22.8	55.7

Lean production: an approach which combines machine-pacing, work standardization, just-in-time materials flow, continuous improvement, problem-solving teams and powerful supervision.

These comparisons were damning, pointing to significant advantages in Japanese methods. At Uddevalla, the training time for team members was high, and the assembly time for each car was twice the European average. Despite favourable working conditions, absenteeism and labour turnover remained high (Wickens, 1993). Womack, Jones and Roos argued that the productivity differences were due to production methods. The Japanese advantage, they claimed, was based on **lean production** methods (Oliver, Delbridge, Jones and Lowe, 1994).

Lean production, or lean organization, combines the following techniques and approaches:

■ machine-paced assembly, with task specialization, placing responsibility on workers to improve the 'one best way' for each task;

■ 'just-in-time' delivery of materials to the point of assembly, replacing the need to hold costly inventories, reducing the need for storage space, and thus shortening the time that elapses between receipt of order and delivery to the customer;

■ continuous improvement or *kaizen* – when the worker identifies an improvement, this is agreed with supervision and engineering staff, and the work procedure sheet is revised;

■ aggressive problem-solving with 'quality circles', a team approach to *kaizen* for addressing quality and manufacturing problems;

■ a ruthless approach to reducing equipment adjustment and retooling times, and eliminating defects. In a Japanese plant, one worker can bring the plant to a halt if a problem arises. The plant is not restarted until the problem is fixed;

■ powerful first-line supervisors who monitor and encourage continuous improvement.

Teamwork in Japanese organizations, therefore, is not the same as teamwork in most Scandinavian, European or American companies (MacDuffie, 1988; Buchanan, 1994a, 1994b, 2000a). The assembler in a Japanese plant carries out a short-cycle repetitive task, under supervisory control, and is under pressure to improve productivity through adjustments to the job or aspects of the manufacturing process. This is quite different from the experience of multiskilled autonomous team members, who decide how to allocate and rotate tasks, and who solve problems in collaboration with each other, at their own pace and discretion. Bram Steijn (2001) distinguishes four work systems in terms of their effects on employees:

	Low autonomy	High autonomy
no teamwork	scientific management	professional work
teamwork	lean teams	autonomous teams

Adapted from B. Steijn 'Work systems, quality of working life and attitudes of workers: an empirical study towards the effects of team and non-teamwork', *New Technology, Work and Employment*, vol. 16, no. 3, 2001, pp. 193. Reprinted by permission of Blackwell Publishing Ltd.

Scientific management, or Taylorism, creates individual job roles with limited autonomy. However, some individual job roles, in for example the professions of accounting, law and medicine, have high autonomy. Teams in lean manufacturing have low levels of autonomy, in contrast with teams organized using socio-technical system design principles.

Is it safe to conclude that the Anglo-American-Scandinavian model of team-based manufacturing has been discredited, and that lean production is a more effective socio-technical paradigm?

The evidence suggests that lean production can also be 'mean' production. The pace and intensity, the demands of *kaizen*, supervisory regulation of methods, and lack of discretion are stressful. Parker and Slaughter (1988) studied a plant run jointly by Toyota and General Motors in California – New United Motors Manufacturing Incorporated (NUMMI). This was publicized as a lean 'industry standard' production approach, but Parker and Slaughter called it 'management by stress', with every worker motion and action timed meticulously to remove waste effort, reduce time and inventory, and streamline production continuously. Hammarstrom and Lansbury (1991) point out that these workplace pressures are typically offset by high pay and job security, and that Japanese transplants are often located in areas of high unemployment and low trade union membership. They conclude that Japanese methods based on scientific management methods appear 'natural' and 'safe' to many managers.

Swedish researchers have been forceful in their defence of Scandinavian socio-technical methods. Christian Berggren, at the Swedish Institute for Work Life Research in Stockholm, has been scathing of the narrow range of measures used in the American research, which focused on final assembly hours and paid less attention to the way in which the overall supply chain, from design to customer, was organized (Berggren, Bjorkman and Hollander, 1991; Berggren, 1993a, 1993b; Berggren, 1995). Berggren also argues that Volvo's decision to close Kalmar and Uddevalla was reached despite company analyses which revealed that these plants were at least as productive as the conventional, but much larger and older, plant at Torslanda. The company had excess production capacity in the early 1990s, and logistics and politics made it expedient to close the smaller, experimental plants located some distance from the company's main facilities.

The ultimate aim of lean manufacturing is to build products only when a customer order is received instead of manufacturing items for storage in warehouses until they are sold. The ability to react instantly to business changes would create the 'real-time enterprise', and this is made possible with information technology. There is a growing demand in the motor manufacturing sector for vehicles tailored to individual requirements, known as 'flexible mass customization'. Manufacturers thus aim for what is known as 'build to order', or BTO. With a con-

Building washers and fridges to order

Bill Beer is head of the appliances division of the American manufacturing company Maytag, based in Iowa. Maytag is in the business of mass customization, making washing machines, dishwashers and refrigerators which sell at around three times the price of mainstream products. The company must be able to offer customers a range of choice, while keeping up with demand. Working towards a build-to-order system, Maytag has developed 'build to replenish'; production of an item only begins when one has been sold. This involves a lean manufacturing system, with close links to the retailers who sell the products:

Walking around the floor of Maytag's washing-machine factory in Iowa is like a lesson in modern industrial archaeology. There are three levels of sophistication on show. One part of the factory makes a traditional basic model in a traditional manner, with one long assembly-line conveyor belt and lots of offline areas in which faulty machines are taken out of the loop for repair. A second line, making more sophisticated products, has a number of smaller production cells instead of a long line, and only a few offline repair areas. Instead of a conveyor belt, machines come along on little pads that stop them at each station for a while. So far, so traditional.

But the third production area, making the most advanced Atlantis washing machines, consists of just seven cells. In these, groups of workers make whole boatloads of washers, which come off the line at the rate of one a minute. The work is less mindless than performing single repetitive tasks, and each operator can see what is going on around him. That means he can stop the line if something is wrong, or move along to help a buddy at the next station when needed. Working in such small cells means that no time is wasted by workers looking around for parts. 'Everything is brought to the worker, as if he were a surgeon', says Art Learmonth, one of Mr Beer's manufacturing lieutenants. The cell arrangement is also more flexible than one long line, in that seven different variations of a washing machine can be turned out at the same time.

A similar reworking of the company's Jackson, Tennessee, dishwasher factory improved quality by 55%, freed up 43,000 square feet and increased capacity by 50%. Such factories can now turn out any model at any hour of the production day, in response to feedback from the department stores that sell Maytag's products.

From 'A long march', *The Economist*, special report on mass customization, 14 July 2001, p. 81.

ventional manufacturing system, the buyer might wait months for delivery. Many companies are now attempting to reduce this to fifteen days or less, using the internet to integrate their supply chains. This improves customer service and reduces supply-chain and manufacturing costs. This approach also requires skills upgrading for assembly workers.

We are faced with a dispute between two socio-technical paradigms, two different ways of organizing people around production. The 'team versus lean' debate is far from resolution, although it appears that some lean approaches depend at least in part for their effectiveness on the use of small and relatively autonomous teams. While the arguments in motor car production may be unresolved, similar methods are being applied and developed in other manufacturing and service sector organizations. This debate is likely to run for some time.

Recap

1. *Explain different uses of the term 'technology'.*

   - Material technology means equipment, machines, apparatus. Social technology means organization structures and processes of co-ordination and control.

2. *Explain why predictions about technology and unemployment are often exaggerated.*

   - The effects of technology on employment are indeterminate because replacement mechanisms (through which jobs are lost) are offset by compensatory mechanisms (through which new jobs are created).

3. *Explain how new technology is changing the nature of work for some people, through teleworking, call centres and increased surveillance.*

   - Teleworkers escape direct management control but can become socially isolated.

   - Call centre workers may be highly skilled, but can suffer high workload and pressure.

   - Technology is increasingly used for covert employee surveillance, through computer monitoring, telephone call logging and closed circuit television. These methods may be legal, but infringe individual privacy and generate resentment.

4. *Demonstrate how the consequences of technological innovation for skill requirements depend on the organization of work, and not simply on technical capabilities.*

   - The impact of technology on work and skills depends on choices concerning equipment and system design, goals and objectives, and the organization of work.

   - New technology has, however, reduced the need for manual labour, creating instead jobs which demand high levels of interpretative and problem-solving skills.

5. *Define the characteristics of mass production and identify approaches to overcome them.*

   - Mass production characteristics include mechanical pacing, no choice of method, repetition, task fragmentation, and minimum use of skills and mental attention.

   - Psychological reactions to work with mass production characteristics include anxiety and tension, hostility, isolation and despair, and social withdrawal which can be overcome to some extent by job enlargement and job rotation.

6. *Apply the socio-technical system perspective to organizational analysis and design.*

   - Socio-technical system design aims to find the best fit between social and technical sub-systems, to achieve joint optimization through minimal critical specification.

7. *Contrast the Scandinavian and Japanese models of team-based work organization.*

   - Scandinavian companies use autonomous work groups. Japanese companies use 'off line' quality circles and problem-solving teams as part of a lean manufacturing approach, which has mass production characteristics.

Revision

1. Why is 'technology' such an important aspect of organizational behaviour, and what are the personal and organizational implications of 'the death of distance'?

2. Japanese and Scandinavian manufacturing companies use teams as part of their organizational design. What are the differences between the Japanese and Scandinavian approaches?

3. Your organization is considering the establishment of a call handling centre to deal with customer enquiries and problems. What are the main managerial benefits and drawbacks of this strategy, and what human resource benefits and problems is it likely to create?

4. What is 'technological determinism' and what are the criticisms of this perspective?

5. What are the characteristics of mass production, what problems do these characteristics generate, and how can these problems be addressed?

Springboard

Boreham, P., Thompson, P. and Parker, R., 2003, *New Technology @ Work*, Routledge, London.

Combining Australian and British authorship, offers a critical and up-to-date examination of the continuing influence of information and communication technology on work and organizations, considering current and future impact.

Bredin, A., 1996, *The Virtual Office Survival Handbook: What Telecommuters and Entrepreneurs Need to Succeed in Today's Nontraditional Workplace*, Wiley, New York.

Entertaining guide to the practical consequences of teleworking.

Cairncross, F., 2001, *The Death of Distance 2.0: How the Communication Revolution Will Change Our Lives*, Harvard Business School Press, Boston, MA.

A positive perspective on the impact of the internet to reduce costs, improve productivity and increase government accountability, balanced with consideration of the internet's 'five Ps': policing, pornography, privacy, protection and property.

Dawson, P., 1996, *Technology and Quality: Change in the Workplace*, International Thomson, London.

Explores the role of technology in changing working conditions, demonstrating the shift to teamworking, computer-based covert controls and individual contracts.

McLoughlin, I., 1999, *Creative Technological Change: The Shaping of Technology and Organizations*, Routledge, London.

Examines relationships between technology and organization from a metaphor-based postmodern perspective in which innovation is a 'configurational process'.

McLoughlin, I. and Harris, M. (eds), 1997, *Innovation, Organizational Change and Technology*, International Thomson, London.

Explores the technology–organizational relationship from a range of perspectives. McLoughlin's entertaining chapter, 'Babies, bathwater, guns and roses', defends technological determinism against a constructivist interpretation.

Daniels, K., Lamond, D.A. and Standen, P. (eds), 2000, *Managing Telework*, Business Press Thomson Learning, London.

Explores a range of practical and theoretical issues concerning the personal and organizational benefits and drawbacks of teleworking, drawing on a range of perspectives including organization culture, personality and organizational learning.

Stredwick, J. and Ellis, S., 1998, *Flexible Working Practices: Techniques and Innovations*, Institute of Personnel and Development, London.

Comprehensive guide to trends in flexible working, including teleworking and call centres, with case studies and practical management advice.

Home viewing

In *The Net* (1995, director Irwin Winkler), Angela Bennett (played by Sandra Bullock) is a teleworker operating from her isolated, technologically cluttered and complex home office. Her job is to identify and fix bugs and viruses in the software which her employers send to her over the internet. One day, she accidentally sees files relating to a criminal syndicate which consequently pursues her, using the internet in an attempt to erase her identity and existence. Angela thus uses her computing skill and knowledge not just to live, but also to survive. Is the internet really a threat to privacy? If teleworking is the future of employment for many people, can this be regarded as a desirable future? How many different ways are computer networks used to intrude on the life of the individual in this film?

OB in literature

Matt Thorne, *Eight Minutes Idle*, Phoenix/Orion Books, London, 1999.

Unable to afford the rent on his flat, Dan moves into the call centre where he works. This novel offers hilarious insights into the nature of the work, relationships with colleagues and management style. Quick Call is a 'multi-client' call centre, and one of Dan's clients is Angel Cruises, a company which has specified the precise script that call centre staff must follow, including the 'salutation'. In his annual appraisal, Dan's team leader, Alice, explains to him that the company wants him to say, 'Hello, Angel Cruises, how *may* I help you', and not 'how *can* I help you'. What else does this novel reveal about work in call centres?

Chapter exercises

1: Technology test

Objective 1. To evaluate popular stereotypes of the impact of technology.

Rate your agreement or disagreement with the ten statements about technology and work on p. 100, ticking the appropriate box in the column on the right.

Calculate your score, between 10 and 50, and compare your score with colleagues.

- If you got a score of 20 or less, consider the extent to which your image of technology has been shaped by media accounts.

- If you got a score of 40 or more, consider why your views are inconsistent with contemporary media images of the role of technology.

	definitely yes (1)	probably yes (2)	unsure (3)	probably no (4)	definitely no (5)
1. Once we know what a technology is capable of, we should be able to predict the work, organizational and social consequences	☐	☐	☐	☐	☐
2. The nature of jobs which rely on technology is determined by the technology	☐	☐	☐	☐	☐
3. Advances in technology are bound to increase unemployment	☐	☐	☐	☐	☐
4. Computers and robots are deskilling work for most people	☐	☐	☐	☐	☐
5. Japanese car manufacturing technology is superior to that used in America and Europe	☐	☐	☐	☐	☐
6. Boring repetitive jobs with 'mass-production characteristics' are a thing of the past	☐	☐	☐	☐	☐
7. Telecommuting, or working from home, will be the pattern of work for most of us in the future	☐	☐	☐	☐	☐
8. The success of Japanese car companies is based on teamwork	☐	☐	☐	☐	☐
9. Covert surveillance of employee behaviour at work is an invasion of privacy, which is illegal	☐	☐	☐	☐	☐
10. Computing power is replacing the need for people to think and to solve problems at work	☐	☐	☐	☐	☐

2: Someone to watch over you

Objectives   1. To consider the possibilities, acceptability and limits of technological surveillance.

2. To assess the balance between an individual's right to privacy and an employer's right to monitor and control employee behaviour at work.

Briefing   Read the following actual case account.

Last year, during a lunch break in the kitchen at Leeds Metropolitan University, cleaning supervisor Ros Johnstone was chatting to colleagues about the possibility of her husband and his friend bumping into her manager at a football match. The pair knew that Johnstone felt she had grievances against her boss and she was wondering aloud whether they would, in her words, 'kick the **** out of him'.

A few weeks later, back in the university's kitchen, Johnstone was again gossiping about how her husband would like to punch her boss. Soon after that, she was arrested by the police on suspicion of drug dealing. The university had received anonymous letters that she had been dealing drugs on campus and, to gather evidence, she had been covertly filmed and taped by management on a hidden microphone and a pinhole video camera secreted in a smoke detector.

Johnstone was not subsequently charged with drug offences, but in the process of gathering what proved to be non-existent evidence, she was arrested on suspicion of conspiracy to commit grievous bodily harm. There were tapes covering more than 1,000 hours of her break-time *tête-à-têtes*, but she was allowed access to a mere ten minutes of the 'damning' proof. The charges were later dropped, but she was suspended from work for six months pending a university hearing. The outcome? Johnstone was given a written warning from the university.

When you have read this account, prepare considered answers to the following questions:

1. To what extent were management in this case justified in the actions which they took covertly to monitor Ros Johnstone's behaviour at work?

2. To what extent have Johnstone's rights to privacy been infringed?

3. From a management perspective, what are the advantages and disadvantages of using technology for covert surveillance of employee behaviour at work, without their consent?

4. From the perspective of the individual employee, do you think that managers have a right to monitor your behaviour at work without consent?

5. From an individual perspective, is surveillance acceptable if it is not covert, if employees are aware that they are being observed while they work?

This case account is from 'Someone is watching you – and it could be your boss', *The Times Magazine*, 6 November 1999, pp. 26–30.

Part 2 Individuals in the organization

A field map of the organizational behaviour terrain

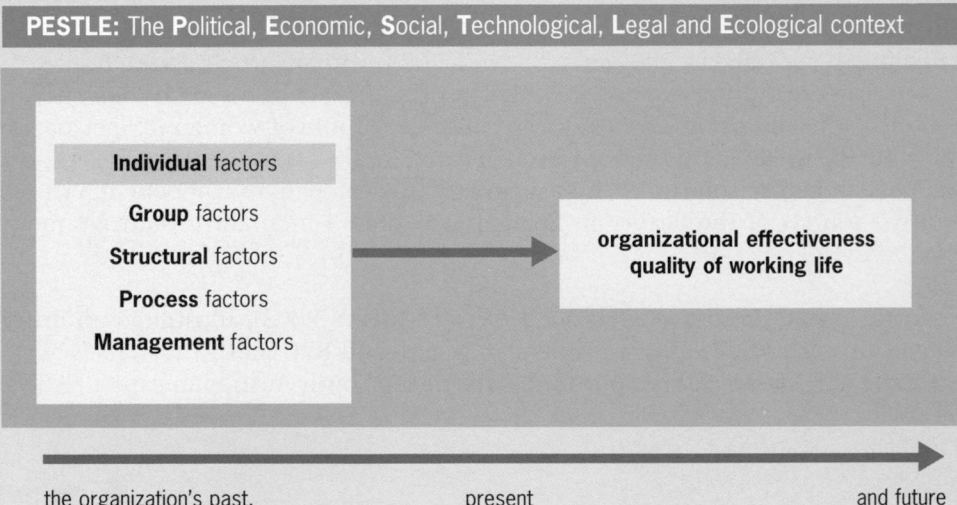

PESTLE: The **P**olitical, **E**conomic, **S**ocial, **T**echnological, **L**egal and **E**cological context

Individual factors
Group factors
Structural factors
Process factors
Management factors

organizational effectiveness
quality of working life

the organization's past,   present   and future

Introduction

Part 2, Individuals in the organization, explores five topics:

- Learning, in chapter 4
- Personality, in chapter 5
- Communication, in chapter 6
- Perception, in chapter 7
- Motivation, in chapter 8

These aspects of psychology are closely related. Each contributes in a different way to our understanding of behaviour in general, to our understanding of behaviour in organizations in particular, and to our analysis of performance at work and quality of working life.

Invitation to see

The first image appeared in *The Times* (8 March 2003) with an article about 'Beauty in Epaulettes 2003', a Russian Army recruiting exercise in which contestants are assessed on their shooting as well as their appearance. The aim of the contest was to raise the profile of women in Spetsnaz, the Russian equivalent of the British SAS. This picture also appeared in *The Daily Telegraph* above the caption 'Guns and poses: Russian female soldiers with Kalashnikov rifles prepare to compete in a shooting match during one of the rounds of the Beauty in Epaulettes contest which aims to attract more women into the Russian army'.

The second image, from the *Financial Times* (21 March 2003), illustrated an article about a merger between Constellation Brands, an American group, and BRL Hardy, Australia's biggest wine producer. The photograph shows Hardy's bottling plant in the South Australian capital, Adelaide.

Russia's glamour brigade aims high
Source: Associated Press, AP

Bottling at BRL Hardy in Adelaide, now home to the world's biggest wine group
Source: Newspix/Chris Crerar

1. **Decoding:** Look at these images closely. Note in as much detail as possible what messages you feel they are each trying to convey. Do they tell a story, present a point of view, support an argument, perpetuate a myth, reinforce a stereotype, challenge a stereotype?

2. **Challenging:** To what extent do you agree with the messages, stories, points of view, arguments, myths or stereotypes in these images? Are these images open to challenge, to criticism, to interpretation or decoding in other ways, revealing other messages?

3. **Sharing:** Compare with colleagues your interpretation of these images. Explore explanations for differences in your respective decodings.

Chapter 4 Learning

Key concepts

learning	cybernetic analogy
behaviourist or stimulus–response psychology	intrinsic and extrinsic feedback
cognitive or information processing psychology	concurrent and delayed feedback
feedback	behaviour modification
positive and negative reinforcement	socialization
punishment	behavioural self-management
extinction	learning organization
Pavlovian (classical or respondent) conditioning	single-loop learning
Skinnerian (instrumental or operant) conditioning	double-loop learning
shaping	tacit knowledge
intermittent reinforcement	explicit knowledge
schedule of reinforcement	knowledge management

Learning outcomes

When you have read this chapter, you should be able to define those key concepts in your own words, and you should also be able to:

1. Explain the characteristics of the behaviourist and cognitive approaches to learning.
2. Explain and evaluate the technique of behaviour modification.
3. Explain the socialization process, and assess the practical relevance of this concept.
4. Explain and evaluate the technique of behavioural self-management.
5. Describe the characteristics of the learning organization and explain why this concept has been popular since the 1990s.

Why study learning?

Learning is important to you personally. As a rule, the higher the level of your qualifications, the higher the salary you will be able to command. Our ability to learn is central to organizational effectiveness. Employees have to know what they are to do, how they are to do it, and how well they are expected to perform. Learning theories have thus influenced several organizational practices concerning:

- the induction of new recruits;
- the design and delivery of job training;
- the design of payment systems;
- how supervisors evaluate performance and provide feedback;
- the design of forms of learning organization.

What is learning all about?

1. Learning is a part of work and work involves learning; these are not separate functions but intertwined; the separation we have made of them is artificial and often does not serve us well.

2. Learning is not only or even primarily about obtaining correct information or answers from knowledgeable others; it is fundamentally about making meaning out of the experience that we and others have in the world.

3. Organizational learning results from intentional and planned efforts to learn. Although it can and does occur accidentally, organizations cannot afford to rely on learning through chance.

4. As a collective we are capable of learning our way to the answers we need to address our difficult problems. It is ourselves we must rely on for these answers rather than experts, who can, at best, only provide us with answers that have worked in the past.

From Nancy M. Dixon, *The Organizational Learning Cycle: How We Can Learn Collectively*, Gower, Aldershot (second edition), 1999, p. xiv.

Theories of learning thus have significant practical implications. However, this is one of the most fundamental and controversial topics in psychology. The extremes of the controversy are explained here, in the form of *behaviourist* and *cognitive* theories of learning.

The concept of the *learning organization* became popular during the 1990s. The learning organization is a configuration of structures and policies which encourage individual learning, with individual and organizational benefits. The organization itself can also be regarded as an entity which is capable of learning. Knowledge has thus become an asset more important than materials and products for many organizations.

Assets not on the balance sheet

The value of a business increasingly lurks not in physical and financial assets that are on the balance sheet, but in intangibles: brands, patents, franchises, software, research programmes, ideas, expertise. Few firms try to measure returns on these assets, let alone publish information on them. Yet they are often what underlines a firm's success. 'Our primary assets, which are our software and our software-development skills, do not show up on the balance sheet at all', says Microsoft's boss, Bill Gates.

From, 'A price on the priceless', *The Economist*, 12 June 1999, p. 94.

Why is the concept of the learning organization now regarded as significant? Competitive advantage means knowing how to produce certain products, knowing how to innovate rapidly, knowing how to bring new products and services quickly to the marketplace, knowing how to meet changing customer needs. The capacity to develop new knowledge has direct consequences for an organization's ability to grow and to survive, as technologies, customer requirements, government policies and economic conditions change. John Burgoyne (1999, p. 40) points out, however, that 'after a decade of working with the learning organization concept, there are distressingly few, if any, case studies of success with the idea on a large scale'. This kind of major transformation, Burgoyne argues, takes time to reveal its full potential, and should not be abandoned simply because of a lack of early results.

The learning process

How do we learn? How do we come to know what we know, and to do the things that we are able to do? These questions lie at the heart of psychology, and our understanding is in a constant state of development. It is therefore not surprising that the student of learning is confronted with different approaches to the topic. This variety helps to maintain controversy, excitement and interest in the subject, which in turn help to generate new ideas and methods.

Psychology is associated with the study of rats in mazes. Rats, and other animals, have contributed much to our understanding of human behaviour, and have been widely used by psychologists concerned with the development of theories of learning. Rat biochemistry is similar to ours. We have to face the fact that we humans are animals in many respects, and that we can learn much about ourselves through studying other creatures.

The ability to learn is not unique to human beings. Animals also learn, as dog owners and circus fans can confirm. One feature that seems to distinguish us from animals is our ability to learn about, adapt to and manipulate our environment for purposes that we ourselves define. Animals can adapt to changes in their circumstances, but their ability to manipulate their environment is restricted, and they appear to have limited choice over their goals. In addition, animals have developed no science, technology or engineering.

Source: © copyright United Feature Syndicate, Inc. Reproduced by permission.

The terms 'skill' and 'training' are used here in a broad sense. Skill to a psychologist covers a range of behaviours, from the trained ability to play tennis, to the routine ability to walk down the street. When the latter skill is analyzed in detail, it turns out to be extremely complex. Training covers not just the acquisition of manual skills, but also the learning of 'correct' attitudes, values, beliefs and expectations.

We hope that when you have finished reading this book you will be able to say that you have learned something. The test of this hope concerns whether or not you will be able to do things that you could not do before. You should, for example, know what the study of organizational behaviour is concerned with, and you should be able to tell others what you know and think about it. You should be able to write essays and answer examination questions that previously you could not tackle.

We are concerned with two related aspects of learning:

1. How we come to know things, through the process of learning.

2. The organization of our ideas, thoughts and knowledge, which constitutes the content of memory.

Learning: the process of acquiring knowledge through experience which leads to an enduring change in behaviour.

We refer to the process as **learning**, and to the result as knowledge.

It is important to note the limits on what counts as learning which are defined by the criteria of durability and experience. Behaviour can be changed temporarily by many factors, in ways which are not described as learning. Factors other than experience which alter our behaviour temporarily include maturation (in children), ageing (in adults), drugs, alcohol and fatigue.

We cannot see what goes on inside your head as you learn. We can only infer that learning has taken place by examining changes in your behaviour. If we assume that behaviour does not alter spontaneously, for no reason, then we can look for experiences that may be causes of behaviour change. These experiences may be derived from inside the body or they may be sensory, arising outside. The task of inferring whether or not learning has taken place may be an obvious one, but observable behaviour may not always reveal learning.

It is helpful to distinguish between two types of learning. Procedural learning, or 'knowing how', concerns your ability to carry out skilled actions, such as riding a horse or painting a picture. Declarative learning, or 'knowing that', concerns your store of factual knowledge, such as an understanding of the history of our use of the horse, or of the contribution of the European Futurist movement to contemporary art.

Changes in behaviour can be quantified using a 'learning curve'. The graph in figure 4.1 shows a typical learning curve for a trainee machine operator.

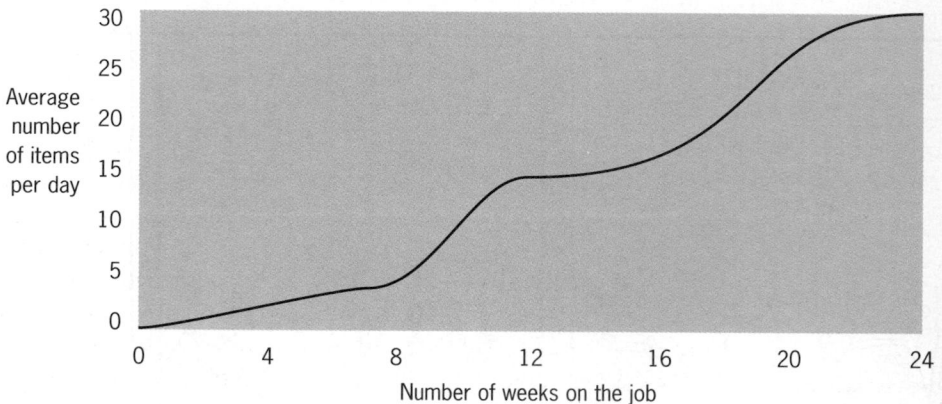

Figure 4.1: The typical manual skills learning curve

A learning curve can be plotted for an individual, for a group of trainees, or even for a whole organization. This (fictitious) learning curve shows that:

1. It takes about six months for machinists to become proficient, and for performance to 'level out' or peak at its maximum.

2. Top output is around 30 items a day.

3. The trainee's ability develops slowly at first, rises sharply during the third month, and hits a plateau during the fourth month of training before starting to take off again.

Most learning curves for manual skills seem to follow this profile, but cognitive skills can develop in the same way. The shape of a learning curve depends, as one would expect, on the characteristics of the task and of the learner. It is often possible to measure learning in this way, to compare individuals with each other, and thus to establish what constitutes good performance. If we know what form a learning curve takes, and if we understand the factors influencing the shape of the curve, we should be able to develop fresh approaches to make learning more effective.

Stop and Criticize

What is the shape of your learning curve for this course? Draw it.

Why is it that shape? Identify factors that you feel determine its form.

Should it be that shape – and what would be your ideal?

What could you do to change the shape of your learning curve?

Behaviourist or stimulus–response psychology: a perspective which argues that what we learn are chains of muscle movements; mental processes are not observable, and are not valid issues for study.

Cognitive or information processing psychology: a perspective which argues that what we learn are mental structures; mental processes are amenable to study even though they cannot be directly observed.

The experiences that lead to changes in behaviour have a number of important features.

First, the human mind is not a passive recorder of information picked up through the senses. We can often recall the plot of a novel, for example, but remember very few of the author's words. This suggests that we do not record experiences in a simple, straightforward way.

Second, we are usually able to recall events in which we have participated as if we were another actor in the drama. We are able to reflect, to see ourselves 'from outside', as objects in our own experience. At the time when we experienced the events, those cannot have been the sense impressions that we picked up. Reflection is a valuable capability.

Third, new experiences do not always lead to behaviour change. Declarative learning, for example, may not be evident until we are asked the right questions. Our experiences must be processed in some way to become influential in determining future behaviours.

Fourth, the way in which we express our innate drives is not merely inherited, but also depends on experience. We do have innate drives, but these are expressed in behaviour in different ways. How they are expressed depends on many factors, including past experiences. Our innate makeup biases our behaviour in certain directions, but these biases can be modified by experience.

This chapter explains two influential approaches to learning, based on **behaviourist psychology** and **cognitive psychology**. These perspectives are in many respects contradictory, but they can also be viewed as complementary. These perspectives have very different implications for organization and management practice.

These perspectives, summarized in table 4.1, are based on the same empirical data, but their interpretations of those data are radically different.

Table 4.1: Behaviourist and cognitive perspectives on learning contrasted

Behaviourist, stimulus–response	Cognitive, information processing
studies only observable behaviour	studies mental processes
behaviour is determined by learned sequences of muscle movements	behaviour is determined by memory, mental processes and expectations
we learn habits	we learn cognitive structures and alternative ways to achieve our goals
problem-solving occurs by trial and error	problem-solving involves insight and understanding
dull, boring, but amenable to research?	rich, interesting, but complex, vague and unresearchable?

The behaviourist approach to learning

Feedback: information concerning the outcomes of our behaviour.

Positive reinforcement: the attempt to encourage desirable behaviours by introducing positive consequences when the desired behaviour occurs.

Negative reinforcement: the attempt to encourage desirable behaviours by withdrawing negative consequences when the desired behaviour occurs.

The oldest theory of learning states that ideas that are experienced together tend to be associated with each other. Behaviourist psychologists speak of the association between stimulus and response. Learning is thus a result of experience. We use knowledge of the outcomes of past behaviour to change, modify and improve our behaviour in future. You learn to write better assignments and get higher grades by finding out how well or how badly you did last time and why. We cannot learn without **feedback**. Behaviourists and cognitive psychologists agree that experience affects behaviour, but disagree over how this happens.

Feedback may be either rewarding or punishing. Common sense suggests that if a particular behaviour is rewarded, then it is more likely to be repeated. If it is punished or ignored, it is more likely to be avoided in future. This observation is encapsulated in the behaviourists' 'law of effect', which states that we learn to repeat behaviours that have favourable consequences and to avoid behaviours that lead to undesirable or neutral consequences. Rats are thus trained to run through mazes at the whim of the psychologist using a combination of food pellets and electric shocks.

Behaviourism makes subtle distinctions relating to reward and punishment. Table 4.2 illustrates these distinctions with examples.

With **positive reinforcement**, desired behaviours lead to positive consequences. With **negative reinforcement**, the negative consequences continue until the desired behaviour is displayed. As one-off **punishment** follows undesirable behaviour, this is different from negative reinforcement. With **extinction**, the undesirable behaviour is simply ignored.

The American psychologist John B. Watson (1878–1958) introduced the term 'behaviourism' in 1913. He was critical of the technique of introspection, in which subjects were asked to talk about their sensory experiences and thought processes, to explore their minds and to tell the psychologist what they found there. Instead, Watson wanted objective, 'scientific' handles on human behaviour, its causes and its consequences. This took him, and many other psychologists, away from the intangible contents of the mind to the

Table 4.2: Reinforcement regimes illustrated

	Behaviour	Reinforcement	Result	Illustration
positive reinforcement	desired behaviour occurs	positive consequences are introduced	desired behaviour is repeated	confess, and we will give you a shorter prison sentence
negative reinforcement	desired behaviour occurs	negative consequences are withdrawn	desired behaviour is repeated	the torture will continue until you confess
punishment	undesired behaviour occurs	a single act of punishment is introduced	undesired behaviour is not repeated	fail to meet your quarterly target and we will fire you
extinction	undesired behaviour occurs	the behaviour is ignored	undesired behaviour is not repeated	supervisor ignores an individual's practical jokes used to gain attention

Punishment: the attempt to discourage undesirable behaviours through the application of negative consequences, or by withholding a positive consequence, following the undesirable behaviour.

study of the relationships between visible stimuli and visible responses. That is why behaviourist psychology is sometimes referred to as 'stimulus–response psychology'.

The behaviourist perspective assumes that what lies between the stimulus and the response is a mechanism that will be revealed as our knowledge of the biochemistry and neurophysiology of the brain improves. This biological mechanism must relate stimuli to responses in a way that governs behaviour. We can therefore continue to study how stimuli and responses are related without a detailed understanding of the nature of that mechanism.

Behaviourists thus argue that nothing of psychological importance happens between the stimulus and the response. Cognitive theory, in contrast, argues that something of considerable psychological importance happens between stimulus and response.

Getting Dennis Rodman in the game

In 1997, the owners of the Chicago Bulls basketball team faced a tricky challenge: they had to negotiate a contract with their controversial star forward Dennis Rodman. Rodman, an immensely talented rebounder, was known for his unpredictable behaviour and, in particular, his propensity to miss games. During the preceding season, for example, Rodman played in only 55 of the Bulls' 82 regular season contests. Because his contract for that season was guaranteed, the Bulls ended up paying him US$2.96 million for games he didn't play in. Understandably, the team was not eager to enter into the same kind of contract again.

Instead, the Bulls signed Rodman with the most incentive-laden deal in the history of the National Basketball Association. Rodman was eligible to earn $10.5 million during the season, but only $4.5 million was guaranteed. The remainder depended on his fulfilment of various performance and behaviour clauses. For instance, he'd get $1 million for playing in all play-off games, $500,000 for winning another NBA rebounding title, $185,000 for each game he played after the 59th game, and $100,000 for maintaining a positive assist-to-turnover ratio.

The contingent contract proved to be a slam dunk for both the Bulls and Rodman. It not only reduced the team's risk but also gave Rodman the incentive to excel. He played in 80 of the season's 82 games, won his seventh rebounding title, and collected $10.1 million of his potential $10.5 million salary. Rodman's performance helped the Bulls win the league championship, providing a windfall for the team's owners.

From Max H. Bazerman and James J. Gillespie, 'Betting on the future: the virtues of contingent contracts', *Harvard Business Review*, vol. 77, no. 5, September–October 1999, p. 160.

Extinction: the attempt to eliminate undesirable behaviours by attaching no consequences, positive or negative, such as indifference and silence.

The development of associations between stimuli and responses happens in two different ways, known as **Pavlovian conditioning** and **Skinnerian conditioning**.

Pavlovian conditioning is also known as *classical* and as *respondent* conditioning. The concept and related conditioning techniques were developed by the Russian physiologist Ivan Petrovich Pavlov (1849–1936).

The best-know response which Pavlov studied concerned a dog salivating at the sight of food. Pavlov demonstrated how this could be associated with a new and completely different stimulus, such as the sound of a bell. Dog owners are still trained in the use of classical conditioning methods. If you show meat to a dog, it will produce saliva. The meat is the stimulus, the saliva is the response. The meat is an unconditioned stimulus because the dog salivates naturally. Similarly, the saliva is an unconditioned response. The dog will produce saliva without any

Pavlovian conditioning (also known as *classical* and as *respondent conditioning*) a technique for associating an established response or behaviour with a new stimulus.

John Broadus
Watson
(1878–1958)

Skinnerian conditioning (also known as *instrumental* and as *operant conditioning*) a technique for associating a response or a behaviour with its consequence.

Ivan Petrovich
Pavlov
(1849–1936)

Burrhus Frederic
Skinner (1904–90)

manipulation by a psychologist. Unconditioned responses are also called reflexes. Your lower leg jerks when you are struck just below the kneecap; your pupils contract when light is shone into your eyes. These are typical human reflexes. Humans also salivate naturally, another unconditioned response, at the sight and smell of food.

Suppose we now ring a bell before we show the meat to the dog. Do this often enough, and the dog will associate the bell with the meat. Eventually the dog will start to salivate at the sound of the bell, without food being present. The bell is a conditioned stimulus, and the saliva is now a conditioned response. The dog has learned, from experience, to salivate at the sound of a bell as well as at the sight of food. It does not have to be a bell. All manner of stimuli can be conditioned in this way. Pavlov discovered this form of conditioning by accident. His research was initially concerned with salivation, but he observed that his dogs salivated at the sight and sound of his laboratory assistants, before they received their meat. He found this more interesting, and switched the focus of his research.

Suppose we now stop giving the meat to the dog after the bell. The dog will continue to salivate at the sound of the bell alone, expecting the bell to signal the arrival of food. If we continue to do this, however, the volume of saliva produced falls, and the association between the conditioned stimulus and conditioned response eventually suffers extinction.

The conditioned response may also be invoked by stimuli similar to the original conditioned stimulus, such as a bell with a different pitch. This phenomenon is called stimulus generalization. A complementary phenomenon, stimulus discrimination, can also be demonstrated by conditioning the dog to salivate at a bell of one pitch, but not at another.

Skinnerian conditioning is also known as *instrumental* and as *operant* conditioning. It is the discovery of the American psychologist Burrhus Frederic Skinner (1904–90). Instrumental conditioning demonstrates how new behaviours or responses become established through association with particular stimuli.

Where the consequence of a particular behaviour is desirable to the individual, then the frequency of that behaviour is likely to increase. Given a particular context, any behaviour that is rewarded or reinforced will tend to be repeated in that context. Skinner put a rat into a box (now known as a 'Skinner box') with a lever inside which, when pressed, gave the animal food. The rat is not taught to press the lever. However, in the process of wandering around the box, the rat eventually nudges the lever. It may sit on it, knock it with its head or push it with a paw. That random behaviour is reinforced with food, and it is likely to happen again.

Classical conditioning has that name because it is the older of the two conditioning methods. Skinnerian conditioning is also called instrumental conditioning because it is related to behaviours that are instrumental in getting some material reward. Skinner's rat has to be under the influence of some drive before it can be conditioned in this way. His rats were hungry when they went into his box, and their behaviour thus led to a desired reward.

Where do the terms 'respondent' and 'operant conditioning' come from? Watson's stimulus–response psychology stated that there was no behaviour, or no response, without a stimulus to set it in motion. One could therefore condition a known response to a given stimulus. In other words, one could attach that response to another stimulus. Such responses are called respondents. Knee jerks, pupil contractions and salivation are well known and clearly identified responses that are amenable to conditioning.

Skinner argued that this was inconsistent with known facts. Animals and humans do behave in the absence of specific stimuli. In fact, he argued, most human behaviour is of this kind. Behaviours emitted in the absence of identifi-

Shaping: the selective reinforcement of chosen behaviours in a manner that progressively establishes a desired behaviour pattern.

able stimuli are called operants. Operant conditioning explains how new patterns of behaviour become established. Respondent conditioning does not alter the animal's behaviour, only the behaviour's timing.

Skinner also introduced the concept of **shaping**, which was achieved by selectively reinforcing desired pieces of behaviour. In this way he was able to get pigeons to play ping-pong and to walk in figures of eight – famous demonstrations of how random, aimless or spontaneous behaviours can be shaped by operant conditioning.

Conditioning at Amazon

Actually it *was* a bit of a sweatshop, or like something from the accounting halls of Dickens' *Bleak House* – a wasteland of cubicle dividers filled with the ceaseless murmuring of order numbers and apologies. If human misery and efficient boredom could be beautiful, there would have been a kind of beauty in the endlessly replicated, hot-desking, rack-mounted workers and their swiftly exchangeable work stations. Lit up by the dead light of our monitors, we would constantly scratch at our keyboards – it could have been sadly romantic, if it hadn't been for the sirens.

Hanging everywhere were readerboards showing the number of calls on hold and the average response time. When the numbers got too high they would turn red and a fearful, piercing whistle would go off, hooting over and over. People developed neurotic aversion to the sound, they shook and looked up like dogs when they heard it.

Msmith explained it to me. 'It's conditioning.'

'What is?'

'The sirens. They actually condition you to work faster.'

'Uh-huh.'

'No, I'm serious. Think about it: what's the most horrible sound you can think of right now?' The siren was blaring right over our head – *eepEEP, eepEEP*.

'I think that would be the siren.'

'Right. They make it so horrible so that you feel intense relief when the siren stops ... Wait for it ...' The siren stopped. 'See? Can you feel that?'

'Holy shit.' Sitting there, I could actually feel my heart rate dropping and my tension beginning to dissolve. 'It's like I'm wired to it.'

'Yeah. I heard they could have gotten a normal alarm, but the workflow analysts they hired said we'd work harder if we had something at stake.'

From Mike Daisey, *21 Dog Years: Doing Time @ Amazon.Com*, Fourth Estate, London, 2002, pp. 78–9.

Intermittent reinforcement: the procedure whereby a reward is provided only occasionally following correct responses, and not for every correct response.

Skinner studied numerous variations on the operant conditioning theme. One important variation concerns the occasional reward of desired behaviour rather than delivering rewards in a continuous and regular manner. This mirrors real life more closely than the laboratory experiment. Why, for example, do gamblers keep playing when they lose much of the time? Why do anglers continue to fish when they catch nothing for hours at a time? There are many such examples of the power of **intermittent reinforcement**. Behaviour can be maintained without regular and consistent reinforcement every time that it occurs.

Schedule of reinforcement: the pattern and frequency of rewards contingent on the display of desirable behaviour.

The pattern and timing of rewards for desired behaviour is known as the **schedule of reinforcement**. The possible variation in schedules of reinforcement is limitless, and Skinner investigated the effects of a number of these (Ferster and Skinner, 1957). However, there are two main classes of intermittent reinforcement, concerning interval schedules and ratio schedules, which are described in table 4.3, contrasted with continuous reinforcement.

Skinner claimed to be able to explain the development of complex patterns of behaviour with the theory of operant conditioning. This shows how our behaviour is shaped by our environment, by our experiences in that environment, and by the selective rewards and punishments that we receive. Thinking, problem-solving and the acquisition of language, he argued, are dependent on these simple conditioning processes. Skinner rejected the use of 'mentalistic' concepts and 'inner psychic forces' in explanations of human behaviour because these were not observable, were not researchable, and were therefore not necessary to the science of human psychology. Why use complicated and unobservable concepts when simple and observable phenomena seem to provide adequate explanations?

Stop and Criticize

In this Alex cartoon, is young Oliver's problem the result of respondent conditioning, or of operant conditioning?

Table 4.3: Schedules of reinforcement

Schedule	Description	Implications
continuous	reinforcement after *every correct response*	can establish high performance, but can also lead to satiation; rapid extinction when reinforcement is withheld
fixed ratio	reinforcement after a *predetermined number* of correct responses	tends to generate high rates of desired responses
variable ratio	reinforcement after a *random number* of correct responses	can produce a high response rate that is resistant to extinction
fixed interval	reinforcement of a correct response after a *predetermined period*	can produce uneven response patterns, slow following reinforcement, vigorous immediately preceding reinforcement
variable interval	reinforcement of a correct response after *random periods*	can produce a high response rate that is resistant to extinction

Adapted from Fred Luthans and Robert Kreitner, *Organizational Behaviour Modification and Beyond*, Scott Foresman, Glenview, IL (second edition), 1985.

Skinner's ambitious project has been enormously influential. It has led to the widespread use of programmed learning, a technique of instruction designed to reinforce correct responses in the learner and to let people learn at their own pace. The *behaviour modification* techniques described later are also based on his ideas. As the behaviour of a conditioned animal is consistent and predictable, this can be used to test the effects of drugs.

It is generally accepted that reinforcing desired behaviour is more effective than punishing undesirable behaviour. However, C.C. Walters and J.E. Grusek (1977), from a review of research, suggest that punishment can be effective if it meets the following conditions:

- the punishment should be quick and short;
- it should be administered immediately after the undesirable behaviour;
- it should be limited in its intensity;
- it should be specifically related to behaviour, and not to character traits;
- it should be restricted to the context in which the undesirable behaviour occurs;
- it should not send 'mixed messages' about what is acceptable behaviour;
- penalties should take the form of withdrawal of rewards, not physical pain.

Stop and Criticize

To what extent should the punishment criteria identified by Walters and Grusek be used by managers when disciplining employees in an organizational context?

The cognitive approach to learning

Norbert Wiener
(1894–1964)

Cybernetic analogy: a perspective which seeks to explain the learning process with reference to the components and operation of a feedback control system.

Why should we look only at observable stimuli and responses in the study of psychology? It is possible to study the internal workings of the mind in indirect ways, by inference. Behaviourism seems to be unnecessarily restrictive, excluding those characteristics that make us interesting, different and, above all, human.

How do we select from all the stimuli that bombard our senses those to which we are going to respond? Why are some outcomes seen as rewarding and others as punishments? This may appear obvious where the reward is survival or food and the punishment is pain or death. However, with intrinsic or symbolic rewards this is not always clear. To answer these questions, we have to consider states of mind concerning perception and motivation.

The rewards and punishments that behaviourists call reinforcement work in more complex ways than conditioning theories suggest. Reinforcement is always knowledge, or *feedback*, about the success of past behaviour. Feedback is information that can be used to modify or maintain previous behaviours. This information has to be perceived, interpreted, given meaning and used in decisions about future behaviours. The feedback has to be processed. Cognitive learning theories are thus also called information processing theories.

This approach draws concepts from the field of cybernetics which was established by the American mathematician Norbert Wiener (1954). He defined cybernetics as 'the science of communication in the animal and in the machine'. One central idea of cybernetics is the notion of the control of system performance through feedback. Information processing theories of learning are based on what is called the **cybernetic analogy**.

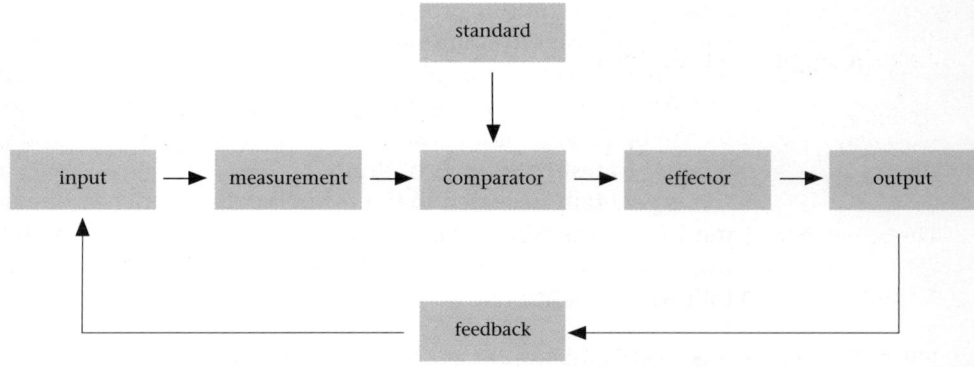

Figure 4.2: The elements of a cybernetic feedback control system

Intrinsic feedback: information which comes from within, from the muscles, joints, skin and other mechanisms such as that which controls balance.

Extrinsic feedback: information which comes from our environment, such as the visual and aural information needed to drive a car.

Concurrent feedback: information which arrives during our behaviour and which can be used to control behaviour as it unfolds.

Delayed feedback: information which is received after a task is completed, and which can be used to influence future performance.

The elements of a cybernetic feedback control system are outlined in figure 4.2.

Consider a domestic heating control system. The temperature standard is set on a thermostat, and a heater (effector) starts to warm up the room. The output of the system is heated air. Changes in temperature are measured by a thermometer. The temperature of the room is continually compared with the standard. When the room reaches the required temperature, the effector is switched off, and when the room cools, it is switched on again.

We will meet this concept later in our discussion of *single-loop* and *double-loop learning*. This example of cybernetic control illustrates single-loop learning. The cybernetic analogy claims that this control loop is a model of what goes on inside the mind. For standard, read motive, purpose, intent or goal. The output is behaviour. The senses are our measuring devices. Our perceptual process is the comparator which organizes and imposes meaning on the sensory data which thus control behaviour in pursuit of given objectives. We have in our minds some kind of 'internal representation' or 'schema' of ourselves and the environment in which we function. This internal representation is used in a purposive way to determine our behaviour. This internal representation is also called the image – also known as the individual's *perceptual world*.

Our behaviour is purposive. We formulate plans for achieving our purposes. The plan is a set of mental instructions for guiding the required behaviour. Within the master plan (get an educational qualification) there are likely to be a number of sub-plans (submit essay on time; pass the examination; make new friends). The organization of our behaviour is hierarchical – a concept which can be illustrated by comparison with a computer program in which instructional routines and sub-routines are typically 'nested' within each other.

However, unlike most computer programs, we can use information on how we are doing – feedback – to update our internal representation and to refine and adapt our plans. Feedback comes in different forms, and can either be self-generated or come from some external source. In other words, feedback can be either **intrinsic** or **extrinsic**.

Independent of the source and nature of the feedback, timing is also an important consideration. Feedback can arrive during or after the behaviour in which we are interested in learning. In other words, feedback can either be **concurrent** or **delayed**.

Stop and Criticize

From your own experience, identify an example of each of the four varieties of feedback identified here. What changes in that feedback would be required for you to be able to improve your performance (on this course, at sport, whatever)?

We need appropriate feedback

Appropriate feedback on work performance is necessary to ensure the learning and development of job skills. But do supervisors always tell their subordinates the truth? Daniel Ilgen and William Knowlton designed an experiment to answer this question.

The researchers asked 40 students each to supervise a group of three workers doing a routine clerical job for two hours. The supervisors were first shown the results of a test which was supposed to measure the abilities of their workers for such a task.

But each group had one worker, a confederate of the researchers, who performed much better or much worse than the others, working either enthusiastically or apathetically. The supervisors were led to believe that the level of performance of this exceptional group member was due either to high or low ability, or to their motivation.

After the work session, the supervisors rated the ability and motivation of all their subordinates on scales ranging from 'unsatisfactory' to 'outstanding'. They then completed a separate 'feedback report form', believing that they would have to discuss it with the exceptional (weak or strong) worker in person.

For the feedback, supervisors were asked to choose one of twelve statements which best described their evaluation of each worker, such as:

- 'You have done very well. I believe I would try to do even better next time if I were you.'

- 'Your performance is not good at all. You really need to put much more into it.'

The supervisors also had to recommend further action for the subordinate, to change either ability or motivation, such as:

- Attend a special training session.
- Concentrate more on the task.
- Try harder.

The supervisors were then told about the deception. There was no feedback session. The researchers wanted to find out how truthful the supervisors would have been with their feedback. As expected, ratings of ability and motivation were higher when supervisors believed that they would have to tell their subordinates this in person. Where low performance was attributed to low motivation, the feedback reflected this accurately. But where low performance was blamed on poor ability, supervisors recommended an inappropriate mix of feedback, directed at effort and skill.

The researchers conclude that supervisors systematically distort their assessments of subordinates and thus inhibit their learning.

Based on Daniel R. Ilgen and William A. Knowlton, 'Performance attributional effects on feedback from superiors', *Organizational Behaviour and Human Performance*, vol. 25, no. 3, 1980, pp. 441–56.

When you submit a written assignment, intrinsic feedback is of limited value. Extrinsic feedback from your instructor is what matters. However, that feedback is delayed. When you are throwing rings over pegs at the fair to win a soft toy, the intrinsic concurrent visual feedback means that you know how well, or how badly, you are performing during the action. Instructors, of course, cannot provide concurrent feedback while you are writing an essay, but the longer the delay, the less effective the feedback is likely to be.

Feedback, rewards and punishments, and knowledge of results, also have a *motivating* effect on behaviour, rather than simply a reinforcing effect. Several writers on motivation have argued that opportunities to learn new skills and knowledge, to understand more, to develop more effective ways of living and coping with our environment are intrinsically motivating. The American psychologist Robert W. White (1959) suggests that we have a motive to develop 'competence' in dealing with our environment and that this gives us satisfaction. As the later section on the *learning organization* demonstrates, the 'urge towards discovery' and the 'will to understand' have triggered a search for novel organizational configurations in which individual and organizational learning are encouraged.

Applications: behaviour modification techniques in practice

> **Behaviour modification**: a technique for encouraging desired behaviours and discouraging unwanted behaviours using operant conditioning.

Behaviourism has led to the development of techniques of **behaviour modification**. These were first used for the treatment of mental disorders, learning disorders, phobias, for psychiatric rehabilitation, and for accident and trauma recovery. Applications have since been extended to organizational settings.

As developed by Fred Luthans (Luthans and Kreitner, 1985; Luthans et al., 1998), organizational behaviour modification, or 'O.B.Mod.', has five mains steps:

1. *Identify* the critical, observable and measurable work performance-related behaviours to be encouraged.

2. *Measure* the current frequency of those behaviours, to provide a baseline against which to measure improvement.

3. *Establish* the triggers or antecedents for those behaviours, and also establish the consequences – positive, neutral and negative – that follow from those behaviours.

4. *Develop* an intervention strategy to strengthen desired behaviours and weaken dysfunctional behaviours through the use of positive reinforcement (money, recognition) and corrective feedback, noting that punishment may be necessary in some instances, for example to inhibit unsafe behaviour.

5. *Evaluate* systematically the effectiveness of the approach in changing behaviour and improving performance compared with the original baseline measurement.

Fred Luthans

Behaviour modification can appear particularly attractive to managers who are often in ideal positions from which to manipulate the reinforcement of certain employee behaviours. Managers also tend to find this approach attractive because it argues that what has to be changed is behaviour, and that to achieve this one needs to know very little about the complex internal workings of the people concerned.

Desirable workplace behaviours could include, for example, speaking courteously to customers, attending training to develop new skills and being helpful to colleagues. Undesirable behaviours could include lateness, the production of poor quality items and being rude to customers. Behaviour modification uses the principles of reinforcement to eliminate undesired behaviour and to increase the frequency of desired work behaviour. Suppose a manager wants more work assignments completed on time and fewer submitted beyond deadline. The behaviour modification options are summarized in table 4.4.

Table 4.4: Behaviour modification options

Procedure	Operationalization	Behavioural effect
positive reinforcement	manager praises employee each time work is completed on schedule	increases desired behaviour
negative reinforcement	unpaid overtime continues to be mandatory until work is completed on schedule, then overtime is rewarded	increases desired behaviour
punishment	manager asks employee to stay late when work is not handed in on schedule	eliminates or decreases undesired behaviour
extinction	manager ignores the employee when work is handed in late	eliminates or decreases undesired behaviour

E. Scott Geller (1983) reports how the Radford Army Ammunition Plant in Virginia, America, used behaviour modification to encourage the wearing of seat belts among employees. The 'treatment' followed twelve days of unobtrusive observation at the three main entrances to the munitions complex, to establish a 'baseline' of seat-belt wearing. 'Incentive fliers' were then distributed, encouraging seat-belt use and offering opportunities to win prizes for those who did. The prizes included gift certificates and dinners at local restaurants, worth around $2 to $15. Only those wearing belts got a 'prize-winning' flier with a special symbol; those without belts got one which read 'next time wear your seat belt and receive a chance to win a valuable prize'. This 'incentive condition' lasted for a month.

Seat-belt use increased from an average of 20 per cent and 17 per cent in the mornings and afternoons respectively to 31 per cent and 55 per cent. After the programme was discontinued, seat-belt use returned to baseline levels. Subsequent observation revealed that 'those individuals who showed the greatest response maintenance also evidenced the highest baseline rate of seatbelt usage' (which implies that those who continued to use their belts were those who used them before anyway). Only nine prizes were claimed at a cost of $126, and four prizes had been donated by other local businesses covering 40 per cent of the expense.

Fred Luthans and colleagues (1998) describe the application of organizational behaviour modification in a Russian textile mill. To improve productivity, two interventions were used. First, workers were offered extrinsic rewards for performance improvement, including valued American products such as adults' and children's clothing, jeans, T-shirts with popular logos, music tapes, and food that was difficult to get in Russia. Second, workers were given 'social rewards' for performing specific actions, such as checking looms, undertaking repairs, monitoring fabric quality and helping others. These rewards involved attention, recognition and feedback from supervisors. The researchers note that this approach had a 'very positive impact' leading to 'highly significant increases in performance' (Luthans et al., 1998, p. 471).

In this case, a participative approach, in which the employees were first asked for ideas for improving performance, failed to work. The researchers argue that the cultural and political climate inhibited workers from making suggestions which could be regarded as criticizing existing methods and colleagues. On this evidence, they argue that behaviour modification 'fits' Eastern European social and organizational cultures and is widely applicable.

From these examples, the typical features of organizational applications of 'O.B. Mod' are:

- It applies to clearly identifiable and observable behaviours, such as timekeeping, carrying out checks and repairs, and the use of particular work methods.

- Rewards are contingent on the performance of the desirable behaviours.

- Positive reinforcement can take a number of forms, from the praise of a superior to cash prizes, to food, to clothing.

- Behaviour change and performance improvements can be dramatic.

- The desired modification in behaviour may only be sustained if positive reinforcement is continued (although this may be intermittent).

Stop and Criticize

How would you feel about being given food, T-shirts and praise from your supervisor for working harder?

Do you regard this approach as realistic, or as demeaning – and why?

Applications: socialization and feedback

When people join an organization, of any kind, they give up some personal freedom of action. That is part of the price of membership. Employees thus accept that an organization can make demands on their time and effort, as long as these demands are perceived to be legitimate. Other members of the organization have to teach new recruits what is expected of them. The process through which recruits are 'shown the ropes' is called **socialization**. Cognitive psychologists regard behaviour modification as simplistic, and turn to more complex social explanations and methods for organizational behaviour change.

This perspective draws on social learning theory which is based on assumptions about human psychology quite different from those behind behaviour modification techniques.

One of the most influential advocates of social learning theory has been Albert Bandura (1977, 1986). Bandura demonstrated that we learn new behaviours by observing and copying the behaviour of others, in the absence of any rewards or punishments. In this perspective, our capabilities for reflection and self-determination are central. We construct, through observation and experience, internal models of our environment, and plan courses of action accordingly. The ways in which we 'model' ourselves on others is particularly apparent in children. However, this propensity to copy or imitate others continues into adulthood.

The argument that we learn through social experience, through observation and modelling, does not deny the importance of reinforcement, which remains a factor in Bandura's social learning theory. Suppose, for example, that we choose to base some of our behaviours (how to handle a job interview, how to make new friends at parties) on a chosen model, presumably someone who appears particularly successful in those domains. Suppose that our new approach does not lead to the desired results; didn't get the job, failed to establish new relationships. In the absence of reinforcement, we are likely to abandon our new behaviours and look for other models and approaches.

How does social learning theory apply to organizational settings? Organizations tend to encourage different standards concerning, for example:

- what counts as adequate and good work performance;
- familiarity in everyday social interactions at work;

Socialization: the process through which individual behaviours, values, attitudes and motives are influenced to conform with those seen as desirable in a given social or organizational setting.

Albert Bandura
(b. 1925)

- the appropriate amount of deference to show to superiors;
- dress and appearance;
- social activities after work;
- attitudes to work, colleagues, managers, unions, customers.

The newcomer has to learn these standards and the ways of behaving and related attitudes that they involve, to become an effective and accepted member. The individual does not have to believe that the organization's standards are appropriate. In order to 'fit in', what matters is that individuals behave *as if* they believed in those norms.

The socialization process is often informal, rather than a planned programme of instruction. Some organizations have formal induction programmes, but these are often brief and superficial, concentrating on mundane matters like organization structures and policies, and health and safety regulations. Often, newcomers learn the ropes simply by watching their new colleagues. Socialization is thus achieved without planned intervention, by giving rewards such as praise, encouragement, privilege and promotion for 'correct' behaviour. It is achieved by negative reinforcements and punishments, like being ignored, ridiculed or fined for behaviour that is 'out of line'. We quickly learn what attitudes to take, what style of language to use, what 'dress code' to obey, where to take lunch and with whom, and so on.

Stop and Criticize	Most organizations plan the punishments and material rewards that members will get, but leave the social and symbolic rewards to chance. From your knowledge of learning theory, what would you predict to be the consequences of such a policy?

Note that some of the 'rewards for good behaviour' offered by organizations are material rewards, in the form of money and desirable working conditions (the bigger office and desk, the subsidized meals, access to free sports and leisure facilities, a space in the car park). Some of the available rewards, on the other hand, are symbolic and social rewards such as prestige, status, recognition and public praise.

Socialization – an alternative to behaviour modification

Social learning theory argues that we learn correct behaviours through experience and through the examples or *role models* that other people provide. While this can happen naturally, some companies prefer not to leave it to chance, and to manage the process instead. For example, some companies use a 'buddy system', pairing new recruits with established employees. However, if you get a job with the American computer software company Trilogy, based in Austin, Texas, you will not be given a buddy, or a one-day induction by your new boss. Instead, you will be sent to Trilogy University (TU) for three months, to join an orientation programme modelled on Marine Corps basic training. This is a 'boot camp', intense and intimidating, designed to challenge new recruits, most of whom are university graduates with an average age of 22. Trilogy wants to familiarize them quickly with appropriate knowledge and job skills, and also with the company's 'vision and values'. Run twice a year, over twelve weeks, for between 60 and 200 recruits at a time, the boot camp has three stages.

Month one

New recruits are assigned to a section, of about 20 people, and to an instruction track. The section leader is an experienced Trilogy employee, and the tracks resemble work in the company. Along with

➤

functional training, constantly evaluated, recruits are given a series of increasingly challenging assignments, which mirror real customer problems but with reduced timescales. Students are stretched beyond the point of failure in order to introduce company values, including humility, creativity, innovation, teamwork, customer problem-solving and risk taking. Another goal is to develop lasting, trusting relationships with colleagues.

Month two

This is project month and recruits are told that 'in order for the company to survive, they have to come up with a frame-breaking great new business idea'. Teams of three to five have to generate an idea, create a business model, build the product, develop a marketing plan and present the results to the Chief Executive. These projects are real, and around 15 per cent are funded. Recruits are expected to learn about the need to set priorities, evaluate probabilities and measure results. Failure to generate a successful idea is not punished.

Month three

Most recruits move on to business-related 'graduation projects', and leave TU as they find sponsors willing to take them on. Graduation involves a meeting between the recruit, the new manager and the section leader, at which the recruit's abilities are reviewed, their personal career objectives are examined, and the manager's three- to five-year goals for the recruit (including further skill development) are agreed. Most graduates find a home in the company, but those few who cannot find a sponsor have to leave.

Since 1995, when TU was founded, projects developed by recruits have generated revenues of US$25 million and have formed the basis for $100 million in new business for the company. These innovative ideas include internet-based motor car retailing and a website which allows shoppers to put products from several different internet retailers into a single purchase. In addition, the section leaders assigned for three months to inspire, motivate, mentor and develop the new recruits develop their leadership and change agency skills.

Based on Noel M. Tichy, 'No ordinary boot camp', *Harvard Business Review*, vol. 79, no. 1, April 2001, pp. 63–70.

Behaviour modification versus socialization

Stop and Criticize

Identify the main characteristics of, and contrasts between, behaviour modification and socialization as management techniques. Which more adequately deals with the realities of organizational life as you understand it – and why?

Is behaviour modification a generally applicable approach to employee learning and the development of appropriate behaviours? The evidence seems to suggest that the answer to this question is a qualified 'yes'. There are two major qualifications.

First, behaviour modification needs careful planning to identify specific behavioural goals, and procedures for reinforcing the behaviours that will achieve those goals. The method can be effective when behaviour and reinforcement are clearly identified and linked; wear your seat belt and we'll give you cash. The method is less effective when this relationship is vague; demonstrate commitment and we'll consider you for promotion.

Second, the 'rewards for good behaviour' method appears broadly consistent with American (and perhaps Eastern European) cultural values and aspirations.

The transfer of this approach to other cultures is questionable. The most often cited practical examples are American.

Behaviour modification is overtly manipulative, potentially ignores internal needs and intrinsic rewards, and can be seen as a threat to individual dignity and autonomy. It can be viewed as a simplistic and transparent attempt at manipulation, invoking only a cynical rebuke as a 'new' behaviour. The technique is thus clearly limited in its application. However, behaviour modification requires the communication of goals and expectations to employees in unambiguous terms. Many would argue that this clarity is highly desirable.

Fred Luthans and R. Kreitner (1985) summarize the problems with behaviour modification:

1. Appropriate reinforcers may not always be available, in limited and boring work settings, for example.

2. We do not all respond the same way to the same reinforcers; what one person finds rewarding may be of little consequence to someone else.

3. Once started, a behaviour modification programme has to be sustained.

4. There may not be enough extrinsic motivators (such as money and luncheon vouchers, for example) available.

They also argue, however, that the technique has made four significant contributions:

Behavioural self-management: a technique for changing one's own behaviour by systematically manipulating cues, cognitive processes and contingent consequences.

1. Behaviour modification techniques put the focus on observable employee behaviour and not on hypothetical internal states.

2. The method shows how performance is influenced by contingent consequences.

3. It supports the view that positive reinforcement is more effective in changing employee behaviour than punishment.

4. There are demonstrable causal effects on employee performance – a feature that is sometimes difficult to establish unequivocally with other behaviour change methods, such as job enrichment.

Behavioural self-management (BSM)

Management attempts to modify the behaviour of others raises ethical questions. Self-improvement, however, is acceptable and fashionable. Fred Luthans and Tim Davis (1979) developed the technique of **behavioural self-management** for individual use.

BSM combines the behavioural focus of 'O.B. Mod' with the cognitive processes central to social learning theory. It is not merely a form of self-imposed behaviour modification. Social learning theory argues that we actively process stimuli and consequences in a self-monitoring fashion, whereas behaviourism sees our behaviour shaped by rewards and punishments.

The practice of BSM involves the following steps:

1. *Identify the undesirable behaviour* that you want to change, develop or improve.

2. *Manage the situational cues* which trigger desired behaviour. Avoid situations which trigger the target behaviour, seek situations which encourage desired behaviour instead. Use 'reminders

and attention focusers', such as notes stuck in prominent places, and 'self-observation data' recording success and lapses. Set personal contracts, establish behavioural goals, post records of these in prominent places.

3. *Provide cognitive support* for the new behaviour. There are three ways to do this. First, through *symbolic coding*, using visual images and acronyms to support the desired behaviour (KISS, MBWA). Second, through *mental rehearsal* of the desired behaviour (a technique used by many successful sports people). Third, through *self-talk*, which is positive and supportive of the desired behaviour change.

4. *Develop self-reinforcement*, which is within your control and which is delivered only on condition that the desired behaviour change is achieved. This can be strengthened by arranging also for positive reinforcement from supportive friends and colleagues.

This web of situational cues, cognitive support and self-reinforcement can be a powerful combination in helping to eliminate target behaviours and establish desired behaviours in their place. Using this technique, Rakos and Grodek (1984) report how American college students successfully modified behaviour problems concerning smoking, lack of assertiveness, poor study habits, overeating, sloppy housekeeping, lack of exercise and moodiness. Luthans and Davis (1979) describe how the technique was used to deal with management behaviour problems such as overdependence on the boss, ignoring paperwork, leaving the office without notifying anybody and failing to fill out expense reports.

Apply behavioural self-management to your own behaviour. Target a behaviour of current personal significance: drinking, smoking, overeating, excessive clubbing, inappropriate study habits. Establish a pattern of situational cues, cognitive support and self-reinforcement. Set a timescale, and use your experience to assess the power and relevance of this technique.

Based on Robert Kreitner, Angelo Kinicki and Marc Buelens, *Organizational Behaviour*, McGraw-Hill, London, 1999, pp. 457–61.

Socialization has the advantage of flexibility. Social learning is dependent on the cultural context, and as a process rather than a specific technique, the general approach is not restricted to one culture. American induction and socialization procedures may be quite different from Swedish, Belgian, Nigerian, Malaysian or Spanish methods.

Socialization is a process that takes place anyway, planned or not. The issue concerns appropriate socialization, with respect to existing organization culture and behavioural preferences. Because it is a 'natural' process, with no clear financial or other material benefit from investing in its operation, it may be difficult to persuade management to give socialization the attention and resource that some commentators advocate. However, as the following section demonstrates, some organizations have started to introduce the apparatus of the *learning organization*. This approach can be regarded as an attempt to socialize an organization's members with respect to attitudes and behaviours related to the acquisition and development of new knowledge, creativity, innovation, flexibility and readiness for change.

Beyond supervisory appraisal: 360-degree feedback

Traditionally, it has been your immediate boss who conducts regular (usually annual) performance appraisals and gives you feedback on how well you are doing and about what you need to do to improve. The limitations of this approach encouraged a number of organizations in the mid- to late 1990s to experiment with multi-source feedback at all levels, including management. The technique that became popular is known as *360-degree appraisal*. In 360-degree appraisal, you are given feedback from your immediate boss, your colleagues, your subordinates and perhaps other senior organizational members, and you may be invited to conduct a self-appraisal as well.

This also means that you get to appraise your manager, in a process called 'upward appraisal'.

Assuming that the feedback is honest and constructive, the individual receives a much wider set of comments that can be used to reflect on and to change behaviour, and to improve work performance. However, as most appraisal schemes involve special forms for recording and monitoring, 360-degree appraisal generates a huge administrative workload.

Based on Mike Thatcher, 'Allowing everyone to have their say', *People Management*, 21 March 1996, pp. 28–30.

Stop and Criticize

What advantages and disadvantages of 360-degree appraisal can you identify, for you as employee and also from a management perspective?

Table 4.5 summarizes one similarity and a number of contrasts between the techniques of behaviour modification and socialization.

Table 4.5: Behaviour modification versus socialization

Behaviour modification	Socialization
feedback needed in both approaches for behaviour to change	
planned procedure	naturally occurring, even if also planned
stimulus determines responses	individual needs determine responses
externally generated reinforcements	internally generated reinforcements
focus on observable behaviour	focus on unobservable internal mental states
focus on tangible rewards and punishments (money, other material rewards)	focus on intangible rewards and punishments (social inclusion, self-esteem)
clear links between desired behaviour and consequences	intangible links between desired behaviour and consequences
compliance required by external agent	conformity encouraged by social grouping

The learning organization

Learning organization: an organizational form that enables individual learning to create valued outcomes, such as innovation, efficiency, environmental alignment and competitive advantage.

The concept of the **learning organization** is derived from the work of Chris Argyris and Donald Schön (Argyris and Schön, 1974, 1978; Argyris, 1982), but became fashionable during the 1990s. Marleen Huysman (1999, p. 61) offers this definition.

A number of factors have stimulated interest in the learning organization concept:

■ the production of goods and services increasingly involves sophisticated knowledge;

■ knowledge is therefore as valuable a resource as raw material;

Chris Argyris
(b. 1923)

- many organizations lost knowledgeable staff through delayering in the 1990s;

- information technologies are knowledge intensive;

- knowledge can have a short life span, made obsolete by innovation;

- flexibility, creativity and responsiveness are now prized capabilities;

- knowledge can thus be a source of competitive advantage for an organization.

Ikujiro Nonaka and Hirotaka Takeuchi (1995) argue that the ability to create knowledge and solve new problems has become a 'core competence' for most organizations. In their view, everyone is a 'knowledge worker', not just those who work with books and computers. Anyone dealing with customers, for example the ticket clerk in a theatre run by the local council, is a valuable source of intelligence on customer perceptions of theatre facilities, productions and pricing. These 'boundary workers' are typically employed in poorly paid jobs (receptionists, porters, sales staff, secretaries) and their customer intelligence is often overlooked as their positions are distant, in terms of physical location as well as organization structure, from management decision-makers.

There's no accounting for organizational knowledge

In an attempt to develop guidelines for the measurement of organizational knowledge, the trade ministry in Denmark asked twenty companies to produce 'intellectual capital reports' for three years. A Danish computer software company, Systematic, publishes information on customer satisfaction, education and average age of staff (83 per cent of whom are under 40) and the company's investment in innovation, which is over 10 per cent of annual turnover. These intellectual capital reports are published alongside traditional financial accounts.

Based on: 'A price on the priceless', *The Economist*, 12 June 1999, pp. 94, 98.

The literature of this topic is preoccupied with refining the way in which learning, knowledge and the learning organization can be conceptualized. Karl Weick and Frances Westley (1996, p. 440) point out that the concepts of 'organization' and 'learning' are contradictory. Organization implies structure, order, stability. Learning implies change, variety, disorganization. The management literature is concerned with models of best practice and with management consulting tools. The management book by Senge et al. (1999) includes an 'owner registration form' at the back, to return after indicating in tick boxes your interest in speakers, seminars, further materials or hiring the authors as consultants.

Stop and Criticize

If we discount the inanimate buildings, equipment and furniture, organizations have no existence independent of their members. So what does it mean to claim that an organization can 'learn'?

Mike Pedler, John Burgoyne and Tom Boydell (1997) identify eleven features of the 'learning company' (table 4.6). Why do they use the term 'company' rather than organization?

The original idea of eating bread together and of creating meaning through relationships, captures the conviviality of working together better than the more mechanical and lifeless 'organization'. As one of our oldest words for a group of people engaged in a joint enterprise, we continue to 'accompany' others and do things 'in company'. (Pedler et al., 1997, p. 5)

This usage assumes, of course, that an organization's members regard themselves as working 'convivially' towards shared outcomes.

Table 4.6: The features of the learning organization

Feature	Explanation
A learning approach to strategy	The use of trials and experiments to improve understanding and generate improvements, and to modify strategic direction as necessary
Participative policy-making	All the organization's members are involved in strategy formation, influencing decisions and values and addressing conflict
Informative	Information technology is used to make information available to everyone and to enable front-line staff to act on their own initiative
Formative accounting and control	Accounting, budgeting and reporting systems are designed to help people understand the operations of organizational finance
Internal exchange	Sections and departments think of themselves as customers and suppliers in an internal 'supply chain', learning from each other
Reward flexibility	A flexible and creative reward policy, with financial and non-financial rewards to meet individual needs and performance
Enabling structures	Organization charts, structures and procedures are seen as temporary, and can be changed to meet task requirements
Boundary workers as environmental scanners	Everyone who has contact with customers, suppliers, clients and business partners is treated as a valuable information source
Inter-company learning	The organization learns from other organizations through joint ventures, alliances and other information exchanges
A learning climate	The manager's primary task is to facilitate experimentation and learning in others, through questioning, feedback and support
Self-development opportunities for all	People are expected to take responsibility for their own learning, and facilities are made available, especially to 'front-line' staff

This image of the learning organization is an ideal, something to which to aspire, rather than a description of any particular organization. These features 'cluster' under the five headings shown in figure 4.3. These clusters concern strategy, structure, looking in, looking out and learning opportunities. Pedler et al. (1997) provide a diagnostic questionnaire for evaluating an organization on these features as a basis for developing them further.

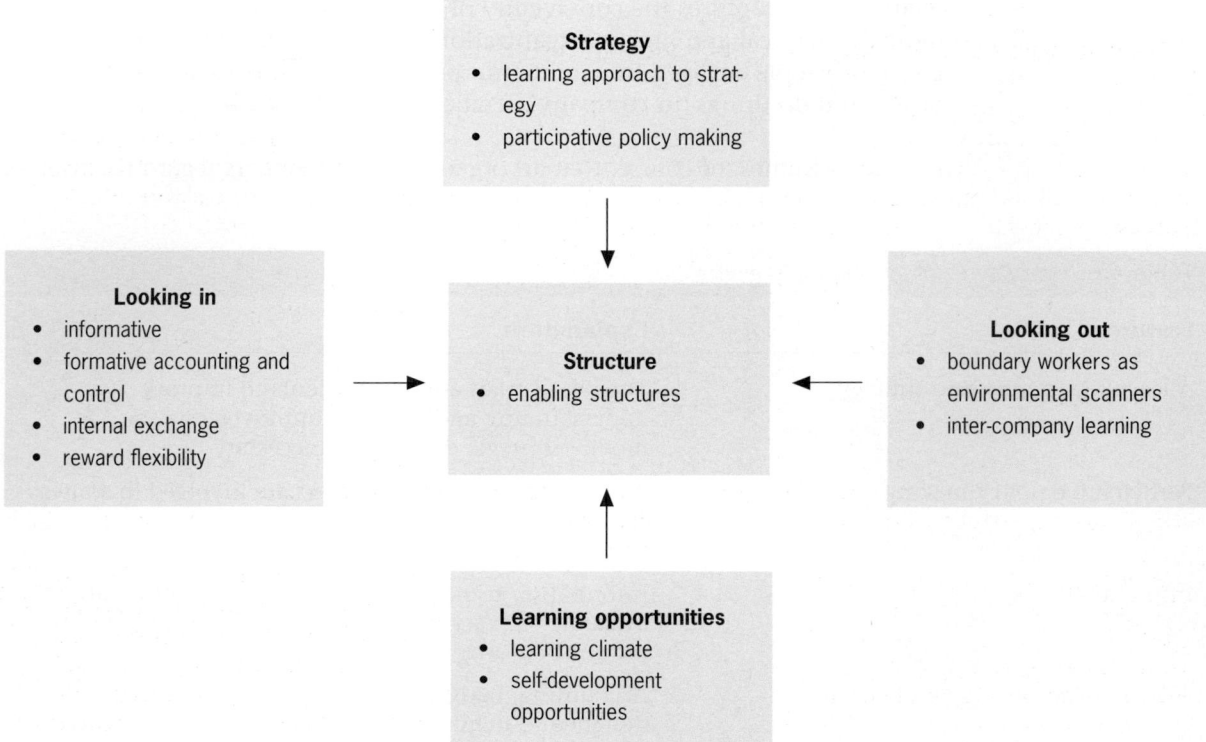

Figure 4.3: Clusters of learning organization features
From Mike Pedler, John Burgoyne and Tom Boydell, *The Learning Company: A Strategy for Sustainable Development*, McGraw-Hill, London (second edition), 1997, p. 37. Reprinted by permission of McGraw-Hill International (UK) Limited.

The learning organization concept was popularized by Peter Senge whose book, *The Fifth Discipline* (1990), became an international best-seller. Senge argues (1990, p. 4) that work must become more 'learningful' at all levels. He identifies five 'learning disciplines' for building organizational learning capabilities. These disciplines are summarized in table 4.7.

Table 4.7: Peter Senge's five learning disciplines

Learning discipline	Explanation
1. Personal mastery	a discipline of *aspiration*, concerning what you as an individual want to achieve
2. Mental models	a discipline of *reflection and inquiry*, concerning the constant refinement of thinking and development of awareness
3. Shared vision	a *collective* discipline, concerning commitment to a common sense of purpose and actions to achieve that purpose
4. Team learning	a discipline of *group interaction*, concerning collective thinking and action to achieve common goals
5. Systems thinking	a discipline which concerns *understanding interdependency and complexity* and the role of feedback in system development

A learning approach to strategy: the management challenge

Challenging your norms and assumptions is difficult. As the terms imply, these everyday structures of individual and corporate lives are taken for granted, not noticed. In effect, they are invisible to those who follow or hold them. They are much more obvious to others who follow different norms and assumptions, who, while similarly blind to their own taken-for-granted norms and assumptions, can ask penetrating and provoking questions about those of others.

Royal Dutch Shell have tried to incorporate this potentially valuable process into their company operations with what they call 'the management challenge'. Every three years, a senior executive from another plant, and usually another country, visits a given location to deliver a challenge to management. He or she spends a week or so at the site, wandering around, reading reports, talking to people before challenging the management team. The challenge itself involves presenting observations, impressions, making suggestions but, above all, asking 'naive' questions that an insider would not ask because the answers are obvious. These questions are basically of the nature 'Why do you do such and such?' or 'How does this and that contribute to plant efficiency?' The local managers must publish the challenge and their response to it.

The management challenge is one way of ensuring that the 'hidden' fundamentals of 'how we do things around here' are questioned on a regular basis. Such questioning seems to be an essential component of 'double-loop learning' or the reframing essential to organizational transformation. You could institute your own management challenge and put in place this vital aspect of organizational learning by inviting different people in to question your operations. Why not start by inviting fellow managers from a sister plant? If you feel up to being more challenged than this, you could invite a customer, a supplier or a stakeholder from the local community.

From Mike Pedler, John Burgoyne and Tom Boydell, *The Learning Company: A Strategy for Sustainable Development*, McGraw-Hill, London (second edition), 1997, pp. 69–70.

Senge's argument is: have realistic goals, challenge your assumptions, commit to a shared vision, teamworking is good. The organizational application of these 'disciplines', however, is problematic, and can be related to our discussion of socialization, to encouraging the 'correct' attitudes, values and beliefs among employees at all levels. The most important of these learning disciplines is 'the fifth discipline', systems thinking, which means understanding how complex organizations function and how they can be changed to work more effectively. The theory is:

> [T]he practice of organizational learning involves developing tangible activities: new governing ideas, innovations in infrastructure, and new management methods and tools for changing the way people conduct their work. Given the opportunity to take part in these new activities, people will develop an enduring capability for change. The process will pay back the organization with far greater levels of diversity, commitment, innovation and talent. (Senge et al., 1999, p. 33)

In other words, the manager who wants commitment, flexibility and creativity from employees is advised to provide them with lots of learning opportunities.

Some commentators argue that a learning organization helps its members to learn. Others claim that the organization itself learns. How can this be? Silvia Gherardi (1997, p. 542) treats the term 'learning organization' as a metaphor which regards an organization as a biological entity, as 'a subject which learns, which processes information, which reflects on experiences, which is endowed with a stock of knowledge, skills and expertise'.

Gherardi supports the view that organizations learn with experience, the proof lying with visible changes in an organization's behaviour. For example, it is known that in the development of manufacturing processes the staff hours required to produce a unit of output decrease with accumulated experience. Another example concerns the ways in which organizations evolve and adapt to 'fit' their environment, introducing internal structural changes in response to environmental opportunities and pressures.

Organizations also have available to them several different types of knowledge, not all of which are dependent on individual expertise (Gherardi, 1997, p. 547). This includes learning from past experience through assessment and evaluation, and learning from the experience of other organizations. There is also knowledge 'built in' to equipment and even raw materials, with formulae, ingredients, recipes, known properties and so on. Standard operating procedures can usually be found in instruction manuals, forms and job descriptions – all ways of codifying knowledge. Many organizations also possess patents and property rights.

Karl Weick and Frances Westley (1996) argue that organizational learning is best understood in terms of *organization culture*. Culture includes values, beliefs, feelings, artefacts, myths, symbols, metaphors and rituals, which taken together distinguish one organization or group from others. Organizations are thus 'repositories of knowledge' independent of their members (Schön, 1983, p. 242). Organizations which accumulate stocks of codified, documented knowledge, independent of their members, can thus be said to learn.

The corporate university: a sign of the learning organization

There are around 1,600 corporate universities in America. Microsoft, Motorola and Disney all have one. The fast-food chain McDonald's established its first 'hamburger university' in 1961, run by the company's own staff and managers, offering courses in human resource management, employment law, accounting and marketing. 'Burger U' today operates on six campuses, including one in London.

Although the idea has been around for some time, the development of corporate universities became more popular during the 1990s. In Britain, in 1996, Anglian Water Services established The University of Water to run a mix of management, engineering and science courses for its 4,000 staff, based at the Whitwell campus on Rutland Water. In 1999, British Telecommunications announced that it was establishing a university centre to offer degrees for its 125,000 employees. Set up in 2000, the Shell Open University had 11,000 students on 600 courses by 2002. Other companies, including British Aerospace, General Electric, Unipart and The Body Shop also have their own universities.

In order to compete effectively, these organizations require highly educated and skilled workforces. This explains such a significant investment in learning, in developing the organization's intellectual capital.

Based on R. Dalton and M. Lynn, 'Companies lead university revolution', *The Sunday Times*, 7 February 1999, p. 3.4; and on Lucie Carrington, 'Oiling the wheels', *People Management*, vol. 8, no. 13, 27 June 2002, pp. 31–4.

Single-loop learning: the ability to use feedback to make continuous adjustments and adaptations, to maintain performance at a predetermined standard.

Weick and Westley (1996) note how different organizational forms are better equipped for learning. The post-modern organization described in chapter 2 adapts to change in its environment in an innovative, creative and responsive manner. This is an organizational form associated with creative thinking and rapid learning, and has also been described as *adhocracy* (see Glossary). Bureaucracy, on the other hand, is concerned with efficiency, with division of labour, with rigid chain of command, with clear distinctions and rationality.

How can 'organizational learning' best be understood? Argyris and Schön

Double-loop learning: the ability to challenge and to redefine the assumptions underlying performance standards and to improve performance.

(1974) developed the distinction between **single-loop learning** and **double-loop learning**.

The concept of single-loop learning, which can be applied to individuals, groups and organizations, is borrowed from cybernetics, where control systems are considered in terms of norms, standards, procedures, routines and feedback (see figure 4.1). The classic example of cybernetic control is the domestic thermostat which, by detecting temperature variations, takes action to correct deviations from a predetermined norm. In single-loop learning, the system maintains performance at that norm, and is unable to 'learn' that the norm is too high or too low. In other words, it is unable to 'learn how to learn', to challenge and rethink its values and assumptions. The system just goes on doing what it has been asked to do. Limited to making small-scale changes and improvements, it can be argued that single-loop learning is not really learning at all.

Stop and Criticize

Let us assume that you are learning through your organizational behaviour course. Is this single-loop learning or double-loop learning? Which of these two types of learning should you be engaged in during your college or university education?

Learning how to learn involves double-loop learning. This means challenging assumptions, beliefs, norms, routines and decisions, rather than accepting them and working within those limitations. In single-loop learning, the question is: how can we better achieve that standard of performance? With double-loop learning, in contrast, the question becomes: is that an appropriate target in the first place? Mary Jo Hatch (1997, p. 372) observes that:

> Double-loop learning, once strictly the domain of strategists and top managers, is increasingly being seen as taking place, or needing to take place, throughout organizations as they hire professionals and skilled technicians to help them adapt to the increasing rates of change they perceive as necessary to their survival. As double-loop learning diffuses, organizational stability is replaced by chaos and new organizational orders emerge from the internal dynamics of the organization rather than at the behest of top management.

When we learn, we acquire knowledge – of organizational behaviour, gardening, guitar playing, accountancy, electrical engineering, and so on. Knowledge, however, is a difficult term to define clearly. For Nonaka and Takeuchi (1995), there are two types of knowledge, **tacit knowledge** and **explicit knowledge**.

Tacit knowledge: knowledge and understanding specific to the individual, derived from experience and difficult to communicate to others.

Tacit knowledge includes insights, intuition, hunches and judgements, and concerns the individual's unarticulated mental models and skills. Tacit knowledge tends to be personal, specific to particular contexts and difficult to communicate. For example, if you are able to drive a motor car with a manual gear shift, then you will know where to position your foot to 'slip the clutch' and prevent the car from rolling on a slope. You will be able to move your foot to that position, accurately and consistently, without much conscious thought. However, expect to run into difficulties when you try to explain this tacit skill to a learner driver.

Explicit knowledge: knowledge and understanding which is codified, clearly articulated and available to anyone.

Explicit knowledge, on the other hand, is articulated, codified, expressed, available to anyone. Nonaka and Takeuchi argue that the Japanese emphasize tacit knowledge, while Westerners emphasize explicit, formal, objective, codified knowledge. In Western cultures, tacit knowledge is undervalued because it is intangible and difficult to measure. However, tacit and explicit knowledge are complementary. Nonaka and Takeuchi are thus concerned with 'knowledge conversion' in which tacit knowledge is made available to the organization, on the

Knowledge management: the conversion of individual tacit knowledge into explicit knowledge so that it can be shared with others in the organization.

one hand, and organizational knowledge becomes the individual's tacit knowledge, on the other (Nonaka, Umemoto and Sasaki, 1999).

Some commentators distinguish between organizational learning and **knowledge management** (Rajan, Lank and Chapple, 1999).

Knowledge management concerns turning individual learning into organizational learning. Amin Rajan and colleagues (1999) describe how some organizations have developed 'intelligent search engines'. These are technology-based systems designed to facilitate access to expertise by creating a catalogue of specialists, each with their own web site in the company intranet, so that their knowledge can be accessed by email or video conferencing. The number of times somebody's expertise is used can be monitored and used to influence pay and promotion decisions (Rajan, Lank and Chapple, 1999, p. 6).

Knowledge management tends to be distinguished from the learning organization concept by the focus on information technology, on the development of databases accessed by internet. The supermarket chain Safeway, for example, gives its 2,500 suppliers for its 20,000 product lines, access to its warehouse information over the internet. Company buyers and their suppliers have much better information and forecasts on which to base purchasing and delivery decisions. Zeneca Pharmaceuticals has developed a system called Concert, to bring together information on new drug discoveries and licences in a highly competitive sector. Managers around the company are responsible for identifying relevant knowledge and for putting it into the system (Coles, 1998). Harry Scarbrough (1999), however, is critical of the emphasis on technological solutions such as these, which tend to overlook the ways in which people develop, use and communicate knowledge as part of their working activity.

Oiling the wheels of knowledge management

Shell International Exploration and Production (SIEP) is a knowledge-intensive global oil company. A problem arising in Nigeria may have already been solved in the North Sea off the coast of Scotland. To put the people with the answers in touch with the people having the problems, the company has developed a knowledge management system. SIEP set up 'New Ways of Working' in 1998, creating three web-based global networks dealing with sub-surface, surface and wells knowledge. Each of these three core business groups allow members to share their knowledge with 3,000 to 4,000 other members.

■ So, for example, when Shell Brazil wanted help to retrieve broken tools from a borehole, engineers asked colleagues in other countries for help. This exchange of ideas saved the well and also saved the company US$7 million.

■ A manager in Shell Malaysia had problems shutting down a gas turbine. Searching for ideas in the archived material on the surface global network, he found that teams in Australia and America had already posted potential solutions.

■ The Shell sales company in Singapore beat bigger rivals to a contract by using the global network to research the company's history with the client and their competitors.

This idea was expanded to eleven knowledge communities covering support functions, human resources, information technology, finance and procurement. Each community has a co-ordinator responsible for controlling content and traffic flow, and encouraging people to contribute. If a particular question receives no answers, the co-ordinator attempts to find an expert in the area. Each community has developed a massive archive of knowledge which is used for personal development, problem-solving and contacting those with specialist information and expertise. Total savings from this initiative were estimated in 2002 to be US$200 million, considering only those instances where savings could be quantified.

Based on Lucie Carrington, 'Oiling the wheels', *People Management*, vol. 8, no. 13, 27 June 2002, pp. 31–4.

Table 4.8: Learning organization positives and negatives

Learning organization positives	Learning organization negatives
a rich, multidimensional concept affecting many aspects of organizational behaviour	a complex and diffuse set of practices, difficult to implement systematically
an innovative approach to learning, to knowledge management and to investing in intellectual capital	an attempt to use dated concepts from change management and learning theory, repackaged as a management consulting project
a new set of challenging concepts focusing attention on the acquisition and development of individual and corporate knowledge	a new vocabulary for encouraging employee compliance with management directives in the guise of 'self-development'
an innovative approach to organization, management and employee development	an innovative approach for strengthening management control
innovative use of technology to manage organizational knowledge through databases and the internet or intranets	a technology-dependent approach which ignores how people actually develop and use knowledge in organizations

Table 4.8 summarizes the main positive and negative aspects of the learning organization and its related concepts of intellectual capital and knowledge management.

The concept of the learning organization has remained fashionable for over a decade. This popularity has been reinforced by the growth of 'knowledge work', by the realization that ideas generate competitive advantage, and by technological developments. However, there are organizational barriers to the implementation of this 'ideal', and it will be interesting to observe whether the learning organization remains fashionable.

Recap

1. *Explain the characteristics of the behaviourist and cognitive approaches to learning.*

   - Behaviourism argues that we learn chains of muscle movements. As mental processes are not observable, they are not considered valid issues for study.

   - Cognitive psychology argues that we learn mental structures. Mental processes are important, and they are amenable to study although they cannot be observed.

   - In behaviourist theory, feedback contributes to learning by providing reinforcement; in cognitive theory, feedback provides information and is motivational.

2. *Explain and evaluate the technique of behaviour modification.*

   - Respondent (or Pavlovian, classical) conditioning is a method by which an established response (good work performance) is associated with a new stimulus (supervisory encouragement).

   - Operant (or Skinnerian, instrumental) conditioning is a method by which a behaviour

(good work performance) is associated with a new consequence (bonus payment).

   - Positive reinforcement, negative reinforcement, punishment and extinction condition the target by manipulating the consequences of desirable and undesirable behaviours.

   - Behaviour modification works well when rewards are linked clearly to specific behaviours, but does not work well when these links are ambiguous and vague; this manipulative approach may not be acceptable in some cultures.

3. *Explain the socialization process, and assess the practical relevance of this concept.*

   - Social learning theory argues that we learn values, beliefs and behaviour patterns through experience, observation and modelling.

   - Socialization can be informal – this happens anyway – or it can be formally organized through induction and training programmes.

4. *Explain and evaluate the technique of behavioural self-management.*

   - Behavioural self-management involves identifying the behaviour you want to change, altering the situational cues which trigger that behaviour, and establishing support and reinforcement for your new behaviour.

5. *Describe the characteristics of the learning organization, and explain why this concept became popular during the 1990s.*

   - A learning organization is characterized by its approach to strategy, to environmental scanning, to the use of information, to the creation of learning opportunities, and to the creation of structures that are flexible and enable employee learning, in contrast to rigid, bureaucratic organizations in which learning is the employee's responsibility.

   - The learning organization concept became popular as managers recognized the strategic need for more highly skilled and trained, flexible and creative workforces.

   - Knowledge management is a technology-based technique for making tacit knowledge available more widely, typically through individual and corporate databases which can be accessed through the organization's intranet.

Revision

1. Why is the psychology of learning a controversial topic, and what are the implications of this controversy for organization and management practice?

2. What are the main distinctions between behaviourist and cognitive perspectives on learning?

3. What is the difference between Pavlovian and Skinnerian conditioning? What relevance do these and their related laboratory-based concepts have in an organizational context?

4. Describe and illustrate the technique of organizational behaviour modification, and identify the advantages and disadvantages of this technique.

5. Why are positive and negative reinforcement usually more effective methods for encouraging behaviour change than punishment? In what circumstances can punishment be effective in encouraging behaviour change?

Springboard

Argyris, C., 1982, *Reasoning, Learning, and Action*, Jossey-Bass, San Francisco.

Classic text on the nature of individual and organizational learning.

Dixon, N.M., 1999, *The Organizational Learning Cycle: How We Can Learn Collectively*, Gower, Aldershot (second edition).

Theoretically informed and readable account of organizational learning in practice. Case illustrations include the US Army, Bank of Montreal, Chaparral Steel, World Health Organization, Johnsonville Foods.

Dixon, N.M., 2000, *Common Knowledge: How Companies Thrive by Sharing What They Know*, Harvard Business School Press, Boston, MA.

Argues that organizations deal with different types of knowledge, which have to be managed in different ways; the 'wrong' methods can block knowledge-sharing.

Easterby-Smith, M., Burgoyne, J. and Araujo, L. (eds), 1999, *Organizational Learning and the Learning Organization: Developments in Theory and Practice*, Sage Publications, London.

Academic critiques of the learning organization concept from different perspectives.

Miller, R. and Stewart, J., 1999, 'Opened university', *People Management*, vol. 5, no. 12, June, pp. 42–6.

An account of how the motor components company Unipart developed a learning organization. Also describes Unipart U, the company university opened in 1993.

Pedler, M., Burgoyne, J. and Boydell, T., 1997, *The Learning Company: A Strategy for Sustainable Development*, McGraw-Hill, London (second edition).

Written for managers, this illustrates the dimensions of the learning organization and provides a diagnostic checklist against which to evaluate progress towards the ideal.

Scarbrough, H. and Swan, J., 1999, *Case Studies in Knowledge Management*, Institute of Personnel and Development, London.

Argues that a focus on technology will fail and that effective knowledge management requires supportive human resource management policies, concerning rewards and trust in particular. Knowledge is power; why should we share it?

Senge, P., 1990, *The Fifth Discipline: The Art and Practice of the Learning Organization*, Doubleday Currency, New York.

The best-seller which popularized the learning organization idea in the early 1990s.

Senge, P., Kleiner, A., Roberts, C., Ross, R., Roth, G. and Smith, B., 1999, *The Dance of Change: The Challenges of Sustaining Momentum in Learning Organizations*, Nicholas Brealey, London.

Presented as a set of ideas and resources for managers developing the learning organization in practice, professionally produced, treads a thin line between a theoretical approach and an advertisement for management consultancy.

Home viewing

A Clockwork Orange (1971 and 2000, director Stanley Kubrick) is based in a future a totalitarian state in which the Droog (thug) Alex (played by Malcolm McDowell) is subjected to aversion therapy to cure him of his addiction to violence, rape, drugs and classical music. An extremely violent film for its time, Kubrick took it out of circulation in 1974 when it was accused of triggering copycat crimes. The film was released again on the anniversary of Kubrick's death, in March 2000. The practical questions are: what kind of conditioning and reinforcement regime is Alex subjected to?; and how effective is this in altering his behaviour? The moral questions concern society's right to interfere with individual behaviour in this way. Fiction? Aversion therapy was used to 'treat' homosexuals in the 1960s.

Full Metal Jacket (1987, directed by Stanley Kubrick) follows the experiences of an American photo-journalist, Private Joker (played by Mathew Modine), during the Vietnam War. The first 45 minutes are set in a Marine Corps training camp in Carolina, and portray the induction of new recruits. Their initiation is directed by Sergeant Hartman, played by R. Lee Ermey, a former marine drill instructor who was hired as a consultant to make sure the training scenes were realistic, but who impressed Kubrick so much he was invited to play the role. Hartman uses a range of tactics to turn 'maggots into marines' who are 'ready to eat their own guts and ask for more', with 'killer instinct that is clear and strong'. Identify the behaviour modification and socialization techniques used and assess their effectiveness.

OB in literature

B. Frederic Skinner, *Walden II*, 1948, Macmillan, London.

Skinner's own novel is based on a fictional community which applies operant conditioning to establish desired humanitarian behaviours and to 'engineer' a better society (along the lines of *A Clockwork Orange*). What application does this vision have to contemporary society – in any culture? What would it be like to live in such a society?

Chapter exercises

1: The learning curve

Objectives
1. To demonstrate the concept of the learning curve.

2. To identify factors affecting the learning process.

3. To identify ways of improving the effectiveness of the learning process.

Learning can be measured in many different ways. The learning of subject matter in an educational context is traditionally measured using examinations, essays, projects or assignments, and oral presentations. The learning process unfolds through time, and we establish whether learning has taken place by identifying changes in behaviour. When estimating how long it will take us to acquire skills in using new computer software, or skills in moving to the next level of a challenging computer game, we often refer to 'moving up the learning curve'. We can therefore assess our rate of learning by considering the extent to which our behaviour may or may not have changed.

Numbers forms: Sheets 1–4

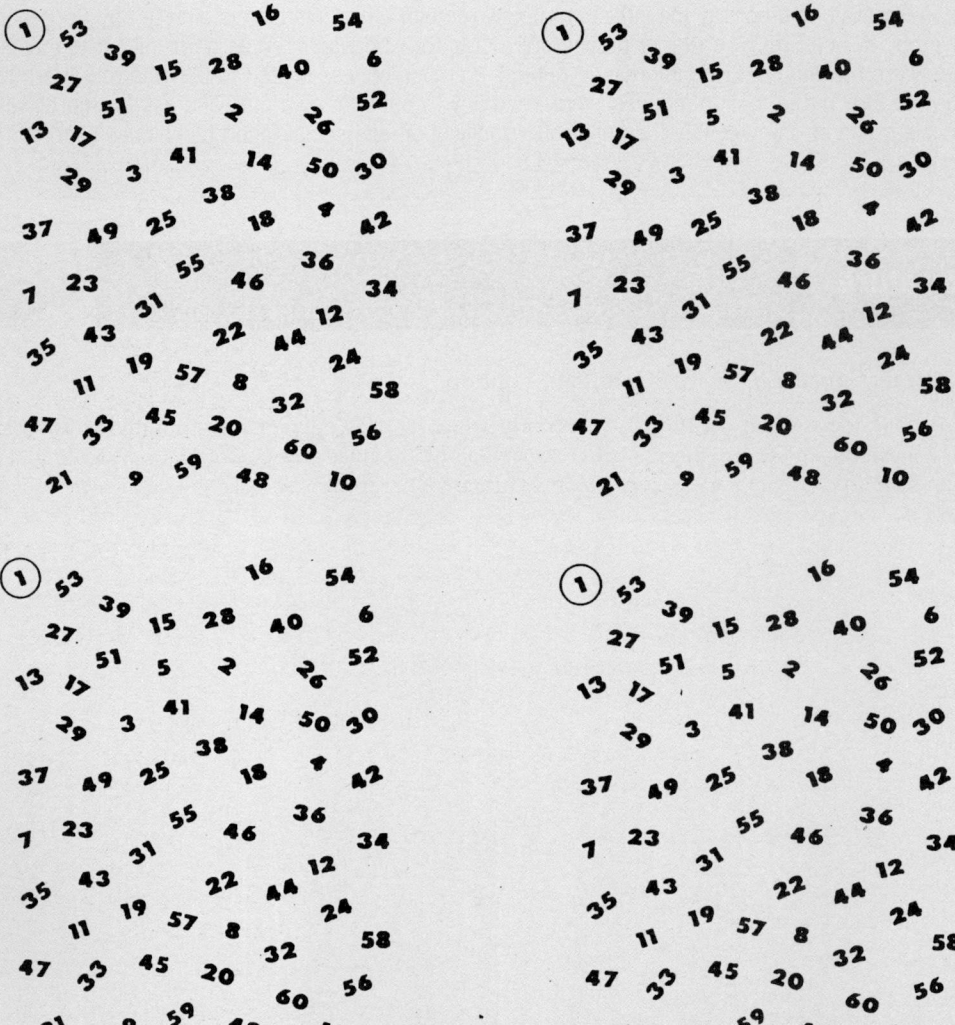

Briefing
1. Cover the Numbers Forms, so that you cannot see the placement of the numbers.

2. When directed by your instructor, remove the cover and, working on sheet 1, use a pen or pencil to circle number 1, then circle number 2, then circle 3, and so on, until your instructor tells you to stop. You will have 30 seconds to do this.

3. You will be asked to do this three more times by your instructor, each time moving to the next sheet on the Numbers Form.

4. Insert your score for each of the four trials on this graph:

highest
number
attained

	trial 1	trial 2	trial 3	trial 4
35				
30				
25				
20				
15				

2: Making modifications

Objectives
1. To demonstrate the practical dimensions of applying behaviour modification techniques.

2. To explore the benefits and limitations of behaviour modification techniques.

The theory and practice of behaviour modification appears to have significant potential in organizational settings. Organizations are concerned with eliciting 'appropriate behaviours' from employees. Managers typically occupy positions from which a range of rewards and punishments can be manipulated. The scope for changing working methods and practices through behaviour modification thus appears to be wide. In this exercise, you are invited to design and assess a behaviour modification approach that deals with specific problems of organizational behaviour, problems with which you may be familiar.

Briefing
1. Ensure that you are familiar with the behaviour modification approach explained in this chapter, including theoretical background and practical applications.

2. Read the 'Making modifications' brief overleaf and, working on your own, make preliminary notes in answer to the questions that follow.

3. In syndicates with three to five members each, design a practical, realistic behaviour modification programme that addresses the issues in the brief. Think *creatively* with respect to appropriate reinforcement regimes.

4. When you have completed your design, make a realistic practical assessment. What are the three main *strengths* of your behaviour modification approach that give it a chance of working as intended? What are the three main *weaknesses* in your approach that might make it less effective? Don't forget to nominate a spokesperson to present your approach and assessment to the whole group.

5. Present solutions and assessments to the whole group. To avoid repetition, perhaps have only two groups present designs, with the third and fourth groups presenting their

strengths and weaknesses respectively, and with the audience each time commenting only on differences between their analysis and that presented.

Making modifications

Your organizational behaviour instructor, Lesley, has been experiencing some problems recently. She has asked you to design a behaviour modification programme to help her.

Lesley is concerned about the increase in undesirable behaviours in one of her student groups. There are around 250 students in this class, and organizational behaviour is one of the first courses they take as part of their qualification. The problems this year seem to be worse than in the past, but otherwise things are running much the same as they always have been. Lesley is not sure what is causing the increase in undesirable behaviours.

Attendance at lectures has been poor, with more than 20 per cent of the class missing on some occasions. Many students arrive late. This is disruptive, as Lesley has to stop for each noisy new bunch of arrivals. This also effectively cuts down the lecture duration, and some material has been covered more superficially than Lesley planned. There has also been an increase in students talking during lectures. This is not confined to the back rows, and there does not seem to be any acoustic problem; Lesley's voice can be heard clearly from all seats in the lecture theatre. The crosstalk is usually quiet, but it is loud enough to be distracting for Lesley and annoying for students listening to the lecture. Students come to tutorial sessions without having done the required background reading and making notes, and are unwilling to get involved in discussion. Lesley uses practical, interesting, stimulating tutorial exercises and is accustomed to much higher levels of student interest and participation.

There are no explanations – or excuses – to be found in the conditions surrounding the course. Lecture rooms are close to each other, so there is little delay in getting from one class to another. Lesley's sessions are not at awkward times (not first thing Monday, not last thing Friday), so students are not particularly tired or preoccupied in her sessions. In summary, we can assume that the undesirable behaviours are within the control of the students themselves, and are thus amenable to behaviour modification.

Questions

1. What target behaviour(s) would it be realistic to consider modifying in this situation?

2. What reinforcement regime could be developed and applied to achieve the desired behaviour change(s)?

3. What behaviour changes would you hope to see?

Chapter 5 Personality

Key concepts

psychometrics

personality

type

trait

nomothetic approach

emotional intelligence

the big five

Type A personality

Type B personality

idiographic approach

self concept

generalized other

thematic apperception test

need for achievement

projective test

reliability

predictive validity

Learning outcomes

When you have read this chapter, you should be able to define those key concepts in your own words, and you should also be able to:

1. Distinguish between type, trait and self theories of personality.
2. Identify the strengths and limitations of formal approaches to personality assessment.
3. Explain the uses and limitations of objective questionnaires and projective tests as measures of personality.
4. Explain the relationship between personality and stress, and identify appropriate individual and organizational stress management strategies.
5. Evaluate the benefits and problems of psychometric assessment as a tool to assist management decision-making, particularly in selection.
6. Assess realistically the main characteristics of your own personality.

Why study personality?

Useful Latin terms

per sonare   to speak through
persona   an actor's mask; a character in a play
persona grata   an acceptable person
persona non grata   an unacceptable person

Who are you? How do you describe your characteristics? How do you differ from others? How can we define and measure those characteristics and differences? Psychologists answer these questions using the concept of *personality*. Many managers think that personality is related to job performance and career success, and personality assessment is a widely used selection tool. What are the foundations of these assessments, and what value are they?

Quick personality check: are you a doormat or a bully?

- Do you dread being asked favours?

- Do you keep quiet when criticized unfairly?

- Would you quietly put up with lukewarm food in a restaurant rather than send it back?

- Do you find it hard to turn away canvassers and door-to-door salespeople?

- Do you tell white lies to avoid hurting friends' feelings?

- Do you sometimes agree to have sex with your partner when you don't feel like it?

- If you hailed a taxi, but someone else got into it, would you just slope off and look for another one?

If you got more than four 'yeses', you are veering towards doormat status. You need to practise being more assertive. One or nil suggests that, even if you think you are firm but fair, friends and colleagues may well regard you as a bit of a shit. Considering other people's needs could mean you get more done in the long run. If you scored two or three yeses, you've got the situation more or less sussed.

From Jerome Burne and Susan Aldridge, 'Who do you think you are?', *Focus Extra*, April 1996, p. 6.

Psychometrics: the systematic testing, measurement and assessment of intelligence, aptitudes and personality.

The term **psychometrics** is now used to refer to the broad range of different types of assessment and measurement, of aptitude, intelligence, and also of personality.

There are numerous tests for aptitudes related to particular occupations, such as aptitude in computer programming, typing ability and arithmetic competence. When measuring aspects of aptitude or intelligence, we can use the term 'test', because a high score is usually better than a low score. When measuring aspects of personality, however, it is more appropriate to use the term 'assessment'. A 'high' score on a personality factor (extraversion, for example), cannot be said to be better or worse than a 'low' score. There are no right or wrong answers in a personality assessment. There are no correct or incorrect personality types or traits.

Psychometric assessment has a wide range of organizational applications in, for example:

- shortlisting and selecting candidates for jobs;

- assessment of suitability for promotion;

- assessment for redeployment purposes;

- evaluation of training potential;

- career counselling and development;

- graduate recruitment, for applicants with limited work experience;

- vocational guidance;

- redundancy counselling.

Psychometric assessments are used to complement less formal and more subjective methods, to help managers reach more widely informed and objective judgements about people. However, these assessments have been widely criticized as unfair and misleading, in gender and cultural terms, and as poor predictors of job performance. Should you wish to practise to improve your scores, or even to 'cheat' on a forthcoming assessment, you will find several 'how to' books on psychometrics and personality assessment on the self-help shelves in your local bookshop. An internet search for 'psychometric tests' will reveal many relevant sites.

We will focus on personality assessment. The testing of intelligence and aptitudes are specialist topics beyond our scope. Two approaches are explained, called *nomothetic* and *idiographic*. Nomothetic approaches form the basis for most contemporary psychometrics. These are usually based on self-report questionnaires, which are easier to administer, to score and to interpret than idiographic methods. The latter use open-ended questioning strategies to capture the individual's unique characteristics. Nomothetic techniques appear to be more objective and quantitative than idiographic methods. However, idiographic techniques rely on radically different assumptions about human psychology. It is on the validity of these assumptions that our judgements of different methods should be based, and not simply on matters of operational convenience.

The definition problem

Personality: the psychological qualities that influence an individual's characteristic behaviour patterns in a stable and distinctive manner.

The concept of **personality** underpins psychology's attempt to identify the unique character of individuals and to measure and understand differences between individuals. The term describes those properties of behaviour which are both enduring and set the individual apart from others. These properties concern the individual's typical ways of coping with life.

Personality is a broad, integrating concept. However, our definition of personality is restricted to properties which set us apart, and which are both stable and distinctive, across different situations and over time.

Stability

Personality theory deals with behaviour patterns that are consistent in different contexts and over time. We are not interested in properties that are occasional and transient. Mood swings and related behaviours caused by illness or the consumption of drugs are not stable and are thus not regarded as personality characteristics, unless they become permanent. However, there is a problem here. Personality appears to be flexible. The manager who is loud and autocratic in the office can be a caring and supporting parent at home. The 'stable' behaviours which we exhibit depend, in part, on social context. Some personality features (as with allergies) may only appear in specific social and physical conditions.

Distinctiveness

Personality theory is concerned with the pattern of dispositions and behaviours unique to the individual, and is not so concerned with properties that all or most other people share. You may be aggressive towards waiters, friendly with librarians, deferential to professors, and terrified of mice. You may share some of these dispositions with a friend who breeds mice.

The study of personality relies on two key propositions. First, we have to accept that behaviour does have stable and distinctive features, and does not change frequently. Most of us recognize consistency in our thought patterns, in our ways of relating to others, in meeting our needs, in solving problems, in our emotional responses, and in coping with stress and frustration. These regularities can be observed and studied. Second, we have to accept that the distinctive properties of individual personality can be measured and compared with the properties of others. Measurement does not necessarily imply quantification, but nomothetic methods do rely on sophisticated statistical analysis.

Some psychologists argue that personality is largely inherited, determined by genetics and the biochemistry of our brains. There is evidence to suggest that, because measures of job satisfaction are fairly stable over time and across different jobs, a predisposition to be content with or frustrated at work may have a genetic component. In this perspective, your personality is fixed at birth, if not before, and life's experiences do little to alter it.

Other psychologists argue that our characters are shaped by environmental, cultural and social factors, that our feelings and behaviour patterns are learned. Social learning theory argues that we learn new behaviours through observing and imitating others. Motivation theory demonstrates how job satisfaction can be influenced by changing job design and other factors such as supervisory style. Every society has distinctive ways of doing things. We cannot possibly be born with this local knowledge. In this perspective, your personality is flexible, changing with experience. Psychological well-being may depend on such adaptability.

The controversy over the relative effects of heredity and environment on personality is known as the 'nature–nurture' debate. Few psychologist if any now hold the extreme positions set out here. Both genetic and situational factors influence behaviour. Theorists disagree over the emphases to be given to these factors, how they should be measured, and how they interact. During the 1960s and 1970s, 'nurture' was the position in vogue. Since the 1990s, biological and genetic evidence have moved thinking in the direction of 'nature'. Steven Pinker (2002) offers a particularly scathing criticism of the view that the mind is a 'blank slate' inscribed by our environment and our experiences, arguing instead for an innate human nature based on discoveries in evolutionary biology, genetics and neurophysiology.

These debates have interesting implications for organizational behaviour. There are many situations in which we want to be able to explain behaviour, and personality characteristics may give us clues. However, there are also organizational settings where it is important to be able not just to explain, but to predict behaviour, such as in job selection and promotion contexts. Personality characteristics offer the promise of helping to make those predictions about someone's future behaviour and performance.

Types and traits

Type: a descriptive label for a distinct pattern of personality characteristics. Examples of personality types include extravert, neurotic and open.

Attempts to describe the components and structure of personality have focused on the concepts of *type* and *trait*. One of the most straightforward ways of describing and analyzing personality concerns the categorization of people into personality **types**.

One of the first personality theorists was Hippocrates ('The father of medicine'), who lived in Greece around 400 BC. He claimed that personality type or 'temperament' was determined by bodily 'humours', generating different behaviour patterns as shown in table 5.1.

Table 5.1: Hippocrates' type theory of personality

Body humour	Temperament	Behaviours
blood	sanguine	confident, cheerful, optimistic, hopeful, active
phlegm	phlegmatic	sluggish, apathetic
black bile	melancholic	depressed, sad, brooding, prone to ill-founded fears
yellow bile	choleric	aggressive, excitable, irritable

Hippocrates
(450–370 BC)

Carl Gustav Jung
(1875–1961)

These temperament labels are still in use today, with the same meanings. Hippocrates' theory, however, is unsound for two reasons. First, what we know about the relationships between body chemistry and behaviour fails to confirm the theory. Second, our personal experience reveals that there are more than four types of people in the world.

A more recent type theory was developed by William Sheldon (1898–1970), who argued that temperament was related to physique, or to what he called *somatotype* (Sheldon, 1942). In other words, your personality depends on your 'biological individuality', your size and shape:

The *ectomorph*, who is thin and delicate, is restrained, inhibited, cautious, introverted, artistic and intellectual.

The *mesomorph* is muscular, strong and rectangular, and is energetic, physical, adventurous and assertive.

The *endomorph* who is fat, soft and round, is also sociable, relaxed, easy-going, and enjoys food.

This typology has intuitive appeal, but it may not be a good model for predicting behaviour. Can you think of an endomorph who is introverted and intellectual? Are you friendly with a mesomorph who is a relaxed gourmet, or with an ectomorph who is sociable and assertive?

The Ayurveda principle

The ancient Indian system of holistic medicine, Ayurveda, is founded on the principle that living matter is composed of earth, water, fire, air and ether, combining to give three basic personality types or *doshas*: *vata*, *pitta* and *kapha*:

Vata (air and ether): Slim, angular and restless. Creative and artistic, leaning towards athletics or dancing. Like to travel, can be flirtatious and emotionally insecure. Dry skin, prone to joint pains, rheumatism and depression.

Pitta (water and fire): Medium build with fair or red hair. Good leaders and executives who get things done. Articulate and impatient, can be irritable. Lunch is a very important meal. Skin is reddish. Prone to acne, rashes, ulcers and urinary infections.

Kapha (earth and water): Stocky, perhaps overweight. Loyal workers, not pushy. Patient, affectionate and forgiving. Smooth and oily skin. Prone to respiratory tract problems, asthma, bronchitis, colds and sinus problems, and to depression.

Each of us is a combination of all three *doshas*, the dominant one determining our physical and spiritual character. The key to health lies in balance, ensuring that one doshic personality is not too prominent. The similarities between Ayurveda and somatotyping are striking.

Based on Sally Morris, 'An Eastern art of healing that is heading West', *The Times*, 26 October 1999, p. 47.

Type theory owes a debt to the Swiss psychologist, Carl Gustav Jung (1875–1961) whose approach is based on *psychological preferences* for extraversion or introversion, for sensation or intuition, for thinking or feeling, and for judging or perceiving (Jung, 1953, 1971). At the heart of this complex theory lie four personality types, plotted across the sensation–intuition and thinking–feeling dimensions in figure 5.1, and described in more detail in table 5.2.

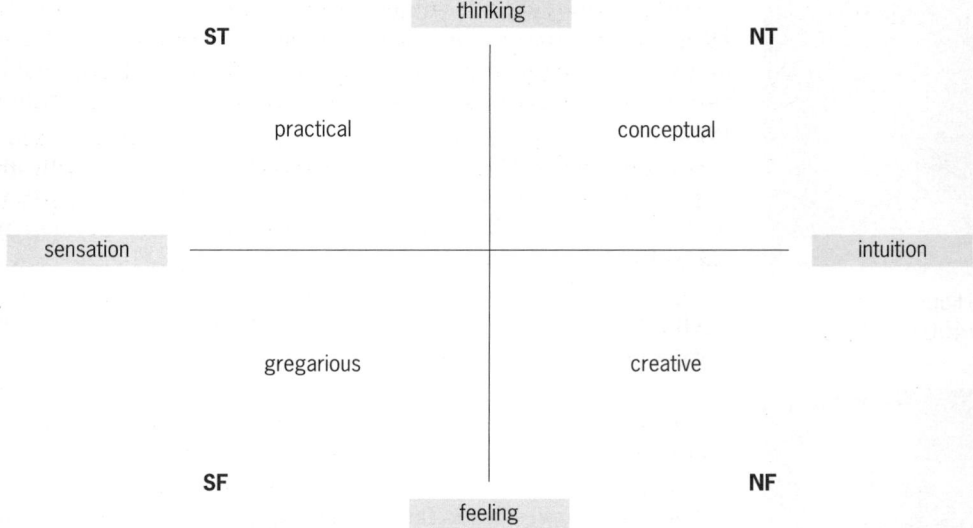

Figure 5.1: Jung's personality type matrix

Table 5.2: Jung's personality types described	
Sensation–Thinking (ST)	Practical, down to earth, impersonal, interested in facts, wants order, precision, no ambiguity, values efficiency and clear lines of authority in an organization.
Intuition–Thinking (NT)	Conceptual and inventive, sees future possibilities through analysis, is comfortable using flow charts and graphs, generates new ideas and change, sparks enthusiasm in others.
Sensation–Feeling (SF)	Gregarious and sociable, interested in facts about people, dislikes ambiguity, likes to establish settings in which people care for and support each other, has no time for reflection.
Intuition–Feeling (NF)	Creative, values imagination and warmth, is enthusiastic, has grandiose goals, dislikes rules, hierarchies and procedures, likes flexibility and open communication, is persistent and committed, can be seen as an idealistic dreamer.

Using this theory, the mother and daughter team of Katherine Briggs and Isabel Myers (Myers, 1962, 1976; Myers and McCaulley, 1985) developed the Myers–Briggs Type Indicator (MBTI), possibly the world's most popular personality assessment. The MBTI makes Jung's theory accessible and practical, rating personal preferences on the four scales:

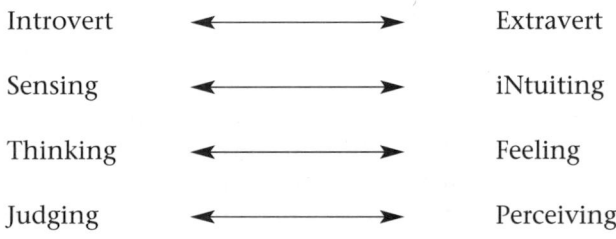

This approach assigns subjects to one side or other of each dimension, establishing 16 personality types, each known by its letter code; iNtuiting is known by the letter N to avoid confusion with introversion. If you are ENFP, you have been typed as Extravert, Intuitive, Feeling and Perceiving. It is useful to remember, however, that the assessments that produce individual scores reveal preferences and tendencies. The resultant profiles do not necessarily mean that individuals are trapped in those categories. While we may have a preference for impersonal analysis (T), we may, when appropriate, be able to use personal evaluations (F); we may prefer to focus on the immediate and concrete (S), while being able when appropriate to consider imaginative opportunities (N)_ (Trompenaars and Woolliams, 2002).

The MBTI has a number of applications. For example, problem-solving and decision-making groups need a complementary personality mix, intuitive types need sensing types, feeling types need thinking types. This echoes the theory of effective group composition developed by Meredith Belbin (1981, 1993a).

Type approaches fit people into categories possessing common behaviour patterns. A personality **trait**, on the other hand, is any enduring behaviour that occurs in a variety of settings. While individuals belong to types, traits belong to individuals. You fit a type, you have a trait. Traits are also defined in terms of predispositions to behave in a particular way.

Examples of traits include shyness, excitability, reliability and moodiness. The study of traits in personality research and assessment, and of how traits cluster to form personality types, is associated with the **nomothetic** approach in psychology.

Nomothetic means 'law setting or law giving'. Psychologists who adopt this approach look for universal laws of behaviour. The nomothetic approach assumes that personality is inherited and that environmental factors have little effect. The nomothetic approach adopts the following procedures.

First, it is necessary to identify the main dimensions on which personality can vary. Trait approaches assume that there is a common set of dimensions on which we can be compared. Traits describe aspects of temperament and character, and reflect the individual's predisposition to behave in particular ways. This approach assumes that your unique personality can be measured and compared with others on the same dimensions.

Second, the personalities of groups of people are assessed, usually through a self-report questionnaire. Popular magazines often use 'fun' versions of these questionnaires. The questions typically ask you to choose between a fixed number of answers. Responses may be confined, for example, to 'true' or 'false', to 'yes' or 'no' or to a rating scale that runs from 'strongly agree' to 'strongly disagree'. These are called 'forced choice' questions, and this procedure assumes that your answers reflect your behaviour.

Third, your personality profile is constructed across the traits measured. Your score on each dimension is compared with the average and the distribution of scores for the whole group. This enables the assessor to identify individuals around the norm, and those with pronounced characteristics that deviate from the norm. Your personal score has little meaning outside the scores of the population with which you are being compared. You cannot have a 'high' or 'low' score; you can only have scores that are high or low when compared with others.

Trait: a relatively stable quality or attribute of an individual's personality, influencing behaviour in a particular direction.

Nomothetic approach to the study of personality: the identification of traits; an approach that looks for systematic relationships between different aspects of personality.

Personality types and sales maximization

Bluewater, a retail park in Kent in Britain, opened in March 1999. Research helped to design the 'customer friendly' features of the centre: wide car park spaces, no shops in 'dead end' corridors, police station for security, natural materials on the floors, poetry on the walls, coffee shops at the entrances with welcoming aromas, and staff trained in positive body language. The research produced a breakdown of the centre's customers into seven personality types. This was used to determine the mix of shops, based on the percentage of each type in the area, and expected sales to that category:

Category	Characteristics	% of population	% of sales
county classics	upmarket, middle-aged women, house proud and arty, shop at 'big name' stores	14.6	25.2
club executives	male equivalent of county classics, impatient, successful, status- and career-obsessed, like 'middle-of-the-road' stores	13.5	21.2
young fashionables	twentysomethings, vain and superficial fashion victims, like 'lifestyle' clothing stores and fashionable brand images	15.6	21.6
sporting 30s	middle-income men, casual, undomesticated, holding on to youth, fighting flab, want special interest stores	13.4	12
young survivors	singles and couples with limited interests, abilities and ambitions – and limited incomes, seek budget stores	15.3	7.4
home comfortables	'cardigans and knitting' types, retired and more at home in the garden than a shopping mall, like 'traditional' stores	14.4	7.1
budget optimists	middle-aged and older women on low incomes, limited horizons, set routines, like 'traditional' clothing and food stores	13.2	5.4

Based on Paul Bray, 'Falling under the psychologist's spell', *The Sunday Times*, 'The Restless Customer' supplement, 13 June 1999, p. 9.

Fourth, the group may be split into sub-groups, say by age, sex or occupation. This produces other reference points, or norms, against which individual scores can be compared. Patterns of similarities and differences among and between sub-groups enable general laws about personality to be formulated. One may find, for example, that successful Scottish male managers tend to be introverted, or that women under the age of 30 employed in purchasing have unusually low scores on shyness. This approach is impersonal, and it is difficult to use the results to predict individual behaviour, even with 'extreme' scores. It may be possible, however, to make probabilistic predictions about groups, in terms of behaviour tendencies.

It may seem odd that one approach to individual personality assessment relies on studies of large groups. However, through this method, one discovers what is normal or average for those groups and compares individuals with that. The terms 'normal' and 'average' are used in the statistical sense. Individuals who 'deviate

Hans Jürgen
Eysenck
(1916–97)

from the norm' are not social outcasts. However, assessments based on this method are often used as a guide to the profile of individuals, especially in employment selection.

One of the most influential trait theories of personality is that of Hans Jürgen Eysenck (1970, 1990), who was born in Germany in 1916 and who worked in Britain until his death in 1997. Following Jung, his research explored the key dimensions on which personality varies, including the extraversion–introversion or 'E' dimension, and the neuroticism–stability or 'N' dimension. However, unlike Jung, Eysenck sought to identify trait clusters.

Eysenck's approach is nomothetic. His sympathies lie with behaviourist psychologists who seek a scientific, experimental, mathematical psychology. Behaviourists claim, however, that behaviour is shaped by environmental influences. Eysenck's explanations of personality, on the other hand, are based on genetics and biology.

Eysenck's model offers a way of linking types, traits and behaviour. He argues that personality structure is hierarchical. Each individual possesses more or less of a number of identifiable traits – trait 1, trait 2, trait 3, and so on. Research shows how individuals who have a particular trait, say trait 1, are more likely to possess another, say trait 3, than people who do not have trait 1. In other words, traits tend to 'cluster' in systematic patterns. These clusters identify a 'higher order' of personality description, which Eysenck refers to as personality types, as figure 5.2 illustrates.

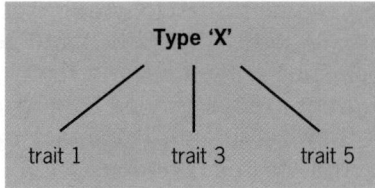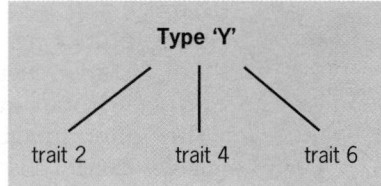

Figure 5.2: A hierarchical model of personality types and traits

This does not mean that every individual who has trait 1 has a Type 'X' personality. It means that questionnaire analysis has shown that individuals with high scores on trait 1 are more likely to have high scores on traits 3 and 5 also, putting them into the Type 'X' category.

Eysenck presents statistical evidence from personality assessments to support the existence of personality trait clusters. However, individuals vary in a continuous distribution on trait scores. The result of an individual assessment using this approach is a personality profile across several traits rather than allocation to a single personality type.

The E dimension divides us into two broad categories of people – extraverts and introverts. American use of these terms refers to sociability and unsociability. European use emphasizes spontaneity and inhibition. Eysenck's account combines these notions. Most of us have a trait profile between these extremes on a continuum, and they are not exclusive categories.

Eysenck argues that seven pairs of personality traits cluster to generate, respectively, the extravert and introvert personality types. These traits are summarized in table 5.3.

Extraverts are tough-minded individuals who need strong and varied external stimulation. They are sociable, like parties, are good at telling stories, enjoy practical jokes, have many friends, need people to talk to, do not enjoy studying and reading on their own, crave excitement, take risks, act impulsively, prefer change, are optimistic, carefree, active, aggressive, quick tempered, display their emotions and are unreliable.

Table 5.3: The trait clusters for Eysenck's extravert and introvert types

Extravert	Introvert
activity	inactivity
expressiveness	inhibition
impulsiveness	control
irresponsibility	responsibility
practicality	reflectiveness
risk taking	carefulness
sociability	unsociability

Introverts are tender-minded, experience strong emotions, and do not need intense external stimuli. They are quiet, introspective, retiring, prefer books to people, are withdrawn, reserved, plan ahead, distrust impulse, appreciate order, lead careful sober lives, have little excitement, suppress emotions, are pessimistic, worry about moral standards and are reliable.

The N dimension assesses personality on a continuum between neuroticism and stability.

Neurotics are emotional, unstable and anxious, tend to have low opinions of themselves, feel that they are unattractive failures, tend to be disappointed with life, and are pessimistic and depressed. They worry about things that may never happen and are easily upset when things go wrong. They are obsessive, conscientious, finicky people who are highly disciplined and get annoyed by untidiness and disorder. Neurotics are not self-reliant and tend to submit to institutional power without question. They feel controlled by events, by others and by fate. They often imagine that they are ill and demand sympathy. They blame themselves excessively and are troubled by conscience.

Stable people are 'adjusted', and are self-confident, optimistic, resist irrational fears, are easy going, realistic, solve their own problems, have few health worries, and have few regrets about their past.

The traits clusters for emotionally unstable and stable types are summarized in table 5.4. The questionnaire that Eysenck used to measure the E and N dimensions has 96 questions, 40 for each dimension and 16 'lie detector' questions. The questions are mainly in the 'yes/no' format. The E and N dimensions are not correlated; if you are extraverted, you could be either stable or neurotic. If you are stable, you could be either extravert or introvert.

Is one personality type more desirable than another? The extravert may be sociable, friendly, cheerful, active and lively. However, extraverts are unreliable, fickle in friendships, and are easily bored with uninteresting or time-consuming tasks. There are positive and negative sides to the extravert personality, as with the introvert. Those with extreme scores have what Eysenck calls an 'ambiguous

Table 5.4: The trait clusters for Eysenck's emotionally unstable and stable types

Emotionally unstable	Emotionally stable
anxiety	calm
guilt	guilt freedom
hypochondriasis	sense of health
lack of autonomy	autonomy
low self-esteem	self-esteem
obsessiveness	casualness
unhappiness	happiness

gift'. If we are aware of such features, however, we may be able to act in ways to control and exploit them to our advantage. It is thus important to be aware of your personality, and to be aware of the characteristics that might be seen by others as strengths and weaknesses. To understand other people, you must begin with an understanding of your own personality and emotions, and the effect that you have on others.

Source: © copyright United Feature Syndicate, Inc. Reproduced by permission.

Emotional intelligence

Surely a stable personality is more desirable than a neurotic one? That is not necessarily the case. Embarrassing in some settings, an open show of emotion is desirable in others. Emotions are a major source of motivation. Inability to display and share feelings can be a handicap. Sharing feelings of frustration and anger can be as important in an organizational setting as showing positive feelings of, for example, praise, satisfaction and friendship. It has been argued that an ability to handle emotions is a particular mental skill. Some commentators regard this mainly as a competence that can be developed with training. Others treat it as a personal quality reflecting a dimension of individual personality.

The concept of **emotional intelligence** was developed by Peter Salovey and John D. Mayer (1990) who argued that the concept of 'rational' intelligence ignores emotional competencies.

This concept has been popularized by Daniel Goleman (1995, 1998), who claims that emotional intelligence is more important to career success than technical skills or rational intelligence. Goleman's dimensions of emotional intelligence are summarized in table 5.5. He argues that emotional intelligence gives anyone an advantage, at work and in social relationships, but that it is particularly important for senior management and leadership roles, where conventional notions of intelligence are taken for granted. At senior levels, high emotional intelligence is a mark of the 'star performer'. There are several assessments available for measuring emotional intelligence (sometimes confusingly called EQ), and some commentators are convinced that emotional intelligence is developed through experience, and can be learned through training (Pickard, 1999).

Emotional intelligence: the ability to identify, integrate, understand and reflectively manage one's own and other people's feelings.

Emotional intelligence is normally regarded as a property of the individual. Vanessa Druskat and Steven Wolff (2001) argue that emotional intelligence also operates at the group level. They identify a series of norms, or 'small acts that make a big difference', that lead to the development of high-performing teams, prescribing behaviours at the level of the individual, the level of the group and between organizational boundaries, to build group emotional intelligence. These behaviours include:

Table 5.5: The five dimensions of emotional intelligence

Dimension	Definition	Hallmarks
1 Self-awareness	the ability to recognize and understand your moods, emotions and drives as well the effect you have on others	self-confidence, realistic self-assessment, self-deprecating sense of humour
2 Regulating feelings	the ability to control and to redirect your disruptive moods and impulses; the propensity to suspend judgement, to think before acting	trustworthiness and integrity, comfortable with ambiguity, openness to change
3 Motivation	a passion to work for reasons beyond status and money; a propensity to pursue goals with energy and persistence	high achievement need, optimism even in the face of failure, organizational commitment
4 Empathy	the ability to recognize and understand the emotional makeup of others; skill in dealing with the emotional responses of others	expertise in building and retaining talent; cross-cultural sensitivity; service to clients and customers
5 Social skills	effectiveness in managing relationships and building networks; ability to find common ground, to build rapport	effectiveness in leading change; persuasiveness; expertise in building and leading teams

At the individual level:

- take time to get to know one another;
- ask quiet members what they think;
- let group members know that their contributions are valued;
- tell teammates what you are thinking and feeling;
- appoint a 'devil's advocate'.

At the group level:

- make time to evaluate team effectiveness;
- openly discuss the 'group mood';
- discuss 'difficult' emotional issues;
- create fun ways to relieve tension and stress;
- create a postive, optimistic, affirmative environment.

At the cross-boundary level:

- find out the concerns and needs of others in the organization;
- discuss the culture and politics of the organization;
- create opportunities for networking;

- provide support for the needs of other teams;

- invite relevant others to your team meetings.

These 'norms of group emotional intelligence' are similar to the guidance which researchers in group dynamics have advocated since the 1950s, expressed in more modern terms, such as 'customer feedback', 'high-performing team', 'group mood', 'affirmative environment' and 'networking'. Some commentators have therefore been critical of the exaggerated claims made for the novelty and power of emotional intelligence. Charles Woodruffe (2001), for example, describes the concept as 'old wine in new bottles'.

It has long been recognized that career success depends on personal and inter-personal skills, including self-confidence, adaptability and the development of others. As chapter 17 describes, the technique of *sensitivity training* was developed in the late 1940s to develop personal and interpersonal emotional awareness. Woodruffe (2001) also notes a paradox concerning the tests used to measure emotional intelligence. Only an emotionally intelligent person, he points out, could recognize whether or not they 'can easily express emotion over the phone', a typical test question. He then asks: 'Is it emotionally intelligent to express the emotion or to be aware that you don't express it?' The person responding 'no' to the telephone test question could be just as emotionally intelligent as the person responding 'yes'. Woodruffe concludes that emotional intelligence is neither a new nor a useful concept, and that its contribution to job performance has been exaggerated. While a number of organizations now provide training programmes to develop emotional intelligence in management and other grades of staff, the debate over their value continues.

The big five

The big five: trait clusters that appear consistently to capture main personality traits: Openness, Conscientiousness, Extraversion, Agreeableness and Neuroticism.

The search for trait clusters has culminated in what is known as **the big five.** The most influential advocates of this approach are Paul Costa and Robert McRae (1992; McRae, 1992). This approach has achieved broad acceptance as a common descriptive system. Research has consistently reproduced these dimensions in different social settings and cultures, with different populations, with different forms of data collection, and in different languages. However, the labelling and interpretation of the factors and sub-traits remains controversial.

The big five, known by the acronym OCEAN, are not personality types. These are sets of factors, 'super traits', which describe common elements among the 'sub-factors' identified as clustering together looking for a heading. Costa and McCrae identify six traits under each of the five headings, giving 30 traits in total. Table 5.6 summarizes the big five personality trait clusters, and one of the exercises at the end of this chapter invites you to profile your own personality using this approach.

The six traits relating to *Openness* (fantasy, aesthetics, feelings, actions, ideas, values) run on a continuum from 'explorer' at one extreme, to 'preserver' at the other. Explorer (O+) traits are useful for entrepreneurs, architects, change agents, artists and theoretical scientists. Preserver (O−) traits are useful for finance managers, stage performers, project managers and applied scientists. Those in the middle of this spectrum (O) are labelled 'moderates' who are interested in novelty when necessity commands, but not for too long.

The traits relating to *Conscientiousness* (competence, order, dutifulness, achievement striving, self-discipline, deliberation) run from 'focused' to 'flexible'. Focused (C+) traits are useful for leaders, senior executives and other high

Table 5.6: The big five personality factors or trait clusters

	← or →	
Openness	**Explorer (O+):** creative, open-minded, intellectual	**Preserver (O−):** unimaginative, disinterested, narrow-minded
Conscientiousness	**Focused (C+):** dutiful, achievement-oriented, self-disciplined	**Flexible (C−):** frivolous, irresponsible, disorganized
Extraversion	**Extravert (E+):** gregarious, warm, positive	**Introvert (E−):** quiet, reserved, shy
Agreeableness	**Adapter (A+):** straightforward, compliant, sympathetic	**Challenger (A−):** quarrelsome, oppositional, unfeeling
Neuroticism (or negative emotionality)	**Reactive (N+):** anxious, depressed, self-conscious	**Resilient (N−):** calm, contented, self-assured

achievers. Flexible (C−) traits are useful for researchers, detectives and management consultants. Those in the middle (C) are 'balanced', and find it easy to move from focus to being flexible, from production to research.

The big five in action

Pierce and Jane Howard (1993) cite the case of Henry, a freelance television sports producer. Henry was rich and miserable, but worn out by work and unable to sleep properly. A sports lover who was good at his job, producing fast-paced live basketball games rattled his nerves and he took a long time to calm down afterwards. What was the problem? His big five personality profile was:

O−   C+   E+   A   N+

His scores for openness (preserver), conscientiousness (focused), extraversion (extravert) and agreeableness (negotiator) were ideal for this job. The problem lay with his high N+ reactive, emotional score. A television producer has to be resilient and calm, monitoring the action and the camera work, giving instructions to produce a smooth programme in a fast-moving and stressful environment with no margin for error. The solution? Henry moved to producing sports documentaries and took a degree in eastern studies, planning to specialize in documentaries on eastern culture (including sport).

The traits relating to *Extraversion* (warmth, gregariousness, assertiveness, activity, excitement-seeking, positive emotions) run from 'extravert' to 'introvert' (surprise, surprise). Extravert (E+) traits are useful in sales, politics and the arts. Introvert (E−) traits are useful for production management, and in the physical and natural sciences. Those in the middle of this spectrum (E) are 'ambiverts' who move easily from isolation to social settings.

The traits relating to *Agreeableness* (trust, straightforwardness, altruism, compliance, modesty, tender-mindedness) run from 'adapter' to 'challenger'. Adapter (A+) traits are useful in teaching, social work and psychology. Challenger (A−) traits are useful in advertising, management and military leadership. Those in the middle of this spectrum (A) are 'negotiators' who move from leadership to followership as the situation demands.

The traits relating to *Neuroticism* or 'negative emotionality' (worry, anger, discouragement, self-consciousness, impulsiveness, vulnerability) run from 'reactive' to 'resilient'. Reactive (emotional) or 'N+' traits are useful for social scientists, academics and customer service professionals, but extreme reactivity interferes with intellectual performance. Resilient (unflappable) or 'N−' traits are useful for air traffic controllers, airline pilots, military snipers, finance managers and engineers. Those in the middle of this spectrum (N) are 'responsives', able to use levels of emotionality appropriate to the circumstances.

This analysis implies that certain traits will lead to success in particular occupations. Reviewing the research, Ivan Robertson (2001) argues that the relationship between personality and performance is not straightforward. In particular, findings suggest that:

- only two of the big five personality factors, conscientiousness and emotional stability, are consistently associated with better performance, in most occupations;

- conscientiousness is a better predictor of work performance than emotional stability;

- although openness, agreeableness and extraversion are not universally important, any of the big five personality factors could be significant in certain occupations;

- the correlations that have been found between personality factors and job performance are not strong, as performance is also affected by a range of other factors.

High conscientiousness cannot always be regarded as a reliable single predictor of someone's suitability for a job. One study showed that employees with low conscientiousness scores were rated by supervisors as innovative and highly promotable (Robertson, 2001, p. 43). Many organizations, particularly those facing high levels of competition and rapid change, are concerned with attributes such as interpersonal skills, motivation, flexibility and adaptability. High conscientiousness may be less relevant in such contexts.

Personality Types A and B

Type A personality: a combination of emotions and behaviours characterized by ambition, hostility, impatience and a sense of constant time-pressure.

Type B personality: a combination of emotions and behaviours characterized by relaxation, low focus on achievement and ability to take time to enjoy leisure.

Personality and health seem to be linked in a way particularly relevant to organizational behaviour. Meyer Friedman and Ray Rosenman (1974) identified two extreme 'behaviour syndromes' which explained differences in stress levels. In other words, they claim to have identified a 'stress prone' personality. Much subsequent research has focused on what Friedman and Rosenman called the **Type A** behaviour syndrome and its opposite, **Type B**.

Table 5.7 summarizes these two personality types.

Friedman and Rosenman found that Type A personalities were three times more likely to suffer heart disease than Type B personalities. The typical Type A thrives on long hours, large amounts of work and tight deadlines. These are socially and organizationally desirable characteristics, as are competitiveness and a high need for achievement. However, those who are extremely Type A may not be able to relax long enough to stand back from a complex problem to make an effective and comprehensive analysis, and may lack the patience and relaxed style required in some management positions. A further problem lies in the fact that their impatience and hostility can increase the stress levels in those who have to work with

Table 5.7: Type A and Type B personality characteristics

Type A personality characteristics	Type B personality characteristics
competitive	able to take time out to enjoy leisure
high need for achievement	not preoccupied with achievement
aggressive	easy-going
works fast	works at a steady pace
impatient	seldom impatient
restless	not easily frustrated
extremely alert	relaxed
tense facial muscles	moves and speaks slowly
constant feeling of time pressure	seldom lacks enough time
more likely to suffer stress-related illness	**less likely to suffer stress-related illness**

them. Like the extravert, although a Type A personality can appear to have many admirable facets, this behaviour syndrome can be dysfunctional for the individual, and for others.

Stop and Criticize

Are you a Type A or a Type B personality?

Do you suffer from any of these symptoms: alcohol abuse, excessive smoking, dizziness, upset stomach, headaches, fatigue, sweating, bad breath? If 'yes', these could be stress responses to your Type A behaviour pattern. Expect your first heart attack before you are 45.

If you don't suffer stress-related symptoms, perhaps you are a Type B. However, do you think that your dozy behaviour could damage your career prospects?

Whichever your response, what are you going to do about it?

Friedman and Rosenman argue that a Type A can change into a Type B, with awareness and the right training, and suggest a number of personal 're-engineering strategies':

- keep reminding yourself that life is always full of unfinished business;
- you only 'finish' when you die;
- learn how to delegate responsibility to others;
- limit your weekly working hours;
- schedule time for leisure and exercise;
- take a course in time management skills.

The problem, of course, is that the extreme Type A personality – the person most at risk – can never find enough time to implement these strategies effectively. Another problem lies with the question of whether you can 're-engineer' your personality this easily.

Stress management: individual and organizational methods

The work of Friedman and Rosenman is important in demonstrating a relationship between personality and health. Negative emotional states such as depression, hostility and anxiety appear to be linked to heart diseases, respiratory disorders such as asthma, and headaches and ulcers. Health risks are greater where negative states are chronic, particularly when they are an aspect of personality. There are a number of other causes of stress that arise from individual factors: difficulty in coping with change, lack of confidence and assertiveness in relationships, poor time management, poor stress management skills (Clarke, 1989).

Is stress a problem?

■ A survey in 1996 by the European Foundation for the Improvement of Living and Working Conditions found that 28 per cent of European workers consider their health to be affected by stress at work, that 'high stress' working conditions are on the increase, and that women suffer to a greater degree than men.

■ The UK Health and Safety Executive estimates that 40 million working days were lost in 2001–02 due to sickness, 13 million the result of stress, anxiety or depression, and that these figures are rising.

■ 75 per cent of managers claim that stress adversely affects their health, happiness, home life and work performance.

■ The Confederation of British Industry estimates that stress costs British industry £7 billion a year, equivalent to 2–3 per cent of gross domestic product.

■ Compensation payments for stress-related injuries are rising, and stress is likely to become the most dangerous risk to business in the early part of the twenty-first century.

Based on Chartered Institute of Personnel and Development, *Key Facts: Stress at Work* (1998) and *Quick Facts: Stress* (2002), CIPD, London; and Z. Roberts, 'Worrying about stress', *People Management*, vol. 9, no. 5, 6 March 2003, pp. 14–15.

Stress has many causes other than personality. The pace of life, work and change in contemporary society generates stress by increasing the range and intensity of the demands on our time. Any condition that requires an adaptive response from the individual is known as a stressor. Typical stressors likely to arise in an organizational context include:

■ *inadequate physical working environment*: noise, bad lighting, inadequate ventilation, lack of privacy, extremes of heat and cold, old and unsuitable and unreliable equipment;

■ *inappropriate job design*: poor co-ordination, inadequate training, inadequate information, rigid procedures, inadequate staffing, excessive workloads, no challenge, little use of skills, no responsibility or participation in decision-making, role ambiguity;

■ *poor management style*: inconsistent, competitive, crisis management, autocratic management, excessive time pressures placed on employees;

■ *poor relationships*: with superiors, with colleagues, with particular individuals, lack of feedback, little social contact, racial and sexual harassment;

■ *uncertain future*: job insecurity, fear of unemployment or redeployment, few promotion opportunities, low-status job;

■ *divided loyalties*: conflicts between personal aspirations and organizational requirements, conflict between job and family and social responsibilities.

Stress can also be arousing and exciting, and can enhance our sense of satisfaction and accomplishment and improve our performance. The term 'eustress' is sometimes used to describe this positive aspect of stress. The prefix 'eu' is Greek for 'good'. This contrasts with distress, which means the unpleasant, debilitating and unhealthy side of stress.

The escalating costs of work-related stress

In 1997 John Walker, a social worker, received an out-of-court settlement of £175,000 from Northumberland County Council following nervous breakdowns resulting from excessive workload. In June 1999, a court awarded Beverley Lancaster, a housing officer with Birmingham City Council, damages of £67,000. The Council allegedly failed to provide training and support when she transferred jobs. Lancaster was seriously injured as a result of work overload, and had to retire on grounds of ill health. In September 1999, Muriel Benson, a teacher, reached an out-of-court settlement of £47,000 with Wirral Borough Council, which failed to act on complaints about her workload which caused her stress-related anxiety and depression and forced her into early retirement. In January 2000, Randy Ingram was awarded £203,000 damages for intense stress and depression caused by lack of management support at Hereford and Worcester Council for his difficult work in caring for residential sites for gypsies. In December 2000, Janice Howell, a teacher, won £250,000 in compensation from a school in Newport following two breakdowns caused by intolerable and stressful working conditions. In March 2001, a London policeman, Richard Parsonson, sued Scotland Yard for £400,000, blaming his breakdown on the stress generated by a 'front line' policing role. Stress is often regarded as a personal problem. These cases show that it is management's responsibility to monitor workloads and stress symptoms, and to respond appropriately.

Based on Mark Whitehead, 'Watch your workloads', *People Management*, vol. 5, no. 14, 15 July 1999, pp. 12–13; Russel Jenkins, '£47,000 for teacher made sick by stress', *The Times*, 1 October 1999, p. 11; *The Times*, 'Council worker awarded £200,000 over stress claim', 11 January 2000, p. 3; Glen Owen, 'Stressed Teacher awarded £250,000', *The Times*, 5 December 2000, p. 9; Stewart Tendler, 'Retired PC seeks £400,000 for stress of going on beat', *The Times*, 21 March 2001, p. 3.

Stress can be episodic. When dealing with life's problems, we get anxious, cope with the problem, and then relax again. Some events can be extremely stressful, such as the death of a close relative or a term in prison. Other experiences can also be stressful, such as getting a poor exam grade, being fined for speeding, or arguing with a parent, but trigger a less extreme response. Each of these episodes on its own is unlikely to cause lasting damage. However, when several of these episodes occur around the same time, the health risk is increased.

Stress can be chronic. This happens when we face constant stress, with no escape, and can lead to exhaustion and 'burnout'. This may be due to the unfortunate coincidence of several unrelated episodes. However, chronic stress also arises from the enduring features of our personal, social and organizational circumstances. If we are always under pressure, always facing multiple and unrealistic demands, always having difficulties with our work, our colleagues and our relationships, then the health risk from stress is likely to increase.

Stress can be a personal response to life's challenges. What you brush aside may be a debilitating problem for someone else. There seem to be three main factors moderating the impact of a stressor on an individual:

Condition You are better able to cope with stress if you are in good health and full of energy.

Cognitive appraisal If you believe that you are not going to cope with a particu-

Hardiness

lar event, this belief can become a 'self-fulfilling prophecy'. The opposite can also be true.

Hardiness is an outlook on life characterized by a welcoming approach to change, commitment to purposeful activity and a sense of being in control. This combination of factors can increase resilience to stressful events.

Stress has many symptoms which, taken on their own, do not appear significant and are not particularly threatening if they are transient. An occasional headache is seldom cause for concern. Many of these symptoms have other causes, so they can be overlooked, and stress passes unrecognized and untreated. Table 5.8 identifies typical symptoms of stress.

Table 5.8: Typical stress symptoms

excessive alcohol intake	heavy cigarette smoking	dependence on tranquillizers
tiredness	low energy	dizziness
headaches	stomach upsets and ulcers	bad breath
high blood pressure	sleep problems	hyperventilation
temper tantrums	irritability	moodiness
loss of concentration	aggression	overeating
excess worrying	anxiety	inability to relax
pounding heart	feelings of inadequacy	memory loss

Stress can have emotional consequences for the individual – anxiety, fatigue, depression, frustration, nervousness, low self-esteem, and so on. At the extreme, stress can contribute to mental breakdown and suicide. Stress also influences behaviour in many ways, from 'comfort tricks' involving alcohol and other drugs and excessive eating, to accident-proneness and emotional outbursts. Stress affects our thinking ability, interfering with concentration, decision-making, attention span and reaction to criticism. There are a number of physiological responses too, such as increased heart rate and blood pressure, sweating, and 'hot and cold flushes'.

The organizational consequences of stress can therefore be highly damaging. The work performance of stressed employees can be poor. This is sometimes revealed in high levels of absenteeism, staff turnover, accidents and wilful sabotage. Stress can cause relationships to deteriorate (although poor relationships may cause stress in the first place), and commitment to work and to the organization are also likely to fall.

There are two broad strategies for reducing stress: problem-focused strategies and emotion-focused strategies.

Problem-focused strategies deal directly with the stressors and include:

- improved selection and training mechanisms;
- staff counselling programmes;
- improved organizational communications;
- job redesign and enrichment strategies;
- development of teamworking systems.

Emotion-focused strategies improve individual resilience and coping skills and include:

- consciousness-raising to improve self-awareness;
- exercise and fitness programmes;

■ self-help training, in biofeedback, meditation, relaxation, coping strategies;

■ time management training;

■ development of other social and job interests.

It is not always appropriate to 'blame' individuals for their experience of and response to stress, despite the known link to personality. Stress is also caused by organizational factors. While individual resilience can be improved, the need for problem-focused organizational solutions is inescapable.

Figure 5.3 summarizes the argument of this section, with respect to the causes of stress, factors that moderate the experience of stress, stress symptoms and coping strategies.

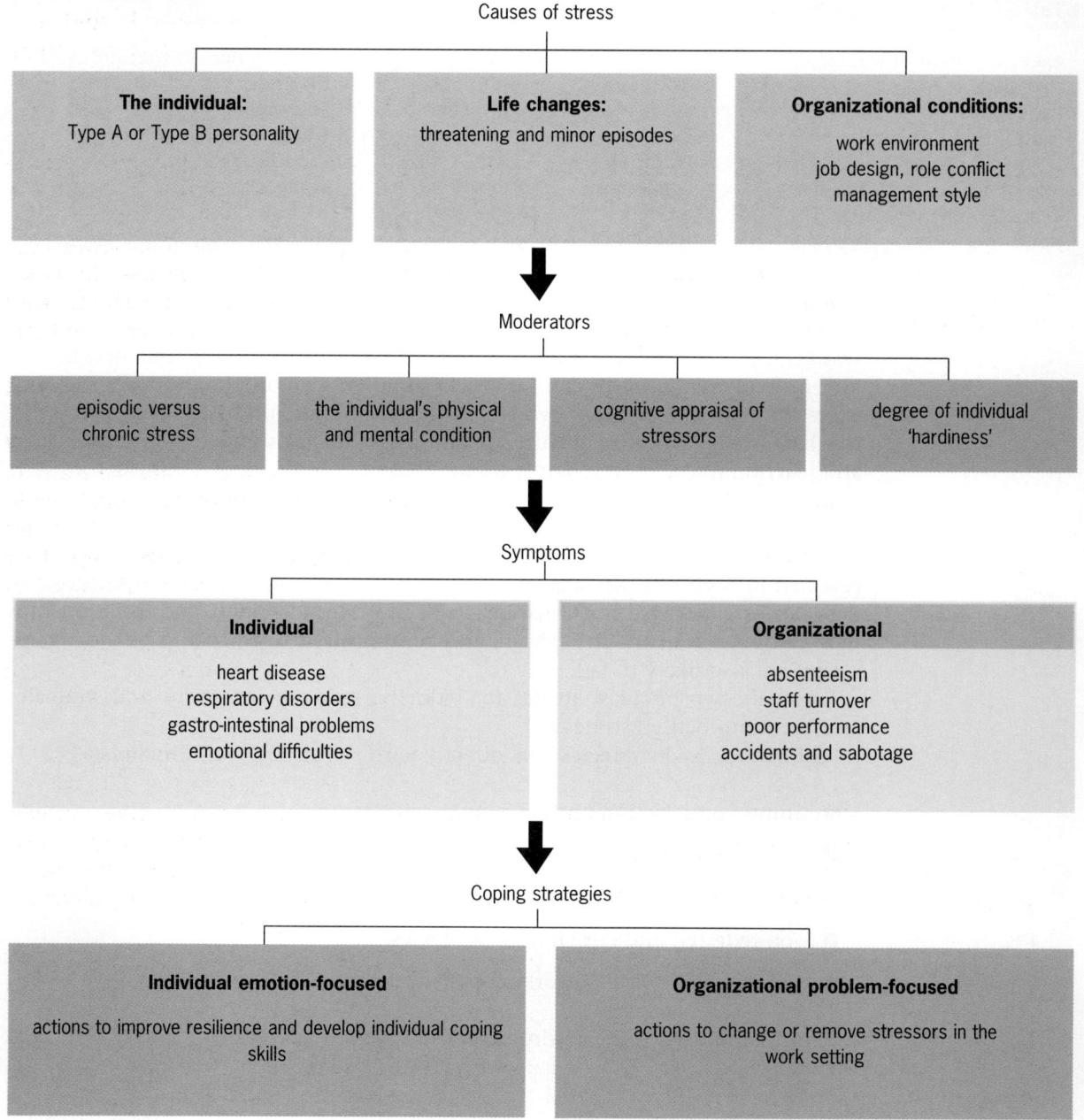

Figure 5.3: Stress causes, moderators, symptoms and coping strategies

The development of the self

The nomothetic approach to the study of personality has been criticized by those who advocate an **idiographic** approach, which contrasts sharply in perspective and implications.

Idiographic means 'writing about individuals'. Psychologists who adopt this perspective begin with a detailed picture of one person. This approach aims to capture the uniqueness, richness and complexity of the individual. It is a valuable way of deepening our understanding, but does not readily lead to the generation of universal laws of behaviour.

The idiographic approach makes the following assumptions.

First, each individual has unique traits that are not comparable with the traits of others. Your sensitivity and aggression are not necessarily comparable with my sensitivity and aggression. Idiographic research produces in-depth studies of normal and abnormal individuals, with information from interviews, letters, diaries and biographies. The data include what people say and write about themselves, and are not restricted to scores on paper-and-pencil tests.

Second, we are not just biological machines driven by heredity. This is only part of our nature. We are also socially self-conscious. Our behaviour patterns are influenced by experience, and by conscious reflection and reasoning, not just by instinct, habit and heredity.

Third, we behave in accordance with the image that we have of ourselves – our self, or **self concept**. We derive this concept or image from the ways in which other people treat us. We learn about ourselves through our interactions with others. We take the attitudes and behaviours of others towards us and use them to adjust our self concept and behaviour.

Fourth, as the development of the self concept is a social process, it follows that personality is open to change through social interactions and experiences. The development of the individual's personality is therefore not the inevitable result of genetic inheritance. It is through interaction with others that we learn to understand ourselves as individuals. We cannot develop self-understanding without the (tacit) help of others. There is no such thing as 'human nature'. We derive our nature through social interactions and relationships. Remember, this view contrasts starkly with the argument that human nature is largely influenced by biology and genetics (Pinker, 2002).

Your self-understanding thus determines your behaviour. For example, confidence in your ability to do something is related to the successful demonstration of that ability. Ability combined with lack of confidence usually leads to failure or poor performance.

The mind's ability to reflect on its own functions is an important capability. We experience a world 'out there' and we are capable of experiencing ourselves in that outer world, as objects that live and behave in it. We can observe, evaluate and criticize ourselves in the same conscious, objective, impersonal way that we observe, evaluate and criticize other people and events, and we experience shame, anxiety or pride in our own behaviour. Our capacity for reflective thought enables us to evaluate past and future actions and their consequences.

The American psychologist Charles Horton Cooley (1864–1929) introduced the concept of the 'looking-glass self'. Our mirror is the other people with whom we interact. If others respond warmly and favourably towards us, we develop a 'positive' self concept. If others respond with criticism, ridicule and aggression, we tend to develop a 'negative' self-image. The personality of the individual is thus the result of a process in which the individual learns to be the person they are. Most of us learn, accept and use most of the attitudes, values, beliefs and expectations of the society or part of society in which we are brought up.

Charles Horton Cooley (1864–1929)

George Herbert
Mead (1863–1931)

In other words, we learn the stock of knowledge available in and peculiar to our society. Red means stop. Cars drive on the left-hand side of the road (in Australia and Britain). An extended hand is a symbol of respect and friendship, not of hostility or aggression. These examples, on their own, are trivial. Taken together, they comprise a vital and 'taken-for-granted' knowledge of how society works. Phenomenologists (see chapter 1 and glossary) call this 'recipe knowledge'. The 'rules' that govern our behaviour are created, recreated and reinforced through our continuing interactions with others based on shared definitions of our reality. We interact with each other competently because we share this broad understanding.

How could we develop such a shared understanding on our own in isolation from society? What we inherit from our parents cannot possibly tell us how to behave in a specific culture. We have to learn how to become *persona grata* through social interaction.

If we all share the same ideas and behaviours, we have a recipe for a society of conformists. This is, of course, not consistent with the available evidence, and the theory does not imply this. George Herbert Mead (1934) argued that the self has two components:

I The unique, individual, conscious and impulsive aspects of the individual
Me The norms and values of society that the individual learns and accepts, or 'internalizes'

Generalized other: what we understand other people expect of us, in terms of our attitudes, values, beliefs and behaviour.

Mead used the term **generalized other** to refer to the set of expectations one believes others have of one. 'Me' is the aspect of self where these generalized attitudes are organized. The 'Me' cannot be physically located. It refers rather to the mental process that enables us to reflect on our own conduct. The 'Me' is the self as an object to itself.

The 'I' is the active, impulsive component of the self. Other people encourage us to conform to current values and beliefs. Reflective individuals also adjust their part in the social process. We can initiate change by introducing new social values. Patterns of socially acceptable conduct are specified in broad and general ways. There is plenty of scope for flexibility, modification, originality, creativity, individuality, variety and significant change.

Stop and Criticize

Make a list of the ten words or phrases that best describe the most important features of your individual identity.

These features could concern your social roles, physical characteristics, intellectual qualities, social style, beliefs and particular skills.

Then make a second list, putting what you regard as the most important feature at the top, and ranking all ten items with the least important at the bottom.

Starting at the bottom of your list, imagine that these items are removed from your personality one by one. Visualize how you would be different without each personality feature. What difference does its absence make to you?

This is the start of the process of establishing your *self concept*. How much more or less valid is this approach than one based on forced-choice questionnaires – and why?

Figure 5.4 illustrates what Carl Rogers (1902–87) called the 'two-sided self'.

Carl Ransom
Rogers (1902–87)

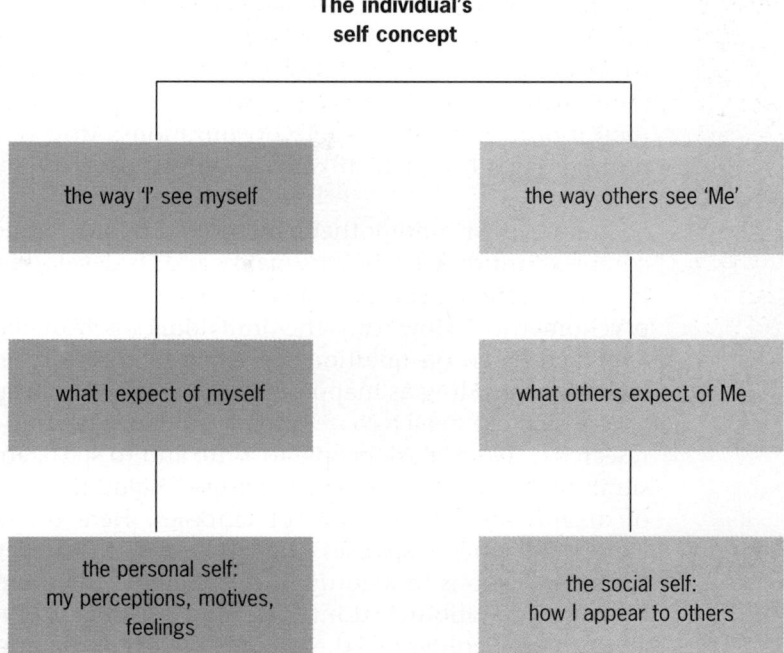

Figure 5.4: The two-sided self

Our self concept gives us a sense of meaning and consistency. But as our perceptions and motives change through new experiences and learning, our self concept and our behaviour change. Personality in this perspective, therefore, is not stable, as the self concept can be reorganized. We have perceptions of our qualities, abilities, attitudes, impulses and so on. If these perceptions are accurate, conscious, organized and accepted, then we can regard our self concept as successful in that it will lead to feelings of comfort, freedom from tension and of psychological adjustment. Well-adjusted individuals thus have flexible images of themselves that are open to change through new experiences.

Personality disorders can be caused by a failure to bring together experiences, motives and feelings into a consistent self concept. We usually behave in ways consistent with our self-images, and when we have new experiences or feelings that are inconsistent we either:

■ recognize the inconsistency and try to integrate the two sets of understanding – the healthy response; or

■ deny or distort one of the experiences, perhaps by putting the blame on someone or something else – an unhealthy defence mechanism.

'Maladjusted' individuals are those who perceive as threatening those experiences and feelings that are not consistent with their self concept. They deny and distort their experiences in such a way that their self-image does not match their real feelings or the nature of their experience. This leads to a build-up of psychological tension as more defence mechanisms are required to keep the truth at a distance.

Rogers argued that at the core of human personality is the desire to realize fully one's potential. To achieve this, however, the right social environment is required, one in which we are treated with what Rogers calls 'unconditional positive regard'. This means a setting in which one is accepted for whatever one is; in which one is valued, trusted, respected, even in the face of characteristics which others dislike. In this kind of environment, the individual is likely to become trusting, spontaneous and flexible, leading a rich and meaningful life with a harmonious self concept. However, this is far from the type of social environment typical of most contemporary organizations. Most of us face highly conditional positive regard, in which only a narrow range of thoughts and behaviours is accepted.

Compared with nomothetic methods, an idiographic approach appears to be a complex, untidy view of personality and its development. It has been influential in phenomenological research, but is conspicuous by its absence in contemporary psychometrics. How can the individual's self-understanding be studied? An approach based on questions designed by a researcher is problematic. You may reject that wording as inappropriate to *your* self concept.

We therefore need a route into an individual's mind that is independent of the researcher. We can ask people to write and to speak about themselves. These and similar techniques are in common use, including free association, interpretation of dreams and the analysis of fantasies. Here the individual has freedom of expression and responses are not tied to predetermined categories. The researcher's job is to identify in this material the themes that reveal the individual's preoccupations and interests, and personality. One successful technique for accessing the content of the mind is the **thematic apperception test**, or TAT.

This concept breaks our rule about not describing personality assessments as 'tests'. However, we have to be consistent with the literature. This is how the TAT works.

First, you are told that you are about to take a test of your creative writing. Then you are shown photographs or drawings, typically including people, and asked to write an imaginative story suggested by what you see. The images do not imply any particular story. Your imaginative accounts are then assessed in various ways. One of these concerns the assessment of **need for achievement** (*n*Ach). This is not a test of your creative or imaginative writing at all.

The assessment procedure first involves determining whether any of the characters in your story has an achievement goal. In other words, does somebody in your story want to perform better? This could involve doing something better than someone else, meeting or exceeding some self-imposed standard of excellence, doing something unique, or being involved in doing something well or successfully. Points are scored for the presence of these features in the story. The more achievement imagery, the higher the score.

The TAT was invented by Henry Murray in 1938 and was subsequently developed by David McClelland (1961; McClelland et al., 1976) as a means of measuring the strength of need for achievement. The TAT is also used to measure the needs for power and affiliation, using a similar scoring procedure, but looking for different imagery. In a full assessment, you would be asked to write stories about between four and 20 pictures.

What can short, creative stories about ambiguous pictures tell us about your distinctive and stable personality characteristics? The thematic apperception test is a **projective** assessment.

The label 'projective' is used because subjects project their personalities into the stories they write. The Rorschach test is a form of projective assessment which uses random inkblots instead of pictures or photographs. McClelland argues that it is reasonable to assume that the person with a strong concern with achievement is likely to write stories with lots of achievement imagery and themes. The evidence seems to support this view.

Need for achievement is important in an organizational context. People with low need for achievement are concerned more with security and status than with personal fulfilment, are preoccupied with their own ideas and feelings, worry

Thematic apperception test: an assessment in which the individual is shown ambiguous pictures and is asked to create stories of what may be happening in them.

Need for achievement (*n*Ach): a general concern with meeting standards of excellence, the desire to be successful in competition; the motivation to excel.

Projective test: an assessment based on abstract or ambiguous images, which the subject is asked to interpret by projecting feelings, preoccupations and motives into their responses.

Henry Alexander
Murray
(1893–1988)

David Clarence
McClelland
(1917–98)

more about their self-presentation than their performance, and prefer bright Scottish tartans. (The Buchanan tartan is bright red and yellow; the author does not wear it.)

People with high need for achievement have the following characteristics:

■ they prefer tasks in which they have to achieve a standard of excellence rather than simply carrying out routine activities;

■ they prefer jobs in which they get frequent and clear feedback on how well they are doing, to help them perform better;

■ they prefer activities that involve moderate risks of failure; high-risk activities lead to failure, low-risk activities do not provide opportunities to demonstrate ability;

■ they have a good memory for unfinished tasks and do not like to leave things incomplete;

■ they can be unfriendly and unsociable when they do not want others to get in the way of their performance;

■ they have a sense of urgency, appear to be in a hurry, to be working against time and have an inability to relax;

■ they prefer sombre Scottish tartans with lots of blues and greens; unobtrusive backgrounds allow them to stand out better.

Organizations want employees with drive, ambition and self-motivation. Can the TAT be used to identify these people? It is not a good assessment for this purpose. Although the detailed scoring is not obvious to the untrained, the definition of achievement imagery is close to popular understanding. So, when you know what the 'test' is all about, it is easy to fake your score. We have here the same problem as with objective questionnaires. Personality assessment scores are not necessarily good predictors of job performance.

The TAT faces other problems as an organizational selection tool. The output of the assessment is hard for the untrained eye to regard as 'objective data'. The scoring procedure involves some subjective interpretation. Expensive training is required in the full technical procedure to produce judges who can reach reliable assessments. With an objective questionnaire, anyone with the scoring key can calculate quickly and accurately the results.

McClelland argues that your achievement need can be increased by teaching you the scoring system, and by helping you to write high-scoring stories. This increases need for achievement by encouraging you to see and to understand daily life more vividly in achievement terms. This retraining in mental habits can thus be translated more readily into action. In other words, the TAT can be used as a personality assessment and also to change personality.

Nomothetic versus idiographic?

The two approaches to the study of personality presented here are summarized in table 5.9.

How should we choose between these perspectives? We can examine the logic of the arguments, consider how the evidence relates to and supports the theories, and consider the comprehensiveness of the explanations. We can resort to practical considerations and assess the methods used to treat personality disorders, and to analyze and predict behaviour. However, these forms of

Table 5.9: Nomothetic versus idiographic

The nomothetic approach	The idiographic approach
Has a positivist bias	Has a phenomenological bias
Is generalizing; emphasizes the discovery of laws of human behaviour	Is individualizing; emphasizes the richness and complexity of the unique individual
Is based on statistical study of large groups	Is based on intensive study of individuals
Uses objective questionnaires	Uses projective assessments (tests) and other written and spoken materials
Describes personality in terms of the individual's possession of traits, and trait clusters or personality types	Describes personality in terms of the individual's own understanding and interpretation of their identity
Views personality as composed of discrete and identifiable elements	Believes that personality has to be understood as an indivisible, intelligible whole
Believes that personality is primarily determined by heredity, biology, genetics	Believes that personality is primarily determined by social and cultural processes
Believes that personality is given at birth and cannot be altered	Believes that personality is adaptable, open to change through experience

judgement miss the point that these different approaches are based on widely conflicting views of human nature. The evidence is such as to leave us debating for a considerable time without satisfactory resolution. We thus have to resort to criteria such as:

- Which theory is more aesthetically pleasing?
- Which approach 'feels' right?
- How does each approach fit with my world view?

Another way to resolve this, however, is to regard these approaches as *complementary*. They offer two broad research strategies, each of which is capable of telling us about different aspects of human psychology. What each alone reveals is interesting, but partial. Perhaps we should use both approaches and not concentrate on one alone? However, contemporary employee assessment and selection methods ignore this advice, and use nomothetic methods.

Selection methods

Choosing the right candidate for a job, or for promotion, is a critical decision. Incorrect decisions lead to frustrated employees and poor performance. Selection procedures are costly and time-consuming, and it is expensive to repeat them to recover from errors.

A selection or a promotion decision is a prediction about the ability of a candidate to perform well in a particular job. Predictions are based on an understanding of the demands of the position to be filled, and on information about candidates. Traditionally, candidate information has come from application forms, the testimony of referees and interviews. The application form provides background, but is impersonal. Referees notoriously reveal only pleasant things about candidates. Research suggests that interviews can also be unreliable.

Psychometric methods promise to strengthen the objectivity of selection and promotion decisions by collecting systematically information that has predictive power. Applications of psychometrics developed rapidly in the last two decades of the twentieth century. There are now over 5,000 such tests and assessments in use.

When choosing a psychometric assessment, for any purpose, a number of criteria are relevant, particularly those concerned with **reliability** and *validity*.

If the same group of people is given the same assessment or test on two or more occasions and the results are the same or similar, then the assessment can be described as reliable. This method for establishing reliability is known as 'test–retest reliability'.

The *validity* of a test or assessment concerns the extent to which it actually measures what it sets out to measure. There are different types of validity, the main ones being *face validity* (does it look right?), *construct validity* (does it relate to other similar measures?), and **predictive validity**. In employee selection, predictive validity is critical.

The key question is, can we predict job performance from personality assessments? This question is readily answered using the following method. First, assess a large applicant group. Second, hire them all regardless of their scores. Third, wait for an appropriate period (say five years). Finally, assess their performance, to see whether those with 'good' profiles became high performers, or not. If they are, then you have a valid test.

The evidence shows varying estimates for the predictive validity of personality assessments, but most suggest that it is low. If a test or assessment score predicts job performance accurately, the predictive validity coefficient will be 1.0. If there is no correlation, the coefficient is zero. Table 5.10 shows the estimates for different types of assessment.

Reliability: the degree to which an assessment or test produces consistent results when repeated.

Predictive validity: the extent to which scores on an assessment or test accurately predict behaviours such as job performance.

Table 5.10: Predictive validity of different employee assessment methods

Measure	Predictive validity
astrology	0.0
graphology	0.0
references	0.13
unstructured interviews	0.31
personality assessments	0.38
biodata	0.40
assessment centres – performance	0.41
ability tests	0.54
work samples	0.55
structured interviews	0.62
assessment centres – promotion	0.68

Based on N. Anderson and V. Shackleton, *Successful Selection Interviewing*, Blackwell, Oxford, 1993.

There are two points to note from these figures. First, any method which has a validity coefficient of less than 0.5 is going to be wrong more often than it is right. Second, personality assessments have relatively low predictive validity. The potential cost of recruitment error has been estimated to lie between £5,000 and £50,000, depending on the seniority of the appointment and the potential for error should the wrong person be hired (Chartered Institute for Personnel and Development, 2001).

Stop and Criticize

The links between personality factors and job performance are difficult to establish. Why should this be the case? Explain your reasoning and share this with colleagues.

If you believe that psychometrics cannot make accurate predictions, then you belong to the two-thirds of job candidates who think the same way (Anderson, 1999).

Personality transplants?

In 1994, a merchant bank in London decided that, to compete in a rapidly changing context, it had to change its autocratic 'command and control' style of management and develop participative team-work instead. One senior manager, 'Mr X', responsible for £500 million of profits a year, had problems shaking off his traditional style: 'He never opened a door with his hands, just kicked it in.' Other staff were afraid to approach or to challenge him. So, the bank hired a consultant to address the problem:

■ First, Mr X was ordered to see the consultant, who met him at 9.00 pm, when Mr X finished work.

■ Mr X completed a series of personality assessments, which showed him to be independent, single-minded, determined, forceful and tough on others.

■ Ten colleagues of Mr X were asked to provide their assessment of him, and they pointed out that he was abrasive and insensitive, that he did not delegate to junior colleagues, and that he humiliated people in meetings.

■ The consultant produced a 25-page report summarizing these assessments.

How did Mr X respond? He enjoyed the report and regarded the comments as 'a problem to solve'. To improve his interpersonal skills, the consultant asked Mr X to keep a diary of his exchanges with others, noting when and how he got into arguments. These incidents were then discussed with the consultant, to demonstrate how the same results could have been achieved by being less abrasive and impulsive. Part of his problem, apparently, was due to overwork. He worked twelve hours a day, six days a week, and took only one week's holiday a year. Mr X had problems delegating because he wished to protect a less than competent assistant, and so did the work himself. He was eventually persuaded to 'let the assistant go'.

Did the 'personality transplant' work? The process lasted two years, at the end of which Mr X was less abrasive, worked as a team member and became more relaxed about work and delegation, and others found him more approachable. The consultant involved argues that the behavioural transformation is stable (implying a personality change) and that Mr X is an effective manager without his traditional aggressive style.

Based on Andrew Rogers, 'Personality transplant tames the boss', *The Sunday Times*, 13 June 1999, p. 7.19.

On the available research evidence, the results of personality assessments should never be used as the sole basis of a selection decision. While this may be a useful complement to other methods, personality assessments are poor performance predictors because:

■ people are flexible and multifaceted, able to develop new skills and behaviours and to adapt to new circumstances; personality assessment captures a fragment of the whole;

■ most jobs are multifaceted in their demands on skill and knowledge, and traits which enhance competence in one task may not improve overall job performance;

- performance depends on many factors: ability, luck, training, payment systems, physical facilities, supervisory style, organization structure, company policies and procedures;

- most jobs change over time, so predictions based on current measures are unreliable;

- nomothetic methods work with populations and large samples, against which individual profiles can be compared; they are not designed to make predictions about individuals;

- in clinical and research settings, most people give honest answers about personality, but these assessment are relatively easy to falsify when job or promotion is at stake.

Structured or situational interviewing is an approach with a relatively high predictive validity. Candidates are presented with a series of work-based problems and asked how they would respond. Situations and questions are based on job analysis which focuses on critical knowledge, skills and abilities. Neal Schmitt and David Chan (1998, p. 31) give examples of situational interview questions used for selecting emergency telephone operators:

1. Imagine that you tried to help a stranger, for example, with traffic directions, or to get up after a fall, and that person blamed you for his misfortune or yelled at you. What would you do?

2. Suppose a friend calls you and is extremely upset. Apparently, her child has been injured. She begins to tell you, in a hysterical manner, all about her difficulty in getting her baby-sitters, what the child is wearing, what words the child can speak, and so on. What would you do?

3. How would you react if you were a salesclerk, waitress or gas station attendant and a customer talked back to you, indicating that you should have known something you did not, or telling you that you were not waiting on him fast enough?

Candidates' responses are rated for communication skills, emotional control and judgement, and can be compared against the actual behaviour of high-level performers in this occupation. It is difficult for candidates to cheat or to practise their responses to a situational interview, not knowing what specific behaviours and replies are being sought by assessors. Companies using these methods report a high success rate (Maurer, Sue-Chan and Latham, 1999).

Robert Sternberg (1988, 1999) has designed measures of successful intelligence, that is the ability to operate effectively in a given environment. Sternberg claims that successfully intelligent people have the three kinds of ability shown in table 5.11. The techniques used to assess this concept in practice are similar to those used in situational interviewing. Sternberg (1999, p. 31) reports this example:

I have developed a test in which a candidate for a sales job would make a phone call and try to sell a product to an examiner. During the call, the candidate has to reply to standardized objections to the sale. Responses to test items are compared against the responses of designated experts in each field, and scoring is done by comparative profile analysis [comparing the profile of the candidate with that of the expert].

Table 5.11: Dimensions of successful intelligence

analytical	analyzing, evaluating, making judgements on abstract data removed from day-to-day practicalities
creative	finding novel, high-quality solutions, going 'beyond the given', 'making do in a rapidly changing world'
practical	the solution of real problems, application of common sense, not dependent on educational qualifications

The most appropriate combination of techniques for employee assessment is through assessment centres, which were first used during the Second World War by the UK War Office Selection Boards. Groups of around six to ten candidates are brought together for one to three days. They are presented, individually and as a group, with a variety of exercises, tests of ability, personality assessments, interviews, work samples, team problem-solving, and written tasks. Their activities are observed and scored. This approach is useful for selection and promotion, staff development, talent spotting, and for career guidance and counselling. The evidence suggests that this combination of techniques significantly improves the probability of selecting and promoting appropriate candidates.

Critics of assessment centres point to the investment in time and money they require to design and operate. Qualified assessors are necessary, and a lack of senior management commitment to the process can give both assessors and candidates inappropriate signals. Methods must be specifically tailored to each organization's needs. The focus on observable and measurable aspects of behaviour overlooks less apparent and less easily assessed skills.

Advocates argue that the information collected is comprehensive and comparable, and candidates have opportunities to demonstrate capabilities unlikely to

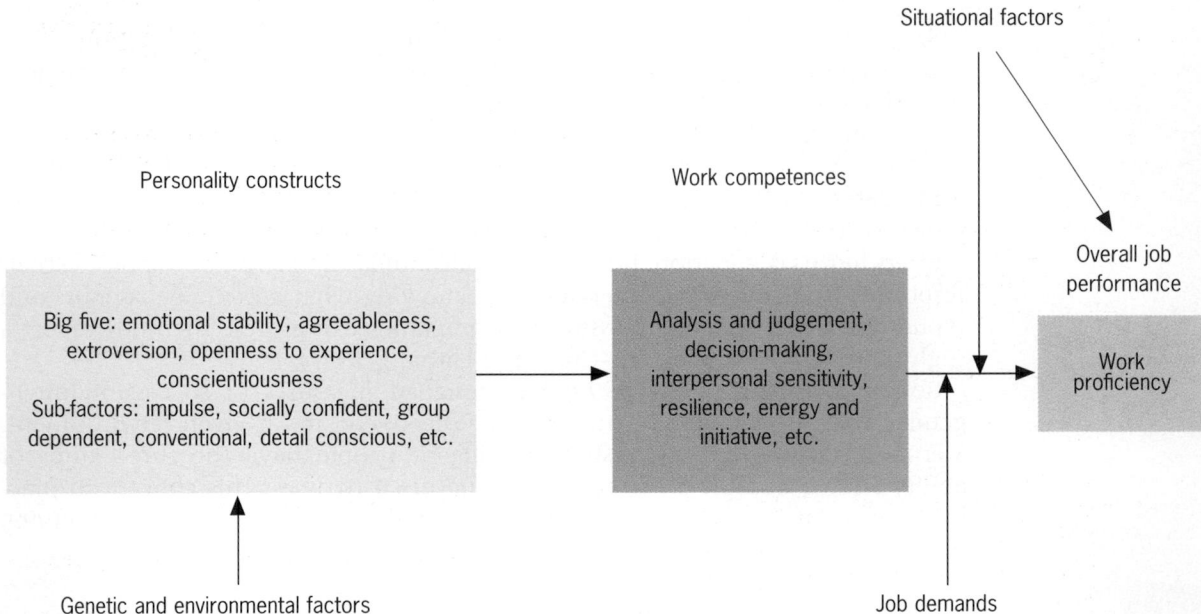

Figure 5.5: Personality and job performance
From I.T. Robertson, 'Personality and personnel selection', in C.L. Cooper and D.M. Rousseau (eds), *Trends in Organizational Behaviour*, 1994, p. 8. Copyright 1994 © John Wiley & Sons Limited. Reproduced with permission.

appear in interviews. The self-knowledge gained can also be valuable to candidates. It is claimed that a well-designed assessment centre using a variety of methods can achieve a predictive validity of 0.8 with respect to job performance (Chartered Institute of Personnel and Development, 2001).

Does personality assessment have a future? The relationships between personality constructs and job performance are modelled by Ivan Robertson (1994), shown in figure 5.5. Robertson argues that the links between personality, performance and career success must be weak. There are too many factors to allow us to make reliable predictions. The model identifies the demands of the job, and factors in the organizational context that can influence behaviour at work independently of, or in interaction with, personality. Robertson argues, however, that it is possible to relate personality measures to specific competencies, such as judgement, resilience, sensitivity and energy. This argument has intuitive appeal. He claims that the evidence supports this view, and that this is where the future research agenda lies. He concludes that 'When the personality constructs involved are clear and thought is given to the expected link between these constructs and work behaviour, it is likely that worthwhile information may be derived from personality measurement' (Robertson, 1994, p. 85).

Recap

1. *Distinguish between type, trait and self theories of personality.*

   - Type theories use a range of perspectives (Hippocrates, Sheldon, Jung) to classify individuals using a limited number of personality categories.

   - Trait theories, based on a nomothetic perspective (Eysenck, Costa and McCrae), seek to profile the individual's personality across a number of different facets.

   - Self theories, based on an idiographic perspective (Cooley, Mead), seek to describe unique individual personalities.

2. *Identify the strengths and limitations of formal methods of personality assessment.*

   - Formal methods offer objective and comprehensive assessments of personality. But they are impersonal and based on group norms, and don't capture individual uniqueness.

   - Formal methods provide further objective information about job candidates, but the links between personality assessment scores and job performance are weak.

3. *Explain the uses and limitations of objective questionnaires and projective tests as measures of personality.*

   - Objective questionnaires are easy to score and offer quantitative rigour, but they can only be interpreted using group norms; individual scores are meaningless.

   - Projective tests capture the richness and uniqueness of the individual, but they have complex scoring, are subjective and individual results cannot easily be compared.

4. *Explain the relationship between personality and stress, and identify appropriate individual and organizational stress management strategies.*

   - Type A personalities (competitive, impatient) are more stress prone than Type B personalities (easygoing, relaxed).

   - Individuals can develop physical and psychological resilience and coping skills.

   - Management has to reduce or remove work-related stressors (job design, management style, adverse working conditions, excessive workload).

5. *Evaluate the benefits and problems of psychometric assessment as a tool to assist management decision-making, particularly in selection.*

   - Psychometrics offer objective, systematic, comprehensive and quantitative information. They are also useful in career guidance, counselling and development.

   - Individual scores are meaningless outside the context of group norms.

   - It is difficult to predict job performance from a personality profile.

   - Personality assessment can identify strengths in specific areas of competence.

6. *Assess realistically the main characteristics of your own personality.*

   - Current thinking profiles personality on 'the big five' trait clusters of Openness, Conscientiousness, Extraversion, Agreeableness and Neuroticism (OCEAN). Self theories argue that the self concept is what is important, not your test scores.

Revision

1. What is 'psychometrics', and what are the main organizational applications? What are the benefits and drawbacks of psychometric assessment in organizational contexts?

2. We all seem to be good implicit personality theorists, but we also seem to be poor judges of personality. How can these two claims be reconciled?

3. What is 'personality' and why is this term difficult to define unambiguously and with precision?

4. What is the difference between 'type' and 'trait' theories of personality? Using at least one example of a trait theory, explain the benefits and problems associated with this approach to personality assessment.

5. Explain the distinction between nomothetic and idiographic perspectives on personality assessment. How do idiographic methods approach the assessment of personality, and what are the advantages and drawbacks of these methods?

Springboard

Chartered Institute of Personnel and Development, 2002, *Quick Facts: Stress*, August, CIPD, London.

Defines and explains the significance of stress, identifies the behavioural signs that indicate someone may be suffering, outlines management strategies for dealing with stress, and provides useful suggestions for further reading, theoretical and practical.

Cooper, C. (ed.), 2000a, *Theories of Organizational Stress*, Oxford University Press, Oxford.

A widely informed and authoritative 'single source' review of various theories of stress, including causes (downsizing, outsourcing, short-term and part-time working, teleworking) and implications (sickness, absence, turnover, premature death, burnout, decreased productivity). Also discusses management interventions.

Doherty, N. and Tyson, S., 1998, *Mental Well Being in the Workplace: A Resource Pack for Management Training and Development*, Health and Safety Executive, London.

Reinforces the argument that stress is an organizational problem, not a private, individual issue, and that management needs to address it as such. Also provides systematic practical management advice.

Goleman, D., 1995, *Emotional Intelligence: Why It Can Matter More Than IQ*, Bloomsbury, London.

The book which turned the concept of emotional intelligence into a management fad, and turned Daniel Goleman into an international management guru. A deceptively easy read, but entertaining if you like this kind of style. One major problem with the argument is that if you are not committed to the organization, to teamworking and to high performance, then you lack emotional intelligence. Is that a valid perspective?

Maslach, C. and Leiter, M.P., 1999, *The Truth about Burnout*, Jossey-Bass, San Francisco.

Argues that, while stress is an employee problem, 'burnout' is a problem particularly associated with management positions, caused by delayering, downsizing, work intensification and demands for increased flexibility, customer retention and profitability. However, they also argue that this is an organizational management problem, not an individual one, requiring organizational solutions.

Pinker, S., 2002, *The Blank Slate: The Modern Denial of Human Nature*, Allen Lane/Penguin, London.

Pinker explores the genetic roots of individual character, combining evolutionary biology and a computational theory of the mind. He presents a complex argument for 'preprogramming' with regard to a range of capabilities on which behaviour depends. For example, while we are not born with a language 'hard wired' into our brains, the evidence shows that a sophisticated 'language learning module' is 'pre-wired', enabling infants to absorb the language that they hear being used around them.

Sternberg, R., 1999, 'Survival of the fit test', *People Management*, vol. 4, no. 24, 10 December, pp. 29–31.

Sternberg is critical of the lack of predictive power of psychometrics and of the lack of development in this field. Proposes instead the development of tests of 'successful intelligence', defined as the ability to function effectively in a given context, so the precise definition of this concept differs from one setting to another (pp. 31–3).

Home viewing

Glengarry Glen Ross (1992, director James Foley) is based in a Chicago real-estate office. To boost flagging sales, the 'downtown' manager Blake (played by Alec Baldwin) introduces a sales contest. First prize is a Cadillac Eldorado, second prize is a set of steak knives, third prize is dismissal. The sales staff include Ricky Roma (Al Pacino), Shelley Levene (Jack Lemmon), George Aaronow (Alan Arkin) and Dave Moss (Ed Harris). In the first ten minutes of the film, note how Blake in his 'motivational pep talk' conforms to the stereotype of the extravert, competitive, successful 'macho' salesman. Observe the effects of his 'pep talk' on the behaviour of the sales team. Does Blake offer a stereotype which salespeople should copy? What is Blake's view of human nature? From a postmodern perspective, the film portrays the construction of individual identity through a 'performance' conditioned by organizational context. This contrasts with a view of identity as genetically determined.

OB in literature

Bret Easton Ellis, *American Psycho*, Random House/Pan Books, New York/London, 1991.

How does the psychopath appear 'ordinary' to casual observers and fit effortlessly into society? What 'normal' personality traits has the author given his 'hero', Patrick Bateman? Here is a character with enormous intellect, but lacking in what Daniel Goleman (1995, 1998) describes as 'emotional intelligence'.

David Ireland, *The Chosen*, Random House, Sydney, 1997.

In drawing personality portraits of 52 diverse Australians in the town of Lost River, what aspects of their lives, appearance and behaviour does the novelist use? Note the personality traits and types described in each portrait. Are they Type A or Type B? Extravert or introvert? Neurotic or stable? Can you give each character an OCEAN profile?

Chapter exercises

1: How stress-prone are you?

Objectives The objectives of this exercise are:

1. To give you an opportunity to assess your personality in terms of propensity to suffer stress-related disease.

2. To assess critically this type of personality assessment method.

Briefing This questionnaire is designed to identify whether you have a Type A or a Type B personality. Here are eight pairs of statements describing aspects of personality and behaviour. For each pair, decide which is more accurate as a description of you, and circle the appropriate point on the seven-point rating scale. Be honest in your ratings. There are no 'right' or 'wrong' answers to this questionnaire.

I am casual about appointments	1 2 3 4 5 6 7	I am never late
I am not competitive	1 2 3 4 5 6 7	I am very competitive
I never feel rushed, even under pressure	1 2 3 4 5 6 7	I always feel short of time
I take things one at a time	1 2 3 4 5 6 7	I try to do too many things at once
I concentrate on finishing what I am doing right now	1 2 3 4 5 6 7	I am always thinking about what I am going to do next
I take my time, do things slowly	1 2 3 4 5 6 7	I do things, even walking and eating, fast
I like to express my feelings	1 2 3 4 5 6 7	I prefer to keep my feelings private
I have many interests	1 2 3 4 5 6 7	I have few interests outside work

When you have finished, calculate your score by totalling the numbers you have circled and multiplying that sum by three. Put your score in this table:

Interpretation

If your points total is:	Your personality type is:
less than 50	B
50 to 89	B+
90 to 119	A−
120 to 145	A
more than 145	A+

Discussion

| | tick the appropriate column | | |
	low	medium	high
How would you rate the reliability of this assessment?			
How would you rate the face validity of this assessment?			
How would you rate the predictive validity of this assessment?			

2: The Big Five Locator

Objectives

1. To assess your personality profile on 'the big five' personality trait clusters.

2. To assess the value of this kind of personality assessment in career counselling and employment selection.

Briefing

A 'big five' personality assessment involves either a short questionnaire (the NEO–FFI with 60 questions covering the five factors) or the 'full facet' version (the NEO–PI–R with 240 questions covering all 30 traits). These assessments can also be used for management development, in leadership and interpersonal skills, and for the assessment of conflict management and decision-making styles (Howard and Howard, 1993).

The Big Five Locator, on the other hand, is an easy-to-use instrument for assessing an individual's personality profile. It can also be used to explore and resolve team conflict. It is presented here for demonstration and discussion, and should be regarded as providing only an approximate measure of individual traits and individual differences.

On the centre scale, circle the point which most accurately describes you between each of the two terms presented. If the two terms are equally accurate in their description, then mark the middle point.

1	Eager	5	4	3	2	1	Calm
2	Prefer being with others	5	4	3	2	1	Prefer being alone
3	A dreamer	5	4	3	2	1	No-nonsense
4	Courteous	5	4	3	2	1	Abrupt
5	Neat	5	4	3	2	1	Messy
6	C autious	5	4	3	2	1	Confident
7	Optimistic	5	4	3	2	1	Pessimistic
8	Theoretical	5	4	3	2	1	Practical
9	G enerous	5	4	3	2	1	Selfish
10	Decisive	5	4	3	2	1	Open-ended

11	Discouraged	5	4	3	2	1	Upbeat
12	Exhibitionist	5	4	3	2	1	Private
13	Follow imagination	5	4	3	2	1	Follow authority
14	Warm	5	4	3	2	1	Cold
15	Stay focused	5	4	3	2	1	Easily distracted
16	Easily embarrassed	5	4	3	2	1	Don't give a damn
17	Outgoing	5	4	3	2	1	Cool
18	Seek novelty	5	4	3	2	1	Seek routine
19	Team player	5	4	3	2	1	Independent
20	A preference for order	5	4	3	2	1	Comfortable with chaos
21	Distractible	5	4	3	2	1	Unflappable
22	Conversational	5	4	3	2	1	Thoughtful
23	Comfortable with ambiguity	5	4	3	2	1	Prefer things clear-cut
24	Trusting	5	4	3	2	1	Sceptical
25	On time	5	4	3	2	1	Procrastinate

Scoring Calculate your **negative emotionality** score by adding the numbers you circled on the first row of each five-line grouping: row 1 + row 6 + row 11 + row 16 + row 21:
score = _____

Calculate your **extraversion** score by adding the numbers you circled on the second row of each five-line grouping: row 2 + row 7 + row 12 + row 17 + row 22:
score = _____

Calculate your **openness** score by adding the numbers you circled on the third row of each five-line grouping: row 3 + row 8 + row 13 + row 18 + row 23:
score = _____

Calculate your **agreeableness** score by adding the numbers you circled on the fourth row of each five-line grouping: row 4 + row 9 + row 14 + row 19 + row 24:
score = _____

Calculate your **conscientiousness** score by adding the numbers you circled on the last row of each five-line grouping: row 5 + row 10 + row 15 + row 20 + row 25:
score = _____

Enter your five scores in the following table, noting the different order (back to OCEAN).

trait	score
openness	_____
conscientiousness	_____
extroversion	_____
agreeableness	_____
negative emotionality	_____

When you have calculated your five scores, transfer them to this interpretation sheet by putting a cross at the approximate point on each scale:

Big Five Locator score interpretation

low openness:	preserver	moderator	explorer	high openness:
practical, conservative, efficient, expert	10	15	20	curious, liberal, impractical, likes novelty
low conscientiousness:	flexible	balanced	focused	high conscientiousness:
spontaneous, fun-loving, experimental, unorganized	10	15	20	dependable, organized, disciplined, cautious, stubborn
low extroversion:	introvert	ambivert	extrovert	high extroversion:
private, independent, works alone, reserved	10	15	20	assertive, sociable, warm, optimistic
low agreeableness:	challenger	negotiator	adapter	high agreeableness:
sceptical, tough, aggressive, self-interested	10	15	20	trusting, humble, altruistic, team player
low negative emotionality:	resilient	responsive	reactive	high negative emotionality:
secure, unflappable, unresponsive, guilt-free	10	15	20	excitable, worrying, reactive, alert

Discussion

1. How accurate, in your view, is your personality profile as revealed by this assessment?

2. Does this assessment indicate that you have one or more 'dominant' traits?

3. Given your profile, what jobs or occupations would you *not* be suitable for?

4. How helpful is this personality assessment in enabling a manager to make predictions about a potential employee's future job performance?

5. How valuable is this personality assessment in enabling a careers guidance counsellor effectively to advise clients on suitable and unsuitable career options?

This exercise is based on:

Pierce J. Howard, Phyllis L. Medina and Jane Mitchell Howard, 'The Big Five Locator: a quick assessment tool for consultants and trainers', *The 1996 Annual: Volume 1, Training*, Pfeiffer & Company, San Diego, CA, 1996, pp. 107–22.

Chapter 6 Communication

Key concepts

communication process   non-verbal behaviour
coding   high-context culture
decoding   low-context culture
perceptual filters   impression management
noise   communication climate
feedback

Learning outcomes

When you have read this chapter, you should be able to define those key concepts in your own words, and you should also be able to:

1. Explain the main components of the interpersonal communication process.
2. Identify the main barriers to effective interpersonal communication.
3. Understand the effective use of different questioning techniques, conversation controls and listening skills.
4. Explain the nature and significance of non-verbal behaviour.
5. Understand the nature and mechanisms of impression management skills and techniques.
6. Understand the ways in which corporate communication can be used to manipulate understanding and encourage compliance with management directions.

Why study communication?

Communication is central to understanding organizational behaviour for several reasons:

1. Communication effectiveness influences organizational performance and individual career prospects.

2. Very few people work alone, and the job of most managers involves interacting with other people, often for more than 90 per cent of their time.

3. Although the topic is relatively well understood, communication continues to be regarded as a problem in many organizations.

4. In an increasingly diverse multicultural society, sensitivity to the norms and expectations of other cultures is vital to effective cross-cultural communication.

5. New technology may radically change patterns of organizational communication.

Organizational communication is now regarded as a discipline in its own right, with its own research traditions (Jablin and Putnam, 2001). We can claim that everything significant that happens in an organization is underpinned by communication: hiring and training employees, providing feedback, purchasing supplies, solving problems, dealing with customers, deciding strategy. It can also be demonstrated, however, that organizations systematically inhibit communication through hierarchical structures, power and status differences, the design and gendered differentiation of jobs, the nature of (part-time, temporary) employment contracts, physical layouts, and rules. The relationship between organization and communication is not straightforward, and many managers regard communication as a major problem.

It has long been recognized that most managers spend most of their time in meetings and in conversation – talking and listening, networking and influencing, gathering information and negotiating. The work of Henry Mintzberg (1973), for example, emphasized the monitoring, informational, decision-making and interpersonal aspects of the work of chief executives.

John Kotter (1982, 1999) found that most general managers spend most of their time in conversation, often on topics not directly related to the business, but central to maintaining networks and relationships, and to developing goals and action plans.

Globalization and greater international mobility mean that we are now likely to find ourselves working alongside people from other countries and cultures. Different cultures have differing norms concerning how conversations should be handled, including appropriate greetings, level of formality, the use of eye contact, suitable topics for discussion, the physical distance between speakers and the interpretation of gestures. Sensitivity to and understanding of cultural diversity has become increasingly important.

How Europe communicates

In France there is an emphasis on written reports rather than oral presentations and on formality in work communication. However, informal networking and 'politicking' are important in actually making things happen.

The Dutch, on the other hand, practise widespread dissemination of information and 'behind the scenes' influence is discouraged.

In Germany, there is a tendency for everything to be put in writing (email flourishes), while use of the telephone is inhibited.

In contrast, in Italy, there is extensive use of all personal channels of communication, including telephone and email, that can be used to bypass the formal structure.

In Spain, communication is mainly oral, face-to-face and one-to-one, especially with the boss.

From Maureen Guirdham, *Interactive Behaviour at Work*, Financial Times/Prentice Hall, Harlow (third edition), 2002, p. 277.

Technological innovations such as the internet and video conferencing have not eliminated the need for people to meet to exchange information. Where information is easily codified (a booking, a bank statement) and transactions are simple (paying a bill, buying a ticket), an exchange can be completed online. However, where transactions are complex and based on judgements ('what is your opinion of this deal?', 'could we do it this way?'), where emotions and feelings are as significant as facts and figures, the social and geographical context, the quality of relationships and interpersonal trust are crucial:

> One of the mysteries of the wired (and wireless) world is that proximity still counts. In spite of September 11th, and the predictions that everyone would travel less and have fewer meetings, people still want to gather to do deals, to drum up new ideas and to court customers. Indeed, in some ways, physical presence counts even more than it used to. Tony Venables, an economist at the London School of Economics, believes that businesses that thrive on face-to-face communications – or what some call F2F – now account for a growing share of economic activity. (*The Economist*, 'Press the flesh, not the keyboard', 24 August 2002, pp. 56–7)

Janet Fulk and Lori Collins-Jarvis (2001) estimate than less than 15 per cent of management meetings are currently mediated by video conferencing, computer conferencing or group support technologies, but claim that mediated meetings will become more common as the technology develops and as new organizational forms generate demand.

Computer-mediated communication (CMC) includes email, instant messaging and computer conferencing, and is a developing research field. Maureen Guirdham (2002) notes that CMC has several characteristics. Non-verbal or 'body language' cues are less important, fears of interpersonal communication can be overcome, receivers are empowered with regard to when and whether to respond, status differences have limited impact, more openness in communication can result, and CMC is widely regarded as democratic and subversive. Research also suggests that CMC benefits those with powerful language styles, can lead to inappropriate openness, can encourage the convergence of attitudes in a user community, and can reduce levels of group identification unless interactions are prolonged. Much depends on how these technologies develop, and the organizational uses to which they are devoted.

SQUAWKS

Communication between different occupational groups can be difficult. SQUAWKS, for example, are problems noted by United States Air Force pilots and left for maintenance crews to fix before their next flight. Here are some complaints logged by pilots and the replies from the maintenance crews.

pilot complaint	maintenance crew response
Test flight okay, except auto land very rough	Auto land not installed on this aircraft
DME volume unbelievably loud	Volume set to more believable level
Friction locks cause throttle levers to stick	That's what they're there for
Number three engine missing	Engine found on right wing after brief search
Target radar hums	Reprogrammed target radar with the words
Aircraft handles funny	Aircraft warned to straighten up and be serious
Dead bugs on windshield	Live bugs on order
Left inside main tyre almost needs replacement	Almost replaced left inside main tyre
Evidence of leak on right main landing gear	Evidence removed
IFF inoperative	IFF always inoperative in OFF mode
Something loose in cockpit	Something tightened in cockpit

From *Focus*, May 1999, p. 18, www.focusmag.co.uk. Reprinted by permission of the publisher.

A model of interpersonal communication: coding and decoding

Conversation: a competitive sport in which the first person to draw breath is declared the listener.

In most cultures, conversation is a social imperative in which silences are discouraged (Finland is different). Normally, as soon as one person stops talking, another takes their turn. The currency of conversation is information. We ask you the time. You tell us the time. Information has been transmitted. Interpersonal communication has been achieved. However, communication is more subtle and interesting than this illustration suggests.

Communication process: the transmission of information, and the exchange of meaning, between at least two people.

We concentrate first on interpersonal communication, because of its significance in understanding organizational behaviour. A more detailed study would recognize the importance of other aspects of communication, including the use of different media, networks and interorganizational communication. The principles that we will explore, however, have wide application. For the moment, let us focus on 'one-on-one' or 'F2F' communication, and examine more carefully our definition of the **communication process**.

Stop and Criticize

We all have experience of ineffective communication. Either the other person misunderstood what you had to say, or you misunderstood what they were tying to tell you. Remember the last time this happened? What went wrong? Can you establish the cause or causes of that communication failure? Share your analysis with colleagues and establish whether there are common causes.

We do not receive communication passively. We process messages to interpret or to *decode* them. To the extent that we interpret communication from others in the manner they intended, and they in turn interpret our communication accurately, then we can claim that our communication is effective. However, communication is an error-prone process.

Communication is an error-prone process

I rang the bell of a small bed-and-breakfast place, whereupon a lady appeared at an upstairs window. 'What do you want?', she asked. 'I want to stay here,' I replied. 'Well, stay there then,' she said and banged the window shut.

Chick Murray, Scottish comedian

Interpersonal communication typically involves much more than the simple transmission of information. Pay close attention to the next person who asks you what time it is. You will often be able to tell something about how they are feeling and about why they need to know, if they are in a hurry, perhaps, or if they are anxious or nervous, or bored with waiting. In other words, their question has a purpose or a meaning. Although it is not always stated directly, we can usually infer that meaning from the context and from their behaviour.

The same considerations apply to your response. Your reply suggests, at least, a willingness to be helpful, may imply friendship, and may also indicate that you share the same concern as the person asking the question (we are going to be late;

context

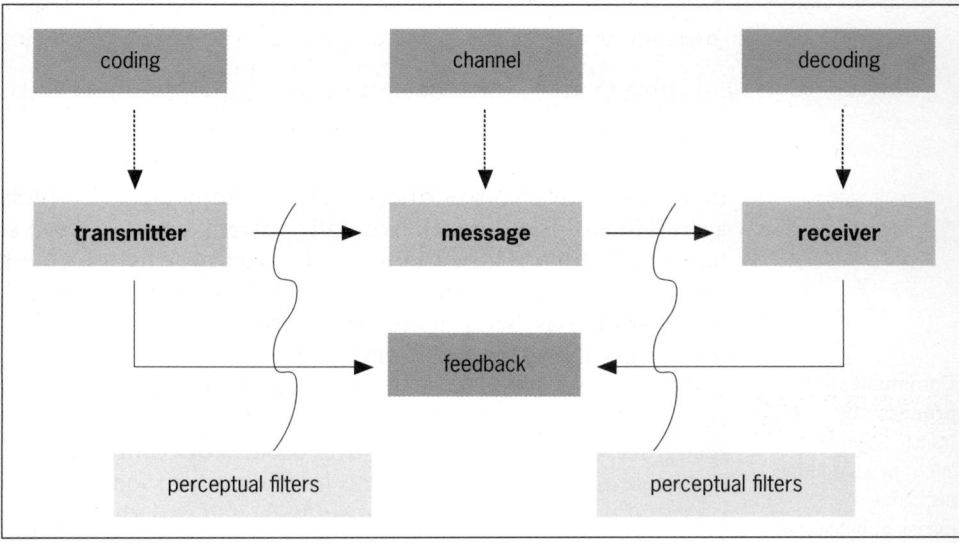

context

Figure 6.1: Exchanging meaning: a model of the communication process

Coding: the stage in the interpersonal communication process in which the transmitter chooses how to express a message for transmission to someone else.

Decoding: the stage in the interpersonal communication process in which the recipient interprets a message transmitted to them by someone else.

Perceptual filters: individual characteristics, predispositions and preoccupations that interfere with the effective transmission and receipt of messages.

when will this film start?). However, your reply can also indicate frustration and annoyance: 'five minutes after the last time you asked me!' Communication therefore involves more than the transmission of information. Interpersonal communication is a process that involves the exchange of meaning.

This process of exchange is illustrated in figure 6.1 which identifies the main elements in the interpersonal communication process. This model is based on the seminal work of Claude Shannon and Warren Weaver (1949), who were concerned with signal processing in electronic systems, rather than with the organizational communication issues explored here.

At the heart of this model, we have a transmitter sending a message to a receiver. We will assume that the channel is face-to-face, rather than over a telephone or through a letter or a video conference or electronic mail. It is useful to think of the way in which the transmitter phrases and expresses the message as a **coding** process; the transmitter chooses words, and also how the message will be expressed (loud and with exasperation, quiet and in a friendly manner, for example). We can say that communication has been successful if the message is accurately **decoded** by the receiver: did they understand the language used and appreciate the exasperation or friendship? We each have our own **perceptual filters** which can interfere with accurate decoding, such as predispositions to hear, or not to hear, particular types of information, and preoccupations which divert our attention elsewhere.

This is a useful way of examining the communication process because it highlights the problems that arise and points to solutions. There are many ways in which coding and decoding can go wrong; some common terms can lead to misunderstandings:

Term	Popular use	Dictionary definition
decimate	devastate	cut by 10 per cent
exotic	colourful, glamorous	from another country
aggravate	to annoy, to irritate	to make worse
clinical	cold, impersonal	caring, at the bedside of the sick
avid	keen, enthusiastic	greedy, desirous

The branch manager who receives from head office an instruction to 'decimate' her or his salesforce would thus be advised to check the original coding of the message before taking action. Using the dictionary definition of the word 'exotic' implies that Daewoo, Hyundai, Skoda and Isuzu sell exotic motor cars in Britain. To be successful, therefore, transmitters and receivers in the communication process need to share a common 'codebook'.

Language is also used to 'soften' or disguise unpleasant events. Employees being made redundant, for example, may be 'given the pink slip', 'downsized', 'right-sized', 'delayered', invited to 'take gardening leave', to 'spend more time with the family', or to 'put their careers on hold'. They may also be 'counselled on', 'repositioned', urged to 'develop their careers elsewhere', or to 'explore other opportunities for their talents', but are rarely 'given the chop'.

Stop and Criticize	From your experience, what other terms and expressions create coding and decoding problems?
	Identify specific examples – which can sometimes be humorous (like the man who asked for wild duck in a restaurant: 'I don't have wild duck, sir', replied the waiter. 'But I can annoy one for you').

The communication process is further complicated by the perceptual filters which affect what we say, and which in turn affect what we hear and how we hear it. When you asked what time it was, did you 'hear' the frustration or friendship in the response? Or did you simply focus on the time issue because that was more important to you? The transmitter of a message has motives, objectives, personality traits, values, biases and prejudices, which colour the content and expression of communication. We decide the information we wish to reveal, and to withhold or conceal from others. We do not always perform this filtering consciously. Similarly, at the receiving end, perceptual filtering can affect what is heard, what is decoded, what is not decoded, and the way in which the message is understood.

There is a further complicating factor: the physical, social and cultural context. The casual remark by a colleague across a restaurant table ('we could all be redundant by Christmas') may be dismissed. The same casual remark by a colleague across an office desk can be a source of considerable alarm. An innocent gesture in one culture causes offence in another. The style and content of our conversation depends often on our relationships with others. Status differences colour our communication. We do not reveal to the boss what we discuss with colleagues. The style and content of communication can change in a striking manner when organizational relationships are 'suspended', such as during an office party.

Noise: factors extraneous to the communication process which interfere with or distract attention from the transmission and reception of the intended meaning.

Electronics engineers use the term **noise** to refer to anything which interferes with a signal in the communication process.

Interpersonal communication suffers from noise, a term which covers more than just the sound of machinery, telephones and other people talking. Noise includes coding and decoding difficulties and errors, perceptual filters, anything else that interferes with the integrity of our chosen channel, and issues arising from our relationships with others. Our motives, emotions and health can constitute noise. For example, the effectiveness of our coding and decoding can deteriorate with anxiety, pressure, stress, and with our levels of enthusiasm and excitement.

Noise constitutes a barrier to effective communication. Our past experiences condition the way in which we see things today, and lead us to filter what we transmit and what we receive. Communication stumbles when transmitter and receiver have different frames of reference and do not share experience and understanding, even where they share a common language. We make judgements about the honesty, integrity, trustworthiness and credibility of others, and decode their messages and act on them (or not) accordingly. People in an organizational setting may have time to reflect, or they may be under considerable time pressure which will affect the care and attention devoted to communication. Some of us, from time to time, suffer from communication overload and our effectiveness can deteriorate for this reason too.

There is a final aspect of our communication model which we have still to consider: **feedback**.

Feedback: the processes through which the transmitter of a message detects whether and how that message has been received and decoded.

When we communicate face to face, we can usually tell if the other person likes us, if they agree with us, and if they are interested in what we have to say – or not. How do we know this? Well, they may simply say, 'that's interesting' or 'I fundamentally disagree with you' or 'I have to catch my bus now'. We can also tell from cues such as the tone of their replies, their facial expression, body posture and limb gestures. We will explore the coding and decoding of *non-verbal behaviour*, or body language, later in the chapter.

When we communicate face to face, we get instant feedback in what others say and in how they say it. Our ability to exchange meaning effectively is assisted by this rich feedback loop. Our communication can be awkward where feedback is delayed or absent. Feedback allows us to check constantly the accuracy of the coding and decoding processes. We ask a question, see the other person look annoyed or puzzled, realize that we have not worded our question appropriately, and 'recode' the message. Face to face, if we are paying attention, this can work well. We can do this to some extent over the telephone, decoding the tone of the other person's voice. With other more formal and distant forms of communication, feedback can be delayed or non-existent, and we need to take much more care over our coding.

Stop and Criticize

Think of the people with whom you communicate regularly. What are the main barriers to effective communication in your experience? What would you have to do to improve the effectiveness of your communication?

We can be careless coders and lazy listeners. What might at first appear to be a simple process can be highly error-prone. Both sides of the exchange, coding and decoding, are subject to error. We cannot confidently assume that receivers will always decode our messages in a manner that leaves them with the meaning that we wanted to transmit. It is obvious to claim that communication processes are central to organizational effectiveness, but this claim has major practical implications. We assume that organizations will function better if communication is open, if relationships are based on mutual understanding and trust, if relationships are co-operative rather than competitive, if people work together in teams, and if decisions are reached in a participative way. These features, however, are not widespread.

Some of the main barriers to effective organizational communication concern:

power differences   research consistently shows that employees distort upward communication, and that superiors often have a limited understanding of subordinates' roles, experiences and problems

gender differences   men and women use different conversational styles which can lead to misunderstanding; men tend to talk more and give information while women tend to listen and reflect more

physical surroundings   room size and layout influence our ability to see others and our readiness to participate in conversations and discussions

language   even within one country, variations in accent and dialect can make communication difficult

cultural diversity   different cultures have different norms and expectations concerning formal and informal conversations; lack of awareness of those norms creates misunderstanding

What guidelines can we derive from this analysis, to improve our communication?

face to face   when we are able to speak with someone directly, we can use the feedback constantly to check the coding and decoding processes, and to correct mistakes and misunderstanding

reality checks   we should not assume that others will necessarily decode our messages in the way we intended, and we should check the way in which our messages have been interpreted

time and place   the right message delivered in the wrong place or at the wrong time is more likely to be decoded incorrectly, or even ignored, so choose the time and place with sensitivity and care

empathetic listening   see things from the other person's point of view, consider the thinking that may have led to their behaviour, decode the message the way they might decode it, listen attentively to feedback (Guirdham, 2002)

Verbal communication: conversation control and listening skills

The word 'verbal' is another term that causes coding and decoding problems. Verbal means 'in words', which can be either spoken or written. The expressions 'verbal agreement' and 'verbal warning' can thus refer either to oral or to written communication, and both are contrasted with non-verbal communication which is the focus of the following section.

Most conversations involve exchanges of information or meaning. How do we get the information we want? We achieve this through a range of questioning techniques. The main types of question are shown in table 6.1, which attaches labels to conversation controls that we all use routinely and unconsciously. However, by using these labels, it becomes easier to analyze the conversation control methods of others, and it also becomes easier for us to make conscious choices about how to conduct our own side of a conversation more effectively.

Table 6.1: Questioning techniques

Question type	Illustration	Uses
closed	Did you enjoy the movie?	to get a 'yes' or 'no' answer; to obtain factual information; to establish conversation control
open	What did you think of that movie?	to introduce a subject; to encourage further discussion; to keep the other person talking
probe	Can you tell me more about that?	to follow up an open question; to get more information; to demonstrate interest
reflective	You thought the acting was poor?	to show interest and concern; to encourage further disclosure of feelings and emotions
multiple	What did you think of the movie, and wasn't the star excellent in that role, and did you think that the ending was rather sudden?	to confuse the listener; to give them a choice of question to which to respond
leading	You didn't see anyone leaving the house?	to get the answer that you expect to hear (so, why ask?)
hypothetical	What would happen if . . .?	to encourage creative thinking

The first basic distinction in questioning strategy is between closed and open questions. Closed questions invite a factual statement in reply, or a simple yes or no response. Open questions, in contrast, invite the person responding to disclose further information. Predict the differences in response to these two questions:

Will you have dinner with me this evening?
What are you doing this evening?

It seems as though closed questions are limited while open questions are more effective. If the purpose is to get the other person to divulge information, then this assessment is correct. However, closed questions are useful in two settings. First, where all that is required is simple factual information: 'Are you coming to the meeting?' Open questions invite the discussion of irrelevant information, for which there may be no time.

Second, interviewers often begin with a short series of closed questions in order to establish the conversation pattern. We have all had experience of conversations where the other person took control, giving us information which we did not want. Closed questioning can avoid this. Consider the following questioning sequence used at the beginning of an interview:

What is your current job title?
How long have you been in your present position?
What was your previous position?

This can help to establish the conversation pattern by signalling to the other person, 'I ask the questions, you give the answers'. Usually, by the time the third or fourth closed question has been answered, the person being interviewed will wait for the interviewer to ask their next question, and will not begin talking about some other issue.

Probes are simply another type of open question. Probes indicate that the listener is interested in what the other person is saying. In most instances, that indication of interest encourages the disclosure of further information.

The reflective statement is a powerful technique for maintaining rapport and for encouraging the disclosure of information, particularly concerning feelings and emotions. Simple in essence, all that you have to do is to mirror or reflect back to the person an emotion that they have 'given' to you. The feeling or emotion expressed can be spoken ('you said that you didn't enjoy your holiday') or it can reflect an unspoken, non-verbal expression ('you look particularly happy this morning'). As with probes, reflective statements signal interest and concern and usually encourage the other person to continue disclosing information.

Multiple questions and leading questions are rarely used by trained interviewers. Multiples are often heard on radio and television, particularly when politicians are being asked about their positions and views on topical subjects. Leading questions are especially ineffective when fresh information is required. Watch a police drama on television, and identify how many times witnesses and suspects are confronted with questions such as:

So you didn't see anyone else leave the house after five o'clock?
So these stolen televisions were put in your garage by somebody else?

Hypothetical questions can be useful in stimulating creative and innovative 'blue skies' thinking. Used in selection interviewing, this technique only reveals how well the candidate handles hypothetical questions, and reveals little about their future job performance.

We also control our conversations through a range of conscious and unconscious verbal and non-verbal signals which tell the parties to a conversation, for example, when one has finished an utterance and when it is somebody else's turn to speak. These signals reveal agreement, friendship, dispute and dislike, emotions which in turn shape the further response of the listener. The four main conversation control signals are explained in table 6.2. Note that the different uses and implications of pauses in conversation depend on the context.

Table 6.2: Conversation control signals

Signal	Example	Meaning
lubricators	'uh huh', 'mmm, mmm' and other grunts and groans	I'm listening, keep talking, I'm interested
inhibitors	'what!', 'really', 'oh' and similar loud interjections	I'm surprised, I don't agree, I've heard enough of this
bridges	'I'd like to leave that and move on to ask you about . . .'	I'd like to make a clean link to the next conversation topic
pauses (1)	about two seconds' silence	in normal conversation: same as lubricators
pauses (2)	silence of three seconds or longer	in a threat context: I'm going to wait until I get an answer
pauses (3)	silence of three seconds or longer	in a counselling context: I'll give you time to think

Record a television police drama, a magazine programme or a news broadcast. Watch somebody being interviewed: police interviewing suspect, host interviewing celebrity, newsreader interviewing politician. Identify the questioning techniques used. What advice can you give the interviewer to help improve their questioning?

Replay the same interview with the sound off. Can you identify any communication barriers which made this exchange less effective than necessary, concerning, for example, physical layout, posture, timing, non-verbal behaviour? What further advice would you give the interviewer to help them improve their technique?

When conversing normally, we use these signals habitually. However, awareness of the methods being used can allow us to bring these under conscious control. Therapists and counsellors, for example, use a range of methods to shape conversations in ways that allow their clients to articulate their difficulties and to work towards identifying appropriate solutions. Managers holding selection, appraisal or promotion interviews need to understand conversation control techniques in order to handle these interactions effectively.

We can also use conversation controls to shape or steer the behaviour of others and to achieve our own preferred ends. Conscious command of these methods increases our ability to manipulate and control others. George R. Walther (1993; see Huczynski, 2004) offers a summary of 'high-power' and 'low-power' conversation tactics. Table 6.3 defines the seven main conversation control strategies used by *Powertalkers*:

Table 6.3: Powertalking strategies

Positive talk	Powertalkers respond positively, make genuine commitments, have high expectations, are optimistic, avoid conditional phrases, seek creative solutions, look for the benefits
Give credit	Powertalkers either alter or ignore their shortcomings, describe their achievements positively, neither apologize nor justify, praise others for their success
Learn from experience	Powertalkers say, 'I learned' instead of 'I failed', seek the positive in the face of setbacks, think positive when feeling low, focus on options rather than on regrets
Accept responsibility	Powertalkers admit their own feelings, accept responsibility for actions, control their use of time
Persuade others	Powertalkers emphasize benefits, keep options open, seek ways to improve relationships, focus on positives, accept ideas of others
Decisive speaking	Powertalkers commit to specific targets, extract detailed information, set realistic goals, decide what to say and then say it
Tell the truth	Powertalkers avoid suspicious and misleading phrases, say 'no' when they mean 'no', avoid self-criticism, respect others with whom they interact – remembering and using others' names

Table 6.4 summarizes conversation styles that signal uncertainty and lack of self-confidence, and which also suggest that the speaker has low power (Huczynski, 2004).

Table 6.4: Low power indicators	
Hedges and qualifiers	'Maybe it has some strengths'
Irritators	'you know', 'sort of', 'kinda'
Intensifiers	'really', 'awfully', 'horrendously'
Tags	'aren't they?', 'didn't you?'
Hesitations	'um, er, ah, uhh, well'
Excessive questions	signal uncertainty and a need for attention

Gender differences also create barriers to effective communication. Deborah Tannen (1990, 1995) argues that boys and girls acquire different linguistic styles, and that these differences affect the career prospects of men and women at work. A linguistic style is a characteristic speaking pattern which includes factors such as tone of voice, speed of speech, loudness, directness or indirectness, pacing and pausing, choice of words, and the extent to which we use jokes, stories, figures of speech, questions and apologies. Tannen (1995, p. 140) claims that '[G]irls learn conversational rituals that focus on the rapport dimension of relationships whereas boys tend learn rituals that focus on the status dimension'.

Boys as they grow up play in large groups, emphasize status and leadership, display their knowledge and abilities, challenge others, take 'centre stage' by telling jokes and stories, and try to acquire status in their group by giving orders to others. Girls focus on a small group of friends, sharing secrets with their best friend, emphasizing similarities and playing down ways in which someone could be better than others. Girls tend to be more modest, appear less self-assured, and ostracize those who claim superiority.

These childhood differences affect adult behaviour in organizational settings. Men tend to think more in hierarchical terms and are concerned with status, power and with being 'one up'. Men strive to retain 'one up' by driving and by interrupting conversations. Men jockey for position by putting others down, appear competent by acting confidently and appear knowledgeable by asking fewer questions. Men tend to give negative feedback quickly and look for opportunities to criticize, rather than pay others compliments.

Women are more likely to avoid putting others down and to act in ways that are face-saving for others. Women can appear to lack self-confidence by playing down their certainty and by expressing doubt more openly. Women also appear less self-assured and knowledgeable by asking more questions, tend to soften criticism by offering positive feedback first, and pay others compliments more often than men do.

These linguistic differences are particularly important when speaking of achievements. Men tend to be more direct and use 'I' more often. Women tend to speak indirectly and speak of 'we' when talking about accomplishments. In summary, men tend to adopt linguistic styles and to behave in ways that are more likely to get them recognized, and that are more likely to earn them attributions of effectiveness and competence. Women who adopt a more 'masculine' linguistic style can be seen as too aggressive. Tannen advises us all to be more aware of these differences in linguistic styles, and to pay attention to the dynamics of our conversations.

Stop and Criticize

Tannen was writing about women in America in the mid-1990s. To what extent does her analysis apply to linguistic and behavioural differences between men and women in your culture today?

Aboriginal culture and communication

Australian Aboriginal culture includes aspects of verbal and non-verbal behaviour which are quite different from most European and North American communication styles.

■ Aborigines value brevity in verbal communication rather than detailed elaboration, and simple 'yes' and 'no' replies are common.

■ There is no word for 'thank you' in Aboriginal languages. People do things for you as an obligation.

■ In some Aboriginal tribes, it is unlawful to use the name of a dead person.

■ The terms 'full-blood', 'half-caste', 'quarter-caste', 'native' and 'part-Aborigine' are regarded as offensive by Aborigines.

■ Long silences in Aboriginal conversation are common and are not regarded as awkward.

■ To some Aboriginal people, it is not acceptable to look another straight in the eye.

■ Some Aboriginal groups do not allow men and women to mix freely.

■ Aborigines do not feel that it is necessary to look at the person who is speaking to them.

■ Aborigines do not feel that it is necessary to attend meetings (an interview, for example) at specific times.

How do these norms and preferences compare with the communication style of your culture?

Based on Richard Nelson-Jones, *Introduction to Counselling Skills*, Sage Publications, London, 2000, p. 54.

The significance of non-verbal communication

Which part of the human anatomy is capable of expanding up to ten times in size when we are emotionally aroused? The answer, of course, is the pupil of the eye. When we look at something we find interesting – an image, a scene, a person – our pupils dilate. When we lose interest, our pupils contract. There is, therefore, a physiological basis in non-verbal behaviour for the 'dark limpid pools' to which romantic novelists refer.

When we interact with others face to face we are constantly sending and receiving messages through the signs, expressions, gestures, postures and vocal mannerisms that we seem to adopt unconsciously. In other words, **non-verbal communication** accompanies our verbal communication. As a general rule, we code and transmit factual information primarily through verbal behaviours. We code and transmit our feelings and emotions, and the strength of our feeling through our non-verbal communication.

The term 'body language' has come into use in recent years as our knowledge of this fascinating side of behaviour has developed. But we use the technical term here for two reasons. First, non-verbal behaviour is extremely rich and varied, and the term 'body language' is inaccurate if it implies a concern only with bodily movements and postures. Second, the term 'body language' seems to suggest that

Non-verbal communication: the process of coding meaning through behaviours such as facial expressions, limb gestures and body postures.

gestures have specific meanings; in other words, we can produce a dictionary of body language. That, as we will demonstrate, is not the case. The technical term has the advantage of including a range of behaviours and also signals our concern with the way these behaviours are embedded in the communication process.

Allan Pease (1985, 1997) implies in the title of his popular books that one can 'read' somebody else's attitudes and emotions from their non-verbal behaviour. Is this possible? Well, if we are careful, sometimes. This 'mind reading' claim deserves cautious support. We are able to exchange meaning with non-verbal codes as long as we evaluate the verbal and non-verbal components together, and pay close attention also to the context.

Non-verbal hints for the job interview

When you sit down, lean forward slightly; this shows interest. Use open-handed gestures – palm upwards – to convey sincerity. Keep regular eye contact, but not for more than 60 per cent of the time, or you'll look mad. However, do it for less than 30 per cent of the time and you may seem shifty or bored.

Don't sit defensively – hands across the body, knees pressed together, hand over your mouth – it can look neurotic or unstable. Equally, don't fidget or play with your hair, or grin maniacally. Above all, don't slouch back in the chair, arms behind your head, with a challenging stare. It threatens the interviewer and makes you look arrogant and difficult.

From Jerome Burne and Susan Aldridge, 'Who do you think you are?', *Focus Extra*, April 1996, p. 4.

The first study of gesture was conducted by the Italian cleric Andrea de Jorio, born in 1769. To help him to decipher the Greek figures excavated by archaeologists at Herculaneum, Pozzuoli and Pompei in the early nineteenth century, he studied the facial and bodily gestures of the people of Naples, a city founded by the ancient Greeks. His book *Gesture in Naples and Gesture in Classical Antiquity* is available in translation (Kendon, 2001).

Early Italian hand gestures

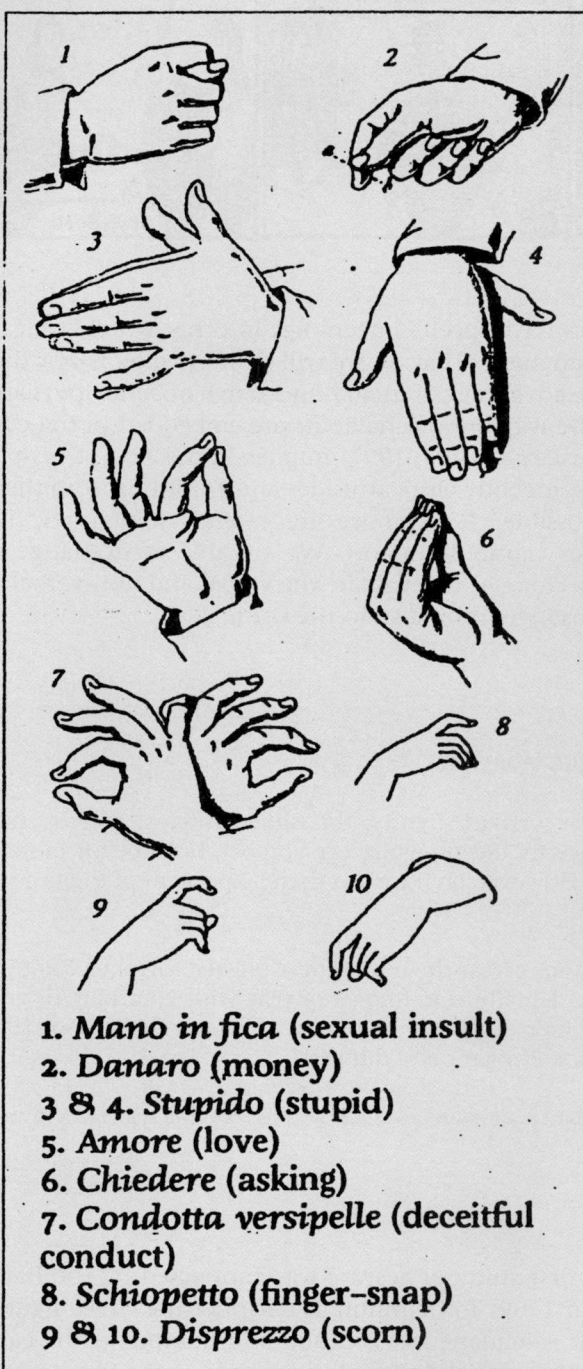

1. *Mano in fica* (sexual insult)
2. *Danaro* (money)
3 & 4. *Stupido* (stupid)
5. *Amore* (love)
6. *Chiedere* (asking)
7. *Condotta versipelle* (deceitful conduct)
8. *Schiopetto* (finger–snap)
9 & 10. *Disprezzo* (scorn)

Reprinted by permission of the Syndics of Cambridge University Library. From Adam Kendon (trans.), *Gesture in Naples and Gesture in Classical Antiquity*, by Andrea de Jorio, Indiana University Press, Bloomington, IN, 2001.

Table 6.5: Dimensions of non-verbal behaviour

- eye behaviour (occulesics)
- facial expressions
- posture
- limb movements (kinesics)
- tone and pitch of voice (paralanguage)
- distance (proxemics)

Non-verbal behaviour is rich and varied. The main dimensions are summarized in table 6.5.

Maureen Guirdham (1995, p. 165) lists 136 non-verbal behaviours, in nine categories. These include what we do with our mouths, eyebrows, eyelids and eyes, gaze, facial expressions, head movements, hands and arms, lower limbs and trunk movements. The sub-heading 'mouth region' lists 40 behaviours, such as tongue out, open grin, yawn, wry smile, sneer, tight lips, lower lip tremble, and so on. The sub-heading 'hands and arms' lists a further 40 behaviours, such as scratch, sit on hands, hand flutter, digit suck, palms up, caress, hand on neck, and so on.

Non-verbal courtship

According to Allan Pease (1997), typical male courtship gestures involving non-verbal behaviour include: preening (straightening tie, smoothing hair), thumbs-in-belt (pointing towards genitals), turning his body to face a female, pointing his foot towards her, holding her gaze, hands on his hips, dilated pupils and the 'leg spread' (crotch display). Women, on the other hand, have a much richer repertoire of non-verbal courtship behaviour which includes:

- preening gestures such as touching hair, smoothing clothing;
- one or both hands on hips;
- foot and body pointing towards the male;
- extended eye contact or 'intimate gaze';
- thumbs-in-belt, but often only one, or thumb protruding from pocket or handbag;
- pupil dilation;
- flushed appearance;
- the head toss, to flick hair away from face (used even by women with short hair);
- exposing the soft smooth skin on the wrists to the male;
- exposing the palms of the hands;
- the sideways glance with drooped eyelids ('you caught me looking at you');
- wet lips, mouth slightly open;
- fondling cylindrical objects (stem of wine glass, a finger);
- the knee point, one leg tucked under the other, pointing to the male, thighs exposed;
- the shoe fondle, pushing the foot in and out of a half-on-half-off shoe;
- crossing and uncrossing the legs slowly in front of the man;
- gently stroking the thighs (indicating a desire to be touched).

How many of these non-verbal courtship gestures, male and female, are illustrated on p. 194?

Source: Colin McDougall, photographer

Another important aspect of non-verbal behaviour is 'paralanguage'. This concerns the rate of speech, and pitch and loudness of our voice, regardless of the words we are using. There are many different ways of saying the same sequence of words; it's not what you say, but the way that you say it. Paralanguage demonstrates some of the overriding power of non-verbal behaviour. Consider the simple statement: 'That was a really great lecture'. Think of the many ways in which you can say this, the differences in gaze and posture as you say it, and particularly the differences in the tone and pitch of your voice. For some of these expressions, listeners will hear you say that you really *did* enjoy the lecture. However, there are a number of ways in which you can 'code' this statement, non-verbally, in such a way that listeners will be left in no doubt that you thought the lecture poor, even though the wording remains as it is written here. Where the verbal and non-verbal messages contradict each other, it is the non-verbal message which is believed, not the verbal message.

Yet another aspect of non-verbal behaviour concerns the way in which we use distance in interpersonal behaviour. The study of this aspect of behaviour is sometimes called 'proxemics'. British culture requires a 'social distance' of about half a metre or more between people in normal conversation. If you cross this invisible boundary and step into someone's 'personal space' they will usually move backwards to maintain the distance; a failure to 'retreat' implies intimacy. The comfortable distance in Arab and Latin (American and European) countries is smaller, and you are likely to be regarded as arrogant and distant by trying to maintain your personal space when interacting with members of those cultures.

It is possible to test the theory of personal space in many social situations. At a social gathering, a party perhaps, move gradually and tactfully into someone else's space, by pretending to reach for a drink, or by moving aside to let someone else past, or by leaning forward to be heard better, and so on. It is possible to move someone across a room in this way. The same result can be achieved while seated, as long as the chairs are easy to move. However, if your target does not retreat as predicted, and you are now in their intimate space, you have a decoding problem, and the textbook can't help you.

Lie detectors

Can we use non-verbal behaviour to detect when someone is lying? Adrian Furnham identifies several verbal and non-verbal 'lie detectors'. However, in other cultures, these cues may constitute normal interpersonal behaviour and may *not* signal deceit.

Verbal cues

■ Response latency	The time between the end of a question and the start of a reply. Liars take longer, hesitate more.
■ Linguistic distance	Not saying 'I', but talking in the abstract: for example, 'one might believe that . . .'.
■ Slow, uneven speech	As an individual tries to think through their lies. They might also suddenly talk quickly, attempting to make a sensitive subject appear less significant.
■ Too eager to fill gaps in conversation	Liars keep talking when it is unnecessary, as if a silence signifies that the other person does not believe them.
■ Too many pitch raises	Instead of the pitch dropping at the end of a reply, it is lifted in the same way as asking a question.

Non-verbal cues

■ Too much squirming	Someone shifting around in their seat is signalling their desire not to be there.
■ Too much eye contact, rather than too little	Liars tend to overcompensate.
■ Micro-expressions	Flickers of surprise, hurt or anger that are difficult to detect. Sudden facial expressions of pain are often giveaways.
■ An increase in comfort gestures	These often take the form of self-touching, particularly around the nose and mouth.
■ An increase in stuttering and slurring	Including what are known as 'Freudian slips'.
■ A loss of resonance in the voice	It tends to become flatter and more monotonous.

Based on Adrian Furnham, *The Psychology of Behaviour at Work*, Psychology Press/Taylor & Francis, Hove, Sussex, 1997, p. 53.

When we are lying, we may unconsciously send non-verbal 'deceit cues', which include rapid shifts in gaze, fidgeting in our seats, long pauses and frequent speech corrections. When lying, it is important to control these cues, ensuring that verbal and non-verbal messages are consistent. Similarly, when we want to emphasize the sincerity or strength of our feelings, it is important that the non-verbal signals we send are consistent with the verbal message.

It's the way that you say it: the power of paralanguage

Change your tone and you change your meaning:

Meaning 1	Why don't I take **YOU** to dinner tonight?	I was going to take someone else.
Meaning 2	Why don't **I** take you to dinner tonight?	Instead of the guy you were going with.
Meaning 3	Why **DON'T** I take you to dinner tonight?	I'm trying to find a reason why I shouldn't take you.
Meaning 4	**WHY** don't I take you to dinner tonight?	Do you have a problem with me?
Meaning 5	Why don't I **TAKE** you to dinner tonight?	Instead of going on your own.
Meaning 6	Why don't I take you to **DINNER** tonight?	Instead of lunch tomorrow.
Meaning 7	Why don't I take you to dinner **TONIGHT**?	Not tomorrow night.

From Michael Kiely, 'When "no" means "yes"', *Marketing*, October 1993, pp. 7–9. Reproduced from *Marketing* magazine with permission of the copyright owner, Haymarket Business Publications Limited.

Maureen Guirdham (2002, p. 184) describes non-verbal behaviour as a 'relationship language'. This is how we communicate trust, boredom, submission, dislike and friendship without stating these feelings directly. When decoding non-verbal behaviour, it is important to pay attention to the context, and to the pattern or cluster of verbal and non-verbal behaviours on display. For example, when someone wishes to indicate liking or friendship, they are likely to turn their body towards you, look you straight in the face, establish regular eye contact and look away infrequently, and to nod and smile a lot, keeping their hands and arms by their sides or in front of them. This cluster conveys friendship, or positive non-verbal behaviour.

We can often identify disagreement or dislike by negative non-verbal behaviour. This cluster includes turning the body away, folding the arms tightly, crossing the legs in such a manner that they point away from the other person, loss of eye contact, wandering gaze, looking at someone else or at the door (suggesting a desire to leave), and a lack of nods and smiles. The cluster of non-verbal behaviours producing this 'closed posture' often mean that we know that someone does not like what we are saying before they state their disagreement in words.

However, awareness of the context is critical to this decoding or 'mind reading'. People also engage in negative non-verbal behaviours when they are unwell, or when they are anxious about something, perhaps unrelated to your conversation and relationship. People also 'close up' and fold their arms when they are cold and uncomfortable.

Interpreting gesture clusters

cluster signals	indicating
flexible open posture, open hands, display of palms and wrists, removing jacket, moving closer to other person, leaning forward in chair, uncrossed arms and legs, smiling, nodding, eye contact	openness
rigid, closed posture, arms and legs tightly crossed, eyes glancing sideways, minimal eye contact, frowning, no smiling, pursed lips, clenched fists, head down, flat tone of voice	defensiveness
drumming fingers, head cupped in palm of hand, foot swinging, brushing or picking lint from clothing, body pointing towards exit, repeatedly looking at watch, the exit, a book	boredom, impatience
small inward smile, erect body posture, hands open and arms extended outwards, eyes wide and alert, lively walk, expressive and well-modulated voice	enthusiasm
knitted forehead, deadpan expression, tentative nodding or smiling, one slightly raised eyebrow, strained voice, saying 'I understand' while looking away	lack of understanding
blank expression, phoney smile, tight posture, arms stiff at side, sudden eye shifts, nervous tapping, sudden mood shifts, speech toneless and soft or too loud and animated	stress

Eye behaviour has also attracted much research. The dilation and contraction of our pupils is largely beyond our direct control, unlike, say, the movements of our hands, but this can convey significant non-verbal information. Our pupils dilate (expand) in low light, and also when we see something or someone in which we have an interest. Dilation conveys honesty, openness and sexual interest. However, our pupils also dilate when we are relaxed, and with the consumption of alcohol and other drugs. Again, a knowledge of context is critical to accurate decoding. Contracted pupils can signify low lighting conditions or lack of interest, or distrust, hatred, hostility, fatigue, stress, sorrow, or perhaps a hangover. It is only possible to decode pupil dilation or contraction with reference to other non-verbal clues and to the context in which this behaviour appears (including, in some circumstances, what the person was doing the previous evening).

The importance of cultural context in communication

The use and interpretation of non-verbal behaviours differ from culture to culture. In Japan, for example, smiling and nodding implies understanding, but not necessarily agreement. In Australia, raising the pitch of your voice at the end of a sentence signifies openness to challenge or question, not a lie. In some Asian cultures, it is impolite to give superiors direct and prolonged eye contact; a bowed head thus signifies deference and not lack of self-confidence or defensiveness. People from north European cultures prefer a lot of personal space and rarely touch each other. French, Italians and Latin Americans, in contrast, stand closer together and touch more often to indicate agreement and friendship. The verbal and non-verbal 'lie detectors' described earlier are specific to British culture.

Simple gestures must also be used with care. Make a circle with your thumb and forefinger, extending the other three fingers. How will this be interpreted (DuBrin, 1994)? In America, it means 'that's OK'. In Japan, it means money. In France, it means zero or nothing. In some Arab countries it signifies a curse. In Germany and Brazil it is obscene.

Edward Hall (1976, 1989) distinguished between **high-context** and **low-context** cultures.

high-context culture	low-context culture
establish relationship first	get down to business first
value personal relations and goodwill	value expertise and performance
agreement based on trust	agreement based on legal contract
slow and ritualistic negotiations	fast and efficient negotiations

China, Korea, Japan and Vietnam are high-context cultures, where people tend to take a greater interest in your position, your business card, your dress, material possessions and other signs of status and relationships. Written and spoken communications are not ignored, but they are secondary. Agreements can be made on a handshake, on someone's word.

North America, Scandinavia, Switzerland and Germany are low-context cultures. Here people pay secondary attention to non-verbal messages. People in German organizations tend to be preoccupied with detailed written rules, and Americans like to have precise legal documents. Agreements are not made until the contract is in writing, signed.

These categorizations reflect tendencies and are not absolutes. Most countries have sub-cultures with very different norms. In addition, men tend to be more high-context than women, but clearly this observation does not apply to all men or to all women. Nevertheless, it is easy to see how misunderstanding can arise when high- and low-context cultures meet, unless those communicating are sensitive to their respective differences.

High-context culture: a culture in which people tend to rely heavily on a range of social and non-verbal clues when communicating with others and interpreting their messages.

Low-context culture: a culture in which people tend to focus on the written and spoken word when communicating with others and interpreting their messages.

Someone who is anxious usually indulges in non-verbal behaviour known as 'self-manipulation'. This includes playing with an ear lobe, stroking lips or chin, or playing with hair or a moustache. Anxiety can also be signalled by shifting direction of gaze. Friendship is conveyed, as we have indicated, by an open non-verbal behaviour cluster. There are a number of other friendship signals, and these can sometimes be amusing to use and to identify. When we meet someone to whom we are attracted, we typically use unconscious 'preening gestures': straightening our clothes, stroking our hair, straightening our posture. Observe a group of friends together and you will often see them standing, sitting and even holding cups or glasses in an almost identical manner. This is known as 'posture mirroring'. Sometimes you can identify the 'outsider' as the one not adopting the similar posture. Friendship groups also copy each other's gestures, known as 'gesture mirroring'.

Neuro-linguistic programming (NLP)

NLP is a technique for improving performance in interpersonal communication. Developed by Richard Bandler and John Grinder (1975, 1979), it is now widely used as a management development tool (Harris, 1992; Dimmick, 1995). The components of the somewhat clumsy name have the following sources:

neuro   the method is underpinned by an understanding of how the human nervous system processes incoming information

linguistic   the method in practice is based on the use of words, tone of voice, timing and gestures to improve the effectiveness of communication

programming   the aim of the method is to base interpersonal communication on systematic, and thus trainable, techniques

The conscious control of behaviour is fundamental to the practice of NLP, which advocates a form of objective detachment known as 'disassociation' from events going on around us. In a disassociated state, which can be achieved with practice, it is possible to observe and monitor one's behaviour during a 'live' conversation, consciously choosing a range of verbal and non-verbal behaviours and evaluating their impact. Feelings can also be directed consciously in a similar manner, by 'anchoring' the emotion of, for example, calmness to a specific event which can be recalled to generate that emotion when required (for example, when called upon to make a presentation to a large audience). These examples of disassociation and anchoring help to explain the 'programming' element of the approach.

On the basis that effective communication is based on rapport, on establishing that 'we are very much alike', NLP advocates a series of techniques known as mirroring or 'matching'. These include, for example, matching the other person's body movements, the volume and rate of speech, breathing pattern, and mood or 'frame of mind'. Any aspect of the other person's behaviour can be matched in order to signal, 'see, I'm a lot like you', as long as it is done carefully and tactfully, and not overdone.

Even the other person's preferred communication style can be matched. This style, according to NLP practitioners, is revealed by eye movements. When someone looks upwards frequently, this usually suggests a preference for *visual* imagery. Matching involves saying things like 'I can see that' or 'That looks right', and showing the person charts and diagrams. When someone looks frequently to the side, this usually suggests a preference for *auditory* signals. Matching involves using words like 'That sounds right' or 'Listen to this' or 'That rings a bell'. Finally, when someone looks downwards frequently, this usually suggests a preference for *kinaesthetic* information, which is information received through actions or feelings. Matching involves using phrases like 'It doesn't feel right' or 'I can grasp that'. To clarify these distinctions, Sally Dimmick (1995) uses the example of 'splitting the bill' with a group of people at the end of a meal in a restaurant. Individuals with different communication style preferences need to be handled in different ways:

visual preference   they want to see the bill for themselves, to work out what each person has to contribute

auditory preference   they don't want to see the bill, they just want to be told the total and how much they have to pay

kinaesthetic preference they will want to do the necessary calculation manually, and will be the first to reach for a pen

To the extent that they are effective, NLP techniques are particularly useful to salespeople (trying to persuade customers to buy more of their product) and to negotiators (trying to gain concessions from their adversaries). The approach is thus open to the criticism that it is overtly manipulative and unethical. However, we all use the techniques of mirroring or 'matching' unconsciously anyway. The conscious, deliberate attempt to improve interpersonal communication is not necessarily devious or damaging. Or is it?

Impression management: form versus substance?

We usually send and receive non-verbal messages unconsciously. However, it is possible both to control most of the non-verbal signals we send and consciously to be aware of and read the cues that others are giving us. This level of conscious attention and control may be difficult for most of us to sustain, but it can be significant in organizational settings.

Impression management: the process whereby people seek to control the image others have of them.

The concept of **impression management** has its foundations in the work of Erving Goffman (1959). Our definition is taken from the more recent work of Paul Rosenfeld, Robert Giacalone and Catherine Riordan (2001). They remark that our impression management methods are extremely rich and varied, incuding:

- what we do and how we do it;
- what we say and how we say it;
- the furnishings and arrangement of our offices;
- our physical appearance, including clothes and makeup;
- non-verbal behaviours such as facial expressions or postures.

Effective impression management means being consciously aware and in control of the cues that we send to others through verbal and non-verbal channels. This suggests that we consciously seek to manipulate the impression or perceptions that others have of us.

Stop and Criticize

Is impression management simply a form of deceit? What in your view are the ethical problems raised by the advice that we consciously seek to manipulate the impression that others have of us through verbal and non-verbal behaviours? What are the practical problems? How long can you keep this up?

As with conversation controls, we can use impression management to manipulate the behaviour of others. We do this, for example, by 'giving off' the impression that we are friendly, submissive, apologetic, angry, defensive, confident, intimidating and so on. The more effectively we manage our impression, the greater the control we can achieve in social interaction, and the greater our power to pursue our preferred outcomes over others.

Gardner (1992) speaks of impression management as 'organizational dramaturgy', and in terms of 'stagecraft': actors, audience, stage, script, performance and reviews. It is not surprising, therefore, that some people regard impression management as a form of acting. The problem with this view is that we 'manage' our impression all the time, whether we like this concept or not. It is hardly possible to avoid sending 'signals' to others through, for example, our style of dress, posture, facial expressions, gestures, tone and pitch of voice, and even location in a room. The only useful distinction here is between conscious (and by implication more effective, for the initiator) impression management and unconscious (and by implication less effective, or even misleading) impression management.

Conscious impression management has many advantages. Interactions run more smoothly when we provide the 'correct' signals to others who in turn accurately 'decode' these signals of our attitudes and intents. Impression management is a critical skill in many organizational contexts, such as counselling, and in selection, appraisal and disciplinary interviewing.

Anita Roddick learns impression management

Anita Roddick started The Body Shop in 1976. At the end of 1999, her company was worth over £200 million and had 1,600 stores in 47 countries. She explains her initial problems:

> The most difficult thing was raising money for the first shop. I knew I had a good idea and a reasonable business plan, and I thought naïvely that this was all that was important. I went to see my bank manager in my Bob Dylan T-shirt with my two small children in tow. I thought my enthusiasm and energy would convince the bank manager to believe in me. But he turned me down, which took me aback. Gordon, my husband, told me to have another go but this time to dress up like a bloke in pinstripes and leave the kids behind. He came, too. After taking this advice I was able to walk out of the same bank with a £4,000 loan.

From Rupert Steiner, 'Pinstripes put Roddick on the right scent', *The Sunday Times*, 24 October 1999, p. 3.15.

Feldman and Klitch (1991) offer advice on how to manage your impression to enhance your career, suggesting six methods for creating a favourable self-image (table 6.6).

Table 6.6: Creating a favourable self-image

Ingratiation	Use flattery, agree with the opinions of others, do favours to encourage people with power and influence to befriend you.
Intimidation	Convey the image of potential danger to those who could stand in the way of your advancement. Use veiled threats of exposure.
Self-promotion	Win respect and admiration of superiors through embellishing your accomplishments, overstating your abilities, displaying awards.
Exemplification	Create an impression of selfless dedication and self-sacrifice so those in positions of influence will feel guilty and offer reward or promotion.
Accounting	Distance yourself from negative events, deny personal responsibility for problems, diminish the seriousness of difficulties.
Supplication	Get those in positions of influence to be sympathetic and nurturing, for example, through requests for 'mentoring' and other support.

They also argue that a 'careerist orientation' to work is based on six beliefs which, incorporating some impression management advice, are that:

1. Merit alone is insufficient for advancement. Creating the appearance of being a winner, or looking 'promotable', is just as important.

2. To advance, it is critical to pursue social relationships with superiors and co-workers. On the surface, these relationships should appear to be social in nature, but in reality they are used instrumentally for job contacts and insider organizational information.

3. Looking like a 'team player' is central. However, you should still pursue self-interest at work through 'antagonistic co-operation', that is appearing co-operative and helpful while simultaneously seeking information about how to beat the other team members.

4. In the long run, your career goals will be inconsistent with the interests of any one organization. Therefore, in order to advance, you must appear to

be loyal and committed to your current employers while 'keeping your options open'.

5. Dishonest or unethical behaviours are sometimes necessary in order to get promoted. Instead of advocating or even acknowledging the existence of such behaviour, you should become adept at inconsistency, and develop the ability to hold public positions that are either mutually inconsistent or inconsistent with past public positions.

6. Much of the 'real work' of many jobs cannot be assessed, nor can relative success be easily validated. Thus it is important to construct the illusion of success through symbols such as dress and office design. These props include locks on file drawers and positioning visitors so the sun is in their eyes and visitors' chairs lower than the occupant's desk.

Will you get that job?

Summarizing research on communication in selection interviews, Fredric Jablin (2001, pp. 749–50) concludes that:

■ Interviewers report that applicants' communication skills are critical to selection decisions, including fluency of speech, composure, appropriate content and ability to express ideas in an organized manner.

■ Interviewers rate more favourably interviewees who display appropriate levels of non-verbal immediacy, including eye contact, smiling, open posture, interpersonal distance and direct body orientation.

■ Interviewers rate more highly and are more satisfied with interviewees who talk more of the time in interview, who elaborate on their answers, and whose discussion of topics closely matches the interviewer's expectations.

■ Interviewers rate more favourably interviewees who display assertive impression management techniques, such as agreeing with the interviewer, emphasizing positive traits, asking positive-closed questions, claiming that they 'fit' the organization, and telling personal stories to confirm that they are competent, hardworking, goal-oriented, confident, adaptable, inter-personally skilled, and effective leaders.

■ Where the interviewer is seen as trustworthy, competent, composed, empathic, enthusiastic and well organized the applicant is more likely to accept the job offer.

Based on Fredric Jablin, 'Organizational entry, assimilation, and disengagement/exit', in Fredric M. Jablin and Linda L. Putnam (eds), *The New Handbook of Organizational Communication: Advances in Theory, Research, and Methods*, Sage Publications, Thousand Oaks, CA, 2001, pp. 732–818.

Organizational communication: commitment and propaganda

In this section, the focus shifts from interpersonal to organizational communication, between management and employees. Although communication is widely recognized as central to individual and organizational performance, many managers regard communication as a major problem (Buchanan, Claydon and Doyle, 1999), and many employees feel that they are not adequately informed about management plans. From a survey of communication concerning organizational restructuring, Katherine Burke (1999) concludes that many companies do not pay enough attention to communication when planning and implementing change, resulting in absenteeism, staff turnover, low productivity and disputes. David Clutterbuck and Sheila Hirst (2003) argue that employee communication has become more important. Why? One reason is the growth in the volume of other information available through the internet. A second reason is the rise in employee expectations to be kept informed and to contribute ideas.

One problem facing most managers lies with persuading employees to work in the interests of the organization as a whole. However, the interests of individuals and organizations do not always coincide. How can employee behaviour be channelled in the desired directions? In their seminal contribution to organizational behaviour, James March and Herbert Simon (1958) argued that management cannot change individual behaviour directly, or by attempting to alter people's personalities. It is more effective and practical, they observed, to manipulate the premises on which people make their own decisions about how they will behave.

How can management manipulate the premises – the underlying assumptions – which influence the day-to-day decisions of employees? This can be achieved in relatively straightforward ways. The basis on which pay is calculated, for example, can influence attendance, timekeeping and work rate (through piece rates and bonuses). Company rules, the way these are enforced, and the vocabularies in use are also symbolic ways of 'signalling' or 'coding' desirable and undesirable behaviours. Desirable behaviours can also be reinforced through the appraisal system which, in a retail store for example, can evaluate employee behaviours such as 'expresses ideas clearly, keeps other informed, shares knowledge, provides timely communication, listens and responds to customers'.

Stop and Criticize	How does your educational institution use rewards and sanctions to influence the decisions you make about the nature and direction of your studies? What 'signals' do teaching staff use to communicate to students how they expect them to behave?

These 'signalling systems' are, in effect, saying 'behave this way and you will be rewarded and/or promoted, but behave that way and you are likely to be overlooked for promotion – or fired'. These systems are often complemented by organization mission statements, vision statement, and by statements of corporate values. Peter Wickens (1999), ex-human resources director for the Nissan Japanese car plant at Sunderland in the north east of England, argues that clear organizational values confer competitive advantage, and he offers a procedure for identifying what these values should be for an individual organization. In the following box, the 'vision and values' statement of a privatized English water utility is described.

Anglian Water Services plc, Huntingdon, England
Vision and Values Statement, September 2003

Vision

purpose	To safeguard public health and the environment whilst providing increased value for our stakeholders
vision	By 2005 Anglian Water Services will be: 'The most highly regarded UK Water Services Company'
strategy	Our strategic objectives define the delivery of our vision and form the basis for an aligned set of performance objectives deployed down and across the organisation. These objectives are:

- Cost effective provision of products and services – delivering high quality services to customers most effectively.

- Establishing a beneficial regulatory position – obtaining a leading position in performance tables for the benefit of all stakeholders.

- Exceeding regulatory expectations – delivering selected services over and above regulators' expectations.

- Delivering sustainable returns to investors – ensuring we satisfy the needs of our lenders and shareholders.

Values

safe	in everything we do
effective	doing the right thing well
competitive	if not in direct competition, then comparative efficiency
responsible	adopting a sustainable approach
responsive	to customers, internal and external
friendly	in our approach to customers and each other

Senior management at Anglian Water Services presented their vision and values statement to employees in a series of meetings held late 1997 and early 1998. In response to a question concerning job security from the floor at one of these meeting a senior manager replied:

> Vision and Values sets out clear guidelines for all employees to demonstrate the core values – to be effective, competitive, responsible, friendly and responsive in the day jobs. Those employees who really live these values will contribute to the growth of Anglian Water and be rewarded accordingly. By contrast, those people who do not take account of Vision and Values will be shown the door. (*Anglian Water News*, April 1998, p. 5).

Barbara Townley (1994) claims that British managers neglect employee communication. Better communication is often advocated by management consultants as a cure for low morale, high absenteeism and turnover, labour unrest and conflict, low productivity and resistance to change. This advice is based on the theory that, if people understand what is going on and why, then they will be more likely to follow management directions. A well-presented case supported with compelling evidence should result in consensus and compliance. Is that always going to be the case? Research considered shortly suggests not.

Organizations use a range of mechanisms for communicating with employees, such as:

- the management chain;
- regular meetings with senior and/or middle managers;
- in-house newspapers and magazines;
- noticeboards;
- videos;
- conferences and seminars;
- employee reports (similar to but different from shareholder reports);
- team briefings, to cascade information through the structure;
- email and intranets (for those with access to terminals).

Those tend to be one-way-downward modes of communication. Two-way exchanges of information are more effectively achieved through methods such as:

- 'speak out' programmes in which problems are taken to counsellors;
- suggestion or 'bright ideas' schemes;
- open door policies;
- the appraisal system;
- quality circles;
- attitude surveys;
- interactive email (where managers guarantee to reply).

Culture differences in organizational communication

In the 'North' [of Europe] the policy is that everyone knows. 'Southern' management discourages an open, critical attitude of younger and 'inexperienced' employees, whereas in the North such an attitude is welcomed. On the corporate information front, five years ago Unilever started 'Cascade', a system to acquaint all employees yearly with information about how the Corporation was doing financially. For this, corporate HQ prepares a big packet full of information, complete with overhead sheets and even videos. All business groups receive the same information and are expected to pass it on to their companies and eventually to all employees. Random checks among employees after the Cascade exercise have shown that in Eastern Europe all employees are very interested in corporate information and that 'coverage' is near 100%; in Western Europe coverage is 'average', some 80%, but in Latin countries coverage is 'difficult', at around 65%, because local management seems to decide that not all information is 'necessary' or fit for their employees.

From C.V. Fourboul and F. Bournois, 'Strategic communication with employees in large European companies: a typology', *European Management Journal*, vol. 17, no. 2, 1999, p. 211.

What evidence is there concerning the ways in which organizational communication is practised? From a major national survey in Britain of around 4,000 employees and 1,000 unemployed, in all occupational grades, Duncan Gallie and colleagues (1998) found that:

- mechanisms for informing the workforce about management decisions and organizational developments are widespread;
- it is more common for employers to distribute information (76 per cent) than to hold meetings in which employees can express their opinions;
- the higher the skill level, the more likely that people will have good access to information;

- more than three-quarters of professional and managerial workers have meetings about organizational issues in which they can express their views;

- less than a half of all manual workers, skilled and non-skilled, have meetings in which they can express their views;

- involvement in communication is better in larger organizations;

- less than half of employees working in small businesses report any type of formal provision of company information at all;

- in larger establishments employing 500 people or more, 92 per cent receive some type of information (84 per cent through meetings) and 71 per cent are able to express their views.

Gallie et al. (1998, p. 98) argue that larger organizations are more likely to have 'administrative sophistication', in the form of adequately resourced administrative or human resources departments to implement communication policies systematically.

Jack Gibb (1961) developed the useful concept of **communication climate**. An open communication climate promotes collaborative working which is discouraged by a closed climate. Gibb argued that, in an open climate, people develop self-worth, feel that they can contribute freely without reprisal, know that their suggestions will be welcomed and that mistakes will be regarded as learning opportunities, and feel trusted, secure and confident in their job and the organization. In a closed communication climate, information tends to be withheld unless it is to the advantage of the sender, and the atmosphere of recrimination, secrecy and distrust can make working life very unpleasant.

The distinction between open and closed climates is summarized in table 6.7. These extremes are not absolutes; most organizations are likely to have a climate which lies on the continuum between open and closed, and the climate may vary between sections or departments.

Communication climate in an organization: the prevailing atmosphere, *open* or *closed*, in which ideas and information are exchanged.

Stop and Criticize

How would you diagnose the communication climate of your educational institution? Of an organization where you have recently worked? Of your current employer?

One recurring theme in contemporary organizational communication concerns the need to improve effectiveness in increasingly turbulent and competitive markets – the 'adapt to survive' argument. Organizations thus require employee commitment. Mere compliance or 'following the rules' is not enough. The need for commitment is often central to organizational communication programmes, is often accompanied by Total Quality Management (TQM) or Continuous Quality Improvement (CQI) methods, and is an aspect of strategic human resource management (SHRM). The vocabulary of this argument revolves around 'survival', 'competitiveness', 'customer service' and 'organizational effectiveness'.

The theory that 'people will comply if they understand' suggests that organizational communication has an educational component. Employees who are better informed about 'economic realities' are more likely to have realistic expectations and make reasonable demands. However, as Townley (1994, p. 611) notes, this argument equates communication with propaganda which attempts to shape attitudes and behaviours in particular directions, to generate consensus on organizational issues and management decisions, 'giving the logic of managerial decision-making a greater legitimacy'. With the widespread use of team briefing

Table 6.7: Open and closed communication climates

Open, supportive communication climate	Closed, defensive communication climate
Descriptive: informative rather than evaluative communication	**Judgemental**: emphasis on apportioning blame, make people feel incompetent
Solution-oriented: focus on problem-solving rather than on what is not possible	**Controlling**: conformity expected, inconsistency and change inhibited
Open and honest: no hidden messages	**Deceptive**: hidden meanings, insincerity, manipulative communication
Caring: emphasis on empathy and understanding	**Non-caring**: detached and impersonal, little concern for others
Egalitarian: everyone valued regardless of role or status	**Superior**: status and skill differences emphasized in communication
Forgiving: errors and mistakes recognized as inevitable, focus on minimizing	**Dogmatic**: little discussion, unwillingness to accept views of others or compromise
Feedback: positive, essential to maintaining performance and relationships	**Hostile**: needs of others given little importance

and teamworking approaches to organizational design, management can bypass trade union representatives by working through team leaders instead.

Townley thus argues that communication in an organization is not 'neutral'. Organizational communication is constructed from a perspective which represents management interests. Organizational power inequalities require management to direct and dominate workforce behaviour. Information is not simply a commodity to be transmitted. Organizational communication mechanisms are tools (not always effective) for manipulating workforce attitudes and behaviours. This argument reflects a postmodern viewpoint which encourages us to ask, 'whose interests are served by this statement, this way of presenting information, this argument?' The 'context' indicated in our model of the communication process, in figure 6.1, must therefore consider not just the physical and interpersonal context, but also the wider social and political context of organizational communication.

Not getting the message: employee responses to corporate communication

Alan Harrison explored employee attitudes to management communication in three British organizations: Royal Mail, GPT (now Marconi Communications) and BT (British Telecommunications). Focus groups of employees recruited through trade union contacts were conducted, in two cases following a union meeting and in one instance at an Indian restaurant before a meal. Each focus group was first invited to discuss management communication in general, then to discuss specific items of company communication, including articles from company magazines and a letter from a managing director about possible redundancies. The discussion revealed some common responses:

- The term 'bullshit' was used to describe management communication in every discussion.

- Most said that they threw away corporate magazines and letters without reading them.

- Team briefings were criticized for containing irrelevant material and for omitting important issues, due to management misunderstanding or to conflict among managers.

- Management briefings in general were criticized for being late, inadequate and 'one way only', with no opportunity to provide feedback.

➤

■ Direct corporate communication to employees was seen as a way of bypassing trade unions; in GPT, for example, issues raised formally in union negotiation meetings were answered months later in the company magazine.

Scepticism about corporate communication was not related to trade union density or level of militancy, as had been expected. Harrison argues that employees have a sophisticated understanding of the management language used in corporate communication, and that they can decode the underlying messages effectively. Management, however, appear not to bring much sophistication to the coding of their corporate messages.

Based on Alan Harrison, 'Getting the message: resistance to corporate communication in three British organizations', Paper presented to the Working Class Academics Conference, University of Arkansas, Little Rock, AR, 1999.

Recap

1. *Explain the main components of the interpersonal communication process.*

   • Communication involves an exchange of meaning, achieved through the processes of coding, transmission, decoding and feedback.

   • Face-to-face communication allows instant feedback, and coding and decoding problems arise with other forms of communication where feedback is delayed or absent.

2. *Identify the main barriers to effective interpersonal communication.*

   • The main barriers to communication include power and gender differences, physical surroundings, language variations and cultural diversity.

   • Barriers can be overcome through face-to-face communication, by checking decoding, by paying attention to the context of communication, and by trying to see things the way the other person does.

3. *Understand the effective use of different questioning techniques, conversation controls and listening skills.*

   • Getting appropriate information from someone else involves the effective use of different questioning methods: open, closed, probe, hypothetical and reflective.

   • Effective communication involves the use of a range of simple conversation controls: lubricators, inhibitors, bridges and pauses.

   • Active listening involves a range of verbal and non-verbal skills.

   • Communication methods differ between high-context and low-context cultures.

4. *Explain the nature and significance of non-verbal behaviour.*

   • Non-verbal behaviour concerns communication through facial expressions, eye behaviour, gesture and posture, distance between ourselves and others, and paralanguage.

   • If the verbal and non-verbal messages which we are sending are inconsistent, the verbal will be discounted and the non-verbal accepted.

   • Lies can be detected in non-verbal behaviour, but many of the clues are culture-specific.

5. *Understand the nature and mechanisms of impression management skills and techniques.*

   • We influence the image that others have of us through verbal and non-verbal signals.

   • Impression management is used to create a favourable self-image through, for example, ingratiation, intimidation, self-promotion, exemplification, accounting and supplication.

   • Impression management can be seen as natural and unconscious, or as a deliberate attempt at deceit.

6. *Understand the ways in which corporate communication can be used to manipulate understanding and encourage compliance with management directions.*

   • Organizations use a range of media for communicating with employees.

   • The communication climate in an organization can be classed as open and supportive, or closed and defensive.

   • Organizational communication is not neutral, but is constructed from a management perspective in an attempt to manipulate the attitudes and behaviour of recipients.

Revision

1. Explain with appropriate examples the various elements of the model of the interpersonal communication process, identifying why this apparently straightforward process is error-prone.

2. What are the main barriers to effective communication, and how can these barriers be overcome?

3. Explain with appropriate examples the questioning techniques which we use to get information from others, and the conversation control methods that we use to ensure that our interactions run smoothly and in our favour.

4. What is non-verbal communication, and what part does this play in human interaction in general and in organizational settings?

5. Why have organizational communications increased in significance, what problems can arise with organizational communications, and what steps can management take to ensure that communications to employees are effective?

Springboard

Guirdham, M., 2002, *Interactive Behaviour at Work*, Financial Times/Prentice Hall, Harlow (third edition).

A comprehensive and clearly written guide to the significant body of research, theory and practice which concerns interaction and interpersonal skills at work, including cross-cultural and technology-mediated communication, and also covering related aspects of learning, personality, perception, motivation, groups, organization politics and leadership. Offers self-assessment exercises, 'how to' practical advice, and discussion and assignment questions.

Huczynski, A., 2004, *Influencing Within Organizations: Getting In, Rising Up and Moving On*, Routledge, London (second edition).

A practical guide to the realities of influence in organizational life, arguing that job competence alone is usually not enough to ensure career advancement. Includes chapters on verbal and non-verbal influencing and on impression management.

Jablin, F.M. and Putnam, L.L. (eds), 2001, *The New Handbook of Organizational Communication: Advances in Theory, Research, and Methods*, Sage Publications, Thousand Oaks, CA.

Comprehensive and authoritative review of this diverse and rapidly developing field, offering a range of critical and postmodern approaches, paradoxes and perspectives, theoretical, methodological and empirical. This is an advanced text, to be approached selectively. Chapters in part IV are particularly relevant.

McNeill, D., 2000, *The Face*, Penguin, Harmondsworth.

A fascinating guide to the 'uncanny semaphore' of the face, illustrating the richness of the signals that we send and that we can read in the facial expressions of others. You may never look at anyone else quite the same way again.

Rogers, C.R. and Roethlisberger, F.J., 1952, 'Barriers and gateways to communication', *Harvard Business Review*, July/August, pp. 28–34.

Classic article on interpersonal communication problems, from the founder of non-directive therapy, Carl Rogers, and one of the founders of the human relations school of management, Fritz Roethlisberger. Some of the examples are dated but the overall argument still rewards reading. Appears in many collections of readings.

Rosenfeld, P., Giacalone, R.A. and Riordan, C.A., 2001, *Impression Management: Building and Enhancing Reputations at Work*, Thomson Learning, London.

Contemporary text on the nature and significance of impression management in organizational settings, demonstrating the progress made since Goffman.

Tannen, D., 1995, 'The power of talk: who gets heard and why', *Harvard Business Review*, vol. 73, no. 5, pp. 138–48.

If you don't have time to read Deborah Tannen's book, *You Just Don't Understand* (1990), then read this article on the subject of male–female differences in approach to social interaction.

Walther, G.R., 1993, *Say What You Mean and Get What You Want*, Piatkus, London.

Walther argues that the 'powertalking' skills summarized in this chapter can be taught, simply because they involve the conscious use of words and phrases that convey a positive and powerful impression of the speaker.

Home viewing

Catch Me If You Can (2003, directed by Steven Spielberg) is a comedy drama based on the true story of the forger and confidence trickster Frank Abagnale Jr (played by Leonardo Di Caprio) and the FBI agent Carl Hanratty (Tom Hanks) who finally apprehends him, but not before Frank has committed millions of dollars worth of fraud. Frank is a master of the art of impression management, effortlessly convincing others that he is, at various stages in his 'career', student newspaper journalist, high school teacher, airline pilot, doctor and lawyer. He is so convincing that, when he does at one point decide to reveal the truth, his fiancée's father (Martin Sheen) does not believe him. Watch how Frank deploys a powerful combination of non-verbal behaviour, courtship techniques, avoidance of lie detection cues, paralanguage and gesture clusters to manage the impression that he conveys to others.

OB in literature

Louis de Bernières, *Captain Corelli's Mandolin*, Secker and Warburg/Vintage, London, 1994.

A love story set on a Greek island during the Second World War. Analyze the cross-cultural communication problems of (Greek) Pelagia and her (Italian) lover Captain Corelli, during and long after the hostilities, using the coding–decoding model of communication in figure 6.1 of this chapter. Note how their respective backgrounds and occupations (Corelli is an officer in the invading Italian army) affect their perceptions of each other and their communication.

Chapter exercises

1: Close Encounters

Objectives
1. To explore the impact of non-verbal behaviour on interpersonal communication.

2. To expose the wide diversity of non-verbal cues that influence the quality and effectiveness of interpersonal communication.

Briefing
1. Imagine you are having a conversation with someone. They display the non-verbal behaviours listed on p. 211. Considering each in turn, does this behaviour make you feel **P**ositive or **N**egative about the other person, or does it leave you **U**naffected? Why?

2. Compare your responses with colleagues and identify and discuss any discrepancies.

3. What other non-verbal cues (including paralanguage) contribute to effective interpersonal communication?

4. In what ways, if any, do you think you need to change your own behaviour in order to communicate more effectively?

	behaviour	P/N/U	why?
1	picks nose		
2	calm manner		
3	leans far back		
4	head very close to yours		
5	tugs at ear		
6	looks towards you		
7	sits on the same level as you		
8	bounces a leg		
9	picks lint off clothes		
10	voice easy to hear		
11	stares at you		
12	facial expression matches what you feel		
13	relaxed seating position		
14	slouches		
15	raises eyebrows		
16	looks alert		
17	smiles when greeting you		
18	sits higher than you		
19	half closes eyes		
20	high-pitched voice		
21	leans slightly towards you		
22	looks clean		
23	comfortable speech rate		
24	monotonous voice		
25	open body posture		
26	flowery arm gestures		
27	has vacant look		
28	has warmth in voice		
29	pauses for you to continue		
30	whispers		

Based on Richard Nelson-Jones, 2000, *Introduction to Counselling Skills*, Sage, London, p. 52.

2: How would you respond?

Objectives

1. To analyze the practical uses of questioning techniques and conversation controls.

2. To explore appropriate management options in dealing with employee grievances.

Briefing

1. Individual analysis. Read these sets of statements on your own, without discussing them with colleagues. In each case, decide how you would assess the choice of responses, what your selection would be or, if appropriate, how you would word an alternative response. Your instructor may ask you to read all three statements with options before moving to syndicates, or you may be invited to tackle these one at a time.

2. Syndicate discussion. Following your instructor's advice on size of syndicate and timing, share your assessments, selections and, where appropriate, alternative responses, and attempt to reach a group consensus.

3. Plenary. Each group presents and explains its conclusions to the group as a whole.

4. Debriefing. Your instructor will lead a discussion of the implications of the different responses in each case, and of the key learning points from this exercise.

Here are three statements from employees.

Assistant Foreman, age 30, computer manufacturing plant

'Yes, I do have a problem. I'd like to know more about what happened with the promotions last month. Charlie got the foreman's job in motherboard assembly and I didn't even know he was interested. Why did you give the job to him? I would like to know more about what you think of my promotion prospects here. I've been doing this job for about three years now, and I've been with the company for almost five years. I haven't had any complaints about my work. Seems to me I've been doing a pretty good job, but I don't see any recognition for that. What do I have to do to get promoted round here?'

1. You'll make a great foreman, Charlie, but give it time. I'll do what I can to make your case. Don't be discouraged, OK? I'm sure you'll get there soon, you'll see.

2. So, you're not sure about how the company regards your work here, Charlie?

3. Charlie, I understand how you feel, but I have to admit it took me five years to make foreman myself. And I guess I must have felt much the same way you do today. But we just have to be patient. Things don't always happen when we'd like them to, do they?

4. Come on, you've been here long enough to know the answer to that one. Nobody got promoted just by waiting for it to happen. Get with it, you've got to put yourself forward, make people stand up and take notice of your capabilities.

Secretary, age 45, insurance company headquarters

'Can I ask you to do something about the calendars that Mr Johnson and Mr Hargreaves insist on displaying in their offices? They are degrading to women and I find them offensive. I know that some of the other secretaries who work on their floor feel exactly the same way as I do. I have to work with these men and I can't stay out of their offices. Don't we have a company policy or something? I'm surprised you've allowed it to go on this long as it is.'

1. You and some of the other secretaries find these calendars insulting?

2. Look, you're taking this all too seriously. Boys' toys, that's all it is, executive perks. Doesn't mean anything, and there's nothing personal behind it at all. You've no cause for concern.

3. You're right, I don't like that either, but we're talking about their own offices here, and I think that they have the right, within reason, to make their own decisions about what pictures to put on the walls, same as you and I do.

4. I'll see if I can't get a chance to have a quiet word with them some time next week, maybe try to persuade them to move their calendars out of sight, OK? I'm sure they don't mean anything by it.

Personnel Officer, age 26, local authority

'I've just about had it. I can't put up with this kind of pressure for much longer. We just don't have the staff to service the level of requests that we're getting and still do a good job. And some of the people we have to deal with! If that old witch in administration calls me one more time about those files that went missing last week, she's going to get a real mouthful in return. How come you let your department get pushed around like this?'

1. You're not alone. Pressure is something that we've all had to endure at some time. I understand that, it comes with the territory. I think it's about developing the right skills and attitudes to cope.

2. You're right, this is a difficult patch, but I'm sure that it will pass. This can't go on for much longer, and I expect you'll see things start to come right at the end of the month.

3. Well, if you can't stand the heat, I suppose you just have to get out of the kitchen. And please don't refer to people who are senior to you in this organization in that manner.

4. Let me check – this is not about Mrs Smith in admin, you're saying the strain is such that you're thinking of leaving us?

Chapter 7 Perception

Key concepts

perception	perceptual set
selective attention	perceptual world
habituation	halo effect
perceptual filters	stereotype
perceptual organization	attribution

Learning outcomes

When you have read this chapter, you should be able to define those key concepts in your own words, and you should also be able to:

1. Identify the main features of the process of perception.
2. Distinguish between the bottom-up processing of sensory information and the top-down interpretation of that information.
3. Understand the nature and implications of selective attention and perceptual organization.
4. Give examples of how behaviour is influenced by our perceptions.
5. Explain and illustrate the main processes and problems in person perception, including false attributions, halo effects and stereotyping.
6. Explain some less widely appreciated sources of discrimination at work, against men and women, arising from characteristics of the person perception and attribution processes.

Why study perception?

Of all the topics covered in this text, perception is perhaps the one which most clearly sets social science apart from natural science. We attach meanings, interpretations, values and aims to our actions. What we do in the world depends on how we understand our place in it, on how we see ourselves and our social and physical environment, on how we perceive our circumstances. We explain our behaviour with terms like 'reason', 'motive', 'intention', 'purpose' and 'desire'. Physicists, chemists and engineers do not face this complication in coming to grips with their subject matter; matter does not possess motives.

We each perceive the world around us in different ways. It is our perception of reality which shapes and directs our behaviour, not some objective understanding of it. If one person on a hillside perceives that it is cold, they will reach for a sweater. If the person standing next to them perceives that it is warm, they will remove their sweater. These contrasting behaviours can occur simultaneously, regardless of the ambient temperature measured objectively by a thermometer. Human behaviour is a function of the way in which we perceive the world around us, and how we perceive other people and events in that world.

Stop and Criticize

Choose a film that you have seen recently, and which you particularly enjoyed. This could, perhaps, be one of the 'home viewing' suggestions in this textbook. Now find a friend or colleague who has seen the same film and hated it.

Share your views of that film. What factors (age, sex, background, education, interests, values and beliefs, political views, past experience) can you identify to explain the differences in perception between you and your friend or colleague?

We often find ourselves unable to understand other people's behaviour. People can say and do surprising things in settings where it is obvious to us that some other behaviour would be more appropriate. If we are to understand why you behaved in that way in that context, we first need to discover how you perceive that context and your place in it. When we are able to 'see it the way you see it', to put ourselves in your position, what initially took us by surprise is likely to become readily understandable. To understand each other's behaviour, we need to be able to understand each other's perceptions. We need to be able to understand why we perceive things differently in the first place.

Selectivity and organization in perception

We do not passively register sense impressions picked up from the world around us. We process and interpret the incoming raw data in the light of our past experiences, in terms of our current needs and interests, in terms of our knowledge, expectations, beliefs and motives.

The main elements in the perceptual process are illustrated in figure 7.1. From a psychological point of view, the processes of sensation, on the one hand, and **perception**, on the other, work together through what are respectively termed 'bottom-up' and 'top-down' processing. The 'bottom-up' phase concerns the way in which we process the raw data received by our sensory apparatus. One of the key characteristics of bottom-up processing concerns the need for selectivity. We are simply not able to attend to all of the sensory information available to us at any given time. Bottom-up processing screens or filters out redundant and less relevant information so that we can focus on what is important.

Perception: the dynamic psychological process responsible for attending to, organizing and interpreting sensory data.

The 'top-down' phase, in contrast, concerns the mental processing that allows us to order, interpret and make sense of the world around us. One of the key characteristics of top-down processing concerns our need to make sense of our environment, and our search for meaning.

This distinction between sensation (bottom-up) and perception (top-down) can be illustrated in our ability to make sense of incomplete, or even incorrect, sensory information. The missing letter or comma, or the incorrectly spelled term does not normally interfere with the comprehension of the human reader:

This sent nce us incorr ct, bit yoo wull stell bi abl to udersta d it.

Our top-down conceptual processing ability means that we are able to fill in the gaps and correct the mistakes, and make sense of 'imperfect' raw data.

We each have a similar nervous system and share more or less common sensory equipment. However, we have different social and physical backgrounds which give us different values, interests and expectations, and therefore different perceptions. We do not behave in, and respond to, the world 'as it really is'. This idea of the 'real world' is somewhat arbitrary. The 'real world' as a concept is not a useful

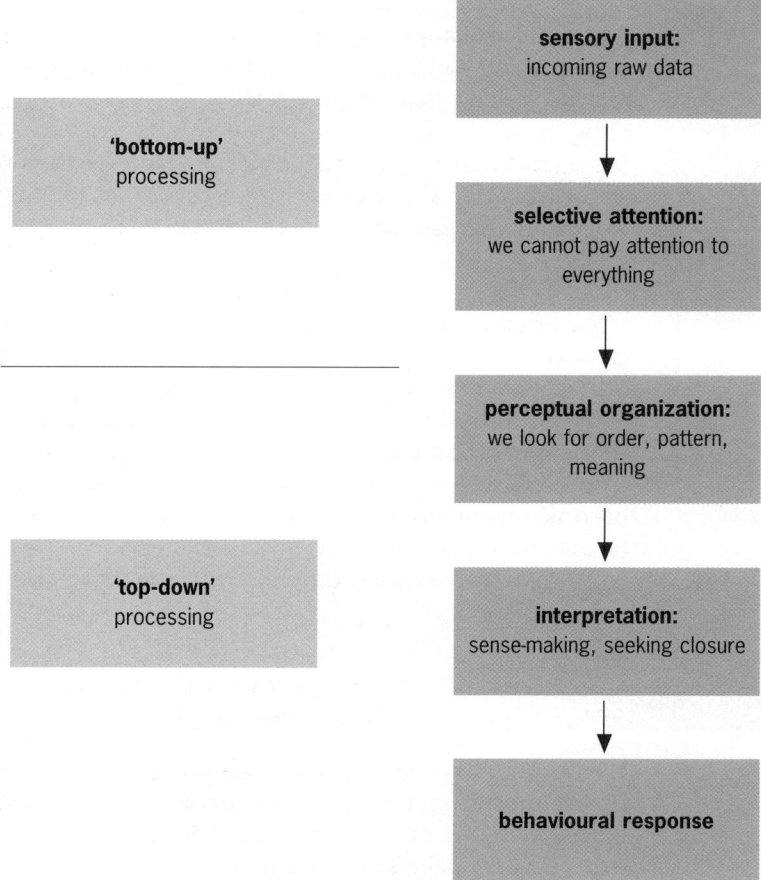

Figure 7.1: Elements in the process of perception

starting point for developing an understanding of human behaviour in general, or organizational behaviour in particular. We behave in, and respond to, the world as we perceive it.

Successful interpersonal relationships depend on some overlap between our perceptual worlds, and on some common perceptions, or we would never be able to understand each other. Our perceptual worlds, however, are in a detailed analysis unique, which makes life interesting, but also gives us problems.

Our perceptual processing is normally carried out without much conscious deliberation or effort. In fact, we often have no effective control over the process and, fortunately, control is not always necessary. We can, however, control some aspects of the process simply by being consciously aware of what is happening. There are many settings where such control is desirable and can help us to avoid dangerous and expensive errors. Understanding the characteristics of perception can be useful in a variety of organizational settings: for example, with the design of aircraft instrumentation and displays for pilots, in the conduct of selection interviews for new employees, in the handling of disputes and employee grievances.

Perception is a dynamic process because it involves ordering and attaching meaning to raw sensory data. Our sensory apparatus is bombarded with vast amounts of information. Some of this information comes from inside the body, such as sensations of hunger, lust, pain and fatigue. Some of this information comes from people, objects and events in the world around us. We do not passively record these sensory data. We are constantly sifting and ordering this stream of information, making sense of it and interpreting it.

Perception, therefore, is an information processing activity which concerns the phenomena of **selective attention** and *perceptual organization*.

Our senses – sight, hearing, touch, taste, smell, and the sensing of internal bodily signals or 'kinaesthesia' – each consist of specialist nerves that respond to specific forms of energy, such as light, sound, pressure, and temperature changes. There are some forms of energy that our senses cannot detect unaided, such as radio waves, sounds at very low and very high pitch, and infrared radiation. Our sensory apparatus has limitations that we cannot overcome without the aid of special equipment. We are unable to hear sound frequencies above 10,000 hertz, but many animals, including dogs and dolphins, have better hearing. We are unable to hear sounds below 30 hertz, but whales can. Owls have much better eyesight than us.

The constraints imposed by our sensory apparatus can be modified in certain ways by experience. The boundary, or threshold, between what we can and cannot detect can be established by experiment. It is also possible to explore individual differences in thresholds across the senses. These thresholds can be altered by experience. If there happens to be a clock ticking in the room where you study, you will almost certainly not be aware of the sound, until somebody mentions it, or the clock stops. Next time you visit a library, close your eyes for few seconds and pay attention to the background noise that you do not usually hear. But surely, you must have heard it, as you must have heard the clock ticking, if your ears were working properly? Our sensory apparatus responds not simply to energy, but to changes in energy levels. Having detected a stimulus, such as a clock, or the hum of air conditioning, the nerves concerned become tired of transmitting the same information indefinitely and give up, until the stimulus changes. This explains our surprise at the sudden silence which follows when machinery stops.

Once stimuli become familiar, they stop being sensed. This phenomenon, in which the perceptual threshold is raised, is known as **habituation**.

Our sensory apparatus has design limitations which filter out some information, such as x-rays and dog whistles. Perception involves other filtering processes, as the phenomenon of habituation suggests. In particular, information that is familiar, non-threatening and unnecessary to the task in hand is screened out of our conscious awareness.

Stand on the pavement of a busy street and pay attention to as much of the available information as you can: the noise of the traffic, the make, colour and condition of passing vehicles, the smell of rubber tyres and exhaust fumes, the pressure of the pavement on the soles of your feet, the breeze across your face, the smell of the perfume of a passing woman, the clothes of the man across the street and the type of dog he is walking, an overheard mobile telephone conversation. When you think you are taking it all in, start to cross the road. If you get across safely, you will find that your heightened awareness has lapsed, dramatically. You would be mown down fairly quickly if this were not the case. Selective attention allows us to concentrate on what is important and significant, and to ignore the insignificant and trivial.

Nancy Adler (2002) offers an excellent example of habituation in our use of language. Read the following sentence, and then very quickly count the number of Fs:

FINISHED FILES ARE THE RESULT OF YEARS OF SCIENTIFIC STUDY COMBINED WITH THE EXPERIENCE OF YEARS

Most people who speak English as a second language see all six Fs. Native English speakers usually pick up only three or four, because they tend to miss out the Fs in 'of'. Native English speakers have been conditioned – habituated – to skip the 'of' because it does not contribute to the meaning of the sentence.

Adler's explanation is that, once we stop seeing the 'ofs', we do not see them again, even as in this example when we are looking for them. There is simply too much information available at any one time for us to pay attention to all of it, so we screen out that which is apparently of little or no value. The image of the world that we carry around inside our heads can only ever be a partial representation of what is 'really out there'. This leads to the conclusion that our behavioural choices are determined not by reality, but by what we perceive that reality to be. Our perception is influenced by what are called **perceptual filters**.

The internal and external factors which affect selective attention are illustrated in figure 7.2.

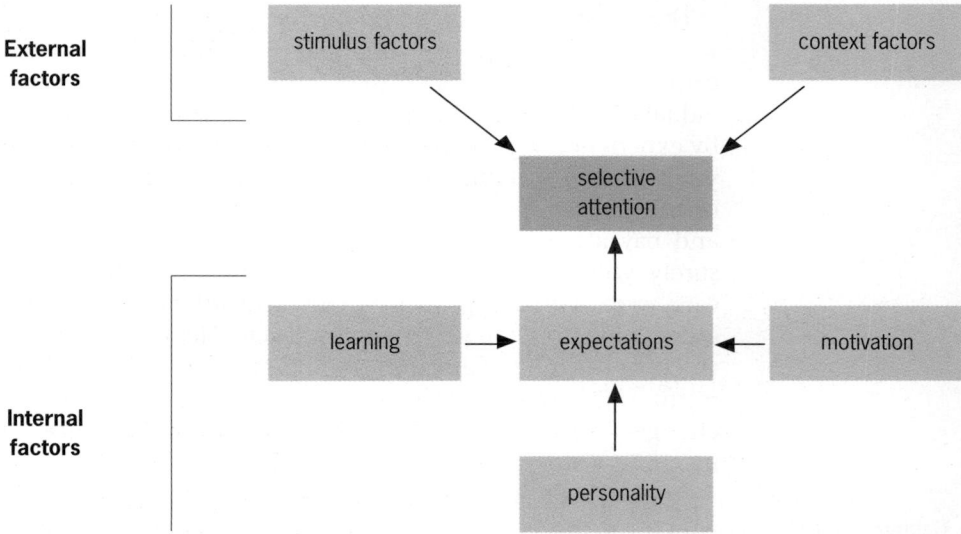

Figure 7.2: The external and internal factors influencing selective attention

The external factors affecting selective attention include stimulus factors and context factors. With respect to the stimulus factors, our attention is drawn more readily to stimuli that are:

large		small
bright		dull
loud		quiet
strong	*rather than*	weak
unfamiliar		familiar
stand out from surroundings		blend with surroundings
moving		stationary
repeated (but not repetitive)		one-off

Note, however, that we do not merely respond to single features, as this list might imply; we respond to the pattern of stimuli available to us.

Stop and Criticize

Identify examples of the ways in which advertisements creatively use stimulus factors to attract our attention, in newspapers and magazines and on billboards and television.

Our attention is also influenced by context factors. The naval commander on the ship's bridge and the cook in the kitchen may both have occasion to shout 'fire', but these identical utterances mean quite different things to those within earshot, and will lead to radically different forms of behaviour (the taking and saving of lives respectively). We do not need any help to make this crucial distinction, beyond our knowledge of the context.

The internal factors affecting perception include:

■ *Learning*: You've heard that argument before, so are you going to listen carefully to it again? Our past experience leads to the development of perceptual expectations or *perceptual sets*, which give us predispositions to pay attention to some stimuli, and to ignore other information.

■ *Personality*: How come you (gregarious, sociable) saw the advertisement for the party, but your friend (reserved, shy) did not? Our personality traits predispose us to pay attention to some issues, events and human characteristics and not others.

■ *Motivation*: Do you get out of the shower to take a telephone call, perhaps expecting a party invitation or a job offer? We are more likely to perceive as important, and thus to respond to, stimuli that we find motivating.

Five ways the supermarket has you sussed

1. Different colours produce different reactions in shoppers. Cool blue, for example, is used at the fish counter to suggest freshness – and, of course, the sea.

2. The order in which a shopper looks over the goods is controlled by the order in which they are displayed. Goods at eye level are inspected first, then attention wanders to lower shelves.

3. Shelves of varying depth put more goods into view. This produces a sense of limitless stocks, and encourages shoppers to notice less well-known products.

4. Strategic positioning of mirrors adds to the impression of abundance that the supermarket trades on ('you'll get everything here'). This is especially the case in the fruit and veg section.

5. Careful design of shelf units holds shoppers' attention. Curved shelving leads seamlessly from one aisle into the next. You probably won't even take your eyes off the displays as you progress through the store.

They say the trick when you are showing prospective buyers around your house is to brew fresh coffee and bake bread, as the smells produce a reassuring, homely atmosphere. Smell is a key tactic for supermarkets too. Coffee shops can create that same desirable smell, while bread smells can be pumped through air vents into the store, and in some cases into the car park so it hits you before you even enter the building. On trial in some American supermarkets is a process called micro-encapsulation, used at the point of sale. As the customer's hand brushes the surface of a pack of, say, coffee or bread rolls, smell capsules that emit the smell of coffee or bread are broken. The capsules can also be triggered by heat, for instance by a neon sign above the display. Smell often affects us below the conscious level – we may not even know that we are responding to a supermarket's subtle manipulations.

From Gillian Drummond, 'Irresistible science of the super-sellers', *Focus*, November 1994, pp. 24 and 26.

Much of perception can be described as classification, or categorization. We categorize people as male or female, lazy or energetic, extrovert or shy. In fact our classification schemes are usually more sophisticated than that. We classify objects as cars, buildings, furniture, crockery, and so on, and we refine our classification schemes further under these headings. However, we are not born with a neat classification scheme 'wired in' with the brain. These categories are learned.

Max Wertheimer
(1880–1943)

Perceptual organization: the process through which incoming stimuli are organized or patterned in systematic and meaningful ways.

They are social constructs. What we learn is often culture bound, or culture specific. An Indonesian visitor to one of our institutions once remarked, 'In your country, you feed the pigeons. In my country, the pigeons feed us.' The British revulsion at the thought of eating dog (classified as pet), the Hindu revulsion at the thought of eating beef (classified as sacred), and the Islamic aversion to alcohol (classified as proscribed by the Koran), are all culturally transmitted emotions based on learned values.

Problems arise when we and others act as if our culture had a monopoly on 'right thinking' on such issues. Different does not imply wrong. Different people within the same culture have different experiences and develop different expectations. The internal factors – our past experience and what we have learned, our personalities, our motivations – contribute to the development of our expectations of the world around us, what we want from it, what will happen in it, and what should happen. We tend to select information that fits our expectations, and pay less attention to information that does not.

Our categorization processes, and the search for meaning and pattern, are key characteristics of perception. This perceptual work is captured by the concept of **perceptual organization**.

The principles by which the process of perceptual organization operates were first identified by Max Wertheimer (1880–1943) in 1923. The 'proximity principle' notes that we tend to group together or to classify stimuli that are physically close to each other and which thus appear to 'belong' together. Note how you 'see' three sets of pairs rather than six blobs here:

The 'similarity principle' notes that we classify or group together stimuli that resemble each other in appearance in some respect. Note how you 'see' four pairs here, not eight objects:

The fact that we are able to make use of incomplete and ambiguous information, by 'filling in the gaps' from our own knowledge and past experience, is known as the 'principle of closure'. These principles of perceptual organization apply to simple visual stimuli. Of more interest here, however, is the way in which these principles apply to person perception. How often do we assume that people are similar just because they live in the same neighbourhood, or work in the same section of the factory or office building (proximity principle), or just because they wear the same clothes or have similar ethnic origins (similarity principle)? How often do we take incomplete information about someone (he's Scottish) and draw inferences from this (closure principle)? This can cause the spread of false rumours in organizations through what is sometimes called 'the grapevine'.

Change blindness: just how selective can we get?

Picture the following, and prepare to be amazed. You're walking across a college campus when a stranger asks you for directions. While you're talking to him, two men pass between you carrying a wooden door. You feel a moment's irritation, but they move on and you carry on describing the route. When you're finished, the stranger informs you that you've just taken part in a psychology experiment. 'Did you notice anything change after the two men passed with the door?' he asks. 'No', you reply uneasily. He then explains that the man who initially approached you walked off behind the door, leaving him in his place. The first man now comes up to join you. Looking at them standing side by side, you notice that the two are of different height and build, and dressed differently, have different haircuts, and different voices.

It sounds impossible, but when Daniel Simons, a psychologist at Harvard University, and his colleague Daniel Levin of Kent State University in Ohio actually did this experiment, they found that fully 50 per cent of those who took part failed to notice the substitution. The subjects had succumbed to what is called change blindness. Rather than logging every detail of the visual scene, says Simons, we are actually highly selective about what we take in. Our impression of seeing everything is just that – an impression. In fact we extract a few details and rely on memory, or perhaps even our imagination, for the rest.

From Laura Spinney, 'Blind to change', *New Scientist*, 18 November 2000, pp. 27–32.

Perceptual sets and perceptual worlds

Perceptual set: an individual's predisposition to respond to people and events in a particular manner.

We have shown how the perceptual process selects incoming stimuli and organizes them into meaningful patterns. We have also argued that this processing is influenced by learning, motivation, and by personality – factors which give rise to expectations, which in turn make us more ready to respond to certain stimuli in certain ways and less ready to respond to others. This readiness to respond is called the individual's **perceptual set**.

A perceptual set is also known as a mental set. As we tend to perceive what we expect to perceive, this can also be called our perceptual expectations. The drawing on the following page was published by an international accounting firm in 1995. Some readers will recognize this as a variant on a drawing published in 1915 by the cartoonist W.H. Hill. What do you see here? An old woman or a young woman? Your answer may be influenced by what you are predisposed to see at the time you are reading this. The reactions of different individuals will not be consistent, and it does not make sense to argue over which perception is correct. We must accept that two people can observe the same thing, but perceive it in quite different ways. Failure to appreciate this feature of the perceptual process creates many organizational problems, and particularly communication problems. Employees may perceive that they face chronic problems, while management perceive that such complaints are trivial and transient. It makes little sense to ask whose perceptions are correct. The starting point for resolving such issues must lie with the recognition that different people hold different, but equally legitimate, views of the same set of circumstances.

Chapter 1 identified two views of human behaviour. The *positivist* perspective sets out to discover 'the world out there, as it really is'. The *phenomenological* perspective sets out to discover how our world is *socially constructed*, and how we experience and interpret that world. The argument in this chapter suggests that 'the world out there' is not a good starting point for developing an understanding of human behaviour. We each have a unique version of what is out there and of our own place in it. We each live in our own **perceptual world**.

Perceptual world: the individual's personal internal image, map or picture of their social, physical and organizational environment.

We each have a perceptual world that is selective and partial, and which concentrates on features of particular interest and importance to us. Through the processes of learning, motivation and personality development, we each have different expectations and different degrees of readiness to respond to objects, people and events in different ways. We impose meaning on received patterns of information; the meanings that we attach to objects, people and events are not intrinsic to these things, but are learned through social experience and are coloured by our current needs and objectives.

Artwork supplied by *The Broadbent Partnership*, London.

Our perceptions, that is the meanings that we attach to the information available to us, shape our actions. Behaviour in an organization context can usually be understood once we understand the way in which the individual perceives that context. Figure 7.3 (based on Dixon, 1999, p. 30) illustrates the links between available information based on observation and experience, the perception based on that information and outcomes in terms of decisions with respect to actions. This example explains why employees would ignore apparently reasonable management requests to become 'team players'.

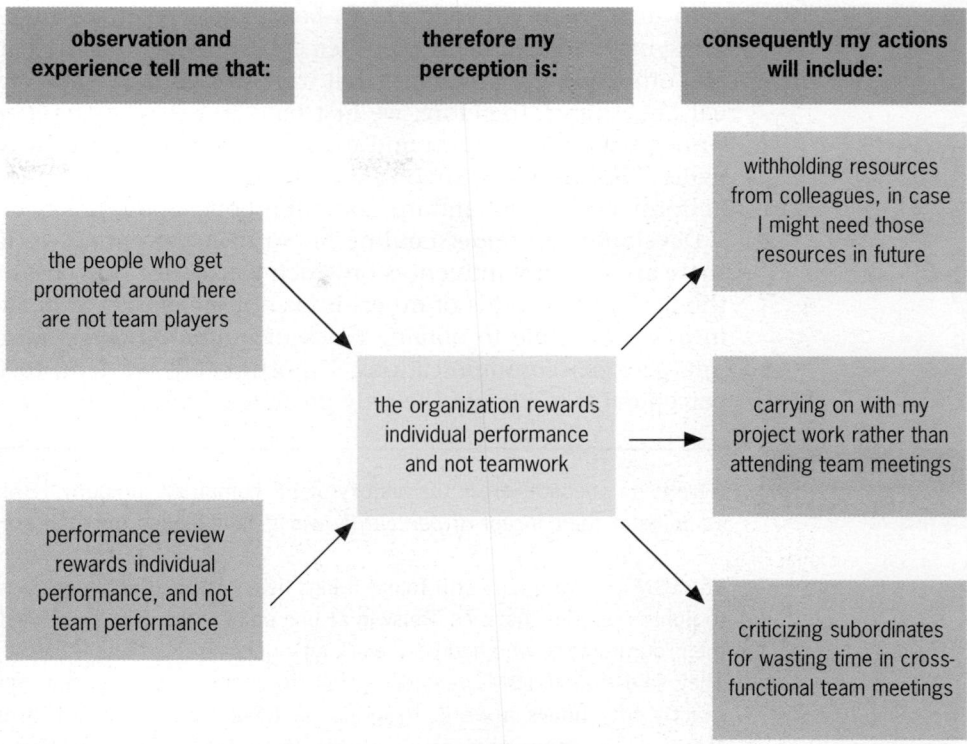

Figure 7.3: The information–perception–actions link

Cultural factors pay a significant role in determining how we interpret available information and experience. You order a meal in a restaurant. Was the service fast or slow? Research into cultural differences in the perception of time suggest that your answer to this question depends to some extent on where in the world you come from. One well-known piece of research (Levine, 1990) compared the pace of life in six countries (Britain, Italy, Indonesia, Japan, Taiwan and the United States) by measuring:

- the accuracy of clocks in city bank branches;
- the speed at which city pedestrians walked;
- the length of time it took to buy a postage stamp.

The research revealed that Japanese cities had the most accurate clocks, the fastest pedestrians and the most efficient post office clerks. Indonesian cities, in contrast, had the least accurate clocks and the slowest pedestrians. Italy, however, had the slowest post office clerks. The overall results of this study were as follows:

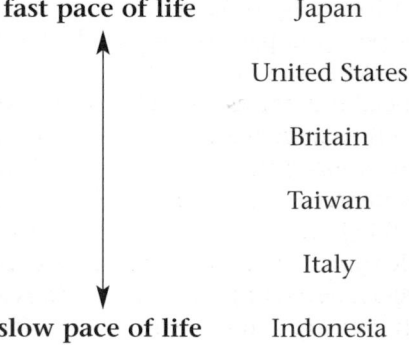

fast pace of life   Japan

United States

Britain

Taiwan

Italy

slow pace of life   Indonesia

To understand an individual's behaviour, therefore, we need to know something of the elements in their perceptual world, and the pattern of information and other cultural influences that have shaped that world. To change an individual's behaviour, therefore, we first have to consider changing their perceptions, through the information and experiences available to them. In the example in figure 7.3, this would involve radical, visible and sustained changes in company performance review, and in promotion policies and practice.

Developing an understanding of our own perceptual world is difficult because there are so many influences of which we are not fully aware. Information about the perceptual worlds of others is even more elusive and, although this is by no means impossible to obtain, a lack of mutual understanding creates barriers to interpersonal communications. Unfortunately, we tend to forget that our own perceptual world is not the only possible or correct one.

Stop and Criticize

Here is an anecdote from the history of the computer company, IBM. How would an understanding of the concept of *perceptual world* have helped the manager, Reiswig?

The IBM programmers still found things heavy-handed at times, despite Reiswig's attempts to lighten up. For instance, Reiswig at one point made fifty-hour weeks mandatory. Some of the programmers, who had been working eighty- to ninety-hour weeks, took that as an insult. They said that if IBM wanted to play those sorts of penny-ante games, then they'd work exactly fifty hours a week. Progress on OS/2 actually *slowed* after extra hours became required. An apocryphal memo began circulating among the IBM programmers about a rowing race that had supposedly taken place between IBM and Microsoft. Microsoft had one coxswain shouting orders while eight people rowed, the memo said. IBM had eight coxswains shouting orders while one rowed. Microsoft won big. So IBM launched several task forces to do some coxswain/oarsman analyses and decided after several weeks that the problem was that the oarsman wasn't rowing hard enough. When the race was rerun and Microsoft won big again, the oarsman was fired.

After a month or so, though, Reiswig figured out what was going on and removed the requirement. Hours soared, and the OS/2 project became one of the most engaging in the history of IBM.

From Paul Carroll, *Big Blues: The Unmaking of IBM*, Orion Books, London, 1994, p. 278.

Do we see to know or know to see?

Fortunately, we as individuals are not as isolated from each other as the argument so far suggests. We do not live in a social and organizational world of constant misunderstanding and failed communication. A high proportion of our interactions are effective, or tolerably so. Why? We are, of course, not wholly unique as individuals, and our personal perceptual worlds overlap. We share the same, or similar, sensory apparatus. We share the same basic needs. We share much of the same background social environment. Within the same society, although there are vast differences in experience, we share some of the same problems and environmental features. All this common ground makes the tasks of mutual understanding and interpersonal communication possible.

We have defined the process of perception in terms of making sense of the information available to us. We are active processors of that information, not passive recipients. However, much of that information is already processed for us. We are bombarded with sensory information, from other people, from books and newspapers and magazines, from street advertising, from radio and television, from the internet, and from various internal organizational sources – annual reports, team briefings, newsletters.

In the contemporary organizational context, employees at all levels have experienced major upheavals in recent years as organizations have introduced initiatives to improve performance. These changes, which have often led to stress, burnout, initiative fatigue and work intensification as well as to improved organizational performance (Buchanan, Claydon and Doyle, 1999), have typically been communicated using arguments like this:

> In order to survive in a rapidly changing, turbulent, and highly competitive environment, we need to become more efficient, more cost conscious, more flexible and adaptable, and more customer-focused. Therefore, we need to implement the following radical changes to organization structures, procedures, and jobs.

There are two ways to read this 'turbulent world' argument.

First, this is an unexceptional and taken-for-granted expression of contemporary organizational reality. There is nothing unusual in this argument about the need for organizational flexibility to deal with external change. People have been saying that for years. It's obvious, isn't it? This is a widely accepted view.

Second, this is an attempt to promote a particular *perception* of organizational reality, based on management values. After all, change is stressful and employees are likely to resist. If we can present a compelling argument that is beyond challenge, resistance can be avoided and the changes can go ahead more smoothly.

The key to this second reading lies with our use of language. One view of language is that we use it as a tool to communicate observations and understanding. An alternative view is that language, particularly the concepts that we use, constructs that understanding. You cannot 'see' twenty different types of snow until you know what they are called and can link those labels to different visual stimuli. In other words, one view of language simply says that we 'see in order to know'. The alternative view is that we need to know first, before we can 'see'. The implication of this second view of language, that 'we know to see', is that perceptions can potentially be influenced, that is can be managed, through language.

Consider the 'turbulent world so we must change' argument. What language typically accompanies this exhortation? Looking through job advertisements and other forms of organizational literature, note how many times the following kinds of statement appear:

- we need to become more *customer oriented*;

- our mission is *excellence*;

- we believe in employee *empowerment*;

- our survival depends on *efficiency* and *cost-effectiveness*;

- *initiative* and *creativity* are key competencies;

- *flexibility* is the key to competitive success;

- we must strive for *continuous improvement*;

- we are a *total quality* organization.

The 'turbulent world' argument is hard to challenge. Communications of this kind have the potential to lead employees to internalize management values as their own, without question. It is difficult to argue that 'there is so little change in the business environment that we should be developing a rigid bureaucracy', or that 'customers don't matter, let's pay attention to our own staff'. However, rapid change can be personally and socially damaging; factory and office closures and relocation, loss of jobs, loss of community. An organization that ignores the well-being of its staff may find that it loses customers who feel that they have been given inadequate or discourteous service.

Language promotes a particular set of perceptions related to a specific set of values. The 'turbulent world' language creates an impression of 'the way things are', of 'it makes sense doesn't it?', of 'that's obvious'. If you can get people to accept this language and these arguments, then language becomes a tool for manipulating perceptions. If we can manipulate perceptions, we can control behaviour because, as this chapter argues, our behaviour depends not on some 'external reality' but on our perception of reality.

This 'second reading' of the 'turbulent world' argument, viewing it as an attempt to manage perception, reflects an aspect of the *postmodern perspective* discussed in chapter 2. This perspective argues that 'reality out there' is not simply waiting to be discovered, but is created in social exchange through language. We don't go out and discover reality. Multiple realities are presented to us through our interactions. What matters is the version of reality in which most people come to believe. The management of perception is thus a tool for 'keeping people in their place' by inhibiting challenge and criticism. You cannot readily challenge something that appears to be, and is widely accepted as natural, obvious or inevitable without appearing deviant or eccentric.

Here we find, as chapter 2 argues, two strengths of the postmodern perspective. First, it highlights the existence and value of differences in perception, of multiple perspectives, arguing that no single perspective should be given the privilege of being correct. Second, it invites us to question the obvious and the taken-for-granted.

Stop and Criticize

The postmodernist argues that we are 'fed' information in language which reinforces the management definition of reality and justifies management decisions in order to make employees compliant. The manager can claim, 'communication is part of my job'. The employee can claim, 'I can tell when managers are trying to fool me'. Are our perceptions so readily manipulated by slick presentation and fancy jargon?

Perceptual sets and assumptions

The concept of perceptual set, or perceptual expectation, applies to the ways in which we see other people, events and objects. To understand the nature of perception is to understand, at least in part, the sources and nature of many organizational problems. There are two related and prominent features of the process of people perception: the *halo effect* and *stereotyping*.

The term **halo effect** was first used by the psychologist Edward Thorndyke in 1920. This is an application of the concept of *selective attention* to our perception of people. It is a natural human response, on meeting a stranger, to 'size them up', to make judgements about the kind of person they are, and whether we will like them or not. We do this to others on a first encounter; they do this to us. It seems as if first impressions really do count, after all (and we don't get a second chance to make a first impression).

Halo effect: a judgement based on a single, striking characteristic, such as an aspect of dress, speech, posture or nationality.

However, faced with so much new information about someone – the physical and social setting, their appearance, what they say, how they say it, their posture, their non-verbal behaviour, how they respond to us – we are forced to be selective with respect to the information to which we pay attention. In terms of the model

Edward Lee
Thorndyke
(1874–1949)

Walter Lippmann
(1889–1974)

of the perceptual process in figure 7.1, therefore, the halo effect is an error at the selective attention stage. Our judgements can thus rely on a single striking characteristic: the sound of their voice or a familiar accent, a perfume, their dress or tie, the car they drive or their hairstyle. If this judgement is favourable, we give the other person a positive halo, regardless of other information that, if we gave it due attention, might lead us to a different, more balanced, evaluation. If our judgement, on the other hand, is not favourable, we give the other person a negative halo (or horn). The halo effect can work in both directions.

The halo effect can thus act as an early screen that filters out later information which is not consistent with our earlier judgement. The problem, of course, is that what we notice first about another person is often not relevant to the judgement that we want to make. A confounding factor is that we tend to give more favourable judgements to people who have characteristics in common with us. However, since when did somebody's voice, hairstyle, deodorant or clothes enable us to predict, say, their ability to design bridges or manage a department in a hotel? Some people feel that they can make such predictions from such limited evidence, based presumably on their own past experiences. The halo effect can apply to things as well as to people. How many examples can you think of where country of origin leads you automatically to believe that the product quality will be good or bad (Australian wine, Belgian chocolates, French perfume, German cars, Italian clothes, Scottish whisky)?

Why job applicants are not hired

A survey of 153 human resource managers in America identified the twenty most common errors made by applicants attending job interviews, listed here in order of importance:

1. Poor personal appearance.
2. Overaggressiveness.
3. Inability to express information clearly.
4. Lack of interest and enthusiasm.
5. Lack of career planning; no purpose and no goals.
6. Nervous, lack of confidence and poise.
7. Overemphasis on money.
8. Unwillingness to start at the bottom.
9. Makes excuses.
10. Lack of tact and courtesy.
11. Immaturity.
12. Condemns past employers.
13. No genuine interest in company or job.
14. Fails to look interviewer in the eye.
15. Sloppy application form.
16. Little sense of humour.
17. Arrives late at interview.
18. Fails to express appreciation for interviewer's time.
19. Fails to ask questions about the company and job.
20. Vague responses to questions.

Each of these behaviours can lead the interviewer to perceive the applicant in negative terms.

From Arthur G. Bedeian, *Management*, CBS International, 1986, p. 376.

Stereotype: a category, or personality type, to which we consign people on the basis of their membership of some known group.

Remember the concept of *perceptual organization*? This phenomenon also applies to person perception. The term **stereotyping** was first used by typographers to made-up blocks of type, and was used to describe bias in person perception by Walter Lippmann in 1922. The concept refers to the way in which we group together people who seem to us to share similar characteristics. Lippmann saw stereotypes as 'pictures in the head', as simple mental images of groups and their behaviour. So, when we meet, say, an accountant, a nurse, an engineer, a poet or a mechanical engineering student, we attribute certain personality traits to them because they are accountants, or students, or whatever. Everybody knows, for example, that Scots are mean and blondes have more fun. In terms of the model in figure 7.1, therefore, stereotyping is an error at the perceptual organization stage in the process of perception.

The pupils' stereotype of mathematicians

A survey of 450 children aged 12 and 13 from seven countries, including Britain, America, Finland and Romania, revealed a common stereotype of mathematicians. School pupils everywhere see them as overweight white males, often with beards and spectacles, who are scruffy, unfashionably dressed, middle-aged, bald or with weird hair, with few friends and no social life. One child in the survey produced this drawing.

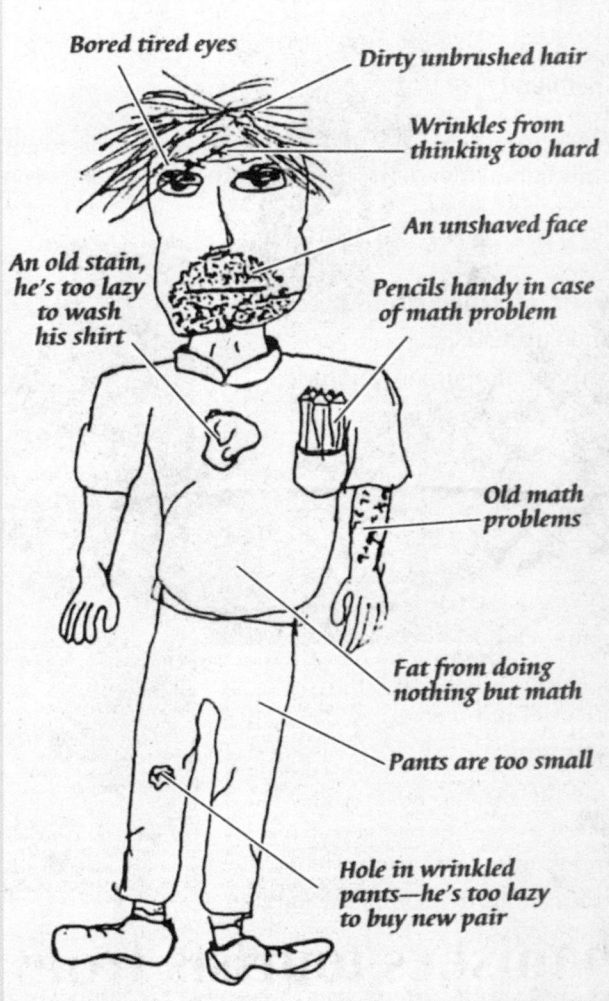

After Picker, S. H. and Berry, J. (2000) 'Investigating pupils' images of mathematicians', *Educational Studies in Mathematics*, 43(1), pp. 65–94. Reproduced by permission of Susan H. Picker.

Explore your own stereotypes by completing each of the following sentences with three terms that you think describe most or all members of the category concerned:

university lecturers are . . .
artists are . . .
mechanical engineers are . . .
trainee nurses are . . .
airline pilots are . . .

You may find it interesting to share your stereotypes with those of colleagues, particularly if some of them have friends or close relatives who are pilots, nurses, mechanical engineers . . .

If we know, or assume, somebody's apparent group membership in this way, our instant categorization allows us to attribute a range of qualities to them. Stereotypes are overgeneralizations, and are bound to be radically inaccurate on occasion. But they can be convenient. By adopting a stereotyped perspective, we may be able to shortcut our evaluation process, and make quicker and more reliable predictions of behaviour. We can have problems, however, with those who fall into more than one category with conflicting stereotypes: the mechanical engineer who writes poetry, for instance.

Stereotyping also works at an international level. See if you can match these stereotyped (not necessarily accurate) images with the right countries:

Culture		Stereotyped image
1 **American**	A	Demonstrative, talkative, emotional, romantic, bold, artistic
2 **English**	B	Manana attitude, macho, music lovers, touchers
3 **French**	C	Inscrutable, intelligent, xenophobic, golfers, group-oriented, polite, soft-spoken
4 **Italian**	D	Conservative, reserved, polite, proper, formal
5 **Latin American**	E	Arrogant, loud, friendly, impatient, generous, hardworking, monolingual
6 **Japanese**	F	Arrogant, rude, chauvinistic, romantics, gourmets, cultural, artistic

Clearly, while some members of each of these cultures may possess some of the attributes of their stereotype, it would be false to claim that every member of a culture shared the same attributes to the same degree. Not all Asians are keen golfers; not all English people are reserved and polite; not all Americans are arrogant and hardworking.

Sex, appearance, attractiveness and discrimination

Attribution: the process by which we make sense of our environment through our perceptions of causality.

We emphasized earlier that the perceptual process is concerned with making sense of and explaining the world around us, and the people and events in it. Our need for explanation and understanding is reflected in the way in which we search for the causes of people's actions. Our perceptions of causality are known as **attributions**.

Fritz Heider
(1896–1988)

Harold H. Kelley
(1921–2003)

An attribution is a belief about the cause or causes of an event or an action. Attribution theory was developed in the 1950s and 1960s by Fritz Heider (1958) and Harold H. Kelley (1971). They argue that our understanding of our social world is based on our continual attempts at causal analysis based on how we interpret experience.

Why is that person so successful? Why did that project fail? Why are those people still arguing? If we understand the causes of success, failure and conflict, we may be able to adjust our behaviour and other factors accordingly. Attribution is simply the process of attaching causes or reasons to the actions and events we see. We tend to look for causes either in people's abilities and personalities, or in aspects of the setting or circumstances in which they find themselves. This distinction is usually described in terms of internal causality and external causality. We may explain a particular individual's success or promotion with reference to their superior skills and knowledge (internal causality), or with reference to luck, friends in high places and coincidence (external causality).

Research has revealed patterns in our attributions. When we are explaining our personal achievements, we point to our capabilities, but when we are explaining our lack of success, we blame our circumstances. This is known as projection. We project blame on to external causes that are beyond our control. However, we tend to attribute the behaviour of others to their disposition, that is to aspects of their personality. In psychology, the tendency to exaggerate the influence of personality when explaining the behaviour of others, and to overlook the effect of contextual factors, is known as the fundamental attribution error.

Attribution theory can explain aspects of discrimination in organizational settings. It has been shown that our sex and appearance affect how we are paid and promoted. Leslie Martel and Henry Biller (1987) demonstrated how the problems of sexism, ageism and racism apply also to 'heightism'. Their research showed how men and women thought that short men, from 5 feet 2 inches to 5 feet 5 inches, were less mature, less positive, less successful, less capable, less confident, less outgoing, more inhibited, more timid and more passive. In other words, short men are judged negatively, as their behaviour and competence are attributed to size and related personality characteristics. Susan Averett and Sanders Korenman (1993) found that the average hourly wage of overweight American women, aged 23 to 31, was 20 per cent lower than that of women of average weight. They also found that underweight women received underweight pay packets. However, the husbands of thin women earned on average 45 per cent more than those of fat ones. Almost the reverse was found to be true for American men. Those who were underweight had the lowest earnings, with slightly overweight men earning as much as 26 per cent more than their lightweight colleagues.

A summary of research in this field by *The Economist* newspaper (1995) argued that the western ideal height for men is now 6 feet 2 inches, and rising. This summary argued that discrimination on grounds of height, or heightism, is well established. In all but three American presidential elections in the twentieth century, the taller man won. President George W. Bush is a rare exception. In 1980, over half the chief executives in America's largest 500 companies were 6 feet tall or higher, and only 3 per cent were 5 feet 7 inches or less. A British study suggested that for each four inches of height in adolescence, earnings rose by 2 per cent in early adulthood.

Short changed in China

In 2002, Jiang Tao brought a court case against the Chengdu branch of The People's Bank of China in Sichuan province for discrimination on the basis of his height. The Bank advertised a job in a local newspaper stating that male applicants should be at least 1.68 metres tall, and that female applications should be at least 1.55 metres. Mr Jiang was three centimetres too short, and this criterion excluded around 40 per cent of the male population of Sichuan.

Height requirements are common in China. The East China University of Politics and Law in Shanghai requires male and female students to be at least 1.70 and 1.60 metres tall respectively, thereby excluding around half of the otherwise eligible students from rural areas where average heights are lower. A teacher in Fujian province was fired because he was found to be four centimetres shorter than the required 1.60 metres.

Height in China is considered to be an important attribute for those in jobs which carry authority, in catering and leisure industries where tall is considered beautiful, and in jobs that involve contact with foreigners, because it is undignified to have to look up to others. Height may not be important in politics. Deng Xiaoping, who ruled China for over a decade, was only 1.50 metres tall.

Based on 'No small matter', *The Economist*, 2 March 2002, pp. 68–9.

In Britain, Barry Harper (2000) studied over 11,000 people (belonging to the long-term National Child Development Study) aged 33 to determine the effects of looks, height and obesity on pay. This study confirmed that attractive people – men and women – earn more, that tall men earn substantially more, but that height is less important for women. Unattractive men earn 15 per cent less than colleagues with average looks, while unattractive women earn 11 per cent less. Tall men earn 10 per cent more than men of average height, but tall women earn only 5 per cent more. Obese women earn 5 per cent less than those of average weight, but obese men are not affected. While widespread, the benefits of height and the costs of being unattractive were more common in 'white-collar' occupations. For women, a 15 per cent penalty for being unattractive was most common in secretarial and clerical jobs. Attractive men in customer-facing sales roles earned 13 per cent more, while tall men in 'high touch' positions earned 25 per cent more. Some commentators are critical of 'beauty bias', putting appearance before capability, as another form of unfair discrimination at work.

The wrong attribution

June 1996 Sharon Wilson, 20, sales assistant at Jacket Racket and Destiny Clothing Company, Clydebank, dismissed for 'becoming too fat and ugly' when pregnant. Wins unfair dismissal claim of £1,049 against employer.

August 1998 Three teenage girls dismissed for being 'too ugly' at a nightclub in South Shields. Reported management wanted to bring in 'models' to hand out flyers.

October 1999 Patrick Carroll, offshore oil worker, dismissed for being 'too fat'. Wins £14,420 compensation after Aberdeen tribunal heard that his medical exam was incomplete.

October 1999 Disc jockey Steve Jackson, 40, sacked by Kiss FM after a change of management, wins unfair dismissal claim. Claimed that both his race and age were a factor, but tribunal accepts only the latter allegation.

►

October 1999 Diana Holland, Transport and General Workers' Union officer for women, race and equality, reports case of three young women who were dismissed from employment at a motorway services restaurant. A new manager told them they were 'not the sort of people we want to employ'. One wore thick glasses, one was 'too quiet' and the other was black.

From Jon Lamb, 'Face value gains credence in "unwritten" HR policies', *People Management*, vol. 5, no. 23, 25 November 1999, p. 15.

Why should appearance influence career progression? Our attributions are related to the phenomenon of stereotyping. We seem to attribute explanations of, or causes for, people's behaviour to aspects of their appearance. Discrimination against particular groups and individuals, on the basis of sex, sexual orientation, age or ethnic background, is now widely recognized. Legislation seeks to address sexual and racial discrimination, and social attitudes towards homosexuals and the elderly in organizational settings do appear, slowly, to be changing. However, attribution research suggests that discrimination, based on our perceptions of causal links between sex, appearance and job performance, are more subtle than this, and less public.

Source: © Jim Unger. Distributed by United Media. Reproduced by permission.

With respect to attractiveness, sex, height and weight, we are dealing with factors which cannot have any meaningful impact on performance for most jobs or occupations. The tall, attractive female computer programmer of average weight may be more effective in her job than the short, overweight male programmer with the unremarkable features. A moment's consideration, however, would probably lead us to reject height, weight and attractiveness as causal factors in this equation, and lead us to look for differences in education, experience and ability instead. The problem seems to be that we make attribution errors by jumping quickly and unconsciously to judgements of this kind, particularly when we have little information about the other person on which to base a more careful assessment.

Any aspect of our appearance is a form of *non-verbal communication*. We cannot control our age or height, but these factors, combined with behaviour that is under our control, send signals that others decode in the light of their experiences (age is related to reliability), expectations (tall and handsome means self-confident and knowledgeable) and prejudices (short and overweight women will deter customers). This also applies to choice of clothing. This is an aspect which is, of course, within our control. Dress can indicate organizational culture, and can contribute significantly to the individual's *impression management*. The way in which we dress can tell others how we want to be seen (as formal, relaxed, creative, businesslike) rather than what we are really like. However, we may not always be aware how others perceive these attempts to manage our impression through our dress style.

Perceptions of personality based on voice quality

We develop perceptions about relationships between the physical characteristics of other people and their behaviour. In other words, we develop implicit personality theories. Perry Hinton (1993) notes that we base these implicit theories, in part, on voice quality, such as:

voice quality high in	male voice	female voice
breathiness	young, artistic	feminine, pretty, petite, shallow
flatness	masculine, cold: same for both sexes	
nasality	having many socially undesirable features: same for both sexes	
tenseness	old, unyielding, cantankerous	young, emotional, high-strung

There is, however, no empirical basis for these judgements. A man with a tense voice is not necessarily old and cantankerous. A woman with a breathy voice is not necessarily petite and shallow. Think of a time when you first spoke to somebody on the telephone. Later, when you met them face to face, did they appear and behave as you expected?

Based on p. R. Hinton, *The Psychology of Interpersonal Perception*, Routledge, London, 1993, p. 16.

Stop and Criticize

Let us consider the styles of dress adopted by the instructors in your educational institution, across all the subjects you may be studying at the moment. (Let us not pick on organizational behaviour instructors in particular.) How does their style of dress influence your perceptions of their:

- approachability;
- subject knowledge;
- professionalism;
- understanding of the world beyond the academic 'ivory tower'?

How would you advise individual instructors to change their style of dress to improve the ways in which they are perceived by students on those criteria?

Is there a student 'dress code' in your institution – a code to which you adhere? What are you personally saying by sticking to this dress code? What messages would you send by deliberately breaking or ignoring this dress code?

Person perception: errors and avoidance

The main sources of errors in person perception seem to include:

1. Not collecting enough information about other people.

2. Basing our judgements on information that is irrelevant or insignificant.

3. Seeing what we expect to see and what we want to see, and not investigating further.

4. Allowing early information about someone to affect our judgement, despite later and contradictory information.

5. Allowing our own characteristics to affect what we see in others and how we judge them.

6. Accepting stereotypes uncritically.

7. Attempting to decode non-verbal behaviour outwith the context in which it appears.

8. Basing attributions on flimsy and potentially irrelevant evidence.

The remedies, therefore, include:

1. Take more time and avoid instant or 'snap' judgements about others.

2. Collect and consciously use more information about other people.

3. Develop self-awareness, and an understanding of how our personal biases and preferences affect our perceptions and judgements of other people.

4. Check our attributions – the assumptions we make about the causes of behaviour, particularly the links we make between aspects of personality and appearance on the one hand and behaviour on the other.

If we are to improve our understanding of others, we must first have a well-developed knowledge of ourselves – our strengths, our preferences, our flaws and our biases. The development of self-knowledge can be an uncomfortable process. In organizational settings, we are often constrained in the expression of our feelings (positive and negative) about other people, due to social or cultural norms, and to the communication barriers erected by status and power differentials. This may in part explain the enduring appeal of training courses in social and interpersonal skills, self-awareness and personal growth designed to help us overcome these problems, to 'get in touch' with other people, and to 'get in touch with ourselves'. Training in interpersonal communication skills typically emphasizes openness and honesty in relationships, active listening skills, sensitivity to non-verbal behaviour, and how to give and receive both critical and non-evaluative feedback.

Adrian Furnham's unlucky thirteen

Adrian Furnham (1997) argues that the process of making evaluations, judgements or ratings of the performance of employees is subject to a number of systematic perception errors. This is particularly problematic in a performance appraisal context:

1. *Central tendency*: Appraising everyone at the middle of the rating scale.

2. *Contrast error*: Basing an appraisal on comparison with other employees (who may have received undeserved high or low ratings) rather than on established performance criteria.

3. *Different from me*: Giving a poor appraisal because the person has qualities or characteristics not possessed by the appraiser.

4. *Halo effect*: Appraising an employee undeservedly well on one quality (performance, for example) because they are perceived highly by the appraiser on another quality (attractiveness, perhaps).

5. *Horn effect*: The opposite of the halo effect. Giving someone a poor appraisal on one quality (attractiveness) influences poor rating on other qualities (performance).

6. *Initial impression*: Basing an appraisal on first impressions rather than on how the person has behaved throughout the period to which the appraisal relates.

7. *Latest behaviour*: Basing an appraisal on the person's recent behaviour, rather than on how they have behaved throughout the appraisal period.

8. *Lenient or generous rating*: Perhaps the most common error, being consistently generous in appraisal, mostly to avoid conflict.

9. *Performance dimension error*: Giving someone a similar appraisal on two distinct but similar qualities because they happen to follow each other on the appraisal form.

10. *Same as me*: Giving a good appraisal because the person has qualities or characteristics possessed by the appraiser.

11. *Spillover effect*: Basing this appraisal, good or bad, on the results of the previous appraisal rather than on how the person has behaved during the appraisal period.

12. *Status effect*: Giving those in higher-level positions consistently better appraisals than those in lower-level jobs.

13. *Strict rating*: Being consistently harsh in appraising performance.

Based on Adrian Furnham, *The Psychology of Behaviour at Work*, Psychology Press/Taylor & Francis, Hove, Sussex, 1997, pp. 507–8.

Recap

1. *Identify the main features of the process of perception.*

   - People behave according to how they perceive the world, not in response to 'reality'.

   - The perceptual process involves the interpretation of sensory input in the light of past experience, and our store of knowledge, beliefs, expectations and motives.

2. *Distinguish between the bottom-up processing of sensory information and the top-down interpretation of that information.*

   - Sensation, or bottom-up processing, determines the data to which we pay attention.

   - Perception, or top-down processing, determines the way in which we organize and interpret perceived information in order to make behavioural choices.

3. *Understand the nature and implications of selective attention and perceptual organization.*

   - Selective attention is influenced by external factors relating to the stimulus and the context, and by internal factors such as learning, personality and motivation.

   - The way in which we organize and interpret sensory data in meaningful ways, even when they are incomplete or ambiguous, is known as perceptual organization.

4. *Give examples of how behaviour is influenced by our perceptions.*

   - We each have our own perceptual world, an internal mental image of our environment.

   - Supermarkets exploit an understanding of selective attention when designing store layout, when positioning goods, and in deciding which odours to use to entice customers.

   - Different cultures lead to differences in perception and consequently in behaviour.

5. *Explain and illustrate the main processes and problems in person perception, including false attributions, halo effects and stereotyping.*

- An attribution is a belief about cause and effect. When speaking about ourselves, we tend to attribute success to personal factors and failure to external factors. When speaking about others, we tend to attribute success and failure to personality features.

- Making an overall favourable judgement of someone on the basis of a single positive characteristic is known as the halo effect, which can be positive or negative.

- Assuming that someone possesses a set of personality traits because they belong to a particular social group is known as stereotyping.

- Errors in person perception can be overcome by taking more time, collecting more information, avoiding personal prejudices and increased self-awareness.

6. *Explain some less widely appreciated sources of discrimination at work, against men and women, arising from characteristics of the person perception and attribution processes.*

- Aspects of behaviour are attributed to appearance, leading to discrimination. You are likely to be paid less at work if you are an overweight or underweight female, a short man, a husband with an overweight wife, or are perceived to be unattractive.

- The fundamental attribution error leads us to emphasize personality and ignore context.

Revision

1. You observe someone behaving in what you perceive to be a highly unusual manner at work, contrary as far as you can observe to 'common sense'. How would you proceed to understand and to make sense of their behaviour?

2. Explain the distinction between sensation and perception, and explain also the significance of this distinction.

3. What is the individual's perceptual world, what factors influence this construct, and how does an understanding of someone's perceptual world help us to understand their behaviour?

4. What is the difference between selective attention and perceptual organization, and what factors influence the latter process?

5. What are the factors influencing selective attention, and how can a knowledge of these factors be exploited in commercial settings?

Springboard

Anderson, D. and Mullen, P. (eds), 1998, *Faking It: The Sentimentalization of Modern Society*, Penguin, Harmondsworth.

A controversial series of essays with a critical theme: the media offer us a 'sentimentalized' view of events and problems including, for example, the treatment of cancer and school education. The authors argue that widespread media sentimentalization distorts our perception of reality, leading us to overlook genuine social and organizational problems. Reading these accounts, consider the extent to which your perception of society and its organizations is influenced by the media.

Goldstein, E., 2001, *Sensation and Perception*, Wadsworth, Belmont, CA.

A comprehensive introduction to the psychology and physiology of sensation and perception. Describes how the senses function in tandem, exposing the complexity of perceptual processes. Uses fascinating illustrations to reinforce the argument.

Pinker, S., 1997, *How the Mind Works*, Penguin, Harmondsworth.

Pinker's explanation relies on evolutionary biology (a version of Darwinism) and the computational theory of mind. The computational theory regards the mind as a modular information processor of considerable complexity. Pinker's investigation of the clues to how our information processor functions is insightful and entertaining, and his style makes complex ideas accessible. Readers develop more than an understanding of perception from his wide-ranging analysis.

Zalkind, S.S. and Costello, T.W., 1962, 'Perception: some recent research and implications for administration', *Administrative Science Quarterly*, vol. 7, pp. 218–35.

A much quoted paper which has been reproduced in many collections of readings. Clearly written and still worth reading, these authors explore the importance of an understanding of perception for management, which in those days was described as 'administration'. It is perhaps also interesting to note how perceptions of administrators have changed, becoming today's professional business managers who would reject that dated term.

Home viewing

The Sixth Sense (1999, director M. Night Shyamalan) concerns the attempts of a disillusioned child psychologist, Malcolm Crowe (played by Bruce Willis), to cure a young boy, Cole (Haley Joel Osment), who is tormented because he sees dead people. Crowe's depression and his eagerness to help Cole are explained at the beginning, when he is attacked at home by an ex-patient who had the same problem but whom Crowe was unable to help. Crowe spends so much time with Cole that he ignores his wife Anna (Olivia Williams). However, this film cleverly manipulates the perceptions and assumptions of the audience. Once you have watched the film to the end, either reflect on the action or watch it again. Notice which clues you 'saw' but either ignored or misinterpreted the first time around. Notice how your interpretation of events relied on the assumptions that you made, or rather the assumptions that you were expected to make. It is only when you know the full plot of the film that you can begin to make 'correct' assumptions and interpretations, based on exactly the same evidence you were presented with the first time around. What does this reveal about the ease with which your perceptions, assumptions and understanding can be manipulated?

OB in literature

Aldous Huxley, *The Doors of Perception/Heaven and Hell*, Flamingo, London, 1994 (first published in 1954 by Chatto and Windus, London).

This is Huxley's account of his experiment, in 1953, with mescalin, a hallucinogenic drug with effects similar to those induced by LSD (and with echoes from the mystical Mexican writing of Carlos Castaneda). In *The Doors of Perception*, Huxley provides a fascinating account of how his perception of reality was altered by this experience, in effect opening up a whole new perceptual world. In *Heaven and Hell*, the sequel, he presents his later reflections on this experience. An interesting place to start questioning what we take to be 'real' with respect to the world around us and our perception and understanding of it.

Chapter exercises

1: Personality perception

Objectives
1. To explore how we make personality assessments based on perceptions of facial characteristics.

2. To consider the validity of these kinds of assessment.

When you meet someone for the first time, you immediately begin to assess what kind of person they are – friendly, hostile, shy, outgoing, warm, cold, helpful, reserved and so on. Facial features and expressions are one of the main sources of clues for this assessment. It is particularly important for politicians to understand how these judgements are made, because they (presumably) want to appear open, honest and sincere and not to be perceived as uncaring, devious and manipulative. Television now plays a significant role in the promotion of political figures, and television typically concentrates attention on the face and voice. How do we make personality judgements based on facial features?

Briefing
First read these two descriptions of different people. As you read these descriptions, imagine what each person looks like, then rate their facial features on the following characteristics, placing an A at the appropriate point on the scale for the first person on each characteristic, and a B on the scale for the second person.

First person (A): This man is warmhearted and honest, has a good sense of humour, is intelligent and is unbiased in his opinions. He is responsible and self-confident with an air of refinement.

Second person (B): This woman is ruthless and brutal. She is extremely hostile, quick-tempered and overbearing. She is known for her boorish and vulgar manner, and is a very domineering and unsympathetic person.

feature		←				→	
directness of gaze	direct gaze	☐	☐	☐	☐	☐	averted gaze
direction of gaze	upward gaze	☐	☐	☐	☐	☐	downward gaze
eyes	wide eyes	☐	☐	☐	☐	☐	narrow eyes
brow	smooth	☐	☐	☐	☐	☐	knitted
nostrils	relaxed	☐	☐	☐	☐	☐	distended
curve of mouth	corners up	☐	☐	☐	☐	☐	corners down

Now compare your ratings with colleagues, and consider the following questions:

1. Did you have difficulties in imagining what these two people could look like, leading you to hesitate in making judgements of their facial features on these characteristics?

2. Are there similarities between you and your colleagues with respect to expectations concerning the different facial characteristics of these two people? Or do you and colleagues have completely different expectations?

3. If you were making this judgement the other way around, inferring personality traits from your perception of facial features, how accurate do you think such personality judgements are likely to be?

2: Waiting for interview

Objectives
1. To examine how perception is influenced by knowledge and past experience.

2. To demonstrate how our individual perceptual worlds are shaped by these factors.

You are about to go for a job interview, but you will be kept waiting in the interviewer's office for a time beforehand. During that time, you can observe clues about your interviewer and perhaps about the company. What clues do you consider to be significant and revealing? Can you identify your own personal experiences that affect how you observe and judge in this kind of setting? How does that past experience colour your perception today?

Briefing
This exercise can be completed in class time but may be more effective if steps 1 to 3 are completed beforehand. If the class lasts for only 50 to 60 minutes, time will be tight without some advance preparation.

Step 1   Read *The manager's room description* which follows to get a feel for the setting in which you find yourself.

Step 2   Complete the analysis sheet.
In the *data* column, record those observations that you find significant and revealing about the kind of person who occupies this room.
In the *experiences* column, record past incidents or events, recent or distant, that you think influence your observation.
In the *inferences* column, note the perceptions or conclusions that you reach from your data.

data I observe in the room	my past experiences	the inferences that I make

Step 3   Using that analysis, write a profile of your interviewer.

Step 4   Finally, record your answers to the following questions:
1. Would you work for this person?
2. What would you expect this person's management style to be like?
3. How confident are you of your analysis, your profile and your responses to the last two questions?
4. Explain how the analysis that you have just completed can be used to illustrate the concepts of selective attention, perceptual organization, perceptual world and stereotyping.

Step 5   Present your findings, according to your instructor's directions.

The manager's room description

You are now in the Acme Holdings company offices, top floor, for your job interview. It sounds like your ideal position. As personal assistant you will be working for the managing director who has asked to interview you. You have arrived on time, but the managing director's secretary apologizes and tells you there will be a delay. The managing director has been called to an important meeting which will take up to 15 minutes. The secretary tells you that you are welcome to wait in the managing director's private office, and shows you in.

You know that you will be alone here for 15 minutes. You look around the room, curious about the person with whom you may be working. The shallow pile carpet is a warm pink, with no pattern. You choose one of six high-backed chairs, upholstered in a darker fabric which matches well with the carpet and curtains, and with polished wooden arms. In the centre of the ring of chairs is a low glass-topped coffee table. On the table there is a large white ashtray, advertising a well-known national brand of beer. There is no sign of cigarettes, but the ashtray holds two books of matches, one from a hotel in Geneva and the other from a local restaurant. On the wall behind you is a large photograph of a vintage motor car, accompanied by its driver in leather helmet, goggles, scarf and long leather coat; you can't make out the driver's face. The window ledge holds four plants arranged equal distances apart; two look like small exotic ferns and the others are a begonia and a geranium in flower.

On the other side of the room sits a large wooden executive desk, with a black leather chair. A framed copy of the company's mission statement hangs on the wall behind the desk, and below that sits a closed black leather briefcase with brass combination locks. The plain grey waste paper basket by the wall beside the desk is full of papers. At the front of the desk sits a pen-stand with a letter opener. To the side is a state-of-the-art laptop computer and a desk lamp. In front of the lamp sits a metal photograph frame holding two pictures. One is of an attractive woman in her thirties with a young boy around eight years old. The other photograph is of a retriever dog in a field to the side of some farm buildings. In front of the frame is a stack of file folders. Immediately in front of the chair, on the desk, is a small pile of papers and a Mont Blanc pen with the Acme company logo stamped on the barrel.

On the other side of the desk is a delicate china mug. In front of it lies what looks like a leather-covered address book or perhaps a diary, and a pad of yellow paper. Beside the pad there is a pile of unopened mail with envelopes of differing sizes. On top of the mail and behind are some half-folded newspapers: *The Guardian*, *The Independent* and *The Financial Times*. You note that there is no telephone on the desk. Behind the desk is a small glass-fronted display case. There are some books lined up on top of the case: *The Pursuit of Wow*, *The Oxford Dictionary of New Words*, *Dealing with Difficult People*, *You Are What You Eat*, and *Shattering the Glass Ceiling*. Also on top of the case sits a small bronze statue of a man sitting with his legs crossed in a Yoga position. There is a cheese plant on the far side of the display case. Inside the case, you see company computing systems manuals and books and pamphlets on employment law, some of which deal with race and sex discrimination issues.

You decide to get up and look out the window. There is a three-seater settee under the window, covered in the same fabric as the armchairs with matching scatter cushions in the corners. From the window you can easily see people shopping and children playing in the nearby park. You turn to another table beside the settee. Several magazines sit in front of a burgundy ceramic lamp with a beige shade. There are two recent copies of *The Economist*, and a copy each of *Asia Today*, *Classic CD* and *Fortune*. As you head back to your chair, you notice that the papers on the desk in front of the chair are your application papers and curriculum vitae. Your first name, obviously indicating your sex, has been boldly circled with the Mont Blanc pen. As the Managing Director may return at any moment, you go back and sit in your chair to wait.

Chapter 8 Motivation

Key concepts

drives	motivator factors
motives	hygiene factors
motivation	vertical loading factors
self-actualization	intrinsic rewards
equity theory	extrinsic rewards
expectancy theory	Growth Need Strength
valence	Job Diagnostic Survey
instrumentality	Motivating Potential Score
expectancy	empowerment
goal-setting theory	high-performance work systems
job enrichment	

Learning outcomes

When you have read this chapter, you should be able to define those key concepts in
your own words, and you should also be able to:

1. Understand different ways in which the term 'motivation' is used.
2. Understand the nature of motives and motivation processes as influences on
   behaviour.
3. Use expectancy theory and job enrichment to diagnose organizational problems and
   to recommend solutions.
4. Explain the renewed interest in this field in the 1990s, with respect to the evolving
   link between organization strategy and high-performance work systems.

Why study motivation?

Douglas Murray
McGregor
(1906–64)

We each have a different reason for getting out of bed in the morning. Our
motives (from the Latin *movere*, to move) are major determinants of our behaviour. If we understand your motives (a desire for more leisure time), we can influence your behaviour (take a day's holiday if you finish that assignment). A recent
survey (Reade, 2003) revealed that students rate job satisfaction more highly than
money. The top two aspects of the ideal job were enjoyment and friendly colleagues. Earning 'enough' came third, followed by passion for the industry, good
location and social life. Armed with this knowledge of applicants' motives,
organizations can adjust their job specifications and payment levels. In other
words, look for job advertisements which seem to suggest 'we don't pay much,
but it's fun'.

Douglas McGregor (1960) set out two sets of propositions about human motivation, which he labelled 'Theory X' and 'Theory Y'. To discover the set of propositions to which you subscribe, complete this questionnaire. Read each pair of
statements, and circle the number that best reflects your view:

the average person inherently dislikes work	1	2	3	4	5	work is as natural as rest to people
people must be directed to work and self-control	1	2	3	4	5	people will exercise self-discretion
people wish to avoid responsibility	1	2	3	4	5	people enjoy real responsibility
people feel that achievement at work is irrelevant	1	2	3	4	5	achievement is highly valued by people
most people are dull and uncreative	1	2	3	4	5	most people have imagination and creativity
money is the only real reason for working	1	2	3	4	5	money is only one benefit from work
people lack the desire to improve their quality of life	1	2	3	4	5	people have needs to improve their quality of life
having an objective is a form of imprisonment	1	2	3	4	5	objectives are welcomed as an aid to effectiveness

If you scored 16 or less, then you subscribe to Theory X. If you scored 32 or more, then you subscribe to Theory Y. So what? One key question for many managers is – how can we motivate people to work harder, or smarter? One answer lies with management style. David Buchanan and Diane Preston (1992, p. 69) quote a foreman in an engineering plant:

People only come to work for money. You're not telling me that if you just left them they wouldn't go and have a chat or sit down and read the newspaper. If you're telling me that wouldn't happen, then one of us is kidding and it isn't me.

In this factory, the machinists pinned up a notice: *The floggings will stop when morale improves*. The foremen kept taking it down, and the machinists pinned it up again. To which theory of motivation do these foremen adhere? How effective is their approach, in your judgement, in stimulating high performance at work? McGregor died in 1964, but his ideas remain influential and are explored in Heil, Bennis and Stephens (2000).

Rank and yank

Some companies, including Ford, General Electric, Cisco Systems, Intel, Conoco, Hewlett-Packard, Microsoft and Sun Microsystems, use Forced Ranking Systems (FRS) to assess employee performance. FRS asks managers to rank employees against each other, evaluating their contributions along a continuum from best to worst. Then, depending on company policy, the worst 5 or 10 per cent are likely to be fired. At General Electric, employees are divided into top 20 per cent, middle 80 per cent and bottom 10 per cent. Advocates claim that this method helps managers to justify difficult decisions about underperforming staff.

This approach is based on the statistical observation that individual differences are normally distributed in the form of a bell curve. FRS ensures that a percentage of employees will fall into the 'worst' category. So, for example, if at Ford you are graded C, the lowest grade in their system, you are not eligible for bonuses that year; two Cs in a row are grounds for dismissal. At Sun Microsystems, FRS is used to identify the lowest-performing 10 per cent of employees who are then given 90 days 'to shape up, find another job inside Sun, or ship out'. One problem is that the criteria for ranking are increasingly qualitative and subjective, involving teamwork and communication skills, for example.

What would you predict will be the impact of this approach on employee motivation? FRS is used by some business schools in America and Europe. How would you respond should your organizational behaviour instructor use 'rank and yank' with your class examination grades?

In 2001, nine employees raised a class action suit against Ford claiming that its forced ranking system discriminates against older workers. In the previous year, cases involving FRS discrimination against blacks and women were raised against Microsoft and Conoco.

Based on Matthew Boyle, 'Performance reviews: perilous curves ahead', *Fortune*, 28 May 2001, pp. 103–4.

Drives, motives and motivation

Motivation can be explored from three distinct but related perspectives:

1. **Goals**: What are the main motives for our behaviour? Wealth, status and power trigger behaviours directed towards their pursuit. This perspective views motivation in terms of desired goals. This question is addressed by *content* theories of motivation.

2. **Decisions**: Why do we choose to pursue certain goals? Why do you study hard to earn distinctions while a friend has a full social life and gets pass grades? This perspective views motivation in terms of the cognitive decision-making processes influencing an individual's choice of goals. This question is addressed by *process* theories of motivation.

3. **Influence**: How can we motivate you to work harder? Managers want to motivate employees to turn up on time and be helpful to customers. This perspective views motivation as social influence and is addressed by *job enrichment* theories.

Drives: the innate, biological determinants of behaviour, activated by deprivation.

Do we inherit the goals that we desire, or are they acquired through experience? If our motives are innate, then it would be pointless to attempt to change them. If they are acquired, then they can be altered. Our behaviour is influenced by our biological equipment. We appear to have an innate need for survival. Our needs for oxygen, water, food, shelter, warmth and sex can be overpowering. These needs are triggered by deprivation and are known as **drives**.

The drives may not be restricted to basic biological needs. Some psychologists claim that we are active sensation-seekers who have the innate cognitive drives listed in table 8.1.

Table 8.1: Innate cognitive drives

curiosity	the need to explore, to play, to learn more
sense-making	the need to impose meaning and order on the world around us
order and meaning	the need for certainty, equity, consistency, predictability
effectance or competency	the need to exert mastery and control over the world around us
self-understanding	the need to know who and what we are

The drives come with the body. We do not have to learn to be cold, or thirsty, or hungry. However, we can *override* these drives. Some religious orders inflict celibacy on willing members. Altruism can overcome personal safety needs in extraordinary circumstances. The idea that our behaviour is pre-programmed is too simplistic. Psychologists once thought that human behaviour could be explained in terms of instincts, but that line of enquiry turns out to be largely false. Animal behaviour, in contrast, is triggered by instincts. Birds and squirrels cannot override their programming, and remain locked into their niches in nature. The ways in which we, on the other hand, seek to satisfy our drives are innumerable, and vary between individuals and across cultures. Consider the differences in eating habits around the world, and the range of things that individuals do to satisfy their sex drives.

Motives: socially acquired needs activated by a desire for their fulfilment.

Motives, in contrast, appear to be acquired through experience.

Polygamy is a crime in most western cultures, but a sign of male achievement, wealth and status in parts of the Arab world. In some Muslim societies, the consumption of alcohol carries severe punishment, while gifts of alcohol are the norm in western cultures. Our choice of goals and behaviours is influenced by the ways of thinking and behaving typical of our society. Those who choose not to conform are often shunned or ridiculed, and are sometimes even imprisoned.

The distinction between drives and motives is summarized in table 8.2.

Table 8.2: Drives versus motives

Drives	Motives
are innate	are learned
have a physiological basis	have a social basis
are activated by deprivation	are activated by environment
are aimed at satiation	are aimed at stimulation

However, this distinction between innate drives and acquired motives is an oversimplification. We seek to satisfy our biological drives in ways acceptable to our society. The potentially innate drives for competency, sense-making and curiosity are socially prized in most cultures. The point is that human behaviour is purposive. We attach reasons to our goals and behaviours. To understand your motives, and to influence your behaviour, we need to understand why you choose particular outcomes and how you decide to pursue them.

Motivation: the cognitive, decision-making process through which goal-directed behaviour is initiated, energized, and directed and maintained.

Motivation can be regarded as a broad concept which includes preferences for particular outcomes, strength of effort (half-hearted or enthusiastic) and persistence (in the face of barriers). These are the factors that we have to understand in order to explain our motivation and behaviour. These are the factors which a manager has to appreciate in order to motivate employees to behave in organizationally desirable ways.

Content theories of motivation

Theories of motivation that focus on the goals to which we aspire are known as content theories, as they reveal the contents of the motives compartment in our mental luggage. Abraham Maslow's (1943, 1954, 1971) content theory of motivation aims to resolve the confusion between drives and motives, arguing that we have nine innate needs or motives.

1. *Biological* needs, for sunlight, sexual expression, food, water, rest and

Abraham Harold
Maslow (1908–70)

oxygen – in other words, needs basic to our individual and collective survival.

2. *Safety* needs, for security, comfort, tranquillity, freedom from fear, and threat from the environment, for shelter, order, predictability, for an organized world.

3. *Affiliation* needs, for attachment, belongingness, affection, love, relationships.

4. *Esteem* needs, for strength, confidence, achievement, self-esteem, independence, and for reputation, prestige, recognition, attention and appreciation – in other words, the need for a stable and high self-evaluation based on capability and the respect of others.

5. The need *to know and to understand*, to gain and to systematize knowledge, the need for curiosity, learning, philosophizing, experimenting and exploring.

6. *Aesthetic* needs, for order and beauty.

7. The need for *transcendence*, a spiritual need, for 'cosmic identification' or 'to be at one with the universe'.

8. The need for *freedom of enquiry and expression*, an essential *prerequisite* for the satisfaction of the other needs.

9. *Self-actualization* needs, for the development of our full potential.

Self-actualization:
the desire for personal fulfilment, to develop one's potential, to become everything that one is capable of becoming.

If our biological and safety needs are not satisfied, we die. If our needs for love and esteem are not satisfied, we feel inferior and helpless, but if these needs are satisfied, we feel self-confident. **Self-actualization** and 'transcendence', Maslow argued, are the ultimate goals. In the organizational behaviour literature, the spiritual, metaphysical concept of transcendence has been largely ignored.

Maslow argued that self-actualized people were rare, and that establishing the conditions for people to develop their capabilities to this extent was a challenging task. The need for freedom of enquiry and expression is also often missing from popular accounts of Maslow's theory. However, this need can be significant, both in a wider cultural context (there are country variations with respect to such freedoms) and in organizational settings, where free enquiry and expression are frequently constrained by procedures, rules and social norms. Maslow argued that these needs are organized hierarchically, with lower-order biological and safety needs at the bottom, and higher-order self-actualization and transcendence needs at the top, as in figure 8.1.

This hierarchy, he argued, has the following properties.

1. A need is not an effective motivator until those lower in the hierarchy are more or less satisfied. You are unlikely to be concerned about the sharks (threat to safety), if you are drowning (biological deprivation).

2. A satisfied need is not a motivator. If you are well fed and safe, we would have difficulty energizing and directing your behaviour with offers of food and shelter.

3. Lack of need satisfaction can affect mental health. Consider the frustration, anxiety and depression that can arise from lack of self-esteem, loss of the respect of others, an inability to sustain relationships and an inability to develop one's capabilities.

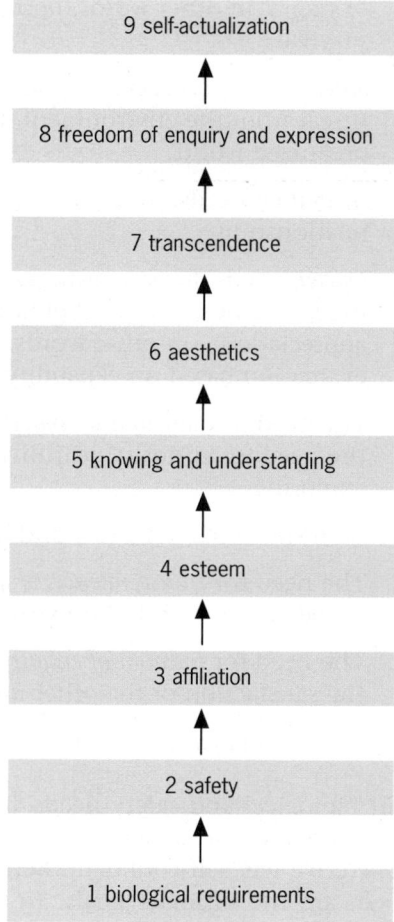

Figure 8.1: Abraham Maslow's needs hierarchy

4. We have an innate desire to work our way up the hierarchy, pursuing the satisfaction of our higher-order needs once our lower-order needs are more or less satisfied.

5. The experience of self-actualization stimulates desire for more. Maslow claimed that self-actualizers have 'peak experiences'. When you have had one of these, you want another. The need for self-actualization cannot be satisfied in the same way as the other needs.

Maslow did not intend this hierarchy to be regarded as a rigid description of the development of human motivation. He offered this as a typical picture of what might happen under ideal (and, therefore, rarely attained) social and organizational conditions.

Maslow's theory has attracted two main criticisms. First, it is vague and cannot readily predict behaviour. Second, it is more of a social philosophy reflecting white, American, middle-class values. Can his theory be dismissed as irrelevant to organizational behaviour in the twenty-first century? No. His thinking remains influential, particularly in the recognition that behaviour depends on a range of motives. His ideas continue to affect management practice in areas such as rewards policy, management style and job design. Many subsequent management fashions such as job enrichment, total quality management, business process re-engineering, self-managing teams, 'the new leadership' and employee empowerment have incorporated his ideas in the search for practical motivational methods.

Is Maslow's theory 'culture bound'?

Scandinavian cultures – Sweden, Norway, Finland, Denmark – place a high value on quality of life and social needs. European and Anglo-American cultures place a high value on productivity, efficiency and individual self-actualization. Chinese culture values collectivism and community activity higher than individualism. Maslow's theory may be 'culture bound':

Maslow's hierarchy	The hierarchy of needs in China
self-actualization	safety and security (personal and national)
esteem	sense of belongingness and love
love and affiliation	esteem, family, tradition
safety and security	self-actualization through fitting in, non-individualistic
physiological	physiological

Based on E. Nevis, 'Using an American perspective in understanding another culture: toward a hierarchy of needs for the People's Republic of China', *Journal of Applied Behavioral Science*, vol. 19, no. 3, 1983, pp. 249–64.

Clayton Paul
Alderfer

Clayton Alderfer (1972) argued that it was more realistic to consider three basic categories of needs which he called Existence, Relatedness and Growth, so this is known as the ERG theory of motivation. Table 8.3 illustrates how ERG and Maslow's theories relate.

Table 8.3: ERG theory

Existence needs	physiological and safety needs
Relatedness needs	affiliation and esteem needs
Growth needs	self-actualization and self-esteem needs

ERG theory says that all three need categories can be present at any one time, in contrast with Maslow's 'progression hypothesis', that we try to work our way up the hierarchy. Alderfer added a 'regression hypothesis', arguing that we drop to a lower category when attempts to satisfy higher needs are frustrated. Maslow was not initially concerned with work motivation, whereas Alderfer's theory is directed at organizational settings. Despite the differences between these theories, the practical managerial implications are similar.

Stop and Criticize

Let us assume that you are not white, American, comfortably affluent and living in the 1940s. From your own observations and experience (the primary research sources for Maslow's theory), devise a five-step need hierarchy that you believe would apply to your own culture today.

Would different need hierarchies apply to particular sub-cultural groups (teenage job seekers, freelance management consultants, single parent families)?

What are the main differences between your theory and that of Maslow?

Sheila Ritchie and Peter Martin (1999, p. xii) argue that 'the task of the manager is to find out what it is that motivates people', to make them 'smile more and carp less'. Observing that there has been little recent development in theories of work motivation, they aimed to devise a fresh approach and a practical tool. Their research identified twelve 'motivational drivers':

1. Interest.

2. Achievement.

3. Recognition.

4. Self-development.

5. Variety and change.

6. Creativity.

7. Power and influence.

8. Social contact.

9. Money and tangible rewards.

10. Structure.

11. Relationships.

12. Physical conditions.

The characteristics of 'high-need' and 'low-need' individuals are defined in table 8.4 (based on Ritchie and Martin, 1999, pp. 11–12 and 245–6). They claim there is little correlation between scores on these factors, suggesting that they are independent of each other.

The twelve factors were derived from the literature and from their observations as management consultants. They developed a questionnaire which produces a motivational profile indicating the relative strength of each factor. This questionnaire was completed by 1,355 managers and other professionals, from several nationalities, mainly participants on the authors' management development programmes. The order in which the factors are listed in table 8.4 is based on the questionnaire scores. In other words, this management group had relatively high levels of need for interest and achievement in their work, moderately high levels of need for creativity, power and influence, and lower levels of need for relationships and good physical working conditions. Notice that money comes ninth out of twelve.

The composition of the sample allowed comparisons to be made between different professional and occupational groups and between nationalities. Ritchie and Martin note, however, that differences in the motivational profiles between individuals are more significant than either occupational or international differences.

What are the practical implications of this perspective? Profiling encourages sensitivity to individual differences, highlighting the need to use a range of different motivational strategies. Managers are advised to respond to the profile of the individual, regardless of the job they are doing or their country or culture of origin.

The motivation profile perspective has a number of strengths:

■ it is based on contemporary data drawn from managers and other professionals;

■ it recognizes a range of individual differences;

■ it offers a diagnostic tool for managers seeking to improve individual and group motivation, by indicating the factors on which to concentrate.

However, this perspective has a number of weaknesses:

■ the derivation of the twelve factors seems arbitrary, relying on a

Table 8.4: The motivation profile

Motivating factor	The high-need individual	The low-need individual
Interest	needs to feel that work is intrinsically interesting and useful	will do work regardless of its intrinsic interest or usefulness
Achievement	need to set self-challenging goals; unhappy if nothing to achieve; requires constant stimulation	no motivation for achievement; world passes them by
Recognition	need for constant recognition and appreciation; can inhibit effectiveness	indifferent to other people's views about them; possibly insensitive to others
Self-development	need to grow and develop; assesses work in terms of its contribution to personal growth	does what is required, does not assess in terms of contribution to personal development
Variety and change	need for constant variety, change and stimulation; high level of arousal and vigilance	happy to tolerate the mundane and boring
Creativity	explorative, creative and open-minded; curious and thinks divergently	little need for creative thinking; lacks curiosity; can be closed minded
Power and influence	strong impulse to influence others, competitive power drive dominates personality	no wish to attempt to exercise influence
Social contact	need for light social contact with a wide range of people	feels no compelling need for company; but is able to work with others if necessary
Money and tangible rewards	need for high salary and tangible rewards; concentrates on monetary rewards	spends little energy thinking about reward; indifferent to money as a motivator
Structure	need for rules and structure, feedback and information; wants procedures	finds rules and structures restrictive; wants freedom; feels no need for compliance
Relationships	need to form and sustain stable long-term relationships with a small number of people	feels no need to maintain deep relationships; is able to work with people if necessary
Physical conditions	needs good working conditions; constantly complains if not physically comfortable	largely indifferent to physical surroundings

combination of judgement and informed guesswork rather than on systematic research;

■ the sample on which the perspective is based is atypical, comprising managers on training programmes run by the authors;

■ it is difficult to identify motivating factors that are not already covered in Maslow's theory.

Ritchie and Martin appear to have developed a practical approach useful in a management training and development context, and also for guiding management action in response to employee motivation issues. As indicated earlier, although Maslow's content theory of motivation may be dated, his influence persists.

"Excellent work, Osgood. Help yourself to some sprinkles."

Source: Cartoon © Mike Shapiro

Good work if you can get it

The popular image of 'new work' is the burger-flipping 'McJob', a boring, repetitive, low pay, low prestige, low dignity, no future role in a service sector organization. Andy Westwood argues that this stereotype does not apply to Asda Wal-Mart. According to a survey by *The Sunday Times* newspaper, the ten best places to work in Britain in 2002 were:

1. Asda Wal-Mart

2. Microsoft

3. Richer Sounds

4. Bain & Company

5. AIT

6. Timpson

7. Cisco Systems

8. Goldman Sachs

9. Bacardi Martini

10. JLT Risk Solutions

Asda has 126,000 employees in Britain, and it pays its front-line 'colleagues' an hourly rate of less than £5, which is not much above the statutory minimum wage. However, all staff get a 10 per cent store discount card, as well as discounts on car purchase, theme parks, cinemas and holidays. There are company pension schemes and share plans (in which over 70 per cent of employees participate), and special mortgage deals, unsecured personal loans and an Asda tax-free individual savings account. There is a Law Club where, for 10 pence a week, all employees have access to legal advice and support on any issue, including employment rights as well as writing wills and dealing with personal or domestic issues. Staff get childcare vouchers, debt advice and medical insurance, and can take leave for almost any purpose such as extended holidays, religious festivals, adoption and children starting school.

All employees are encouraged to reach higher levels of pay and responsibility through a 'So You Want To Be' approach to career development, and all stores carry posters and information advertising development opportunities, with clear requirements for each promoted position. There are few status symbols, with no business cards, no large offices, no reserved parking spaces, no differential dress codes and no 'top management attitudes', and all incentives and benefits are equally available to all staff. Behind the scenes, everyone is on first name terms, buying tea and sandwiches with the same charge card.

Based on Andy Westwood, *Is New Work Good Work?*, The Work Foundation, London, 2002.

Process theories of motivation

Theories of motivation that focus on how we make choices with respect to desired goals are known as process theories. Unlike content theories, process theories give the individual a cognitive decision-making role in selecting goals and the means by which to pursue them.

Do we really come into the world with mental luggage labelled 'motives', containing goals that we are predestined to pursue? Individuals are motivated by different outcomes. Cultures encourage different patterns of motivation. We appear to have some choice of motives, and the means of achieving them. Content theories fail to recognize either individual choice or social influence. Maslow's is a universalist theory, which applies to everyone, and thus cannot readily explain differences between individuals and between cultures.

We will explore three process theories of work motivation, *equity theory*, *expectancy theory* and *goal-setting theory*.

Equity theory

Equity theory: a process theory which argues that perception of unfairness leads to tension, which then motivates the individual to resolve that unfairness.

Several theorists have argued that we seek what we perceive to be a just or equitable return for our efforts. The calculation of what is just or equitable depends on the comparisons we make with others. **Equity theory** is thus based on our perceptions of fair treatment. The most influential statement of this theory comes from the work of Stacy Adams (1963, 1965), who argued that we are motivated to act in situations which we perceive to be inequitable or unfair. Inequity occurs when you get either more, or less, than you think you deserve. The argument is based on perceptions of *in*equity, but is traditionally called *equity* theory.

This theory bases explanations of behaviour on perceptions of social comparisons. Equity theory argues that the more intense the perceived inequity, the higher the tension and the stronger the motivation to act. Adams argues that we respond differently to 'over-reward' and 'under-reward'. We tend to perceive a modest amount of over-reward as 'good luck', and do nothing, while a modest under-reward is not so readily tolerated.

How do you calculate inequity? Adams proposed that we compare our rewards (pay, recognition) and contributions (time, effort, ideas) with the outputs and inputs of others. Equity thus exists when these ratios are equal:

$$\frac{\text{my rewards (minus my costs)}}{\text{my effort and contribution}} = \frac{\text{your rewards (minus your costs)}}{\text{your effort and contribution}}$$

J. Stacy Adams

Rewards can include a range of tangible and intangible factors, including pay, status symbols, fringe benefits, promotion prospects, satisfaction and job security. Inputs similarly relate to any factor that you believe you bring to the situation, including age, experience, skill, education, effort, loyalty and commitment. The theory says nothing about the relative priority or weighting of these various factors. That depends on the individual's perception.

Table 8.5: Strategies for reducing inequity

Strategy	Example
1. Alter your outcomes	I'll persuade the manager to increase my pay
2. Adjust your inputs	I won't work as hard as Annika
3. Alter the comparison person's outcomes	I'll persuade the manager to cut Annika's pay
4. Alter the comparison person's inputs	I'll leave the difficult tasks to Annika
5. Compare with someone else	Lars gets the same as I get
6. Rationalize the inequity	Annika has worked here for much longer
7. Leave	I'll get another job

How do you resolve inequity? Let's imagine that you are working in a restaurant in Gamla Stan (the Old Town) in Stockholm and you discover that Annika is earning 12 Swedish kroner (about US$1.5) an hour more than you for the same work (about $50 a week more than you). Table 8.5 lists Adams's seven strategies for reducing this inequity.

Choice of strategy is a sensitive issue, and equity theory does not predict which strategy an individual will choose. Each option has different short-term and long-term consequences. Arguing with your manager, reducing your input or making Annika do the difficult work may reduce inequity in the short term, but could have long-term consequences for your relationships and employment at this location.

The theory's causal chains for over-reward and under-reward are shown in figure 8.2.

Research evidence from laboratory studies in the 1960s supports the theory, and also confirms that people who are overpaid reduce their perceived inequity by working harder. Further studies in real settings have continued broadly to confirm equity theory predictions. Interestingly, from a management perspective, perceived equity seems to lead to greater job satisfaction and organizational commitment (Sweeney et al., 1990).

Equity theory has some problems. A number of quantitative and qualitative variables have to be considered when calculating an equity ratio. These variables

Figure 8.2: Equity theory – causal chains

are dependent on individual perception and are difficult to weight or measure. Different people use different timescales when calculating fairness; short-term calculations may be different from long-term implications. There are individual differences in tolerance levels, and not everyone will respond in the same way to a particular level of inequity. The extent to which you believe that there is a valid explanation for inequity will also moderate your response.

Equity theory, as a psychological perspective, ignores the wider social and organizational context in two ways. The first concerns the basis of our social comparisons, which can be extremely varied. Some of us compare our situations with immediate colleagues, while others make comparisons with people in other organizations, sectors and countries. There is no rationale for preferring one basis of comparison to another. The second way in which equity theory ignores social context concerns the systemic inequities in capitalist economies. You and I, close colleagues, may receive the same treatment from our employing organization (perception of equity) while being exploited by relatively invisible individuals in positions of wealth, influence and power (perception of inequity). However, the latter expression of inequity is a 'normal' feature of capitalist society, and is thus difficult to challenge.

Stop and Criticize

What actions would you take if you were earning a little more than Annika in our earlier example from the Stockholm restaurant?

What actions would you take if you were earning much more than Annika?

To what extent do you think equity theory can make accurate predictions of your behaviour in inequitable situations?

Edward Chace Tolman (1886–1961)

Expectancy theory: a process theory which argues that individual motivation depends on the *valence* of outcomes, the *expectancy* that effort will lead to good performance, and the *instrumentality* of performance in producing valued outcomes.

Equity theory has significant implications for management practice. For example, it is important to recognize that employees compare pay (even in organizations that insist on pay secrecy) and inequity quickly generates predictable resentment. Comparisons are often subjective and imprecise, particularly where information is lacking and employees rely on rumour. It is important for management to recognize that perceptions of inequity can generate tension, even where actual inequity is limited. The circulation of accurate information about rewards, and the links between effort and rewards, is thus crucial.

Expectancy theory

A motive is an outcome that has become desirable. The process through which outcomes become desirable is explained by the **expectancy theory** of motivation. This is a *process* theory which does not assume that we come complete with a package of pre-defined goals.

Cognitive theories in psychology assume that we are purposive and aware of our goals and actions. Expectancy theory is a cognitive theory, and was first developed by the American psychologist Edward C. Tolman in the 1930s as a challenge to the behaviourist views of his contemporaries. Tolman argued that behaviour is directed by the expectations that we have about our behaviour leading to the achievement of desired outcomes.

For high motivation, productive work has to be seen as a path to valued goals. If you need more money, and if you expect to get more money for working hard, then we can predict that you will work hard. If you still need more money, and if you expect that hard work will only get you happy smiles from the boss, then we can predict that you will decide not to work hard, unless you place a high value

Valence: the perceived value or preference that an individual has for a particular outcome – it can be positive, negative or neutral.

Instrumentality: the perceived probability that good performance will lead to valued rewards – it is measured on a scale from 0 (no chance) to 1 (certainty).

Expectancy: the perceived probability that effort will result in good performance – it is measured on a scale from 0 (no chance) to 1 (certainty).

Victor Harold Vroom (b. 1932)

Stop and Criticize

on happy smiles. The theory thus assumes that we behave in ways that are instrumental to the achievement of valued goals.

The American psychologist Victor H. Vroom (1964) developed the first expectancy theory of work motivation, based on three concepts: **valence**, **instrumentality** and **expectancy**. This is therefore known as *valence–instrumentality–expectancy theory* – expectancy theory for short.

Instrumentality and expectancy are both known as subjective probabilities, as what is important is what the individual estimates to be the likelihood of good performance leading to valued rewards, and of effort leading to good performance, respectively.

The force (F) of your motivation to work hard is the result of the product (multiplication) of these three variables and not the sum (addition), because if one of the variables is zero, then, despite the value of the other two, the product, F, will be zero, and that is what we would expect. This cumbersome explanation is expressed in *the expectancy equation*:

$$F = V \times I \times E$$

What is the effect of a low 'V' value? If you do not care what grade you get for your next essay or examination, then you will not be motivated to work hard for it.

What is the effect of a low 'E' value? If you believe that long hours in the library will not lead to a high essay or examination grade, then you will not be motivated to work hard.

What is the effect of a low 'I' value? If you believe that a good grade will not lead to a chosen qualification, job or career, then you will not be motivated to work hard.

Only when all three of the terms in the expectancy equation are positive will the motivating force be positive. However, behaviour typically has a number of outcomes. Working hard affects our work performance, levels of fatigue, social life, today's pay and tomorrow's promotion prospects. The expectancy equation thus has to be summed for all possible outcomes. The full expectancy equation is:

$$F = \Sigma (V \times I \times E)$$

The sign Σ is the Greek letter sigma, which means 'add up all the values of the calculation in the brackets'. Note that there will be only a single E value, concerning the probability that high effort will lead to high performance. However, there will be several different I values, one for each rated outcome, concerning the probability that these will be obtained.

Measure the force of your motivation to get a high grade in organizational behaviour:

What are your V values? Identify the range of outcomes from working hard for this subject. Rate the value of each of these to you, as 1 (positive), 0 (ambivalent) or −1 (negative).

What are your I values? For each outcome, estimate the subjective probability of that occurring (you could get a high grade, you could ruin your social life).

What is your E value? Estimate the subjective probability that high effort will produce a high grade in this subject. This probability will be between 0 (little or no chance) and 1 (certainty of high grade).

Sum the calculation across all your outcomes and compare your score with colleagues. If the

Lyman W. Porter

Edward Emmett Lawler III

theory is correct, those with higher F scores are more highly motivated to get a good grade for the organizational behaviour course.

Consider the process through which you have just worked. To what extent is this a realistic picture of the cognitive decision-making process that we undertake when deciding on aspects of our behaviour?

Expectancy theory is more complex than content theory. In summary:

- Expectancy theory states that behaviour results from a conscious decision-making process based on expectations, measured as subjective probabilities, that the individual has about the results of different behaviours leading to performance and to rewards.

- Expectancy theory helps to explain individual differences in motivation and behaviour, unlike Maslow's universal content theory of motivation.

- Expectancy theory provides a basis for measuring the strength or force of the individual's motivation to behave in particular ways.

- Expectancy theory assumes that behaviour is rational, and that we are conscious of our motives. As we take into account the probable outcomes of our behaviour and place values on these outcomes, expectancy theory attempts to predict individual behaviour.

Lyman Porter and Edward Lawler (1968; Lawler, 1973) developed Vroom's expectancy theory into a more comprehensive theory of work motivation. Their theory is illustrated in figure 8.3 which identifies the factors contributing to job performance (box 6).

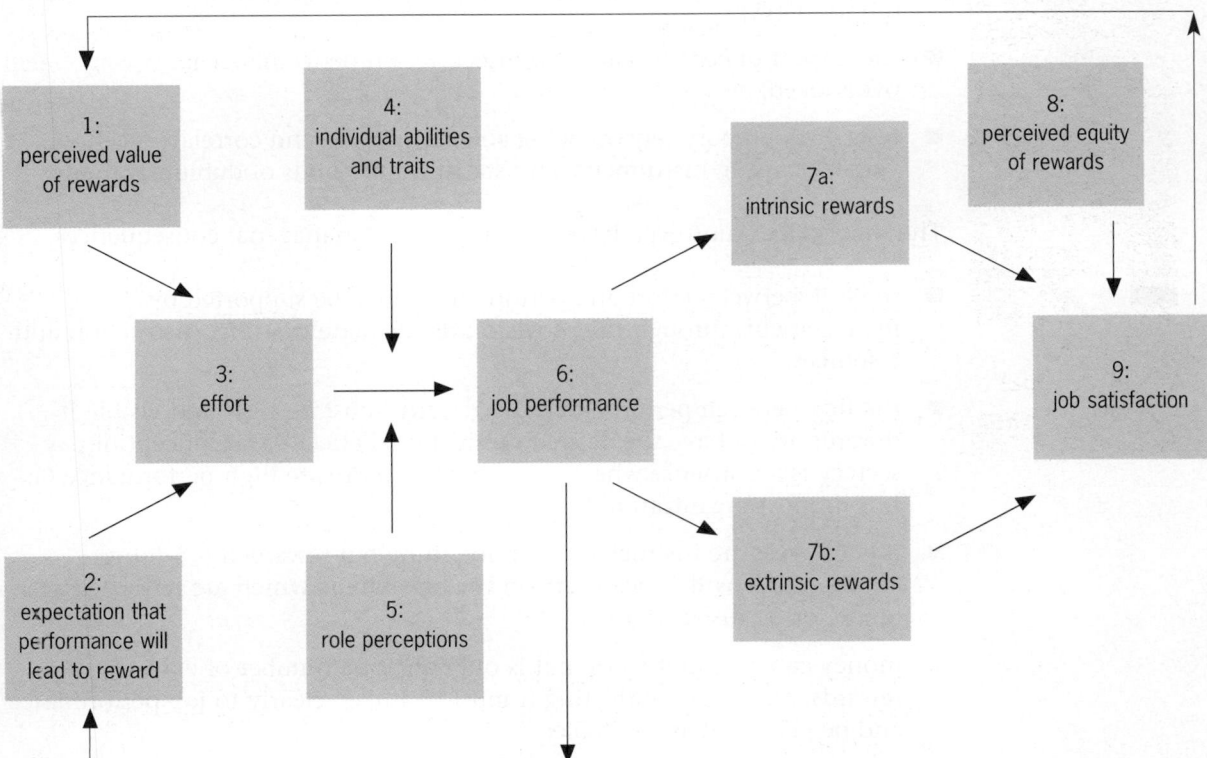

Figure 8.3: The Porter–Lawler model of work motivation (based on Porter and Lawler, 1968)

The effort expended on a task (box 3) depends on the rewards for performing well (box 1), and on the expectation that those rewards follow (box 2) perform-ance (box 6). In this model, what Vroom called instrumentality becomes a feed-back loop to effort through what is labelled the likelihood that performance will lead to rewards. What Vroom called expectancy, or the effort–performance link (will high effort lead to good performance?), is seen to depend not just on indi-vidual perceptions, but also on abilities and traits (box 4) and on role perceptions (box 5), or the degree to which the individual feels that what they are required to do is consistent with their perception of their role. Your performance may suffer if you are asked to do something which you feel is not consistent with the job and your expertise.

This integrative approach takes into account job satisfaction (box 9), based on perceptions of intrinsic and extrinsic rewards (boxes 7a and 7b), and also incor-porates equity theory (box 8). Satisfaction also influences the perceived value of rewards, and thus has a feedback effect.

This model argues that performance affects satisfaction, and not the other way around. Why? Satisfaction depends on need fulfilment. Need fulfilment is in turn dependent on the range of intrinsic and extrinsic rewards which come from job performance. Job satisfaction may or may not be associated with good job per-formance. Job satisfaction is only one attitude, or set of related attitudes, poten-tially linked with performance. Good performance, however, appropriately rewarded, is likely to lead to job satisfaction.

This theory has intuitive appeal; it has face validity; it feels right. Research by the authors and others appears to support it. However, the theory faces a number of criticisms:

- the theory covers a range of interrelated variables and is complex;

- the assumption that we make decisions using such a detailed calculus is questionable;

- the impact of coercion and job insecurity on performance is overlooked;

- tests of the theory rely on being able to measure and correlate all those variables, using instruments and statistical methods of dubious validity.

The theory does, however, have several practical managerial consequences:

- the link between effort and performance must be supported by management, through the provision of adequate training, instruction and resources;

- the link between performance and rewards must be clear and visible if rewards are to have the desired motivational effect – the concept of pay secrecy is a nonsense where pay is used to motivate high performance (as it is in most organizations);

- if employees are instructed to do one thing but rewarded for doing another, they will concentrate on the behaviours which are rewarded and ignore other instructions;

- money can be a motivator, but is only one of a number of extrinsic rewards, and to be motivating it must be linked clearly to job performance and be perceived as equitable;

- performance standards must be clear and unambiguous, otherwise employees will not know how best to direct their efforts;

- there is no point in offering rewards which employees do not value, or which are not valued highly enough to influence behaviour;

- if different employees value different kinds of reward, it may be necessary to introduce a cafeteria benefits or 'flex benefits' scheme, offering choices of medical insurance, health club memberships, car breakdown cover, bus passes, shopping vouchers, cinema tickets, bicycle allowances, financial planning advice and travel insurance, for example;

- the value of different rewards may change with time and has to be monitored;

- inconsistent or ambiguous performance ratings are a major potential source of inequity, and management must establish accurate and consistent ratings systems;

- the theory has been developed into a job enrichment technique.

In other words, to ensure low motivation and poor performance:

1. keep performance goals vague and ambiguous;

2. provide inadequate advice and resources for goal achievement;

3. reward behaviour other than good job performance;

4. offer rewards which employees do not value;

5. concentrate on financial rewards and ignore other intrinsic and extrinsic rewards;

6. make sure performance ratings are subjective and inconsistent.

Goal-setting theory

Goal-setting theory: a process theory which argues that work motivation is influenced by goal difficulty, goal specificity and knowledge of results.

Goal-setting theory is now regarded as a process theory of motivation. However, the main advocate of this approach, Edwin Locke (1968; Latham and Yukl, 1975), argues that 'goal-setting is more appropriately viewed as a motivational technique rather than a formal theory' (Locke, 1975, p. 465). This technique relies on a series of propositions which allow us to explain and to predict work behaviour, so it is entitled to be described as theory.

Goal theory has established four main propositions which are well supported by research:

1. *Challenging goals* lead to higher levels of performance than simple and unchallenging goals. Difficult goals are also called 'stretch' goals because they encourage us to try harder (unless the goal is beyond our level of ability).

2. *Specific goals* lead to higher levels of performance than vague goals such as 'try harder' or 'do your best'. It is easier for us to adjust our behaviour when we know precisely what is required of us, and goal specificity avoids confusion. A popular acronym states that goals should be SMART: specific, measurable, attainable, realistic and time-related.

3. *Participation* in goal-setting, particularly when this is expected, can improve performance by increasing commitment to those goals, but managerially assigned goals that are adequately explained and justified can also lead to high performance.

4. *Knowledge of results* of past performance – feedback – is necessary for

Edwin A. Locke

effective goal achievement. Feedback contains information and is also motivational.

The theory has been tested mainly in situations where short-term targets can be expressed in clear and quantifiable terms. It is unclear if the theory applies to longer-term goals, say over a period of years, as targets are likely to be more qualitative and to change as circumstances alter. It is also unclear whether this applies where goals are difficult to measure, such as in most types of managerial work. Another problem is that the theory and its applications concentrate on individual goals and performance rather than on teamwork.

Goal-setting for lumberjacks

Responding to criticism that goal-setting had been tested mainly in laboratory settings, Locke (1975, pp. 466–7) cited four studies in real organizational settings. In two separate studies of independent pulpwood producers, high productivity was maintained when a supervisor remained on the job with the men and set production goals for them.

In a third study of sawing crews, output per man was higher over a three-month period when specific and moderately difficult goals were assigned to the sawyers; this was not the case with other sawing crews where no specific goals were assigned.

In a fourth study, loggers were given the goal of loading trucks to 94 per cent of the legal maximum; the old average was only 60 per cent. Performance improved immediately, and loading weights remained high, averaging 90 per cent, for the next 15 months, saving a quarter of a million US dollars, as the purchase of additional trucks was avoided.

Locke points out that, in all four cases, performance improvements were quickly obtained without the offer of financial rewards for goal attainment or penalties for failure.

The main positive feature of goal-setting theory is the clarity of the practical management implications (Locke and Latham, 1990). These include:

- *Goal difficulty*: set goals for work performance at levels which will stretch employees, but which are not beyond their ability levels.

- *Goal specificity*: express goals in clear and precise language, if possible in quantifiable terms, and avoid setting vague and ambiguous goals.

- *Participation*: allow employees to take part in the goal-setting process to increase the acceptability of and their commitment to goals.

- *Acceptance*: if goals are set by management, ensure that they are adequately explained and justified, so that those concerned understand and accept them.

- *Feedback*: provide information on the results of past performance to allow employees to adjust their behaviour, if necessary, to improve future performance.

Goal-setting theory thus has implications for the design and conduct of staff appraisal systems, and for the technique of 'management by objectives' which focuses on the achievement of agreed or negotiated performance targets.

Stop and
Criticize

Yo! Sushi, a small Japanese restaurant chain, offers its staff financial bonuses of up to 20 per cent of annual salary every three months. To earn this bonus, staff have to meet restaurant targets, which include the number of customers, the average bill amount and profitability. Staff also have individual performance targets which are documented and reviewed quarterly, and which affect the bonus. One of the chain's restaurant managers, Tony Pay, claims that the scheme is effective because bonuses are frequent (not annual), and targets are agreed upon by management and staff.

What are the strengths of this scheme from the perspective of goal-setting theory?

What potential problems does this approach have, for management, for employees, and perhaps also for customers?

How would you advise management to adapt and improve this scheme?

Based on Sally Patten, 'Incentives prove key method of keeping staff', *The Times*, 12 October 1999, p. 38.

The social process of motivating others

In addition to the two perspectives considered so far in this chapter, concerning goals and decision-making, motivation can be regarded as a social influence process. The broad question is, how do we motivate or persuade others to do what we want them to do? The specific management problem is, how do we motivate employees to perform well?

A significant number of manual jobs in factories and clerical jobs in offices are still designed using methods advocated by an American engineer called Frederick Winslow Taylor (1911). Taylor's *scientific management* approach to designing jobs is as follows:

1. Decide on the optimum degree of *task fragmentation*, breaking down a complex job into a sequence of simple steps.

2. Decide the *one best way* to perform the work, through studies to discover the most effective method for doing each step, including workplace layout and design of tools.

3. *Train* employees to carry out these simple fragmented tasks in the manner specified.

4. *Reward* employees financially for meeting and exceeding specified performance targets.

Stop and
Criticize

You are employed on a job in which you repeat precisely the same simple task every fifteen seconds, perhaps wiring plugs for lamps, 9.00 am until 5.30 pm, every day (with a lunch break), five days a week. Maybe you have done work like this before?

Describe your emotional responses to work of this kind.

Do you think that it is inevitable that some jobs just have to be like this, given the nature of work and technology, and the need to keep quality high and costs low?

The advantages of task fragmentation include:

- employees do not need expensive and time-consuming training;

- specialization in one small task makes employees very proficient through repetition;

- lower pay can be given for such unskilled work;

- some of the problems of achieving controlled performance are simplified.

The disadvantages, however, include:

- repetitive work can be extremely boring;

- the individual's contribution to the organization is meaningless and insignificant;

- monotony leads to apathy, dissatisfaction and carelessness;

- the employee develops no skills that might lead to promotion.

Job enrichment: a technique for broadening the experience of work to enhance employee need satisfaction and to improve work motivation and performance.

Motivator factors: aspects of work which lead to high levels of satisfaction, motivation and performance, including achievement, recognition, responsibility, advancement, growth and the work itself.

Hygiene factors: aspects of work which remove dissatisfaction but do not contribute to motivation and performance, including pay, company policy, supervision, status, security and working conditions.

Taylor's approach to job design appears logical and efficient, but it creates jobs that do not stimulate motivation and performance. Taylor had a simplified view of human motivation, regarding 'lower-level' employees as 'coin operated' and arguing that the rewards for working as instructed should be financial. Taylor's methods are more likely to encourage absenteeism and sabotage than commitment and flexibility. Managers are thus interested in theories of motivation as sources of alternative methods for encouraging motivation and high performance. During the 1960s and 1970s, these concerns created the Quality of Working Life (QWL) movement whose language and methods are still influential.

One popular QWL technique derived from work motivation theory as an antidote to Taylorism is **job enrichment**.

The concept of job enrichment was first developed by the American psychologist Frederick Herzberg (1966, 1968). To discover what factors influenced job satisfaction and dissatisfaction, 203 Pittsburgh engineers and accountants were interviewed, and were asked two 'critical incident' questions. They were asked to recall events which had made them feel good about their work, and events which had made them feel bad about it.

Analysis of these critical incident narratives showed that the factors which led to job satisfaction were different from those which led to job dissatisfaction. Herzberg called this a 'two factor theory of motivation', the two sets of factors being **motivator** and **hygiene factors**, summarized in table 8.6. Motivators are also known as (job) content factors, while hygiene factors are known as (organizational) context factors.

Herzberg (1987) claims that this pattern of motivation has been identified in Finland, Hungary, Italy, Israel, Japan and Zambia. In South Africa, however, while managers and skilled workers, black and white, produced the expected

Frederick Herzberg (1923–2000)

Table 8.6: Motivator and hygiene factors

Motivator factors (job content)	Hygiene factors (organizational context)
achievement	pay
advancement	company policy
growth	supervisory style
recognition	status
responsibility	security
the work itself	working conditions

Vertical loading factors: methods for enriching work and improving motivation by removing controls, increasing accountability and providing feedback, new tasks, natural work units, special assignments and additional authority.

Intrinsic rewards: valued outcomes or benefits which come from the individual, such as feelings of satisfaction, competence, self-esteem and accomplishment.

Extrinsic rewards: valued outcomes or benefits provided by others, such as promotion, pay increases, a bigger office desk, praise and recognition.

Growth Need Strength: a measure of the readiness and capability of an individual to respond positively to job enrichment.

results, unskilled workers' satisfaction appeared to be dependent on hygiene. Herzberg claims that 'the impoverished nature of the unskilled workers' jobs has not afforded these workers with motivators – thus the abnormal profile'. He also cites a study of unskilled Indian workers who were 'operating on a dependent hygiene continuum that leads to addiction to hygiene, or strikes and revolution'.

The redesign of jobs to increase motivation and performance should thus focus on motivators or content factors. Improvement in the hygiene or context factors, Herzberg (1968) argued, will remove dissatisfaction, but will not increase motivation and performance. He advocated the application of **vertical loading factors**, to achieve job enrichment.

The way in which a job is designed determines the rewards available and what the individual has to do to get those rewards. It is useful to distinguish **intrinsic** and **extrinsic rewards**.

Intrinsic rewards are valued outcomes within the control of the individual, such as feelings of satisfaction and accomplishment. For some of us, and for some actions, the outcome is its own (intrinsic) reward. Mountaineers, poets, athletes, painters and musicians are usually familiar with the concept of intrinsic reward; few people ever get paid for climbing hills, and there are few wealthy poets on this planet. *Extrinsic rewards* are valued outcomes that are controlled by others, such as recognition, promotion and pay increases. The relationships between performance and intrinsic reward are usually more immediate and direct than those between performance and extrinsic reward. Edward Lawler (1973) thus argues that intrinsic rewards are more important influences on our motivation to work.

The Job Characteristics Model, shown in figure 8.4, is the basis of the job enrichment strategy of the expectancy theorists Richard Hackman and Greg Oldham (1974; Hackman, Oldham and Purdy, 1975). This model sets out the links between the features of jobs, the individual's experience, and outcomes in terms of motivation, satisfaction and performance. This model also takes into account individual differences in **Growth Need Strength**, a concept based on Maslow's concept of self-actualization.

Growth Need Strength (GNS) is an indicator of your willingness to welcome personal development through job enrichment. The causal chain, from job design, through individual experience, to performance outcomes, depends on GNS. With employees whose GNS is low, enriched jobs will not lead to positive performance outcomes. This is a contingent model, not a universal one.

At the heart of this model is the proposition that jobs can be analyzed in terms of five *core dimensions* which are defined as follows:

1. *Skill variety*: the extent to which a job makes use of different skills and abilities.

2. *Task identity*: the extent to which a job involves a 'whole' and meaningful piece of work.

3. *Task significance*: the extent to which a job affects the work of others.

4. *Autonomy*: the extent to which a job provides independence and discretion.

5. *Feedback*: the extent to which performance information is related back to the individual.

Stop and Criticize

Your manager offers to enrich your job. However, you see this as a way of getting you to take on more responsibility and work harder for no extra pay, and you turn down the offer. Familiar with the Job Characteristics Model, your manager describes you as 'low in Growth Need Strength'. How do you feel about this judgement?

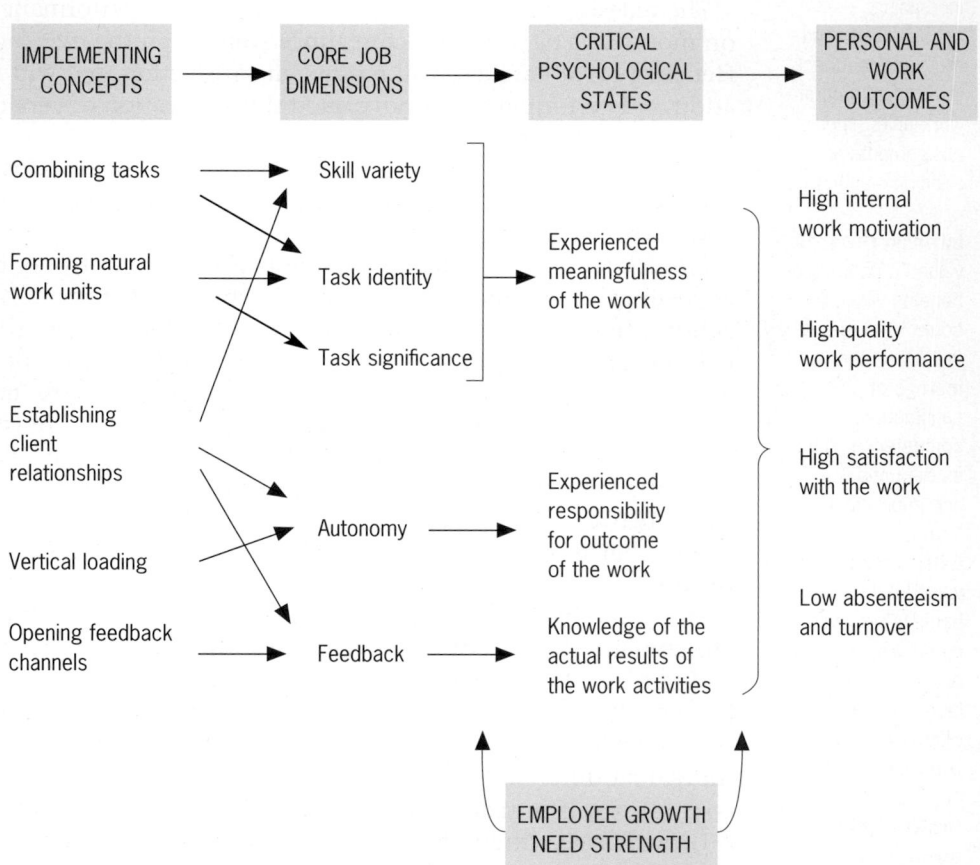

Figure 8.4: The job characteristics model
From J.R. Hackman, G. Oldham, R. Janson and K. Purdy, 'A new strategy for job enrichment'. Copyright © 1975, by The Regents of the University of California. Reprinted from the *California Management Review*, vol. 17, no. 4. By permission of The Regents.

Eat what you kill: do incentive schemes improve motivation and performance?

Performance-related payment schemes continue to flourish as managers try to find new ways to motivate employees by linking rewards to the achievement of performance targets. Alfie Kohn claims that these 'eat what you kill' incentive schemes are doomed to fail because:

- Money helps us to meet many of our needs, but research reveals that money is not an overriding concern for most people.

- Pay that is dependent on performance ('If they have to bribe me to do this') is manipulative, and heightens the perception of being controlled.

- Competition for rewards can disrupt relationships between individuals whose collective performance would be improved by co-operation, and is damaged by rivalry.

- Dependence on financial incentives to improve productivity diverts attention from attempts to understand and solve the underlying problems facing an organization.

■ Incentive schemes discourage risk-taking, experiment and creative exploration, by sending the signal 'do exactly what you are told'.

■ Rewards that are contingent on particular levels of performance undermine interest in the job itself, whereas intrinsic motivation is usually the real basis of exceptional work.

Kohn concludes that performance-related pay schemes are based on a misunderstanding of extrinsic and intrinsic motivation. These two aspects of motivation cannot be 'added', and it is not simply a case of 'targeting' the behaviours that will attract additional bonuses. Extrinsic rewards buy compliance and do not encourage long-term commitment. People do not necessarily perform better when paid more, and may even perform worse:

The more we experience being controlled, the more we will tend to lose interest in what we are doing. If we go to work thinking about the possibility of getting a bonus, we come to feel that our work is not self-directed. Rather it is the reward that drives our behaviour. [A]nything presented as a prerequisite for something else – that is, as a means toward another end – comes to be seen as less desirable. (1993, p. 62)

Based on Alfie Kohn, 'Why incentive plans cannot work', *Harvard Business Review*, vol. 71, no. 5, 1993, pp. 54–63, and *The Economist*, 'Just deserts', January 1994, p. 77.

Job Diagnostic Survey: a questionnaire designed to assess the degree of skill variety, task identity, task significance, autonomy and feedback in jobs.

Jobs can be assessed on these core dimensions. Richard Hackman and Greg Oldham (1974; Hackman, Oldham and Purdy, 1975) developed an opinion questionnaire called the **Job Diagnostic Survey** (JDS) for this purpose.

Skill variety and autonomy are measured in the JDS by questions such as:

How much *variety* is there in your job? That is, to what extent does the job require you to do many different things at work, using a variety of your skills and talents?

How much *autonomy* is there in your job? That is, to what extent does your job permit you to decide *on your own* how to go about doing the work?

Motivating Potential Score: an indicator of how motivating a job is likely to be for an individual, considering skill variety, task identity, task significance, autonomy and feedback.

Respondents rate their answers to each these questions on a seven-point scale. The JDS thus provides *operational definitions* (see glossary) of the variables in the Job Characteristics Model. The core job dimensions are *independent variables*, and critical psychological states and performance outcomes are *dependent variables* (see glossary). Growth Need Strength, also operationalized in the JDS, is a mediating variable in this causal chain. The JDS can be used to establish how motivating a job is by permitting the calculation of a **Motivating Potential Score** (MPS), from answers across groups of employees on the same job.

The MPS is calculated using the following equation, where the values of the variables have been measured using the JDS:

$$\text{MPS} = \frac{(\text{skill variety} + \text{task identity} + \text{task significance})}{3} \times \text{autonomy} \times \text{feedback}$$

Autonomy and feedback are considered more important in their motivating influence than the other three core job dimensions. The equation is designed to reflect this, by treating them as separate components, and by treating as one component the arithmetic mean of the ratings for skill variety, task identity and task significance. If one of the three main components in this equation is low, then the MPS will be low. A near-zero rating on either autonomy or feedback, for example, would pull the score down disproportionately (five plus zero equals five, but five times zero equals zero). A near-zero rating on variety, identity or significance would not have a significant effect on the overall score.

The five core dimensions stimulate three psychological states critical to high work motivation, job satisfaction and performance. These critical psychological states are:

1. *Experienced meaningfulness*: the extent to which the individual considers the work to be meaningful, valuable and worthwhile.

2. *Experienced responsibility*: the extent to which the individual feels accountable for the work output.

3. *Knowledge of results*: the extent to which individuals know and understand how well they are performing.

Jobs with high MPS are more likely to lead to the experience of critical psychological states than jobs with low scores. Expectancy theorists argue that all three critical states must be present if the personal and work outcomes on the right-hand side of the model are to be achieved. One or two is not good enough. It is important to recall that individuals who put a low value on personal growth and development will not respond in the way suggested by the model. No point, then, in offering them enriched jobs, unless one believes that the experience of personal development can in itself stimulate growth need.

The model also shows how the motivating potential of jobs can be improved by applying five *implementing concepts*. These (including vertical loading, from Herzberg) are:

1. Combining tasks
Give employees more than one part of the work to do. This increases the variety of the job, and increases the contribution that the individual makes to the product or service. For example, train call centre staff to handle a broad range of customer questions and problems rather than having them specialize in specific and narrow areas.

2. Forming natural work units
Give employees meaningful patterns of work. This increases individual contribution and task significance. For example, create teams which build the whole motor car engine, rather than assigning individual assembly workers to fragmented and repetitive tasks.

3. Establishing client relationships
Give employees responsibility for personal contacts. This increases variety, gives the person freedom in performing the work, and also increases the opportunities for receiving feedback. For example, staff working in a hospital pharmacy can deal directly and consistently with staff and patients on nominated wards, rather than responding on a 'first come first served by whoever is free at the time' basis.

4. Vertical loading
Give employees responsibilities normally allocated to supervisors. Such additional responsibilities include granting discretion for:

work scheduling	work methods	problem-solving
quality checks	training others	cost control
work times and breaks	deciding priorities	recruitment decisions

This gives individuals more autonomy, and can be achieved by removing the supervisory role, or by redesigning it to involve activities other than direct supervision, such as training, coaching and liaising with other departments.

5. Opening feedback channels

Give employees performance summaries and corporate information, as well as establishing client relationships. This improves opportunities for feedback of results. Feedback tells people how well they are doing and provides a basis for improvement.

A number of successful applications of job enrichment were reported during the 1960s and 1970s. In America, the best publicized applications were at American Telephone and Telegraph (AT&T) which conducted nineteen job enrichment projects between 1965 and 1969 affecting over 1,000 blue- and white-collar employees (Ford, 1969). The company was concerned mainly with the rising costs of employee dissatisfaction and labour turnover, which were attributed to monotonous, meaningless jobs. In Britain, the best publicized applications of job enrichment were at ICI, a chemicals company. Paul and Robertson (1970) reported eight applications between 1967 and 1968, mainly with white-collar groups, including sales representatives, design engineers, foremen and draughtsmen. The popularity of job enrichment waned during the 1980s, as the economies of Europe and America became preoccupied with unemployment. However, job enrichment methods have enjoyed renewed popularity since the 1990s, based on teamworking approaches.

Can the theory and practice of job enrichment now be abandoned? On the contrary. The language and the method have become a taken-for-granted aspect of contemporary management practice. Applications of job enrichment no longer carry novelty value, and thus pass unreported. The concept of job enrichment has been 're-invented' by Timothy Butler and James Waldroop (1999) under the label 'job sculpting'. However, practice in many organizations has gone beyond the enrichment of individuals jobs, to encompass teamworking, organizational culture change and other forms of employee empowerment.

Source: © Copyright United Feature Syndicate, Inc. Reproduced by permission.

Job sculpting and staff retention

Timothy Butler and James Waldroop argue that educated high-achievers are mobile because they can succeed in just about any job. They move on when work does not match their deeply embedded life interests, which are a stable part of personality (not hobbies or enthusiasms). Research with 650 'professionals' revealed eight main life interests:

Life interests	How to recognize them
application of technology	the person who is intrigued by the inner working of things, reads software manuals for fun
quantitative analysis	the 'quant jock' who excels at numbers, designs optimum production schedules for fun
theory development and conceptual thinking	the person who enjoys talking about abstract ideas, wants the 'helicopter' view, reads academic journals for fun
creative production	the imaginative thinker, good at inventing novel solutions, wears unconventional clothes for fun
counselling and mentoring	the person good at counselling, mentoring and guiding, gets satisfaction from feeling needed and helping others
managing relationships	the person interested in managing people for results, deals with others, face-to-face, for fun
enterprise control	the responsibility-seeker and decision maker who wants to control things, runs projects and manages teams for fun
influence through ideas	the person who is fulfilled when writing or speaking, wants to persuade, negotiate or just communicate for fun

Butler and Waldroop argue that, to motivate people to perform well and to stay with the organization, managers have to use *job sculpting*. This involves:

■ listening carefully to discover what really challenges, excites and motivates people;

■ understanding the individual's embedded life interests;

■ designing both the job and the individual's career path to match those interests;

■ using assignments as opportunities to sculpt the job for the person;

■ reviewing performance regularly to ensure that work and career interests are consistent.

A salesperson with an interest in quantitative analysis could be assigned to market research. An engineer with an interest in influence through ideas could help design sales support materials and manuals. A bank lending officer, good at customer services but with a life interest in theory development and conceptual thinking, was about to leave the company until it moved him to a role in competitive analysis and strategy formulation.

Based on Timothy Butler and James Waldroop, 'Job sculpting: the art of retaining your best people', *Harvard Business Review*, vol. 77, no. 5, 1999, pp. 144–52.

Enrichment, high-performance systems and empowerment

In the 1960s, an executive of American Telephone and Telegraph, concerned about low levels of staff commitment to the company, complained that 'we have lost too many people who are still with us' (Ford, 1969). AT&T employees expected interesting, meaningful work, which was not on offer, and performance consequently suffered. Those expectations do not appear to have changed. A well-educated, media-informed, knowledge-based workforce, conscious of individual rights and social comparisons, is much less willing to tolerate bureaucratic control, and is more ready openly to challenge management decisions and actions.

Empowerment: a general term describing organizational arrangements that give employees more autonomy, discretion and unsupervised decision-making responsibility.

High-performance work system: a form of organization that operates at levels of excellence far beyond those of comparable systems.

As a result, many organizations during the 1990s reconsidered job enrichment and other approaches to improve quality of working life, through employee **empowerment**.

Specific techniques for improving motivation and performance through empowerment fall into two broad categories: individual job enrichment and self-managing or autonomous teamwork. This chapter concentrates on individual motivation and jobs. Chapter 12 explores teamwork. These approaches to empowerment converge in **high-performance work systems**.

The features of high-performance work systems were first explored by Peter Vaill (1982, p. 25). Organizations or sub-groups qualify for the title 'high-performance system' if they:

1. Perform excellently against a known external standard.

2. Perform beyond what is assumed to be their potential best.

3. Perform excellently in relation to what they did before.

4. Are judged by observers to be substantially better than comparable groups.

5. Are achieving levels of performance with fewer resources than necessary.

6. Are seen to be exemplars, as a source of ideas and inspiration.

7. Are seen to achieve the ideals of the culture.

8. Are the only organizations that have been able to do what they do at all, even though it might seem that what they do is not that difficult or mysterious a thing.

At the heart of the high-performance system is the self-managing or autonomous team, empowered to make most its own decisions about how work is carried out, without having to refer issues to management. Claiming significant performance improvements on a range of criteria, many organizations developed high-performance systems, including Digital Equipment Corporation (Perry, 1984; Buchanan and McCalman, 1989). Similarly, empowered employees can also be found in The Body Shop, Unipart, Frizzell Financial Services, Ciba UK and Harvester Restaurants (Pickard, 1993). Garment makers in Hong Kong adopted self-managing work groups (Li, 1992). Many American companies have publicized their autonomous teams, including Shenandoah Life Insurance, Harley-Davidson, Compaq, Cummins Engine Company, Procter and Gamble and General Motors (Hoerr et al., 1986; Hoerr, 1989). In most cases, the role of the first line supervisor changed radically, from 'policeman to coach', and has in some cases been removed (Peters, 1987; Dumaine, 1990).

Do we need to use more empowerment?

Toby Wall and Stephen Wood argue that empowerment can be an effective management tool. Their study of 80 manufacturing companies found that empowerment had a more significant impact on performance than new technology or research and development. Empowerment is not effective in every setting. It works better where there is uncertainty in the production process, and employees have to deal with variable demands and ambiguity. Where jobs are standardized and routine, performance is unaffected by empowerment.

Empowerment seems to improve performance by encouraging new ideas and by allowing employees to work more effectively. Empowerment itself is not motivating. The wider research revealed international differences in the use of such management tools:

➤

management preferences (per cent)	Britain	Japan	Australia	Switzerland
empowerment	23	21	34	47
teamworking	35	22	45	50
total quality management	42	61	55	54
just-in-time methods	41	40	39	61

Based on Toby Wall and Stephen Wood, 'Delegation's a powerful tool', *Professional Manager*, vol. 11, no. 6, November 2002, p. 37.

Autonomous teamworking thus involves changes to the role of management. Edward Lawler (1986, 1995) argues that, in what he calls 'new design plants', 'almost no aspect of the organization is left untouched'. New design plants are characterized by:

■ common entrance and car parking, with no reserved top management slots;

■ common eating and restaurant areas, with no executive dining room;

■ salaried status for all staff, no 'hourly paid' employees;

■ self-managing teams performing 'whole' work processes with elected leaders;

■ flat management hierarchy, no foremen;

■ team responsibility for goals, task allocation, quality control and absenteeism;

■ team responsibility for selecting and training new members;

■ some support functions performed within teams;

■ other support staff become consultants and trainers.

Lawler (1986) claims that new design plants are 'a new kind of organization'. Are the claims for high-performance work systems justified? While work redesign methods have remained the same, and theories of motivation have seen little development since the 1970s, the organizational context to which these theories and techniques are applied has changed dramatically. The distinctions between the quality of working life (QWL) approach and the high-performance work systems (HPWS) approach are summarized in table 8.7.

Empowerment has become a broad term applied to any organizational arrangements which pass decision-making responsibilities from managers to lower-level employees. Tim Claydon and Mike Doyle (1996) argue that empowerment is more myth than reality, as organizational changes introduced under this heading are often cosmetic, and managers are reluctant to relinquish power. Have competitive pressures and the need for cost cuts, improved quality and flexibility eroded that management reluctance? Anna Psoinos and Steve Smithson (2002) mailed a survey questionnaire to the human resource managers of the top 450 manufacturing companies in Britain. The findings suggest that empowerment, in some form, is widely developed. Of the 103 companies which replied:

■ 91 (88 per cent) had introduced organizational changes that could lead to empowerment, such as delayering, downsizing, total quality management and process re-engineering;

Table 8.7: QWL versus HPWS

QWL in the 1970s	HPWS today
aimed to reduce costs of absenteeism and labour turnover and increase productivity	aims to improve organizational flexibility and product quality for competitive advantage
increased autonomy improves quality of work experience and job satisfaction	increased empowerment improves skill, decision-making, adaptability and use of new technology
had little impact on management functions	involves redefinition of management function, particularly for supervision
'quick fix' applied to problematic groups	takes time to change the organizational culture, attitudes and behaviour
personnel administration technique	human resource management strategy

- of those 91 companies, 79 (87 per cent) had delegated decisions to lower-level staff, such as quality responsibility, problem-solving, job and shift allocations, quality control, production and maintenance scheduling, and plant modifications and improvements;

- of those 79 companies, 25 per cent said that empowerment was unsuccessful, while 18 per cent said that information was not available, or that it was too soon to tell;

- empowerment was seen as successful in 60 per cent of companies where it was used.

One manager who was subsequently interviewed said (Psoinos and Smithson, 2002, p. 139):

I think empowerment to [this company] is actually giving employees flexibility and the room to manoeuvre, to actually do their job and to do their job to a high standard. It's about providing them with the right training, providing them with the right skills and the right tools to actually look at their job and see how they're doing their job, and are they doing their job in the best way. And giving them scope to actually make decisions and have some impact on what they're doing.

However, another manager argued:

That doesn't mean to say that everybody can do what they like. You've got to have a process to say yes, this is a good idea, and you put it in, in a way that enables you to control the changes.

The main reasons for introducing empowerment concerned quality, productivity, flexibility and cost reduction, not concern for quality of working life. The main constraints on empowerment were traditional job and status demarcations, hierarchical structures, organization culture, middle management resistance and complex production systems. However, organization culture and middle managers facilitated empowerment in successful contexts, along with employee skills and decision-making capabilities.

The argument of this chapter is summarized in figure 8.5. This begins with demands for involvement autonomy in work, and with the challenge and personal development that we desire. These needs seek fulfilment in contexts facing multiple socio-economic pressures. Addressing these needs and pressures involves individual job enrichment, self-managing teamwork and other approaches to empowerment. The emphasis on personal development and continuous improvement improves adaptability, product quality and customer care, leading to improved organizational effectiveness and quality of working life.

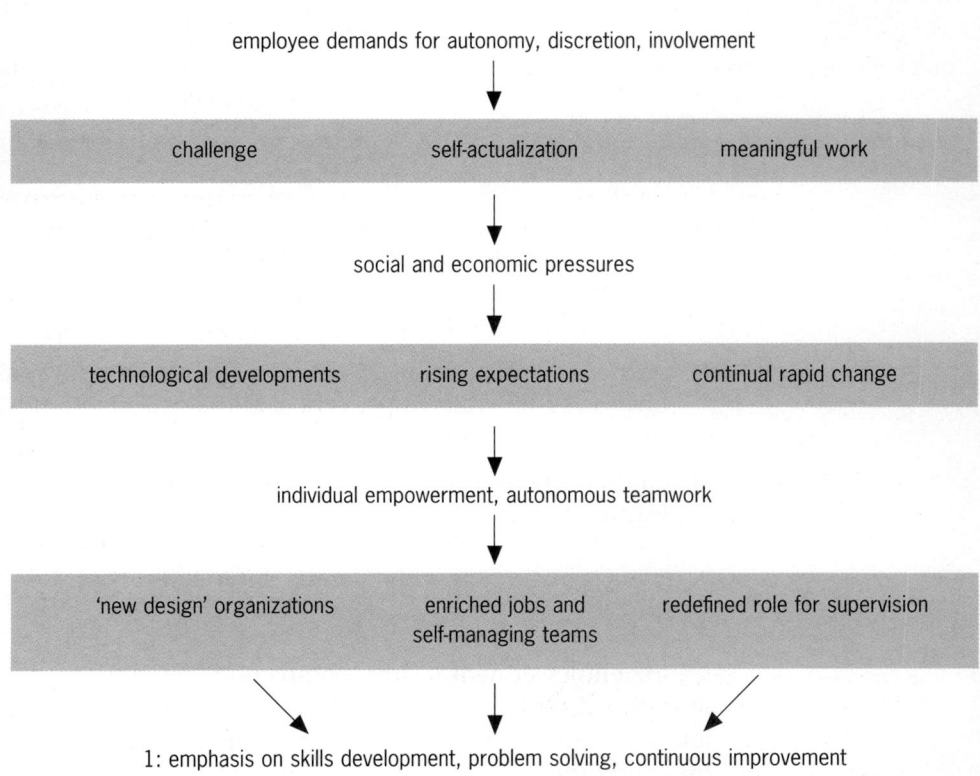

Figure 8.5: The case for the 'new design' organization

Some commentators argue that job enrichment, high-performance work systems, new design plants and empowerment constitute a radical transformation in organization design and in management–employee relationships.

Some commentators argue that these initiatives are cosmetic, having no effect on the power and reward inequalities and exploitation in contemporary organizations.

What are arguments for and against these extreme positions – and where do you stand on this debate?

Recap

1. *Understand different ways in which the term 'motivation' is used.*

   - Motivation can refer to desired goals which we as individuals have or acquire.

   - Motivation can refer to the individual decision-making process through which goals are chosen.

   - Motivation can refer to social influence attempts to change the behaviour of others.

2. *Understand the nature of motives and motivation processes as influences on behaviour.*

   - Motives as desirable goals can be innate (drives) or acquired (socially learned).

   - Content theories of motivation explain behaviour in terms of innate drives and acquired motives.

   - Equity theory explains motivation in terms of perceived injustice or unfairness.

   - Expectancy theory explains motivation in terms of valued outcomes and the subjective probability of achieving those outcomes.

   - The Porter–Lawler model of work motivation combines expectancy theory with equity considerations in explaining job performance levels.

   - Goal-setting theory explains behaviour in terms of goal difficulty and goal specificity.

3. *Use expectancy theory and job enrichment to diagnose organizational problems and to recommend solutions.*

   - A job will only be motivating if it leads to rewards which the individual values.

   - Rewards motivate high performance when the link between effort and reward is clear.

   - Hygiene factors can overcome dissatisfaction but do not lead to motivation.

   - Content factors lead to job satisfaction, motivation and high performance.

   - Jobs can be enriched by applying vertical job loading factors.

   - The motivating potential of a job can be increased by improving skill variety, task identity, task significance, autonomy and feedback.

   - Job enrichment will not improve the performance of individuals with low Growth Need Strength.

4. *Explain the renewed interest in this field in the 1990s, with respect to the evolving link between organization strategy and high-performance work systems.*

   - An educated, informed, knowledge-based workforce expects more participation in management decisions and opportunities for self-development.

   - In a rapidly changing competitive business environment, organizations need to motivate employees to be flexible, adaptable, committed and creative, not just to turn up on time and follow instructions.

   - High-performance work systems use combinations of individual job enrichment, autonomous teamworking, facilitative, coaching supervisory style, and other forms of delegation to empower lower-level employees.

Revision

1. Why is it difficult to make a clear distinction between innate drives and socially acquired motives, and what are the practical implications of this argument?

2. Explain the distinction between content and process theories of motivation. Explain an example of a content theory of motivation, its implications for organizational practice, and its limitations.

3. Abraham Maslow meets Frederick Winslow Taylor; needs hierarchy meets scientific management. What criticisms would each of these gentlemen offer to the other, and how would they each defend their respective positions when faced with such criticisms?

4. How does equity theory seek to explain motivation and behaviour, and how can equity theory be used to diagnose and improve employee motivation?

5. Explain what is meant by the expectancy equation. How does this equation help to explain employee behaviour at work, and what criticisms can be levelled against this approach?

Springboard

Harvard Business Review, 2003, 'Motivating people: how to get the most from your organization', Special issue, vol. 81, no. 1, January.

In addition to new articles on leadership styles, organizational forms based on 'citizenship' and motivating 'problem people', five previously published articles are included, from Frederick Herzberg's famous paper, 'One more time: how do you motivate employees?' (1968).

Lawler, E.E., 1996, *From the Ground Up: Six Principles for Building the New Logic Corporation*, Jossey-Bass, San Francisco.

Argues that single techniques for improving organizational effectiveness are not effective and argues that a range of methods have to be integrated to achieve success.

Lawler, E.E., Mohrman, S.A. and Ledford, G.E., 1998, *Strategies for High Performance Organizations*, Jossey-Bass, San Francisco.

Describes how Fortune 1000 companies use employee involvement, quality management and reengineering to improve organizational effectiveness.

Locke, E.A. and Latham, G.P., 1990, *A Theory of Goal Setting and Task Performance*, Prentice-Hall, Englewood Cliffs, NJ.

Comprehensive overview of what appears to be one of the most robust motivational theories in work psychology – an important and influential treatment.

Maslow, A.H., 1943, 'A theory of human motivation', *Psychological Review*, vol. 50, no. 4, pp. 370–96.

The original statement of Maslow's need hierarchy theory, essential (and not too difficult) reading for all those who believe that his theory mentions only five needs.

Pfeffer, J., 1996, *Competitive Advantage Through People: Unleashing the Power of the Work Force*, Harvard Business School Press, Boston, MA.

Attacks Taylor's scientific management and offers a range of techniques and management behaviours (which go beyond the more narrowly focused material on motivation in this chapter) for stimulating motivation and performance.

Pfeffer, J., 1998, *The Human Equation: Building Profits by Putting People First*, Harvard Business School Press, Boston, MA.

Describes high-performance management methods to improve motivation and performance. Gives detailed evidence to persuade sceptical managers.

Porter, L.W. and Lawler, E.E., 1968, *Managerial Attitudes and Performance*, Irwin, Homewood, IL.

Clear explanation of the Porter–Lawler model, theoretical background, underpinning evidence and practical managerial implications. Seminal and still widely cited.

Ritchie, S. and Martin, P., 1999, *Motivation Management*, Gower, Aldershot.

A content theory of motivation, based on a motivational profile of the individual rather than a universalistic approach. Written for a practising management audience rather than a theoretical academic one. British, not American, in style.

Home viewing

Bringing out the Dead (1999, director Martin Scorsese) is based around three night shifts in the working life of a New York paramedic, Frank Pierce (played by Nicolas Cage). He is burned out and exhausted, an alcoholic and insomniac, haunted by the memory of a girl he was unable to save, and desperate to leave the job. He is unable to save many patients as they are either crazy, dead or dying by the time the ambulance reaches them. His supervisor won't accept his resignation, even when he turns up late, because they are short of ambulance drivers. On each night, Frank tours the city streets with a different partner. Larry (John Goodman) likes fast food. Marcus (Ving Rhames) preaches the gospel. Tom (Tom Sizemore) likes to beat up patients for excitement when the pace is slack. Identify which of the needs on Maslow's hierarchy Frank and his colleagues display in their behaviour. Identify the motivational profile of each of the ambulance drivers. Use the Porter–Lawler model of work motivation to explain Frank's low job satisfaction, and advise management on how to improve the motivating potential of ambulance work.

American Beauty (1999, director Sam Mendes) is a story of 'the perfect family' falling apart. Lester Burnham (played by Kevin Spacey) quits his dead-end management job to work serving burgers in Mr Smiley's, while his wife Carolyn (Annette Bening) has an affair with her local competitor in the real estate business. The story displays the corrosive effects of dissatisfying, demotivating work on family, personal identity and relationships. Also of interest is the way in which the main characters define 'success' in life.

The Office (2002, written and directed by Ricky Gervais and Stephen Merchant) is a television comedy based in a paper merchants' office in Slough, England. The Regional Manager, David Brent (played by Ricky Gervais), is not familiar with McGregor's Theories X and Y. Can you identify the set of propositions, about human nature, employee motivation and leadership style, which define 'Theory Brent'?

OB in literature

David Ireland, *The Unknown Industrial Prisoner*, Angus and Robertson/Vintage, Sydney, 1971.

A poignant and hilarious account of factory life, this award-winning novel is based on the 'Puroil Refining Termitary and Grinding Works' in Sydney, Australia. 'Termitary' because of the ant-like behaviour in the administration block. 'Grinding Works' because of what long-term employment does to those who work there. The opening chapter, 'One day in a penal colony', sets the tone. The jobs are designed in the best traditions of scientific management. Dealing with autocratic managers and hazardous working conditions, note how employee motivation is systematically destroyed and how performance suffers. Note the employee strategies for coping with this environment, including practical jokes, sabotage, sex and alcohol. Identify the motivational profiles, and the embedded life interests, of the plant employees as you read this.

Michael Bracewell, *Perfect Tense*, Vintage, London, 2001.

A cynical and comical story about the dull grey meaningless routine of office life, punctuated by occasional excitement provided by other characters, and not the work. At one point, Bracewell writes (p. 140): 'boredom leads to neglect of duties, which leads to mistakes, which leads to censure, which leads to lack of confidence, which leads to more mistakes, more censure, lack of motivation and more boredom'. Bracewell also introduces the concept of 'compensatory pleasures' which he defines as 'all the rewards, big and small, which we give to ourselves to keep us going' (p. 142). Office work does have intrinsic rewards after all?

Chapter exercises

1: Growth need and job characteristics

Objectives
1. To assess the Motivating Potential Score of a particular job or jobs.

2. To determine which core job characteristics would need to change to improve the MPS of that job or those jobs.

3. To identify your personal Growth Need Strength and by implication your preference for enriched or empowered work.

(a)   Applying the Job Characteristics Model

To measure the Motivating Potential Score (MPS) for a given job, researchers developed the Job Diagnostic Survey (JDS). The JDS is a lengthy questionnaire, which takes time to complete and analyze in full. However, here is a short version. This allows job design deficiencies to be identified and triggers ideas for job redesign.

Complete this analysis for a job in which you are currently employed (full- or part-time), or for a job that you have performed recently. The JDS is designed for completion by the job holder and not by an observer. For each of the twelve items, indicate whether it is an accurate or an inaccurate description of the chosen job, and give it a rating using this scale:

1 = very inaccurate

2 = mostly inaccurate

3 = somewhat inaccurate

4 = uncertain

5 = somewhat accurate

6 = mostly accurate

7 = very accurate

The job chosen for analysis is:

Item	Rating	
1	_____	supervisors often let me know how well they think I am performing
2	_____	the job requires me to use a number of complex high-level skills
3	_____	the job is arranged so that I have the chance to do a complete piece of work from beginning to end
4	_____	just doing the work required by the job provides many chances for me to work out how well I am doing
5	_____	the job is not simple and repetitive
6	_____	the job is one where a lot of other people can be affected by how well the work is done
7	_____	the job does not deny me the chance to use my personal initiative or judgement in carrying out the work
8	_____	the job gives me the chance to completely finish the pieces of work I begin

9 _____ the job itself provides plenty of clues about whether or not I am performing well

10 _____ the job gives me considerable opportunity for independence and freedom in how I do the work

11 _____ the job itself is very significant and important in the broader scheme of things

12 _____ the supervisors and co-workers on this job almost always give me feedback on how well I am doing in my work

Scoring

Work out the average of the two items that measure each job characteristic:

job characteristic	item numbers	average score
skill variety	2 and 5	_____
task identity	3 and 8	_____
task significance	6 and 11	_____
autonomy	7 and 10	_____
feedback from the job itself	4 and 9	_____
feedback from others	1 and 12	_____

To calculate the MPS for this job, first add your scores for the two feedback characteristics, and divide by two to give the average. Then put all of the scores into the MPS formula:

$$\text{MPS} = \frac{(\text{skill variety} + \text{task identity} + \text{task significance})}{3} \times \text{autonomy} \times \text{feedback}$$

If you have completed this analysis alone:

■ assess the strengths and weaknesses of this job in terms of its motivating potential;

■ identify recommendations for redesigning this job to improve the MPS;

■ assess the difficulties in implementing these recommendations, given the nature of the work and the organizational context in which it is performed.

If you have completed this analysis alongside colleagues:

■ share the results of your analysis with colleagues;

■ pick the job in your group that has the lowest MPS;

■ identify redesign options for improving the job's MPS (you will first need to ask the job holder for a detailed description of the job);

■ assess the difficulties in implementing these recommendations, given the nature of the work and the organizational context in which it is performed.

(b) Assessing personal Growth Need Strength

We know that there are individual differences with respect to work preferences. Here are twelve pairs of statements of job characteristics. Taking each pair of characteristics, decide which kind of job you would prefer from the choice offered (these are not all opposing choices) by circling a number on the five-point rating scale.

a job that offers little or no challenge	1 2 3 4 5	a job that requires you to be completely isolated from co-workers
a job that pays very well	1 2 3 4 5	a job that allows considerable opportunity to be creative and innovative
a job that requires you to make important decisions	5 4 3 2 1	a job in which there are many pleasant people to work with
a job with little security in an unstable organization	5 4 3 2 1	a job in which you have limited opportunities to influence decisions affecting your work
a job in which greater responsibility is given to those who do the best work	5 4 3 2 1	a job in which greater responsibility is given to those who are loyal and have seniority
a job with a supervisor who is sometimes highly critical	5 4 3 2 1	a job that does not make too many demands on your abilities
a routine and undemanding job	1 2 3 4 5	a job in which your co-workers are not very friendly
a job with a supervisor who respects you and treats you fair	1 2 3 4 5	a job that provides constant opportunities for learning
a job that gives you a chance to develop yourself personally	5 4 3 2 1	a job with excellent vacations and fringe benefits
a job in which there is a real chance you could be laid off	5 4 3 2 1	a job with very little chance to do challenging work
a job with little freedom and independence to do the work the way you think best	1 2 3 4 5	a job with poor working conditions
a job with very satisfying teamwork	1 2 3 4 5	a job that allows you to use your abilities to the fullest extent

To calculate your individual Growth Need Strength, simply add up the numbers that you have circled and divide that total by 12.

A score of 3.5 or above suggests that you have high Growth Need Strength, and that you would respond positively to job enrichment leading to the critical psychological states in the Job Characteristics Model.

A score of 2.5 or less suggests that you would not find enriched jobs satisfying or motivating.

Scores between 2.5 and 3.5 suggest that you would find some job enrichment satisfying, but that you also welcome some structure and management control over your work.

2: The 'best place to work' blueprint

Objectives 1. To provide practice in applying motivation theory to a real-life organizational context.

2. To analyze critically the approach of one particular organization.

3. To reflect critically on one particular theoretical model of work motivation and job performance.

Briefing First, familiarize yourself with the Porter–Lawler model of work motivation (figure 8.3) and the expectancy theory of work motivation from which this is derived. Then, read the following (real) case, without discussion with colleagues, and turn to the case analysis.

After the merger – the best place to work? Commercial Union and General Accident merged in 1998 to become CGU, one of the largest insurance companies in Britain. As part of the process of creating a new company, a two-day conference was organized for 420 first line managers and technical specialists, 80 managers, and union representatives. Conference participants were asked what would make CGU 'the best place to work'. Here is their blueprint:

Alignment

■ I value knowing the big picture and having the support that enables me to 'own' it.

■ I value knowing that our individual and team targets are clearly aligned to the key result areas (KRAs) and balanced business scorecard (BBS) objectives.

■ I value knowing where I fit in terms of how my accountabilities and responsibilities help to achieve the KRAs and BBS objectives.

■ It is important to me that I feel I belong to my team and to the organization.

Performance

■ It is important to me to work for managers who acknowledge success and deal fairly and promptly with failure.

■ I expect a fair reward that is aligned with my achievements and efforts.

■ I value having the right skills, tools and authority to do my job.

■ It is important for me to work for managers who are good at managing people and the business we are in, and who have the right level of technical knowledge.

■ I value managers who consult me on issues that affect me, but who are also prepared to take decisions quickly.

■ I value working in a team that maintains a strong customer focus.

Support

■ It is important for me to have leaders who inspire my confidence and trust.

■ Give me structures, processes and practices that enable me to deliver.

■ I value a stimulating, friendly, open working environment.

■ I value company policies that enable me to balance my home life with work.

■ I value focused and lively feedback about my work and the way I behave.

■ I value responsibility, but within clear boundaries that stretch as I develop.

■ I want to work for a company that has a long-term, structured approach to career planning, succession planning and personal development.

This 'blueprint' was based on employees' views and not on any theoretical framework.

Case analysis

Make notes for yourself in response to these five questions:

1. Compare this blueprint with the Porter–Lawler model of work motivation. If management at CGU are able to implement this blueprint, what would be your prediction? Will this motivate employees to high or low performance, or will it have no impact? And why?

2. What does the model, and expectancy theory, recommend that is missing from the blueprint? What advice would you give to the company based on this analysis?

3. What does the blueprint specify that is missing from the Porter–Lawler model? What advice would you give to Porter and Lawler based on this analysis?

4. What problems would you expect management to face in implementing this blueprint in a highly competitive and rapidly changing environment? How would you advise management in dealing with these issues?

5. Job enrichment – is this a genuine attempt to improve working conditions, employee skills development, career opportunities and the quality of working life, or is this just a cosmetic attempt to disguise the systemic power inequalities and exploitation in contemporary organizations?

When asked by your instructor, compare your answers with those of colleagues. Try to reach a consensus on each question, and be prepared to present your answers to your group.

This case is based on Tony Clarry, 'Premium Bonding', *People Management*, vol. 5, no. 17, 2 September 1999, pp. 34–9.

Part 3 Groups and teams in the organization

A field map of the organizational behaviour terrain

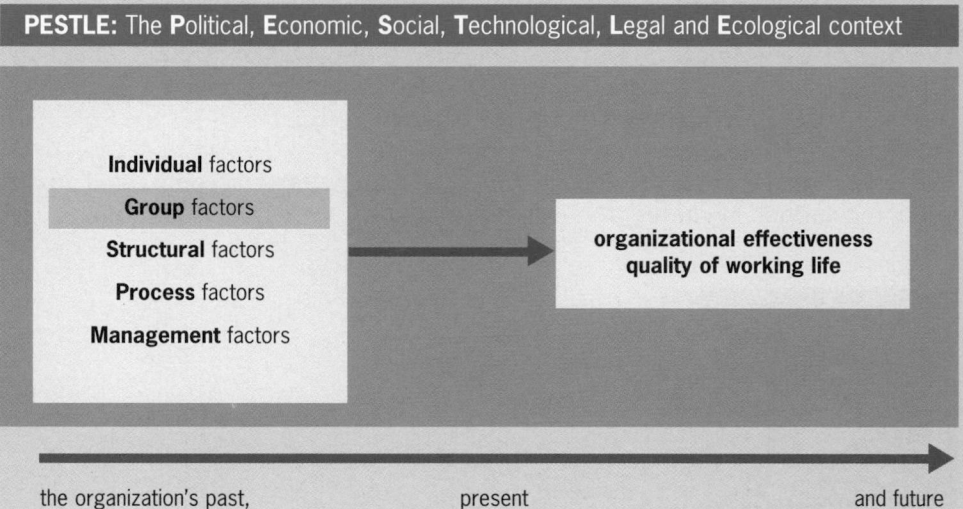

PESTLE: The Political, Economic, Social, Technological, Legal and Ecological context

Individual factors
Group factors
Structural factors
Process factors
Management factors

organizational effectiveness
quality of working life

the organization's past,   present   and future

Introduction

Part 3, Groups and teams in the organization, explores the following four topics:

- Group formation, in chapter 9
- Group structure, in chapter 10
- Individuals in groups, in chapter 11
- Teamworking, in chapter 12

These topics reflect the progress of collections of people over time within the organizational context. Thus, a number of individuals may informally develop into a group, or a team may be formally established by management and given a task. Each then develops its own internal structures to allow its members to work together. The group influences the attitudes and behaviours of its members, and the individual within it can affect the group as a whole. Meanwhile, management's ambition is to get individuals working together as a single, effective team. Groups and teams offer a distinct but related level of analysis between the individual and the organization structure and its processes.

Invitation to see

The first of these images, from the *Financial Times* (17 March 2003, Graduate Recruitment Special Report), illustrated an article about the changing nature of policing, including increased pay, and a High Potential Development scheme for graduate recruits.

The second image, from *The Sunday Times* (16 March 2003), accompanied an article about health and safety regulations, including the risks associated with firefighters climbing ladders.

Forceful talent: cadets relish 'intelligence-driven' policing
Source: North News and Pictures

Fire chiefs are believed to have been threatened over the risk of ladders
Source: www.shoutpictures.com

1. **Decoding:**   Look at these images closely. Note in as much detail as possible what messages you feel they are each trying to convey. Do they tell a story, present a point of view, support an argument, perpetuate a myth, reinforce a stereotype, challenge a stereotype?

2. **Challenging:**   To what extent do you agree with the messages, stories, points of view, arguments, myths or stereotypes in these images? Are these images open to challenge, to criticism, to interpretation or decoding in other ways, revealing other messages?

3. **Sharing:**   Compare with colleagues your interpretation of these images. Explore explanations for differences in your respective decodings.

Chapter 9 Group formation

Key concepts

group relations

psychological group

aggregate

additive task

conjunctive task

disjunctive task

Hawthorne effect

informal organization

Human Relations approach

formal group

informal group

group self-organization

activities

interactions

norms

sentiments

virtual team

synchronous communication

asynchronous communication

Learning outcomes

When you have read this chapter, you should be able to define those key concepts in your own words, and you should also be able to:

1. List the key characteristics of a psychological group.
2. Distinguish between different types of group task.
3. Name the four research phases of the Hawthorne studies.
4. Distinguish between a formal and an informal group.
5. Outline Homans' theory of group formation.
6. Enumerate the five stages of Tuckman and Jensen's model of group development.
7. Summarize Katzenbach and Santamaria's distinction between a team and a single-leader working group.

Why study group formation?

Marion Hampton (1999, p. 113) summarized both the symbolic and practical aspects of groups:

> Groups embody many important cultural values of Western society: teamwork, co-operation, a collective that is greater than the sum of its parts, informality, egalitarianism and even the indispensability of the individual member. Groups are seen as having a motivating, inspiring influence on the individual, drawing the best out of him or her, enabling him or her to perform feats that would be beyond him or herself as a detached individual. Groups can have a healing effect on individuals, bolstering their self-esteem and filling their lives with meaning.

Groups play an important role in our lives. It has been estimated that the average person belongs to five or six different groups, and about 92 per cent of members are in groups of five people or less. These may include the quality control circle, the new product team, the local women's group and the sports team. Groups and teams are terms which are now used interchangeably, and readers are advised to read carefully to pick out the author's definition. People join groups because of common needs, interests or goals, physical proximity or cultural similarity, or may be assigned to them by management.

Much organizational work is performed in teams. Their performance thus affects the success of the organization as a whole. Being able to work productively with others is so important that companies place an emphasis on their recruits being good 'team players'. To ensure this, they invest in team development activities to develop their teamworking abilities. Hayes (1997, p. 1) noted that, 'To an ever-increasing extent, modern management has become focused on the idea of the team. Management consultants propose organizational restructuring to facilitate teamwork; directors make policy statements about the importance of the team to the organization; and senior managers exhort their junior staff to encourage teamworking in their departments'. Proctor and Mueller (2000b, p. 7) summarized the most recent statistics which reveal the remorseless organizational trend towards group and teamworking all around the world, and in virtually all industries. Thus, since the chances of either working in a team or managing one are so high, it is prudent to know how they operate.

- In the USA, 54 per cent of 600 leading enterprises used self-directed teams (Osterman, 1994).

- The EPOC survey of European workplaces showed that some sort of teamwork existed in 36 per cent of them (Benders and Van Hootegem, 2000; Benders et al., 2001).

- The British 1998 Workplace Employee Relations Survey found that 54 per cent of employees in the core workforce who manufactured a product or provided a service, worked in some form of a team (Culley et al., 1998).

- In Australia, the percentage of employees working in formal teams rose from 8 per cent to 47 per cent in the 1988–91 period (Ozaki, 1996). By 1995, 47 per cent of manufacturing workplaces with over 100 employees reported that they had some form of semi-autonomous teamworking (Morehead et al., 1997).

To boldly go . . . in groups

Again and again we have seen that Star Trek views [humankind] as the ultimate social animal, thriving in groups, and utterly unable to exist alone or in isolation. Isolation in Star Trek is always the breeding ground for delusion, madness or megalomania. All the mad scientists in the series hatch their schemes in lonely corners of the galaxy. Entering human society and becoming a part of it is the sum and substance of the series' many fables of identity.

From T. Richards, *Star Trek in Myth and Legend*, Orion Books, London, 1997, pp. 91–2.

"I'll begin by reading the minutes from our last meeting: Higgins: 'If I don't get out of this room my head will explode.' Jenkins: 'I feel like I'm trapped in a Kafka-like nightmare.' Milbrook: 'This is two hours of my life I'll never get back'..."

Source: Cartoon © Mike Shapiro

Group and teamworking has been an aspect of organizational life for a long time, yet remains controversial. The management literature promotes the benefits of group working, and stresses the commonality of interests between individual workers, organized by management into teams, and the goals of the 'organization as a whole', that is, of senior management. Critics, in contrast, contend that the extent of group-management conflict has been misinterpreted, underplayed or simply ignored.

Stop and Criticize

Suggest reasons why group working has become so popular in organizations.

What benefits does it offer to individual employees? To management?

Definitions of groups

Interpersonal behaviour builds up into group behaviour that in turn sustains and structures future interpersonal relations. Groups develop particular characteristics, affecting not only the behaviour of the individuals within them, but also their relation to other groups in the organization. Because of the importance of **group relations**, social psychologists have studied them extensively. The idea of a group is well known to most people who work, live and play in groups. Very often we may refer to persons standing at a bus stop or in a queue as a group. However, it has a more specialist and restricted meaning.

Group relations: the interactions within and between groups, and the stable arrangements that result from them.

It is important to maintain a distinction between mere aggregates of individuals and what are called psychological groups. The latter are so called because they exist not only through the (often visible) interactions of members, but also in the (not observable) perceptions of their members. The term **psychological group** is thus reserved for people who consider themselves to be part of an identifiable unit, who relate to each other in a meaningful fashion and who share dispositions through their shared sense of collective identity.

Stop and Criticize

Why would only *one* of the following be considered to be a psychological group? In what circumstances could one of the other aggregates become a psychological group?

- People riding on a bus
- Blonde women between 20 and 30 years of age
- Members of a football team
- Audience in a theatre
- People sheltering in a shop doorway from the rain

Psychological group: two or more people in face-to-face interaction, each aware of their membership in the group, each aware of the others who belong to the group, and each aware of their positive interdependence as they strive to achieve their goals.

Aggregate: a collection of unrelated people who happen to be in close physical proximity for a short period of time.

In the above example, only the football team would fulfil our criteria for a group. We can usefully adopt Johnson and Johnson's (1991) definition in order to distinguish it from an **aggregate**.

These definitions enable us to exclude aggregates of people who are simply individuals who happen to be collected together at any particular time. Like the bus travellers, theatre audience or rain shelterers, they do not relate to one another in any meaningful fashion, nor consider themselves a part of any identifiable unit, despite their temporary physical proximity. By the same token, the definition allows one to exclude classes of people who may be defined by physical attributes, geographical location, economic status or age. Even though a trade union in an organization may like to believe it is a group, it will fail to meet our definition if all of its members do not interact with each other, and if they are not aware of each other. This need for all members to interact has led to the suggestion that, in practice, a psychological group is unlikely to exceed twelve or so persons. Beyond that number, the opportunity for frequent interaction between members, and hence group awareness, is considerably reduced.

It is possible for small aggregates of people to be transformed into a psychological group through outside circumstances. In fact, a whole series of 'disaster movies' in the cinema have been made in which people fight for their lives on board sinking ships, hijacked aeroplanes and burning skyscraper buildings. The story typically involves aggregates of people setting out at the start of the film. The danger causes them to interact with one another, and this increases their awareness of one another and leads them to see themselves as having common problems. By the end of the film, the survivors demonstrate all the characteristics of the psychological group as defined here. The disaster movie example helps us to understand some of the characteristics of a psychological group:

1. *A minimum membership of two people:* There is no 'official' size, and different authors discuss groups that range from two to thirty individuals. However, the greater the number of group members, the higher the number of possible relationships between them, the greater the level of communication that is required, and the more complex the structure needed to operate the group successfully.

2. *A communication network:* Each group member must be capable of communicating with every other member. In this communication process, the aims and purposes of the group are exchanged. The mere process of communication interaction satisfies some of our social needs, and it is used to set and enforce standards of group behaviour.

3. *A shared sense of collective identity*: Each member must identify with the other members of their group, and not see themselves as an individual acting independently. They must all believe themselves to be participants in the group which itself is distinct from other groups.

4. *Complementary goals*: Members have individual objectives which can only be met through membership of and participation in the group. Their goals may differ but are sufficiently complementary that members feel able to achieve them through participation in the group. They recognize the need to work collectively and not as individuals.

5. *Group structure*: Individuals in the group will have different roles, for example initiator/ideas person, suggestion-provider, compromiser. These roles, which tend to become fixed, indicate what members expect of each other. Norms or rules exist which indicate which behaviours are acceptable in the group and which are not (for example, smoking, swearing, late coming).

Groups will differ in the degree to which they possess such characteristics. To the extent that they do have them, it will make the group more easily recognizable by others as a group, and this will give it more power with which to influence its members. The topic of influence and control in groups is dealt with in a later chapter. What will be said in the remainder of this chapter and this part of the book will refer only to psychological groups. For this reason we shall use the shorthand label of group to refer to a psychological group (Guzzo, 1996).

Stop and Criticize

The groups to which you belong provide you with shared goals and a sense of identity, and meet your social needs. However, they can also constrain your thinking, stifle your freedom of expression, limit your behaviour and restrict your freedom of expression. What is your opinion?

As the size and complexity of modern organizations has increased, the need to integrate the work of different individuals within groups, and groups within organizations, has also grown. Mohrman et al. (1995) list the benefits of working in groups:

■ They allow organizations to develop and deliver products and services quickly and cost-effectively while maintaining quality.

■ They enable organizations to learn and retain that learning more effectively.

■ Cross-functional groups promote improved quality management.

■ Cross-functional design groups can undertake effective process re-engineering.

■ Production time can be reduced if tasks performed concurrently by individuals are performed concurrently by people in groups.

■ Group-based organization promotes innovation because of the cross-fertilization of ideas.

■ Organizations with flat structures can be monitored, co-ordinated and directed more effectively if the functional unit is the group rather than the individual.

■ Groups can handle the rise in organizational information-processing requirements caused by increasing complexity better than individuals.

Types of group task

The tasks that groups and teams are asked to perform vary greatly. Their nature is an important variable in their performance. Tasks can be divided in different ways. One simple dichotomy to be discussed is that of simple–complex. Research showed that this had an impact on the group's communication structure (see chapter 10), and affected an individual's performance in the presence of others, as described in the discussion on social facilitation. Ivan Steiner (1972) classified group tasks on the basis of the type of interdependence that they required.

Additive task: a task whose accomplishment depends on the sum of all group members' efforts.

Additive task

With this type of task, all group members do basically the same job, and the final group product or outcome (group performance) is the sum of all their individual contributions. The final outcome is roughly proportional to the number of individuals contributing. There is low interdependency between these people. A group working together will normally perform better than the same number of individuals working alone, provided that all group members make their contribution. Social loafing can, however, reduce performance on an additive task. Examples of additive tasks are tug-of-war contests and pedestrians giving a stalled car a push-start (Littlepage, 1991).

Conjunctive task: a task whose accomplishment depends on the performance of the group's least talented member.

Conjunctive task

In this task, one member's performance depends on another's. There is high interdependency. Thus, a group's *least* capable member determines performance. A successful group project at university depends on one member finding the information, a second writing it up and a third presenting it. All three elements are required for success and hence co-ordination is essential in conjunctive tasks. Groups perform less well on conjunctive tasks than lone individuals. Examples of conjunctive tasks include climbing a mountain, running a relay race and playing chamber music (Steiner and Rajaratnam, 1961).

Disjunctive task: a task whose accomplishment depends on the performance of the group's most talented member.

Disjunctive tasks

In this type of task, once again, one member's performance depends on another's. Again there is high interdependency. However, this time, the group's *most* capable member determines its performance. Groups perform better than their average member on disjunctive tasks, since even the best performer will not know all the answers, and working with others helps to improve overall group performance. Diagnostic and problem-solving activities performed by a group would come into this category. Co-ordination is important here as well, but in the sense of stopping the others impeding the top performers (Diehl and Stroebe, 1991). Examples of disjunctive task performers are quiz teams (*University Challenge*, pub quiz) and a maintenance team in a nuclear power generating plant.

Groups will tend to outperform the same number of individuals working separately when working on disjunctive tasks rather than on additive or conjunctive tasks. This is provided that the most talented member can convince the others of the correctness of their answer. The attitudes, feelings and conflicts in a group setting might prevent this from happening.

Team tasks and Extreme Programming

Give a computer programmer complete freedom and he or she will code in their own idiosyncratic way. When software changes or a different programmer needs to repair it, he will have to pore over his colleague's indecipherable code. In contrast, teach programmers some discipline and they will code logically and clearly. This is the idea behind Extreme Programming (XP), invented in 1996 by Kent Beck, Ward Cunningham and Ron Jeffries when they were working to rescue the Chrysler Comprehensive Compensation (C3) software project from collapse. They formulated a set of directions for keeping code 'elegantly written'. XP's tenets include a rule forbidding any individual from taking exclusive responsibility for any piece of programming. Another rule specifies that programmers must work in pairs, on a single terminal, on each bit of code. Two programmers working together are more than twice as fast and think of more than twice as many solutions as two working alone. They achieve a higher level of defect prevention and removal, leading to a higher quality product. Since software developers treat programming methodologies as rules of personal ethics, XP has provoked heated debate. XP sceptics suggest that the best coders are probably 100 times more productive than the worst, and stories of 'Top Gun', heroic (individual) programming which kept projects on schedule abound. They add that pairing such 'cowboy coders' slows each one down and undercuts the team's overall efficiency. In their defence, XP proponents argue that the approach saves money in future programming time because code changes can be made by anybody. Many companies are keen to have software developers use XP. They believe that it helps to develop products quickly and cost-effectively, maintains quality and enables organizations to retain their learning. Extreme measures, it appears, are good for extreme times.

Based on Laurie A. Williams and Robert R. Kessler, 'All I really need to know about pair programming, I learned in kindergarten', *Communications of the ACM*, vol. 43, no. 5, May 2000, pp. 108–14.

The Hawthorne studies

George Elton Mayo (1880–1949)

Fritz Jules Roethlisberger (1898–1974)

In the United States, during the 1920s and 1930s, the Hawthorne studies led to the creation of the human relations movement and a highly influential school of academic and practical management thinking. In that period, factories used natural daylight or candles to illuminate the workspace of their workers. In an attempt to promote the sales of light bulbs in the early 1920s, the General Electric (GE) company paid for a series of experiments to try to demonstrate a positive correlation between the amount of light and worker productivity. The original experiments therefore examined the effect of physical changes, originally illumination and later room temperature and humidity, on worker productivity (Gillespie, 1991).

The experiments were conducted at the Hawthorne plant of the Western Electric Company, the manufacturing subsidiary of the American Telephone and Telegraph Company (AT&T) which supplied telephones to the entire Bell System (figure 9.1). The factory was located in Cicero, Illinois. In November of 1924, the initial experiments began examining productivity improvements from a scientific management perspective, assessing the effect of physical factors. Later, Professor George Elton Mayo of the Harvard Business School was invited to bring an academic research team into the factory. Team members included Fritz Jules Roethlisberger, who later become the first Professor of Organizational Behaviour (holding his post in the Harvard Business School), and William J. Dickson. It was through their book, *Management and the Worker* (1939), that the results of the Hawthorne studies were communicated to the world. The Hawthorne research revolutionized social science thinking. Four particular studies that were conducted stand out: illumination experiments; the Relay Assembly Test Room experiments; the interviewing programme; and the Bank Wiring Observation Room experiments.

Figure 9.1: The Hawthorne plant of the Western Electric Company, *c.* 1925
Source: AT&T Archives.

The illumination studies (1924–27)

William J. Dickson
(1904–73)

These explored the relationship of the quality and quantity of illumination to efficiency (figure 9.2). No correlation was found between production output obtained and the lighting provided. Production even increased when the light intensity was reduced. The conclusion was that lighting was only one of several factors affecting production, and perhaps a minor one. A more controlled study of fewer workers was needed to identify and control for the effect of any single variable on output.

Figure 9.2: Relay Assembly Department, Hawthorne works, *c.* 1925
Source: AT&T Archives

Relay Assembly Test Room

Selected results

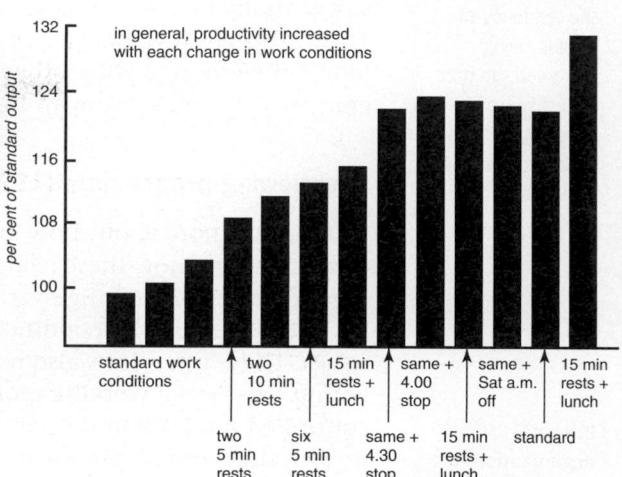

Figure 9.3: Relay Assembly Test Room, *c.* 1929
Source: Property of AT&T Archives. Reprinted with permission of AT&T.

Based on data from Roethlisberger and Dickson (1939). From *Behavior in Organizations*: 6/E by Greenberg/Baron, © 1997. Reprinted by permission of Pearson Education, Inc., Upper Saddle River, NJ.

Relay Assembly Test Room experiments (1927–33)

Six self-selected female workers, drawn from the regular workforce of the Relay Assembly Department, were placed in a separate room for closer observation (figure 9.3). They had been working a 48-hour week, including Saturdays, with no tea breaks. A researcher was in the room with them, keeping a note of what happened, maintaining a friendly atmosphere by listening to their complaints, and telling them what was going on. This experiment focused on questions of fatigue, rest pauses, length of working day; equipment change effects; attitudes to their work and the company. A total of thirteen periods were studied during which changes were made to rest pauses, hours of work and breaks for refreshment.

As figure 9.3 shows, there was a nearly continuous increase in output. This increase began when employee benefits such as rest periods and early finishes were added, but was maintained even when they were withdrawn and the women returned to a 48-hour week. The reasons offered for the increases in output included:

■ the motivating effect of acquiring a special status through their selection for and involvement in the experiment;

■ the effect of participation as the women were consulted and informed by the experimenter;

■ the effect of observer friendliness which improved their morale;

■ a different and less intense form of supervision which reduced their stress while increasing their productivity;

■ the self-selected nature of the group, creating higher levels of mutual dependence and support appropriate for group working.

One of these explanations has even established itself as a concept in social science research. This says that the changed behaviour of the women was just the result of being observed by the researchers, and that the manipulation of the aforementioned variables played no part. This is now referred to as the **Hawthorne effect**. The researchers were convinced that the women were not solely motivated by money or by improvements in their working conditions. Their attitudes towards and achievement of increased output seemed to be affected by the group to which they belonged. These results led management to study employee attitudes using an interviewing programme.

Hawthorne effect: the tendency of people being observed, as part of a research effort, to behave differently than they otherwise would.

Interviewing programme (1928–30)

To find out more about how employees felt about their supervisors and working conditions and how these related to morale, management instituted an interviewing programme involving over 20,000 interviews. The information obtained went beyond issues of work conditions and supervision, extending to family and social issues. These interviews also revealed the existence of informal, gang-like groups within the formal working groups. Each had its own leaders and 'sidekicks', who controlled production output. The existence of the **informal organization** with its own rules and hierarchy of positions was revealed, and became the focus of the Bank Wiring Observation Room experiments.

Informal organization: the network of relationships that spontaneously establish themselves between members of an organization on the basis of their common interests and friendships.

Bank Wiring Observation Room experiments (1931–32)

The interviews revealed that groups exercised a great deal of control over the behaviour of their members. To test this, a group of men were observed in another part of the company. The Bank Wiring Observation Room consisted of fourteen men who were formally organized into three sub-groups, each of which contained three wirers and one supervisor (figure 9.4). In addition, two inspectors moved between the three groups. There were two major findings. First, the detailed observation of interactions between the men revealed the existence of two informal groups or 'cliques' within the three formal groups. The membership of these transgressed the formal group boundaries. These two cliques are shown in figure 9.5.

It was found that these cliques developed informal rules of behaviour or 'norms', as well as mechanisms to enforce these. The total figure for the week would tally with the total week's output, but the daily reports showed a steady,

Bank wirers at work	Norms and sanctions
	Norms: • Don't be a rate-buster, chisler or squealer • Don't act officious Sanctions: • 'Binging' – tap on upper arm • Ridicule • Exclusion

Figure 9.4: Bank Wiring Observation Room, *c.* 1932
Source: AT&T Archives

The figure below shows the formal structure of the group as devised by the company's management. This consisted of three trios of workmen, each directed by their own supervisor. Two inspectors assessed the work of these three formal groups. The researchers noted which individuals interacted with whom, and who participated in whose work-time games. This revealed the friendship relations that existed between the men in the Bank Wiring Room.

Within these three formal groups, the researchers identified two informal groups or 'cliques'. The curving lines indicate the boundary of each informal group or clique. One clique consisted of a supervisor, his three wirers and a lone wirer from the adjacent group. The other clique consisted of a supervisor, two of his wirers (his third one was 'semi-detached'), and a different, lone wirer from the adjacent group. In addition, this clique included one of the inspectors. The three remaining individuals did not appear to be members of either clique.

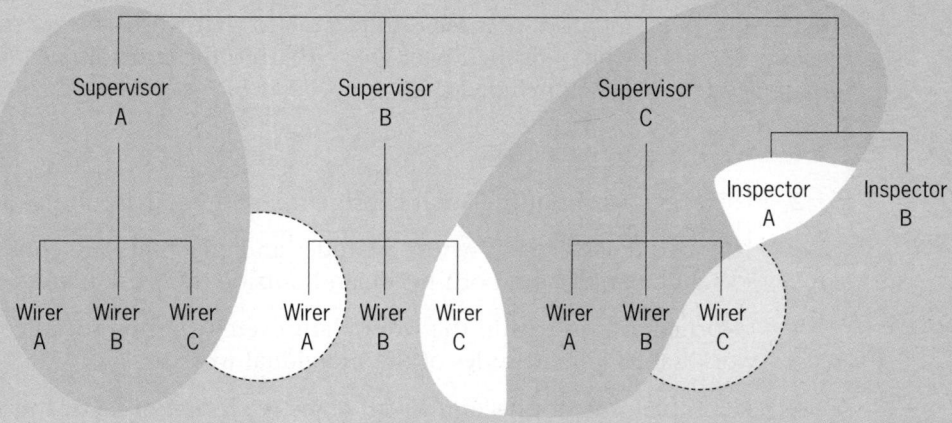

Figure 9.5: The informal as opposed to the formal organization of the groups in the Bank Wiring Observation Room

Based on Fritz J. Roethlisberger and William J. Dickson, *Management and the Worker*, Harvard University Press, Cambridge, MA, 1939, pp. 501, 507 and 509.

level output regardless of actual daily production. The researchers decided that the group was operating below its capability and that individual group members were not earning as much as they could. The norms under which the group operated were found to be the following (Roethlisberger and Dickson, 1939, p. 522):

■ You should not turn out too much work. If you do, you are a *rate-buster*.

■ You should not turn out too little work. If you do, you are a *chisler*.

■ You should not tell a supervisor anything that might get a colleague into trouble. If you do, you are a *squealer*.

■ You should not attempt to maintain social distance or act officiously. If you are an inspector, for example, you should not act like one.

The researchers discovered that members of the Bank Wiring Observation Room were afraid that if they significantly increased their output, the unit incentive rate would be cut and the daily output expected by management would increase. Layoffs might occur and men could be reprimanded. To forestall such consequences, the group members agreed between themselves what was a fair day's output (neither too high nor too low). Having established such a output norm, they enforced it through a system of negative sanctions or punishments. These included:

■ ridicule, as when a group member was referred to as 'The Slave' or 'Speed King';

■ 'binging', in which a norm-violator was tapped on the upper arm;

■ total rejection or exclusion of the individual by the group as a whole.

Roethlisberger and Dickson (1939, pp. 523–4) wrote that: 'The social organization of the bankwiremen performed a twofold function (1) to protect the group from internal indiscretions and (2) to protect it from outside interference ... nearly all the activities of this group can be looked upon as methods of controlling the behaviour of its members.' These results showed that workers were more responsive to the social forces of their peer group than to the controls and incentives of management. Mayo concluded that:

1. Work is a group activity.

2. The social world of the adult is primarily patterned around work activity.

3. The worker is a person whose attitudes and effectivity are conditioned by social demands from both inside and outside the work plant.

4. Informal groups within the work plant exercise strong social controls over work habits and attitudes of the individual worker.

5. A complaint is not necessarily an objective recital of facts; it is commonly a symptom that is manifesting disturbance of an individual's status position.

6. Group collaboration does not occur by accident; it must be planned and developed. If group collaboration is achieved, the human relations within a work plant may reach a cohesion which resists the disrupting effects of an adaptive society.

7. The change from an established society in the home to an adaptive society in the work plant resulting from the use of new techniques tends continually to disrupt the social organization of a work plant and industry generally.

Human Relations approach: a school of management thought which emphasizes the importance of social processes at work.

Those conclusions led to the **Human Relations approach** to management, which held that work should be a source of social relationships for individuals, a way of meeting their need for belonging and for group membership, and even a focus for their personal identity. As Rose (1988, p. 104) noted:

Within work-based social relationships or groups ... behaviour, particularly productivity or cooperativeness with management, was thought to be shaped and constrained by the worker's role and status in a group. Other informal sets of relationships might spring up within the formal organization as a whole, modifying or overriding the official social structure of the factory, which was based on purely technical criteria such as division of labour.

Stop and Criticize	How might the Hawthorne studies have been conducted differently if they had been:

■ 'Pure academic' research, with Mayo a bearded sociologist in corduroy trousers, woolly cardigan and scruffy notebook, with band of graduate research students in tow?

■ 'Pure management' research, with Mayo as a management consultant with an expensive suit and tie, executive briefcase and a team of smart associate consultants to support this work?

How might the findings and recommendations have differed from those actually obtained?

Group-oriented view of organizations

In his book, *The Social Problems of an Industrial Society* (1945), Elton Mayo went on to propose a social philosophy which placed groups at the centre of understanding human behaviour in organizations. He stressed the importance of informal groups, and encouraged managers to 'grow' them. He discussed *natural groups* of three to six workers and *family groups* of between eight and thirty members. These would develop into one, large *organized group*, consisting of a plant-wide network of family groups, each with its natural groups. Mayo's vision was of a community organization in which all or most employees were members of well-knit, natural groups, which were linked together in common purpose. These were not the formal groups discussed earlier. Mayo invited managers to act somewhat like gardeners rather than engineers, and to use their skills, intelligence and experience to deliberately integrate individuals within groups.

Back to the future: Work as the new community?

Eighty years on from Mayo, the idea of the workplace taking on the functions of the community is back in vogue. For example, the workers at *Google*, the internet search engine company, are not offered a job but 'the chance to be part of a community of people doing meaningful work. It is not the role so much as belonging that is the key; employees are consumers of a collective experience.' Companies such as this allow staff to bring their children to work, play roller hockey, use the gym or sauna, have a massage or play the piano, all on company time and premises. Work, it appears, can give us friends, lovers, identity, childcare and dry cleaning. Researchers have documented a renewed appetite for community and belonging in western democracies, and 'corporate communities' and 'company families' are developing to fill the gap. Many social issues are currently being tackled through the suffix 'at work' – bullying, racism, stress, drugs. Some employers are acting as quasi-national states, offering healthcare, eye-tests and playgroups.

The work-as-community theory reflects the fact that employees spend more time at work than previous generations. For many staff, it is the most important time in their lives. Hochschild (1997) suggests that individuals are working longer not because of employers' demands but because they find greater satisfaction at work than where they live. Work gives them order, a degree of stability and involvement in teamwork, which replaces family relationships. In contrast, home is dysfunctional and certainly makes work a place to which to escape. Critics respond by saying that in addition to applying to a tiny section of the professional middle class anyway, the work-as-community view merely betrays a desire to put a positive gloss on the 'long hours' culture. It's a nice motherhood notion that makes work seem worthwhile.

Based on Stephen Overell, 'A home from home', *Personnel Today*, 21 May 2002, p. 13; Stephen Overell, 'Work moves to home ground', *The Financial Times*, 2 August 2002, p. 16; Arlie Russell Hochschild, *The Time Bind: When Home Becomes Work and Work Becomes Home*, Owl Books, New York, 1997.

Rensis Likert
(1903–81)

Another famous psychologist, Rensis Likert (1961) echoed the idea that organizations should be viewed and managed as a collection of groups rather than individuals. He felt that group forces were important both in influencing the behaviour of individual work groups with regard to productivity, waste, absence and the assembly line, and also in affecting the performance of the entire organization. In his book chapter entitled 'The principle of supportive relationships', Likert, like Mayo, attempted to derive a theory of organizational design with the group as the basic building block. He argued that:

1. Work groups are important sources of individuals' need satisfaction.

2. Groups in organizations that fulfil this psychological function are also more productive.

3. Management's task is therefore to create effective work groups by developing 'supportive relationships'.

4. An effective organizational structure consists of democratic-participative work groups, each linked to the organization as a whole through overlapping memberships.

5. Co-ordination is achieved by individuals who carry out 'linking functions'.

Likert (1961) is also remembered for proposing the concept of the overlapping group membership structure. This he termed a 'linking pin' process. The overlapping works vertically by having the leaders of related subordinate groups as members of the next higher group, with their common superior as leader and so on up the hierarchy. The organization is therefore conceived as consisting of many overlapping groups. This is shown in figure 9.6. In his view, an organizational design based around groups rather than individuals improves communications, increases co-operation, provides more team member commitment and produces faster decision-making.

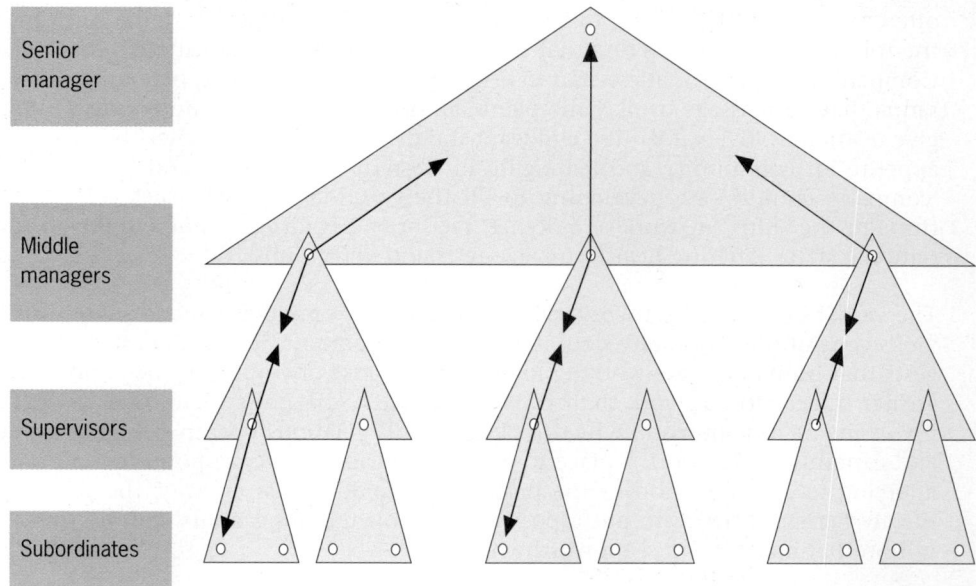

Figure 9.6: Rensis Likert's linking pin model
Based on Rensis Likert, *New Patterns of Management*, McGraw-Hill, New York, 1961, p. 105. Reprinted by permission of The McGraw-Hill Companies.

While Likert's 'linking pin' concept focused on *vertical* co-ordination, today the stress is placed upon *horizontal* integration in the form of cross-functional teams. Nevertheless, most people in an organization are now members of several teams. This overlap of groups in organizations, due to matrix structures and cross-functional teamworking, means that an individual can be a member of a project team and a geographical group all at the same time. This will hinder their ability to identify with any one distinct group.

In addition to Likert, a succession of well-known academics and consultants have followed Mayo in promoting the cause of organizations built around groups, rather than just including them. In the 1970s, Leavitt (1975) asked management to use small groups as the basic building blocks for an organization. Ouchi and Johnson (1978) echoed Mayo's thesis that people in society lacked social support and anchors which made life tolerable, and recommended that large organizations should be organized around 'clans' (similar to Mayo's natural groups) which could provide associational ties and cohesion for their employees. In the 1980s, Tom Peters (1987, p. 296) said that: 'The modest-sized, task-oriented, semi-autonomous, mainly self-managing team should be the basic organization building block.' In the 1990s, Katzenbach and Smith (1993) proposed their own team-based organizational model, as did Jenkins (1994).

Stop and Criticize

Your employer tells you that you will become 'part of the team', that you will be a 'member of one big happy family here'. How do you feel about the organization as your 'psychological home' in this respect?

When managers say that they want you 'to belong' what do they *really* mean?

From this analysis can you explain why the concept of teamworking has been so consistently popular with managers interested in improving employee performance?

Formal and informal groups

Workplace behaviour can be considered as varying along a continuum from formally to informally organized. At one extreme, formal behaviour is organized to achieve the collective purpose of an organization. This may be to make washing machines, provide a repair service, earn £200,000 profit a year or achieve a 5 per cent return on investment. To achieve such collective purposes, the organization is structured in such a way as to use the limited resources it has at its disposal as efficiently and effectively as possible. It does this by creating what is called a formal organization. The overall collective purpose or aim is broken down into sub-goals and sub-tasks. These are assigned to different sub-units in the organization. The tasks may be grouped together and departments thus formed. Job requirements in terms of job descriptions may be written. The subdivision continues to take place until a small group of people is given one such sub-goal and divides it between its members. When this occurs, there exists the basis for forming the group along functional lines. This process of identifying the purpose, dividing up tasks and so on is referred to as the creation of the formal organization. The groups that are formed through this division of labour are labelled **formal groups**.

Managers make choices as to how technology and organization will be combined to create task-oriented (formal) groups. The purpose of the sub-groups in the production department may be to manufacture 100 cars a day, while that of the group in the design department may be to draw up a set of construction plans.

Formal group: one which has been consciously created to accomplish a defined part of an organization's collective purpose. The formal group's functions are the tasks which are assigned to it, and for which it is officially held responsible.

Whatever type of formal group we are interested in, they all have certain common characteristics:

■ they are task-oriented;

■ they tend to be permanent;

■ they have a formal structure;

■ they are consciously organized by management to achieve organizational goals;

■ their activities contribute directly to the organization's collective purpose.

Formal groups can be distinguished by the duration of their existence. There are permanent formal groups, such as a staff group providing specialist services (for example, a computer unit, a training section). There are also likely to be temporary formal groups: for example, a task group that is formally designed to work on a specific project. What makes a formal group permanent or temporary is not the actual time it exists, but how it is defined by the company. Some temporary groups may last for years. What is important is whether or not the group's members feel that they are part of a group that might be disbanded at any time.

Alongside these formal groups, and consisting of the same employees, albeit arranged differently, will be a number of informal groups. These emerge in an organization and are neither anticipated nor intended by those who create the formal organization. They emerge from the informal interaction of the members of the formal organization. These unplanned-for groups share many of the characteristics of the small, social or leisure groups. These function alongside the formal groups. An **informal group** develops during the spontaneous interaction of persons in the group as they talk, joke and associate with one another.

Informal group: a collection of individuals who become a group when members develop interdependencies, influence one another's behaviour and contribute to mutual need satisfaction.

Why do informal groups exist and what purpose do they serve? Ackroyd and Thompson (1999) introduced the concept of group self-organization to help our understanding of the nature of formal and informal groups. Group self-organization refers to the tendency of groups to

■ form interests;

■ develop autonomy;

■ establish identities.

Group self-organization: the tendency of groups to form interests, develop autonomy and establish identities.

In the case of the men in the Bank Wiring Room in the Hawthorne studies, their interests centred around restricting their output. In so doing, they gained a degree of personal control: that is, they increased their autonomy *vis-à-vis* management. The two cliques that emerged each developed their own, separate identities. Self-interest and self-identity interact and reciprocate. These processes have implications for the behaviour of the groups concerned. This phenomenon is termed **group self-organization**.

Interests encompass the human needs. Among these are those for love, esteem and safety. Love needs are concerned with belongingness and relationships; esteem needs focus on recognition, attention and appreciation; while safety needs concern security of employment. The failure to satisfy these needs may result in our inability to feel confident, capable, necessary or useful members of society. These needs concern our relationships with others. The time that we do spend at work remains considerable, and we frequently seek to satisfy these needs through our relationships with work colleagues. The difficulty is that the organizations are not primarily designed to allow individuals to meet such needs at work.

A formal organization is ostensibly designed on rational principles and is aimed at achieving the collective purpose of the organization. It thus limits employees' behaviour in order to be able to control and predict it. The individual brings their hopes, needs, desires and personal goals to their job. While the company may not be interested in these, the employee will nevertheless attempt to achieve their personal ambitions while at work by manipulating the situation to fulfil their unmet needs. Most other staff will generally be seeking to do the same, so it will not be difficult to set up series of satisfying relationships. These relationships in turn will lead to the formation of informal groups. Because of our social nature, we have a tendency to form informal groups. The task-oriented, formal groups rarely consider the social needs of their members. Indeed, these needs are frequently considered to be dispensable and counterproductive to the achievement of the formal purpose of the organization.

Stop and Criticize

Consider how your educational institution contributes to the satisfaction of your social needs while studying through your membership of social groups (class, tutorial groups, self-help and study groups, clubs and societies, sports teams). On the other hand:

How are other aspects of your institution's structure, rules, procedures and policies blocking your satisfaction?

How could your institution meet your social needs and those of your fellow students more effectively through different forms of group arrangement – and would these be consistent with good teaching and learning practice?

How would instructors evaluate your recommendations? What would be their impact on your own academic performance?

There is also the issue of the group autonomy: that is, avoiding direct control by management or developing a group's economic interests. This can be seen as meeting members' safety needs. The group in the Bank Wiring Observation Room at the Hawthorne works sought to defend itself from outside interference. There is the issue of identity and the group, and this has two aspects. First, there is each person's *individual identity*, which comes in part from his or her group membership. Second, there is *group identity*, which distinguishes one group from another. All groups develop informal hierarchies which, in turn, become the basis for building both types of identity. They distinguish or differentiate themselves from other, similar groups in the neighbourhood or organization. Street gangs in London and New York have their own, unique labels, as do company improvement teams. Groups use ritual 'fazing' techniques, initiation ceremonies and ongoing practical jokes (which management would define as 'misbehaviour') to socialize new members. Within the group, its members develop their own identities.

Banana time

The development of identity and control is present in even the most rudimentary groups. In a pioneering paper written in 1958, Donald Roy reports on a very small group of unskilled workers engaged in 'repetitive manual work'. He records the way in which the working day was divided by the group into a series of intervals demarcated by specific 'times'. Thus, 'peach time' marked one break from work followed by 'banana time', 'Coke time', 'fish time' and so on, the intervals being named after the kind of refreshment taken at each interval. Roy argued that these designated times broke up long periods of extremely tedious work, providing intervals of rest and diversion. They helped to 'kill the beast of monotony'. But this designation of 'times' is not simply a matter of marking the passage of time. The interludes are given meaning by their association with particular events. Clearly, too, these meanings are intertwined with the creation and re-creation of group relationships. The 'banana time', which provides the title of Roy's journal article, is not simply a regular break time defined by members eating bananas. In fact, it is a relatively arbitrary time interval marked by the pilferage and consumption of a banana belonging to one worker by another.

According to Roy, each and every day, a worker called Ike would steal and consume a banana belonging to a co-worker called Sammy. 'Each morning, after making the snatch, Ike would call out "banana time!" and proceed to down his prize, while Sammy made futile protests and denunciations. George (the charge hand) would join in with mild remonstrations, sometimes scolding Sammy for making so much fuss. The banana Sammy had brought in for his own consumption at lunch time. He never did get to eat his banana, but kept bringing one for his lunch. At first, the daily theft startled and amazed me. Then I grew to look forward to the daily seizure and the verbal interaction that followed (Roy, 1960: 159)'. The continued daily provision of the banana must have been to some extent a voluntary matter for Sammy. The banana must be regarded as some kind of quasi-voluntary tribute or gift, perpetually provided and perpetually 'stolen'. However, its summary but, after a few occasions, entirely predictable seizure, clearly defined relative positions in the group, as well as providing entertainment and diversion ... Roy's report is interesting because he shows that, even in a very mundane work situation, subtle processes of self-regulation and group formation exist.

From Stephen Ackroyd and Paul Thompson, *Organizational Misbehaviour*, Sage Publications, London, 1999, pp. 65–6.
Used with permission.

In any company, there will be numerous formal groups which interlink with each other, and also many informal groups which form a network. To distinguish these two different collectivities, they are referred to respectively as the *formal organization* and the *informal organization*. The two are not separate since the composition, structure and operation of the different informal groups which make up the informal organization will be determined by the formal arrangements that exist in the company. These provide the context within which social relationships are established and within which social interaction can take place. Such formal contextual constraints can include plant layout, work shifts, numbers of staff employed and the type of technology used.

Commentators recommend that whenever possible, management should design groups in a way that informal and formal overlap. Even when this happens, the effect of the former on the latter can be considerable. In the end, however, when individuals have to choose between following the informal or the formal group, research has shown that they will tend to choose the former. To summarize, therefore, one can say that the informal group can meet some of their higher-level needs in Maslow's hierarchy, while formal groups exist to meet organizational objectives and fulfil the individual workers' lower-level needs.

Homans' theory of group formation

George Caspar Homans offered a theory explaining the formation of groups. He had been a junior member of Elton Mayo's research team in the Hawthorne

George Caspar
Homans
(1910–89)

studies. In his book, *The Human Group* (Homans, 1951), he used the general term 'behaviours' to refer to concrete, observable phenomena such as the interactions between individuals and their activities. He argued that every group (he used the term *social system*) exists within an environment which affects the group. The group, in turn, seeks to influence the environment within which it exists. The mutual interactions between a group and its environment shape the characteristics of the group. Let us consider his model in more detail (see figure 9.7).

Background factors

These provide the context in which group activity takes place. Homans termed this the *external system*. It can be seen as representing the 'stage' upon which group activity occurs, and consists of five elements:

- *physical context* refers to the spatial arrangement of physical objects and human activities: for example, office architecture and furniture, assignment of workers to positions on an assembly line;

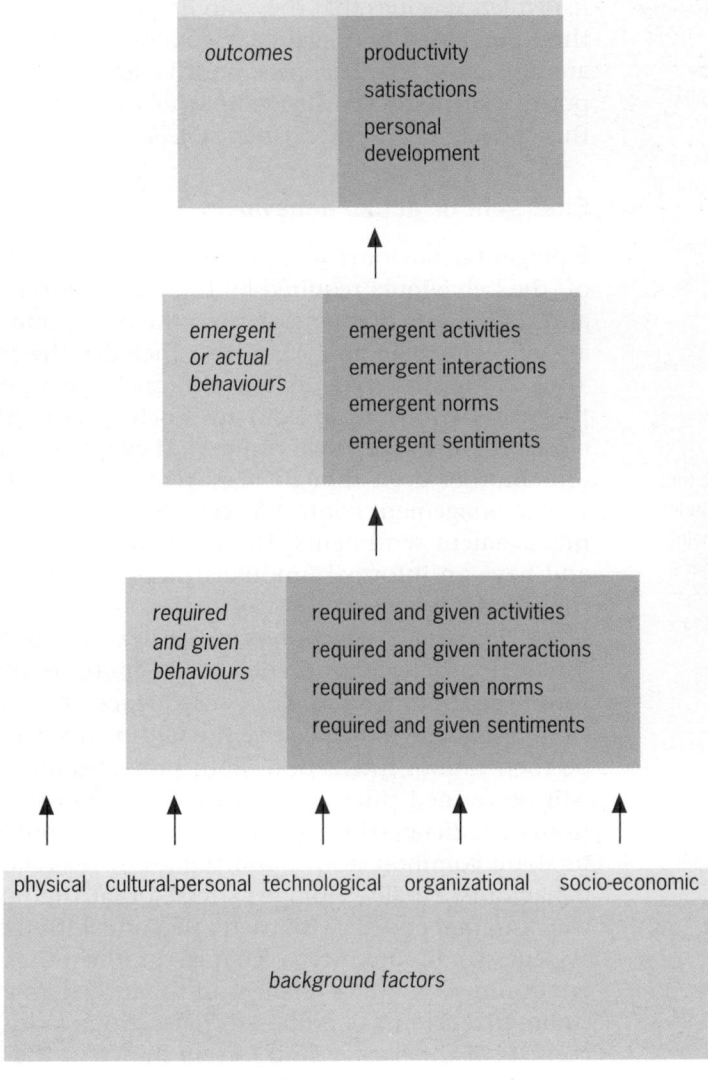

Figure 9.7: Homans' model of group formation

- *cultural-personal context* refers to the aspects of the individuals themselves, specifically the norms, values and goals that make up their shared understanding within which the group will function;

- *technological context* refers to the facilities that the group will have access to while pursuing its activities;

- *organizational context* refers to company policies, practices and rules related to the way work is performed: for example, bonus system, staff appraisal;

- *socio-economic context* refers to the economic situation as it affects the company: for example, profitability, government legislation and so on.

Required and given behaviours

These are behaviours which the managers require or expect of their employees. From the employees' perceptive, they are 'given' these. The organization requires individuals to perform certain **activities**, to have certain **interactions** with others, to adhere to certain **norms** or rules, and to hold certain **sentiments** or feelings towards their work. For example, all supermarket checkout operators are required to scan the customers' purchases (required activities). They are also given a checklist which specifies that they should greet the customer verbally before processing their purchases, and again say goodbye at the end (required interactions). They are also expected to appear positive and friendly towards customers, and hold positive attitudes to their employer (required sentiments). Homans referred to this collectively as the *external system*.

Emergent or actual behaviours

Emergent behaviours are those actions that members do in addition to, or in place of, the behaviours required by the organization. They are activities, interactions and sentiments that emerge from the background factors, and from the required and given behaviours. They also includes the norms that develop from these. Thus, if the job is repetitive (technical context), operators might see how quickly they can perform it, so as to give their work more challenge. If employees are in close proximity (physical context), they might relieve their boredom by talking to one another even though management rules prohibit this. They may come to view management control (organizational context) negatively, and develop anti-management sentiments. The group will quickly develop informal norms (rules) and have an informal (unofficial) leader. Homans referred to this collectively as the *internal system*.

For Homans, interaction is at the heart of model. The higher the frequency of interaction between individuals, the more positive the attitudes that they have towards each other and, as a consequence, the better the relations between them. Conversely, the more positive the sentiments between individuals, the higher will be their rate of interaction. Both processes increase the likelihood that a group will be formed. Increased interaction develops sentiments (attitudes and emotions) not dictated by the external (organizational) system. Hence, members come to share common norms and frames of reference. These in turn stimulate new behaviours. Finally, Homans stressed that the internal and the external systems were interdependent with each other and with the environment. A change in one system would produce a change in the other. Additionally, changes in the environment produce changes in the formal and informal work organization. To summarize, Homans proposed that a group exists within an environment which consists of the background factors shown at the base of the model in figure 9.7. These interacted with each other to produce what he termed the *required* behaviours of the group and, ultimately, also its *emergent* behaviours.

Activities: in Homans' theory, the physical movements and verbal or non-verbal behaviours engaged in by group members.

Interactions: in Homans' theory, the two-way communications between group members.

Norms: expected modes of behaviour.

Sentiments: the feelings, attitudes and beliefs held by group members.

Stop and Criticize

Identify and explain the emergent behaviours in a work group that you are able to observe.

How would group members explain and assess these emergent behaviours?

How would management respond to these emergent behaviours?

Bull Dogs and Red Devils: an empirical study of group formation

Muzafer Sherif studied how a collection of individuals without previous ties formed themselves into a group. He studied 12-year-old boys attending a summer camp in northern Connecticut in the summer of 1949. Twenty-four boys were carefully selected and matched to eliminate any possible bases for group formation (for example, background, education, ethnicity, religion, friendship). Having arrived in camp, they were separated into two groups. From then on, for five days, the two sets of boys were on separate schedules, sleeping in different bunkhouses and eating at different times. Sherif considered that a common group goal was essential for group formation to occur. He predicted that, as members interacted to achieve this, the boys would produce a group organization with hierarchical status and role relationships, and develop common, unwritten rules (norms) of behaviour which would serve as the basis for individual members' attitudes.

Sherif discovered that two groups formed over time. After a few days' interaction, the top and bottom status within the two groups became stabilized. The lower positions established as it became obvious that some of the boys were not contributing to the task, were playing around, or lacked interest or skill. The boys jockeyed for positions, and ultimately the status structure of each of the two groups had fully stabilized. The early development of leadership showed that one person had begun to co-ordinate and initiate plans in a variety of different situations. Certain boys were more popular than others and gained undisputed authority over others. As the structure formed within each group, their members' attitudes to their group became positive and norms were established. One of these was the naming of the groups – 'Red Devils' and 'Bull Dogs'. Another was the conferment of nicknames on group members, 'Baby Face' and 'Lemon Head'. Each group came to prefer certain songs and developed its own jargon, special jokes, secrets and preferred places. Each group also had its special ways of performing tasks, such as braiding lanyards and preparing meals, which was consistently followed by group members. Methods of praise and punishments were standardized in each group. Wayward members who failed to do the 'right' things or who did not contribute to the common effort found themselves receiving reprimands, ridicule, 'silent treatment' or even threats. Sherif concluded that when individuals who have no established relationships are brought together to interact in activities with common goals, they produce a group structure with hierarchical positions and roles within it. The interaction process produces common goals, which constitute the basis of individual members' attitudes in matters important to the group.

Based on Muzafer Sherif and Caroline W. Sherif, *Groups in Harmony and Tension*, Harper and Brothers, New York, 1953.

Stages of group development

Since we have been using the terms 'formal group' and 'informal group', it is important to relate these to our organizational definition of the 'psychological group'. While an informal group is always also a psychological group, a formal group may not necessarily be a psychological group. Consider for a moment the staff in a company finance office. As a task-oriented formal group they have a responsibility for the control of the company finances, costing and control. Of the twenty individuals who compose it, half may have been there for over twenty years, while others will have joined the company when it merged. Consider also the definition of the psychological group. There is no reason why these staff

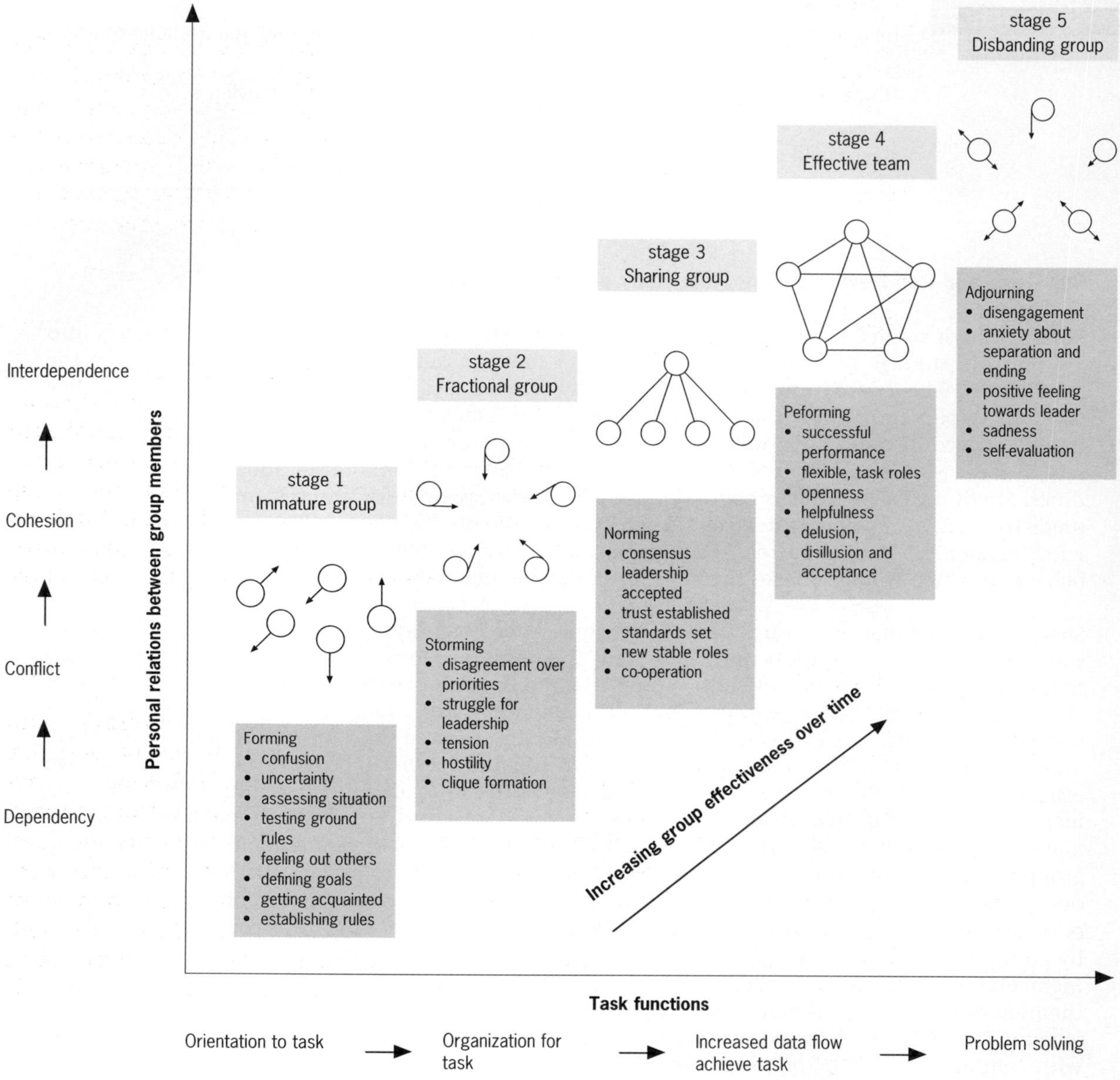

Personal relations between group members

Interdependence

Cohesion

Conflict

Dependency

**stage 1
Immature group**

Forming
• confusion
• uncertainty
• assessing situation
• testing ground rules
• feeling out others
• defining goals
• getting acquainted
• establishing rules

**stage 2
Fractional group**

Storming
• disagreement over priorities
• struggle for leadership
• tension
• hostility
• clique formation

**stage 3
Sharing group**

Norming
• consensus
• leadership accepted
• trust established
• standards set
• new stable roles
• co-operation

**stage 4
Effective team**

Peforming
• successful performance
• flexible, task roles
• openness
• helpfulness
• delusion, disillusion and acceptance

**stage 5
Disbanding group**

Adjourning
• disengagement
• anxiety about separation and ending
• positive feeling towards leader
• sadness
• self-evaluation

Increasing group effectiveness over time

Task functions

Orientation to task → Organization for task → Increased data flow achieve task → Problem solving

Figure 9.8: Stages of group development
Based on B.C. Tuckman, 'Development sequences in small groups', *Psychological Bulletin*, vol. 3, no. 6, 1965, pp. 384–99;
J.E. Jones, 'Model of group development', *The 1973 Annual Handbook for Group Facilitators*, Pfeiffer/Jossey-Bass, San Francisco,
1973, pp. 127–9; and B.C. Tuckman and M.A.C. Jensen, 'Stages of small group development revisited', *Group and Organization
Studies*, vol. 2, no. 4, 1977, pp. 419–27.

Bruce Wayne
Tuckman (b. 1938)

should all necessarily interact with each other or perceive themselves to be a single group. The finance department, as a formally established unit, may consist of different informal groups. The question then arises as to how a collection of individuals becomes a psychological group.

Groups of whatever type do not come into existence fully formed. Bruce Tuckman and Mary Ann Jensen suggested that groups pass through five clearly defined stages of development which they labelled forming, storming, norming, performing and adjourning (Tuckman, 1965; Tuckman and Jensen, 1977) (see figure 9.8). Of course not all groups develop through all the stages and some get stuck in the middle and remain inefficient and ineffective. Progress through the stages may be slow, but appears to be necessary and inescapable.

Forming

This is the orientation phase, at which the set of individuals has not yet gelled. Everyone is busy finding out about each other's attitudes and backgrounds, and establishing ground rules. Members are also keen to fix their personal identities in the group and make a personal impression on the others. In the personal relations area, members are *dependent* on some leader to provide them with structure in the form of ground rules and an agenda for action. Task-wise, they seek *orientation* as to what they are being asked to do, what the issues are and whether everyone understands the task.

Storming

This is a conflict stage in the group's life and can be an uncomfortable period. Members bargain with each other as they try to sort out what each of them individually, and as a group, want out of the group process. Individuals reveal their personal goals and it is likely that interpersonal hostility is generated when differences in these goals are revealed. Members may resist the control of other group members and may show hostility. The early relationships established in the forming stage may be disrupted. The key personal relations issue in this stage is the management of *conflict*, while the task function question is *organization* – how best to organize to achieve the group objective.

Norming

In this cohesion stage, members of the group develop closer relationships with each other. The questions of who will do what and how it will be done are addressed. Working rules are established in terms of norms of behaviour (do not smoke) and role allocation (Jill will be the spokesperson). A framework is therefore created in which each group member can relate to the others and the questions of agreeing expectations and dealing with a failure to meet members' expectations are addressed. The personal relations within the group stress *cohesion*. Members feel that they have overcome conflict, have 'gelled' and experience a sense of 'groupiness'. On the task side, there is an *increase in data flow* as members are prepared to be more open about their goals.

Performing

By this stage the group has developed an effective structure and it is concerned with actually getting on with the job in hand and accomplishing objectives. The fully mature group, which can get on with its work, has now been created. Not all groups develop to this stage but may become bogged down in an earlier and less productive stage. In personal relations, interdependence becomes a feature. Members are equally happy working alone, in sub-groups or as a single unit. Collaboration and functional competition occur between them. On the task side, there is a high commitment to the objective, jobs are well defined and problem-solving activity ensues.

Adjourning

In this final stage the group may disband, either because the task has been achieved or because the members have left. Before they do so, they may reflect on their time together and ready themselves to go their own ways.

Tuckman and Jensen's stages need not occur in sequence. While groups do pass through these different stages, they have been found to go through a more iterative process. They cycle back and forth between the different stages. They may pass through one stage several times or become frozen in a certain stage for a period of time. Some groups pass through certain stages more quickly than others. Moreover, progress through to any given stage is not inevitable (Gersick, 1988, 1989).

| **Stop and Criticize** | Identify a group to which you currently belong – a sports club, drama society, tutorial group, project group, etc.

Identify which stage of development it has reached.

What advice would you give to this group, based on your analysis of its development? |

Tuckman and Jensen's model has been verified by research and, to complement it, Jones (1973) has described the personal relations issues that affect group members and the task functions that are addressed at each of its five stages. The combined framework is shown in figure 9.8. Its value is that it can help us to explain some of the problems of group working. A group may be operating at half power because it may have failed to work through some of the issues at the earlier stages. For example, the efficiency of a project team may be impaired because it had not resolved the issue of leadership. Alternatively, people may be pulling in different directions because the purpose of the group has not been clarified and its objectives not agreed. Members might be using the group to achieve their personal and unstated aims (so-called hidden agendas). For all these reasons, effective group functioning may be hindered.

A group can be considered as a society in miniature. A college department or company sales team will have a hierarchy with leaders and followers. It will have rules, norms and traditions, as well as goals to strive for and values to uphold. It will change and develop, and will also adapt to and create changes in the environment and its members. Like a society it may experience a period of difficulty and decline. It is in such mini-societies as the family and the work group that an individual learns about and is socialized into the wider society. It has been argued that small groups will reflect the social changes in the wider society. It is likely that the individual will most directly experience these through the small group. For example, as there are changes about the value and organization of work, these may be reflected in changes in job design and work group organization.

Groups influence the behaviour, beliefs and attitudes of their members. While we may like to believe that we are all free agents, and would resent being told that we are influenced by others or conform to others' views, research shows that this is in fact the case. In varying degrees and under certain circumstances, we are all influenced by others when we are in a group. If it is any consolation, we can remember that we in turn play an important role ourselves in influencing and controlling other group members. This is the topic of a later chapter in this part of the book.

Table 9.1: Issues facing any work group

Issue	Questions
1. Atmosphere and relationships	What kinds of relationship should there be among members? How close and friendly, formal or informal?
2. Member participation	How much participation should be required of members? Some more than others? All equally? Are some members more needed than others?
3. Goal understanding and acceptance	How much do members need to *understand* group goals? How much do they need to *accept* to be *committed* to the goals? Everyone equally? Some more than others?
4. Listening and information sharing	How is information to be shared? Who needs to know what? Who should listen most to whom?
5. Handling disagreements and conflict	How should disagreements or conflicts be handled? To what extent should they be resolved? Brushed aside? Handled by dictate?
6. Decision-making	How should decisions be made? Consensus? Voting? One-person rule? Secret ballot?
7. Evaluation of member performance	How is evaluation to be managed? Everyone appraises everyone else? A few take the responsibility? Is it to be avoided?
8. Expressing feelings	How should feelings be expressed? Only about the task? Openly and directly?
9. Division of labour	How are task assignments to be made? Voluntarily? By discussion? By leaders?
10. Leadership	Who should lead? How should leadership *functions* be exercised? Shared? Elected? Appointed from outside?
11. Attention to process	How should the group monitor and improve its own process? Ongoing feedback from members? Formal procedures? Avoiding direct discussion?

From Allan R. Cohen, Stephen L. Fink, Herman Gadon and Robin D. Willits, *Effective Behavior in Organizations*, 6th Edition, Irwin, Homewood, IL, 1995, p. 142. Reprinted by permission of The McGraw-Hill Companies.

Groups and teams

In the literature, the terms 'group' and 'team' are used interchangeably, with the personal preference of writers and tradition guiding the choice of word, rather than conceptual distinction. For example, the 'how-to-do-it' books aimed at a management audience tend to refer to teams in organizations, while, for historical reasons, discussions about shop-floor working arrangements refer to autonomous work groups. Authors who are management consultants frequently use the term 'team' metaphorically: that is, they apply this label to a collection of employees to which it is imaginatively, but not literally, appropriate. Hayes (1997) noted that the idea of the team must be one of the most widely used metaphors in organi-zational life. These same writers also use the term normatively: that is, to describe a collection of people as what they *should* be, or what they would *prefer* them to be, rather than as they actually are.

In their examination of the managerial practices used by the US Marine Corps to engage the hearts and minds of its front-line troops, Jon Katzenbach and Jason

Table 9.2: Teams and groups – it pays to know the difference

	Team	Single-leader work group
Run by:	The members of the team best-suited to lead the tasks at hand; the leadership role shifts among the members	One person, usually the senior member, who is formally designated to lead
Goals and agenda set by:	The group, based on dialogue about purpose; constructive conflict and integration predominate	The formal leader, often in consultation with a sponsoring executive; conflict with group members is avoided and the leader integrates
Performance evaluated by:	The members of the group, as well as the leader and sponsor	The leader and sponsor
Work style determined by:	The members	The leader's preference
Most appropriate business context:	A complex challenge that requires people with various skill sets working together much of the time	A challenge in which time is of the essence and the leader already knows how best to proceed; the leader is the primary integrator
Speed and efficiency:	Low until the group has learned to function as a team; afterwards, however, the team is as fast as a single-leader group	Higher than that of teams initially, as the members need no time to develop commitment or to learn to work as a team
Primary end-products:	Largely collective, requiring several team members to work together to produce results	Largely individual and can be accomplished best by each person working on his or her own
Accountability characterized by:	'We hold one another mutually accountable for achieving the goals and performance of the team'	'The leader holds us individually accountable for our output'

Reprinted by permission of *Harvard Business Review*, Exhibit, p. 114, from 'Firing up the front line' by Jon R. Katzenbach and Jason A. Santamaria, May–June, 1999. Copyright © 1999 by the Harvard Business School Publishing Corporation; all rights reserved.

Santamaria (1999) contrasted the characteristics of a team with that of a single-leader work group. These are summarized in table 9.2. The authors describe the training of marines, and note that the highly cohesive groups produced by this process learn when and how to function as a real team and when to rely on a single leader.

Most commonly, writers focus on the transformation of a group into a team. They see the difference between the two as being in terms of a group being 'stuck' in the forming, storming or norming stage of Tuckman and Jensen's model, while a team is a group that has successfully arrived at the performing stage. From the point of view of management, a team is a group which possesses extra, positive features. As a group comes to acquire these positive characteristics, it is seen as progressing towards the team-end of the continuum. These positive 'team traits' include co-operation, co-ordination, cohesion and so on. From this perspective, a group turns into a team once it has organized itself to fulfil a purpose. This implies a process of conscious self-management by the group's members during which they assign tasks, develop communication channels and establish decision-making processes. Thus, the transition from a group to a team is the result of a learning process.

Stop and Criticize

Management has just told you that you are not a 'real team' and that you are certainly not a 'high-performance team'. How do you feel about that and what are you going to do about it?

Mayo's 'Human Relations approach' and Katzenbach and Santamaria's managerial practices to create teams are separated by over seventy years but have remarkable similarities. Both:

- are directed at managers who design jobs and structure organizations;

- promote the virtues of teams and groups over individuals;

- assume that teams and the individuals share common goals and interests;

- ignore or explain away areas of conflict or dissent;

- seek to use the power of the team in management's interest.

Management's practical interest grew, and they became interested not just in observing groups but in designing and building effective teams. The general theme of making group behaviour contribute to management goals has been lately re-discovered at the level of the shop floor by the interest in Japanese-style teamworking. Writers have argued that the managerial belief that links all these contemporary writers with Elton Mayo back in the 1920s is that of the creation of a compliant and programmable workforce.

Virtual team: a group of people who work closely together even though they are geographically separated, and are usually cross-functional work groups brought together to tackle a project for a finite period of time through a combination of technologies (Henry and Hartzler, 1998).

Virtual teams

Synchronous communication: occurs when people are online at the same time, engaging in a real-time conversation with others, somewhat similar to normal face-to-face discussions.

Asynchronous communication: occurs when participants start a discussion topic (or thread) and post replies to each other. After delays, individuals read to catch up with the discussion. It is similar to a dialogue conducted by post.

Increasing competition and globalization is forcing organizations to speed up their development and production of new products and services. Simultaneously, advancing communications hardware is allowing individuals to interact with others anywhere in the world, on the move, via laptop or mobile phone. Additionally, project-management software ('groupware') links the members of a team electronically, and allows them instantly to share and analyze project information. This combination of market-push and technology-pull has led companies to explore new types of working arrangement and organizational form. One such development is the **virtual team**. Here, the term 'virtual' implies the use of technology to create a common workplace, rather than the use of simultaneous physical presence.

The members of these teams are connected by the various technological hardware, collaborative software and group support systems. The differences in time and location associated with different forms of information exchange possibilities were summarized by James Bowditch and Anthony Buona (2001) and are shown in figure 9.9. According to this table, the members of a team may be present in the same place (co-located) or present in different places (distributed) when receiving or giving information. Similarly, their communication may be **synchronous** or **asynchronous**. Many studies examining their operations are in progress (Hughes et al., 2001).

		PLACE	
		Same	**Different**
TIME	**Same**	**Co-located/Synchronous** • Face-to-face meetings • Technography • Decision-support rooms I	**Distributed/Synchronous** • Audio (telephone) • Video conferencing • Distance whiteboarding II
	Different	III **Co-located/Asynchronous** • Resource centre • Team rooms • 'War' room	IV **Distributed/Asynchronous** • Voice mail, email • Computer conferencing • Groupware and intranets

Figure 9.9: Time and place dimensions of team information exchange
From James L. Bowditch and Anthony F. Buono, *A Primer on Organizational Behavior*, 2001, p. 170. Copyright © 2001 John Wiley & Sons, Inc. This material is used by permission of John Wiley & Sons, Inc.

Virtual teamworking: not as easy as it looks

A series of empirical studies have uncovered a range of problems associated with different varieties of virtual teamworking. Research by Hughes et al. (2001) examined the structural changes involved in the centralization of 'back office' (non-customer) processing and the creation of specialist centres to deal with lending, service and securities. These served the bank's customer service branches, at a distance, in towns and cities around the country. They found that virtual teamwork placed a particular emphasis on communication between units, and the development of 'awareness skills' on the part of workers. They were encouraged to complete their tasks in a way that enabled other workers, at other sites, to complete theirs.

However, the increased geographical dispersion of the specialist centres led to a culture of 'passing the blame', with poor communication affecting teamworking across the organizational divide. Locating all staff dealing with a single task at a single centre (co-location) created and encouraged strong group loyalties and an 'us' and 'them' attitude ('them' being any other organizational unit).

Nandhakumar (1999) investigated a large multinational organization whose virtual teamworking project involved geographically dispersed team members interacting online. He focused on the issue of trust. He found that to operate this virtual working arrangement, team members had to develop personalized trust relationships. These provided them with the 'backstage' where they could exchange feelings and emotions with one another. Such relationships not only were seen as psychologically rewarding, but also helped to exchange favourable attitudes and positive expectations. Normally, these types of relationship are established through face-to-face interaction and socialization, and they are sustained through participants' interactions. The study showed that the technology used by the team neither maintained nor reproduced these vital trust relationships. As a result, some participants lacked the confidence to share their informal knowledge of the organization with other members, while others were unable to engage in virtual teamworking at all because they lacked sufficient confidence in their fellow workers, based at different locations, to permit continuous interaction with them.

Carletta and her colleagues (2000) focused on online, collaborative engineering work, rather than the more frequently studied business meetings. They investigated the operation of two virtual teams formed by an original equipment manufacturer (OEM) for the purpose of collaborative design with its first-tier suppliers. They confirmed Nandhakumar's finding that the technology the groups used decreased sociability (social talk), thereby reducing group solidarity and hence the likelihood of open communication, particularly among low-status members. They added that the teams were affected by, and had to overcome, the status differences inherent in their traditional hierarchical structures so as to share information and authority more widely. Finally, Mortensen and Hinds (2001) found that shared team identity helped distributed teams (but not co-located ones) to manage conflict.

Based on John A. Hughes, Jon O'Brien, Dave Randall, Mark Rouncefield and Peter Tolmie, 'Some "real" problems of virtual teamwork', *New Technology, Work and Employment*, vol. 16, no. 1, 2001, pp. 49–64; Joe Nandhakumar, 'Virtual teams and lost proximity', in P. Jackson (ed.), *Virtual Working*, Routledge, London, 1999, pp. 46–56; Jean Carletta, Anne H. Anderson and Rachel McEwan, 'The effects of multimedia communication technology on non-collocated teams: a case study', *Ergonomics*, vol. 43, no. 8, 2000, pp. 1237–51; Mark Mortensen and Pamela Hinds, 'Conflict and shared identity in geographically distributed teams', *The International Journal of Conflict Management*, vol. 12, no. 3, 2001, pp. 212–38.

Organizations are increasingly taking advantage of electronic media to support group work activity, using email, online discussion forums and conferences, and a variety of software tools that allow group members to engage in voting, sorting, prioritizing, collaborative document editing, online chatting, interactive video and collective decision-making. The effectiveness of virtual work groups is a significant issue, and we need to know how the quality of the working life of their members, as well as their dynamics and productivity, are affected by members not being in face-to-face contact with each other. Why are organizations experimenting with virtual teams? Townend et al. (1998) offer a number of reasons:

- the transnationalization of trade and business activity;

- heightened worker expectations about participation and involvement;

- the increasing prevalence of flat or horizontal organization structures;

- environmental pressures that require interorganizational co-operation;

- the ongoing shift from production to service and knowledge-based environments.

Information and communication technologies can potentially increase the effectiveness of teamworking by removing barriers of place and enabling individual team members to work together across organizational and geographical boundaries. However, it is more difficult for a virtual team to be successful since there is a greater potential for misunderstandings to arise and for more things to go wrong. Bowditch and Buona (2001) explain that while team leaders are skilled in dealing with Quadrant I interactions (same time/same place), they lack the experience and expertise to guide and facilitate interactions in the other three quadrants (see figure 9.9). These authors believe that the only way to build trust and resolve conflicts between individuals, especially in the early stages of projects, is to give them the full sensory information that only person-to-person interactions provide. Bowditch and Buona report that some companies are experimenting with 'hybrid meetings' where one part is physical and the other is virtual. Some members are physically present in the room, while the others are 'attending' from their offices via desktop video conferencing and instant messaging technologies. They conclude that moving virtual teams beyond being just vehicles for information-sharing mechanisms and towards having them complete organizational tasks and resolve project-related issues raises unique challenges for managers and their organizations.

Teamworking: physical or virtual?

If a virtual working environment can be created to represent the outside world on a computer screen, why do personnel need to be physically centralized in control rooms when they can be removed from the plant itself or from the operations that they are supervising? Power stations already have remotely maintained gas turbine stations, and the trend to automation and remote monitoring may be followed by more manufacturing companies in the future. Neville Stanton and his colleagues (in press) studied the control room operations of energy distribution companies. Their research highlighted the limitations of the current virtual world. They found that in these work situations, people worked much better together than in isolation, and that even the best of the new technologies, video conferencing, did not compensate for the benefits gained from working shoulder-to-shoulder with one's colleagues.

Their study found that people working in close physical proximity as a team dealt more effectively with problems than a team whose members worked at a distance from each other, and who were linked by computer and video conferencing. The team whose members were physically congregated showed superiority in terms of better performance, reduced costs, greater group identity, enhanced motivation and greater tactical control. Physical proximity produces better communication. Half of the teams working at a distance had long periods of non-interaction between their members, while teams working physically together in a single room had no such interaction gaps. The research concluded that people work more effectively when they are together because group contact increases the three key elements of effective teamworking – familiarity, respect and trust.

Based on N.A. Stanton, M.J. Ashleigh, A.D. Roberts and F. Xu, 'Testing Hollnagel's contextual control model: assessing team behaviour in a human supervisory control task', *International Journal of Cognitive Ergonomics*, vol. 5, no. 1, 2001, pp. 21–33; N.A. Stanton, M.J. Ashleigh, A.D. Roberts and F. Xu, 'Virtuality in human supervisory control', *Ergonomics* (in press).

Recap

1. *List the key characteristics of a psychological group.*

   - The key characteristics are: two or more people, in face-to-face interaction, each aware of their membership in the group, each aware of the others who belong to the group, and each aware of their positive interdependence as they strive to achieve mutual goals.

2. *Distinguish between different types of group task.*

   - Groups can be assigned many different tasks, many of which can be categorized under the headings of additive, conjunctive and disjunctive.

3. *Name the four research phases of the Hawthorne studies.*

   - The Hawthorne studies consisted of four major phases – illumination experiments, Relay Assembly Test Room experiments, interviewing programme, and the Bank Wiring Observation Room experiments.

4. *Distinguish between a formal and an informal group.*

   - Formal groups can be distinguished from informal groups in terms of who creates them and the purposes that they serve.

5. *Outline Homans' theory of group formation.*

   - George Homans' theory of group formation uses the concepts of background factors, required and emergent activities, interactions, sentiments, to explain how individuals come to form groups.

6. *Enumerate the five stages of Tuckman and Jensen's model of group development.*

   - Tuckman and Jensen distinguish five stages through which groups typically proceed, which they name forming, storming, norming, performing and adjourning.

7. *Summarize Katzenbach and Santamaria's distinction between a team and a single-leader working group.*

   - Katzenbach and Santamaria distinguish between a team and a single-leader working group.

   - They contrast the two on the basis of who runs it, who sets the goals, performance evaluation, work style, business context, speed and efficiency, primary end products and accountability.

Revision

1. Why have the Hawthorne studies remained so important? Of what value are they to working in and managing groups today?

2. In what ways does a group link an individual to the organization?

3. Think of two different groups that you joined in the past. In each case, identify what motivated you to join. To what extent have your needs been met or objectives realized?

4. Why do companies recruiting new graduates stress the importance of their being 'team players'?

5. 'Informal groups can be detrimental to management but beneficial to individual members.' Do you agree or disagree? Explain your view.

Springboard

Ackroyd, S. and Thompson, p. , 1999, *Organizational Misbehaviour*, Sage Publications, London.

A highly entertaining, academic study of organizational misbehaviour (time wasting, absence, sabotage, pilferage, fiddling, joking rituals, sex games) examined from a sociological perspectives. Considers the part played by groups in initiating and sustaining these.

Gillespie, R., 1991, *Manufacturing Knowledge: A History of the Hawthorne Experiments*, Cambridge University Press, Cambridge.

At one level, this book provides a historical account of the Hawthorne studies, complete with photographs. At another level, it addresses the question of how knowledge is generated within the social sciences, and explains how interpretations of data become official versions.

Homans, G.C., 1984, *Coming to My Senses*, Transaction Books, New Brunswick, NJ.

Roethlisberger, F.J., 1977, *The Elusive Phenomena: An Autobiographical Account of My Work in the Field of Organizational Behaviour at the Harvard Business School*, Harvard University Press, Cambridge, MA.

Two autobiographies of academics directly involved in the Hawthorne studies, the human relations movement, and the development of organization behaviour as a distinct field of academic study.

Jackson, p. (ed.), 1999, *Virtual Working*, Routledge, London.

Chapter 4 considers virtual teams and the effect of proximity on trust relationships.

O'Connor, E., 1999, 'Minding the workers: the meaning of "human" and "human relations" of Elton Mayo', *Organization*, vol. 6., no. 2, pp. 223–46.

A consideration of Mayo's ideas from a contemporary perspective.

Sinclair, A., 1992, 'The tyranny of team ideology', *Organization Studies*, vol. 13, no. 4, pp. 611–26.

Critical review of the concept of team in managerial and organizational writings.

Sonnenfeld, J., 1985, 'Shedding light on the Hawthorne studies', *Journal of Occupational Behaviour*, vol. 6, pp. 111–30.

A critique of the Hawthorne studies which looks in-depth at all six studies and reviews the contributions of those who have attacked and defended it.

West, M.A. (ed.), 1998, *Handbook of Work Group Psychology*, Wiley, Chichester.

Contains writings on group and team behaviour. Provides an overview of the field and current theoretical and research directions.

Wren, D.A., 1994, *The Evolution of Management Thought*, Wiley, New York.

Sets the Hawthorne studies and the human relations approach in its wider historical context. Demonstrates how the current popularity of teamworking of all kinds owes its debt to this research.

Home viewing

The Breakfast Club (1984, directed by John Hughes) is set in the library of an American high school where five students have been sent to spend a whole Saturday in detention, under a teacher's less than watchful eye. Apart from the teacher and the school janitor, there are only five main characters in the film, representing different stereotypes:

Character	Stereotype	Played by
Andrew Clark	sports 'jock'	Emillo Estevez
Claire Standish	prom queen	Molly Ringwald
Aillson Reynolds	weirdo	Ally Sheedy
Brian Johnson	nerd	Anthony Michael Hall
Judd Nelson	lout	John Bender

These five high school students have never met each other before, and each is being punished by this detention for a different act of organizational misbehaviour (see Ackroyd and Thompson, 1999). Shut in together in the school library for the day, they are forced to get to know each other. As the film unfolds, can you:

1. Identify the 'break points' in the action when the students move from *forming* to *storming* to *norming* and, finally, to *performing* as a group?

2. Identify examples of *norming* during the *group forming* stage?

3. Identify examples of *performing* during the group *storming* stage?

4. Establish where and why the *leadership* of this student group moves from one character to another?

5. Identify examples of organizational misbehaviour, not only among the five students, and also determine the purpose, objective or motive for that behaviour?

Two classic disaster movies, *The Poseidon Adventure* (1972, directed by Ronald Neame) and *Towering Inferno* (1972, directed by John Guillermin), both show aggregates of individuals becoming transformed into psychological groups. What circumstances in the movie turn the former into the latter? How is the interaction between the individuals changed?

OB in literature

Thomas Keneally, *Flying Hero Class*, Hodder and Stoughton, London, 1991.

This is a story of an airline hijack. How does the plot illustrate the distinction between mere aggregates of people and psychological groups? How does the 'aggregate' of people on an aeroplane become a 'psychological group'?

Graham Greene, 'The Destructors' (short story written in 1954), in *Twenty-one Stories*, Penguin, Harmondsworth, 1975, pp. 7–23.

How does this short story demonstrate Homans' theory of group formation?

Chapter exercises

1: Group development stages questionnaire

Objectives   1. Introduce Tuckman and Jensen's model of group development.

2. Determine which stage of development a given group is at.

Briefing   1. Think of a group of which you are a member. This may be your university tutorial or syndicate group, a project team at work, or some other regularly meeting group such as a social club, sports club or society. This group should have some kind of objective to achieve.

2. Keeping the behaviour of this group in your mind as a focus, circle Y (= Yes) or N (= No) for each statement in relation to your group, in the group development stages questionnaire.

3. Score the questionnaire as directed by your instructor.

Group development stages questionnaire

1. Members are unclear as to what the group's goals are.	Y N
2. At each meeting there is always a lot of talk about who is supposed to do what.	Y N
3. Members frequently look to the official chairperson or informal leader for guidance.	Y N
4. There is rarely, if ever, any discussion of how members feel about things.	Y N
5. When direction is provided by someone in the group, the others are reluctant to follow.	Y N
6. Members seems reluctant to tell others what they really think about things.	Y N

Total: F

7. People are discussing what part each will play in meeting the goal.	Y N
8. The group has developed a 'game plan' for achieving its priority objectives.	Y N
9. Measures are being produced to allow the checking of progress.	Y N
10. Group members look to others for direction as to what to do next.	Y N
11. Members argue a lot about what the group should be doing.	Y N
12. There are at least two people who want to be the group leader.	Y N

Total: S

13. Members comment intermittently on how well or badly the group is operating.	Y N
14. Relevant information is widely shared, and little is kept hidden by individuals.	Y N
15. Most people are working for the group, rather than for themselves.	Y N
16. There is a sense of 'togetherness' among the group.	Y N
17. Members trust and support each other.	Y N
18. Relationships between group members are for the most part amicable.	Y N

Total: N

19. The group is becoming good at identifying obstacles to achieving its goal.	Y N
20. We can diagnose problems in the way we work as a team and fix them.	Y N
21. We often develop creative solutions to achieve our objectives in different ways.	Y N
22. In this group, I feel able to risk expressing new ideas.	Y N
23. I can feel able to express my disagreement without others taking it personally.	Y N
24. Members take the lead as the situation requires it.	Y N
Total: P	

2: Types of task

Objectives 1. Distinguish between the different types of task that a group may perform.

2. Recognize how type of task affects group process.

Briefing 1. Form into groups of four or five members.

2. You have 15–20 minutes to complete four tasks which vary in their nature. Groups may consult references, etc., at their discretion.

3. The tasks are:
  ■ Task 1 – Generate words that rhyme with the 15 words listed;
  ■ Task 2 – Produce synonyms or antonyms for the 15 words listed;
  ■ Task 3 – Solve the equation;
  ■ Task 4 – Suggest the best route between here and the nearest coastal town or city.

4. Groups compare their answers and are provided with the correct answers.

5. All the groups then:
  ■ identify the unique characteristics of each type of task they performed;
  ■ provide other examples of each type of task;
  ■ consider the effect of task type on their group decision-making processes.

Task 1 – Generate words that rhyme with the 15 words listed below:

feast	beard	battle	flowers	hissed
hurried	profit	world	orange	load
sorrow	song	accounting	great	smiles

Task 2 – Produce synonyms or antonyms for the 15 words listed below:

celebrity	diminutive	traditional	moveable	sweet
fearful	crescendo	agitation	deliver	borrow
quietly	circuitous	paltry	foolish	indeterminate

Task 3 – Solve the following equation:

$$\text{Find } x, y, z \text{ and } w \text{ if } 3 \begin{pmatrix} x & y \\ z & w \end{pmatrix} = \begin{pmatrix} x & 6 \\ -1 & 2w \end{pmatrix} + \begin{pmatrix} 4 & x+y \\ z+w & 3 \end{pmatrix}$$

Task 4 – Suggest the best route between here and the coastal town or city that is nearest to your educational establishment.

Inspired by Diane Dodd-McCue, 'Led like sheep: an exercise for linking group decision-making to different types of task', *Journal of Management Education*, 1991, vol. 15, no. 3, pp. 335–9.

Chapter 10 Group structure

Key concepts

group structure	sociometry
group process	sociogram
power	communication network analysis
reward power	comminigram
coercive power	communication pattern analysis
referent power	communication pattern chart
legitimate power	interaction process analysis
expert power	social role
formal status	team role
social status	group leadership

Learning outcomes

When you have read this chapter, you should be able to define those key concepts in your own words, and you should also be able to:

1. List the six dimensions of group structure.
2. Identify the sources of power within the group.
3. Distinguish between two common uses of the concept of status.
4. Understand how emotional relationships within a group can be represented symbolically.
5. Distinguish between communication network analysis, communication pattern analysis and IPA analysis.
6. Distinguish between task, socio-emotional and individual classes of roles within a group.
7. Distinguish Belbin's team roles.
8. Give examples of three leadership styles identified by White and Lippitt.
9. Distinguish between a task and a socio-emotional group leader.

Why study group structure?

Abraham Zaleznik (1993, p. 180) has argued that:

> While Americans admire the 'hero', the individual who has the 'right stuff', they worry about his (sic) recklessness, his willingness to take risks that endanger others. Frequently the 'hero' is suppressed in favour of the team player who values the performance of the group over individual recognition.

However, how the group as a whole performs depends very much on the behaviour and contribution of its individual members. Within organizations, a great deal of work is done by individuals working with others in groups and teams. Because it is so important, management monitors how groups work in order to pinpoint any problems and rectifies them so as to raise team effectiveness. When there is a problem with a motor car, it is taken into a garage and the mechanic drives it around, listens to the engine, feels the gear changes and attends to the smoothness of the ride. The individual parts of the car are then inspected, to ensure that all of them are performing their respective tasks and are working together satisfactorily in combination. Individual faulty or worn-out parts are replaced. Linkages between the parts, which may have become loosened, are tightened. The mechanic checks that the vehicle is performing satisfactorily and can be returned to its owner.

This analogy is a useful way of introducing the concept of group structure from a management perspective. In this view, structure is an important aspect of 'engineering the group'. When a group or team is performing poorly, a consultant may be brought in to observe its operation and to evaluate its outputs. The consultant will focus on individual team members, assessing their performance of their roles, and ensuring that everyone is working well together as a team. Individuals who are not contributing or who do not 'fit in' may be replaced by others. The consultant checks that communication between team members is timely and effective, and that leadership within the group is contributing towards the achievement of the goal.

Social scientists in general, and social psychologists in particular, are less directly concerned with improving team effectiveness and more concerned with understanding how the structure of a group develops; how it affects the individuals who comprise the groups and how it impacts on group functioning.

Team problem

There were four team members named Everybody, Somebody, Anybody and Nobody.

There was an important job to do and Everybody was asked to do it.

Everybody was sure Somebody would do it.

Anybody could have done it, but Nobody did.

Everybody was angry about that, because it was Somebody's job.

Everybody thought Anybody could do it, but Nobody realized that Everybody wouldn't.

In the end, Everybody blamed Somebody when Nobody did what Anybody could have done.

Source unknown.

Group structure

A central idea in helping us to examine the nature and functioning of groups is that of structure. **Group structure** refers to the way in which members of a group relate to one another. The formation of group structure is one of the basic aspects of group development. When people come together and interact, differences between individuals begin to appear. Some talk while others listen. These differences between group members serve as the basis for the establishment of group

Group structure: the relatively stable pattern of relationships among different group members. There is no single group structure and the concept can be expressed in several and overlapping ways.

structure. As differentiation occurs, relations are established between members. Group structure is the label given to this patterning of relationships.

Group structure carries with it the connotation of something fixed and unchanging. While there is an element of permanency in terms of the relationships between members, these do continue to change and modify. Group members continually interact with each other and, in consequence, their relationships are tested and transformed. As we describe the structure of any group, it is useful to view it as a snapshot photograph, correct at the time the shutter was pressed, but to acknowledge that things were different the moment before and after the photo was taken. Differences between the members of a group begin to occur as soon as it is formed. This differentiation within a group occurs along not one but several dimensions. The most important of these are:

- power;
- status;
- liking;
- communication;
- role;
- leadership.

There are as many structures in a group as there are dimensions along which a group can be differentiated. Although in common usage we talk about the structure of a group, in reality a group will differentiate simultaneously along a number of dimensions. Group members will be accorded different amounts of status and hence a group will have a status hierarchy. They will be able to exert differing amounts of power and thus a power structure will emerge. In examining group functioning, social scientists have found it useful to consider differences among group members in terms of their liking for each other, status, power, role and leadership. While it is possible to examine each structural dimension of the group in turn, we need to remember that all are closely related and operate simultaneously in a group setting. Cartwright and Zander (1968) suggest that a group's structure is determined by:

1. The requirements for efficient group performance.
2. The abilities and motivations of group members.
3. The psychological and social environment of the group.

Why does a group have structure?

Why does a patterning of relationships between individuals in a group occur and what purpose does it serve? Robert Bales (1950a) offered a psychological explanation based on the individual's desire for stability, 'need for order' and 'low tolerance of ambiguity'. He argued that meeting and dealing with other people within a group can cause an individual stress. It is the potential uncertainty and unpredictability in the actions of others that causes this. If the behaviour between group members can be made predictable, this can reduce the tension for all concerned. This, he explained, is what group structure does.

A sociological explanation would point to structure as a manifestation of power, with structure 'imposed' on groups (as a natural aspect of efficient functioning, of course!) to maintain the power position of key players in the organization. All groups are overlaid with the power and cultural patterns of the organization within which they exist. This also raises gender issues concerning male domination.

Whether a group's structure results from its members' basic need for predictability or is imposed by powerful outsiders, the effect in either case is to create differences between the individuals within the group along several dimensions at the same time (for example, status, role, power). One person will therefore simultaneously have high status and power since each person stands at the intersection of several dimensions. The combination of all of these for each group member is referred to as their position in the group structure. A group's structure will be affected by **group process**. A group's process refers to the group activity which occurs over time, specifically to the verbal and non-verbal contributions of group members. Examples of a group's process include:

- direction of communication (who talks to whom);
- quantity of communication (number of times each group member speaks);
- content of communication (type of verbal utterance made);
- decision-making style (how decisions are made in the group);
- problem-solving style (how problems are approached and solved).

The structure of a group can affect its process. For example, when an individual is appointed the leader of a formal group, they will tend to speak more often and will be listened to more closely. Being group leader will therefore determine the direction, frequency and content of their communication with others in the group. Conversely, group process can determine group structure. In an informal group, the individual who speaks most often to all fellow members may come to be liked the most. Their status will rise in the eyes of the other members, and they may be given permission to take on a leadership role within the group.

When seeking to improve the performance of a group through the use of team-building activities, management consultants often focus on group processes in order to locate problems in group functioning and to suggest solutions. They look at *how* a group does things and not on *what* it does. They may decide that a group is performing poorly because its members are not communicating with each other sufficiently, that there is an absence of goal clarity, that leadership within the group is poor or that the way decisions are reached antagonizes members and fails to secure their commitment. Inevitably, they will recommend that the group should become aware of its processes and manage them better in order to achieve improved outcomes.

Power structure

Individual members of a group differ in terms of how much **power** they each possess, and hence in their ability to direct the behaviour of other members. For this reason, it becomes necessary for the group to have established control relations between members. By having a power structure the group avoids continued power struggles that can disrupt its functioning. It can also can link goal achievement activities to a system of authority which is seen as legitimate.

Various writers have defined power in terms of influence (Weber, 1947; Dahl, 1957). Power is an aspect not only in relationships between individuals within a group, but also in leadership relations and political issues. We shall therefore re-visit the work of these authors several times in a later chapter. For now, we can draw upon the classic work of John French and Bertram Raven (1958), who saw

---

Group process: the patterns of interactions between the members of a group.

Power: the capacity of individuals to overcome resistance on the part of others, to exert their will and to produce results consistent with their interests and objectives.

Reward power: the ability of a leader to exert influence based on the belief of followers that the leader has access to valued rewards which will be dispensed in return for compliance.

Coercive power: the ability of a leader to exert influence based on the belief of followers that the leader can administer unwelcome penalties or sanctions.

Referent power: the ability of a leader to exert influence based on the belief of followers that the leader has desirable abilities and personality traits that can and should be copied.

power as a property not of the individual but of the relationship. These authors distinguished five types of power, which are defined here: **reward power, coercive power, referent power, legitimate power** and **expert power**.

Saying that power is a property of the relationship and not of the individual means that, for example, it is not having rewards to distribute or sanctions to exercise that matters, it's being *perceived* to have them. So you have reward power when others think that you have rewards up your sleeve, even when you don't.

Stop and Criticize

Who gains from having a stable power in a group and why?

Who loses? How and why?

Make the argument for having an *unstable* power structure in a group.

Status structure

Legitimate power: the ability of a leader to exert influence based on the belief of followers that the leader has the authority to issue orders which they in turn have an obligation to accept.

Expert power: the ability of a leader to exert influence based on the belief of followers that the leader has superior knowledge relevant to the situation and the task in hand.

Formal status: a collection of rights and obligations associated with a position, as distinct from the person who may occupy that position.

Social status: the relative ranking that a person holds and the value of that person as measured by a group.

Status is a prestige ranking within a group that is independent of formal status or position. It is closely related to leadership. As an individual's higher status is accepted by others within the group, they can influence, control or command those around them. Status ranking indicates the group's 'pecking order'. Some writers argue that status is important because it motivates people and has consequences for their behaviour. This is particularly the case when individuals perceive a disparity between their own perception of themselves and how others perceive them to be. Each position in a group has a value placed upon it. Within the organization, a value is ascribed to a position by the formal organization (for example, chief executive officer, vice-president, supervisor) and can be labelled formal status. **Formal status** is best thought of as being synonymous with rank, as in the police or the armed forces, and reflects a person's position on the organizational ladder.

A second way in which value is placed on a position is the social honour or prestige that is accorded an individual in a group by the other group members. In this second sense, the word 'status' is prefixed by the word 'social', indicating the degree of informally established value accorded to that position, as compared with other positions that are perceived by both the formal and the informal group. While one can view **social status** as a sort of badge of honour awarded for meritorious group conduct, it can also be viewed as a set of unwritten rules about the kind of conduct people are expected to show one another. It can indicate the degree of respect, familiarity or reserve that is appropriate in a given situation.

One of the powers possessed by an informal group is its ability to confer status on those members who meet the expectations of the group. These members are looked up to by their peers not because of any formal position they may hold in the organization, but because of their position in the social group. Many people actively seek status in order to fulfil their need for self-esteem. The granting of it by the group provides them with personal satisfaction. Similarly, the withholding of status can act as a group control mechanism to bring a deviant group member into line. The status accorded by the group to a member is immediate in terms of face-to-face feedback. The recognition and esteem given to group members reinforces their identification with the group and increases their dependence upon it.

Turning to consider a formal group or team, individual members will be accorded formal status within it based on hierarchical position and task ability. The organization is made up of a number of defined positions arranged in order of their increasing authority. The formal status hierarchy reflects the potential ability of the holder of the position to contribute to the overall goals of the organization. It differentiates the amount of respect deserved and simultaneously ranks positions on a status scale. The outward symbols associated with formal status (for example, size of office, quality of carpet) are there to inform other members in the organization of where exactly that person stands on the 'organizational ladder'. This topic leads ultimately to a consideration of organization structure, to which we shall return later.

What effect does the status structure have on group behaviour? Research shows that, as one would expect, higher-status people in a group have more power and tend to be more influential than lower-status ones (Greenberg, 1976). Knowing this, individual members may take steps to enhance their status in the eyes of their colleagues, and thereby be able to get the group to make the decisions that they want.

Stop and Criticize

Consider a group of which you are currently a member. What action could you take to change your status in this group and what impact would this have on your relationships and friendships?

Status and authority in an aeroplane cockpit

In an aircraft, cockpit members comprise teams with a designated leader and clear lines of authority and responsibility. Status comes with position. The status ranking is captain, first officer and second officer. To fly safely, team members need to engage in the verbal behaviours of enquiry, advocacy and assertion: for example, *enquiring* why one member is taking certain actions, *advocating* alternative options, and *asserting* their views on matters. The accident literature is full of examples when this had not been done.

In a study of a major airline conducted by Harper et al. (1971), captains feigned incapacitation at a predetermined point during final approach in simulator trials which involved landing in poor visibility. They discovered that 25 per cent of the flights 'hit the ground' because, for some reason, the first officers did not take control even when they knew that their plane was well below glide slope. The authority–status dynamic surrounding the role of the captain in a cockpit crew is extremely powerful and has a dramatic effect on overall group performance.

Based on C.R. Harper, G.J. Kidera and J.F. Cullen, 'Study of simulated airplane pilot incapacitation. Phase LL: subtle or partial loss of function', *Aerospace Medicine*, vol. 42, 1971, pp. 946–8.

Interaction with others perceived as lower in status can be threatening because of the potential identification of the person with the group or individual being associated with. Status is abstract and ascribed through the perceptions of others. One's status is therefore always tenuous. It may be withdrawn or downgraded at any time. The reference group, with which one identifies and whose values and behaviour one adopts, plays an important part in establishing and maintaining one's status. To preserve that status, one cannot leave the reference group for a lower-status reference group.

Status in cyberspace

The phenomenon of *status equalization* occurs when a group interacts over the internet. It refers to the tendency for one person's ideas to carry greater weight than their socio-economic position. Wallace explained that status is much more difficult to read over the internet. Since it is difficult to determine an individual's status in an online conversation, you tend to think of the person with whom you are communicating as possessing a status equivalent to your own. This is particularly the case if you find their ideas appealing. For this reason, there is a tendency for perceptions about members' statuses to converge. Whereas in face-to-face situations status tends to be ascribed or linked to acquired characteristics, within the internet context it becomes linked more closely to a person's experience or expertise.

Based on Patricia M. Wallace, *The Psychology of the Internet*, Cambridge University Press, Cambridge, 1999.

Hells Angels' status structure

The Hells Angels were first organized in San Bernadeno, California, in 1948 by Second World War veterans. They received national attention in the movies when Marlon Brando played an angst-ridden gang leader in the 1953 film, *The Wild One*. At the same time as cultivating their rebel image, they became more businesslike. They have 1,000 members worldwide organized into 70 local clubs called 'chapters'. There is a tight management structure, a communications system and paramilitary discipline. Each chapter has its own strict status structure as depicted here.

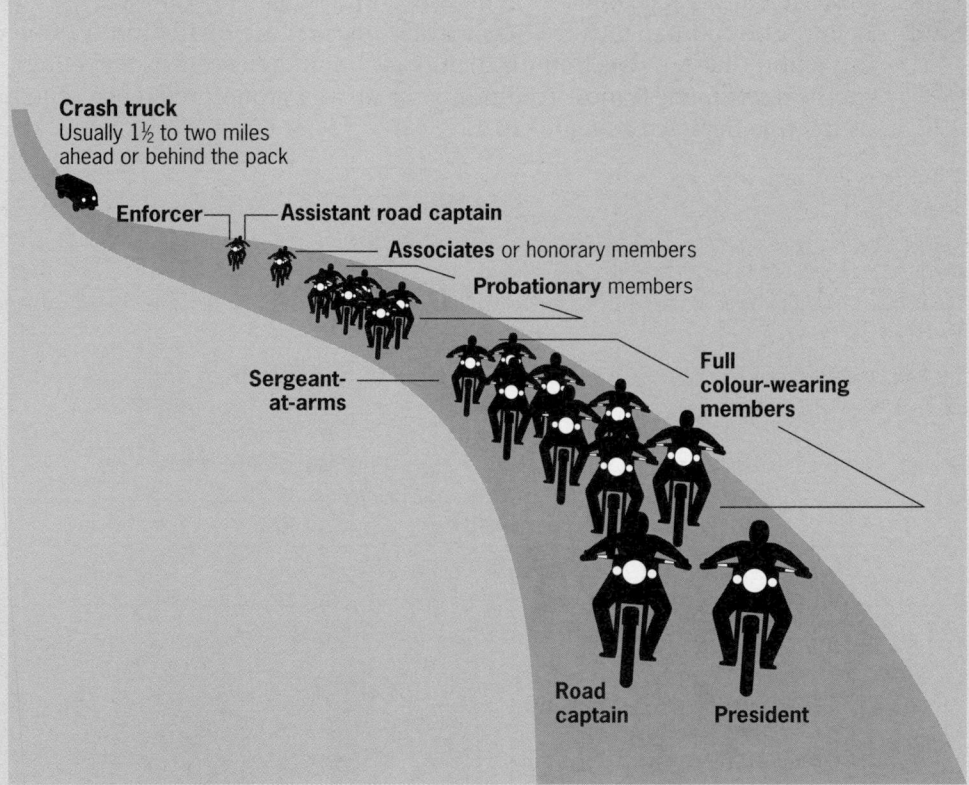

Crash truck
Usually 1½ to two miles ahead or behind the pack

Enforcer

Assistant road captain

Associates or honorary members

Probationary members

Sergeant-at-arms

Full colour-wearing members

Road captain

President

Source: Linda Eckstein for *Fortune*, from 'The Hellish Angels' devilish business', *Fortune*, 30 November 1992, pp. 84–90. © 1992 Time, Inc. All rights reserved.

Liking structure

Sociometry: the study of interpersonal feelings and relationships within groups.

Jacob Levy Moreno
(1889–1974)

Within a group, individual members will like, dislike or be indifferent to other members, in varying degrees. Their combined feelings towards each other represent their group's liking structure. This can be studied using the technique of **sociometry**. The term derives from the Latin *socius* (companion) and the Greek *metron* (measure). Sociometry was devised by Jacob Moreno who coined the term in his book, *Who Shall Survive?* (Moreno, 1953). Moreno and his colleagues originally used the technique in their research in the New York Training School for Girls in the 1930s. They mapped the friendship choices among girls in reformatory cottages.

Sociometry diagrammatically maps the emotional relationships between individual members in a group on the basis of their personal choices of selection and rejection of other group members using a few standard symbols. This network of a group's interpersonal feelings is exposed by the use of sociometric tests. These reveal the spontaneous feelings and choices that individuals in a group have and make towards each other. Moreno asked individuals to complete the test shown below. The spontaneous feelings within a person are divided into three classes – attraction (liking), rejection (disliking) and indifference (neutral feeling). A sociometric assessment is most commonly set up as a group preference schedule, such as the one depicted in figure 10.1.

Below are eight boxes.

■ In the box marked 'Work With – Yes', write the name of two people in your class whom you prefer to work with.

■ In the box marked 'Work With – No', write the name of two people in your class whom you prefer not to work with.

Repeat this with the remaining boxes marked 'Study With', 'Play With' and 'Live With'.

Work With	
Yes	No

Study With	
Yes	No

Play With	
Yes	No

Live With	
Yes	No

Figure 10.1: Sociometric assessment

Sociogram: a chart which shows the liking (social attraction) relationships between individual members of a group.

After analyzing the answers, Moreno calculated how many times an individual had been chosen as a comrade by the other members of the group for the activity in question. This feeling, the sociometric term for which is *tele*, may be one of attraction (positive tele) or repulsion (negative tele). Alternatively, there may merely be indifference. Group members' choices are depicted on a **sociogram**, which reveals the existence of any sub-groupings within the main group.

A sociometric assessment can reveal the 'stars', 'isolates', 'neglectees', 'rejectees', and 'mutual pairs' and 'mutual trios' in a group. These are defined as:

Star	recipient of a large number of choices, sometimes described as 'over-chosen'
Isolate	person who makes no choices at all and is not chosen: that is, has a relationship of mutual indifference with the remainder of the group
Neglectee	person who, although he or she makes choices, receives none at all
Rejectee	person who is not chosen by anyone and who is rejected by one or more persons
Mutual pair or mutual trio	individuals who choose one another

Stop and Criticize

Below is a sociogram. Identify a 'star', an 'isolate', a 'neglectee', a 'rejectee' and a 'mutual pair'.

———▶ Positive choice

----------▶ Rejection

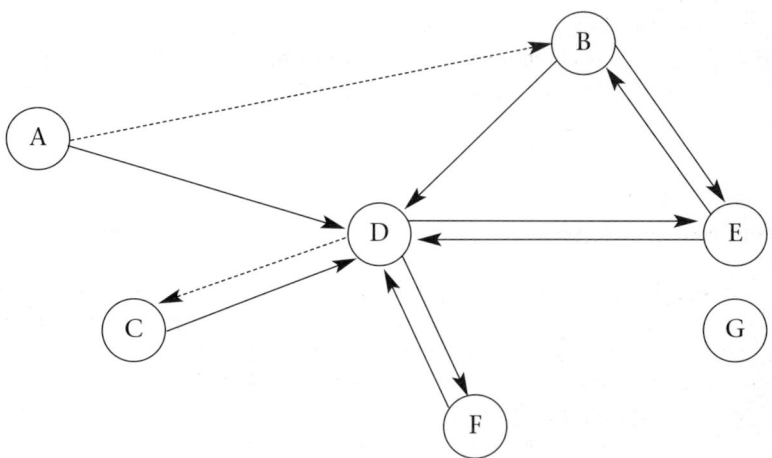

How might a researcher create a sociogram without having individuals complete a sociometric questionnaire? How reliable would such information be? For what purposes might sociograms be used in an organization?

How are sociometric assessments and sociograms used? Originally developed as a research method by sociologists, they were later used in industry (Jacobs, 1945). Sociometry continues to be applied in organizations today under the label *social network analysis*. Sociograms can be used for:

1. *Mapping the informal organization*
   Problems and opportunities in an organization can be located in its informal organization. The company's formal organization structure is depicted in its organizational chart but its informal organization is only revealed through a sociogram.

2. *Selecting group members*
   Sociograms have been used to determine the right mix of work team

members to avoid personality clashes, raise group cohesion and increase group performance. Sociograms have been used to design flight crews (Zeleny, 1947).

3. *Revealing feelings*
   Sociograms can reveal people's feelings towards one another. Sociograms have been used in schools to reveal the existence of unhappy pupil isolates who have not adjusted to the class group, as well as isolate workers who have not adjusted to their work team.

4. *Modifying the group structure*
   Sociograms of productive and unproductive teams can highlight areas where other aspects of group structure require modification (see Cross and Prusak, 2002).

5. *Other*
   Sociograms have also been used in the selection and training of group leaders, to increase co-operation, productivity and morale among employees in a group and to anticipate turnover and conflict problems.

Stop and Criticize

Think of an organization of which you are or have been a member. Identify two individuals with whom you would *not* like to work in this group. List the reasons why you would enter their names under the 'Work With – No' category. Describe your feelings towards them.

Informal group structure

Informal organizations consist of networks of relationships that employees form across functions and divisions. Using a case study approach, David Krackhardt and Jeffrey Hanson (1993) studied how these operated in the banking industry. From a managerial viewpoint, such networks can be positive, cutting through reporting procedures, re-starting stalled initiatives and meeting ambitious deadlines, or negative, sabotaging their goals by blocking communications and fomenting opposition to change. The authors carried out a social network analysis which consisted of a questionnaire that asked employees about who interacted with whom about what. The results obtained were cross-checked to ensure a consensus of the group, and then drawn on to a network map. This activity revealed three types of relationship:

- *advice* networks ('who depends on whom' to solve problems and provide information);
- *trust* networks (in which employees share potential information and back each other in a crisis);
- *communication* networks (in which employees regularly talk to each other on work-related matters).

Such analyses can reveal the influence of the central figures in informal networks – who wields the power and how various coalitions of employees function. For example, one bank's 80 per cent staff turnover problem was not due to difficulties in its formal organization. Instead, the tellers had key informal relationships with others in the trust network, and when these people left the company, so did the tellers.

Krackhardt and Hanson argue that revealing the hidden aspects of the informal organization can both address company problems such as turnover, poor communication and bad decision-making, and also suggest solutions. For example, they analyzed the functioning of a bank's task force team, which was failing to make progress. They found that while its leader held a central position in the advice network (many employees relying on him for technical advice), he had only one trust link with a colleague. Having understood the cause of the problem, senior management wanted to avoid labelling the team a failure or embarrassing a valued employee by dismissing him as team leader. Instead, it re-designed this task force to reflect the inherent strengths of the trust network by adding a person in the trust network to share responsibility for the group leadership role.

In a second example, the analysis of the informal communication structure of a bank branch showed that it had divided itself into two distinct cliques, with the tellers, loan officers and administrative staff distributing themselves between the two. Because of their different working times, the two clique cultures rarely interacted and therefore never clashed. In the end, it was customer complaints which stimulated the branch manager to unify the two groups and their cultures. He did this not by re-vamping the branch's formal structure, but by expanding the informal organization to integrate both groups. He intentionally mixed members of the two cliques on training courses; temporarily changed their work schedules so that members of one group would interact with the other; substituted a member from the other clique where there was a staff absence; and scheduled meetings so that all staff could attend. The level of customer satisfaction rose.

Krackhardt and Hanson recommend that managers should re-vamp their formal organizational structure to allow the informal one to thrive. By letting the formal organization complement the informal one, the latter can be made to help solve problems, improve performance and generally support the achievement of company goals.

Based on David Krackhardt and Jeffrey R. Hanson, 'Informal networks: the company behind the chart', *Harvard Business Review*, vol. 71, no. 4, July–August 1993, pp. 104–11.

Status and communication structure in an orchestra

In their study of two freelance orchestras, Kwiatkowski and Lawrence (1996) reported that status in an orchestra was denoted by geographical location on the concert hall stage. The further forward and closer to the outside one was (and therefore more easily seen), the higher was one's status. Considering the communication structure, they noted that if there was any technical disagreement within a section of the orchestra (for example, brass) or if there was uncertainty about what the conductor wanted, this would be referred to the principal of that section for a decision. If a musician asked the principal and the principal was unsure, he or she would ask the conductor. The researchers observed that if any of the principals had to ask the conductor a question, they would do it in a deferential manner or else make it into a light-hearted joke.

Based on Richard Kwiatkowski and Susannah Lawrence, 'Orchestral metaphors and organizational reality: or "Taylor rides again", Paper presented at the British Psychological Society Conference, Occupational Psychology section, 1996.

Communication structure

To understand the communication structure of a group, it is necessary to know the pattern of positions: that is, the role and status of every member, and the duration and direction of communication from position to position. Each group member depends on information provided by others. Solving a problem, making a decision or reaching agreement all require information exchange between individuals. The members of a group may work closely together, interacting frequently and attending regular meetings. Alternatively, they may be physically dispersed within a building or located in different buildings, and therefore only be able to come together occasionally to attend a meeting. Increasingly, different members of the same group may be located in different countries (globally dispersed groups) and interact through video conferencing. Whatever the situation, there are different ways to determine a group's communication structure.

Communication network analysis

When group members come physically together and participate in a meeting around a table, a **communication network analysis** of the event can be conducted. The observer of the group makes a note of how often each group member speaks, and to whom they direct their comments. The outcome is a creation of a **communigram** which in some ways resembles a sociogram discussed earlier. This details the participation, quantity and direction of the verbal communication between the group's members. Essentially, it answers the question of who spoke to whom and how often (see figure 10.2).

Communication pattern analysis

When group members are physically dispersed around the same building or around different buildings, or are located in different countries, it is still possible to determine the source, frequency and direction of their communication with

Communication network analysis: a technique that uses direct observation to determine the source, direction and quantity of verbal communication between congregated members of a group.

Communigram: a chart that indicates the source, direction and quantity of verbal communication between the congregated members of a group.

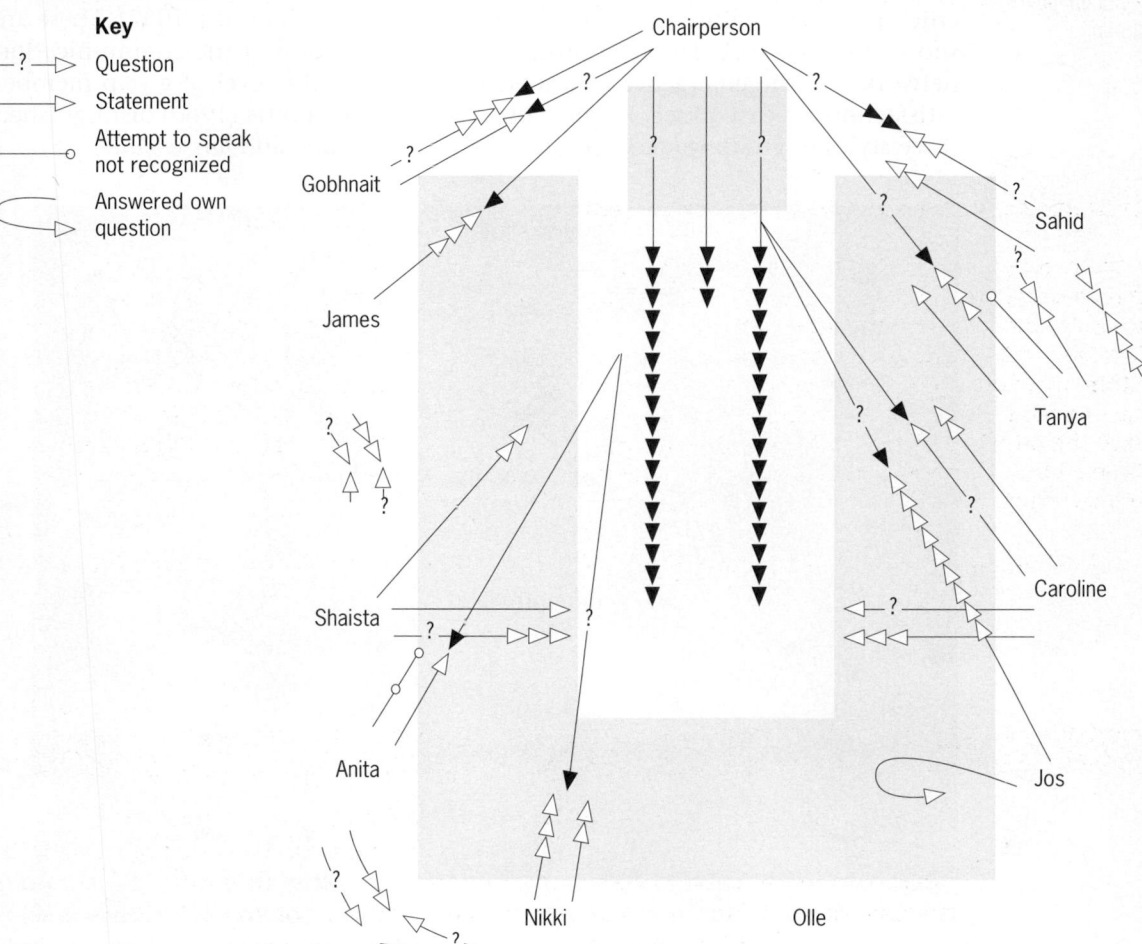

Figure 10.2: Communigram showing participation at a meeting

Communication pattern analysis: a technique that uses analysis of documents, data and voice mail transmission to determine the source, direction and quantity of verbal and written communication between the dispersed members of a group.

Communication pattern chart: indicates the source, direction and quantity of verbal and written communication between the dispersed members of a group.

each other by using **communication pattern analysis**. Instead of observing the interactions between individuals, which is impossible, the researcher would note the initiation and direction of telephone conversations, memos, faxes and emails between the group's members. These are depicted on a **communication pattern chart**.

For example, the information flow between the members of a group can take the form of a chain. A tells B, B tells C and so on. In his classic study, William Foote Whyte (1948) described one such chain pattern in a restaurant in which customers gave their orders to a waitress, who passed it to a runner, who passed it to a pantry worker, before it was finally delivered to the cook. This communication network could produce a distortion in the message. When information arrived through this route, the cook was unable to check it, had no opportunity to negotiate with the customer and hence was unable to discuss any problems.

The aforementioned 'chain' is only one of several communication networks used by groups. To discover the full range, and the effectiveness of each, Shaw (1978) conducted a laboratory experiment to test if certain group communication networks impeded or facilitated the performance of a task by its group. While all the communication networks studied were adequate for the group to do the task, he discovered that some were superior in terms of standing up to disruption, and in encouraging the emergence of leadership. Shaw studied the effects of five group communication networks on task performance and member satisfaction, and these are shown in figure 10.3.

Another study on group communication structure, this time by Alex Bavelas and Dermott Barrett (1951), compared the five communication networks on four criteria, so as to highlight the differences between them (Bavelas, 1967). These are shown in table 10.1. The relationships between the form of the communication network and the emergence of leadership style, and the level of group member satisfaction are easy to see. Ralph White and Ronald Lippitts (1960) distinguished three styles of group leadership – autocratic, democratic and *laissez-faire*.

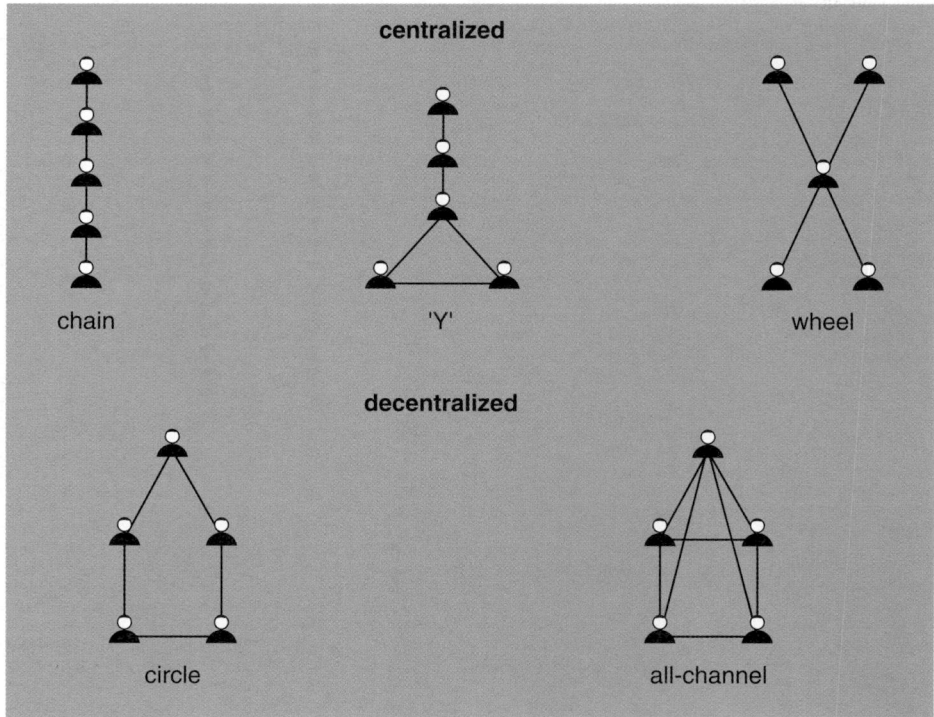

Figure 10.3: Centralized and decentralized communication networks in groups
Reprinted from Marvin E. Shaw, 'Communication networks fourteen years later', in *Group Processes*, edited by Leonard Berkowitz, pp. 351–61. Copyright © 1978, with permission from Elsevier.

Table 10.1: Types of communication network

Criteria	Channel				
	Chain	'Y'	Wheel	Circle	All-channel
Speed	Moderate	Moderate	Fast	Slow	Fast
Accuracy	High	High	High	Low	Moderate
Leader emergence	Moderate	Moderate	High	None	None
Member satisfaction	Moderate	Moderate	Low	High	High

Based on A. Bavelas and D. Barrett, 'An experimental approach to organizational communication', *Personnel*, March, 1951.

Autocratic leadership was accompanied by a wheel communication net, and the democratic style with the all-channel network. The *laissez-faire* leadership style generated a somewhat fragmented communication pattern. Shaw noted that in centralized networks (chain, wheel and 'Y'), group members had to go through a person located at the centre of the network in order to communicate with others. This led to unequal access to information in the group, because the person at the centre had more access to information than did persons at the periphery. In decentralized networks (circle and all-channel), information could flow freely

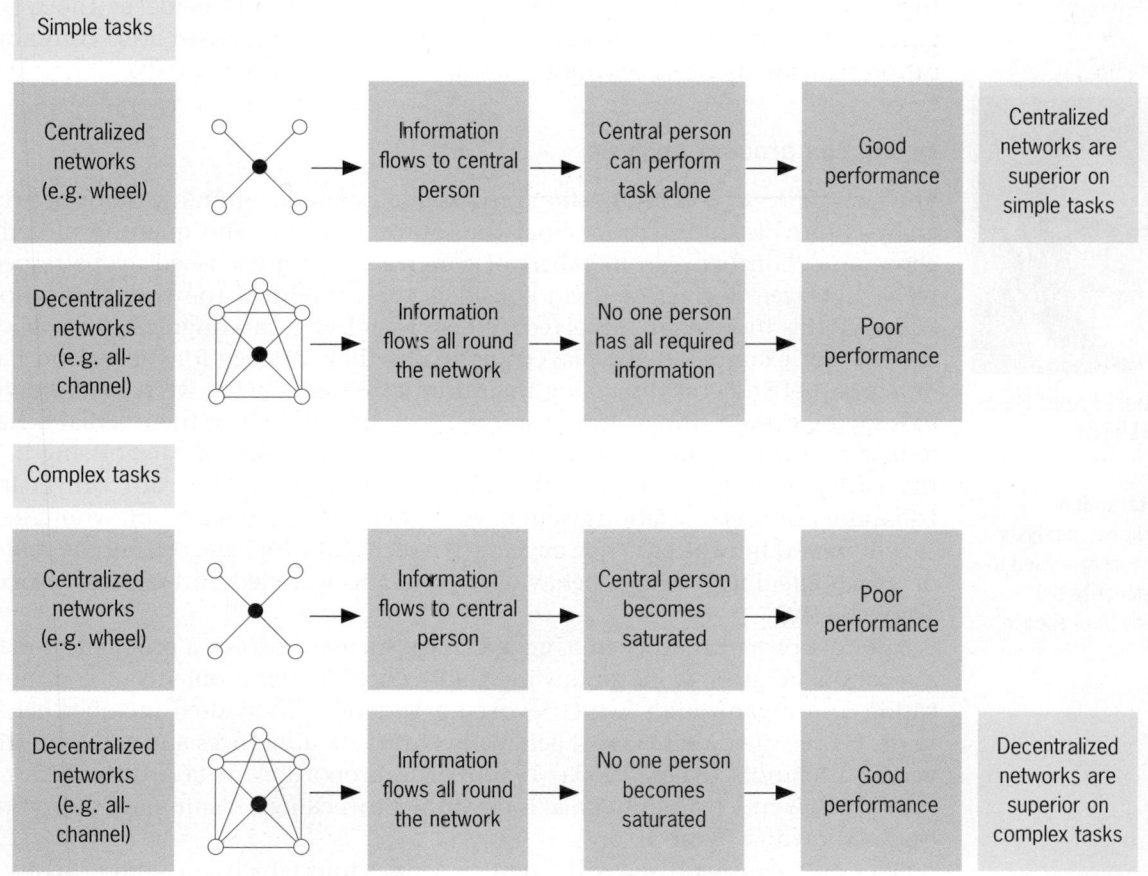

Figure 10.4: Task type and communication network performance
From *Behaviour in Organizations*: 6/E by Greenberg/Baron, © 1997. Reprinted by permission of Pearson Education, Inc., Upper Saddle River, NJ.

between members without having to go through a central person, thus equalizing access to information.

The way in which different communication networks affect group functioning in terms of group performance, structure and member satisfaction continues to be a subject of interest. Jerald Greenberg and Robert Baron (1990) studied the differences in performance between centralized and decentralized networks. The focus of their study was upon the type of task that a group was required to complete. The previous chapter distinguished between additive, conjunctive and disjunctive tasks. Greenberg and Baron distinguished between 'simple' and 'complex' tasks. They concluded that centralized networks are superior on simple tasks (top) and decentralized networks are superior on complex tasks (bottom). These are summarized in figure 10.4. Managers in organizations are interested in ensuring that a group's communication network supports rather than impedes the achievement of its task. Hence, by first identifying the type of network used, and then assessing its effect, they can take steps to match the type of network with the type of group task.

Communication network research conducted in the 1950s by Robert Bales on all-male groups revealed a relationship between group size, seniority of status, and direction and quantity of communication. The most senior status individual ('top man') in groups larger than five members tended to speak more to the group as a whole than to specific individuals. Other members, in contrast, spoke more often to specific individuals, and particularly to the 'top man', rather than to the group as a whole. As group size increased, a larger percentage of the comments came to be addressed to the top man, and a smaller percentage to other members; and the top man increased the percentage of the remarks that he made to the whole group. The researchers concluded that as group size increased, the communication structure became centralized around the leader (Bales, 1953).

Interaction process analysis

Robert Freed Bales
(b. 1916)

Interaction process analysis: a technique used to categorize the content of speech.

The techniques of communication process analysis and communications network analysis provide information about the source, direction and quantity of verbal communication between members of congregated and dispersed teams respectively. However, neither of them considers the content of the communications between the individuals involved. When we observe a congregated group in action – for example, rugby players discussing their strategy for the second half, or a group of students discussing their tutorial system – what we see are individuals saying certain things. If we want to study the content of their verbal behaviour within that group, we need a precise and reliable way of categorizing it. In the late 1940s, Robert Freed Bales and his colleagues at Harvard University's Laboratory of Social Relations went beyond their original research on who-talked-to-whom and how-often. They developed a technique for categorizing the *content* of group members' verbal behaviours (utterances) called **interaction process analysis** (IPA).

Bales discovered that when assigned a task such as to solve a problem or make a recommendation, work groups inevitably encountered problems of communication and organization, which evoked a variety of individual member behaviours. He classified these verbal behaviours into task utterances and socio-emotive verbal utterances (Bales, 1950a, 1950b). The proportion of task utterances can indicate how much an individual is directing proceedings. A summary of his findings is shown in figure 10.5.

Bales distinguished twelve different categories into which one could classify or 'code' each person's verbal statements or utterances. For example, category 1 is 'shows solidarity, raises other's status, gives help, reward'. So, if one group member said, 'That's an excellent idea from Lucy', that would be an example of a

The figure shows the twelve categories that Bales used to classify the verbal behaviours (utterances) of group members whom he observed. He grouped them into four general categories.

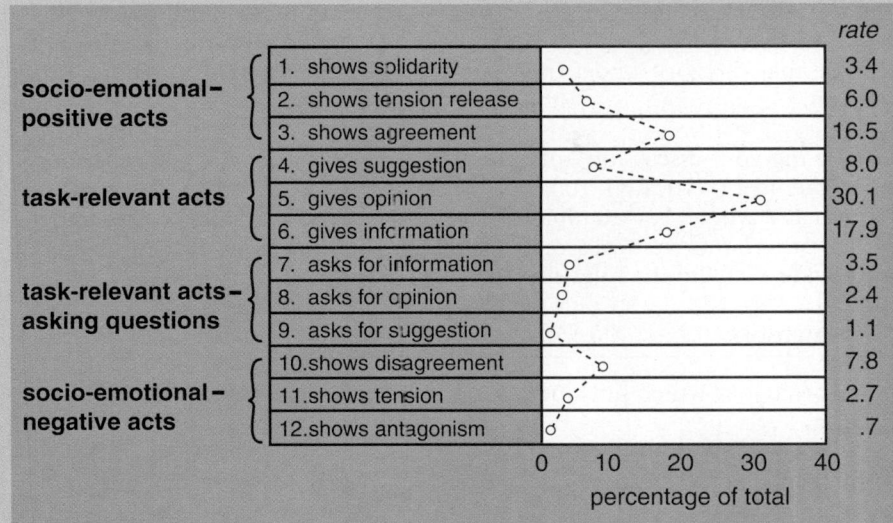

		rate
socio-emotional–positive acts	1. shows solidarity	3.4
	2. shows tension release	6.0
	3. shows agreement	16.5
task-relevant acts	4. gives suggestion	8.0
	5. gives opinion	30.1
	6. gives information	17.9
task-relevant acts– asking questions	7. asks for information	3.5
	8. asks for opinion	2.4
	9. asks for suggestion	1.1
socio-emotional– negative acts	10. shows disagreement	7.8
	11. shows tension	2.7
	12. shows antagonism	.7

percentage of total

Figure 10.5: Bales' categories and summary of psychological events in small groups

The data are based on 71,838 observations of 24 groups in 96 different sessions. The behaviour profile shown here can be regarded as typical of many small groups. Of all the behaviours of these group members, 30.1 per cent are of the giving opinions type, while less that 1 per cent show overt antagonism.

Based on R.F. Bales. 'How people interact in conferences', *Scientific American*, vol. 192, 1955, pp. 31–5.

category 1 utterance. In contrast, category 12 is, 'shows antagonism, deflates other's status, defends or asserts self'. If another member said, 'Jill's report was pathetic! I could do one that was twice as good in half the time', that would be an example of category 12 utterance. Bales felt that with his twelve categories, one could classify most utterances that were likely to be made by individuals in a group when they engaged in verbal interaction. In his original experiments, his researchers, acting as observers, watching groups from behind a two-way mirror.

Stop and Criticize

Becoming a competent verbal interaction 'coder' takes a little time and practice. To develop your skill, videotape a five-minute sequence from any television programme or film that involves four or five people together having a discussion. Rewind the tape to the start of the sequence and use the verbal interaction scoring sheets on pages 348–9 at the end of this chapter to categorize their speech utterances into the appropriate categories. Rewind the tape and repeat the procedure to check your accuracy, or ask a friend to do the same and then compare your results. Then analyze your data by totalling your observations.

After carrying out this exercise, assess the value of this information and of your analysis, to you as an observer of the group and to the group as a whole.

If you were a group *member*, how would you use this information?

If you were a group *consultant* or facilitator, how would you use this information?

Here is a simplified version of Bales' interaction process analysis (IPA) verbal behaviour classification scheme. It consists of six verbal behaviour categories, and each has an explanation alongside. Also provided is a chart for categorizing group members' verbal contributions (pp. 348–9). There is a space for their initials along the top row. Next time you are present at a group discussion, listen to what each individual says. Every time they speak, decide in which verbal category their utterance belongs, and place a tick or dot beside that category, under their name. Continue to do this, building up a record of the whole discussion.

After you have finished observing your discussion, total up your ticks or dots in the columns (horizontally) and for each group member (vertically). Your horizontal score total gives you an indication of the behaviour of the group as a whole. For example, is this a group whose members are competing or co-operating with each other? Your vertical scores contrast the contributions of the individual group members, and can provide a clue to the roles they are playing in the group.

Verbal category	Explanation
Proposing	Any behaviour which puts forward a new suggestion, idea or course of action.
Building	Any behaviour which develops or extends an idea or suggestion made by someone else.
Supporting	Behaviour which declares agreement or support with any individual or idea.
Disagreeing	Any behaviour which states a criticism of another person's statement.
Giving information	Any behaviour which gives facts, ideas or opinions or clarifies these.
Seeking information	Any behaviour which asks for facts, ideas or opinions from others.

Figure 10.6: Analyzing verbal interactions

Bales' IPA is the most refined and exhaustive (empirically usable) method yet developed which can be used to study the content of the verbal communication between individuals in groups. It has been extensively tested, and has achieved an acceptably high level of agreement between different observer-coders. Bales' research, conducted in the 1940s and 1950s, provided the first rounded picture of what happens in face-to-face groups. He used the data gathered with this technique to develop a theory of group functioning. He argued that group behaviour could be explained by showing how groups dealt with certain recurring problems such as orientation, evaluation, control, decision, tension management and integration (Bales, 1953). His theory of group functioning thus pre-dates the Tuckman and Jenson model discussed previously.

Stand back, I'm a social scientist!

To get its researchers from different fields to push new technologies through the research and development (R&D) pipeline, the Science and Technology Center for Environmentally Responsible Solvents and Processes at Chapel Hill in North Carolina, USA, included a social scientist in each of its research teams. The idea was to analyze communication patterns between the team participants, to suggest improvements and to make the teams more effective. The researchers were organized in teams according to the technical application they were pursuing. For example, one team was developing polymers that dissolved in liquid carbon dioxide, thereby not only solving an environmental problem, but also allowing wafers to be coated with much thinner films. Getting this process to work in practice requires a range of skills and techniques. Diane Sonnenwald, the social scientist from the University of North Carolina, mapped out the pattern and level of communication between the researchers in the team. She conducted interviews to discover which colleagues within the team could most usefully collaborate.

The team leader acknowledged that Sonnenwald's input led him to appreciate the abilities of other members of the team, thereby highlighting complementary team skills. It also closed the gap between theorists and experimenters on the team. The two were stereotyped respectively as haughty high priests and pugnacious pragmatists. In fact, it was more a case of one researcher not understanding another's jargon, being afraid to ask stupid-sounding questions or hesitating about giving up vital and hard-won information to a distant colleague. Sonnenwald was able to dismantle these types of barrier between the research team members, leading to greater co-operation between theorists and experimenters. It may be too early to judge how much this analysis of group process has accelerated development of liquid carbon-dioxide technology. However, the funding bodies are responding positively. In a similar way that sports teams have hired psychologists to produce a winning mind set, future technology teams may include a social scientist to help them find the shortest route from the laboratory to the marketplace.

Based on 'Of high priests and pragmatist', *The Economist Technology Quarterly*, 23 June 2001, p. 16.

Role structure

Social role: the set of expectations that others hold of an occupant of a position.

It is a short step from identifying the main class of verbal contributions that an individual makes in their group to identifying their team member role. The occupants of every position in the group are expected to carry out certain functions when the members of the group interact with one another. The expected behaviours associated with a position within the group constitute the social role of the occupant of that position. **Social role** is the concept which relates the individual to the prescriptive dictates of the group. People's behaviour within the organization is structured and patterned in various ways. An understanding of role helps us to see and explain how this happens.

Social role is the set of expectations that others hold of an occupant of a position in an organization structure: for example, shop manager, bishop, head of the production department, and so on. These expectations presume attitudes, relationships and behaviours. A role can be thought of rather like a script which actors are given. The same actor changes their roles, and can act out different parts in front of different audiences. The topic of role within the context of organizational structure will be discussed later. Here, our concern is with the different roles that are played out by various members of a group or team.

Totalling vertically each individual's verbal contributions in figure 10.6 reveals that group members contributed in different ways to the discussion. Bales found that individuals played different roles (role differentiation) within their groups, and that this was a universal feature of face-to-face interaction in groups. As the group deals with its problems, individual members begin to 'specialize' in certain types of behaviour, taking on different 'roles' within the group. Bales also found that as roles become more differentiated, some of them contributed to the progress and welfare of the group while others seemed to add little or nothing to either its happiness or success. The former set of roles come to be more highly regarded than the latter, and are generally referred to as leadership roles. The idea of leadership as a set of behavioural acts was considered by Edwin Fleishman and Ralph Stogdill at about the same period, and will be examined later.

Group member roles

Within a group activity, such as a staff meeting or a tutorial discussion, some people will show a consistent preference for certain behaviours and not for others. The particular behaviour or set of behaviours that a person demonstrates in a group can lead them to be seen to be playing a particular role within the group. Bales showed that individuals adopted specific roles within their groups. Kenneth Benne and Paul Sheats, who distinguished the roles that were played by members

Table 10.2: Benne and Sheats' 27 roles commonly played by members in a group

Group task roles

1.	Initiator-contributor	Recommends new solutions to group problems.
2.	Information seeker	Attempts to obtain necessary facts.
3.	Opinion seeker	Asks for clarification of values related to the group task or to a suggestion made.
4.	Information giver	Offers facts and generalizations.
5.	Opinion giver	Shares own opinions with others.
6.	Elaborator	Spells out suggestions in terms of examples.
7.	Co-ordinator	Clarifies connections between various ideas; pulls them together; links activities of various members.
8.	Orienter	Defines position of group with respect to their goals.
9.	Evaluator-critic	Measures group achievements against standards.
10.	Energizer	Stimulates group into action when interest sags.
11.	Procedural technician	Does routine tasks for the group.
12.	Recorder	Writes down suggestions.

Group building and maintenance roles

13.	Encourager	Praises and encourages others.
14.	Harmonizer	Mediates in group conflicts.
15.	Compromiser	Within a conflict situation, offers compromise by yielding status, admitting error.
16.	Gatekeeper and expediter	Keeps communication channel open between members and suggests ways to help group operate more smoothly.
17.	Standard setter	Expresses standards for the group to strive for, evaluates process using these.
18.	Group observer and commentator	Keeps records of group process, allowing group to evaluate its own procedures.
19.	Follower	Goes along with the movement of the group passively, accepting the ideas of others and serving as their audience.

Individual roles

20.	Aggressor	Jokes aggressively, attacks group's problem.
21.	Blocker	Acts stubbornly and resists group.
22.	Recognition-seeker	Tries to call attention to him/herself by boasting, etc.
23.	Self-confessor	Uses audience to express personal feelings, insights or ideology.
24.	Playboy	Displays lack of involvement through cynicism, nonchalance.
25.	Dominator	Asserts authority or superiority by manipulating group or certain members of it.
26.	Help seeker	Seeks sympathy response by expressing insecurity, confusion or self-deprecation.
27.	Special interest pleader	Cloaks own prejudices or biases in stereotype that best fits their need.

Based on Kenneth Benne and Paul Sheats, 'Functional roles of group members', *Journal of Social Issues*, vol. 4, 1948, pp. 41–9. Reprinted by permission of Blackwell Publishing Ltd.

of a group, developed Bales' work. They listed a total of 27 different group roles which are shown in table 10.2.

Looking at that table, one sees that Benne and Sheats grouped their 27 roles under three main headings. The first of these was *group task roles*, which are principally directed towards achieving the group's task. Roles under the second heading, *group maintenance and building roles*, are concerned primarily with establishing and sustaining good relations between individual members so as to ensure the group as a whole can work together. Both of these two categories of roles help the group to achieve its objective. In contrast, the third category, *individual roles*, impedes the group's efforts to achieve its aims. This distinction between behaviour that is oriented towards achieving the task and behaviour that is focused upon individuals was originally made in the 1940s and 1950s. It has become the foundation for many subsequent teamwork theories and training techniques, and has also laid the foundation for many theories of leadership.

Following Benne and Sheats' list of 27 roles, many writers offered their own lists of team roles or team-player roles, which vary in number from four to fifteen (Woodcock, 1989; Margerison and McCann, 1990; Parker, 1990; Davis et al., 1992; Spencer and Pruss, 1992). All proponents of the team role concept claim to have observed the behaviours typical of that role being manifested in a variety of teams in different organizations.

Team role: an individual's tendency to behave in particularly preferred ways which contribute to and interrelate with other members within a team.

Belbin's team role theory

R. Meredith Belbin
(b. 1926)

A very popular and widely used framework for understanding roles within a group or team was developed by Meredith Belbin and his colleagues in the late 1970s (Belbin, 1981, 1993a, 1996). It was derived from observations that he conducted of general managers on training courses at the Administrative Staff College, Henley. These managers completed a number of personality assessments (for example, 16PF personality inventory) before participating in a team simulation exercise. Belbin observed their behaviour during the exercise using Bales' IPA. From the information obtained, he produced a self-report questionnaire known as the Belbin Team Role Self-Perception Inventory (team role questionnaire) and distinguished nine (originally eight), team roles. Each **team role** is listed and defined in figure 10.7.

Source: © copyright United Feature Syndicate, Inc. Reproduced with permission.

Belbin argued that:

1. Within an organization people are generally appointed to a functional role on the basis of their ability or experience: for example, marketing. They are rarely selected for personal characteristics that would fit them to perform additional tasks within a team. In an ideal world, a person's functional role and their team would coincide.

2. The personal characteristics of an individual fit them for some roles within a team, while limiting the likelihood that they will be successful in other roles. For Belbin, therefore, team roles are *individual preferences* based on personality, and not the *expectations of others*, as discussed earlier in this chapter with respect to social role.

roles and descriptions – team role contribution	allowable weaknesses
 **Plant** Creative, imaginative, unorthodox. Solves difficult problems.	Ignores details. Too preoccupied to communicate effectively.
 **Resource investigator** Extrovert, enthusiastic, communicative. Explores opportunities. Develops contacts.	Over-optimistic. Loses interest once initial enthusiasm has passed.
 **Co-ordinator** Mature, confident, a good chairperson. Clarifies goals, promotes decision making, delegates well.	Can be seen as manipulative. Delegates personal work.
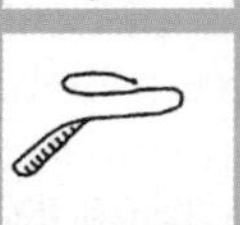 **Shaper** Challenging, dynamic, thrives on pressure. Has the drive and courage to overcome obstacles.	Can provoke others. Hurts people's feelings.
 **Monitor–evaluator** Sober, strategic and discerning. Sees all options. Judges accurately.	Lacks drive and ability to inspire others. Overly critical.
 **Teamworker** Co-operative, mild, perceptive and diplomatic. Listens, builds, averts friction, calms the waters.	Indecisive in crunch situations. Can be easily influenced.
 **Implementer** Disciplined, reliable, conservative and efficient. Turns ideas into practical actions.	Somewhat inflexible. Slow to respond to new possibilities.
 **Completer** Painstaking, conscientious, anxious. Searches out errors and omissions. Delivers on time.	Inclined to worry unduly. Reluctant to delegate. Can be a nit-picker.
 **Specialist** Single-minded, self-starting, dedicated. Provides knowledge and skills in rare supply.	Contributes on only a narrow front. Dwells on technicalities. Overlooks the 'big picture'.

Strength of contribution in any one of the roles is commonly associated with particular weaknesses. These are called allowable weaknesses. Executives are seldom strong in all nine team roles.

Figure 10.7: Belbin's nine team roles
From R. Meredith Belbin, *The Coming Shape of Organization*, Butterworth-Heinemann, London, 1996, p. 122. Reprinted by permission of Belbin Associates.

3. Individuals tend to adopt one or two team roles fairly consistently.

4. The roles that individuals are naturally inclined towards can be predicted through personality assessments and the team role questionnaire.

5. In an ideal ('dream') team, all the necessary roles are represented, and the preferred roles of members complement each other, thereby avoiding 'gaps'. This does not mean that every team has to consist of nine people. A single member can 'double up' and play several roles, thereby enabling the overall size of the team to be reduced.

6. The assessment, selection, placement and guidance of individual employees by management is the way to improve team effectiveness. Once management knows employees' team role preferences, it can use them to compose teams in which all the required role preferences are represented.

Stop and Criticize

Many TV serials about the police, hospitals, people sharing a flat, for example, depict individuals operating as part of a group or team. Many children's novels also recount the adventures of a gang: for example, *The Famous Five*. Select a TV or book series and identify which character is most closely depicted as playing which of Belbin's team roles?

How easy or difficult was it for you to determine their team role preferences through observing or reading about their behaviour?

If you needed each of your characters to complete a Belbin team role questionnaire, to what extent could you trust the scores that you obtained from them? Why?

Critique of team role theory

Because of its widespread popularity and use, Belbin's theory has been extensively researched and continues to receive a great deal of critical assessment (Belbin, 1993b; Furnham et al., 1993a, 1993b; Dulewicz, 1995; Fisher and Macrosson, 1995; Broucek and Randell 1996; Fisher et al., 1996, 1997, 1998, 2000; Hayes, 1997; Manning, 1997; Senior, 1997; Butcher and Bailey, 2000). The main criticisms of the theory are summarized below. Writers variously claim that:

■ There is little empirical evidence to support his theory and it is difficult to devise objective measures of team success that can be objectively related to team composition. It is difficult to say that a given team succeeded because it possessed all nine roles or failed because it lacked some of them.

■ The questionnaire is based on respondents' self-reporting. Self-perceptions are a poor basis upon which to select team members. A more objective measure might be obtained through the use of peer ratings and an established personality assessment questionnaire.

■ The questions are vague and inconsistent, and potentially open to creating misunderstandings. The more experience respondents have of working in diverse teams, the more unreliable the results are likely to be.

■ The team role profiles derived from forced-choice personality and adjective checklists do not allow for a sufficiently detailed exploration of role-related issues. There is a difference between assessing an individual's *potential* to play various team roles, and the *actuality*, which is influenced by their degree of autonomy in, and commitment to, those roles.

■ How individuals see their team roles is influenced as much by the roles they habitually play, especially in teams, and what is expected of them in such roles. Thus the questionnaire scores reflect not only an individual's personality traits, but also their social learning of roles.

■ The theory takes an excessively psychological perspective on role, neglecting the sociological dimension of the social position they habitually adopt, and on what is expected of them in such positions by others.

■ The questions in the Belbin self-completion questionnaire describe vague situations. Some of them do not mention teams at all. Individuals behave differently in different circumstances and in different groups – for example, project team at work, in the family at home – so specification of team context of behaviour is essential.

■ The theory does not sufficiently take into account differences in the type of task that the team is being asked to perform. Additive, conjunctive and disjunctive tasks may require different combinations of team roles to achieve success.

■ The theory underplays the impact of wider, environmental factors. For example, team performance may be impeded by limited company resources.

■ Performance is affected by a variety of different factors such as strategy and leadership, structure and management style and interpersonal skills. Focusing exclusively on team composition leads to ignoring these other critical factors.

■ The concepts of team role and personality have become intertwined, being treated as interchangeable rather than as separate but interrelated. Team roles and individual personality differences have been insufficiently related.

Butcher and Bailey (2000) questioned the idea that a 'dream team' is one in which all members were fully committed to the team's goals; where they were all present when decisions were taken and where all members worked closely together. They felt that this was both impractical and undesirable. Managers who worked on several projects did not have time to develop close relationships, could not give full commitment to a team, and were not able to be present at all its meetings. The authors recommended instead that the task allotted to a team should indicate the required performance criteria, and it should be explained to members how they are to work together. Butcher and Bailey concluded that organizations could benefit by understanding how teams operated in real life, rather than how they ought to work, and they rejected the idea that a team should conform to some ideal, regardless of the organizational circumstances.

Stop and Criticize

You and your fellow team members have completed the Belbin Team Role Self-Perception Inventory and been supplied with the results and analysis. You now know your individual role preferences, and your team knows which roles are overrepresented and underrepresented within it.

How do you exploit the information about yourself?

Can the team compensate by asking its members to switch to their second or third preferences. What might be the issues involved?

Roles within social networks

Social networks (the 'informal organization') are generally considered to be unobservable and ungovernable by most corporations, and are consequentially treated as an 'invisible enemy'. In consequence, managers frequently try to work around or ignore them. Even where the network's existence is acknowledged and valued, managers tend to rely on intuition to nurture this social capital, but commonly misunderstand the links between their members. Cross and Prusak (2002), who conducted a study into the social networks that existed within 50 large organizations, argue that it is possible for managers to develop informal networks systematically in order to enhance their effectiveness. The first step is for them to identify and map the many different informal networks of people within a company, which can be done using a graphical tool called *social network analysis* described by Krackhardt and Hanson (1993). The next step is for the managers to focus their attention on just a few role-players in the network, whose performance is critical to the entire organization. Their research revealed four such key roles:

- *Central connectors* link most of the people within an informal network to one another. Despite not being formal leaders, they know who possesses the critical information or expertise required to get the work done.

- *Boundary spanners* connect the informal organization with other parts of the company or with similar networks in other organizations. They consult and advise individuals from many different company departments, regardless of their own functional affiliations.

- *Information brokers* keep different sub-groups in an informal network together. Failure to communicate across sub-groups would lead to their splintering into smaller, less effective segments.

- *Peripheral specialists* are those members within an informal network to whom anyone can turn for specialized expertise.

To transform an ineffective informal network into a productive one, Cross and Prusak recommend focusing on these key individuals, and determining whether they themselves are performing their roles effectively or being allowed to. For example, are the central connectors hoarding information? Are boundary spanners talking to the right people outside the group? Do the peripheral specialists need to be drawn more closely into the network? The authors recommend making social networks more effective and aligning them with organizational goals.

Based on Rob Cross and Laurence Prusak, 'The people who make organizations go – or stop', *Harvard Business Review*, vol. 80, no. 6, June 2002, pp. 104–12.

Leadership structure

There are many jobs to be done in a group if it is to be both productive and satisfying for its members. The emergence of a leader within any group is a function of its structure. Usually, a group makes a leader of the person who has some special capacity for coping with the group's particular problems. They may possess physical strength, shrewdness or some other relevant attribute. The leader and the members all play roles in the group. Through them, a group atmosphere is created which enables communication, influence and decision-making to occur. In much of the management literature, leadership is considered exclusively as a management prerogative. Authors write about 'management style' rather than 'leadership style'. This material will be dealt with in a later chapter.

Group atmosphere and leadership style

Kurt Lewin
(1890–1947)

Ronald O. Lippitt
(1914–86)

Task leaders in groups do not all perform their roles in exactly the same way. They use different approaches which have different effects on group members' performance and satisfaction. One of the most famous leadership studies was carried out by Kurt Lewin, Ralph White and Ronald Lippitt. Beginning in 1938, a series of studies designed to investigate group functioning under experimentally induced group atmospheres or social climates was carried out under the general direction of Lewin, and continued throughout the 1950s. One major study in the series was conducted at the Iowa Child Welfare Research Station by White and Lippitt.

It involved four groups of ten-year-old boys operating in a natural setting. Each group was a genuine hobby club that met after school and comprised five members. Each group's members had been matched on characteristics such as age, personality, IQ, physical and socio-economic status, to be as similar as possible. Four adult leaders were trained to proficiency in the three leadership styles (see below), and shifted from club to club every six weeks. The clubs met in the same place and engaged in similar activities (arts-and-crafts, primarily the making of masks) with similar materials. The characteristics of each leadership style are summarized below.

Authoritarian leadership: The primary focus was upon achievement. The leader gave orders and praised or criticized the boys without giving reasons. He behaved in a distant and impersonal way, discouraging communication between the boys themselves.

Democratic leadership: The primary focus was on the boys' choices. When the leader made comments, he explained them. He used discussions to help the boys plan their projects, allowed them to choose their own work mates and permitted them to communicate freely with each other. He also participated in the group activities himself.

Laissez-faire leadership: The primary emphasis was minimal involvement. The leader left the boys to themselves; only gave advice and help when directly asked; and provided no praise, blame or any other comments.

The researchers found that the autocratic leadership style led to high productivity, but only in the presence of the leader. It also created an aggressive but dependent atmosphere among the boys. The democratic leadership style led to relatively high productivity, to the boys liking of their leaders most, to the creation of a friendly atmosphere and to the boys proceeding with their work, irrespective of the presence or absence of the leader. The laissez-faire leadership style led to low productivity which only increased when the leader was present. It created a friendly but play-oriented atmosphere.

Based on Ralph White and Ronald Lippitt, *Autocracy and Democracy*, Harper & Row, New York, 1960.

Group leadership:
the performance of those acts which help the group achieve its objectives.

It has been found that the type of leadership exercised affects group performance and member satisfaction. Activities are performed and actions are taken by the leader. There has been an increasing interest in **group leadership** as opposed to the individual leadership. One can distinguish between a leader and acts of leadership. If we accept Raymond Cattell's (1951) view that the leader is any group member who is capable of modifying the properties of the group by their presence, then we can acknowledge that any member of the group can perform acts of leadership, and not just a single, designated individual. The group leadership approach considers the characteristics of small groups, seeking to understand the organizational context in which they exist and the objectives that they seek to achieve. It therefore seems more useful to view leadership as a set of behaviours that change their nature depending on circumstances, and which switch or rotate between group members as circumstances change, rather than a static status associated with a single individual.

The relationship between the group's leader, at a given point in time, and the followers may be thought of as one of social exchange. The leader provides rewards for the group by helping its members to achieve their own and the group's goals. They in turn reward the leader by giving the individual heightened status and increased influence. However, members can rescind that influence at any time if they feel that the leader is no longer worthy of their respect. Viewed as a social exchange process, the leader has power in terms of their ability to influence the behaviour of those around them. Nevertheless, it is the group members who give the leader the power to influence them.

One group, two leaders

When people think of leadership, they usually imagine a single person. Robert Bales and Philip Slater used a laboratory research design with which to study the patterns of leadership that emerged in small, unstructured groups. The subjects of the study were fourteen separate groups of Harvard University undergraduates, each consisting of between three and six men. They were selected so that they were strangers to each other, and were paid to spend one hour a day solving an administrative case study problem that they were supplied with. Their interactions were recorded and analyzed in terms of Bales' twelve categories.

Source: Robert F. Bales.

The researchers found that at the end of the first day, the group member whom the others rated as having the best ideas – that is, who was most helpful in moving the group towards a solution – was also rated as the most liked. However, after the first day, this person's equally high rating for best ideas *and* most liked dropped sharply. From then on, two leaders seemed to emerge. One was the *task leader* who specialized in making suggestions, giving information, expressing opinions and generally contributing most to helping the group achieve its objective. The second to emerge was the *socio-emotional leader* who helped other group members to state their ideas, expressed positive feelings towards them, made jokes and released tensions in the group. The socio-emotional leader generally acted to maintain the group as a functioning entity.

Bales and Slater thus discovered that leadership in a group split into two. Although there was some rivalry, the two group leaders, *task* and *socio-emotional*, typically co-operated and worked together well. Beyond the laboratory situation, such division of leadership can be seen in families when one parent assumes task leadership while the other deals with socio-emotive issues. The researchers discovered that split leadership only occurred after the task leader had been identified and agreed upon. They argued that it was only after the group knew who would lead it to achieve its external goals that it could afford the luxury of a socio-emotional leader. Thus, the researchers did not view leadership as a single role, but as applying to several roles within the group. A well-organized group, in which the leadership functions were being satisfactorily performed, would have both a task leader and a socio-emotional leader.

Based on Robert F. Bales and Philip E. Slater, 'Role differentiation in small group decision-making groups', in T. Parsons and R.F. Bales (eds), *Family, Socialization and Interaction*, Routledge, London, 1956, pp. 259–306.

Contemporary team structure

The original theoretical developments in the area of group structure and process occurred between the 1930s and 1950s. Many were conducted in non-organizational contexts, and frequently involved children and university students. Their findings were then applied to companies. The more recent developments have been practical rather than theoretical. They have been accompanied by a linguistic change within the research and management literature where the predominant term is now 'team' rather than 'group'. While western companies may have been reluctant formally to structure their organizations around groups, they have been prepared to train their managerial and technical staff to work more effectively in teams. Thus, team-building or team development activities have established themselves as a major element in both management training and organizational development (OD) activities.

Recap

1. *List the six dimensions of group structure.*

   - The six main dimensions along which the members of a group differ are power, status, liking, communication, role and leadership. A person may be placed high on one dimension and simultaneously low on another.

   - The group's structure acts to increase the predictability of behaviour between the group's members.

2. *Identify the sources of power within the group.*

   - There are six bases or types of power – reward, coercive, referent, legitimate, expert and informational power.

3. *Distinguish between two common uses of the concept of status.*

   - The status structure of a group is determined by how much status an individual member possesses. There is formal status and social status.

4. *Understand how emotional relationships within a group can be represented symbolically.*

   - The liking (emotional) structure of a group is revealed through the use of sociometry, a technique developed by Jacob Moreno.

5. *Distinguish between communication network analysis, a communication pattern analysis and IPA analysis*

   - Communication network analysis of a group maps the direction and quantity of verbal communication in a group. It is depicted on a communigram.

   - Communication pattern analysis analyzes documents, data and voice mail transmission to determine the source, direction and quantity of both verbal and written communication between the dispersed members of a group. It is depicted as a 'chain', a 'Y', a 'wheel', a 'circle' or 'all-channel').

   - Interactional process analysis (IPA) classifies the content of verbal communications between group members. It was developed by Robert Bales.

6. *Distinguish between task, socio-emotional and individual classes of roles within a group.*

   - The role structure of a group can differentiate those members who perform task-focused roles, relations-oriented roles and individual roles. This distinction was made by Benne and Sheats.

7. *Distinguish Belbin's team roles.*

   - Meredith Belbin's team role theory distinguishes the roles played by the members of a team. They are Plant, Resource investigator, Coordinator, Shaper, Monitor, Teamworker, Implementer, Completer and Specialist.

8. *Give examples of three leadership styles identified by White and Lippitt.*

   - White and Lippitt distinguished three leadership styles which they labelled authoritarian, democratic and laissez-faire.

9. *Distinguish between a task and a socio-emotional group leader.*

   - Bales and Slater suggested that groups often have a task leader and a socio-emotional leader. The first drives the group towards task achievement, the second maintains the group as a co-operative working unit.

Revision

1. Group members may possess as much power as the group leader. Give examples of the kind of power possessed and suggest how it can help or hinder group performance.

2. Select any two techniques for measuring an aspect of a group's structure (for example, power, communication, liking, roles and leadership). List and define three criteria on which they can be compared. Then contrast your two chosen techniques using your three criteria.

3. Describe situations in which a team role analysis and a sociogram would be relevant to improve group functioning. How would you apply these two techniques? How would you use the results?

4. What are the strengths and weaknesses of Belbin's team role theory as a guide for the manager wishing to construct a team that will be effective?

5. What are some of the problems that a new leader of a group faces? How can they be overcome?

Springboard

Belbin, R.M., 1981, *Management Teams: Why They Succeed or Fail*, Heinemann, London.

This is the original work on team role theory which explains each role in greater depth.

Brotherton, C., 1999, *Social Psychology and Management*, Open University Press, Buckingham.

Written from a social psychological perspective, this text considers how the discipline can benefit from considering the contexts in which management is exercised.

Brown, R., 2000, *Group Processes*, Blackwell, Oxford.

Provides a recent review and assessment of the theory and research on group processes.

Furnham, A., Steele, H. and Pendleton, D., 1993, 'A psychometric assessment of Belbin's team role self-perception inventory', *Journal of Occupational and Organizational Psychology*, vol. 66, no. 3, pp. 245–57.

Senior, B., 1997, 'Team roles and team performance: is there "really" a link?', *Journal of Occupational and Organizational Psychology*, vol. 70, no. 3, September, pp. 241–58.

Two empirical studies critically evaluating Belbin's team role theory.

Hayes, N., 1997, *Successful Team Management*, Thompson Business Press, London.

A book which blends past and present academic research and theory on groups and teams, and offers practical recommendations for improving team performance.

Parkinson, M., 1999, *Using Psychology in Business*, Gower, Aldershot.

Taking a practical approach, this book considers what psychology has to offer business. Draws upon the theories and techniques that have been applied in a variety of organizational contexts.

Turniansky, B. and Hare, A.P., 1998, *Individuals and Groups in Organizations*, Sage Publications, London.

Offers a range of approaches for looking at the way in which people interact in organizational life. Considers the individual in the group, the group in the organization and the organization in the environment.

Wheelan, S.A., 1999, *Creating Effective Work Teams*, Sage Publications, London.

Using a version of the Tuckman and Jensen framework, the author offers a range of strategies for building and supporting well-managed, high-performing teams. The book is more of a practical guide than a theoretical discourse.

Home viewing

Aliens (1986, directed by James Cameron) is a science fiction thriller set in the distant future on the planet LV–426. It is the sequel to the film *Alien*, in which the crew of the spaceship *Nostromo* is plagued by a creature which is described as a 'pure killing machine'. The lone survivor of this encounter, Ellen Ripley (Sigourney Weaver), spends 57 years in suspended animation drifting through space. After returning to earth, she reluctantly agrees to return to LV–426 because contact has been lost with the colonists who settled there.

The first part of the film begins with Ripley's return to earth and ends with the space marines' landing-craft crashing on to the planet's surface, leaving the investigation party marooned on the plant. The characters featured in this segment include Lieutenant Gorman, the senior officer of the space marines, Sergeant Apone and Corporal Hicks. Other individuals identified by name are Vasquez and Hudson. In addition to these military personnel, there is Burke, who represents the Weyland–Yutani Corporation (motto: 'Building Better Worlds'). This company built and owns the facilities on planet LV–426 and employs Ripley.

As you watch this first sequence of the film, use French and Raven's five power-base classification to decide which of the seven aforementioned characters possesses which types of power within the group. Also assess who gains and who loses what type of power. How does this happen? What does this tell us about the power in an organization in general and the power structure of a group in particular?

OB in literature

William Golding, *Lord of the Flies*, Faber & Faber, London, 1954.

In this novel (also a film), a party of schoolboys are marooned following an aeroplane crash. They form a society-in-microcosm. What group norms and sanctions develop? What aspects of group structure, group power and conflict are illustrated?

J.G. Ballard, *Cocaine Nights*, Flamingo/HarperCollins, London, 1996.

Which social psychological theory of group cohesion is illustrated by the events and characters in this novel? Does your personal experience confirm this?

Chapter exercises

1: Tutorial pie

Objectives
1. To distinguish between different dimensions of group structure.
2. To analyze the structure of one group on a given dimension.

Background
Group structure can be a somewhat abstract concept, yet each person who is a member of a group automatically and unconsciously rates the other members on the basis of some criteria. Having done so, they then interact with them accordingly. This rating or ranking of group members is at the heart of the concept of group structure. However, there is a misconception that a group can only have one structure. In reality, there are a number of different but simultaneous ranking systems operating within any group, and a person high on one ranking scale may be low on another.

Briefing
Imagine that the circle below is a pie-chart which represents the members of your tutorial or syndicate group. This group is scheduled to meet several times a semester or term, and you will have already participated in some of the group's discussions.

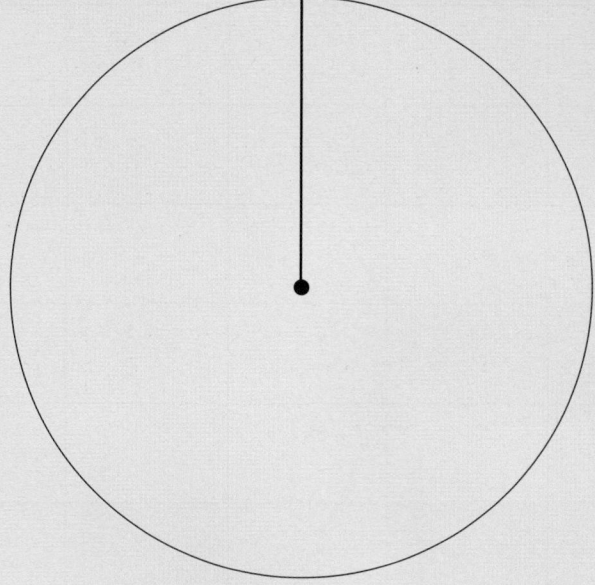

Divide the pie into slices – one for each of the members of your tutorial group. Be sure to include a slice for yourself and for the group's tutor. The size of each slice should represent each person's contribution to the class. Label each slice by inserting the individual's name or initials. Having done this, form a pair with the person sitting next to you. Take turns to explain the division of your pie-chart to them. Your explanation should focus on the following four questions:

■ What criteria did you use to decide on the size of each person's 'contribution slice' to the tutorial class?

■ Describe the way in which you divided up the pie.

■ Which three people did you give the largest slices to?

■ How did you evaluate yourself in relation to the others in your tutorial group?

Verbal Interaction Scoring Sheet

Record sheet 1

	Names (initials)					Totals
Verbal category						
Proposing						
Supporting						
Disagreeing						
Giving information						
Seeking information						
Totals						

Record sheet 2

	Names (initials)					Totals
Verbal category						
Proposing						
Building						
Supporting						
Disagreeing						
Giving information						
Seeking information						
Totals						

Record sheet 3

Category	**1**	**2**
Proposing		
Building	—	
Supporting		
Disagreeing		
Giving information		
Seeking information		
Totals		

2a: Belbin's team role exercise

Objectives

1. To introduce Belbin's team role theory.
2. To identify your preferred team roles.

Briefing

Individually: below is a brief description of each of Belbin's nine team roles. Read them all through first and decide which two or three roles you tend to regularly play when you are a member of a group or team. Next, rank these in order.

Team roll	Description	Rank
Plant	Creative, imaginative, unorthodox. They come up with novel solutions, solve difficult problems. Normally, they prefer to work alone. They are not social, and respond strongly to praise and criticism.	
Resource-investigator	Extrovert, enthusiastic, communicative. Explores opportunities, develops contacts, a good networker. An outgoing manner helps them negotiate, and elicits a warm response from others. They get bored easily however.	
Co-ordinator	Mature, confident, a good chairperson. Clarifies goals, promotes decision-making, delegates well. Can recognize individual members' abilities, and brings them in. Keeps the group moving, on track, towards its objective.	
Shaper	Challenging, dynamic, thrives on pressure. Being highly motivated, they display drive and the need to achieve. Can appear to others as aggressive or pushy, as they overcome obstacles to achieve the team goal.	
Monitor-evaluator	Sober, strategic and rarely excessively enthusiastic. Sees the options, and their pros and cons, more clearly than others. Has good critical abilities, and judges slowly but accurately. They prefer analysing problems and evaluations proposals.	
Teamworker	Mild, co-operative, perceptive and diplomatic. They provide support for the team. Listening and building on others' contributions, they avoid conflict, calm the waters, and allow others to contribute to the task.	

Implementer	Disciplined, reliable, conservative and efficient. Possessing a practical orientation, they turn the team's ideas into practical actions. Enjoys routine and dealing with problems systematically.	
Completer	Painstaking, conscientious, anxious. They follow-through and finish-off projects. They give tremendous attention to detail, rely on themselves, without requiring outsiders to meet their high standards and deliver on time.	
Specialist	Single-minded, self-starting and dedicated. Possesses specific technical skills required by the team to achieve its goal. Their primary focus is meeting professional standards demanded by their work. Less interested in the team's work and its members.	

Divide into groups of 4–5.

1. Remind yourself of each of Belbin's nine team roles.

2. Compare and contrast your own team role rankings with those of the other members of your group.

3. Reflect on your past experiences of participation in teams. Give specific examples of times when you played these roles.

4. Decide to what extent your preferred team roles are a reflection of your personality.

5. Identify which roles in this team are preferred and which are avoided, rejected or are missing? If this was a real management or project team, what could be done to cover the avoided or rejected roles?

6. Decide whether certain roles are more important in particular phases of a team's operation? For example, which two team roles are likely to be crucial in the getting-started phase of a team's work; the generating-ideas phase; the developing-the-ideas phase; and the implementing-the-decision phase?

2b: Structural problems in groups and teams

Objectives
1. To analyze the problems of a functioning real group or team.
2. To suggest recommendations to improve its performance.

Background
Many students are a member of some formal group or team. It may be a sports team, a social club, a choir, or a cross-functional or project team. Some teams work well, but the majority either perform poorly, or else can only manage a satisfactory performance and could do a lot better. This exercise invites students to analyze a group/team of which they have detailed knowledge, in terms of its structural features, with a view to identifying its deficiencies and suggesting ways in which they can be rectified.

Briefing
1. Form into groups of 4–5.

2. Go round, with each member in turn stating which formal groups they are members of. The aim here is to identify one or two formal groups which are performing poorly or which could be functioning more effectively. These will form the basis of the subsequent discussion.

3. The student whose group is being discussed takes the role of problem-owner, while the remainder of the members act as consultants.

4. The problem-owner explains how poorly the group is performing, providing objective measures (missed deadlines, over budget) or problem symptoms (cliques, failure to agree), if possible.

5. The consultants ask the problem-owner for additional information about the group – its members, goals, organizational context, etc.

6. Focussing on the structural features of group – power, status, liking, communication, role and leadership – they assess whether any of these, singly or in combination, might be the cause of the poor performance.

7. If there is agreement from the problem-owner that the suggested causes might indeed be valid, the consultants move on to offering a solution e.g. modifying the group's power structure, changing its communication network, clarifying or redefining members' roles, etc.

8. If the structural features of the group do not offer a complete problem explanation or solution, consultants identify what non-structural group aspects may be pertinent (referring to the Sundstrom, De Meuse and Futrell ecological framework for analysing work team effectiveness to be found in Chapter 12, pp. 390–1).

9. If time permits, a second group performance issue, described by a different problem-owner, can be tackled.

2c: Leadership styles, managerial roles and communication networks

Objectives
1. To distinguish different group leadership styles and management roles.
2. To relate the different styles and roles to communication networks.

Background
From their research, Lewin, Whyte and Lippitt distinguished three types of leadership styles which they labelled authoritarian, democratic and laissez-faire (see p. 342). Later, Henry Mintzberg, identified three groups of managerial roles that rely on effective and accurate communication: interpersonal, informational and decisional (see Chapter 14, pp. 494–5).

Before proceeding, you should review the material on these two pieces of research, as well as on the five types of communication networks (Chapter 10, pp. 330–1).

Briefing   The purpose of this exercise is to examine the different leadership styles and managerial roles, and to recommend which of the five communication networks would be most useful to the managers concerned. The following two charts list the leadership styles and managerial roles.

Work in groups on each chart in turn. First, consider which network would be the most useful for managers using one of the three leadership styles listed. Then, turning to the second chart, determine which one is the most effective for each of the three management roles. Your discussion should address the following issues:

1. Justify each of your choices, indicating the advantages and disadvantages of what you have recommended.

2. In practice, do you think managers select a communication network on the basis of their preferred leadership style or managerial role that they are playing? If they do not, what are the costs of staying with one type of network regardless of their style or role?

Communication Networks					
Leadership style	*Chain*	*'Y'*	*Wheel*	*Circle*	*All channel*
Autocratic					
Democratic					
Laissez-faire					

Communication Networks					
Managerial role	*Chain*	*'Y'*	*Wheel*	*Circle*	*All channel*
Interpersonal					
Informational					
Decisional					

Developed from Exercise 4.7, 'Managerial Roles and Communication Networks' in R.W. Griffin and T.C. Head, 1987, *Practicing Management*, second edition, Houghton Mifflin, Boston, MA, pp. 193–4.

Key concepts

self concept	peripheral norms
social identity	group sanction
self-esteem	conformity
social representations	obedience
shared frame of reference	group cohesion
social influence	group socialization
synergy	organizational socialization
social facilitation	deindividuation
social loafing	compliance
group norms	conversion
pivotal norms	

Learning outcomes

When you have read this chapter, you should be able to define those key concepts in your own words, and you should also be able to:

1. Explain the basic tenets of social identity theory and social representation theory.
2. Distinguish between social facilitation and social loafing.
3. Understand why groups develop norms and use sanctions to regulate the behaviour of their members.
4. Understand the process of group socialization of individuals.
5. Explain why individuals conform to the dictates of their group.
6. Distinguish between conformity and conversion.

Why study individuals in groups?

Marion Hampton (1999, p. 113) warns:

> Yet groups are also endowed with a darker side, one which is highlighted in mobs and crowds. They are seen as taking over the individual's mind, depressing intelligence, eliminating moral responsibility and forcing conformity. They can cause their members a great deal of suffering and despair and can perpetuate acts of great cruelty. If groups are capable of great deeds, they are also capable of great follies.

There is now extensive research evidence that demonstrates the power of groups to affect the behaviour of their individual members. This was originally revealed in the research conducted by Elton Mayo at the Hawthorne plant in the 1920s. Since that time, managements have harnessed this power by creating groups and teams which police and discipline their own members, keeping their behaviour in line with organizational (management) objectives. The most developed form of such management-initiated group control is to be found in Japanese teamworking, which will be described in the next chapter. However, this chapter introduces the basic concepts of group norms, socialization and sanctions, and reports some research from an American multinational plant in Scotland.

The power of the group to affect the perceptions, performance and attitudes of its individual members is well established. However, since the 1980s, there has also been a growing body of research that shows how a lone individual can have an influence on a majority. The two concepts of compliance and conversion have generated a great deal of interest in this field.

Stop and Criticize

Think of three things that you do alone that you would not do if someone else was with you at work.

- Why would you not do these things in the presence of others?
- What would be the consequences in each case if you did?

Is such self-control to the benefit of yourself, your employer or both? Explain how.

The individual and the group

Henri Tajful and John Turner (1986) argued that as long as individuals see themselves as more important than the group, then the latter cannot function effectively. Tajfel and Turner maintain that in order to achieve this, individuals have to stop seeing themselves as individuals, and instead identify themselves as group members, treating the group's values as their own. Such an individual attitudinal 'switch' and commitment facilitates the long-term existence and success of the group. This question of how much an individual should be part of the group (for their own well-being, for that of their group, and for their organization) and how much separate from it (to remain creative and critical and for their own mental health) is a continuing debate in the literature.

Integration in the Borg

In the TV and film series *Star Trek*, the Federation comes up against its most powerful adversary, the Borg, a collective species with no distinct individuals. Part human and part machine, they seek to transform all other species into Borg, ending their will to resist by destroying their identities as individuals. In the story, Captain Picard and his staff realize that they are dealing not with an individual mind, but with the collective minds of all the Borg. As a collective culture, the Borg have to continue consuming individuals in order to remain a collective. The Borg threaten to multiply, and spell the end of human individuality. Picard asks them what their objective is, to which they reply, 'We wish to improve ourselves.'

Based on Thomas Richards, *Star Trek in Myth and Legend*, Orion Books, London, 1997.

Let us first consider some theories which seek to explain the relation between the individual and their group. *Social identity* (or identification) *theory* was developed by Henri Tajfel and focuses on those aspects of our identity which derive from our group membership (Tajfel and Turner, 1986). Group formation can be seen as an adaptive process as one moves from feeling and thinking as an individual (personal identity) to feeling and thinking as a representative of a group (social identity). It holds that group membership affects people's sense of who they are. The groups or social categories to which we belong (for example, student course member, management team member, parent or sports club secretary) are an integral part of our **self concept**. Our own self concept is the way in which we see ourselves, the set of perceptions that we have about ourselves. It affects both how we feel about ourselves and how we act within a group. This is because joining a group lowers our self-awareness and raises our group awareness. The roles that we play within different groups, especially those that are important to us, influence and shape our attitudes and behaviours.

That part of their self concept which comes from their membership of a group is called **social identity**. Social identity fulfils two functions. First, it defines and evaluates a person (for example, 'she's a member of the design team'). Such definition and evaluation is done both by others and by the person themselves. Second, it prescribes appropriate behaviour for them. They think and behave in characteristically 'design team' ways. How this happens is through social comparison. According to Tajfel, in order to evaluate their own opinions and abilities, individuals not only compare themselves to other individuals with whom they interact, but also compare their own group with similar, but distinct, out-groups. The dimensions that are used to make these comparisons are called social categorizations. Categorization leads to assumptions of similarity among those who are categorized together. It minimizes the perceived differences between members of the in-group and maximizes the differences between the in-group and out-groups. The out-groups will tend to be stereotyped. When this happens, the individuals who are part of the in-group will have assumed social identity, and this represents the standpoint from which they will view other people.

We all see ourselves as members of various social groupings, which are distinguishable and hence different from other social groupings. The consequence is that by identifying with certain groupings but not others, we come to see the world in terms of 'us and them'. There are two benefits for us from this. First, our understanding of the world is enhanced by classifying everybody this way. Second, our **self-esteem** can be maintained or even enhanced. Membership of a high-status group gives us prestige, which in turn raises our self-esteem. We are highly motivated and feel proud to belong to the group of which we are members. If we cannot achieve this feeling of pride, we will either try to change the group's perceived status or detach ourselves from it. Although such social identification can potentially lead to conflict between different groups within an organization, it can also be effectively managed in a way that improves the performance of both groups.

Categorizing people into groups and identifying with some of these groups appears to be a fundamental human characteristic, which derives from the fact that human beings are social animals. Because of these two basic needs for differentiating themselves from others and for belonging, individuals expose themselves to the control of others. Within the organizational context, we offer control to fellow group members who wish to direct our attitudes, thoughts and ideas in line with what the group considers appropriate; and also to managers who seek both to motivate and to control us through instituting various teamworking arrangements.

Self concept: the way in which we view ourselves; the set of perceptions that we have about ourselves.

Social identity: that part of the self concept which comes from our membership of groups; it contributes to our self-esteem.

Self-esteem: the part of the self which is concerned with how we evaluate ourselves.

Which group memberships do you cite when you introduce yourself to others? From the 'us and them' perspective, who are 'us' and who are 'them', for you?

Has this helped your own group improve its performance? Has it raised your own self-esteem?

Has the management in your organization used this distinction to motivate or control your group? How?

Group influences on individuals' perceptions

Social representations: the beliefs, ideas and values, objects, people and events that are constructed by current group members and which are transmitted to its new members.

How does a group affect the perceptions of its individual members? One explanation is provided by social representations theory, which was formulated by Serge Moscovici (1984). This refers to the finding that when individuals join a new group, its members will construct and transmit complex and unfamiliar ideas to them, in straightforward and familiar ways. This process creates what are termed **social representations**, which come to be accepted, in a modified form, by the new members of a group, and these help the new recruits to make sense of what is going on around them within the group and the organization. The explanation of some occurrence is simplified, distorted and ritualized by the group, and becomes a 'common sense explanation' which is accepted as orthodoxy among its members, and is then communicated to new members. Social representations are theories about how the world works and are used to justify actions.

In an exclusive ladies clothes shop in the centre of Glasgow, every day the sales staff had two meetings. The first of these followed their breakfast together. Before starting their shift, and in the presence of managers who brought a flipchart, sales staff met to discuss, as a group, their objectives for the day. The second meeting occurred at the end of the day when, once again as a group, they discussed what had happened and whether they had achieved their stated objectives.

At the start of the book, the *social construction of reality* perspective was introduced. This argued that our social and organizational surroundings possess no ultimate truth or reality, but are determined instead by the way in which we experience and understand those worlds which we construct and reconstruct for ourselves, in interaction with others. Among these important 'others' with whom we interact, and with whom we experience and understand the world, are the members our psychological group. The prefix 'social', in both phrases, reminds us about the collective way in which representations are created and accepted, and how they come to form a shared, manufactured reality.

Shared frame of reference: a set of assumptions that are held in common by group members, which shape their thinking, decisions, actions and interactions while being constantly defined and reinforced through those interactions.

As a new company recruit, you discuss your role in the group with existing members. During these interactions, representations are presented, developed, adapted and negotiated before being incorporated into your own, existing, belief framework. This happens during the period of socialization shortly after you join the group. It is not a matter of you, as a new recruit, being given and accepting a bundle of existing group assumptions, ideas, beliefs and opinions to absorb. Moscovici's theory emphasizes the interactive nature of the process between you as an individual and the other group members. Once incorporated, the group representations are revealed in all members' speech and actions.

Through these social representations, group members gain a **shared frame of reference**. Over time, new-joiners learn about the different assumptions, ideas, beliefs and opinions held by their fellow group members about their common work situation. Some agreement on perception and meaning is essential among the members of a group if they are to interact, communicate, agree on goals and generally act in concert on a common task. Such a shared view is essential for a group if it is to continue and develop. Moreover, as we work in groups we find that our views coalesce with those of other members of the group. A shared frame of reference and social representations suggest a group-level equivalent of the concept of organizational culture. Together, these determine the meaning that group members attach to events and other people's behaviour.

Multicultural perceptions

Increasing numbers of organizations create groups, whose members are of different nationalities and ethnic backgrounds, in the hope of producing cross-cultural collaboration. These groups possess differences in language, culture and historical sensitivity. Kenwyn Smith and David Berg (1997) observed that every member of newly formed multicultural groups had their own understanding of how best to contribute to it so as to make it effective. These beliefs reflect the norms of their own culture. The authors found that expectations about how to contribute to the group's process varied along eight dimensions or 'polarities'. These are presented as questions to which individuals from different cultural backgrounds will have different answers:

1. *Confrontation v. conciliation*: When differences arise, do they confront each other, or do they overlook or discuss the aggravations that come from these differences?

2. *Individuality v. collectivity*: Is the individual paramount, with the work group providing the context for people to make their personal contribution to a common goal, or is the work group central, with the individual merely a component of the collective?

3. *Participative v. autocratic*: Are individuals expected to express their views and thereby contribute to a quality decision, or are they expected to keep quiet, 'buy-into' the vision of the 'legitimate authority' and be told how to implement it?

4. *Spontaneous v. orchestrated*: Does the group actually make a decision, or is it a sounding board or way of communicating already-made decisions to which members have previously been exposed?

5. *Task v. process*: Is the group's primary focus *what* it does, or *how* it does it? Is productivity (task output) or the quality of the internal interactions (process) the key indicator of a group's value?

6. *Quality v. quantity*: Is the best indicator of the group's performance to be the quality or the quantity of the work it produces?

7. *Criticism v. diplomacy*: Will group members criticize each other directly in public or will they seek more diplomatic, less overt ways of communicating their dissatisfaction?

8. *Productivity v. receptivity*: Is creativity recognized in terms of ideas implemented, problems solved or capabilities developed, or more abstractly in terms of light-shedding, energy-releasing or potential development?

Smith and Berg recommend that while single-culture group members can use what they have in common as the basis of their collective functioning, those in multicultural groups should use their differences as the basis for their shared actions. The latter might usefully begin their deliberations by sharing their own cultural assumptions about group process and outcomes with their colleagues. The objective is to help individuals learn from each other, in order to make the group function effectively.

Based on Kenwyn Smith and David Berg, 'Cross cultural groups at work', *European Management Journal*, vol. 15, no. 1, 1997, pp. 8–15.

Group influences on individuals' performance

Social influence: the process where attitudes and behaviour are influenced by the real or implied presence of others.

Synergy: the positive or negative result of the interaction of two or more components, producing an outcome that is different from the sum of the individual components.

The presence of another person or a group of people changes our attitudes and behaviour. **Social influence** refers to the process where attitudes and behaviour are influenced by the real or implied presence of others. What type of student behaviour does the presence of a university invigilator in an examination hall seek to influence? For familiar, well-learned activities such as assembly line work and similar repetitive tasks, the presence of co-workers is likely to improve performance, and the presence of an observer such as a manager is unlikely to hinder it, unless it carries a message of distrust or punishment. In contrast, a person who is attempting to perform a complex, unfamiliar task will find that observation by others may cause them to make more mistakes, and their performance will decline. Hence the presence of others can improve or reduce an individual's performance. Elliott Aronson and his colleagues (Aronson et al., 1994) suggested two alternative reactions by an individual to having one or more people present when performing a task – *social facilitation* and *social loafing*. Their model stresses the importance of evaluation, arousal and task complexity (figure 11.1).

How might an individual's performance be improved by the presence of others? The biological concept of **synergy** helps us to do this. Strictly defined, synergy is the positive or negative result of the interaction of two or more components, producing an outcome that is different from the sum of the individual components. In the field of management and organization behaviour, 'individuals' have replaced 'substances', and the concept has been suitably amended. It is important to emphasis the word 'different' in the definition because it indicates that the effect may be positive or negative.

Positive synergy is a fundamental concept which underpins all kinds of group working in organizations. In particular, it supports the use of cross-functional teams. Positive synergy is the belief that the final output produced by a group of individuals working together, rather than separately, will equal more than the

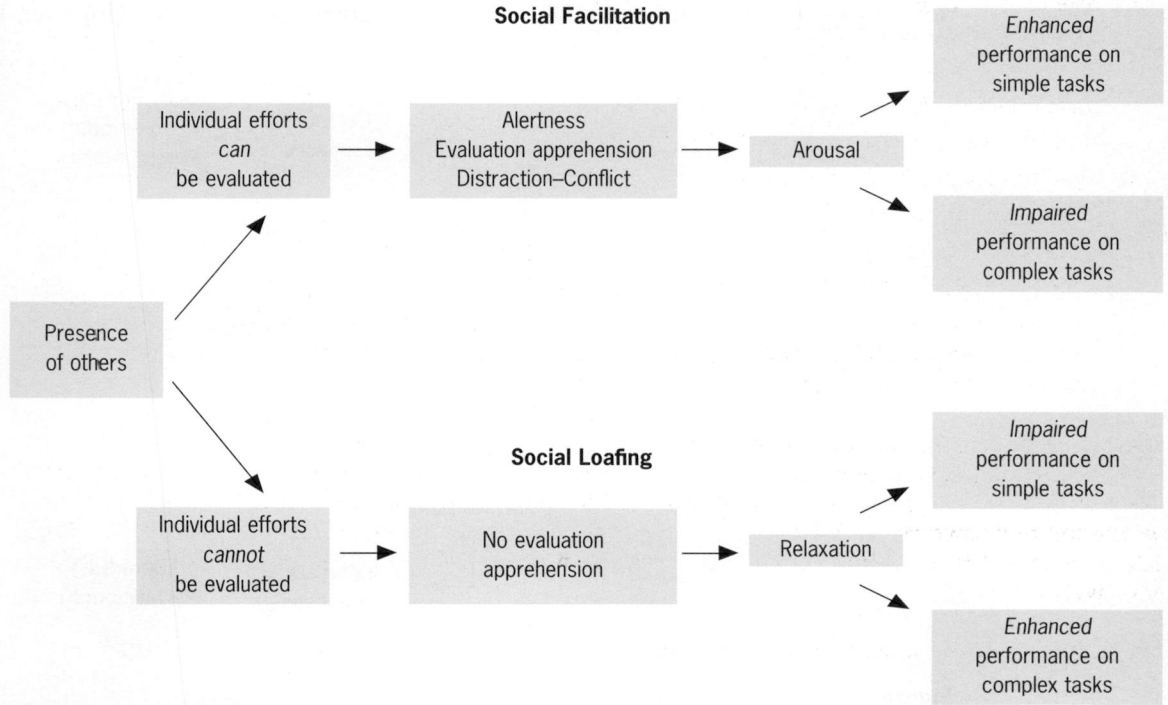

Figure 11.1: Social facilitation and social loafing
From Elliot Aronson, Timothy D. Wilson and Robin M. Akert, *Social Psychology*, HarperCollins College Publishers, New York, 1994, p. 332.

sum of the individual members' abilities and efforts. A popular short-hand term for this is 2 + 2 = 5. It has been argued that the designated purpose of group tasks should necessarily *require* more than its members are able to offer working as individuals, so as to benefit from the positive aspects of group dynamics.

Early research investigated individuals performing various physical tasks. Norman Triplett (1898) studied children winding fishing reels and cyclists racing. The children were found to turn the reels faster when other children were present, and the cyclists performed 20 per cent faster when accompanied by a pacemaker than when alone, even in a non-racing situation. He found that they performed better in the presence of another person (a co-actor). Later studies focused on non-physical tasks. Floyd Allport (1920) discovered that students completed mathematical calculations faster in the company of other students than when alone, and coined the term **social facilitation** to indicate that the task was made easier, or was 'facilitated', by the presence of others.

Social facilitation appears to be the result of two fundamental, psychological processes. First, when in the presence of others, individuals experience increased emotional arousal, feeling more tense and excited. Second, when aroused, people perform their most dominant response: that is, their most likely behaviour in that setting, which is also likely to be a correct one. In contrast, if the behaviour in question is newly learned and hence not established, the dominant response is likely to be incorrect. Robert Zajonc's *drive theory of social facilitation* combines these two ideas (Zajonc, 1965, 1980). It states that whatever you do well, you are likely to do it even better in front of an audience; whereas what you normally find difficult to do you will find virtually impossible to do, when others are watching. The theory stresses the strengthening of the dominant (prevalent or most likely) response due to the presence of others (Myers, 1993, p. 306).

Drive theory of social facilitation states that the arousing presence of others enhances the tendency to perform dominant responses. When these responses are correct (as when well learned), performance will be improved; if these responses are incorrect (when the task is novel), performance will be impaired (figure 11.2). The theory recommends that learning new and difficult material is usually best done alone, but once it is known, it is best demonstrated in public. However, it

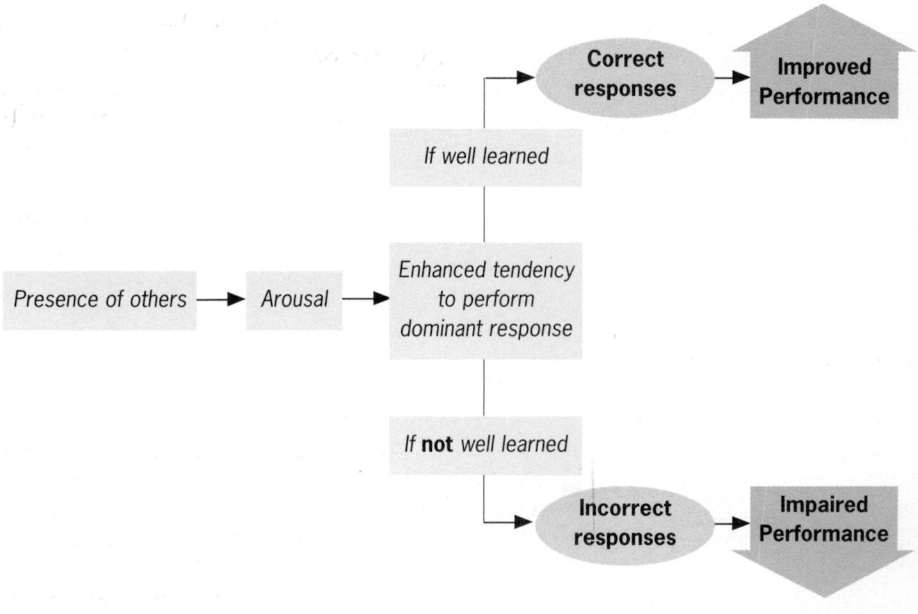

> **Social facilitation**: a strengthening of the dominant (prevalent or likely) responses due to the presence of others.

Figure 11.2: Drive theory of social facilitation
From *Managing Behaviour in Organizations, 2/E* by Jerald Greenberg, © 1999. Reprinted by permission of Pearson Education, Inc., Upper Saddle River, NJ.

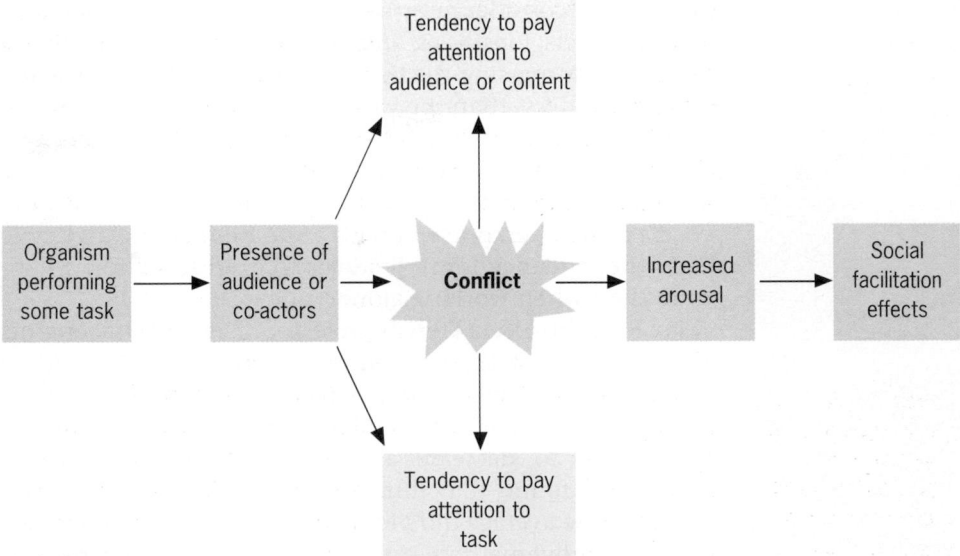

Figure 11.3: Distraction–conflict theory of social facilitation
From Baron, *Social Psychology*, 9/e. Published by Allyn and Bacon, Boston, MA. Copyright © 2000 by Pearson Education. Reprinted by permission of the publisher.

does not explain why the presence of others increases drive. Two explanations have been offered as to why this occurs.

Distraction–conflict theory of social facilitation states that the presence of an audience or co-actors increases arousal by inducing conflicting tendencies between (1) paying attention to the audience and (2) paying attention to the task being performed. This arousal increases the tendency to perform dominant responses. This explanation holds that the presence of others creates a conflict between the competing demands of attending to the task in hand and to those present (Baron, 1986). Such conflict is arousing and increases the tendency for us to perform our dominant response. Increased arousal in such situations may be instinctive as others who are present may be unpredictable, requiring us to be alert and ready to react in case of danger (figure 11.3).

The evaluation–apprehension explanation of social facilitation holds that the dominant behavioural responses result from our fear of being evaluated by an audience which is present (Cottrell et al., 1968). However, it is not clear whether it is the audience's presence, their judgement of us, or both, which is the crucial variable. The acquired arousal (drive) results from our learning in childhood that rewards and punishments are based on others' evaluations of us.

To monitor or not?

The productivity of employees performing a novel clerical task at a computer was measured in one of three ways. Under the first condition, they completed the task alone. In the second, someone stood behind and watched them. Under the third, they worked alone, but were monitored remotely. Performance was found to considerably lower among those who were being monitored, either personally or remotely. The findings confirm the drive theory of social facilitation.

Based on J.R. Aiello and C.M. Svec, 'Computer monitoring of work performance: extending the social facilitation framework to electronic presence', *Journal of Applied Social Psychology*, vol. 23, 1993, pp. 537–48.

Let us now consider negative synergy. Teamwork of all kinds is fraught with tensions, conflicts, obstacles and problems. If these are not managed effectively, rather than surpassing the best member's capabilities, the total group output may actually equal *less* than the weakest members' efforts. This is caused by various so-called 'processes losses' which can hinder effective group functioning (Steiner, 1972). The mathematical equivalent would be $2 + 2 = 3$. This challenges the idea that 'unity is strength'. If the aforementioned group process losses exceed group process gains, then one will have a situation of negative synergy. One example of this is the tendency for individuals to exert less effort when working as part of a group than when working alone.

Max Ringelmann, a French professor of agricultural engineering, conducted the original studies in the late 1920s on subjects pulling ropes (Kravitz and Martin, 1986). Research suggests that when individuals perform additive tasks (that is, where members perform similar tasks and their output is pooled), individual effort tends to decrease as the size of the group increases (figure 11.4). Ringelmann found that three people pulling together only achieved two and a half times the average individual rate, while eight 'pullers' achieved less than four times the individual rate. Ingham et al. (1974) later repeated these experiments and reported an 18 per cent variation in effort. The 'Ringelmann effect' was renamed **social loafing** in the 1970s by Bibb Latane following investigations at Ohio University to confirm Ringelmann's original work (Latane et al., 1979).

Suggestions have been offered at the individual group member level to account for social loafing (George, 1992; Karau and Williams, 1993; Comer, 1995). The process losses in a group have been ascribed to different causes:

Social loafing: the tendency for individuals to exert less effort when working as part of a group on an additive task than when working alone.

■ equity of effort ('others are not contributing, why should I?');

■ dispersion of responsibility ('I'm hidden in the crowd, no one will notice me');

■ negative effect of group reward ('everyone will get the same, why should I work harder?');

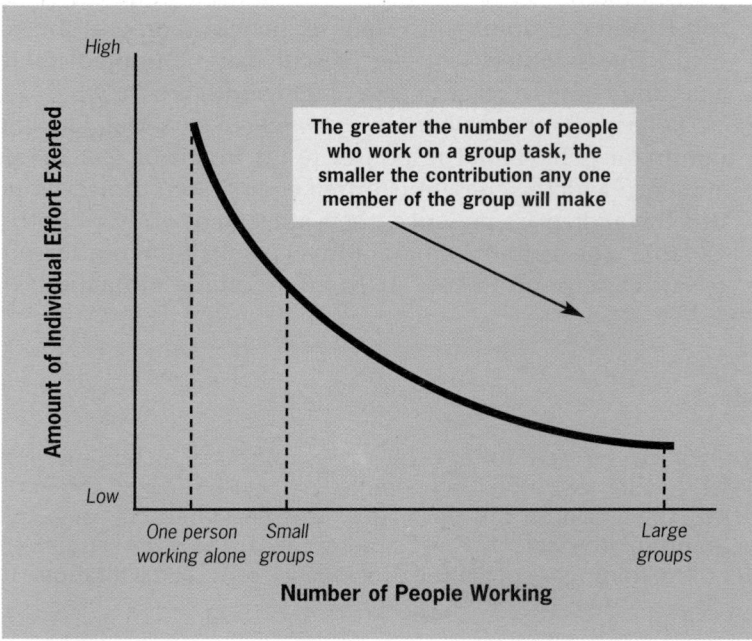

Figure 11:4: The social loafing effect
From *Managing Behaviour in Organizations*, 2/E by Jerald Greenberg, © 1999. Reprinted by permission of Pearson Education, Inc., Upper Saddle River, NJ.

■ problems of co-ordination ('people are getting in each other's way').

Additionally, Latane's *social impact theory* explains the phenomenon of social loafing in terms of a force acting upon a group, such as the task needing to be completed. Such a force becomes divided equally among the available members. The greater the size of the group, the lower will be the impact of that force upon any one member, and vice versa. As group size increases, responsibility for task completion becomes diffused more widely among all members and the pressure on each individual declines. Each person will thus feel less responsibility for acting responsibly (Latane and Nida, 1980).

The *collective effort model* is an expectancy theory of social loafing. It holds that social loafing is the result of participants' realization that their performance cannot be evaluated on an individual basis. It led them to withhold their full effort when contributing to additive group tasks (Karau and Williams, 1993). Laboratory studies have revealed key situational factors. Social loafing was found to occur most often when the:

■ task was perceived as unimportant, simple or boring;

■ group members thought their individual output was not identifiable;

■ nature of each person's contribution was similar to that of the others;

■ group members expected their colleagues to loaf.

Additionally, self-reliant individualists appeared to be more social loafers than group-oriented collectivists, and more men engaged in it than women (Kugihara, 1999). This individual finding has a cultural equivalent. Studies have found that individualist societies which are dominated by self-interest (like the Americas, Britain, Australia) have more social loafing than collectivist societies whose members are motivated by in-group goals. The Israelis and Chinese performed better in a group than when working alone (Earley, 1989, 1993). The solutions offered to managers to overcome social loafing assume that it is our natural state, and that something has to be added to a situation to avoid it. Suggestions include (Greenberg and Baron, 1999; Baron and Byrne, 2000):

Make the work more involving	Keep people interested, thereby increasing their commitment to successful task performance, and hence encouraging them to perform at a high level.
Upgrade task	Increase the perceived importance of the task in the group members' eyes.
Identify workers	Point out each member's individual contribution; it prevents their getting away with a 'free ride'.
Reward contributions to the group	Reward members for helping others achieve the common goal, and not just for their individual contributions.
Threaten punishment	Fear of punishment prevents loafing and gets members to 'pull their weight' in the group.
Strengthen group cohesion	Make the group size small, make membership attractive and stable, have common goals and facilitate member interaction.

How many pickles could a pickle packer pack if pickle packers were only paid for properly packed pickles?

What are the problems facing production line workers in a pickle factory? A key job is stuffing dill pickle halves into jars. Only dill halves of a certain length can be used. Those that are too long will not fit and those that are too short will float and dance inside and look cheap and crummy. The dill halves and jars are carried on separate high-speed conveyor belts past the contingent of pickle stuffers. If the stuffers don't stuff quickly enough, the jars pile up at the workers' stations while they look for pickles of the appropriate length, so stuffers have a great temptation to stuff whichever pickles come to hand. The individual outputs of the stuffers are unidentifiable, since all jars go into a common hopper before they reach the quality control section. Responsibility for the output cannot be focused on one worker. This combination of factors leads to poor performance and improper packing. This research suggests making individual production identifiable and raises the question: 'How many pickles could a pickle packer pack if pickle packers were only paid for properly packed pickles?'

Based on Kipling Williams, Stephen Harkins and Bibb Latane, 'Identifiability and social loafing: two cheering experiments', *Journal of Personality and Social Psychology*, vol. 40, no. 2, 1981, pp. 303–11.

Stop and Criticize

Are you a social loafer in an educational or work context? How is social loafing reducing or improving your studying or work performance? What advice would you give your instructor or manager on improving your performance and that of your colleagues, either through social facilitation or by discouraging social loafing in relation to particular tasks or activities?

Group norms: expected modes of behaviour and beliefs that are established either formally or informally by a group. Norms guide behaviour and facilitate interaction by specifying the kinds of reaction that are expected or acceptable in a particular situation.

Pivotal norms: socially defined standards relating to behaviour and beliefs which are central to a group's objective and survival.

Peripheral norms: socially defined standards relating to behaviour and beliefs which are important but not crucial to a group's objective and survival.

Group influences on individuals' behaviour

Elton Mayo originally noted the existence of **group norms**, and their enforcement through sanctions, during the Bank Wiring Observation Room studies at the Hawthorne works. The men there restricted their output to conform to a group-agreed norm or standard. In another study which has now become a classic in experimental social psychology, Muzafer Sherif (1936) showed how group norms emerged. He demonstrated that the way an individual perceives motion can be affected by what others present at the time claim to see. Few of the subjects who took part in Sherif's experiments felt conscious that others had influenced their judgements.

Sherif's work showed that in a situation where doubt and uncertainty exist, and where first-hand information is lacking, a person's viewpoint will shift to come into line with those of other group members. In essence, this situation leads to the creation of a group norm. This occurs quickly among group members who have had little previous experience of the group's work, but it also occurs among those who have had experience, although somewhat more slowly. Sherif's work suggested that in order to organize and manage itself, every group developed a system of norms. Norms are behavioural expectations and they serve to define the nature of the group. They express the values of the members of the group and provide guidelines to help the group achieve its goals. A group may develop them consciously or unconsciously.

Not all group norms have equal importance. **Pivotal norms** guide behaviour which is central to the group: for example, the level of output or the amount of work preparation done. In contrast, **peripheral norms** guide behaviour that is important but not essential: for example, the choice of clothing or break-time activities. Group members who violate pivotal norms can impede group objectives or endanger its survival. Therefore the consequences for transgressing individuals are severe. In contrast, violation of peripheral norms, although frowned upon, has fewer negative consequences for the offender.

Bloody beefers and hanging beef tongues

Over a nine-week period, William Thompson used the observational data collection method to study the day-to-day activities of assembly-line workers in a beef processing plant in the American Midwest. He reported that 'working in the beef plant is "dirty" work, not only in the literal sense of being drenched with perspiration and beef blood, but also in the figurative sense of performing a low-status, routine and demeaning job'. Thompson and his fellow workers had to hang, brand and bag between 1,350 and 1,500 beef tongues during an eight-hour shift. The work was both monotonous and routine.

Thompson described the camaraderie that existed among the 'beefers' as they called themselves. Because of the noise, the need for earplugs and the isolation of certain work areas, it was virtually impossible for the men on the assembly line to speak to each other. Instead, they communicated using an elaborate system of non-verbal and paraverbal symbols. These included exaggerated gestures, shrill whistles, 'thumbs up' and 'thumbs down', and the clanging of knives against stainless steel tables and tubs. Thompson observed that 'in a setting which apparently eliminated it, the workers' desire for social interaction won out and interaction flourished'.

To reduce the feeling of alienation and retain a sense of humanity, the beefers developed certain coping mechanisms. They replaced the formal, managerially imposed norms of the workplace with their own informal ones. At certain times, instead of working at a steady speed which matched the line speed, they would work at a frantic pace and get ahead of the line. While such behaviour added a few precious minutes to their scheduled break-time, its importance was primarily symbolic in that it challenged the company's dictates concerning the speed of the line and it gave them a small measure of control over the work process.

The informal group norms also encouraged certain types of rule breaking. Indeed, Thompson noted that the 'workers practically made a game out of doing forbidden things simply to see if they could get away with it'. For example, at Thompson's workstation, despite strict rules to the contrary, workers covered in beef blood, washed their hands, arms and knives in a tub of water which was reserved for cleaning tongues. In addition, workers often cut out pieces of meat, and threw them at other employees. If not noticed by the supervisor or inspector, the thrown meat chunks might be picked up off the floor and put back on the line – a blatant violation of hygiene rules. Thompson concluded that such 'artful sabotage served as a symbolic way in which workers could express a sense of individuality, and hence self-worth'.

Based on William E. Thompson, 'Hanging tongues: a sociological encounter with the assembly line', *Qualitative Sociology*, vol. 6, Fall, 1983, pp. 215–37.

Muzafer Sherif
(1906–88)

Why do norms develop within a group? David Feldman (1984) argued that their purpose was to:

■ *Facilitate group task achievement or group survival*: Groups develop norms which increase their chances of being successful and protect themselves from outsiders.

■ *Increase the predictability of group members' behaviours*: Predictability means that, internally, members can anticipate and prepare for the actions of colleagues, thereby smoothing social interaction. Externally, it allows them to relate appropriately to outsiders.

■ *Reduce embarrassing interpersonal problems for group members:* Knowing what to do and say in a group (and what not to) increases an individual member's comfort.

- *Express the group's core values and define their distinctiveness*: Norms allow members to gain a sense of the essence of the group.

Discovering the norm

In a now classic study, Donald Roy, a researcher who acted as a participant observer in a factory, described the pressures that were placed on an individual to adhere to the group norm. Roy's earnings, and those of others, were based on a piece-rate system. The more he produced, the more he earned.

From my first to my last day at the plant I was subject to warnings and predictions concerning price cuts. Pressure was the heaviest from Joe Mucha, who shared my job repertoire and kept a close eye on my production. On November 14, the day after my first attained quota, Joe Mucha advised: Don't let it go over $1.25 an hour, or the time-study man will be right down here! And they don't waste time, either! They watch the records like a hawk! I got ahead, so I took it easy for a couple of hours. Joe told me that I had made $10.01 yesterday and warned me not to go over $1.25 an hour ... Jack Starkey spoke to me after Joe left. 'What's the matter? Are you trying to upset the applecart?' Jack explained in a friendly manner that $10.50 was too much to turn in, even on an old job. 'The turret-lathe men can turn in $1.35', said Jack, 'but their rate is 90 cents and ours is 85 cents.' Jack warned me that the Methods Department could lower their prices on any job, old or new, by changing the fixture slightly or changing the size of the drill. According to Jack, a couple of operators ... got to competing with each other to see how much they could turn in. They got up to $1.65 an hour, and the price was cut in half. And from then on they had to run that job themselves, as none of the other operators would accept that job. According to Jack, it would be all right for us to turn in $1.28 or $1.29 an hour, when it figured out that way, but it was not all right to turn in $1.30 an hour.

Well now I know where the maximum is – $1.29 an hour.

From Donald Roy, 'Quota restriction and goldbricking in a machine shop', *American Journal of Sociology*, vol. 57, no. 5, 1952, pp. 430–1.

Feldman (1984) also noted that group norms developed in four ways:

- *Explicit statement by a supervisor or co-worker*: This person may explicitly state certain expectations. The project leader may tell the newcomer that the group meeting starts promptly on the hour, when all members are expected to be present.

- *Critical events in the group's history*: A shop-floor employee makes a suggestion for an improvement to his supervisor who criticizes and ridicules him. Group members ensure that in the future none of them offers any more suggestions.

- *Initial pattern of behaviour*: The first behaviour pattern that emerges in a group can establish group expectations. For example, if the first speaker shares his feelings and anxieties with the other group members, the discussion of emotions in a group can become a norm.

- *Transfer behaviours from past situations*: When individuals carry over behaviours from past situations, they can increase the predictability of group members' behaviours in new settings. For example, instructors and students transfer constant expectations from class to class.

Sherif's study of the emergence of group norms

Muzafer Sherif placed a group of three subjects in a darkened room and presented them with a small spot of light. He then asked them to track the apparent movement of the spot and to say, aloud, each in turn, the direction in which they thought that the light was moving. The apparent movement is an optical illusion known as the 'autokinetic effect'; the light does not move. Sherif's subjects made three series of 100 estimates on successive days. Initially, there were quite wide individual differences in the response to this situation. Some subjects saw little movement while others saw a lot. However, Sherif discovered that they started to agree on the amount of apparent movement quite quickly. Having exchanged information on their judgements, their behaviour changed. They began seeing the light moving in the same direction as those who had spoken earlier.

subject trial:	individual first	1st group	2nd group	3rd group
estimates	100	100	100	100

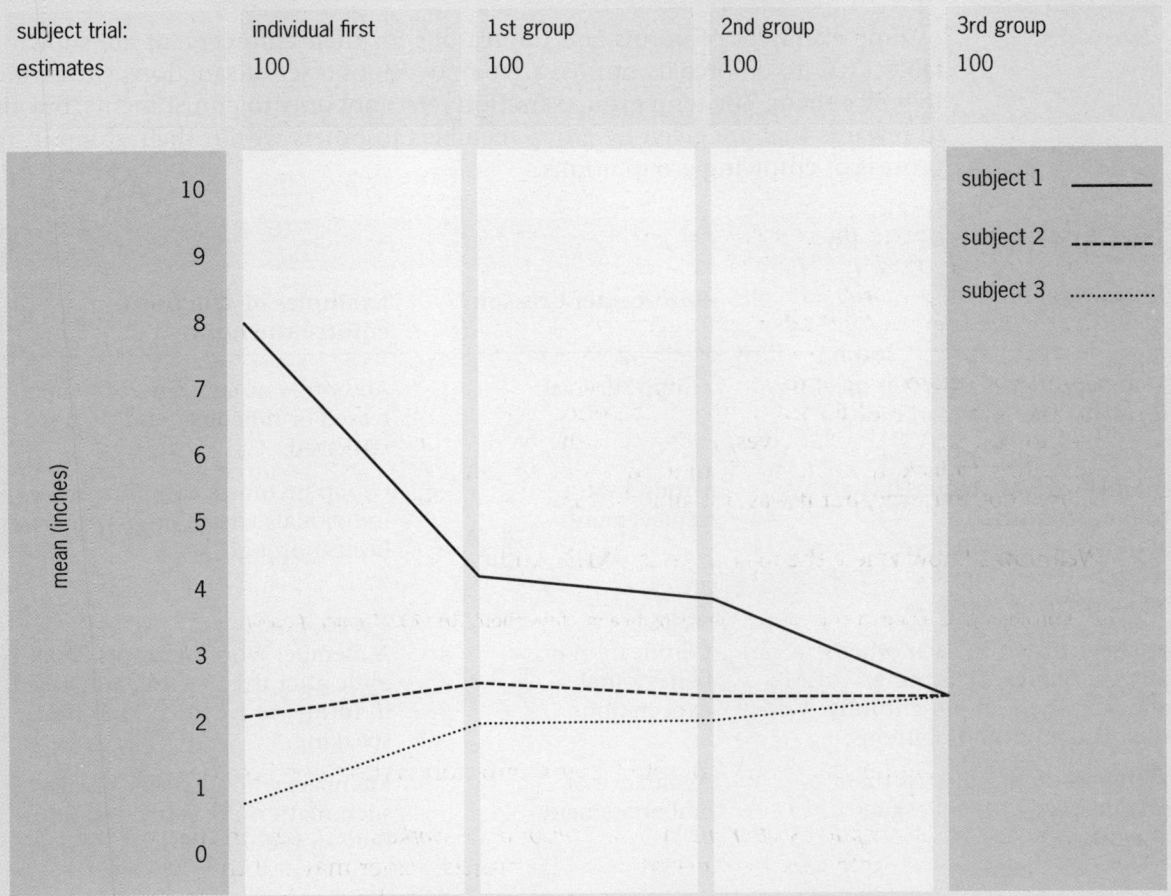

Gradually, all the members came to see the light as moving in the same direction at the same time. There was of course no 'real' movement of the light. Each individual began to see the light in the same way as the group saw it. The results Sherif obtained with two-person and three-person groups are shown in the diagram above. When a group norm emerged it was found that it became the basis for subsequent judgement when subjects were re-tested independently. The group norm therefore became a relatively permanent frame of reference for behaviour.

Based on Muzafer Sherif, *The Psychology of Social Norms*, Harper & Row, New York, 1936.

It appears that once established, group norms are difficult to change. Since the group members originally created the norms, it is they who ultimately change them. Members will tend to resist any attempts by managers or outsiders to

Group sanction: both punishments and rewards given by members to others in the group in the process of enforcing group norms. Punishments are a negative sanction and rewards are a positive sanction.

modify their group's norms. Once a group has established a set of norms, it will enforce them in order to:

- ensure its survival;

- help it achieve its task;

- clarify or simplify how members are to behave;

- avoid embarrassing situations between members;

- clarify its central values or unique identity.

Some examples of norms and the reasons for their enforcement are shown in table 11.1. To enforce its norms, a group develops a set of sanctions with which to police them. The term **group sanction** refers not only to punishments, but also to rewards that are given by group members to others within their group in the process of enforcing group norms.

Table 11.1: Norms and sanctions

Norm	Enforcement reason	Examples of sanctions to enforce the norm
Members attend all group meetings regularly and arrive on time.	Group survival	Absentees or latecomers are first teased or ridiculed, and then criticized.
All members are required to prepare written work particularly before the group meetings to avoid delay at meetings.	Group task achievement	Group members compliment individuals whose preparation has been thorough.
Members listen to each other's ideas without interrupting, allowing them to present fully their thoughts and opinions.	Clarification of behavioural expectations	A member who interrupts is taken aside after the meeting and asked, in future, to let the person finish speaking.
Members do not discuss their private lives with colleagues at work.	Avoidance of embarrassment	Members who insist on discussing such matters are ostracized until they stop doing so.

The earliest examples of negative sanctions exercised in groups were revealed by the Bank Wiring Observation Room phase of the Hawthorne studies. The researchers discovered that persons who broke the group norm – for example, producing either over or under the group norm – were 'binged'. This involved a group member flicking the ear of the norm transgressor or tapping him on the upper part of the arm. Both actions were intended to indicate physically to the man that his behaviour was unacceptable to the other group members. Other negative sanctions can also be used by the group, and can be placed in ascending order of severity, as shown in figure 11.5. If negative sanctions represent the 'stick' to enforce group norm compliance, then the positive sanctions represent the 'carrot'. Such carrots for the conforming individual include accolades from other members, emotional support, increase in social status and acceptance of their ideas by others (Doms and van Avermaet, 1981).

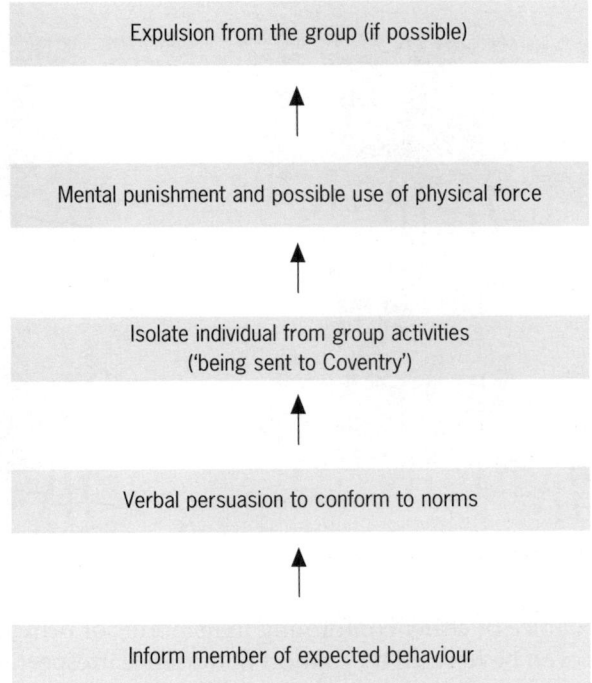

Figure 11.5: Increasing group pressure to secure individual conformity to group norms

Sent to Coventry

Being 'sent to Coventry' means becoming a social outcast. Individuals in a group can be punished in this way by their colleagues, who ignore them, refuse to speak to them, and isolate them from group activities. During the English Civil War (1642–51) fought between the Royalists and the Parliamentarians, the city of Coventry was a strong outpost of parliamentary support. Royalist prisoners who were captured in the Midlands were frequently sent to the city of Coventry, where the local population would have nothing to do with them.

Conformity: a change in belief or behaviour in response to real or imagined group pressure when there is no direct request to comply with the group or any reason to justify the behaviour change (Zimbardo and Leippe, 1991).

Obedience: a situation in which individuals change their behaviour in response to directions from others.

Conformity with norms tends to increase under certain conditions. An increase in norm conformity is associated with a decrease in the size of the group; and also with an increase in the group's homogeneity and visibility, and a stable experience. Members who perceive themselves to have low status within the group will tend to conform more and feel that they have to 'earn' the right to be deviant. High conformers are also those who feel that they are not fully accepted by the others. Diagnosing a team's norms and its members' conformity to them can help to explain group behaviour (Rothwell, 1992). Conformity can be contrasted with **obedience**, a situation in which individuals change their behaviour in response to directions from others.

If you want to deviate from a group norm you have several options. You can try to persuade others of the force of your position, and thereby alter the group norm to accommodate what you want to do. Of course, the other members may respond by persuading you to conform to the existing norm. The higher your status, and hence your power in the group, the more likely you are to be successful in changing the behaviours and beliefs of other members, and the less likely they are to change your own. If neither of these alternatives takes place, then something else will happen. If you are free to leave the group, and the group is of little importance to you, you may leave it. Conversely, if you are of little importance to the group, you may be faced

Source: © The New Yorker Collection 1976 Lee Lorenz from cartoonbank.com. All Rights Reserved.

with the choice of either conforming to its norms or being rejected by its members. You may even be rejected by your act of deviance irrespective of whether or not you are willing to recant. If, however, you are of importance to your group because you are a high-status member possessing power, popularity or special skills, then the group may tolerate your deviant behaviour and beliefs in order to avoid the threat of losing a valued member. Hence, the power that a group has to influence its members towards conformity to its norms depends on three main factors:

■ the positive and negative sanctions (rewards and punishments) that the group has at its disposal;

■ the member's desire to avoid negative sanctions such as social and physical punishments or expulsion from the group;

■ the degree to which individual members value their membership of the group and its accompanying rewards (for example, recognition, status, prestige, financial inducements).

Group cohesion: the number and strength of mutual, positive attitudes towards group members.

This last factor, the attraction that the group has for an individual, and the attraction that group members have for each other, is defined as **group cohesion**. It is the sum of all the forces that influence members to remain part of a group (see table 11.2).

Table 11.2: Group cohesion – contributors and consequences

Contributors to group cohesion	Consequences of group cohesion
Small size	
External threat	
Stable membership	Group success
Past success of group	Member satisfaction
Difficulty of entry to the group	Productivity high or low
Members sharing common goals	Greater conformity by members
Opportunity to interact with others	Members' evaluations become distorted
Attractiveness of group to individuals	Increased interaction between members
Fairness of rewards between members	Increased group influence over members
Members' agreement about their statuses	Co-operative behaviour between individuals

Stop and Criticize

Consider a group of which you are a member, and its norms and sanctions. Reflect on a situation in which a member (perhaps yourself) broke a norm and received a sanction.

Assess the positive and negative outcomes of this occurrence for the individual group member concerned and the group as a whole.

Group socialization: the process whereby members learn the values, symbols and expected behaviours of the groups to which they belong.

Organizational socialization: the process through which an individual's pattern of behaviour and their values, attitudes and motives are influenced to conform with those seen as desirable in a particular organization.

Having established a set of norms and the sanctions to enforce them, a group has to communicate these to new individuals who join the group. The new group member 'learns the ropes', and is shown how to get things done, how to interact with others and how to achieve a high social status within the group. An important aspect of achieving such status is to adhere to the group's rules or norms. Initial transgressions will be gently pointed out. However, the continued violation of norms by a group member puts the cohesion of the group at risk. When there is disagreement on a matter of importance to the group, the preservation of group effectiveness, harmony and cohesion requires a resolution of the conflict. Hence pressure is exerted on the deviating individual through persuasive communication to conform. The name given to this 'educational' process which the new member undergoes is **group socialization** and it occurs within most groups in all types of organization.

If new recruits are thoroughly socialized, they are less likely to transgress group norms and require sanctions to be administered. However, while such pressure to go along with the majority of other members may be beneficial in many respects for the group, it also carries costs. If conformity is allowed to dominate and individuals are given little opportunity to present alternative and different views, there is the danger of the group collectively making errors of judgement, leading them to take unwise actions. A later chapter will consider the concept of group-think which, through internal conformity and external group pressure, leads individual members collectively to make poor decisions.

It is important to remember that while a work group will be attempting to get its new member to adopt its own values, symbols and expected behaviours, the organization which recruited the person will be endeavouring to do the same. Some companies, such as Disney and McDonald's, are famous for and put much time, money and effort into getting their new-joiners to adopt the 'company way' of doing things. This equivalent process is called **organizational socialization**, and it too will be investigated in greater detail in a later chapter.

Employees phone home!

Alan McKinley and Phil Taylor (2000) investigated the use of teamworking in the Scottish plant of the American electronics multinational which manufactured cell phones. The company's self-managing team members learned a variety of tasks, and rotated between them. The work involved was neither skilled nor routine labour. The company produced sophisticated components using high-tech production lines. Moreover, 80 per cent of workers were male, which represented a 'masculization of production' from the female-dominated assembly of the past.

The company had an ambitious objective based on a 'management sanctioned team ideology' to produce 'a "socially individualized" pro-company workforce'. Management's ambition was to have individuals working together in groups or teams without their acquiring the characteristics of psychological groups. The research study revealed how teamwork was used by the organization for purposes of mutual control, self-surveillance, peer pressure and review.

The authors described how teams took on the tasks of disciplining and policing norms through the use of what they termed 'peer review', which formed the basis of an intensive system of internal control. In this process, individual team members were required by management to rate each other on various attitudinal and production dimensions, and to assess the behaviour of their fellow members. In essence, the company's management sought to harness the well-known power of groups to control and modify their members' behaviour (revealed in research by Mayo, Sherif, Asch and Janis) to achieve organizational goals.

McKinley and Taylor found that the company's work teams became increasingly variable and erratic. Not surprisingly, team members were initially distrustful of this process of peer review. Later, as the mutual scoring system became increasingly punitive, team members' dislike of it hardened and the workers sought to 'trade' and equalize their scores. In this way, the process of group policing of individual behaviour conceived and instigated by management was tamed.

Based on Alan McKinley and Phil Taylor, *Inside the Factory of the Future: Work, Power and Authority in Microelectronics*, Routledge, London, 2000.

Table 11.3: Comparison of stages of group development to stages of socialization

	Group development	Organizational socialization
Stage 1: Orientation	1. Forming • Establish interpersonal relationships • Conform to organizational traditions and standards • Boundary testing in relationships and task behaviours	1. Getting in (anticipatory socialization) • Setting of realistic expectations • Determining match with the newcomer
Stage 2: Redefinition	2. Storming • Conflict arising because of interpersonal behaviours • Resistance to group influence and task requirements	2. Breaking in • Initiation to the job • Establishing interpersonal relationships • Congruence between self and organizational performance appraisal
Stage 3: Co-ordination	3. Norming • Single leader emerges • Group cohesion established • New group standards and roles formed for members	3. Setting in (role management) • The degree of fit between one's life interests outside work and the demands of the organization • Resolution of conflicts at the workplace itself
Stage 4: Formalization	4. Performing • Members perform tasks together • Establishing role clarity • Teamwork is the norm	

From *A Diagnostic Approach to Organizational Behaviour*, 4/E by Gordon, © 1993. Reprinted by permission of Prentice-Hall, Inc., Upper Saddle River, NJ.

Group influences on individuals' attitudes

Why do members conform to group pressure? Group norms allow individual members to avoid chaos in their lives. They let them get on with their business by ensuring the survival of the group; focusing on achieving its task; increasing the predictability of the behaviour of others; and avoiding individuals embarrassing each other. These might be termed 'external' for conformity to group norms: for example, speaking or dressing in a particular way. Observing norms is of such personal benefit to us that we are prepared to suppress any personal desires and are thus willing to limit our individual freedom and abide by them. Moreover, we punish those who violate the norms and reward those who do not. The earliest experimental studies into conformity to group norms were carried out by Solomon Asch. Alongside these external reasons, there are 'internal' ones. One such internal reason is that we each have a desire for order and meaning in our lives, making attempts to 'make sense' of seemingly unconnected facts or events. For many human beings, uncertainty is disturbing and is something that should be reduced to the absolute minimum. We like to know 'what's going on' and to be in control of the situations in which we find ourselves. Norms, and the adherence to norms, offer a contribution to the predictability which most human beings desire.

Asch's study of conformity to group norms

The experimenter and his study

In the early 1950s, Solomon E. Asch conducted a laboratory experiment into individual conformity in groups.

The situation

Seven men sat around a table supposedly to participate in a study on visual perception.

The subject

Only no. 6 was a real subject (second from the right). The remainder were Asch's paid accomplices.

The task

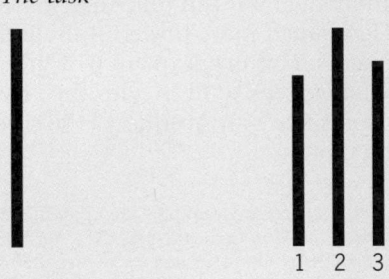

The task was an easy one. To judge which of three lines was equal in length to one they had seen earlier.

➤

The problem

The results

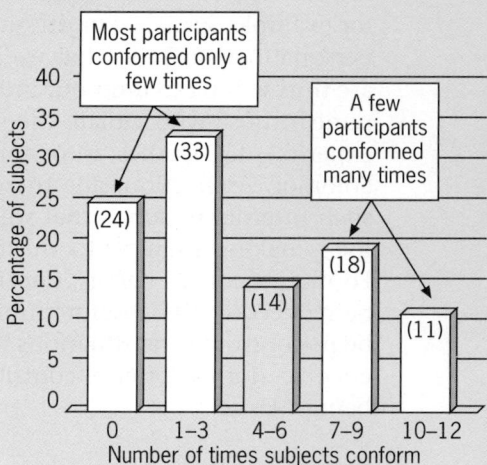

In the experimental conditions, the accomplices had been instructed to lie about which line was correct. Under pressure, the subject (no. 6) shows signs of conflict, of whether to conform to the group judgement or give the response he judges to be correct.

Most subjects conformed to group judgements at least once. However, most resisted group pressure most of the time. 58 per cent conformed three times or less, on the twelve occasions when accomplices gave false answers.

The conclusion

Overall in twelve trials, involving 123 subjects, approximately 75 per cent of experimental subjects conformed at least once; 5 per cent conformed all the time; and 25 per cent never conformed; the average for conformers was 37 per cent. Later Asch found that three subjects were sufficient to create the effect. Large numbers did not increase conformity. A second dissenter cut the conformity rate by 25 per cent, even when the dissenter disagreed with the subject.

■ Conformity increased if the group member was regarded as being of high status.

■ Conformity decreased if subjects were not face-to-face.

■ Conformity increased when the group members had to continue working together in the future.

The research indicates how difficult it can be for individuals to express their opinions when these are not in accord with those of other team members. It is interesting to consider the pressure that a group can exert on an individual if it can influence something as unambiguous and familiar as judging the length of lines. How much more powerful the influence if individuals have to make subjective and unfamiliar judgements. This may explain why groups are ineffective. The best decisions are not made because group members seek to fit in with the views of others rather than work for the best solution to the problem. Doms and van Avermaet (1981) replicated Asch's studies and obtained results similar to Asch's original ones.

Based on Solomon E. Asch, 'Effects of group pressure upon the modification and distortion of judgements', in H. Guetzkow (ed.), *Groups, Leadership and Men*, Carnegie Press, New York, 1951, pp. 177–90. Photographs (the situation, the subject and the problem) from S.E Asch 'Opinions and social pressure', *Scientific American*, vol. 193, no. 5, pp. 31–5, offprint 450. Figures reprinted from *Groups, Leadership and Men*: 'The task' and 'the results' from Asch, S.E. 'Effects of group pressure upon the modification and distortion of judgements' by permission of Carnegie Press © 1951 by H. Guetzkow.

Solomon Asch (1951, 1952, 1956) found that those subjects who yielded to group pressure did so for different reasons. He distinguished three types of yielding.

Distortion of perception

These subjects seem to have convinced themselves that they actually did see the lines the way the other group members stated in their judgements. Yielding at the perceptual level was rare, and occurred primarily among those who displayed a lack of trust in themselves. They were unaware that their estimates had been displaced or distorted by the majority.

Distortion of judgement

These subjects yielded either because they were unsure that they understood the task set for them, or because they did not want to 'spoil the experiment'. They suffered from primary doubt and lack of confidence. The factor of greatest importance was their decision that their perceptions were inaccurate, and that those of the majority were correct (akin to independence without confidence). Distortion of judgement occurred frequently.

Distortion of action

The subjects did not suffer a modification of perception, nor did they conclude that they were wrong. They yielded because they feared being excluded, ostracized or considered eccentric. These subjects suppressed their observations and voiced the majority position with a full awareness of what they are doing.

Asch's experiment was replicated more than thirty years later, this time with five individuals using PCs who were told that they had been linked together. Whereas Asch had found that the number who refused to conform to the group in any trial was just 25 per cent, in the repeat study, 69 per cent of the subjects made no errors. Maybe a computer-mediated communication environment reduces our tendency to conform to a unanimous group position.

Stop and Criticize

Think of an occasion when you have given an opinion or supported a decision contrary to your own feelings and judgement, but consistent with those around you at the time.

How can you live with yourself for acting in such a socially compliant and submissive manner? What is your pathetic excuse for having done so?

Milgram's 'electric shock' experiments

Stanley Milgram, experimenter (1933–84)

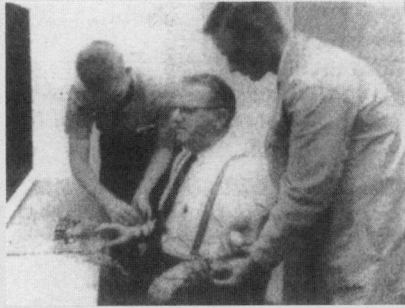

Volunteer subject, accomplice 'learner', accomplice experimenter

A study by Stanley Milgram showed that a group can aid the individual to defy authority. Would you torture another person simply because you were told to do so by someone in authority? Of course not, you would probably reply with little hesitation. In a series of now famous and highly controversial experiments, Stanley Milgram examined people's level of obedience to authority. The research involved ordinary people of different ages, sexes, races and occupations. A group of psychiatrists, post-graduate students and social science lecturers were asked by Milgram to predict how many of the research subjects would actually obey the experimenter's order. There was a high agreement that virtually all subjects would refuse to obey. Only one in a hundred would do it, said the psychiatrists, and that person would be a psychopath.

Milgram's experiment involved volunteer subjects participating in a learning experiment. They were to act as teachers of people who were trying to learn a series of simple word pairs. As teachers they were told to punish the student when he failed to learn by giving him an electric shock. At the start the shocks were small in intensity but every time the learner made a mistake, the teacher was told to increase the size of the shock. In carrying out the experiments Milgram found that two out of every three subjects tested administered the electric shocks up to a level which was clearly marked 'fatal' simply because an authority figure told them to do so. In fact, no electric shocks were ever actually given although the volunteer 'teachers' believed that the learners were really receiving the shocks they administered. An earlier experiment by Asch had shown that it only needed one other person to agree with a deviant for the conformity effect to be counteracted. In one variation of his experiment, Milgram placed two of his accomplices alongside the subject, so that the testing of the wired-up learner would be done by a group and not by a single subject. This experimental situation is thus similar to Asch's.

The experiment began with one of the accomplices administering the shocks. He then refused to continue, argued with the experimenter and withdrew, sitting in the corner of the room. The second accomplice then took over, continued for a bit and then refused, just as the previous one had done. The real subject now remained to administer the shocks himself. Milgram repeated this procedure forty times, each with a different subject. In thirty of these forty cases, he found that once the subjects had seen their group colleagues defy the experimenter, they also defied him. When group pressure (or support) for such defiance was lacking, only fourteen subjects defied the authority figure. Milgram concluded that peer rebellion is a very powerful force in undercutting the experimenter's authority. Milgram offered seven explanations of why the group was effective in helping the individual to do this. The reasons are the same as those which explain the power the group has over the individual:

1. Peers instil in the subject the idea of defying the experimenter.

2. The lone subject has no way of knowing if defiance is a bizarre or common occurrence. Two examples confirm that it is a natural reaction.

3. The act of defiance by the accomplice defines the act of shocking as improper. It provides social confirmation for the subject's suspicion that it is wrong to punish a subject against his will, even in a psychological experiment.

4. By remaining in the room, the accomplices' presence carries with it a measure of social disapproval for the subject.

5. As long as the accomplices participate in the experiment, there is dispersion of responsibility among group members for the shocking. As they withdraw, the responsibility focuses on the subject.

6. The subject witnesses two instances of disobedience and observes that the consequences of defying the experimenter are minimal.

7. Failing to keep the accomplices performing as required diminishes the experimenter's power.

Based on Stanley Milgram, *Obedience to Authority*, Tavistock, London, 1973. Milgram experiment photo from S. Milgram, *Obedience to Authority*, Tavistock, 1973.

Deindividuation

Deindividuation:
an increased state of anonymity that loosens normal constraints on individuals' behaviour, reducing their sense of responsibility, and leading to an increase in impulsive and antisocial acts.

Social facilitation explains how groups can arouse individuals, while social loafing shows that groups can diffuse and hence diminish individual responsibility. Together, arousal and diffused responsibility combine to decrease normal, social inhibitions and create deindividuation. **Deindividuation** refers to a person's loss of self-awareness and self-monitoring. It involves some loss of personal identity and greater identification with the group.

The writings of Gustave LeBon led to the theory of deindividuation which was first proposed by Leon Festinger, Albert Pepitone and Theodore Newcombe (1952). However, it is Marion Hampton (1999, p. 112) who neatly captures the experience of deindividuation when she writes:

> There are moments when we can observe ourselves behaving irrationally as members of crowds or audiences, yet we are swept by the emotion, unable to check it. In smaller groups too, like committees or teams, we may experience powerful feelings of loyalty, anxiety or anger. The moods and emotions of those around us seem to have an exaggerated effect on our own moods and emotions.

The influence of the crowd in history

Gustave LeBon stated that the crowd is 'always intellectually inferior to the isolated individual ... mob man is fickle, credulous and intolerant, showing the violence and ferocity of primitive beings'. He observed events during a period of great upheaval in France, reading accounts of crowd behaviour in the French Revolution of 1789 and in the Paris Commune of 1871. In his book, *The Crowd*, originally published in 1895, he hypothesized that humans had a two-part personality. The upper half was conscious and unique to each individual, and contained dignity and virtue. The lower half, in contrast, was unconscious, was shared with everyone else, and contained bad desires and instincts. In normal circumstances the conscious part guided a person's behaviour, but in a group or a crowd situation, it somehow stopped functioning, and allowed the lower half to take over. LeBon attributed this primitive behaviour to three things:

Anonymity   Individuals cannot be easily identified in a crowd.

Contagion   Ideas and emotions spread rapidly and unpredictably.

Suggestability   The savagery that is just below the surface is released by suggestion.

Based on Gustave LeBon, *The Crowd: A Study of the Popular Mind*, Unwin, London, 1908 (first published in 1895 by Ernest Benn).

Social information processing theory tells us that individuals use information from their immediate environments to interpret events, develop appropriate attitudes and understand expectations about their behaviour and its consequences. Bandura's social learning theory reminds us that role models can direct such non-inhibited behaviour in various ways within the organization (O'Leary-Kelly et al., 1996). Edward Diener (1979) argued that when people were in a deindividuated state, they experienced:

- an inability to monitor or regulate their own behaviour;
- a reduction in the normal restraints against impulsive behaviour;
- a heightened sensitivity to emotional states and situational cues;

- a reduced concern with social approval of actions;

- a reduction in the capacity for rational planning.

In his novel, *Lord of the Flies* (1954), William Golding describes how a group of boys marooned on a desert island, through their shouting, clapping and face painting, 'hype themselves up' and reduce their self-consciousness, turning themselves into a single organism, within which the individual members lose their identity. The unrestrained behaviours are provoked by the power of the group. In certain kinds of group situation, attention is drawn away from the individual, their anonymity is increased, and they are more likely to abandon their normal restraints and to lose their sense of individual responsibility. Edward Diener (1979, 1980) extended the original work on deindividuation. He specified the conditions within a group in which individuals lose their personal identities and merge into it (figure 11.6).

Studies have found that two factors encourage deindividuation.

Group size

Within a group, members consider themselves unidentifiable, and their own actions to be those of the group. As group size increases, the more its members lose self-awareness and the more willing they become to commit antisocial actions. In these circumstances, self-awareness and self-monitoring plummet.

Anonymity

Anonymity lessens inhibitions. It can lead to prosocial behaviour, such as making people more intimate or playful, or antisocial behaviour, such as attacking a person as a mob. For example, warriors in a tribe paint their faces and wear masks; military personnel wear uniforms; and companies increasingly require staff to dress in standardized 'workwear'. The positive aspect is that they associate with the company, but it can also increase anonymity.

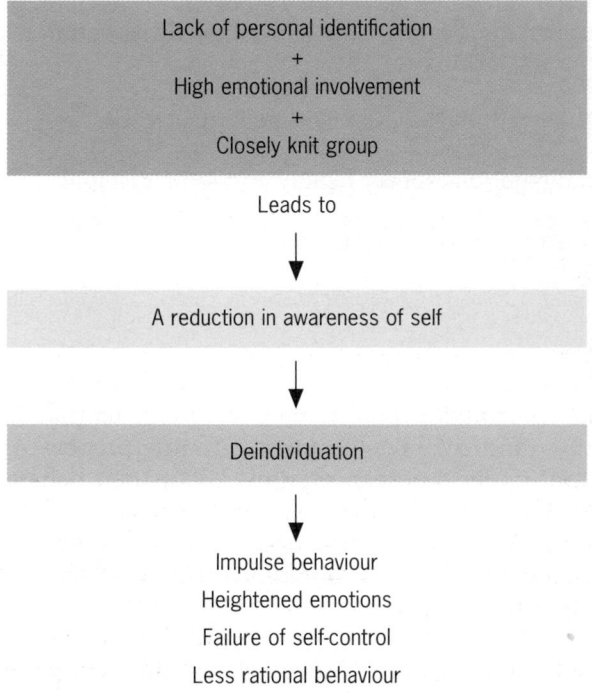

Figure 11.6: The process of deindividuation
From Tony Malim and Ann Birch, *Social Psychology*, 2nd Edition, Macmillan, 1997. Reproduced with permission of Palgrave Macmillan.

All these writings make the point that an individual's mental processes are radically altered when they become part of a crowd. They come to share the emotional experience of others; and the forces of emotion and the unconscious against the forces of reason. LeBon contributed to a number of core concepts in group theory, as suggested by Hampton (1999, pp. 115–16):

- The group as a distinct level of analysis in a kind of nested hierarchy of human systems (the individual, the group, the organization, the society), each level requiring its own theories and means of analysis and not being reducible to its constituents.

- The 'boundaries', mostly invisible, psychological, but also spatial and temporal – features that differentiate groups from each other and from their environments.

- The temporary character of groups, which implies that these social systems have a life span, with a beginning, a maturity and an end.

Studies of deindividuation on the internet suggest that when dispersed members communicate using computers, there is a higher frequency of insults, swearing and name-calling between them. When working in computer-mediated mode, there tends to be more hostility than when individuals are in face-to-face interaction. Much internet communication occurs under conditions in which participants, rightly or wrongly, believe that they cannot be personally identified. However, once names are attached to members' messages, the number of uninhibited remarks tends to fall significantly.

Stop and Criticize

What deindividuating tendencies can you identify in the organizations with which you are familiar? Are these being created consciously or unconsciously? What effect are they having on organizational employees and clients?

A great number of different factors influence conformity to norms. The personality characteristics of individuals play a part in predisposing them to conform to group norms. The kinds of stimulus eliciting conformity behaviour are also important. That people conform to norms when they are uncertain about a situation was demonstrated by the Sherif experiments. He also discovered that a person with a high degree of self-confidence could affect the opinions and estimates of other group members.

Upbringing also plays an important part. A value which is particularly salient in Jordan, for example, is the subordination of one's personal interests and goals to the welfare and needs of one's family or group. Group-centredness can be seen in Arab cultures where the individual is regarded as subservient to the group. Berger (1964, p. 33) alluded to this trait when he wrote: 'Through most of their history, despite the recent introduction of Western political forms, Arab communities have been collections of groups rather than individuals. The family and the tribe have been the social units through which the individual has related himself to others and to governments.' Formal education can be considered a part of the process of upbringing and child socialization. In this context, Japan is particularly noted for the group orientation of its youngsters, although at the start of the twenty-first century this is slowly beginning to change (*The Economist*, 2000).

The amount of conformity to a group standard generally corresponds strongly to the degree of ambiguity of the stimulus being responded to. Situational factors are also involved. The size of the group, the unanimity of the majority, and its structure all have an effect. It has been found that conformity increased as the group size increased. It is also affected by a person's position in the communication structure of a group, with conformity being greater in a decentralized network than in a centralized one. Finally, there are the intra-group relationships referred to earlier. The kind of pressure exerted, the composition of the group, how successful it has been in the past, and the degree to which the member identifies with the group, are all examples of this.

Stop and Criticize

Is such conformity by the individual within organizations a bad thing that should be eliminated? Or is it a good thing that should be encouraged?

Monkey see, monkey do

Sandra Robinson and Anne O'Leary-Kelly studied antisocial actions in organizations. These were defined as behaviours which could potentially harm the individual or organizational property. Such actions included sexual harassment, stealing, insubordination, sabotage, rumour spreading, withholding effort and absenteeism. The researchers studied 187 employees from 35 groups in 20 organizations. They examined the extent to which individual employees' antisocial actions were shaped by the group in which they worked.

They found that as the richness of the group experience increased, members became more likely to match their individual level of antisocial behaviour to that of the group in general. The stronger the group's antisocial behaviour climate, the more it affected an individual's actions. Where individuals in the group relied on each other to complete a task, their behaviour was more strongly related to the level of antisocial behaviour exhibited by the group. Where an individual exhibited less antisocial behaviour than the group in general, they were less satisfied with their co-workers. Groups can display high levels of either antisocial or prosocial behaviour, and can encourage similar behaviour from their members. The group thus provides a social context to an individual's interpretation of organization-level systems, and this context has a significant effect on the individual's antisocial behaviour in the organization.

The authors also point to the group-induced, *contagion effect* which explains the spread or clustering of aggressive acts in particular organizations or industry. They conclude that antisocial groups encourage antisocial individual behaviour, and that isolating or ignoring them is unlikely to change them. They found that the likelihood of punishment was more effective than closeness of supervision in weakening the group–individual behaviour link.

Antisocial behaviour was thus not solely an individual-level phenomenon. Although individual characteristics such as personality, prior learning of aggressive behaviour, family background and upbringing all played part, they argued that the social context of the work group exerted a major influence on whether individuals behaved in an antisocial way at work. Managers had both the ability and the responsibility to influence antisocial behaviour by shaping work group dynamics.

Based on Sandra L. Robinson and Anne M. O'Leary-Kelly, 'Monkey see, monkey do: the influence of work groups on the antisocial behaviour of employees', *Academy of Management Journal*, vol. 41, no. 6, 1998, pp. 658–72.

Individual influences on group attitudes and behaviour

So far, the focus has been on the group influencing its members. Does this mean that an individual can never influence their group? Clearly not, since history recounts numerous instances of individuals – revolutionaries, rebels, radical thinkers, religious zealots – who created minority groupings, and as minorities successfully persuaded majorities. Indeed, leadership can be considered an

Compliance: a majority's influence on a minority.

Conversion: a minority's influence on a majority.

example of minority influence. The theoretical underpinning to the process of a minority's influence on a majority is provided by Serge Moscovici's (1980) social influence theory. He used the term **compliance** to describe what happens when a majority influences a minority, through its possession of various kinds of power and its ability to implement positive and negative sanctions. He applied the term **conversion** to describe a minority's influence on a majority. The concept of conversion is illustrated every time an employee persuades their company to adopt a new product or create a new division.

Moscovici stressed the importance of consistency in the conversion process. The individual persuading the group has to stick unswervingly to their point of view. Moscovici's original work on conversion has stimulated much research, and we now possess a growing body of research and an understanding of how a minority can influence a majority (Nemeth, 1986). These different writings have been summarized by Huczynski (2004), who listed what the minority influencer of a majority has to do:

Become viable	Take a position that others are aware of, make yourself heard, get yourself noticed, and generally overcome the illusion of unanimity.
Create tension	Motivate those in the majority to try to deal with your ideas.
Be consistent	Stick unswervingly to the same position. Do not take a variety of positions that disagree with the majority.
Be persistent	Restate your consistent position in the face of others' opposition to you.
Be unyielding	Being firm and unyielding involves digging your heels in and not compromising.
Be self-confident	This is conveyed by one's consistency and persistence. It raises self-doubts among the majority, leading it to reconsider its position.
Seek defectors	Defections from the majority increases the self-doubt of the remaining majority and frees its doubters, who may have self-censored themselves to speak out, perhaps encouraging more converts.

Before the 1980s, the idea that a minority could influence a majority was not a widely held view among social psychologists. However, through their research and publications, Moscovici and his colleagues presented an alternative view that possessed all the above characteristics. Minority influencing is now becoming an accepted and recognized phenomenon which regularly features in social psychology texts.

The eyes have it

In an online work group, how are minority opinions expressed and received by the majority? Will a dissenter feel freer to express their opinion than in a face-to-face situation? Research by Poppy McLeod and her colleagues (1997) gave partial information about three different companies to group members who discussed it either face-to-face or in a synchronous chat. Their task was to share the information to make the best investment decision. The data were organized in such a way that if all the information was made available to all the members, company A would be recognized as the best choice. However, the most revealing piece of information was provided to only one of the group's members, ensuring that they would be the minority opinion holder. These individuals were found to

➤

be particularly vocal when their contributions were online and anonymous, but they were ineffective at changing the majority's opinion. In consequence, the online work groups made poor decisions and bad investments. The researchers highlight the role of 'pain–gain'. In a face-to-face setting, a minority opinion holder has to stick their neck out and risk censure when voicing their opinions, and this alone may make the others pay attention to them. In contrast, online, the dissenter's pain is considerably reduced, particularly if their contributions are anonymous, so the gain will be lower as well.

Based on p. L. McLeod, R.S. Baron, M.W. Marti and K. Yoon, 'The eyes have it', *Journal of Applied Psychology*, vol. 82, no. 5, 1997, pp. 706–18.

Recap

1. *Explain the basic tenets of social identity theory and social representation theory.*

   - Social identity theory holds that aspects of our identity derive from the membership of a group.

   - Groups construct social representations consisting of beliefs, ideas and values which they transmit to their new members.

   - Such representations, together with group socialization, lead to all members sharing a common frame of reference.

2. *Distinguish between social facilitation and social loafing.*

   - Individual behaviour is variously modified by the presence of others or by being a part of a group.

   - The concepts of social influence, social facilitation, synergy and social loafing distinguish the direction and nature of such modifications.

3. *Understand why groups develop norms and use sanctions to regulate the behaviour of their members.*

   - Social norms guide the behaviour of individuals in a group. They can be pivotal or peripheral.

   - Social norms are established in four ways – explicit statement, critical events, initial behaviour and transfer behaviour.

   - Sanctions are administered by members to those individuals who transgress or uphold the group's norms. Sanctions can therefore be negative (verbal abuse) or positive (praise). Groups possess an escalating hierarchy of ever-stronger negative sanctions.

4. *Understand the process of group socialization of individuals.*

   - Groups teach new members about their norms and incorporate them in their shared frame of reference through the process of group socialization.

5. *Explain why individuals conform to the dictates of their group.*

   - As individuals, we tend to conform to group norms because of benefits for us individually if others abide by the agreed rules, our desire for order and meaning in our lives, and a need to receive a satisfying response from others.

   - The 'cost' to the person who is a member of a group is the deindividuation that membership entails. Group membership brings with it anonymity and becoming 'lost in the crowd'. This can reduce our sense of individual responsibility, lower our social constraints and lead us to engage in impulsive, antisocial acts.

6. *Distinguish between conformity and conversion.*

   - Group orientation differs depending on the culture in which an individual lives.

   - Research shows that a majority influences an individual (called *conformity*) and that a minority can influence a majority (called *conversion*).

Revision

1. Consider the advantages and disadvantages at work of being (a) 'one of the gang', (b) a 'lone wolf' – loner, or (c) somewhere in between.

2. Your instructor is proposing to set a student group assignment as part of the continuous assessment for this course. However, you are concerned about the effect that social loafing might have on your group's overall performance, the likely contributions of your other group members, and the equitable award of marks among the individual group members. How would you respond to your instructor's proposal?

3. Is conformity by the individual within organizations a bad thing that should be eliminated? Or is it a good thing that should be encouraged?

4. Critically evaluate the empirical research on individual conformity to group pressure.

5. Suggest how an individual might go about persuading a majority.

Springboard

Diener, E., 1979, 'Deindividuation, self-awareness and disinhibition', *Journal of Personality and Social Psychology*, vol. 37, no. 7, pp. 1160–71.

Article describing the theory and research into deindividuation.

Doms, M. and van Avermaet, E., 1981, 'The conformity effect: a timeless phenomenon?', *Bulletin of the British Psychological Society*, vol. 36, pp. 180–8.

These authors replicated Solomon Asch's classic studies on individual conformity in groups and obtained similar results.

Hogg, M.A. and Vaughan, G.M., 1998, *Social Psychology*, Prentice Hall, Hemel Hempstead.

An introductory textbook for social psychology. Chapter 7, entitled 'Basic group processes', provides more detailed, experimental description and discussion of the concepts briefly considered in this chapter.

Huczynski, A.A., 2004, *Influencing Within Organizations: Getting In, Rising Up and Moving On*, Routledge, London (second edition).

This book discusses various aspects of influencing. One of the chapters concentrates on influencing a group, summarizing Moscovici's research findings and complementing them with other techniques to influence groups of people.

Latane, B., Williams, K. and Harkins, S., 1979, 'Many hands make light work: the causes and consequences of social loafing', *Journal of Personality and Social Psychology*, vol. 37, no. 6, pp. 822–32.

This is a full account of the recreation of the Ringelmann experiment which first revealed the existence of the phenomenon of social loafing.

McKinlay, A. and Taylor, P., 2000, *Inside the Factory of the Future: Work, Power and Authority in Microelectronics*, Routledge, London.

Considers work, power and authority in a microelectronics plant and highlights how group pressure is used to affect the performance of individual workers.

Home viewing

In *Twelve Angry Men* (1957, directed by Sidney Lumet) a jury retires to deliberate and to decide on the guilt or innocence of a youth from a slum background. At the outset, eleven of the twelve jurors are convinced of the boy's guilt and are keen to find him guilty without further discussion. Only one member of the jury, played by Henry Fonda, has reservations and persuades the other members to take the time to review the evidence. Fonda manages to change the guilty votes of the other eleven jurors, and persuades them to acquit the young defendant. The film illustrates the concept of *conversion*. Watch Fonda's behaviour carefully. At first sight it appears that it is random. But then, you'll see a pattern. What is that pattern? What influencing tactics does he use? Which types of power are possessed by which characters in the film?

OB in literature

Fred Voss, *Goodstone*, Bloodaxe Books, Newcastle upon Tyne, 1991.

Poems by a machinist who works on the shop floor of a US company which manufactures aircraft parts. The verses describe his experiences with groups of fellow workers and managers – sometimes informative, sometimes cynical, but always thought-provoking.

Chapter exercises

1: Discovering the norms

Objectives 1. To raise your understanding of the effect of group norms on behaviour in an organizational environment.

2. To demonstrate the link between behaviour in groups and the creation of group norms, and group norm enforcement strategies.

Background Often group norms are implicit rather than explicit, and are difficult to identify. Nevertheless, individuals' behaviour may be influenced by norms of which they may not be fully conscious. The more people become aware of the norms that affect them, the more they are able to understand their own behaviour. This activity seeks to make group norms explicit.

Briefing Step 1: Write down in the space below, ONE important norm that operates in your place of work, university class or tutorial group.

Step 2: Make a note of the following:

■ How was that group norm communicated to you?

■ What happens if you break this group norm? How did the group 'police' this norm?

■ How does the norm affect your performance?

Step 3: In pairs, compare and discuss your answers to these questions.

2: Changing the norms

Objectives 1. To raise your understanding of the effect of norms on behaviour in individual groups.

2. To consider the relationship of group and leadership behaviour.

Briefing Step 1: Read the case, 'Getting the group into line'.

Step 2: Consider the four questions at the end.

Step 3: Re-read the case, noting your responses to each question.

Step 4: Be prepared to discuss your answers with fellow course members.

Getting the group into line

To save a little money for skiing I worked for six weeks on a hydroelectric construction project at Lake Pukaki. . . . My job was surveyor's lineman. The pay was good; but not good enough, I decided, so I took a second job at night and became a tally clerk with a pile driving gang. . . .

The first night I joined the four-man gang after dinner and we walked through the frosty air to a large muddy pond on the down-river side of the dam. There was a dinghy on the shore of the pond and we used it to row out to a floating platform supporting a tall tower. The task was a simple one: to test the depth and consistency of the clay in the pond by driving a succession of steel pipes into it. The hammer was a great iron contraption suspended from the tower and pulled up by hand. My job was to take a tally of the number of blows required to drive a foot of pipe into the clay.

The four-man team was not an impressive group. They ranged from a small, wizened character with a bitter, debauched face to an enormous Maori workman who seemed to lack the customary good humour. Work commenced – if you could call it work – and the four men pulled the weight to the top of the tower with the greatest of ease and duly let it fall with an almighty clunk – and I made a notation in my book. At the end of an hour nobody had achieved a sweat and they had driven the pipe down a total of twelve feet.

'OK, that's the lot for tonight', said the little man, and the four of them got back in the dinghy. 'Coming mate?'

Somewhat dazed I asked for an explanation, and got it. They were working on contract – so much a foot of pipe – and someone had made a mistake. Twelve feet of pipe a night was enough to give them all a substantial pay packet so that's all they did. No point in spoiling a good contract, was there? What they did was really none of my business – I got paid wages for an eight-hour shift irrespective of how much pipe was driven – so we rowed ashore and went to a small hut which was already crammed with a dozen other men. A stove was red hot in the corner and a game of cards was going strong. For six hours I listened to crude stories and idle chatter and I have rarely been more bored. At the end of the eight-hour shift I was more than happy to escape back to bed.

The second night was as cold and frosty as the first. Out we went to the platform and this time it took us nearly two hours to knock the pipe down twelve feet. We went ashore and the gang headed for the hut but I stayed behind. I couldn't stand another six hours of dirty jokes, and didn't I have some responsibility to my employers? I jumped into the dinghy and rowed out to the platform again. In the next six hours I operated the hammer by myself and drove in another thirty feet of pipe, recording it all in my notebook. At the end of the shift I went off to bed feeling a lot happier.

I was back on the survey job next morning and felt none the worse for the night's work. During the afternoon I felt a jab in the ribs, and there was the little man.

'The fellas aren't too happy about last night,' he hissed out of the side of his mouth in best Mafia fashion. 'If you do it again they are going to throw you in the lake.'

I grabbed his jacket and pulled him close until we were eyeball to eyeball. 'You plan to throw me in the lake?' I queried.

'Not me mate!' he hastened to assure me. 'It's the other fellas.' I released him and he slunk off back to his hut.

Nobody said anything that night as we rowed out to the raft but there was tension in the air. It took two and a half hours to drive the pipe down twelve feet – the clay was much tougher – but finally the job was done.

'Let's go ashore,' said someone, but nobody moved.

'Coming mate?' one of them asked me.

This was it, I knew, and I braced myself.

'Not me, friend!'

For a few seconds nothing was said and the atmosphere quivered with violence. It was the big Maori who made the first move.

'Let's knock the bloody thing down a bit further,' he suggested. 'I've had a gutsful of sitting in that hut . . .' And knock it down we did – eighty feet that night. I can't say I ever became bosom buddies with this quartet, but over the next few weeks we didn't spend another hour in the hut. Finally the 'bosses' caught up with the contract and had it modified – but the men had made a fortune before the change came.

1. How did the managerial context affect group norms and behaviour? From this story, how would you evaluate the behaviour of 'the bosses'?

2. What methods did the group try to use to influence Hillary to adopt its norms?

3. Usually individuals fall into line with the groups they join. In this case the reverse occurred. Why?

4. What would you have done if you had found yourself in Hillary's situation? Why?

E. Hillary, *Nothing Venture, Nothing Win*, 1975, Coronet, London. Questions from G. Elkin and K. Inkson, *Organizational Behaviour in New Zealand*, 2000, Prentice Hall, Auckland, pp. 185–7.

Chapter 12 # Teamworking

Key concepts

team	high-performance work system
team autonomy	autonomous teamworking
advice team	total quality management
quality circles	just-in-time systems
action team	Japanese teamworking
project team	external work team differentiation
cross-functional team	internal work team integration
production team	team performance
empowerment	team viability

Learning outcomes

When you have read this chapter, you should be able to define those key concepts in your own words, and you should also be able to:

1. Understand why 'team' is a contested concept in the organizational literature.
2. List the nine dimensions of team autonomy.
3. Differentiate between four major types of team and give an example of each.
4. Discuss the types of obstacle to effectiveness experienced by each type of team.
5. Contrast Western with Japanese concepts of teamworking.
6. List the four main variables in the ecological framework for analyzing work team effectiveness.
7. Understand the increasing importance of virtual teamworking.

Why study teamworking?

Research shows that 70 per cent of airline disasters are caused by failures in teamworking rather than by individual human errors or mechanical breakdown. Studies into space travel have concluded that a smoothly functioning team contributes to mission success and survival in an emergency. A study into the design of a lunar laboratory stated that the primary limiting factor for all extraterrestrial activities is the problem of interpersonal relationships. Dr Oleg Gazenko, medical director of Soviet and Russian space programmes, noted that the limitations of life in space are not medical but psychological (Stuster, 1996). If poor teamworking does not kill you, it can seriously reduce your work motivation and raise your level of job stress. Yet teamworking has also been found to increase productivity and increase job satisfaction, to the benefit of both the organization and the employee. Managers want to know how they can obtain the benefits of teamworking without its costs.

The potential of teamworking to contribute to these organizational (management) goals has been rediscovered at the level of the shop floor by the interest in

Japanese teamworking, seen by many critics as a means of creating a compliant and programmable workforce. The teamwork literature reveals a continuing, worldwide, organizational trend towards the introduction of teamworking. Senior management appears to believe that teams are an effective way of:

- improving performance;

- reducing production costs;

- speeding up innovations;

- improving product quality;

- increasing work flexibility;

- introducing new technologies;

- increasing employee participation;

- achieving better industrial relations;

- meeting the challenge of global competition;

- identifying and solving work-related problems.

Indeed, some critics claim that teamworking is seen as a simple solution to virtually all organizational problems. Much management research, consultancy work and money has been, and continues to be, spent on making teams work well in companies (Veloutsou and Panigyrakis, 2001). With the current popularity of teamworking in organizations, it is important to assess critically the suggestions, research and prescriptions on offer.

The T-word and team job design

Team: a psychological group whose members share a common goal which they pursue collaboratively. Members can only succeed or fail as a whole, and all share the benefits and costs of collective success or failure.

The word **team** derives from the old English, Fresian and Norse word for a bridle and thence to a set of draught animals harnessed together and, by analogy, to a number of persons involved in joint action (Annett and Stanton, 2000). Nicky Hayes saw teams as a sporting metaphor used frequently by managers and consultants. It stressed both inclusiveness and similarity – members sharing common values and co-operating to achieve common goals – while also emphasizing differences, as various individuals play distinct, albeit equally valuable roles, and have different responsibilities. She wrote that (Hayes, 1997, p. 27):

The idea of 'team' at work must be one of the most widely used metaphors in organizational life. A group of workers or managers is generally described as a 'team', in much the same way that a company or department is so often described as 'one big family'. But often, the new employee receiving these assertions quickly discovers that what was described as a 'team' is actually anything but. The mental image of cohesion, co-ordination and common goals which was conjured up by the metaphor of the team, was entirely different from the everyday reality of working life.

Jos Benders and Geert Van Hootegem (1999a, 1999b) too felt that after decades of experimentation, teams had finally achieved the status of 'good management practice' in Western organizations. Echoing Hayes' point, they wrote that 'team is a word for managers': that is, an appealing word used as a rhetorical strategy through which managers hope to achieve their goals. Sainsbury's, a large British supermarket, has the employee job title of 'checkout captain'. Academics and practitioners around the world had developed different notions of what was meant by teamworking. Benders and Van Hootegem went on to distinguish three different meanings of the word 'team', as used by Japanese managers working in Western countries:

Team as collective spirit

The appealing label 'team work' is used to convey the necessity of the desired co-operative spirit when establishing Japanese transplants in Western countries (for example, 'Team Toyota' in its plant in Kentucky, USA). Employees are socialized into an organization's cultural, 'community-of-fate'.

Teams as the hallmark of lean production

Based on the book, *The Machine That Changed the World* (Womack et al., 1990), teams are assigned a critical role in lean production's superior performance, and are presented as a break with European and American 'Fordist' production practices.

Teams as quality control circles

Quality control circles are groups of employees who meet to improve their work situation. These were widely adopted in Europe and America during the 1980s. However, their popularity was short-lived as they failed to deliver quick performance improvements. Although QC circles were, in theory, considered to be distinct from work units, in practice there was considerable overlap between the two.

Despite this semantic confusion, Jon Annett and Neville Stanton suggest that the key distinction between a group and a team is that the members of the latter share a common goal that they pursue collaboratively. Moreover, they can only succeed or fail as a whole, and the members of that team share the benefits and costs of success or failure. In contrast, the members of a (psychological) group may share a number of common features that are listed in chapter 9, and each has their individual goals, but if they lack a common goal, they will be in competition with each other. Thus, a team is a group, but not all groups are teams (Annett and Stanton, 2000).

Assigning a task to a team of people rather than to a single individual is a relatively recent practice. More is known about individual-based than team-based job design. J. Richard Hackman (1983, 1987, 1990), a major contemporary contributor to the theory and practice of work organization, is also an active promoter of teamworking. Writing about job design in the context of teamworking, he argued that the Job Characteristics Model recommendations were as valid at the team level as they were at the individual level. He also offered guidelines for the effective functioning of work teams:

1. The task is one that is appropriate for a work team.

2. The team is recognized as such by its own members and others in the organization.

3. The team has clear authority over the task (for example, a team must not be 'second guessed' by management).

4. The structure of the team, including the task, the team members and the team norms, needs to promote teamwork.

5. The organization must support the team through policies and systems that help meet its needs.

6. Expert coaching and feedback are provided to the teams when needed and when team members are ready to receive it.

Table 12.1: Types of team and their outputs

Types and examples	Degree of differentiation from other work units	Degree of co-ordination with other work units	Degree of technical specialization	Work cycles/time frame	Typical outputs
ADVICE Committees Review panels and boards Quality control circles Employee involvement groups Advisory councils	Low	Low	Low	Work cycles can be brief or long; one cycle can be a team life span	Decisions Selections Suggestions Proposals Recommendations
ACTION Sports teams Entertainment groups Expeditions Negotiating teams Surgery teams Cockpit crews Military platoons and squads	High	High	High	Work cycles brief, repeated under new conditions	Competitive events Expeditions Contracts Lawsuits Concerts Surgical operations Flights Combat missions
PROJECT Research groups Planning teams Architect teams Engineering teams Development teams Task forces	High	Low (for traditional units) or High (for cross-functional teams)	High	Work cycles typically differ for each new project; one cycle can be a team's life span	Plans Designs Investigations Prototypes Reports Findings
PRODUCTION Assembly teams Manufacturing cells Mining teams Flight attendant crews Data processing groups Maintenance crews	Low	High	High	Work cycles typically repeated or continuous process; cycles often briefer than team life span	Food Chemicals Components Assemblies Retail sales Customer service Equipment repairs

Adapted from Eric Sundstrom, Kenneth De Meuse and David Futrell, 'Work teams', *American Psychologist*, 1990, vol. 45, no. 2, February, p. 125. Copyright © 1990 by the American Psychological Association. Adapted with permission.

Types of team

Many different types of team operate within organizations. Eric Sundstrom, Kenneth De Meuse and David Futrell (1990) distinguished four types of team, based on their objectives and type of output produced. These are summarized in table 12.1, and are labelled advice, action, project and production. Each team type is further differentiated along four dimensions:

1. *Degree of technical specialization*: Are members required to apply special, technical skills acquired through higher education or extensive training (high differentiation); or do they draw upon their members' general experience and problem-solving ability (low differentiation)?

2. *Degree of co-ordination*: Is its work closely related to and intertwined with that of other work units within the organization (high co-ordination); or does it operate relatively independently (low co-ordination)?

3. *Work cycles*: How much time does the team need to achieve its aims? Does it perform short, repetitive work cycles, or a single, long one?

4. *Typical outputs*: What does the team produce as its output?

Table 12.2: Team task areas, levels of team input and team autonomy levels

Team task area/dimensions
1. Selection of the team leader
2. Acceptance of a new member into the team
3. Distribution of work
4. Time flexibility
5. Acceptance of additional work
6. Representation outside the team
7. Production methods (choice of)
8. Production goals (output determination)
9. Production goals (quality determination)

Team input levels
1. *None*: No team participation and total management control. Managers make all the decisions and teams implement them. Team members have no input into the decision-making process; there is no element of participation, not even in the form of suggestions or requests.
2. *Some*: Teams have some input into decisions concerned with their immediate working environment. They can make suggestions and requests and have discussions with management who may adopt their ideas.
3. *Joint*: A situation of co-decision-making, in which teams share decision-making power with management, having an equal role in the taking and implementing of decisions.
4. *Autonomy*: Teams are fully trusted by management, the teams are truly autonomous, reaching their decisions with no input from management whatsoever. They are accepted by management as full and equal partners.

Team autonomy level

low-autonomy teams	moderate-autonomy teams	high-autonomy teams
assembly line workers	quality circles	autonomous work groups
supermarket checkouts	semi-autonomous groups	high-performance teams
		self-directed teams
		self-designing teams

Based on Jan Gulowsen, 'A measure of work-group autonomy', in L.E. Davies and J.C. Taylor (eds), *Design of Jobs*, Goodyear, Santa Monica, CA (second edition), 1979, pp. 206–18.

Team autonomy: the extent to which a team experiences freedom, independence and discretion in decisions in the performance of its tasks.

Teams differ in terms of how much autonomy management grants them. **Team autonomy** refers to the extent to which a team experiences freedom, independence and discretion in decisions related to the performance of its tasks.

Jan Gulowsen (1979), a Norwegian researcher, provided a framework which enabled more specific assessments to be made about team autonomy for comparative purposes (table 12.2). He distinguished nine 'task areas' or dimensions in a team's working which offered the potential for autonomy. Within each area, he specified four possible levels of team input. This allows teams to be distinguished in terms of the level of autonomy that they possess.

Stop and Criticize

An external management consultant has suggested giving greater autonomy to (choose a work team with which you are familiar) to improve its morale and performance. Looking at this as (i) a manager, (ii) a trade union (labour) representative, and (iii) an employee in the team, what are the advantages and disadvantages of giving this team high (level 4) autonomy on these nine task areas?

How much team autonomy in automobile manufacture?

Thomas Murakami (1997) investigated the degree of autonomy possessed by different manufacturing teams in the car industry. Nineteen final assembly automobile plants were studied, which were owned by fourteen different car companies: Toyota and Nissan in Japan; Nissan, Ford (Engines), Rover, Vauxhall, Rolls-Royce and Peugeot in the UK; GM-Bochum, GM-Eisenach, GM Opel-Russelsheim, Mercedes-Benz-Bremen, Mercedes-Benz-Sindelfingen, VW–Wolfsberg, BMW–Bavaria, Ford–Cologne in Germany; GM in Vienna, Austria; and GM Saab in Usikapungi in Finland.

Murakami assessed the degree of autonomy given to teams by management to influence decisions within their immediate work areas. Unlike some similar studies which surveyed company managers, asking them to state which traditional management functions their teams performed, Murakami interviewed team leaders and personnel managers in these car plants, used observation during personal visits and cross-checked using secondary sources. Using Gulowsen's nine, key 'task areas of decision-making' and his four 'levels of autonomy' framework, Murakami calculated an 'arithmetic mean' level of team autonomy for each area.

1 = None – no team participation/pure management decision.

2 = Some – team participation/suggestion, request, discussion.

3 = Joint – co-decision-making/equal power with management.

4 = Autonomy – a team decision/no management involved.

Team task area	Average score
1. Selection of the team leader	2.5
2. Acceptance of new member into the team	1.4
3. Distribution of work within team	2.7
4. Time flexibility	1.4
5. Acceptance of additional work	1.0
6. Representation outside the team	2.1
7. Methods of production (choice of)	2.0
8. Production goals (output)	1.6
9. Production goals (quality)	2.3

The figures indicate that few teams scored much above 2.0. Murakami ranked the work teams at GM-Eisenach (2.7) and at GM's Finnish Saab plant (2.6) as the most autonomous, but that just indicated the suggestion-request level of input. The other German work teams averaged 2.2, slightly ahead of the Japanese who were on or just below 2.0. British work teams were the least autonomous, scoring only 1.6 on average.

In none of Gulowsen's nine task areas was the average work team granted full autonomy. However, in two aspects, *self-organization* (combination of dimension 1: team leader selection, plus dimension 6: representation outside the team) and *production* (combination of dimension 3: distribution of work, plus dimension 9: production goals quality and, to a lesser extent, plus dimension 7: production methods choice), they had somewhat more autonomy.

Murakami's view was that while the work teams studied lacked any real autonomy, they could influence management decisions to some degree, and management had departed from sole decision-making responsibility in many areas. On the basis of this empirical study, he concluded that management's power in prime task areas of production remained unchallenged, despite the introduction of teamworking.

Based on Thomas Murakami, 'The autonomy of teams in the car industry – A cross-national comparison', *Work, Employment and Society*, vol. 11, no. 4, 1997, pp. 749–58.

Advice teams

Advice team: a team created primarily to provide a flow of information to management to be used in its own decision-making.

Quality circles: groups of shop-floor employees from the same department, who meet for a few hours each week to discuss ways of improving their work environment.

Advice teams are created primarily to provide a flow of information to management for use in its own decision-making. Depending on organization circumstances, an advice team may be given authority to implement solutions to the problems that it has identified. It requires little in the way of co-ordination with other work units in the company. Following a major accident or disaster, governments often set up committees of experts and eminent people to advise it on future action. The committee reviews the events that occurred, makes recommendations about improvements, and suggests changes in the law.

In organizations, the **quality circle** (also known as a *Kaizen* team) has been the best known and most publicized advice team of recent times. The original concept was of a team of six to twelve employees from the shop floor of the same manufacturing department, meeting regularly to discuss quality problems, investigating their causes, and recommending solutions to management. In practice, a wide range of different arrangements were established under this label. Circles varied in terms of the number of members; were applied in service as well as manufacturing contexts; included supervisory staff; discussed non-quality issues; and some had authority to implement their suggestions. All these matters depended on the basis upon which the circle was established by management in the particular organization.

Quality circles are a Japanese export, and have been used worldwide. They were introduced into the West during the 1980s in an effort to emulate Japanese successes. The first quality circle in the United States is claimed to have been at the Lockheed Missile and Space Company at Sunnyvale in California in 1974. The first one in Britain appeared at Rolls-Royce in Derby in 1978. Although originally used in manufacturing, quality circles have been applied extensively in the service industries, government agencies, voluntary sector, the British National Health Service, and many other types of organization. Despite their differences, which were mentioned earlier, quality circles do possess some common features:

- membership is voluntary, and members are drawn from a particular department;

- no financial rewards are given for team suggestions;

- members receive training in problem-solving, statistical quality control and team processes;

- their problem-solving domain is defined by management (often, but not always, quality, productivity and cost reduction);

- meetings are held weekly, usually in company time, often with trained facilitators helping members with training issues and helping them to manage the meetings;

- the decision to install quality circles is made at the top of the organization, and the circles are created at the bottom;

- management's objectives for introducing quality circles vary greatly. They include quality improvement, quality enhancement and employee involvement. Although an organization may claim to have introduced quality circles, even at the height of their popularity, only a small proportion of the employees ever took part (Marchington, 1992);

- circles were developed in a largely atheoretical manner, and whatever underpinning theory they have is either implicit or was developed *post hoc* by their promoters;

- quality circles represent one of the largest experiments in the use of advice teams to improve organizational performance during the 1980s. During the 1990s quality circles began to be superseded by the 'total quality movement' (Hill, 1991).

Using the British Workplace Industrial Relations Survey (WIRS3), McNabb and Whitfield (1999) found that during the 1990s, quality circles ranked only seventh out of ten work organization innovations, being used by 31 per cent of the companies surveyed.

Action teams

Action team: a team that executes brief performances which are repeated under new conditions. Its members are technically specialized, and the team has a great need to co-ordinate its output with that of other work units.

Action team members are specialized in terms of the knowledge and skill they possess and contribute to achieving their team's objective. The 'performance' of an action team is brief, and is repeated under new conditions each time. Additionally, both the specialized inputs of the various team members and the need for individuals to co-ordinate with other team members is high.

If a football player sustains a serious injury, an action team consisting of an accident and emergency (A&E) unit in a hospital may deal with him. While there, he may be given surgery by another action team in the operating theatre. Finally, when recuperating, he may attend a theatre play or symphony concert performed by yet another action team. In all these situations, action team members have to exhibit peak performance on demand.

One example of an action team is a *crew*. This term is frequently used to refer to employees who work on aircraft, boats, spacecraft and film sets. A distinguishing feature of a crew is that it is equipment- or technology-driven. If the technology is changed, then so too is the nature of the crew. A crew depends on its technology, which transforms difficult, cognitive tasks into easy ones. The crew's 'tools' affect the division of labour among its members, and crew members use various techniques to co-ordinate their activities (Hutchins, 1990; Hare, 1992).

Ginnett (1993) reported how, on a Boeing 727 aircraft, the crew members' roles were determined by the location of their seats in the cockpit. The captain sat in the left seat, from which he tested all the emergency warning devices. He was the only one who could taxi the aircraft since the nose wheel gear steering was located on that side of the cockpit. The first officer, who started the engines and who communicated with the tower, occupied the right-hand seat. The flight engineer sat sideways, facing a panel that allowed him to monitor and control the various sub-systems in the aircraft. He was the only one able to reach the auxiliary power unit. In other transportation craft, the relationship of roles to equipment would be different. Two crews can be considered as existing, those inside the cockpit – the cockpit crew (pilots, flight engineers) – and those outside it – the cabin crew (flight attendants). Between 1959 and 1989, 70 per cent of all severe aircraft accidents were at least partly attributable to flight crew behaviour (Weiner et al., 1993). Thus, it is a more common cause than either pilot error or mechanical failure.

Mending a broken heart

During cardiac surgery, a patient is rendered functionally dead – the heart stops beating, the lungs stop pumping air – while a surgical team repairs or replaces damaged arteries or valves. A week later, the patient walks out of the hospital. The team that performs this task is as important as the technology that allows it to do it. It consists of different specialists – a surgeon, an anaesthesiologist, a perfusionist and a scrub nurse – working closely and co-operatively together. It exemplifies an *action team* where a single error, miscommunication or slow response by any member can result in failure. Individuals are in *reciprocal interdependence* with each other, *mutually adjusting* their actions to match those of fellow members.

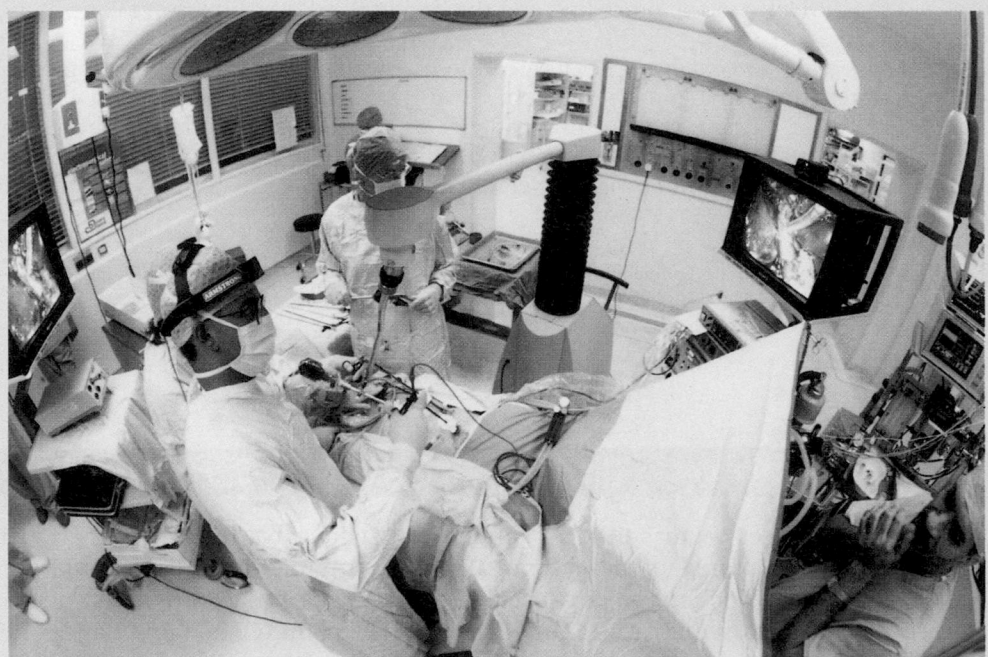

Source: Armstrong Healthcare Ltd.

Since this type of team performs hundreds of cardiac operations annually, it establishes a sequence of individual tasks that become very well defined and routine.

Indeed, team members often need only to look at, rather than speak to, one another to signal the initiation of the next stage of the procedure. The change from traditional, open-heart surgery procedures to minimally invasive ones involved several changes. The new procedure not only required individual team members to learn new, unfamiliar tasks, but also necessitated that a number of familiar tasks occurred in a different order. Thus, team members had to unlearn old routines before learning ones. Additionally, the new technology required a greater degree of interdependence and communication between team members. For example, the surgeon relied more on team members for essential information than before. This not only disrupted the team's routine, but also changed the surgeon's role as order-giver in the operating room's tightly structured hierarchy.

The authors studied surgical teams at sixteen medical centres, which were implementing this new and difficult surgical procedure. While the rate of death and serious complications did not rise, operations were found to be taking two to three times longer than conventional ones. Long operations put patients at increased risk, strain the operating team members both mentally and physically, and reduce the total number of operations that can be performed annually in the hospitals. While all teams became faster the more they performed the procedure, the pace of improvement between the teams differed significantly. The researchers studied what contributed to the accelerated speed of learning. They found that the team's design and its management were the key factors. The teams which learned the new procedures fastest, shared three key features:

Team designed for learning: Team members were consciously and carefully selected, on the basis not only of their competence, but also on ability to work with others, willingness to deal with new, ambiguous situations, and confidence in offering suggestions to higher-status team members. Once selected, the team that remained intact (no substitutions) became faster.

Members motivated to learn: Team leaders treated the implementation of the new technology as an organizational challenge rather than as a technical one. Emphasis was placed both on new ways of working together (rather than just acquiring new individual skills), and on the fact that changes in relationships would necessitate inputs from all members. Leaders of teams with positive attitudes acknowledged the difficulty of the procedure and the importance of each person's contribution.

Psychological safe learning environment: Because of the many interactions between members, teams improve through real time, trial-and-error learning. Fast-learning teams experimented with different approaches to save time without endangering patients. By creating an environment in which members felt comfortable making suggestions, trying out things that might not work, making mistakes and pointing out problems, learning was accelerated. Such a climate was fostered by the words and actions of surgeons acting as team leaders.

Based on Amy Edmondson, Richard Bohmer and Gary Pisano, 'Speeding up team learning', *Harvard Business Review*, vol. 79, no. 9, October 2001, pp. 125–32.

Project teams

Project team: a collection of employees from different work areas in an organization brought together to accomplish a specific task within a finite time.

A **project team** consists of individuals who have been brought together for a limited period of time from different parts of the organization to contribute towards a management-specified task. The task may be developing a product, refining a service or commissioning a new plant (Cohen and Bailey, 1997). Once this has been completed, the team is either disbanded or its members are given new assignments. Project teams are created when:

■ creative problem-solving is required involving the application of different types of specialized knowledge;

■ there is a need to co-ordinate closely the work on a specific project: for example, design and development, production and testing of a new product.

Every university has hundreds of project teams conducting research. Most of their members are on two- or three-year contracts which span the period of the research project. Team members are recruited on the basis of their specialist knowledge, and their output is a research report and book and journal publications.

Within the organizational context, one of the best-known and most common types of project team is the **cross-functional team** (see figure 12.1). Jack Gordon (1992) reported the spread of work teams in the United States. His report showed that, across all sizes of organization (with a workforce greater than 100 employees), 82 per cent of employees were members of a working group identified as a team, and of these 18 per cent of employees belonged to a cross-functional team. Another survey, this time by the Hay Group, revealed that approximately 25 per cent of US companies had implemented cross-functional teams, with variations across industries (Leshner and Brown, 1993, p. 39).

Traditionally, organizations have been divisionalized into tall, functional 'boxes' or 'chimneys'. It has been argued that by forming teams consisting of people from these different boxes, organizations can break down the boundaries between their functions (for example, accounting, marketing, research, product design, human resources), improve co-ordination and integration, release the creative thought of their employees, and increase the speed and flexibility of their responses to customers. They are established with the objective of combining a wide range of expertise in order to reach a more informed and rounded outcome than would otherwise be possible.

Cross-functional teams comprise employees who traditionally work in different departments or work areas. Sometimes they may also include customers, suppliers

> **Cross-functional team**: a team composed of employees from about the same hierarchical level but from different work areas or functions in the organization, who are brought together to complete a particular task.

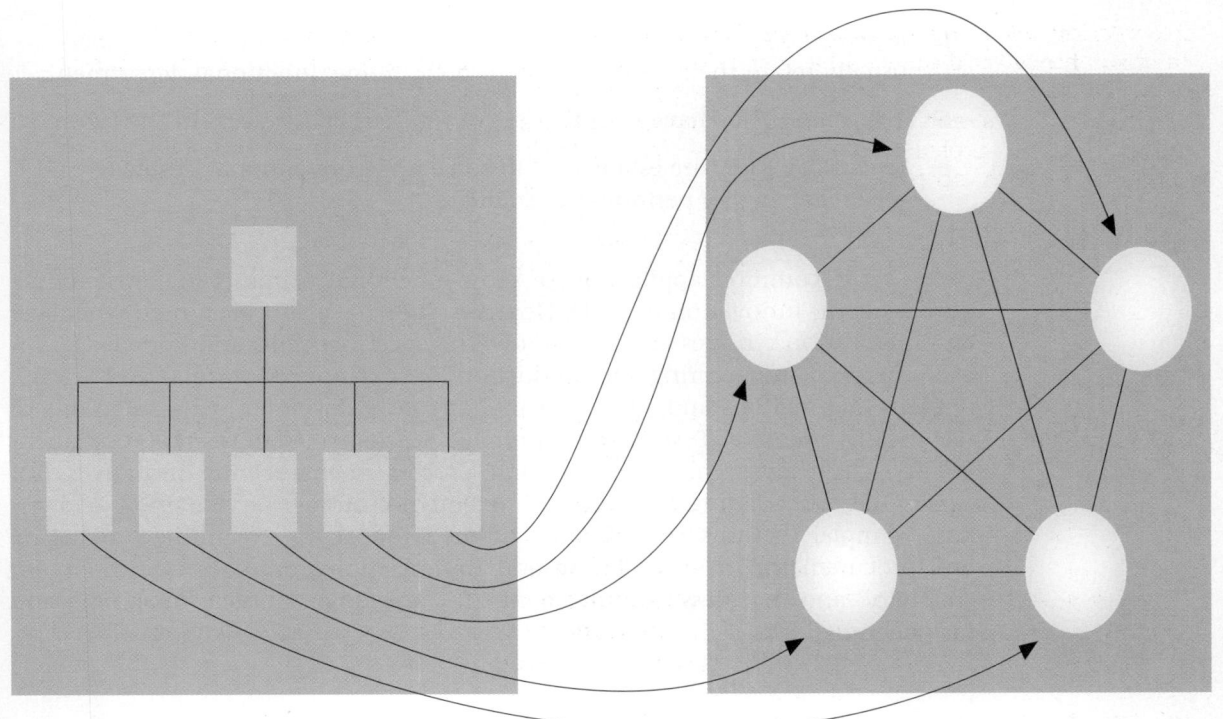

Figure 12.1: Cross-functional team

and external consultants. They are supported by their organization's structures, systems and skills, which enable the teams to operate successfully as a more independent unit (less bound by functional ties) towards goals which transcend the combined abilities of individual members.

Proponents of cross-functional teams claim that they are beneficial to their customers and employees and to the organization as a whole. Customers obtain more attractive and customized products, and have their needs met more rapidly. Team members benefit through having more challenging and rewarding jobs with broader responsibilities, greater opportunities for gaining visibility in front of senior management, increased understanding of entire processes across the organization, a 'fun' working environment and closer relationships with colleagues. The organization gains through:

- increasing productivity;

- improving co-ordination and integration;

- significantly reducing processing times;

- improving market and customer focus;

- reducing the time needed to develop new products;

- improving communications by spanning boundaries between functions.

In effect, therefore, the cross-functional team resembles a 'mini-company'. They most commonly take the form of teams which are located towards the bottom of the hierarchy. The project teams are overlaid upon the existing functional structure of the organization, and hence are an addition to it. Cross-functional teams differ from other types of team in three important respects:

- *Representative*: They are representative in that their individual members usually retain their position back in their 'home' functional department.

- *Temporary*: They have a finite life, even if their end is years in the future.

- *Innovation*: They are established to solve non-conventional problems and meet challenging performance standards.

The most common application of cross-functional teams is in new product development, innovation or R&D. However, they have also been used whenever an organization requires an input of diverse, specialist skills and knowledge: for example, in manufacturing and production (for example, Motorola); in IT development, automation and support, simultaneously developing the soft skills of technically-oriented IT staff (for example, Procter & Gamble); to implement quality, cost, speed improvements and process re-engineering initiatives (for example, USAir, Hallmark Cards); to implement customer service improvements (for example, Unisys Client Server Systems Groups); to streamline purchasing and procurement; in streamlining and optimization; for market research; for creativity and business improvement (for example, Konica Imaging); and for benchmarking.

Organizational context and cross-functional teams

For cross-functional teams to exist within an organizational environment they must first define their role in relation to upper management and resolve inherent conflicts between the functions ('chimneys') represented in them. An example drawn from an interview in one product development team shows how difficult this can be:

> The total amount of electrical power in a vehicle is determined by the capacity of an alternator. This power must serve 20 subsystems, such as the stereo, the engine, the instrument panel, and so on. These subsystems are developed and controlled by separate 'chimney' organizations, and power allocations must be made for each system. The problem was, in this vehicle programme, when all the requirements of all the chimneys and teams were added up, they equalled 125 percent of the capacity of the alternator. Keith, who had recently taken over as head of this vehicle programme, which had made changes in direction and was behind schedule to begin it, called a meeting of the Programme Steering Team designed to resolve this conflict and reach a compromise. However, many of the chimney representatives, who were the members of the team, came to this meeting with instructions from their bosses (who, incidentally, did their performance appraisals . . .) *not* to make any compromises, but to make certain that their chimney 'got what it needed' and 'didn't lose out'. After Keith presented the group with the problem and the need to reach a compromise solution, their response surprised him: 'It's not *our* problem', they replied, 'it's *your* problem'. Keith soon changed his job again. (p. 1011)

> From Daniel Denison, Stuart Hart and Joel Kahn, 'From chimneys to cross-functional teams: developing and validating a diagnostic model', *Academy of Management Journal*, vol. 39, no. 4, 1996, pp. 1005–23.

It has been argued by critics that cross-functional team members, since they are representatives, owe their true allegiance to their home, functional (chimney) department; that the chances of pressure and conflict are higher than in other teams; and that their temporary nature puts strain on members who have quickly to develop stable and effective working group processes. Cross-functional teams place great demands on the organizational support system and can have a negative effect on the individual team member. They suggest that organizations and managers need to define clearly cross-functional team assignments in order to maintain order and accountability.

Critics of cross-functional teams also acknowledge the restrictions on information flow and knowledge, and therefore on performance and the internal battles over intra-company territories, that functional boundaries cause. They offer the example of sales managers who never see their impact on distribution costs when offering a service frequency promise to clinch sales. This view encapsulates the main tensions many researchers perceive in a shift to increased cross-functional team application. Nevertheless, in total, current literature projects at best a mixed, at worst a biased set of findings.

Management cross-functional teams at Nissan

Following the strategic alliance between Renault and Nissan in 1999, Carlos Ghosn went to Tokyo to lead Nissan back to profitability. He wanted to introduce changes that went against both the company's long-standing operating practices and some of the behavioural norms of Japanese society. Rather than imposing these changes from the top, he established a number of cross-functional teams (CFTs) comprising Nissan's middle management, and made these the centrepiece of his turnaround plan. While executives prefer working in teams with those of 'their own kind', Ghosn wanted them to look beyond the functional or regional boundaries that defined their direct responsibilities, and to ask difficult questions. Cross-functional teamworking would, in his view, encourage his managers to think in new ways and to challenge existing practices. In this organizational context, the teams would also provide a means for explaining the need for change, and for communicating difficult messages across the whole company. Ghosn quickly established nine CFTs, each with its own area of responsibility: business development; purchasing; manufacturing and logistics; research and development; sales and marketing; general and administrative; finance and cost; phase out of products and parts complexity management; and organization.

Together, the CFTs addressed all the key drivers which determined Nissan's performance. Each team consisted of about ten middle managers, and created its own sub-teams to investigate some issues in greater depth. To give each CFT authority within the company, two 'leaders' (to prevent a single function's perspective predominating) from the executive committee were appointed to it. They served as that team's sponsors, helping to smooth its path and removing institutional obstacles to its work. To avoid charges of top-down, imposed change, these leaders took a back seat and rarely attended team meetings, leaving the real work to the team's 'pilot', who progressed the work and led the discussions.

All the CFTs were given three months, and asked to review the company's operations, and recommend ways of returning Nissan to profitability and uncovering opportunities for future growth. None of them had any decision-making responsibility. The outcome was a detailed blueprint for the Nissan Revival Plan developed by Nissan's own executives. They proposed major changes to some Nissan business practices (for example, in engineering specifications and reducing some quality standards) and 'harsh medicine' in the form of plant closures and headcount reductions (which challenged Japanese business traditions).

Based on Carlos Ghosn, 'Saving the business without losing the company', *Harvard Business Review*, vol. 80, no. 1, January 2002, pp. 37–45.

Stop and Criticize	You are a middle manager at Nissan who has been a member of one of the nine cross-functional teams (see box). Do you feel pleased to have been given the responsibility to participate in setting the company's future direction, or resentful that the senior management seems to have manipulated you and your colleagues, through the means of cross-functional teams, into proposing unpalatable solutions that they should have had the courage to make themselves?

Production teams

Production team: a stable number of individuals in a relationship involving shared and recognized production goals, with work status defined through a system of social roles and behavioural norms supported by a set of incentives and sanctions.

Typically, a **production team** consists of individuals who are responsible for performing day-to-day, core operations. These may be product-oriented teams such as those assembling a computer on a factory floor; construction workers placing a bridge in position across a motorway; or teams assembling sound and light systems for a pop concert. The degree of technical specialization required of the team members varies from medium to low, depending on the nature of the duties performed. However, the degree of required co-ordination, both between the members of each team, and between the team and other work units, is high. It is these other units that are either responsible for providing support activities such as quality control and maintenance, or who provide the inputs to, or receive the outputs of, that team.

The modern concept of teamworking goes back to Eric Trist and Ken Bamforth (1951) who analyzed the psychological and emotional responses to underground working by miners. The socio-technical paradigm was developed during the

Suitable autonomous work team settings

There are different teams and many different types of work task and work setting. Some are suitable for autonomous teamworking, while others are not. Louis Davis and George Wacker cited situational factors which they believed facilitated autonomous group working.

1. When the work is not entirely unskilled.

2. When the work group can be identified as a meaningful unit of the organization, and when inputs and outputs are definable and clearly identifiable and the groups can be separated by stable buffer areas.

3. When turnover in the group can be kept to a minimum.

4. When there are definite criteria for performance evaluation of the group and group members.

5. When timely feedback is possible.

6. When the group has resources for measuring and controlling its own critical variances in work-flow.

7. When the tasks are highly interdependent, so that group members must work together.

8. When cross-training is desired by management.

9. When jobs can be structured to balance group and individual tasks.

From Louis E. Davis and George J. Wacker, 'Job design', in G. Salvendy (ed.), *Handbook of Human Factors*, Wiley, New York, 1987.

Empowerment: organizational arrangements that give employees more autonomy, discretion and unsupervised decision-making responsibility.

High-performance work system: a form of organization that operates at levels of excellence far beyond those of comparable teams.

Autonomous teamworking: a process whereby management gives formal groups the right to make decisions on how their work is performed on a group basis without reference to management.

1960s, but became more widely known through applications in the late 1960s and 1970s. It was upon this basis that teamworking was established.

The focus of 1970s' experiments into employee participation and industrial democracy sought to raise productivity by providing employees with more interesting and varied work. In contrast, team-based working innovations of the 1990s represent a greater concern with efficiency and effectiveness. They were stimulated by the need of companies to remain successful in a fiercely competitive, global environment. The rationale is that in the race to improve service quality or reduce new product cycle times, technology only gives an organization a short advantage, and one which can be copied anyway. It is the way that human resources are organized and developed that is more critical.

Management's interest in production teams has always been in finding ways of improving employee motivation and performance. Employee participation in decision-making can take the form of increasing their autonomy. Bram Steijn distinguished between individual autonomy for the employee who was not part of a team – for example, in the form of job enrichment (see chapter 8) – and the autonomy given to a team of workers, which is 'the (collective) autonomy for the workers *as a team* to do a task' (Steijn, 2001, p. 193). It is the latter that is considered in this chapter. The individual and the teamworking approaches, both examples of **empowerment** (figure 12.2), have converged in practice in what has become known as the **high-performance work system**.

Alan Jenkins (1994) argued that management had become preoccupied with autonomous (or self-managed) teamworking, and that such teams had come to be seen as the basis for effective organizational designs. Other authors have noted some of the social and historic processes that have led to the emergence of **autonomous teamworking**. The concept continues to receive attention to this day (Langfried, 2000; Kirkman et al., 2001; Chansler et al., 2003). Table 12.3 summarizes the two historical phases of interest in teams.

Ajax Football Club, Amsterdam

Ajax seemed majestic and invincible in their golden age ... [*in the early 1970s*]

... Johan Cruyff and Piet Keizer had a remarkable degree of authority on the pitch. ... The freedom the players enjoyed is probably without parallel at the highest level of the modern game. Even in the post-Bosman era, in which power has shifted sharply from clubs to players, there has been nothing to compare with the giddy, unintended experiment in football democracy. It was probably as close as anyone has ever come to running a major football club like a workers' co-operative: not only did the team practically pick itself, but the players also determined most of their own tactics and decided which friendly matches they would play. ... It was the custom every year of the captain of Ajax to be chosen by the players without the presence of the coach. ... Teamwork in Dutch football is based on the quality of the players. ... For the team to work, the team has to be the star, not the players.

From David Winner, *Brilliant Orange: The Neurotic Genius of Dutch Football*, Bloomsbury, London, 2001, pp. 73–74 and 80.

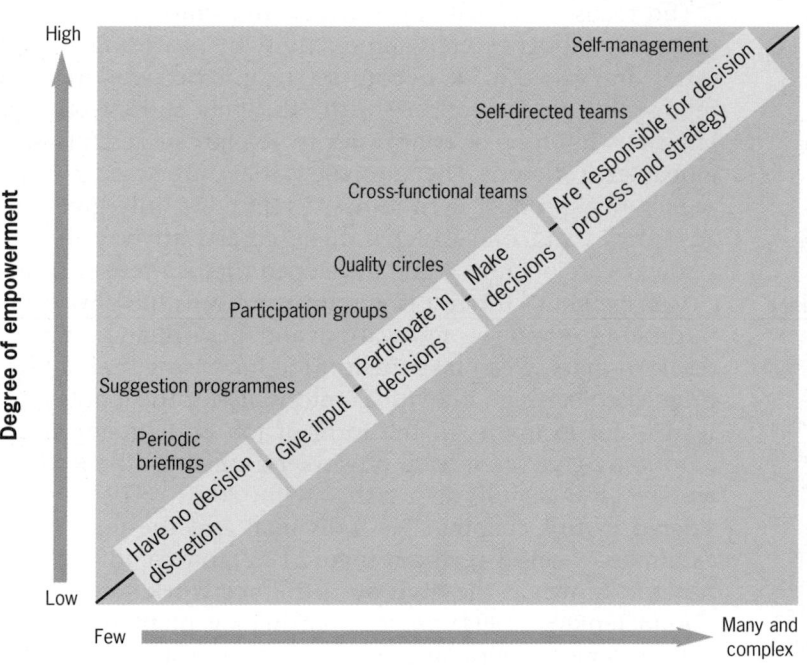

Figure 12.2: A continuum of empowerment
Source: R.L. Daft and R.A. Noe, 2001, *Organizational Behaviour*, International Thomson Publishing, London, 2001, p. 218; Robert C. Ford and Myron D. Fottler, 'Empowerment a matter of degree', *Academy of Management Executive*, vol. 9, no. 3, 1995, pp. 21–31; Lawrence Holpp, 'Applied empowerment', *Training*, February 1994, pp. 39–44; and David P. McCaffrey, Sue R. Faerman and David W. Hart, 'The appeal and difficulties of participative systems', *Organization Science*, vol. 6, no. 6, November–December, 1995, pp. 603–27.

Table 12.3: Historical changes in management's interest in autonomous teamworking

1970 to 1985	1985 to 1994
Focus on strategic organizational change	
■ Break with negative consequences of assembly-line type (Taylorist) work design. ■ Aim to increase productivity, attendance, job satisfaction and quality of working life. ■ Other techniques include job enlargement, job rotation and, occasionally, workplace democracy. ■ Organizational designs *included* autonomous teams.	■ More integrated organizational design. ■ Highly skilful, responsible workers possess adaptability and flexibility. ■ They are capable of using IT to increase productivity and quality. ■ Organizational designs *built around* autonomous groups.
Scale and scope of management involvement in team activities	
■ Many time-limited autonomous group experiments, but only in specific and linked areas of operation. ■ 'Islands of autonomy' in a sea of orthodox, Taylorist theory and practice, lacking top management support. ■ Neither extension of experiments nor equivalent changes in human resource areas like compensation, recruitment, training, etc.	■ Teamworking initiatives part of an overall strategy of delayering to create flatter, 'leaner' organization structures. ■ Recognition of the need to change managerial roles to fit these new structures. ■ Greater recognition of the time and financial resources required to achieve such organizational redesign.
Increased union and worker acceptance of the greater job flexibility needed for group organization	
■ Initial concern that teamworking would destroy job demarcation and replace a job focus with a task or team focus.	■ Union acceptance of the need for the greater job flexibility that team organization requires.
Types of organization considered appropriate settings for autonomous groups	
■ Initial focus on shop-floor manufacturing and production teams. Often, greenfield sites of electronics and automotive sector companies.	■ Extension of autonomous groups to different types of organization and to different hierarchical levels. Contexts now include customer care, healthcare, prison service, technical support, etc.

Original source unknown.

Toyota Way teamwork

The 1,300 workers in Toyota Motor Corporation's Tianjin plant in China assemble Vios. To teach them 'Toyota 101', the company has despatched experienced technical hands from its most productive Japanese plants to serve as factory drill sergeants. The new assembly-line workers first build their own workbenches to learn teamwork and responsibility. They practise assembling and dismantling prototypes. All new hires go through a week-long course on Toyota culture, plus wrist exercises to build up muscles used on the line. The company selects younger workers, whose average age is 21, which Toyota officials said make for a more malleable workforce, amenable to learning 'Toyota Way' teamwork, respect for authority, and the techniques of *kaizen* or continuous improvement.

Based on Chester Dawson, 'Roaring into China', *Business Week*, 7 April 2003, pp. 76–7.

Total quality management: a philosophy of management that is driven by customer needs and expectations, and which is committed to continuous improvement.

Just-in-time systems: methods of managing inventory (stock) in which items are delivered when they are needed in the production process instead of being stored by the manufacturer.

Japanese teamworking: teamworking that uses scientific management principles of minimum manning, multi-tasking, multi-machine operation, pre-defined work operations, repetitive short-cycle work, powerful first-line supervisors and a conventional managerial hierarchy.

Japanese teamworking (also known as *Toyotaism*) refers to a particular form of work organization that is based on the Japanese production model. It possesses four distinguishing characteristics as described by Masaya Morita (2001):

1. Multiskilled workers

2. Workers' continuous skill development.

3. Assignment of tasks to work units rather than individual workers.

4. Supervisors' roles as models for workers and a buffer between labour and management.

It is called lean production because, compared with other mass-production plants, it has higher labour flexibility by using multiskilled employees who operate different machines; fewer workers not directly involved in product manufacture; a minimum of unfinished products (work in progress/process); and requires very little rectification of work already carried out. In a Toyota production system, work operations are highly standardized. After three days, new workers are able to perform any particular job specified on a standard operation sheet. These highly standardized jobs are combined with similarly standardized ones, so as to extract the maximum amount of effort from employees with minimum labour input. Japanese teamworking also incorporates **total quality management** (TQM) and **just-in-time systems** (JIT).

Japanese teamworking is not the same as the teamworking that came to prominence in most Scandinavian and American companies during the 1960s and 1970s (MacDuffee, 1998). The differences are summarized in table 12.4.

There has been confusion about the use of the concept of teamworking in different countries. Western teamworking emphasizes enhanced employee control and job satisfaction through participation, and represents an example of worker empowerment. Japanese teamworking, in contrast, operates at the other end of the autonomous teamworking continuum. It uses the scientific management principles of 'minimum manning, multi-tasking, multi-machine operation, pre-defined work operations, repetitive short-cycle work, powerful first-line supervisors, and a conventional managerial hierarchy' (Buchanan, 1994, p. 219). Japanese work teams tend to be advice teams mistaken for production teams. They meet and function as teams 'off-line' (outside the production context) in contrast to autonomous work groups which function as teams 'on-line' (inside the production context).

A key aim of the Toyota production system has been not only to minimize the inventory (stockholding) required, but also to eliminate wasted effort and

Table 12.4: A comparison of Japanese and Swedish approaches to the organization of production and work

Variables	Japan: Toyota	Sweden: Volvo
Production flow design	Trimmed lines JIT techniques	Socio-technical design Job enrichment
Relations between groups	High degree of sequential dependence Elimination of buffers	Group control of boundaries Independence through buffers
Supervision	High-density production Emphasis on the authority and role of the supervisor	Low-density production Emphasis on planning and coordination by supervisors
Administrative control	Leading hands appointed by management Suggestions are encouraged but decisions are hierarchically determined to ensure standardization	Leading hands appointed by the group Job rotation
Workload and performance	Intensive peer and supervisory pressure for maximum job performance and low absenteeism	Regulated by union–management agreements
Role of unions	Management exclusively decides about work organization and wage systems Weak union influence	Job content and wage system regulated by agreement Union involvement in production design and development

From Olle Hammarstrom and Russell D. Lansbury, 'The art of building a car: the Swedish experience re-examined', *New Technology, Work and Employment*, vol. 6, no. 2, 1991, p. 89. Reprinted by permission of Blackwell Publishing Ltd.

employees. Martin Parker and Jane Slaughter (1988) were critical of Japanese teamworking, describing it as part of an overall management package which they labelled 'management-by-stress'. In their view, what appears to be participation is in fact a new form of exploitation.

Innovations like the 'team concept' increase the pace and pressure of work, despite the rhetoric of worker empowerment. The innovation expands management's control by getting workers to 'participate' in the intensification of their own exploitation. The outcome is a low-skill, repetitive ('lean and mean') mass-production system. Japanese teamworking contains the following elements (Parker and Slaughter, 1988, p. 5, cited in Garrahan and Stewart, 1992, p. 88):

1. A rewritten contract announcing that a new relationship exists between the company and its workforce.

2. Interchangeability, meaning the workers are required or induced (through pay-for-knowledge) to be capable of doing several jobs.

3. Drastic reduction of classifications, giving management increased control to assign workers as it sees fit.

4. Less meaning for seniority. In most cases seniority is explicitly undermined or modified. For example, if classifications are eliminated,

opportunities to transfer to different classifications by seniority are also eliminated.

5. Detailed definition of every job step, increasing management control over the way jobs are done.

6. Workers' participation in increasing their own workload.

7. More worker responsibility, without more authority, for jobs previously performed by supervisors.

8. A management attempt to make workers aware of the interrelatedness of the plant's departments and the place of the individual in the whole; an attempt by union and management to get away from the 'I just come to work, do my job and mind my own business' outlook.

9. An ideological atmosphere that stresses competition between plants and workers' responsibility for winning work away from other plants.

10. A shift towards enterprise unionism, where the union sees itself as a partner of management.

Karen Legge (1995) asked why there was not more overt opposition from these production-line workers, who were colluding in their own subjugation. She offered the first three explanations, to which Ruth Milkman (1998) adds a fourth.

1. *Careful selection of employees*: On green-field sites, new staff are chosen on the basis of their behavioural traits (rather than relevant skills) and for having the 'right attitude' towards teamworking and flexibility.

2. *Team leader's role*: The role of the trade (labour) union representative on the shop floor has been marginalized through developing the role of the team leader. This individual is responsible both for achieving production targets and for the social organization of the group.

3. *Innate appeal*: the appealing aspects of this teamworking approach – mutual support, limited participation, collective endeavour, emphasis on consensus – coupled with the company's 'family orientation', the potential to enhance job satisfaction and to save jobs, all make it appealing to recruits.

4. *Contrast with past*: Workers who have experienced both the traditional, authoritarian management system and the new, participatory initiatives prefer the latter despite some criticism of it.

Several researchers have highlighted the contradictions between management desire for control and attempts to increase team autonomy. Anna Pollert (1996) studied the imposition of teamworking on a repetitive, low-skill assembly line manufacturing chocolate. She described how the managers sought to gain employee commitment to the company in a situation in which work intensification and job rationalization engendered feelings of alienation, and where management values stressed cost control. Andrew Scott's (1994) study of a frozen food processing plant revealed how management conceded team autonomy provided that the shop-floor employees agreed to accept greater discipline and exert extra effort. Once employees exercised this new autonomy by increasing their control over the work process, the management responded by re-establishing their own direct control.

Sony goes Swedish

Last summer Sony did something unusual. It brought production of camcorders destined for the US market back from China to Japan. The move highlights the success of a wide-ranging revamp of Sony's global manufacturing and distribution system. Japan's largest consumer electronics group derives more than 60 per cent of its revenues from manufacturing consumer electronics hardware. Yet the commodification of electronics and the rapid speed of change in its markets have made it difficult for Sony and many of its Japanese competitors to make profits by churning out electronic boxes. Sony has been under intense pressure to improve its ability to respond flexibly and speedily to market demand. 'Digitalization has made the product life cycle even shorter than before,' says Tadakatsu Hasebe, President of Sony Logistics. 'In the past, because the market was growing, it was fine to make as much product as you had the capacity [for]. But now it is necessary to adjust product to market demand as closely as possible.'

Source: © Tom Wagner/CORBIS SABA.

An important step towards that goal has been the introduction of cell-based manufacturing, whereby products are manufactured in small lots by small groups or cells. This system makes it easier to control the volume of production than traditional mass-production factory lines, which are difficult to stop once they are started. Cell-based manufacturing makes it possible to shift quickly from making one camcorder model to another. This is important as Sony makes 200–300 models of camcorder. It takes only 30 minutes to put together a digital camera and 240 minutes to assemble a camcorder. If the order is in the United States, the product is air-freighted, so a customer can place an order for a camcorder accessory online and receive the product, which is made in Japan, 48 hours later.

From Michiyo Nakamoto, 'A speedier route from order to camcorder', *Financial Times*, 12 February 2003, p. 11.

Andy Danford also discussed the contradictions of applying this type of teamworking to repetitive, low-skill, assembly-line work. Teamworking espouses team participation and empowerment, but managers simultaneously seek to retain traditional control. His own case study research of a firm in South Wales which manufactured large pressed steel sub-assemblies such as car doors, subframes and dashboards for the auto industry (Danford, 1998) challenged the positive assessments of Japanese teamworking provided by earlier authors (Womack et al., 1990; Kenney and Florida, 1993). He argued that management could exploit labour flexibility by using a form of teamworking which actually *disempowered* workers. He reported how temporary employee upskilling and team autonomy came to be replaced by a strengthening of management control. He pointed to the impact of external factors, specifically supplier–customer relations, management's wish to exert unfettered control over labour utilization, and its desire to have a co-operative and motivated workforce who were employed in an alienating, mass-production environment. These inherent conflicts and contradictions appeared to be a feature of attempts to implement Japanese teamworking in lean production environments (Blyton and Bacon, 1997).

Stop and Criticize

What problems is Sony likely to experience if it attempts to apply the Swedish approach to teamworking to the Japanese version?

Ecological framework for analyzing work team effectiveness

Historically, attempts to understand the factors influencing team performance have used an input-process-output model. Its advantage is that it is easy to understand since it looks at the team from within, and all of us have been team members. However, this 'inside-out' approach, although still influential (Kretch et al., 1962; West et al., 1998), underplays the interdependencies of teamworking. In contrast, Eric Sundstrom, Kenneth De Meuse and David Futrell's (1990) ecological framework for analyzing work team effectiveness provides an 'outside-in' perspective which looks at teams as embedded within their organization (see figure 12.3).

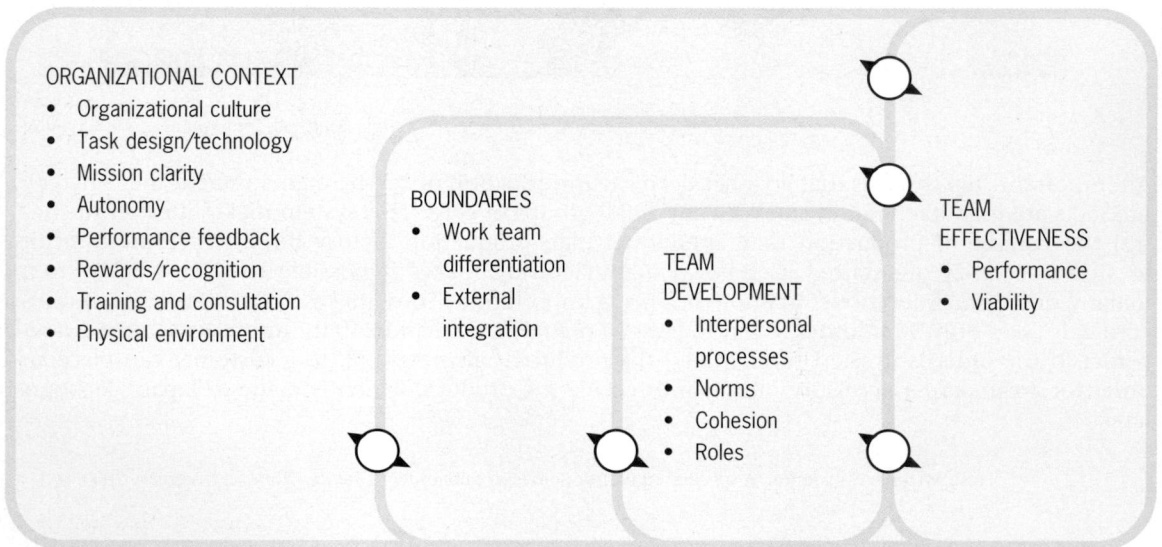

The spiked circular symbols signify reciprocal interdependence between the four variables.

Figure 12.3: An ecological framework for analysing work team effectiveness
From Eric Sundstrom, Kenneth De Meuse and David Futrell, 'Work teams', *American Psychologist*, vol. 45, no. 2, February 1990, p. 125. Copyright © 1990 by the American Psychological Association. Reprinted with permission.

The framework emphasizes the interactions between a team and the different aspects of its environment. It also provides a reminder that the organization can facilitate or impede a team achieving effectiveness. It therefore offers a way to consider factors contributing to effectiveness. The framework holds that the effectiveness of any work team is best understood in terms of both its external surroundings and its internal processes – external to the team, but internal to the organization. The framework is intentionally vague about causation and timing, seeing team effectiveness as more of an ongoing process than a fixed end-state. The framework also makes extensive use of the concept of boundary. Boundaries both separate and link the work team with its other work units and the organization as a whole. They act to:

- distinguish (differentiate) one work unit from another;

- present real or symbolic barriers to the access or transfer of information, goods or people;

- serve as points of external exchange with other teams, customers, peers, competitors or other entities;

- define what constitutes effectiveness for the team within its particular organization context.

The framework suggests that, at any point in time, a team's effectiveness is the outcome of team development and the organizational context, mediated by the team's boundaries. Each of these four sets of variables will now be described.

Organizational context

The first major variable in Sundstrom et al.'s (1990) framework is the organizational context of the work team. This refers to those features of an organization which are external to the work team but which are relevant to the way that it operates. The framework lists a total of eight such features.

1. Organizational culture
Every team operates within an organization that has its own culture and a wider, national cultural context. How do these values and beliefs impact on team effectiveness? Certain companies have a multi-stakeholder culture (for example, Germany) where teamworking is more likely to succeed than in a shareholder culture (for example, USA, Britain).

2. Task design and task technology
Every team works to complete its given task in a particular way. How do different types of task affect team effectiveness? Task technology refers to the way of working that is permitted or required. Technology may dictate a social organization of individual team roles.

3. Mission clarity
If a team has a clearly defined mission or purpose within the organization, it can assist those work units which are closely related to, or synchronized with, the team's work. How clear is the team's mission and how effectively has it been communicated to others?

4. Autonomy
Externally, management will determine a team's autonomy. Internally, it will

depend on the role of the leader and how they delegate their authority within the team. Every effective team has to co-ordinate and integrate the contributions of its individual members. Which type of team leadership best achieves this?

5 Performance feedback
Does the team receive accurate, timely feedback on its performance from dependable measurement systems?

6 Rewards and recognition
These can be anything from financial rewards to verbal praise. Are the two sufficiently connected so that individual performance contributes to team effectiveness?

7. Training and consultation
Training and consultation in technical skills and interpersonal processes is seen as a key element in achieving team effectiveness. Cross-training in technical skills is very often a pre-requisite for job rotation, which itself can be an aspect of autonomous group working.

8. Physical environment
The proximity of team members to one another affects both their ability to communicate and their level of team cohesion. Whether communicating across a table during a meeting or between workstations on a factory shop floor, territories can reinforce team boundaries and encourage or inhibit exchanges. Physical environments are therefore central to group boundaries (Sundstrom and Altman, 1989).

Tenerife air disaster

At 5.01 pm on 27 March 1977 at Tenerife airport in the Canary Islands, two 747–100 jets began taxiing on the runways, their captains in communication with the airport's traffic controllers. Four minutes later, Pan Am 1736 and KLM 4805 collided on the tarmac when the Dutch aircraft took off without permission. It led to the death of 583 people, to this day one of the biggest air fatalities in history. A number of contextual factors came together, interrupting the routines of the cockpit and air-traffic control crews, generating stress. These were Dutch law, difficult manoeuvres and unpredictable weather. In this stressful setting, the interaction of the KLM cockpit crew broke down.

More stress improves team performance but reduces individual performance by lowering task complexity. Hence the importance of the cockpit crew coalescing into a team with a distinctive entity, rather than falling apart and acting more like individuals. Weick stated that it was unclear whether the KLM crew experienced negative synergy, defined as a form of interaction between team members which causes a failure of co-ordination within the team that is so severe that nobody knows what they are supposed to be doing, or whether the three individuals in the cockpit acted in parallel rather than as a team, falling back on their most familiar and well-rehearsed response routines.

Their normal operating procedures were interrupted, inducing in them high levels of arousal, which reduced their cognitive information processing abilities and led them to ignore important cues. As a result, the flight and air-traffic control crews made the wrong responses, which resulted in the deadly crash. This was an example of the context influencing individuals and teams, who responded in a way that changed as the events unfolded. A well-functioning, high-integrated cockpit crew might have responded to the increased stress with increased performance.

Based on Weick, K.E., 'The vulnerable system: an analysis of the Tenerife air disaster', *Journal of Management*, vol. 16, no. 3, 1990, pp. 571–93.

Work team boundaries

The second major variable in Sundstrom et al.'s framework is the set of work team boundaries. The boundary for a team is like the fence around a piece of property. It allows its members to know who is a member and who is not. It defines both physically and psychologically on whom group members can rely, and thereby indicates when it may be necessary for them to go beyond their own team for assistance and resources. For example, the boundary for an aircraft cockpit crew is physically defined by the design of the aircraft. A Boeing 727 has seats for three cockpit members and hence there is an expected boundary of three for the crew of that aeroplane.

Technological developments can change boundaries. On a C–141 aircraft, while there is space for a workstation and a seat for a navigator, the incorporation of an inertial navigation system has eliminated the need for a navigator (Ginnett, 1993). Thus, changes in technology, physical layout and member roles are constantly modifying team boundaries, thereby changing the interactions of members within and across them.

While working to complete an assigned task (for example, improving a procedure, designing a new product, winning a match), a team has to meet the needs of the larger organization within which it is embedded (external integration). At the same time, it has to secure enough independence to allow it to get on with its own work (external differentiation). These two features define every team's boundary, and boundary management refers to the process by which teams manage their interactions with other parts of their organization. How successfully a team manages its boundaries will affect its performance.

External work team differentiation refers to the team as a whole in relation to the rest of the organization (team–organization focus). For example, a temporary team may be assembled by management and given resources to deal with a crisis. This team thus stands out, and hence *differs* from other work units within the company by virtue of containing an identifiable collection of people (membership), working in a specific place (territory), over a set period of time (temporal scope), on a unique task.

These four features define the team's boundary, distinguishing it from other work units within the organization:

Team membership	The identity of the individuals treated as members by both the team and organization is crucial. Who decides the composition and size of a work team?
Team territory	A work team has its 'own turf' to establish its identity and manage its external relations, especially in teams whose missions demand both external integration and differentiation.
Temporal scope	The longer a work team exists and the more time its members spend co-operating, the greater will be its temporal scope and differentiation as a work unit.
Team task	The task given to the team may be *additive* (accomplishment depends on the sum of all members' efforts), *conjunctive* (it depends on the performance of the least talented member) or *disjunctive* (it depends on the performance of the most talented member).

Internal work team differentiation refers to the degree to which a team's members possess different skills and knowledge that contribute towards the achievement of the team's objective. A team may have high differentiation with its members having special, perhaps unique, skills, such as the cockpit crew in an

External work team differentiation: the degree to which a work team stands out from its organizational context, in terms of its membership, temporal scope and territory.

Internal work team differentiation: the degree to which a team's members possess different skills and knowledge that contribute towards the achievement of the team's objective.

External work team integration: the degree to which a work team is linked with the larger organization of which it is a part. It is measured in terms of how its goals and activities are co-ordinated and synchronized with those of other managers, peers, customers and suppliers.

aircraft, or it may have low differentiation, when the knowledge and contributions of members tend to be similar, as in a quality circle team.

External work team integration refers to the fact that a work team also has, to some degree, to be linked, that is *integrated*, with the larger organization of which it is a part. External integration refers to this team–organization fit. The degree to which a team's goals and activities need to be co-ordinated and synchronized with those of other work units will depend on the type of team and its task.

A systems perspective sees the team as receiving materials or information from outsiders, transforming or adding value to them in co-operation with managers, peers and staff, and then delivering an output to its customers. These 'customers' may be internal (for example, other work units or individuals within the same organization), or external (for example, shoppers in the marketplace).

Team boundary management

Deborah Ancona and D. Caldwell (1990) studied the boundary management activities of 45 new product teams in five high-technology companies. They found that team members engaged in four types of intergroup activity:

- *Ambassador*: representing the team to others – for example, protecting it from interference, 'talking it up' to obtain outside resources, reporting its progress to higher management and checking threats or opposition.

- *Co-ordinating*: communicating laterally to co-ordinate the team's effort on its task with other work units – for example, discussing problems, negotiating, obtaining feedback on team progress and securing information on the progress of other teams.

- *Scouting*: scanning the team's immediate environment – for example, gaining information on what was going on elsewhere in the organization.

- *Guarding*: keeping information and resources within the group – for example, preventing another team or individual from acquiring its resources.

The researchers also found that the teams' boundary management activities differed over the period of the product development cycle. In the first, creation, phase members were exploring issues, and hence ambassador, co-ordinating and scouting activities were high. In the second, development, phase members were exploiting the information and resources that they had acquired. Task co-ordinating remains high, while ambassador and scouting activities are reduced. In the third, diffusion, phase members were exporting the work that they had completed and convincing others to make their product a priority. External interaction levels were highest in this phase.

The third finding was that high-performing new product teams carried out more external activity than low-performing teams, even when controlling for the project cycle phase. They not only responded to, but also initiated, communications with other work units. While internal group operations to integrate information gained from outside are important, it is the organization and management of interactions with other groups that appears critical.

Based on Deborah Ancona and D. Caldwell, 'Improving the performance of new product teams', *Research Technology Management*, vol. 33, no. 2, March–April 1990, pp. 25–9.

Team development

The third major variable in Sundstrom et al.'s framework concerns the internal development of the team. Four factors are relevant here: interpersonal processes, roles, norms and cohesion.

1. Interpersonal processes

A group of individuals moves through a series of stages before achieving effective performance at the performing stage. Tuckman and Jensen's (1977) model describes the characteristics of each stage – forming, storming, norming, performing and adjourning.

2. Roles

Roles in general are a defining feature of a team, and the role of a leader is much studied. Are the required member roles being performed given the group's tasks, and are the task and interpersonal aspects of the leadership role being fulfilled?

3. Norms

Are the norms and rules of behaviour which are agreed on by the team members supportive or in conflict with effective performance? Can organizational culture be used to modify team norms?

4. Cohesion

Team cohesion can engender mutual co-operation, generosity and helping behaviour, motivating team members to contribute fully. However, it can also stifle creative thinking as individuals seek to 'fit in' and not 'rock the boat'. Small group size, similar attitudes and physical proximity of workspaces have all been found to encourage cohesion. Does the level of cohesion aid or impede the team's effectiveness?

Team effectiveness

The final, dependent variable in the framework is the level of team effectiveness. Sundstrom et al. offer two criteria for measuring team effectiveness – performance and viability. **Team performance** is externally focused and concerns meeting the needs and expectations of outsiders such as customers, company colleagues or fans. It is assessed using measures such as quantity, quality and time. Meanwhile, **team viability** is the social dimension, which is internally focused and concerns the enhancement of the group's capability to perform effectively in the future. Team viability indicators include the degree of group cohesion, shared purpose and member commitment. The two are closely related since there is a possibility that a team may get a job done but self-destructs in the process.

Team performance: performance that is externally focused and concerns meeting the needs and expectations of outsiders such as customers, company colleagues or fans. It is assessed using measures such as quantity, quality and time.

Team viability: the social dimension which is internally focused and concerns the enhancement of the group's capability to perform effectively in the future. It is assessed using measures such as group cohesion and mutual liking.

Communities of practice

Knowledge has become the unique distinguishing factor, and companies use cross-functional teams, customer- and product-focused business units and work groups to capture and spread ideas. A new organizational form is emerging to complement these organizational forms and radically galvanize knowledge-sharing, learning and change. It is called the community of practice. It consists of a group of people informally bound together by shared experience and a passion for joint endeavour. Wenger and Snyder (2000) cite engineers from different companies all engaged in deep-water drilling and consultants from different firms specializing in strategic marketing. One might add academics with a common research interest. Some communities of practice meet regularly and physically, at a conference or for lunch, while others interact using the email network. Members of such communities share their experience and knowledge in free-flowing ways that foster new approaches to problems.

In one sense, they appear to be a version of the existing professional association, which attracts members from a variety of organizations, industrial sectors and organizational levels. What is different is that, for the first time, companies are attempting to 'install' and nurture them. However, they are neither easy to build nor easy to sustain within the rest of a typical organization. Their organic, spontaneous and informal nature makes them resistant to supervision and interference. They have to be cultivated rather than organized by managers.

Communities of practice may emerge as a result of a reorganization into a team-based structure, and employees with functional expertise may want a way to maintain connections with their peers. They may emerge as a response to environmental changes, such as the rise of e-commerce or a company providing a new service. A community of practice can exist wholly within a single business unit, stretch across divisional boundaries or be composed of members employed by different companies. It may involve tens or hundreds of people. The table below contrasts them with other organizational forms.

Organizational form	What's the purpose?	Who belongs?	What holds it together?	How long does it last?
Community of practice	To develop members' capabilities; to build and exchange knowledge	Members who select themselves	Passion, commitment and identification with the group's expertise	As long as there is an interest in maintaining the group
Informal network	To collect and pass on business information	Friends and business acquaintances	Mutual needs	As long as people have a reason to connect
Project team	To accomplish a specific task	Employees assigned by senior management	The project's milestones and goals	Until the project has been completed
Formal work group	To deliver a product or service	Everyone who reports to the group's manager	Job requirements and common goals	Until the next reorganization

Communities of practice are informal, establishing their own agenda and leadership. Members are self-selected and may invite others to join. The role of company managers is to cultivate them, which they can do in three ways: first, by identifying potential communities of practice in the company that could enhance its strategic capabilities (for example, technicians, product-delivery consultants) and bringing the potential members into proximity of each other; second, by providing infrastructure that will support and enable them to apply their expertise effectively (for example, introducing the concept, sponsoring them, and granting time for participation); and third, by measuring their value to the organization using non-traditional methods (for example, by systematically gathering anecdotal evidence).

The authors recommend that managers understand what these communities are and how they work; appreciate that they represent a hidden source of knowledge development in the company that can meet the challenge of the knowledge economy; and recognize the paradox that these informal structures require managerial effort to develop and to become integrated within the organization so as to maximize their potential benefits.

Based on Etienne C. Wenger and William M. Snyder, 'Communities of practice: the organizational frontier', *Harvard Business Review*, January–February 2000, pp. 139–45.

So why no neat summary? Why no big picture? When analyzing any organizational innovation, whether quality circle or autonomous teamworking, a careful balance is needed because of both the complexities of the phenomenon itself and the process of its diffusion between organizations. Paul Thompson and Chris Warhurst (1998, p. 8) have reviewed workplace initiatives (including teamworking) and concluded that:

The banal but simple truth is that there is no simple or universal direction. Look in detail at case study research across companies and countries and we find the usual suspects of mediation by institutional factors; noticeably national industrial relations systems and labour markets, as well as strategic choices by firms themselves. This should be obvious, but runs counter to the investment in high theory and epochal breaks by those whose job description is to draw the 'big picture', resulting in too many commentators continuing to insist on a coherent transformation package.

Teamworking in Europe

Jos Benders, Fred Huijgem and Ulrich Pekruhl surveyed workplaces in ten European Union countries to ascertain the extent of team (group) working. Their study consisted of 5,786 organizations, and assessed the level of direct participation that these organizations permitted their work groups. They considered eight group decision (-making) rights, mostly similar to those described by Gulowsen (1979), but they also included two additional ones – group's 'control of attendance and absence' and 'improving work processes'. The authors placed workplaces into one of three categories, depending on the number of rights possessed by their teams. They labelled these three: group-based organizations, medium group decision and weak group decision. The study revealed three clusters of group decision rights:

1. Allocation of work, scheduling of work and improving work processes.

2. Quality of work, time-keeping and co-ordination.

3. Attendance and absence, and job rotation.

The group's decision rights that were found to be most widespread were those most closely linked to planning and improving work. A total of 55 per cent of groups scheduled their own work and improved their work processes; 47 per cent allocated work themselves; and about 40 per cent made decisions on their work quality, time keeping and co-ordination with other groups. Managements were less inclined to delegate the control of activities to groups, and only 29 per cent were allowed to decide on attendance and absenteeism issues.

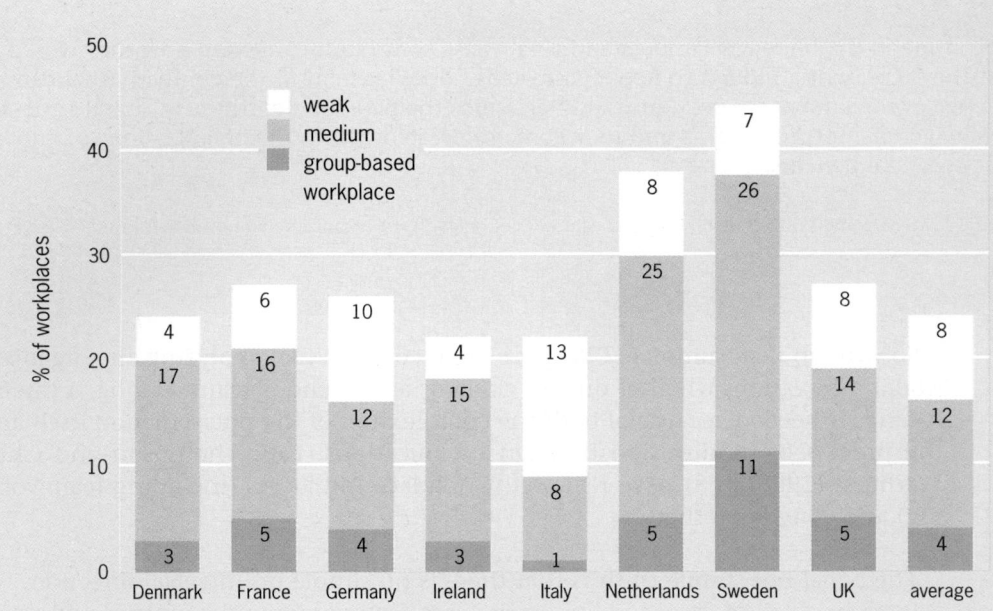

Group delegation

The authors contrasted the incidence of group delegation in different countries. As shown above, Sweden had the highest score for group delegation in general, but also for the top, group-based workplace category. The Netherlands came second on group delegation in general, but their score of 5 per cent for group-based workplace placed them alongside France and the UK, both of whom had lower general delegation scores. Portugal (not shown in the diagram), achieved a higher group-based score of 6 per cent. Summarizing the results, the authors pointed to the lower levels of workplace delegation in southern European countries. The high Swedish and Dutch scores may be associated with their established socio-technical traditions. The high score for France came as a surprise.

Based on Jos Benders, Fred Huijgem and Ulrich Pekruhl, 'Measuring group work: findings and lessons from a European survey', *New Technology, Work and Employment*, vol. 16, no. 2, 2001, p. 209. Reprinted by permission of Blackwell Publishing Ltd.

Recap

1. *Understand why 'team' is a contested concept in the organizational literature.*

   - Teamworking is being increasingly adopted as a favoured form of work organization in different companies and industries around the world.

   - The different purposes and ways in which managers have introduced this innovation have meant that the term 'team' is used to describe a wide range of radically different working arrangements.

2. *List the nine dimensions of team autonomy.*

   - Gulowsen's nine dimensions of team autonomy are: selection of the team leader; acceptance of a new member into the team; distribution of work; time flexibility; acceptance of additional work; representation outside the team; production methods (choice of); production goals (output determination); production goals (quality determination).

3. *Differentiate between four major types of team and give an example of each.*

   - Teams in organizations can be classified as advice teams (quality circles), action teams (for example, surgery team), project teams (cross-functional team) or production teams (autonomous work team).

4. *Discuss the types of obstacle to effectiveness experienced by each type of team.*

   - Advice teams frequently lack authority to implement their recommendations. Action teams can fail to integrate their members' contributions sufficiently closely. Project team members can suffer 'divided loyalties' between their team and their home department. Production teams may lack autonomy required for job satisfaction.

5. *Contrast western with Japanese concepts of teamworking.*

   • The Western concept is based upon principles of empowerment and online teamworking, while the Japanese concept is based upon management principles of individual working online and teams advising offline.

6. *List the four main variables in the ecological framework for analyzing work team effectiveness.*

   • Team development, work team boundaries and organizational context all affect team effectiveness.

7. *Understand the increasing importance of virtual teamworking.*

   • Dispersed team members, located at different physical locations and interacting through email, video conferencing and similar technologies, have experienced problems due to insufficient non-verbal communication, misreading of status signals and deindividuation effects.

Revision

1. What is the relationship between a work team and the organization of which it is a part?

2. What impact can technology have on the behaviour and performance of teams? Discuss positive and negative effects, illustrating your answer with examples.

3. 'Autonomous team is a relative term.' Discuss the concept of team autonomy, explaining why similarly labelled teams may, in practice, operate very differently, and consider why management might have difficulty in increasing the autonomy that it gives to a team.

4. Highlight briefly the main differences between West European and Japanese-style teamworking. Then, using references to the literature, consider the positive and negative aspects of both systems for EITHER shop-floor workers OR management.

5. Discuss the reasons why Japanese-style teamworking has become widely adopted around the world.

Springboard

Durand, J.-P., Stewart, p. and Castillo, J.J. (eds), 1999, *Teamwork in the Automobile Industry: Radical Change or Passing Fashion*, Macmillan Business, Basingstoke.

A collection of chapters which contrast four types of teamworking: traditional Fordist; Toyota-Japan; out-side-Japan; and Swedish–German.

Human Relations, 2000, Special Issue, vol. 53, no. 11.

New Technology, Work and Employment, 2001, Special Issue, vol. 16, no. 3.

Personnel Review, 2002, Special Issue, vol. 31, no. 3.

The above special issues of these journals have been devoted to the most recent research on teams in organizations.

Proctor, S. and Mueller, F. (eds), 2000b, *Teamworking*, Macmillan, Basingstoke.

The individual contributions consider teamworking from many different angles and perspectives, and different organizational contexts. Reporting research, theories and frameworks, it brings together current thinking on teamworking.

Sinclair, A., 1992, 'The tyranny of a team ideology', *Organization Studies*, vol. 13, no. 4, pp. 611–26.

Jenkins, A., 1994, 'Teams: from "ideology" to analysis', *Organization Studies*, vol. 15, no. 6, pp. 849–60.

Two articles respectively attacking and defending management's obsession with teams.

Tjosvold, D., 1996, *Team Organization: An Enduring Competitive Advantage*, Wiley, Chichester.

A widely cited managerially-oriented text on the topic of effective teamworking based on his research and theoretical work.

Winner, D., 2001, *Brilliant Orange: The Neurotic Genius of Dutch Football*, Bloomsbury, London.

Fascinating account of the rise and decline of Dutch football teams, which can be analyzed using the Sundstrom et al. (1990) framework.

Womack, J.P., Jones, D.T. and Roos, D., 1990, *The Machine that Changed the World: The Triumph of Lean Production*, Macmillan, New York.

The classic, influential book that extolled the virtues of Japanese production arrangements and was influential in changing Western manufacturing practices. Commentators have criticized its pro-management bias.

Home viewing

The Great Escape (1963, directed by John Sturges) is a story of American and British airmen set in a German prisoner-of-war camp during the Second World War. It features Steve McQueen, James Garner, Richard Attenborough, James Coburn, David McCallum and Donald Pleasance.

Apply Sundstrom et al.'s (1990) ecological framework to this work team. What represents team performance and team viability? Identify the eight aspects of the organizational context in which this team operates (culture, task design, task technology, etc.). Finally, use the same model to comment on the interpersonal processes within the team, its norms, roles and level of cohesion. Use the concepts of external integration, external differential and internal differential to analyze the team within the context of the whole camp. What constituted its boundaries?

OB in literature

Tracy Kidder, *The Soul of a New Machine*, Random House, New York, 1997.

This is a true story which has been 'fictionalized'. It is based on how teams worked together to design and build a new computer. What aspects of effective teamworking and work team management does the story illustrate?

Chapter exercises

1: Team autonomy assessment

Objectives
1. To apply Gulowsen's autonomy framework to a team with which you are familiar.

2. To identify areas of a team's work where it would be beneficial to increase autonomy.

Briefing
1. Below are Gulowsen's task areas/dimensions of team autonomy. Select a team and rate it on each of the nine dimensions. Your chosen team can be:

   (a) A team of which you have been, or currently are, a member, or,
   (b) Your tutorial group at university or college

Your team autonomy score will range between 9 (no autonomy) and 36 (high autonomy).

2. Discuss in which task areas/dimensions the team's autonomy can be increased. What benefits do you envisage from such a change?

Team (name/organization)					
Team task area/dimensions	**Level of team participation**				
	None	*Some*	*Joint*	*Autonomy*	*Total*
1. Selection of the team leader	1	2	3	4	
2. Acceptance of a new member into the team	1	2	3	4	
3. Distribution of work	1	2	3	4	
4. Time flexibility	1	2	3	4	
5. Acceptance of additional work	1	2	3	4	
6. Representation outside the team	1	2	3	4	
7. Production methods (choice of)	1	2	3	4	
8. Production goals (output)	1	2	3	4	
9. Production goals (quality)	1	2	3	4	
TOTAL TEAM SCORE					

2: Self-managing teams: costs and benefits

Objectives
1. To assess the degree of autonomous teamworking within an organization.

2. To identify conditions favouring and impeding the introduction of empowerment.

Briefing
1. Divide into groups of three to five.

2. Read the case study and, using Gulowsen's checklist, identify the degree of team autonomy possessed by Patchwork's self-directed team members. Score each of the nine areas/dimensions on a four-point scale – none, some, joint, autonomy.

3. Discuss what features of the company's present situation are conducive to implementing the empowerment of employees. What company changes in the future, either inside or outside the company, could make the current working arrangements difficult to sustain?

4. Consider the views and reactions of Margaret Carter and her employees. What issues do they raise about the introduction and operation of empowerment within the workplace?

The Patchwork Traditional Food Company

Patchwork is a small company consisting of ten employees based in the Clwyd region of North Wales. It produces a range of pies, chutneys, jams and patés and other foods made with fresh ingredients to traditional recipes targeted at a niche market. Its owner, Margaret Carter, saw a gap in the market for handmade, low-volume, high-quality foods, which could be sold at a premium price. By personally ensuring the highest standards, she hopes to retain and increase her company's market share. As the business developed, Margaret needed to be out on the road a lot more, promoting her products to potential customers. She is responsible for taking the orders. These have varied considerably from month to month, but she has personally ensured that all products are delivered to customers in good time. This is one reason why she transformed her group of employees into a self-managing team. She explained that 'Everybody is empowered to make their own decisions and be in control of their day, in their working environment.' Margaret Carter realized that it was unnecessary for her employees to seek permission from her office to do what needed to be done in the production area. As a team, she felt, they already knew that better than anyone else. However, after being given the power by her to make their own decisions, her employees' first reaction was one of uncertainty and fear. The workers were anxious that now they had nobody to blame but themselves if something went wrong. Obviously, this was an issue which had to be discussed and resolved between all concerned.

After the team had overcome their initial doubts, they went about making the new arrangements work. While they each knew their individual jobs, they were less familiar with the day-to-day running of the factory. They felt that they needed someone who could take an overview of the whole situation. Their past experience had taught them that everybody in the factory tended to do the jobs that they liked, while leaving the less pleasant tasks to others. Also, receiving advice from one person rather than two would eliminate differing priorities and would avoid conflict. To meet this need, the self-managing team turned to Chris, one of their co-workers. Although Chris felt that her colleagues saw her as a supervisor, she sees herself as a team leader. She explains, 'I'm here for anybody to come to me if they need advice or help with their job, and I'm here to train up new members who come to work with us. I'm there if they need me, like a mother.'

Since what is produced is determined by how it is produced, Margaret had very clear ideas as to how her patés, soups and other products should be made. Her views are based on her own experience of cooking. As production volumes have increased, team members have commented that the prescribed cooking methods are difficult to operate. Following a series of meetings, she and her staff have now agreed modifications to the original practices which, while addressing the need for higher production volumes, also maintain her quality standards. The team runs the factory without the involvement of any management. Staff are responsible for ordering stock, recruiting staff and deciding their own working hours and holidays. Every morning, they get together to talk about what they've got to do that day.

What is the reaction of employees and the management to this empowering of a self-managing team? Company workers seem generally positive about the change: 'It works very well because we all have a sense of what needs to be done, and when it needs doing.' 'It's more enjoyable because you get more job satisfaction out of being involved in everything yourself.' 'Everybody knows what everybody else is doing, what you have got to do, and it's much nicer.' However, they are aware of differences in response. One employee stated: 'Some of us enjoy taking on responsibilities, but there are a few who have not got into that yet. These are early days, but we shall get there eventually. I think that some people are just slightly frightened. They are doing it gradually, and they are all picking it up a bit at a time, and I think taking on the new responsibilities will come to them quite easily after a length of time.'

Speaking as the owner-manager of the company, Margaret Carter noted that the change has given her time to find new markets for her products, providing job security for the team; it has also enabled her to spend more time developing new recipes with one of the other team members, Penny. She commented that 'I would not have implemented a self-directed team if I did not fully trust my people, which, in my view, is one of the most important factors. The main upside of the new work arrangement is that it has become a really happy team. I believe that this team happiness goes right through to our suppliers, to our product and to our customers. Her view about empowerment is that it needs to be total. 'You have to genuinely and completely let go, not half-heartedly and not pretending that you are letting go, because it will not work!'

Based on *20 Steps to Better Management*, 'Letting go', BBC Enterprises Ltd, London, 1996.

Part 4 Organization structures

A field map of the organizational behaviour terrain

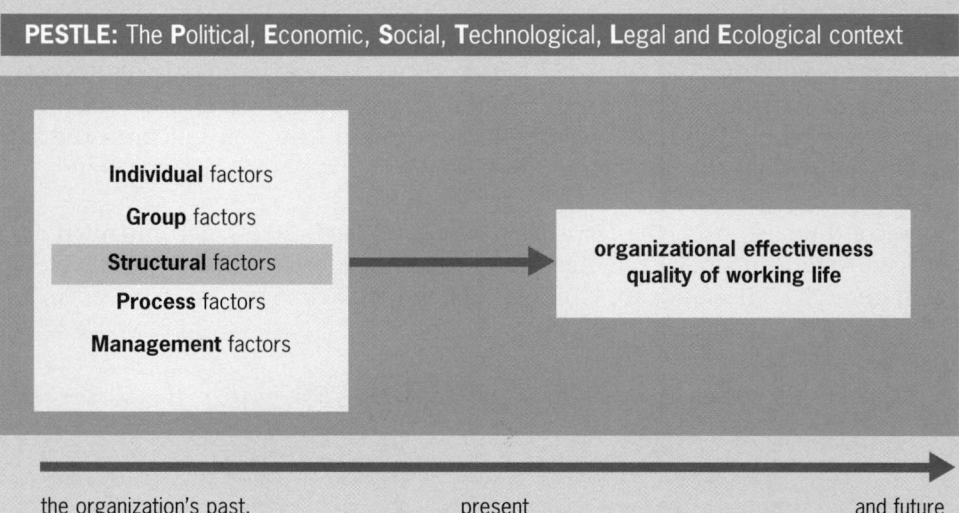

PESTLE: The **P**olitical, **E**conomic, **S**ocial, **T**echnological, **L**egal and **E**cological context

Individual factors
Group factors
Structural factors
Process factors
Management factors

organizational effectiveness
quality of working life

the organization's past,   present   and future

Introduction

Part 4, Organization structures, explores the following four topics:

- Traditional work design, in chapter 13
- Elements of structure, chapter 14
- Early organization design, in chapter 15
- Organization strategy and design, in chapter 16

These topics consider how the way in which work is designed and defined affects employee behaviour in organizations. Chapter 13 on traditional work design provides a historical foundation for chapter 3 on technology. It links technology to structure by highlighting how choices about the former have an impact on design decisions concerning the latter. Chapter 14 on elements of structure provides an introduction to the key concepts, theories, models and authors in the field. This 'vocabulary' is then applied to provide an understanding of early organization design, particularly in the work of Weber, Fayol, Burns and Stalker, and Mintzberg. The final chapter explains how contemporary thinking about structures in the field of organization behaviour has merged with discussions about corporate strategy and strategic management. It also brings the consideration of structural forms up to date by discussing the networked, virtual organization. The structural perspective offers a separate but related level of analysis after individuals and groups.

The first image, from *The Times* (27 March 2003), shows the managing director, a director and three members of staff from Anything Left Handed, a company which manufactures household goods for left-handed people. Without looking at the caption, can you tell from the photograph who is the director and who is the managing director? Why?

The second image, from the *Financial Times* (27 March 2003), accompanied an article about conflict between American stock exchanges and brokers over fee structures. This style of trading is known as 'open outcry'. CME stands for Chicago Mercantile Exchange.

Left to right: Debbie Kilby, behind camera; director Lauren Milsom, managing director Keith Milsom, Arthur Haines and Denis Zekic with some of the left-handed products from the Sutton-based mail-order company Anything Left Handed
Source: The Times/John Cassidy/NI Syndication

Traders in the CME's Eurodollars futures
Source: Associated Press, AP

1. Decoding: Look at these images closely. Note in as much detail as possible what messages you feel they are each trying to convey. Do they tell a story, present a point of view, support an argument, perpetuate a myth, reinforce a stereotype, challenge a stereotype?

2. Challenging: To what extent do you agree with the messages, stories, points of view, arguments, myths or stereotypes in these images? Are these images open to challenge, to criticism, to interpretation or decoding in other ways, revealing other messages?

3. Sharing: Compare with colleagues your interpretation of these images. Explore explanations for differences in your respective decodings.

Key concepts

rationalism	control concept
scientific management	McDonaldization
systematic soldiering	intrinsic motivation
functional foremanship	extrinsic motivation
initiative and incentive system	instrumental orientation to work
time and motion studies	introjection
Fordism	identification
systems concept	concertive control

Learning outcomes

When you have read this chapter, you should be able to define those key concepts in your own words, and you should also be able to:

1. Understand how scientific management met the needs of its historical context.
2. Describe the main objectives and principles of the scientific management approach.
3. Critically assess Taylorism.
4. Enumerate the contributions of the Gilbreths and Gantt to scientific management.
5. Understand how Fordism developed out of Taylorism.
6. Understand the deskilling debate, and the contribution of Braverman and Ritzer.
7. Provide examples of scientific management in contemporary society.

Why study traditional work design?

Only a handful of theories can claim to be truly revolutionary, and to have had an enduring and worldwide impact on organizational thought and management practice. Frederick Winslow Taylor's scientific management is one of them. Many textbooks only mention this topic briefly, locating its place in history, before implying that his ideas are no longer relevant to our modern, hi-tech, organizational lives. This chapter will argue the complete opposite. Specifically, it contends that scientific management is having a wider and more pervasive impact on society today than it did in Taylor's day.

Developments in information technology have increased rather than reduced its relevance. One needs only to look at the current interest in Total Quality Management, ISO 9000 and the other management techniques for bringing greater discipline into manufacturing, clerical and professional work (including education) to realize that Taylorism is alive and well and thriving at the start of the twenty-first century (Wilson, 1995; Jones, 1997). For example, one current academic debate focuses on whether the virtual organization is a new organizational arrangement or a refinement of scientific management thinking.

Taylorism affects us all as students, employees, consumers and citizens. It is just that most do not realize this. By pointing out examples of it in contemporary life, we hope to raise readers' awareness.

Why is the topic of job design being considered in a chapter on organization structures? Buchanan (1994, p. 86) argued that 'It has . . . become increasingly unrealistic to distinguish between work design on the one hand and organization design on the other. The former now implies the latter.' Work design and organization design are now interminably linked (Procter and Mueller, 2000a). Taylor focused his attention on shop-floor workers, the design of the manual tasks that they performed, and their motivation. Taylor's approach to prescribing the appropriate organization structure was 'bottom-up'. Beginning with the task, he established working practices for shop-floor workers before considering the question of appropriate supervision and the implications of all this for senior management. Taylor stands in contrast to other organization structure designers such as Max Weber and Henri Fayol, who were 'top-down' and looked at organization from the perspective of top management. Their contributions will be considered later.

Birth of scientific management

Between 1880 and 1910, the United States underwent major and rapid industrialization, including the creation of the first large corporations. Complex forms of organization were emerging, with new technologies of production and large workforces. Many of today's well-known organizations, such the Standard Oil Trust (Esso), United States Steel, General Motors and Ford, were created at that time. The workers in these new factories came from agricultural regions of America, or were immigrants from Europe. Directing the efforts of workers with little knowledge of the English language, few job skills and no experience of the disciplined work of a factory was a key organizational problem. Scientific management offered a solution, and represented one of the first organizational practices capable of being applied to different companies.

Before the 1880s, work organization on the factory shop floor was based upon the authority of subcontractors and supervisors. Owners employed workers indirectly, and it was labour masters and gang bosses who recruited, paid and disciplined them. However, these informal, personal methods of control created inefficiencies. During this period of economic growth, scientific management ended such internal contracting, enabling owners to employ workers directly, and thereby introduced a formal system of industrial discipline. In this period, most products were hand-made by skilled operators who handcrafted items using general-purpose machine tools such as lathes. It took these craftsmen years of training to acquire the necessary skills and experience. They could read a blueprint and visualize the final product, and possessed a level of hand–eye co-ordination and gentleness of touch that allowed them to manufacture the required item (Littler, 1982). However, there were insufficient numbers of them to permit mass production.

It was against this background that Frederick Taylor and Henry Ford developed and implemented their ideas. They and their supporters all shared a belief in **rationalism** which is the theory that reason is the foundation of certainty in knowledge. They believed that if one understands something, one should be able both to state it explicitly and to write a law or a rule for it. They held that the human mind could discover innate laws that governed the workings of the universe. The consequence of developing and applying rules, laws and procedures is to replace uncertainty with predictability, in both the human and non-human spheres.

Rationalism: the theory that reason is the foundation of certainty in knowledge.

Scientific management: a form of job design theory and practice which stresses short, repetitive work cycles; detailed, prescribed task sequences; a separation of task conception from task execution; and motivation based on economic rewards.

All manufacturing involves three separate activities: the transformation of work pieces (for example, turning a piece of wood into a chair leg); the transfer of work pieces between workers and operations; and the co-ordination and control of these two processes, ensuring sufficient raw material is available to operators to work on, and that finished pieces flow smoothly through assembly. Originally, each of these processes was performed manually, and the history of work transformation has involved the mechanization of each one. The first major approach to work rationalization, that of scientific management or Taylorism, focused on the first of these stages, the transformation of the work piece (Gill, 1985). Taylor's approach is known by two names. **Scientific management** is the collective term for his ideas, coined by his supporters. *Taylorism* is an eponym which, although applied by his supporters, was used mainly by his opponents, who regarded the other term as specious. In this chapter, the two terms are used interchangeably.

Taylorism

Frederick Winslow Taylor (1856–1915)

Systematic soldiering: the conscious and deliberate restriction of output by operators.

Frederick Winslow Taylor was born into a wealthy Quaker Philadelphia family in 1856. Philadelphia was the industrial heart of 1800s America. It contained many manufacturers who had ready access to the Pennsylvanian coal and iron mines. Taylor became an apprentice machinist in a firm of engineers before joining the Midvale Steel Company in 1878 where he developed his ideas. The company manufactured locomotive wheels and axles, and it was here that he rose to the position of shop superintendent by 1887. In this role, he observed that workers used different, and mostly inefficient work methods. He also noticed that few machinists ever worked at the speed of which they were capable. He contrasted natural soldiering (that is, the inclination to take it easy) with what he labelled **systematic soldiering**. Taylor attributed systematic soldiering to a number of factors:

- the view among the workers that an increase in output would result in redundancies;

- poor management controls which enabled them to work slowly, in order to protect their own best interests;

- the choice of methods of work was left entirely to the discretion of the workers, who wasted a large part of their efforts using inefficient and untested rules-of-thumb.

Soldiering

Robert Kanigel (1997) explained that the word 'soldiering' had nautical roots. It related to soldiers who, when transported by ship, acted as privileged passengers. They were exempt from the work on board that the seamen had to perform. To the sailors, such work avoidance came to be known as 'soldiering'. Frederick Taylor distinguished, on the one hand, the tendency of workers to take it easy. This he labelled 'natural soldiering'. He considered it unfortunate, but almost excusable. On the other hand, and more insidious in his view, was 'systematic soldiering' which was the organized, collective behaviour of workers in the whole workshop, who restricted their production, prevented their employers knowing how fast they could work, and thus were able to pursue their own narrow self-interest.

Based on Robert Kanigel, *The One Best Way: Frederick Winslow Taylor and the Enigma of Efficiency*, Little Brown and Company, London, 1997.

Appalled by what he regarded as the inefficiency of industrial practices, Taylor took steps to increase production by reducing the variety of work methods used by the workers. He set out to show how management and workforce could both benefit from adopting his more efficient work arrangements. His objectives were to achieve:

■ *efficiency*, by increasing the output per worker and reducing deliberate 'underworking' by employees;

■ *predictability* of job performance – standarizing tasks by dividing up tasks into small, standardized, closely specified sub-tasks;

■ *control*, by establishing discipline through hierarchical authority and introducing a system whereby all management's policy decisions could be implemented.

Table 13.1: Frederick Taylor's five principles of scientific management

1. A clear division of tasks and responsibilities between management and workers.

2. Use of scientific methods to determine the best way of doing a job.

3. Scientific selection of the person to do the newly designed job.

4. The training of the selected worker to perform the job in the way specified.

5. Surveillance of workers through the use of hierarchies of authority and close supervision.

Taylor's approach involved studying each work task. He chose routine, repetitive tasks performed by numerous operatives where study could save time and increase production. A wide range of variables was measured, such as size of tools, height of workers and type of material worked. His studies tried to answer the question: 'How long should it take to do any particular job in the machine shop?' He wanted to replace rules-of-thumb with scientifically designed working methods. Taylor experimented with different combinations of movement and method to discover the 'one best way' of performing any task.

His approach involved the use of analysis and synthesis. Analysis involved the job being divided up into its elementary motions, discarding non-essential motions, examining the remaining motions to determine the quickest and least wasteful means of job performance, and describing, recording and indexing these.

Table 13.2: Scientific approach to shovelling

1. Select a suitable job for study which has sufficient variety without being complex, which employs enough men to be worthwhile and will provide an object lesson to all when installed.

2. Select two good steady workers.

3. Time their actions.

4. Get them to use large shovels on heavy material. Total amount within a set time period is weighed and recorded.

5. Shovel size reduced so that weight of shovel-load is decreased, but total amount shovelled per day rises.

6. Determine best weight per shovel-load, identify correct size of shovel for all other materials handled.

7. Study actual movements of arms and legs.

8. Produce 'science of shovelling', which shows correct method for each material and amount which should be shovelled per day by a first-class man.

Synthesis consisted of determining the proper sequence of motions, recombining those motions in that sequence for optimal job performance, and presenting that information to the employees.

It was not only shop-floor workers who had their jobs fragmented. Taylor felt that every employee in an organization should be confined to a single function. He proposed a system called **functional foremanship**, which never became popular. The job of the general foreman was to be divided and distributed among eight separate individuals. Each of these would oversee a separate function of the work, and would be called:

1. Inspector	5. Gang boss
2. Order of work and route clerk	6. Speed boss
3. Time and cost clerk	7. Repair boss
4. Shop disciplinarian	8. Instruction card clerk

Functional foremanship: an approach devised by Frederick Taylor in which the job of the general foreman was divided into its constituent parts. Each of the main parts was given to a different individual who would oversee and be responsible for that aspect of a worker's job.

Stop and Criticize

You are a product line manager in a large factory in the English Midlands making chocolate biscuits. This guy, Frederick Taylor, a management consultant, has told you that what you need in your factory to improve efficiency is functional foremanship. In replying, 'I don't think so, Mr Taylor', give four reasons for rejecting his professional advice.

Machine Shop No. 2 at Bethlehem Steel Works in Bethlehem, Pennsylvania, USA
Source: Reprinted by permission of Bethlehem Steel Corporation.

In 1898, Taylor was hired by the Bethlehem Iron Company (later part of the Bethlehem Steel Corporation) to improve work methods. For many years, the product of the company's blast furnaces had been handled by 75 pig iron handlers, who loaded an average of twelve and a half tons [tonnes] per man per day. Taylor estimated that a first-class pig iron handler ought to handle between 47 and 48 long tons [tonnes] per day. Taylor introduced his experimental changes; raised productivity by a factor of four; and increased workers' wages by 60 per cent. The savings achieved with his improved work plan were between $75,000

Pig iron handlers at the Bethlehem Steel Works.
Source: Reprinted by permission of the Bethlehem Steel Corporation.

and $80,000 per annum at 1911 prices. The cost of handling pig iron dropped substantially, and the employed men did the work previously done by many more. Taylor's 'deal' with his workers was as follows: 'You do it my way, by my standards, at the speed I mandate, and in so doing achieve a level of output I ordain, and I'll pay you handsomely for it, beyond anything you might have imagined. All you do is take orders, give up your way of doing the job for mine' (Kanigel, 1997, p. 214). It was among the first attempts to align the goals of the workers with those of management.

Taylor's scientific management was a powerful and largely successful attempt to wrest the organization of production from the workers and place it under the control of management. Before Taylor, the use of the **initiative and incentive system** within the company involved management specifying production requirements, providing workers with incentives in the form of a piece rate bonus and leaving them to decide how to organize their work. In Taylor's view, not only did this result in wasted effort but also, and more importantly, workers kept their craft secrets to themselves and worked at a collectively agreed rate that was below their ability. Taylor argued that management should exercise responsibility for the planning, co-ordinating and controlling of work (management functions), thereby leaving workers free to execute the tasks (shop-floor work).

Initiative and incentive system: a form of job design practice in which workers are given a task to perform by management who also provide them with a financial incentive. Workers are then left to use their initiative as to how to complete the task and which tools to use.

Taylor's view of workers, groups, unions and management

Taylor's views have often been misrepresented in numerous textbooks, yet they are clearly detailed in his own book, *The Principles of Scientific Management* (Taylor, 1911). As regards individual workers, Taylor sought to 'isolate' them, as far as possible, from their work mates. He neither ignored groups, nor considered them as unimportant, as is sometimes claimed. On the contrary, his experience of systematic soldiering showed him exactly how individuals behaved when part of a group. His solution to the problem of output restriction was to eliminate collusion between workers and to introduce best practice. It is true, however, that his interest in securing a docile workforce led him to take a negative, one-dimensional view of groups in the workplace.

Taylor recommended 'not dealing with men in masses'. Instead, he stressed the importance of talking to, and dealing with, only one worker at a time, since each employee possessed their own special abilities and limitations. Again, contrary to popular myth, Taylor did not regard the workers as simply robots. Instead, he wanted workers to progress on the basis of their abilities. He sought to develop individual workers to their highest state or rate of efficiency and prosperity. He felt that the objective of management should be to maximize the prosperity for both owners and employees, and contended that the prosperity of the former should not be at the cost of the latter.

The popular misconception that Taylor considered workers to be machines may have been perpetuated in the term that scientific management is also known by – 'modern machine theory'. He has been criticized for his view of workers as 'coin operated' beings, responding directly to financial incentives and being guided in their actions by a pleasure–pain calculation that would lead them to exert effort in proportion to the rewards available. Taylor's concern about the effects of groups on individual workers made him suspicious of unions. His individually oriented approach had no place for them. By their nature, unions emphasized group solidarity, common rules, and standardization of wages and conditions. This was contrary to his belief in the individual assessment of workers, matching their abilities to job requirements, fulfilling their personal desires and enabling them to 'better themselves' in line with the Protestant work ethic. Many of these criticisms ignore the historical context of Taylor's work, which took place at a time in which any social welfare system was absent, and one in which workers focused more on economic issues than perhaps they do today.

PAY DAY

Source: © 2003 Mike Stevens from cartoonbank.com. All Rights Reserved.

Management–worker relations, in Taylor's eyes, should be co-operative rather than adversarial. He saw the two pulling together to produce as much product as possible for their mutual benefit. His techniques were meant to improve the efficiency and social harmony of industrial life, and they required, in his phrase, a 'Mental Revolution' by both parties. By this he meant the application of the principles of science to determine the best way to perform any given task and the acceptance of the results obtained thereby, by both workers and management. He also believed that his 'scientific' approach would end arbitrary management decisions. Management would plan and organize the work, and labour would execute it, all in accordance with the dictates of science. Once his methods had been introduced within a company, trade unions and collective bargaining would become redundant. Scientific assessment would eliminate all ambiguity and argument.

Workers were concerned that scientific management just meant 'work speed-up': that is, getting more work for less pay. Taylor was adamant that after the implementation of his methods, workers would be rewarded by large pay increases and managers would secure higher productivity and profits. Sometimes workers complained about the inequality of pay increases, as when a 300 per cent productivity increase resulted in a 30 per cent pay increase. Taylor argued that his approach enabled people to do more work, in less time, using less effort because of the more efficient physical movements. Since they were expending less effort, this had to be taken into account when calculating their wage increases. The efficiency savings also led to the requirement for fewer workers. Would existing workers be re-deployed or made redundant? In later years the unions became reconciled with work-study, and accepted it, especially if financial benefits followed.

Taylor felt that managers who introduced his innovations deserved compensation for the costs of studying them, the purchase of special tools and the costs of reorganization. Nevertheless, his approach was resisted as much by managers (who resented the way that it diluted their prerogatives) as by workers (who were concerned about job intensification and redundancy). Taylor's approach was meant to be thorough, rigorous and systematic. However, 'scientific' implies objectivity, a methodology and an impartiality. These had no place in his thinking and techniques. Thus Taylor's claim that his approach to work design was 'scientific' was challenged both by his opponents at the time and by succeeding generations of academics.

Symphonic engineering

Here is the way in which a literal-minded industrial engineer reported on a symphony concert.

For considerable periods the four oboe players had nothing to do. The number should be reduced and the work spread more evenly over the whole concert, thus eliminating peaks and valleys of activity. All the twelve violins were playing identical notes, this seems unnecessary duplication. The staff of this section should be drastically cut. If a larger volume of sound is required, it could be obtained by means of electronic apparatus. Much effort was absorbed in the playing of demi-semi-quavers; this seems to be an unnecessary refinement. It is recommended that all notes be rounded up to the nearest semi-quaver. If this were done, it would be possible to use trainees and lower-grade operatives more extensively.

There seems to be too much repetition of some musical passages. Scores should be drastically pruned. No useful purpose is served by repeating on the horns something which has already been handled by the strings. It is estimated that if all redundant passages were eliminated the whole concert time of two hours could be reduced to twenty minutes and there would be no need for an intermission. In many cases the operators were using one hand for holding the instrument, whereas the introduction of a fixture would have tendered the idle hand available for other work. Also, it was noted that excessive effort was being used occasionally by the players of wind instruments, whereas one compressor could supply adequate air for all instruments under more accurately controlled conditions.

Finally, obsolescence of equipment is another matter into which it is suggested further investigation could be made, as it was reported in the programme that the leading violinist's instrument was already several hundred years old. If normal depreciation schedules had been applied, the value of this instrument would have been reduced to zero and purchase of more modern equipment could then have been considered.

From Robert M. Fulmer and Theodore T. Herbert, *Exploring the New Management*, Macmillan, New York, 1974, p. 27.

Taylorism was used extensively in the Soviet Union though its effectiveness was questionable (Merkle, 1980). In 1918, the newspaper *Pravda* quoted Lenin as saying that every scientific suggestion of the Taylor system should be tried out. Perhaps most significantly, Taylor's book was translated into Japanese in 1912.

Critics of Japanese teamworking argue that it contains more elements of Taylorism than of employee empowerment.

Criticisms of Taylorism

The following criticisms are commonly found in textbooks and historical accounts of Taylorism:

1. It assumed that the motivation of the employee was to secure the maximum earnings for the effort expended. It neglected the importance of other rewards from work (achievement, job satisfaction, recognition), which later research has found to be important.

2. It neglected the subjective side of work – the personal and interactional aspects of performance, the meanings that employees give to work and the significance to them of their social relationships at work.

3. It failed to appreciate the meanings that workers would put on new procedures and their reactions to being timed and closely supervised.

4. It had an inadequate understanding of the relation of the individual incentive to interaction with, and dependence on, the immediate work group. Taylor did attribute 'underworking' to group pressures but misunderstood the way in which these worked. He failed to see that these might just as easily keep production and morale up.

5. It ignored the psychological needs and capabilities of workers. The one best way of doing a job was chosen with the mechanistic criteria of speed and output. The imposition of a uniform manner of work can both destroy individuality and cause other psychological disturbances.

6. It had too simple an approach to the question of productivity and morale. It sought to keep both of these up exclusively by economic rewards and punishments. However, the fatigue studies of the Gilbreths during the 1920s did signal the beginnings of a wider appreciation of the relevant factors than had initially been recognized by Taylor. Incentive approaches under the scientific approach tended to focus on the worker as an individual and ignored his social context.

7. Functional foremanship was deemed to be too complex and unwieldy a mode of supervision.

Stop and Criticize

You have travelled back through time and are able to meet Taylor. What three things would you congratulate him for, and what three things would you criticize him for?

Development of Taylorism: the Gilbreths and Gantt

Frank Bunker Gilbreth had participated in a meeting held in 1910 in Laurence Gantt's apartment where, with Jim Dodge and Louis Brandies, the group adopted the term 'scientific management'. His background resembled Taylor's in that both were practising engineers and managers. Gilbreth's experience was in the construction industry, and his most famous experiments involved bricklayers. His main contribution was to refine the techniques for measuring work. His wife Lillian was a trained psychologist and her contribution was in the area of the human aspects of work.

Lillian Moller Gilbreth (1878–1972) and Frank Bunker Gilbreth (1868–1924)

- *Motion study*: This refers to the investigation and classification of the basic motions of the body, regardless of the particular and concrete form of labour in which those motions are used. Gilbreth develop motion study, including job simplification. Taylor had looked mainly at time, and had not focused as closely on motions. Gilbreth sought to rectify this omission and to determine the fundamental units of work. His views were published in his book *Motion Study* in 1911.

■ *Research techniques*: To implement motion study, Gilbreth devised techniques to study and improve workers' body movements. He used *stroboscopic pictures* which involved keeping the camera lens open to show changing positions assumed by the worker. Small electric lamps were attached to workers' fingers, hands and arms, and their motions were photographed at slow shutter speeds. This method left paths of light, indicating acceleration and deceleration, on the photographic plate as a series of dots. The outcome was a *chronocyclegraph*, which was a photograph of the workplace with motion paths superimposed. From these he made wire models which allowed the work task to be analyzed in detail, and redesigned to be performed more efficiently. He used also used *motion picture cameras* to record a worker's movements in the performance of a task. A clock, calibrated in hundredths of a minute within the film frame, enabled the worker's motions, the time taken and the conditions surrounding the job to be all recorded simultaneously.

■ *Therbligs*: In motion and time study, the elementary movement was visualized as the building block of every work activity. Gilbreth developed a comprehensive system of noting such elementary movements (see 'Gilbreth's contributions' box), each with its own symbol and colour. They are called 'therbligs' – a variation of his name spelt backwards. Like dance, all the movements of the worker's body performing a particular task are noted down using the therbligs notation. In addition, Gilbreth developed a standard time for each job element, thereby combining time study with motion study. This was used for designing wage payment systems whose universal application Gilbreth advocated. Process charts continue to be used in business process re-engineering. **Time-and-motion studies** are conducted to this day.

Time-and-motion studies: measurement and recording techniques which attempt to make operations more efficient.

Like Taylor, Gilbreth gave detailed rules on how to find out the best way of doing any job. He discovered that eighteen separate movements were made in laying each brick. By reorganizing the work pattern, he was able to reduce the movements to five, and increase the bricklayers productivity from 120 to 350 bricks an hour. Additionally, in order to control work carried on building sites far from head office, he devised the 'Field System'. This was a set of written rules and procedures intended to establish uniform practice on all work sites. It detailed how to mix concrete, transport materials, train apprentices, erect scaffolding, and so on.

Lillian Gilbreth's contribution came from psychology. Her book, *The Psychology of Management* (1916/1973), highlighted the importance of human factors in organizations and was published in 1916. Her work complemented her husband's. The study of motions and the elimination of unnecessary and wasteful actions sought to reduce the fatigue experienced by workers. Since all work produced fatigue for which the remedy was rest, the aim was to find the best mixture of work and rest to maximize productivity. The Gilbreths distinguished between *necessary fatigue*, which was a consequence of work that must be done to complete a task, and *unnecessary fatigue*, which resulted from effort that did not need to be expended at all. Through the use of motion study linked with the redesign of work, they sought to eliminate unnecessary fatigue and minimize necessary fatigue.

To do this, they focused on the total working environment, and not just on selecting first-class workers as Taylor had done. They shortened the working day,

Gilbreth's contributions

Micro-motion studies and chronocyclegraphic models

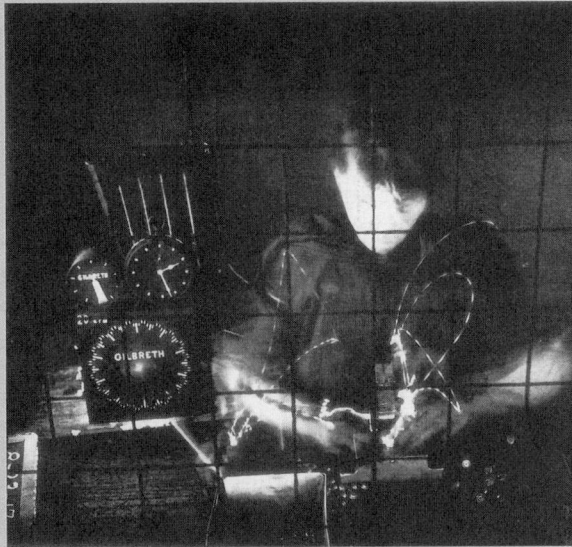

Source: Smithsonian Institution, National Museum of American History.

Therblig symbols and colours

symbol	name	colour
	search	black
	find	grey
	select	light grey
	group	red
	hold	gold ochre
	transport loaded	green
	position	blue
	assemble	violet
	use	purple
	disassemble	light violet
	inspect	burnt ochre
	pre-position	pale blue
	release load	carmine red
	transport empty	olive green
	rest for overcoming fatigue	orange
	unavoidable delay	yellow
	avoidable delay	lemon yellow
	plan	brown

Source: H.R. Pollard, *Developments in Management Thought*, Heinemann, London, 1974.

Henry Laurence Gantt
(1861–1924)

introduced rest periods and chairs and instituted holidays with pay. They studied jobs to eliminate fatigue-producing elements. Changes were also made to heating, lighting and ventilation. The final ingredient was termed the 'betterment of work'. It included introducing rest rooms, canteens, entertainment and music into the factory. In the work of the Gilbreths we see the first realization that workers may have a variety of different needs. They thought that individual work performance depended on attitudes, needs and the physical environment as well as correct work methods and suitable equipment. In 1916, the Gilbreths published their book *Fatigue Study*, which linked Frank's development of Taylor's scientific management ideas with Lillian's work in industrial psychology.

Midvale Steel Company

In 1887, Henry Laurence Gantt joined the Midvale Steel Company as an assistant in the Engineering Department. A year later, he became assistant to the

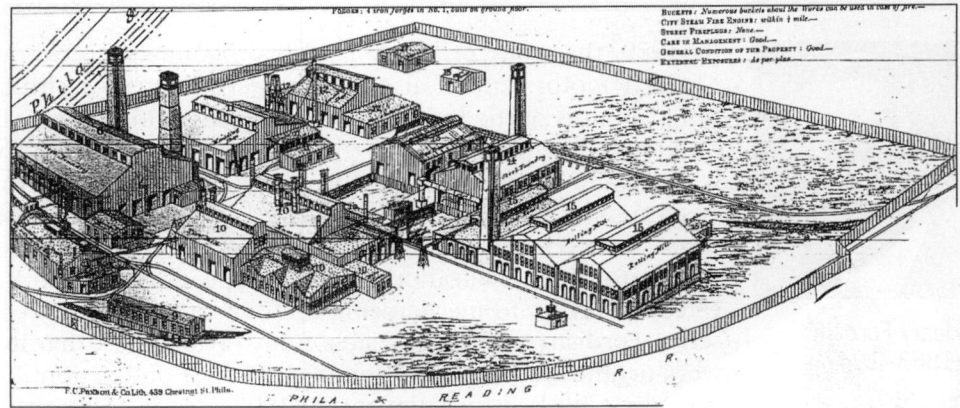

Midvale Steel Company
Source: Reprinted by permission of Free Library of Philadelphia, Map Collection.

company's chief engineer – F.W. Taylor. Gantt supported Taylor's approach, but he did much to humanize scientific management to make it more acceptable (Gantt, 1919). He tempered Taylor's work with greater insight into human psychology, and stressed method over measurement. He believed that Taylor's use of incentives was too punitive and lacked a sensitivity to the psychological needs of the workers. He believed in consideration for and fair dealings with employees. He felt that scientific management was being used as an oppressive instrument by the unscrupulous. He made three major contributions:

- *Best known way at present*: Gantt's system was based on detailed instruction cards in the best scientific management tradition. However, he replaced Taylor's 'one best way' with his own 'best known way at present'. This involved a much less detailed analysis of jobs than Taylor had suggested.

- *Task-and-bonus payment scheme*: He replaced Taylor's differential piece-rate wage system with his own task-and-bonus scheme. Each worker was set a task, and received a set day rate and an additional 20–50 per cent bonus.

- *Gantt chart*: He developed a bar chart used for scheduling (that is, planning) and co-ordinating the work of different departments or plants. His chart depicted quantities ordered, work progress and quantities issued from store. Although he never patented it, it is still in use today, and bears his name (see figure 13.1).

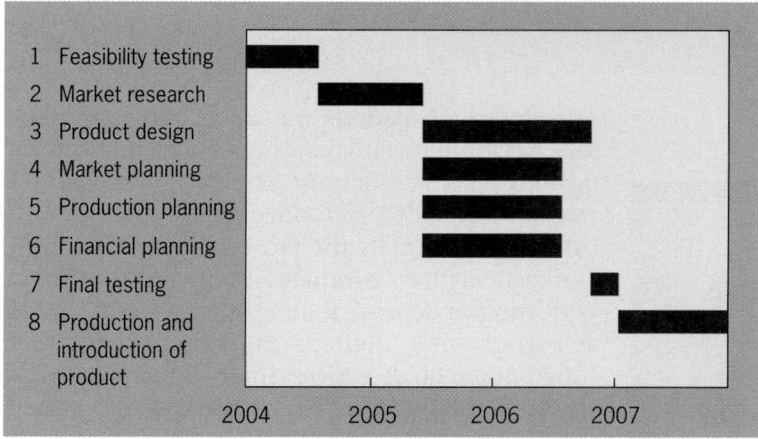

Figure 13.1: Gantt chart for new product development plan beginning 2004

Fordism

Henry Ford
(1863–1947)

By 1920, the name of Henry Ford had became synonymous not only with his Model T motor car, but also with his revolutionary techniques of mass production. In terms of the three separate manufacturing activities listed by Gill (1985) on page 429, Ford developed the last two – the transfer of work pieces between workers and operations; and the co-ordination and control of these processes, ensuring that sufficient raw material was available to operators and that finished pieces flowed smoothly through assembly. Thus he moved on from the mechanization and rationalization of work on the individual work piece or object pioneered by Taylor, to mechanizing the flow of objects between operatives. In this sense, **Fordism** is distinguishable from Taylorism in that it represents a form of work organization designed for efficient mass production.

Ford established his company in 1903. In the 1890s, it was skilled craftsmen who built motor cars. Ford claimed that there were not enough of them to meet

Fordism: the application of scientific management principles to workers' jobs; the installation of single-purpose machine tools to manufacture standardized parts; and the introduction of the mechanized assembly line.

the level of car production that he wanted, and that was why, in his view, deskilling of work was necessary. Others argue that deskilling made labour easier to control and replace. Ford's goal was 'continuous improvement' rather than the 'one best way'. Ford's objective was to increase his control by reducing or eliminating uncertainty (Ford and Crowther, 1924). Among his major innovations were:

■ analysis of jobs using time-and-motion techniques;

■ the installation of single-purpose machine tools to manufacture standardized parts;

■ the introduction of the assembly line.

Analyzing jobs

Ford applied the principles of scientific management to remove waste and inefficiency. He established a Motion Picture Department that filmed work methods in different industries so as to learn from them. He applied the principles of work rationalization: employees were allocated simple tasks, all of which had been carefully designed to ensure maximum efficiency. Ford's approach was entirely experimental, very pragmatic and always open to improvements – try it, modify it, try it again, keep on until it's right. The Ford mechanic, originally a skilled craftsman, became an assembler who tended his machine, only performing low-grade tasks. For example, the wheelwright's job was divided into almost a hundred operations, each performed by a different man using specialized equipment.

Installation of single-purpose machine tools to produce standardized parts

Ford used rigid and heavy machine tools, carbon alloy tool steels and universal grinding machines. This ensured that each part was exactly like the next, and hence interchangeable. This facilitated the division of labour and increased certainty. The single-purpose machines in his factory were called 'farmer machines' because farm boys, coming off the land, could be quickly trained to use them. Their operators did not have to be skilled, just quick. The skill was now incorporated within the machine. This eliminated the need for skilled mechanics, as the unskilled could now assemble an automobile.

Introduction of the assembly line

Despite the aforementioned innovations, employees could still work at their own speed. In 1913 it still took ninety minutes to assemble a car. To overcome this problem, instead of moving the men past the car, the car was moved past the men. The assembly line imposed upon employees the working speed that Ford wanted. By 1914, the plant had installed a continuous automatic conveyer that met Ford's technical and philosophical objectives. The engineers arranged work in a logical order. The materials and semi-completed parts passed through the plant to where they were needed. The conveyor belt took radiator parts to assemblers, and then carried their work away to solderers, who finished off the product (Gartman, 1979).

After integrating other production processes, Ford's engineers produced a continuously moving line fed by overhead conveyors. Each worker was feeding, and being fed by, the assembly line. In 1908, when the Model T was introduced, production ran at 27 cars per day. By 1923, when the River Rouge plant had been completed, daily production had reached 2,000 cars. More than quantity of production, the assembly line involved, in Ford's words, 'the focusing upon a manufacturing process of the principles of power, accuracy, economy, system, continuity, speed and repetition'.

The credit for the original concept of the assembly line (manual and mechanically paced) is disputed. A Spanish visitor to the Arsenal of Venice in 1436 reported galleys passing along a 'street' (canal), and being loaded with munitions and equipment, which were passed through the windows of adjacent houses, as they progressed. They exited the street fully loaded. Some stories tell of Henry Ford getting the idea at an abattoir where beef carcasses, suspended from moving hooks, were being disassembled. Other accounts have him visiting a watch plant, and seeing the staged assembly process of timepieces (Collier and Horowitz, 1987). Although Henry Ford claimed the authorship of the assembly line in the

First moving assembly line

The photograph below shows men working on the first moving assembly line at Ford's Highland Park factory, 1913.

Source: Reprinted by permission of Ford Motor Company.

Many songs were written about Ford's assembly lines. One was sung to the tune of the Battle Hymn of the Republic. Its first verse and chorus ran:

Mine eyes hath seen the glories of the making of a Ford,
It's made under conditions that would offend the Almighty Lord,
With a most ungodly hurry, and amidst wild uproar,
The production rushes on.

Hurry, hurry, hurry, hurry,
Hurry, hurry, hurry, hurry,
Hurry, hurry, hurry, hurry,
Production rushes on.

Collection of Henry Ford Museum and Greenfield Village.

manufacturing plant at Highland Park near Detroit, there is strong evidence to suggest that credit for it should be given to others (Heizer, 1998).

Taylor's ambition had always been to wrest control of the production process from the workers and place it into the hands of management. Under Fordism, this was broadly achieved. Ford's objective was to allow unsophisticated workers to make a sophisticated product in volume. He sought to make his workforce as uniform and interchangeable as the parts they handled. This created an authoritarian work regime with closely monitored, machine-paced, short-cycle, unremitting tasks. Ford made other, less publicized innovations, including the introduction of highly co-ordinated logistics systems, greater bureaucratic control through job classifications with uniform wage scales, and he placed a limit on the prerogatives of supervisors and line managers.

The speed of the assembly line was increased with Henry Ford being labelled the 'Speed-up King'. This, plus the monotonous work, meant that in 1913 the company had an astronomical turnover rate. Newly hired workers stayed an average of only three months. Indeed, over 70 per cent of the men who left Ford were categorized as '5 day men': that is, they walked off the job without any formal notification and were simply presumed to have quit after missing five days' work. Since it cost $100 to train each worker, this level of turnover was costing the company $3 million a year (Wilson, 1995).

Partly in response to this, Ford cut the working day from nine to eight hours and doubled the minimum wage from $2.50 to $5.00 a day. This was twice that was offered by any other motor car company. He believed that higher wages would lead to higher production and higher profits. As a result, turnover reduced, absenteeism fell from 10 per cent to 0.5 per cent and Henry Ford became a hero overnight. The workers who had cursed him now wore their company identification badges as tie-pins on Sundays with pride. Ford knew that they could use the extra money to buy his cars. However, he was concerned that this wage increase could lead some workers to depravity. Hence, this wage increase was dependent on workers showing sobriety and industry. But who was to judge this?

Ford's legacy continued to dominate twentieth-century organization. He showed his successors how the world could be organized to solve problems using the closely related concepts of **system** and **control**. What Ford built was not just a factory, but an entire production system. This system included the factory, but went beyond its walls. What made that system so effective was the nature and the degree of control that he exerted upon it. It has been said that Ford was determined to gain complete control of all aspects of the manufacture and sale of his car. That he nearly succeeded testified to his genius (Zaleznik and Kets de Vries, 1975). His control over the manufacturing process was achieved through the logical organization of his plants. The output of one group of workers became the input of others. The production system was like a giant river fed by the tributaries that constantly flowed into it.

Control over the worker was exerted through task specialization and assembly-line working. Such control was both invisible and non-confrontational. It was the system not the supervisor that told the employee to work faster. It de-personalized the authority relationship to such a degree that workers were no longer aware that they were being directed. Control over the environment was achieved through purchase of vital raw materials. Ford experienced production hold-ups when his suppliers had strikes. To avoid this he sought to control all aspects of the production process. In the Brazilian rain forest, he carved out rubber plantations the size of Connecticut which were called 'Fordlandia'. He bought coal mines in Kentucky, iron mines in Michigan, as well as glassworks, shipping lines and railways. He was determined to control every element of the manufacturing process, both inside and outside his factory.

Systems concept: a management perspective which emphasizes the interdependence between the various parts of an organization, and also between the organization and its environment.

Control concept: the process of imposing a pattern on previously haphazard activities, such as the operation of machinery, the interaction of machinery with people or the interactions between individuals.

Fordist model of work organization

1. Prescribed tasks and compulsory operational methods.

2. Timings based on time-and-motion method with little modification.

3. Centralized Engineering Department organizes the shop floor.

4. Unskilled operators are relieved by 'multiskilled' workers.

5. Role of supervisors primarily disciplinary.

6. No motivation system, no local goals, respect for discipline.

7. System emphasizes discipline.

Based on Jean-Pierre Durand, Paul Stewart and Juan Jose Castillo (eds), *Teamwork in the Automobile Industry: Radical Change or Passing Fashion*, Macmillan Business, Basingstoke, 1999, p. 16.

The debate about Henry Ford's legacy continues to this day. On the positive side, there is agreement about his contribution to productivity. In 1913, before the assembly line, it took twelve and a half hours to put together a Model T. In 1914, Ford's 13,000 workers produced 267,720 cars while the other American motor companies, with a combined workforce at the time of 66,000 employees produced 287,770 cars. Further improvements were to occur. By 1920, one Ford car rolled off the line every minute, and by 1925, the figure was one every ten seconds. In 1935, Ford's River Rouge plant in Dearborn on the outskirts of Detroit, spread over 1,096 acres, had 7.25 million square feet of floor space, possessed 235 acres of glass windows and 90 miles of railway track, employed 100,000 men, and built 2 million cars each year. Little wonder that it was called the *Cathedral of Industry*.

Ford's giant River Rouge plant, *c*. 1935.
Source: Popperfoto.com

Ford's contribution to raising people's standard of living is also acknowledged. Having shown that something as complicated as a motor car could be built using the techniques of mass production, it was recognized that the manufacture of other, simpler products was also possible. Mass production led to mass consumption, and gave more people more access to more goods than ever before in history. In the fifty years to 1970, the standard of living of Americans sky-rocketed. Other countries which adopted Ford's system of manufacturing production also benefited.

Critics have argued that Ford destroyed craftsmanship and deskilled jobs. He did indeed change the work process by introducing greater amounts of rigidity and regulation, thereby affecting the skill content of jobs. Others argue that since there were insufficient numbers of skilled workers available to do the original jobs, Ford had to redesign the tasks so that the existing, pre-industrial labour force could cope with them. In their view, it was less a question of forcing a highly-skilled, high-priced employee to accept a cheapened, dead-end job, and more an issue of identifying tasks appropriate for unskilled people to do who would otherwise have performed even less enjoyable, back-breaking work. The same critics also assert that short-cycle, repetitive jobs have caused worker alienation and stress, and have subjugated human beings to the machine. The assembly line is vilified for exerting an invidious, invisible control over the workers. The debate over the balance of costs and benefits of Fordism and its precursor, Taylorism, continues to this day, as the next section illustrates.

Cathedral of Industry

In the 1930s, the Mexican artist, Diego Rivera (1886–1957), was commissioned by the Detroit Institute of Art to paint frescos devoted to the city's motor car industry. His panels feature Ford's River Rouge plant. Rivera was an independent artist with a Marxist perspective. He painted the factory workers and the machines they used. The ethnic mix of the workforce is depicted. The panels show various stages in the production of the automobile. The men in the murals are depicted as sullen and angry, working amid the clamour and din of the machinery around them. The strength shown in their faces was perceived as intimidating by some observers, who accused Rivera of producing left-wing propaganda.

Detroit Industry (South Wall), Diego Rivera, 1932–33.

The machines themselves are shown as perfect designs, as part of a system that is so complicated and so intimidating that it dwarfs ordinary human beings. The murals exalt the sophistication of the production system, saying to the on-looker, 'Look at this incredible achievement'. They depict the triumph of rationality over nature's apparent disorganization; of new forms of manufacturing over old; and of the new order over the old. However, one obvious thing is missing from the pictures.

Look at the picture again carefully. Can you see a completed car? The panels convey the awe-inspiring nature of Ford's technology – as something that helps human beings, but which simultaneously dominates them.

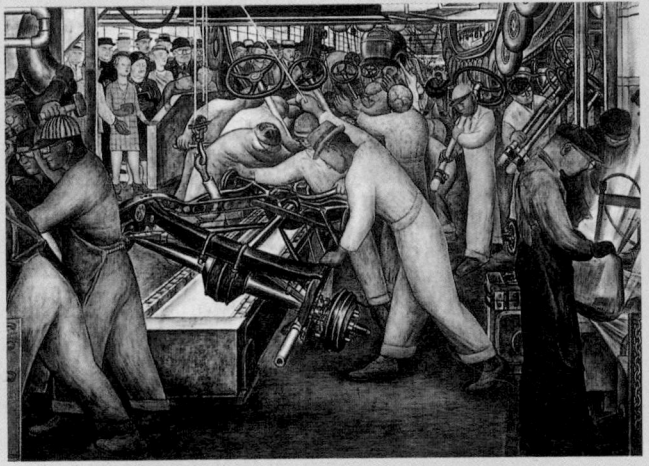

Source: (both images) Detroit Industry, South Wall (detail), 1932–33, Diego M. Rivera. Gift of Edsel B. Ford. Photograph © 1991 The Detroit Institute of Arts.

Was Fordism a development of Taylorism, or were the two merely historically coincidental? David Hounshell (1984) felt that if by Taylorism is meant rationalization through the analysis of work (time-and-motion studies to eliminate wasteful motions) and the 'scientific' selection of workmen for prescribed tasks, then indeed, Ford's engineers did 'Taylorize' his Highland Park plant. They seemed to have followed broad scientific management principles, if not necessarily a specific programme. Hounshell listed the following as evidence: within the plant, the standardization of work routines following an analysis of jobs and work flow patterns; the widespread use of special-purpose machine tools; the careful selection of skilled and unskilled workers to operate these machines; the establishment of a work standards department to conduct time-and-motion studies to establish a 'fair day's pay'; and the clear division of labour between management and labour, with machine tenders leaving the maintenance of their machines to specialists. In contrast, Hounshell considers that, within the factory, there is little evidence that scientific management contributed significantly to the assembly-line system that Ford created within it. There were, however, three fundamental differences between Taylorism and Fordism, as listed in table 13.3.

Table 13.3: Differences between Taylorism and Fordism

	Taylorism	Fordism
Approach to machinery	Organized labour around existing machinery	Eliminated labour with new machinery
Technology and the work design	Took production process as given and sought to reorganize work and labour processes	Used technology to mechanize the work process; workers fed and tended machines
Pace of work	Set by his workers or the supervisor	Set by machinery – the speed of the assembly line

After Ford: the deskilling debate

The idea of fragmenting work tasks and simplifying jobs was begun by Taylor and developed by Ford. Since that time, has this process of deskilling work continued and been extended to other occupations and types of worker? Or, on the contrary, has work become more complicated, have employees been better trained and educated, and are the jobs that they do more skilled? Taylor and Ford placed the issue of job skill at the centre of all subsequent discussions about work transformation and work organization. The deskilling debate provides a useful perspective from which to consider the plethora of theoretical, empirical and prescriptive writings produced by academics, managers and consultants during the twentieth century on the topics of work design.

Mike Noon and Paul Blyton (2002) provide a clear exposition of the deskilling debate, and this section draws heavily upon their explanatory structure. It also incorporates additional, more recent contributions. However, it leaves untouched their basic contention that deskilling theory has failed to provide a satisfactory explanation of the diverse empirical evidence obtained by researchers. Instead, these authors offer an exploratory framework. We shall see how Noon and Blyton reached their conclusion; how recent studies confirm their assessment; and we shall apply their framework. Before proceeding, however, we need to go back briefly in time.

The last half of the twentieth century witnessed two seemingly contradictory trends in work design. From the 1950s, in both the United States and Europe, there was a reaction against Taylorism, and a steady and consistent interest in more 'people-oriented' approaches. Labels like human relations, socio-technical systems, quality of working life, organization development and human-centred manufacturing reflected this inclination. Then, during the 1970s, Japanization, and in particular the success of Japanese 'lean production' manufacturing techniques and Japanese teamworking, became prominent. The contradiction was very apparent. On the one hand, lean production involved many features of Taylorist and Fordist work designs, while on the other, it appeared to incorporate numerous people-oriented features like teamworking. This paradox generated much research and debate.

At the same time, the gathering pace of information technology signalled the increasing importance of knowledge-based jobs, and of the need for so-called 'knowledge workers' to fill them. The necessity of having a well-educated and trained workforce to perform these more technically complex jobs was widely discussed. The question asked by many commentators was whether a fundamental change was taking place in the nature of work, and if so, whether it was resulting in people being deskilled, and their work degraded, or upskilled (or enskilled), and their work and working lives enriched.

This then is the 'deskilling debate'. Although the deskilling and upskilling positions stand in opposition to one another, the deskilling one has, to date, generated the greatest amount of research and literature. Indeed, it has created its own sub-field in sociology, that of labour process theory. Within this camp, debates have mostly occurred between the deskilling 'agnostics' and 'sympathizers'. In contrast, the upskilling position has been promoted primarily by business writers, management consultants and business school academics who are keen to identify abrupt and dramatic shifts and new trends in work, the workplace and the economy. There have been fewer inter-positional discussions between the 'deskillers' and 'upskillers' so far, but this may be changing.

The deskilling position

Crudely summarized, the deskilling of work thesis holds that the principles and practices of Taylorism and Fordism continue to be ever more widely applied within modern organizations. The thesis first appeared in 1974 in the book, *Labour and Monopoly Capital: The Degradation of Work in the Twentieth Century*. The book was written by Harry Braverman (1920–74), an American theorist, who had originally been trained as a craftsman coppersmith, and who had worked in naval shipyards, railway repair shops and steel plants before becoming a journalist and sociologist. Braverman died shortly after his book was published, and he was not around to enjoy the reputation that his book brought, or to contribute to the debate – the labour process debate – that his work triggered (Littler and Salaman, 1982).

The Braverman deskilling thesis

There is a long-run tendency through fragmentation, rationalization and mechanization for workers and their jobs to become deskilled, both in an absolute sense (they lose craft and traditional abilities) and in a relative one (scientific knowledge progressively accumulates in the production process). Even when the individual worker retains certain traditional skills, the degraded job that he or she performs does not demand the exercise of these abilities. Thus, a worker, regardless of his or her personal talents, may be more easily and cheaply substituted in the production process.

From Andrew S. Zimbalist, *Case Studies on the Labour Process*, Monthly Review Press, London, 1979, p. xv.

The 'Braverman thesis', as it came to be known, has stimulated a wide-ranging debate among labour process theorists. It was based on Marxist economic theory and the crisis of capitalism in industrial societies. Braverman saw scientific management as a method of direct employee control. Managers removed the surplus value of their employees' labour (the difference between the sales price and production cost) and realized that value when the good was sold. He called this process *valorization*. To increase their own control, managers reduced the autonomy and discretion exercised by workers in how they performed their jobs, thereby deskilling their work. Braverman contrasted two types. The first type, *organizational deskilling*, involved Taylor's separation of task conception from task execution. Workers no longer planned their work or solved their problems since these were now dealt with by managerial or technical staff. The second type, *technological deskilling*, involved using technology, in the form of software development and equipment replacement, to do the same thing. This trend, he felt, was growing in all forms of capitalist enterprises, and was being extended to clerical, administrative and other occupational (non-shop floor) groups (Braverman, 1974).

Braverman sought to counter the popular view in social science and business literature that Taylorism has been superseded by human relations and other, more sophisticated approaches, and that it no longer determines work design or management methods. On the contrary, he argued that, far from being superseded, Taylorism was institutionalized and formed the basis of production control within organizations. Following this impetus, researchers rushed to study organizations to test the thesis. They conducted case studies to determine the existence and nature of deskilling in a wide range of different organizations in both production and service industries. The Braverman deskilling thesis was proposed in 1974, but by the 1990s it was discussed as the **McDonaldization** thesis. This followed the publication of George Ritzer's *The McDonaldization of Society* (Ritzer, 1993).

McDonaldization: an approach to work organization based on efficiency, calculability, predictability and control, using sophisticated technology to enhance these objectives by limiting employee discretion and creativity.

In his book, Ritzer argued that the process of McDonaldization was affecting many areas of our social and organizational lives. He has no particular complaint against McDonald's hamburger restaurants; he merely used this fast food chain as an illustration of the wider process which was the real focus of his attention. For Ritzer, the new model of rationality, with its routinization and standardization of product and service, and represented by McDonald's, had replaced the bureaucratic structures of the past, as described by Max Weber. Ritzer saw the McDonald's approach as possessing four key elements:

1. *Efficiency*: high speed of product manufacture or service provision.

2. *Calculability:* high value and minimum waste.

3. *Predictability*: of product or service irrespective of time or location.

4. *Control*: staff perform a limited range of tasks in a precisely detailed way.

Ritzer's argument is that the process of McDonaldization is spreading and that, while it yields a number of benefits, the associated costs and risks are considerable. His own view is that this trend is undesirable. He looks at the issue primarily from the point of view of what the consumer, client or citizen is receiving – a uniform, standardized product or service. However, he recognizes that to achieve this, the jobs of producers have to be deskilled. In addition to the simplified jobs that McDonald's employees perform, their work is also limited by the sophisticated technology of fast food preparation, which gives them little or no discretion in how they prepare and deliver food to customers. Given our definition of action teams, it is perhaps appropriate that McDonald's restaurant employees are referred to by the company as 'crew members'. Crews are a form of action team which is equipment- or technology-driven, and if that technology changes, then so too does the nature of the crew.

Hamburger grilling instructions are precise and detailed, covering the exact positioning of burgers on the grill, cooking times, and the sequence in which burgers are to be turned. Drinks dispensers, french-fry machines, programmed cash registers all limit the time required to carry out a task and leave little or no room for discretion, creativity or innovation on the part of the employee. Such discretion and creativity would of course subvert the aims of efficiency, calculability, predictability and control. Fiona Wilson (2004) summarizes some of the other key features of McDonald's work design:

> The McDonald's 'Counter Observation Checklist' is used to ensure that employees welcome customers in the prescribed way. For example. 'Greeting the customer': 1. There is a smile. 2. Greeting is pleasant, audible and sincere. 3. Looks customer in the eyes (quoted in Fineman, 1995). Similar checklists exist for other processes in the restaurants.

Stop and Criticize

Robin Leidner's (1993) research revealed that McDonald's workers do not say that they are dissatisfied with their jobs. Do you find this disturbing or expected? Suggest an explanation for this finding.

The significance of this development is that much of current literature about the nature of work and workplace organization is discussed in terms of Ritzer and his McDonaldization thesis, rather than in terms of Braverman and his deskilling and work degradation thesis. The key point, however, is that both writers address broadly the same issues. Warhurst and Thompson (1998) reported that Ritzer acknowledged the links between his own work and that of Braverman, and between Max Weber's theory of rationalization and Karl Marx's theory of exploitation. There have been many criticisms of Braverman and his deskilling thesis. These include the following (Fincham and Rhodes, 1998; Noon and Blyton, 2002):

Ignores alternative management strategies

It ignores management's ability to choose between using Taylorism to deskill a job and empowering workers to create responsible autonomy. Leaving employees with some discretion can be to management's advantage. Thus, employee empowerment facilitates greater worker interchangeability, thereby allowing better assembly-line balancing. These employees are not deskilled, but management nevertheless continues to control the labour process. This suggests that deskilling is neither inevitable nor necessarily always desirable.

Underestimates skill changes caused by technology

Technological developments are constantly creating new skills, specialists and entire occupations. If the economy and technology can create such new skills, there is no simple process of deskilling. There are many examples of both reskilling (the growth of wholly new skills) and of upskilling (the enhancement of existing skills).

Overstates management's objective of controlling labour

The thesis underestimates the diversity and complexity of management objectives and plurality of interests, many of which may be competing (Buchanan and Boddy, 1983; Child, 1985). Marketing, technological, financial and political considerations may have as much, if not more, impact on work organization. The cost of

- success depends more on 'brains than brawn' (Barley, 1996);

- the information age has replaced the machine age (Hamel and Prahalad, 1996);

- locating vital information and using it to help understand what is happening in a turbulent environment has become a major determinant of organizational success (Quah, 1997);

- providing services is more important than making tangible products;

- a small group of core workers with steady jobs and fixed salaries will be outnumbered by a growing number of 'portfolio workers' offering their skills to clients (Handy, 1984);

- the work of symbolic analysts who trade and manipulate symbols is too complex, domain-specific and esoteric to be subjected to managerial control (Reich, 1993).

Noon and Blyton (2002) list some of the criticisms of the upskilling thesis:

1. One cannot establish a causal relationship between technical change and rising skill levels.

2. Advanced technology does not always require increased skill levels.

3. The growth of the service sector does not necessarily lead to the creation of high-skill jobs.

4. Existing mass production methods are likely to continue supplying mass markets.

5. Because of multinationals, upskilling needs to be considered at global and national levels.

Stop and Criticize

The obvious way to resolve the deskilling debate is to ask individual employees whether they think that their job now possesses a higher or lower level of skill requirement and responsibility compared to five years ago. Or, if they have a new job, whether that requires more skill to perform it than their previous job. Why is this approach unlikely to provide a reliable answer?

To determine whether or not Taylorist and Fordist practices are being introduced or replaced, one might give up the search for any general tendencies and look instead for specific trends in skill changes on the basis of survey data. This is what Gallie (1991) did on UK data obtained in the 1980s from the Social Change and Economic Life Initiative (SCELI). He found that:

- within institutional classes, those who remained in the same job experienced less upskilling than those who moved;

- within sectors, the general trend was towards upskilling rather than deskilling, with non-skilled workers in manufacturing experiencing more upskilling than those in the service sector;

- in every occupational class, work with advanced technology was associated with higher skill demands;

- overall deskilling was rare, and the most common experience was upskilling;

- the evidence most strongly supports the argument that skills are being polarized, being associated most closely with skill differentials, advanced technology and gender.

Chris Warhurst and Paul Thompson (1998) quote an OECD *Jobs Study* (1994) which showed that 'new professionals', like scientists, engineers and marketers, now form the largest occupational group in the UK. They refer to 'technicization', a situation in which theoretical knowledge now infuses previously tacit-knowledge-only jobs. However, this still leaves students without a way of critically evaluating the empirical evidence on work organizations, which predominantly comes not from surveys but from case studies of single-occupational groups, single-site or single-industry case studies. What is needed is a conceptual frame-work with which to analyze and then map the case accounts that are available. Noon and Blyton (2002, pp. 166–8) offer just such a conceptual framework, which is capable of being developed into an analytical tool. These authors conceptualize the work performed by employees as varying along two dimensions – *range of work* and *discretion in work*. These are shown in figure 13.2.

Range of work
The vertical range of work dimension distinguishes, at one extreme, those workers who repeatedly perform a single task: for example, operators attaching a wheel on a car on an assembly line. Their work range would be narrow. At the other end of this dimension, there might be a shop assistant serving staff, re-stocking shelves, stocktaking and changing window displays. Since they performed many different tasks, their range of work would be wide.

Discretion over work
The horizontal control over work dimension distinguishes, at one extreme, workers who, because of the specificity with which their work is defined, have little or no discretion as to how to perform it. For example, our assembly-line operator who attaches a wheel on a car will follow a detailed, written specification

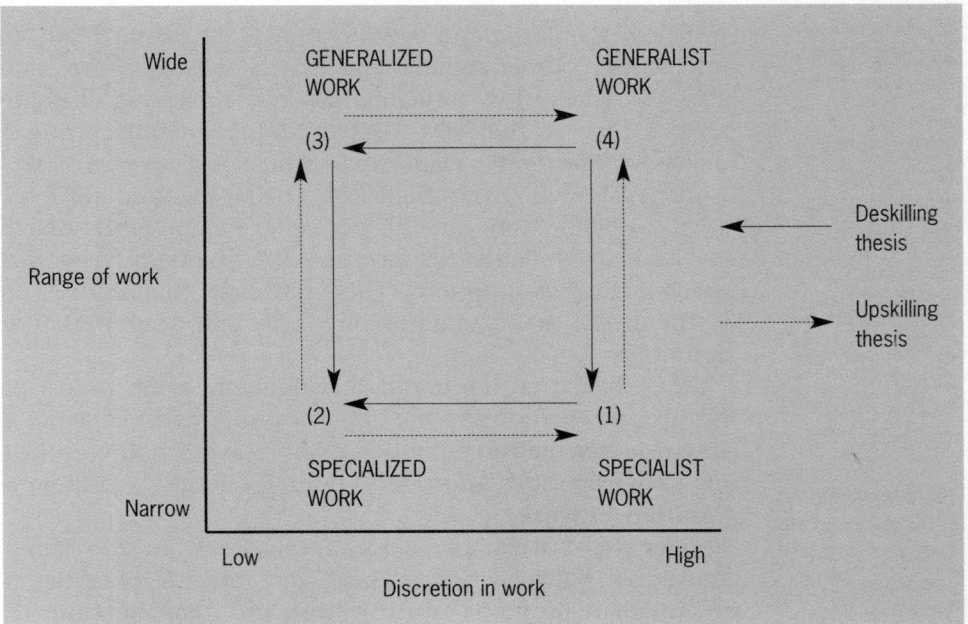

Figure 13.2: Work categorization framework and trends in skill change
From Mike Noon and Paul Blyton, *The Realities of Work*, Palgrave, Basingstoke (second edition), 2002, p. 167. Reproduced with permission of Palgrave Macmillan.

Intrinsic motivation: a form of motivation that stresses valued outcomes or benefits that come from within the individual, such as feelings of satisfaction, competence, self-esteem and accomplishment.

of how they should perform their job. Their work control would be labelled low. At the other end of this dimension would be a person who had wide discretion as to how to perform their work: for example, a potter, a plumber or a doctor. Their control over their work would be high. Noon and Blyton's framework distinguishes four classes or types of job that they label as follows:

1. Specialist work: high discretion over a narrow range of work.

2. Specialized work: a narrow range of prescribed tasks.

3. Generalized work: a wide range of prescribed tasks.

4. Generalist work: high discretion over a wide range of tasks.

Stop and Criticize

Consider an organization with which you are familiar – a school, university, church or current employer. Give one example of *specialist, specialized, generalized* and *generalist* work. What effect did it have on your satisfaction and motivation?

Extrinsic motivation: a form of motivation that stresses valued outcomes or benefits provided by others, such as promotion, pay increases, a bigger office desk, praise and recognition.

The framework can be used both to trace trends in skill changes and to compare different work organization initiatives described in empirical case studies. Noon and Blyton depict the deskilling trend with the solid arrows, from high to low on the range of work dimension, and from high to low on the control over work dimension. Its most extreme position is labelled (1) specialist work. The upskilling trend is shown with dotted arrows in the opposite direction, with its extreme position labelled as (4) generalist work. Instead of looking for any general trends, Noon and Blyton's 'map' allows a single group, workplace, industry or industrial sector to be represented.

Instrumental orientation to work: an attitude that sees work as an instrument to the fulfilment of other goals.

Back to the future?

Introjection: a formerly external regulation or value that has been 'taken in' and is now enforced through internal pressures such as guilt, anxiety or related self-esteem dynamics.

Just how alienating and demotivating is Taylorism? Paul Adler (1999) offers an interesting counter-argument to this established view, claiming that Taylorism actually represents a fundamental emancipatory philosophy of job design. He reports that at the New United Motors Manufacturing Inc. (NUMMI) auto plant in Freemont, California, which uses a classical Taylorist approach, workers show relatively high levels of motivation and job commitment (Adler, 1993a, 1993b). How can this be? Adler's argument is that his research findings reveal two fundamental flaws in the standard view that is based on two psychological assumptions. These are, first, that work is only truly motivating to the extent that it resembles free play and, second, that workers have to have autonomy.

Adler states that the standard critique of Taylorism just presents extrinsic and intrinsic motivation as polar opposites, and holds that since Taylorized work lacks **intrinsic motivation** potential, it only leaves employees the possibility of obtaining **extrinsic motivation**. In so doing, it develops in them an **instrumental orientation to work**.

Identification: the incorporation of the thoughts, feelings and actions of others into one's self-esteem or to reduce the threat from powerful others. Typically, it takes the form of 'I want'.

Adler draws upon the work of Richard Ryan and James Connell (1989) to argue that between the extrinsic and intrinsic polarities, there are two other intermediate positions – **introjection** and **identification**. These are presented in table 13.4.

Table 13.4: Four bases of motivation

Extrinsic	Introjection	Identification	Intrinsic
■ Following rules	■ Self- and other-approval	■ Self-valued goal	■ Enjoyment
■ Avoidance of punishment	■ Avoidance of disapproval	■ Personal importance	■ Fun
■ Because I'll get into trouble if I don't	■ Because I want the teacher to think I'm a good student	■ Because I want to understand the subject	■ Because it's fun
■ Because that's what I'm supposed to do	■ Because I'll feel bad about myself if I don't	■ Because I want to learn new things	■ Because I enjoy it
■ So the teacher won't yell at me	■ Because I'll feel ashamed of myself if I don't	■ To find out if I'm right or wrong	
■ Because that's the rule	■ Because I want other students to think I'm smart	■ Because I think it's important to	
	■ Because it bothers me when I don't	■ Because I wouldn't want to do that (negative behaviour)	
	■ Because I want people to like me		

From Paul S. Adler, 'The emancipatory significance of Taylorism', in M.P.E. Cunha and C.A. Marques (eds), *Readings in Organization Science – Organizational Change in a Changing Context*, Instituto Superior de Psicologia Aplicada, Lisbon, 1999, p. 9.

Adler argues that job design at NUMMI taps into the identification motivation base. This focuses upon the internalization of company values and goals, and the means by which these are absorbed and adopted. Instead of motivating through 'free play', NUMMI employees are motivated through:

■ the desire for excellence, the instinct of craftsmanship and a job well done;

■ their 'psychological maturity', which recognizes the reality of the competitive situation, encouraging them to compete on quality and productivity with other autoworkers around the workplace;

■ respect and trust shown to them by management that elicits reciprocal commitment.

Adler then considers the autonomy issue at the individual and team levels. Critics of Taylorism hold that the choice over work methods and pace of work is crucial for sustaining high levels of motivation and involvement. Adler argues that his research suggests it is not as important as claimed. NUMMI's use of the Japanese form of teamworking offered little in the way of team autonomy. The teams were organized by engineers, managers and workers, and they were tightly coupled with other teams, both upstream and downstream, through just-in-time *kanban* systems, and with teams on other shifts. Yet workers endorsed such interdependence (low autonomy) as an effective way of managing. Adler (1999, p. 12) quotes one worker:

The work teams at NUMMI aren't like the autonomous teams you read about in other plants. Here we're not autonomous, because we're all tied together really tightly. But it's not like we're getting squeezed to work harder, because it's us, the workers, that are making the whole thing work – we're the ones that make the standardized work and the *kaizen* suggestions. We run the plant – and if it's not running right, we stop it.

Adler argues that when workers establish a feeling of organization-wide responsibility for the effectiveness of their work, and they come to perceive their Taylorized jobs as an effective way of accomplishing the necessary interdependent tasks, then low individual and team autonomy can co-exist with high morale.

Thompson and McHugh (2002) argued that companies had been persuaded of the financial advantages of teamwork, less as a way of enhancing employees' quality of working life, but more as a way of facilitating greater flexibility, problem-solving and continuous improvement. Unlike Taylor or Ford, who were wary of the effect of group dynamics, modern management has found that it can be directed towards organizational goals and outcomes. Promoters see teams facilitating cohesion, co-operation and productivity, while critics highlight self-surveillance, peer pressure and socialization of members into the organization's culture. They refer to the work of Barker (1993) and Tompkins and Cheney (1985) who discuss the concept of **concertive control**, which is exerted not by management but by the workers themselves. In this way, external values become internalized and managerial control becomes social control. The team achieves first accommodation, then assimilation, then identification, and finally internalization. The process described by Barker is interesting:

Concertive control: control that is exercised by the workers themselves, who collaborate to develop the means of their own control by negotiating a consensus which shapes their own behaviour according to a set of core values such as those of the corporate vision statement (Barker, 1993).

1. Group members have discussions and develop a consensus over values, based on their company's 'vision statement'.

2. This value consensus is then translated into group rules or norms of behaviour.

3. Guidelines on how members are to behave are specified (to provide a sense of stability and predictability for members).

4. These devised norms, rules and guidelines are easily understood by new group members, who subject themselves to them.

What is most interesting is that, as Barker (1993, p. 433) notes, '[t]he teams were said to be their own masters and their own slaves'. The teams ended up doing management's work for them by dealing with their uncommitted workers by making them 'feel unworthy as a team mate' (p. 436).

Stop and Criticize

Is concertive control a totally new form of control over employees, or does it represent a modification and updating of traditional Taylorist and Fordist ideas?

Recap

1. *Understand how scientific management met the needs of its historical context.*

   - At the start of the twentieth century, European emigration to the United States and internal migration from rural to urban areas produced a large workforce with poor English language skills which lacked work discipline.

   - The same period saw the establishment of large corporations and the development of technology that permitted, for the first time, mass manufacture of products. These factories required a large workforce.

2. *Describe the main objectives and principles of the scientific management approach.*

   - The objectives are efficiency, by increasing the output per worker and reducing deliberate 'underworking'; predictability of job performance – standarizing tasks by dividing them up into small and closely specified sub-tasks; and control by establishing discipline through hierarchical authority and introducing a system whereby all management's policy decisions could be implemented.

   - The principles are: a clear division of tasks and responsibilities between management and workers; the use of scientific methods to determine the best way of doing a job; the scientific selection of employees; the training of the selected worker to perform the job in the way specified; and the surveillance of workers through the use of hierarchies of authority and close supervision.

3. *Critically assess Taylorism.*

   - It has been criticized for its assumptions about human motivation: neglecting the subjective side of work; ignoring the impact of the work group; disregarding the psychological needs and capabilities of workers: and taking too simple an approach to the question of productivity and morale.

4. *Enumerate the contributions of the Gilbreths and Gantt to scientific management.*

   - Frank Gilbreth's contributions were micromotion study, the chronocyclegraph and the 'therbligs' notation system. Lillian Gilbreth contributed fatigue study based on physiological and psychological principles.

   - Laurence Gantt supplied the 'best-known-way-at-present' approach to job design, the task-and-bonus payment scheme and the 'Gantt chart'.

5. *Understand how Fordism developed out of Taylorism.*

   - Ford developed the analysis of jobs, installed single-purpose machine tools to produce standardized parts and established the mechanically-paced assembly line.

   - The twin concepts of system and control underpinned his approach.

6. *Understand the deskilling debate, and the contribution of Braverman and Ritzer.*

   - The 'Braverman thesis' holds that there is a long-term tendency for workers and their jobs to become deskilled through fragmentation, rationalization and mechanization.

   - Some argue for the deskilling thesis, while others reject it claiming that technological developments have upskilled both workers and jobs and created new, high-skill industries.

   - The deskilling debate is often discussed in the context of Ritzer's McDonaldization process, which refers to an approach to work design based on efficiency, calculability, predictability and control.

7. *Provide examples of scientific management in contemporary society.*

   - Apart from fast food restaurants, the process of credit-granting through credit card; semesterization and modularization of university courses; television programmes; food packaging.

Revision

1. Taylorism has been much criticized. Which criticisms do you feel are valid and which are not? Give reasons for your assessment.

2. Have quality and flexibility requirements in modern organizations rendered Fordism redundant?

3. To what extent are performance-based pay, just-in-time (stock) inventory and business process re-engineering just modern-day applications of Frederick Taylor's scientific management?

4. Identify non-food examples of the McDonaldization process. Analyze them in terms of Ritzer's four central dimensions.

5. 'The very uncertainty that inevitably accompanies the human element, in itself often provided by relatively unqualified labour, drives management to *standardize* the encounter as a means of ensuring "quality" or at least consistency' (Warhurst and Thompson, 1998, p. 5). Discuss the application of Taylorism in employee–customer, face-to-face work situations such as supermarket checkouts, hotels and call centres. Does this need for quality and consistency make the application of Taylorism more or less vital?

Springboard

Braverman, H., 1974, *Labour and Monopoly Capital: The Degradation of Work in the Twentieth Century*, Monthly Review Press, New York.

This book initiated the deskilling debate and the labour process school.

Durand, J.-P., Stewart, p. and Castillo, J.J. (eds), 1999, *Teamwork in the Automobile Industry: Radical Change or Passing Fashion*, Macmillan Business, Basingstoke.

Wide-ranging, critical assessments of the application of teamworking in automobile manufacturing in Europe, Japan and the United States.

Kanigel, R., 1997, *The One Best Way: Frederick Winslow Taylor and the Enigma of Efficiency*, Little Brown and Company, London.

A biography of Frederick Taylor, providing fascinating detail which links his personal and professional lives.

Millman, R., 1997, *Farewell to the Factory: Autoworkers in the Late Twentieth Century*, University of California Press, Berkeley, CA.

A critical assessment of automobile production plants which use the 'lean production' approach.

Noon, M. and Blyton, P., 2002, *The Realities of Work*, Palgrave, Basingstoke, Chapter 6.

Introduces the Braverman debate for those wishing to join in.

Parker, M. and Slaughter, J., 1988, *Choosing Sides: Unions and the Team Concept*, South End Press, Boston, MA.

Critiques the Taylorist principles and practices within 'lean production' manufacturing environments in the (NUMMI) Inc. plant in Freemont, California.

Ritzer, G., 1993, *The McDonaldization of Society: An Investigation into the Changing Character of Contemporary Social Life*, Pine Forge Press, Thousand Oaks, CA.

Ritzer, G., 1995, *Expressing America: A Critique of the Global Credit Card Society*, Pine Forge Press, Thousand Oaks, CA.

Ritzer, G. (ed.), 1998, *The McDonaldization Thesis*, Sage Publications, London.

Three books which build on the Braverman deskilling thesis and bring the debate up to the present day.

Schlosser, E., 2002, *Fast Food Nation*, Penguin, Harmondsworth.

Considers the impact of assembly-line food manufacture on politics, the environment and consumers.

Thompson, P. and McHugh, D., 2002, *Work Organizations: A Critical Introduction*, Palgrave, London (third edition).

A critical introduction to work organization.

Thompson, P. and Warhurst, C. (eds), 1998, *Workplaces of the Future*, Macmillan Business, Basingstoke.

A set of chapters that challenge the current accepted rhetoric about 'new' work organization by using empirical research to demonstrate just how much these are based on traditional, Taylorist principles.

Home viewing

Modern Times (1936, directed by Charlie Chaplin) is a satire of the automated age. It stars Chaplin himself and Paulette Goddard. In the opening sequence, Chaplin is a comic victim of the assembly line in a huge manufacturing plant in the 1930s. Watch the first fifteen minutes of the film. Identify as many different aspects of Taylorism and Fordism as you can.

OB in literature

Aldous Huxley, *Brave New World*, Chatto and Windus, London, 1932 (Penguin, Harmondsworth, 1955).

Where in the plot are the techniques of Frederick Taylor and Henry Ford effectively deployed in the society which Huxley describes? This story also illustrates Pavlovian conditioning in action. Which aspects of Huxley's fictional account are found in some form in contemporary society?

Jacqueline Briskin, *The Onyx*, Grafton Books, London, 1983.

A story of the creation of the first mass-produced motor car in the world. It mixes fact with fiction, and business with romance.

Chapter exercises

1: Assembly line simulation

Objectives
1. To introduce you to the concept of assembly-line production.

2. To highlight some of the key issues and debates about this form of work organization.

Briefing
1. While remaining in your lecture theatre seats, identify yourself as part of a group of six, counting off from the aisles. Your groups will consist of six people in a row, sitting next to each other. Each lecture theatre row will have a number of such sixes. However, a group may have one or more of its members in the row immediately in front of or behind them.

2. Nominating the person nearest the aisle as A, assign letters B, C, D, E and F in order to the other members of your group who are sitting next to one another.

3. Your instructor will brief all the groups in the lecture theatre to perform the same assembly-line task. He or she will 'train' you, explaining what each group member has to do.

4. After your training, you will have a practice production run, followed by one or more real production runs.

5. After you have completed the simulation, consider the following questions.
   - What was the physical arrangement of group members? Did this help or hinder your task?
   - In what direction did the work 'flow'? Did it affect left- or right-handed members?
   - How many seconds did it take to complete your part of the task (cycle time)?
   - How would you feel if you had to do this for eight hours every day?

2: McDonaldization

Objectives
1. To introduce you to the concept of McDonaldization.

2. To encourage you to recognize non-food examples of the McDonaldization process.

3. To allow you critically to evaluate the costs and benefits of McDonaldization.

Introduction
In his book, *The McDonaldization of Society* (1993), George Ritzer argues that the process of *McDonaldization* is affecting many areas of our social and organizational lives, and that this trend is undesirable (see also Ritzer, 1998; and Smart, 1999).

Ritzer has no particular complaint against McDonald's hamburger restaurants; he merely uses this fast food chain as an illustration of the wider process which is the real focus of his attention. The argument is that the process of McDonaldization is spreading and that, while it yields a number of benefits, the costs and risks are, in Ritzer's view, considerable. This exercise is based on what Ritzer identifies as the four central dimensions of McDonaldization. You are then invited to consider for yourself the benefits of this trend, and the associated costs and risks. Finally, using some of Ritzer's ideas as a basis, we will consider whether and how such an organizational trend can be subverted by individual action.

Everybody knows McDonald's, the fast food chain which has outlets in most towns and cities of any size on the planet. The McDonald's large yellow 'M' logo (Golden Arches) is one of the most widely recognized company symbols in the world (along with Holiday Inn and Coca-Cola). Ritzer argues that the McDonald's approach has four central dimensions:

1. *Efficiency*, with respect to the speed with which you are transformed from being hungry to being fed, including the drive-through option.

2. *Calculability*, with respect to high-value meals for discounted prices – quarter pounders, Big Macs, large fries, all ordered, delivered and consumed with a minimum waste of time.

3. *Predictability*, as the Big Mac in New York is the same as the Big Mac in Helsinki which is the same as the Big Mac in Singapore – no surprises, but nothing special either.

4. *Control*, as the staff who work in McDonald's are trained to perform a limited range of tasks in a precisely detailed way, and customers are similarly disciplined with queues, limited menu options and the clear expectation that they will eat and then leave.

In addition to the simplified jobs which McDonald's employees perform, their work is also limited by the sophisticated technology of fast food preparation. Their job specifications give them little or no discretion in how they prepare and deliver food to customers. Hamburger grilling instructions are precise and detailed, covering the exact positioning of burgers on the grill, cooking times and the sequence in which burgers are to be turned. Drinks dispensers, french-fry machines and programmed cash registers are all used to limit the time required to carry out tasks, and leave little or no room for discretion, creativity or innovation on the part of the employee. Discretion and creativity would, of course, subvert the aims of efficiency, calculability, predictability and control.

Analysis questions

1. What are the benefits of this approach – to the company, to the employee, to the customer, to society as a whole?

2. What are the disadvantages of this approach?

3. Identify examples of McDonaldization from sectors other than fast foods – work, travel, family, medical care and commerce.

4. To what extent is higher education susceptible to McDonaldization? Is your university currently being McDonaldized? Explain how.

Chapter 14 Elements of structure

Key concepts

organization structure	functional relationship
job definition	formal organization
job description	informal organization
organization chart	departmentalization
hierarchy	matrix structure
span of control	role
authority	role set
responsibility	self-fulfilling prophecy
accountability	role conflict
line employees	centralization
chain (or line) of command	decentralization
staff employees	

Learning outcomes

Once you have read this chapter, you should be able to define those key concepts in your own words, and you should be able to:

1. Explain how organization structure affects human behaviour in organizations.
2. List the main elements of organization structure.
3. Relate the concept of span of control to the shape of the organization hierarchy.
4. Identify line and staff relationships on an organization chart.
5. Describe six different criteria on which jobs might be departmentalized.
6. Distinguish between the formal and the informal organization of a company.
7. Distinguish Mintzberg's five organizational parts, five types of organization structure and ten managerial roles.

Why study elements of structure?

Organizational social scientists are interested in studying three related questions. *What* are organizations trying to do? *How* are they trying to do it? *Why* are they trying to do it that way? Roy Payne (1996) explains that the 'what' question begins by classifying organizations according to their goals or purposes, and leads to a consideration of why these goals are chosen and how. This is the area of corporate strategy or strategic management. The question of why organizations choose to pursue some goals in certain ways leads to a consideration of organization culture. The consideration of how organizations attempt to achieve their goals is the domain of organization structure. As Payne points out, strategy, structure and culture are closely related, although rarely considered together.

Other social scientists, particularly sociologists, are interested in organization structure for another reason. They claim that people's attitudes and behaviour are shaped as much by the structure of the company within which they work as by the personalities that they possess. The constraints and demands of the job, imposed through the roles that they play, can dictate their behaviour and even change their personalities. For this reason, it is impossible to explain the behaviour of people in organizations solely in terms of individual or group characteristics. Alan Fox argued that, in seeking to make such explanations, the structural determinants of behaviour should be considered (Fox, 1966). He was critical of those who insisted on explaining human behaviour in organizations exclusively in terms of personalities, personal relationships and leadership. Such explanations were highly appealing to common sense. This was partly because such variables were clearly visible, while the effects of structure were often hidden.

A consideration of organization structure is likely to be encountered by students in two ways. First, it will be considered on a corporate strategy course, as a vehicle for achieving organizational goals (Johnson and Scholes, 2002). Second, it will be considered on an organization behaviour course, in which the logical and rational elements of organizations are emphasized, while people's preferences or feelings are underplayed. The structural approach stands in contrast to the psychologistic approach which holds that it is the internal (individual) factors that are the main determinants of human behaviour in organizations.

Stop and Criticize	Consider the behaviour of the instructor teaching this course. Identify aspects of their behaviour which you like and do not like. Decide if these positive and negative behaviours are influenced by that person's personality or by the organization structure within which they work.

Organization structuring

Organization structure: the formal system of task and reporting relationships that controls, co-ordinates and motivates employees so that they work together to achieve organizational goals.

At the start of the book, organizations were defined as social arrangements for achieving controlled performance in pursuit of collective gaols. One aspect of this 'arrangement' is the creation of a structure. The purpose of **organization structure** is, first, to divide up organizational activities and allocate them to sub-units and, second, to co-ordinate and control these activities so that they achieve the aims of the organization.

A popular way of depicting the structure of any large organization is that of a pyramid or triangle, as in figure 14.1. This is only one of many possible shapes for a structure (several others will be presented later in the chapter). For the time being, we can note that the pyramid form shows that an organization has both a vertical and a horizontal dimension. Its broad base indicates that the vast majority of employees are located at the bottom, and are responsible for manufacturing the product or providing the service (for example, making refrigerators, selling insurance). Proponents of the formal system claim that the reporting relationships co-ordinate, motivate and control employees, so that they work together to achieve organizational goals. Child (1984, p. 8) identified the five main questions that any organization structure designer needs to answer:

1. *Specialization*: Should jobs be broken down into narrow areas of work and responsibility, so as to secure the benefits of specialization? Or should the degree of specialization be kept to a minimum in order to simplify communication and to offer members of the organization greater scope and responsibility in their work?

2. *Hierarchy*: Should the overall structure of an organization be 'tall' rather than 'flat' in terms of its levels of management and spans of control? What are the implications for communication, motivation and overhead costs of moving towards one of these alternatives rather than the other?

3. *Grouping*: Should jobs and departments be grouped together in a 'functional' way according to the specialist expertise and interests which they share? Or should they be grouped according to the different services and products which are being offered, or the different geographical areas being served?

4. *Integration*: Is it appropriate to aim for an intensive form of integration between the different segments of an organization or not? What kind of integrative mechanisms are there to choose from?

5. *Control*: How should management maintain control over work done? Should it centralize or delegate decisions, and all or only some of the decisions? Should a policy of extensive formalization be adopted in which standing orders and written records and rules exist for control purposes? Should work be subject to close supervision?

The answers to these questions will have a major impact on the nature of the jobs of all employees working within that structure. For example, a highly centralized structure with little delegation means that senior managers will spend more of their time making decisions, while junior staff may feel power-less and demotivated. Choices about organization structure and the content of individual employees' jobs (both managers and non-managers) are intimately related.

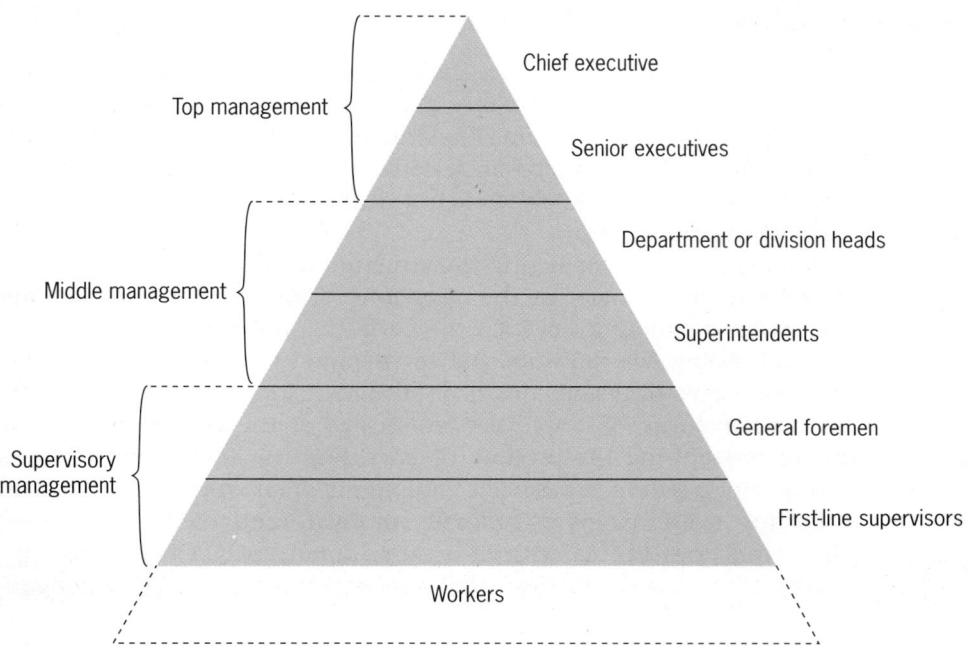

Figure 14.1: Organization structure

In figure 14.1, each of the six successive levels above the workers represents a layer of management. On the left-hand side of the diagram, the managerial ranks are divided into three groupings: supervisory or first-line management; middle management; and senior or top management. The diagram's right-hand side lists the commonly used job titles of managers who are members of each grouping. The layers also represent differences in status. While most people will recognize an organization structure, they are less clear about its purpose. Robert Duncan (1979, p. 59) said that:

> Organization structure is more than boxes on a chart; it is a pattern of interactions and co-ordination that links the technology, tasks and human components of the organization to ensure that the organization accomplishes its purpose.

For him, the purpose of a structure was two-fold. First, it facilitated the flow of information within the company in order to reduce the uncertainty in decision-making which was caused by information deficiency. Second, a structure achieved effective co-ordination–integration of the diverse activities occurring within the firm, integrating the actions of individuals, groups and departments, especially those which were interdependent, so that all became co-ordinated. The structure of an organization signals the behaviour expected of its members (table 14.1).

Table 14.1: Elements of structure

Concerned with	Involves	Exemplified in
how the work of the organization is divided and assigned to individuals, groups and departments	■ allocating tasks and responsibilities to individuals (e.g. how much choice they have about how they work)	■ organization chart ■ job descriptions ■ establishing boards, committees and working parties
how the required co-ordination is achieved	■ specifying and defining jobs ■ designing the formal reporting relationships ■ deciding on the number of levels in the hierarchy ■ deciding on the span of control of each supervisor and manager	■ rules and policies ■ hierarchy ■ goal clarification ■ temporary task forces ■ permanent project teams ■ liaison roles ■ integrator roles

Harold Leavitt has suggested that organizations can be viewed as complex systems which consist of four mutually interacting independent classes of variables: organizational objectives company structure, technology used and people employed. All of these are affected by the firm's environment such as the economic, political or social situation. The differences in organization structure can be partly accounted for by the interactions of these elements (see figure 14.2).

Types of job

An important series of decisions on organization design relate to what types of job should be created. How narrow and specialized should these be? How should the work be divided and what should be the appropriate content of each person's job? The detailed answer will of course depend on the type of job considered. Is it the job of a nurse, engineer, car assembly worker, teacher or politician that is being designed?

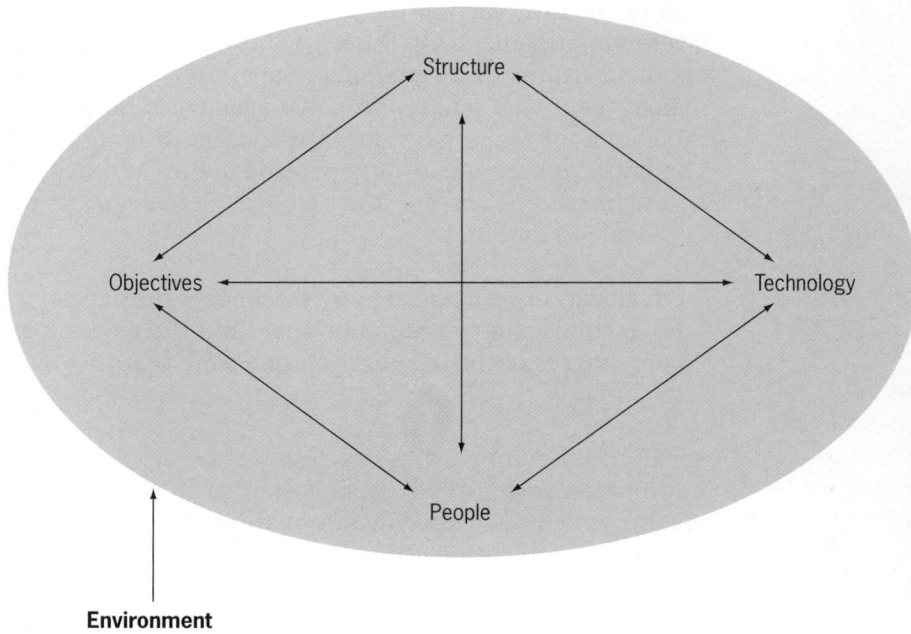

Figure 14.2: Leavitt diamond

Specialization is a feature of knowledge, clerical and manual jobs. After their general medical training, some doctors become paediatricians, while on the assembly line some workers fit car tyres while others fix on the doors. The choice concerning the extent and type of specialization depends on criteria used by the organization designer. These will be affected by their values, beliefs and preferences. It may be a case of trading off efficiency of production against job

HANDS ON CHIEF EXECUTIVE

To bring bags of presence and enormous energy to a unique global distribution operation

A package with bells on + sleigh **Far North**

This intensely private operation, which has a brand that is recognised throughout the world, has carved a unique position in a highly seasonal business. Its President and owner, who has always maintained a close personal involvement in every aspect of the operation, has decided that it's time to hand over the reins. The opportunities and challenges presented by technological change, and the potential threat of imitators, are issues which call for fresh ideas, new perspectives and, candidly, younger eyes. Ideal candidates, probably entering their second century and quite possibly retired recruitment consultants, will have the maturity which goes with white hair, the vision to penetrate the darkest night, a lightness of touch, and the leadership to direct a diminutive yet dedicated team. Skills in more than one language and sensitivity to a wide range of cultures will be essential, and experience of working with quadrupeds, especially reindeer, will help. Above all, we will be looking for the humour to overcome the intense seasonal pressures and the ability to appear to be in several places simultaneously. Please post full career details, quoting reference WE2512, up the nearest chimney, and share the joy, mystery, and magic of this special time with those you value most—with best wishes to our readers, candidates and clients, Ward Executive Limited, 4–6 George Street, Richmond-upon-Thames, Surrey TW9 1JY.

WARD EXECUTIVE
LIMITED
Executive Search & Selection

From *Daily Telegraph*, Appointments, 31 December 1998. Reprinted by permission of Ward Executive Ltd.

satisfaction. A value position might be to seek to maximize both elements. Too rigid a specialization can lead to demarcation disputes. Once the elements of the job have been decided, it is possible to advertise the post.

How well defined ought a job to be? There is a school of management thought which argues that newly appointed staff should know exactly what their duties are in detail. They suggest that this high degree of **job definition** helps to motivate employees by letting them know exactly what is expected of them. Such detail can also assist in the appraising of their past performance.

Others commentators believe that, far from being motivating, a high level of job definition acts to control people's behaviour and sets minimum performance standards. What is needed, they argue, is for the employees to create their own jobs. In practice, a detailed job definition is provided to those doing low-level manual and clerical jobs, while at more senior levels there is a greater degree of own job-making. The physical manifestation of the choice about how much to define the job is the piece of paper on which is written the **job description**. Individuals who request more information about a job advertised in the newspaper are usually sent a job description and an application form. A job description will usually contain the following information:

- job title and the department in which it is located;

- job holder's position in the hierarchy;

- to whom the job holder is responsible;

- the objectives of the job;

- duties required of the job holder (regular, periodical and optional);

- liaison with other workers, staff, supervisors and managers;

- authority to carry out the task – the degree of freedom permitted to exercise one's own judgement in carrying out the job.

The specialization of work activities and the consequent division of labour are features of all large, complex organizations. Once tasks have been broken down (or 'differentiated') into sub-tasks, these are allocated to individuals in the form of jobs. Persons carrying out the jobs occupy positions on the organization's hierarchy. Particular levels of responsibility and authority are allocated to these positions. The division of labour and the relationship of one position to another is reflected in the organization chart, which can act as a guide to explain how the work of different people in the organization is co-ordinated and integrated.

Job definition: the task requirements of each job in the organization; it is the first decision in the process of organizing.

Job description (or post profile): a summary statement of what an individual should do on the job.

The name game

In the past, an employee's post or job title used to indicate neatly their role, level and career progression. There was a period in some Anglo-American cultures when trendy titles were in vogue, such as 'director of emerging thought', 'goddess of invention' or 'manager of mischief'. These were particularly popular among dot.com companies as a means of both countering the pecking order of traditional hierarchical structures and encouraging a new organization culture. Some of these have survived with the traditional title on one side ('retail operations director') and the funkier one on the reverse ('chief cheerleader').

In status-conscious Latin American countries, however, job titles carry their own nuances, implicitly signalling social privileges. A person called 'senior executive' will expect to be provided with a club membership and a chauffeur – it goes automatically with the job (title). Qualified professionals are

➤

also addressed by their titles both inside the workplace and outside in the community. This extends beyond medical doctors (Dr Suarez) and academics (Professor Suarez) to include qualified lawyers, referred to as 'Licenciado' Suarez (not Señor Suarez), and to engineers, 'Ingeniero' Suarez.

In both Latin America and Asia, the job title reflects an individual's location in the social hierarchy. In Japanese organizations, the more senior an employee, usually indicated by age, the higher the job title and the more respect they receive. The higher in the pecking order someone is, the lower the *kurtow* (bow) he would expect to get from subordinates. In Asia, job title is possibly more important than name. On Japanese business cards, job title often appears above the name. Far East Asian cultures are impressed by job titles and letters after a name. In Japan, Singapore and Hong Kong, managers may turn down a position if they feel that the job title insults them.

In culture where 'face' is important, employees will accept a better job title in place of a pay rise. It is easier to flaunt on a business card. This has, however, led to the problem of 'uptitling' – the creation of longer and more impressive-sounding job titles in order to retain and motivate staff when budgets are stretched. Many of these only served to obfuscate what jobs were performed: Senior Vice-president Global Procurement (office manager); Yield Improvement Manager (stock controller); and IT Strategic Sourcing Analyst (computer programmer).

Based on Pepi Sappel, 'The name game', *Personnel Today*, 9 April 2002, pp. 28–9.

WINDWORTH UNIVERSITY BUSINESS SCHOOL
JOB DESCRIPTION

Post title School Clerk

Position in the university Reporting to School Registrar

Main purpose of the post To provide an efficient and effective clerical/secretarial support for the wide-ranging activities of the Business School office.

Main duties

- ■ To provide clerical support to the various committees and sub-committees, including:
  - – Preparation and circulation of agendas and minutes
  - – Dealing with correspondence and related work falling within the scope of the School Office
  - – Booking of accommodation and hospitality arrangements for committees and meetings
- ■ To provide clerical support to the wide range of activities of the School Office, including:
  - – Quality Assurance processes and procedures
  - – Research
  - – Marketing
  - – Programmes
  - – Finance
- ■ Maintenance of management information systems
- ■ Maintenance of filing systems and records, both electronic and manual
- ■ To carry out such duties as may be assigned from time to time by the Registrar or Dean

Profile of expected competencies

- Excellent communication skills both written and oral. Ability to liaise with colleagues at all levels within the university and with external contacts

- Excellent organizational skills, including:
  - ability to work in a team and independently without supervision
  - ability to carry out tasks efficiently and effectively
  - motivated and enthusiastic team player

- Excellent IT skills, must be fully conversant with Microsoft Office, including spreadsheets, databases and Microsoft mail

- HNC qualification is desirable

- Knowledge of university administration desirable, but not essential as training will be given

As a term of employment, staff may be required to undertake such other duties and/or hours of work at any Windworth University establishment as may be required to meet the needs and exigencies of the university.

The Job Description by Bertie Ramsbottom

I trod, where fools alone may tread,
Who speak what's better left unsaid,
The day I asked my boss his view
On what I was supposed to do;
For, after two years in the task,
I thought it only right to ask,
In case I'd got it badly wrong,
Ad-hoc'ing as I went along.

He raised his desultory eyes,
And made no effort to disguise
That, what had caused my sudden whim,
Had equally occurred to him;
And thus did we embark upon
Our classic corporate contretemps,
To separate the fact from fiction,
Bedevilling my job description.

For first he asked me to construe
A list of things I really do;
While he – he promised – would prepare
A note of what he thought they were;
And, with the two, we'd take as well
The expert view from Personnel,
And thus eliminate the doubt
On what my job was all about.

But when the boss and I conflated
The tasks we'd separately stated,
The evidence became abundant
That one us must be redundant;
For what I stated I was doing
He claimed himself to be pursuing,
While my role, on his definition,
Was way outside my recognition.

He called in Personnel to give
A somewhat more definitive
Reply, but they, by way of answer,
Produced some vague extravaganza,
Depicting in a web of charts,
Descriptive and prescriptive parts,
Of tasks, the boss and I agree,
Can't possibly refer to me.

So, hanging limply as I am,
In limbo on the diagram,
Suspended by a dotted line
From functions that I thought were mine,
I feel it's maybe for the best
I made my innocent request;
I hopefully await their view
On which job of the three I do!

From Ralph Windle, *The Poetry of Business Life: An Anthology*, Berrett-Koehler, San Francisco, 1994, pp. 80–2.

Organization chart: a pictorial record which shows the formal relations which the company intends should prevail within it.

Hierarchy: the number of levels of authority to be found in an organization.

Let us consider the **organization charts** in figures 14.3a and 14.3b, since an examination of them can help to clarify some of the basic aspects of an organization's structure that are introduced in this chapter. These include chain of command; formal communication channels; division of labour; departmentalization; span of control; and levels of hierarchy. **Hierarchy** refers to the number of levels of authority to be found in an organization. In a company that has a flat organization structure, such as that shown in Figure 14.3a, only one level of hierarchy separates the managing director at the top from the employees at the bottom. In contrast, the organization structure depicted in Figure 14.3b has four levels in between the top and the employees at the bottom.

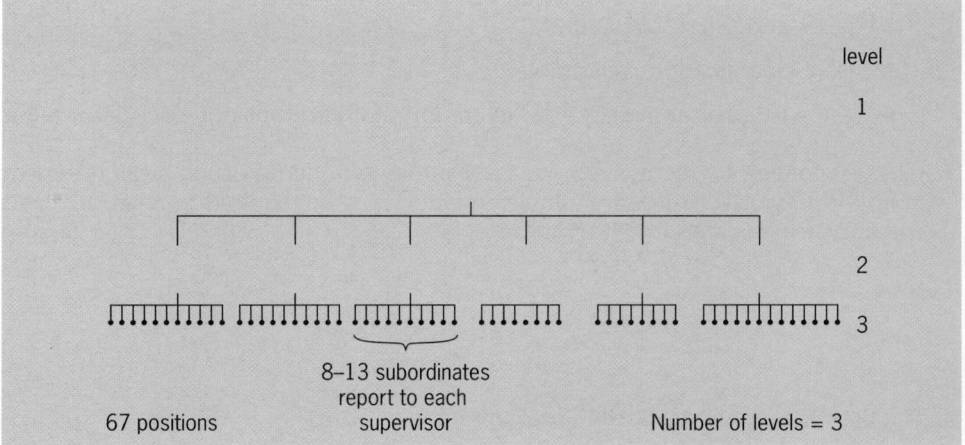

Figure 14.3a: Flat organization structure

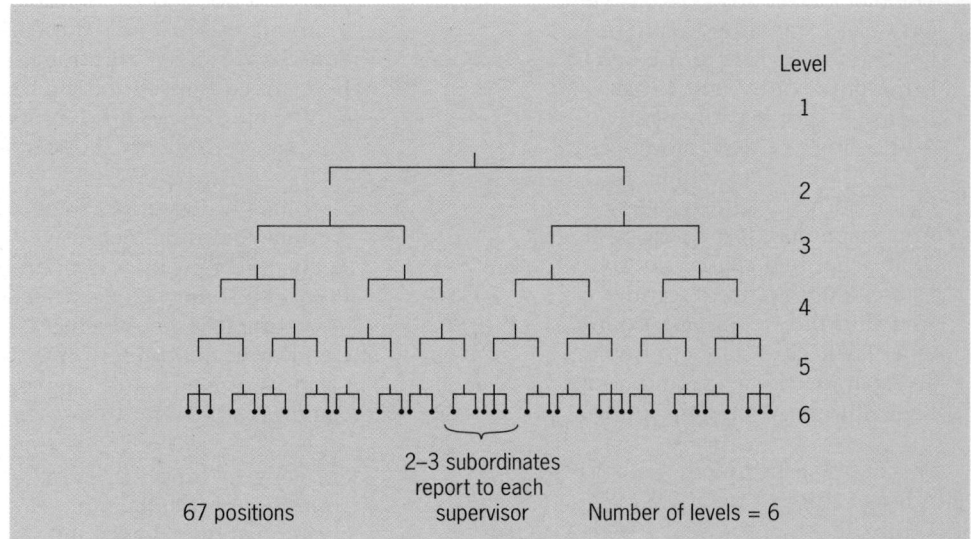

Figure 14.3b: Tall organization structure

It is useful to distinguish between organizations which have many levels in their hierarchy, such as the armed forces, the police and the civil service (referred to as having a 'tall' hierarchy), and organizations which manage to operate with relatively few levels of hierarchy, such as small businesses and universities (referred to as possessing a 'flat' hierarchy). The Catholic Church, which has 800 million members and has been in existence for over fifteen hundred years, operates with five hierarchical layers – parish priest, bishop, archbishop, cardinal and Pope.

The five organization charts below all show the same eleven positions (numbered 1, 21, 22, 23, etc.) in the same relationships to one another. They only differ in the way that they visually depict those relationships.

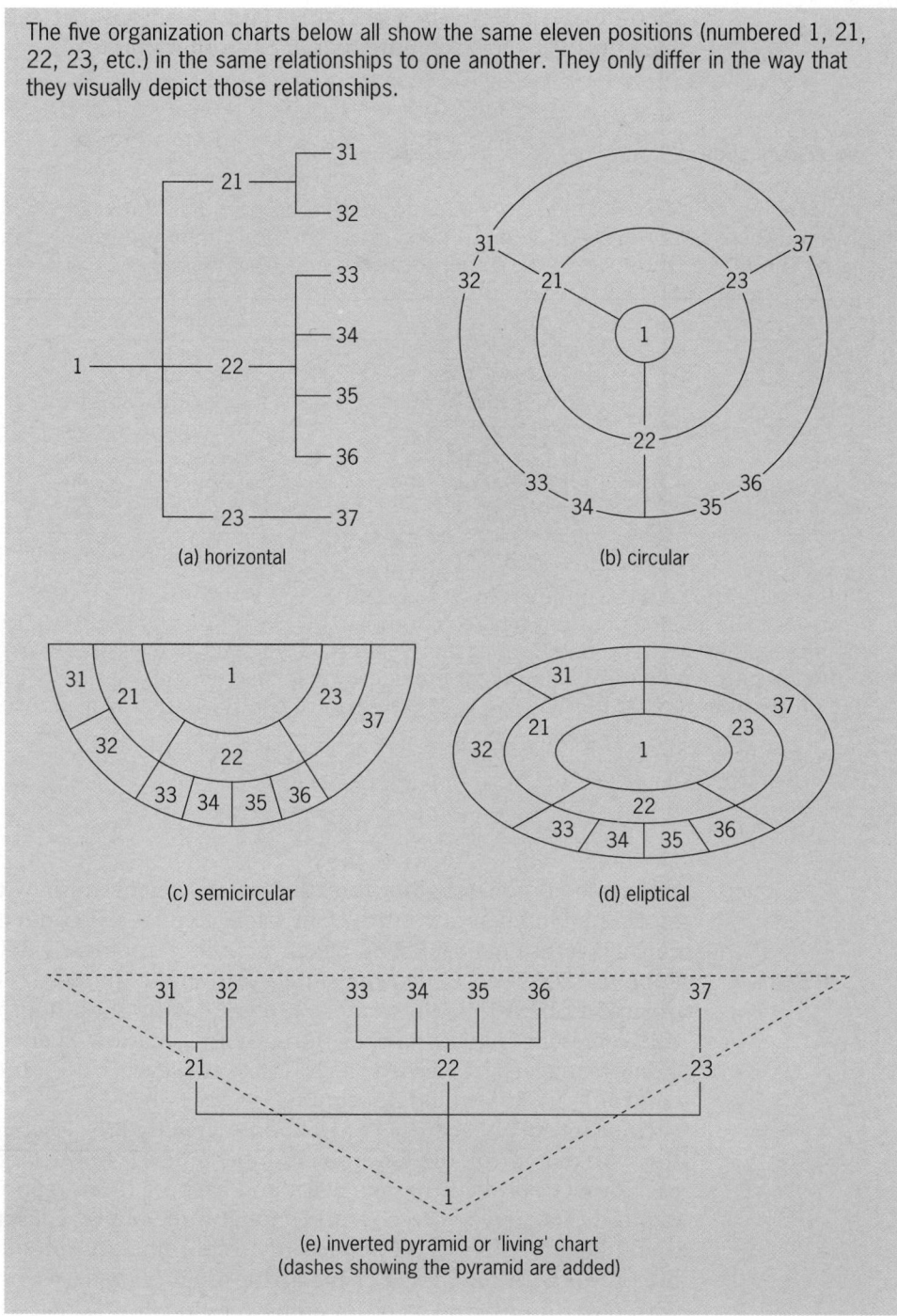

Figure 14.4: Variations in organization charting

Span of control refers to the number of subordinates who report to a single supervisor or manager and for whose work that person is responsible. Comparing the two organization charts in figure 14.3, it can be seen that in the one with a flat hierarchy there are many employees reporting to each supervisor. Hence, that person has a broad span of control. In a tall organization structure, fewer employees report to each manager and hence the span of control of each of the managers is narrow. The larger the number of subordinates reporting to one manager, the more difficult it is for them to supervise and co-ordinate the subordinates effectively. General Sir Iain Hamilton once said that 'No one brain can effectively control more than 6 or 7 other brains.'

The army's span of control

The principle is to have a chain of command, so that each soldier knows to whom they are responsible and there can be units of different managerial sizes for different purposes. For example, according to Xenophon counting on the fingers of two hands, the divisions of Cyrus's army were:

	Form	Under	
5 men	1 squad	corporal	5
2 squads	1 sergeant's squad	sergeant	10
5 sergeant's squads	1 platoon	lieutenant	50
2 platoons	1 company	captain	100
10 companies	1 regiment	colonel	1,000
10 regiments	1 brigade	general	10,000

With modifications in the numbers in different units, this is the principle on which armies have been organized. The general does not have to control 10,000 men directly; he controls the ten regimental colonels, and so on. In modern armies this would be considered an excessive span of control and two or three armies would form an army group, but the principle remains. Split the task up into manageable proportions and do not have an excessive span of control so that real control is lost.

From Frank R. Jervis, *Bosses in British Business*, Routledge and Kegan Paul, London, 1974, p. 87. Reprinted by permission of Thomson Publishing Services.

Harold Koontz (1966) wrote that if an organization with 4,000 employees broadened its span of control from 4-to-1 to 8-to-1, it could eliminate two hierarchical layers of management, which translates into nearly 800 managers. Stephen Robbins (2003) explained the simple arithmetic involved. Figure 14.5 shows an organization with 4,096 workers at level 7 – the shop floor. All the levels above this represent managerial positions. With a narrow span of control of 4-to-1, 1,365 managers are needed (levels 1–6). However, with a broader 8-to-1 span of control, only 585 would be required (levels 1–4).

The concepts of span of control and hierarchy are closely related. The broader the span of control, the fewer the number of levels in the hierarchy. At each level, the contact between the managers and each of those reporting to them will be reduced. A supervisor responsible for eight operatives will have less contact with each operative than if they were only responsible for only four. This broad span of control with few levels of hierarchy produces a flatter organization structure with fewer promotion steps for employees to climb. However, it is likely that the communication between the levels will be improved as there are fewer of them for any message to pass through.

With a narrow span of control, of one supervisor to four workers, the daily contact between the boss and the staff will be closer. This narrower span creates vertical differentiation and a taller hierarchy. Although it provides more steps in a career ladder for employees to rise through, communication tends to deteriorate as the message has to go through an ever-increasing number of layers both upwards and downwards. Because resources are always limited, they restrict the decision-making process.

Although flat hierarchies imply a broader span of control and fewer promotion opportunities, they also force managers to delegate their work effectively if they

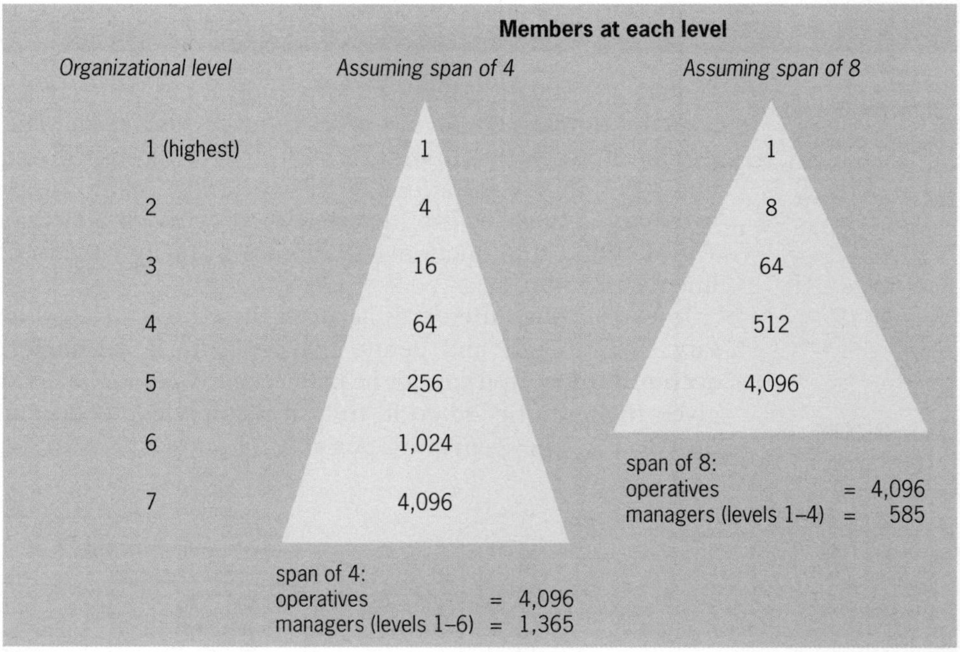

| | Members at each level | |
Organizational level	Assuming span of 4	Assuming span of 8
1 (highest)	1	1
2	4	8
3	16	64
4	64	512
5	256	4,096
6	1,024	
7	4,096	

span of 8:
operatives = 4,096
managers (levels 1–4) = 585

span of 4:
operatives = 4,096
managers (levels 1–6) = 1,365

Figure 14.5: Contrasting spans of control
From *Organizational Theory 3/E* by Robbins, © 1990. Reprinted by permission of Prentice-Hall, Inc., Upper Saddle River, NJ.

are not to be faced with an intolerable workload. Evidence suggests that individuals with high self-actualization needs prefer flat hierarchies, while those who emphasize security needs tend to gravitate towards organizations with tall hierarchies. Hierarchy is a co-ordinating and integrating device intended to bring together the activities of individuals, groups and departments which were previously separated by the division of labour and function.

To recap, an organization structure performs three functions. First, it designates the formal reporting relationships, specifying both managers' spans of control and the number of hierarchical levels. Second, it groups together individuals into departments and departments into the whole company. Finally, it specifies systems within the firm, to ensure that the communication, co-ordination and integration between different departments is effective.

Structure at Amazon.com

Our lives were structured around the 'quad', a term of unknown origin that signified a manageable clump, the size of a squad or platoon. CS [customer service] management broke us up into these groups to manage workflow and make certain that everyone had someone with an eye on them, but mostly it just helped create job positions above email gerbil to which people could aspire. Each quad had a 'quad leader' and the quad leader had two lieutenants known as 'leads' who were there to provide guidance and to be leaders-in-training with ill-defined job descriptions. In addition, quads had six Tier 1s (greenhorns) and six Tier 2s (veterans). It was much like a combat team, *sans* guns, combat and machismo. The weirdest thing about the entire structure was how totally unnecessary it was. We never spoke to anyone on our team with regard to our work. You were surrounded by co-workers, but you never needed to have a meeting or 'interface' with anybody. The only people you spoke with were four to six hundred customers a shift, on the phone and via email. Every couple of days you might have a question, but you just asked whoever was next to you, and they'd tell you what to do. ... We named our quads after pop-culture detritus: Graceland, Route 66, Area 51, *Barberella* – the list was endless. I lived in Dagobah, Yoda's camp.

From Mike Daisey, *21 Dog Years: Doing Time @ amazon.com*, Fourth Estate, London, 2002, p. 21.

Line, staff and functional relationships

Authority: the right to guide or direct the actions of others and extract from them responses that are appropriate to the attainment of an organization's goals.

Responsibility: an obligation placed on a person who occupies a certain position in the organization structure to perform a task, function or assignment.

Accountability: the obligation of a subordinate to report back on their discharge of the responsibilities which they have undertaken.

Within any organization structure, individuals will have different relationships with one another. These can be *line*, *staff* and *functional*. The line relationship is a feature of every organization, irrespective of its size or simplicity. The staff and line types are modifications of this basic line relationship which have become necessary because of the increased complexity of an organization's operations. The staff and the functional relationship usually exist in combination with the line relationship.

To explain the differences between these types of relationship, it is first necessary to introduce and define the concepts of **authority**, **responsibility** and **accountability**. You cannot be held accountable for an action unless you are first given the authority to do it. In a situation where your manager delegates authority to you, they remain responsible for your actions to senior management.

'Actually madam, I don't know how you managed it, but you are talking to someone in authority'

Source: © Telegraph Group Limited 2000

Authority is vested in organizational positions, not in the individuals who occupy them. Military personnel salute the rank, not the person holding it. Authority is accepted by subordinates who comply because they believe the position holder has a legitimate right to exercise the authority. Authority flows down the vertical hierarchy of the organization, existing along the formal chain of command.

The **line relationships** in an organization are depicted vertically, and connect the positions at each level with those above and below it. It is this set of manager–subordinate relationships that are collectively referred to as the organization's chain of command. Using the analogy of a river, the line relationships are the designated channels through which authority flows from its source at the top of the organizational pyramid, through the middle management ranks, down via the supervisors, to employees at the desk or on the factory floor. Thus the most junior employee has some linkage to the most senior manager. All non-managerial employees have some authority within their jobs, which may be based on 'custom and practice' or formally defined in their job descriptions.

Line employees: those workers who are directly responsible for manufacturing goods or providing a service.

Source: Cartoon by Austin. Copyright Pressdram Limited 2002. Reproduced by permission.

Every organization possesses line relationships if it has formally appointed leaders who have subordinates who report to them. All individuals in an organization report to a 'manager' from whom they receive instructions, help and approval. Managers have the authority to direct the activities of those in positions below them on the same line. Thus in the organization chart shown in figure 14.6, the Operations Manager (Completions) has the authority to direct the activities of

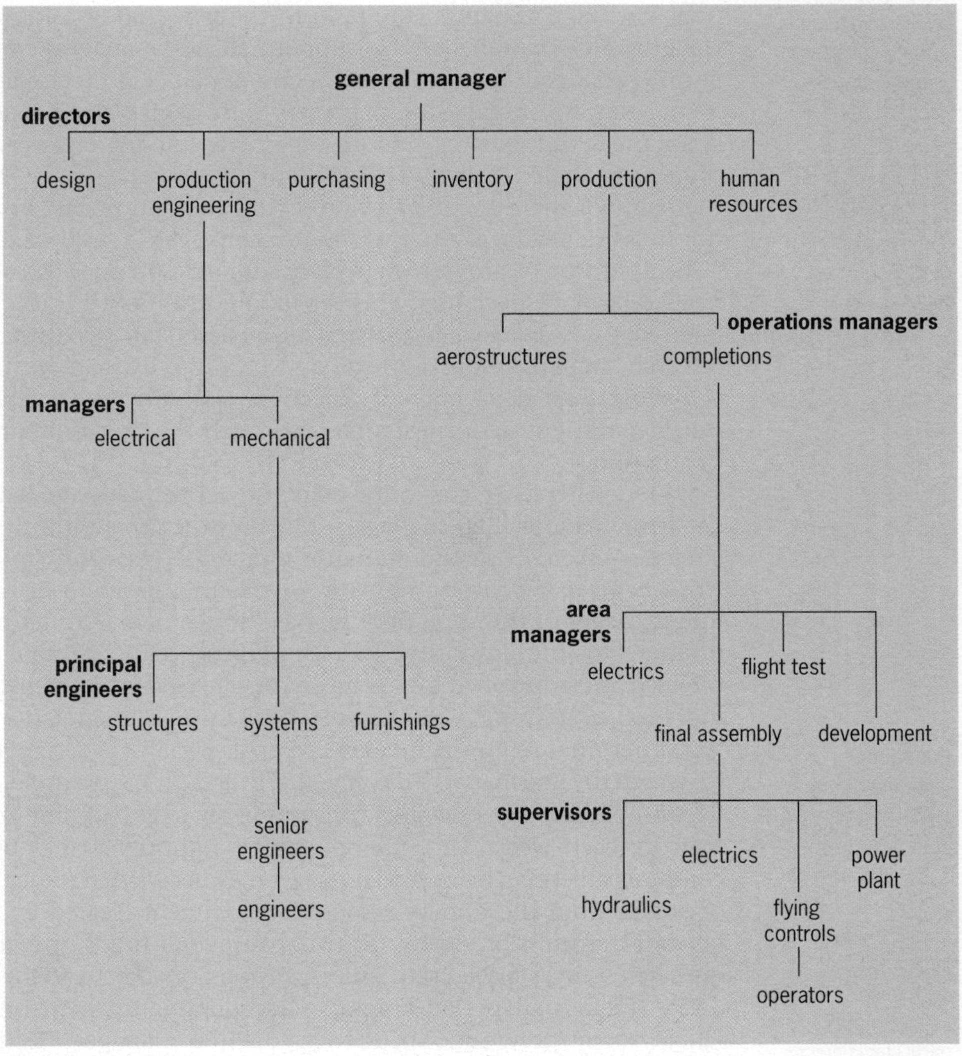

Figure 14.6: Line relationships

the four Area managers. The Operations Manager (Completions) in turn can be directed by the Director of Production. All the aforementioned individuals are in the same line relationship. The line relationships in a company are found within departments and functions. Line managers are responsible for everything that happens within their particular department.

Given the pyramidal nature of companies, managers located towards the top of an organization have more authority to control more resources than those below them. For this reason, lower-level managers are forced to integrate their actions with those above them by having to ask their bosses to approve some of their actions. In this way, managerial control is exercised down through the organization by the **chain of command**.

The line structure is the oldest and most basic framework for an organization, and all other forms are modifications of it. It is indispensable if the efforts of employees are to be co-ordinated. It provides channels for upward and downward communication, and links different parts of the company together with the ultimate source of authority. As long as an organization is small and simple, and its managers can exercise effective direction and control, then an organization based exclusively on line relationships will be adequate. However, once a company becomes large and more complex, requiring perhaps an expert in human resources, in advertising or in buying, then some modifications to its existing structure will be required. These new activities support, but do not directly progress, the company's core task. In the way that an old man may lean on his walking stick or staff pole for support, so line managers can lean on their **staff employees** or specialists for advice and guidance on technical matters.

One way to provide line managers with advice and support is to appoint an 'assistant to' an existing line manager. The line manager can delegate tasks and projects to their assistant. The assistant has no authority of their own, but acts in the name of their line manager and with their authority. Because the assistant is not in a line relationship, they do not constitute a level in the hierarchy.

Another way of providing advisory support is to establish separate departments headed by staff specialists. This is a modification of the basic line structure and is referred to as a *line-and-staff structure*. These staff departments, such as market research, human resources, legal and training, exist to aid the line managers in achieving their departmental objectives. As with the 'assistant to' example, the staff department performs its tasks through the line structure, and not independently of it.

Staff departments can only plan for, recommend to, advise or assist other departments and their managers, but they lack the authority to insist that their advice is taken. Thus the human resources department cannot direct shop-floor workers, even when dealing with a personnel problem. It has to work with the line manager of the shop-floor workers concerned. Staff authority is usually subordinate to line authority, and its purpose is to facilitate the activities being directed and controlled by the line managers. Each staff department, like computing, legal or training, will of course have its own line relationships within it.

A **functional relationship** exists when a specialist is designated to provide a service which the line manager is compelled to accept. For example, the human resources department issues instructions concerning the length of time employees are allowed to work each week. The staff specialist's authority comes by delegation from a common superior. The general manager may decide that rather than have each piece of advice from the human resources department cleared by them personally for onward transmission down to her departmental heads, it is more efficient for the human resources specialist to issue an instruction directly to the departmental heads.

The functional specialists remain accountable to their functional manager, in whose name they issue instructions to line managers. If the general manager requires functional assistance to be given to their subordinates in an area such as

Chain (or line) of command: the unbroken line of authority that extends from the top of the organization to the bottom and clarifies who reports to whom.

Staff employees: workers who are in advisory positions and who use their specialized expertise to support the efforts of line employees.

Functional relationship: a situation where staff department specialists have the authority to insist that line managers implement their instructions concerning a particular issue.

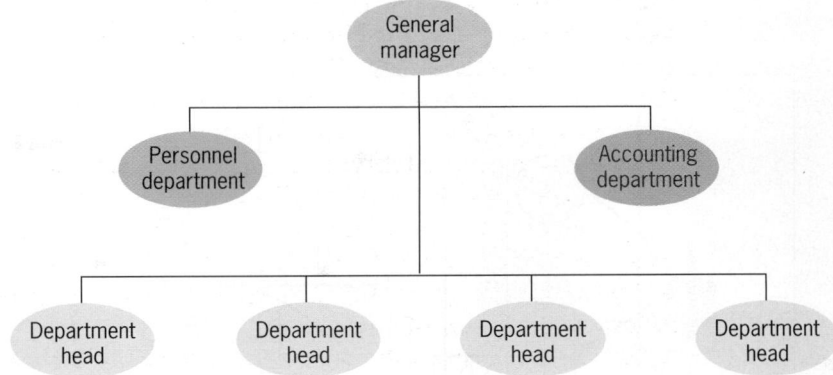

Figure 14.7: Functional relationship

training, they have to delegate some of their own authority to the functional specialist concerned. The organization chart will thus look like that shown in figure 14.7.

The formal and the informal organization

Formal organization: the collection of work groups that have been consciously designed by senior management to maximize efficiency and achieve organizational goals.

Decisions about job descriptions, organization charts, types of authority and so on all relate to designing the formal organization. However, to understand and explain the behaviour of people in organizations it is necessary to become familiar with the informal organization. There are two main problems with organization charts. First, they are static and do not show the ever-changing aspects of organizational life. Second, being depictions of how formal relations should prevail, they do not show the informal, social relations that actually do exist between company employees. The key differences between the **informal** and the **formal organization** are shown in table 14.2.

Informal organization: the network of relationships that spontaneously establish themselves between members of the organization on the basis of their common interests and friendships.

Design or evolution of structure

An organization can acquire a particular structure almost unconsciously. When a group of computer programmers hire an administrator and a secretary to 'deal with the paperwork' while they are doing their jobs, they are in fact designing structure. When a newly appointed chief executive of a multinational corporation centralizes the previously dispersed research and development activities into one location, they are consciously restructuring the company. Between these two extremes, incremental, *ad hoc* changes can be made. The point is that the structure of organizations evolves as often as it gets 'designed', and both can be messy processes.

There are many different types of organization – businesses, hospital trusts, schools, local authorities, football clubs and trade unions. All of these have a purpose and hence a policy. Those who design them, or change their design, can be seen as attempting to translate that policy into practices, duties and functions which are allocated as specific tasks to individuals and groups. Different organizations will have different structures. These differences partly represent

L'organigramme

Un organigramme représente sous forme de graphique l'orga-nisation des responsabilités et des fonctions d'une organisation.

La préparation de l'organigramme

On répertorie tous les organismes qui doivent figurer sur l'organigramme. Les différentes directions, les différents secteurs, les différents services...

On les désigne de manière cohérente en mentionnant trois informations:
-- le niveau de l'organisme (Division, Département, Secteur..);
-- la fonction de l'organisme (Production, Finances, Commercialisation..);
-- le nom du responsable de l'organisme.

Le dessin de l'organigramme

On visualise la nature et l'activité de l'organisme. La forme que l'on donne au cadre dans lequel on inscrit l'organisme (rond, rectangle, ovale...) doit permettre de différencier:
--l'organisme d'état-major: Comité de direction, Comité financier, Comité social...;
--l'organisme fonctionnel: Service finance, Service personnel, Service planification...;
--l'organisme opérationnel: Département achats, Département production...

La hiérarchisation des composants

Verticalement, on détermine les niveaux de la structure. On visualise cette hiérarchie en diminuant la taille des cadres au fur et à mesure que leur nombre augmente.

Horizontalement, la place de l'organisme est située à son niveau hiérarchique. Elle est établie logiquement par le degré d'autonomie de l'organisme. On place côté à côté des organismes de même niveau qui entretiennent des relations dans le temps (le Service conditionnement se trouvera au côté du Service expédition).

Les types de relations entre les organismes

Relations opérationnelles: des traits continus épais relient les cadres. Ils constituent la charpente de l'organigramme.
Relations fonctionnelles: elles sont établies par des traits plus fins qui se greffent sur les relations opérationnelles.
Relations informelles de collaboration ou de conseil: lorsqu'elles existent, ce qui n'est pas tonjours le cas, elles sont souvent représentées en pointillés.

Le rôle de l'organigramme

Il est essentiellement destiné a donner une image de l'organisation d'un groupe. Il permet de situer précisément un service particulier dans ses relations avec les autres. C'est un moyen de savoir exactement qui est responsable de quoi.

Exemple d'organigramme classique

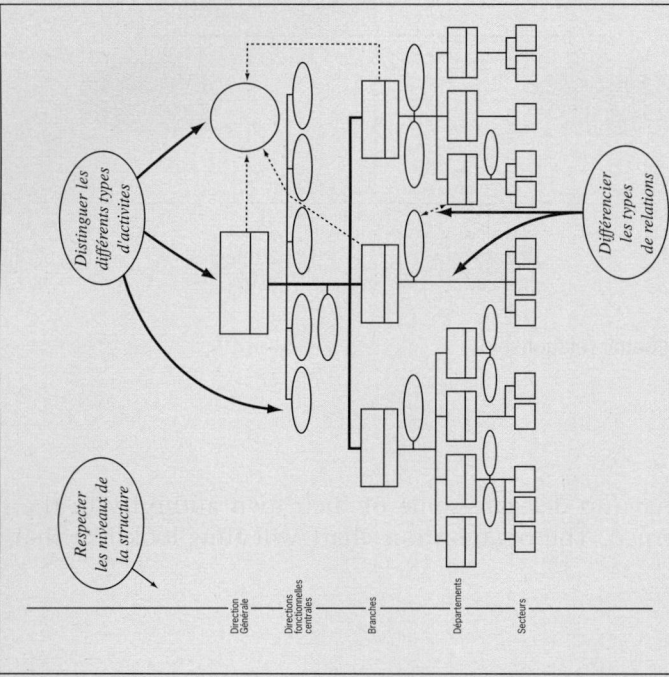

Distinguer les différents types d'activités

Respecter les niveaux de la structure

Différencier les types de relations

Direction Générale
Directions fonctionnelles centrales
Branches
Départements
Secteurs

Exemple d'organigramme classique

Les niveaux de la structure sont presentes sur l'organigramme. Le plus important figure en haut de la pyramide. La hierarchie est marquee par la place dans la pyramide et par la grandeur du cadre.

Les différents types d'activités apparaissent dans la forme du cadre. Dans les rectangles sont inscrits les différentes branches d'activités. Dans les ovales figurent les directions. Dans le cercle, on trouve l'organisme de controle.

Les traits continus forts indiquent une relation de dependance entre differentes branches. Les traits fins marquent une relation de fonction. Les traits pointilles indiquent une collaboration occasionnelle entre les services.

From Christiane Cadet, Rene Charles and Jean-Luc Galus, *La Communication par Limage*, Nathan, Paris, 1990, pp. 66–7.

Table 14.2: The formal and the informal organization compared

	Formal organization	Informal organization
A structure		
(a) origin	planned	spontaneous
(b) rationale	rational	emotional
(c) characteristics	stable	dynamic
B position terminology	job	role
C goals	profitability or service to society	member satisfaction
D influence		
(a) base	position	personality
(b) type	authority	power
(c) flow	top down	bottom up
E control mechanism	threat of firing or demotion	physical or social sanction (norms)
F communication		
(a) channels	formal channels	grapevine
(b) networks	well defined, follow formal lines	poorly defined, cut across regular channels
G charting	organizational chart	sociogram
H miscellaneous		
(a) individuals included	■ all individuals in work group	■ only those 'acceptable'
(b) interpersonal relations	■ prescribed by job description	■ arise spontaneously
(c) leadership role	■ assigned by organization	■ result of membership
(d) basis for interaction	■ functional duties or position	■ personal characteristics status
(e) basis for attachment	■ loyalty	■ cohesiveness

Based on *Organizational Behaviour: Concepts and Applications* by Gray/Starke, © 1977. Reprinted by permission of Prentice-Hall, Inc., Upper Saddle River, NJ.

divergences between goals and policies of the enterprises concerned. The organization structure that emerges results from the choices made about the division and grouping of tasks into functions, departments, sections and units.

Having decided on the degree of job specialization and job definition, there is the need to group the jobs into sections, place the sections into units, locate the units within departments and co-ordinate the departments. A department designates a distinct area or branch of an organization, over which a manager has authority for the performance of specified activities. Thus job grouping or the **departmentalization** of jobs constitutes a second major area of organization design. Jobs can be grouped on several criteria, and usually an organization will use a mixture of such grouping criteria.

Function (e.g. marketing, engineering, production or finance)
Grouping of jobs based on the function which they perform. For example, the jobs in a manufacturing organization will be grouped according to production, marketing, sales, finance and so on. In a hospital grouping they will be physiotherapy, nursing, medical physics.

Product or service (e.g. car insurance)
Traditionally, educational institutions are structured on the basis of the service. Thus all lecturers teaching management subjects in a university or college are located in its business school. Within that school, they are further divided into subject specialisms (corporate strategy, quantitative methods, accounting).

Departmentalization: the process of grouping together employees who share a common supervisor and resources, who are jointly responsible for performance, and who tend to identify and collaborate with each other.

The two diagrams below show the same set of managers and workers. The top one identifies the positions and departments by name (for example, president, personnel), while the lower one identifies the same ones by numbers (for example, 1 = president, 2 = head of accounting, etc.).

The top one also depicts the formal relationships (the formal organization) as specified by senior management and as depicted in the organization chart. The lower diagram depicts the informal relationships (the informal organization). That is, it shows how these same people actually interact on a day-to-day basis. To obtain these data, the researcher would either have to observe their interactions over a period of time or ask them to complete a sociometric questionnaire which asks them with whom they prefer to lunch, car share, play cards, drink and share leisure time.

(a) formal organization

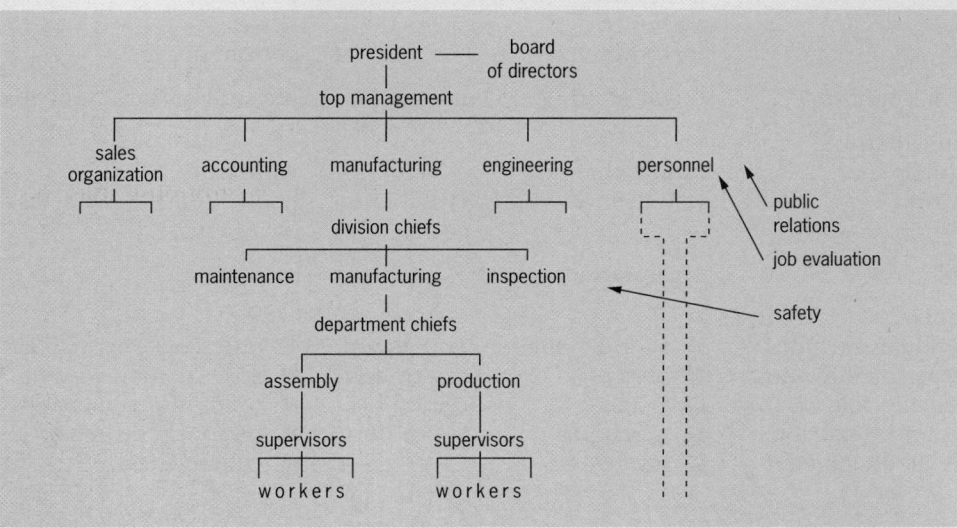

(b) informal organization

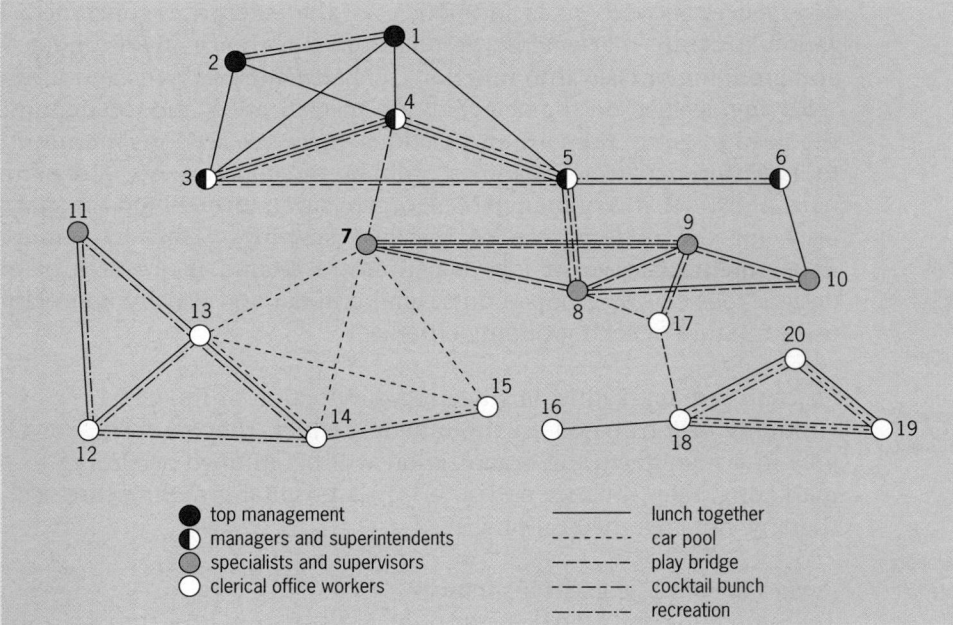

Figure 14.8: The formal and the informal organization

Customer (e.g. retail, wholesale)
Separate groups are organized for different types of customer. Thus, an educational publishing company may have separate divisions for schools, colleges, universities and general readers.

Geography or territory (e.g. Northern England, Scotland)
Grouping on this basis is used where the service is most effectively or economically provided within a limited distance. Companies offering repair and maintenance services will be geographically divided to ensure that customer problems can be solved rapidly.

Time (e.g. shift, non-shift)
Hospitals and factories offering a 24-hour service or producing round the clock will have different groups for different shifts.

Technology or equipment used (e.g. small batch, mass production, process)
The type of technology employed can be a criterion, especially when several different types are used in a single plant.

An organization chart shows which type of grouping has been adopted (figure 14.9).

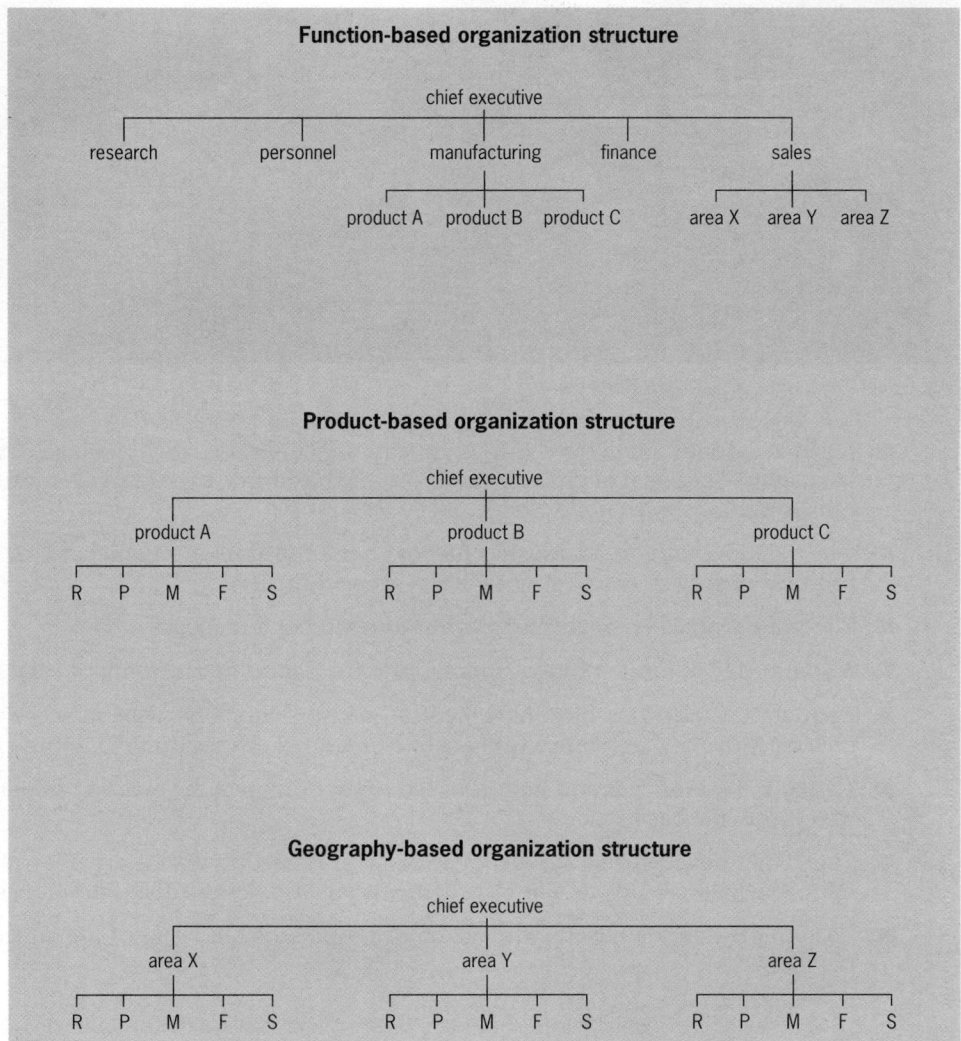

Figure 14.9: Function-, product- and geography-based organization structures

The Lifeboat Service: how it works

The Royal National Lifeboat Institution (RNLI) is a charity which saves lives at sea. It provides, on call, the 24-hour service necessary to cover search and rescue requirements up to 50 miles (80 kilometres) out from the coast of the United Kingdom and Republic of Ireland. There are over 230 lifeboat stations, their lifeboats are launched over 7,500 times every year and rescue over 7,000 people.

Source: Royal Bank of Scotland/Peter Bentley

- Lifeboat stations are divided into six operational divisions, each managed by an inspector and his deputy. Specialist engineers, surveyors and electronic experts make routine and emergency calls to stations in their divisions.

- Every station with an all-weather lifeboat has a full-time mechanic and, in some cases, also a full-time coxswain. The rest of the crew are volunteers.

- The honorary secretary authorizes the launching of a lifeboat.

- A committee of local volunteers looks after the day-to-day running of each lifeboat station.

- Each station also has honorary medical advisors (doctors) who may go to sea aboard the lifeboat if medical assistance is likely to be required. They also help with first aid training.

- Nearly 1,500 branches and guilds, in ten fundraising regions, work to raise the money needed to run the lifeboat service.

- The RNLI's headquarters and depot at Poole in Dorset (England) provides administrative back-up to the lifeboat service. The new lifeboats are also designed and developed there.

- A Committee of Management made up of people from all walks of life directs overall policy of the RNLI.

From 'What is the RNLI?', *Lifeboats*, Royal National Lifeboat Institution, Poole, Dorset, UK, 2002.

Matrix structure

Matrix structure:
a type of organization design that combines two different, traditional types of structure, usually a functional structure and a project structure, which results in an employee being part of both a functional department and a project team, and, in consequence, having two reporting relationships.

The distinguishing feature of a **matrix structure** is that the employees within it report to two bosses rather than the traditional one. There is thus a dual, rather than a single, chain of command. This occurs because in a matrix, one type of structure has been superimposed upon another one. The matrix structure was developed in the late 1950s to cope with increasingly complex technological problems and rates of change. Some writers discuss the matrix structure alongside line, staff and functional ones, while others treat it as yet another form of departmentalization.

Simon Ramo, the co-founder of TRW Inc., is credited with introducing the first matrix structure in 1957. As an aerospace company, TRW found that joint military–industrial projects, such as the manufacture of Minuteman, Atlas and Titan missile systems, could not be co-ordinated through the use of traditional functional or product departmental groupings. These projects were so complex that it was not possible to make a single manager responsible for their entire execution.

The most common type of matrix combination is departmentalization by product and by function simultaneously. Maybe your course is organized using such a structure. Table 14.3 shows a matrix structure within a university. In this example, the programmes or courses to be taught are listed horizontally, while the academic departments in which the instructors are based are shown vertically. In the case of the aerospace example quoted earlier, the matrix structure would combine projects or rockets to be manufactured (Titan, Delta) and company functions (engineering, marketing, research, testing).

The matrix structure chart in table 14.3 shows that the individual instructors report to two different bosses. One of these is responsible for the function, in this case the university academic department of accounting, economics or psychology. Their other 'boss' is the director of the product – in this example, the educational programme being provided, whether undergraduate, master's or doctoral. Both the heads of departments and the programme directors may, in turn, report to a common boss, who co-ordinates the activities of the academic functions and the educational programmes. This may be the dean of the faculty.

Table 14.3: Example of a matrix structure for university course teaching

	PRODUCTS (*Educational programme*)		
	Director	Director	Director
	Undergraduate Programme	Master's Programme	Doctoral Programme
SUBJECTS (*Academic departments*)			
Head: Accounting	A	B	C
Head: Economics	D	E	
Head: Psychology	F		

A: Department of Accounting lecturer teaching undergraduates.
B: Professor of accounting teaching a postgraduate programme.
C: Senior lecturer from the Accounting Department teaching doctoral students.
D: Economics lecturer teaching undergraduate students.
E: Professor of economics teaching master's degree students.
F: Psychology lecturer teaching undergraduates.

One consequence of having a matrix structure is that employees simultaneously belong to two different groups. Instructor D is both a member of the Economics Department group (with colleague E and others), while at the same time, she is a member of the undergraduate programme teaching group (with colleagues A and F). Instructor D reports to two superiors. Her permanent functional boss is the head of the Economics Department and her temporary boss, as long as she contributes to undergraduate courses, is the director of the undergraduate programme. In industry, the latter is commonly referred to as the 'project manager'.

Thus in every matrix, there are three sets of unique relationships. These exist between the top manager who balances the dual chains of command; the directors of programmes and heads of functions who share the subordinates; and the employees who report simultaneously to their department head and to the programme director. Although the integration of product and function structures is the most common form of matrix organization, any two forms of departmentalization are capable of being combined: for example, product and geography.

Companies use matrix structures when they have to be responsive to two sectors simultaneously (for example, technology and markets); when they face uncertainties that require information to be quickly exchanged between all those involved; and when they are strongly constrained by financial or human resources. The aim of the matrix structure is to gain the benefits of the two previously separate structures (Davis and Lawrence, 1978).

There are at least three advantages of the matrix structural arrangement in organizations:

- it avoids the duplication of overhead costs since the same employees can contribute to different company projects or programmes;

- being members of a project team, employees from different departments and with different backgrounds can focus more directly on the project;

- it leaves heads of department free to develop and deploy their staff members, while programme directors become responsible for delivering the service to customers.

There are at least three disadvantages of the matrix structure:

- occupying two roles can cause team members ambiguity and conflict, leading to stress;

- it may be difficult to demonstrate their individual contribution as they change from team to team;

- their opportunities for promotion may be limited because movement is lateral.

Stop and Criticize

Can you think of any *other* advantages and disadvantages of the matrix structure for (a) the individual team member, (b) their organization?

Organigraphs

Henry Mintzberg and Ludo van der Heyden highlighted the deficiencies of traditional organization charts. To outsiders, such charts reveal little about a company's products, processes, customers or line of business – 'using an organization chart to "view" a company is like using a list of municipal managers to find your way around a city'. To its employees, a chart does not tell them which parts connect to which; how people and processes should come together; or whose ideas should flow to where. To overcome these deficiencies, organigraphs have been developed. Although they do not totally eliminate little boxes, they do include 'sets', 'chains', 'hubs' and 'webs', which are forms that better reflect the way in which people organize themselves at work today.

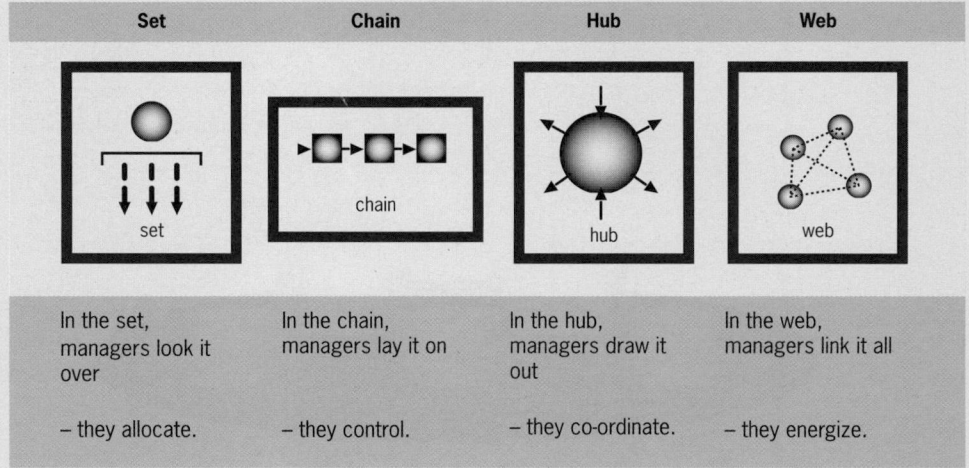

The organization chart treats everybody and everything as an independent box connected by a vertical chain – a chain of authority. In contrast, drawing an organigraph requires managers to create a customized picture of their company using sets, chains, hubs and webs and other meaningful symbols like 'funnels' (to depict transformations). Organigraphs have less to do with names, titles and formal authority, and more to do with relationships and processes. The diagram below shows, in contrast, an organization chart and an organigraph for the same newspaper.

Newspaper organization chart

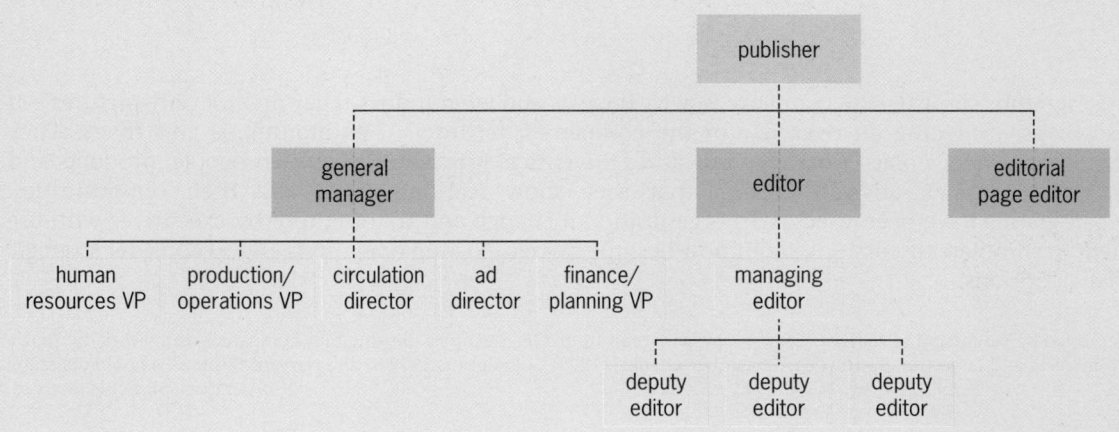

Newspaper organigraph

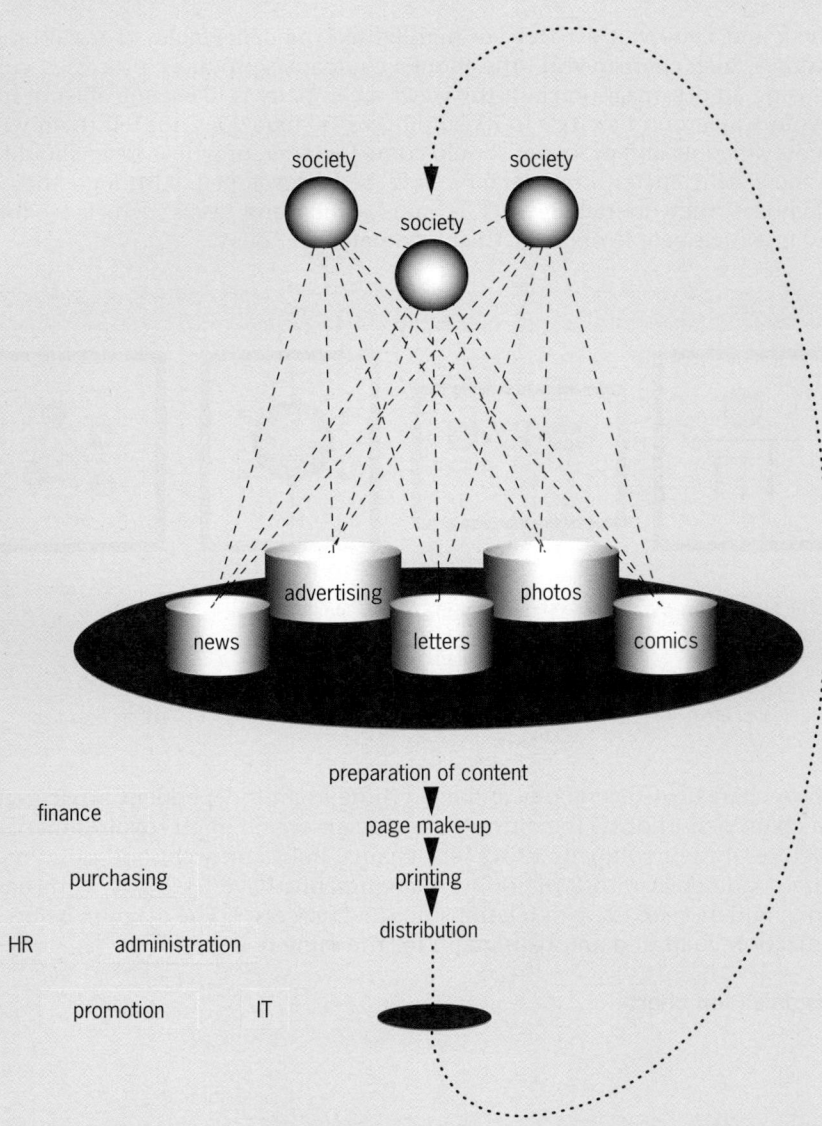

Organigraphs show what a company is, why it exists and what it does. They are not only pictures but also maps, providing an overview of the company's 'territory' – its mountains and rivers. They demonstrate *how* a place works by indicating the critical interactions between people, products and information. Their advocates claim that they show real businesses and their opportunities. Organigraphs have been used as an organizational change and training tool by executives who use them to stimulate discussions about how best to manage existing operations and to consider strategic change options.

Roles in organizations

Role: the pattern of behaviour expected by others from a person occupying a certain position in an organization hierarchy.

Roles are a central feature of every organization structure, and are specified in the organization hierarchy. All organization structuring occurs through the specification of the roles that employees are expected to play. It follows that if individuals occupying different positions in the hierarchy have mutual and complementary expectations, then the patterning and predictability of their behaviour is increased. The formal positions identified on an organization chart of a company imply the expectation of certain behaviour by any person occupying that office. This becomes the person's 'role'. Roles are thus associated with positions in the organization and are involved in interactions.

Role set: the collection of persons most immediately affected by the focal person's role performance, who depend upon the focal person for their own role performance and who therefore have a stake in it.

A single office holder, such as an engineer, will have regular interactions with a limited number of other office holders such as workers, the department manager, trade union officials and so on. Each individual in an organization therefore has their own particular **role set** (figure 14.10). This refers to the collection of persons who are most immediately affected by how the role incumbent (the focal person) performs their role. They depend upon the focal person for their own role performance, and therefore have a stake in it. Because of this, they mobilize instructions, encouragement, assistance, rewards and penalties to direct and elicit the role performance. The role incumbent is surrounded by expectations of their role set as to how they should behave. Their desire for approval from role set members encourages compliance to their expectations. Finally, one can note that a single person plays many different and sometimes conflicting roles in life, both sequentially and simultaneously (for example, mother, team leader, trade union official).

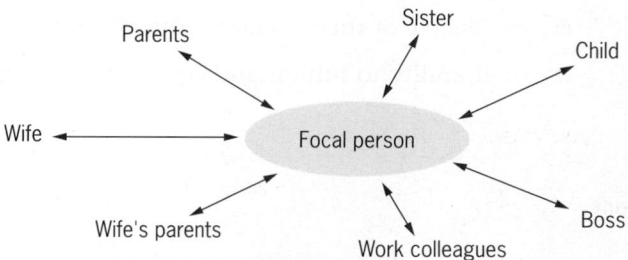

Figure 14.10: Role set

People's roles in organizations are ranked by status. Individuals occupying the role of manager are generally accorded more status that those occupying that of cleaner. In other companies, the ranking of roles is less obvious. John van Maanen (1991) described the rank ordering of occupations at Disneyland:

1. Disneyland Ambassadors and Tour Guides. These were the upper class, prestigious, bilingual women in charge of ushering tourists through the park.

2. Ride operators who either performed skilled work such as live narration, or who drove costly vehicles such as antique trains, horse-drawn carriages or the Monorail.

3. All the other ride operators.

4. Sweepers who kept the concrete grounds clean were designated as *proles*.

5. There was a still lower, fifth category of *sub-prole* or peasant status.

6. The 'lowest of the low' included food and concession workers, pancake ladies, peanut pushers, coke blokes, suds drivers and soda jerks.

Organizations are, to a degree, co-operative arrangements that are characterized by give and take, mutual adjustment and negotiation. Their members get on with one another, often without explicit guidance, instruction or direction. The concept of role aids our understanding of this aspect of organizational life by stressing that employees monitor and direct their own work behaviour in the light of what they know is expected of them.

Stop and Criticize

It is common for people to refer to an organizational title or position (e.g. supervisor, scientist, manager) as the supervisor's role, scientist's role and manager's role, as though it were merely an established way of referring to these positions. What assumptions and problems does this use of the concept fail to appreciate?

Philip Zimbardo
(b. 1933)

Many of the tasks involved in the job are learned and assimilated so well that they become accepted as being part of the person. This raises the question of whether, in behaving in a certain way, we are ourselves or just conforming to what the organization (and society) expects of us. Role relationships therefore are the field within which behaviour occurs. People's behaviour at any given moment is the result of:

■ their personalities;

■ their perception and understanding of each other;

■ their attitudes to the behavioural constraints imposed by the role relationship;

■ the degree of their socialization with respect to constraints;

■ their ability to inhibit and control their behaviours.

Prison experiment

To what extent do our attitudes, values and self-image affect the way we play roles in organizations such as student, lecturer, doctor, nurse or doorman? To what extent are our attitudes, values and self-image determined by the organizational roles we play?

Philip Zimbardo and two graduate-student colleagues from the Department of Psychology at Stanford University in California created their own prison to examine the roles of prisoner and guard. Advertising in the Palo Alto city newspaper, they selected 21 young men from the 75 whom they interviewed. These individuals were screened to ensure that each was a mature, emotionally stable, normal, intelligent North American male student from a middle-class home with no criminal record. Each volunteer was paid $15 a day to participate in a two-week study of prison life. A toss of a coin arbitrarily designated these recruits as either prisoners or guards. Hence, at the start of the study, there were no measurable differences between the two groups assigned to play the two roles (10 prisoners and 11 guards).

Those taking the role of guards had their individuality reduced by being required to wear uniforms, including silver reflector glasses which prevented eye contact. They were to be referred to as Mr Correction Officer by the prisoners, and they were given symbols of their power which included clubs, whistles, hand-cuffs and keys. They were given minimal instructions by the researchers, being required only to 'maintain law and order'. While physical violence was forbidden, they were told to make up and improvise their own formal rules to achieve the stated objective during their eight-hour, three-man shifts.

 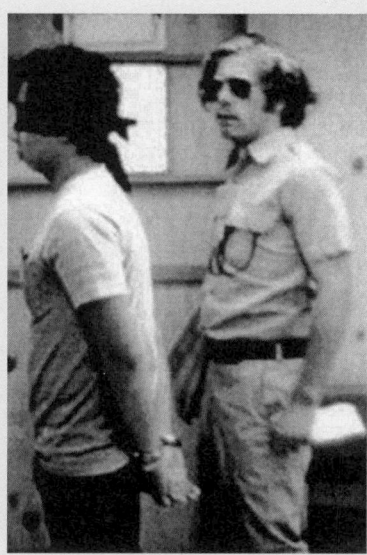

Those who were assigned the role of prisoners were unexpectedly picked up at their homes by a city policeman in a squad car. Each was searched, hand-cuffed, finger-printed, booked in at the Palo Alto police station, blindfolded and then transferred to Zimbardo's 'Stanford County Prison' which was located in the basement of the university psychology building. Each prisoner's sense of uniqueness and prior identity was minimized. They were given smocks to wear and had nylon stocking caps on their heads to simulate baldness. Their personal effects were removed, they had to use their ID numbers; and they were housed in stark cells. All this made them appear similar to each other and indistinguishable to observers. Six days into the planned fourteen-day study the researchers had to abandon the experiment. Why?

In a matter of days, even hours, a strange relationship began to develop between the prisoners and their guards. Some of the boy guards began to treat the boy prisoners as if they were despicable animals, and began to take pleasure in psychological cruelty. The prisoners in turn became servile, dehumanized robots who thought only of their individual survival, escape and mounting hatred of the guards. About a third of the guards became tyrannical in their arbitrary use of power, and became quite inventive in developing techniques to break the spirit of the prisoners and to make them feel worthless. Having crushed a prison rebellion, the guards escalated their aggression, and this increased the prisoners' sense of dependence, depression and helplessness.

Within 36 hours, the first 'prisoner' had to be released because of uncontrolled crying, fits of rage, disorganized thinking and severe depression. He was Doug Korpi (Prisoner No. 8612) and he suffered a mental breakdown. 'I've never screamed so loud in my life. I've never been so upset,' he said. Three more prisoners were released on consecutive days with the same symptoms. A fifth left after developing a psychosomatic rash. Others begged to be paroled and nearly all were willing to forfeit their money if the guards agreed to release them.

Zimbardo and his colleagues were surprised by the changes in the behaviour and attitudes of their experimental subjects. The researchers attributed these changes to a number of causes. First, the creation of a new environment within which both groups were separated from the outside world. New attitudes were developed about this new 'mini-world', as well as what constituted appropriate behaviour within it.

A second explanation was that within this new 'mini-world' of the prison, the participants were unable to differentiate clearly between the role they were asked to play (prisoner or guard) and their real self. A week's experience of imprisonment (temporarily) appeared to undo a lifetime of learning. Human values and self concepts were challenged, and the pathological side of human nature was allowed to surface. The prisoners became so programmed to think of themselves as prisoners that when their requests for parole were refused, they returned docily to their cells, instead of feeling capable of just withdrawing from an unpleasant psychological research experiment.

This study raises many different issues. Of particular interest is Zimbardo's conclusion that individual behaviour is largely under the control of social and environmental forces, rather than being the result of personality traits, character or willpower. In an organizational context such as a prison, the mere fact of assigning labels to people and putting them in situations where such labels acquire validity and meaning is sufficient to elicit a certain type of behaviour. The power of the prison environment was stronger than each individual's will to resist falling into his role. In the light of these research findings, what undesirable behaviours might be elicited by assigning the labels of student, lecturer, doctor, nurse or doorman to individuals?

Based on Craig Haney, Curtis Banks and Philip G. Zimbardo, 'A study of prisoners and guards in a simulated prison', *Naval Research Reviews*, Office of Naval Research, Department of the Navy, Washington, DC, September 1973; and P. G. Zimbardo et al., 'A Pirandellian prison', *The New York Times Magazine*, 8 April 1973. Photographs reprinted by permission of Philip G. Zimbardo.

Self-fulfilling prophecy: an expectation that leads to a certain pattern of behaviour whose consequences confirm the expectancy.

The roles that we play are part of our self concept, and personality theory tells us that we come to know ourselves through our interactions with others. We play different roles throughout our lives, and these require us to use different abilities, thereby adding more aspects to our self-image. Which roles we play and how successfully we play them during our adulthood affects our level of self-esteem. Thus the roles that we play both inside and outside the organization affect our self-image and self-esteem. In his research, Philip Zimbardo showed that people possess mental concepts of different roles and conform to them when asked or required to do so (Zimbardo et al., 1973).

A related concept is that of the **self-fulfilling prophecy**, which is ascribed to the sociologist, Robert Merton. It refers to a prediction that comes true solely because it is made. For example, a rumour (prophecy) that a bank is about to collapse leads people to withdraw their money from it all at the same time, and then the bank does indeed collapse. If a teacher expects children to work hard and do well at school, they will do so (Rosenthal and Jacobson, 1968). Interest in this study relates to whether supervisor behaviour may improve employee output through performance expectations. Rosenthal (1973) identified four factors which produced the effect:

Climate: Supervisors' expectations lead them to treat workers differently. Such differences are manifested in their eye contact, smiling, nodding, posture and tone of voice. Their expectation is transmitted in this way.

Feedback: More detailed and accurate information is given to workers about their performance. Supervisors can say how workers can improve, rather than just giving a general 'well done'.

Input: Supervisors give the workers more demanding tasks to perform which stretches them.

Output: Supervisors give the developing workers cues to respond to – for example, asking questions.

Psychologists have explained what must happen before the self-fulfilling prophecy can occur. This is shown in figure 14.11.

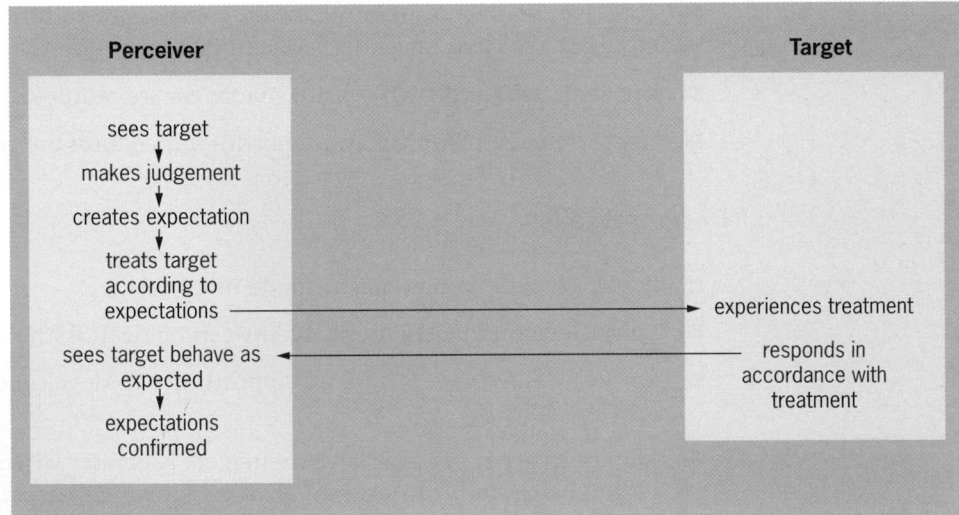

Figure 14.11: Self-fulfilling prophecy

Role conflict: the simultaneous existence of two or more sets of role expectations on a focal person in such a way that compliance with one makes it difficult to comply with the others.

The woman who is both a manager and a mother may experience **role conflict** when the expectations in these two important roles pull her in opposite directions.

Stop and Criticize

Identify any three roles that you currently occupy simultaneously in three different social contexts: for example, work, home, leisure. Identify any two conflicts that you regularly experience as a result of such multiple role occupancy.

Centralization: the concentration of authority and responsibility for decision-making power in the hands of managers at the top of an organization's hierarchy.

Decentralization: authority and responsibility for decision-making being dispersed more widely downwards and given to the operating units, branches and lower-level managers.

Some senior company executives like to retain decision-making power in their own hands, and thus run highly centralized organizations. Others prefer to delegate their power, and give more junior managers a greater responsibility to make decisions. Their organizations are more decentralized in their structure. The question of whether and how much to centralize has been one of the major topics discussed in organization structuring.

Arthur Bedeian and Raymond Zammuto (1991) argued that the balance between **centralization** and **decentralization** changes on an ongoing basis. It does so, in their view, in response to changes in company size, market opportunities, developments in new technology and, not least, changes in the quality of existing decision-making. On the one hand, it is possible to observe decentralization increasing as companies in new and developing markets, such as Central and Eastern Europe and China, leave decisions for their managers on the spot. On the other hand, developments in new technology have meant that banks and building societies have increased centralized decisions and shed thousands of staff in the process. Somewhat more cynically, Anthony Jay (1970) felt that whichever of the two is currently the fashion, it will be superseded by the other in due course. This may occur for no other reason than that the incoming chief executive wishes to make a highly visible impact on their managers, employees, shareholders and financial analysts. The advantages and disadvantages of each approach have been widely considered and are listed by Bedeian and Zammuto (1991, p. 139):

Centralization

■ A greater uniformity in decisions possible.

■ Top-level managers are more aware of an organization's future plans and are more likely to make decisions in its best interests.

■ Fewer skilled (and highly paid) managers are required.

■ Less extensive planning and reporting procedures are required.

Decentralization

■ Lower-level decisions can be made more easily.

■ Lower-level management problems can be dealt with on the spot.

■ Lower-level managers have an opportunity to develop their decision-making skills.

■ The motivation of lower-level managers is greater when they are entrusted to make decisions rather than always following orders issued at a higher level.

■ An organization's workload is spread so as to allow top-level managers more time for strategic planning.

Organization structures and managerial roles

Henry Mintzberg
(b. 1939)

Henry Mintzberg, a Canadian business academic, has contributed widely to the field of management theory and research. In addition to being active in the field of strategic management, he has made a major contribution to two topics within the field of organization behaviour. One of these relates to a consideration of the different forms that an organization's structure can take. The other concerns the range of roles performed by managers. Both will be considered in this section.

Forms of organization structure

The concepts introduced so far provide a vocabulary that can be used to discuss the strengths and weaknesses of different structures of organizations. Mintzberg (1979, 1983a, 1989) provided a framework to help us engage in 'conversations' about them. He distinguished five basic parts of an organization, which he termed *strategic apex*, *operating core*, *middle line*, *technostructure* and *support staff*. He also suggested ways in which these parts could be co-ordinated. He used these five parts and five co-ordinating mechanisms to describe five different 'ideal' types of organization structure. This explains the title of his book, *Structure in Fives* (Mintzberg, 1983a).

Strategic apex contains those individuals who direct the organization. It consists of senior management, whether in the form of chief executive officers, archbishops or generals. It is here that policies are decided, plans are made, resources are allocated and instructions are given. These individuals ensure that the organization meets its objectives, including the needs of stakeholders, such as shareholders, lenders, employees and congregation members. They also manage the boundary relations between the organization and its links with the outside world.

Operating core refers to those who receive inputs and transform them into products or services. Functional, core employees are located at the heart of every organization. This core may take raw materials and process them into motor cars, or ill patients and transform into well patients. Thus, in one company, the operators can be semi-skilled, blue-collar workers, while in another, they may be highly trained professionals like doctors and nurses.

Middle line employees and their departments are located between the strategic apex at the top and the operating core at the bottom. This layer consists of middle managers and supervisors who are responsible for carrying out orders and ensuring the policies are pursued. The middle line links the senior management to the operators, usually through a single line of authority or chain of command. These managers pass information up and down the hierarchy, make decisions, deal with internal disturbances to smooth running and manage the relationships across the company boundary with suppliers, customers, media and other groups.

Technostructure consists of the technical support staff. The analysts and technical advisors who comprise it serve those at all levels in the organization but are separate from them. The job of these technicians is to standardize the work throughout the entire organization. Technostructure activities include designing systems and procedures, redesigning work processes, providing information and library services, providing market information and building financial systems.

Staff support refers to individuals who provide administrative and clerical support for the different levels. For example, by providing personnel and human resource management, security, catering, public relations, building maintenance, paying bills, delivering mail, and other, similar services.

To these five building blocks of organization design, Mintzberg added ideology or 'culture of the organization'. This refers to the values, beliefs and taken-for-granted assumptions that underpin the way that parts and co-ordinated mechanisms can be configured. These are only possibilities, but not his recommendations:

Mutual adjustment: as people communicate with one another verbally and visually, they adjust to one another and to changing circumstances. An operating team in a hospital theatre or a basketball team on the court does this. For this co-ordinating device to be effective, individuals have to be committed to each other and to the organization's goals, be personally competent and trust the others.

Direct supervision: as its name suggests, the supervisor will stand over or will frequently check what the employee has done. Such close monitoring will ensure that the task is being carried out as the manager desires, and thereby fits in with what others are doing.

Standardize the input focuses on who gets things done. It ensures that the individuals who are selected either already possess or are trained to have the skills and knowledge necessary to achieve the standard of performance required. This co-ordination strategy is commonly used with professionals. They have to be trusted to provide the required service or product on time and to quality stardards.

Standardize the work processes focuses on how things get done. Using technology in its broadest sense, work can be organized to incorporate rules and operating procedures that restrict employees' choice of behaviour and monitor their performances to ensure objectives are achieved. For this form of co-ordination to work, the operating and business processes must be well designed.

Standardize the output focuses on what gets done. This form of co-ordination involves the strategic apex specifying the quality, quantity and delivery of a product or service. Here, production standards and deadlines have to be clearly specified, together with sanctions for non-compliance.

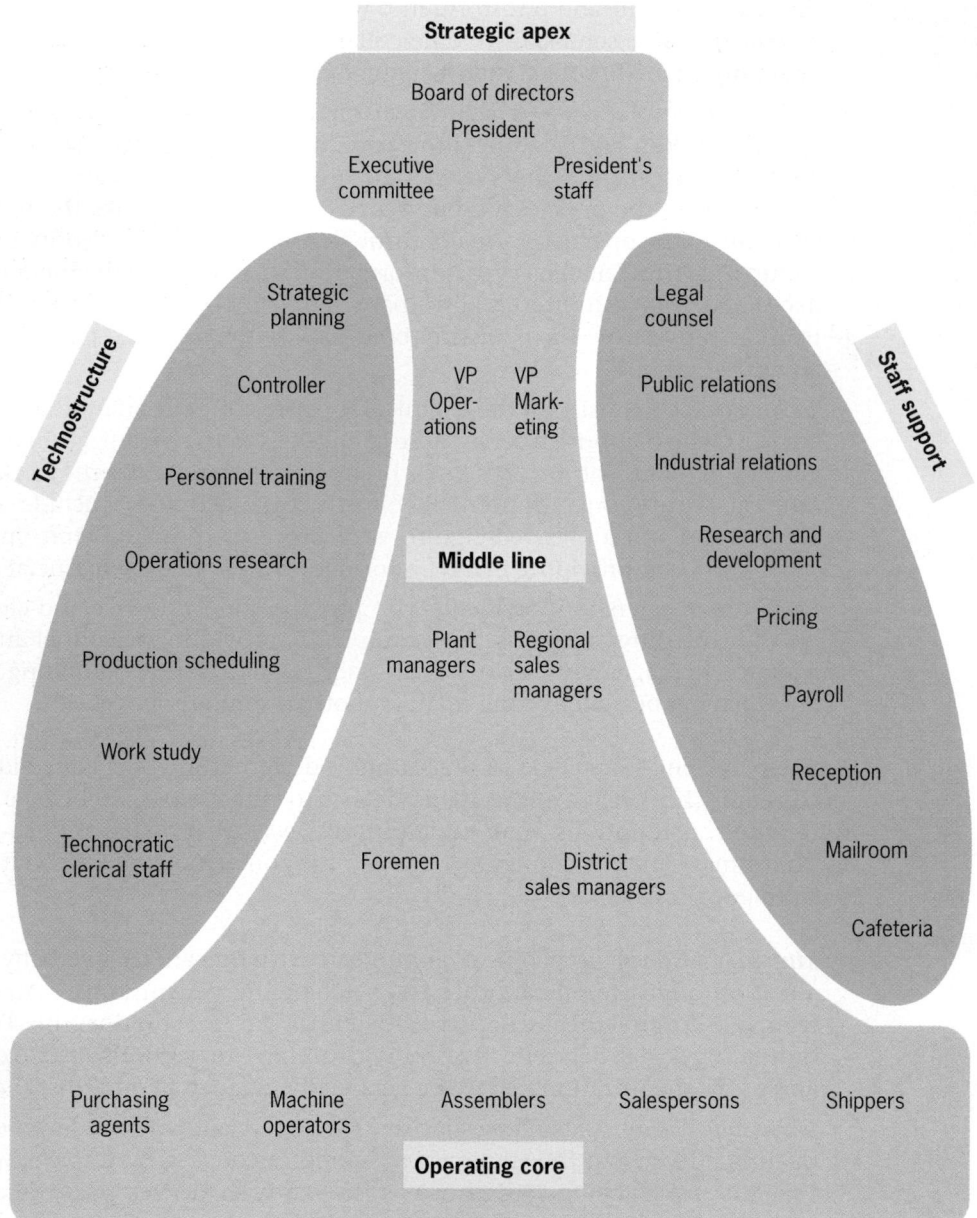

Figure 14.12: Mintzberg's five organizational parts
Based on Henry Mintzberg, *The Structure of Organizations*, Prentice-Hall, Englewood Cliffs, NJ, 1979; Henry Mintzberg, *Structure in Fives: Designing Effective Organizations*, Prentice-Hall, Englewood Cliffs, NJ, 1983a; and Roy Payne, 'The characteristics of organizations', in P. Warr (ed.), *Psychology at Work*, Penguin, Harmondsworth, 1996, pp. 383–407.

Having distinguished five organization parts and five co-ordinating mechanisms, Mintzberg proposed five ideal or pure types of organization structure. The relative importance and size of each of the organization parts within each structure type differed. So too did the relationships between the parts. The five organization parts are shown in figure 14.12.

Simple structure

This consisted mainly of just two of the parts – the strategic apex and the operating core. It has little or no technostructure, few support staff, a short hierarchy and minimal differentiation between departments. A garage owner and his team of mechanics would be an

example. The owner, who can see the entire operation, achieves co-ordination through direct supervision. Being simple, the structure is flexible and adaptable. It is one possessed by nearly all-new, entrepreneurial, owner-managed firms. Its weakness is that it relies on one individual who can both block and initiate change, or die.

Machine structure

Most decisions are made at the strategic apex; daily operations are controlled by middle managers directly, using standard procedures and rules. The technostructure and administrative support staff are large in this structure. Co-ordination is achieved mainly through standardizing work processes. Efficient and effective, this structure provides customers with a guaranteed, unvarying, product or

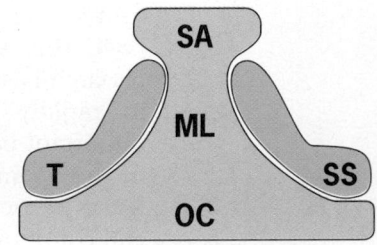

service. The problem for their managers is motivating the staff in the operating core where the work is standardized and repetitive, yet creativity and challenge could undermine the consistency and uniformity of the product or service. A difficulty for the strategic apex is that it receives problems up the chain of command for solution, but being distanced from the situation, its suggested solutions may not meet local needs.

Professional structure

This has a large operating core, with few levels between the strategic apex and the professional employees. Decentralized and therefore flat, it is run by hierarchical authority, but stresses the power of expertise. Co-ordination is achieved predominantly through

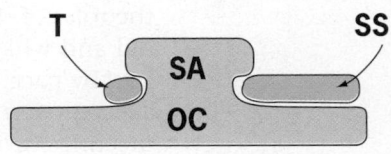

the standardization of input. The professional employees (for example, doctors, lawyers, engineers) have received extensive professional training and indoctrination. The technostructure is small, but the administrative support staff is substantial. The task of the latter is to serve the professionals. By insulating their members from external interference, the professional structure has problems of adapting to change and maintaining quality. Professional autonomy makes it difficult to implement changes and to deal with professional incompetence.

Divisional structure

Quasi-autonomous divisions perform the bulk of the work here. In consequence, the middle line and operating core are large, while the technostructure and support structures are small. The internal structure of these divisions can take any of the forms described in this section, but machine struc-

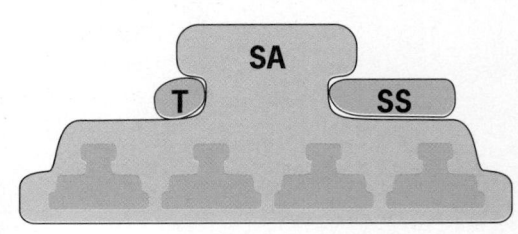

tures tend to be most common. Each division serves its own market and houses its own functions. It enjoys a high degree of autonomy, but in return, has to meet sales, profit and return-on-investment targets. Co-ordination is thus achieved predominantly through the standardization of outputs. While overall company rules and regulations exist, it is the managers in the middle line in each division who provide the direction and exert control. While offering potential for economies of scale and responsiveness, this structural form can experience a struggle for control between the operating core and the strategic apex.

Ad hoc structure

This is a loose, flexible, self-renewing organic form, which frequently includes experts from different backgrounds and disciplines. A small film or music company, advertising agency, 'think tank' or computer software firm may have this structure, or indeed, any young, research-based company that needs to innovate in rapidly changing conditions. The most

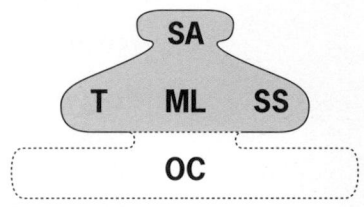

important parts are the support staff in research and development, as well experts in the operating core. It groups its highly trained specialists into mixed project teams in the hope of generating new ideas. Co-ordination is achieved through lateral communication and by members' directly co-operating and mutually adjusting to each other. Its form is both organic and decentralized.

Managerial roles

Mintzberg's second major contribution was to conduct empirical research into how managers actually spend their time within these different organization structures. Although structures do not determine the roles that individuals play in an organization, they do greatly influence them. Mintzberg's work led to a re-assessment of the nature of managerial work within organizations and a redefinition of the roles of the manager. It revealed a difference between what managers actually did and what they say they did. He showed that a manager's job was characterized by pace, interruptions, brevity and fragmentation of tasks. In addition, managers preferred to communicate verbally, and spent a great deal of time in meetings or in making contacts with others outside meetings. Mintzberg (1977) distinguished ten managerial roles which he classified under the three headings of *interpersonal*, *informational* and *decisional* (table 14.4).

Mintzberg argued that the ten roles that he identified could describe the nature of managerial work more accurately than other frameworks. The concept of role was introduced earlier in this chapter. One aspect of it is that any role holder can choose how to carry it out. In the case of a manager, they can decide how they wish to blend the ten listed roles, taking into account organizational constraints and opportunities. A consequence of this is that management becomes more of an art, rather than a teachable science that can be reduced to a set of prescriptions which can be easily taught.

Table 14.4: Mintzberg's ten managerial roles

Role	Description
Interpersonal	
Figurehead	Symbolic head; obliged to perform routine duties of a legal or social nature.
Leader	Responsible for the motivation and activation of subordinates for staffing, training and associated duties.
Liaison	Maintains self-developed networks of outside contacts and informers who provide favours and information.
Informational	
Monitor	Seeks and receives wide variety of special information (much of it current) to develop thorough understanding of organization and environment; emerges as nerve centre of internal and external information of the organization.
Disseminator	Transmits information received from outsiders or from other subordinates to members of the organization; some information is factual, some involving interpretation and integration of diverse value positions of organizational influences.
Spokesperson	Transmits information to outsiders on organization's plans, policies and actions, results, etc.; serves as expert on organization's industry.
Decisional	
Entrepreneur	Searches organization and its environment for opportunities and initiates 'improvement projects' to bring about change; supervises design of certain projects as well.
Disturbance handler	Responsible for corrective action when organization faces important unexpected disturbances.
Resource allocator	Responsible for the allocation of organizational resources of all kinds – in effect making or approving all significant organizational decisions.
Negotiator	Responsible for representing the organization at major negotiations.

From Henry Mintzberg, *The Nature of Managerial Work*, Prentice-Hall, Englewood Cliffs, NJ, 1980, pp. 92–3.

Patterns of general management behaviour

More recent research by John Kotter adds to our understanding of management roles. Like Henry Mintzberg, he studied management behaviour using various methods, including interviews, observation, questionnaires, inspecting relevant documents, and interviews with colleagues. His analysis of the work of the general manager is as follows:

➤

They spend most of their time with others	Average managers spend 25 per cent of their time alone; some spend 90 per cent with others
They spend time with many people in addition to their direct subordinates and their bosses	They regularly meet with people who appear to be unimportant outsiders
The breadth of topics in their discussions is extremely wide	Not limited to management concerns, managers discuss virtually anything
General managers ask a lot of questions	In a half-hour conversation, some managers ask literally hundreds of questions
During conversations, general managers rarely seem to make 'big' decisions	So why is 'decision-making' considered such a key part of the manager's role?
Their discussions usually contain a fair amount of joking and often concern topics not related to work	Humour is often about others in the organization or sector; non-work discussions are usually about families
In more than a few of these encounters, the issue discussed is relatively unimportant to the business or organization	General managers regularly engage in activities even they regard as a waste of time
In these encounters, managers rarely give orders in a traditional sense	So why is 'giving direction' considered such a key part of the manager's role?
Nevertheless, general managers often attempt to influence others	Instead of telling people what to do, they ask, request, cajole, persuade, intimidate
General managers often react to others; much of the typical day is unplanned	Even those with a heavy schedule spend a lot of time on topics not on their formal agenda
General managers spend most of their time with others in short, disjointed conversations	Discussions of single questions or issues rarely last more than ten minutes; not unusual to cover ten unrelated topics in five minutes
They work long hours	Average is 60 to 90 hours a week; but how can they apparently waste so much time?

Based on John P. Kotter, 'What effective general managers really do', *Harvard Business Review*, vol. 77, no. 2, 1999, pp. 145–59.

Stop and Criticize

What extra insights about management roles do Kotter's findings provide over Mintzberg's? What personal and professional advice would you give general managers on the basis of this work?

Recap

1. *Explain how organization structure affects human behaviour in organizations.*

   - The procedures employees are required to follow and the rules by which they are required to abide by, both control and direct their behaviour in specified directions.

   - The roles that people play and the expectations that others have of role holders both direct the behaviour of employees. Indeed, in the long term, these may even lead to a change in the personality of the employee.

2. *List the main elements of organization structure.*

   - The main elements include: chain of command; hierarchical levels; line employees; rules; staff employees; role expectations; span of control; departmentalization; authority; and job description.

3. *Relate the concept of span of control to the shape of the organization hierarchy.*

   - The narrower the span of control, the taller the organization hierarchy (and vice versa), and the greater the consequences for employees of having one or the other.

4. *Identify line and staff relationships on an organization chart.*

   - Line relationships are depicted vertically on a organization chart, indicating that those above possess the authority to direct the behaviours of those below.

   - The former have responsibility for the work of the latter, while the latter are responsible for their work to the former.

   - Staff relationships are depicted horizontally on an organization chart, indicating that those who possess specific expertise (for example, in personnel or computing matters) advise those in line positions.

5. *Describe six different criteria on which jobs might be departmentalized.*

   - Function (for example, production, marketing, personnel); product or service (for example, type of motor car); type of customer (for example, health, computer, hospitality sector); geography (for example, Europe, North America, Pacific); time (for example, front shift, back shift); and technology used (for example, small batch, mass production).

6. *Distinguish between the formal and the informal organization of a company.*

   - The formal organization refers to the collection of work groups that have been consciously designed by senior management to maximize efficiency and achieve organizational goals, while the informal organization refers to the network of relationships that spontaneously establish themselves between members of the organization on the basis of their common interests and friendships.

   - The two forms consist of the same people, albeit arranged in different ways.

7. *Distinguish Mintzberg's five organizational parts, five types of organization structure and ten managerial roles.*

   - Mintzberg's five organizational parts consist of the strategic apex, middle line, operating core, technostructure and support staff.

   - His five types of organization structure are simple structure, machine structure, professional structure, divisional structure and ad hoc structure.

   - His ten managerial roles are figurehead, leader, liaison, monitor, disseminator, spokesperson, entrepreneur, disturbance handler, resource allocator and negotiator.

Revision

1. Is hierarchical control an inevitable part of organization design or a just a management convenience? Discuss.

2. The question of how many levels of hierarchy to have is one that has exercised managers and management writers for nearly a century. Why should it be so important?

3. How does the informal organization of a company contrast with the formal one? Can the informal organization ever be managed by senior company executives?

4. Distinguish the different bases upon which an organization can be departmentalized. Selecting TWO of these, compare the advantages and disadvantages of each, and suggest the type of company or circumstance which would make it most appropriate.

5. Suggest how the relative importance of each of Mintzberg's ten managerial roles might be affected by the seniority of the post, type of organization or its size.

2: The Big Chip Electronics Company: function or product organization structure?

Objectives   1. To give you the opportunity to compare the effects of a function-based and product-based organization structure on company functioning.

Briefing   There are several different ways to organize work. Managers can often decide what form of organization structure they would like to have. However, each different form of structure has some advantages and disadvantages associated with it. In choosing a form of organization, a manager really is deciding which set of problems they want to live with. Read the description of the Big Chip Electronics Company. When you are finished answer the questions that follow. Base your answers on your own knowledge, guesses and common sense.

1. What is your choice of organization structure? Functional or product?

2. What are the reasons for your preference?

Big Chip Electronics (BCE)

Big Chip Electronics (BCE) manufactures and markets computers and peripheral electronic equipment for the UK and European markets. The company has been in business for the past 35 years and has established a major reputation in its industry. They have also been quite successful in marketing their products. Up until now BCE has been a family business run by Alan Demerera, whose father and uncle started the business. He has had his son Clive working as his assistant since his own business was wound up. Basically there are three major sets of activities that must be accomplished to manufacture and market BCE's products. One group of workers and managers produce the computer systems, using the latest technology to populate printed circuit boards, test systems and meet manufacturing schedules. Another group of workers and managers work in development research. This group largely comprises scientists who attempt to improve the current products and introduce future additions to the BCE range of systems.

Marketing is handled by several sales personnel who call on wholesalers and distributors in the UK and Europe. The sales staff is very large and has been, like all other employees, very effective. Alan and Clive have been managing BCE without many formal policies and procedures. The company has few set rules, procedures or job descriptions. Alan believes that once people know their job, they should and would do it well. However, BCE has grown fairly large and Alan and Clive believe that it is now necessary to develop a more formal organization structure. They have invited D.A. Buchan, a noted management consultant, to advise them. D.A. has told them that they basically have two choices. One is a functional organization structure and the second is a product-based organization structure. These two different forms are shown on p. 501.

Functional

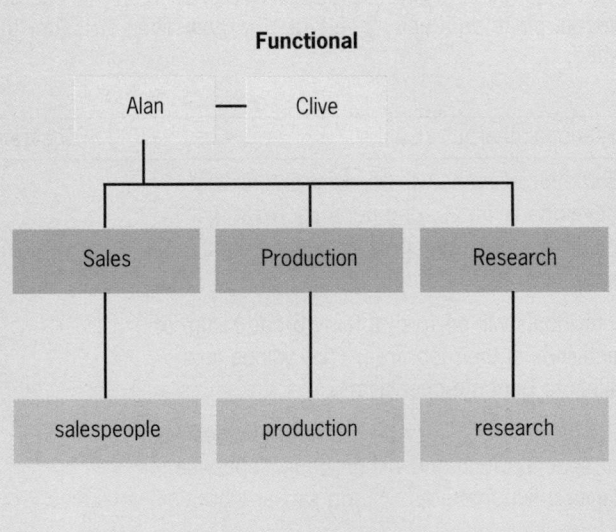

Product

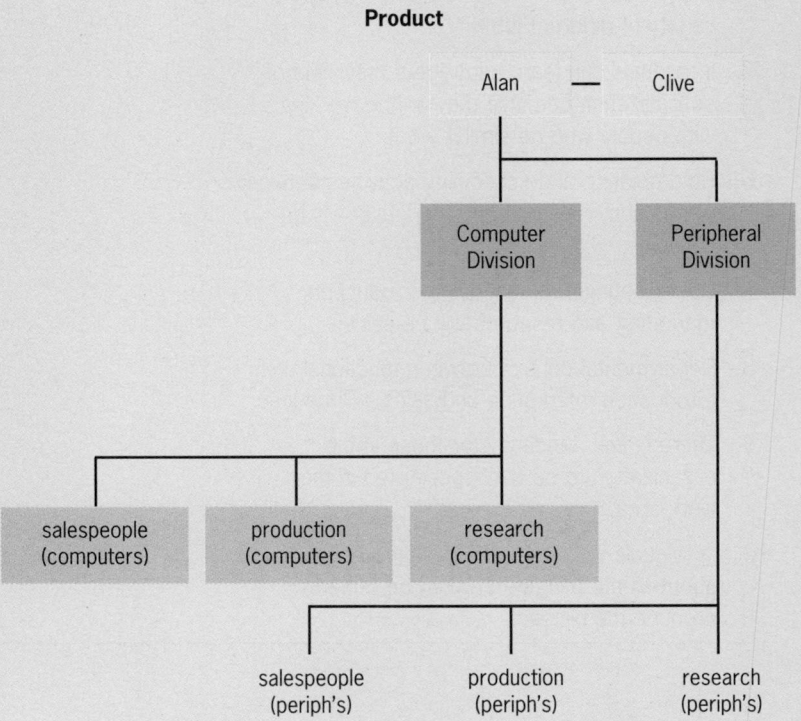

Big Chip Electronics Company: alternative organization structures
From H.L. Tosi and J.W. Young, *Management: Experiences and Demonstrations*, Irwin, London, 1982, pp. 75–8, using A. Filley, *The Complete Manager: What Works When*, Research Press, Champaign, Ill., 1978.

Read the description of organization characteristics, conditions or problems. For each description, place an X under the type of organization structure that fits the organization described.

Organizational characteristic	Functional	Product
1. Job specialization will be most extensively developed; that is, one person might specialize in correspondence and another in word processing.		
2. Individuals will perform a fairly broad range of activities in their job area. They will be less likely to become specialists.		
3. People will very likely be promoted in their field of specialization and will probably supervise several subordinates who do similar work.		
4. Managers of major departments are more likely to have subordinates who do a wide variety of different jobs.		
5. Individuals can learn a lot about their field of specialization because they will be working with people who do similar work.		
6. Co-ordinating and scheduling activities between production, research and marketing will be difficult.		
7. Co-ordinating and scheduling production, marketing and research will be easier.		
8. Departmental conflict between functional units (production, marketing and sales) will be less.		
9. There is less tendency for those in the organization to be over-specialized in their work area.		
10. Individuals will tend to learn a good deal more about all the things that must be done to produce the product.		

Key concepts

traditional authority	technological interdependence
charismatic authority	mediating technology
legitimate authority	long-linked technology
bureaucracy	intensive technology
rules	task variety
formalization	task analyzability
machine bureaucracy	environmental determinism
professional bureaucracy	environmental complexity
time span of responsibility	environmental dynamism
contingency approach	mechanistic structure
to organization structure	organic structure
technological determinism	differentiation
technical complexity	integration

Learning outcomes

When you have read this chapter, you should be able to define those key concepts in your own words, and you should be able to:

1. Distinguish between charismatic, traditional and legitimate forms of authority.
2. State the main characteristics of a bureaucratic organization structure as specified by Max Weber.
3. Summarize the approach and main ideas of the classical management school.
4. Identify the writers who comprise the early contingency approach and state their main individual contributions.
5. Discuss the strengths and weaknesses of early ideas on the design of organization structure and the practice of management.
6. Identify the influence of early organization design ideas on contemporary organizations.

Why study early organization design?

Organization design refers to the process by which managers select and manage various dimensions and components of organization structure so that it achieves their goals. Organization design affects what they and others do, and how they spend their time. Many textbooks mention early twentieth-century writings on organization design only briefly, before turning to explore team-based, network, virtual and similar contemporary developments in organization structure. This chapter will demonstrate that these early ideas, far from being either out of date

Traditional authority: authority that is based on the belief that the ruler has a natural right to rule. This right is either God-given or by descent. Kings and queens enjoy this type of authority.

Charismatic authority: authority that is based on the belief that the ruler has some special, unique virtue, either religious or heroic. Religious prophets, charismatic politicians and pop and film stars all wield this type of power.

or superseded, continue to exert a pervading influence on organizational life. In addition, their source and form exercise a similar, enduring influence on modern management and organizational thinking.

Max Weber's ideas on bureaucracy were developed at the start of the twentieth century and implemented from that time onwards. Today, the vast majority of employees in industrial societies around the world continue to work in bureaucratic organizations whose structures Weber would easily recognize. Moreover, they will continue to work under these structural arrangements for the foreseeable future. It is most likely that your own university is structured in this way. In contrast, at present, your chances of joining a so-called network or virtual organization are relatively slim. A significant feature of early management thought was its source and form. Little of it was based on systematic, empirical research. Max Weber was himself a historian and philosopher, while his contemporary, Henri Fayol, was a colliery manager. Fayol and his successors developed an approach to management knowledge which was based wholly on the experiences of mainly successful managers. Moreover, the form it took was of principles based on that experience. Organization structure designs conceived in the past, which may have been updated, continue to have a significant impact upon the present. This raises a number of questions:

- What are the benefits and costs of a bureaucratic organization structure?

- Why have the early structure arrangements remained so influential?

- In what ways has bureaucracy become modified?

- What does this imply for the nature of jobs?

Max Weber and bureaucracy

Max Weber
(1864–1920)

Legitimate authority: authority that is based on formal, written rules which have the force of law. The authority of present-day presidents, chief executive officers and cardinals is based on the position that they hold.

The interesting aspect of bureaucracy is its widespread adoption as an organizational form and its continuing popularity. The literal meaning of bureaucracy is 'rule by office or by officials', and it is primarily with the German sociologist and philosopher, Max Weber, that one associates this concept. His work on the topic was carried out at the turn of the twentieth century and stemmed from his interest in power and authority. In this textbook, the term 'power' is used to refer to the capacity of individuals to overcome resistance on the part of others, to exert their will, and to produce results consistent with their own interests and objectives. Weber studied societies in history and distinguished three different types of authority – **traditional**, **charismatic** and **legitimate authority**. Legitimate authority, which most concerns us here, carries with it position power.

Because of the process of rationalism in modern society (the belief that the human mind can discover innate laws which govern the workings of the universe), legitimate authority has predominated. Within a **bureaucracy**, we do what managers, civil servants and university lecturers tell us, not because we think that they have a natural right to do so, or because they possess some divine power, but because we acknowledge that their exercise of power is legitimated and hence supported by two factors:

- The demonstrably logical relevance of their requests, directions and instructions to us. Their commands must seem rational by being justified through their relevance to the tasks of the bureaucracy and, ultimately, to its objectives.

- A shared belief in the norms and rules of the bureaucracy which have

Bureaucracy: the legal-rational type of authority. It is a form of organization structure that is characterized by a specialization of labour, a specific authority hierarchy, a formal set of rules, and rigid promotion and selection criteria.

been arrived at rationally (not based on tradition or personal whim) and which possess a law-like character.

Weber believed that an organization based on legitimate authority would be more efficient than one based on either traditional or charismatic authority. This was because its continuity was related to formal structure and positions within it, rather than to a particular person who might leave or die. Not every formal organization will possess all the characteristics that Weber identified. However, the more of them that it has, the more closely it approximates to the 'ideal type' that he had in mind. Weber's description of bureaucracy is known as an 'ideal type'. It is not meant to describe any particular existing organization, but rather it represents a model or a checklist, against which to compare and assess real organizations.

Characteristics of Weberian bureaucracy

1. *Job specialization*: Jobs are broken down into simple, routine and well-defined tasks. Clear definitions of authority and responsibility are legitimated as official rules.

2. *Authority hierarchy*: Positions are in a hierarchy of authority, with each position under the authority of a higher one. There is a clear chain of command and workers clearly know to whom they are responsible.

3. *Employment and career:* All personnel are selected and promoted on the basis of their technical qualifications and offered a full-time career.

4. *Recording*: Administrative acts and decisions are recorded in writing. Record keeping provides an organizational memory and continuity over time.

5. *Rules and procedures:* All employees are subject to rules and procedures that ensure reliable, predictable behaviour.

6. *Impersonality:* Procedures and rules are impersonal, and apply to managerial and non-managerial employees alike.

Based on Max Weber, *The Theory of Social and Economic Organizations*, Trans. and ed. A.M. Henderson and T. Parsons, Oxford University Press, Oxford, 1947, pp. 328–37.

"I'd like to think of you as a person, David, but it's my job to think of you as personnel."

Weber used the term 'bureaucracy' to describe a particular type of organization structure and was concerned with how work was divided, co-ordinated and controlled. It was a structure that was both impersonal and rational. Whereas in the past, authority had been based on nepotism, whim or fancy, in bureaucratic organizations it was based on rational principles. For this reason, it offered the possibility of being the most efficient ever, in comparison with what had preceded it. Bureaucracy for him was a form of organization which emphasized speed, precision, regulation, clarity, reliability and efficiency. This was achieved through creating a fixed division of tasks, imposing detailed rules, regulations and procedures, and monitoring through hierarchical supervision.

Many aspects of Weber's model reflected the organizational circumstances at the time in which he was writing. In the early twentieth century, establishing employment relationships on the basis of professional selection and creating continuity of employment and career structures were important when the methods commonly used at the time were amateur, personal and haphazard. Because they were adopted so widely, so long ago, it is difficult to believe that there was a time when organizations did not keep detailed written records.

Ford's pre-1979 bureaucracy

In their investigation of managers' experiences of working for Ford of Europe, Starkey and McKinlay vividly contrast that company's pre-1979, ideal type bureaucratic organization with its post-1980 'After Japan' organization, which introduced employee involvement and participation. Historically, prior to 1979, Ford had been an archetypal 'machine bureaucracy', which was the classic, institutional form of twentieth-century big business. The design of its management structure mirrored its assembly lines, it was specialized, hierarchical and rigidly controlled. Following a 1945 reorganization modelled on General Motors, a managerial bureaucracy was created in which managers became the cogs in Ford's machine. Just like the specialized workers down on the assembly line, Ford's managers were operators of company procedures. A British systems manager reported:

> When I joined the company, it was full of empty boxes and you could put anybody with any intelligence at all in any one of those boxes, give him a statement of functions, the relevant procedure manuals, and he could read through these and do the job. The whole company was structured that way. There were a large number of people involved in writing policy manuals to make sure it was all up to date.

The same Ford structure, systems, philosophy and culture were so strong that managers could be rotated around Ford plants all over the world. The boxes on the organization chart not only provided certainty of task and responsibility, but also meant it was possible to know exactly who to blame if there was a problem. It was a highly controlled environment in which the relationships between the functions, especially between sales and manufacturing, became aggressive and confrontational. The Fordist bureaucracy was developed by Robert McNamara and was designed to ensure that neither divisional nor functional managers had access to information or made decisions that could challenge the hegemony of the Detroit headquarters.

This pre-1979, ideal-type 'machine bureaucracy' was perfectly suited to a stable environment but represented a major handicap in a more dynamic market setting. What were earlier perceived as the cardinal virtues of Ford's managerial bureaucracy came later to be understood as its dysfunctions. One manager reported: 'The clarity of structure was terrific – the rigidity of it was terrible.' The exhaustive 'checks and balances' were redefined as counterproductive control mechanisms. As one manager put it: 'There were so many rules and regulations that you spent half your time administering routines rather than managing. Innovation was pointless. Managers knew that bureaucracy would review the hell out of any initiative anyway.'

Ford's traditional bureaucracy came to be considered too slow and inflexible for a dynamic market environment over which the corporation had little control. The traditional Ford approach had been to manage *through* hierarchical levels and tasks. It changed to managing *across* levels and projects. It had to give up its enormous bureaucracy based on the fetish that it had to police everything.

Based on Ken Starkey and Alan McKinley, 'Managing for Ford', *Sociology*, vol. 28, no. 4, 1994, p. 4.

The strength of bureaucracy lay in its standardization. Employee behaviour was controlled and made predictable. In Weber's conception, this was achieved not through time-and-motion study, but through the application of rules, regulations and procedures. Bureaucratic organizations have a reasonably consistent set of goals and preferences. They devote few resources to time-consuming information searches or the analysis of current activities to check if these are meeting stated goals. Instead, they rely on rules, tradition, precedent and standard operating procedures. Little time is spent on decision-making since decisions follow from the established routines, and few action alternatives are considered. The ideological emphasis is on stability, fairness and predictability (Pfeffer, 1981). Weber was struck by how the bureaucratic structure of a company routinized the processes of its administration, in a way similar to how a machine routinized production. Weber's ideas developed independently, but they neatly complement those of Frederick Taylor. While Taylor focused on the worker on the shop floor, Weber's interest lay in a body of knowledge, administrative rules and organization hierarchy, progressing from the top of the organization downwards. Nevertheless, Weber would have approved of the disciplining, rational conditioning and training of workers proposed by Taylor.

In modern usage, bureaucracy has acquired a pejorative meaning among the public and the media: for example, when people come up against red tape and obstructiveness in any aspect of organizational life. Weber's view was in direct opposition to this. For him, bureaucracy was the most efficient form of social organization precisely because it was so coldly logical and did not allow personal relations and feelings to get in the way of achieving goals. On the one hand, rules and other bureaucratic procedures provided a standard way of dealing with employees, avoiding favouritism and personal bias. Everyone knows what the rules are and receives equal treatment. On the other hand, there is frustration at having to follow what appear to be seemingly illogical rules, and thereby experience delays. This change in meaning has occurred because the principles of bureaucracy, originally designed to maximize efficiency, also resulted in inefficiencies. These negative aspects, costs or 'dyfunctions' of bureaucracy were the focus of debates in both organization behaviour and bureaucracy during the 1950s and 1960s (Merton, 1940; Gouldner, 1954; Blau, 1966).

Research conducted during the 1960s and 1970s recognized that bureaucracy should be treated as a continuum. Thus the question changed from whether or not an organization was a bureaucracy to one that asked to what degree any given organization was 'bureaucratized'. For example, the Aston studies (Pugh and Hickson, 1976; Pugh and Hinings, 1976; Pugh and Payne, 1977; Hickson and McMillan, 1981) measured the bureaucracy of companies on a number of dimensions, as shown in table 15.1. Using these criteria, the Aston studies distinguished three types of bureaucratic structure:

■ *Full bureaucracies*, which approximated to Weber's ideal type. These tended to be rare and were found in central government.

Table 15.1: Bureaucratic dimensions of an organization

Specialization	To what degree are tasks subdivided into separate jobs?
Formalization	Are there laid-down standard rules, standards and procedures?
Standardization of practices	Are there standardized practices: for example, employment, discipline?
Centralization	To what extent is the authority to make decisions located at the top of the management hierarchy?
Configuration	What is the 'shape' of the organization's structure measured by: managers' chain of command – long or short? managers' span of control – wide or narrow? number of specialized support staff – many or few?

- *Workflow bureaucracies*, which combined tight structuring of manufacturing with more decentralized authority.

- *Personnel bureaucracies*, which combined employment relationships which were bureaucratized with lower structuring of activities, allowing more personal forms of control. These were to be found in small branch plants and parts of local government.

global village a weekly posting from cyberspace

Bureaucratium ▶

Scientists have discovered the heaviest element known to science. This startling new discovery has been tentatively named Bureaucratium Bm.

This new element has no protons or electrons, thus having an atomic number of 0. It does, however, have 1 neutron, 125 assistant neutrons, 75 vice-neutrons and 111 assistant vice-neutrons, giving it an atomic mass of 312.

These 312 particles are held together by a force called morons, and are surrounded by vast quantities of lepton-like particles called peons.

Since it has no electrons, Bureaucratium is inert. However, it can be detected as it impedes every reaction with which it comes into contact. According to the discoverers, a minute amount of Bureaucratium causes one reaction to take more than four days to complete when it would normally take less than a second.

Bureaucratium has a normal half-life of approximately three years; it does not decay but instead undergoes a reorganisation in which a portion of the assistant neutrons, vice-neutrons, and assistant vice-neutrons exchange places. In fact, a Bureaucratium sample's mass will actually increase over time, since with each reorganisation some of the morons inevitably become neutrons, forming new isotopes.

This characteristic of moron promotion leads some scientists to speculate that bureaucratium is spontaneously formed whenever morons reach a certain quantity in concentration. This hypothetical quantity is referred to as the "Critical Morass".

● From: robert.nel@entegria.com. If you have a favourite global, please e-mail it to **global.village@the-times.co.uk**

Source: The Times 7.10.2000

Organizational rules

Rules: procedures or obligations that are explicitly stated and written down in organization manuals.

A defining characteristic of every bureaucratic structure are its **rules**. From the 1930s, senior managements in large organizations increasingly adopted systems of bureaucratic (rule-governed) control. These complemented the control exercised through machinery and replaced those exercised through supervisor commands. Rules serve to regulate and control what individuals do and, to the extent that employees comply with company rules, they can ensure the predictability of human behaviour within organizations. Both parties benefited. For employees, rational and fair rules avoided managers' personal bias. This was true despite the fact that the rules were devised and policed by management, who could relax or ignore them at their discretion. Unions used rules to restrict the arbitrary power of employers, and demarcation rules protected jobs. Although rules can cause frustration to employees, they also reduce role ambiguity and offer them high organizational identification, and low self-estrangement.

Management also benefits from rules, using them to co-ordinate the activities of different employees and to establish conformity among employees. **Formalization** refers to the degree to which an organization possesses rules. It can be high or low. Bureaucratic structures created job hierarchies with numerous job titles, each with its own pay rate. Elaborate formal rules, and apparently 'objective' criteria, provided a basis for evaluating employee performance and determining rewards, allowing results to be traced back to the individual employee. This was all part of management's attempt to 'routinize' tasks which, together with the use of forecasting, planning, creating buffer stocks and so on, sought to remove the uncertainties involved in dealing with its environment. Provided that that environment was stable and unchanging, it was an effective strategy.

> **Formalization**: the degree to which formal procedures and rules exist and are used within an organization.

"I was just going to say, 'Well, I don't make the rules.' But, of course, I do make the rules."

Source: © The New Yorker Collection 1986 Leo Callum from cartoonbank.com. All rights reserved.

Pyramid working

In modern discussions, an organizational structure is often both referred to and shown as a pyramid. The ancient Egyptians, who built the original pyramids, relied neither on complex machines nor animals for any of their labour. To build such monumental structures they needed a highly organized workforce. From tomb inscriptions and labourers' instructions, researchers can draw a modern organizational chart of these ancient workers. 'Every project, like a pyramid, had a crew of workers', explains Ann Roth, an Egyptologist who has studied groups of workers in detail. 'And each group was responsible for one part of the pyramid complex. There was one group for building the interior granite roofs, and separate groups for raising the chamber walls. Each crew of workers was divided into four or five smaller units which Egyptologist call *phyles* (after the Greek for 'tribe'). Each phyle carried a name such as 'Great One' or 'Green One'. The phyles too were broken up into forces of 10 or 20 men, and these had names like 'Endurance' and 'Perfection'.'

Source: Ancient Art and Architecture Collection Ltd.

They had to be very organized to build these things as they did. To construct a pyramid in a time period of twenty years, the workers had to set a stone in place every two minutes, a phenomenal pace! To keep that kind of workforce functioning at top speed, a highly developed support system was also needed to feed and house the workers. Tombs have been found bearing the titles of middle- and senior-level managers, which demonstrates the tight organization of the ancient Egyptian workforce. These administrators had to co-ordinate the arrival of rotating teams of labourers and shipments of supplies from all over Egypt. What really blossomed in the fourth dynasty was not the realization of how to work large blocks of stone, but rather the discovery of how to organize a large labour force. Raising the pyramids was as much a feat of organization as of engineering.

Based on Virginia Morell, 'The pyramid builders', *National Geographic*, November 2001, pp. 78–99.

Stop and Criticize	Think of some of the rules that you have encountered in organizations to which you currently belong or used to belong. How effective are they in directing the behaviour of individuals? What problems do they cause, and what advantages did they offer, and for whom?

Strengths and weaknesses of bureaucratic organization structures

The writers who are critical of bureaucracy have argued that the challenge for management is to create work environments in which employees have the opportunity to grow and to mature as individuals. In their view, this means moving away from bureaucratic organization forms and towards some other type of organization design. They say that in the twenty-first century the bureaucratic organization will be too expensive to maintain, will be incapable of responding sufficiently quickly to change, and will not be using the innovative resources of its members. Failure to achieve profit targets will result in company collapse and large-scale redundancies. Their argument is that now that the slimming down has been completed in many companies, the new-look, leaner organizations are experimenting with radically different forms of structures which overcome the dysfunctions of bureaucracy.

Table 15.2: Positive and negative consequences of a bureaucracy

Characteristic	Positive consequences	Negative consequences	
		For the individual	**For the organization**
1. Job specialization	Produces efficient, repetitive working	Over specialization of employees' skills and knowledge prevents them recognizing or caring about problems not in their domain	Inhibits rotation and hence flexible use of personnel, and thus can reduce overall productivity
2. Authority hierarchy	Clarifies who is in command	Prevents employees contributing to decisions	Allows errors to be hidden
3. Employment and career	Most appropriate person appointed to a position	Can restrict the psychological growth of the individual in their job	Individuals throughout the company are promoted to their level of incompetence
4. Recording	Creates an organization history that is not dependent on individual memory	Employees come to see record-keeping as an end in itself rather than a means to an end	Recorded precedents stifle attempts at company innovation Inhibits flexibility, adaptability and responsiveness
5. Rules and procedures	Employees know what is expected of them	Introduces delays; stifles initiative and creativity	Leads to individual and sub-unit goals replacing organization objectives; rules define *minimum* levels of acceptable performance
6. Impersonality	Fosters efficiency, reduces bias	Dehumanizes those it purports to serve – officials prevented from responding to unique features of clients who are treated as standard cases	Creates a climate of alienation through the firm as employees come to see themselves as small cogs in a wheel

In contrast, there are other writers who are supportive of bureaucratic organization structures, in part or in whole. They note that most large organizations possess many of the features of Weber's model, and that their longevity and continued existence confirms that they can achieve an acceptable level of efficiency. In contrast, they cite example of companies which have not adopted bureaucratic features and have failed. There is a prevailing view that organizations should be structured on the basis of rationality. This means that organization designers should accept that a hierarchical structure is more likely to produce rational decisions and better control within the organization than any other structure of authority (for example, one based on teams).

Wot, *more* organization hierarchy?

Adrian Furnham commented on one aspect of the continuing trend to de-bureaucratization, that of reorganizing structures to reduce the number of levels in hierarchies and thus create flatter organization structures. While supposedly aimed at securing the benefits of improved customer service, faster communication, better quality inspection and lower personnel costs, this strategy also resulted in many negative consequences both for the organization and for its employees. This was particularly so when the organization concerned did not know the optimum number of hierarchical levels that it should have. Removing levels and making the managers within them redundant has a number of consequences.

First, the number of duties to be performed by each of the surviving managers is necessarily increased, as is their span of control. With more to do and an increased number of subordinates to manage, these managers communicate less and more slowly with each one. Second, there is a particular problem in providing regular, two-way, manager–subordinate communication that is sufficiently specific, personalized and regular to allow the correction of errors and to motivate staff.

Furnham challenges the view that the percentage of managers grows in proportion to the increase in the size of the company. Indeed, by using standard procedures and systems that are relevant and supported by new technology, managers save themselves time and are able to supervise more people, while delegating more specialized work to support staff. In consequence, as organizations grow their hierarchies actually become more efficient and flatter, he claims. A company of 800 employees may thus have the same number of personnel staff as one of 8,000.

Furnham says that there are limits to which technology can replace middle managers who have been made redundant. Technology deals well with routine, rule-based work but is inappropriate for tasks that possess an innovative, strategic or political dimension. He stresses the difference between over-manning and optimal manning. In his view, a hierarchy is actually a good way to control work processes. This is because it defines who is responsible to whom for what. It encourages specialization throughout the entire organization, allowing those who possess the most knowledge and skill to perform the task. Top management level and shop-floor level decision-making have very different time frames, needs and objectives, and are unlikely to be performed well by a single individual. Ineffective decision-making may be due more to poor selection of managers than to an inappropriate organization structure.

Furnham contends that the complexity of the size of an organization and the complexity of the work performed within it determines the number of levels in any hierarchy. Thus, if a company's work needs to be closely supervised or cannot be made routine, or if the employees performing it are physically distanced, then closer supervision, and hence a narrower span of control and a taller hierarchy, will be necessary (and vice versa). Many organizations which have made many of their middle managers redundant after business process re-engineering (BPR) exercises have found that they have had to rehire many of them as consultants at twice their pay and half their responsibility.

Based on Adrian Furnham, 'Anti-hierarchy gurus fall flat on their faces', *Daily Telegraph*, 'Appointments Section', 1 April 1999, p. A3.

Machine bureaucracy: a type of organization which possesses all the bureaucratic characteristics. The important decisions are made at the top, while at the bottom standardized procedures are used to exercise control.

'Post-industrial' does not necessarily mean 'post-bureaucratic'. Bureaucracy has adapted and survived. In the original **machine bureaucracy**, control was exercised through rules, technology and the supervisor's command. This made the behaviour of people within large, complex organizations highly predictable. Since that time, environmental conditions have changed and authority has increasingly become based on knowledge. In response, **professional bureaucracy** has developed. Rational discipline has become internalized by professional employees like teachers, doctors, social workers, accountants and similar groups, through a

Professional bureaucracy: a type of organization which possesses all the bureaucratic characteristics. In addition, there are few levels between the strategic apex and the operating staff, control of which is achieved through professional indoctrination.

process of socialization, rather than being imposed externally. Thus, self-regulation through internalized professional standards has replaced external rules and controls or authority from above.

Professional bureaucracies modify the principle of centralized control and thus allow their staff a greater autonomy. This is appropriate for working in relatively stable conditions in which tasks are relatively complicated. Universities and hospitals are examples of professional bureaucracies whose staff possess key skills and abilities. Until recently in the UK, these occupational groups enjoyed a large degree of freedom and discretion in how they did their work. However, professional staff in both types of organization are being increasing monitored and subjected to 'quality control and assurance' procedures. These have been instituted by government and have been implemented by senior managements.

All over in a flash

The first thing the three technicians pouring the uranium oxide solution into a precipitation tank at Tokaimura on September 30, 1999 noticed was a blue flash. Then they began to experience waves of nausea and some difficulty in breathing. What they did not realize was that they had accidentally dumped in more than six times as much fissile uranium as they had meant to, and had therefore triggered a runaway chain reaction. . . . In one sense, they were lucky. They poured in 16kg of the solution. Had they poured in 40kg, they could have built themselves an amateur nuclear bomb. (*The Economist*, 1999)

Popular management and media writers consistently condemn the effects of bureaucracy, calling instead for employees to use their initiative, not be bound by rules, to look for the 'bigger picture', avoid rigid, programmed behaviour, etc. However, the moment that an accident occurs, be it rail, road, aircraft, space or, as in this case, nuclear, the search is on for those who failed to adhere strictly to the rules and procedures that had been set down. A consideration of the main features of bureaucracy illustrates that it was precisely such occurrences that this form of organization structure sought to anticipate and avoid. In the case of the uranium-processing plant in Tokaimura, Japan, initial reports identified four causes of the accident:

1. The company had illegally compiled a manual that encouraged workers to cut corners in order to reduce costs. Instead of using the tower, they mixed the material by hand.

2. The workers making the fuel lacked the knowledge and experience to do it correctly and safely.

3. Because the workers were allowed to bypass the time-consuming mixing process in the tower, with its automatic controls for preventing such things happening, they were free to dump their material into a vessel that was not designed to take it. This further aggravated the problem.

4. The company procedure did not anticipate the possibility of such an accident occurring, and hence lacked any containment facility.

Two of the three workers inside the plant received more than the lethal dose of seven sieverts (a sievert is the unit that measures the intensity of radiation's impact on the body). One of them has since died. A further 46 employees were exposed to radiation as they sought to contain the problem. The International Atomic Energy Agency classified the accident in Tokaimura as level four on a seven-point scale, making it the world's most serious since the level-seven disaster at Chernobyl in the Ukraine in 1986.

Based on *The Economist*, 'All over in a flash', 9 October 1999, p. 142; *The Economist*, 'The land of disappointments', 4 March 2000, pp. 115–17.

Elliot Jaques
(b. 1917)

Elliot Jaques and the time span of responsibility

Elliot Jaques (1990) is an uncompromising supporter of bureaucracy who rejects the current fashion for teams and teamworking. The essence of bureaucracy is the hierarchically stratified employment system in which employees are accountable to their managers for the work that they do. He agrees with the need to release employee energy and improve morale in order to increase productivity. However, he rejects the fashionable team-based organization designs (for example, autonomous work teams) as neither feasible nor necessary, and doomed to failure. He contends that bureaucracy is the only viable structural form for a large organization.

For him, the managerial hierarchy is 'the most efficient, hardiest, and in fact the most natural structure ever devised for large organizations' (Jaques, 1990, p. 127). He contends that the admitted deficiencies of hierarchy and the 'flight to groups' are not due to any inherent deficiency in the bureaucratic model itself, but to the fact that it has been poorly understood and badly applied. That failure stems from a misunderstanding of how a managerial hierarchy functions, how it relates to the complexities of work and how it can be used to encourage employee talent and stimulate their energy. Hierarchies in organizations should be neither tall nor flat, but requisite. He suggests that there is an optimum number of hierarchical levels for every organization (Jaques, 1989).

Time span of responsibility: the time period for which an individual's decisions can commit an organization.

To explain this thinking, he uses the concept of the **time span of responsibility**. This refers to the time period for which an individual's decisions can commit an organization. The assembly-line operator who bolts on wheels commits the organization over a period of seconds or minutes; the supervisor drawing up rosters commits the organization for a period of days or weeks; materials acquisition people potentially commit the organization to contracts lasting for months up to a year; a chief executive can commit an organization to a strategy for five to ten years (Jaques, 1976, 1982). This can be related to the time interval in which supervisors check subordinates; middle managers check supervisors; senior management checks the material acquisitions department; and the board of directors checks the chief executive's performance. For Jaques, the key to making bureaucracy efficient is ensuring a match between a manager's responsibility and the time span for their position in the hierarchy.

Jaques found that efficient bureaucracies operated with seven basic steps or strata of increasing time-spans. These corresponded with levels of thinking capability, from concrete thinking at the bottom to abstract thinking and envisioning at the top. The inefficiencies of bureaucracy (for example, duplication) stemmed

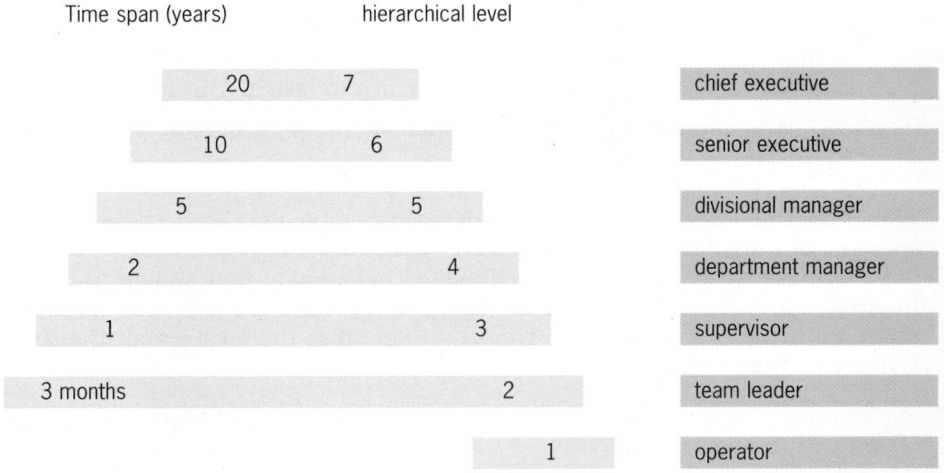

Figure 15.1: Elliot Jaques' time span of responsibility

from the insertion of additional, unnecessary levels (for example, for political purposes), to accommodate extra pay bands or to provide career ladder steps. The seven layers with their associated time spans is shown in figure 15.1.

The creative, motivational aspect of bureaucratic organization occurred when employees worked at a hierarchical level that corresponded to their current time-span capacity but which allowed them to progress to their maximum time-span capacity. Jaques extended his thinking on the seven-strata idea in two directions – assessing what employees should do (job evaluation) and how much they should be paid to do it (financial remuneration) (Jaques, 1956). Jaques offered something unusual in organizational behaviour – a theory that links organizations and individuals. It has far-reaching implications for grading and payment systems, organization structuring, work organization and programming, staff training and development, and decision-making.

Stop and Criticize	A company about to embark on a restructuring programme (possibly including the use of teamworking) has asked you to evaluate Jaques' ideas before it goes ahead with its changes. Assess the strengths and weaknesses of his ideas for senior management.

Henri Fayol and classical management theory

Henri Fayol
(1841–1925)

Classical management theory resembles bureaucracy even though it originated in France in the early twentieth century with the work of Henri Fayol. Fayol qualified as a mining engineer in 1860, after which he joined the Commentary-Fourchambault combine, a company in which he was to spend his entire working life. In 1866, he became manager of the Commentary collieries and in 1888, at the age of 47, he was appointed to the general manager position at a time when the financial position of the company was critical. By the time he retired in 1918, he had established financial stability in the organization. Fayol's list of managerial activities provides a definition of management. Indeed, he is credited with 'inventing' management: that is, distinguishing it as a separate activity, and defining its constituent elements. Interestingly, the word 'management' is not translatable into all languages, nor does the concept exist in all cultures. Managing of course occurs, but is not always treated as anything special or separate.

It was in 1916, the year before Frederick Taylor died, that Fayol's book, *General and Industrial Administration*, was published (see also Gray, 1987). In it, Fayol put down in a systematic form the experience that he had gained while managing a large organization. He stressed methods rather than personalities, seeking to present the former in a coherent and relevant scheme. This formed his theory of

Table 15.3: Fayol's six managerial activities

Forecasting	Predicting what will happen in the future
Planning	Devising a course of action to meet that expected demand
Organizing	Mobilizing materials and resources by allocating separate tasks to different departments, units and individuals
Commanding	Providing direction to employees, now more commonly refereed to as *directing* or *motivating*
Co-ordinating	Making sure that activities and resources are working well together towards the common goal
Controlling	Monitoring progress to ensure that plans are being carried out properly

organization. While Taylor focused on the worker on the shop floor – a bottom-up approach – Fayol began from the top of the hierarchy and moved downwards. However, like Taylor, he too believed that a manager's work could be reviewed objectively, analyzed and treated as a technical process which was subject to certain definite principles which could be taught. Fayol's list of management activities, originally developed some eighty years ago, remains broadly intact to this day. Only minor modifications have been made to the labels that he used. His six managerial activities are listed in table 15.3.

The six management activities are interrelated. For example, a company management team begins by *forecasting* the demand for its product: for example, steel wire. It requires a sales forecast and will use market research to develop one. Once it is clear that there is a market for the product, the next activity, *planning*, will take place. For Fayol, planning involved 'making a programme of action to achieve an objective'. He collectively referred to the two activities, forecasting and planning, as *purveyance*. Because they are so closely related, some authors and books treat them as a single management activity.

Having made the plan, the third activity to be performed is *organizing*. This involves bringing together the money, materials and people needed to achieve the objective. It also involves breaking down the main task into smaller pieces and distributing them to different people. In a company structured along functional lines (accounting, production, marketing), the organizing of people may involve creating a special, temporary project team, consisting of members from the different functions. This is the matrix structure that was introduced in chapter 14.

Fayol used the word '*commanding*' to describe his fourth management activity. It has been defined as 'influencing others towards the accomplishment of organizational goals'. We would now refer to it as either *directing* or *motivating*. Whichever term is chosen, performing this activity involves the manager ensuring that employees give of their best. To do this, managers must possess a knowledge of both the tasks to be done and the people who are to do them. This management activity is mainly, although not exclusively, performed in a face-to-face situation.

Earlier, organizing involved distributing task elements to various individuals. Now those separate elements have to be brought together. This represents the *co-ordinating* activity. Co-ordination can be achieved through memos, meetings and personal contacts between the people carrying out their unique activities. The sixth and final activity of managers is *controlling*. This involves monitoring how the objectives set out in the plan are being achieved, with respect to the limitations of time and budget that were imposed. Any deviations are identified and action is taken to rectify them. It may be that the original plan will have to be amended. Although the six managerial activities have been presented as a sequence, in reality they occur simultaneously in a company. However, forecasting and planning tend to be primary. There are also loops when original plans have to be changed because certain resources are found to be unavailable (when organizing) or when cost overruns are discovered (through controlling).

Fayol's second major contribution was to identify fourteen 'principles of management'. They included division of work, authority, discipline, unity of command, scalar principle, unity of direction, interest subordination, remuneration, centralization, order, equity of treatment, stability of employment, opportunity for initiative and *esprit de corps*. These were not based on any systematic research but on his personal reflections and his experience of management. The principles continue to be used today. They are referred to by chief executives as 'best practice'. They contain rules and guidelines, but most are devoid of any empirical research backing.

Fayol's ideas are referred to as *classical management theory* (also dubbed *scientific administration*.) Many felt that these mirrored, at the macro-organizational level, what scientific management offered at the micro-organization level. Classical management considered that there is one best organization structure which would suit all organizations, irrespective of their size, technology, environment or employees. This structure was based on the application of certain key principles that reflected the 'logic of efficiency', which stressed:

- functional division of work;

- hierarchical relationships;

- bureaucratic forms of control;

- narrow supervisory span;

- closely prescribed roles.

Stop and Criticize

What are the advantages and disadvantages of having management principles based on the experience of successful managers?

Criticism of classical management

When considering classical management theory, it is important to locate it in its historical content. The managers of the period were dealing with larger, more complex organizations than had existed hitherto. At the beginning of the twentieth century many new companies developed. They employed vast numbers of people, had numerous plants and employed new technologies. All of this needed co-ordinating. With no model or experience to fall back on, those who managed these organizations had no choice but to develop their own principles and theories as to what to do to run them well. Inevitably these principles were grounded in their day-to-day experience of managing, and owed much to the models offered by military, religious and governmental organizations. Over the years, various writers have criticized Fayol's principles (March and Simon, 1958; Child, 1969; Peters and Waterman, 1982; Thomas, 2002). Their criticisms include the following:

- misleadingly proposed a single, standardized organizational model as the optimum one;

- promoted a militaristic, mechanistic organization, which stressed discipline, command, order, subordinates and *esprit de corps*;

- overlooked the negative consequences of tight control and narrow task specialization which can demotivate employees and hinder efficiency;

- over-emphasized an organization's formal structure, while neglecting processes such as decision-making and communication;

- underestimated the complexity of organizations;

- were based on unreliable personal knowledge rather than systematic research evidence;

- lacked a concern with the interaction between people;

- underestimated the effects of conflict;

- underestimated the capacity of individual workers to process information;

- misunderstood how people thought;

- were overrated in that there was no one best way of organizing a company.

Gareth Morgan (1989) presents a continuum of different organization structural forms, ranging from a bureaucratic one possessing classical features at one extreme, to a flexible, organic network at the other (see figure 15.2). He stated that a bureaucracy could probably evolve from numbers 1 to 3, and perhaps even number 4, but for an organization to move to 5 or 6 would require a major revolution. Such a transformation would require not only a structural change, but also a cultural and a political one. If achieved, it would mean a loss of its bureaucratic features. Why do the bureaucratic-classical structural features described in this chapter continue to be a feature of the majority of large companies to the present day? Stephen Robbins (1990) suggested seven reasons to account for their continued existence.

1. *Success*: For the most part, over the last 100 years, irrespective of technology, environment and people, and irrespective of whether it has been a manufacturing, medical, educational, commercial or military organization, it has worked.

2. *Large size*: Successful organizations survive and grow large, and the bureaucratic form is most efficient with large size.

3. *Natural selection favours bureaucracy*: Bureaucracy's natural features, the six identified at the start of this chapter, are inherently more efficient than any others, and thus allow the organization to compete more effectively.

4. *Static social values*: The argument is that Western values favour order and regimentation, and bureaucracy is consistent with such values. People are goal-oriented and comfortable with authoritarian structures. For example, workers prefer clearly defined job responsibilities.

5. *Environmental turbulence is exaggerated*: The changes currently being experienced may be no more dynamic than those at other times in history. Management strategies can also reduce uncertainty in the environment.

6. *Emergence of professional bureaucracy*: Bureaucracy has shown its ability to adjust to the knowledge revolution by modifying itself. The goal of standardization has been achieved in a different way among professional employees.

7. *Bureaucracy maintains control*: Bureaucracy provides a high level of standardization, coupled with centralized power, which is desired by those in command. For this reason senior managers who control large organizations favour this organization design.

In modern organizations, power and authority continue to lie with those at the top. Robbins' seventh reason to explain the appeal of bureaucratic structures among senior management is that it centralizes power in their hands, which appeals to them. Those people at the bottom of the hierarchy are strictly controlled by those above them. In the end, the decision to replace bureaucracy may be a political one.

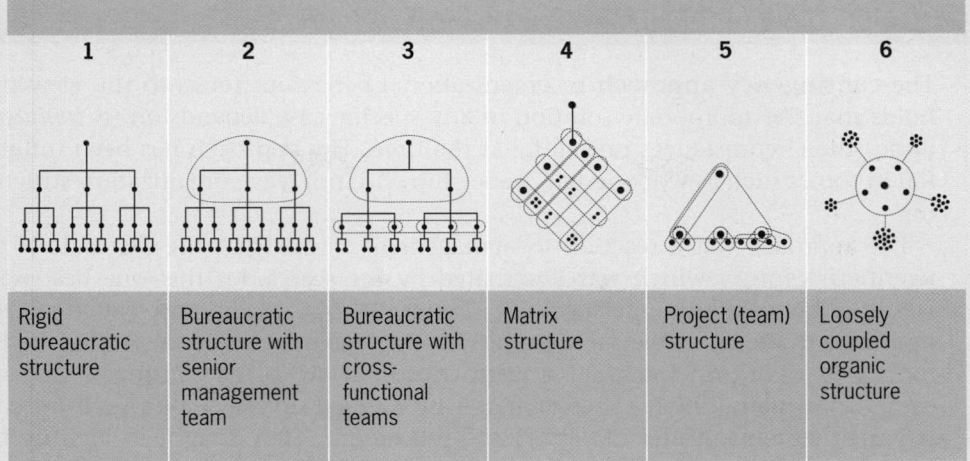

1	2	3	4	5	6
Rigid bureaucratic structure	Bureaucratic structure with senior management team	Bureaucratic structure with cross-functional teams	Matrix structure	Project (team) structure	Loosely coupled organic structure

Figure 15.2: Types of organization structure
From Gareth Morgan, *Creative Organization Theory*, p. 66. Copyright © 1989. Reprinted by permission of Sage Publications, Inc.

Rigid bureaucratic structure

This is Weber's classic bureaucratic structure. The organization operates in a very stable environment. Its structure is pyramid-shaped and is under the control of a single chief executive. Since all important principles have been codified and since every contingency is understood and has been anticipated, it is unnecessary for the executive to hold meetings.

Bureaucratic structure with senior management team

The environment is generating novel problems which cannot be anticipated and for which responses cannot be codified. The chief executives creates a management team of departmental heads who meet regularly to deal with non-routine problems. Department heads have authority over their areas of responsibility.

Bureaucratic structure with cross-functional teams

For problems requiring an interdepartmental view, a team is assembled consisting of lower-level staff from different departments. Members attend discussions as departmental representatives. They give the 'departmental view', report back on developments to their department head, delegate problems and information up to that person and receive decisions down. They operate as a less rigid bureaucracy.

Matrix structure

This is the matrix structure described in chapter 14. It attaches as much importance to functional departments, such as marketing and production, as to projects or customer groups. It offers the benefits previously discussed.

Project team structure

In this design, the majority of the organization's core activities are tackled through project teams. If functional departments do exist, they play a background role. The task consists of completing a series of projects, and the vehicle for task achievement is the team. These teams are given the freedom to manage themselves within the strategic parameters defined by senior management. The organization possesses more of the features of a network of interaction than of a bureaucratic structure.

Loosely coupled organic structure

A small core staff represent the organization and set its strategic direction. They form its 'inside' centre and sustain a network which is joined to others located 'outside'. They use contracting to get key operational activities performed. This network of firms is held together by its current product or service. The firm is really an open-ended system of firms, ideas and activities. It lacks a clear organization structure and a definable boundary, making it difficult to determine what or who is inside or outside.

Contingency approach

Contingency approach to organization structure: a perspective which argues that an organization, to be effective, must adjust its structure in a manner consistent with the main type of technology it uses, the environment within which it operates, its size and other contextual factors.

The **contingency approach** in organizational behaviour refers to the view that holds that the appropriate solution in any specific case depends on (is *contingent* upon) the circumstances prevailing at the time. The approach has been influential in topics such as work design, leadership and, not least, organization structuring.

The approach was a reaction to management thinking in the first half of the twentieth century which was dominated by the search for the 'one best way'. Despite their differing perspectives, Taylor, Weber, Mayo and Fayol all recommended single, universal solutions to management problems, often in the form of laws or principles. Subsequent contributions to the contingency school came from many different researchers who studied diverse topics such as wage payment systems, leadership styles and job design. They sought to identify the kinds of situation in which particular organizational arrangements and management practices appeared to be most effective. Applied to structuring, the contingency approach recommends matching an organization's structure to the contingencies that it faces. Richard Whittington (2002) listed five key contingencies:

Technology	Type of production process used by the organization (Woodward, 1965; Thompson, 1967; Perrow, 1970)
Environment	Degree of change in the environment within which the organization exists (Burns and Stalker, 1961/1994; Lawrence and Lorsch, 1967)
Size	Number of employees in the organization or volume of sales (Pugh and Hickson, 1976; Greiner, 1998)
Diversification	Number of different businesses which an organization runs (Chandler, 1962)
Internationalization	Number of different countries in which an organization operates (Stopford and Wells, 1972)

The contingency approach holds that organizational success will be secured when a company achieves a match between its situation, its corporate strategy and its organization structure. Thus, the bureaucratic structure described earlier in this chapter is said to be appropriate for (matches) a stable environment, while a turbulent environment requires a more flexible or organic structure. A few other aspects of the contingency approach distinguish it from perspectives to be considered in the next chapter:

■ it operates on a cause-and-effect basis (for example, '*if* your technology, environment, size, history or employees are like this, *then* your structure should be that');

■ the causal connections are held to run in one direction (for example, one type of environment will require a particular organization structure);

■ it assumes that approximately the same cause will have approximately the same effect (for example, it does not envisage a situation in which a small difference between two causes can escalate to cause radically different outcomes for a company);

■ it assumes success to be the achievement of a state of equilibrium. Since successful firms are all held to be close to equilibrium, the future time paths of successful companies are held to be predictable.

Determinism versus strategic choice

The main debate within the contingency approach to organization structuring is between two of its sub-schools – the determinists and the strategic choice thinkers. The determinists assert that 'contextual' factors, like an organization's size, ownership, technology or environment, impose certain constraints on the choices that their managers can make about the type of structure to adopt. If the structure is not adapted to context, then opportunities will be lost, costs will rise and the organization's existence will be threatened. They view the aforementioned variables as determining organizational characteristics. Meanwhile, strategic writers contend that a company's structure is always the outcome of a choice made by those in positions of power within organizations. Linked to the question of the shape of the organization's structure is that of its performance and efficiency. Both sub-schools are interested in discovering if certain structural arrangements are more conducive to organizational success than others.

Contingency and technological determinism

Technological determinism: the argument that technology can explain the nature of jobs, work groupings, hierarchy, skills, values and attitudes in organizational settings.

Joan Woodward, James Thompson and Charles Perrow are the leading figures in the school of **technological determinism**. They all agree that technology requires that certain tasks be performed, and that this in turn determines jobs, organization structures and attitudes and behaviours. However, they differ in both the way in which they classify technologies and in how they conceive of the relationship between technology and organization structure.

Joan Woodward and technological complexity

Joan Woodward was a British academic whose work from the 1950s continues to have an impact today for at least three reasons. First, she created a typology for categorizing and describing different technologies, which gives us a 'language' with which to discuss them. Second, by discovering that no single organization structure was appropriate for all circumstances, she ended the supremacy of classical management theory and ushered in the modern, contingency approach to the design of organization structures. Third, by recognizing the impact of technology on organization design, she began a research tradition that has enhanced our understanding of the relation of new technologies to organizational forms.

Joan Woodward
(1916–71)
The Times, London

Technical complexity: the degree of predictability about, and control over, the final product permitted by the technology used; it is usually related to the level of mechanization used in the production process.

Woodward studied 100 firms in south-east England. Having established their levels of performance, she correlated them with various aspects of organization structure which had been proposed by Weber, Fayol and other classic writers: for example, with the number of hierarchical levels, with the span of control, the level of written communication, and so on. She had expected her analysis to reveal the relationship between some of these aspects of organization structure and the level of company performance, but it failed to do so. In her search for an alternative explanation she noted that her firms used different technologies. She classified their technologies, producing a ten-step categorization based on three main types (unit, mass and process) which was based on increasing **technical complexity** (1 = least complex; 10 = most complex) as shown in figure 15.3. In unit production, one person works on a product from beginning to end, for example, a cabinet maker producing a piece of hand-built furniture. In mass production, the technology requires each worker to make an individual contribution to a larger whole: for example, fitting a bumper on a car assembly line. In process production, workers do not touch the product, but monitor machinery and the automated production processes: for example, chemical plants and oil refineries.

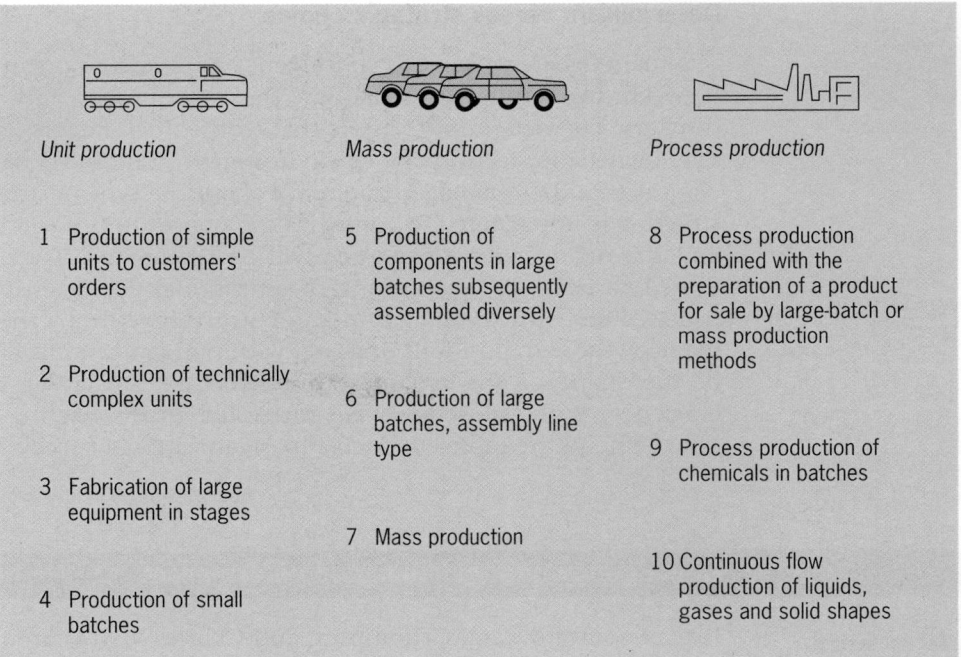

Figure 15.3: Woodward's classification of 100 British manufacturing firms according to their systems of production
From Joan Woodward, *Management and Technology*, HMSO, London, 1958, p. 11. Crown copyright material is reproduced under Class Licence Number C01W0000039 with the permission of the Controller of HMSO and Queen's Printer for Scotland.

Stop and Criticize

Woodward's classification of technologies is based on the manufacture of products. How well does it fit the provision of services? Consider services such as having your windows cleaned, buying a lottery ticket, insuring your car, having a dental check-up, etc. What alternative classification system would you need for these?

Woodward discovered that a firm's organization structure was indeed related to its performance, but through an important, additional variable – technology. Thus, the 'best' or most appropriate organization structure – that is, the one associated with highest performance – depended on (or was *contingent* upon) the type of technology employed by that firm. Thus, it was Woodward (1965) who first introduced the notion of the technological imperative – the view that technology determines the organization's structure. Specifically, she held that it was the complexity of the technology used that determined the structure.

Woodward identified differences in the technical complexity of the process of production, and examined the companies' organization structures. She found that as the technology became more complex (going from type 1 through to type 10), two main things occurred. First, the length of the chain of command increased, with the number of management levels rising from an average of three to six. The proportion of managers to the total employed workforce rose, as did the proportion of indirect to direct labour. Her second major finding was that the increasing complexity of technology meant that the chief executives' span of control increased, and that of the supervisors. The span of control of first-line supervisors was highest in mass production and lowest in process production. Span of control refers to the number of subordinates supervised by one manager and represents one of the ways of co-ordinating the activities of different employees.

Woodward argued that a relationship existed between a company's economic performance and its technology. Her conclusion was that 'there was a particular form of organization most appropriate to each technical situation' (Woodward, 1965, p. 72). The reasoning underlying this conclusion is that the technology used to manufacture the product, or make available the service, places specific requirements on those who operate it. Such demands (for example, in the need for controlling work or motivating staff) are likely to be reflected in the organization structure. The technology–structure link is complemented by the notion of effective performance which held that each type of production system called for its own characteristic organization structure.

James Thompson, technology and interdependence

The second contributor to the technological determinist school was a sociologist, James Thompson (1967). He was not interested in the complexity of technologies (as with Woodward), but in the characteristic types of **relationship of interdependence** that each technology created (figure 15.4). His argument was that different types of technology create different types of interdependence between individuals, teams, departments and firms. These specified the appropriate type of co-ordination required which, in turn, determined the structure needed.

Mediating technology created pooled interdependence
Mediating technology allows individuals, teams and departments to operate independently of each other. Pooled task interdependence results when each department or group member makes a separate and independent contribution to the company or team performance. The individual outputs are pooled: for example, lecturers running their own courses, secretaries in a firm, sales representatives on the road, insurance claim units, and supermarket checkout operators. In each case, the individual contributor's performance can be easily identified and evaluated, and hence the potential for conflict between departments or individuals is low.

James David Thompson (1920–73)

Technological interdependence: the extent to which the work tasks performed in an organization by one department or team member affects the task performance of other departments or team members. It can be high or low.

Mediating technology: technology that links independent but standardized tasks.

Type of technology	Form and degree of task interdependence	Main types of co-ordination used	Cost of co-ordination	Examples
Mediating	'Pooled' A B C D Low interdependence	*Categorization* standardization rules and procedures	low	Bank and branches University departments Baseball teams
Long-linked	'Sequential' A → B → C → D Medium interdependence	*Planning* scheduled meetings, committees	medium	Assembly line Fast food restaurants American football teams
Intensive	'Reciprocal' A ⇄ B ⇄ C ⇄ D High interdependence	*Mutual adjustment* unscheduled meetings, face-to-face discussions, physical proximity, interdepartmental teams	high	Hospitals Airports Basketball teams

Figure 15.4: Thompson's typology of technology, interdependence and co-ordination

Thus, pre-determined rules, common forms and written procedures act to co-ordinate the independent contributions of different units and separate employees, while clearly defined task and role relationships integrate the functions. This produces a bureaucratic organization form in which the costs of co-ordination are relatively low.

Long-linked technology created sequential task interdependence

Long-linked technology requires specific work tasks to be performed in a pre-determined order. Sequential task interdependence results when one department or individual group member must perform their task before the next can complete theirs. For example, in an organizational behaviour course taught by three lecturers, sequential task interdependence means that the first one has to complete their sessions on individual psychology, before the second can teach group psychology, who is then followed by the third, who presents the material on organization structure. In a car factory, a car has to be assembled before it can be painted. Sequential task interdependence means that a department's or a group member's performance cannot be easily identified or evaluated as several individuals, groups or departments make a contribution to a single product or service.

At the company level, co-ordination is achieved through planning and scheduling which integrates the work of different departments. At the group level, co-ordination is achieved by the close supervision of workers, forming work teams consisting of employees with similar levels of skills, and motivating by rewarding group rather than individual performance. The relative cost of co-ordination with this type of technology is medium.

Intensive technology created reciprocal task interdependence

With reciprocal interdependence under **intensive technology**, all the activities of all the different company departments or all the team members are fully dependent on one another. The work output of each serves as the input for another. For example, in an organizational behaviour course which uses the group project method, a group of students can call upon different lecturers to provide them with knowledge or skill inputs to enable them to solve the project problems. Each lecturer would notice what the other had done and contribute accordingly. For this reason, with reciprocal task interdependence the sequence of required operations cannot be predetermined.

Thus, the mechanisms of co-ordination include unscheduled meetings, face-to-face contacts, project groups, task forces and cross-departmental teams. This in turns necessitates a close physical grouping of reciprocally interdependent units so that mutual adjustment can be accomplished quickly. Where this is impossible, then mechanisms like daily meetings, email and teleconferencing are needed to facilitate communication. The degree of co-ordination required through mutual adjustment goes far beyond what is necessary for the other technologies discussed, and is thus the most expensive of the three.

Charles Perrow, technology and predictability

Charles Perrow is the third contributor to the technological determinist school. He saw technology's effect on organization structure as working through its impact on the predictability of providing the service or manufacturing a product. He considered two dimensions. The first he labelled **task variety**. This referred to the frequency with which unexpected events occurred in the transformation (inputs to outputs) process. Task variety would be high if many unexpected events occurred during a technological process. The second, he termed **task analyzability**. This term referred to the degree to which the unexpected problems could be solved

---

Long-linked technology: technology that is applied to a series of programmed tasks performed in a predetermined order.

Intensive technology: technology that is applied to tasks that are performed in no predetermined order.

Task variety: the number of new and different demands that a task places on an individual or a function.

Task analyzability: the degree to which standardized solutions are available to solve the problems that arise.

Charles Perrow

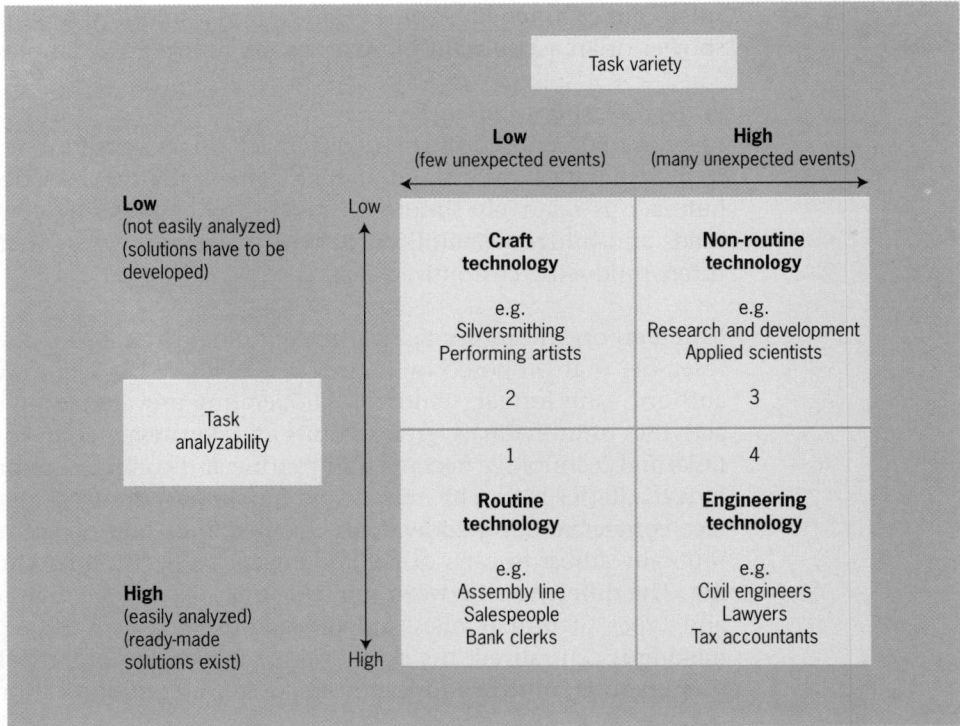

Figure 15.5: Perrow's model of technology
After C. Perrow, *Organizational Analysis: A Sociological View*, 1970, p. 78.

using readily available, off-the-shelf solutions. Task analyzability would be low if individuals or departments had to search around for a solution and rely on experience, judgement, intuition and problems-solving skills (Perrow, 1970) (see figure 15.5).

Types of technology

On the basis of these two dimensions, Perrow categorized technologies into four types (figure 15.5), and discussed the effects of each one upon an organization's structure. He was particularly interested in co-ordination mechanisms, discretion, the relative power of supervisors and the middle managers who supervise them.

1. Routine technology

Located at one extreme in cell 1 are tasks which are simple and where variety is low (repetitive task). Task analyzability is high (there are standard solutions available). Examples include supermarket checkout operations and fast food hamburger restaurants.

3. Non-routine technology

At the other extreme in cell 3 are complex and non-routine tasks where task variability is high (with many new or different problems encountered) and task analyzability is low (finding a solution to the problem is difficult). The tasks performed by research chemists, advertising agencies, high-tech product designers and top management teams are all examples of non-routine technology.

2. Craft technology

Between the extremes in cell 2 is craft technology, characterized by low task variety and low task analyzability. The number of new problems encountered is small, but each requires some effort to find a solution. A plumber fitting a bath or shower or an accountant preparing a tax return are examples.

4. Engineering technology

Also located between the extremes in cell 4 is engineering technology, character- ized by high task variety and high task analyzability. Many new problems crop up, but each is relatively simple to solve. Civil engineering companies which build roads and bridges exemplify this type of technology, as well as motor manufac- turers producing customized cars.

When an organization's tasks and technology are routine, its structure is likely to resemble that proposed by Weber and Fayol. With a tall hierarchy, channels of authority and formal, standardized operating procedures are used to integrate the activities of individuals, groups, units and departments. In contrast, when a firm's tasks and technology become non-routine and complex, an organization will tend to use a flatter hierarchy, more cross-functional teamworking, and greater face-to- face contact to allow individuals, groups, units and departments to observe and mutually adjust to each other, and engage in decision-making and problem-solv- ing. The differences between the two structures will be manifested in the number and types of formal rules and procedures used, the degree to which decision- making is centralized, the skill levels of workers employed, the width of supervi- sors' span of control, and the means used for communication and co-ordination.

Contingency and environmental determinism

Environmental determinism: a perspective which claims that internal organizational responses are wholly or mainly shaped, influenced or determined by external factors.

Environmental complexity: the range of external factors relevant to the activities of the organization; the more factors, the higher the complexity.

Environmental dynamism: the pace of change in relevant factors external to the organization; the greater the pace of change, the more dynamic the environment.

The second strand of determinism in organization structuring has been environ- mental. Researchers supporting **environmental determinism** have had an interest in the relationship between a company's environment and its structure. Some of them argue that success depends on securing a proper 'fit' or alignment between itself and its environment. For these environmental determinists, environment determines organization structure. One prominent environmental determinist, Paul Lawrence, even said: 'Tell me what your environment is and I shall tell your what your organization ought to be' (Argyris, 1972, p. 88).

The environmental determinists see the organization as being in constant inter- action with the environment within which it exists (figure 15.6). That environ- ment consists of 'actors' or 'networks' (for example, competitors, investors, customers). It includes the general economic situation, the market, the competi- tive scene and so on. Each organization has its own unique environment. The more actors or networks that are relevant to a given company, the more complex its environment is said to be. Organizations vary in the relative degree of their **environmental complexity** (Duncan, 1972, 1973, 1974, 1979).

Those same actors and networks in an organization's environment can also change a great deal or remain the same. They thus differ in their degree of **environmental dynamism**. Different industries vary widely in their degree of dynamism. At one extreme of stability is the mainframe computer industry where new players must confront the barriers of an entrenched set of standards and the costs of switching are high. Here, the concepts of market segmentation, economies of scale and pre-emptive investment are all still important. Mainframe computers are not immune to change, as the mini-computer and PC revolutions showed, but there are periods of considerable stability. In the middle of the range, one finds businesses like branded consumer goods. Substitution ranges from medium to high, and new entrants can replace established ones but not overnight. Survival and success depend upon capabilities and network relation-

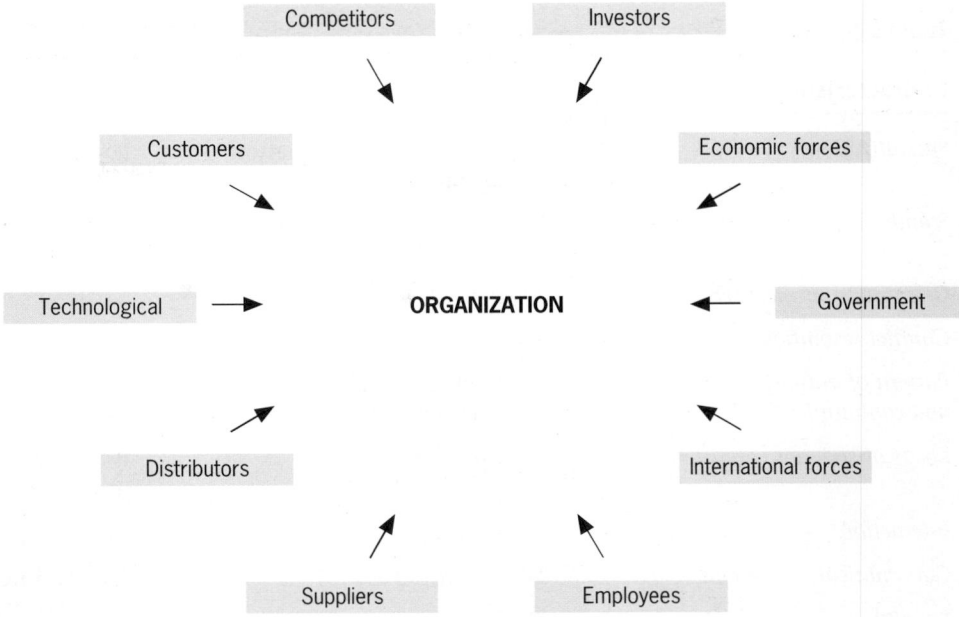

Figure 15.6: An organization depicted in its environment, consisting of different actors, stakeholders and 'networks'

ships. Most industries are located in this middle ground. At the extreme of turbulence is a situation where customers can constantly and easily substitute. It consists of networks of players whose positions and prospects change suddenly and unpredictably. Many internet businesses are located at this end of the spectrum.

Environmental determinists argue that because a company is dependent on its environment for its sales, labour, raw materials and so on, that environment constrains the kinds of choice an organization can make about how it structures itself. As the environmental situation changes, the organization–environment relationship also changes. Hence, to be effective, a company has to structure and restructure constantly to maintain alignment. The environmental determinists use the key concepts of environmental uncertainty and complexity in their explanations. These will be considered later.

Tom Burns, George M. Stalker, mechanistic and organic organization structures

In the late 1950s in Britain, Tom Burns and George McDonald Stalker studied the behaviour of people working in a rayon mill. Rayon is a yarn or fibre produced by forcing and drawing cellulose through minute holes. They found that this contented, economically successful company was run with a management style which, according to contemporary wisdom about 'best' management practice, should have led to worker discontent and inefficiency. Some time later, the same authors studied an electronics company. Again it was highly successful, but used a management style completely different from that of the rayon mill studied earlier. This contradiction gave the authors the impetus to begin a large-scale investigation to examine the relationship between the management systems and the organizational tasks. They were particularly interested in the way management systems changed in response to changes in the commercial and technical tasks of the firm (Burns and Stalker, 1961/1994).

The rayon mill had a highly stable, highly structured character which would have fitted well into Weber's bureaucratic organizational model. In contrast, the

George McDonald Stalker (b. 1925)

Table 15.4: Characteristics of mechanistic and organic organization structures

Characteristic	Rayon mill (mechanistic)	Electronics (organic)
Specialization	High – sharp differentiation	Low – no hard boundaries, relatively few different jobs
Standardization	High – methods spelled out	Low – individuals decide own methods
Orientation of members	Means	Goals
Conflict resolution	By superior	Interaction
Pattern of authority, control and communication	Hierarchical – based on implied contractual relation	Wide net based upon common commitment
Locus of superior competence	At top of organization	Wherever there is skill and competence
Interaction	Vertical	Lateral
Communication content	Directions, orders	Advice, information
Loyalty	To the organization	To project and group
Prestige	From the position	From personal contribution

Based on J.A. Litterer, *The Analysis of Organizations*, John Wiley & Sons Inc., 1973, p. 339.

electronics firm violated many of the principles of classical management. It discouraged written communications, it defined jobs as little as possible, and the interaction between employees was on a face-to-face basis. Indeed, staff even complained about this uncertainty. In contrast, the authors gave the label mechanistic to the first form of organization structure and organic to the second (table 15.4). These represented ideal types at opposite ends of a continuum. Most firms would be located somewhere in between.

Burns and Stalker argued that neither form of organization structure was intrinsically efficient or inefficient, but rather that it all depended on the nature of the environment in which a firm operated. In their view, the key variables to be considered were the product market and the technology of the manufacturing process. These needed to be studied when the structure of a firm's management system was being designed. Thus, a **mechanistic structure** may be appropriate for an organization which uses an unchanging technology and operates in relatively stable markets. An **organic structure** can be more suitable for a firm which has to cope with unpredictable new tasks.

Paul Roger
Lawrence
(b. 1922)

Paul Lawrence, Jay Lorsch, organization design and environmental needs

During the 1960s, Paul Lawrence and Jay Lorsch (1967) built on the work of Burns and Stalker, using the concepts of **differentiation** and **integration**. Differentiation refers to the process of a firm breaking itself up into sub-units, each of which concentrates on a particular part of the firm's environment. A university differentiates itself in terms of different faculties and departments. Such differentiation inevitably leads to the sub-units developing their own goals, values, norms, structures, time frames and interpersonal relations that reflect the job that they have to do and the uncertainties with which they have to cope.

Jay William Lorsch
(b. 1932)

Differentiation: the degree to which the tasks and the work of individuals, groups and units are divided up within an organization.

Integration: the required level to which units in an organization are linked together, and their respective degree of independence. Integrative mechanisms include rules and procedures and direct managerial control.

Considering differentiation first, Lawrence and Lorsch found that effective organizations increased their level of differentiation as their environment became more uncertain. This was because it allowed staff to respond more effectively to the specific sub-environment for which they were responsible. On the other hand, however, the more differentiated the sub-units became, the more their goals would diverge, the more they would perceive the same things differently, and hence the more conflict there would be between them.

Turning next to integration, Lawrence and Lorsch use this term to refer to the process of achieving unity of effort among the previously differentiated sub-systems in order to accomplish the organization task. It is thus equivalent to co-ordination. Having divided the university into faculties and departments, there is the need to ensure that all contribute to the goals of high-quality research, excellent teaching and income generation. The authors found that as environmental uncertainty increased, and thus the degree of differentiation increased, so organizations had to increase the level of their integration (co-ordination) between people in different departments if they were to work together effectively towards a common goal.

When environmental uncertainty is low, differentiation is correspondingly low. Because the units share common goals and ways of achieving them, the hierarchy of authority in a company and standard procedures are sufficient to integrate the activities of different units and individuals. However, as uncertainty increases, so does the need for integration, and so too do the number of integrative devices used. Lawrence and Lorsch argued that the level of uncertainty in the environment that a firm has to cope with will determine the organization structure that is most appropriate for it.

Stop and Criticize

How well are the activities performed by your educational institution differentiated and integrated? Identify the problems and recommend solutions that would improve organizational performance from the student perspective.

Contingency and organizational size

As organizations evolve and grow, passing through different phases of their life-cycle, changes occur in their goals, innovation level and control systems that have an impact on their structures. Large and small organizations, as measured by the number of employees or volume of sales, usually have very different organization structures. For example, large ones tend to have specialist staff located in functional departments (for example, human resources, finance, research and development) and more levels of hierarchy. Larry Greiner (1998) distinguished five phases of company growth. He argues that each was characterized by a dominant management style that was used to achieve growth. This created a dominant management problem, which required an appropriate structural solution if growth was to continue. The solutions to the problems in each phase created their own problems in turn. Hence the cyclical nature of the model as summarized in table 15.5.

Creativity

In the first phase, the entrepreneurs focus on making and selling their new product. Staff numbers are small, product volumes are low and communications are informal. With growth comes the need for greater technical expertise, better procedures for control and a different way of managing the larger workforce. This *crisis in leadership* leads to the owner-entrepreneurs appointing a business manager.

Table 15.5: Organizational practices in five phases of growth

Category	Phase 1	Phase 2	Phase 3	Phase 4	Phase 5
Phase	Creativity	Direction	Delegation	Co-ordination	Collaboration
Top-management style	Individualistic and entrepreneurial	Directive	Delegative	Watchdog	Participative
Management focus	Make and sell	Efficiency of operations	Expansion of market	Consolidation of organization	Problem solving and innovation
Organization structure	Informal	Centralized and functional	Decentralized and geographical	Line, staff and product groups	Matrix of teams
Management in crisis	Leadership	Autonomy	Control	Red tape	Employees
Problem created	Insufficient control and communication	Conflict between procedure-following and initiative-taking	Loss of control over diversified field operations	Lack of confidence between employees and in systems and procedures	Emotional and physical exhaustion of employees caused by intensity of teamwork and continued need for innovative solutions
Management solution	Locate and install a business manager	Delegate responsibility to lower-level managers	Use of special co-ordination techniques	Use of teams and confrontation of interpersonal differences	Creation of structures allowing employees to rest, reflect and revitalize themselves

Direction

In the second phase, the introduction of a functional structure groups activities by creating departments, and makes job assignments more specialized. Communication becomes more formal and impersonal as the hierarchy of positions and number of job titles grow. Top management assumes responsibility for company direction, removing decision-making power from functional specialists. The new, directive techniques used in this phase enhance growth. However, junior employees possessing greater market knowledge than their leaders are torn between following procedures and using their own initiative, thereby creating a *crisis in autonomy* which leads to the creation of a decentralized organization structure.

Delegation

In the third phase, headquarters management deal only with exceptional problems, giving plant managers greater responsibilities over their plants and market territories. These lower-level managers are motivated to expand the company by penetrating larger markets, responding faster to customers' needs, and developing new products more quickly. After a time, senior management come to feel that they are losing control over what has become a highly diversified field operation, resulting in a *crisis in control*. The use of special co-ordination techniques is preferred to recentralization.

Co-ordination

In the fourth phase, senior executives introduce formal systems to co-ordinate the activities. Decentralized units are merged into product groups and extra staff are hired to work in cross-departmental, liaison roles. Company growth continues by the more efficient use of limited resources. Local field managers are forced to overcome their parochial attitudes and interests. They continue to possess much decision-making responsibility, but now have to justify decisions to a watchdog audience located at headquarters. A lack of confidence develops between line and staff members, and between headquarters and field employees, together with the many systems and procedures outliving their usefulness, thereby causing a *red tape crisis*.

Collaboration

In this fifth and final phase, social control and self-discipline founded upon a behavioural approach to management are used to replace formal control. The focus is upon solving problems through team action, using cross-functional teams to solve specific problems, reassigning headquarters staff experts to work within disciplinary teams and using matrix structures. Many companies are currently in this phase, and Greiner considers that the upcoming crisis will centre around the psychological saturation of employees who grow emotionally and physically exhausted from the intensity of teamwork and the pressure upon them to come up with innovative solutions. He proposes an organization structure that allows employees to rest, reflect and revitalize themselves through the use of manager job rotation, sabbaticals, four-day working weeks, and similar devices.

Greiner proposed that, as every organization evolved and grew, it encountered problems caused by an increase in size. These problems, which are predictable and occur at set times, must be solved by an appropriate modification to the company's existing structure. If this occurs, the company's growth and increase in size can continue. If at a given point in time, a firm has insufficient structure or the wrong type of structure, growth may slow and the company's future may be endangered. Greiner therefore offers a contingency theory of organization structure because he argues that company size, as signified by its current phase of development, should be of a particular type in order to maximize the performance of that organization. Structures are essential for all kinds of businesses, whether traditional manufacturing like motor car production, knowledge-intensive service industry like management consulting or internet start-up like *Lastminute.com*.

Washington's mega-merger

It will be one of the biggest mergers ever. The newly consolidated business will have an annual turnover of US$37 billion and 169,000 employees. The chief executive is babbling about synergies, benefits of rationalization and economies of scale. The track record of ordinary mergers, involving

➤

two companies, is poor – and this one consolidates twenty-two units from twelve different companies. Meanwhile, in the background the shareholders or their representatives are bickering and the unions are suspicious. If this were a real corporate merger, Wall Street would already be discounting the share price. So the first question to ask about America's new Department of Homeland Security is whether the basic [*organizational structure*] design (see below) is the right one. It will bring most of the main functions of domestic security under one roof. Huge agencies will be seized from other departments – the Immigration and Naturalization Service (39,500 employees) from Justice, the Coast Guard (43,600) from Transportation, the Customs Service (21,700) from the Treasury. Other independent entities, like the Federal Emergency Management Agency (5,100), will be gobbled up whole.

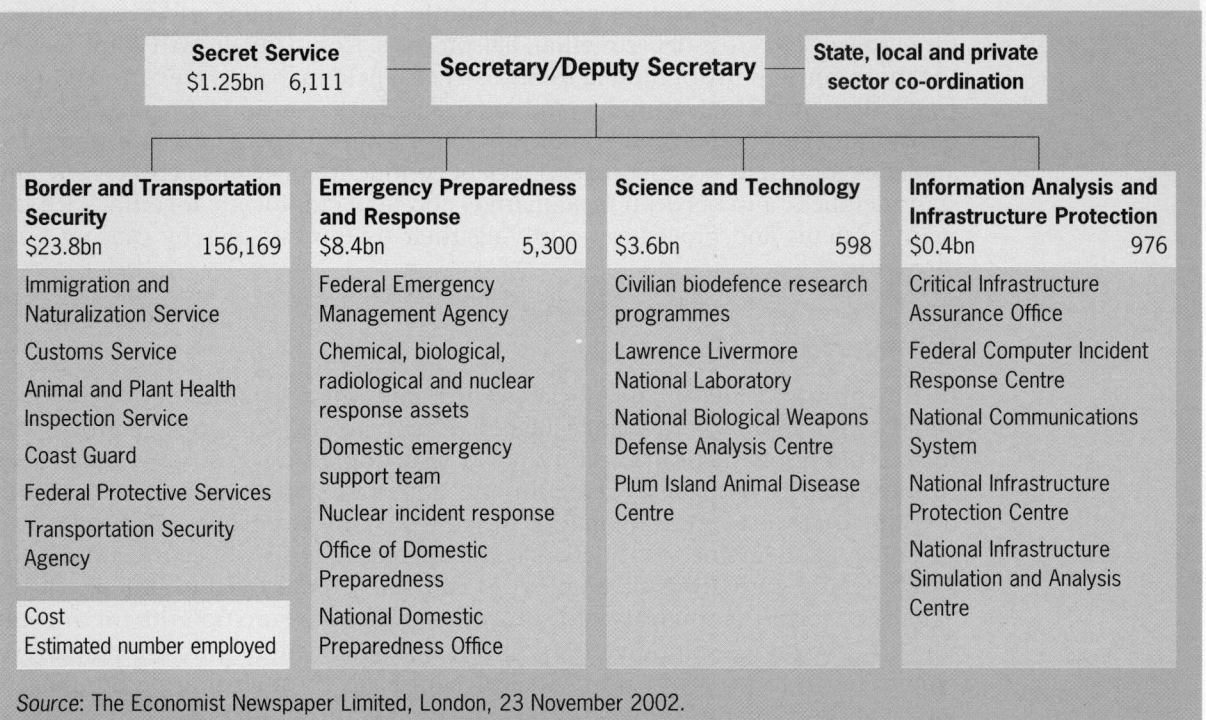

Source: The Economist Newspaper Limited, London, 23 November 2002.

With such an immense job of co-ordination to do, having a single department with budgetary control looked necessary. However, the bill that has been approved vests the powers of the various units in the department heads, in order to eliminate duplication and enforce the adoption of common standards. The department heads can delegate authority back to the bits as they see fit. The bill vests much administrative discretion in one person. What were the alternatives? To have folded everything into a single, traditional, giant department would have been logical but impractical, as the job requires specialization and expertise. To have left agencies scattered around would have been no good either. Consider two examples. If there were a chemical or biological attack now in the United States, health advice would come from no fewer than twelve federal agencies, to say nothing of local government ones. If there were an attack on a nuclear power plant, one agency would distribute anti-radiation treatment if you lived within ten miles, a different one if you lived outside that circle, a third controls the drug stockpile and a fourth takes over if the attack also happens to be within ten miles of a nuclear-weapons facility. So it was not surprising that the president came round to seeing the benefits of rationalization.

The new department will begin operating a year after the president signs the bill. To get the last comparable governmental reorganization right – the establishment of the Department of Defence – took forty years and several congressional interventions. This top-down reform to improve security occurs at a time when the most useful protection comes from the bottom-up, such as a security guard noticing something strange at a power plant. Even after the new mega-merger, it is these guards, as well as alert customs officers and vigilant passengers, who will keep America's homeland secure.

From 'Washington's mega-merger', *The Economist*, 23 November 2002, pp. 51–3.

Recap

1. *Distinguish between charismatic, traditional and legitimate forms of authority.*

   - Traditional authority is based on the belief that the ruler had a natural right to rule.

   - Charismatic authority is based on the belief that the ruler had some special, unique virtue, either religious or heroic.

   - Legitimate authority is based on formal written rules which have the force of law.

2. *State the main characteristics of a bureaucratic organization structure as specified by Max Weber.*

   - Job specialization; authority hierarchy; employment and career; recording and keeping all administrative acts and decisions; rules and procedures to which all employees are subject; and the impersonality of those rules and procedures, meaning that they apply to all equally.

3. *Summarize the approach and main ideas of the classical management school.*

   - Based on the experience of managers and consultants rather than researchers.

   - Distinguished six managerial activities: forecasting, planning, organizing, commanding, co-ordinating and controlling.

   - Distinguished fourteen principles of management: division of work, authority, discipline, unity of command, scalar principle, unity of direction, interest subordination, remuneration, centralization, order, equity of treatment, stability of employment, opportunity for initiative and *esprit de corps*.

4. *Identify the writers who comprise the early contingency approach and state their main individual contributions.*

   - Contingency writers challenged Max Weber and Henri Fayol's view that there was one best way to structure an organization.

   - They held that there was an optimum organization structure that would maximize company performance and profits, and that this structure would differ between firms.

   - Technological contingency theorists, Joan Woodward, Charles Perrow and James Thompson, saw technology determining appropriate organization structure.

   - Environmental contingency theorists, Tom Burns and G.M. Stalker, Paul Lawrence and Jay Lorsch, saw the environment determining appropriate organization structure.

5. *Discuss the strengths and weaknesses of early ideas on the design of organization structure and the practice of management.*

   - Provides a rationally designed, organizational model that allows complex tasks to be performed efficiently. Persons who are best qualified to do it, carry out the work. It provides safeguards against personal bias and individual favouritism.

   - It creates dysfunctional consequences of members who are only interested in their own jobs, following rules obsessively and who are slow to respond to changes. Bureaucracies perpetuate themselves.

6. *Identify the influence of early organization design ideas on contemporary organizations.*

   - Modern organizations continue to possess the features described by Weber and Fayol over a century ago.

   - Early design principles have been successful; have helped large organizations to survive; reflect the static social values of many nations and cultures; are capable of withstanding environmental turbulence; and allow senior management to retain power.

Revision

1. Commentators argue that both too much and too little bureaucracy in an organization demotivates employees and causes them stress. How can this be?

2. How does uncertainty affect the successful operation of rationally designed organization structures such as those proposed by Weber and Fayol?

3. Which of Fayol's principles of management emphasize human relations? Which emphasize production efficiency? Which emphasize the organizational or administrative aspects of management?

4. Define and distinguish differentiation from integration. Using an example from your experience or reading, illustrate these two processes in operation, and highlight some of the problems that can be encountered.

5. Explain how technology and environment might influence the structure of an organization. Consider their effect on co-ordinating activities.

Springboard

Bauman, Z., 1991, *Modernity and the Holocaust*, Polity Press, Cambridge.

The Holocaust was unique among genocides in history because it involved the large-scale extermination of vast numbers of people in concentration camps such as Auschwitz using bureaucratic means. Bauman argues that the organization structure of bureaucracy, with its emphasis on the division of labour, impersonality, rule following and abrogation of personal responsibility, made the Holocaust possible.

Burns, T. and Stalker, G.M., 1994, *The Management of Innovation*, Oxford University Press, Oxford (first published in 1961 by Tavistock, London).

This 1961 classic has been re-published. It is one of the most influential books in organization theory and industrial sociology. Its central theme is the relationship between an organization and its environment, particularly technological and market innovations.

Du Guy, P., 2000, *In Praise of Bureaucracy*, Routledge, London.

Explores and analyzes the positive and creative potential of bureaucracy in a time of complexity, uncertainty and disorder.

Jaques, E., 1990, 'In praise of hierarchy', *Harvard Business Review*, vol. 68, no. 1, January–February, pp. 127–33.

An article summarizing his thoughts on managerial accountability, hierarchy and the time span of discretion for a managerial audience. A good starting point from which to move on to some of his more complex books.

Kanter, R.M., 1985, *The Change Masters: Corporate Entrepreneurs at Work*, International Thomson Business Press, London.

Her discussion about various organization structures introduces the terms 'integrative' and 'segmentalist', echoing similar distinctions from the past.

Miller, E.J. (ed.), 1999, *Tavistock Institute Contribution to Job and Organizational Design* (2 vols), Ashgate, Aldershot.

Provides a historical overview and assessment of the theories, models and authors from the Tavistock Institute in London who contributed extensively to thinking about organization change and design.

Thomas, A.B., 2002, *Controversies in Management: Issues, Debates, Answers*, Routledge, London (second edition).

Chapter 5 discusses the principles of management to assess if they are valid or vacuous.

Whittington, R., 2002, 'Organizational structures', in D.O. Faulkner and A. Campbell (eds), *Oxford Handbook of Strategy. vol. 2: Corporate Strategy*, Oxford University Press, Oxford, Chapter 28, pp. 319–48.

This chapter develops the contingencies theme and considers the effect of diversification, internationalization and networks upon company structures.

Home viewing

Crimson Tide (1995, director Tony Scott) is the story of how a global emergency provokes a power play on a nuclear submarine between a pair of US senior naval officers, the battle-hardened Captain Frank Ramsay (played by Gene Hackman) who 'goes by the book', and his Executive Officer, Lt Commander Ron Hunter (Denzil Washington). When an order is issued, but is only half received, concerning a nuclear strike, Hunter demands confirmation while Ramsay insists on unquestioning obedience to the rules.

List the different aspects of bureaucratic organization structure portrayed. Which of the two senior officers, Ramsay or Hunter, subscribes more to Weber's principles? Does adhering to bureaucratic principles 'save the day' or nearly cause disaster? Beyond the concern with bureaucracy, can you identify the formation of cliques? On what basis do they form? Are there examples of group pressure being exercised?

OB in literature

David Feintuch, *Midshipman's Hope*, Orbit/Little Brown and Company, Boston, MA, 1996.

This science fiction novel, set in AD 2194, concerns intergalactic travel and highlights aspects of power and authority, personality, staff and line relationships, organization culture, interpersonal relations, and bureaucracy and roles.

Chapter exercises

1: Personal orientation test

Objectives

1. To allow you to assess your preference for working within a bureaucratic organization structure.

2. To introduce you to the characteristics of Max Weber's bureaucracy.

Briefing For each statement, tick the box that best represents your feelings.

Statement	Agree	Disagree
1. Job descriptions should be detailed and complete so that everyone knows exactly what they are supposed to do.		
2. I like a predictable organization.		
3. Organization charts should be constructed so that everyone understands where they fit into the organization's structure.		
4. Relations with colleagues should be formal in nature.		
5. Rules, policies and procedures provide me with guidance, avoiding the danger of my making a mistake.		
6. Authority should be clearly related to position in each department so that higher-level positions have authority over lower-level ones.		
7. Senior managers should set objectives and communicate them down the hierarchy.		
8. Before accepting a job, I would like to see an exact job description.		
9. Work roles should be specialized with each person making their unique, expert contribution.		
10. Promotion should be based on demonstrated technical competence.		

2: Managerial activities quiz

Objectives

1. To allow you to distinguish between Henri Fayol's six managerial activities.

Briefing Indicate, by placing a tick under the appropriate heading in the table on p. 536, which one of Fayol's managerial activities is being described.

F: Forecasting:	P: Planning	O: Organizing
M: Motivating	CD: Co-ordinating	CN: Controlling

	Managerial activity					
	F	P	O	M	CD	CN

1. Government inspectors visit schools to assess their performance against a checklist and grade each one.

2. The lecturer explains to students how working hard to get a good degree will help them to get a good job.

3. The national census data will determine how many old people there are, and what residential care facilities will be needed.

4. The government decides to increase the number of university students by 50 per cent, and considers how and over what time period to do this.

5. The introductory course is divided among a number of staff, each of whom gives a number of lectures.

6. Course team members meet periodically to ensure that their individual contributions complement each others' and that there are no gaps.

3: Learning the rules

Objectives 1. To introduce you to the concepts of tacit knowledge and basic rules.

2. To illustrate how Socratic questioning and problem-solving is used by Toyota to teach its workers that knowledge.

Briefing 1.   Read the following case.

2.   Divide into groups and apply the same approach to (a) tying a shoelace and (b) writing an essay.

How Toyota's workers learn the rules

If the rules of the Toyota production system aren't explicit, how are they transmitted? Toyota's managers don't tell workers and supervisors specifically how to do their work. Rather they use a teaching and learning approach that allows their workers to discover the rules as a consequence of solving problems. For example, the supervisor teaching a person the principle of the first rule ['All work shall be highly specified as to content, sequence, timing and outcome'] will come to the work site and while the person is doing his or her job, ask a series of questions:

■ How do you do this work?
■ How do you know you are doing this work correctly?
■ How do you know that the outcome is free of defects?
■ What do you do if you have a problem?

This continuing process gives the person increasingly deeper insights into his or her own specific work. From many experiences of this sort, the person gradually learns to generalize how to design all activities according to the principles embodied in rule one. All the [four Toyota] rules are taught in a similar Socratic fashion of iterative questioning and problem solving. Although this method is particularly effective for teaching, it leads to knowledge that is implicit. Consequently, the Toyota production system has so far been transferred successfully only when managers have been able and willing to engage in a similar process of questioning to facilitate learning by doing.

From Steven Spear and H. Kent Bowen, 'Decoding the DNA of the Toyota production system', *Harvard Business Review*, vol. 77, no. 5, September–October 1999, p. 99.

Chapter 16

Organization strategy and design

Key concepts

configuration	merger
complementarities	acquisition
strategic choice	strategic alliance
enacted environment	joint venture
managerial enactment	outsourcing
vertical integration	unilateral agreement
bounded instability	network organization
explosive instability	virtual organization
stable equilibrium	

Learning outcomes

When you have read this chapter, you should be able to define those key concepts in your own words, and you should also be able to:

1. Appreciate the reciprocal relationship between corporate strategy and organization structure.
2. Discuss theories that explain managerial changes in corporate strategy and organization structure with respect to the environment.
3. Distinguish between bounded instability and non-linearity, and state their implications for corporate strategy.
4. Define a 'transaction' and distinguish three major types of institutional arrangement for the conduct of transactions.
5. Differentiate between the main types of mutual interorganizational arrangement.
6. Identify the distinguishing features of a virtual organization.

Why study organization strategy and design?

After more than two decades of being in the shadow of more popular management topics such as leadership and teamwork, the subject of organization structure has re-emerged as the 'hot topic', high on the executive agenda. Whittington, Mayer and Smith (2002b) ascribe this both to the increasing scale of business (the US retailer Wal-Mart has 1.2 million employees worldwide) and to the intensity with which knowledge flows through it (Unilever, a consumer goods group, processes 1 million emails daily). These writers note that business is too big and too complex to allow bad organizational design to interfere. Commentators are in agreement that a new form of organization is emerging which differs from its classical predecessors and which has been dubbed 'post-bureaucratic'.

Exactly what shape (or shapes) the new form will take is still not clear. However, flexibility and indirect, internalized controls exercised on the basis of cultural and ideological values are likely to be its distinguishing features. The new concept of

Configuration: the structures, processes, relationships and boundaries through which an organization operates.

organization sees it as 'a combination of both external circumstances and internal dynamics' (Adcroft and Willis, 2000). Gerry Johnson and Kevan Scholes observed that while a particular structure itself would not ensure the success of a company's corporate strategy, an inappropriate structure could impede its achievement. More recently, the focus has turned to matching organization structure, processes, relationships and boundaries to achieve strategic objectives. The authors refer to this as **configuration** (Johnson and Scholes, 2002, p. 420).

Corporate strategy and organization structure

An organization's strategy and its structure are mutually interdependent. Organization structure can be seen as the vehicle for implementing and administering its corporate strategy. The direction in which an organization moves is influenced by the decisions that are made about its strategy. Since corporate strat-

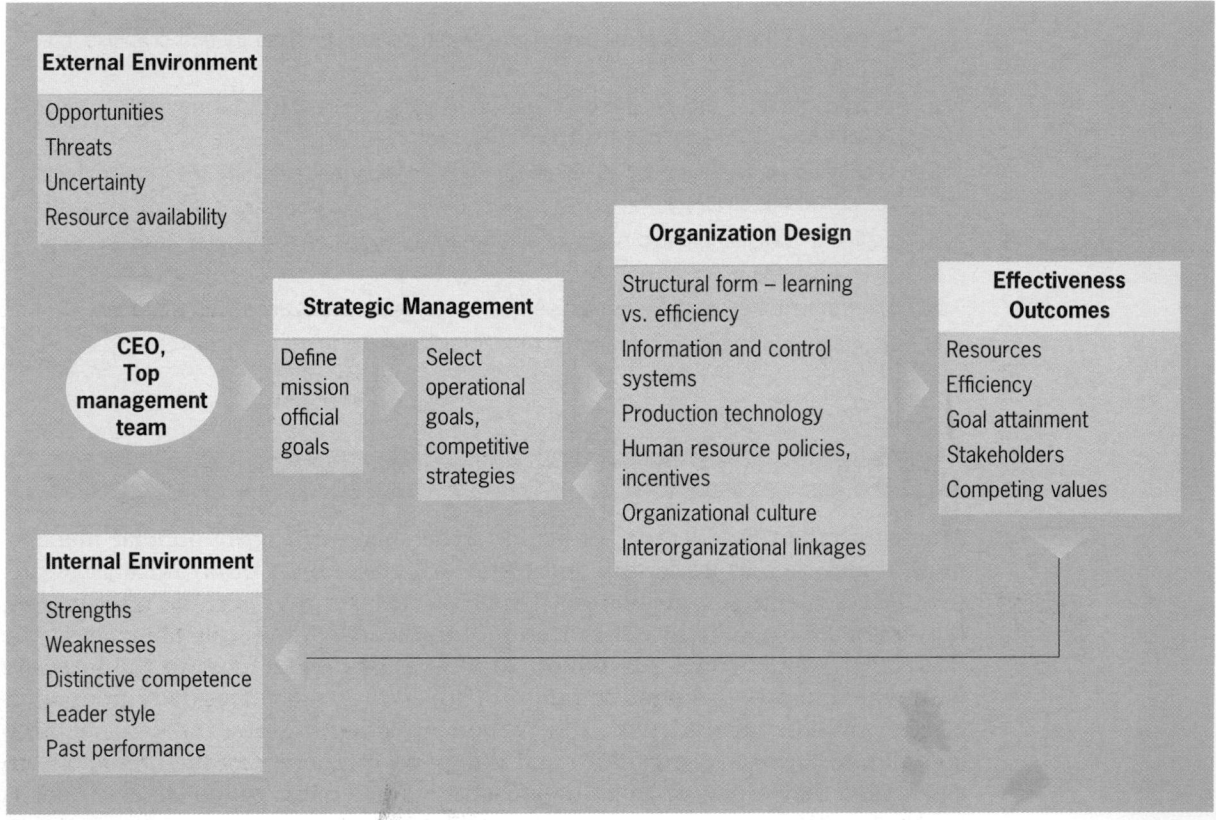

Figure 16.1: Top management's role in organizational strategy and organizational design

From *Organizational Behaviour* 1st edition by Daft. © 2001. Reprinted with permission of South-Western, a division of Thomson Learning: www.thomsonrights.com. Fax 800 730-2215. Adapted from Arie Y. Lewin and Carroll U. Stephens, 'CEO attributes as determinants of organization design: an integrated model', *Organization Studies*, vol. 14, no. 2, 1994, pp. 183–212.

egies are determined by senior management operating within an existing organization structure, that structure may limit the company's strategic options. However, there are many examples of organizational goals being selected, and strategy being implemented, on the basis of environmental needs, and top management then redesigns the structure of the organization to achieve this. The relationship is summarized in figure 16.1.

The terms 'corporate strategy', 'business strategy' and 'strategic management' are often wrongly used interchangeably. Although they are connected, they refer to different things.

Corporate strategy	Addresses the question of 'what business are we in?' It is concerned with the determination of the future direction and scope of the entire organization and is performed by top management. In Virgin Ltd, Richard Branson and his senior management team decide this question.
Business strategy	Relates to that part of the corporate strategy which is relevant to one of the company's divisions or business units. Thus Branson and his senior managers will set the corporate strategy of Virgin Ltd. Within that, Virgin Entertainment, Virgin Travel and the other Virgin business units that together make up the company will each have their own business strategies.
Strategic management	Refers to the ongoing process performed by managers which seeks to develop strategy while keeping the company matched to its environment. Virgin Ltd's executives are expected to manage strategically.

The lion's friendly approach

As the chairman of ING, one of Europe's biggest financial services companies, Godfried van der Lugt likes clarity. He pulls out a slide, littered with colourful shapes, showing its activities around the world. The red circles, he explains, mark areas of market leadership while green squares signal the need for organic growth. And the blue triangles? 'That's where we're planning acquisitions', he replies, his eyes twinkling. 'You don't get strategy much clearer than that.'

From 'The lion's friendly approach', *The Economist*, 18 December 1999, p. 149.

An organization's goals typically include growth, profitability and return on investment. Companies failing to achieve their goals will either go out of business or else become targets for take-overs. Historically, organizations have tended to pursue their strategic goals and manage their dependence on their environment unilaterally. The conventional wisdom held that strategic success criteria had to do with consistency, regularity and stability – the paradigm of the stable equilibrium organization. From this perspective, installing organization structures to implement the strategy to achieve goals involved designing hierarchical reporting, information and control systems, defining roles, allocating responsibilities, drawing up organization charts, etc. Such an 'internal' focus was the norm. Robert Grant (2002) summarized the evolution of corporate strategy during the second half of the twentieth century (table 16.1).

Table 16.1: The evolution of corporate strategy

Period	1950s	1960s	Early–mid 1970s	Late 1970s and early 1980s	Late 1980s and early 1990s	Late 1990s and early 2000s
Dominant theme	Budgetary planning and control	Corporate planning	Corporate strategy	Analysis of industry and competition	The quest for competitive advantage	Strategic innovation and the new economy
Main issues	Financial control through operational and capital budgeting	Planning growth	Diversification and portfolio planning	Choice of industries, markets, and segments, and positioning within them	Sources of competitive advantage within the firm	Competitive advantage through strategic innovation Competing on knowledge Adapting to the new, digital, networked economy
Principal concepts and techniques	Financial budgeting Investment planning Project appraisal	Business forecasting Investment planning models	Synergy Strategic business units Portfolio planning matrices	Experience curve and returns to market share Analysis of industry structure Competitor analysis PIMS analysis	Resource analysis Analysis of core competencies	Organizational flexibility and speed of response Knowledge management and organizational learning Competing for standards Early-mover advantage
Organizational implications	Financial management the key	Rise of corporate planning departments and medium-term formal planning	Diversification Multidivisional structures Quest for global market share	Greater industry and market selectivity Industry restructuring Active asset management	Corporate restructuring and business process reengineering Refocusing and outsourcing	The virtual organization The knowledge-based firm Alliances and networks The quest for critical mass

From Robert M. Grant, *Contemporary Strategy Analysis: Concepts, Techniques and Applications*, Blackwell, Oxford (fourth edition), 2002, p. 22. Reprinted by permission of Blackwell Publishing Ltd.

The first three rows of Grant's table – those to do with 'dominant theme', 'main issues' and 'principal concepts and techniques' – relate primarily to corporate strategy issues. The fourth row, however, the one that deals with organizational implications, concerns organization structure. The final, right-hand column summarizes the currently related concerns in these two fields. Reading across those columns, from left to right, three contrasts are evident:

From	*To*
'good, old stable then'	'turbulent now' management rhetoric
an internal focus on the organization	external focus on its environment
organization operating alone	organization operating in some relationship with others

Raymond E. Miles

Charles C. Snow

Raymond Miles and Charles Snow (1986) conceived more of a two-way influence between strategy and structure. Managers made strategic choices based on their perceptions of the environment and of their organization's capabilities. The success of these choices rested on how well their chosen competitive strategy matched the environmental conditions and management processes. They argued that, historically, strategy and structure have evolved together. Each advance in structural form was stimulated by the limitations of the previous form; and each new form built upon the previous form, highlighting its predecessors' strengths and weaknesses. Simultaneously, each development in structure permitted new competitive strategies to be pursued by the company. Innovative organization forms were thus developed to cope with new environmental conditions. They distinguished the most common generic strategies – Prospectors, Defenders, Analyzers and Reactors (table 16.2). They argued that each strategic orientation also specified the major structural and managerial features needed by the company to support it.

Richard Whittington, Andrew Pettigrew and their colleagues (Whittington et al., 1999a) developed Miles and Snow's 'equal partners' idea of strategy and structure, arguing that the new organizational 'fit' involves not only these two variables, but all the other processes within an organization. In their view, these variables should not be interlocked in a static way, but should be in a 'continuous co-evolution of a complex whole'. Their notion of the new fit is

Table 16.2: Strategy and structure

Corporate strategy	Organization structure
Prospector 'First-to-the-market', innovation-oriented, finding, developing and exploiting new opportunities; see their products as short-term ventures. They are better at developing prototypes than long-term, efficient production.	Flexible structure, which uses autonomous work groups or product divisions for planning and control, is highly decentralized. Permits market responsiveness but not at the expense of overall specialization and efficiency.
Defender Offers a limited, stable product line. They are cost-effective, maintain quality and use price competition to create barriers and defend their position against potential competitors.	Mechanistic structure which relies on a functional form with centralized decision-making and control, vertical integration and high degrees of technical specialization.
Analyzer Combines the strengths of defenders and prospectors. Pursue a 'second-in' strategy, imitating and improving on their competitors' product offerings, producing a range of high-quality products at lower cost.	Mixes functional and divisional structures to create a matrix where project or brand managers act as integrators between resource groups and project units. Internal differentiation allows some parts flexibility and change, while other parts remain traditional and stable.
Reactor Not a strategy at all since reactors respond to environmental threats and opportunities in an *ad hoc* fashion. Top management has not defined either goals or a long-term plan, taking instead any actions that appear necessary.	No clear structural approach since the company has no clear direction or approach to design. The characteristics of the company's structure may shift abruptly depending on the current needs.

Based on R.E. Miles and C.C. Snow, 'Organizations: new concepts for new forms', *California Management Review*, vol. 28, no. 3, 1986, pp. 62–73; and C.C. Snow, R.E. Miles and H.J. Coleman, 'Manging twenty-first century network organizations', *Organizational Dynamics*, vol. 20, no. 3, 1992, pp. 5–20.

Complementarities: the potential for mutually reinforcing effects when one or more business practices are operated in parallel or simultaneously. Practices are said to be complementary when doing more of one increases the returns for doing more of another.

based on **complementarities**. These refer to the potential for mutually reinforcing effects when one or more business practices are joined together. Practices are said to be complementary when doing more of one increases the returns for doing more of another. Research suggests that within a company, there is a need to link strategy and structure to process. For example, the introduction of a just-in-time system needs to be complemented by appropriate manufacturing, information and human resource systems. More recently, Whittington has stressed that a critical aspect of the concept of complementarities is in the negative effects of non-complementarity for an organization. This refers to the dangers of *dysynergy* rather than simply the benefits of *synergy* (Pettigrew and Whittington, 2001).

The INNFORM project

This research used an international survey to compare new forms of organizing in Europe between 1992 and 1996. A total of 450 large and medium-sized European companies responded. While finding no evidence of revolutionary change, the researchers discovered, as predicted by complementarity theory, that 'whole system' change was required for success. To reap the benefits of organizational innovation companies had to think and act holistically, making carefully aligned innovations in:

- *Structures*: delayering; decentralization of operations, although not strategic decisions; and greater use of project-team structures to increase horizontal knowledge- and resource-sharing; and new human resource practices.

- *Processes*: investments in information technology and intranets to support internal networking to share knowledge horizontally and spread accountability vertically. Investments were also made in training and team- and mission-building.

- *Boundaries*: a focus on core competences, increasing use of outsourcing, joint ventures and alliances, but limited diversification.

New forms of organizing: the multiple indicators

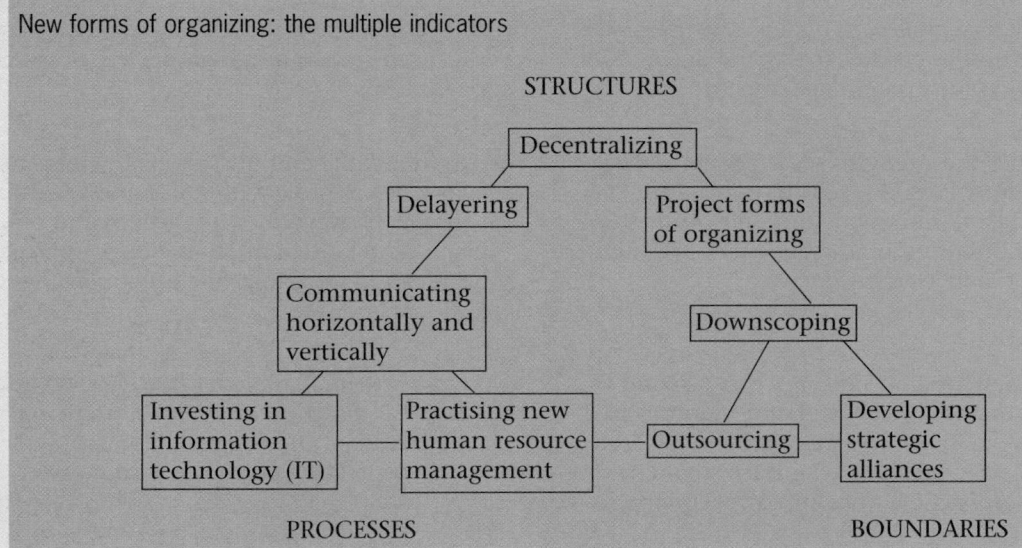

Source: A.M. Pettigrew, Organizing to improve company performance', *Hot Topics*, vol. 1, no. 5, February 1999, Warwick Business School, Warwick University.

Researchers concluded that high performance was obtained when change was implemented in many of the 9 elements detailed in the diagram. Piecemeal changes (with the exception of IT) produced little performance benefit. Indeed, singular innovations frequently produced loss of performance. Few European firms simultaneously changed their structures, processes and boundaries. However, the 5 per cent which did so in a complementary way gained an average performance premium of 60 per cent. The change element that singly produced the greatest benefit was investment in information technology.

The authors noted that while many companies were moving towards flatter and more flexible ways of organizing, few were doing so coherently. They concluded that it was only those which innovated coherently that reaped the rewards. Piecemeal initiatives typically cost more than they were worth.

Based on A.M. Pettigrew, Organizing to improve company performance', *Hot Topics*, vol. 1, no. 5, February 1999, Warwick Business School, Warwick University; R. Whittington, A.M. Pettigrew, S. Peck, E. Fenton and M. Conyon, 'Change and complementarities in the new competitive landscape: a European panel study, 1992–1996', *Organizational Science*, vol. 10, no. 5, 1999a, pp. 583–600; R. Whittington, A.M. Pettigrew and W. Ruigrok, 'New notions of organizational "fit"', *Financial Times*, 'Mastering Strategies' supplement, 29 November 1999b, pp. 8, 10; W. Ruigrok, A.M. Pettigrew, S. Peck and R. Whittington, 'Corporate restructuring and new forms of organizing in Europe', *Management International Review*, vol. 39, no. 2, 1999 pp. 41–64; A.M. Pettigrew, 'Success and failure in corporate transformation initiatives', in R.D. Galliers and W.R.J. Baets (eds), *Information Technology and Organizational Transformation*, Wiley, Chichester, 1998, pp. 271–89; A.M. Pettigrew and E.M. Fenton (eds), *The Innovating Organization*, Sage Publications, London, 2000.

Strategic choice and environments

Strategic choice: the view that holds that environments, markets and technology of an organization are the result of senior management decisions.

The debate about contemporary organization design involves a consideration of the decisions that managers make about their organizations within their environments. Thus, strategic choice and environment are central concepts. Both Tom Burns and George Stalker (1994) and Paul Lawrence and Jay Lorsch (1967) stressed the importance of an organization's environment. Their original contributions were concerned primarily with the market conditions and took a deterministic perspective. Their critics, however, pointed to the neglect of **strategic choice** in decisions about organization structure. John Child (1972) rectified this omission, arguing that there was no one best organization structure and that companies could have different structures. However, he disagreed with the contention that those structures were *determined* by 'external, operational contingencies'. Instead, he stressed the part played by powerful leaders and groups, who exerted their influence to create organizational forms which suited their particular values and preferences.

Strategic choice holds that decisions about the number of hierarchical levels, the span of control, etc., are ultimately based on the personal beliefs and political manoeuvrings of those who make them. Strategic choice researchers continue to focus on companies' environments, but they became interested in how senior managers make the choices that link their firms' strategies to their organization structures. These commentators have criticized the deterministic writers on a number of issues:

1. *The idea that an organization should 'fit' its environment.* That is, while there are choices about organization structure design, these will be relatively limited. Thus, for two similar companies operating in a stable environment to succeed, each would make similar choices about the shape of its organization structures. However, there are examples of companies making very different structural choices in the same circumstances and both succeeding.

2. *The idea that cause and effect are linked in a simple (linear) manner*. This ignores the fact that organizations are part of a larger, complex environmental system consisting of other organizations with which they interact. Managers can create their own environments, and the idea that organizations merely adapt to their environment is too simple a view.

3. *The assumption that the choice of organization structure is an automatic reaction to the facts presented*. Studies show that such decisions are made by managers on the basis of the interpretations that they have made about the nature of their environment. The same environment can be perceived in different ways by various managers, who might implement different structures which can be equally successful.

4. *The view that choices of organization structure are not political*. Linked to the previous point, political factors will impinge on choices about structure as much as issues of perception and interpretation.

Child suggested that organization structuring was a political process in which power and influence were used to decide on the types of job, levels of hierarchy, spans of control, etc. that were to be adopted and, by implication, also which markets to enter and with which companies to link up. His work stimulated discussion in three main areas (Child, 1997):

- the human agents (individuals or groups) who exercise choice in the design of organizations;

- the nature of the environment within which an organization exists;

- the relationships between organizational agents (for example, managers) and that environment.

Enacted environment: the environment of an organization that exists for members by virtue of the interpretations they make of what is occurring 'outside' the organization, and the way their own actions influence or shape those occurrences.

The first of the two major strategic choice perspectives was presented by Karl Weick (1979), who introduced the concept of **enacted environment**. This is the notion that organization and environment are created together (enacted) through the social interaction processes of key organizational participants – usually managers (Smircich and Stubbart, 1985; Westwood and Clegg, 2003). The environment within which managers work and make decisions does not consist of a simple set of objective conditions which are just 'given'. Here we use Tony Watson's (2002) definition of the concept.

He explained that the environment of an organization exists for its members by virtue of the interpretations that they make of what is occurring 'outside' the organization, and the way in which their own actions influence or shape those occurrences. He illustrates it with the example of a market and a product (Watson, 2002, p. 203). A business organization does not go out and 'find' a market which it then satisfies in order to stay in business. Instead, its managers first strategically identify the *possibility* of a market relationship with certain would-be customers outside the organization. They then work at their product in the light of the possibilities and potentials that they envisage. Next they present the product to the would-be customers in a way that will *persuade* them to trade with the organization, again in the light of their *interpretations* of the inclinations of these potential customers. Active sense-making is central to all this.

Ian Brooks offered another example of enactment, this time from the football industry. He noted that a number of football teams are relegated annually from the higher divisions and commented that, according to press reports, many had given up the struggle well before the end of the season. He noted that they stopped spending money on new players and prepared themselves for leaner times in lower divisions. By doing this, they increased their chances of being relegated since, without new players or the motivation to stay up, their performance remained poor, or even declined, and they were indeed relegated. When this happened, the clubs looked back and said that since they knew that they were going down, they did the sensible thing and saved their money and energy for the following season. He asked whether these football clubs could have stayed up had they adopted a different strategy. Did they enact their environment (Brooks, 2003)?

Thus in Weick's view, managers *enact* rather than *react* to their environments. That is, they *create* their organization's environment, making it easier for them to understand and modify it. This **managerial enactment** view differs from that of the environmental determinist school discussed in the previous chapter. However, the fact that managers make choices about their organization's strategy, processes, structures and relationships with other firms does not tell us *how* they do so or why. Watson, however, answers the 'why' question, describing the choices and contingencies in organizational shaping (see box below).

> **Managerial enactment**: the active modification of perceived and selected parts of the organization's environment by managers.

Managerial argument, negotiation and choice

The contingencies of the organization's size, technology or environment are not given 'things' that directly and straightforwardly 'affect' the organization. Managers always interpret them, and 'what they are' is partly an outcome of the interpretations that managers make. For example, an organization is not unequivocally and objectively 'large' or 'small', and therefore needing to be pushed towards a more or a less bureaucratic structure and culture to achieve a 'fit' between contingencies and organizational shape. Managers will typically differ on just what a small, medium or large company is. For example, an argument was witnessed in a management meeting along the lines:

'We are becoming a rather large business now and need to think of the implications of this for our efficiency.'

'Oh no, I wouldn't say that. We have a long way to go before we start to worry about size.'

Moreover, managers may choose to act upon the perceived 'contingent factor' (in this case, size) and change it, rather than make some structural change to accommodate it. The first manager in the above conversation, for example, went on to argue that what he took to be 'bigness' of the organization meant that some more formal operating procedures were going to be needed to avoid 'things getting out of control'. The other managers disliked his ideas, one of whom expressed a personal 'hatred of big bureaucracy'. The discussion then proceeded along the lines that that it would be preferable to try to 'keep things small' than to move in the direction of tighter bureaucracy. They then discussed ways of splitting the organization into two smaller ones. In so doing, the contingency of size was tackled, rather than a structural arrangement made to 'fit' with that contingency. This case illustrates the process of managerial argument, negotiation and choice.

The managers start off by identifying the 'contingency' of large size – a circumstance that does not fit with what we can take to be currently a fairly loosely bureaucratized structure and culture. But their interpretation of the salience of this contingency differs. Some personal values, like one person's 'hatred of big bureaucracy', are then brought into the argument. It does appear, though, that the discussion then proceeded in a direction whereby the managers agreed that there was an issue about size. But instead of *reacting* to the 'contingency' of larger size, they considered acting upon the contingency itself. In effect, they were contemplating 'getting rid' of 'bigness' by splitting up the organization and retaining 'smallness'. This possibility is recognized by the double-headed arrow between the managerial argument and the enacted contingencies boxes in the diagram on p. 546.

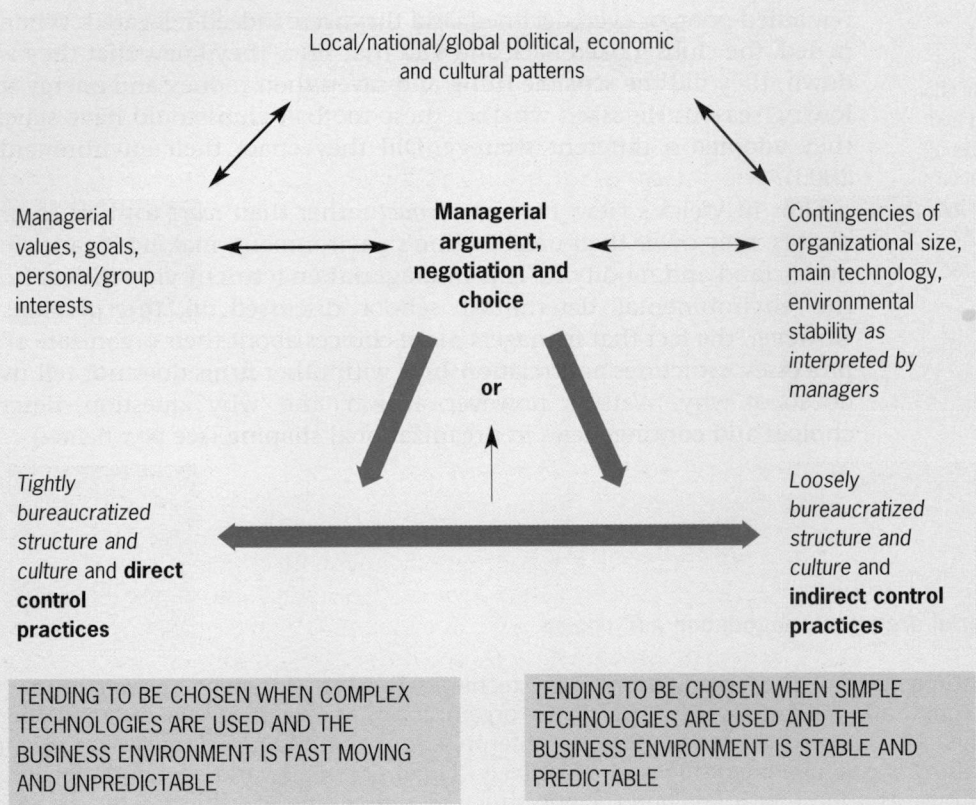

Local/national/global political, economic and cultural patterns

Managerial values, goals, personal/group interests

Managerial argument, negotiation and choice

Contingencies of organizational size, main technology, environmental stability *as interpreted by managers*

or

Tightly bureaucratized structure and culture and **direct control practices**

Loosely bureaucratized structure and culture and **indirect control practices**

TENDING TO BE CHOSEN WHEN COMPLEX TECHNOLOGIES ARE USED AND THE BUSINESS ENVIRONMENT IS FAST MOVING AND UNPREDICTABLE

TENDING TO BE CHOSEN WHEN SIMPLE TECHNOLOGIES ARE USED AND THE BUSINESS ENVIRONMENT IS STABLE AND PREDICTABLE

The double-headed arrow between *managerial argument* and *managerial values* recognizes that managers' values and interests are themselves emergent and enacted phenomena. Managers develop their values, goals and interests within the arguments and negotiations that they have with other managers, and do not simply bring them, performed, into those debates. The remaining double-headed arrows remind us that organization structures and cultures must always be seen in a wider social, economic and political context. However, this context is not just one that makes an 'input' in processes of organizational shaping. The way managers generally attempt to shape organizations is equally an input into the shaping of the societies and changing global relationships of which organizations are a part. Organizations make societies and societies make organizations, we might say, to put it very simply.

Based on Tony J. Watson, *Organising and Managing Work*, Financial Times/Prentice Hall, Harlow, 2002, pp. 257–9. Figure (p. 259) reprinted by permission of Pearson Education Ltd. © Pearson Education Limited 2002.

Jeffrey Pfeffer

An answer to the question of 'why' managers make choices is provided by the second major strategic choice perspective – *resource dependence theory*. It was developed by Jeffrey Pfeffer and Gerald Salancik (1978). Their theory sees every organization as being at the mercy of its environment, needing resources from it in the form of employees, equipment, raw materials, knowledge, capital and outlets for its products and services. The environment which gives it power also controls access to these resources. It makes the firm dependent on its environment. Hence the name of the theory. The environment (in the form of customers, suppliers, competitors, government and other stakeholders) uses its power to make demands upon the organization to provide not only desirable products and services at competitive prices, but also efficient organization structures and processes.

Pfeffer and Salancik argue that although organizations are dependent on their environments, their managers have still to achieve their chosen objectives. To do this, they need to identify the critical resources needed – defined as those without which the company cannot function. They then trace these back to their sources in their environment, and identify the nature of their dependence. For practical reasons, only the most critical and scarce resources are focused on. While it is possible to distinguish and discuss a single dependency relation between an organization, in practice, a firm will be experiencing a complex set of dependencies between itself and the various elements in its environment. When costs or risks are high, companies will team up to reduce their dependencies and risks of bankruptcy.

For example, for McDonald's fast food restaurants, having beef, buns and cheese is critical, having plastic customer seating is not. Scarcity refers to how widely available that resource is in the organization's environment. Control of resources that are most critical and scarce gives environmental elements the greatest power over a company. Pfeffer and Salancik state that the first step in applying the approach is to understand the organizational environment with respect to criticality and scarcity of resources. The second step is for managers to find ways of reducing that dependency, eliminating it altogether, or making the others dependent on their organization. Companies use their power differences to avoid excessive dependence on their environment, in order to maintain control over required resources and thereby reduce uncertainty and increase their autonomy.

There are a number of dependence-reduction strategies. If you are a manufacturer, you could develop long-term contracts with suppliers, have several suppliers for your crucial components, purchase part-ownership of your suppliers, establish a joint venture or simply buy up all the resources that are critical to your company. In the case of a motor manufacturer, these would mean steel for car bodies, rubber for tyres, coal to fire factory furnaces, and ships and railways to transport this material. In order to secure access to the critical resources that he needed, we know that Henry Ford bought iron mines, coal mines, rubber plantations, shipping lines and railways. This corporate strategy, which involves acquiring related businesses assimilated into the purchaser, is called **vertical integration**. Although a popular strategy, mergers and acquisitions are only one of many kinds of relationship that one company can have with another as it seeks to reduce its dependency on its environment.

Vertical integration: a situation where one company buys another in order to make the latter's output its own input, thereby securing that source of supply through ownership.

Stop and Criticize

Select an organization that you have read about or have first-hand experience of. What is its strategy? How effective is it? What advice or recommendations would you make to its chief executive and the company board?

Bounded instability and non-linearity

Both Miles and Snow's and Pfeffer and Salancik's theories describe organizational environments that are unchanging enough to be understood and acted upon by their managers. By about the mid-1990s, however, such thinking had changed. Commentators noted how organizations' environments, both in the private and public sectors, had become more complex, more prone to sudden unexpected changes, and would continue to be so in the future. Neil Glass (1996) summarized some of these features which are shown in table 16.3.

Glass's assertion is one that is reinforced by the management rhetoric. It holds that the past was more predictable, and that such predictability has now disappeared. On the other hand, business historians who have studied the 'capitalist era' that began between the eighteenth and nineteenth centuries challenge this view. Indeed, some of the management literature from the early twentieth

Table 16.3: Organizations: past assumptions and current realities

Past assumptions	Current realities
Closed systems The organization is almost a simple 'closed system'. Generally, what it decides to do will take place without too much disruption from outside events.	*Open systems* Organizations are complex 'open systems' constantly, deeply influenced by and influencing their environments. Often, intended actions will be diverted off-course by external events or even by internal, political or cultural processes of the organization itself.
Stable environment The operating environment is stable enough for management to understand it sufficiently well to develop a relevant, detailed strategy and for that strategy to be relevant by the time it comes to be implemented.	*Turbulent environment* The environment is changing so rapidly (continuously throwing up new opportunities and threats) that top management cannot expect to have sufficient sense of what is happening to formulate very detailed strategies. Moreover, by the time a strategy moves from concept to being operationalized, key aspects of the environment have often changed.
Predictable causality In an organization or an economy, there are a series of levers that you can apply to cause a known response (for example, if you cut staff numbers, profitability should go up; if you increase interest rates, the value of your currency will rise).	*Unpredictable causality* The simple linear models of cause and effect have broken down and many actions can lead to quite unexpected (positive or negative) effects.

Based on *European Management Journal*, vol. 14, no. 1, Neil Glass, 'Chaos, non-linear systems and day-to-day management', pp. 98–106, Copyright 1996, with permission from Elsevier.

century talks about 'an era of unprecedented social and technological change'. What we now refer to as the 'globalization' of trade was, in many instances, as widespread in 1900 as it is today. Hence, one cannot take it for granted that the past consisted of 'good old, stable days', whereas the organizations of today increasingly face turbulent environments (see Thompson and Davidson, 1995).

Stop and Criticize

How does the rhetoric of 'turbulent environments' serve the interests of different groups? Consider this question from the point of view of managers, management consultants and the media.

Bounded instability: a state in which there is a mixture of order and disorder, there are many unpredictable events and changes, and an organization's behaviour has an irregular pattern.

Bounded instability has a very specific scientific meaning. It refers to a state in which there is a mixture of order and disorder, but in which a basic pattern of the systems behaviour can be discerned. It can be contrasted with **explosive instability**, which is a state in which there is no order or pattern whatsoever. Glass (1996) argued that over the last twenty years car markets had been affected by changes in oil prices, environmental pressure and consumer tastes. In 2000, the British government's Competition Commission's report into car prices, the selling of cars by the Consumers' Association and P&O Stenna Ferries, plus the start of internet car shopping in general, have increased industry uncertainty. In such a situation, motor manufacturers will tend to abandon long-term forecasts and instead will seek to identify and exploit general trends.

Explosive instability: a state in which there is no order or pattern.

Stable equilibrium: a state in which the elements are in a balanced state or quickly return to a state of balance.

Historically, the concept of bounded instability is understood in relation to that of a **stable equilibrium**. The latter is a state whose elements are always in, or which will quickly return to, a state of balance. Central heating systems with pre-set thermostats provide a domestic illustration of the concept. For many years, motor car and soap powder markets were in stable equilibrium. Product improvements and advertising affected sales of one company's product for a while before the market shares of competitors returned to broadly the same percentages.

Commentators argue that, for many organizations, bounded instability has replaced stable equilibrium. Airlines have found that denationalization, followed by greater competition, dramatically changed their working environment (Colling, 1995). In Britain, banks were first challenged by legislation opening up competition from building societies, then by telephone banking and, shortly after, by internet banking. Competitors can come from nowhere to dominate a market. A linear system is one in which a given action will cause a directly predictable outcome. Turn on a tap and water flows out. In non-linear systems, actions tend to have both expected and also unexpected outcomes (both positive and negative) because changes or complex interactions of factors tend to amplify consequences. Hence, in complex, non-linear systems, small actions can very quickly create unforeseen consequences, which are self-reinforcing. Actions can produce outcomes which are both unexpected and directly opposite to those intended.

Complexity and non-linearity in Cumbria, England

In February 2000, the British Nuclear Installations Inspectorate (NII) published a damning report into the falsification of safety data concerning Mox pellets destined for Japanese reactors by staff at the Sellafield nuclear reprocessing plant in Cumbria in North West England. Following this disclosure:

- John Taylor, the chief executive of BNFL, resigned;

- in March, equipment in the vitrification unit of the plant was sabotaged and detectives were interviewing employees;

- BNFL's biggest customer, Japan, insisted on returning the processed fuel rods that were accompanied by the false data. It warned that it would impose a permanent boycott of the company;

- Germany, Sweden and Switzerland instituted similar boycotts, and the United States planned to send a team of safety inspectors;

- the Irish and Danish governments then began discussing a bid to have BNFL shut down because of the environmental damage caused by its discharges into the North Sea;

- the British government was considering ending all nuclear reprocessing at Sellafield;

- plans for the partial privatization of BNFL by the government were shelved.

The cause of the data falsification was that workers were said to have become bored by the repetitive process of measuring the uranium-plutonium oxide pellets. Their work was tedious, repetitive and not strictly necessary as computers had already performed the task. However, BNFL's Japanese customers insisted that it was done to ensure quality control. These employees simply copied the results of the previous tests to save themselves work. The full consequences of their actions are continuing to have an impact on the company.

Based on Cathy Cooper, 'Management blasted at nuclear plant', *People Management*, vol. 6, no. 6, 19 March 2000, pp. 16–17; *The Economist*, 'Running scared', 8 April 2000, p. 37.

In an unpredictable environment, where it is difficult or impossible to plan, strategic intent replaces strategic planning. This involves setting a fairly clear direction, then continuously adapting the detail to cope with specific events, threats and opportunities. One needs entrepreneurial and creative people who are constantly on the lookout for small advantages.

However insignificant these advantages may appear to be at the time, they can often be quickly amplified into self-reinforcing, positive outcomes for the company. The stress is upon *creating self-renewal*, never-ending improvement, and on rewarding change agents. In other words:

contextual → organization → human resource → organization
change   strategy   requirements   structure

Structuring and managing endemic uncertainty

Complexity theory has been applied to business to understand the behaviour of large complex systems. The problem for managers is determining how all the different forces and elements interact to shape the overall system, especially in a situation where minor events can have enormous consequences because of the chain reaction that they trigger off. Chaos theorists argue that since radical uncertainty is now endemic, traditional, analytically driven strategies to shape the needs of the business are obsolete. The best management structures, they claim, do not adapt to their environment but emerge from it. The *survival* of the fittest has been replaced by the *arrival* of the fittest.

Sherman and Schultz (1998) wrote that the shift to a non-linear world means that the organization structure of any business works best when it is self-organized. Rather than imposing a given structure upon a company, senior management should allow the organization of effort and people to evolve in response to ongoing messages from customers. According to Brown and Eisenhardt (1998), peak performance at the edge of chaos comes from establishing a few simple rules (hard-and-fast rules that define direction without confining it) and adopting an approach which allows different businesses to co-evolve by sharing resources and capabilities. The latter involves rewarding individual business performance and maintaining porous boundaries, allowing a multiplicity of volutary collaborations within and between businesses (Eisenhardt and Galunic, 2000).

Being a complex system, the market reflects intricate, low-level interactions, and the best solutions to problems come from those who are constantly communicating with one another at ground level, rather than being issued with directives by those on high. The invisible hand of the market replaces the visible hand of the manager. 'Try something and see what happens' is the guiding principle.

Based on Thomas M. Hout, 'Are managers obsolete?', *Harvard Business Review*, March–April 1999, pp. 161–8; H. Sherman and R. Schultz, *Open Boundaries: Creating Business Innovation Through Complexity*, Perseus Books, Reading, MA, 1998; S.L. Brown and K.M. Eisenhardt, *Competing on the Edge: Strategy as Structured Chaos*, Harvard Business Review Press, Boston, MA, 1998; K.M. Eisenhardt and D.C. Galunic, 'Co-evolving: at last a way to make synergies', *Harvard Business Review*, vol. 78, no. 1, January–February 2000, pp. 91–101.

Market, hierarchy and interorganizational relationships

The environmental volatility discussed earlier has led many organizations to abandon isolation in favour of establishing interorganizational relationships. Discussions of organization structure have therefore increasingly focused on co-operative relationships between organizations, intended to develop new, joint strategies. Table 16.4 contrasts three 'ideal-type' organization forms. These do not describe any particular existing organization. Instead, each represents a model or provides a checklist against which to compare and assess real organizations.

On the far right of the table, the market portrays a particular 'perfect' market situation. Economists define this as a situation in which buyers and sellers possess full (perfect) knowledge of prices. On the left of the table is the hierarchical form which is best represented by Max Weber's bureaucratic arrangements. In the centre are interorganizational relationships characterized by various co-operative arrangements between organizations. Here it is important to identify those organizations that are networked (via technology or by an umbrella organization perhaps) and whose relationships typify the characteristics of the true network form, which emphasizes trust, common needs, etc. Not all examples of the interorganizational form – alliances, joint ventures or networks – will necessarily be governed or co-ordinated in a way that fits with the descriptors shown in table 16.4. In reality, a single organization will often exhibit all three types of arrangements because hierarchy, interorganizational forms and market are ideal-type concepts, and are not found in a pure form or in isolation.

Market

This perspective from market economics contrasts the relationship between the 'unplanned' nature of market relations between individuals, groups and organizations and the 'planned' nature of hierarchical, bureaucratic organizational life. Institutional economists like Oliver Williamson (1975) and business historians like Alfred Chandler (Chandler, 1962; Chandler et al., 1999) start from the perspective of a world without organizations, and ask how and why they should arise. They then focus on the exchanges that take place between individuals, which they call 'transactions'. The selling of an item by one party and its purchase by another represents a 'transaction'. The authors consider how these can be achieved at the lowest cost to those involved. Back in 1937, Ronald Coase, a Nobel prize-winning economist, argued that setting up companies made sense when the 'transaction costs' associated with buying things in the market exceeded the costs of establishing and maintaining a bureaucracy (hierarchy). Modern technology is shifting the balance of advantage away from companies and towards markets.

Individuals could obtain all goods and services that they needed through the marketplace. The market will work to the benefit of all concerned, except when it 'fails': that is, becomes inefficient. In these circumstances, transactions are removed from the marketplace and placed instead within organizations (which Williamson chooses to call 'hierarchies'). The interest of these writers was solely upon these two structural forms (markets and hierarchies), and was focused on the reasons why transactions occurred in one or the other and why they move between them. The market model sees the co-ordination of social activity as being accomplished through private dealings between individuals, groups or organizations. Once a transaction is completed between the parties, it does not imply any repetition in the future. Markets are a way of bringing together buyers and sellers. A free competition market has the following features (Colebatch and Lamour, 1993, pp. 19–20):

- there are a large number of buyers and sellers;
- they know what they want;
- they are able to pay for it;
- they act independently of each other;
- they are free to enter and leave the market;
- information about products and processes is free and accessible;
- there are no costs on making deals.

Table 16.4: Contrasting organization arrangements

	Hierarchy	Interorganizational relationships (includes *some* alliances, joint ventures, consortia and network organizations, including virtual)	Market
Organizational boundaries	Single administrative authority	Blurred boundaries between firms	Distinct boundaries between firms
Flexibility	Low	Medium	High
Resource/asset management	Resources are managed within the organization	Resources are complementary and may be jointly owned. Firms can influence the management of one another's resources	Resources can be the basis of competition between firms and are used to gain competitive advantage
Communication and co-ordination	Actors communicate within the framework of a formal bureaucracy in which activities are co-ordinated through a clear organizational hierarchy in which actors have degrees of authority. Communication is exercised through routines, rules and procedures	Actors communicate on an open, often informal basis and activities are negotiated between parties. Communication may be face to face, articulated through contracts and/or electronically mediated. Activities are co-ordinated through mutual agreement and often interorganizational teams which span individual firm boundaries	Actors communicate on a formal basis and through contracts.
Information exchange	Information is widely shared within the organization in accordance with departmental and individual relationships depicted in the organization's structure chart/diagram	Information is exchanged between parties on an ongoing basis. This is one of the key characteristics of network forms and is often a key motive for engaging in collaborative relations	Information is exchanged largely through the price mechanism and relates to the product/service, not to any internal aspects of the organization (for example, the methods of production, costs etc.)
Relationship between actors	The basis of actor relationships is the employment contract. There is a medium to high degree of trust between parties and actors exhibit a high degree of dependency upon the employing organization	Parties are interdependent. There is an expectation that the relationship between firms will endure for some time and that mutual trust will be developed over time	Parties are independent of one another. The basis of their relationship is mainly competitive and does not advocate open exchange of information. There is no expectation of an enduring relationship

Developed by Moira Fischbacher.

British National Health Service: from hierarchy to market?

In the early 1990s, under the Conservative government of Mrs Margaret Thatcher (now Lady Thatcher), the British National Health Service (NHS) was reorganized. At that time, it represented an example of a bureaucratic, hierarchical organization, and possessed all its advantages and disadvantages. In an effort to improve the efficiency of healthcare delivery, the government introduced the element of market discipline, thereby seeking to change its organizational form from hierarchy to that of market.

Specifically, this meant that general practitioners (GPs) and health authorities were given funds to purchase certain health services from hospital and community providers. These were services which had previously been provided by the health authorities themselves. Hospitals were reorganized into non-profit hospital trusts, thereby giving hospital and community health providers autonomous status. Separating the purchasing of services from their provision and encouraging purchasers to respond to price signals created a market.

Research into this political-economic innovation has revealed a variety of responses. In some situations, the NHS hospital trust's contract with the local health authority was an exceedingly detailed and formalized affair. In other situations this was less so. Moira Fischbacher's case study, conducted in the Glasgow area, found that contracts were neither as detailed nor as specified as elsewhere. She argued that a network rather than a true market had developed. The purchasers and providers established long-term relationships (relational contracting) which were based on mutual trust, and they relied on social relationships rather than formal, annual contracts to organize the activities and exchanges between themselves. She concluded that this case demonstrated the move from a hierarchy to a network, rather than to a market, as the Conservative government had wanted. In the late 1990s, the Labour government decided to modify the NHS structure once again, and removed the purchasing function and contracting system from GPs and health boards, thereby returning the NHS to a more unified structure or hierarchical form.

Based on Moira Fischbacher and Arthur Francis, 'Purchaser–provider relationships and innovation: a case study of GP purchasing in Glasgow', *Financial Accountability and Management*, vol. 14, no. 4, 1998, pp. 281–98.

Stop and Criticize

To what extent is there a market in higher education at the present time? What are the costs and benefits for students and for the university, if the former act as 'buyers' and the latter behave as 'sellers'?

Hierarchy

This is the structural arrangement that most people think of when someone says 'organization'. In this context, the term 'hierarchy' is used in two different, albeit related ways. First, following Williamson, it refers to a situation in which some transactions are removed from the marketplace and take place instead within the boundaries of a single organization: when, for example, a company decides to stop contracting out its cleaning and provides the service itself. Institutional economists would say that an organization hierarchy arises when the boundary of a firm expands to bring within it the flow of transactions and resources that were previously conducted in the marketplace. A fully integrated corporation, in the traditional style, is then created in order to (Chandler, 1962, 1990):

■ co-ordinate administrative activities;

■ reduce risk and the cost of transactions;

■ take advantage of the economies of scale and scope.

The second and more familiar usage of the term 'hierarchy' refers to the traditional, structural arrangement whose various forms and typically mechanistic features were discussed earlier. This is the most integrated and most formal arrangement. It is neither interorganizational nor co-operative. The organization is a single entity, although it may be divided into parts. The National Health Service in the UK is a single organization, but consists of NHS trusts. Nevertheless, its members share many of the same values and norms, follow its practices and procedures, and exchange information about problems to be dealt with. The two concepts of hierarchy come together when, for example, having decided to end outsourcing of its catering, a company establishes its own catering department and appoints a catering manager who then appoints assistant managers, supervisors and restaurant staff. That is, a hierarchical structural arrangement is established to provide the service.

Music direct?

Consider the changing marketplace for music at the start of the twenty-first century. Music buyers used to visit their local music stores in the city centre to buy pre-packaged disks. How do they get their music now? In particular, what effect has the internet had on music purchase?

Think about the effect of the changes that you observe on the artists, recording companies, music publishing houses and music retailers. Are we close to reaching direct source-to-consumer selling in this retail sector or is there still some way to go?

Merger: a situation in which two companies voluntarily join together, pooling the ownership interests of the two sets of shareholders to own the new combined entity.

Acquisition: a situation in which one firm buys the equity stake or assets of another. A major control acquisition is called a 'take-over' and may be friendly or hostile.

A single hierarchy arrangement can result from two companies merging, or from one company acquiring another. A corporate **merger** pools the ownership interests of shareholders of the previously separate companies, whereas in an **acquisition**, one firm buys the equity stake or the assets of another. Whichever form of combination is adopted, the assets of the two organizations are integrated and managed jointly, while their personnel are assigned positions within a single organization hierarchy. Mergers and acquisitions are most likely to occur when the assets of the two companies cannot be easily separated, where joint management is required or where there is a high risk of assets being appropriated by one of the companies. The advisability of mergers (Haspeslagh, 1999) and of acquisitions (Anand, 1999) to form such a single, hierarchical organization have been the focus of much debate in corporate strategy. Some industrial sectors are more prone to mergers than others (for example, telecommunications); media (movies, records, magazines, newspapers); financial (investment and commercial banks, insurance companies); chemicals and pharmaceuticals; autos; oil and gas; and industrial machinery.

Contrasting markets with hierarchy, markets work best when:

■ the transactions are straightforward;

■ they are non-repetitive;

■ they do not require specific investment in the transaction;

■ all the necessary information needed is conveyed by price and is sufficient.

Hierarchies work best when the transactions between parties:

■ are certain;

- occur frequently;
- require specific investments of time, money, energy, equipment and technology;
- are not easily transferred out to the market.

Stop and Criticize

You are the manufacturer of an internationally famous brand of alcoholic drink. A large part of your product's image and success is based on the packaging that surrounds your bottle and its contents. It is this that shoppers see first on the supermarket shelves. To obtain this, you are currently considering either establishing your own in-house printing-packaging department or tendering out your requirements to sub-contractors. List the advantages and disadvantages of each option.

Japanese mergers

A major obstacle to structural reform in Japanese industry is employees' reluctance to transfer loyalty to a new company. While an American or European merger may be concluded within two or three months of announcement, Japanese ones take typically between two and three years. Moreover, they tend to create much post-merger discord and bitter internal rivalries. A major reason for this is the need to 'save face'. Even when there are clear disparities in strength and size of the companies involved, such as in the merger between Japan Airlines, the country's top carrier, and Japan Air Systems, a domestic carrier, the merger is billed as occurring in a 'spirit of equality'. Preserving this balance creates false expectations and problems.

When in 1996 Tokyo Bank merged with Mitsubishi Bank, a bigger but less prestigious bank, Tokyo Bank employees were outnumbered three-to-one. Many left and others complained of being sidelined. The merged Bank of Tokyo–Mitsubishi still contains unofficial Tokyo Bank 'societies' where disgruntled employees air their grievances to each other. Despite Nissan Motor's merger with Prince Motor in 1966, older employees in the 1980s still identified themselves as belonging to one or other of the companies. When Dai-Ichi Bank merged with Nihon Kangyo Bank in 1971, the new organization, Dai-Ichi Kangyo Bank (DKB), kept two personnel departments for twenty years, for each of the two sets of employees.

Based on 'Marriage in name only', *The Economist*, 2 March 2002, pp. 72–3.

Interorganizational relationships

Between hierarchy and markets one finds intermediate examples of interorganizational relationships in which two or more organizations share resources and activities to pursue a common strategy. Interest has hugely expanded in these in recent years (Oliver and Ebers, 1998). Walter Powell (1987, p. 67) noted that: 'By looking at the economic organization as a choice between markets and contractual relations on one side, and at conscious planning within a firm on the other, we fail to see the enormous variety that forms of co-operative arrangements can take.' He concluded that these non-market, non-bureaucratic organizational relationships were becoming highly significant features of the modern organizational landscape. Rubery et al. (2002) suggested three main reasons for the growth of these complex or permeable organizational forms:

1. *Reduced transaction costs*: The costs of managing outsourced or shared activities have declined due to cheaper new technologies. This reduces the

transaction costs associated with running less integrated firms (Williamson, 1985; Seminger, 1991; Schendel, 1995; *The Economist*, 2001a, 2001b).

2. *Priority on competences*: Organizations focus on the things in which they excel and hand (outsource) all other non-core activities to equally focused specialists. They also link up with firms to expand into new areas (Penrose, 1959; Montgomery, 1995).

3. *Source of learning and knowledge*: These arrangements provide a way of acquiring knowledge and learning in situations where these are significant factors in competitiveness (Cooms and Ketchen, 1999).

Other literature reviews have identified a wide range of internal and external triggers that lead organizations to form networks with others. The main ones are summarized in table 16.5.

Table 16.5: Triggers for interorganizational collaboration

Internal triggers
- Ensure the survival of the firm
- Increased profitability potential
- Limited finance for development
- Limited technological know-how
- Collecting information about competitor
- Collecting information about a competitor
- Realization that a partner can produce a good more efficiently
- Realization that market opportunities cannot be exploited solo
- Limited management expertise/desire to buy in management talent
- Lack of resources for marketing products and services to best advantage
- Limited essential expertise and knowledge in foreign markets and cultures
- Finding a means to replace the market mechanism (rather than trading in a market setting, the firm enters into a longer-term networking arrangement which effectively supersedes the market)

External triggers
- Regional policy to 'lift the game' of a depressed region
- Government encouragement (for example, grants, allowances)
- Spreading business risk by diversifying out of a single economy
- Overcoming pressure generated by customers in the marketplace
- Overcoming prejudice in a market by joining with an indigenous partner
- Generating national or global flexibility by being able to join and leave networks
- Taking advantage of a naturally occurring phenomenon (for example, the opportunity to regenerate an area following a flood)

From Ewa Buttery, Liz Fulop and Alan Buttery, 'Networks and inter-organizational relations', in Liz Fulop and Stephen Linstead, *Management: A Critical Text*, Macmillan Business, London, 1999, pp. 416–17. Reproduced with permission of Palgrave Macmillan.

Strategic alliance: an arrangement in which two firms agree to co-operate to achieve specific commercial objectives.

Powell noted how many organizations had revamped their relationships with trading partners, suggesting a 'wholesale stampede into various alliance-type combinations'. His use of the phrase 'alliance-type' exposes the inconsistency and ambiguity of the existing terminology in the literature. The term 'interorganizational relationships' is used here to refer generically to the wide range of different co-operative relationships entered into between two or more organizations. The most common examples will be distinguished, defined and exemplified.

One popular example of an interorganizational form is the **strategic alliance**. This is a tight, formalized, contractual relationship with a legal element, in which two firms co-operate to achieve certain commercial objectives for mutual advantage. An alliance may relate to supply or purchase agreements, to marketing or distribution agreements or similar areas. Alliances tend to be established over a single, specific initiative, although they may be later extended to cover other activities between the two companies. In a strategic alliance, companies merge a limited part of their domain with each other, and attempt to achieve, with their existing respective value chains, the competitive advantage that might have individually eluded them.

One recent example of an alliance in the financial services industries took place between Standard Life and the Royal Bank of Scotland. The former, a life assurance company at the time, owned 30 per cent of the latter, a retail bank. The two undertook to cross-sell each other's products and services. When a customer indicates an interest in a mortgage, the Bank of Scotland branch will deal with all aspects of the mortgage up to the point where they need to address the endowment. At this stage, the customer is referred to a financial consultant, an independently employed and regulated agent, who works with Standard Life on the endowment side of the mortgage. Another example is the Star Alliance in the airline industry, and involved code sharing. The airlines sell each other's connecting services on a single ticket. Alliances have been popular in uncertain industries such as biotechnology, as well as in distant geographical markets (Reuer, 1999).

Source: © United Feature Syndicate, Inc. Reproduced by permission.

One reason that strategic alliances are created by companies is to bring about organizational learning. Rather than the partners being involved in skill substitution (one produces, while the other sells), they are interested in learning from each other, thereby strengthening the areas in which each is weakest. The primary reason for alliance creation is to secure specific competencies and resources to survive and succeed in globalizing markets, particularly those in which technologies are rapidly changing. Research shows, however, that often they end in disappointment for the organizations involved (Koza and Lewin, 1999).

Constant re-structuring

'Getting organization design correct' may be critical for senior management, but 'keeping it correct' can be problematic. Good design can lift a company's stock price (12 per cent in the case of DuPont's division into five business units in early 2002, raising its worth by US$7billion) or lower expectations (as in the case of Procter & Gamble's failure to implement a fully integrated structure by the summer of 2000). Acquisitions, mergers, customer realignments and rationalizations all involve, to a greater or lesser degree, the modification of a company's structure. Thus, one might speak more accurately of 'organizational structur*ing*' as an ongoing process dedicated to keeping structure aligned with strategy. Microsoft has reorganized four times in the last five years. An Oxford University study of 50 top UK companies in the 1991–2000 period revealed that, at the start of that decade, 20 per cent underwent major reorganizations to their structures annually, a figure that rose to 30 per cent by the end

➤

of the period. It concluded that, at present, the average business could expect a major reorganization every three years.

Whittington, Mayer and Smith's survey (conducted in association with the Chartered Institute of Personnel and Development) of 300 chief executives and 500 human resource professionals revealed 800 reorganization initiatives, ranging from corporate transformations at one extreme through to mergers of departments at the other. In half the cases, the reorganization occurred immediately after the installation of a new chief executive; half were linked to major changes in top management membership, leadership culture and style changes; and in 90 per cent of cases either chief executives or unit heads were represented on reorganization steering committees. The authors draw several conclusions. First, reorganizations have only about a 40 per cent chance of being on time and a 50 per cent chance of success; 60 per cent meet external objectives such as improving market share or customer responsiveness; under half meet internal effectiveness targets such as increased flexibility, or morale and retention of key employees (33 per cent). Second, the chief executive's personal credibility is put on the line during reorganizations, leaving them exposed and vulnerable. Third, reorganizations are now tightly managed. Those undertaken with clear objectives, timescales, milestones, project champions, regular reviews and detailed budgeting are more likely to be completed on time, to budget, and to meet their objectives and raise efficiency.

Based on R. Whittington, M. Mayer and A. Smith, 'Restructuring roulette', 'Mastering Leadership' supplement, *Financial Times*, 8 November 2002, pp. 6, 8; R. Whittington, and M. Mayer, *Organizing for Success in the Twenty-First Century: A Starting Point for Change*, Chartered Institute of Personnel and Development, London, 2002; R. Whittington, M. Mayer and A. Smith, *Organizing for Success in the Twenty-first Century: Practice and Performance*, Chartered Institute of Personnel and Development, London, 2002c.

Stop and Criticize

For whom are strategic alliances more beneficial – the producer or the consumer? Consider their advantages and disadvantages for each group.

Joint venture: an arrangement in which two or more companies remain independent but establish a new organization that they jointly own and manage.

Outsourcing: a situation in which an organization subcontracts to another supplier work that it was previously performing in-house.

A second form of interorganizational relationship is the **joint venture** and the consortium. Here, two (joint venture) or more (consortium) companies remain independent but establish a new organization which they jointly own and manage. The relationships between them are formalized, either through shareholding arrangements or by agreements specifying asset-holding and profit distribution. For example, the Swiss company Nestlé established a joint venture with America's General Mills in the specific field of breakfast cereals. Both parties' other businesses remained separate from this venture (Anand, 1999; Mitchell, 1999). During the early 1990s, West European companies set up joint ventures with companies in the ex-Soviet block. The former provided investment and expertise, while the latter supplied labour and entry to markets. The arrangement continues to be popular with Western companies operating in China.

A third example of interorganizational relationship is sub-contracting or **outsourcing**. This involves one organization selecting outside companies to perform some of the tasks that it requires to be done. In many cases, the company itself might have previously performed such tasks: for example, cleaning, transport logistics (delivering goods). The contracting organization is not likely to own its sub-contractor. In recent years, this has been the most common change to take place in organizations. After outsourcing their cleaning, catering, training, payroll and buildings management, companies are now outsourcing their business processes. Among the first to go was the human resource/personnel function. The next in line appears to be procurement (corporate purchasing). In Powell's (1987) view, such contracting was blurring [firms'] established boundaries and engaging in forms of collaboration that resemble neither the familiar 'arm's length' market contract, nor the former, hierarchical, vertically integrated one. These include linking large, generalist firms with specialist, entrepreneurial start-ups, and large firms with other large firms into global strategic partnerships.

Outsourcing the HR function

BP Amoco signed a record £370 million, five-year deal to contract out the bulk of its human resource (HR) function to Exult, a US-based company. BP Amoco has 82,000 staff and, under the deal, the HR spend was set at £90 per head per year. Exult will administer nearly of all BP Amoco's HR functions, including training, employee relations policy, recruitment and legal compliance. The core strategic HR function will remain in-house. The 300–350 BP Amoco staff who will transfer to Exult will eventually be working on contracts for other firms. A spokesman for the oil firm said that the deal would free in-house managers to concentrate on strategy, and would mean their taking on greater amounts of higher-level HR work for BP Amoco. Other UK organizations, which have signed similarly comprehensive outsourcing deals, include the local government councils of Westminster (in London) and Lincolnshire (in Eastern England). Exult had to standardize 150 different payroll schemes and forty different appraisal systems. In the first year of operation, BP has cut its annual spend on HR support from US$350 million to $250 million. The human resource profession fears that if such outsourcing deals become widespread, the HR function in major corporations will be fatally downgraded and its contribution marginalized.

Based on Katie Hawkins, 'BP makes $100m saving since handing HR to Exult', *Personnel Today*, 19 June 2001, p. 3; Jane Pickard, 'The truth is out there', *People Management*, vol. 6., no. 3, 3 February 2000, pp. 48–50.

Unilateral agreement: a co-operative arrangement in which one firm provides another with a service on a fairly intimate basis in exchange for money.

Network organization: a collection of essentially equal agents or agencies which are in informal relationships with each other based on affiliation.

A fourth type of interorganizational relationship can be found in **unilateral agreements**. Here, one firm provides another with a service on a fairly intimate basis, in exchange for money. Examples include provision of consultancy advice, training courses, marketing and technical transfer agreements and relational subcontracting. A minority investment of a large company in a small one would also be an instance. Since the relationship is strictly financial – the service is being provided for payment – the level of interdependence between the parties is very limited indeed. A company that ends a relationship with one supplier can establish a new one with another.

A fifth and increasingly popular form of interorganizational relationship is the **network organization**. Network organizations frequently grow due to the fact that knowledge and resources are difficult to locate within the boundaries of a single organization. The capabilities needed are more likely to be distributed across a network of different businesses and contractors. The network of organizations is a collection of essentially equal agents or agencies which are in informal relationships with each other, based on affiliation (Thompson et al., 1991). The expectation is of a long-term relationship, openness of information, mutual dependency and long-term rather than short-term gains, all underpinned by mutual trust. In order to understand all the ramifications of a network, it must be viewed simultaneously from the perspective of its individual components and from the perspective of the whole (Ebers, 1999).

Various commentators have drawn upon the personal relationship analogy to describe an interorganization network. They see it as being more like a marriage than a one-night stand, but without a marriage licence. There is no common household and no pooling of assets. Being neither a market transaction nor a hierarchical governance structure, it is a different mode of exchange which possesses its own logic. Within this arrangement, the network partners work in collaboration for their mutual advantage on the basis of trust rather than on the basis of a formalized, contractual relationship,

In one sense, networks have been with us continuously from the moment that business people engaged in repeated transactions with their suppliers, distributors, employees and customers, and decided whether to outsource any of their production (Child and Faulkner, 1998b). Such early networks required verbal and written communication between their members, and the development of trust in each other through experience and over time. Developments in electronic communications between a company and its suppliers and customers have transformed the previous arm's length relationship. The suppliers have become electronically linked to the company and now work as close partners. Customers have also been provided with online information, allowing them to compare the prices of products on different company web sites. The new relationships are summarized by table 16.6.

Table 16.6: Key characteristics of traditional versus interorganizational relationships

	Traditional	Emerging
Suppliers ⟶	*Arm's length relationship* Use of telephone, post, some electronic data interchange for ordering and invoicing	*Interactive electronic relationships* Electronic ordering, invoicing, paying
Customers ⟶	*Limited communication with manufacturer* Mixture of telephone response, post, hard-copy information	*Direct access to manufacturer, real-time information exchange* Electronic access to product information, consumer ratings, customer service data

From 'Corporate Strategy in the Digital Age', *strategy+business*, Issue 15, 2nd Quarter 1999, Booz Allen Hamilton. www.strategy-business.com

A survey of 458 companies across Europe revealed an increase in the horizontal linkages that they had established with others in the form of joint purchasing, as well as the sharing of research and development (R&D) and marketing information. Outsourcing and strategic alliance were also up by about 60 per cent (Pettigrew and Fenton, 2000). Within the United Kingdom, a study of 2,700 firms showed a 61 per cent increase in those sharing knowledge with suppliers and 41 per cent sharing it with 'other organizations in the network'. In the United States, General Electric collaborates with its major suppliers, sharing monthly sales data with twenty-five of them. They plan jointly, co-ordinating data on sales, scheduling, production and design, and can thus respond quickly to demand changes and production schedules (Storey, 2001).

In another sense, networks, and the organizations which comprise them, represent a distinct structural form which has been discussed from the 1980s onwards (Miles and Snow, 1986; Powell, 1990; Snow et al., 1992; Hinterhuber and Levin, 1994; Ebers, 1999). Networks can range along a continuum from 'dominated' to 'equal-partner', as shown in figure 16.2 (Child and Faulkner, 1998b). The 'dominated' network has a single downsized, delayered, core competencies-based, 'lean-and-mean' firm at its centre. This hub-company relies on outsourcing its production functions except those deemed to be strategically vital and close to its core competence: for example, Marks & Spencer controls quality and supply. The distinguishing feature of a dominated network is the limited amount of communication that occurs *between* the smaller node-companies. Instead, most of the

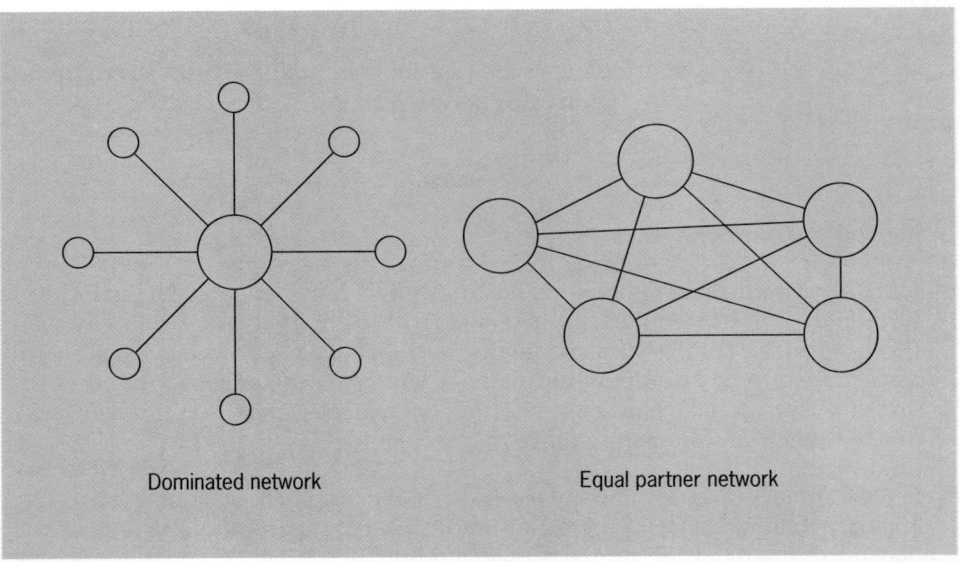

Dominated network   Equal partner network

Figure 16.2: Dominated and equal partner networks

communication is in the form of a series of one-to-one, hub–node interactions. The relationship between Ford or General Motors and its suppliers would be an example of a dominated network.

At the other extreme of the continuum there is an equal partner network, consisting of a collection of similarly sized companies. Its three distinguishing features are:

■ no single partner has set up or controls the network's activities;

■ partners have varying amounts of power which change constantly;

■ the network structure does not represent a substitute for the integrated (hierarchical) firm which is retained.

The relationships between these component firms create a sub-structure that forms the basis for a co-operative, organizational entity: for example, small firms developing computing and biotechnology in Silicon Valley in California. Nohria (1992) reports how these organizations have established a network of lateral and horizontal linkages within and between each other. They have sought to replace an arm's length, competitive relationship with a more collaborative one, through the use of a network. Whether dominant or equal partner, all networks involve a collection of organizations loosely coupled together, each of which retains its autonomy and choice.

Child and Faulkner (1998b) took the 'organic' concept from contingency theory where it was applied to intra-organizational arrangements and extended it to interorganizational arrangements. They noted that in a turbulent and global economic world with fast-changing markets, companies have to adopt structural arrangements that emphasize strategic flexibility, involving simultaneous co-operation and competition. The formation of a network involves companies whose domains overlap in terms of products, markets, operating modes or territories, contacting one another and recognizing the benefits of co-operation.

■ Network firms are linked with their suppliers, distributors and customers.

■ The network is open, flexible and dynamic, allowing members to enter and leave.

- Members are concerned with future rather than immediate benefits.
- Members seek to establish, maintain and strengthen the quality of the relationships between them.

Managing a network organization

John Storey warns that conducting relationships through a supply chain or through a network makes hierarchical control impractical. The relationships become more complex than in market transactions. With the shift from a product-based mode to a process-based one, narrow job descriptions usually have to be abandoned. In place of hierarchy, the process-focused organization increasingly uses cross-functional teams, taskforces and outsourcing. This raises fundamental questions about corporate strategy and human resource management.

On the strategy side, a company can lose its expertise and capabilities with respect to the performance of certain activities if these are sub-contracted. Indeed, it may become 'hollowed out' and thus dependent upon outside contractors and consultants, relying on them for strictly delineated services. From the HRM perspective, how does one manage people who, as a result of outsourcing, become service providers and are no longer direct employees? Should they be included or excluded from internal company communications, invited to meetings or involved in commitment-building activities? How does one develop and maintain relationships between traditional boundaries, both within the organization and between organizations? The new organizational forms require new ways of influencing behaviour. Procedures and rules are inappropriate when corporations are increasingly fashioned around devolved, empowered business units.

Based on John Storey, 'When internal boundaries become network relationships', 'Mastering People' supplement, Part 6, *Financial Times*, 12 November, pp. 6, 8.

Spontaneous organization

Raymond Miles and Charles Snow propose the spherical organizational structure as a way of more effectively arranging and managing the internal resources within network organizations. Increasingly, managers are promoting spontaneous co-ordination of activities to facilitate the flexibility, responsiveness and innovation essential for company renewal. This contrasts with the use of top-down, vertical control exercised through planned co-ordination of activities in hierarchical, bureaucratic structures, or even horizontal co-ordination of activities through cross-functional teams and interdepartmental liaison roles.

These authors recommend replacing the organizational pyramid with a rotational sphere structure. The pyramid suggests that wherever problems and opportunities enter the hierarchy, they are routed to the top for consideration, with solutions eventually leaving at prearranged locations at lower levels. The sphere, in contrast, can arrange and rearrange resources to meet unique needs of its network partners and its customers both flexibly and rapidly. When a request (problem, opportunity) confronts the organization, the sphere rotates, allowing the initiator to access the company's entire array of resources. Such interaction can begin at any angle, with any member becoming responsible for seeing the request through to completion. The sphere will rotate again in response to the next opportunity or problem. A spirit of partnership, co-operation and entrepreneurial opportunity prevails.

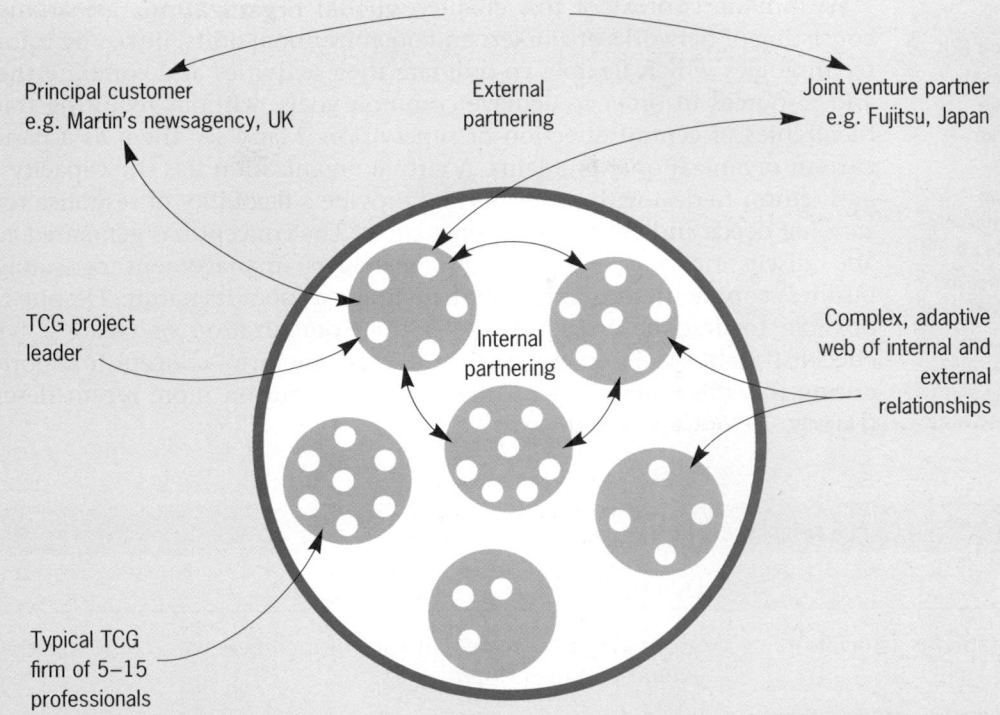

Diagram from M. Brown and D. Beech, 'Spontaneous organization', *Directions: The Ashridge Journal* (Ashridge Web document: /directions/2000–1/04), reprinted by permission of Ashridge.

Technical and Computer Graphics (TCG) is a group of twenty-four small companies based in Sydney, Australia. These confederated firms are hooked together in a voluntary, co-operative network of 'cells', each of which consists of between five and fifteen dispersed, technical professionals. Each cell is co-ordinated by knowledge-sharing protocols. The forms are self-organizing, self-managed teams of professionals, primarily oriented to project-based management development. As shown in the diagram above, within TCG, new product development (and hence network expansion) involves 'triangulation', a three-cornered partnership between the major customer (for example, Martin's news agency), a TCG firm and a similar technology-based firm outside (for example, Fujitsu). The last of these provides funding, technological skills and distribution channels. Any firm in the internal TCG network can take the lead in initiating a project. When TCG staff see a new entrepreneurial opportunity, they can draw upon experience and expertise in other cells and seek out outside partners. The triangular product development process involves five stages: identify the market niche; find a development partner; locate a major customer; involve other TCG firms; and extend the triangulation in new directions.

Based on Martin Brown and David Beech, 'Spontaneous organization', *Directions: The Ashridge Journal*, 2000 (Ashridge web document: /directions/2000–1/04); Raymond E. Miles and Charles C. Snow, 'The new network firm: a spherical structure built on human investment philosophy, *Organizational Dynamics*, vol. 23, no. 4, Spring, 1995, pp. 5–18; John Mathews, 'TCG R&D networks: the triangulation strategy', *Journal of Industry Studies*, October 1993, pp. 64–74.

Virtual organization (1): several conventional companies working very closely together (even fronting the market as one organization) with electronic channels or even common systems of communication.

Virtual organization

Social scientists have used a wide variety of adaptive, electronic, futuristic and cybernetic terms to conceptualize emerging organizational forms. For example, 'cyberspace corporation' (Pruitt and Barrett, 1991), 'learning organization' (Senge, 1990), 'modular corporation' (Clegg and Hardy, 1996) and 'mobius strip' organization (Sabel, 1991); 'cyber-world' and 'info-institution'. However, the most popular analogy remains that of the *virtual organization* (Groth, 1999, pp. 246–7).

Virtual organization (2): an organization where a large number of the organization members use electronic channels as their main (or even only) medium of contact with each other, and with the rest of the organization.

Within the context of this chapter, **virtual organizations** are arrangements consisting of networks of workers and organizational units, linked by information technologies which flexibly co-ordinate their activities and combine their skills and resources in order to achieve common goals, without requiring traditional hierarchies of central direction or supervision. Many see them as a panacea for current organizational problems. A virtual organization has the capacity to form and reform to deal with problems and provide a flexibility of response to organizational needs and changing circumstances. The concept has generated considerable discussion and debate among managers, management consultants and business commentators, although they disagree about its nature. Despite this, it is possible to describe an 'ideal-type' virtual organization or create a 'virtuality checklist' (table 16.7) on the basis of the 'flexible firm' concept first popularized during the 1980s and 1990s (Atkinson, 1985) and on more recent descriptions (Handy, 1995; Carr, 1999).

Table 16.7: Features of a virtual organization

Feature	Description
1. Spontaneous association	Spontaneously created alliance of members who come together to exploit a market opportunity.
2. Lack of physical structure	It is defined in terms of a network of members collaborating, rather than in terms of its physical space like its buildings.
3. Division of task	The total task is fragmented, given to separate individuals who perform it in geographical isolation from one another, and the outputs are reintegrated in different ways.
4. Mobile working	Transfer of work from traditional office spaces to remote locations has increased the chances of its being performed in non-traditional ways.
5. Knowledge workers	Individuals are typically 'knowledge workers' (a controversial term) whose value as employees depends primarily on what they know.
6. Expertise	Members contribute their core competencies (those deemed essential to the company) to create a value-adding alliance.
7. Contracting out	Core competencies are retained (for example, research, development, design), while non-essential ones are contracted out.
8. Electronically linked	Uses highly sophisticated information and communication technologies, allowing faster linking.
9. Reliance on communication technologies	People, assets and ideas are linked electronically much faster than ever before.
10. Switching	Ability of a firm to shift rapidly between suppliers.
11. Meta-management	A central management hub which co-ordinates these outsourced functions between the different suppliers, thereby creating supply chains.
12. Appearance of unity	Despite being individual network members, they act, in all appearances, as a single, organizational unit.

Based on W. Davidow and M. Malone, *The Virtual Corporation*, HarperCollins, New York, 1992; A. Mowshowitz, 'Virtual organization: a vision of management in the information age', *The Information Society*, vol. 10, 1994, pp. 267–94; and N. Venkatramen and J.C. Henderson, 'Real strategies for virtual organizing', *Sloan Management Review*, vol. 40, no. 1, Fall, 1998, pp. 38–44.

The promise and appeal of the virtual organization is that by dispersing its operations through information technology it can speedily adapt and reconfigure itself in response to the ever more common state of bounded instability. Specifically, it is able to adopt new information technologies; speed product development; raise quality; improve management–employee relations; and engender new collaborative links between suppliers, producers and customers. Some observers see this organizational form as being modelled on the internet itself which, after all, was designed to sustain itself in the event of a nuclear strike on the United States. All this is being implemented through processes of rationalizing, downsizing and the flattening of hierarchies (delayering). Increasingly, one reads about company *'disembodiment'* or *'hollowing out'* which has been reflected in new configurations between work practices, employee relations and organization designs.

Just how revolutionary is the virtual organization as an organization design? Andrew Burnett (2000) noted that some evolutionists would argue that the concept goes back at least four decades to include 'organic' structure (Burns and Stalker, 1961), 'innovative adhocracy' (Mintzberg, 1983a), and the 'loosely coupled network' (Weick, 1977; Morgan, 1989). They would also see it as comparable to flexible specialization, lean production and business process re-engineering (Harris, 1998). In retrospect, the judgement that the structural forms used by companies like Benetton and Toyota were fledgling virtual organizations was based solely on their focus on a dense network of suppliers rather than communications technology (Faulkner, 1996).

However, the virtual organizational model of today would be inconceivable and impractical without the increasingly sophisticated information technology. This has provided the opportunity to automate work fully, disperse it across wide geographical areas, and allow it to be performed in a non-synchronized,

Table 16.8: Contrasting views of the virtual organization

Postmodernist model of the future?	Scientific management model of the past?
Radical, paradigm shift.	Provides old-style management control and work intensification in a new guise.
Offers flexibility and success for the company and empowerment and job satisfaction for its employees.	The freedom and speed with which elements can be combined through 'switching' allows ever more fragmented production to be managed.
New developments in the technological and social arena allow managers to organize in distinct and novel ways.	Virtualization, with its emphasis on rational planning, control and the achievement of economic advantage through cheaper production, represents a further and superior stage of Taylorization.
Allows the relaxation of geographical and organizational boundaries.	Isolates individuals, making them more dependent on organizational fiat.
Loosens the constraints upon co-operation, co-ordination and control for both managers and employees.	Stimulates the application of more sophisticated forms of monitoring and employee surveillance.
It thus provides the possibility for employees to take greater responsibility and control of their own work, producing new multi-skilled and therefore more intrinsically rewarding work.	Rationalistic, Theory X-oriented, managerial control device that continues the Taylorist/Fordist models of production rather than shifting to 'high-trust' organizational forms.
Offers efficiency and cost benefits on an unprecedented scale.	Offers efficiency and cost benefits on an unprecedented scale.

non-linear fashion while, at the same time, effectively integrating and controlling it. In this sense, the virtual organization does represent a revolutionary step beyond traditional, and also the network, organization design. Some promoters see the virtual organization as representing an epochal shift in the way we think about organizing work, and an example of the post-modern organization of the future, owing no debt to the technologically primitive past. Does it represent a postmodern model for the future? Others view it as a case of 'back to the future'. For them, the virtual organization is a throwback to scientific work design of the past and in particular to the scientific management of Frederick Taylor. Andrew Burnett and Chris Warhurst (1999) argue that the virtual organization is a manifestation, and even perhaps the apotheosis of, scientific management. In their view, it is not just a technical practice, but also a manifestation of the politics of production. The two opposing views are summarized in table 16.8.

Stop and Criticize

Some of the new forms of organization structure discussed in this chapter have been charted using four, separate dimensions. Consider each dimension in turn, and assess the authors' accuracy in placing it there.

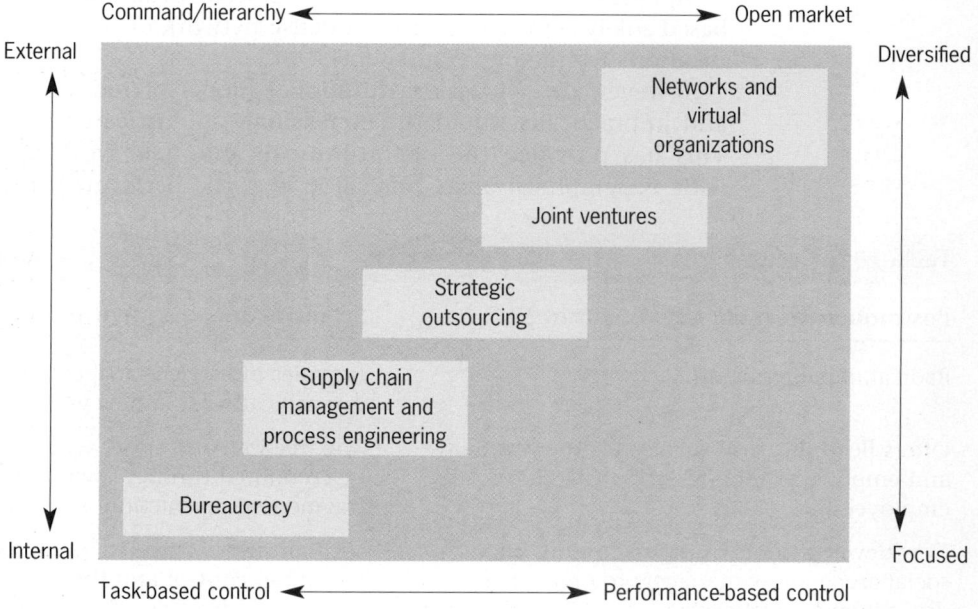

From Christopher Mabey, Graeme Salaman and John Storey, *Human Resource Management: A Strategic Introduction*, Blackwell, Oxford (second edition), 1998, p. 236. Reprinted by permission of Blackwell Publishing Ltd.

The interest in post-Fordism, the flexible form, the virtual organization and all the other new social and organizational arrangements represents a major theme in the application of postmodernist thinking. Discussions of post-modern organizational forms feature increasingly in management magazines, but have only just begun to be studied by academics. As Stuart Clegg (1990) noted, on the one hand, these organization designs offer the opportunity for the progressive development of industrial democracy and skill enhancement, and on the other hand, tight job specification and high levels of control. Since, so far, few of us have first-hand experience of these 'new age' organizations, our ability to make a judgement about them is based on the information and views supplied to us by others. Whether employees or students, we need to be sceptical and questioning about the data provided by the commentators on this currently fashionable topic.

William Gibson, the futuristic novelist and author of the book *Neuromancer*, and creator of the term 'cyberspace', has described this medium as a 'consensual hallucination'.

In what way might the virtual organization be similarly conceived as the consensual hallucination of organizational theorists, management journalists, practising managers and management gurus?

Recap

1. *Appreciate the reciprocal relationship between corporate strategy and organization structure.*

   - Structure can follow strategy (for example, Miles and Snow's Prospector, Defender, Analyzer and Reactor).

   - Structure complements process and boundaries (for example, Whittington, Pettigrew).

2. *Discuss theories that explain managerial changes in corporate strategy and organization structure with respect to the environment.*

   - Strategic choice theory holds that all organization design choices are management decisions (Child).

   - Managers' perceptions of their organizations' environments provide the basis for their choices (Weick).

   - Organizations seek to reduce their dependency on aspects of their environment (Pfeffer and Salancik).

3. *Distinguish between bounded instability and non-linearity, and state their implications for corporate strategy.*

   - Bounded instability is a state mixing order and disorder, but one in which a basic pattern of the systems behaviour can be discerned. Non-linearity represents a state in which actions have both expected and unexpected outcomes, and in which small actions can quickly escalate, producing unexpected consequences.

   - In such unpredictable environments, planning is less possible and is replaced by setting a fairly clear direction, then continuously adapting the detail to cope with specific events, threats and opportunities.

4. *Define a 'transaction' and distinguish three major types of institutional arrangement for the conduct of transactions.*

   - Any 'exchange' between actors (for example, buying and selling; providing information and making a decision based upon it) is a transaction.

   - Transactions can be conducted in a hierarchy, a market or a mutual relationship.

5. *Differentiate between the main types of mutual inter-organizational arrangement.*

   - Strategic alliance, joint venture, unilateral agreement and network organization.

6. *Identify the distinguishing features of a virtual organization.*

   - A virtual organization is one example of a network organization.

   - A virtual organization possesses many of the following features: spontaneous association, lack of physical structure, division of task, mobile working, knowledge workers, expertise, contracting out, electronically linked, reliance on communication technologies, switching, meta-management and appearance of unity.

Revision

1. Why might Max Weber and Henri Fayol be surprised by developments in contemporary organization design arrangements?

2. Why do organizational behaviour academics increasingly have to take corporate strategy into account in their considerations of the design of organization structures?

3. Select an organization with which you are familiar. Identify three significant environmental actors or agencies that are making demands on it at the present time. Suggest what type of power the latter have over the former. What is the nature of the dependency relationship between them. Suggest ways in which it could be reduced or eliminated.

4. How would organizing and managing a company which operated in a state of bounded instability differ from one that operated in a state of stable equilibrium?

5. Why are network and virtual structures preferred by managers seeking to encourage entrepreneurship and innovation?

Springboard

Chandler, A.D., Hagstrom, P. and Solvell, O. (eds), 1999, *The Dynamic Firm: The Role of Technology, Strategy, Organization and Regions*, Oxford University Press, Part 2: 'Strategy and Organizations'.

Contributions consider the relationship between corporate strategy and organization structure from a strategy perspective.

Child, J., 1997, 'Strategic choice in the analysis of action, structure, organizations and environment: retrospective and prospective', *Organization Studies*, vol. 18, no. 1, pp. 43–76.

An overview of the strategic choice debate which sets it within a contemporary context. A challenging read for those wishing to understand current thinking about organization structuring.

Child, J. and Faulkner, D., 1998, *Strategies of Co-operation: Managing Alliances, Networks and Joint Ventures*, Oxford University Press, Oxford.

Provides a discussion of organization structures which moves beyond the boundary of the firm to include a consideration of other agencies and actors.

Ebers, M. (ed.), 1999, *The Formation of Inter-Organizational Networks*, Oxford University Press, Oxford.

Considers interorganizational networks, how they form and what their strengths and weaknesses are.

Fulop, L. and Linstead, S. (eds) 1999, *Management: A Critical Text*, Macmillan Business, London.

Chapters 10 and 11 by Browne et al., and Buttery et al. respectively, address the issues of strategy and interorganizational relations from a critical organizational behaviour perspective.

Parker, M., 2000b, 'Postmodernizing organizational behaviour: new organizations or new organization theory', in J. Barry, J. Chandler, H. Clark, R. Johnston and D. Needle (eds), *Organization and Management: A Critical Text*, Thomson Learning, London, pp. 36–50.

Introduces contemporary thinking about new forms of organization structuring.

Spector, R., 2000, *Amazon.com: Get Big Fast*, Random House Business, New York.

A clear and readable description of the origins and early growth of probably the best-known virtual organization.

Smircich, L. and Stubbart, C., 1985, 'Strategic management in an enacted world', *Academy of Management Review*, vol. 10, no. 4, pp. 724–35.

Contrasts three models for knowing the organizational environment – objective, perceived and enacted.

Thompson, G.F., 2003, *Between Hierarchies and Markets*, Oxford University Press, Oxford.

Examines the widely used (and abused) concept of networks, and considers it as a separate form of socio-economic mechanism of co-ordination and governance, which possesses its own internal logic.

Whipp, R., 1999, 'Creative deconstruction: strategy and organizations', in S.R. Clegg, C. Hardy and W.R. Nord (eds), *Managing Organizations: Current Issues*, Sage Publications, pp. 11–25.

A book chapter which provides a brief historical background to the rising importance of corporate strategy to contemporary organization studies.

Home viewing

Other People's Money (1991, director Norman Jewison) shows how the inability of a firm to react to an external threat leaves it vulnerable to a hostile take-over. It raises management and leadership issues related to corporate restructuring. New England Wire and Cable (NEWC) is an old-fashioned manufacturing company, paternalistically led for 26 years by Andrew Jorgenson (played by Gregory Peck) who values stability and predictability. He is unaware of the developing problems in one of his company's divisions which requires urgent re-engineering and diversification. Meanwhile, Garfield Investment Corporation (GIC), headed by Lawrence Garfield (played by Danny DeVito) is using modern technology to scan the environment for firms that are ripe to be taken. GIC exemplifies the quintessential Wall St firm, with its chrome, leather furniture, glass building and Manhattan location. Garfield expects to make a substantial profit by taking over and liquidating NEWC.

Once you have watched the entire film, consider the following. What are some of the reasons why corporate restructurings take place? How do Jorgenson's leadership and decision-making style leave his company vulnerable to a take-over? What skills do you think are most useful for managers in the organizations of the future?

OB in literature

Mario Puzo, *The Godfather*, Arrow Books, London, 1998

Originally published in 1969, this book (also a film) tells the story Don Corleone and the New York Mafia. What are his 'Family's' (organization's) objectives, strategy and structure? It operates using both a hierarchy and interorganizational (network) relationships. Consider these within the context of trust, mutual respect, reciprocity and collaboration for mutual advantage between the individuals, groups and Families involved. How did the leading Mafia families regulate the conflict of interests between them?

Chapter exercises

1: Career progression

Objectives   1. To introduce the differences between different organization designs.

Briefing   You are a middle manager in a large organization and have been in the same job for three years. You are dissatisfied with your current position and want a more senior job that pays you more money.

- How do you go about getting a better job?

- What are the advantages and disadvantages of each option?

Devised by Moira Fischbacher.

2: Municipal airport

Objectives   1. To identify problems in a situation of inter-firm collaboration and sub-contracting relationships.

Task
Read the case study on pp. 570–1 and make notes on the two questions: What are the sources of the problems in this organizational arrangement? How might they be solved?

Municipal airport

Research was carried out at a large municipal airport in the United Kingdom. The airport company introduced a high level of internal competition for all aspects of the airport work. This led to complex and multiple sub-contracting arrangements between the providers of these services. Contractors tendered to provide specific services – passenger handling, baggage handling, catering, cleaning, fuelling, etc. There were over 270 employers with nearly 3,900 employees, all operating side-by-side on the same site, providing services for the landing and dispatching of aircraft. The majority of these workers were in low-level jobs, working unsociable hours and earning less than €9.40 (£6) per hour.

To operate safely and meet regulations, a very high degree of co-ordination and interorganizational working is required. Aircraft at airports stop for a 'minimum ground time' of between 45 and 90 minutes. In that period, all the activities essential to the turn-around of an aircraft have to take place, most of them simultaneously. The employees of different contractors work alongside each other, performing their different functions within this limited time. Each group of workers has its own priorities and objectives.

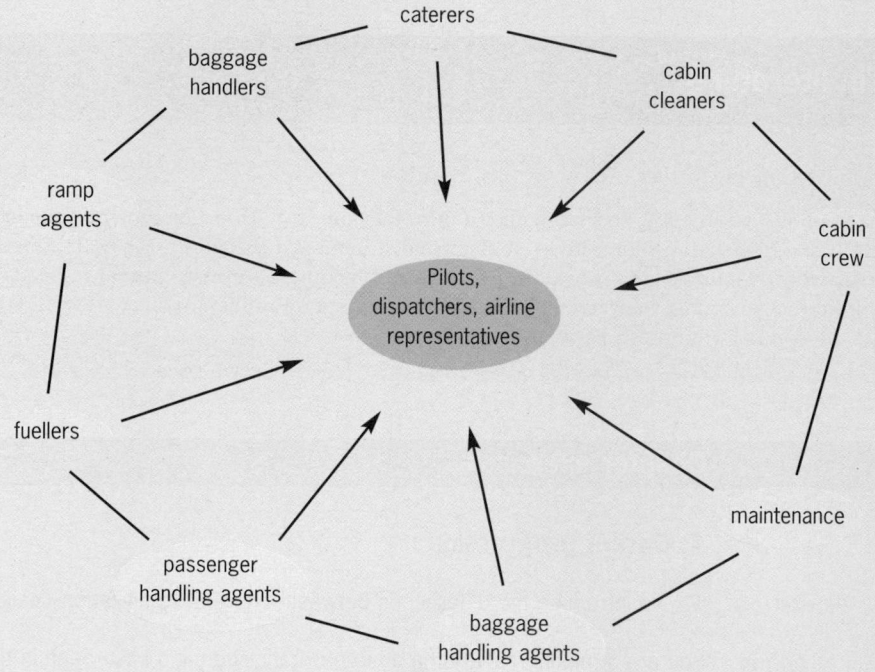

The different contract teams shared a higher goal of minimizing aircraft turnaround time and ensuring punctual departures. However, each had their own goals, whether cabin cleaning or replacing catering items. All had their performances monitored by service level agreements (SLA) and key performance indicators (KPI). In the short term, failure to meet targets could result in a contractor having to pay the airport compensation if they were deemed to be responsible for a delay. In the longer term, team performance affected the renewal of a firm's contract, most of which were negotiated annually. After an aircraft had landed, the various teams each performed their different tasks at the same time, often in the same place. Even though members often got in each other's way, there was evidence, at some times, of their helping each other. This occurred on a voluntary basis, and depended on the situation and personalities of those involved. At other times, they apportioned blame for failures. The employees worked at the airport but were employed by a contractor, by whom they were paid. Some airlines had arranged for these contract employees to wear their uniforms instead of those of their employers. The airlines also rewarded good performance by giving free flights to some contract workers, while offering employment to others.

Each service-providing organization (for example, cleaning, baggage handing) officially had its own authority hierarchy, with its own workers being directed by and reporting to their own management. It was the 'dispatcher' who co-ordinated all their work, ensuring that all the service deliverers appeared and performed their duties. Dispatchers were employees of the large handling firm, so were employees in the same organization as some of the service deliverers whom they co-ordinated, but in a different one from that of the other contract staff whom they directed. The researchers found that, unofficially, the employees of one contractor were monitored, controlled and appraised by managers and even junior employees of a different company. Power relationships intersected authority relationships. The most powerful firms at the airport are the airlines. They were found to be regularly intervening in the affairs of handling suppliers, despite the fact that such interventions were not permitted by the contractual agreements. Contractors' employees were required to accept the control and discipline of these 'non-employers' in the form of the airlines' representatives.

These representatives used the power possessed by their airlines to manage the activities of the contracted handling firms, despite lacking the authority to do so. Their interventions were made on their own initiative, derived from the power that the airlines had as a customer. They exercised their power without accepting responsibility for the consequences of their interventions. This combination of formal and informal work practices between the two parties was used as a way of 'getting the job done'. The handling employees complained that different agents wanted them to do different things. However, the workers clearly identified the airlines as the ultimate providers of their jobs, and recognized that they should keep them happy. However, the managers in the handing firms were less sure. They were willing to do favours for, but not take orders from, the airline representatives. On occasions, dispatchers from the handling firm had to ask their managers to negotiate with the airline managers to get their airline representatives to stand back and let the dispatchers get on with their work.

Based on Jill Rubery, Fang Lee Cooke, Jill Earnshaw and Mick Marchington, 'Contracts, co-operation and employment relationships: working in a multi-employer environment', *British Journal of Industrial Relations*, in press.

Part 5 Organization processes

A field map of the organizational behaviour terrain

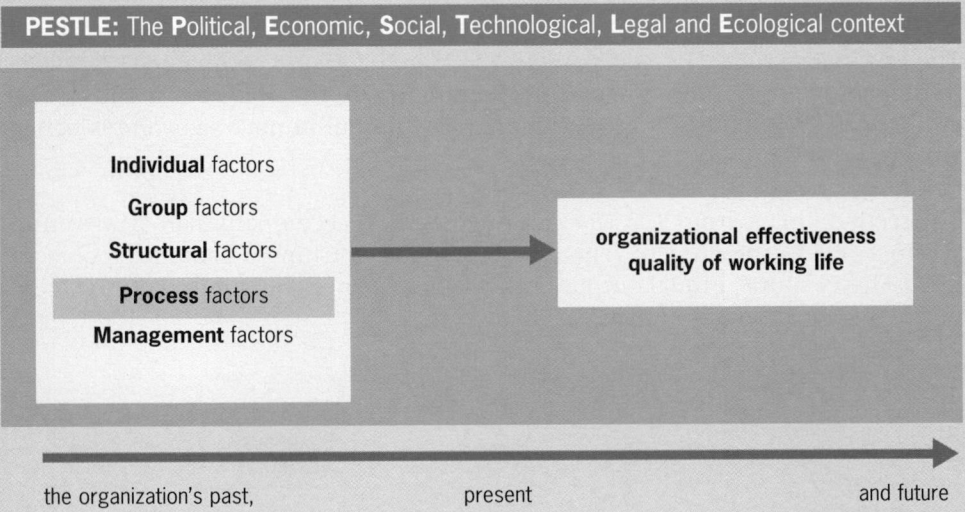

PESTLE: The **P**olitical, **E**conomic, **S**ocial, **T**echnological, **L**egal and **E**cological context

Individual factors
Group factors
Structural factors
Process factors
Management factors

organizational effectiveness
quality of working life

the organization's past,   present   and future

Introduction

Part 5, Organization processes, explores the following four topics:

- Organization development, in chapter 17
- Organizational change, in chapter 18
- Organizational culture, in chapter 19
- Human resource management, in chapter 20

These are overlapping areas of organization processes which contribute in different modes to the ways in which organizations change, develop and evolve. These processes also contribute in significant ways to organizational effectiveness and quality of working life.

The first image, from *The Sunday Times* (23 March 2003), accompanied an article about a proposed rise in the national minimum wage. Chris Remington, in the foreground, runs a care home for the elderly and employs 28 staff, half of whom are paid the minimum wage. She is concerned that a wage rise will cut profits and lead to job losses.

The second, image from *The Times* (4 August 2003) accompanies an article entitled 'Chinese in bid to sell foie gras to the French'. The article describes a Chinese company's objective of exceeding three times France's total annual output of this delicacy, and selling it back to the French who consume 90% of the world's production of it.

Tough times: Chris Remington says her business is surviving but a minimum wage of £4.85 would make it unprofitable
Source: Chris Bourchier, photographer.

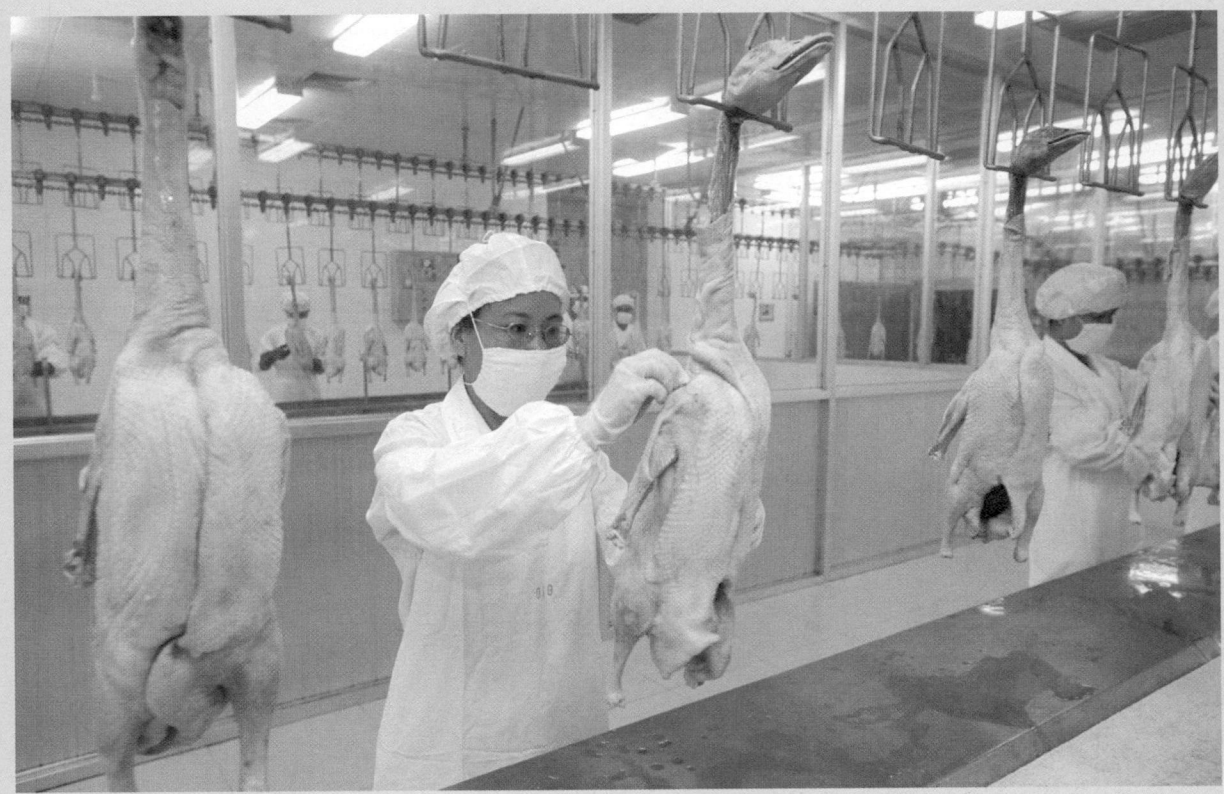

Lucrative luxury: Chen Xiuhong's factory in Beihai, Guangxi province. The price of liver in China is £5, a quarter of what his French competitors pay.
Source: Sinopix.

1. Decoding: Look at this image closely. Note in as much detail as possible what messages you feel the image is trying to convey. Does it tell a story, present a point of view, support an argument, perpetuate a myth, reinforce a stereotype, challenge a stereotype?

2. Challenging: To what extent do you agree with the message, story, point of view, argument, myth or stereotype in this image? Is this image open to challenge, to criticism, to interpretation or decoding in other ways, revealing other messages?

3. Sharing: Compare with colleagues your interpretation of this image. Explore explanations for any differences in your respective decodings.

Organization development

Key concepts

organization development (OD)	survey feedback
OD intervention	team building
force field analysis	intergroup development
action research	role negotiation
sensitivity training	Grid OD
process consultation	

Learning outcomes

When you have read this chapter, you should be able to define those key concepts in your own words, and you should also be able to:

1. Explain the goals of OD.
2. Understand the values underpinning the OD movement.
3. Understand the main OD interventions, how they work, and what they aim to achieve.
4. Assess critically the difficulties in evaluating the effectiveness of OD interventions.
5. List the main skills and areas of knowledge required by an OD consultant.

Why study organization development?

Organization development (OD) offers a comprehensive, systematic and practical approach to improving individual and organizational effectiveness. Although this is an American perspective developed in the 1960s, it deserves study today for several reasons:

1. The perspective remains influential, change programmes incorporating OD principles and methods are common, and there is healthy demand for change agents with OD skill, knowledge and experience.

2. The values and techniques which underpin OD distinguish this approach from the general field of organizational change management.

3. Most other change implementation methodologies have been influenced by the values, concepts and frameworks of OD.

4. OD has contributed to the organization culture change issues explored in chapter 19.

5. OD values and methods are similar to those advocated by the Human Resource Management (HRM) movement.

6. The perspective invites critical inspection, as the quasi-religious values which underpin OD can be seen either as caring management or as an attempt to disguise the nature of conflict in organizations.

Many commentators have expressed criticism of the way in which management ideas and methods come into and go out of fashion, like clothing (Micklethwait and Wooldridge, 1996; Shapiro, 1996; Collins, 2000). Andrzej Huczynski (1993) identified the ingredients of management ideas which made them popular, and turned their originators into wealthy management 'gurus'. Business process re-engineering (BPR) is one example. The approach was brought to management attention in 1990, but by 1995 critics claimed that it had been discredited because it was not novel, not radical and not effective.

In other words, it took only five years for the BPR fashion to fade. OD, in sharp contrast, has endured for over half a century, and continues to influence management thinking and practice. OD has been widely adopted, and has many devotees among managers and management consultants. An understanding of the organizational change issues introduced in chapter 18, and the organization culture issues explored in chapter 19, is not complete without an understanding of OD principles and methods, which have also influenced human resource management practice, explored in chapter 20.

The OD agenda: goals and processes

Chapter 1 introduced the concept of the *organizational dilemma* – the problem of meeting individual employee needs and aspirations while meeting the performance, survival and growth needs of the organization as a whole. Rapid developments in social science methodology and knowledge after the Second World War led to a growth in confidence in the practical application of that knowledge to organizational problems. During the 1960s in America, this confidence generated a movement committed to the design and use of social science techniques for the development of organizational effectiveness *and* the development of an organization's members. In other words, the OD movement can be regarded as a long-running confrontation with the organizational dilemma.

OD dates back to the 1960s, when the term first began to find currency. OD practitioners believe that the conflicting interests of organizations and their members can be reconciled through appropriate interventions. We have the social science understanding, and we have the change techniques, through which problems and conflicts can be diagnosed and resolved. OD also claims to enhance an organization's independent capability to address and resolve its own problems, and thus to reduce dependence on OD 'experts' beyond an initial intervention. The field of OD has its own literature, with its own conceptual, theoretical and empirical bases, its own specialized journals, conferences and societies, and its own specialized higher degrees. It can therefore be seen as a distinct organization studies discipline or sub-discipline, dealing with a specific set of issues, goals and problems.

OD also has some of the features of a religious movement, which may help to explain the durability of this perspective. In addition to the belief that conflict in organizations can be managed through appropriate intervention, the approach adheres to a series of underpinning social values, the pursuit of which may be regarded as valuable, independent of any implications for productivity or financial performance.

The term **organization development** was probably coined by Richard Beckhard (1969) while looking for a label for a consulting programme in which he was involved with Douglas McGregor in 1960. They did not want to describe their work as 'management development', because the whole organization was involved, and they wanted to avoid the term 'human relations training' as that was too narrow. The term 'organization development' was used instead. One of

Warren G. Bennis

Organization development: a systematic process in which applied behavioural science principles and practices are introduced towards the goals of increasing individual and organizational effectiveness.

the other founders of the movement was Warren Bennis (1969) who defines OD as: 'a response to change, a complex educational strategy intended to change the beliefs, attitudes, values and structure of organizations so that they can better adapt to new technologies, markets, and challenges, and the dizzying rate of change itself.' Our definition is based on that of Wendell French and Cecil Bell (1999).

The organizational boundaries and focus of an OD intervention are a matter of judgement. The approach can be applied to one or more sections of an organization, but OD practitioners like to 'get the whole system in the room'. This implies an attempt to understand and to influence the entire organization, involving everyone about everything.

It is important to note that the objectives of OD include individual development and organizational effectiveness. Interventions to achieve these goals are deliberate, planned and systematic. OD seeks to apply social and behavioural science knowledge and techniques in a manner that will enhance both organizational effectiveness and the quality of work experience for the organization's members. In pursuit of these twin goals, OD has a clear and prescriptive value orientation. These values relate to an individual's experience of employment, and to the manner in which the organization treats and relates to its members.

| **Stop and Criticize** | Consider the manager who wants a more compliant and committed workforce, which will welcome and not resist organizational change. One route to achieving these outcomes involves reassuring employees that 'we all share common interests', that 'our conflicts and disagreements can be resolved', and that 'the changes we are about to make are in your interests because they will enhance the quality of your working life'. |

Now listen to these reassurances from the perspective of the employee who sees fundamental power inequalities and conflict between management and workforce.

To what extent can OD be used to exert management control over a workforce by appealing to values like openness, trust and harmony that are difficult to challenge?

Stephen Robbins (2001, p. 553) outlines the values underpinning most OD efforts as follows:

■ the individual should be treated with respect and dignity;

■ the organization climate should be characterized by trust, openness and support;

■ hierarchical authority and control are 'de-emphasized';

■ problems and conflicts should be confronted, and not disguised or avoided;

■ people affected by change should be involved in its implementation.

Some practitioners argue that this agenda is worth pursuing in its own right, independent of attempts directly to enhance organizational functioning. Others argue that an organization cannot be productive, efficient and effective unless it adopts these values. The committed OD practitioner asks, can an organization be effective without mutual trust and confidence, honesty, open communications, sensitivity to the feelings and emotions of others, shared goals, and a commitment to addressing and resolving conflict?

Table 17.1: Characteristics of the effective and the ineffective organization

Effective organization	Ineffective organization
clearly defined goals	ill-defined or unknown goals
structure related to goals	no link between goals and structure
flexible forward planning	focus on immediate pressing problems
consistent, clear procedures which evolve purposefully	bureaucratic rigidity, or constant change without rationale
meaningful, varied work with learning opportunity	narrow, repetitive jobs with little learning opportunity
commitment to personal growth (planned skills development)	contempt for individuals and groups (the POPOS: pissed on, passed over)
power recognizing mutual influence	politicking and defensive cliques
flexible, participative decisions	'what the boss says, goes'
information openness	secrecy, gossip, failure to listen
mutual trust, support, respect	the FUJIAR syndrome: 'fuck-you-Jack-I'm-all-right'
accurate, timely performance feedback	unclear signals: 'what did the boss mean by that?'
just and equitable rewards	apparently arbitrary rewards
constant scanning of environment and appropriate adaptation	failure to perceive and act on critical environmental changes
initiative in external relations	reactive, selective responses
well-defined concept of social responsibility	'don't care' attitude to community values

From D. Dunphy, *Organizational Change by Choice*. McGraw-Hill, Sydney, 1981, pp. 26–8.

Note that a definition of 'effective' in this context depends on who is using the term. Effectiveness can be considered in terms of profitability, the pursuit of organizational goals (at whatever cost), or in terms of quality of life for those involved. Some of the general characteristics of the 'effective' organization are set out in the table 17.1, from Dexter Dunphy (1981, reprinted 1993, pp. 26–8). See how many of these you agree with.

Thomas Cummings and Christopher Worley (2001) claim that early practitioners in this field were more interested in projects which concerned 'people problems', such as interpersonal relationships and group dynamics, and were less concerned with productivity issues. However, as French and Bell (1999) point out, the values and assumptions supported by the OD movement in the 1960s represented a radical departure for most organizations at that time. Managers in that era did not think in terms of involving their employees in decision-making, or of inviting their ideas and contributions. Most managers did not recognize a link between interpersonal relationships, self-awareness and the exchange of emotions and feelings, on the one hand, and the performance of their businesses, on the other.

Since the 1960s the OD movement has been associated with the argument that 'bureaucracy is bad' and that the caring, sharing, empowering organization is not only a better place to work, but is financially and materially more effective. The 'bureaucracy-busting' agenda of OD relies on the diagnosis of problems and solutions summarized in table 17.2.

OD practitioners claim that bureaucratic diseases can be cured in commercial settings, but have been concerned that the public sector is resistant. Warren Burke

Table 17.2: Bureaucratic diseases and OD cures

Bureaucratic disease	Symptoms	OD cures
rigid functional boundaries	conflict between sections, poor communications	team building, job rotation, change the structure
fixed hierarchies	frustration, boredom, narrow specialist thinking	training, job enrichment, career development
information only flows down	lack of innovation, minor problems escalate	process consultation, management development
routine jobs, tight control	boredom, absenteeism, conflict for supervisors	job enrichment, job rotation, supervisory training

(1980) claimed that the use of OD in government and healthcare organizations resembled the confrontation of 'David and Goliath' except, he argued, 'we are not as skilful as David'. Public sector bureaucracies are now probably more in need of OD intervention, as government policies and demographic trends encourage them to become more flexible and responsive. This is now happening in healthcare in Britain (Bate, 2000) and in America (Martin and Huq, 2002) where OD interventions are being combined with other change approaches with evident success.

The OD matrix: levels and modes of intervention

The OD toolkit includes a large and expanding number of intervention techniques or strategies (Huczynski, 2001). In fact, many of the approaches to organizational improvement covered in earlier chapters – job enrichment, assessment centres, team building, participative management – have been used as **OD interventions**. The first step in any OD project, however, concerns diagnosis. Until one is clear about the nature of the problem and its roots, it is not possible effectively to select an appropriate strategy.

Problems in organizations can arise at different levels:

OD intervention: a technique used to effect change in the target organization or section of the organization to improve organizational effectiveness.

- organizational level;
- intergroup level;
- group level;
- individual level.

An individual may have problems at work: too complex, not challenging enough, boring, no prospects. A group may not be functioning effectively: lack of leadership, poor relationships, personality clashes, team lacking cohesion. Two or more groups may find themselves in (intergroup) conflict for some reason: unwilling to co-operate or liaise, differences in outlook, physical distance, conflict of priorities. The whole organization may experience low morale, be out of touch with its environment, lack an effective structure, lack a clear strategy.

The first step in problem diagnosis thus concerns identifying the level at which the problem has arisen. In most complex organizations, as one might expect, problems are likely to be caused and reinforced by factors at more than one level. For example, those unhappy individuals may be concerned with their positions in the structure, and with a lack of understanding of the organization's strategic purpose, as well as with fellow section or group members and the lack of challenge in their own individual repetitive tasks. Problem diagnosis, therefore, is not always a straightforward step. The selection of an appropriate intervention strategy, or more often a solutions package, can thus be a complex choice.

To help with these issues of diagnosis and choice, Derek Pugh produced the OD matrix shown in table 17.3. This matrix first outlines problems that can arise at each of the four levels, with respect to behavioural factors, organization structural factors and wider contextual factors. Each cell in the matrix identifies relevant OD interventions. If the problem lies with the individual, and the cause or causes are structural, then a job redesign approach may be relevant. If the problem lies at the organizational level, and the cause or causes are contextual, job enrichment is going to be of limited value and a change of organization strategy or location may be necessary.

Table 17.3: The Pugh OD matrix for organizational diagnosis and choice of OD intervention

	behaviour what is happening?	structure what is the system?	context what is the setting?
organizational level	poor morale, pressure, anxiety, suspicion, weak response to environmental changes *survey feedback, organizational mirroring*	inappropriate and poorly defined goals, strategy unclear, inappropriate structure, inadequate environmental scanning *structure change*	geography, product market, labour market, technology, physical working conditions *change strategy, change location, change conditions, change culture*
intergroup level	sub-units not co-operating, conflict and competition, failure to confront differences, unresolved feelings *intergroup confrontation, role negotiation*	no common perspective on task, difficult to achieve required interaction *redefine responsibilities, change reporting relations, improve liaison mechanisms*	differences in sub-unit values and lifestyles, physical barriers *reduce psychological and physical distance, exchange roles, arrange cross-functional attachments*
group level	inappropriate working atmosphere, goals disputed, inappropriate leadership style, leader not trusted or respected, leader in conflict with peers and superiors *process consultation, team building*	task poorly defined, role relations not clear, leader overloaded, inappropriate reporting structures *redesign role relations, autonomous groups, socio-technical system redesign*	lack of resources, poor group composition, inadequate physical facilities, personality clashes *change the technology, change the layout, change group membership*
individual level	individual needs not met, frustration, resistance to change, few learning and development opportunities *counselling, role analysis, career planning*	poor job definition, task too easy, task too difficult *job restructuring or redesign, job enrichment, clear objectives*	poor individual–job 'fit', poor selection or promotion, inadequate training, inadequate recognition and reward *improve personnel procedures, improve training, align recognition and reward with objectives*

Source: Pugh, D.S. (1986) 'The Pugh Organizational Development Matrix' in *Planning and Managing Change* (p769), Block 4, Open University Business School, page 6.1. Reprinted by permission of Professor D.S. Pugh.

It is important to recognize that an intervention strategy, or package of strategies, cannot simply be 'read' mechanically from a matrix. This is simply a useful diagnostic and planning guide. A knowledge of the organizational context is also required. The approach that is relevant, practical and acceptable is part systematic diagnosis, part local context knowledge and part judgement.

The relationship between OD practitioner or consultant, and the target or host organization, has generated much discussion. Consultants, of course, work for clients. In an OD setting, defining 'the client' is not always straightforward. The person who invited the OD consultant into a preliminary discussion (the 'gatekeeper') may not be the person (the 'problem owner') who represents the section with the difficulty to be resolved. Someone else (the 'paymaster') may eventually settle the consultant's invoice. The problem may actually lie, for example, with two groups of relatively low-status employees whose poor interaction is adversely affecting organizational performance. Can these groups be regarded as 'clients'? To make matters more complex, the consultant is also likely to become involved in the organization's political system. Those with the most status and influence in the organization (the 'powerbrokers') may not be the clients, gatekeepers, problem owners or paymasters.

We can examine this issue from a theoretical and from a practical perspective. From a theoretical point of view, once engaged, the consultant quickly becomes involved in a complex and ongoing series of relationships within the host organization. It is useful, then, to consider the consultant interacting with, and intervening in, a 'client system', a term which captures the complexity and variety in the OD consultant's net of relationships. Some parts of the client system will be critical, others less so. Some will collaborate willingly while others will manifest resistance to creative interventions. Action that will affect one part of the client system may create 'knock on' or 'ripple effects' in other parts of the system.

In practice, however, the term 'client system' obscures and confuses a critical issue for the OD consultant as a temporary employee in the host organization. In this respect, identifying clearly and without ambiguity the person or group responsible for settling invoices and writing cheques may be vital. But the simplicity of this mercenary stance has to be set against the need to recognize that the OD consultant may have many different clients, with different needs and expectations, within the same organization. It may be appropriate to identify the client differently for different activities and stages of the OD process.

Stop and Criticize

As OD consultant, you have been asked by the plant human resources director to conduct an attitude survey in a branch plant of a multinational electronics company in the Netherlands with over 200 employees on site. There seems to be a problem with morale which may be affecting shop-floor productivity. You are doing this through a combination of questionnaire and structured 'focus group' discussions with ten to twelve employees at a time. Individual employees are guaranteed anonymity, and management are happy with this approach. Four groups from one section of the site have independently asked you to represent their strong and critical views about supervisory and middle management style and behaviour to senior management on their behalf. They see this as the purpose of the attitude survey, and see this also as a legitimate aspect of your neutral OD consulting and advisory role. Other employee groups, however, have not made this special request.

In this assignment, who is your client?

How should you, as external OD consultant, handle the attempt to recruit you to a specific cause? (This account is based on a real case.)

How should an OD intervention take place? Kurt Lewin (1951, pp. 228–9) argued that the process of change must pass through three stages of unfreezing, transition and refreezing:

> A change toward a higher level of group performance is frequently short lived; after a 'shot in the arm', group life soon returns to the previous level. This indicates that it does not suffice to define the objective of a planned change in group performance as the reaching of a different level. Permanency of the new level, or permanency for a desired period, should be included in the objective. A successful change therefore includes three aspects: unfreezing (if necessary) the present level L^1, moving to the new level L^2, and freezing group life on the new level. Since any level is determined by a force field, permanency implies that the new force field is made relatively secure against change.

Force field analysis: a technique for assessing the balance of factors that respectively encourage and resist movement towards a desired target situation.

OD interventions can be considered in terms of how they help with the unfreezing, transition and refreezing states of the change and development process. Lewin also developed the technique of **force field analysis**, noting that the nature and pace of change depend on the balance of driving and restraining forces in relation to a particular 'target situation'.

A force field analysis involves assessing the factors supporting and impeding movement towards a given target situation. This can indicate the viability of the change, and suggest action to alter the balance of forces if necessary. A typical force field analysis looks like this:

target situation: emigrate from Britain to Australia	
driving forces ————→>>>	<<<———— **restraining forces**
friendly natives	family in Scotland
inexpensive lifestyle	high cost of moving
the wide open spaces	the long journey to anywhere
the beer, the wine	the mosquitoes, the spiders
clear skies, sunshine, beaches	sunburn, skin cancer, sharks

If the driving forces are overwhelming, then the change can probably go ahead without any significant problems. If the resisting forces are overwhelming, then the change may have to be abandoned until conditions have improved. The factors can be weighted or scored, say from 1 (weak) to 10 (strong), to provide a rough guide to the balance.

If the driving and restraining forces are more or less in balance, then the force field analysis can be used to determine appropriate action. Lewin suggested concentrating on weakening or overcoming resisting forces, as attempts to strengthen driving forces could simply strengthen resistance, and the force field would remain where it was, but at a higher level of tension. The durability of Lewin's thinking is reflected in the work of Peter Senge et al. (1999, p. 10), who describe what they call 'the dance of change', but use the same argument:

> We need to understand the nature of growth processes (forces that aid our efforts) and how to catalyze them. But we also need to understand the forces and challenges that impede progress, and to develop workable strategies for dealing with these challenges. We need to appreciate 'the dance of change', the inevitable interplay between growth processes and limiting processes.

The weighting of factors gives the technique a spurious air of scientific validity. Clearly, the extent to which a force field is balanced is a matter of judgement.

Used in a group setting, however, the technique helps to structure discussion of what can often be a large and untidy collection of issues, and the scoring procedure can stimulate lively and valuable debate.

Stop and Criticize

Your educational institution plans dramatically to extend the use of objective testing of students in business and management studies. This will replace conventional essay-style assignments and exams with multiple choice tests, and one-word and other short-answer tests. Multiple choice tests, of course, can be scanned and marked electronically, avoiding the need for tedious essay marking.

Draw the force field, identifying the driving and resisting forces.

Assess the balance of forces, and the ease or difficulty of introducing this change.

Construct a brief action plan for *implementing* this change.

Construct a brief action plan for *blocking* this change.

What does this exercise reveal about the strengths and limitations of force field analysis as a diagnostic and action planning tool?

What approaches are used by OD to implement planned change? Thomas Cummings and Christopher Worley (2001) outline two intervention models – the planning model and the action research model. The planning model, summarized in table 17.4, assumes that change can be implemented in seven related stages.

Table 17.4: The planning model of OD intervention

1: **Scouting**	consultant and client share information and ideas with respect to problems and the appropriate approach
2: **Entry**	a formal consulting or helping relationship is established
3: **Diagnosis**	information gathering to define the problem and identify causes
4: **Planning**	jointly establish the goals of intervention and the proposed approach
5: **Action**	intervention strategies are implemented
6: **Stabilization**	change is stabilized (refreezing) and outcomes are assessed
7: **Termination**	the consultant withdraws or moves on to another OD project

In practice, change rarely unfolds in such a straightforward manner. The original plan is always subject to modification and refinement. The seven steps are not always followed in precisely this sequence. Some stages may be omitted or passed over quickly, or revisited several times during the change process. This does not invalidate the model, which remains a useful guide or route map for participants in the OD process.

Action research: a model of OD consulting that involves the feedback of findings from interventions to help design and implement further improvements.

The **action research** model differs from the traditional planning model in two respects.

First, action research is a cyclical or iterative process. This simply means that the results from an intervention are fed back in such a way that further changes and improvements can be implemented. Of course, this can happen with a planning model too, but in action research, this intention is designed into the approach from the beginning.

Second, *research* here signals the aim of generating knowledge that can be applied in other organizational settings. This means that action research is a different kind of consulting model, and also a different kind of organizational research model, which aims to produce not just theoretical, academic understanding, but also actionable knowledge.

Action research can also be defined as a model of organizational research in which generalizable knowledge is produced from attempts actively to change and improve organizational functioning, rather than from passive observation. Action research is sometimes seen as a recent development, which gained acceptance during the 1990s. However, applications of this approach date from the mid-1940s.

Consistent with the overarching goals of OD, action research in practice is a collaborative method, involving consultant and organization members in joint planning, diagnosis, implementation, evaluation and further planning. The outline stages of an action research programme are therefore likely to include:

1. problem identification

2. preliminary diagnosis

3. data gathering from the client group

4. data feedback to the client group

5. joint evaluation of data

6. joint action planning

7. action or implementation of proposals for change

8. repeat the cycle – fresh data gathering and feedback of results of change

As with the traditional planning model, action research is unlikely always to unfold in such a tidy manner in practice. Once again, the model is simply a useful guide. The main differences between the planning and action research models lie with their respective emphasis and goals. Action research emphasizes the cyclical nature of organization development and change, whereas the planning model presumes a 'one-off' intervention. The goals of the planning model are improved personal and organizational effectiveness. Action research adds the goal of generating new knowledge and insights for application elsewhere.

OD techniques: the toolkit

Designing a package of OD interventions is a creative assignment. The approach has to be tailored to fit the culture and problems of the client system. In any particular organization, some approaches are likely to be more appropriate, and perhaps more acceptable, than others. An examination of the OD toolkit has to bear this in mind. The main techniques are these.

Sensitivity training

Sensitivity training: a technique for enhancing individual self-awareness, and for changing behaviour, through unstructured group discussion.

If you join a **sensitivity training** programme, you will find yourself in a room with other participants, but without an agenda or discussion topic, or other obvious purpose. The aim is to allow participants to discuss themselves, to observe and discuss the ways in which they interact together, and to exchange feedback on each other and their interactions.

Probably the oldest OD intervention, sensitivity training sessions are also known as laboratory training, encounter groups and T-groups, where T stands for training or therapy.

The sensitivity training group may have a facilitator, but sometimes participants are brought together without anyone 'in charge' and are left to create their own conversation. When a facilitator is present, he or she rejects a leadership role, pushing any such requests back to the group to discuss and resolve. Without an agenda beyond 'talk about yourselves', the discussion can quickly turn to feelings and emotions. This may begin with the expression of how participants feel about being in such an unstructured setting. This can then evolve into an emotionally charged discussion about how individuals feel about themselves, about other participants, and about the facilitators being responsible for this awkward situation. The feelings and emotions exposed in this setting can be personal, confrontational and embarrassing.

Some participants who have undergone sensitivity training experience profound insights about themselves and how they relate to others. Some, however, find the lack of structure and the open sharing of emotions threatening and stressful. Critics argue that the method can cause psychological damage (Guest, 1984, pp. 201–3 reviews the evidence).

The history of sensitivity training predates the founding of OD. The technique was invented, by accident, in the summer of 1946 when the Connecticut State Inter-Racial Commission asked Kurt Lewin at the Research Center for Group Dynamics at Massachusetts Institute of Technology to run a training programme for community leaders. Lewin's team designed a programme of lectures, role plays and group discussions. During the evenings, the trainers met to share their observations and assessments of the programme and its participants. However, some participants were staying in the training centre, and asked if they could observe these evening discussions. Lewin gave them permission to do this, although the other trainers were hesitant.

Kurt Lewin
(1890–1947)

One evening, one participant, listening to the training staff discussing her behaviour during the day, interrupted to challenge their interpretations and to describe what had happened from her perspective. Lewin immediately recognized the potential of this exchange, and an increasing number of participants started to join the evening discussions. Soon the evening sessions were proving as valuable in learning terms as the regular daytime sessions were supposed to be. In other words, participants became more sensitive to their own behaviour, to the effects they had on others, and to how others saw them and related to them.

This method was soon being applied in organizational settings to support change programmes. Its first reported use was by the oil company Esso (now Exxon) in its refineries in Louisiana and Texas. Managers were given three-day training laboratories in order to help them develop and to change to a more participative management style. Sensitivity training is one way to develop *emotional intelligence* (Goleman, 1995, 1998), which has become a more fashionable term for self- and other-awareness (chapter 5).

Change the structure

There are numerous ways in which the structure or design of an organization can be changed (see Part 4). Examples include the techniques of *job rotation*, *job enlargement* and *job enrichment*, which target individual jobs, and *autonomous teamwork* which targets groups of employees. The techniques of socio-technical systems analysis and organizational design (including autonomous groups) have become part of the OD toolkit too. *Business process re-engineering* also leads to structural changes affecting organizational processes. It is possible to change the degree of centralization or decentralization in an organization, or to flatten or

Edgar Henry
Schein (b. 1928)

Process consultation: an OD intervention in which an external consultant acts in a facilitating and catalytic capacity to enhance an organization's diagnostic, conceptual and action planning skills.

Survey feedback: an OD intervention in which the results of an opinion survey are fed back to respondents to trigger problem-solving concerning issues highlighted by the findings.

Team building: an OD intervention to help team members to understand their own roles more clearly, and improve their interaction and collaboration.

extend the organization structure, or to change the basis of the organization design from region to product, or vice versa. Rules and procedures can be relaxed or tightened up.

Apparently simple structural changes can have profound implications. Structure has a significant influence over access to information and other resources, over work experience and career opportunities, and over degrees of individual autonomy. Structure also signifies which departments are marked for growth and which for decline, and structural changes can be used to signal shifts in the organization's future direction and priorities.

Process consultation

In **process consultation**, an external consultant is engaged by the organization in an advisory role, helping individuals to improve their understanding of problems and to identify problem-solving actions. One of the main advocates of this approach has been Edgar Henry Schein (1969).

The role of the process consultant is to 'give the client insight', or rather to help clients to develop their own insights. This requires a great deal of skill, sensitivity and tact, and there are no standard procedures to follow. The process consultant may or may not be knowledgeable with respect to the problems facing the organization. The critical skills for a process consultant are in diagnosis and in forming a supportive, helping relationship. The diagnostic and problem-solving activities of the process consultant are, by definition, joint activities, carried out with the client or clients. The focus is on process, which explains the label. Process consultation contrasts with the conventional view of the consultant as an 'expert' where the client is buying specific knowledge and expertise to fill gaps in the organization, and also to address and resolve a particular problem.

Survey feedback

Survey feedback means just what the term implies. The results of an employee opinion survey are fed back (anonymously) to managers and employees, to help identify action that will improve performance. A typical opinion survey includes questions on leadership and management style, aspects of organization culture such as communications, motivation and decision-making, and member satisfaction with the organization, their job, their supervisor, their pay and their work group.

A survey can cover the whole organization or just a section of it. Those responding may be invited to contribute to the initial design of the questionnaire, suggesting items and indicating significant issues. Opinion surveys typically reveal differences in perception around an organization and usually highlight problem areas. These findings are then used to trigger discussion about ways to resolve differences and solve problems. The most popular approach for achieving this is through group discussions in task forces, working parties, laboratories or project teams, each working on a particular set of themes or issues, or directing their attention to a particular section of the organization.

Team building

Mentioned several times throughout this text, teamwork is fundamental to organizational functioning and has attracted a lot of attention from OD practitioners. The first application of **team building**, according to French and Bell (1999), was by Robert Tannenbaum in the early 1950s at the Naval Ordnance Test Station in California.

There are many different approaches to team building. One popular technique is based on the work of Meredith Belbin (1981, 1996), who argued that teams work most effectively when nine interdependent roles are covered – Plant, Resource investigator, Co-ordinator, Shaper, Monitor-evaluator, Teamworker, Implementer, Completer and Specialist. Belbin developed a self-assessment questionnaire to help you to identify your personal team role preference(s). Once you have identified your preferred role, you can then play to that strength. Once the team has identified which roles are present, and which are absent, it may be possible for it to compensate for any imbalance. One or more individuals, for example, may be invited to 'hold back' a preferred role if it is overrepresented in the group. One or more individuals may be invited to 'cover' roles that are not among their strong preferences, but which are missing from the group's overall profile.

Another popular team-building technique involves the simple process of group effectiveness rating. Members rate their team on criteria such as clarity of goals, willingness to share ideas, time management, focus on achieving results, willingness to listen to others, ability to allow all team members to contribute, and so on. The rating questionnaire is first completed individually, and these scores are then discussed in a team meeting. The combined ratings from the questionnaires can be used to identify and address differences in perception in the team, to highlight problems affecting teamwork, and to trigger a discussion of how the team is going to overcome those problems and improve performance.

Some training organizations offer team-building programmes based on 'outward bound' or 'outdoor training' techniques. Participants are typically subjected to a series of challenges, involving, for example, rock climbing, sailing, orienteering and mountain walking, preferably in appalling weather to heighten the sense of challenge. The activities are designed to require teamwork, and to encourage the development of interpersonal trust, group decision-making, communication skills and an awareness of leadership roles.

© 1993 Farcus Cartoons   WAISGLASS/COULTHART   www.farcus.com

"We've had a few complaints that you're not a team player."

Intergroup development

It is common to find that sections, functions or departments in an organization develop their own unique perspectives and behaviours, which prevent effective interdepartmental communications and collaboration. The functional boundaries that exist between, for example, the finance and personnel departments of a large retailing store, or between the inorganic chemistry and marketing departments in a university, can lead to dysfunctional conflict. Within a single unit or function, groups with different goals, backgrounds and working practices may find it difficult to work together when required. OD has devised methods to improve intergroup relationships and working arrangements. These include **intergroup development**, which is also known as *intergroup confrontation* and *peacemaking*.

How does one create harmony between two organizational groups (cost accountants and mechanical engineers) that have negative stereotypes and perceptions of each other? In the 'mutual expectations' approach to intergroup development, the two groups first meet separately and are asked to note:

Intergroup development: an OD intervention to change the perceptions and attitudes that different groups hold with respect to each other, and improve their interaction and collaboration.

■ how they see themselves;

■ their expectations of the other group;

■ what they think the other group expects from them.

The groups exchange these lists, then meet to explore the similarities and differences in their perceptions and expectations. Such an exchange can be confrontational. If the meeting is deliberately designed as confrontational, special facilitation skills are required on the part of the OD consultant, to keep the discussion under control and to achieve a positive outcome. Once the differences between conflicting groups are known, their causes can be explored and action can be taken to reduce or remove barriers to effective integration and collaboration.

One variant of this technique is known as 'organizational mirroring'. This involves the 'target group' seeking feedback from other groups in the organization on how it is seen and perceived. In this approach, several groups may be concerned, and representatives from the other groups are only involved in providing information and ideas, rather than in full negotiation or confrontation with the target group members.

Role negotiation

Role negotiation: an OD intervention to change the perceptions and attitudes that different individuals in an organization hold with respect to each other, to improve their interaction and collaboration.

Role negotiation can be a useful way to reconcile differences between two individuals whose working relationship is ineffective. The approach is similar to intergroup development.

The technique assumes that interpersonal friction is caused by a lack of mutual awareness and understanding. The aim in role negotiation, therefore, is to make individual perceptions and mutual expectations explicit, so that differences can be identified and resolved.

Other approaches: change systems and procedures

Just about any tool, technique or approach for changing attitudes, behaviour and performance can be regarded and used as an OD intervention. In addition to the intervention techniques described so far, OD uses a range of other methods to change organizational culture, to encourage individual growth, to foster intergroup collaboration, and to improve organizational effectiveness. For example, job definitions, work organization and group relationships can be significantly affected by *technological innovation*, in both office and manufacturing settings. Goals, priorities and behaviours can be altered by making appropriate changes to the organization's *payment system*.

The whole range of *human resource management* policies and practices, including recruitment, selection, placement, training and development, promotion and career planning systems, can be used to influence attitudes and behaviour at work. The organization sends signals about what behaviour is valued through the design of its staff *appraisal system*, where individuals discuss their goals and their performance at least once a year with their manager. The effects of appraisal can be supported by planned *career counselling and development* systems designed to reinforce the same messages. Required changes in skills, knowledge, attitudes and behaviour can be encouraged through specially tailored *training and development* programmes. Communications and working relationships can be improved through a range of mechanisms, such as *conferences, forums, workshops, discussion groups* and *project teams*. These mechanisms can focus on particular groups or they can bring together staff from different sections and levels of the organization structure.

Grid Organization Development

Grid Organization Development: an organization-wide diagnostic approach to the development of effective management style based on a structured, six-phase change model.

Robert R. Blake

Grid Organization Development, invented by Robert Blake and Jane Mouton (1964, 1968, 1969) is probably one of the most widely known OD interventions. The evidence that they collected from around 200 American, British and Japanese companies suggested that the two main barriers to business excellence were planning and communications. One of the main objectives of Grid OD, therefore, is to improve business planning by identifying the strategic organizational goals and policies that will guide decisions and actions. The second objective concerns the development of effective supervisory management style.

Blake and Mouton developed the Leadership Grid, shown in figure 17.1, to help managers to identify and improve their interpersonal management style. The Leadership Grid assumes that management style has two critical dimensions. The first is concern for production, emphasizing task accomplishment. This can cover a wide range of factors, including efficiency and work load, units of output, number of units processed, number of creative ideas suggested, and so on. The second is concern for people, emphasizing the needs of employees. This can cover involvement, commitment, working conditions, concern for personal worth, job security, fair rewards, and good social relationships at work.

The 'nine by nine' Leadership Grid is used to locate a manager's approach to interpersonal relationships in one of 81 possible variations. Blake and Mouton concentrate for simplicity on the four corner positions, and on the style represented by the middle of the Grid.

Style 1,1: Impoverished management

This style is based on the belief that conflict should be avoided by avoiding people and by maintaining a neutral position in disputes. Combining a low concern for production with a low concern for people, managers using this style exert minimum effort, keep out of trouble, avoid rocking the boat, focus on their own job security and can be described as defeatist, having abdicated management responsibility.

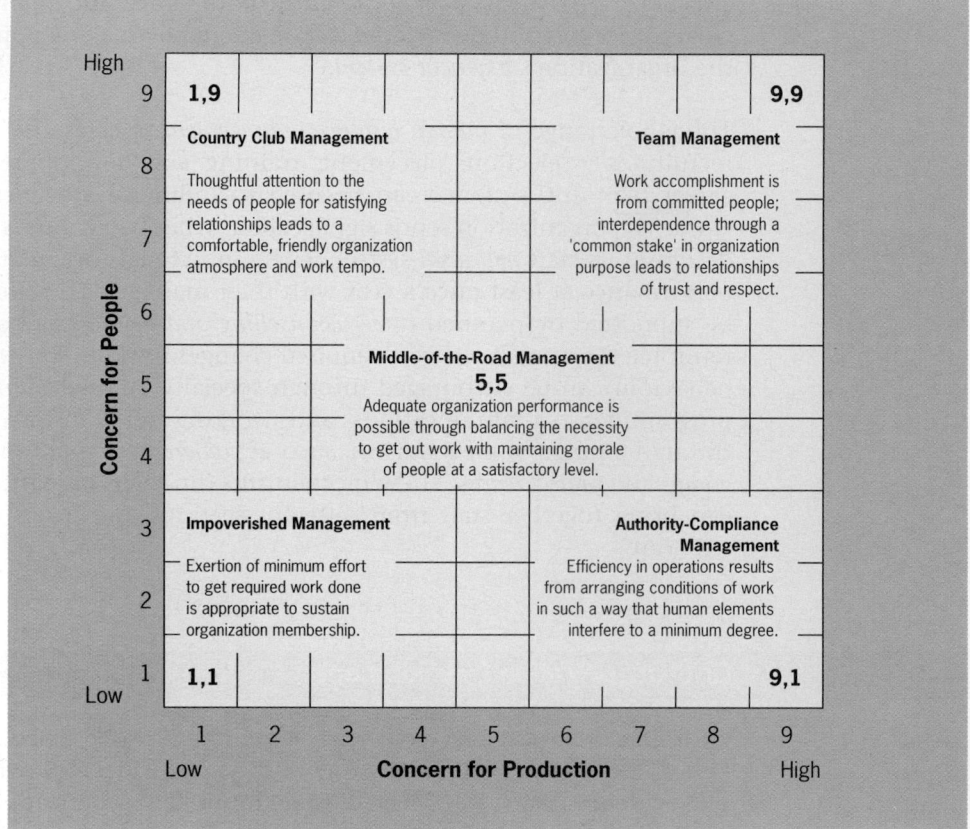

Figure 17.1: The Blake and Mouton Leadership Grid
From E.E. Blake and A.A. McCanse, *Leadership Dilemmas: Grid Solutions*, Gulf Publishing, Houston, 1991, p. 29. Reprinted by permission of Grid International, Inc.

Style 9,1: Authority-compliance management

This style is based on the belief that employees will perform well if they are supervised and controlled closely. Combining a high concern for production with low concern for people, managers using this style assume conflict between organizational and employee needs, and concentrate on maximizing output, ignoring employee attitudes, feelings, needs and ideas.

Style 1,9: Country club management

This style is based on the belief that high work performance depends on treating employees in a friendly manner. Combining a high concern for people with low concern for production, managers using this style concentrate on employee needs, attitudes and feelings, seeking to provide secure and comfortable working conditions potentially at the expense of work output.

Style 9,9: Team management

This style is based on the belief that organizational and employee needs are inherently compatible. Combining high levels of concern for both people and production, managers using this style share information and involve employees in management decisions. The '9,9' manager aims to develop cohesive teamwork to achieve high productivity and high morale.

Style 5,5: Middle-of-the-road management

This style is based on the belief that it is necessary to compromise when employee and organizational needs conflict with each other. Combining moderate levels of concern for both production and people, managers using this style seek workable compromises between employee and organizational needs, attempting to keep employees relatively satisfied while getting the job done to an adequate standard.

The five main styles identified in the Leadership Grid differ on one other major factor, and this concerns the underlying assumption concerning the nature of organizational conflict. The '9,9' manager, according to Blake and Mouton, believes that there is no inherent conflict between employee and organizational needs, and that these can be integrated using an appropriate managerial style. Managers adopting the other four styles believe that such conflicts are inevitable, and their different approaches thus reflect different ways of dealing with those conflicts. The basic assumption of OD, of course, and therefore of the Grid OD approach, is that conflict is unnecessary and undesirable, a result of poor management.

Blake and Mouton claim that the '9,9 team management' style is the most effective. The '9,9' manager gains support for organizational plans by involving employees and thus overcoming communication barriers by openly sharing information. Discussion and debate about decisions, it is assumed, lead to higher levels of commitment than requests for blind obedience. This participative approach to organizational change implementation is fundamental to most of the approaches discussed in chapter 18 on organizational change.

Blake and Mouton advise that the Grid OD approach is applied in a six-phase process, which can take from three to five years to complete, to overcome planning and communications barriers to organizational effectiveness. The six phases, in summary, are as follows:

Phase 1, The grid seminar: Over a full week, participants identify their management style from the Leadership Grid, and learn about communication, problem-solving and teamworking methods from colleagues who have been through special 'prephase' training. The aim, of course, is to learn how to become a '9,9' manager.

Phase 2, Teamwork development: Participants develop further and perfect their teamwork with superiors and with subordinates, focusing on current organizational problems.

Phase 3, Intergroup development: Groups in the organization which have to interact regularly, but which may have developed negative stereotypes of each other, share their perceptions of each other and meet to establish more effective working relationships by specifying the actions that each will in future take with respect to the other.

Phase 4, Developing a strategic organizational model: The emphasis now shifts to strategic planning. Top management develop definitions of financial goals, organizational activities, their customers and markets, the organization structure, decision-making policies and a growth strategy. The aim is to describe what the organization would be like if its performance were truly excellent. This step alone can take up to one year to complete.

Phase 5, Implementing the strategic model: By this stage, if the previous four steps have been effective, barriers to implementation have been removed and communications problems resolved. Planning teams responsible for implementing the model in detail are now appointed for each business unit.

Phase 6, Systematic critique: Progress towards the 'ideal' strategic model is reviewed, using a range of formal and informal measures to assess the quantity and quality of progress, also identifying further organizational development needs and goals.

"*You know what I think, folks? Improving technology isn't important. Increased profits aren't important. What's important is to be warm, decent human beings.*"

This is unlike any of the organization change methodologies discussed in the following chapter, for four reasons. First, this is designed as an organization-wide intervention, so it is time consuming (and expensive) and can be difficult. It can be applied to individual units or departments, but the potential impact is reduced if planning and communication barriers persist in and between departments. Second, the approach recommends one universally effective style of management, not an approach that is contingent on the nature, scale or pace of the change in hand. The exploration of leadership styles in chapter 21 will suggest, in contrast, that the most effective style depends on the context. Third, while most other change advice offers only outline guidance, the Grid approach prescribes in great detail how each phase is to be carried out. We have provided only an overview here. Finally, the organization does not have to follow all six phases. Phases 1 to 3 deal mainly with communication barriers and can be used on their own, without 'follow-through' into the planning phases.

When presenting the work of Blake and Mouton, many organizational behaviour textbooks focus on their model of leadership styles. Some readers will thus look for that model in our chapter on leadership. However, that is a misrepresentation of their contribution. The Leadership Grid is one tool in the systematic OD package which they advocate.

OD applications: the evidence

OD thus has two important features. First, it is potentially wide in its scope and implications for the organization and its members. Second, the design of an OD programme involves constructing an appropriate *package* of interventions, which will be different for each organization. Constructing the package requires judgement, creativity and knowledge of the context. An appropriate package cannot be designed by reading solutions off a matrix.

Bloody battles to harmonious partnership

Paul Bate describes how OD transformed the culture of a British hospital where morale was low, communication was poor, infighting was common, and relationships between management and doctors were 'embittered and hostile'. Staff comments, such as 'disaster ready to happen' and 'this is a sick organization', expressed the sense of crisis. The chief executive wanted a radical new structure, but this would not change the culture of conflict.

A change management group was created, and the researchers were engaged for two years in an action research role. First, over six months, staff opinions across the hospital were surveyed to agree a new 'cultural vision'. This was to move from a rigid, hierarchical and inward-looking 'them and us' culture, to one which was collaborative, flexible and outward-looking, with better communication and exchange of knowledge.

Implementing these changes was difficult because senior management were reluctant to give up power and status. At an off-site meeting, the doctors planned a 'showdown', intending to call for a vote of no confidence in management, but they changed their minds:

> We have decided to stop talking about getting rid of you, and find a way of working with you. We have come to the conclusion that *we* don't want to 'manage', we want you to do that and free us up so that we can treat patients. We want the partnership to become such that the 'chief executive' becomes the 'chief facilitator'. We want a much greater say in setting the priorities and operating the hospital. We will do the leading and you will do the managing. We don't want control of the organization. We all have to learn how to provide different resources and support for each other. It's not a question of them working for us, we are all working for each other.

The result was a power-sharing 'partnership of hierarchies' between management and clinical groups. Temporary flexible arrangements replaced the rigid old hierarchy. The management board, 'scene of many bloody battles', became a multidisciplinary advisory forum, and the executive group was broadened to include doctors and nurses. The chief executive and some senior colleagues resigned. Management became more facilitative, interacting widely with groups inside the hospital and across the local community.

This OD programme used a combination of action research, survey feedback, intergroup development, role negotiation and structure change. Bate concludes that the approach was successful because it was 'home grown', designed in collaboration with those directly involved, not following any preconceived model.

Based on Paul Bate, 'Changing the culture of a hospital: from hierarchy to networked community', *Public Administration*, vol. 78, no. 3, 2000, pp. 485–512.

It is not difficult to see a set of underpinning assumptions reflected in the OD toolkit:

■ individual and organizational goals are compatible;

■ conflict is caused by misunderstandings;

■ conflict can be resolved by openly confronting differences in perception;

■ the open display of emotions and feelings is valuable;

■ people have capacity and desire for personal growth;

■ working relationships can be improved by enhancing self-awareness;

■ collaboration and trust are better than conflict and secrecy.

This is why Warren Bennis described OD as a 'truth, trust, love and collaboration approach'. OD interventions rely on the free and open sharing of information and emotions. Where these values are compromised, the OD agenda may also be endangered. One of the other main criticisms of OD is that, although it claims to confront organizational conflict, the role of trade unions in representing employees and bargaining on their behalf for improved conditions is excluded from consideration.

Stop and Criticize

From a critical perspective, some commentators argue that OD is a powerful set of symbolic techniques for manipulating employee attitudes and behaviour. OD thus seeks to disguise the fundamental conflict of interests between the individual and the organization, between employees and management, in a false language of consensus, co-operation and conflict resolution. This is not a principled approach to humanistic management. OD from this perspective is highly devious and manipulative.

Where do you stand on this argument? OD as a cunning, underhand management plot, or OD as a sincere attempt to improve the quality of working life?

OD practitioners and their clients are preoccupied with the question 'does it work?'. However, OD is a package of approaches to improving organizational effectiveness rather than a well-specified technique; it is 'more of a process than a step-by-step procedure', as Warren Burke (1987, p. 1) notes. The package is configured in different ways to suit different organizational contexts. It is therefore difficult to conduct systematic research that allows comparisons to be made between interventions and across organizational settings.

The factors which OD seeks to change include a broad spectrum of attitudes and values as well as numerous quantitative indicators of organizational performance. The target of a typical OD programme may be the improvement of teamwork or the enhancement of working relationships between groups or departments, or improvement of the performance of the organization as a whole. Interventions can target interpersonal, group and organizational issues simultaneously. There may even be disagreement about which measures or indicators are most significant.

In rigorous research methodology terms (see glossary), the *independent variables* (OD interventions) are loosely defined and inconsistently applied, and the *dependent variables* (measures of organizational effectiveness) are similarly difficult to establish, and may be disputed. These problems are compounded when an action research model is used. Here the 'researcher' is both intimately involved with, and actually seeks to influence, the very interventions and consequences which are the focus of study. How can one adequately assess cause and effect when all the research rules about objectivity and rigour are broken?

Systematic evaluation of the organization-wide approach of Grid OD is especially difficult. There are several individual, group, intergroup and organizational factors to consider, and the full process can take years to complete. Determining cause and effect, unambiguously, is almost impossible. The mainstream OD texts (French and Bell, 1999; Cummings and Worley, 2001) are agnostic, claiming that the approach seems to work well in some settings and that further research is required to settle the matter. Nevertheless, advocates of OD have sought to defend the approach with empirical evidence from across a range of applications, over a number of decades of experience. Don Warrick (1984), for example, lists ten potentially positive results from OD interventions:

1. Improved organizational effectiveness, including better productivity and morale.

2. Better management throughout the organization.

3. Commitment to and involvement in making the organization successful.

4. Improved teamwork.

5. Better understanding of organizational strengths and weaknesses.

6. Improved communications, problem-solving and conflict resolution.

7. Creativity, openness, opportunities for personal development.

8. Decrease in dysfunctional behaviour – politicking, playing games.

9. Increased ability to adapt to changing circumstances.

10. Increased ability to attract and retain quality people.

French and Bell (1999) work through a 'review of reviews', presenting evidence from a broad range of studies and organizational settings. They claim that the literature of the field does demonstrate that OD programmes produce positive changes at the organizational and individual levels. Much of the literature, of course, is produced by OD practitioners who are in turn responsible for publishing the reviews of other reported OD interventions.

It is further interesting to note that French and Bell highlight the *faith* that OD practitioners have in the power of OD interventions. Faith plus data should be reassuring, they point out, suggesting that, for many practitioners, faith alone is probably good enough. Is this an unsatisfactory conclusion? It was suggested earlier in the chapter that OD has some of the properties of a religious movement. The goals and values of OD concern, in part, the development of individuals through improving conditions of work across a number of dimensions. Improving quality of working life may be seen as a valuable outcome of OD interventions, even where the measurable performance of the organization from an accountant's point of view remains unaffected.

| **Stop and Criticize** | David Collins (1998) points out that when considering how best to sell a product or service, organizations typically think in terms of market segmentation. In other words, it is usually necessary to tailor the product, or the service, or the marketing message differently for different segments of the market.

However, when 'selling' change, OD talks about the need for everyone in the organization to 'share the same vision'. Does this imply that an organization's members have common interests, values, perceptions and goals to a degree that surpasses the untidy differences among people outside the organization?

What does this observation suggest about the practicality of the OD perspective and the validity of the underpinning assumptions?

OD assumes that major change is difficult and takes time, that there is 'no quick fix'. However, as the perceived pace of change increased through the 1990s, many commentators sought to challenge that assumption. Many organizations found that they needed to change much more rapidly than OD seemed to allow. OD appears to offer the somewhat elusive promise of improved effectiveness in the long run, but it is probably difficult to measure, following an extended and probably expensive programme of activities which initially address intangible factors like beliefs, values and attitudes. This is not a compelling promise in a fast-moving, competitive world where even public sector organizations are required to deliver improvements within tight and non-negotiable timescales.

Robert Schaffer and Harvey Thomson (1992, p. 80), both harsh critics of OD, argue that:

> The performance improvement efforts of many companies have as much impact on operational and financial results as a ceremonial rain dance has on the weather. While some companies constantly improve measurable performance, in many others, managers continue to dance round and round the campfire – exuding faith and dissipating energy.
>
> This 'rain dance' is the ardent pursuit of activities that sound good, look good, and allow managers to feel good – but in fact contribute little or nothing to bottom-line performance. These activities, many of which parade under the banner of 'total quality' or 'continuous improvement', typically advance a managerial philosophy or style such as interfunctional collaboration, middle management empowerment, or employee involvement. [. . .] Companies introduce these programs under the false assumption that if they carry out enough of the 'right' improvement activities actual performance improvements will inevitably materialize. At the heart of these programs, which we call 'activity-centred', is a fundamentally flawed logic that confuses ends with means, processes with outcomes.

Schaffer and Thomson argue for the advantages of what they call 'results-driven programs' compared with the 'activity-driven programs' of OD. Results-driven programmes aim to produce significant, short-term, measurable performance improvements in areas where long-term benefits can also be achieved. Results-driven programmes are built on ambition and impatience, on a desire to see tangible results, now. OD in contrast requires sustained commitment to the pursuit of intangible goals such as attitude change and new sets of values. This does not necessarily mean, however, that results-driven programmes and OD are incompatible. The teams or task forces searching for those rapid performance gains are going to encounter barriers. As they try to overcome those barriers, their actions may well parallel OD interventions to produce culture change. Schaffer and Thomson do not present their approach as 'fast-track' OD, but clearly the techniques of OD can be combined with a results-driven emphasis to generate such an approach.

If French and Bell (1999) are correct in their prediction that flatter, organic structures are replacing those based on the traditional paradigm of hierarchical, bureaucratic control, then OD will continue to play a central role in organizational change and improvement. The values and interventions that OD advocates appear as relevant in the twenty-first century as they have been since the 1960s. As they claim, the future for OD appears to be bright.

To be an OD consultant

What does it take to be an OD consultant? Warren Burke (1987, p. 143) opens his discussion of this question as follows:

> To be seen as a consultant is to have status, and thus many people aspire to the label and the role. A consultant is one who provides help, counsel, advice, and support, which implies that such a person is wiser than most people.

Burke also lists the personal attributes that the effective OD consultant should possess:

- ability to tolerate ambiguity;

- influencing skill;

- ability to confront difficult issues;

- skills in supporting and nurturing others;

- ability rapidly to recognize one's own feelings and intuitions;

- conceptual skills;

- ability to mobilize self and others;

- ability to teach and to create learning opportunities;

- a sense of humour, to maintain perspective;

- self-confidence;

- a sense of mission about working as an OD consultant.

Stop and Criticize

Could you be an effective OD consultant?

Assess yourself against Burke's list of personal attributes and identify your own strengths and weaknesses. Do you want to be a consultant in this field? To what extent do you think this specification is 'superhuman' and beyond the reach of one individual? Is there a place for humility in the consultant's toolkit?

French and Bell (1999) argue that the OD consultant's role is unique because it is based on a collaborative relationship with the client organization. The OD practitioner, in their view, is 'a facilitator, catalyst, problem solver, and educator'. This makes the OD consultant a peculiar kind of expert – an expert on process, but not necessarily an expert on the content of change. The OD consultant who diagnoses and then prescribes the solution is not helping the client organization to develop its own diagnostic and problem-solving capability. In brief, you do not help someone to learn by simply giving them the right answers all the time.

The traditional approach to management consultancy is based on a 'doctor–patient' model, where the consultant is the expert diagnostician who investigates and prescribes a cure. In contrast, the OD consultant works together with clients, designing interventions that help organization members to diagnose and resolve their own problems more effectively. The medical model is self-perpetuating. The next time you get sick, you still need to call the doctor. The OD model is self-developmental. If the intervention worked the last time, then you will be equipped to develop your own cure the next time you become ill.

OD consultants in particular, and management consultants in general, use a range of styles, distinguished by their reliance on their own skills and knowledge, or on their clients' skills and knowledge. The continuum of styles or approaches is illustrated in table 17.5.

Identifying the skills and knowledge of the effective OD practitioner, Cummings and Worley (2001) identify four critical areas.

Intrapersonal skills

These may also be described as self-management capabilities. They include conceptual and analytical skills, integrity and moral judgement, being in touch with your own goals and values, learning skills and stress management. The OD

Table 17.5: Consultant knowledge versus client knowledge

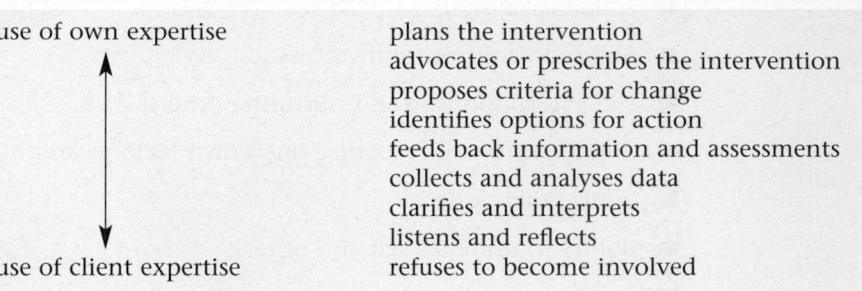

use of own expertise	plans the intervention
	advocates or prescribes the intervention
	proposes criteria for change
	identifies options for action
	feeds back information and assessments
	collects and analyses data
	clarifies and interprets
	listens and reflects
use of client expertise	refuses to become involved

consultant role can be stressful, characterized by ambiguity, time pressure, conflict, emotional outburst and uncertainty. This requires resilience and an ability to manage one's own emotions and stress responses. The intrapersonal skills are not always visible, but they can be critical.

Interpersonal skills

These include general communication skills, listening, establishing trust and rapport, giving and receiving feedback, negotiation, counselling and coaching. This area also includes 'aptitude in speaking the client's language', which is essential in building rapport and credibility, and in maintaining effective helping relationships.

General consultation skills

These include diagnostic capability and skills in designing and implementing appropriate OD intervention packages. The latter involves action planning, customizing the package to fit the organization, and presenting ideas in a way that gains commitment and collaboration. Remember that this also involves understanding when and how effectively to involve the organization's members in collaborative diagnostic and implementation activities. This is a more subtle, complex and difficult skill than individual diagnosis and autocratic implementation would involve. The OD consultant should also be knowledgeable and skilled in the use of process consultation methods.

Organization development theory

The OD consultant should be familiar with OD theory and research, and have an understanding of the planned change and action research models. A knowledge of the range of interventions is useful, along with a knowledge of research findings concerning their application. A conceptual understanding of the role of the OD consultant is also valuable.

These skills and knowledge areas could be applied to many organizational positions. They certainly apply to both internal and external consultants working in an organization. Most of these skills also apply to members of internal project teams, working parties, task forces or steering groups. Even though we do not carry the job title 'management consultant', many of us find ourselves from time to time involved in organizational data gathering, diagnosis, action planning and change implementation. These qualifications should not be seen as belonging exclusively to the professional OD practitioner or consultant.

The OD consultant may not be an expert in a particular organizational area, function, system or problem. However, the range of relevant process expertise is wide, and it may be difficult to find many individuals who are appropriately skilled and knowledgeable. The role of the OD consultant does seem to be one with plenty of variety and challenge.

Recap

1. *Explain the goals of OD.*

   - OD aims to apply social science knowledge to solve organizational problems and improve individual well-being through a comprehensive approach to planned change.

2. *Understand the values underpinning the OD movement.*

   - OD is underpinned by a set of values, principles and beliefs concerning mutual respect, integrity, trust, honesty and support.

   - OD assumes that individual and organizational goals are compatible, that conflict is caused by misunderstandings, that the open display of emotions and feelings is valuable, that working relationships can be improved by enhancing self-awareness, and that collaboration and trust are better than conflict and secrecy.

3. *Understand the main OD interventions, how they work, and what they aim to achieve.*

   - OD interventions begin with diagnosis, to identify the level or levels at which the problem or problems arise – individual, group, intergroup or organizational.

   - Force field analysis is used to assess the factors driving and resisting change so that these forces can be managed.

   - The OD planning model works through a logical, linear series of steps, including scouting, entry, diagnosis, planning, action, evaluation and termination.

   - The OD action research model works through an iterative series of steps involving data collection and joint problem-solving which also generates new knowledge.

   - OD uses a range of intervention methods, including sensitivity training, structure change, process consultation, survey feedback, team building, intergroup development, role negotiation, and changes to other human resource management practices.

   - The most comprehensive intervention method is Grid OD, an approach which aims to improve strategic planning, interpersonal and interdepartmental communications, and organizational effectiveness through a systematic six-phase model of change, based on a leadership style emphasizing high levels of concern for both people and output.

4. *Assess critically the difficulties in evaluating the effectiveness of OD interventions.*

   - From a practical managerial perspective, critics have argued that organizations should target quick, ambitious, measurable performance improvements instead. OD interventions take too much time to deliver unquantifiable benefits.

   - From a critical theoretical perspective, OD can be regarded as a devious and manipulative plot to dupe employees into the belief that their interests are actually aligned with those of management and the organization, thus submerging power inequalities and genuine conflicts of interest. OD is thus a cunning management control mechanism.

5. *List the main skills and areas of knowledge required by an OD consultant.*

   - The OD practitioner requires a range of skills and knowledge concerned mainly with the process rather than the substance of change, and particularly in social and interpersonal skills such as communicating, negotiating, influencing and conflict resolution.

   - OD practice varies in style. At one extreme is the 'medical' model in which the consultant diagnoses and prescribes. At the other extreme, the role of the consultant as 'facilitator' is to help client organization members diagnose and resolve problems for themselves.

Chapter exercises

1: What's the cause? What's the solution?

Objectives
1. To identify different perceptions of the causes of the same behavioural event.

2. To assess the range of causal explanations offered.

3. To highlight the importance of matching the solution to the cause of the problem.

Briefing
We know that people often perceive the same event or situation differently. In the case of an organizational problem, how we attribute cause determines, or at least influences, the choice of solution to the problem. In such settings, two reactions are common. First, people often jump to conclusions about causes without having first analyzed the situation. Second, the conclusions to which they jump often tend to be narrow in scope.

Read the following 15-word incident report:

> An elderly woman in a nursing home is found dead; she
> has apparently committed suicide.

In the space provided, write four alternative hypotheses – possible explanations or causes – for this tragic event:

1: _____

2: _____

3: _____

4: _____

Be prepared to share your explanations with colleagues, and with your instructor.

Note: This activity was first developed by Professor Jack Denfeld Wood, IMD, Lausanne, Switzerland to illustrate the generation of alternate hypotheses along different behavioral levels of analysis. Used with permission.

2: What the chief executive wants – OD consultants in action

Objectives
1. To explore the tensions and dilemmas that can surface in practical OD consulting work.

2. To expose the ethical dimensions of OD consulting.

Briefing
As you read through the following incident report, based on a real case, consider the following questions:

1. If you were a member of the consulting team, how would you have acted differently in these circumstances, and why?

2. On the evidence of this account, what advice would you give to this consulting team?

3. What advice would you give to the chief executive?

This incident was reported by a member of an external consulting team working for a local authority in Central Scotland. The OD assignment was to introduce structural and cultural change to an organization that had operated in much the same style since the early

1970s. A new chief executive had recently been appointed with this remit. The leader of the consulting team was a long-standing personal friend of the new chief executive.

The annoying thing was, we got this assignment against stiff competition, because we didn't want to sell any one particular solution. They were impressed by our flexibility. Local council, they wanted a review of their twenty-year-old office and member organization structures. In fact they wanted us to present options, maybe simple, maybe radical, from which they could choose, within the constraint of a no redundancy policy. We won the assignment in a presentation to [a policy and resources] sub-committee, mainly councillors, with a couple of senior officers present. The leader of our consulting team was an ex-colleague and friend of the council's new chief executive.

The following week, we were invited to a meeting with the chief executive, to launch the project, agree our liaison mechanisms, find a room to work in, and so on. We spent a couple of hours discussing the logistics, then he asked us if we would have some lunch, and sandwiches and stuff were trayed in. However, as we were hoovering this lot up, he produced a seven-page document and gave the four of us copies. He worked through this, line by line, for about an hour. This set out what he wanted to see in our final report. Some of this had been in the original brief for the assignment, set out in general terms, and here it was again with some specific recommendations and markers for action, concerning parts of the organization structure and named individuals in specific posts who were not expected to survive the review. We didn't have as much flexibility as we had thought.

The project rolled out over that year, and our recommendations got firmed up as we collected more information. Basically, this was an autocratically managed, hierarchical, rigid, bureaucratic organization, with lots of time and money wasted on unnecessary procedures and rule-following, and with poor staff morale. So our recommendations were going to be about cutting hierarchy, empowering people, changing the management style, making procedures more flexible, getting decisions taken more quickly, and the chief executive was behind all this. The main client was the sub-committee to which we reported, about every quarter. But not before the chief executive had, at his request, seen an advance copy of the report, commented on it and suggested changes. Quite reasonable, as he would be directly affected by any recommendations about the structure, and also saw himself as a client for our services. This put us in an awkward position. We knew his thinking, and other managers would ask us about that, and we had to fudge answers like, 'that's one of the issues still under consideration'. This also meant we had to build his ideas into our reports, finding some rationale for supporting them, which was important because if questions came up in committee, we would have to explain and defend the point, although he might chip in and voice some agreement with and sympathy for our view from time to time.

Then we started getting bother from one of the councillors, who saw himself as an expert in organization theory. He came up with a proposal for a matrix structure with multidisciplinary teamworking. The teamworking was our idea too, partly to address some communications problems, but the matrix wasn't going to fit their business. We got nowhere with the guy in the full committee, so two of us asked him if we could meet him the next day, maybe over lunch, to kick this around. It turned out his concern was not with a matrix at all, but with the way the new director roles would be specified, that they would be like the previous management group (which he didn't trust), just with new titles. So we built the teamworking ('great idea, thanks for that') and a revised role spec into the report, and he bought that.

The chief executive even sub-edited our final report, making changes to the recommendations which we then had to justify. What if we hadn't been able to roll with these pressures? We would have upset the chief executive, who saw our ability to incorporate his thinking as a reflection of our consulting expertise, and we would probably get no more work with this client. If we hadn't handled these individuals, and others, in this sort of way, the whole project could have been at risk, and the time and contributions of a lot of other staff would have been wasted.

From David Buchanan and Richard Badham, *Power, Politics and Organizational Change: Winning the Turf Game*, Sage Publications, London, 1999a.

Chapter 18 Organizational change

Key concepts

trigger of change

strategic change

adhocracy

future shock

the coping cycle

The Yerkes–Dodson law

resistance to change

stakeholders

readiness for change

processual/contextual theory

business process re-engineering

change agent

Learning outcomes

When you have read this chapter, you should be able to define those key concepts in your own words, and you should also be able to:

1. Outline the contemporary debate concerning repeat change and painless change.
2. Identify the main external and internal triggers of organizational change.
3. Understand the typical characteristics of human responses to change.
4. Understand the nature of resistance to change and approaches to overcoming it.
5. Explain the advantages and limitations of participative methods of change management.
6. Explain the strengths and weaknesses of the processual/contextual perspective on change.
7. Outline the skill requirements for an effective change agent.

Why study organizational change?

Richard Whittington and Michael Mayer (2002) argue that 'adaptive reorganization', the ability to redesign structures frequently, is now critical to organizational performance. Their initial research followed the top 50 companies in Britain from 1992 to 2000 and found that, in the 1990s, they reorganized every five years. By 2000, major changes were taking place on average every three years, with regular minor changes in between. In April 2002, Microsoft announced its fourth major 'reorg' in five years. This pattern of 'repeat change' is driven by:

■ intensified competition and stockmarket turbulence in the private sector, consumerism and government pressures in the public sector;

■ the pace of technological innovation;

■ increased knowledge-intensity, as organization design affects information flows.

Their later research found that the results of major changes were often disappointing. Improvements in flexibility and responsiveness were accompanied by poor financial returns and lower morale and staff retention. With major change, expensive new information systems and complex new structures attract most attention, while people are forgotten. When asked about the aims of their reorganizations, managers emphasized customers, market share and internal efficiency, and ranked improving employee morale and retention lowest. Despite commitment to communication, there was little employee participation in the design and implementation of change (Whittington, Mayer and Smith, 2002a, p. 31). Reporting similar findings, Doyle, Claydon and Buchanan (2000) describe the typical management assessment of change as 'mixed results, lousy process'.

Human resource policies can affect change processes and outcomes in a number of ways. Can staff with the right capabilities be recruited? Can employees be trained and rewarded in such a way that they will be motivated to perform well and to stay? Are change agents trained in implementation, and are they able to handle sensitive emotional responses? Will senior management succession plans produce a new top team which shares the same objectives and methods? A more important issue may concern whether the organizational culture is receptive to change or not. Change may be unsuccessful if human resource policies and practices concerning recruitment, training, reward, retention, management development, succession planning and career management policies are not supportive.

However, only one in five of the organizations studied involved human resource management in a lead role in change. Whittington and Mayer (2002) argue that, for change to be successful, the 'soft' human issues need to be integrated with 'hard' structures and systems. This requires skilled change agents, and organization characteristics such as a culture which welcomes change, appropriate management styles and supportive human resource policies. In this chapter, after a more detailed consideration of the nature of organizational change, we will:

- explore some of the 'soft' issues, including emotional responses to change and causes of resistance;

- consider different perspectives on change, including implementation methods and processes;

- finally explore the expertise required of the change agent.

The links between human resource management policies and organizational performance are explored in chapter 20.

The paradoxical nature of change

Stop and Criticize

How would you respond to these three 'true or false' questions?

'People have a natural resistance to change.'   true or false?

'People get bored with routine and seek out new experiences.'   true or false?

'Older people are more resistant to change.'   true or false?

Did you answer 'true' to all three statements? A moment's reflection should suggest that these positive responses are inconsistent with each other, and contradict the evidence. For example, many people when they retire from work take up radically new activities and hobbies: painting, acting, community involvement, learning a musical instrument. We cannot have natural resistance to change and seek new experiences at the same time.

Change is a recurring theme throughout this text. In Part 1, we noted how environmental and technological trends encourage particular kinds of organizational change. In Part 2, we considered the possibilities of changing human learning, personality, communication skills, perceptions and motivation. In Part 3, we examined how individual behaviour changes in group settings, and how group functioning can be changed to improve performance. In Part 4, we explored trends in organization design. In Part 5, we explore four organizational processes, including change, and in Part 6 we consider how leaders can change employee behaviour, and also consider whether leaders themselves can change their styles.

The need for organizational change can be prompted or initiated by many different **triggers**.

External triggers for organizational change can include:

Trigger of change: any disorganizing pressure indicating that current systems, procedures, rules, organization structures and processes are no longer effective.

- new technology;

- new materials;

- changes in customers' requirements and tastes;

- activities and innovations of competitors;

- legislation and government policies;

- changing domestic and global economic and trading conditions;

- shifts in local, national and international politics;

- changes in social and cultural values.

Internal triggers for organizational change can include:

- new product and service design innovations;

- low performance and morale, high stress and staff turnover;

- appointment of a new senior manager or top management team;

- inadequate skills and knowledge base, triggering training programmes;

- office and factory relocation, closer to suppliers and markets;

- recognition of problems triggering reallocation of responsibilities;

- innovations in the manufacturing process;

- new ideas about how to deliver services to customers.

Listing triggers in this way makes organizational change sound like a reactive process. Clearly this is not always the case. In some instances, it will be appropriate to anticipate events and trends, and to be proactive in introducing appropriate organizational changes.

One of the best-known metaphors for change was developed by Kurt Lewin (1951), who argued for the need to *unfreeze* the current state of affairs, to *move* to a desired new state, then to *refreeze* and stabilize those changes. However, refreezing no longer seems to be an option. 'Repeat change' is the norm. Permanent thaw is perhaps a more appropriate metaphor. Many organizations now face a 'high velocity' environment (Eisenhardt and Bourgeois, 1988; Buchanan, 2000b) in which turbulent external conditions are translated into a complex stream of initiatives affecting work and organization design, resource allocation, and systems and procedures in a continuous attempt to improve performance. The environment for most organizations seems likely to remain volatile, or to become even more turbulent.

Organizational change problems will thus remain on the management agenda for some time. The study of change, however, is paradoxical for several reasons:

- as the triggers and consequences of organizational change are many and complex, establishing cause and effect is problematic;

- organizational change has to be studied at different levels of analysis – individual, group, organizational, social – which are interrelated in complex ways;

- organizational change has to be studied as a process, in terms of a series of unfolding events, and not as a static or time-bounded event, raising questions concerning the appropriate time frame for analysis;

- change that affects a large number of different stakeholders is difficult to evaluate as there may be no agreed criteria on which to base judgements;

- change can only be understood in relation to continuity, with respect to what has not changed.

This latter point, concerning continuity, is fundamental and controversial. The rapid pace and wide scale of contemporary technological, organizational and social change appear to be obvious. Whole industries collapsed and almost disappeared (coal mining, steel making) in the twentieth century while others blossomed (computer software, mobile telephony). Many of the technologies that shape the nature of medicine, communications and home entertainment, for example, were not available five years ago. These technologies potentially affect the design of jobs, the experience of work, the progress of individual careers, and organization structures.

Change has never been so fast

That this is an age of change is an expression heard frequently today. Never before in the history of mankind have so many and so frequent changes occurred. These changes that we see taking place all about us are in that great cultural accumulation which is man's social heritage. It has already been shown that these cultural changes were in earlier times rather infrequent, but that in modern times they have been occurring faster and faster until today mankind is almost bewildered in his effort to keep adjusted to these ever increasing social changes. This rapidity of social change may be due to the increase in inventions which in turn is made possible by the accumulative nature of material culture [i.e., technology].

From William Fielding Ogburn, *Social Change: With Respect to Culture and Original Nature*, B.W. Huebsch, New York, 1922, pp. 199–200.

Henry Mintzberg (1994) argues that our preoccupation with change is exaggerated. We are impressed by technological innovation, the significance of which is overstated by enthusiastic journalists seeking apocalyptic predictions. Each new generation, Mintzberg argues, discovers change as something unique to itself, which previous generations have not had to endure.

The point is that, when considering change, we must also be aware of what is not changing. It is not difficult to list features of technology, jobs, organizations and society in the first decade of the twenty-first century that have barely changed since the beginning of the twentieth. Personal transport still relies on internal combustion engines fuelled by petrol. Securing employment remains a social norm and is central to most people's definition of personal identity. If you commit a serious crime in Britain, you will still be tried by a jury in a sombre courtroom with a judge wearing a funny wig. Some observers have remarked that British railways, in private ownership then as they are now, were more reliable in the early twentieth century.

Another paradox related to continuity has recently emerged in this field. The literature on organizational change during the twentieth century was exclusively concerned with making things happen, and happen faster. An opposing concern at the beginning of this century is that we need to slow things down, perhaps keep some things the same. Behind this switch in emphasis lie the problems caused by high-velocity, adaptive reorganization.

One problem is *initiative decay*, where the benefits of previous change are lost as the organization moves on to deal with fresh initiatives. The British National Health Service Modernization Agency (2002) criticizes the 'improvement evaporation effect', where new processes and increased performance are not maintained. Robert Reisner (2002) examines why the United States Postal Service, radically transformed and successful during the 1990s, was again making a loss by 2001. Paul Green and Paul Plsek (2002) note that American hospitals cannot maintain innovations in step with their changing environment. Alongside the need for change, therefore, there is concern with how to *sustain* changes and improvements that are already in place (Gollop, 2002a; Sharpe, 2002; Whitby, 2002; Jones, 2003).

Another problem is *initiative fatigue*, as people become tired of constant demands to do things differently, work better, work smarter, work harder. Research suggests that initiative decay is widespread, and affects all organizational levels, including management (Buchanan, Claydon and Doyle, 1999). Initiative fatigue lowers enthusiasm for and commitment to more change.

Eric Abrahamson (2000) presents a compelling argument for 'painless change' based on 'dynamic stability'. This involves small and continuing changes such as the redesign of existing practices and business models rather than creating new ones. To change successfully, Abrahamson argues, organizations should stop changing all the time, because this generates cynicism and burnout. Change needs to be carefully paced, with major initiatives interspersed with periods of smaller changes, implemented by 'tinkering' and 'kludging':

Tinkering	This means 'fiddling with the nuts and bolts of what we already have' to create inspired solutions to contemporary problems, rather than trying to create something new from scratch. Abrahamson cites the example of a helicopter manufacturer that handled diversifying customer demand by designing a 'base' helicopter to which a range of accessories could be added.
Kludging	This means 'tinkering on a larger scale', perhaps by creating new divisions or businesses. Abrahamson cites the example of internet book retailers which have combined conventional procurement and merchandising with software and marketing knowledge.

Nick Morgan (2001, p. 3) describes the contemporary workplace as 'one continual change initiative', in which change fatigue is rampant. Like Abrahamson, he argues for 'a quieter, more evolutionary approach to change'. His solution is to reduce the number of change initiatives, abandon the preoccupation with large-scale transformation, and focus on incremental improvements instead.

The arguments about organizational change which follow thus need to be seen in the context of a debate in which some commentators make the case for repeat change, while others argue for more stability and continuity. Those who argue for more stability have not abandoned the need for major changes, but express concern with the number and timing of such initiatives, and their relationship to other changes that may be taking place at the same time.

Strategic change: the contemporary imperative

We need to be clear what kind of change we are discussing. Some changes are major, long-term, expensive and risky, while others are more straightforward. One way of distinguishing different types of change is to consider how deeply they penetrate the organization. This approach, based on the work of Roger Collins (personal communication) is illustrated in figure 18.1. The nature of the change management task shifts as one progresses down this classification. The job of fine tuning is more straightforward than implementing deep change.

In practice, in most organizations, a number of change initiatives are likely to be under way simultaneously, at different levels. This classification does not lead to an argument that 'all change must be deep change'. Deep change is appropriate when dealing with 'deep problems', while 'fine tuning' is a more appropriate response to minor concerns.

Stop and Criticize

If you aspire to a high-flying, fast-track career, you are unlikely to get far if you focus your energies on shallow changes. Shallow changes do not contribute much to organizational performance and will not enhance your visibility and reputation. You would be better advised to work on deep changes, as long as they are successful.

To what extent does this argument lead to the cynical conclusion that major changes are introduced in the interests of progressing individual careers?

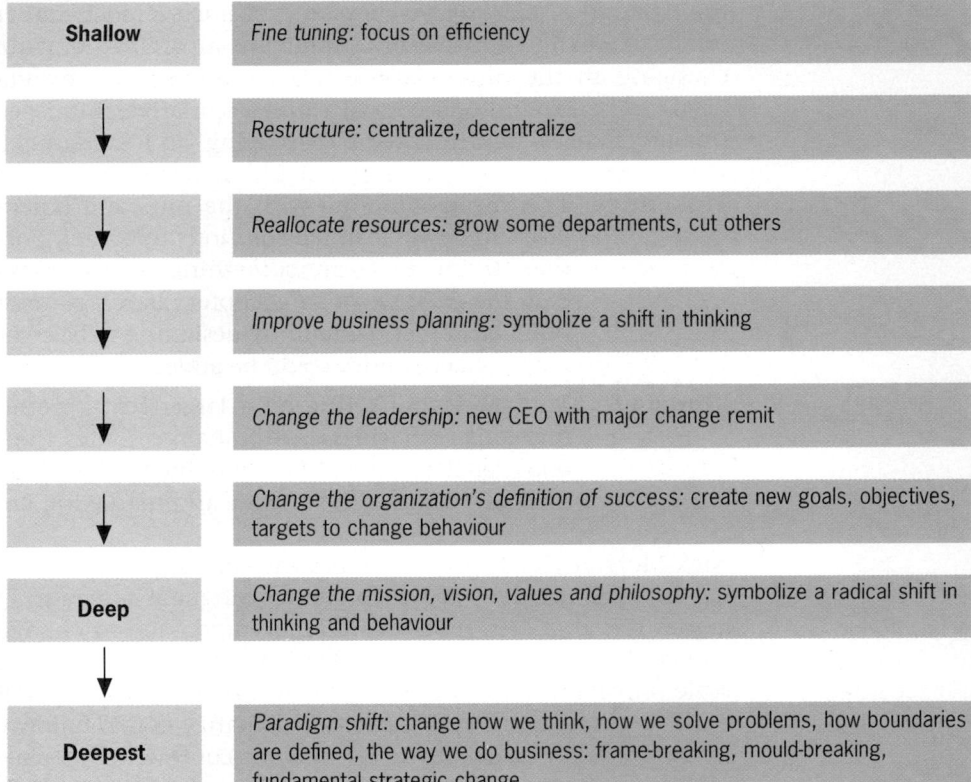

Shallow	Fine tuning: focus on efficiency
	Restructure: centralize, decentralize
	Reallocate resources: grow some departments, cut others
	Improve business planning: symbolize a shift in thinking
	Change the leadership: new CEO with major change remit
	Change the organization's definition of success: create new goals, objectives, targets to change behaviour
Deep	Change the mission, vision, values and philosophy: symbolize a radical shift in thinking and behaviour
Deepest	Paradigm shift: change how we think, how we solve problems, how boundaries are defined, the way we do business: frame-breaking, mould-breaking, fundamental strategic change

Figure 18.1: Depth of organizational intervention

Alvin Toffler

Strategic change: organizational transformation that is radical, frame-breaking, mould-breaking or paradigmatic in its nature and implications.

Adhocracy: a type of organization design which is temporary, adaptive and creative, in contrast with bureaucracy, which tends to be permanent, rule-driven and inflexible.

Many commentators argue that organizational change is a **strategic** imperative. This means that major or radical shifts in organizational design and functioning are required in order to cope with the many and unpredictable changes happening in the wider social, economic, political and technological environment. If you are studying strategic management or corporate strategy as part of your course, you will be familiar with this argument.

The term 'strategic' denotes scale, magnitude or depth. Deciding whether change is strategic or not depends on organizational circumstances. What is strategic in one context may be routine in another. This strategic imperative is usually expressed in terms of the need for organizations to become more flexible, more adaptable, more 'fluid' and more responsive. Warren Bennis (1969) has consistently argued that the pace of change makes traditional forms of organization obsolete. Bureaucratic structures, he claims, cannot cope with complexity, unpredictability, the diversity of specialist expertise required in many organizations, and humanistic participative management styles. Bureaucratic structures work better with impersonal, autocratic management style, and with stability and routine.

Bennis spoke of 'adaptive structures'. Tom Burns and George Stalker (1994) distinguished between rigid, *mechanistic* management systems and fluid, *organic* systems. Alvin Toffler (1970) used the term *adhocracy*. Rosabeth Moss Kanter (1985) contrasted rigid *segmentalist* structures with *integrative* approaches. The concept of the flexible *post-modern* organization was fashionable in the 1990s (Clegg, 1990). These commentators appear to have considered broadly the same issues and concepts, and to have adjusted their labels.

Adhocracy is similar to the concepts of *organic* and *integrative* organizational styles. Bureaucracy equates with *mechanistic* and *segmentalist* approaches.

Organization and management theorists have been remarkably consistent in their advocacy of flexible approaches to coping with uncertainty. Cynics might observe that the main innovations in this research tradition have been in the labels given to the 'old' and 'new' approaches.

As noted earlier, one recently recognized problem concerns the need for organizations that are flexible enough to adapt to change, but that are also stable enough to sustain those changes. In theory, the *ad hoc*, organic organization may be an appropriate vehicle for handling unpredictability. However, these kinds of structure can be extremely insecure and uncomfortable places in which to work, and may not deliver in terms of performance. Doug Stace and Dexter Dunphy (2001, p. 99) identify organizations which they describe as 'prudent mechanistics', which have retained traditional structures, avoided the 'organizational fashion show', survived and performed well. Harold Leavitt (2003) argues that while rigid bureaucratic structures encourage 'authoritarianism, distrust, dishonesty, territoriality, toadying, and fear', they also provide ways of handling complexity, give us structure and predictability, and offer 'psychological rewards' by fulfilling needs for order and security.

Out with the segmentalist, in with the integrative

I found that the entrepreneurial spirit producing innovation is associated with a particular way of approaching problems that I call 'integrative': the willingness to move beyond received wisdom, to combine ideas from unconnected sources, to embrace change as an opportunity to test limits. To see problems integratively is to see them as wholes, related to larger wholes, and thus challenging established practices – rather than walling off a piece of experience and preventing it from being touched or affected by any new experiences. . . .

Such organizations reduce rancorous conflict and isolation between organizational units; create mechanisms for exchange of information and new ideas across organizational boundaries; ensure that multiple perspectives will be taken into account in decisions; and provide coherence and direction to the organization. In these team-oriented co-operative environments, innovation flourishes. . . .

The contrasting style of thought is anti-change-oriented and prevents innovation. I call it 'segmentalism' because it is concerned with compartmentalizing actions, events, and problems and keeping each piece isolated from the others [. . .]. Companies where segmentalist approaches dominate find it difficult to innovate or to handle change.

From Rosabeth Moss Kanter, *The Change Masters: Corporate Entrepreneurs at Work*, International Thomson Business Press, London, 1985, pp. 27–8.

The strategic imperative of radical change thus needs to be treated with caution. Conventional wisdom claims that organizations must be able to respond rapidly to external changes through radical and mould-breaking restructuring. The mould to be broken is the bureaucratic approach to organization structure. The new structures emphasize flexibility, creativity and participation. However, these new methods may not be capable of sustaining desirable changes, and may lose the benefits of more stable structures.

Change and the individual

Future shock: the stress and disorientation suffered when people are subjected to excessive change.

Rapid change can have psychological consequences. Echoing some more recent debates, Alvin Toffler (1970) argued that the rate of change was out of control, and that society was 'doomed to a massive adaptational breakdown'. Toffler believed that there is a limit to the amount of change individuals can handle. He argued that 'the shattering stress and disorientation that we induce in individuals by subjecting them to too much change in too short a time' is unhealthy. He described this 'disease of change' as **future shock**.

Stop and Criticize

Think of the changes – technological, personal, social, organizational, political, economic – that you have experienced over the past two years. Do you feel disorientated and stressed as a result? How about family members and friends – are they displaying signs of disorientation as a result of too much change? From your observations, do you think Toffler's diagnosis of the 'disease of change' was correct?

Coping cycle: a human emotional response to trauma and loss, suggesting that individuals typically experience first denial, then anger, bargaining, depression and finally acceptance.

Our responses to change are neither as simple nor as predictable as Toffler implied. One influential approach to understanding this topic comes from studies of the ways in which we cope with traumatic personal loss, such as the death of a close relative. Elizabeth Kubler-Ross (1969) argued that we deal with loss by moving through a series of stages, each characterized by a particular emotional response. This **coping cycle** has been used to understand responses to radical organizational change.

The five typical stages in the Kubler-Ross coping cycle are illustrated and defined in table 18.1. As with all such models, this universal sequence obscures individual differences. We may not all experience the same five sets of responses. We may omit particular stages, revisit some stages, or pass through them more or less quickly than others. From an organizational perspective, this can be a useful explanatory and diagnostic tool. If we can detect where in the response cycle a person may be, in the face of change, we can be better placed to provide appropriate guidance and support.

The Yerkes–Dodson law: a psychology hypothesis which states that performance increases with arousal, until we become overwhelmed, after which performance falls.

Just how much pressure can we take from organizational change? Psychology has long suggested that the relationship between arousal or sensory stimulation, on the one hand, and human performance, on the other, varies systematically in the form of an 'inverted U' function. This is known as **the Yerkes–Dodson law**, after the originators Robert M. Yerkes and John D. Dodson (1908), and is illustrated in figure 18.2.

Table 18.1: The coping cycle

Stage	Response
denial	unwillingness to confront the reality; 'this is not happening'; 'there is still hope that this will all go away'
anger	turn accusations on those apparently responsible; 'why is this happening to me?'; 'why are you doing this to me?'
bargaining	attempts to negotiate, to mitigate loss; 'what if I do it this way?'
depression	the reality of loss or transition is appreciated; 'it's hopeless, there's nothing I can do now'; 'I don't know which way to turn'
acceptance	coming to terms with and accepting the situation and its full implications; 'what are we going to do about this?'; 'how am I going to move forward?'

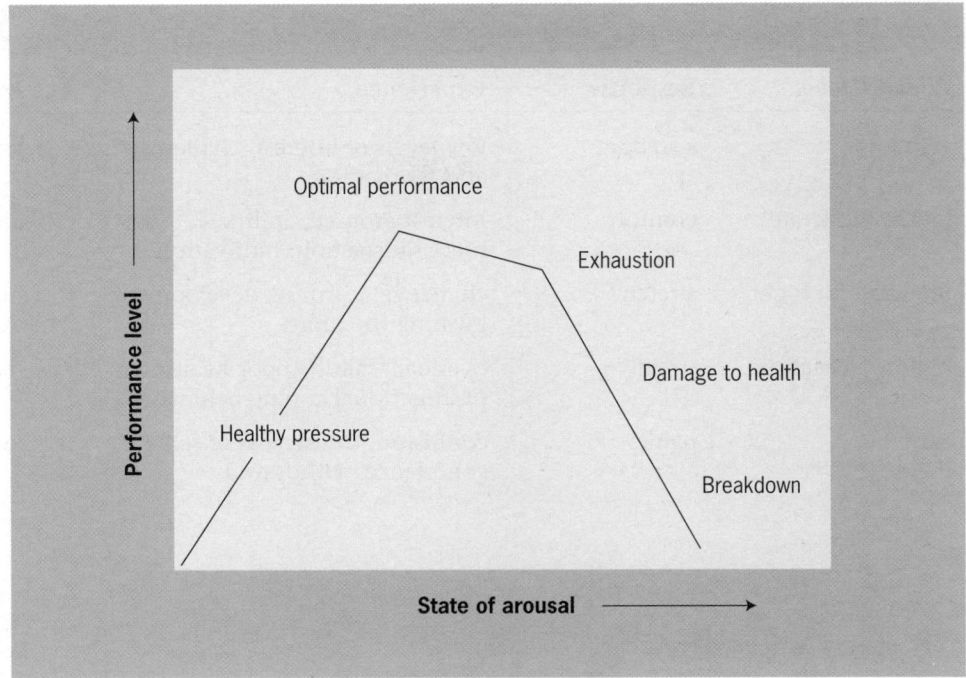

Figure 18.2: Pressure and performance – the inverted-U function

The Yerkes–Dodson hypothesis argues that human task performance is increased by arousal, stimulation and pressure. This explains why, for example, the time you spend on revision work for examinations seems to become more productive as the dates of those examinations draw closer. Here is the basis for the claim: 'I work better under pressure'. However, this hypothesis also argues that, if the pressure continues to mount, the individual will eventually reach a point at which they become stressed and exhausted, and performance will start to fall. This explains why, for example, when you delayed all of your revision for the examination until the night before, you flunked it the following day.

This implies that work performance is likely to be low if arousal is low, perhaps because the task is repetitive and boring. Performance can sometimes be improved in such settings with background music, conversation and frequent job rotation. Now suppose that the job is enriched and becomes more interesting, responsible and demanding, making more use of the individual's skills and knowledge. As the level of pressure increases, performance is likely to increase. However, a point will eventually be reached where the pressure becomes so great that it is perceived not as stimulation but as overwhelming. At this point fatigue and stress set in, and eventually ill-health and breakdown can occur if the pressure continues to escalate.

Can organizational change induce such pressure? Buchanan, Claydon and Doyle (1999) found that over 60 per cent of managers said that people in their organizations were suffering from initiative fatigue. In a second study (Doyle, Claydon and Buchanan, 2000), just under half of respondents claimed that the pace of change was causing middle management 'burnout'. With each change, people have to spend time learning new tasks, implementing new systems and procedures, developing new knowledge, using new skills and behaviours, and all of this, typically, under severe time pressure because the organization cannot stop functioning while this happens. Where change initiatives are frequent, individual arousal levels may be driven beyond their optimum performance points.

Table 18.2: The pressure–performance relationship explained

Pressure level	Response	Experience	Performance
very low	boredom	low levels of interest, challenge and motivation	low, acceptable
low to moderate	comfort	interest aroused, abilities used, satisfaction, motivation	moderate to high
moderate to high	stretch	challenge, learning, development, pushing the limits	high, above expectations
high to unrealistic	stress	overload, failure, poor health, dysfunctional coping behaviour	moderate to low
extreme	panic	confusion, threat, loss of self-confidence, withdrawal	low, unacceptable

Managers' emotional responses to change

Mike Broussine and Russ Vince (1996) asked 86 senior and middle managers in six public sector organizations (local government and healthcare) to 'draw a picture which expresses your feelings about change at work in your organization'. This use of visual imagery is novel in organizational research, and potentially allows respondents to reveal ideas and emotions that would be more difficult to express in language. The organizations from which these managers came had experienced considerable upheaval in the few years before this study.

Analysis of the managers' drawings displayed a range of emotions about change.

Emotional responses	Typical drawings
anxiety, fear, dread	organizational ship swamped by tidal wave, hospital being demolished
fear of personal catastrophe	gravestones, menacing clouds, unhappy faces, football team with three dead members
anger, violence, revenge	organization as decapitated maiden, castle blown apart by cannon
opportunity for personal development	ugly duckling becoming a swan, smiling face on strong body, flourishing tree
denial and rationalization	holiday scenes, oasis, idyllic surroundings
paradox, optimism and pessimism	angry politician pushing boulder uphill along with a ship sailing towards sunset and a gold cup for a prize, double-edged sword, *kamikaze* and astronaut
powerlessness and debility	piles of paperwork, long queues of people, computer spewing out information, very small tree in an empty landscape with a single acorn
destabilization, alienation	manager on a treadmill with sign reading 'business as usual during alterations'
a journey to endure	castles in the air, beach scenes, horse and cart in an ominous valley, vaulting barriers, boats tossed on shark-infested ocean close to tropical island

The researchers conclude that this approach reveals 'the paradoxical, sometimes contradictory and generally messy emotional reality that managers experience in a period of tremendous change' (p. 65). The category with the smallest number of illustrative drawings was the one concerned with opportunity for personal development.

Based on Mike Broussine and Russ Vince, 'Working with metaphor towards organizational change', in Cliff Oswick and David Grant (eds), *Organization Development: Metaphorical Explorations*, Pitman, London, 1996, pp. 57–72.

The Yerkes–Dodson hypothesis applied to work settings is summarized in table 18.2, which plots typical changes in response, experience and performance for escalating pressure levels. There are two qualifications to make to this explanation. First, determining the optimal level of pressure can be hazardous because this depends on the individual. Second, appropriate levels of stimulation also depend on the difficulty of the task. The easier the task, the higher the level of appropriate stimulation. This explains why music can destroy our concentration during a chess game, but may be enjoyed while backing up computer files.

Many laboratory experiments have explored the pressure–performance relationship across a range of settings and factors. How can this theory be used in practice? How can we tell what levels of pressure people are experiencing or when people are getting 'close to the edge'? The obvious answer is to ask them, but that may not always be appropriate or tactful. Fortunately, there are many useful proxy measures which indicate pressure levels. The proxy measures that can indicate when people are suffering excessive pressure include high staff turnover, sickness rates and unexplained absences, and increases in accidents and mistakes, customer complaints and employee grievances. Physical appearance changes as people become stressed and interpersonal relationships become strained. There are therefore a number of observable signs which can indicate that people are suffering overload, thus triggering action to reduce the pressure.

Resistance to change: causes and management solutions

Resistance to change: an inability or an unwillingness to discuss or to accept changes that are perceived to be damaging or threatening to the individual.

It is often possible to anticipate responses to organizational change, and to use that knowledge both to develop support for change and also to address **resistance to change** at an early stage.

Change has both positive and negative aspects. On the one hand, change implies experiment and the creation of something new. On the other hand, it means discontinuity and the destruction of familiar arrangements and relationships. Despite the positive attributes, change can be resisted because it involves confrontation with the unknown and loss of the familiar. It is widely assumed that resistance to change is a common and a natural phenomenon. Many people find change, or the thought of change, painful and frustrating. Arthur Bedeian (1980) cites four common causes of resistance to organizational change.

Parochial self-interest

We understandably seek to protect a *status quo* with which we are content and which we regard as advantageous to us in some way. Change may threaten to move us out of our 'comfort zone', away from those things which we prefer and enjoy.

We develop vested interests in the perpetuation of organization structures and accompanying technologies. Change can mean loss of power, prestige, respect, approval, status and security. Change can also be personally inconvenient for many reasons. It may disturb relationships and other arrangements that have taken much time and effort to establish. It may force an unwelcome move in location. It may alter social opportunities. Perceived as well as actual threats to interests and values are thus likely to generate resistance. We may identify ourselves more closely with our specific functions and roles than with the organization as a whole. We then have a personal stake in our specialized knowledge and skills, and may not be willing readily to see these made redundant or obsolete.

Misunderstanding and lack of trust

We are more likely to resist change when we do not understand the reasoning behind it, or its nature and possible consequences. Resistance can thus be reduced through improved understanding. If managers have little trust in their employees, information about change may be withheld or distorted. If employees distrust managers, information about changes proposed by management may not be believed. Incomplete and incorrect information creates uncertainty and rumour. This has the unfortunate result of increasing perceptions of threat, increasing defensiveness, and reducing further effective communication about the change. The way in which change is introduced can thus be resisted, rather than the change itself.

Contradictory assessments

We each differ in the ways in which we perceive and evaluate the costs and benefits of change; a major disruptive threat for me can be a fresh and stimulating challenge for you. Our personal values ultimately determine which changes are welcomed, promoted and succeed, and which fail. Our contradictory assessments are more likely to arise when communication is inadequate, and where those concerned lack the relevant information. Bedeian points out that contradictory analyses of change can lead to constructive criticism and improved proposals. Resistance to change is not necessarily dysfunctional, but can in some circumstances lead to more effective forms of change and change implementation.

Low tolerance for change

We differ in our abilities to cope with change, to face the unknown and to deal with uncertainty. Change that requires people to think and behave in different ways can challenge the individual's self concept. We each have ideas about our abilities and our strengths. One response to change may thus be self-doubt: 'can I handle this?'. Some people have a low tolerance for ambiguity and uncertainty. The anxiety and apprehension that they suffer may lead them to oppose even potentially beneficial changes.

Are there only four reasons for resistance to change? no. Bedeian summarized the main causes. Tony Eccles (1994) lists thirteen possible sources of resistance:

ignorance	failure to understand the problem
comparison	an alternative is preferred
disbelief	the proposed solution will not work
loss	unacceptable personal costs
inadequacy	rewards are not sufficient
anxiety	fear of being unable to cope
demolition	threat to existing social arrangements
power cut	influence and control will be eroded

contamination	new values and practices are repellent
inhibition	willingness to change is low
mistrust	management motives are suspicious
alienation	other interests are more highly valued
frustration	change will reduce power and career opportunities

Stakeholder:
anyone concerned with how an organization operates, and who is going to be affected by an organizational change or programme of changes.

There is some overlap across these headings; 'comparison' and 'contamination' sound as though they mean much the same thing, as do 'power cut' and 'frustration'. The main point, however, lies with the observation that there are potentially as many different reasons for resisting change as there are individuals affected.

How can resistance be managed? One approach concerns stakeholder analysis. Not everyone in an organization will respond in the same way to change proposals. Different individuals and groups are likely to be affected in different ways, and are therefore likely to react differently. Anticipating these reactions becomes possible when one identifies and understands the **stakeholders** concerned with a particular change.

Contemporary change barriers and success factors[*]

Top ten barriers	%	Top ten success factors	%
Competing resources	48	Ensuring top sponsorship	82
Functional boundaries	44	Treating people fairly	82
Change management skills	43	Involving employees	75
Middle management	38	Giving quality communications	70
Long IT lead times	35	Providing sufficient training	68
Communication	35	Using clear performance measures	65
Employee opposition	33	Building teams after change	62
HR issues (people, training)	33	Focusing on culture and skill change	62
Initiative fatigue	32	Rewarding success	60
Unrealistic timetables	31	Using internal champions	60

[*]Findings from interviews with key change managers in a global sample of 500 companies. With 70 questions, the survey covered 150 companies in Britain, 150 in America, 150 in Europe, and 50 in the Far East and Australia.
Adapted from PriceWaterhouse Coopers Consulting (PWC) and Market Opinion Research International (MORI), *Global Change Management Study*, 1997.

Stakeholder analysis is a useful first step in planning change. The process is:

1. Draw up a list of stakeholders affected by the changes proposed.

2. Establish what each will gain or lose if the change goes ahead.

3. Use the potential benefits to strengthen support for the proposals.

4. Find ways to address the concerns of those who feel they will lose out, by altering the nature of the changes proposed or offering to reduce losses in other ways.

Gerard Egan (1994) identifies nine typical categories of stakeholder:

■ your *partners*, who support your agenda;

■ your *allies*, who will support you, given encouragement;

- your *fellow travellers*, passive supporters, committed to the agenda, but not to you;

- the *fencesitters*, whose allegiances are not clear;

- *loose cannons*, dangerous because they can vote against agendas in which they have no direct interest;

- your *opponents*, players who oppose your agenda, but not you personally;

- your *adversaries*, players who oppose you and your agenda;

- *bedfellows*, who support the agenda, but may not trust you;

- *the voiceless*, who will be affected, but have little power to promote or oppose, and who lack advocates.

Egan argues that different stakeholders must be managed differently. Partners and allies need to be encouraged, to be 'kept on side'. Opponents need to be converted. Adversaries have to be discredited and marginalized. Egan suggests that the needs of 'the voiceless' should be addressed in case they are recruited by adversaries and used against the change agenda.

In an influential article that has been widely cited and reprinted, John Kotter and Leo Schlesinger (1979) identify six techniques for managing resistance:

1. Education and commitment

Managers should share their perceptions, knowledge and objectives with those affected by change. This can involve a major and expensive programme of training, face-to-face counselling, group meetings, and the publication of memos and reports. People may need to be informed about the nature of the problems necessitating change. Resistance may be based on misunderstanding and inaccurate information. It therefore helps to get the facts straight, and to identify and reconcile opposing views. Managers can only use this approach if they trust their employees, and if in return management appear credible to the employees.

2. Participation and involvement

Those who might resist change should be involved in planning and implementing it. Collaboration can have the effect of reducing opposition and encouraging commitment. This helps to reduce fears that individuals may have about the impact of changes on them, and also makes use of individuals' skills and knowledge. Managers can only use this approach where participants have the knowledge and ability to contribute effectively, and are willing to do so.

3. Facilitation and support

Employees may need to be given counselling and therapy to overcome fears and anxieties about change. It may be necessary to develop individual awareness of the need for change, as well as the self-awareness of feelings towards change and how these can be altered.

4. Negotiation and agreement

It may be necessary to reach a mutually agreeable compromise, through trading and exchange. The nature of a particular change may have to be adjusted to meet the needs and interests of potential and powerful resistors. Management may have to negotiate, rather than impose, change where there are individuals and groups who have enough power to resist effectively. However, this can create a precedent for future changes, which may also have to be negotiated, although the circumstances surrounding them may be quite different.

5. Manipulation and co-optation

This involves covert attempts to sidestep potential resistance. Management puts forward proposals that deliberately appeal to the specific interests, sensitivities and emotions of the key groups or stakeholders involved. The information disseminated is selective, emphasizing the benefits to particular stakeholder groups and ignoring or playing down the disadvantages. Co-optation involves giving key resistors direct access to the decision-making process, perhaps giving them well-paid, high-status management positions.

6. Implicit and explicit coercion

Where there is profound disagreement between those concerned with the change, and where there is little chance of anyone shifting their ground, it may be appropriate for management to abandon attempts to achieve consensus, and resort to force and threat (not violence). It may be sufficient to offer to fire, transfer or demote individuals, or to block their career prospects.

Stop and Criticize

Egan advises that 'adversaries' should be discredited and marginalized. Kotter and Schlesinger suggest using manipulation and coercion. Other authors advocate the use of political tactics to neutralize resistance. Are there circumstances in which such management behaviour can be considered professional, ethical or effective?

Kotter and Schlesinger suggest that these methods can be used in combination. The choice depends on the likely reactions of those involved, and on the long-term implications of solving the immediate problem in that way. While a participative, supportive approach may be the norm, there may be circumstances in which manipulation and coercion are appropriate. David Buchanan and Richard Badham (1999a, 1999b) argue that the change agent who is not politically skilled in dealing with adversaries and opponents will fail. Rosabeth Moss Kanter (1985) also argued that 'power skills' in influencing others are necessary attributes of the effective change agent. We will explore organization power and politics in chapter 24.

Readiness for change: a predisposition to welcome and embrace change.

Are we ready for this?

From a practical change implementation perspective, it is usually useful to ask the question: Are the conditions right, or do we have to do some preliminary work before we go ahead? One approach to preparing the ground is based on the concept of **readiness**.

Where readiness is high, change may be straightforward. When readiness is low, some 'groundwork' may be required to increase readiness among those affected. Tony Eccles (1994) identifies eight preconditions for successful change. These are:

1. Is there *pressure* for this change?
2. Is there a clear and shared *vision* of the goal and the direction?
3. Do we have effective *liaison and trust* between those concerned?
4. Is there the *will and power* to act?
5. Do we have enough *capable people* with sufficient resources?
6. Do we have suitable *rewards* and defined *accountability* for actions?

7. Have we identified actionable *first steps*?

8. Does the organization have a *capacity to learn* and to adapt?

Where the answers are 'yes', the organization's readiness for change is high and resistance is likely to be localized and insignificant. Where the answers are 'no', readiness is low and change is likely to be correspondingly more difficult to implement.

The concept of readiness draws attention to two other practical issues. The first concerns timing. Some readiness factors may improve by waiting. The second concerns action, to manipulate readiness factors, to heighten the impatience for change, or to strengthen a welcoming predisposition. In other words, these readiness factors can be managed.

The benefits and limitations of participative change management

In 1999, when the Bacardi Group took over John Dewar & Sons, a Scotch whisky distilling company, management wanted to change aspects of the organization culture and working practices. They negotiated an agreement with the trade unions, which represented around 200 employees, committing both sides to a partnership based on consultation, skills development, flexible working, and sharing information about company performance and management plans (Margolis, 2001). This participative approach to change is now conventional practice.

This approach dates back over half a century to the experiments of Lester Coch and John French (1948) at the Harwood Manufacturing Corporation in Marion, Virginia. The company made pyjamas, and employees were complaining about frequent changes in work methods and pay rates. Absenteeism was high, efficiency was low, output was restricted deliberately, and employees were aggressive towards supervisors. Managers were sensitive to the welfare needs of employees, and had used financial incentives to encourage transfer to new jobs. However, the problems persisted, and Coch and French set out to discover why.

The company employed about 500 women and 100 men, with an average age of twenty-three, and most employees had no previous industrial experience. The company's time-study experts set out standards for all the jobs in the factory. Each employee's output was calculated daily and everyone's performance was made public in a daily list with the best producers at the top. High output led to more money and higher status. Most of the grievances concerned the fact that, as soon as they had learned a new job and started to earn bonuses, they were moved to another task. This meant that they lost the bonus and had to start learning all over again.

Coch and French designed an experiment with three production groups, each with a different level of participation in introducing the changes.

The non-participation group

A group of eighteen 'hand pressers' changed the way in which they stacked their finished work. The production department announced the change and the time-study department announced the new standard work rate. The changes were explained to the pressers, but they were not allowed to participate in any of the decisions surrounding this change. There was immediate resistance. The group showed no improvement in efficiency. They argued with the time-study engineer, were hostile to the supervisor, deliberately restricted their output, and some left. This group was eventually split up and allocated to other tasks around the factory.

The representation group

A group of thirteen pyjama folders had to fold trousers and jackets, having performed only one of these tasks before. They were given a demonstration of the need to reduce costs. The purpose of the meeting at which the demonstration was given was to get approval for a plan to improve work methods. Three representatives from the group were then trained in the new methods, and they subsequently trained the other folders. The representatives were interested and co-operative, and offered useful suggestions for further improvements. This group adopted a co-operative attitude and their efficiency ratings rose rapidly. Nobody argued with the time-study engineer or the supervisor, and nobody left the group.

The total participation groups

Two groups of seven or eight pyjama examiners changed their inspection routine. They had a preliminary meeting, as with the representation group, but everyone took part in the design of the new job and in the calculation of the new time standard. Coch and French remarked that: 'It is interesting to observe that in the meetings with these two groups suggestions were immediately made in such quantity that the stenographer had great difficulty recording them.' These groups recovered their efficiency ratings rapidly, to a level higher than before the change. There was no conflict or resignations.

Two and a half months later, the remaining thirteen members of the initial non-participation group were brought together again for a new pressing job. This time, however, they followed the 'total participation' procedure, which resulted in a rapid increase in efficiency, with no aggression and no resignations. This result confirmed that it was not the people involved but the way in which they were treated that affected resistance to or acceptance of change.

Employee participation has, since that study, been standard advice for managers seeking to encourage a welcoming and creative approach to change and resistance avoidance. Richard Pascale, Mark Millemann and Linda Gioja (1997) more recently urged managers to involve 'every last employee'. However, participative methods have been challenged by the work of two Australian researchers, Dexter Dunphy and Doug Stace (1990; Stace, 1996; Stace and Dunphy, 2001). First they define the scale of change using four categories:

fine tuning	refining methods, policies and procedures, typically at the level of the division or department
incremental adjustment	distinct modifications to strategies, structures and management processes, but not radical enough to be described as strategic
modular transformation	restructuring departments and divisions, potentially radical, but at the level of parts of the organization and not the whole
corporate transformation	strategic change throughout the organization, to structures, systems, procedures, mission, values and power distribution

Then they identify four categories of change leadership style:

collaborative	widespread employee participation in key decisions affecting their and the organization's future
consultative	limited involvement in setting goals relevant to employees' areas of responsibility

directive   the use of managerial authority in reaching decisions about change and the future and about how change will proceed

coercive   senior management impose change on the organization

Plotting scale of change against change leadership style produces the matrix shown in figure 18.3.

Style of change leadership	Scale of change			
	Fine tuning	Incremental adjustment	Modular transformation	Corporate transformation
Collaborative	Type 1		Type 2	
Consultative	Participative evolution		Charismatic transformation	
Directive	Type 3		Type 4	
Coercive	Forced evolution		Dictatorial transformation	

Figure 18.3: Scale of change and leadership style

This matrix identifies four strategies: participative evolution, charismatic transformation, forced evolution and dictatorial transformation. Continuing the categorization theme, four types of change leader are identified. *Coaches* are people-centred, inspirational communicators who lead participative evolutions. *Captains* are systematic, task-oriented authority figures who lead forced evolutions. *Charismatics* are 'heroic' figures committed to their own dramatic and challenging vision who lead (you guessed) charismatic transformations. *Commanders* are purposeful, decisive, tough-minded and forceful, able and willing to neutralize or remove resistance, to implement dictatorial transformations. Of the four types, Commanders tend to be recruited externally.

Dunphy and Stace argue that participative strategies are time-consuming as they can surface conflicting views that are difficult to reconcile. They suggest that where organizational survival depends on rapid and strategic change, dictatorial transformation is appropriate:

> Perhaps the toughest organizational change program in Australia in recent years has been the restructure of the New South Wales Police Force. The person leading that restructure and playing a classic Commander role is Police Commissioner Peter Ryan. Ryan was appointed from the United Kingdom to stamp out corruption in the force and modernize it. In his own words, he initially adopted a management style that was 'firm, hard and autocratic, and it had to be that because that is what the organization understood'. Ryan has made a major impact on the Force but admits that he and his team still have a long way to go to create the highly skilled, community focused organization he believes it should be. (Stace and Dunphy, 2001, p. 185)

The approach to change implementation which Dunphy and Stace advocate is summarized in figure 18.4. This is a contingency model which recommends using an approach which fits the context. For example, where circumstances suggest that it is appropriate for senior management to adopt a dictatorial approach, middle managers implementing changes may find a more collaborative style useful.

	Incremental change strategies	**Transformative change strategies**
	Participative evolution	*Charismatic transformation*
Collaborative–consultative modes	Use when the organization needs minor adjustment to meet environmental conditions, where time is available, and where key interest groups favour change	Use when the organization needs major adjustments to meet environmental conditions, where there is little time for participation, and where there is support for radical change
	Forced evolution	*Dictatorial transformation*
Directive–coercive modes	Use when minor adjustments are required, where time is available, but where key interest groups oppose change	Use when major adjustments are necessary, where there is no time for participation, where there is no internal support for strategic change, but where this is necessary for survival

Figure 18.4: The Dunphy–Stace contingency approach to change implementation

Stop and Criticize

Dictatorial transformation? Coercion to encourage organizational change? Surely this kind of approach is more likely to generate hostility and resistance to change, reducing organizational performance? What arguments would you use to support dictatorial transformation, on the one hand, and to criticize it, on the other?

The argument of Dunphy and Stace thus offers a significant challenge to the universal and oversimplified prescription of participative change management. The argument has intuitive appeal, as any form of consultation and involvement takes time, and time may not always be available in a rapidly changing environment. However, Dunphy and Stace also have empirical evidence from Australian organizations to support their case.

N-step recipes for change

The six phases of a project

1. enthusiasm
2. disillusionment
3. panic
4. search for the guilty
5. punishment of the innocent
6. praise and rewards for the non-participants

Although change is a familiar feature of the organizational landscape, it does not appear to have become any easier to implement. However, much is known about the factors which contribute to effective change, and also about the barriers. That knowledge has been codified by numerous authors advising on 'best practice'.

One influential approach to change is project management. This approach revolves around the concept of the phased project 'life-cycle'. The typical project life-cycle involves: identify problem, gather data, analyze data, generate solutions, select the best solution, plan the implementation, implement and test, monitor and evaluate. This makes the change process sound like a neat, tidy, rational, logical sequence of discrete and identifiable steps. One account (Hussey, 1998) uses the acronym 'EASIER' to argue that effective change involves just six steps: Envisioning, Activating, Supporting, Installing, Ensuring and Recognizing.

The influential American consultant and academic John Kotter (1995a) outlines 'eight steps to transforming your organization':

1. Establish a sense of urgency.
2. Form a guiding coalition.
3. Create a vision.
4. Communicate the vision.
5. Empower people to act on the vision.
6. Create 'short-term wins'.
7. Consolidate improvements to produce further change.
8. Institutionalize new approaches.

There are many such phase models in the management literature, and they all say much the same things about vision, leadership, communication and involvement. David Ulrich (1998) advocates a seven-step guide to change, which includes clear leadership, understanding benefits, a shared vision, mobilizing commitment, changing systems and structures, monitoring progress, and 'making it last'. Tony Eccles (1994) presents fourteen factors in four categories concerning clarity of purpose, effective communication, leadership style which involves and empowers people, and 'building on success'.

David Collins (1998) refers to these prescriptions as 'n-step guides' or simple 'recipes'. Various contributors compete to offer checklists of different lengths, but with broadly similar content. These models of change have one striking feature in common. As with project management, they seem to assume that planned change unfolds in a logical sequence. Solutions are not identified until the problem has been clearly defined. The best solution is not chosen until the options have been evaluated. Implementation does not begin until there is agreement on the solution. The key actors in the process each have clearly defined roles and responsibilities. Implementation is monitored and deviations from plan are corrected. The process is bounded in terms of resources (people, money, space) and time, and has a clear completion date.

The underlying assumptions of rationality and linearity in these accounts of the change process have attracted much criticism. Organizations rarely operate in such a tidy and predictable manner, particularly with respect to strategic (major, messy, radical) change. Bernard Burnes (2000) argues that there can be no 'one best way' or simple recipe, and develops instead an approach based on the wide range of choices in change implementation. Collins (1998) also argues that n-step guides fail on three counts. First, they offer oversimplified universal prescriptions that do not take into consideration the unique circumstances of the organization.

Second, they do not capture the complex, untidy and iterative nature of the change process. Third, they do not encourage a critical perspective with regard to what is being changed, outcomes, and the ways in which organizational change can maintain and reinforce power differences. In other words, these accounts are contextually, processually and politically naive. Collins advises managers to take a more theoretically sophisticated approach, and urges academics to take a more critical stance.

These 'recipe-based' approaches to change implementation have two main advantages:

1. They codify what research and practical experience suggest are the main factors contributing to effective change, even if many of the factors (established the need, clear goals, communications) seem to be common sense.

2. They offer a framework, a checklist of required actions, for those involved in planning a change implementation, perhaps even more useful when accompanied by stakeholder analysis and readiness analysis.

However, these approaches have two major limitations:

1. They are theoretically weak, and rely heavily on retrospective accounts and analyses of 'what went well' and 'what went wrong' in change. There is nothing intrinsically wrong with this research method. However, such an analysis does not contribute to the development of our theoretical understanding of organizational change processes and of how these processes may themselves be changing.

2. While research and experience confirm that change is untidy, politicized, iterative and apparently irrational in terms of the way events unfold, these approaches assume that change either is or should be a rational linear process. There is a presumption that, if change is messy, then it must be because managers have 'failed to follow the textbook'. That may not be the case at all if change is intrinsically untidy.

The process and context of change

**Processual/
contextual theory**:
a perspective
claiming that it is
necessary to
understand how the
substance, context
and process of
organizational
change interact to
generate the
observed
outcomes.

The theoretical sophistication advocated by Collins (1998), among others, can be found in **processual/contextual theory**, which has dominated the debate on change since the 1990s.

Our definition implies that there is one processual/contextual theory. That is not the case. The label applies to a range of processual perspectives on various aspects of organizational functioning (Langley, 1999; Pentland, 1999; Denis, Lamothe and Langley, 2001). Patrick Dawson (2003a) describes the history of processual accounts. Here we will focus on commentators who have applied this perspective to the organizational change process.

Andrew Pettigrew (1973, 1985, 1987a, 1987b, 1988), another critic of n-step guides, cautions against looking for single causes and simple explanations for change. He points instead to the many related factors – individual, group, organizational, social and political – that influence the nature and outcomes of change. Pettigrew argues that change is a complex and 'untidy cocktail' of rational decisions, mixed with competing individual perceptions, stimulated by visionary leadership, spiced with 'power plays' and attempts to recruit support and build coalitions behind particular ideas.

Pettigrew argues that the unit of analysis should be 'the process of change in context', highlighting two related issues. First, this means paying attention to the flow of events and not thinking of change as static or as neatly time-bounded. Second, this means paying attention to the wider context in which change takes place, and not thinking in terms of a particular location in time or geographical space (this new machine in this factory bay). Pettigrew's concept of context is different from the notion of an organization's environment, encountered in chapter 2. It is more elaborate, with three dimensions.

1. The *internal context* includes the structure and culture of the organization, which influence patterns of behaviour and attitudes towards change initiatives.

2. The *external context* lies outside, including customer demands, competitor behaviour and economic conditions, which create opportunities and threats to be exploited or addressed.

3. *Past and current events* and experiences condition current and future thinking.

The organization's history is critical, and relates to our earlier discussion of change and continuity in two ways. First, it is easy to forget how previous events have shaped current perceptions and responses when the focus is on current changes. Second, it is also easy to forget the continuities, to ignore those aspects of the past which have not changed and which are still with us, and which again condition our current thinking.

Pettigrew argues that the change agent must be willing to intervene in the political system of the organization. He argues that the main management problem is to legitimize change proposals in the face of competing ideas. The management of change is thus equated with 'the management of meaning', or with symbolic attempts to establish the credibility of particular definitions of problems and solutions, and to gain consent and compliance from other organization members. Part of the management task, therefore, is to do with 'the way you tell it' or, more accurately, with 'the way you *sell* it' to other organization members.

The processual/contextual perspective has been developed by Patrick Dawson (1994, 1996, 2003a). His approach 'is based on the assumption that companies continuously move in and out of many different states, often concurrently, during the history of one or a number of organizational change initiatives' (Dawson, 2003b, p. 41). He argues that, to understand this complex and untidy organizational change process, we need to consider:

1. The past, present and future context in which the organization functions, including external and internal factors.

2. The substance of the change itself, which could be new technology, process redesign, a new payment system, changes to organization structure and culture.

3. The transition process, tasks, activities, decisions, timing, sequencing.

4. Political activity, both within and external to the organization.

5. The interactions between these factors.

Dawson's argument is illustrated in figure 18.5, emphasizing the interaction of the context, substance and process of change, and highlighting the role of internal and external politics. Dawson identifies five aspects of the internal context: human resources, administrative structures, technology, product or service,

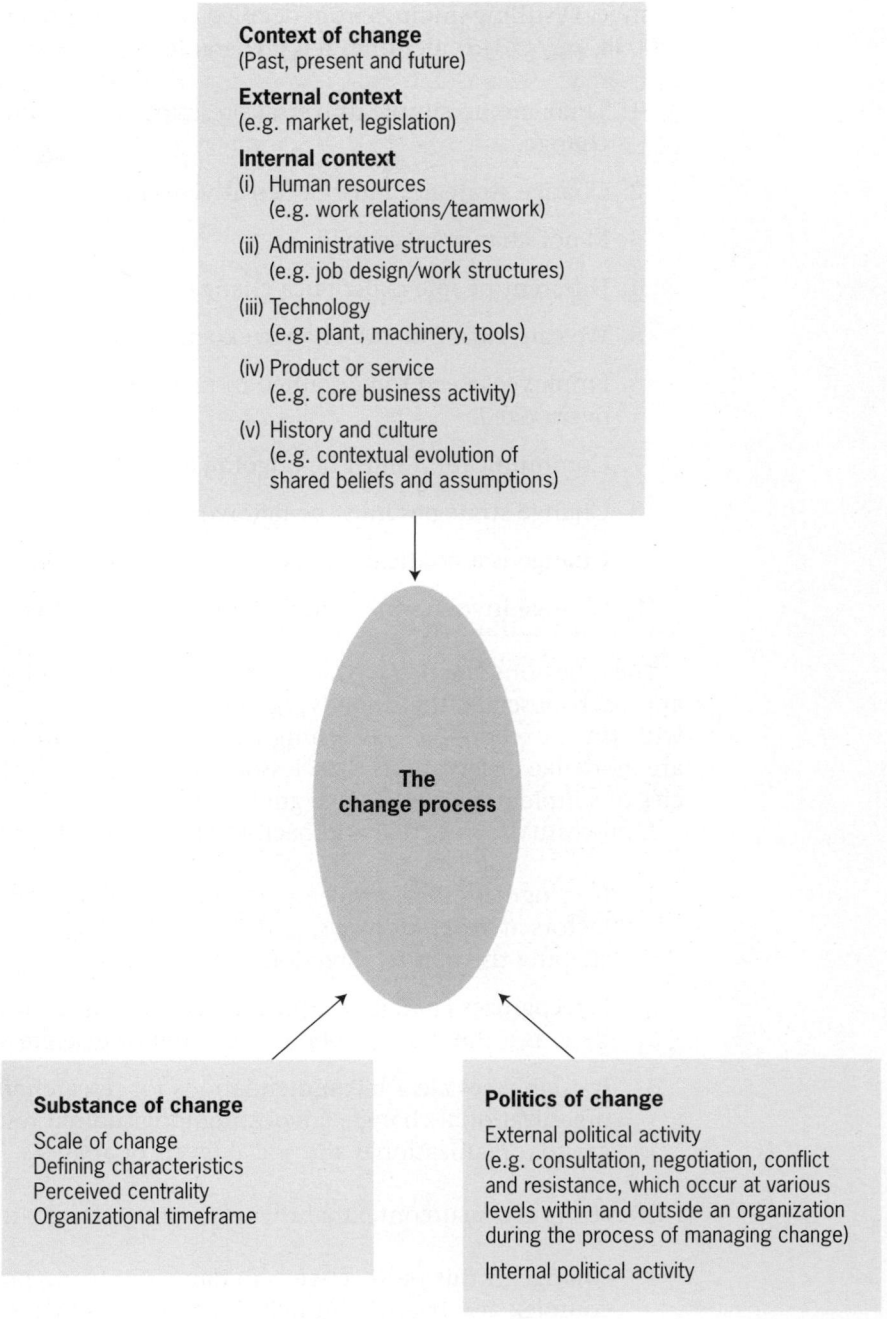

Figure 18.5: Determinants of organizational change
From P. Dawson, *Teaching and Quality: Change in the Workplace*, International Thomson Business Press, 1996, p. 27.

and the organization's history and culture. He also identifies four key features of the substance of change: the scale, its 'defining characteristics', its perceived centrality, and the timeframe of change initiatives. The substance of change influences the scale of disruption to existing structures and jobs. The transition process may be slow and incremental, or rapid. In addition, managers can draw upon evidence from the context and substance of change to marshal support and to legitimate their own proposals through political action. It is the interaction between context, substance and political forces which shapes the process of organizational change. Distilling findings from detailed case studies of change processes, Dawson (2003b, pp. 173–5) identifies ten 'general lessons':

1. There are no simple universal prescriptions for how best to manage change.

2. Change strategies must be sensitive to people and context.

3. Major change takes time.

4. Different people experience change in different ways.

5. We can learn from all change experiences, not just the successful ones.

6. Employees need to be trained in new methods and procedures, often overlooked.

7. Communication must be ongoing and consistent.

8. Change strategies must be tailored to fit the substance and context.

9. Change is a political process.

10. Change involves the complex interaction of often contradictory processes.

These 'lessons' are prefaced with a warning that, while potentially valuable, this approach obscures the underlying complexity of the change process. However, with three exceptions, concerning training, communication and tailoring, these are more like observations than lessons, alerting the practitioner to the inadequacies of simple packaged change guidance.

A processual/contextual approach to change has three main strengths:

1. It recognizes the complexity of change, drawing attention to the many factors at different levels, and the interaction between these factors, shaping the nature, direction and consequences of change.

2. It recognizes change as a process with a past, a present and a future, rather than as a static or time-bounded event or discrete series of events.

3. It establishes clear recommendations for researchers studying organizational change, advocating longitudinal research across individual, group, organizational and social levels of analysis.

However, processual/contextual theory seems to have three limitations:

1. Change in this perspective is in danger of being presented as over-complex and overwhelmingly confusing, and thus as unmanageable.

2. The people involved in the change process (in Pettigrew's account, much less so in Dawson's) tend to be portrayed as minor characters on a broad tapestry of factors and events, relegated to the role of pawns controlled by wider social and organizational forces rather than as proactive 'movers and shakers' in the process.

3. This perspective does not lend itself readily to the identification of practical recommendations for the more effective management of change, beyond generalized advice such as 'recognize complexity' and 'think processually'.

Business process re-engineering

Business process re-engineering: the radical redesign of work activities to achieve dramatic improvements in critical measures of performance.

One of the most controversial developments in the field of organizational change in the 1990s was **business process re-engineering** (BPR).

Processual theory and BPR must not be confused. BPR has no relationship whatsoever with the processual/contextual theory of change. On the contrary, these two perspectives could not be further apart in argument or prescription.

BPR has polarized opinion. Some commentators argue that rapid and radical process improvement is essential to enable organizations to deal with increasing environmental turbulence. Some organizations have reported significant improvements in performance as a result of applying re-engineering methods. Other commentators dismiss the approach as a futile and irrelevant repackaging of traditional management methods. Research suggests that re-engineering has a high failure rate. In America, re-engineering quickly earned a 'slash and burn' reputation for the job losses or 'downsizing' that applications typically caused.

The 'inventors' of business process re-engineering (BPR) include Michael Hammer and James Champy (1993; Hammer, 1990), and Thomas Davenport (1993). Their approach has two main ingredients. First, they advocate a fresh start to organization redesign. In other words, when considering change, start with a blank sheet of paper and redesign from scratch. Second, they advocate a process orientation to the analysis and redesign of work.

The fresh start, blank sheet approach ignores past history and current practice in favour of considering how best to structure the organization and design work to meet the needs of today's business and customers. This conflicts with the advice of the processual/contextual theorists such as Dawson and Pettigrew. BPR is not a 'context sensitive' approach.

The process orientation also represents a departure from most traditional approaches to organizational analysis. A process is simply a set of activities that delivers a product or a service to a customer. The customer may be the eventual user of the product or service, or it could be an 'internal customer' – the person or section responsible for the next set of activities in the overall process. This is potentially radical because it requires a horizontal analysis of work along an activity chain. Most organizations are structured vertically, around functions such as purchasing, warehousing, production, finance, personnel, and marketing.

A typical business process re-engineering project has four main stages:

process mapping	draw a flow-chart of the work activity sequence
identify 'moments of truth'	decide which steps are critical, add value, introduce errors
generate redesign proposals	streamline the process, avoiding duplication and overlap
implementation	put the redesign into effect

Re-engineering at Leicester Royal Infirmary NHS Trust

Leicester Royal Infirmary NHS Trust (LRI) is a large acute hospital in the English East Midlands, with 1,100 beds and 4,200 staff. In a typical year, the hospital deals with 400,000 outpatient visits, 120,000 accident and emergency cases, and 103,000 inpatient and daycase episodes. As one of two National Health Service pilot projects, LRI launched a re-engineering programme in 1994. Around 140 projects were introduced, affecting the whole hospital, to make dramatic improvements to the delivery

▶

of patient care and to provide a working environment in which staff could use their skills and abilities most effectively.

Patients typically move from one department to another, and process mapping showed that:

■ 30 to 70 per cent of staff activity does not contribute directly to patient care;

■ up to 50 per cent of process steps involve a 'handoff' (or handover) to another member of staff, leading to errors, duplications and delays;

■ individual jobs are narrow and fragmented;

■ nobody is responsible for the patient's 'end to end' experience of treatment.

One typical example of a process re-engineered to follow the patient's needs and experience was the development of the outpatient testing service. As testing was fragmented across different locations in the hospital, patients could have a long and anxious wait for results, and clinic staff had problems with lost test results. Re-engineering streamlined the flow of work by bringing test services, staff and equipment to one location. This results were:

	Before	After
average test turnaround	79 hours	5 hours
distance patient travels	650 paces	90 paces
times patient undresses	up to 3	1

Re-engineering improved the quality of patient care in other ways:

■ the number of patients in eye casualty seen within five minutes increased from 5 per cent to 97 per cent;

■ time from referral to bed for emergency admissions was reduced from 160 to 40 minutes;

■ treatment waiting time for rectal bleeding was cut from four weeks to one hour;

■ diagnosis of hypertension was reduced from five weeks to three hours.

Annual cost savings were around £900,000. Re-engineering also brought 'hidden' benefits, including team-based working and problem-solving, improved teaching and research opportunities, improved working relationships, improved skills development, and more timely management decision-making. Staff from all organization levels joined 're-engineering laboratories', absorbing new responsibilities, developing new skills and discovering new career opportunities (Buchanan, 2004).

Re-engineering raised some problems. An attempt to analyze 'core processes', as in a commercial setting, was abandoned in favour of one based on different patient groups. The timescale was longer than anticipated due to the degree of the changes to clinical practice, organization design and management style. The 're-engineers' in some cases found their roles stressful, and some lost friends in their 'home' occupational groups.

Based on *Re-engineering in Healthcare: The Leicester Royal Infirmary Experience*, The Leicester Royal Infirmary NHS Trust, September 1997.

The first step in BPR concerns defining and mapping an existing work process. For example, David Buchanan and Bob Wilson (1996a, 1996b) map the activity chain, or 'patient trail', in a hospital for patients undergoing elective surgery. The main stages in this process include: outpatient appointment, outpatient clinic preparation, clinic attendance, adding patient to theatres waiting list, attendance at a pre-assessment clinic (for tests), admission to a ward, operating theatre procedure, recovery, and finally (if all went well) discharge. In this process, the patient can come into contact with 50 to 150 different members of hospital staff and will become temporarily the responsibility of most of the hospital's departments along the way.

Many of the problems in this situation arise from the fact that staff are concerned primarily with what happens at their own step on the trail and are not always aware either of what has gone before or what will happen afterwards to the patient. This process fragmentation leads to unnecessary duplication of some activities and the unwitting transmission of problems 'down the trail'. This lack of process orientation is typical for an organization structured vertically, into distinct functions, rather than horizontally around work processes.

Process fragmentation also occurs in commercial manufacturing. What does re-engineering advocate in such situations? Hammer and Champy propose the following general principles:

- dismantle functional departments and create process teams;

- customers should deal with a 'case manager' rather than being passed from one member of staff to another;

- empower people and give them enriched jobs with discretion;

- provide training and education to allow people to perform expanded roles;

- flatten the organization hierarchy;

- measure people on the results they achieve, not just on the activities performed;

- promote people on the basis of ability;

- turn senior managers into leaders, not scorekeepers.

Stop and Criticize

Flatten the hierarchy? Enrich jobs? Encourage teamwork? Empower people? Overcome functional barriers? Are these radical recommendations? This advice is similar to that discussed in chapter 8, where we explored approaches to motivation through organization and work redesign.

These recommendation echo those of the organization development movement from the 1960s. Other criticisms of BPR concern its 'slash and burn' impact on job security, and the observation that this is not a new technique. Many commentators have noted that horizontal process analysis is a conventional method that has been used by production and operations management specialists, and socio-technical systems analysts for decades (Buchanan, 1996).

These criticisms may be overstated. Under the label 'redesign', aspects of BPR are today finding application in healthcare (Locock, 2001). The technique of process mapping appears to be particularly powerful in persuading doctors, traditionally sceptical of management methods and suspicious of criticism, to reconsider their working practices in the context of the long-term government aspirations for healthcare 'modernization' (Gollop, 2002b).

The expertise of the change agent

The new agents of change: athletes not cowboys

Our new heroic model should be the athlete who can manage the amazing feat of doing more with less, who can juggle the need to both conserve resources and pursue growth opportunities. This new kind of business hero avoids the excesses of both the corpocrat and the cowboy. Where the former rigidly conserves and protects, the latter relentlessly speculates and promotes. But the business athlete has the strength to balance somewhere in the middle, taking the best of the corpocrat's discipline and the cowboy's entrepreneurial zeal. Business athletes need to be intense, lean and limber, able to stretch, good at teamwork, and in shape all the time.

From Rosabeth Moss Kanter, *When Giants Learn to Dance: Mastering the Challenge of Strategy, Management and Careers in the 1990s*, Simon & Schuster, London, 1989, p. 361.

Change agent: any member of an organization seeking to promote, further, support, sponsor, initiate, implement or help to deliver change.

What does it take to be an effective agent of organizational change? Two trends make this question urgent. First, most managers now combine change responsibilities with their regular duties. Despite the use of project managers and external consultants, many functional managers are also key **change agents**. The second trend concerns the increased involvement of all levels of organizational membership on change teams. This dispersal of change agency means that more people need to have the skills and knowledge required (Buchanan, Claydon and Doyle, 1999). Much of the literature concentrates on external change agents or management consultants. The role of internal change agents is equally important.

Change agents are not necessarily senior managers and do not need formal job titles. Change agents who are formally appointed are often selected for their expertise in the substance of the change. IT specialists, for example, are typically chosen to manage IT projects. However, rather than technical expertise, change agents require interpersonal and managerial skills, in communication, presentation, negotiation, influencing and selling, organization politics and in managing the change process. This is consistent with the way in which change is portrayed by processual/contextual theory: untidy, many factors, many players, politicized.

Rosabeth Moss Kanter (1989) identifies seven essential change agency skills:

Rosabeth Moss Kanter (b. 1943)

1. Ability to work independently, without management power, sanction and support.

2. An effective collaborator, able to compete in ways that enhance co-operation.

3. The ability to develop high trust relationships, based on high ethical standards.

4. Self-confidence, tempered with humility.

5. Respect for the process of change, as well as the content.

6. Able to work across business functions and units, 'multifaceted and ambidextrous'.

7. The willingness to stake reward on results and gain satisfaction from success.

Kanter's 'person specification' for the change agent seems to be consistent with what is known about flexible, organic organization structures, about participative management, and about the practice and implications of process re-engineering. Kanter speaks of this 'superhuman' change agent, with wide-ranging expertise, as a 'business athlete'. Jon Katzenbach (see the box below) distinguishes 'good managers' who analyze, organize, monitor and control from 'real change leaders' who create, innovate, experiment and take risks.

Good managers (GMs) versus real change leaders (RCLs)

Key issues	GMs	RCLs
Basic mindset	*Analyze, leverage, optimize, delegate, organize, and control it – I know best*	*Do it, fix it, try it, change it – and do it all over again; no one person knows best*
End-game assumptions	1. Earnings per share 2. Market share 3. Resource advantage 4. Personal promotions **Always make the numbers**	1. Value to customers, employees and owners 2. Customer loyalty 3. Core skills advantage 4. Personal growth **Satisfy customers and workers**
Leadership philosophy	1. Strategy driven 2. Decide, delegate, monitor and review 3. Spend time on important matters 4. Leverages his/her time **A few good people will get it done for me**	1. Aspiration driven 2. Do real work 3. Spend time on what matters to people 4. Expand leadership capacity **I must get the best out of all my people**
Sources of productivity and motivation	1. Investment turnover 2. Superior technology 3. Process control 4. Leverage people **People = exploitable resource**	1. Productivity 2. Superior people 3. Process innovation 4. Develop people **People = critical resource**
Accountability measures	1. Comprehensive measures across all areas 2. Clear individual accountability **I hold you accountable**	1. A few critical measures in the most critical areas 2. Individual and mutual accountability **We hold ourselves accountable**
Risk–reward trade-offs	1. Avoid failure and mistakes at all cost 2. Rely on proven approaches 3. Limit career risks 4. Analyse until sure **I cannot afford to fail, or leave**	1. Expect, learn from, and build on 'failures' 2. Try whatever appears promising 3. Take career risks 4. If in doubt, try it and see **I can work here, or elsewhere**

Adapted from Table in *Real Change Leaders: How You can Create Growth and High Performance at Your Company* by Jon Katzenbach & The Real Change Team (1997) – published by Nicholas Brealey Publishing, London (0207 239 0360).

Source: © copyright United Feature Syndicate, Inc. Reproduced by permission.

Stop and Criticize

Are you an athlete or a cowboy? Are you a good manager or a real change leader? Do you have the personal qualities required to make you an effective change agent? Match your expertise against Kanter's and Katzenbach's lists.

What further skills development do you think you need if you are to be effective in a change management role?

The effective change agent seems to be someone with a broad and well-developed range of skills and qualities. In a large organization, this can be a lonely and vulnerable role. However, the personal and career rewards can be significant. The high-flying, fast-track career is more readily built on contributions to strategic organizational change. Very few management careers are made by introducing minor, slow, incremental changes.

There are a number of trends evident in this field. Change has become a central management issue. While participative methods remain socially and ethically appropriate, there is a willingness to accept directive methods, accompanied by increasing recognition of the role of organization politics (e.g., Butcher and Clark, 2001). There is also recognition of the need for rapid and continual adjustment to events and trends. Change is no longer something which periodically disturbs the stable fabric, but is an ever present feature of organizational life. However, some commentators argue that repeat change is damaging, and that the initiative stream should be more carefully timed and paced. The significance of context factors in shaping the opportunities for and directions of change is now better understood and appreciated. Finally, while change may still be relevant to improving effectiveness, the organizational capability to change rapidly and often is viewed by many as a factor contributing to competitive advantage and survival. These trends are summarized in table 18.3.

Table 18.3: Trends in organizational change

Change in the late twentieth century	Change in the twenty-first century
one organizational theme among many	an organizational preoccupation
importance of participation and involvement	significance of political motives and actions
rational-linear model of project management	messy, untidy cocktail of reason and motive
content skills are critical	process skills are critical
implementation method is critical	implementation must be tailored to context
change as periodic adjustment	change as continuous upheaval
change must be frequent and fast	need to consider timing and pacing with care
aimed at organizational effectiveness	aimed at competitive advantage and survival

Recap

1. *Outline the contemporary debate concerning repeat change and painless change.*

   - Some commentators argue that constant adaptive reorganization is necessary to compete and survive in a rapidly changing and unpredictable environment.

   - Some commentators argue that constant change causes initiative decay and initiative fatigue which damage organizational performance.

   - While rapid and continuing 'repeat change' may appear necessary, 'painless change', where initiatives are timed and paced more carefully, may be more effective.

2. *Identify the main external and internal triggers of organizational change.*

   - Change can be triggered by a range of factors internal and external to the organization, and can also be proactive by anticipating trends and events.

   - Organizational changes vary in depth or penetration, from shallow fine tuning, to deep paradigmatic or strategic change.

   - The broad direction of change in most organizations is towards becoming less mechanistic and bureaucratic, and more adaptive, responsive and organic.

3. *Understand the typical characteristics of human responses to change.*

   - Individual emotional responses to traumatic changes differ, but the typical coping cycle passes through the stages of denial, anger, bargaining, depression and acceptance.

   - The Yerkes–Dodson law states that the initial response to pressure is improved performance, but that increasing pressure leads to fatigue, and ultimately to breakdown.

   - The evidence suggests that continuous organizational changes do lead to work intensification, burnout and 'initiative fatigue'.

4. *Understand the nature of resistance to change and approaches to overcoming it.*

   - Resistance to change has many sources, including self-interest, lack of trust and understanding, competing assessments of the outcomes and low tolerance of change.

   - One technique for addressing possible resistance to change, as well as identifying and strengthening support for change, is stakeholder analysis.

   - The main prescribed approach for avoiding or dealing with resistance is participative management, in which those affected are involved in implementation.

   - The use of manipulation and coercion to implement change is advocated by some commentators, but the 'political' role of management in change is controversial.

5. *Explain the advantages and limitations of participative methods of change management.*

   - Participative methods can generate creative thinking and increase employee commitment to change, but this process is time consuming.

   - Some commentators argue that rapid and major corporate transformations are more successful when implemented using a dictatorial or coercive style.

6. *Explain the strengths and weaknesses of the processual/contextual perspective on change.*

   - Processual/contextual theory emphasizes the interaction of the substance, process, politics and context of change, at individual, group, organizational and social levels of analysis, and considers how past events shape current and future thinking and actions.

   - Processual/contextual theory is analytically strong, but is weak in practical terms.

7. *Outline the skill requirements for an effective change agent.*

   - The change agent has to be more skilled in managing the change process than knowledgeable with respect to the substance of the change in hand. This involves the 'soft' management skills of communication, presentation, selling, negotiating, influencing, and providing feedback and support.

Revision

1. What value do practical '*n*-step guides' have for managers attempting to implement organizational change, and what are the limitations of this kind of advice?

2. What are the main sources of resistance to organizational change, and how can resistance be overcome?

3. While some commentators argue that 'repeat change' is a strategic imperative, others claim that this is damaging. Why, and what is the alternative?

4. The typical individual response to change is not necessarily negative. Why not, and how can individual responses to change be assessed and understood?

5. What are the benefits and limitations of a participative approach to the implementation of organizational change?

Springboard

Boddy, D., 2002, *Managing Projects: Building and Leading the Team*, Financial Times/Prentice Hall, Harlow (second edition).

Demonstrates the continuing popularity of project management approaches to organizational change, focusing on the roles and skills of project team members and human resource issues. Offers theoretical underpinning and links to practice.

Burnes, B., 2000, *Managing Change: A Strategic Approach to Organizational Dynamics*, Financial Times/Prentice Hall, Harlow, Essex (third edition).

Comprehensive, well-informed and clearly written textbook on change which sets the topic in the wider context of organizational strategy, behaviour and management.

Collins, D., 1998, *Organizational Change: Sociological Perspectives*, Routledge, London.

Surveys the field and is critical of '*n*-step guides'. Criticizes managers for avoiding theory and academics for accepting managerial perspectives on change.

Dawson, P., 2003a, *Reshaping Change: A Processual Approach*, Routledge, London.

Provides an introduction to the history and nature of processual theories of change, including case studies illustrating the interaction of context, substance, process and politics in well-known organizations. Also discusses processual research methods.

Dawson, P., 2003b, *Understanding Organizational Change: The Contemporary Experience of People at Work*, Sage Publications, London.

Reviews perspectives on change, advocating the strengths of a processual approach, critical of change recipes. Case studies illustrate human aspects of change.

Knights, D. and Willmott, H. (eds), 2000, *The Reengineering Revolution: Critical Studies of Corporate Change*, Sage Publications, London.

A collection of chapters assessing critically the impact of re-engineering on management thinking and practice, revealing that this 'fad' has not been abandoned.

Kotter, J.P., 1995a, 'Leading change: why transformation efforts fail', *Harvard Business Review*, vol. 73, no. 2, pp. 59–67.

An American example of an '*n*-step guide', Kotter lists eight steps for successful transformation. He published a book with a similar title.

McCalman, J. and Paton, R., 2000, *Change Management: A Guide to Effective Implementation*, Sage Publications, London (second edition).

Offers a theoretically informed and comprehensive practical framework for applying different perspectives on organizational change. Clearly written with illustrative cases.

Preece, D., Steven, G. and Steven, V., 1999, *Work, Change and Competition: Managing for Bass*, Routledge, London.

An insightful 'insider' account of change in Bass from a processual perspective which covers triggers for change, management strategy and messy politics.

Senior, B., 2001, *Organizational Change*, Pitman, London.

Another well-written text, which explores 'soft' and 'hard' approaches to understanding and managing change.

Home viewing

Lean on Me (1989, director John G. Avildsen) is a school drama based on a true story. Joe Clark (played by Morgan Freeman) is an autocratic and controversial New Jersey high school principal who cleans up his school, East Side High. He institutes a programme of change which elicits various reactions from both the school staff and the students. Identify the trigger of change which prompts the Mayor to appoint Clark as principal. Using the Dunphy and Stace matrix, what is the scale of the change that Clark attempts to introduce? What change leadership style does Clark adopt? Which of Kanter's seven change agent skills does Clark demonstrate? Which change implementation methods are demonstrated? Draw a diagram showing the stakeholders affected by this change, inside and outside the school. Which of the techniques explained by Kotter and Schlesinger does Clark use to overcome resistance?

OB in literature

Jeff Torrington, *The Devil's Carousel*, Martin, Secker & Warburg/Minerva, London, 1996.

Set in the Main Assembly Division (MAD) of the Chimeford plant of the Centaur Car Company. Among the many colourful characters, the crimson-collared overalls of the senior foremen earn them the nickname Rednecks, while Greybacks are junior foremen wearing all-grey overalls to distinguish their lower rank. Senior managers are called Martians by the shop-floor employees. Identify the symptoms and causes of resistance to change in Centaur cars. What factors explain the plant closure? What strategic changes could management have implemented to save the plant? In implementing those changes, would it have been more appropriate to use dictatorial transformation or participative evolution, and why?

Chapter exercises

1: Resistance is futile

Objectives
1. To examine the causes of individual resistance to change.

2. To explore the management problems in overcoming resistance to change.

Briefing   Your instructor will ask your class to engage in a short change experiment. When this is complete, consider your response to your instructor's requests using the following guide:

I resisted this change due to:

cause of resistance	applies to me (√)
parochial self-interest: 'I don't want to be pushed out of my comfort zone'	
misunderstanding and lack of trust: 'why are you asking me to do this?'	
contradictory assessments: 'you might think this is good, but I don't'	
low tolerance of change: 'I can't cope with the uncertainty and the anxiety'	

Compare your responses with those of colleagues:

■ What does this experiment reveal about you as a person?

■ What does this experiment reveal about your colleagues?

■ What does this reveal about the problems that can be associated with even simple organizational changes?

2: Implementation planning

Objectives

1. To apply change implementation theory to a practical setting.

2. To assess the practical value of 'best practice' textbook advice on how to implement change effectively.

Briefing

Due to a combination of space constraints and financial issues, your department or school has been told by senior management to relocate to another building seven kilometres from the existing site within the next three months. Your management have in turn been asked to draw up a plan for managing the move, which will affect all staff (academic, technical, secretarial, administrative), all students (undergraduate, postgraduate), and all equipment (classroom aids, computing). The new building will provide more space and student facilities, but offices for academic staff are smaller, the building is on a different bus route, and car parking facilities are more limited. Senior management have reassured staff that email will allow regular contact to be maintained with colleagues in other departments which are not being moved.

You have been asked to help management with their planning. Your brief is as follows:

1. Conduct a stakeholder analysis, identifying how each stakeholder or stakeholder group should be approached to ensure that this move goes ahead smoothly.

2. Conduct a readiness for change analysis, identifying any 'groundwork' that may have to be done to ensure the move goes ahead smoothly.

3. Determine a change implementation strategy. Is a participative approach appropriate, or is dictatorial transformation required? Justify your recommendation by pointing to the advantages and limitations of the various options you have explored.

4. Using one or more of the *n*-step guides described in this chapter, draw up a creative and practical action plan for implementing this change effectively.

Prepare a short presentation of your results to colleagues.

In discussion, identify what this analysis reveals about the problems of turning organizational change theory and 'best practice' advice into practical management action.

Chapter 19 Organizational culture

Key concepts

Organizational culture	Integration (unitary) perspective
Surface manifestations of culture	Differentiation perspective
Organizational values	Fragmentation (conflict) perspective
Basic assumptions	Power–distance
Organizational socialization	Uncertainty avoidance
Pre-arrival stage of socialization	Individualism–collectivism
Encounter stage of socialization	Masculinity–femininity
Role modelling	Long-term–short-term orientation
Metamorphosis stage of socialization	

Learning outcomes

When you have read this chapter, you should be able to define those key concepts in your own words, and you should also be able to:

1. Account for the popularity of organizational culture among managers, consultants and academics.
2. List, describe and exemplify Schein's three levels of culture.
3. List the stages of organizational socialization.
4. Contrast managerial and social science perspectives on organizational culture.
5. Assess the link between organizational culture and economic performance.
6. Distinguish different national culture dimensions.

Boozing with the boss

Koreans will soon be able to claim compensation for liver damage caused by heavy after-work boozing sessions. Drinking with the boss is an established part of corporate culture in South Korea, but it takes its toll on workers' families lives and health. So in March, the government will start classifying drink-related illness as an industrial accident. 'The change is not related to our drinking habits [national culture], but to unique corporate culture and working conditions' says a government official. Job-induced asthma, skin diseases, hepatitis, stress depression and 'death by overwork' will also be covered.

From *New Scientist*, 'Boozing with the boss', 26 January 2002, p. 7.

Why study organizational culture?

When you walk into a hotel, a bank, a nightclub, a shop, a country pub, the office of a solicitor, what do you notice first? What do 'first impressions' tell you about the organization that you have just entered? How friendly it will be? How expensive it will be? What kind of behaviour is expected of you? How will the staff approach and deal with you? Now look more carefully at the physical surroundings. What positive and negative signs, symbols and signals do you get? How exactly are these being transmitted to you? These are all aspects of organizational culture. The nature of that culture is thus significant, both for those who work there and also for customers and clients. Culture seems to vary from organization to organization, and there is an argument that says that culture affects organizational performance, and hence managers must control and change the culture when necessary. Is culture that important? Can it be managed?

Culture derives from the idea of cultivation, mostly of land, but also of gods. The concept evolved to conceptualize humankind's diversity. It asserts that we socially construct different understandings of nature and hence of the reality that surrounds us. An organization's culture focuses on the values, beliefs and meanings used by its members to grasp how its uniqueness originates, evolves and operates. It has often been considered within the context of corporate strategy and organization structure (Scholtz, 1987). Organizational culture has been a popular concept since the early 1980s. First adopted by senior executives and management consultants as a quick-fix solution to virtually every organization problem, it was later used by academics as an explanatory framework with which to understand behaviour in organizations (Morgan et al., 1983; Meek, 1988).

The concept of organizational culture has retained its place within business life and academic study. For many companies, interest in the topic has been sustained and indeed raised by three factors: first, increasing globalization, which has placed organizational culture sharply into focus alongside national culture; second, the enduring assumption that organizational performance depends on employee values being aligned with company strategy; third, the contentious view that management can consciously manipulate culture to achieve organizational (change) objectives (Ogbonna and Harris, 2002). Culture also possesses an appeal for academics who have researched and taught it for over two decades. In many organizational behaviour and management textbooks, the 'culture perspective' or the 'symbolic approach' now ranks alongside others, as an alternative way of understanding behaviour in organizations (Deal and Kennedy, 2000; Parker, 2000a; Alvesson, 2001; Martin, 2001).

The rise of the organizational culture concept

Organizational (or corporate) culture remains a controversial concept. Some writers argue that just as one can talk about French culture, Arab culture or Asian culture, so too it is possible to discuss the organizational culture of the British Civil Service, McDonald's, Microsoft or Disney. Others reject this notion. David Needle (2000, p. 101) wrote:

> The treatment of culture at the level of the firm varied considerably, ranging across the banal, the simplistic, the misleading, the highly complex, the impenetrably academic and the highly critical.

Organizational culture: the collection of relatively uniform and enduring values, beliefs, customs, traditions and practices that are shared by an organization's members, learned by new recruits, and transmitted from one generation of employees to the next.

Tom J. Peters
(b. 1942)

Robert H. Waterman
(b. 1936)

Terrence E. Deal

Its antecedents go back through anthropology, sociology, psychology and early management thought. In general, it is recognized that organizations have 'something' (a personality, philosophy, ideology or climate) which goes beyond economic rationality, and which gives each of them a unique identity. One writer referred to it as 'The way we do things around here' (Deal and Kennedy, 1982), while another saw it as 'the collective programming of the mind' (Hofstede, 2001). Then, as now, there was no consensus about its definition. Competing definitions abound, and do more to confuse than to clarify. Although a definition of **organizational culture** is offered here, readers are encouraged to devise their own on the basis of the discussion presented in this chapter and their own further reading.

Martin Parker (2000a) argued that the original references to culture go back to the work of human relations researcher Elton Mayo (1933, 1945), who was interested in the social engineering of 'sentiments': that is, the non-logical rationalizations for actions. Mayo argued that executives could manage better if they understood the irrationalities of ordinary employees. The cultural perspective therefore represents a break with the earlier rational-mechanistic view of organization, which sees employees as tools for achieving an organization's goals. Many assumed that the hard 'scientific' management of companies could be replaced by a softer approach that relied on a more humane understanding of people's values, beliefs and feelings that focused on the non-rational aspects.

The current debates about culture are traceable to the early 1980s when four books catapulted the concept to the forefront of management attention: William Ouchi's *Theory Z* (1981), Richard Pascale and Anthony Athos's *The Art of Japanese Management* (1982), *In Search of Excellence* (1982), written by Tom Peters and Robert Waterman, and Terrence Deal and Allan Kennedy's *Corporate Cultures* (1982). These publications suggested that a strong culture was a powerful lever for guiding workforce behaviour. They conceived a company's culture as consisting of values and beliefs, myths, heroes and symbols that possessed meaning for all employees. In addition to these books, other factors also stimulated an interest. These included Japan's industrial success during the 1970s and 1980s; the view that intangible (soft) factors such as values and beliefs impacted on financial (hard) ones; the belief that managers could change cultures to achieve greater organizational effectiveness; and the belief that culture might weaken union power.

Originally introduced to managers by consultants, it was not long before academics started to take an interest in it as well. Some business school professors attempted to refine the concept, seeking to operationalize it for research purposes. Edgar Schein (1985) was among the first of these. His and competing definitions established the basis for later research into the concept. The role of academics has been to research the concept and develop it theoretically. As Majken Schultz (1995, p. 5) observed:

> Opposed to the study of both formal and informal organization behaviour, a cultural way of studying organizations is to study the meaning of organizational behaviour – or more specifically, the meanings and beliefs which members of organizations assign to organizational behaviour and how these assigned meanings influence the ways in which they behave themselves.

Culture: surface manifestations, values and basic assumptions

Edgar Schein's model of culture is among the most widely discussed. It considers organizational culture in terms of three levels, each distinguished by its visibility to and accessibility by individuals (figure 19.1). According to Schein (1985, p. 14):

Allen A. Kennedy

Edgar Henry
Schein (b. 1928)

Organization culture is the pattern of basic assumptions which a group has invented, discovered or developed in learning to cope with its problems of external adaption and integration, which have worked well enough to be considered valid, and therefore to be taught to new members as the correct way to perceive, think and feel in relation to problems. ... Culture is not the overt behaviour or visible artefacts that one might observe if one were to visit the company. It is not even the philosophy or value system which the founder may articulate or write down in various 'charters'. Rather it is the assumptions which lie behind the values and which determine the behaviour patterns and the visible artefacts such as architecture, office layout, dress codes and so on.

Schein's fundamental view is that culture is the sharing of meanings and the sharing of 'basic' assumptions among organizational employees (level 3). He also implies that an organization's senior executives can manage these basic assumptions if they understand what culture is and how it operates.

Schein's first level is the **surface manifestation of culture**. It refers to the visible things that a culture produces. It includes both physical objects and also behaviour patterns that can be seen, heard or felt. They all 'send a message' to an organization's visitors, customers and employees. For him this is not the organization's culture itself, but only its most apparent and most accessible aspect that can be perceived by people.

Surface manifestation of culture: culture's most visible and accessible forms, which are the visible and audible behaviour patterns and objects.

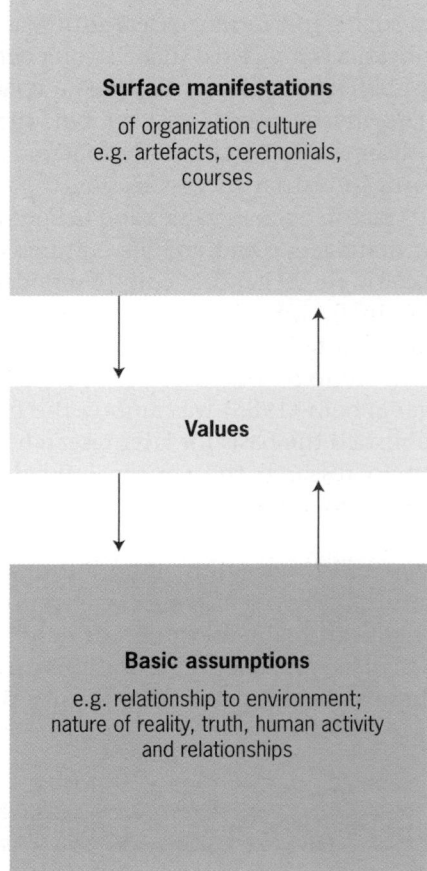

Figure 19.1: Schein's three levels of culture
From Edgar H. Schein, Organizational Culture and Leadership, 1985, p. 14. Copyright © 1985. This material is used by permission of John Wiley & Sons, Inc.

At this level, culture is manifested in company-specific objects, architecture, rituals and language. It has received a great deal of attention in the literature. Over the years, our own students have enthusiastically participated in 'culture spotting' and have shared with us examples from the organizations with which they have been involved. The various elements of organizational cultures naturally change, but here are a few past and present examples of their surface manifestations:

Artefacts are material objects created by human hands to facilitate culturally expressive activities. They include tools, furniture, appliances and clothes ('work wear').

- Open-plan offices, with their absence of doors and personal private space, are intended to convey less of an 'us and them' message.

Ceremonials are systems of rites connected within a single event.

- The Loyalty Group in Canada has an annual 'Funday', which all of its 700 employees attend. Elements of the Funday include a picnic, speeches, team games, dinner and an award ceremony.

Courses are sets of instructions for induction, orientation and training that are used to educate new members.

- McDonald's (the US fast food restaurant chain) established its full-time training centre in 1961. Called Hamburger University, it offers a 'degree' in 'hamburgerology'.

- Airlines have four- to five-week induction courses for cabin staff, incorporating a course on grooming, including how to apply make up. Head of Appearance & Grooming carries out formal, random appraisals on individual crew members.

Gestures are movements of parts of the body used to express meaning.

- In military organizations, junior ranks salute senior ranks in a gesture that acknowledges the higher rank rather than its occupant.

Heroes are characters, living or dead, who personify the values and beliefs; who are referred to in company stories, legends, sagas, myths and jokes; and who represent role models that current employees should emulate.

- In B&Q (British home improvements retailer), Mr Block and Mr Quale were said to have had a vision which is still being followed today.

- Bill Harley and John Davidson still embody the spirit of owning a Harley–Davidson motorbike.

Jokes are humorous stories intended to cause amusement but whose underlying themes may carry a message for the behaviour or values expected of organizational members.

Language is the particular form or manner in which members use vocal sounds and written signs to convey meaning to each other. It includes both specialist technical vocabulary related to the business (jargon), as well as general naming choices.

- Wal-Mart has *associates*; McDonald's has *crew members*; Disney has *cast members*; Asda, Tesco and Sainsbury's have *colleagues*; B&Q has *team players*; Starbucks has *partners*; Brook Street Employment Agency has *recruitment consultants*.

■ Among staff and management, the McDonald's restaurant is known as the 'store', not the restaurant. Thus, each has a 'store manager', not a restaurant manager.

■ In call centres, single words, such as 'confirm' or 'sale', are used between staff members but are not mentioned to customers.

Legends are handed-down narratives about wonderful events based on history, but embellished with fictional details. These fascinate employees and invite them to admire or deplore certain activities.

Mottoes are maxims adopted as rules of conduct. Unlike slogans, mottoes are rarely, if ever, changed.

■ John Lewis Partnership (British department store chain): 'Never knowingly undersold'

■ Special Air Services (SAS) (British military): 'Who dares wins'

Myths are dramatic narratives of imagined events, usually used to explain origins or transformations. They offer an unquestioned basis for a behaviour or techniques that are not supported by demonstrated fact.

■ A staff member at Disneyland Paris dressed as Mickey Mouse was sued by the company after taking off his costume in front of tourists.

Norms are expected modes of behaviour that are accepted as the compay's ways of doing things, thereby providing guidance for employee behaviour.

■ In the British Army officer's mess, one addresses others as Mr or Miss, as a sign of respect.

Physical layout concerns things that surround people, providing them with immediate sensory stimuli as they carry out culturally expressive activities.

■ The headquarters at Nike (sportswear manufacturer) have a Hall of Fame of famous athletes who wore Nike equipment, down which all employees must pass each morning before arriving at their offices.

Rites are relatively elaborate, dramatic sets of activities that consolidate various forms of cultural expression into one event. They are formally planned, though not necessarily officially sanctioned (Trice and Bayer, 1984).

■ Every morning before moving into their sales territory, each Southwestern (book selling company) salesperson performs a dance to motivate themselves.

Rituals are a repetitive patterns of activities that occur in specific circumstances or at particular times in an organization. They are intended to help employees to manage their anxieties.

■ Asda (British food supermarket) staff are encouraged to slap their back pockets while chanting A-S-D-A in unison (Lewis, 2002, p. 22).

■ When a new shift takes over in the Berlin Fire Brigade, all new shift members shake hands with those going off duty.

Sagas are historical narratives describing the unique accomplishments of a group and its leaders. They usually describe a series of events that are said to have unfolded over time and which constitute an important part of an organization's history (Watson, 2002).

Slogans are short, catchy phrases which are regularly changed. They are used for both customer advertising and also to motivate employees.

- Nike: 'Just do it'.
- British Army: 'Be the best'.
- Asda: 'Asda price' jingle.
- Coca-Cola: 'Always Coca-Cola'.

Stories are simple narratives describing how individuals acted and the key decisions they made that affected the company's future. Stories are usually based on true events but can include a mixture of both truth and fiction (Feldman, 1991; Weick, 1995).

- Procter and Gamble's story: an employee noticed that the labels on a product at his local supermarket were mounted off-centre. He bought the whole stock assuming that P&G would reimburse him, which it did.

Symbols refer to any act, event, object, quality or relation that serves as a vehicle for conveying meaning.

- Coca-Cola and IBM logos, Nike 'swoosh', *G* for Gucci and *x* for Coco Channel; McDonald's 'Golden Arches'.
- The Red Cross' symbol is a red cross on a white background, which is the reverse of the Swiss flag and means neutrality.
- Intel's 'Intel inside' symbol on computers.

Corporate anthems

Now you can singalongwith ... AT&T, Hewlett Packard, Fujitsu, Ernst and Young, Philips, KPMG and many other companies. Anthem composition appears to be an established practice in a large number of Western, blue-chip companies. The popularity of corporate anthems has increased in recent years, and web site visitors can now download their favourite tunes. McKinsey & Co's song, entitled *McKC*, has proved to be among the most popular and has notched about 26,000 downloads. 'Anthems are a form of industrial folklore', says Peter Judge. 'While the enjoyment is partly ironic, it's none the less real.' And who's to say what great things might have been achieved had the McKinsey anthem gone on general release? 'Challenges engage us/Nothing really phases us/Come hell or high water/You can count on us.' Embarrassed by its chart-topping success, McKinsey claimed that this was not an official company anthem: 'It's just a group of people in our research and information unit getting together to have some fun.' Few things in the world can equal the power of music, but it is unclear whether company staff are taught these songs or are required to sing them at work. Lyrics from a sample of company songs give their flavour:

➤

We're AT&T, one big happy family We're AT&T, all the business units and me We're AT&T, everything you want it to be We are family, the one and only AT&T	Oh happy day (Oh happy day) Oh happy day (Oh happy day) When Ernst & Young (When Ernst & Young) When Ernst & Young (When Ernst & Young) Showed me a better way (Oh happy day) Oh happy day (Oh happy day)
Philips was my first love And it will be my last Philips is my future And it will ever last	KPMG, we're strong as can be A team of power and energy We go for the gold Together we hold onto our vision of global strategy

Based on Jane Lewis, 'Back on song', *Personnel Today*, 19 November 2002, p. 22.

Organizational values: those things that have personal or organizational worth or meaning to the founders or senior management. Values are typically based on moral, societal or religious precepts that are learned in childhood and modified through experience.

Schein's second level concerns **organizational values** and beliefs. Values are broad tendencies to prefer certain states of affairs over others. They are often unspoken but can mould members' behaviours. They can be both consciously and unconsciously held, and thus reflect relatively general beliefs. They are typically based on moral, societal or religious precepts that are learned in childhood and modified through experience. Again, in his view, this is not the organization's culture itself. These are located below the surface manifestations and underpin them. While values are not visible, individuals can be made aware of them. Many commentators agree that these values are the elements that distinguish the organization from other firms, since they affect the basic assumptions that Schein sees as truly being an organization's culture.

Tom Peters and Robert Waterman's *In Search of Excellence* (1982) proposed the McKinsey 7-S Framework© to organizational success, whose variables are shown in figure 19.2. Values were positioned at the centre of that framework, holding the other elements together, and were thus considered to be a key element in achieving high organizational performance. Values are said to provide a common direction for all employees and act as guidelines for their behaviour. 'People way down the line know what they are supposed to do in most situations because the handful of guiding values is crystal clear' (Peters and Waterman, 1982, p. 76).

Where do organizational values come from? As indicated by Schein's earlier quotation, some authors see values representing organizational solutions to problems experienced in the past. Another source of values are the views of the original founder, as modified by the company's current senior management (Schein, 1983). Originally, a single person (founder) has an idea for a new company and brings in other key people to create a core group who share a common vision with the founder. This group creates an organization, brings in others and begins to build a common history. Stephen Robbins (2003) described senior management as an organization's 'culture carriers'. Thus one can argue that organizational values are the values of the current company elite (senior managers), rather like 'organizational goals' represent the preferred aims of the same group. Values are operationalized into company practices and procedures, as detailed in the surface manifestations. Although senior management might like their employees to adopt the organization's (that is, its) values, this is not only unlikely but also unnecessary. Employees only need to follow the specified, values-based practices and manifest expected responses. For example, they do not need to enjoy a company's 'Elvis Day', only participate enthusiastically in it and just act as if they were having a good time (figure 19.3).

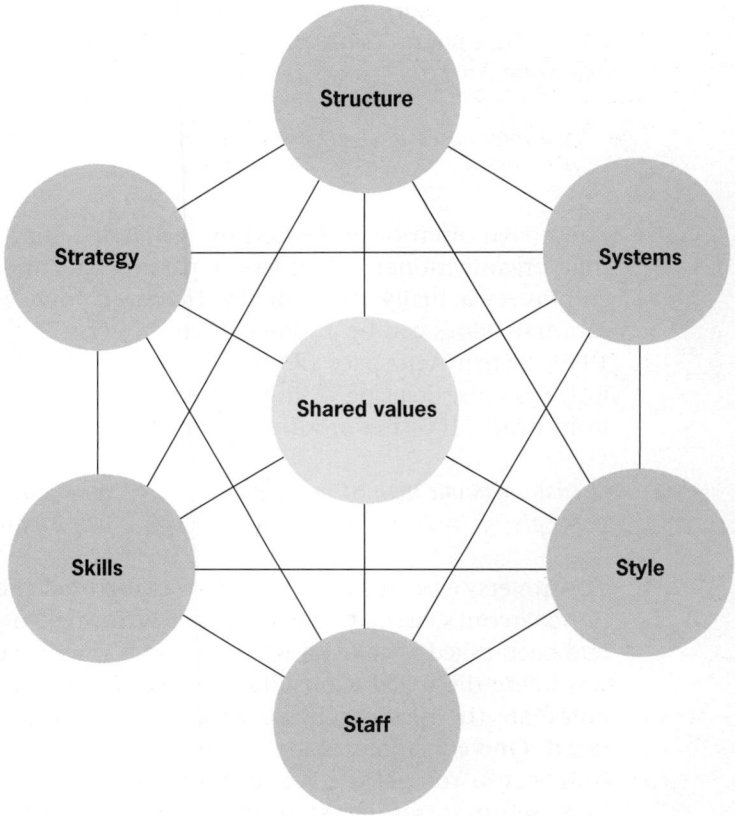

Figure 19.2: McKinsey 7-S Framework©
From Thomas J. Peters and Robert H. Waterman, *In Search of Excellence*, Harper & Row, New York, 1982, p. 10.

In a sense, therefore, organizational values are always backward looking, despite being developed to contribute to the future development of the company. For a organizational culture to form, a fairly stable collection of people need to have shared a significant history, involving problems, which allowed a social learning process to take place. Organizations which have such histories possess cultures that permeate most of their functions (Schein, 1985).

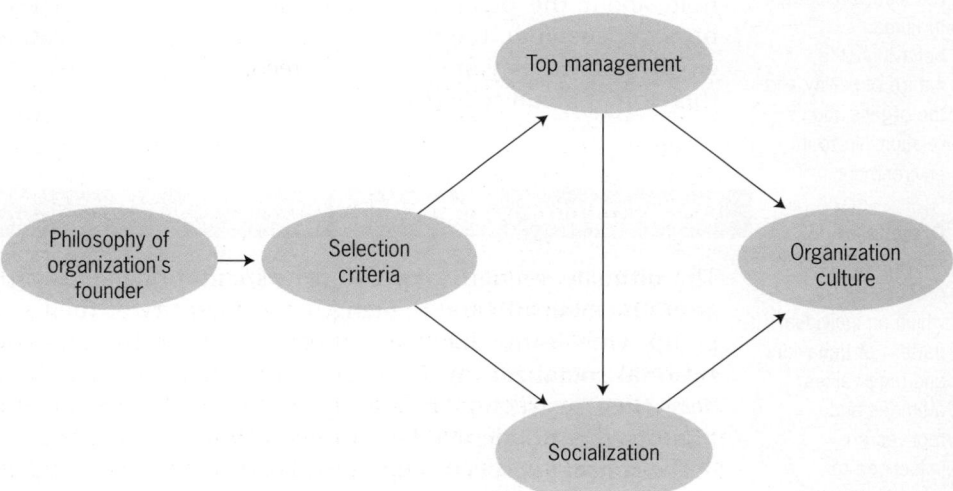

Figure 19.3: Where does organizational culture come from?

Company values come in lists. They are to be found printed in company reports, framed on company walls and published on organizational web sites. For example, Amazon's six core values are:

customer obsession	*ownership*	*bias for action*
frugality	*high hiring bar*	*innovation*

They have often been devised by teams of senior managers. Some cynics argue that organizational values are a passing fad and have little impact on what employees actually think or do. However, there is some evidence that organizational values can be a source of controversy (Buono et al., 1985). In November 1999, British Aerospace (BAe) and Marconi Electronics Systems merged to form BAE Systems, creating a single organization with 100,000 employees, operating from nearly 100 sites around the world. The merged company's values are:

customers our highest priority	*innovation & technology partnership*
people	*performance*

Controversy was aroused when it was reported that BAe's company values, and not Marconi's, would shape the newly formed organization. Marconi directors had been asked to take on BAe's values in the new organization when the merger was being discussed. Consultants warned that this would mean that BAe would dominate the new organization and ex-Marconi employees would be disadvantaged. One consultant said: 'In my experience, one side is always the winner in these cases. You get the best of both companies by merging, so buying into one side's set-up is not necessarily the best way' (*Personnel Today*, 1999).

Stop and Criticize

Basic assumptions: invisible, preconscious and taken-for-granted understandings held by individuals with respect to aspects of human behaviour, the nature of reality and the organization's relationship to its environment.

Visit the web sites of some large European and American companies (for example, Nokia, The Body Shop, Hewlett Packard, Amazon, Accenture, Eriksson, IBM) and locate their list of values. Also, look at some non-profit organizations like universities, local government councils, Greenpeace, Amnesty International, Red Cross and Médecins Sans Frontières. What purposes do these lists of values serve and for whom?

Finally, **basic assumptions** are located at Schein's third level and are, in his view, the organization's culture. They include the assumptions that individuals hold about the organization and how it functions. They relate to aspects of human behaviour, the nature of reality and the organization's relationship to its environment. They are invisible, preconscious and 'taken for granted'. They are therefore difficult to access.

Organizational socialization

Organizational socialization: the process through which an individual's pattern of behaviour and their values, attitudes and motives are influenced to conform with those seen as desirable in a particular organization.

The ultimate strength of a company's culture depends on the homogeneity of group membership and the length and intensity of their shared experiences in a group. One learns about a company's culture through the process of **organizational socialization**. It includes the careful selection of new company members, their instruction in appropriate ways of thinking and behaving, and the reinforcement of desired behaviours by senior managers.

The concept of socialization has already been considered at the level of the individual and the group. Socialization is important because, as John van Maanen and Edgar Schein (1979) argue, new organization recruits have to be taught to see the

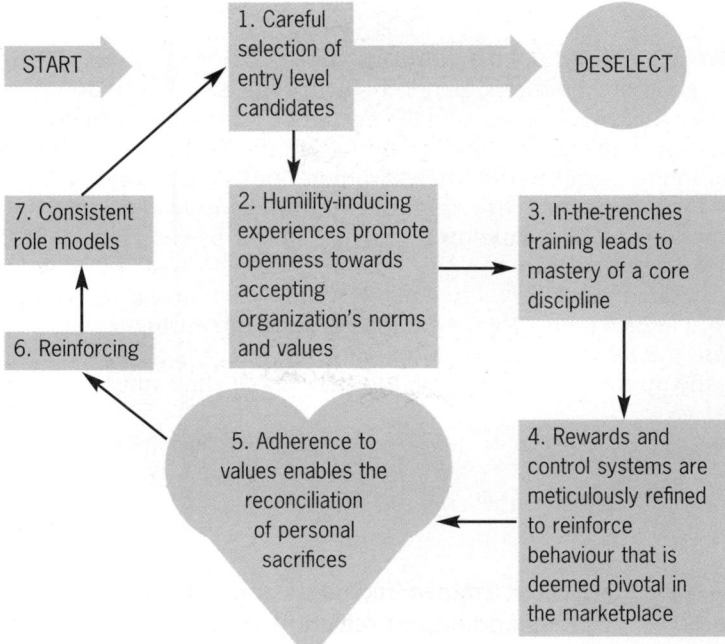

Figure 19.4: Seven steps of organizational socialization
From Richard T. Pascale, 'The paradox of "corporate culture": reconciling ourselves to socialization'.
Copyright © 1985, by The Regents of the University of California. Reprinted from *California Management Review*, vol. 27, no. 2. By permission of The Regents.

organizational world as their more experienced colleagues do, if the tradition of the organization is to survive. Socialization involves newcomers absorbing the values and behaviours required to survive and prosper in an organization. It reduces variability of behaviour by imbuing employees with a sense of what is expected of them and how they should do things. By providing an internal sense of how they should behave, plus a shared frame of reference, socialization standardizes employee behaviour, making it predictable for the benefit of senior management. Richard Pascale (1985) distinguished seven key steps or elements in the process of organizational socialization, which are shown in figure 19.4.

Interviewing for Amazon.com

My first meeting with the recruiter was a revelation. She was a polite and talkative lady with thick glasses and an overbite. . . . She had called me on the phone right away, she told me, because of my background.
'My background?'
'Your degree.'
'Oh, I'm sorry about that –' I began, preparing to launch into my standard corporate apology for not having a background in human resources or political science and why I was still employable, please. Give me a chance, I won't let you down.
'I think you are exactly what we are looking for.'
That stopped me dead. No one had ever said that. I thought for a moment about what this job was: customer service. Selling books over the Internet. Unless there was a hidden element of art criticism to the job, I couldn't see how aesthetics applied.
'Oh', I said. . . .
'Amazon is about broadening horizons, interfacing with technology, and taking a can-do approach to corporate solutions.'

'I like technology . . . I like horizons.' Jesus, I was giving a terrible interview. I was normally very good at interviews, better at them than at actually doing work, but I still couldn't believe that this woman actually thought I was qualified to do something. . . .

'Amazon is always telling us to find them freaks. They want the freaks, you know, people who might not fit in elsewhere. So then I saw your résumé . . . ah . . .' She lost track of her tact for a moment. 'Ah . . . I thought you would really find a home here. People need a home to work in, you know?'

'Well, I agree with that.'

She nodded vigorously, I nodded as well. . . We both sat there, nodding at each other, like a couple of windup toys, working through our hiring script. I was nodding to say: *Yes, please give me a job.* Her nodding said: *Yes, you are a freak.* We nodded all the way to signing me up for an informational meeting about the company and the job.

From Mike Daisey, *Twenty-one Dog Years: Doing Time @ Amazon.com*, Fourth Estate, London, 2002, pp. 16–18.

Pre-arrival stage of socialization: the period of learning in the process that occurs before an applicant joins an organization.

Selection: Trained recruiters carefully select entry-level candidates seeking traits using standardized selection methods. The entrants are not 'oversold' on a particular position because the companies rely on applicants 'deselecting' if they find that the organization does not fit in with their personal styles and values. It is also referred to as the **pre-arrival stage of socialization**.

Humility-inducing experiences: Once working, the organization encourages new entrants to question their past behaviour, beliefs and values. It does this by assigning them more work than they can possibly cope with or giving them menial tasks to perform. The aim is to reduce their self-complacency, increase their self-examination and prepare them to accept the organization's own norms and values. This is also the first step in the **encounter stage of socialization**.

Encounter stage of socialization: the period of learning in the process during which the new recruit learns about organizational expectations.

In-the-trenches training: The training received by recruits focuses on their achieving mastery of the core disciplines of the company's business. These extensive and carefully reinforced job experiences seek to imbue them with the organization's way of doing things.

Rewards and control systems: New members' performances are carefully assessed and rewarded. The organization uses systems that are comprehensive and consistent, and which link to competitive success and its values.

Role modelling: a form of socialization in which an individual learns by example. The learner observes established members, acquires a mental picture of the act and its consequences (rewards and punishments), and then acts out the acquired image.

Adherence to values: The employees identify with the common organizational values, allowing them to reconcile the personal sacrifices they have made in order to be a member of the organization. This creates the foundation of trust between them and their organization, and often involves linking company goals with significant higher-level goals – not making profits from selling PCs but connecting humanity!

Reinforcing folklore: New entrants are exposed to the organizational stories, myths and symbols as they interact with their managers and colleagues within the workplace. These provide them with a code of conduct that clarifies 'how we do things around here' and, by implication, how they should do it as well.

Consistent role models: Entrants also learn through **role modelling**. They are shown personnel who are judged by the company to be 'winners': that is, who possess the traits, demonstrate the behaviours and achieve the results that are rec-

Metamorphosis stage of socialization: the period in which the new employee adjusts to their organization's values, attitudes, motives, norms and required behaviours.

ognized and valued by the firm. This step may mark the **metamorphosis stage of socialization** in which the new employee adjusts to their organization's values, attitudes, motives, norms and required behaviours.

Employees tend to respond to a new culture in one of three ways. They can *collude* and submit entirely and enthusiastically to the cultural values; they might *capitulate*, changing their outward behaviour but not their internal values ('faking it'); or they may be *defensive* and resist the culture. Where the gap between expectation and reality cannot be breached, the individual may leave the job by resigning. Some organizations might want their new employees to the follow the instructions, printed in English, in a hotel elevator in Paris: 'Please leave your values at the front desk'.

Beyond the induction period which, in some large companies, may last up to a year, performance-based appraisal systems and formal training programmes are also instituted by a company to signal visibly which goals new-joiners should be striving for and how. Finally, senior management's behaviour in promoting, censoring and dismissing employees also sends information to employees about company values, expectations about norms, risk-taking, acceptability of delegation, appropriate dress, topics of discussion, and so on.

Disney-fication of new employees

Disney begins tugging on the heartstrings of employees even before they are hired. Think about the typical recruiting office in the hospitality industry – a windowless cubby-hole in the sub-basement between the laundry and the boiler room. Then walk into Disney's capacious 'casting centre' and you're in Wonderland. Well, not exactly, but the doorknobs on the entrance do replicate the ones Alice yanked during her adventures. . . . Ascend a gentle sloping hallway, whose walls are decorated with whimsical murals, and you're in a vast anteroom where the centrepiece is the original model of Snow White's castle.

Some 50,000 aspiring employees funnel through the Lake Buena Vista casting centre every year seeking jobs that start with pay as low as $5.95 per hour (Disney's other theme parks in California, Japan and France do their own hiring). What are Disney World's 40 interviewers – all of whom started as front line workers – most interested in? . . . Says Duncan Dickson, director of casting: 'We're looking for personality. We can train for skills. We want people who are enthusiastic, who have pride in their work, who can take charge of a situation without supervision.'

. . . Disney has overhauled its approach to orientation, putting less emphasis on policies and procedures, and more on emotion. *Traditions*, the two-day initial training session attended by all new cast members, is part inculcation, part encounter group. Guided by two unfailingly upbeat cast members, neatly dressed neophytes seated at round tables in a small classroom discuss their earliest memories of Disney, their visions of great service, their understanding of teamwork.

Next comes the movie, a panegyric to Walt Disney himself. The film depicts the founder as a creative risk taker who overcame setbacks (his first character, destined for obscurity, was named Oswald the Lucky Rabbit), believed in teamwork (he and his brother Roy were partners), and preached the importance of exceeding expectations of his guests. Yes, Walt actually embraced that concept, now being peddled as a new management mantra, way back in 1955. By encouraging . . . spurts of spontaneity . . . Disney World tries to instil verve in jobs that are otherwise tightly regimented. The 36-page cast members' appearance guide, for example, includes excruciatingly detailed ukases on length and style of hair, colour and quantity of cosmetics, and hues and textures of hosiery. . . . Disney World, where the average age of cast members is 37, loses only about 15% of its front line employees to attrition each year, compared with a rate of 60% for the hospitality industry as a whole. Wages are competitive . . . but don't underestimate the power of sentiment. Listen to Rick Anderson, 20, a host in Tomorrowland: 'Sometimes, you get hot in your costume, you get fed up dealing with angry guests who are tired of waiting in line. But then a kid asks you a question, you answer it, and she breaks into a smile. You can make someone happy.'

From Ronald Henkoff, 'Finding and keeping the best service workers', *Fortune*, 3 October 1994, pp. 52–8.

Ford culture

A Detroit-based human resources advisor described his socialization into the pre-1980s Ford culture. He reported that a partial list of the advice that he received from long-serving personnel went something like this:

- Don't disagree with the boss.
- Don't rock the boat.
- Look busy, even if you aren't.
- Don't smile, let alone laugh too much.
- Be obsessive about getting your numbers right; estimates won't do.
- If a colleague gets into trouble with the boss – don't help; be grateful it's not you.
- Observe the dress code.
- CYA (Cover your ass).

From Ken Starkey and Alan McKinlay, 'Managing for Ford', *Sociology*, vol. 28, no. 4, 1994, p. 979.

Perspectives on culture contrasted

The debate about organizational culture takes place between two camps. The managerial writers and consultants believe that there is a relationship between a strong culture and organizational performance. They hold that 'a well-developed and business-specific culture in which management and staff are thoroughly socialized ... can underpin stronger organizational commitment, higher morale, more efficient performance, and generally higher productivity' (Furnham and Gunter, 1993, p. 232). Ranged against them are mainly academic social scientists who believe that organizational culture is a term that is 'overused, over-inclusive but under-defined'. Although there are many debates taking place about organizational culture at many different levels, we have chosen to contrast the managerial perspective with the social science one. We do this so as to enable readers to assess for themselves the discussions of culture in both American and British management-oriented textbooks and management 'self-improvement' books, and compare these to the 'critical' contributions of mainly European academics.

The description of organizational culture described on the preceding pages is a managerial perspective. Its distinguishing feature is that it is both normative and prescriptive. As Needle (2000, p. 101) explained:

> It makes assumptions about employees that it does not explore and constitutes a set of beliefs and values that are deliberately created as part of a management strategy, and which are used to guide behaviour and processes within the organization.

This perspective is less concerned with explaining what the contemporary culture of any given organization actually is, accounting for its elements or assessing its significance. Instead, it takes a more pragmatic, even utopian approach, recommending what it should be, suggesting how it might be changed so as to encourage greater efficiency and even encouraging managers to act as if that preferred culture already existed (Bernick, 2001).

The social science perspective uses culture to explain differences between organizations. It attempts to counter the euphoric and uncritical adoption of the concept. Initially, social scientists sought to operationalize key concepts and conduct meaningful research. Later, they adopted a more critical perspective, questioning both its value and its very existence as a phenomenon. The managerial and social science debate about organizational culture can be considered under five headings:

Managerial		Social science
Culture *has*	v.	Culture *is*
Integration culture	v.	Differentiation culture
Consensual culture	v.	Fragmentation culture
Culture managed	v.	Culture tolerated
Symbolic leadership	v.	Management control

Culture 'has' versus culture 'is'

The *has* view holds that every organization possesses a culture, just as it has a strategy, structure, technology and employees. It is also called a *functionalist perspective*. It sees organizational culture constituting an objective reality of artefacts, values and meanings that academics can quantify and measure. The culture, being an attribute of the organization, is 'given' to its members when they join, and they do not participate in its formation. From this perspective, culture is acquired by employees, and is thus a variable and hence represents a lever for change which senior management can use (Smircich, 1983). The writers most associated with this view are the management academic and consultants mentioned earlier in the chapter (Ouchi, 1981; Deal and Kennedy, 1982; Pascale and Athos, 1982; Peters and Waterman, 1982; Schein, 1985).

The contrasting view presents organizational culture as something that the organization *is*. From this standpoint, culture constitutes a subjective reality of rites, rituals and meanings. It is also known as the *symbolic*, *social constructionist* or *shared cognitions perspective*. It thus rejects the notion that culture possesses any objective, independent existence which imposes itself on employees. Instead, it believes that culture cannot be easily quantified or measured, and that academics must study it holistically in the way that anthropologists study tribes. Culture is produced and reproduced continuously through the routine interactions between organization members. Hence organizational culture exists only in, and through, their social (inter)actions. It shapes both their actions and the outcome of the process of social creation and reproduction.

Culture as what an organization *does*

James Barker (1999) argued that neither the functionalist nor the symbolic perspectives on organization culture explained the fluid and dynamic processes used to create meaning in organizations. He offered a third perspective, presenting culture not as what an organization *has*, or *is*, but as what it *does*. Here culture represents a system for generating meanings in employees, shaping work activity, encouraging members to choose to act in ways that appear functional for the organization (senior management), as they negotiate everyday life at work. This viewpoint focuses not just upon meanings, but on the processes whereby these are constructed, reconstructed and deconstructed. For Barker, these 'organizing processes' are what culture does, and he offers the following illustration:

Joyce and Bob are on their coffee break when Joyce looks at her watch and exclaims, 'Oh my God, it's five past ten. Toni [her boss] will have a fit.' As she is saying this, she sets her cup down and runs back to the office with a wave to Bob, who says, 'See you later.'

In this example, both Joyce and Bob called on cultural knowledge to 'negotiate' their interaction. When Joyce noticed that she was late, several discourses of cultural knowledge were invoked. Within her's and Bob's interaction environment, Joyce was late from her coffee break; she had to get back because being late was 'wrong' in her particular company; and her boss would react negatively to her being late. These all represent aspects of cultural knowledge that are specific to Joyce and Bob's organization, and they influence the form and direction that their interactions take.

Based on James R. Barker, *The Discipline of Teamwork*, Sage Publications, London, 1999, p. 32.

Companies are sources of social relationships and meanings for their members. If these individuals all suddenly vanished, so would the culture. However, this view does not totally reject the influence of leaders, since they are themselves involved in interactions and thus contribute to culture-shaping. They see it as a way of understanding social relations within organizations, and reject the notion that culture may be managed or manipulated. It is useful to note the names of the researchers taking this position. They include Ackroyd and Cowley (1990), Anthony (1990), Gagliardi (1986), Harris and Ogbonna (1999), Knights and Willmott (1987), Krefting and Frost (1985), Legge (1994), Martin (1985, 1992), Meyerson and Martin (1987), Ogbonna (1993), Ray (1986), Weick (1979) and Willmott (1993).

DaimlerChrysler

Many commentators believe that differences of culture at Daimler and Chrysler made its merger more difficult. DaimlerChrysler believed that the two cultures could be combined relatively easily. Cultural issues seemed only to be addressed when executives made statements about differences in the companies. Either they did not realize the implications of cultural differences or they chose to focus on operational and business synergies, hoping that culture would sort itself out. During the initial stages, Chrysler president Thomas Stallkamp indicated that Daimler intended to adopt Chrysler's product development methods, which emphasized teamwork. Chrysler in turn would adopt Daimler's rigid adherence to timetables and its methodological approach to problem-solving. However, evidence of the lack of co-operation soon emerged – demonstrated by Daimler executives' refusal to use Chrysler parts in Mercedes vehicles.

As recently as August 2000, Daimler's chief of passenger cars, Jürgen Hubbert, was quoted in *The Economist*: 'We have a clear understanding: one company, one vision, one chairman, two cultures.' Although DaimlerChrysler may be one company in name, separate operational headquarters were maintained. Business operations continued to be separate. ... Each had its own agenda on different aspects of the market, making it difficult to discern a unified vision for the company. Finally, with the acknowledged existence of two cultures, how could DaimlerChrysler truly become one company with one vision? Dieter Zetsche, a trusted Daimler executive with extensive US experience, is now running Chrysler. His background may give the best opportunity yet to meld the cultures.

From Randall Sculler and Susan Jackson, 'HR issues and activities in mergers and acquisitions', *European Journal of Management*, vol. 19, no. 3, 2001, pp. 239–53; and Randall Sculler and Susan Jackson, 'Seeking an edge in mergers', *Financial Times*, 'Mastering People' supplement, 22 October 2001, pp. 6, 8 and 10.

Integration versus differentiation cultures

Integration (or unitary) perspective: a view which regards culture as monolithic, characterized by consistency, organization-wide consensus and clarity. It holds that these integrating features will lead to improved organization effectiveness through greater employee commitment and employee control, as measured by productivity and profitability.

Differentiation perspective: a view which regards an organization as consisting of sub-cultures. Each represents a fenced-in island of localized consensus, beyond which ambiguity reigns.

The managerial approach to culture takes an **integration or unitary perspective**. The controversial notion of a 'strong' culture is defined by three characteristics. These are the existence of a clear set of values, norms and beliefs; the sharing of these by the great majority of members; and the guidance of employees' behaviour. The focus is upon the consistencies and explores cultural consensus within organizations. It has dominated the managerial literature on organizational culture and forms the basis of consultancy prescriptions and management development.

This view holds that an organization possesses a single, unified culture and hence that it is possible to create a typology of different organizational cultures and assign companies to it on the basis of their cultural features. Adrian Furnham and Barrie Gunter (1993) listed four such typologies (table 19.1). They commented on their similarity and simplicity, added that there was little evidence to demonstrate their veracity and described them as 'interesting intuitions that might or might not be validated'.

In contrast, the social science approach views organizational culture as differentiated or pluralistic. Organizations are seen as consisting of diverse interests which have different objectives (for example, management v. labour; staff v. line; marketing v. production). The aim is to understand the lack of cultural consensus within organizations. Interest is centred upon the way in which organization reality is constructed and reconstructed. Thus, the **differentiation perspective** sees 'cultural pluralism' as a fundamental aspect of all organizations; seeks to understand the complexity and the interaction between frequently conflicting sub-cultures; and therefore stands in direct contrast to the managerial integration or unitary perspective.

Culture is seen as the product of group experience and will be found wherever there is a definable group with significant shared history, values and beliefs. Given the existence of many different groups, one can expect there to be many different sub-cultures within a single organization. Schein acknowledged the existence of a managerial culture, various occupation-based cultures within functional units and worker cultures based on shared hierarchical experiences. The social science perspective sees organizations as composed of interacting sub-cultures, divided both laterally (marketing, accounting) and vertically (shop-floor workers, supervisors, senior managers).

Occupational sub-cultures were also recognized as being based around work since different types of work require different sets of values. Alvin Gouldner (1957) distinguished two social identities which he labelled *cosmopolitans* and *locals*. Cosmopolitans had low loyalty to their employing organization, had a high commitment to their specialized role skills and were likely to use an extra-organization reference group. Locals, in contrast, were high on company loyalty, had low commitment to specialized role skills and were likely to use an in-company reference group. Charles Handy (1979) distinguished four function-based cultures, each of which possessed its own type of structure (role, task or power). He distinguished four different sets of activities which he labelled: steady state, innovative/developmental, breakdown and policy. Tony Watson (1994) suggested that official and unofficial cultures existed in parallel.

Stop and Criticize

You are an assistant bar manager in a fashionable city-centre establishment. In terms of your orientation to work, would you describe yourself as a local or a cosmopolitan? With regard to the bar staff you manage, would you like them to be cosmopolitan or local? If you were one of the bar staff, what would you be a cosmopolitan or a local?

Table 19.1: Alternative organization culture typologies

Authors	Deal and Kennedy (1982)	Schein (1985)	Graves (1986)	Harrison (1972) Handy (1979) Williams et al. (1989)
Contrast between	Amount of risk (high/low) v. Speed of feedback (slow/fast)	Individualistic v. Collectivistic	Bureaucratic–Anti-bureaucratic v. Managerial-Ego-driven	Formalization (high/low) v. Centralization (high/low)
Culture labels *Culture feature*	*Tough guy culture* ■ Risk-taking ■ Individualistic	*Power culture* ■ Entrepreneurial ■ Ability values	*Barbarian* ■ Ego-driven ■ Workaholic	*Power-oriented* ■ Competitive ■ Responsibility to person rather than expertise
	Work/play hard ■ Persistent ■ Sociable	*Achievement culture* ■ Personal ■ Intrinsic	*Presidential* ■ Democratic ■ Hierarchical	*People-oriented* ■ Consensual ■ Rejects management control
	Bet your company ■ Ponderous ■ Unpressurized	*Support culture* ■ Mutuality ■ Trust	*Monarchical* ■ Loyalty ■ Doggedness	*Task-oriented* ■ Competency ■ Dynamic
	Process culture ■ Bureaucratic ■ Protective	*Role culture* ■ Order ■ Dependable	*Pharoanic* ■ Ritualized ■ Changeless	*Role-oriented* ■ Legality ■ Legitimacy ■ Pure bureaucracy

From A. Furnham and B. Gunter, 'Corporate culture: definition, diagnosis and change', in C.L. Cooper and I.T. Robertson (eds), *International Review of Industrial and Organizational Psychology*, Volume 8, Chapter 7, 1993, p. 247. © John Wiley & Sons Limited. Reproduced with permission.

Consensual versus fragmentation cultures

The unitary, managerial view of culture emphasizes consensus. The possibility of conflict is acknowledged, but is attributed to failures in communication and is capable of being managed through change interventions. The assumption is that senior management's articulation of their organization's culture is identical to the actual culture. The focus is on what the culture should be (in management's view), rather than explaining what the culture actually is and assessing its significance. Most problematically, it encourages managers to act *as if* their preferred culture (with its attributes) already existed, leading them to believe that acting out their cultural myth will create their desired organizational reality. The different perspectives are contrasted in table 19.2.

The social science view, in contrast, views organizations as a collection of frequently opposed groupings (for example, management v. labour; staff v. line; production department v. marketing department) which are rarely reconciled. It thus assumes the inevitability of conflict and focuses on the variety of interests and opinions between different groups and upon power in organizations. It is therefore critical of managers and management consultants who underplay the differences that exist between individuals, groups and departments within a company. The **fragmentation (or conflict) perspective** sees organizations as being in constant flux with reality, constantly being constructed and reconstructed due to

Fragmentation (conflict) perspective of culture: a view which regards an organization as consisting of a loosely structured and incompletely shared system that emerges dynamically as cultural members experience each other, events and the organization's contextual features.

Table 19.2: Martin's contrasting perspectives on organizational culture

	Cultural perspective		
Features	Integration	Differentiation	Fragmentation
Orientation to consensus	Organization-wide consensus	Sub-cultural consensus	No consensus – multiplicity of views
Relations between different cultural elements	Consistent	Inconsistent	Complex
Orientation to ambiguity	Exclude it	Channel it outside sub-culture	Focus upon it

From *Cultures in Organizations: Three Perspectives*, by Joanne Martin, copyright 1992 by Oxford University Press, Inc. Used by permission of Oxford University Press, Inc.

human interactions and environmental changes. This view sees conflict rather than consensus as the norm within organizations; and it challenges the value of the concept of organizational culture itself. It offers no comfort for either managers or academics who seek clarity (Cohen et al., 1972; Becker, 1982).

Culture managed versus culture tolerated

Since the managerialist perspective sees culture as something that an organization *has*, it further assumes that it is capable of being created and modified by organizational founders and corporate leaders. This has sparked three debates. First, it promotes a discussion between 'weak' and 'strong' cultures, considering how managers can turn their company's culture from the former into the latter. Second, it has stimulated a related discussion concerning 'inefficient' and 'efficient' cultures, which assesses the ability of an organizational culture to innovate and to adjust rapidly and appropriately to changes in the strategic direction of the firm. Third, it assumes that leaders' visions make a distinctive contribution to cultures, and that they have a crucial role to play in 'culture management'.

> the unique and essential function of leadership is the manipulation of culture. (Schein, 1985, p. 317)

> changing organizational culture is an outcome of transformational leadership which impacts on followers' levels of effort and performance. (Bass, 1985a; Bass and Avolio, 1990)

This view assumes that senior company executives can and should exercise cultural leadership. Culture leadership is seen as having a *maintenance* and an *innovation* dimension (Trice and Beyer, 1984, 1993). Leaders may be required to maintain and reinforce the original culture established by a company's founder. Or, they may be required to modify (and hence innovate) that culture, if it has become a liability in changed environmental circumstances. Indeed, culture change has become a popular organizational change strategy.

In either case, their responsibility is to maintain a 'fit' between the organization's culture and its chosen strategy. This essentially involves leaders creating a culture that anticipates and responds to changes. Leaders either transmit the organization's culture (dispersing what is already there) or mould it (based on their own values), in both cases with a view to affect how members are to think about the organization and their roles within it. Culture management is achieved through human resource management policies, which use culture change programmes with organization development, and are complemented with a modified leadership style.

Symbolic leadership versus management control

Symbolic leadership (or the management of organizational culture) is one way of encouraging employees to feel that they are working for something worthwhile, so that they will work harder and be more productive. It treats managers as heroes, symbolizing the organization both internally to their employees and externally to customers, governments and others (Smircich and Morgan, 1982). These managers, said Carol Ray (1986, p. 362), 'possess direct ties to the values and goals of the dominant elites in order to activate the emotion and sentiment which may lead to devotion, loyalty and commitment to the company'. The idea of the manager as an inculcator of shared company values goes back to the 1930s, when Chester Barnard, one of the early classical theorists, wrote: 'the inculcation of belief in the real existence of a common purpose is an essential executive function . . . [the manager] is primarily an expert in the promotion and protection of values' (Barnard, 1938, pp. 28, 87–8). The managerialist view holds that employees can be helped to internalize organizational values.

The social science perspectives, in contrast, argues that symbolic leadership represents an attempt to internalize managerial control. People enter organizations with different motivations, experiences and values. These natural individual differences tend to direct their behaviours in numerous, often divergent directions. To accomplish its goal and present itself as a unified entity to outsiders, management has to find ways of controlling and reducing the variability of employee behaviour. One such way is through culture. Carol Ray (1986) distinguished different types of management control in history (figure 19.5).

She noted the move away from *bureaucratic control* towards *humanistic control*. The former focuses on the external, overt control of employees through rules, procedures, close supervision, appraisal and reward. Frederick Taylor, Henry Ford, Max Weber and Henri Fayol all recommended this rationalist approach to direct the behaviour of employees towards organizational goals. It was expensive in terms of the supervisory manpower required, it frequently caused resentment, and elicited grudging compliance from the workers. In contrast, humanistic control sought to satisfy employees' needs by providing a satisfying work task or a pleasant working group to promote internal control. Promoted by Mayo (1933, 1945), the hope was that individuals would willingly meet organization goals by meetings their individual ones (van Maanen and Barley, 1984).

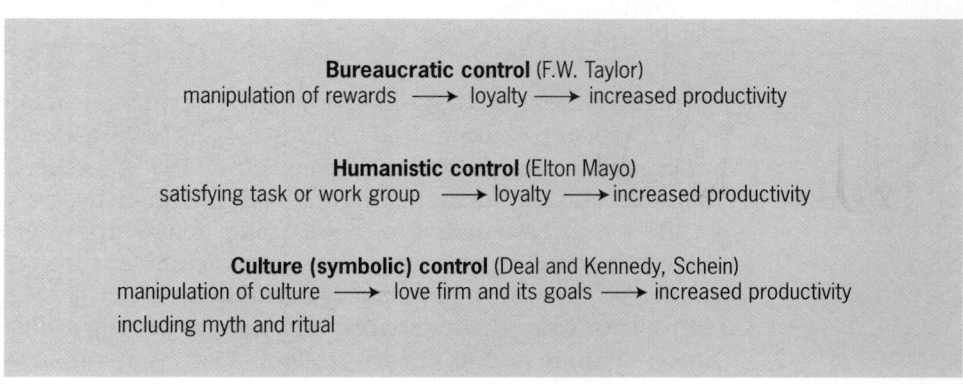

Bureaucratic control (F.W. Taylor)
manipulation of rewards ⟶ loyalty ⟶ increased productivity

Humanistic control (Elton Mayo)
satisfying task or work group ⟶ loyalty ⟶ increased productivity

Culture (symbolic) control (Deal and Kennedy, Schein)
manipulation of culture ⟶ love firm and its goals ⟶ increased productivity
including myth and ritual

Figure 19.5: Contrasting forms of organizational control
From Carol Axel Ray, 'Corporate culture: the last frontier of control?', *Journal of Management Studies*, vol. 23, no. 3, 1986, pp. 287–97. Reprinted by permission of Blackwell Publishing Ltd.

Ray suggested that managers saw the possibility of using organizational culture as an effective control tool. This control by company norms sought to change people's emotions or what they thought, believed and valued: 'control by corporate culture views people as emotional, symbol-loving and needing to belong to a superior entity or collectivity' (1986, p. 295). It was something that had previously only been attempted by religious organizations. A manager at a high-tech, US company summarized the approach: 'Power plays don't work. You can't make 'em do anything. They have to want to. So you have to work through the culture. The idea is to educate people without [their] knowing it. Have the religion and not know how they got it' (quoted in Kunda, 1992, p. 5)

The use of organizational culture involving the selective application of rites, ceremonials, myths, stories, symbols and legends by managers to direct the behaviour of employees is called *symbolic management*. This form of control appeals to managers as, potentially, it can be cheaper, avoids resentment and builds employee commitment to the company and its goals. This theme of 'internalized control' is at the heart of the work of Michel Foucault (1979), whose ideas will be considered in greater depth later. Critics like Willmott (1993) saw this as an attempt at 'colonizing the minds' or 'engineering the soul' (Rose, 1990) of organization members, to encourage them to internalize desired company values and norms. External control is replaced by self-control, such as that used by professionals such as doctors, teachers, lawyers and priests. Colin Hales (1993, p. 216) wrote:

> The power of organizational culture resides in the fact that it is not just another management 'technique' which can be applied at will, but is, rather, an influence upon behaviour which is not recognized as overt 'management'. The beliefs and values which shape employee behaviour are internalized, taken for granted and accepted as unobjectionable; therein lies their force. Culture can therefore exercise the most powerful and insidious form of control because it combines *de facto* compulsion with perceived freedom from coercion.

Source: © copyright United Feature Syndicate, Inc. Reproduced by permission.

Organizational culture, performance and change

Ogbonna and Harris (2002) summarize the research into the impact of culture on organizational performance from the early 1980s. They distinguish the 'trait writers' who proposed which cultural traits a firm needs in order to be successful (for example, 'closeness to the customer'). Attempts by companies to implement these findings met with limited success, and by the end of that decade academic studies were sceptical about the culture–performance link and critical of the traits approach itself. Thompson and McHugh (2002) reviewed this first generation of studies which made the dual claim that strong cultures not only exist but also are the reason for better or even excellent company performance. They pointed to the same, small number of US and UK companies being repeatedly cited (for example, IBM and Marks & Spencer). They noted the emphasis on anecdotal evidence and the use of a dubious research methodology which linked qualitative beliefs with the firm's economic performance, and attributed any superior results to strong cultures, without a reference to market or environmental variables. Much of what passes for evidence comes from interviews with managers who report how their efforts to create commitment met with a positive response from employees and produced a significant improvement in performance.

Referring to more recent studies into culture–performance links, Ogbonna and Harris (2002) comment that although some researchers still defend an association, they temper their claims with caveats. For example, they state that the linkage between the two is dependent upon a firm possessing certain cultural traits which are adaptable as well as strong. Contemporary views suggest that sustainable competitive advantage comes from an organization possessing competencies which are both superior to those of their competitors and cannot be copied. They say that if a firm's culture is to represent a source of competitive advantage, it must be rare, adaptable and non-imitable (Barney, 1986, 1991). Whatever the future research, it is unlikely that one will ever obtain a definitive answer. This is because the concept of culture is difficult to operationalize; the factors affecting company performance are many and varied, and isolating the contribution of culture is difficult if not impossible; it is in the interests of both management consultants and managers to maintain that 'culture makes a difference'.

How successful have culture change initiatives been in instilling corporate ideology into company employees? Thompson and Findlay (1999) observe that the answer to this question depends on what exactly is being changed, and there is confusion about this. They note two different views represented in the literature. The first sees culture as the creation of a vision or set of shared values to guide change; the second sees it as a set of practices or behaviours. Taking the first approach, some large companies have undertaken generalized change programmes under a 'changing culture' banner to give them legitimacy and direction. These have involved employees questioning their current beliefs, behaviours and values. Taking the second approach, other firms have introduced more specific initiatives, such as customer care programmes in the service sector, which have entailed providing workers with scripts which they speak in face-to-face or telephone interactions with customers.

After reviewing the empirical research evidence spanning the last decade, Thompson and Findlay reported that management were not yet able to 'govern the souls' of their employees. Staff responses to such cultural change initiatives included distancing behaviour, cynicism, deep acting and resigned behavioural compliance rather than internalization of values or attitudes. While Coopey's (1995) review found no attitudinal transformation, Hope and Hendry (1995) reported that change initiatives focusing on behaviour were more successful than those attempting to inculcate shared values. There is a danger that such culture change initiatives may result in unintended consequences, leading to a no-win situation for all concerned. This point is picked up by Ogbonna and Harris (2002) who report that many theorists now argue that while organizational culture can and *does* change, the direction and impact of the change cannot be subject to the conscious action of management.

As an attempt at social engineering in the contemporary workplace, how effective are culture change programmes likely to be? In terms of identifying with and learning to love your company and its superordinate goals, they are likely to be limited. Thompson and Findlay (1999) suggest three reasons for this. First, the majority of companies experience enough difficulties managing their operations successfully let alone managing their employees' 'hearts and minds'. Second, there is a high degree of employee awareness of management's motives in instituting these programmes, much of it translated into dissatisfaction and distrust. Third, since the 1990s, the supporting conditions within the workplace environment, which encourage long-term commitment, have been absent or are reducing. For managers, the increased monitoring and personal insecurity impacts on their assessment of the price of their continued loyalty. Professionals, like managers, have experienced increased pressures, reduced autonomy, and greater questioning of their status and expertise. They in turn have questioned their own commitment, taking a more instrumental or calculative approach. For both these groups, as well as for lower-level employees, the new business climate, characterized by delayering, downsizing and outsourcing, interspersed with revelations about corporate frauds which result in redundancies and pension losses, is hardly conducive to fostering a positive company spirit.

National cultures

Geert Hofstede
(b. 1928)

The controversy that surrounds the nature and impact of organizational culture on individual employee behaviour and company performance is to some extent echoed in the discussions of the effect of national (societal) cultures on organizational ones. National cultural stereotypes are well established: Scots are mean; Americans are brash; Germans are humourless; French are romantic; Japanese are inscrutable. However, researchers have studied how national cultures might affect organizational cultures in specific country settings. They have been interested to see how attempts to establish a common organizational culture in a multinational firm can be undermined by the strength of national cultures. Fombrun (1984) saw organizational culture being partly the outcome of societal factors, while Laurent (1989) argued that the cultures of countries were more powerful and stable than those of organizations.

Cultural sensitivity

Awareness and understanding of cultural differences are key skills for everybody in the organization. There are two reasons why they are often neglected. Many people believe that, underneath, everybody is fundamentally the same. This belief is reinforced by the impression that cultures are merging. The success of global companies such as Disney, Coca-Cola and others can convince us that the world is becoming more alike. Although convergence may exist, it is at a superficial level, and cultural differences remain. Pascal, the French philosopher, noted: 'There are truths on this side of the Pyrenees, which are falsehoods on the other.' Even that archetypal global brand McDonald's

➤

encounters cultural obstacles as it covers the world. When it opened in Japan, it found that Ronald McDonald's clown-line white face did not go down well. In Japan, white is associated with death and was an unlikely lure to persuade people to eat Big Macs. It also found that Japanese people had difficulty in pronouncing the 'R' in Ronald, so the character was transformed in Donald McDonald.

Based on Jean Vanhoegærden, 'Sense and sensitivity', *Directions: The Ashridge Journal*, Ashridge corporate web site, 1999–2000, August (http://www.ashridge.com/web/ashridge.nsf/articles)

Power–distance: the extent to which an unequal distribution of power is accepted by members of a society.

Uncertainty avoidance: the extent to which members of a society feel threatened by ambiguous situations and have created beliefs and institutions which try to avoid these.

Individualism–collectivism: the tendency to take care of oneself and one's family versus the tendency to work together for the collective good.

Masculinity–femininity: the extent to which highly assertive masculine values predominate (acquisition of money at the expense of others) versus showing sensitivity and concern for others' welfare and the quality of life.

At both levels of the cultural debate, the organizational and the national, one sees not only attempts to identify specific traits, but also attempts to classify organizations and countries into types. This creation of trait lists and typologies parallels work in personality discussed in chapter 5. In the 1980s, Geert Hofstede (1986, 1991, 2001) carried out a cross-cultural study of 116,000 employees of the same multinational company located in forty countries. Working later with Bond (Hofstede and Bond, 1988), Hofstede distinguished five dimensions of differences (predominant traits) between national cultures. These were labelled **power–distance**, **uncertainty avoidance**, **individualism–collectivism**, **masculinity– femininity** and **long-term–short-term orientation**. Like personality assessment, each of the dimensions represents a different continuum, so that each country can be rated from high to low and placed somewhere along each one, and not just at the ends.

Since 1993, Hofstede's pioneering work has been incorporated, updated and extended by the Global Leadership and Organizational Behaviour Effectiveness (GLOBE) research programme. This is a longitudinal study of leadership and organizational culture of 825 organizations located in 62 countries (Javidan and House, 2001). Whereas Hofstede's was a one-off, snapshot survey, GLOBE is a longitudinal study reporting changes over time. GLOBE contrasts national cultures on nine dimensions, which include, but also go beyond, those proposed by Hofstede.

GLOBE framework for assessing national cultures

Assertiveness: Encouraged to be tough, confrontational, competitive and assertive, as opposed to modest and tender.

Future orientation: Extent to which future-oriented behaviours such as planning, investing and delaying gratification are encouraged and rewarded.

Gender differentiation: Extent to which gender role differences are maximized by society.

Uncertainty avoidance: Extent to which society relies on social norms and procedures to alleviate the unpredictability of future events.

Power–distance: Degree to which members of society expect power to be equally shared.

Individualism–collectivism: Degree to which individuals are encouraged by societal institutions to be integrated into groups.

In-group collectivism: Extent to which society members value their membership of small groups (family, friends and employing organizations).

Performance orientation: Degree to which society encourages and rewards its members for performance improvement and excellence.

Humane orientation: Degree to which society encourages and rewards its members to be fair, altruistic, generous, caring and kind to others.

Table 19.3 lists the three highest- and lowest-ranking countries on each of GLOBE's nine dimensions, as well as those located in the middle.

Stop and Criticize

Are interpersonal skills, motivation, group behaviour, leadership style, conflict management, structure, predominant leadership style, training and HRM practices all culturally relative?

Table 19.3: GLOBE country rankings

Dimension	Countries scoring high	Countries scoring medium	Countries scoring low
Assertiveness	Spain, USA, Greece	Egypt, Ireland, Philippines	Sweden, New Zealand, Switzerland
Future orientation	Denmark, Canada, Netherlands	Slovenia, Egypt, Ireland	Russia, Argentina, Poland
Gender differentiation	South Korea, Egypt, Morocco	Italy, Brazil, Argentina	Sweden, Denmark, Slovenia
Uncertainty avoidance	Austria, Denmark, Germany	Israel, USA, Mexico	Russia, Hungary, Bolivia
Power–distance	Russia, Spain, Thailand	England, France, Brazil	Denmark, Netherlands, South Africa
Individualism–collectivism*	Greece, Hungary, Germany	Hong Kong, USA, Egypt	Denmark, Singapore, Japan
In-group collectivism	Egypt, China, Morocco	Japan, Israel, Qatar	Denmark, Sweden, New Zealand
Performance orientation	USA, Taiwan, New Zealand	Sweden, Israel, Spain	Russia, Argentina, Greece
Humane orientation	Indonesia, Egypt, Malaysia	Hong Kong, Sweden, Taiwan	Germany, Spain, France

* A low score indicates collectivism.

Another attempt to highlight differences between national cultures focuses on countries' values, and attempts to clarify how different countries view the world. This can affect how their citizens view each other within the workplace. The World Values Survey, run by the University of Michigan, addresses the question of whether shared values are more important that contested values. The university has been polling for the past twenty-five years and now covers 78 countries containing 78 per cent of the world's population. It arranges its replies along two value dimensions: *traditional–secular-rational* and *self-expression–survival* (University of Michigan, 2003).

In the first of these dimensions, *traditional values* are defined as those of religion, family and country. Traditionalists hold that religion is important in their lives; have a strong sense of national pride; think children should be taught to obey; and think the first duty of a child is to make their parents proud. They do not feel that abortion, euthanasia, divorce or suicide are ever justified. At the other end of the spectrum are secular-rational values which emphasis the opposite qualities. The traditional and sector-rational values are located on the vertical axis in figure 19.6. The second dimension considers 'quality of life' attributes. At one extreme are the values that people hold when the struggle for survival is a priority for them. They say that economic and physical security are more important than self-expression. People who cannot fulfil their basic needs dislike foreigners, homosexuals and those with AIDS. They are wary of any form of political activity (even signing a petition) and think men make better political leaders than women. *Self-expression values* are the opposite. The *self-expression–survival* values are located along the horizontal axis in figure 19.6. This schema is underpinned by the notion that industrialization turns traditional societies into secular-rational ones, while post-industrial development brings about a shift towards values of self-expression.

As one would expect, poor countries with low self-expression and high levels of traditionalism appear at the bottom left of the figure, while the richer European ones appear in the top right corner. What is perhaps the most unusual finding is the location of America. On the horizontal axis, it resembles Western European countries, being more self-expressive than Catholic France or Italy and a little less than Protestant Sweden or the Netherlands. It therefore shares with Western Europe the common values of democracy and freedom. However, on the vertical axis, the United States is far more traditional than any Central or East European country. It is thus a strange mixture of tradition and self-expression. America is the most patriotic country in the survey (alongside India and Turkey). Since religious attitudes are seen as the most important, single component of traditionalism, Americans are closer to Nigerians and Turks than to Germans or Swedes in this respect. Since the first survey in 1981, all Western countries, including America, have shifted towards greater self-expression. However, in that period, America seems to be becoming more traditional, not less. On average, therefore, the values gap between the United States and European countries seems to be widening (*The Economist*, 2003).

The World Values Survey contributes to the debate as to whether organizations around the world are becoming more similar or whether they are maintaining their cultural differences. Having reviewed cross-cultural studies, John Child (1981) found two equally reputable groups of scholars, each promoting opposite positions. Further investigations revealed that those research findings supporting the convergence thesis focused on macro-level issues such as organization structure and technology. Those arguing for the divergence view addressed micro-level issues, particularly the behaviour of people in organizations. It appears that while organizations around the world are becoming more similar, the behaviour of the people within them remains culturally unique.

What about the related question of whether organizational culture erases or diminishes the influence of national culture? Research by Lubatkin et al. (1998)

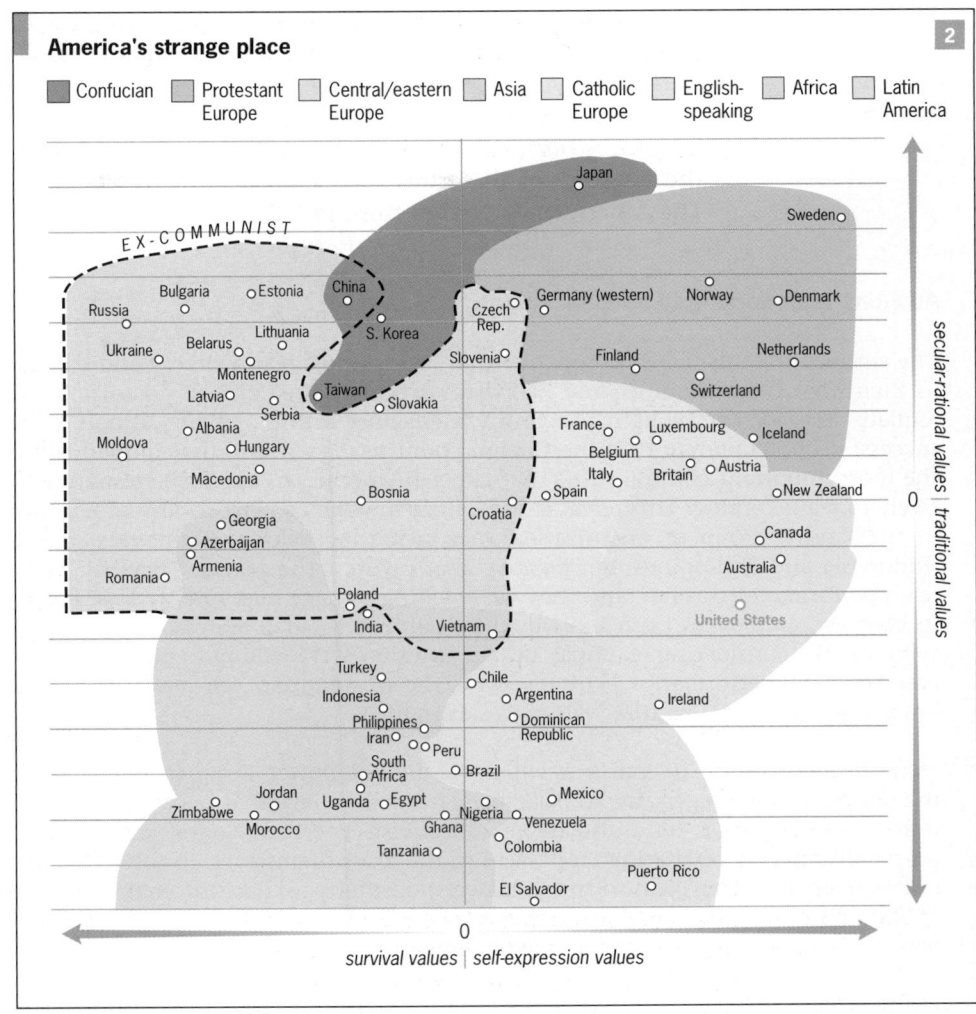

Figure 19.6: America's strange place
From *World Values Survey*, University of Michigan, reproduced in 'Living with a superpower', *The Economist*, 4 January 2003, p. 21. © The Economist Newspaper Limited, London, 4.1.03.

suggests that both company managers and employees bring their cultural background and ethnicity into the workplace. In Hofstede's study, national culture explained more of the differences than did role, age, gender or race (Hofstede, 2001). Laurent (1983) also found more pronounced cultural differences among employees from around the world working within the same multinational company than among those working for companies in their native lands. The company's culture did not replace or eliminate national differences. Nancy Adler (2002) suggested that pressure to conform to the culture of a foreign-owned company brought out employees' resistance, causing them to cling on more strongly to their own national identities. By adulthood, she claimed, national culture may be so ingrained that a company's organizational culture cannot erase it. Catherine Tinsley (1998) found that different cultures had different ways of resolving conflicts, which was a problem if multinational teams worked together. Her studies of three nationalities distinguished the following:

Status model: Assumes that, in a situation of conflict, one should defer to status power within the group. This gives the person with the highest status within the group power to create and enforce solutions for the others, and these will be accepted and respected. The Japanese preferred this model.

Apply regulations: This method emphasized referring back to pre-existing, independent regulations, rules and policies to shape the resolution of conflict. The Germans favoured this model.

Integrating interests: This style of conflict resolution involves bringing together the concerns of all parties so as to create an outcome favoured by all members. The Americans preferred this model.

Adapting teamworking to national culture

The authors investigated US companies that had adopted teamworking and self-managed work teams in their home organizations, and had then 'exported' this form of organizational structure to their affiliates abroad. They sought to identify the factors within a given cultural context which affected successful implementation in the foreign country. They found that individualism–collectivism was the most important cultural value that affected whether an employee responded positively or negatively to teamworking. This refers to the extent to which a person values their own welfare over that of the family, group or organization to which they belong. Employees in collectivist countries (Indonesia and Philippines) felt positive about working in teams. They believed that pay based on team performance was fair, and they were willing to have over one-third of their pay based upon it. In contrast, employees from individualist countries (United States, Finland and Belgium) were less sympathetic, considering team pay unfair, and they were willing to have only 10–25 per cent of pay based on team performance. With respect to the acceptance of self-managed work teams (SMWT), the impact of three other cultural values was examined.

Power–distance. People in countries which are high on power–distance tend to behave submissively in the presence of managers, avoid disagreements and believe that bypassing their boss is insubordination. Those countries tend also to be collectivist. The behavioural self-management requires low power–distance, necessitating employees to think for themselves, to solve their own problems without management intervention and to take responsibility for decision-making. There is less acceptance of SMWT among people high in power–distance, and also a reluctance to confront fellow team members, with a need to 'save face' and avoid embarrassment.

Doing–being orientation: Doing is defined as the extent to which employees value work activities over non-work activities. In contrast, those with a being-orientation prefer spending time outside work with their families. When the former are given a pay rise they will work harder. When the latter receive one, they work less because they can earn the same amount of money in less time and devote the extra time to being with family and friends. Since working in SWMT requires workers to accept greater responsibility, which translates to more work and thus to more time on the job, those who were more accepting of SMWT were more 'doing-oriented'.

Determinism–free will orientation: Determinism is the extent to which employees believe their outcomes or success are due to forces they cannot control. In contrast, free will-oriented employees believe that it is their own actions, taken in their environment, which determine outcomes in work and personal life. As a cultural value it has similarities with the concept of locus of control. Self-management relies on free will as it involves self-set goals and adjustments made to one's own behaviour. Free will-oriented employees accepted the self-management aspects of SMWT.

Considering all these dimensions, the authors concluded that France represented the most challenging country in which to implement SMWTs because it was both highly individualistic and high in power–distance. Costa Rica, on the other hand, with its highly collectivism and low power–distance, may represent the easiest. Employees in countries falling into the collectivistic–deterministic category (China, Singapore) would be receptive to teamworking but less to SMWT, while those in the individualistic–free will category (Australia, the Netherlands, Ireland) will be more receptive to self-management but less accepting of teamwork.

Based on Bradley I. Kirkman, Christina B. Gibson and Debra L. Shapiro, 'Exporting teams: enhancing the implementation and effectiveness of work teams in global affiliates', *Organizational Dynamics*, vol. 30, no. 1, 2001, pp. 12–29.

Recap

1. *Account for the popularity of organizational culture among managers, consultants and academics.*

   - For managers, the concept offered the route to economic success to match that enjoyed by Japanese organizations of the time.

   - For consultants, the concept provided an appealing, easy-to-grasp, quick-fix solution to sell to managers wishing to improve their organization's performance.

   - For academics, it offered an alternative perspective with which to research and theorize about organizations and provided a new context within which to explore postmodernist ideas.

2. *List, describe and exemplify Schein's three levels of culture.*

   - Schein distinguished surface manifestations of culture at level one (e.g. artefacts, rites, ceremonials); organizational values at level two (e.g. customer obsession); and basic assumptions at level three, which actually was the culture (e.g. nature of reality and truth).

3. *List the stages of organizational socialization.*

   - The stages of organizational socialization are pre-arrival, encounter and metamorphosis.

4. *Contrast managerial and social science perspectives on organizational culture.*

   - Is organizational culture something that a company has, or is it what a company is?

   - Is an organizational culture a single, integrated entity, or is it differentiated, consisting of multiple, different sub-cultures?

   - Is there a consensus among organization members as to the company values, or do different groups possess their own?

   - Can an organization's culture be managed by its leaders, or is it beyond their direct control and does it instead have to be tolerated by them?

   - Does culture signal a new era of symbolic leadership which relies on internalized forms of employee direction, or is it old-style management control under a new guise?

5. *Assess the link between organizational culture and economic performance.*

   - Few research studies have been conducted which explicitly test a causal link between an organization's culture and its economic performance.

   - Those that have been conducted do not illustrate any direct causal relationship between a 'strong' culture and high economic performance, suggesting, at a minimum, that other, more intermediate variables are more significant.

   - There are anecdotal data as well as a logical argument to suggest that organizations possessing a strong culture at a time of required change may be less flexible, less able to change, and hence less likely to perform well economically.

6. *Distinguish different national culture dimensions.*

   - Hofstede suggested that national culture could be differentiated along four (later five) dimensions: power–distance; uncertainty avoidance; individualism–collectivism; masculinity–femininity; (and later) short-term–long-term perspective.

   - The GLOBE framework for assessing national culture incorporates and extends Hofstede's dimensions and includes: assertiveness; future orientation; gender differentiation; uncertainty avoidance; power–distance; individualism–collectivism; in-group collectivism; performance orientation; and humane orientation.

Revision

1. 'A strong organizational culture which can be used as a tool of management control helps to motivate staff, improves company performance, and should therefore be encouraged.' Discuss.

2. 'As a way of understanding the behaviour of people in organizations, the concept of organizational culture is more of a hindrance than a help.' Discuss.

3. What guidance does the theory and research into national culture offer managers working around the world for global, multinational corporations?

4. 'Managers and academics have totally different approaches to, and interests in, the concept of organizational culture.' Discuss.

5. To what extent, and in what ways, might a national culture affect an organization's culture?

Springboard

Alvesson, M., 2001, *Understanding Organizational Culture*, Sage Publications, London.

Explores alternative perspectives on culture, and relates them to leadership and change.

Daisey, M., 2002, *Twenty-one Dog Years: Doing Time at Amazon.com*, Fourth Estate, London.

A bottom-up view of this dot.com retailer's organizational culture by an insider.

Gannon, M.J. and Newman, K.L. (eds), 2001, *The Blackwell Handbook of Cross-cultural Management*, Blackwell, Oxford.

Considers the influence of national cultures on managerial and employee behaviour, as well as on strategy, structure and interorganizational relationships; human resources, motivation, rewards and leadership; interpersonal processes and organizational culture.

Hawkins, P., 1997, 'Organizational culture: sailing between evangelism and complexity', *Human Relations*, vol. 50, no. 4, pp. 417–40.

Provides a review of the general literature on organizational behaviour.

Hickson, D.J. and Pugh, D.S., 2002, *Management Worldwide: The Impact of Societal Culture on Organizations Around the Globe*, Penguin, Harmondsworth (second edition).

Builds on Hofstede's work on the impact of different societal cultures on organizational behaviour.

Linstead, S., 1999, 'Managing culture', in L. Fulop and S. Linstead (eds), *Management: A Critical Text*, Macmillan, London, pp. 82–121.

Provides a critical assessment of the concept of organizational culture pitched at an introductory level and offers a comprehensive bibliography.

Martin, J., 2001, *Organizational Culture: Mapping the Terrain*, Sage Publications, London.

Provides an updated, interdisciplinary overview showing how and why researchers have disagreed on fundamental aspects of this concept.

Needle, D., 2000, 'Culture at the level of the firm: organizational and corporate perspectives', in J. Barry, J. Chandler, H. Clark, R. Johnston and D. Needle (eds), *Organization and Management: A Critical Text*, Business Press Thompson Learning, London, pp. 101–18.

An introductory, critical consideration of the organizational culture concept.

Ogbonna E. and Harris, L.C., 2002, 'Organizational culture: a ten-year, two-phase study of change in the UK food retailing sector', *Journal of Management Studies*, vol. 39, no. 5, pp. 673–706.

Reviews past studies of organizational culture change literature, and the theoretical and practical justifications for interest in the topic, and summarizes perspectives on the feasibility of culture management.

Parker, M., 2000a, *Organizational Culture and Identity*, Sage Publications, London.

Considers organizational culture from the critical symbolism perspective, focusing on how organizations shape their members' identities, and asks whether it is right for them to do so.

Schultz, M., 1995, *On Studying Organizational Cultures: Diagnosis and Understanding*, De Gruyter, Berlin.

Considers how the theoretical concepts of organizational culture can be applied to an analysis of organizations. Evaluates different frameworks for an understanding of culture, so as to discover the strengths and weaknesses of each.

Thompson, P. and Findlay, P., 1999, 'Changing the people: social engineering in the contemporary workplace', in L. Ray and A. Sayer (eds), *Culture and Economy after the Cultural Turn*, Sage Publications, London, pp. 162–88.

A critical, historical review of organizational culture within change management programmes.

Thompson, P. and McHugh, D., 2002, *Work Organizations*, Palgrave, Basingstoke (third edition).

Chapter 13, 'Corporations and culture: reinventing organization man?', pp. 191–209, provides an extensive critique of the organizational culture literature.

Home viewing

Gung Ho (1986, director Ron Howard) concerns the conflict of national cultures. A Japanese car manufacturer, Assan Motors, acquires an American motor car company. When the Japanese management team take over, confrontations, conflicts and adjustments ensue. Hunt Stevenson (played by Michael Keaton), a working-class hero, is intent on salvaging Hadleyville, the struggling Rust Belt town where he lives. After acting as an emissary to bring the Japanese to the town, he is co-opted by the new management to be their spokesperson to the workers. The film uses a tongue-in-cheek approach to raise questions of perception and conflict. It uses outrageous stereotypes of both Japanese and American cultures, which it links to considerations of organizational culture. Identify the key stereotypical elements that are presented. Consider how these can lead to similarities being overlooked and racial bias displayed. In several places, the film strays seriously from reality. Can you find these? Finally, it considers individualistic versus group approaches to task performance, and raises issues of leadership style, ethics and discipline.

OB in literature

Mike Daisey, *Twenty-one Dog Years: Doing Time @ Amazon.com*, Fourth Estate, London, 2002.

This highly amusing autobiography concerns Daisey's application to, recruitment by, and short period working in Amazon.com in Seattle. It describes the sequences of organizational socialization and highlights many aspects of this organization's culture, and how it affects him and the other company employees.

Chapter exercises

1: Learning the ropes

Objectives 1. To highlight the process of organizational socialization.

Briefing Think of an organization that you recently joined, or one that you remember joining. This may be a new employer, a church, sports club, or even your university. In the space below, write down an example of a surface manifestation of culture from this organization. What purpose does it serve for the organization?

Cultural surface manifestation	Example	Organizational purpose?
Artefact		
Ceremonial		
Course		
Folktale		
Gesture		
Joke		
Hero		
Language		
Legend		
Motto		

Cultural surface manifestation	Example	Organizational purpose?
Myth		
Norm		
Physical layout		
Rite		
Ritual		
Saga		
Slogan		
Story		
Symbol		

2: Metaphors for culture

Objectives 1. To contrast students' metaphors for national culture.

2. To assess how these help to identify cultural problems and suggest solutions.

Briefing A metaphor says that one thing is something else: 'an eye is a camera' or 'the brain is a computer'. Metaphors can be used as diagnostic tools to help understand organizational problems and offer possible solutions. This two-part exercise does this.

1. Students in the class, individually, complete the sentence 'Culture is . . .'. They then make notes explaining why they chose that particular metaphor.

2. They form into groups of three to five people.

3. Within the groups, they explain their chosen metaphor to the other members. Group members then consider the implications of the selected metaphor for the following: how people learn and motivate themselves, factors affecting relationships between individuals, leadership styles, how groups work and other aspects.

4. Once all group members have had the opportunity to explain and discuss their own metaphor, members read the following case study and, selecting each metaphor in turn, assess how it helps to identify the problem and offer a solution.

In 1993, IBM established a joint venture research team to develop a revolutionary new chip design for the next century. The other companies in the group were Siemens AG of Germany and Toshiba Corporation of Japan. Engineers from all three companies were set up in Long Island at one of IBM's research affiliates. The project was expected to last several years. People who were initially worried that the more than 100 scientists from the three countries would have difficulties working together proved to be correct. Problems began almost immediately. Individuals wanted to associate only with fellow country members, thus jeopardizing the project's success. An observer noted that the Japanese disliked the office set-up, which consisted of many small offices and few open spaces, and they had difficulty conversing in English. The Germans covered the glass walls of their offices to maintain privacy, thus offending both the Japanese and Americans. The Japanese liked to go out drinking after work, during which time they tended to develop strong group norms. The Americans, however, preferred to go home to their families. Furthermore, the Americans complained that the Germans planned too much and that the Japanese would not make decisions.

From Martin J. Gannon, 2001, *Working across Cultures: Applications and Exercises*, Sage Publications, London, pp. 11, 108–11.

Human resource management

Key concepts

employment cycle

personnel management

human resource management

psychological contract

hard HRM

soft HRM

Learning outcomes

When you have read this chapter, you should be able to define those key concepts in your own words, and you should also be able to:

1. Explain why most medium-sized and large organizations have specialized personnel or human resource management functions.

2. Understand the distinction between personnel management and human resource management.

3. Explain the distinctions between different models of human resource management.

4. Explain the strategic contribution which the human resource function potentially makes to organizational effectiveness.

5. Identify the main criticisms levelled against human resource management as a concept and as a management function.

Why study human resource management?

Human resource management has a direct personal impact on us as employees, in shaping, for example, the nature of our work, our pay and our career prospects. The reputation that an organization develops, as a 'good employer', helps to attract and to retain quality employees. The 'people management' activities of an organization are usually handled by a specialized function. However, two labels are now in use: *personnel management* and *human resource management*. Is there a distinction, or are these simply different labels for the same thing?

Some commentators argue that human resource management is just a grander term for a mundane function, representing 'old wine in new bottles'. Others argue that human resource management reflects a fundamental shift in employment relations, made necessary by changes in the organizational environment. In this second view, personnel and human resource management are quite distinct in perspective and in practice. Many organizations claim that 'employees are our most important asset'. Human resource management appears to represent a distinctive approach to managing that asset.

The debate about the distinction between personnel and human resource management is conceptually complex. It also has profound practical implications for the way in which the function, whatever it is called, is organized and operates. We will explore the terms and implications of this debate later in the chapter. First, we will use the term 'personnel management', explaining the nature and background of the function, while reserving the term 'human resource management' for subsequent sections.

"The new approach is still about people, it's just that before
we were for them and now we're against them."

Source: © 2002 P.C. Vey, originally appeared in *Harvard Business Review*. Used by permission.

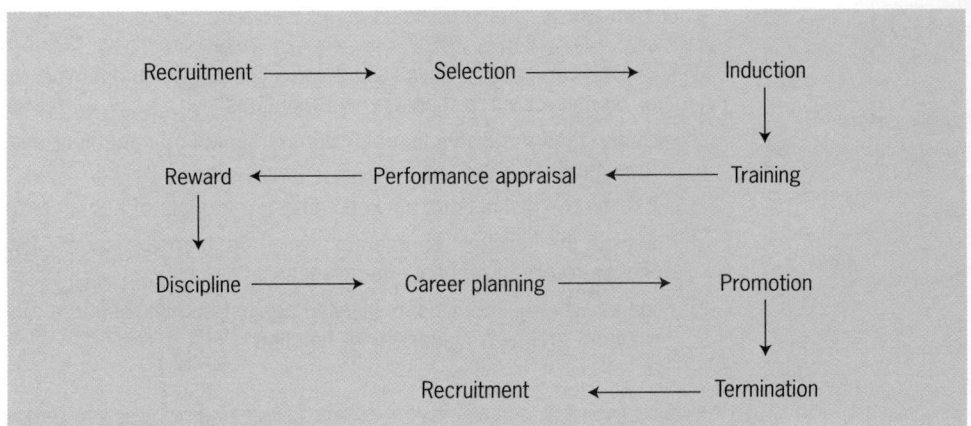

Figure 20.1: The employment cycle

Employment cycle: the sequence of stages through which all employees pass in each working position they hold, from recruitment and selection to termination.

Personnel management: the specialist management function which determines and implements policies and procedures which affect the stages of the employment cycle.

You cannot escape from the personnel management function. Figure 20.1 identifies the main stages of the **employment cycle**. Whatever the job, occupation or profession you are engaged in, you will encounter all or most of these steps at some point in your working life.

The stages of the employment cycle define the activities of the personnel function. All organizations need to recruit, train, reward and motivate employees. It follows that all organizations have a personnel function responsible for the employment cycle. However, the way in which personnel policies are determined and applied varies from one organization to another, and between different countries. In small organizations, without specialist personnel departments, line managers deal with people issues as they arise. Even in large organizations, line managers perform personnel functions, typically with the support of a central department.

Personnel policies need to be framed in a manner that contributes both to the well-being and quality of working life of employees and to organizational effectiveness. The definition of **personnel management** here omits a range of other areas in which the function is involved. These include employee communication, collective bargaining, organizational change, health and safety, and a range of employee welfare services. The employment contract is increasingly shaped by legal constraints. From a management viewpoint, a wrong decision, a failure to act, or the insensitive handling of a situation, can lead to expensive litigation, damaging the organization's reputation and the careers of the managers concerned. Employment law is a specialist subject beyond the scope of this text. However, the manager needs to know enough about employment law to recognize when to seek specialist legal advice.

Stop and Criticize

Why should organizations incur the staff and overhead costs of maintaining a specialist personnel department when line managers can do most of this work themselves?

Some commentators argue that the personnel function should be devolved to line managers, saving the salary and office costs. The function's contribution, however, can be central. Technology, a product design or a service profile can be copied. However, the ways in which employees are managed are difficult to copy, and personnel policy can thus be a source of sustained competitive advantage. Personnel management is also fundamental to the quality and cost-effectiveness of public services. Most public services are labour-intensive. For example, payroll represents around 80 per cent of the annual cost of running a hospital.

What is the link between personnel management and organizational behaviour? Personnel management can be seen as 'organizational behaviour in practice'. An

Table 20.1: Personnel management and organizational behaviour

Personnel functions	Issues and activities	OB topics
recruitment, selection, induction	getting the right employees into the right jobs; recruiting from an increasingly diverse population; sensitivity to employment of women, ethnic minorities, the disabled, the elderly	environmental turbulence; personality assessment; communication; person perception; learning; new organizational forms
training and development	tension between individual and organizational responsibility; development as a recruitment and retention tool; coping with new technology	technology and job design; new organizational forms; learning; the learning organization; motivation; organizational change
performance appraisal and reward	annual appraisal; pay policy; fringe benefits; need to attract and retain staff; impact of teamwork on individual pay	motivation; expectancy theory; equity theory; group influence on individual behaviour; teamworking
managing conduct and discipline	sexual harassment, racial abuse, drug abuse, alcohol abuse, health and safety; monitoring misconduct; using surveillance; formulation and communication of policies	surveillance technology; learning; socialization; behaviour modification; organizational culture; managing conflict; management style
participation and commitment	involvement in decisions increases commitment; design of communications and participation mechanisms; managing organizational culture; tap ideas, release talent, encourage loyalty	communication; motivation; organization structure; organization culture; new forms of flexible organization; organizational change; leadership style
organization development and change	the personnel/human resource management role in facilitating development and change; flexible working practices	organization development and change; motivation and job design; leadership style

appreciation of organizational behaviour is important if you want to become a personnel practitioner. However, while the two subjects are clearly related, their agendas are different. Organizational behaviour is concerned with understanding a range of related micro- and macro-organizational phenomena, at individual, group, organizational and contextual levels of analysis. Personnel management has a more focused concern with theories and techniques which can develop the contribution of the personnel function to organizational effectiveness.

It is, however, possible to map organizational behaviour topics against personnel management functions, as table 20.1 illustrates.

Personnel: traditional rationale and image

Personnel management in Britain has its roots in the industrialization of the latter half of the nineteenth century, when welfare workers were employed to meet the concerns of paternalistic employers for their workers. Factories concentrated large numbers of workers in a relatively small number of workplaces, and poor conditions were visible to large numbers of people. Previously, workers had been dispersed, working mostly in their homes.

The term 'personnel management' came into use during the Second World War. The British Institute of Personnel Management (IPM) produced the first agreed definition of the function in 1945 (Crichton, 1968, p. 26). This definition is worth considering in full, as a benchmark against which recent debates about the role of human resource management can be assessed:

> Personnel management is that part of the management function which is concerned with human relationships within an organization. Its objective is the maintenance of those relationships on a basis which, by consideration of the well-being of the individual, enables all those engaged in the undertaking to make their maximum potential contribution to the effective working of that undertaking.
>
> In particular, personnel management is concerned with:
>
> Methods of recruitment, selection, training and education, and with the proper employment of personnel; terms of employment, methods and standards of remuneration, working conditions, amenities and employee services.
>
> The maintenance and effective use of facilities for joint consultation between employers and employees and between their representatives and of recognized procedures for the settlement of disputes.

As we shall see later, this definition from 1945 appears to capture many of the 'distinctive' features of the 'new' human resource management perspective of the 1990s.

Pressures for a specialized personnel function

■ Recruitment, selection, job grading and employee record-keeping become critical with the growth in organizational size and complexity, and with increased task specialization among all employees, including management.

■ The availability of advice and guidance on personnel issues become critical with state intervention in the form of employment law and regulations affecting, for example, working conditions, health and safety, discrimination, trade union rights and obligations, and management rights to discipline employees and to terminate employment contracts.

- Employee motivation and commitment become critical as the competitive climate intensifies the need for cost-effectiveness, for increased productivity, and for improved product quality and quality of customer service.

- Negotiation and communication skills become critical with the development of industrial relations systems involving trade union recognition and collective bargaining.

- The public image of the personnel function, and the reputation of individual practitioners, is reinforced by the development of a professional body.

Based on Sarah Vickerstaff (ed.), *Human Resource Management in Europe: Text and Cases*, Chapman and Hall, London, 1992.

The IPM revised its definition in 1963, emphasizing the role of teams, noting that general management as well as specialists had personnel duties, and recognizing the function's role in dealing with organizational and economic change. However, personnel specialists in most organizations did not hold director posts, and were rarely members of the senior management team. Tony Watson (1977) argued that the personnel role was an ambiguous one, lacking in credibility. Karen Legge (1978) argued that personnel managers lacked the power and influence to implement their initiatives, and advocated the use of a range of strategies, including 'deviant innovation' to strengthen the function.

Why is this historical background significant today? There are three reasons:

1. **The administrative image survives**: Personnel management has not fully shed the traditional image of a mundane administrative function. Clint Eastwood as Dirty Harry in the film *The Enforcer* (1976) complains that 'personnel is for assholes'. Wickham Skinner (1981) describes personnel managers with the unkind phrase 'big hat, no cattle'.

2. **We need to assess claims about novelty**: Human resource management tends to be defined in terms of how it differs from personnel management, and not just in its own terms. It is therefore hard to assess claims as to what is distinctive about the 'new' human resource management perspective without an understanding of the way in which the personnel function has performed and developed previously.

3. **The function still seeks recognition**: A persistent theme in the history of the function is the pursuit of power, influence and professional status (Kamoche, 1994). This aspiration fuelled the human resource debate in the 1990s and triggered research to 'prove' the contribution of the function to organizational effectiveness. Accountants can quantify *their* contribution to cost reduction and profits. All large companies have a finance director, but only 30 per cent have a human resources director (Purcell, 1995). In Britain, this aspiration culminated in July 2000 with the award of a Royal Charter to what is now the Chartered Institute for Personnel and Development, granting its members a status equivalent to that held by chartered accountants and engineers.

The four distinctive factors which the personnel management function thus brings into the present from its history are:

- **The welfare factor**: It is rooted in a welfare tradition which was associated with industrial betterment at the turn of the twentieth century. Personnel management is the 'corporate conscience', representing the interest of workers to management.

- **The status factor:** The profession spent the twentieth century in pursuit of a clear identity. Personnel management has also sought credibility and status as a function based on its specialist knowledge and expertise.

- **The finance factor:** The boards of large organizations tend to be dominated by the finance and accounting function, which pushes 'soft' personnel voices aside and which traditionally focuses on short-term organizational performance measures, relating to share price movements which directly influence top management rewards and careers.

- **The Cinderella factor:** The profession retains the stereotype of a support function out of touch with commercial imperatives. It thus has 'Cinderella' status, with relatively low status and credibility, represented at board level in only a minority of organizations, and called upon to resolve the messy people problems left behind by other functions.

One estimate suggests that three-quarters of large organizations do not have a human resource director on their main board, and that only 25 per cent of other board members are aware of research findings that link HR practices to profitability (Higginbottom, 2002). The pursuit of status and identity is clouded by at least three paradoxes surrounding the work of the function. First, how can the role of 'employee voice' be combined with management functions of controlling employee behaviour and performance? Second, how can a specialist role be maintained when it is acknowledged that general and line management also have personnel management responsibilities? Third, the claim to be a repository of expertise concerning the employment relationship is undermined by the dilution of the function with many other weakly-related responsibilities. These paradoxes are summarized in table 20.2.

Table 20.2: Personnel management paradoxes

On the one hand	On the other hand
the personnel function is the voice of the employee, championing the employee cause with respect to working conditions, material rewards, health and safety, training and development and career progression	personnel is a management function, providing the right numbers of skilled employees, monitoring their performance and behaviour, ensuring compliance with management policies, rules and procedures
personnel is the specialist function responsible for the employment relationship, covering policy and practice affecting the stages of the employment cycle	all general and line managers perform personnel functions relating to, for example, recruitment, selection, training, performance appraisal, pay review, discipline, counselling
the personnel function is a repository of unique expertise, underpinned by social and behavioural science research, theory and method, requiring understanding of organization development, collective bargaining and employment legislation	the personnel function has been diluted with responsibility for pay systems, counselling, sports clubs, training programmes, company canteen, health and safety, leisure facilities, trade union negotiations, newsletters – more like 'jack of all trades'

Transformation: contemporary problems and solutions

Human resources defined

A disturbingly distant phrase for 'people'. It is not necessarily innocent jargon: it may be that you can treat 'human resources' differently from the way you treat 'people'. If you talk about your requirement for human resources, it sounds as if a **rational** economic decision is being made, without moral or personal overtones. It may be easier for a manager to release human resources than it is to sack people. If you are the human resource in question, you will not be able to detect the difference. Human Resource Management (or HRM) is the phrase which turns this dehumanizing language into an academic subject, covering the areas previously known as personnel management and industrial relations.

From David Sims, Stephen Fineman and Yiannis Gabriel, *Organizing and Organizations: An Introduction*, Sage Publications, London, 1993, p. 256.

Human resource management: a managerial perspective which argues the need to establish an integrated series of personnel policies to support organization strategy.

The pessimistic picture of the personnel profession developed in the previous section was transformed during the 1990s as the ways in which people are managed, rewarded and motivated came to be recognized as fundamental to organizational survival and competitive advantage. That decade witnessed a series of trends, including globalization, intensified competition and technological innovation. The emphasis on product quality, responsiveness and quality of customer service in turn increased the emphasis on people management.

Personnel administration does not address these strategic issues. The emphasis of the role has thus switched to support organization strategy. This is reflected in the widespread use of the term *human resource management* (HRM), sometimes also called *strategic* **human resource management** (SHRM) to reinforce the shift in the emphasis and contribution of the role. Commentators have struggled to articulate and agree a definition of human resource management. No single authoritative version has appeared. On the contrary, Tom Keenoy (1990, 1999) argues that the term has a 'brilliant ambiguity', which enables users to define it in a manner that suits their purpose, and is better understood with the metaphor of 'HRM as hologram', an image which depends on and changes with the standpoint of the viewer.

The overarching purpose of HRM (or SHRM) is to contribute to organizational effectiveness through the development of an integrated range of policies which can enhance the quality of working life and encourage high commitment, flexibility and high performance from employees. The concept of HRM thus has a theoretical dimension, based on the proposition that there is a causal chain linking particular people policies, with employee behaviours, to organizational outcomes. The concept thus also has profound practical implications.

It is no longer adequate for the personnel function to operate as administrative tool and employee voice independently of commercial realities. The effectiveness of the human resource management function becomes central to the strategic and financial success of the organization. The personnel manager may have sat in an isolated office. The human resource director should sit on the organization's Board of Directors.

The broad argument supporting these developments goes like this (based on Sisson, 1994):

- management thinking has moved away from the traditional concepts of mass production, hierarchy, bureaucracy, task fragmentation and deskilling, as these methods were more suited to a world which changed slowly;

■ with rapid change, volatile trading conditions, fewer trade barriers and competition from countries with low labour costs, organizational effectiveness relies on targeting niche markets, on flat structures, on flexible working and on the development of skill and motivation through teamworking;

■ social trends have produced a better educated workforce which is more willing to challenge management decisions, has higher expectations of quality of working life and lacks loyalty to individual employers;

■ the provisions of the Social Charter (Holden, 2001, p. 685) improve employee rights and harmonize employment legislation across the European Community;

■ technological developments have created an organizational world of near instant, low-cost communications and information flows, encouraging new forms of organization and new ways of doing business (e-commerce);

■ as the competition can copy product designs and service specifications, and acquire the same technology, the main source of competitive advantage lies with people, and with the policies and practices that develop and motivate employees to high levels of individual and organizational performance;

■ therefore, the ways in which people are recruited, selected, trained, organized, managed, appraised, rewarded, developed, disciplined and motivated are strategic issues, fundamental to organizational effectiveness.

Psychological contract: an implicit set of obligations and expectations concerning what the individual and the organization expect to give to and receive from each other.

A related issue prompting a rethink of personnel management methods concerns the **psychological contract** between employee and organization (Rousseau, 1990, 1995).

It is not possible to specify every aspect of the employment relationship in a formal contract. The organization expects, for example, loyalty and commitment, while employees expect fair treatment, a degree of security and personal development. Much of our behaviour is thus based on tacit, unspoken beliefs. This concept was first developed by Chris Argyris (1960) and became a renewed focus for research during the 1990s.

The psychological contract is a vague concept, relying on unspoken expectations. David Guest (1998), however, argues that it deserves attention as it may be significant in terms of organizational effectiveness. Guest presents a model of the psychological contract (figure 20.2) which shows the potential links between organization policy and practice, and the experience and responses of employees.

antecedents	the state of the contract	consequences
organization climate	fairness	positive employment relations
human resource practices	trust	job satisfaction
trade union membership	delivery of 'the deal'	commitment
individual experiences		motivation
individual expectations		

Figure 20.2: A model of the psychological contract
From D. Guest 'International relations and human resource management' in J. Storey (ed.) *Human Resource Management: A Critical Text*, 2nd Edition, Thomson Learning, London, 2001, p. 107. Reprinted by permission of Thomson Publishing Services.

At the heart of this model lies the 'state' of the psychological contract. Do people feel that they are being fairly treated? Do they trust management? Do they feel that their expectations are being met? If 'the deal is delivered', and the answers to these questions are favourable, then the outcomes are likely to be favourable, for job satisfaction, commitment to the organization, motivation and non-adversarial employment relations. The factors, or antecedents, which lead to this favourable state include the organization climate or culture, 'high commitment' or 'high-performance' human resource policies and trade union presence.

Survey findings from the late 1990s, Guest argues, suggest that most employees have broadly favourable views of the psychological contract. For example, in 1998:

82 per cent	believe their organization has promised to ensure fair treatment by supervisors and managers
66 per cent	believe that they are fairly rewarded for their effort
60 per cent	believe that their organization has made them a promise about careers
45 per cent	trust their organization 'somewhat' to keep promises and commitments
32 per cent	trust their organization 'a lot' to keep promises and commitments

According to Guest (2001), this pattern of results does not appear to vary much from year to year, and is broadly favourable. However, on some issues, up to one-third of the workforce are less happy about the state of their psychological contract. Problems clearly arise when the contract is perceived to be broken. Robinson and Rousseau (1994) found that 55 per cent of their management sample said their psychological contract had been broken by their employer. The consequences are damaging for both the individual and the organization, and include low job satisfaction, poor performance, high staff turnover, feelings of anger and betrayal, and the erosion of trust. Maintaining the psychological contract in a favourable state is therefore a fundamental HRM responsibility.

The implications of these arguments for HRM include:

- HRM must be part of the strategic management of the organization – it must be involved in major strategic decisions and not confined to administrative support functions;

- organization structures should be flat and decentralized, based on autonomous business units producing high-quality, high-value-added goods and services for carefully defined niche markets;

- management style must emphasize mutual trust, respect and autonomy, not rigid rules and procedures, and should encourage flexibility, co-operation, commitment and high performance;

- integrated human resource policies must emphasize flexibility, teamwork, customer focus, total quality, empowerment, learning and skills development.

David Guest (1989, 1990) thus observes that, in contrast with personnel management, the policy objectives of human resource management include high commitment, high quality, flexibility and strategic integration. He then argues (1989, p. 51):

Only when a coherent strategy, directed towards these four policy goals, fully integrated into business strategy and fully sponsored by line management at all levels is applied will the high productivity and related outcome[...] industry be achieved. Such a strategy is only likely to exist where t[...] is in place in the form of supportive leadership from the top, reflec[...] organization's culture and backed by an explicit strategy to utilize [...] resources.

HR practices are a matter of life and death

Patients seeking the best hospital care traditionally consider the success rates of the doctors who could be treating them. Research suggests that patients should also examine hospital human resource practices because these appear to be linked to mortality rates.

A survey was conducted of 61 hospitals in England, along with ten detailed case studies (West and Johnson, 2002). Chief executives and human resource directors were asked about their hospital's characteristics, HR strategy, employee involvement and HR practices covering all clinical, administrative, support and managerial staff groups. The survey also asked about training policies, teamworking and staff performance appraisals.

Data were then collected on the numbers of deaths following emergency and non-emergency surgery, admission for hip fractures and heart attacks, and re-admission. Care was taken to account for variations in mortality due to region, local population and hospital size. The ratio of doctors to patients affects mortality, as having more doctors around can mean fewer deaths. Analysis showed that mortality rates were significantly lower in hospitals with comprehensive HR practices concerning:

- **appraisal**: extensive and sophisticated appraisal systems;
- **training**: well-developed training policies and budgets;
- **teamwork**: high numbers of staff working in teams, and trained to do so.

These relationships were even stronger where the HR director was a full voting member of the hospital management board, a position of power and influence from which systematic policies could be implemented. However, it is the skills and knowledge of doctors and surgeons which affect patient care and survival, and medical staff were suspicious of these research findings. How can HR practices applied to staff who are not involved in patient diagnosis and treatment affect mortality rates? West and Johnson (2002, p. 35) reply:

> Our answer is simple, though it may seem strange to those who deal with individuals rather than organizations. If you have HR practices that focus on effort and skill; develop people's skills; encourage co-operation, collaboration, innovation and synergy in teams for most, if not all, employees, the whole system functions and performs better. If the receptionists, porters, ancillary staff, secretaries, nurses, managers and, yes, the doctors are working effectively, the system as a whole will function effectively.

The impact of HR practices, therefore, is systemic. A hospital is a work community which depends on the interaction of all its members. Although clearly important, the skills and performance of doctors is not the only factor which affects the quality of patient care.

Based on Michael West and Rebecca Johnson, 'A matter of life and death', *People Management*, vol. 8, no. 4, 21 February 2002, pp. 30–6.

Table 20.3 outlines typical 'high-commitment–high-performance' human resource management practices concerning employee influence, human resource flow, reward systems and work systems. This illustrates the shift from personnel to HRM, and these four areas are the basis for one of the models considered in the following section.

Table 20.3: Typical human resource policy and practice

HRM policy areas	High-commitment–high-performance practices
employee influence	wide participation and involvement in change and management decisions generally; extensive two-way communication; problem-solving groups
human resource flow	selection based on attitudes and values in addition to skills and experience; policies which deliver flexibility in *numbers* of employees, with a more stable core complemented as required by a flexible 'peripheral' workforce, and also flexibility in timing, with a range of part-time, annual hours and flexible hours practices
reward systems	open and participative appraisal with two-way feedback; performance-based pay; individual and group-based rewards; skills-based pay; profit sharing; share options; flexible 'cafeteria' benefits; lateral as well as upward promotions; equal opportunities
work systems	excellence, quality and continuous improvement are dominant values; emphasis on 'beyond contract' and 'can do'; visible, facilitating, inspirational leadership; flat, decentralized structures; cross-functional project teams; autonomous teams with task flexibility

The following sections answer three key questions. What are the links in theory between HRM and organization strategy and effectiveness? How well does HRM work in improving organizational performance? Is HRM really 'new'?

Stop and Criticize

Human resource management practices seem to assume that employers and employees are equal partners with the same interests and goals.

Where in your view do these interests coincide? Where do they differ?

Why is employee training a strategic issue?

ISS is a successful Danish cleaning services company. The cleaning industry is characterized by low-skilled workers and high staff turnover. ISS is an exception, and it achieves high service quality and high employee loyalty through its approach to training.

Even in cleaning, customer satisfaction depends on the behaviour of front-line employees. Contracts are lost when cleaners do a poor job, irrespective of marketing and pricing strategies. ISS thus has a continuing stream of programmes to train employees and to encourage customer-friendly service.

Because ISS is a large international company, with an annual revenue in 1997 of US$1.8 billion, it can bid for large contracts with factories, offices and hospitals. Highly efficient cleaning staff are required to service these clients well and profitably. Efficiency means saving time and cleaning supplies, improving service quality and avoiding accidents. In complex settings, such as hospitals and process plants, for example, the skills and equipment required are quite sophisticated. Cleaners also need to be able to identify and handle the different needs and expectations of different customers.

Here is the training programme for new recruits at the ISS small business services operation:

- recruits first undergo a six-month training programme in cleaning techniques and safety;
- they are then trained to interpret contracts so they understand how profitable they are;

- after a year, trained staff are promoted to team leader posts;

- training is extended to customer handling and coaching skills for developing new staff.

How are staff motivated and rewarded?

- staff are organized into two- or three-person 'hit squads' who work together regularly, even though many contracts could be handled by one person;

- cleaning shifts overlap half an hour with site employees, so they get to know each other;

- team leader performance targets include customer retention and profitability;

- the company pays above industry average wages to encourage retention.

The results? The company share price trebled between 1996 and 1998. In 1997, ISS won the contract to clean the hotel rooms at Disneyland Paris, a company famous for attention to detail. Company profits in 1998 were forecast to grow 15 per cent annually.

Based on, 'Service with a smile', *The Economist*, 25 April 1998, pp. 85–6.

Models of human resource management

Hard HRM: a human resource management perspective which emphasizes the full utilization of employees in a formal, calculating and dispassionate manner, to be treated in a manner similar to any other resources available to the organization.

Soft HRM: a human resource management perspective which emphasizes the need to develop the potential and resourcefulness of employees in order to encourage commitment and high performance in pursuit of shared organizational goals.

The IPM definition of personnel management was couched in structural terms; personnel management is an organizational function, a department. HRM, in contrast, is defined as a perspective. It is possible for an organization to adopt an HRM perspective (however defined) without having a personnel (or HR) department. Indeed, many human resource management initiatives seem to have been initiated by general management (Storey, 1992).

John Storey (1989, 1992, 2001), one of the leading contributors to the HRM debate, argues that the term is difficult to define for at least two main reasons.

1. The term is used in different ways by different commentators. Some use it in a *descriptive* sense, reporting developments in practice. Others use it in a *prescriptive* manner, advocating a particular approach to employee relations. The term is also used in a *theoretical* sense, setting out causal links to aid understanding.

2. Some commentators use the term 'human resource management' in a loose or *weak* sense, as a modern-sounding label applied to any approach to the management of employment relations, while others use it in a *strong* manner, to imply a specific set of management practices with a particular philosophical underpinning.

Storey argues for a distinction between **hard** and **soft** versions of human resource management, depending on the emphasis given to goals and their achievement.

Thus, as Storey (1992, p. 26) points out, the same term can be used to describe contradictory sets of beliefs and practices. Hard HRM can be viewed as instrumental and exploitative, but with a clear focus on organizational performance goals. Soft HRM can be viewed as compassionate and humane, but as woolly and inappropriate in a commercial setting.

Hard HRM is quantitative and calculating, emphasizing the management of headcount and focusing on strategic issues. Hard HRM incorporates any practice that contributes to organization strategy, including task fragmentation, job insecurity and low pay. Soft HRM is people-oriented, rooted in human relations thinking, emphasizing motivation, communication and leadership. Soft HRM rules out practices that would deskill jobs and damage motivation.

This hard–soft distinction is similar to that explored in chapter 21 on leadership, between *initiating structure* (a task-oriented style) and *consideration* (a people-oriented style). The evidence suggests that the leaders who get the best performance from people emphasize both structure and consideration. For effective leaders, this is not an 'either/or' choice.

Similarly, the human resource manager, to be effective, may have to find ways simultaneously to reduce labour costs and increase employee commitment, motivation and performance. The distinction between hard and soft HRM may thus be difficult to sustain in practice. Keith Sisson (1994, p. 14) also notes that 'there must be the danger that managers will be tempted to use the language of "the HRM organization" to cover the reality of what they are doing'. In other words, the language of soft HRM may be used to disguise a hard approach, to make it appear more legitimate, acceptable and palatable (see table 20.4).

Table 20.4: Soft rhetoric hiding hard reality in human resource management

Rhetoric	Reality
Customer first	Market forces supreme
Total quality management	Doing more with less
Lean production	Mean production
Flexibility	Management can do what it wants
Core and periphery	Reducing the organization's commitments
Devolution/delayering	Reducing the number of middle managers
Down-sizing/right-sizing	Redundancy
New working patterns	Part-time instead of full-time jobs
Empowerment	Someone else taking risk and responsibility
Training and development	Manipulation
Employability	No employment security
Recognizing individual contributions	Undermining trade union bargaining
Teamworking	Reducing the individual's discretion

From Keith Sisson, 'Personnel management: paradigms, practice and prospects', in Keith Sisson (ed.), *Personnel Management in Britain*, Blackwell, Oxford, 1994, p. 15. Reprinted by permission of Blackwell Publishing Ltd.

Stop and Criticize

How do you feel about being described as a 'human resource' or as a 'human asset'?

Does it matter? What are the practical advantages and disadvantages to you personally, as an employee, of being labelled in this way?

Various commentators have sought to identify what makes HRM distinctive in relation to personnel management, and as a management perspective in its own right. John Storey (2001, p. 7) helpfully summarizes HRM in terms of four distinguishing elements (table 20.5). The first element is 'beliefs and assumptions', concerning the significance of the way in which people are managed. The second element is 'strategy', concerning the links between HRM policies and business goals. The third element is 'line management role', concerning the involvement of non-specialist managers in the implementation of HRM practices such as team briefings and performance appraisals. The fourth element is 'key levers', concerning techniques for implementing HRM. As Storey (2001, p. 6) observes, this model is a combination of description, prescription and logical deduction.

Table 20.5: The HRM model

1. Beliefs and assumptions
- That it is the human resource which gives competitive edge.
- That the aim should be not mere compliance with rules, but employee commitment.
- That therefore employees should, for example, be very carefully selected and developed.

2. Strategy
- Because of the above factors, HR decisions are of strategic importance.
- Top management involvement is necessary.
- HR policies should be integrated into the business strategy, stemming from it and even contributing to it.

3. Line management role
- Because HR practice is critical to the core activities of the business, it is too important to be left to personnel specialists alone.
- Line managers are (or need to be) closely involved as both deliverers and drivers of HR policies.
- Much greater attention is paid to the management of managers themselves.

4. Key levers
- Managing culture is more important than managing procedures and systems.
- Integrated action on selection, communication, training, reward and development.
- Restructuring and job redesign to allow devolved responsibility and empowerment.

HRM is thus based on the belief that people make the difference with respect to organizational performance; that people decisions are strategic decisions; that all managers must be able consistently to implement HRM practices; and that HRM policies must support each other and corporate strategy in an integrated manner. In other words, to find out if an organization is practising HRM or not, just ask four questions:

1. Do you regard your employees as costs or as assets?

2. Does your human resource director sit on the organization's main board?

3. Are line managers skilled in and committed to implementing human resource policy?

4. Are human resource policies integrated and mutually supportive?

What are the links between HRM policies and organizational performance? To answer this question, we will explore five models of HRM, each explaining these relationships in different ways, with different emphases, using the locations of their authors to label them:

1. The Michigan model

2. The Harvard model

3. The Rutgers model

4. The Warwick model

5. The Bath model

These models make the basic claim illustrated in figure 20.3. They argue that, *if* you design human resource policies in a particular way, *then* performance will improve (Guest, 1989, 1997). Human resource policies are *independent variables* in this relationship, and the quality of working life and organizational effectiveness are *dependent variables* (see glossary).

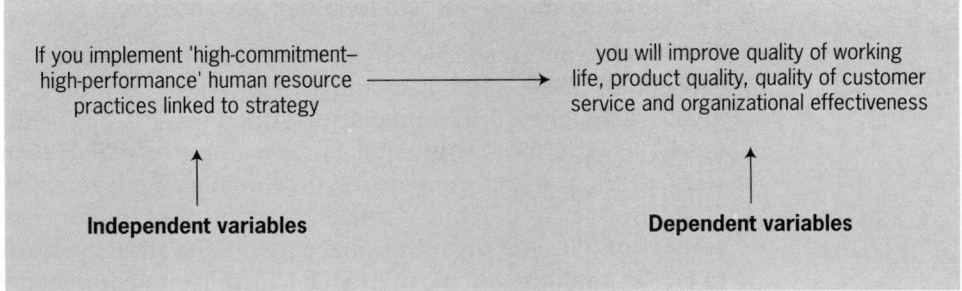

Figure 20.3: A basic model of HRM

The Michigan model – a 'matching' perspective

The Michigan model developed by Charles Fombrun, Noel Tichy and Mary Anne Devanna (1984) emphasizes the 'resource' element, arguing that people should be managed like any other resource, 'obtained cheaply, used sparingly and developed and exploited as fully as possible' (Sparrow and Hiltrop, 1994, p. 7). They also argue that personnel policies, to be effective, must match, or be aligned with, the organization's strategy.

The Michigan model (figure 20.4) is based on the 'human resource cycle', emphasizing the contribution of selection, appraisal, rewards and development to employee performance. These issues reflect elements in the employment cycle, defined earlier. These factors must be linked to organization strategy, and they must also be consistent with each other in 'sending the same messages'. There would be no point in rewarding employees for following rules and procedures if the organization strategy involved innovation and change or if selection and appraisal systems emphasized initiative and discretion.

One of the problems with this model concerns its narrow focus on aspects of human resource management. The model ignores the industrial relations context, the role and interests of trade or labour unions, management style, and the organization of work which could involve task fragmentation, deskilling, job enrichment or teamworking. For the model to work in practice, organizational strategy would have to be fairly stable and well understood. That is not always the case, particularly in a rapidly changing competitive environment.

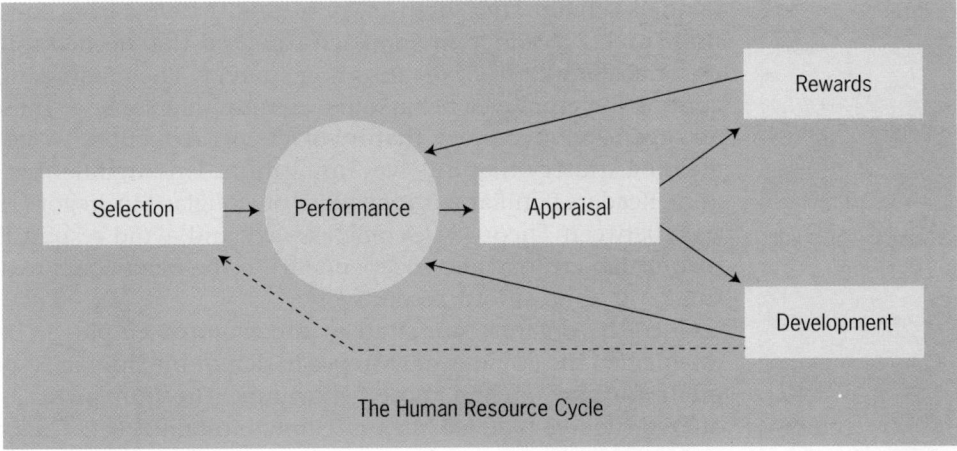

Figure 20.4: The Michigan model of human resource management
From C.J. Fombrun, N.M. Tichy and M.A. Devanna, *Strategic Human Resource Management*. Copyright © 1984. This material is used by permission of John Wiley & Sons, Inc.

The Harvard model – a 'stakeholder' perspective

This model, developed by Michael Beer and his colleagues at Harvard University (Beer et al., 1984, 1985; Beer and Spector, 1985), is probably the best known and most widely cited of the models described here. It has been particularly influential in Britain and continental Europe (Sparrow and Hiltrop, 1994, p. 12). The Harvard 'map of the human resource management territory' is shown in figure 20.5. As with the Michigan model, it argues that human resource policy must be consistent with the organizational context and strategy. It considers a wider range of factors than the Michigan model. Critically, it demonstrates how policy choices are shaped and constrained by context factors and by stakeholder groups whose interests have to be managed and reconciled through a series of 'trade-offs'.

This is a *stakeholder* model which presents a causal chain linking the practice of human resource management to organizational performance and quality of working life. There are four policy areas at the heart of the Harvard model:

- employee influence;
- human resource flow;
- reward systems;
- work systems.

These are the same four policy areas used in table 20.3 to illustrate a typical human resource management approach leading, in this model, to high commitment, high competence, cost-effectiveness, and to a high degree of congruence between individual and organizational goals. The precise nature of these causal links, however, remains vague.

Mike Noon (1992) reminds us that the model was developed as a structure for the Harvard MBA syllabus in human resource management in 1981. It was a framework for organizing teaching and thinking, and was not intended to be either an explanatory or a prescriptive model. However, it is not difficult to see how it can be treated either as a theory of how to manage human resources effectively or as a prescriptive guide to best practice.

Randall S. Schuler

The Rutgers model – a 'contingency' perspective

Randall Schuler and Susan Jackson (1987, 1996), from Rutgers University, New Brunswick, NJ, adopt an approach based on the 'needed role behaviours' to support different kinds of organization strategy. They first identify a series of twelve contrasting employee behaviours, arguing that some of these are appropriate for an organization strategy that involves cost reduction, while others are appropriate for a strategy that involves innovation. This argument is summarized in table 20.6. Readers familiar with the work of Douglas McGregor (1960) will see his contrast between Theory X (people are lazy and avoid responsibility) and Theory Y (people are creative and independent) in the behaviours required for 'cost reduction' and 'innovation', respectively.

Once the organization strategy and required employee behaviours have been established the obvious next step is to determine human resource practices appropriate for encouraging those behaviours. The human resource manager is now offered the five practice 'menus', shown in table 20.7. The criterion of choice for each item rests on the degree of fit or alignment with organization strategy. Of course, the organization strategy has to be clearly articulated before the appropriate choices from the human resource 'menu' can be established. If the organization's strategy changes, then it may be necessary to adjust some of the menu items.

Susan E. Jackson

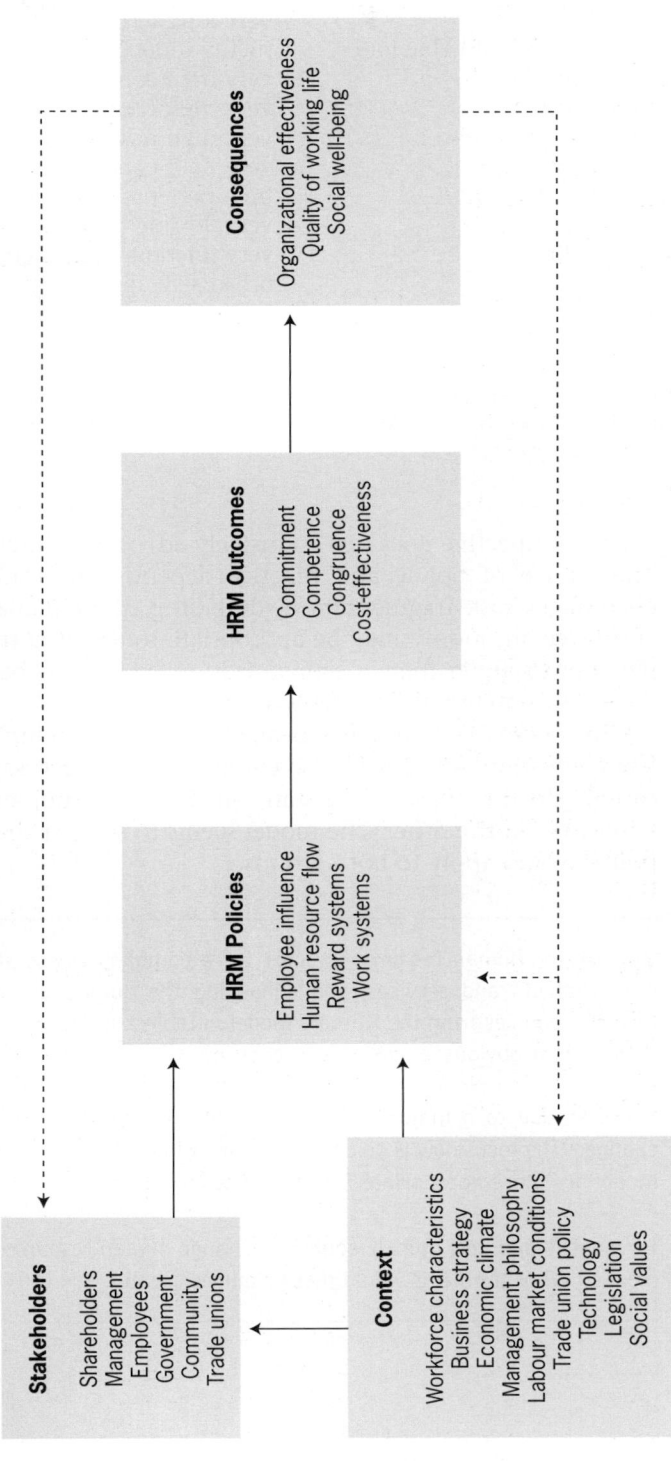

Figure 20.5: Map of the human resource management territory
From Michael Beer, Bert Spector, Paul R. Lawrence, D. Quinn Mills and Richard E. Walton, *Managing Human Assets*, Free Press, New York, 1984. Copyright Michael Beer and Bert Spector, reprinted by permission of Michael Beer and Bert Spector.

Table 20.6: Organization strategy and employee behaviour

Behaviours required for a cost-reduction strategy	Behaviours required for an innovation strategy
highly repetitive, predictable behaviour	highly creative, innovative behaviour
very short-term focus	very long-term focus
highly co-operative, interdependent behaviour	highly independent, autonomous behaviour
very low concern for quality	very high concern for quality
very low concern for quantity	very high concern for quantity
very low risk taking	very high risk taking
very high concern for process	very high concern for results
high preference to avoid responsibility	high preference to assume responsibility
very inflexible to change	very flexible to change
very comfortable with stability	very tolerant of ambiguity and uncertainty
narrow skill application	broad skill application
low job involvement	high job involvement

From 'Linking competitive strategies with human resource management practices', *Academy of Management Executive* by R.S. Schuler and S.E. Jackson. Copyright 1987 by Academy of Management. Reproduced with permission of Academy of Management in the format Textbook via Copyright Clearance Center.

This perspective does not exclusively advocate a 'high-commitment' approach. The choice of policy and practice depends on strategy. An approach which encourages task fragmentation, deskilling, tight management control and low employee autonomy may be appropriate to a cost-cutting strategy. It is also not possible to argue that one organization strategy is better than another as this depends on external, competitive conditions.

This model has intuitive appeal. Consider, for example, the choices concerning 'compensation' and how these choices might differ, say, for the management of casual part-time bartending staff, on the one hand, and for laboratory research scientists, on the other. The model seems to suggest that the same compensation policy would apply to both groups.

Stop and Criticize

You are the human resource director for a company whose strategy involves innovation in new products and services, and enhancing the quality of customer care. Which human resource policies from the Rutgers model in table 20.7 are more appropriate for this organization? Is it obvious, or difficult to choose?

However, due to a major shift in the competitive environment, the company strategy has changed. The focus now is on cost reduction. Which human resource policies from the Rutgers model are more appropriate for these new conditions?

How easily and how quickly could you change human resource policies as the model recommends? What problems would these changes create?

Table 20.7: The Rutgers model of human resource management

Planning practice choices

Informal	------------	Formal
Short-term	------------	Long-term
Explicit job analysis	------------	Implicit job analysis
Job simplification	------------	Job enrichment
Low employee involvement	------------	High employee involvement

Staffing practice choices

Internal sources	------------	External sources
Narrow paths	------------	Broad paths
Single ladder	------------	Multiple ladders
Explicit criteria	------------	Implicit criteria
Limited socialization	------------	Extensive socialization
Closed procedures	------------	Open procedures

Appraising practice choices

Behavioural criteria	------------	Results criteria
Purposes: development, remedial, maintenance		
Low employee participation	------------	High employee participation
Short-term criteria	------------	Long-term criteria

Compensating practice choices

Low base salaries	------------	High base salaries
Internal equity	------------	External equity
Few perks	------------	Many perks
Standard, fixed package	------------	Flexible package
Low participation	------------	High participation
No incentives	------------	Many incentives
Short-term incentives	------------	Long-term incentives
No employment security	------------	High employment security
Hierarchical	------------	Egalitarian

Training and development practice choices

Short-term	------------	Long-term
Narrow application	------------	Broad application
Productivity emphasis	------------	Quality-of-work-life emphasis
Spontaneous, unplanned	------------	Systematic, planned
Individual orientation	------------	Group orientation
Low participation	------------	High participation

From 'Linking competitive strategies with human resource management practices', *Academy of Management Executive* by R.S. Schuler and S.E. Jackson. Copyright 1987 by Academy of Management. Reproduced with permission of Academy of Management in the format Textbook via Copyright Clearance Center.

At the heart of the Rutgers model is the concept of 'behavioural consistency'. If the organization has an innovation strategy, then it will be appropriate to encourage creativity, long-term focus, high levels of co-operation and interdependence, risk taking, and tolerance for ambiguity and uncertainty. In this case, the policies which will apply include:

- job enrichment;

- multiple career ladders;

- high employee participation;

- many and flexible incentives;

- quality of working life emphasis.

This is a contingency model of human resource management. Policy and practice have to be tailored to organizational circumstances. There is no 'one best way' to manage human resources. This presumes, of course, that human resource managers are able to make the choices implied in the model, unconstrained by other organizational and contextual factors.

The Warwick model – a 'contextual' perspective

The models explored up to this point are American. From a European perspective, human resource management is an American import. These models reflect American cultural traditions, management styles, politics and industrial relations. European organizations are more accustomed to collective bargaining with trade unions. American human resource management practices, in contrast, tend to focus on individual employees.

Chris Hendry, Andrew Pettigrew and Paul Sparrow (1989; Hendry and Pettigrew, 1990), all researchers at the Centre for Corporate Strategy at Warwick Business School, extended the Harvard model to take into account the wider organizational context in which human resource policies are designed and implemented. The Warwick model is shown in figure 20.6.

This complex model has five elements. First, in 'HRM content', the model identifies the Harvard policy areas of human resource flows, work systems, reward systems and employee relations (see table 20.3 and figure 20.5). Second, the model identifies the external context of the organization (suggesting a PEST analysis of external political, economic, social and technical factors). Third, it recognizes how the external context influences the inner context of the organization, with respect to organization structure and culture, leadership, technology and business results. Fourth, the inner context both influences and is influenced by the 'HRM context' which concerns the way in which the organization defines the role and specifies the structure of the function and the outputs expected of it. Finally, as with the other models considered so far, human resource policies are also seen to depend on the business or organization strategy. The arrows in the model illustrate lines of mutual influence.

This model was used to analyze data from over twenty organizations in Britain in a study of how strategic change had affected human resource management. This approach highlights the influential role of the strategic change management process, often over a number of years (fifteen to twenty), in developing different approaches to human resource management. The research also highlighted the conceptual and process skills required to implement the human resource management approach effectively (see table 20.8). This is a significant departure from the traditional personnel management portfolio which might have included welfare work, counselling, running sports and canteen facilities and administering

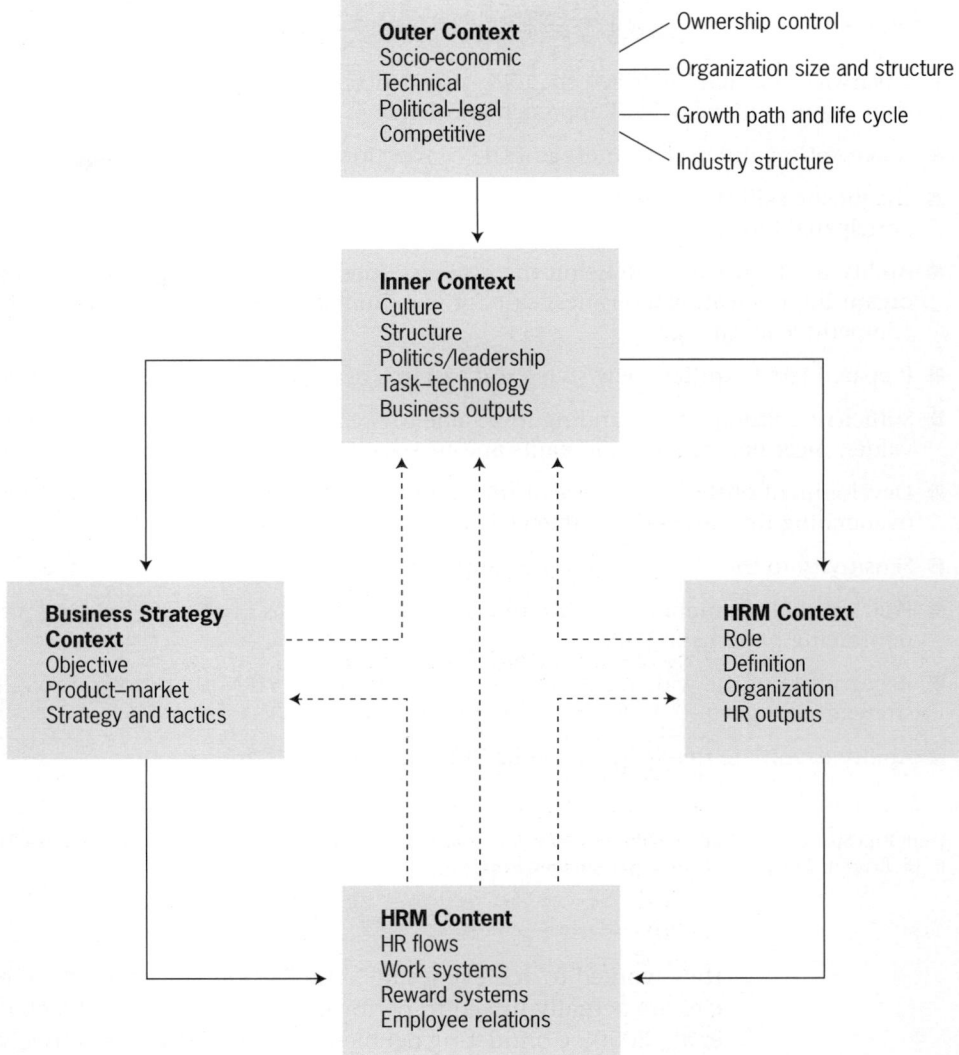

Figure 20.6: The Warwick model of strategic change and human resource management
From C. Hendry and A.M. Pettigrew, 'Human resource management: an agenda for the 1990s',
International Journal of Human Resource Management, vol. 1, no. 1, 1990, pp. 17–43. Reprinted by
permission of Taylor & Francis Ltd, http://www.tandf.co.uk/journals.

employee payroll and personal records. This range of tasks and skills explains
why, as indicated earlier, HRM is sometimes referred to as *strategic* human resource
management or SHRM.

The Warwick model draws attention to the wider context (inner and outer) in
which the human resource management function works. Space prohibits a fuller
consideration of how contextual factors impinge on the human resource function. However, it is important to recognize, first, that the function does not operate free from contextual constraints, and second, that the topic should not be
viewed merely as a contest between competing models.

The Bath model – a 'process' perspective

The Bath People and Performance Model was developed at the University of Bath
in the UK by John Purcell and his colleagues Nick Kinnie, Sue Hutchinson, Bruce
Rayton and Juani Stuart (2003; Sloman, 2002). Most previous research has simply
identified the range of HR policies used in an organization without exploring how

---

Table 20.8: Conceptual and process skills for implementing HRM

The Warwick research identified the following conceptual and process skills required to implement the human resource management approach effectively:

- A perception and understanding of the connections between business and HRM.

- Diagnostic skills to audit and take stock of existing skill bases in organizations in the light of anticipated business and technological changes.

- Ability to identify and advise on the business opportunities afforded by the existing skill base of the organization, creating a business case for why human resources are a perceived source of competitive advantage.

- Preparedness to initiate new styles and patterns of HRM activity in advance of business changes.

- Sufficient cultural understanding to be able to preserve what is valuable from previous missions and values, meet new task requirements and be sensitive to individual satisfaction and career needs.

- Development of the power base of the personnel management function by linking its activities to overarching information, commercial and financial policies.

- Sensitivity to the changing internal situation during major periods of change.

- Political skills to mobilize the internal and external forces of change, creating increasingly self-reinforcing patterns of HRM.

- Recognition of the wide range of pressure points within HRM that can be brought to bear in a strategic change.

- Ability to initiate timely adjustments in HRM agreements and practices.

From Paul Sparrow and Jean-M. Hiltrop, *European Human Resource Management in Transition*, Prentice Hall, Hemel Hempstead, 1994, p. 18. Reprinted by permission of Pearson Education Ltd.

---

they worked to achieve results. The Bath model attempts to explain how HR policies are actually linked to performance, the so-called 'black box problem' (Purcell et al., 2000). Conducting detailed case study research in twelve organizations, this approach focuses on the underlying processes through which HR policies influence employee behaviour and performance. Rather than identifying 'best practices', the model, summarized in figure 20.7, tries to discover 'best processes'.

Purcell and his colleagues first observe that, for people to perform beyond the minimum requirements of a job, three factors, labelled 'AMO', are necessary:

Factor	Employees must
Ability	have job skills and knowledge, including how to work well with others
Motivation	feel motivated to do the work, and to do it well
Opportunity	be able to use their skills and contribute to team and organizational success

If one of these factors is weak or missing, then an individual's performance is likely to be poor. You may have the skill and enthusiasm, but if your supervisor watches you closely and prevents you from sharing ideas with colleagues or deviating from standard procedure, then your performance is unlikely to excel. You will probably not 'go the extra mile'.

Central to this argument is the concept of 'discretionary behaviour'. Most employees have some choice over how, and also how well, they perform their jobs. A sales assistant, for example, can decide to adopt a casual and unsympa-

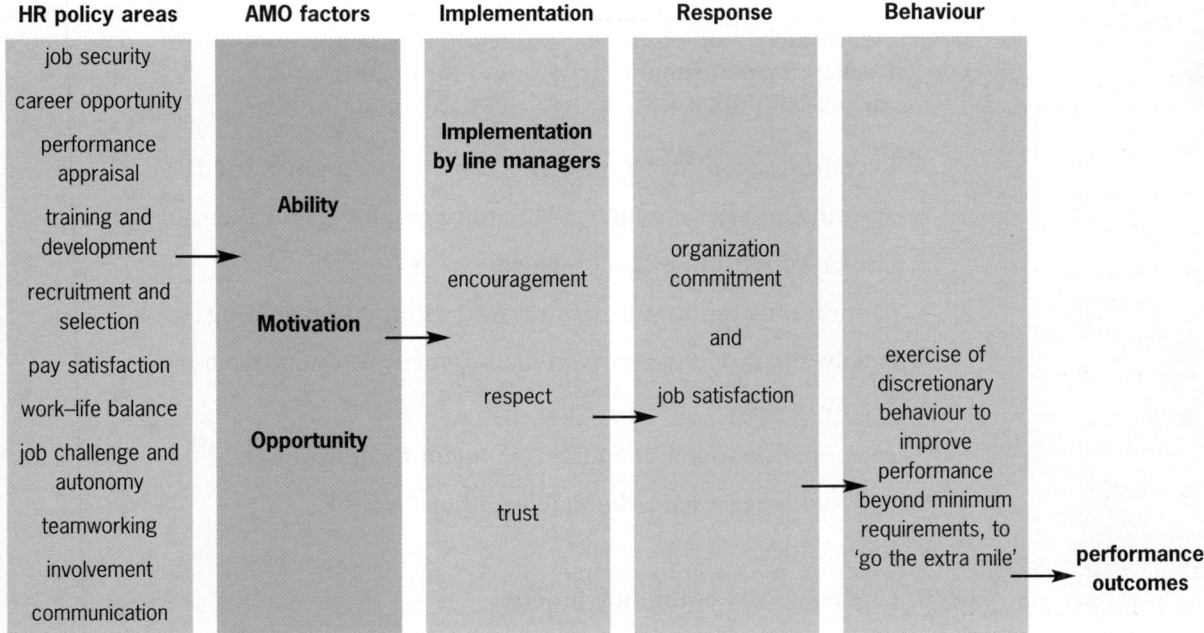

HR policy areas	AMO factors	Implementation	Response	Behaviour

job security
career opportunity
performance appraisal
training and development
recruitment and selection
pay satisfaction
work–life balance
job challenge and autonomy
teamworking
involvement
communication

Ability

Motivation

Opportunity

Implementation by line managers

encouragement

respect

trust

organization commitment

and

job satisfaction

exercise of discretionary behaviour to improve performance beyond minimum requirements, to 'go the extra mile'

performance outcomes

Figure 20.7: The Bath People and Performance Model
Adapted from J. Purcell, N. Kinnie, S. Hutchinson, B. Rayton and J. Swart, *Understanding the People and Performance Link: Unlocking the Black Box*, CIPD, London, 2003, p. 7. Reprinted by permission of Chartered Institute of Personnel and Development.

thetic tone, rather than make customers feel that their concerns have been handled in a competent and friendly way. Negative, uncaring behaviours are often a response to an employee's perception that the organization no longer cares about them. When one member of staff annoys a customer, and management finds out, then that employee has a problem. However, if staff collectively withdraw their positive discretionary behaviours, this can seriously damage organizational performance.

What then encourages employees to 'go the extra mile' and exercise their discretion in ways that improve their job performance? The answer lies in the process orientation of the model that establishes a causal chain consisting of four main steps.

1. Basic HR policies are required to produce the Ability, Motivation and Opportunity central to any level of performance.

2. The line managers who implement and 'bring these policies to life' have to communicate trust, respect and encouragement. This is achieved, for example, in the way that they give directions and respond to suggestions.

3. The combination of HR policies with line management behaviours must lead to feelings of job satisfaction and employee commitment. Otherwise, the policies themselves will have little or no impact on behaviour and performance.

4. People tend to use positive discretionary behaviours when they experience pride in where they work, and want to stay there. Commitment and job satisfaction thus encourage employees to use discretionary behaviour to perform better.

In other words, while those HR policies must be in place, it is the process through which they are implemented, and their impact on commitment and satisfaction, that matters. The same policies, with inconsistent or half-hearted management implementation, could lower commitment and satisfaction, leading to a withdrawal of positive discretionary behaviours, with predictable consequences for performance (Guest and King, 2001).

The eleven HR policy areas identified by the model are:

1. Recruitment and selection that is careful and sophisticated.

2. Training and development that equips employees for their job roles.

3. Career opportunities are provided.

4. Communication that is two-way and information-sharing.

5. Involvement of employees in management decision-making.

6. Teamworking.

7. Performance appraisal and development for individuals.

8. Pay that is regarded as equitable and motivating.

9. Job security.

10. Challenge and autonomy in jobs.

11. Work–life balance.

One problem with this approach is that concepts such as 'careful selection', 'individual performance appraisal' and 'teamworking' can be translated into practice in many different ways in different settings. The model is vague about precisely what forms of selection, appraisal and teamworking will have the desired impact. Each of those practices can affect more than one AMO component. Teamwork, for example, can enhance motivation ('I don't want to let the team down'), can create opportunities to participate, and may improve skills through the sharing of knowledge. Purcell and colleagues thus argue that, although difficult to prove, the concept of a 'bundle' of HR practices has an intuitive appeal. This proposition suggests that a 'positive bundle' of policies which reinforce each other will produce a greater impact than the sum of individual policies. However, it is easier to demonstrate the impact of a 'deadly combination' of policies which compete with and weaken each other. Such a combination could include, for example, financial rewards for individual contribution and appraisal and promotion systems which encourage collective teamworking.

These five models all have various degrees of empirical research support, some convincing and some less so. In the following section, we will explore the criticisms of these perspectives and also consider the results of research which has asked the question 'Does human resource management really contribute to organizational performance?'

The models described here are not only controversial, but are also potentially confusing. Table 20.9 offers a summary of the main strengths and weaknesses of each.

Administrative processes, strategic impact

To help as well as impress their clients, management consulting organizations such as Arthur Andersen, the Saratoga Institute and PriceWaterhouseCoopers have been trying to link human resource practices with profitability. Concerned that their profits were being affected, Quest Diagnostics, the largest clinical testing company in America with 23,000 employees, asked the consultants William Mercer to study their annual staff turnover rate of 23 per cent.

Staff turnover creates costs, but these are difficult to measure. When employees leave, output is lost. Costs are then incurred in advertising and interviewing, then training the new recruits. Turnover is often a symptom of low morale, which can reduce corporate profitability by depressing staff performance. However, individual contributions can be measured in terms of the value added per employee, which may be physical output, customer service or other measures of productivity. Separate business units within the organization can then be compared with each other. The next step is to examine the business context and human resource management practices to identify why some units are more effective. At Quest Diagnostics, analysis showed that the main problems leading to staff turnover arose in the company's selection and promotion procedures, which were changed.

William Mercer was able to demonstrate to Quest Diagnostics that if staff turnover were reduced by just five percentage points, this would make an annual profits contribution of US$31 million (UK£22.7 million). Faced with this evidence, managers who had been complacent about the company's staff turnover were shocked into action, particularly those whose units appeared on the internal league table to have higher staff turnover.

Based on Cathy Cooper, 'In for the count', *People Management*, vol. 6, no. 20, 12 October 2000, pp. 28–34.

Table 20.9: HRM models' strengths and limitations summarized

Model	Strengths	Limitations
The Michigan matching model	■ based on personnel policies affecting the employment cycle ■ emphasizes consistency of approach in supporting strategy	■ focuses on limited set of personnel policies ■ ignores context, organization design, industrial relations
The Harvard stakeholder model	■ comprehensive, systematic and prescriptive causal map ■ recognizes the influence of a range of stakeholders	■ not designed as prescriptive but regarded as such ■ nature of causal links unclear
The Rutgers contingency model	■ exposes a wide range of choices for personnel policy ■ advocates a clear link with organization strategy	■ strategy has to be known before choices can be made ■ managers are not always free to make these choices
The Warwick contextual model	■ recognizes that strategic change is a dynamic iterative process ■ takes into account the shaping role of many contextual factors over lengthy periods of time	■ provides explanations for *past* events, and is complex and difficult to test ■ provides limited change guidance for practitioners
The Bath process model	■ focuses on a bundle of practices which affect employee discretionary behaviour ■ emphasizes the key mediating role of line management in implementing HR policies	■ focuses on internal organizational process, but overlooks the wider social and organizational context ■ HR policy dimensions are open to interpretation in a number of different ways

Criticisms

Human resource management has attracted much criticism. One criticism concerns the definition of the term itself, which is ambiguous. It is used in 'strong' and 'loose' senses to describe 'hard' and 'soft' approaches to employee relations. Storey (2001) complains that while the concept of HRM has developed a distinct definition, the term now tends to be used indiscriminately and carelessly. A second related criticism concerns the potentially cynical use of the term to give a more modern 'up beat' tone to the profession, to give the impression of change and progress. Such image-building is assisted by the addition of 'strategic' to the label human resource management (SHRM), symbolizing a shift in emphasis from personnel administration, and also symbolizing a shift in the function's aspirations concerning status.

There are two other major substantive criticisms of the movement. These concern:

1. The *treatment of conflict*, which tends to be ignored in American models.

2. The *treatment of strategy*, which tends to be treated as a 'given'.

Conflict

Human resource management relies on policies which encourage commitment, loyalty, a strong culture, shared goals and values (Guest, 1990). This is a *unitarist* perspective which assumes that an organization's members are united behind a common purpose (see chapter 23). This overlooks the potential inconsistency between an individual's needs and desires and the needs of the organization. This is the *organizational dilemma* explored in chapter 1. A unitarist perspective also ignores the argument that employee interests and organizational needs are fundamentally irreconcilable, that conflict is inevitable, and that the trade union role is to protect employee interests through collective representation and bargaining.

A 'high-commitment–high-performance' human resource management strategy is only likely to work where the industrial relations climate is sympathetic to notions of shared goals and values. In an adversarial climate (management propose, unions oppose), such a strategy is more likely to be seen as a cynical management attempt to disguise the realities of organizational conflict. American management models do not 'travel' well, particularly to cultures which have different industrial relations histories and socio-cultural contexts.

Strategy

The models that we have explored also argue that human resource management policies should be mutually reinforcing and linked to organization strategy. Personnel management historically operated in relative isolation from strategic concerns, only hiring more people when required and laying them off again when they were no longer needed. The strategy argument is thus central to the distinction between personnel and human resources.

Keith Sisson (1994) identifies a number of difficulties with this argument.

First, organization strategy is rarely as systematic and ordered as these tidy models require. Strategy tends to be 'emergent', not rationally planned. This means that strategy tends to emerge over time from the various actions, successes and failures across the organization. HRM models assume that human resource management choices follow logically from formal organization strategy choices. HRM is thus placed in a reactive mode, not involved with helping to shape and develop strategy in the first place. However, developments in employee availability and skills, in organization culture and structure, or in other aspects of human resource management may shape an organization's strategic thinking and opportunities. The problem remains, how is it possible to develop an integrated human resource management approach to support an emergent strategy which develops more or less slowly and which changes unpredictably? This point is highlighted by the Warwick model, which draws attention to the range of contextual factors which are likely to affect human resource management practice over extended periods of time. This point is to some extend sidestepped by the Bath model, which implicitly assumes the need for discretionary behaviour and high performance regardless of a particular organization strategy.

Second, other senior managers may not accept that human resource management is strategically vital. Given today's aggressively hostile, competitive and volatile international markets, approaches such as task fragmentation, deskilling, increased management control and cost reduction can also look like good human resource management strategies. Taylorism and Fordism look like easier and less riskier options, particularly where there is limited evidence to show a return on investment from a shift to human resource management.

Third, 'full-blown' human resource management can be expensive in terms of set-up costs and support mechanisms, such as specialist staff and training for line managers. Consider the costs involved in implementing the shift from personnel to human resource management identified by John Storey (1992) and summarized in table 20.5. Consider the relative costs of the policy choices in the Rutgers model of HRM from Schuler and Jackson (1987) in table 20.7. Consider the time and costs involved in implementing 'sophisticated' versions of the eleven HR policies identified in the Bath model in figure 20.7. Even if these policy choices were considered appropriate, serious investment in human resource management may be beyond the financial capability of many organizations.

Source: © Copyright United Feature Syndicate, Inc. Reproduced with permission.

Does it work?

The question 'does it work?' is of more than theoretical interest. Proof that human resource management can indeed contribute to 'the bottom line', affecting an organization's costs and profitability, has fundamental implications for whether or not an organization can afford to implement HR policies in the first place. Proof of return on investment also has implications for the status and power of human resource practitioners. Practitioners and their professional institutes, therefore, have paid considerable attention to that research and to its findings.

As the previous section suggests, there are sound theoretical reasons as to why human resource management may not work as well in practice as it does in textbooks. However, research findings suggest that the contribution of a human resource management approach to organizational effectiveness can be both positive and measurable. Here we will consider the work of Mark Huselid and of the University of Sheffield Group (Britain).

Mark Huselid

Mark Huselid

The contribution of Mark Huselid (Rutgers University, New Jersey) to this debate has been to establish a quantifiable link between human resource management practices and an organization's financial performance. Huselid (1995) used a survey questionnaire to measure the extent to which the organizations studied used 'high-performance work practices', and the degree to which these were aligned with their competitive strategies. The main hypothesis for the study was that high-performance work practices aligned with strategy would reduce labour turnover, increase productivity and increase financial performance.

Huselid's questionnaire, to which almost 3,500 replies were received, was sent to senior human resource professionals in a cross-sectoral sample of American organizations with more than 100 employees. A measure of the use of high-performance work practices was developed based on thirteen items in two categories – 'employee skills and organization structures' and 'employee motivation'. Huselid also obtained information on company performance from published accounts.

The main findings of this research were:

■ organizations using high-performance work practices had higher levels of productivity and corporate financial performance;

■ organizations using high-performance work practices in the employee skills and organization structure category had lower employee turnover;

■ a significant proportion of the impact of high-performance work practices on financial performance was due to lower labour turnover, or higher productivity, or both;

■ high-performance work practices contributed US$18,500 per employee in shareholder value and almost $4,000 per employee in additional profits (1995 prices).

Investment in human resource management practice can thus bring a demonstrable financial return in the form of reduced employee turnover, improved productivity and profitability. What of the argument that such practices are only appropriate in some contexts? Huselid points to the substantial impact of high-performance work practices, independent of the internal and external contexts. The findings support the argument that high-performance work practices improve financial performance regardless of the organization's strategy.

At least five criticisms can be levelled at this work:

1. A survey provides only a snapshot in time, making it difficult to establish causality, and lacks longitudinal data of the kind suggested, for example, by the Warwick model.

2. There are technical problems in subjecting straightforward survey questionnaire data to sophisticated (parametric, multivariate) statistical analysis.

3. The findings are based on commercial American firms which differ in their operations from companies in Europe and from public sector organizations in particular.

4. Organizational performance is defined in terms of financial indicators, and individual and social well-being are not considered to be relevant.

5. The definition of high-performance work practices omits other approaches and techniques, and does not permit the assessment of single methods or clusters of methods.

Nevertheless, Huselid's findings present a significant challenge to those who would dismiss human resource management as commercially irrelevant, and to those who seek to develop a more detailed understanding of the links between practice and organizational effectiveness.

High-performance work practices

Mark Huselid designed a questionnaire which gave each organization studied a score measuring its use of thirteen high-performance work practices in two categories.

Employee skills and organizational structures were measured on the following factors:

1. Formal information-sharing programmes

2. Formal job analysis

3. Internal appointments for promoted posts

4. Workforce attitude surveys

5. Quality of work life programmes, quality circles and participative teams

6. Company incentive and profit-sharing plans or gain-sharing plans

7. Training hours per typical employee

8. Formal grievance procedures and/or complaint resolution systems

9. Employment testing for new recruits

Employee motivation was measured on the following factors:

10. Performance appraisals used to determine financial reward

11. Formal performance appraisals

12. Promotion based on merit or performance rating, not seniority

13. The number of qualified applicants for the five most often recruited posts

These are the policies which encourage the 'desired employee behaviours' identified in the Rutgers model of HRM (Schuler and Jackson, 1987) shown in table 20.7. They also overlap with the HR policies in the Bath model (Purcell et al., 2003) shown in figure 20.7.

Based on Mark Huselid, 'The impact of human resource management practices on turnover, productivity, and corporate financial performance', *Academy of Management Journal*, vol. 38, no. 3, 1995, pp. 635–72.

The impact of people management policies

Jeffrey Pfeffer argues that human resource practices can raise an organization's stock market value by US$20,000 to $40,000 per employee. He claims that 'profits through people' are produced by seven people management policies:

1. Emphasis on job security

2. Recruiting the right people in the first place

3. Decentralization and self-managed teamworking

4. High wages linked to organizational performance

5. High investment in employee training

6. Reducing status differentials

7. Sharing information across the organization

Pfeffer's evidence, however, is anecdotal and fragmented.

Based on Jeffrey Pfeffer, *The Human Equation: Building Profits by Putting People First*, Harvard Business School Press, Boston, MA, 1998.

The Sheffield Group

Malcolm Patterson, Michael West, Rebecca Lawthorn and Stephen Nickell (1997) at the Institute for Work Psychology at the University of Sheffield have also explored the contribution of human resource management to organizational effectiveness, in a study which was commissioned by the Chartered Institute of Personnel and Development. The findings again reveal a measurable impact of human resource management on productivity and profitability. In a departure from Huselid's approach, this study also sought to establish the contribution to performance of other management strategies and tactics, none of which had the same positive impact on business performance as human resource management.

The findings are the result of a ten-year longitudinal study of management practice in over 100 manufacturing organizations in Britain. Senior managers were interviewed every two years, and half the companies took part in a survey of employee attitudes to various aspects of company functioning, including job satisfaction and organizational commitment. Company performance data were collected from company and management accounts. This study also used thirteen 'human resource management variables', broadly comparable with those used by Huselid to define 'high-performance work practices'. The adoption of these high-performance work practices varied considerably, as did management attitudes, across this sample.

The findings revealed that two 'clusters' of 'high-performance' human resource management practices in particular are significantly related to organizational productivity and profitability. The labels are different, but these clusters are broadly similar to the two main factors in Huselid's list of thirteen high-performance work practices:

1. **Skills development**: the acquisition and development of employee skills, through selection, induction, training and the use of performance appraisal systems.

2. **Job design**: the design of jobs, including skill flexibility, job responsibility, variety and the use of teams.

Some of the detailed findings include:

- high overall job satisfaction and organizational commitment are positively linked to high company profitability (but satisfaction is not clearly related to performance at an individual level);

- an organization culture that demonstrates concern for employee skill development and well-being is linked to high productivity and profitability;

- skills development and job design practices such as teamworking are positively linked to increased productivity and profitability;

- human resource management practice is a good predictor of performance: quality emphasis, corporate strategy, technological sophistication and investment in research and development contribute weakly to productivity and profitability.

Treat employees well, therefore, and profits will increase. Comparative research by this team has also revealed that British manufacturing companies place less emphasis on empowering and capturing the ideas of employees, and on adopting HR practices than, for example, Australia, Japan and Switzerland. Problems of productivity and innovation thus lie with work organization and management processes.

The Sheffield research is open to criticisms similar to those aimed at Huselid. In particular, the sample included only small to medium-sized manufacturing organizations (with up to 1,000 employees) and the findings do not necessarily apply to larger or public sector organizations. However, the longitudinal approach overcomes the 'snap shot' problem of single surveys, and non-financial indicators (satisfaction, commitment and management attitudes) are considered.

Despite the criticisms of human resource management, the use of the label, its definition, its substance and its treatment of particular issues, the Huselid and Sheffield studies provide positive, quantifiable evidence for its impact and value that is difficult to ignore. Richardson and Thompson (1999) offer a critical overview of this and similar research. Human resource management practitioners at last have hard data with which to justify their activity when confronted by the scepticism of their colleagues in other functions.

Stop and Criticize

The human resource management perspective based on high-performance work practices can be seen in two ways. These are enlightened management methods which empower, develop and emancipate employees, leading to individual and organizational gains, and sophisticated management controls which limit individual freedom by encouraging and rewarding 'good behaviour' to create a compliant workforce.

What are the arguments for and against these contrasting perspectives?

Is it new?

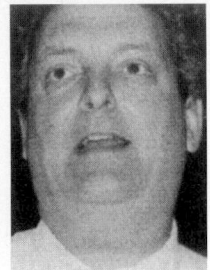

David Ulrich

Some commentators argue that human resource management is facing a crisis of identity and that a 'new agenda' is called for (Sparrow, 1998; Ulrich, 1997, 1998). David Ulrich (1998) argues that the 'new' role for human resource management has four elements:

1. The function should work in partnership with line managers in strategy execution.

2. The function should deliver organizational expertise to reduce costs and improve quality.

3. The function should be 'a champion for employees', representing their concerns to management and working to increase employees' contribution to performance.

4. The function should be 'an agent of continuous transformation', developing the organization's capacity for change.

Randall Schuler, Susan Jackson and John Storey (2001, p. 127) similarly argue that the HR professional has four key responsibilities – as 'strategic partner', 'innovator', 'collaborator' and 'change facilitator'. The problem is that personnel managers have always worked with line managers, although the focus has now moved to strategy. Job redesign and work organization have been central facets of the personnel role, even from an administrative point of view (job descriptions and classifications, job grading, job enrichment, teamworking). The welfare workers of the nineteenth century saw their role, in part, as being the 'employee voice'. In 1963, the Institute of Personnel Management recognized the profession's role in organizational change. It can therefore be argued that this radical 'new' HR agenda has very deep roots.

John Storey (1992) developed a classification of human resource management roles that is based on two considerations. Does the function perform a strategic or a tactical role? Is the function consultative or interventionist? The resulting four main roles are illustrated in figure 20.8.

The first welfare workers were handmaidens. Personnel management during and after the Second World War had a regulatory role. The aspiration of human resource managers combines strategic advisory and change-making roles. In this respect, human resource management has indeed acquired a new emphasis and new responsibilities.

Human resource management has been widely described as a new 'paradigm' – a new philosophy – of people management. How realistic is this claim? The evidence suggests that the adoption of high-performance work practices is not widespread (Storey, 1992; Bach and Sisson, 2000). Table 20.10 summarizes the findings of a major survey of workplaces in Britain in 1998. Only 2 per cent of workplaces reported using ten or more high-performance work practices. However, the survey also found that organizations reporting the use of new practices were more likely to report high productivity (Cully et al., 1998, p. 25). David Guest (2000) investigated eighteen HR practices, surveying more than 1,000 chief executives and HR directors in 237 companies. This study found that only 25 per cent of companies used more than half of those practices, and only 1 per cent used more than twelve or thirteen of them.

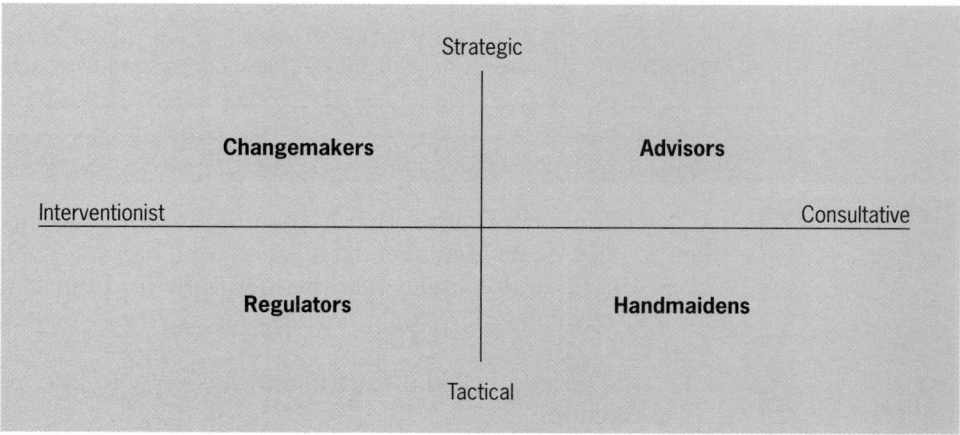

Figure 20.8: Four roles for human resource management

In other words, these 'best practices' are not as commonplace in practice as they are in textbooks. Why not? David Guest and Zella King (2001) suggest five reasons:

- managers may not be aware of the research;

- managers may feel that research evidence does not apply to their organization;

- managers may believe that they already have appropriate practices;

- there may be constraints from more pressing priorities;

- implementation skills may be lacking.

In a previous paper, Guest (1989) identified five conditions for the success of HRM. First, there must be senior management support. Second, there must be a shared management view that human resources are linked to corporate strategy. Third, job redesign must not be constrained by technology. Fourth, employees must not have instrumental attitudes to work and trade unions must not be adversarial. Finally, appropriate policies must be effectively advocated and implemented by HR specialists. These preconditions are formidable and perhaps also help to explain the relatively poor uptake of HRM.

There is further cause for concern, raised when claims for a 'new paradigm' are set against 'old' research, theory and organizational behaviour prescriptions. Here we will consider the four sets of practices which are used to define the content of human resource management in the Harvard and Warwick models of HRM. These practices concern employee influence, human resource flow, reward systems, and work systems (see table 20.3).

Employee influence

Joint consultation gained widespread popularity in the 1940s. Participative management has its roots in research carried out during the 1940s. Employee communication and 'considerate' leadership were features of the human relations school and theories of leadership behaviour in the 1950s. Problem-solving groups became popular during the 1960s and 1970s through the development of 'quality circles' by Japanese organizations. Teamworking is a technique based on the work of socio-technical systems theorists in the 1960s.

Human resource flow

Managing the size of the workforce by using part-time and temporary employment contracts is a long-established tradition. In the nineteenth century, it was common practice in shipbuilding (on the river Clyde in Scotland, for example) for shipyard workers to be employed intensively while a ship was being built, to be laid off on the day the ship was launched, then to be hired again when another order was secured. 'Flexitime', as a formal management practice, dates from the 1970s.

Reward systems

Frederick Taylor's scientific management, from the early twentieth century, was based on an individual pay-for-performance system: follow management instructions and meet and exceed targets and you got paid a high rate with a bonus. The concept of customizing rewards to individual needs and performance is an aspect of the expectancy theory of motivation, developed during the 1960s. Profit- and gain-sharing schemes also date from the 1960s.

Work systems

The role of goal-setting in improving performance, and in particular the concept of 'stretch goals', is another well-known motivational technique from the 1960s and 1970s. Interest in the personality traits of charismatic, inspirational leaders dates back to the beginning of the twentieth century and attracted renewed interest in the 1990s in the form of 'transformational leaders' and 'superleaders'. Alvin Toffler and Warren Bennis, among others, have argued since the late 1960s that tall, hierarchical, bureaucratic structures are ineffective in dealing with environmental change and that flat, flexible decentralized structures perform better. The use of autonomous, self-managing teams is a work design technique which became popular in the 1960s and has been in use ever since.

Personnel management has a new title, advocates 'high-performance work practices' and aspires to a strategic organizational role. The name may be new. The strategic contribution and increased status and influence may be new. However, the practical, prescriptive dimension of the human resource management paradigm repackages what organizational behaviour research has been prescribing for most of the twentieth century – and beyond.

Table 20.10: Percentages of workplaces using high-performance work practices

Appraisal and reward (non-managerial employees)	%
performance appraisal	56
performance-related pay	11
share ownership	15
profit sharing	30
Involvement and participation	
joint consultative committee	28
regular meetings of workforce	37
problem-solving groups, such as quality circles	42
staff attitude surveys	45
team briefing	61
work teams	65
Training and development	
at least five days training per employee a year	12
supervisors trained in employee relations skills	27
Status and security	
no compulsory redundancy policy and guaranteed job security	14
single status between managerial and non-managerial employees	41
selection based partly on aptitude tests	22

Adapted from Table in Bach, S. and Sisson, K., *Personnel Management: A Comprehensive Guide to Theory and Practice*, Blackwell Publishers, 2000, p. 22. Data source M. Cully, A. O'Reilly, N. Millward, J. Forth, S. Woodland, G. Dix and A. Bryson, *The 1998 Workplace Employee Relations Survey: First Findings*, Department of Trade and Industry, London, 1998.

Recap

1. *Explain why most medium-sized and large organizations have specialized personnel or human resource management functions.*

   - Increased organizational size and complexity, the growth in employment legislation, and the contributions of skilled, motivated and committed people to organizational effectiveness make this an area of specialist knowledge and expertise.

   - Wartime production pressures exposed general management weaknesses and heightened concern for employee welfare, strengthening the specialist role of the function.

2. *Understand the distinction between personnel management and human resource management.*

   - Personnel management is traditionally seen as a reactive, background function concerned with the administration of the employment cycle (hiring, training, paying, firing).

   - Human resource management is more concerned with the proactive design and implementation of integrated employment policies aligned with organization strategy.

3. *Explain the distinctions between different models of human resource management.*

   - The Michigan model argues that the elements in the human resource cycle must be integrated and matched to organization strategy.

   - The Harvard model argues that human resource policies are shaped by stakeholders and that effective policies lead to organizational, individual and social gains.

   - The Rutgers model argues that there is a range of human resource policy choices which are contingent on the organization's competitive strategy.

   - The Warwick model argues that human resource policies are shaped over extended periods of time through a dynamic process influenced by a range of contextual factors.

   - The Bath model argues that discretionary behaviour to go beyond minimum requirements relies on a combination of HR policies and effective line management implementation.

4. *Explain the strategic contribution which the human resource function potentially makes to organizational effectiveness.*

   - High-performance work practices demonstrably increase organizational profitability by decreasing employee turnover and improving productivity.

   - Two 'clusters' of high-performance practices are significant, concerning the way in which skills are developed and the way in which jobs are designed.

5. *Identify the main criticisms levelled against human resource management as a concept and as a management function.*

   - Definitions of HRM are ambiguous, practitioners suffer from a lack of commercial credibility, the 'new' high-performance practices reflect existing organizational behaviour thinking, and human resource 'best practices' are not in widespread use.

Revision

1. Why do most medium-sized and large organizations have specialist personnel or human resource management departments?

2. What factors contributed to the development of the personnel or human resource function as a distinct management profession during the twentieth century?

3. What factors in the second half of the twentieth century strengthened the argument that 'people are assets not costs' in an organizational context?

4. What is the distinction between personnel and human resource management? Why is this distinction important?

5. Many commentators argue that it is crucial to align human resource policies with the organization's strategy. Explain the strengths and weaknesses of this argument, and show how it works in practice using one of the models of human resource management which takes this approach.

Springboard

Bach, S. and Sisson, K. (eds), 2000, *Personnel Management: A Comprehensive Guide to Theory and Practice*, Blackwell Business, Oxford (third edition).

Authoritative overview with an academic emphasis, covering the context of personnel management, planning and resourcing, employee development, pay and performance, and work relations. Does not use 'human resource management' in its title.

Beardwell, I. and Holden, L. (eds), 2001, *Human Resource Management: A Contemporary Perspective*, Financial Times/Prentice Hall, Harlow (third edition).

A comprehensive introductory text which covers issues, trends and debates. There are sections on the HRM context, resourcing, training and development, the employment relationship (contracts, rewards, involvement) and international human resource management. See in particular the three chapters by Len Holden on international and comparative HR, and on HR in Europe and Asia.

Legge, K., 1995, *Human Resource Management: Rhetorics and Realities*, Macmillan Business, Basingstoke.

A critical survey of contemporary debates from an author whose contributions in this field are seminal and always interesting. Challenging and clearly written.

Redman, T. and Wilkinson, A., 2001, *Contemporary Human Resource Management: Text and Cases*, Financial Times Prentice Hall, Harlow.

A clearly written introductory text (competition for Beardwell and Holden) covering 'fundamentals' and 'contemporary themes'. Includes teaching cases, role plays and other exercise materials.

Richardson, R. and Thompson, M., 1999, *The Impact of People Management Practices on Business Performance: A Literature Review*, Institute of Personnel and Development, London.

Clear, thorough and critical review of research into the contribution of high-performance work practices to organizational effectiveness. Also short at 78 pages. Companion publication to the research findings in Patterson et al. (1997).

Schuler, R.S. and Jackson, S.E. (eds), 1999, *Strategic Human Resource Management*, Blackwell Business, Oxford.

An excellent reference collection of twenty-four previously published papers exploring the human resource management debate of the 1990s. Wide-ranging in content, this is unusual in combining work from European and North American commentators.

Storey, J. (ed.), 2001, *Human Resource Management: A Critical Text*, Thomson Learning, London.

This is a definitive collection of chapters on strategic issues, 'key practice areas', international human resource management and future prospects. Chapter authors include many of the main British and American contributors to the HRM debate.

Torrington, D. and Hall, L., 1998, *Human Resource Management*, Prentice Hall, London (fourth edition).

Competition for Beardwell and Holden and more practitioner-oriented, covering contemporary debates and also exploring personnel techniques in some detail.

Home viewing

The Enforcer (1976, director James Fargo) is another 'Dirty Harry' movie in which the uncompromising San Francisco cop is played by Clint Eastwood. For his apparently indiscriminate slaughter of criminals (he is supposed to arrest some of them) Harry is disciplined by being transferred to the personnel department, where he is involved in the selection process for his next partner who turns out to be – shock, horror – a woman, Kate Moore (played by Tyne Daly). Sadly, Kate doesn't survive the movie. In the scenes concerning Harry's transfer, what image of personnel work is being reinforced? What explicit and implicit criticisms of personnel management work are being exposed?

OB in literature

Floyd Kemske, *Human Resources: A Business Novel*, Nicholas Brealey, London, 1996.

A caricature of exploitative management, based on the methods of Pierce, the 'turn-around manager' hired to change the fortunes of Biomethods Inc, a struggling biotechnology company. Pierce, however, is a vampire (spot the symbolism). The company's human resource manager, Norman, survives Pierce's purge of top management because he has a skill that Pierce lacks – he 'affiliates'. Despite his title, Norman is a traditional administrator whose personnel procedures do not seem to fit with the faster and more flexible re-engineered style preferred by Pierce. Whose management methods are more effective?

Chapter exercises

1: Hard or soft?

Objectives   1. To identify individual differences in perceptions of the role of personnel or human resource management.

2. To examine the links between the concepts of 'hard' and 'soft' HRM and other theories of organizational behaviour.

Briefing   John Storey (2001) argues that the term 'human resource management' is used in a number of contradictory ways. What is your perception of the role of the function? Read each of the following ten statements, rating your agreement with each on the five-point scale on the right.

	strongly disagree	disagree	neutral	agree	strongly agree
1 human resource management must ensure that employees are treated like any other asset	❏	❏	❏	❏	❏
2 human resource management is about ensuring that all employees share the same goals	❏	❏	❏	❏	❏
3 one key human resource management job is to control headcount and payroll	❏	❏	❏	❏	❏
4 human resource management's task is to design policies that encourage commitment	❏	❏	❏	❏	❏
5 deskilling and task fragmentation are necessary steps to control labour costs	❏	❏	❏	❏	❏
6 employees should be encouraged to develop to their full potential	❏	❏	❏	❏	❏
7 human resource management must design work practices that fully exploit employees' potential	❏	❏	❏	❏	❏
8 the key aspect of human resource management concerns developing employee resourcefulness	❏	❏	❏	❏	❏
9 employees should be given performance targets and be expected to meet them	❏	❏	❏	❏	❏
10 human resource policies should be designed to encourage high individual performance	❏	❏	❏	❏	❏

Scoring

Use this scoring key:	Your 'hard' score:	Your 'soft' score:
strongly disagree = 1 disagree = 2 neutral = 3 agree = 4 strongly agree = 5	Add your scores for the odd-numbered items: Hard score: _____	Add your scores for the even-numbered items: Soft score: _____

2: To dismiss or not to dismiss

Objectives

1. To examine the circumstances in which it is legitimate to dismiss employees for misconduct of some kind and when it is not legitimate to act in this way.

2. To consider the nature of human resource management expertise.

Briefing

As a professional human resource manager, you are frequently asked for advice on a number of matters. One of the most sensitive and difficult issues concerns employee misconduct, which can potentially lead to the dismissal of those concerned.

The following five cases of apparent employee misconduct are based on real examples. Consider, for each case, the following questions:

■ As a human resource manager who believes in 'soft' HRM, what action would you recommend?

■ As a human resource manager who believes in 'hard' HRM, what action would you recommend?

■ In both cases, on what grounds (commercial, managerial, humanitarian, other) would you justify your decision? Ignore legal considerations for the purposes of this exercise. The law differs from country to country. Concentrate on the other grounds on which you would justify your 'soft' and 'hard' decisions.

1. You are the human resource manager for a fast food chain. One of your employees tells you that the manager of one of your outlets is often seen eating a rival brand of fried chicken.

2. You are the human resource manager for a major airline. You discover that one of your stewardesses is a member of a stripping and spanking service called Hot Sex.

3. You are the human resource manager for a small printing firm. You discover that the managing director's (male) chauffeur has a habit of flashing (and we don't mean his headlights) at motorists and was found recently standing by the M40 wearing a bra, stockings and suspenders.

4. You are the human resource manager for a publishing company. You read in the local press that one of your advertising executives has been found guilty of using recreational drugs at home.

5. You are the human resource manager for a multinational toy company. You read in one of the 'sensationalist' Sunday papers that your chief executive has been having sex seven times a night with a woman from an escort service.

This exercise is based on Paul Simpson, 'Blurred boundaries', *Personnel Today*, 16 November 1999, p. 31.

Part 6 Organization management

A field map of the organizational behaviour terrain

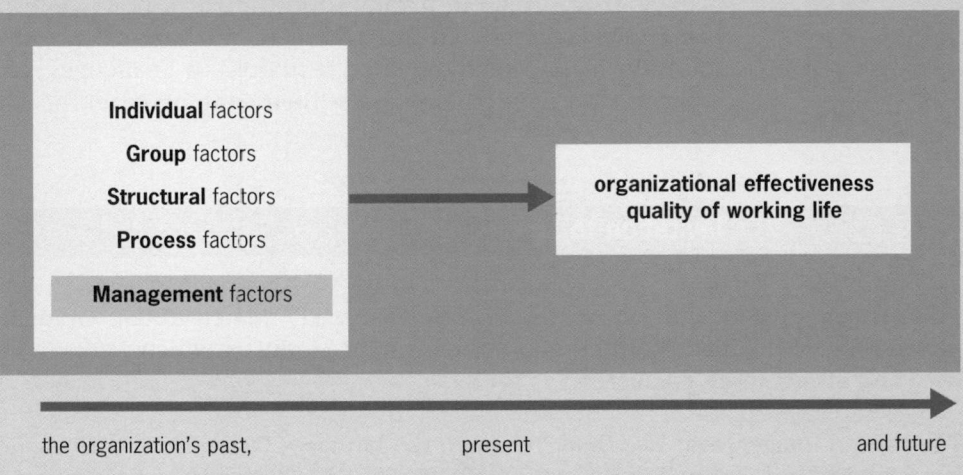

PESTLE: The **P**olitical, **E**conomic, **S**ocial, **T**echnological, **L**egal and **E**cological context

Individual factors
Group factors
Structural factors
Process factors
Management factors

organizational effectiveness
quality of working life

the organization's past,   present   and future

Introduction

Part 6, Organization management, explores four topics:

- Leadership in chapter 21
- Decision-making in chapter 22
- Conflict in chapter 23
- Power and politics in chapter 24

Each of these topics has an enormous impact on how employees are managed, how they experience their work environment and how successful their organization is in achieving its goals. Each topic concerns the process of 'managing', which involves both managers and non-managers. Thus, the most junior of employees may be called upon to exercise their leadership skills, become involved in group decision-making, attempt to resolve a conflict between colleagues, while engaging in political behaviour in order to increase their power.

Chapter 21 on leadership begins with a historical introduction to the topic which identifies common themes in different leadership theories and highlights contemporary debates about the nature of leadership. Chapter 22 on decision-making considers different models of decision-making, different types of decisions, different decision-makers and different problems in decision-making. It challenges the notion that most decisions are made logically for the benefit of the organization by managers who possess the necessary information and authority. Chapter 23 on conflict considers the topic from the point of view of contrasting perspectives on conflict, and stresses how the way you perceive a situation influences what actions you take. It examines how the way a company is organized

itself engenders conflicts which, in turn, have to be managed through the incorporation of conflict resolution devices. Finally, chapter 24 addresses the highly abstract but possibly the most crucial of all the concepts used to explain the behaviour of people in organizations – that of power and politics. The political perspective provides an alternative to the rational standpoint predominantly found in managerially oriented textbooks. It challenges readers to go back over earlier chapter topics, to re-assess their contents from this alternative viewpoint.

Invitation to see

The first of these images, from the *Financial Times* (17 March 2003, 'Graduate Recruitment' supplement), accompanied an article about the insurance industry which wants to improve its reputation with and attract more graduates.

The second image, from *The Daily Telegraph* (26 January 2001), shows a Hugo Boss Sales Adviser at a launch party in London demonstrating a new range of 'executive womenswear'. There was no article with this photograph, only an extended caption which also reveals that, '[a]ccording to the designer, the Boss woman is "an achiever, who can juggle the demands of family and career with skill and self-assurance".'

Lloyd's of London has had its share of disasters
Source: © Reuters 2001. Reuters news picture service photograph by Michael Crabtree 26/09/2001.

Sales Advisor Heather Padua shows fashion designer Hugo Boss's new range of executive womenswear in the City of London yesterday with a launch party at its flagship Queen Street store.
Source: The Daily Telegraph/Marina Imperi.

1. **Decoding:** Look at these images closely. Note in as much detail as possible what messages you feel they are each trying to convey. Do they tell a story, present a point of view, support an argument, perpetuate a myth, reinforce a stereotype, challenge a stereotype?

2. **Challenging:** To what extent do you agree with the messages, stories, points of view, arguments, myths or stereotypes in these images? Are these images open to challenge, to criticism, to interpretation or decoding in other ways, revealing other messages?

3. **Sharing:** Compare with colleagues your interpretation of these images. Explore explanations for differences in your respective decodings.

Chapter 21 Leadership

Key concepts

leadership	consideration
great man theory	initiating structure
power	contingency theory of leadership
reward power	least preferred coworker score
coercive power	structured task
referent power	unstructured task
legitimate power	situational leadership
expert power	new leader
information power	superleader
affiliation power	transactional leader
group power	transformational leader

Learning outcomes

When you have read this chapter, you should be able to define those key concepts in your own words, and you should also be able to:

1. Explain the apparent difference between the concepts of leadership and management.
2. Understand why there is little relationship between personality traits and effective leadership.
3. Understand the bases of a leader's power and the role of followers in creating and supporting leaders.
4. Understand why effective leaders either adapt their style to fit the organizational and cultural context in which they operate or find contexts which fit their personal style.
5. Explain contemporary trends in this field concerning new leadership, the dispersal of leadership and the argument that leaders are unnecessary.

Why study leadership?

Leadership appears to be a critical determinant of organizational effectiveness, whether we are discussing an army, an orchestra, a hockey team, a street gang, a political party, a group of rock climbers or a multinational corporation. It is not surprising to find, therefore, that leadership is the subject of intense academic research and debate, and journalistic commentary. Historically, this interest is a relatively recent phenomenon. Frank Heller (1997, p. 340) notes that in 1896, the United States Library of Congress had not one book on the subject of leadership. The global literature on the subject is now vast and diverse.

Why is leadership such a controversial topic? This is a subject with many paradoxes. We hear the complaint that 'we need more leadership'. However, the organizational hierarchy and formal authority that underpin leadership positions are increasingly being challenged. We tend to equate leadership with positions of power, influence and status. However, acts of leadership can be observed at all levels of the organization structure. Leaders have job titles and working conditions which symbolize their status. However, flat structures, team-based working, the growth of knowledge work, and virtual and networked organizational forms, all weaken traditional leadership positions based on hierarchy and organizational symbolism.

One influential researcher, Ralph Stogdill (1950, p. 3) defined **leadership** as an influencing process aimed at goal achievement.

Stogdill's definition has three key components. First, it defines leadership as an interpersonal process in which one individual seeks to shape and direct the behaviour of others. Second, it sets leadership in a social context, in which the members of the group to be influenced are subordinates or followers. Third, it establishes a criterion for effective leadership in goal achievement, which is one practical objective of leadership theory and research. Most definitions share these processual, contextual and evaluative components.

> **Leadership**: the process of influencing the activities of an organized group in its efforts towards goal-setting and goal achievement.

Stop and Criticize

Consider those whom you would call leaders, including business and political figures, alive now or in recent decades.

What characteristics, skills, abilities and personality traits do they have in common?

In your judgement, which of these leaders have had a positive impact on society and its organizations, and which have had a negative impact?

Your list of leaders might include:

Megawati Sukarnoputri	Usama Bin Laden	Anita Roddick
Richard Branson	Benazir Bhutto	George W. Bush
Mother Teresa	John Howard	Margaret Thatcher
Nelson Mandela	Aung San Suu Kyi	Bill Gates

As Frank Heller (1997) asks, how can the single term 'leader' be applied to such a diverse set of personalities, whose behaviours have had a range of different consequences? This chapter explores six perspectives on the study of leadership:

1. **Trait-spotting:** Attempts to identify the personality traits and other related attributes of the effective leader in order to facilitate the selection of leaders.

2. **Style-counselling:** Attempts to characterize different leadership behaviour patterns to identify effective and ineffective leadership styles in order to improve the training and development of leaders.

3. **Context-fitting:** Contingency theories which argue that the effectiveness of particular leadership behaviours is dependent on the organizational and cultural setting, which can also facilitate leadership awareness and training.

4. **New leadership:** Prescriptive approaches which identify 'new leaders', 'superleaders' and 'transformational leaders' as heroic and inspirational

visionaries who give purpose and direction to others, with an emphasis on senior executives and politicians whose motivational role is said to be central to organization strategy and effectiveness.

5. **Dispersing the role:** A perspective which observes that leadership behaviour is not confined to those with formal leadership roles but can be observed across the organization hierarchy, and thus one aspect of the 'new superleadership' role is to develop self-leadership skills in others.

6. **Who needs leaders:** Argues that leaders can destabilize an organization by driving too much change too quickly, causing burnout and initiative fatigue, and that managers with change implementation skills are more effective.

Alan Bryman (1996) notes that these perspectives developed chronologically. Trait-spotting was popular until the 1940s when inconsistent research findings led to disillusionment. Style-counselling was then popular until the late 1960s, but appeared oversimplified in the face of the contingency theories which dominated thinking until the early 1980s. At that point, the 'new leadership' movement developed. Towards the close of the twentieth century, recognition of the dispersed nature of leadership behaviour attracted more attention. Then, during the opening years of the twenty-first century, several commentators challenged the value of leadership, observing that 'celebrity bosses' in particular were responsible for the rapid and radical change that caused initiative fatigue and organizational destabilization.

It would be incorrect to regard these shifts in emphasis as replacing earlier accounts. On the contrary, much current commentary has returned to trait-spotting. Organization development methods still rely on style-counselling theories and techniques. Contingency theories, arguing that an effective leadership style depends on the context, still offer useful prescriptive accounts of leadership behaviour for management development programmes. Much of the historical material in this chapter therefore continues to have a contemporary relevance.

Leaders are men with special qualities

Discussion of leadership is so often overloaded with vague but emotive ideas that one is hard put to it to nail the concept down. To cut through the panoply of such quasi-moral and unexceptionable associations as 'patriotism', 'play up and play the game', the 'never-asking-your-men-to-do-something-you-wouldn't-do-yourself' formula, 'not giving in (or up)', the 'square-jaw-frank-eyes-steadfast-gaze' formula, and the 'if ... you'll be a man' recipe, one comes to the simple truth that *leadership is no more than exercising such an influence upon others that they tend to act in concert towards achieving a goal which they might not have achieved so readily had they been left to their own devices.*

The ingredients which bring about this agreeable state of affairs are many and varied. At the most superficial level they are believed to include such factors as voice, stature and appearance, an impression of omniscience, trustworthiness, sincerity and bravery. At a deeper and rather more important level, leadership depends upon a proper understanding of the needs and opinions of those one hopes to lead, and the context in which the leadership occurs. It also depends on good timing. Hitler, who was neither omniscient, trustworthy nor sincere, whose stature was unremarkable and whose appearance verged on the repellent, understood these rules and exploited them to full advantage. The same may be said of many good comedians.

From Norman F. Dixon, *On the Psychology of Military Incompetence*, Pimlico, London, 1994, pp. 214–15 (emphasis added).

Leadership versus management

What is the difference between leadership and management? Some commentators argue that these terms are synonymous, as leadership is simply one facet of the management role. Other commentators argue that this distinction is significant, as leaders and managers play different roles and make different contributions – leaders have followers, managers have subordinates.

Those who make the distinction portray the leader as someone who develops visions and drives new initiatives, and portray the manager as someone who monitors progress towards objectives to achieve order and reliability. Warren Bennis and Burt Nanus (1985, p. 21) observe that managers do things right, while leaders do the right thing. The leader is prophet, catalyst, mover-shaker, focused on strategy. The manager is operator, technician and problem-solver, concerned 'with the here-and-now of goal attainment' (Bryman, 1986, p. 6). The distinguishing feature here is orientation to change (Zaleznik, 1977).

John Kotter's (1990) contrast between the functions of leaders and managers is summarized in table 21.1. The leader establishes vision and direction, influences others to sign up to that vision, inspires them to overcome obstacles, and produces positive and sometimes radical change. The manager establishes plans and budgets, designs and staffs the organization structure, monitors and controls performance, and delivers order and predictability.

Joseph Rost (1991) argues that this is a 'good guys, bad guys' caricature. Kotter's perspective elevates leadership and denigrates management. If you really want to find out just how much people value the consistent, predictable manager, Rost suggests:

- deliver payroll cheques late;

- cut off the supplies and services which people need to do their jobs;

- run the buses, trains and planes late and switch off traffic lights;

- deliver unworkable products to customers;

- base promotions and salary increases on arbitrary criteria.

Table 21.1: Leadership versus management

	Leadership functions	Management functions
Creating an agenda	*Establishing direction*: vision of the future, develop strategies for change to achieve goals	*Plans and budgets*: decide actions and timetables, allocate resources
Developing people	*Aligning people*: communicate vision and strategy, influence creation of teams which accept validity of goals	*Organizing and staffing*: decide structure and allocate staff, develop policies, procedures and monitoring
Execution	*Motivating and inspiring*: energize people to overcome obstacles, satisfy human needs	*Controlling, problem solving*: monitor results against plan and take corrective action
Outcomes	Produces positive and sometimes dramatic change	Produces order, consistency and predictability

Based on John p. Kotter, *A Force for Change: How Leadership Differs from Management*, Free Press, New York, 1990.

Rost concludes that 'Down with management and up with leadership is a bad idea.' Many commentators ignore this advice. What is the value of order, predictability and consistency in today's turbulent, hostile organizational context in which innovation is at a premium? Setting visions and strategies is much more fun than planning and budgeting.

If they are not leaders, what do managers do? From his observation of how managers spend their time, Henry Mintzberg (1977) distinguished ten roles under three main headings:

interpersonal roles   leader, figurehead, liaison

informational roles   monitor, disseminator, spokesperson

decisional roles   entrepreneur, disturbance handler, resource allocator, negotiator

Mintzberg's research suggested that, in practice, the distinction between leadership and management is blurred. The roles overlap. Leadership is one dimension of a multifaceted management role. The effective manager requires at least some leadership qualities. The neat conceptual distinction between leader and manager does not translate neatly into practice.

Patterns of management behaviour

John Kotter studied management behaviour using interviews, observation, questionnaires and documents. His analysis of the work of the general manager is as follows:

They spend most of their time with others	The average manager spends 25 per cent of his or her time alone; some spend 90 per cent with others
They spend time with many people in addition to their direct subordinates and their bosses	They regularly meet with people who appear to be unimportant outsiders
The breadth of topics in their discussions is extremely wide	Not limited to business issues, managers discuss virtually anything
General managers ask a lot of questions	In a half-hour conversation, some managers will ask literally hundreds of questions
During conversations, general managers rarely seem to make 'big' decisions	So why is 'decision-making' considered such a key part of the manager's role?
Their discussions usually contain a fair amount of joking and often concern topics not related to work	Humour is often about others in the organization or sector; non-work discussions are usually about families and hobbies
In many encounters, the issue discussed is relatively unimportant to the organization	General managers regularly engage in activities even they regard as a waste of time
In these encounters, managers rarely give orders in a traditional sense	So why is 'giving direction' considered such a key part of the manager's role?
Nevertheless, general managers often attempt to influence others	Instead of telling people what to do, they ask, request, cajole, persuade, intimidate
General managers often react to others; much of the typical day is unplanned	Even those with a heavy schedule spend a lot of time on topics not on their formal agenda

➤

| General managers spend most of their time with others in short, disjointed conversations | Discussions of single questions or issues rarely last more than ten minutes; it is not unusual to cover ten unrelated topics in five minutes |
| They work long hours | Average is 60 to 90 hours a week; but how can they apparently waste so much time? |

Based on John p. Kotter, 'What effective general managers really do', *Harvard Business Review*, vol. 77, no. 2, 1999, pp. 145–59.

Trait-spotting: the search for personality markers

For the first half of the twentieth century, researchers assumed that they could identify the personality traits and other qualities of leaders. It would then be possible to select individuals who possessed those markers, and to promote them into leadership positions.

A profile of the superior chief executive

A study carried out by *Fortune* magazine on leading American executives revealed eight qualities that characterize 'the champs':

1. *Integrity, maturity and energy.* This is the foundation on which everything else is built.
2. *Business acumen.* Understanding the business and a strong profit incentive.
3. *People acumen.* Leading teams, coaching people, cutting losses when necessary.
4. *Organizational acumen.* Engendering trust, sharing information, decisive and incisive.
5. *Curiosity, intellectual capacity, global mindset.* External focus, hungry for knowledge.
6. *Superior judgement.*
7. *An insatiable appetite for accomplishment and results.*
8. *Powerful motivation to grow and convert learning into practice.*

Based on Ram Charm and Geoffrey Colvin, 'Why CEOs fail', *Fortune*, vol. 139, no. 12, 21 June 1999, pp. 69–78.

Great man theory: a historical perspective which argues that the fate of societies and organizations is in the hands of powerful, idiosyncratic (male) individuals.

This search for the qualities of good leaders was influenced by the **great man theory**.

Great man theory focused on political figures, arguing that leaders reach positions of influence from which they dominate and direct the lives of others by force of personality. It is interesting to note that there is no equivalent 'great woman theory'. Great men are born leaders, and emerge to take power regardless of the social, organizational or historical context. Research thus focused on identifying the traits of these special people. Ralph Stogdill reviewed hundreds of trait studies (1948; 1974, p. 81) and compiled this typical list:

- strong drive for responsibility;
- focus on completing the task;
- vigour and persistence in pursuit of goals;
- venturesomeness and originality in problem-solving;

Ralf M. Stogdill
(1904–78)

- drive to exercise initiative in social settings;

- self-confidence;

- sense of personal identity;

- willingness to accept consequences of decisions and actions;

- readiness to absorb interpersonal stress;

- willingness to tolerate frustration and delay;

- ability to influence the behaviour of others;

- capacity to structure social systems to the purpose in hand.

Rosemary Stewart (1963) cites a study in which American executives were asked to identify indispensable leadership qualities. They came up with the following fifteen traits:

judgement	initiative	integrity
foresight	energy	drive
human relations skill	decisiveness	dependability
emotional stability	fairness	ambition
dedication	objectivity	co-operation

It is difficult to challenge these qualities cited by either Stogdill or Stewart. Can we say that leaders should lack judgement, be undependable, lack drive, ambition, creativity and integrity, and have little foresight? Both identify 'drive' as a key trait. However, Stogdill lists venturesomeness, self-confidence, stress tolerance and system structuring as traits, which Stewart omits. Stewart identifies foresight, fairness, integrity and co-operation, which are missing from Stogdill's list.

This line of research was unable to establish a consistent set of leadership traits. As research developed, covering a wider range of settings, larger numbers of leadership qualities were identified. Different studies generated different lists. A total of almost eighty characteristics were reported from a review of twenty studies of leadership traits (Bird, 1940). More than half of these traits had been identified in only one study, very few appeared in four or more investigations, and only 'intelligence' was reported in at least half of the studies reviewed. A further problem is that many of these traits are vague. Willingness to tolerate delay? Capacity to structure social systems? Human relations skill? Ambition? It is difficult to see how trait-spotting can be used in a leadership selection context, as originally intended.

It was therefore clear by 1950 that there was limited value in trying to identify leadership traits, although some weak generalizations did emerge (Shaw, 1976, p. 275; Fraser, 1978, p. 192). Leaders tend to score higher on average on measures of:

ability	intelligence, relevant knowledge, verbal facility
sociability	participation, co-operativeness, popularity
motivation	initiative and persistence

Trait-spotting was abandoned as researchers switched attention, first to leadership behaviour patterns, and then to dimensions of the organizational context. However, despite the known problems, the belief persists that the special traits of leaders can be identified. We have, therefore, seen a recently renewed search for the personality markers of leaders (Leigh and Walters, 1998; Kamp, 1999). Paradoxically, trait-spotting is a contemporary perspective.

Still trait-spotting after all these years

The British National Health Service, concerned with implementing ambitious government plans for healthcare modernization, commissioned Hay Group, a management consultancy, to identify the qualities required of senior leaders. Based on research involving 150 chief executives and directors, the *NHS Leadership Qualities Framework* identifies, in three clusters, the fifteen qualities that distinguish 'effective and outstanding leaders':

Personal qualities

- self-belief

- self-awareness

- self-management

- drive for improvement

- personal integrity

Setting direction

- seizing the future

- intellectual flexibility

- broad scanning

- political astuteness

- drive for results

Delivering the service

- leading change through people

- holding to account

- empowering others

- effective and strategic influencing

- collaborative working

In addition to 'leadership profiling for recruitment and selection', this framework is intended to be used for personal development, career mapping, succession planning, performance management and appraisal, and to 'assess corporate leadership capacity and capability'.

Based on Department of Health, *NHS Leadership Qualities Framework*, Modernization Agency, The NHS Leadership Centre, London, 2002.

Trait-spotting entrepreneurs

Most leadership research is based on studies of large (typically American) organizations. However, in the 1990s, 96 per cent of British employers had fewer than twenty employees, and firms with fewer than 100 employees accounted for 50 per cent of all employment. The evidence suggests that small firms are growing in number, and that they create more jobs than their large (often 'downsizing') cousins (Murphy, 1996, pp. 3–4).

A small business has a number of distinguishing features:

1. The owner-manager has an overwhelming influence, more than any single manager in a large organization.

2. The small firm is unlikely to be able to influence its market, in particular its prices and the range of services and products which it can provide, which makes the business risky.

3. The small firm is likely to be dependent on a small number of customers, which heightens the vulnerability of the business.

4. Small firms often have problems raising capital, which constrains growth.

So what are the personality traits of a successful entrepreneur? Summarizing the research, Burns and Jewhurst (1996, pp. 48–9) identify five characteristics:

High need for achievement: This can mean, for example, making your first million, producing a work of art or employing your hundredth person.

Internal locus of control: Entrepreneurs believe that events, or their 'destiny', are within their personal control. People with an external locus of control believe in 'fate' and are less likely to risk starting their own business.

Risk taking: Entrepreneurs are 'measured risk takers', rarely pursuing business opportunities which have a low chance of success, but are prepared to put themselves into risky positions which will contribute to enterprise growth.

Independence: Entrepreneurs want to be their own boss, control their own destiny and have problems working for anybody else (they make 'difficult employees').

Innovation: Entrepreneurs are more likely to do things that are different or to combine known business elements in new ways, rather than use truly innovative ideas.

Based on Paul Burns and Jim Jewhurst (eds), *Small Business and Entrepreneurship*, Macmillan Business, Basingstoke (second edition), 1996, pp. 48–9.

Power: what is it, and how can I get more?

Power: the capacity of individuals to overcome resistance on the part of others, to exert their will and to produce results consistent with their interests and objectives.

Leadership is about influencing the behaviour of others. One cannot be a leader without followers, and followers must be willing to obey. To understand why people are influenced by some individuals and not others, we need to understand the nature of compliance.

Power is a useful concept with which to explain the social process of interpersonal influence. Power is a critical dimension of leadership, and we can define power in much the same way that we have defined leadership; power is the ability of an individual to control or to influence others, to get someone else to do something that they would perhaps not otherwise do (Astley and Sachdeva, 1984; Pettigrew and McNulty, 1995).

Reward power: the ability of a leader to exert influence based on the belief of followers that the leader has access to valued rewards which will be dispensed in return for compliance.

Coercive power: the ability of a leader to exert influence based on the belief of followers that the leader can administer unwelcome penalties or sanctions.

Referent power: the ability of a leader to exert influence based on the belief of followers that the leader has desirable abilities and personality traits that can and should be copied.

Legitimate power: the ability of a leader to exert influence based on the belief of followers that the leader has authority to issue orders which they in turn have an obligation to accept.

Expert power: the ability of a leader to exert influence based on the belief of followers that the leader has superior knowledge relevant to the situation and the task in hand.

John French and Bertram Raven (1958) identified five main bases of power: **reward**, **coercive**, **referent**, **legitimate** and **expert power**.

Referent power is also known as charisma. Legitimate power is also described as position power, as it relies on the individual's formal organizational role and title. Table 21.2 summarizes the more recent contribution of Robert Benfari, Harry Wilkinson and Charles Orth (1986), who identify eight power bases, adding **information**, **affiliation** and **group power**.

Table 21.2: The effective use of power

Power base	Explanation	Perceived as
Reward	remuneration, awards, compliments, symbolic gestures of praise	*P+*
Coercion	physical or psychological injury, symbolic gestures of disdain, demotion, unwanted transfer, withholding resources	*P−*
Authority	management right to control, obligation of others to obey, playing 'the boss' and abusing authority	*P−*
	exercise of leadership in times of crisis or need	*P+*
Referent	identification based on personal characteristics, sometimes on perception of charisma; or reciprocal identification based on friendship, association, sharing information, common interests, values and preferences	*P+*
Expert	possession of specialized knowledge valued by others, used to help others, given freely when solicited	*P+*
	unsolicited expertise creates barriers; expertise offered condescendingly is coercive; withholding expertise in times of need	*P−*
Information	access to information that is not public knowledge, because of position or connections; can exist at all organizational levels; secretaries and personal assistants to executives often have information power and can control information flows	*P−*
Affiliation	'borrowed' from an authority source – executive secretaries and assistants act as surrogates for their superiors	*P+*
	acting on their own self-interest; using negative affiliation power by applying accounting and personnel policies rigidly	*P−*
Group	collective problem-solving, conflict resolution, creative brainstorming; group resolution greater than the individual contribution	*P+*
	a few individuals dominating the proceedings, 'groupthink'	*P−*

Based on Robert C. Benfari, Harry E. Wilkinson and Charles D. Orth, 'The effective use of power', *Business Horizons*, vol. 29, May–June 1986, pp. 12–16.

Information power: the ability of a leader to exert influence based on the belief of followers that the leader has access to information that is not public knowledge.

Affiliation power: the ability of a leader to exert influence based on the belief of followers that the leader has a close association with other powerful figures on whose authority they are able to act.

Several points follow from these definitions.

First, as indicated in the right-hand column of table 21.2, the exercise of power is not always perceived in negative terms (P−). Rewards are usually welcomed (P+). The exercise of authority or 'strong leadership' in a crisis is usually welcomed. Referent power is, by definition, positively perceived. When expertise is given freely to help those in difficulty it is perceived positively, but it can be perceived negatively when used in a condescending or intrusive manner. The exercise of affiliation and group power can also be either positive or negative depending on how the leader uses them.

Second, these power bases depend on the beliefs of followers. A leader may be able to control rewards and penalties and have superior knowledge. However, if followers do not believe that the leader has these attributes, then they may not be compliant. Similarly, leaders may be able to persuade followers that they possess power which they do not have. Power is thus a property of the relationship between leader and followers, not a property of the leader.

Third, these power bases are linked. The exercise of one may affect a leader's ability to use another. The leader who resorts to coercion may, for example, lose referent power. The leader may be able to use legitimate power to enhance both referent and expert power.

Finally, a leader can operate from multiple bases of power, using different bases in different contexts and at different times. Few leaders may be able to rely on a single power base.

Stop and Criticize

Which combination of power bases would you expect to be most effective for an organization leader? What are the power bases of your organizational behaviour instructor(s)? What countervailing power bases do students possess?

Group power: the ability of a leader to exert influence based on the belief of followers that the leader has collective support from a team or group.

Prestige job titles no longer confer legitimacy on bosses' orders. Employees have their own sources of power, which they can use to undermine a leader's position. The most effective leadership style seems to be one in which power is shared with followers. Some managers feel that more power for subordinates means less power for them. However, power sharing can increase both subordinate satisfaction and confidence in the leader. Granting discretion and access to information are also symbolic rewards. Leaders who appear to 'give power away' can thus strengthen, and not weaken, their influence over those followers.

Building your referent power

Robert Benfari, Harry Wilkinson and Charles Orth argue that *referent power* is both important and under-utilized in organizational settings, observing that:

[C]onflict is an everyday occurrence. The key to conflict resolution is the ability to negotiate workable psychological contracts with colleagues who have no formal reporting obligations. The use of threats (coercive power) or appeals to upper authority can lead to long-term conflict. The party under siege can, at some time in the future, make use of affiliation power to retaliate. Acquiring and using referent power effectively is important not only to managers in matrix organizations but also to all managers at any level in any organization.

They offer suggestions for building your referent power:

■ get to know the motives, preferences, values and interests of your colleagues;

- build relationships using shared motives, goals and interests;

- respect differences in interests and don't attack another person's style;

- give 'positive strokes', use reward power, confirm others' competence;

- invite reciprocal influence, show that you respect the opinions of others;

- share information, give your expertise, particularly where you stand to benefit;

- minimize concerns with status, put signs of office aside, people relate to equals;

- develop communication skills, people value clear and consistent messages;

- get to know how people react to stress and crisis;

- get to know the informal political structure of your organization.

Benfari and colleagues describe the use of 'positive strokes', for example, as a 'cheap and easy way to build a relationship', involving little time and no money.

Based on Robert C. Benfari, Harry E. Wilkinson and Charles D. Orth, 'The effective use of power', *Business Horizons*, vol. 29, May–June 1986, p. 16.

Jobs for the boys?

Leadership commentary, until the 1980s, has assumed that leaders were *men* with special qualities, and most of the research in this area has been conducted by men whose subjects were men. Women are poorly represented in the ranks of management and were largely ignored in leadership research until the 1990s. That position has changed. Fiona Wilson (2002) argues that we may be witnessing a 'feminization of management' as flatter, decentralized organization structures require skills in communication, collaboration, participation, consensus decision-making, teamwork, shared responsibility, networking, developing others – qualities more closely associated with women than with men. However, Marjorie Scardino, chief executive of Pearson Education, the company which publishes this text, is the only woman running one of Britain's top 100 companies.

Career and family

Does career success for women mean sacrificing family life? Sylvia Ann Hewlett surveyed over 1,100 successful women in America in two age groups, 28 to 40, and 41 to 55. She defined high achievers as those earning between US$55,000 and US$65,000, and ultra-achievers as those earning more than US$100,000. For comparison, 470 men were also included in the research. Her findings showed that:

	percentage childless between ages 41 and 55
high-achieving women	33
corporate women	42
high-achieving men	25
ultra-achieving men	19
ultra-achieving women	49

High- and ultra-achieving women were also less likely to be married than their male colleagues. Hewlett quotes a young professional woman whom she met in a focus group:

I know a few hard-driving women who are climbing the ladder at consulting firms, but they are single or divorced and seem pretty isolated. And I know a handful of working mothers who are trying to do the half-time thing or the two-thirds-time thing. They work reduced hours so they can see their kids, but they don't get the good projects, they don't get the bonuses, and they also get whispered about behind their backs. You know, comments like, 'If she's not prepared to work the client's hours, she has no business being in the profession.

Around one-third of high- and ultra-achieving women were working more than 55 hours a week (thirteen hours a day when commuting is included), and some were occasionally working 70 hours. Hewlett argues that, for many women, 'the brutal demands of ambitious careers, the asymmetries of male–female relationships, and the difficulties of bearing children late in life conspire to crowd out the possibility of having children'.

Based on Sylvia Ann Hewlett, 'Executive women and the myth of having it all', *Harvard Business Review*, vol. 80, no. 44, April 2002, pp. 66–73.

Rosabeth Moss Kanter (1977, 1979) argued that women are rendered 'structurally powerless' in being restricted to routine, low-profile jobs, as well as facing discrimination in promotion decisions. Deborah Tannen (1990, 1995) argued that women and men acquire different linguistic styles in childhood. Girls learn conversation rituals that focus on rapport, while boys focus on status. Men thus think in hierarchical terms and of being 'one up'. They are more likely to jockey for position by putting others down and appear confident and knowledgeable. Women are more likely to avoid putting others down, and do so in ways that are face-saving. Women can also appear to lack self-confidence by playing down their certainty and openly expressing doubt. Women adopting a 'masculine' linguistic style are regarded as aggressive.

Tanya Arroba and Kim James (1988), in contrast, argue that women have innate attributes that can be exploited to their advantage. These include intuition, sensitivity, observation and a willingness to engage with feelings. Women, they argue, should put to one side their distaste for organizational politics and the use of power. Getting involved in the politics game, they note, is tough, but not getting involved means staying put.

Sandi Mann (1995) similarly argues that women are underrepresented in leadership and management roles because they are less successful in acquiring power. Organizations which encourage long hours of work disadvantage women with family responsibilities. Failure to participate socially – the late drinks – can also lead to exclusion, exacerbated by inadequate childcare facilities. Meetings are scheduled at difficult times for women, who are excluded from informal male meetings in inaccessible locations (the locker room at the gym). Male conversation is dominated by topics in which women do not share an interest. 'Passive strategies', she argues, are not as effective as self-promotion in terms of career progression.

Comparative data on women in management in different countries are difficult to obtain, but Susan Vinnicombe (2000, p. 10) cites figures from an International Labour Organization study, summarized in table 21.3. This shows that while women account for just under half of the workforce in the six countries covered, they occupy only between one-fifth and one-third of administrative and managerial jobs.

Table 21.3: Women's share of administrative and managerial jobs (%)

Country	Administrative and managerial jobs	Total employment
Austria	22	43
Finland	25	47
Israel	25	47
Norway	32	46
Switzerland	28	40
United Kingdom	33	45

Stop and Criticize

What power bases can women exploit in order to strengthen their organizational positions and achieve promotion to more senior managerial positions?

The future for women in management

Peter York cites Yve Newbold, once Company Secretary for the conglomerate Hanson, as saying, 'I'll only be happy when there are as many mediocre women running organizations as there are mediocre men.' He studied a number of ('forty- and fifty-something') women who had broken through 'the glass ceiling' into top corporate and public sector jobs:

> These women had got through the glass ceiling because they didn't believe it was there – or so they told us. They had a highly developed self-belief, often derived from supportive parents who'd told them anything was possible for girls. They didn't believe in role-playing – from kittens to nannies – any more than they believed in being an 'honorary man'. All those gambits were hopelessly outdated in their view. What they did concede was that there had been a need to network more intelligently, to make yourself useful and be assiduous in the early stages of your career.

York concludes that '[t]he future of management everywhere just has to be a lot more female'.

From Peter York, 'The gender agenda', *Management Today*, October 1999, pp. 56–63.

Marilyn Davidson and Cary Cooper (1992) point out that women are not disqualified from management roles by ability, personality or aspiration. The single main beneficial change to expand opportunities for women in management, they argue, would be in male attitudes. They also argue, however, that it is not necessarily effective for the ambitious woman to adopt a masculine style of behaviour. In contrast, the solution they suggest is to adopt a flexible combination of masculine and feminine attributes. This combination, known as androgyny, means being decisive and emotionally expressive, independent and tender, aggressive and gentle, assertive and yielding. This involves flexible, adaptive behaviour and the rejection of traditional, simple stereotypes – 'typical female' or 'one of the boys'.

Davidson and Cooper (1992) argued that the pace of change for women was slow. A more recent study challenges this pessimism (MacDonald, 1999; York, 1999). The results from the 200 replies, half men and half women, are outlined in table 21.4.

Women saw male bosses as decisive and as team leaders, but also as insensitive. Men saw female bosses as considerate, open-minded and team players. Are men

Table 21.4: Changing beliefs about women in management

Belief	Agreement (%)
Women use their time more effectively than men	70
Women tend to praise their staff more frequently	70
I would trust a female boss not to take credit for my work	60
I would trust a male boss not to take credit for my work	40
Men make better bosses than women (whole sample)	40
Men make better bosses than women (women only)	30

more likely to inspire confidence in staff? Overall, 60 per cent rejected this, and 72 per cent of women rejected it.

These findings suggest that women are now more likely to be promoted for their leadership and management attributes and skills, and are less likely to be discriminated against on grounds of sex and so-called 'feminine' traits.

Beating men at their own game

Several commentators predict that women will assume more leadership positions because they score higher on transformational leadership involving motivation and support. Men score higher on transactional leadership involving traditional command and control methods. Shere Hite (2000) advocates a new 'emotional-psychological landscape', arguing that sexual politics prevent women reaching senior management positions. Her research shows that female managers are admired by male executives for:

■ relative indifference to status symbols;

■ not playing office politics;

■ innovative ways of thinking;

■ understanding of service industries;

■ higher intellectual achievements;

■ greater productivity;

■ 'soft' skills such as communication and networking.

However, women still attract male criticism for taking time off work to have children, not fighting hard enough for power, not making themselves visible and disliking competition. Val Singh at the Centre for Developing Women Business Leaders at Cranfield School of Management argues that women pursuing management careers should use these methods:

■ ingratiation, building your relationships with superiors;

■ window dressing, displaying your competence;

■ taking credit for achievements beyond your contribution;

■ keen, ready and attentive body language;

■ adopting the style and mannerisms of the next management level up;

■ 'good organization citizenship' behaviour such as conscientiousness and courtesy;

■ actively repairing damage to your image;

■ volunteering for extra responsibility.

These are the impression management tactics that work for men so why should women not use them too? Cranfield research in 1999 also found that:

1. More than half of top and middle female managers use impression management methods.

2. More women (53 per cent) than men (38 per cent) admitted that they used impression management.

3. Women said that men used impression management more than women.

4. 25 per cent of women, compared with 10 per cent of men, said that they would not try to impress.

Based on Rebecca Johnson, 'Ascent of woman', *People Management*, vol. 6, no. 1, January 2000, pp. 26–32; and Shere Hite, *Sex and Business*, Financial Times/Prentice Hall, Harlow, 2000.

Style-counselling: the search for effective behaviour patterns

Disillusionment with the traits approach meant that leadership, management and supervisory style became a major focus for research. Attention switched from selecting leaders on personality traits, to training and developing leaders in appropriate behaviour patterns. This research tradition argues that a considerate, participative, democratic and involving leadership style is more effective than an impersonal, autocratic and directive style.

Two projects, the Michigan and Ohio studies, underpinned the investigation of management style. The work of the Survey Research Center in Michigan in the 1940s and early 1950s (Katz, Maccoby and Morse, 1950), identified two dimensions of leadership behaviour:

1. *Employee-centred behaviour*, focusing on relationships and employee needs.

2: *Job-centred behaviour*, focusing on getting the job done.

This work ran concurrently with the influential studies of Edwin Fleishman and Ralph Stogdill, at the Bureau of Business Research at Ohio State University (Fleishman, 1953a, 1953b; Fleishman and Harris, 1962; Stogdill, 1948, 1950; Stogdill and Coons, 1951). Foremen in the International Harvester Company, and employees in other organizations, were asked to rate the frequency with which their superiors behaved in the ways described in a Leadership Behaviour Description Questionnaire.

Consideration: a pattern of leadership behaviour that demonstrates sensitivity to relationships and to the social needs of employees.

Consistent with the Michigan studies, the Ohio results identified two categories of leadership behaviour, **consideration** and **initiating structure**. The considerate leader is needs and relationships-oriented. The leader who structures work for subordinates is task-oriented. The considerate leader is interested in and listens to subordinates, allows participation in decision-making, is friendly and approachable, helps subordinates with personal problems and is prepared to support them if necessary. The leader's behaviour indicates genuine trust, respect, warmth and rapport. This enhances subordinates' feelings of self-esteem and encourages the development of communications and relationships in a work group. The researchers first called this leadership dimension 'social sensitivity'.

Initiating structure: a pattern of leadership behaviour that emphasizes performance of the work in hand and the achievement of product and service goals.

The leader who initiates structure plans ahead, decides how things are going to get done, structures tasks and assigns work, makes expectations clear, emphasizes deadlines and achievement, and expects subordinates to follow instructions. The leader's behaviour stresses production and the achievement of organizational goals. This type of behaviour can stimulate enthusiasm to achieve objectives as well as encouraging and helping subordinates to get the work done. This is the

		Initiating Structure	
		High	**Low**
Consideration	**High**	High performance	Low performance
		Few grievances	Few grievances
		Low turnover	Low turnover
	Low	High performance	Low performance
		Many grievances	Many grievances
		High turnover	High turnover

Figure 21.1: The Ohio State leadership theory predictions

kind of emphasis that the scientific management school encouraged, except that here it is recognized that task orientation can have a positive, motivating aspect. The researchers first called this leadership dimension 'production emphasis'.

The Michigan and Ohio studies developed the dichotomy between democratic and autocratic leadership, dimensions which have been confirmed in numerous other studies. This dichotomy also underpins the *Grid Organization Development* perspective developed by Robert Blake and Jane Mouton (1964, 1968, 1969), who argue that effective leaders are those who combine what they call 'concern for production'with 'concern for people'.

Consideration and structure are independent behaviour patterns and do not represent the extremes of a continuum. A leader can emphasize one or both. Job satisfaction is likely to be higher, and grievances and labour turnover lower, when the leader emphasizes consideration. Task performance, on the other hand, is likely to be higher when the leader emphasizes the initiation of structure. Inconsiderate leaders typically have subordinates who complain and who are more likely to leave the organization, but can have comparatively productive work groups if they are high on initiating structure. This theory is summarized in figure 21.1.

The influential work of another Michigan researcher, Rensis Likert (1961), reinforced the benefits of considerate, performance-oriented leadership. He interviewed 24 supervisors and 419 clerks in an American insurance company. He found that supervisors in highly productive sections were more likely to:

- receive general as opposed to close supervision from their superiors;

- give general as opposed to close supervision to their subordinates;

- enjoy their responsibility and authority;

- spend more time on supervision;

- be employee rather than production oriented.

Rensis Likert
(1903–81)

Likert and his team identified four systems of leadership, finding that effective supervisors adopted either system 3 or system 4, which he called an 'alternative organizational life style':

System 1: *Exploitative autocratic*, in which the leader

- has no confidence and trust in subordinates;

- imposes decisions, never delegates;

- motivates by threat;
- has little communication and teamwork.

System 2: *Benevolent authoritative*, in which the leader

- has superficial, condescending trust in subordinates;
- imposes decisions, never delegates;
- motivates by reward;
- sometimes involves subordinates in solving problems.

System 3: *Participative*, in which the leader

- has incomplete confidence and trust in subordinates;
- listens to subordinates but controls decision-making;
- motivates by reward and some involvement;
- uses ideas and opinions of subordinates constructively.

System 4: *Democratic*, in which the leader

- has complete confidence and trust in subordinates;
- allows subordinates to make decisions for themselves;
- motivates by reward for achieving goals set by participation;
- shares ideas and opinions.

One of Rensis Likert's less effective supervisors

'This interest-in-people approach is all right, but it's a luxury. I've got to keep pressure on for production, and when I get production up, then I can afford to take time to show an interest in my employees and their problems.'

One of Rensis Likert's more effective supervisors

'One way in which we accomplish a high level of production is by letting people do the job the way they want to so long as they accomplish the objectives. I believe in letting them take time out from the monotony. Make them feel that they are something special, not just the run of the mill. As a matter of fact, I tell them if you feel that job is getting you down get away from it for a few minutes. . . . If you keep employees from feeling hounded, they are apt to put out the necessary effort to get the work done in the required time.

'I never make any decisions myself. Oh, I guess I've made about two since I've been here. If people know their jobs I believe in letting them make decisions. I believe in delegating decision-making. Of course, if there's anything that affects the whole division, then the two assistant managers, the three section heads and sometimes the assistant section heads come in here and we discuss it. I don't believe in saying that this is the way it's going to be. After all, once supervision and management are in agreement there won't be any trouble selling the staff the idea.

'My job is dealing with human beings rather than with the work. It doesn't matter if I have anything to do with the work or not. The chances are that people will do a better job if you are really taking an interest in them. Knowing the names is important and helps a lot, but it's not enough. You really have to know each individual well, know what his problems are. Most of the time I discuss matters with employees at their desks rather than in the office. Sometimes I sit on a waste paper basket or lean on the files. It's all very informal. People don't seem to like to come into the office to talk.'

From Rensis Likert, *New Patterns of Management*, McGraw-Hill, New York, 1961, pp. 7–8.

Context-fitting: the development of contingency theories

The Michigan and Ohio perspectives offer leaders 'one best way' to handle followers, by adopting the 'high-consideration, high-structure' ideal. This advice is supported by the fact that most people *like* their leaders to be considerate, even when they are performance-oriented as well. The main criticism of this perspective lies with the observation that one leadership style may not be effective in all circumstances.

Departing from 'one best way', Robert Tannenbaum and Warren Schmidt (1958) presented the autocratic–democratic choice as a continuum, from 'boss-centred leadership' at one extreme to 'subordinate-centred leadership' at the other. This is illustrated in figure 21.2.

The steps in this continuum are presented as alternatives for the leader; Tannenbaum and Schmidt's article was subtitled, 'should a manager be democratic or autocratic – or something in between?'. Tannenbaum and Schmidt argue that the answer depends on three sets of forces:

forces in the manager   personality, values, preferences, beliefs about employee participation, confidence in subordinates

forces in the subordinates   need for independence, tolerance of ambiguity, knowledge of the problem, expectations of involvement

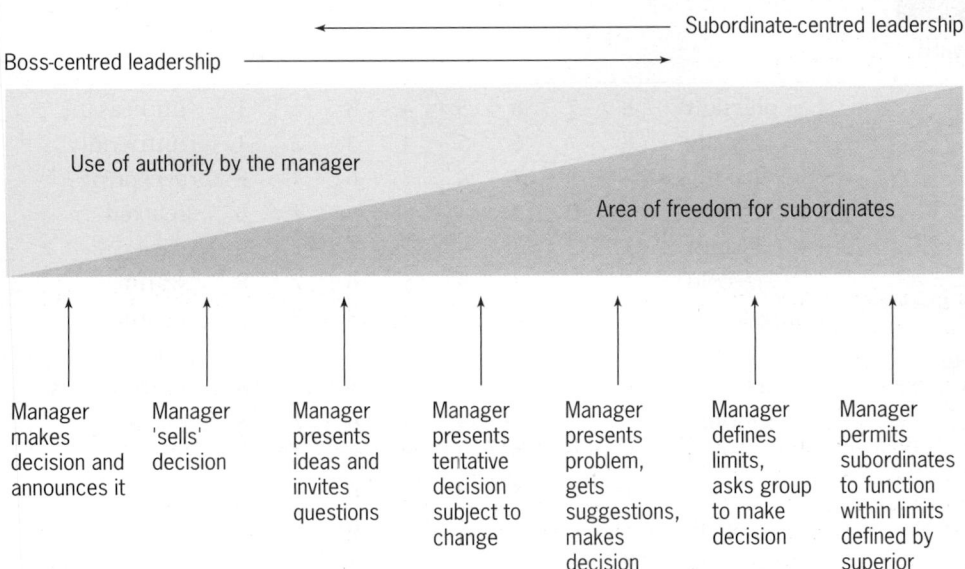

Figure 21.2: The Tannenbaum–Schmidt continuum of leadership behaviour
Reprinted by permission of *Harvard Business Review*. Exhibit from 'How to choose a leadership pattern' by R. Tannenbaum and W.H. Schmidt, Vol. 37, March–April, 1958, reprinted in May–June, 1973. Copyright © 1958 by the Harvard Business School Publishing Corporation; all rights reserved.

Contingency theory of leadership: a perspective which argues that leaders must adjust their style in a manner consistent with aspects of the context.

forces in the situation organizational norms, size and location of work groups, effectiveness of teamworking, nature of the problem

Having concentrated on 'forces in the manager', and having challenged the notion of 'one best way' to lead, research now turned to consider aspects of the context in which the leader was operating. These included the people being led, the nature of the work they were doing and the wider organizational setting. This perspective suggests that leaders must be able to 'diagnose' the context, and then to decide what behaviour will 'fit'. As the best style is contingent on the situation, this approach is known as the **contingency theory of leadership**.

Stop and Criticize

Leadership research and theory seems to be consistent in arguing that a considerate, employee-centred, participative and democratic style is more effective.

Least preferred coworker score: an assessment of the kind of person with whom a leader feels they cannot work effectively.

What factors in an organizational context would make an inconsiderate, goal-centred, impersonal and autocratic leadership style more effective?

The contingency theory of Fred Fiedler (1967; Fiedler and Chemers, 1974, 1984) provides a systematic approach to diagnosing contextual factors. Fiedler worked with groups whose leaders were clearly identified and whose performance was easy to measure, such as basketball teams and bomber crews. Fiedler first developed a new measure of a leader's basic approach to managing people – the leader's **least preferred coworker** (LPC) **score**.

This concept is best understood by completing the LPC assessment. Think of somebody you have had problems working with. It does not matter whether you like this person. Rate them on the following scale (based on Fiedler and Chemers, 1984), and then identify whether your total score is consistent with the high and low LPC leader profiles summarized in table 21.5. A score of 57 or less suggests that you are task-oriented or 'low LPC'. A score of 64 or higher suggests that you are 'high LPC' and that you are relationships-oriented.

Frederick Edward Fiedler

										score
pleasant	8	7	6	5	4	3	2	1	unpleasant	_____
friendly	8	7	6	5	4	3	2	1	unfriendly	_____
rejecting	1	2	3	4	5	6	7	8	accepting	_____
tense	1	2	3	4	5	6	7	8	relaxed	_____
distant	1	2	3	4	5	6	7	8	close	_____
cold	1	2	3	4	5	6	7	8	warm	_____
supportive	8	7	6	5	4	3	2	1	hostile	_____
boring	1	2	3	4	5	6	7	8	interesting	_____
quarrelsome	1	2	3	4	5	6	7	8	harmonious	_____
gloomy	1	2	3	4	5	6	7	8	cheerful	_____
open	8	7	6	5	4	3	2	1	guarded	_____
backbiting	1	2	3	4	5	6	7	8	loyal	_____
untrustworthy	1	2	3	4	5	6	7	8	trustworthy	_____
considerate	8	7	6	5	4	3	2	1	inconsiderate	_____
nasty	1	2	3	4	5	6	7	8	nice	_____
agreeable	8	7	6	5	4	3	2	1	disagreeable	_____
insincere	1	2	3	4	5	6	7	8	sincere	_____
kind	8	7	6	5	4	3	2	1	unkind	_____
									Total	_____

Table 21.5: High- and low-LPC leaders

The low-LPC leader	The high-LPC leader
self-esteem based on task completion	self-esteem based on interpersonal relations
puts the task first	puts people first
is hard on those who fail	likes to please others
considers competence a key attribute	considers loyalty a key attribute
likes detail	is bored with detail

Fiedler appears to have found with the LPC score another way to uncover a manager's predispositions towards consideration and initiating structure. It should not be surprising, therefore, to find that Fiedler's attempts to correlate the LPC scores of leaders with the performance of their groups was not successful. This led Fiedler to the argument that effectiveness is influenced by three sets of factors:

1. The extent to which the task in hand is structured.

2. The leader's position power.

3. The nature of the relationships between the leader and followers.

Tasks vary in the degree to which they are **structured** or not.

Stop and Criticize

Would you describe the task of writing an essay for your organizational behaviour instructor as structured or unstructured?

As a student, would you prefer this task to be more or less structured, and how would you advise you instructor to achieve this?

Structured task: a task with clear goals, few correct or satisfactory solutions and outcomes, few ways of performing it and clear criteria of success.

Unstructured task: a task with ambiguous goals, many correct solutions and satisfactory outcomes, many ways of achieving acceptable outcomes and vague criteria of success.

Fiedler identifies three typical sets of conditions under which a leader may have to work.

Condition 1

■ The task is highly structured.

■ The leader's position power is high.

■ Subordinates feel that their relationships with the boss are good.

Task-oriented (low-LPC score) leaders get good results in these favourable circumstances. The task-oriented leader in this situation detects that events are potentially under their control, sets targets, monitors progress and achieves good performance.

Relationships-oriented (high-LPC score) leaders get poor results in these circumstances. They try to build and maintain good relationships with and between their subordinates. However, when relationships are already good, and the other conditions are favourable, the leader may take subordinates for granted and start to pursue other personal objectives.

Condition 2

■ The task is unstructured.

- The leader's position power is low.

- Subordinates feel that their relationships with the boss are moderately good.

Relationships-oriented (high-LPC) leaders get better results in these moderately favourable circumstances where the maintenance of good relationships is important to the leader's ability to exert influence over subordinates and to getting the work done. In contrast, the task-oriented (low-LPC) leader ignores deteriorating relationships and, as the task lacks structure and the leader lacks position power, the results are likely to be poor.

Condition 3

- The task is unstructured.

- The leader's position power is low.

- Subordinates feel that their relationships with the boss are poor.

Task-oriented (low-LPC) leaders get better results in these very unfavourable conditions. In contrast, the relationships-oriented (high-LPC) leader is unwilling to exert pressure on subordinates, avoids confrontations that might upset or anger them, gets involved in attempts to repair damaged relationships and ignores the task. Meanwhile, the task-oriented leader gets impatient, tries to structure the situation, ignores resistance from subordinates, reduces the ambiguity surrounding the work and achieves good performance.

The research to support Fiedler's contingency theory is positive but weak. There seem to be four problems.

1. The key variables, task structure, power and relationships are difficult to assess. The leader who wants to rely on this framework to determine the most effective style for a given situation has to rely more on intuition than on systematic analysis.

2. The concept of the 'least preferred coworker' is unusual, negatively worded and confusing. It is not clear just what this measures. It looks like another indicator of employee-centred versus task-centred behaviour.

3. The framework does not take into account the needs of subordinates.

4. The need for a leader to have relevant technical competence is ignored.

Paul Hersey

Kenneth H. Blanchard

This theory has two strengths. First, it confirms the importance of contextual factors in determining leader behaviour and effectiveness. It reinforces the view that there is no one ideal set of traits or best behavioural pattern. Second, it provides a systematic framework for developing the self-awareness of managers concerned about their leadership style.

Most contingency theories argue that leaders should change their style to fit the context. However, Fiedler felt that most managers and supervisors have problems in changing their leadership style. To be effective, he argued, *leaders have to change their context*, choosing conditions in which their preferred style was most likely to be effective. This could mean changing work group or department, or even moving to another organization.

Another influential contingency theory of leadership was developed by Paul Hersey and Ken Blanchard (1988). Like Fiedler, they argue that the effective leader 'must be a good diagnostician' and adapt style to meet the demands of the situ-

Situational leadership: an approach to determining the most effective style of influencing, considering the direction and support a leader gives, and the readiness of followers to perform a particular task.

ation in which they operate. Unlike Fiedler, they believe that leaders can alter their style to fit the context. Hersey and Blanchard call their approach **situational leadership**.

Their theory of situational leadership is summarized in figure 21.3.

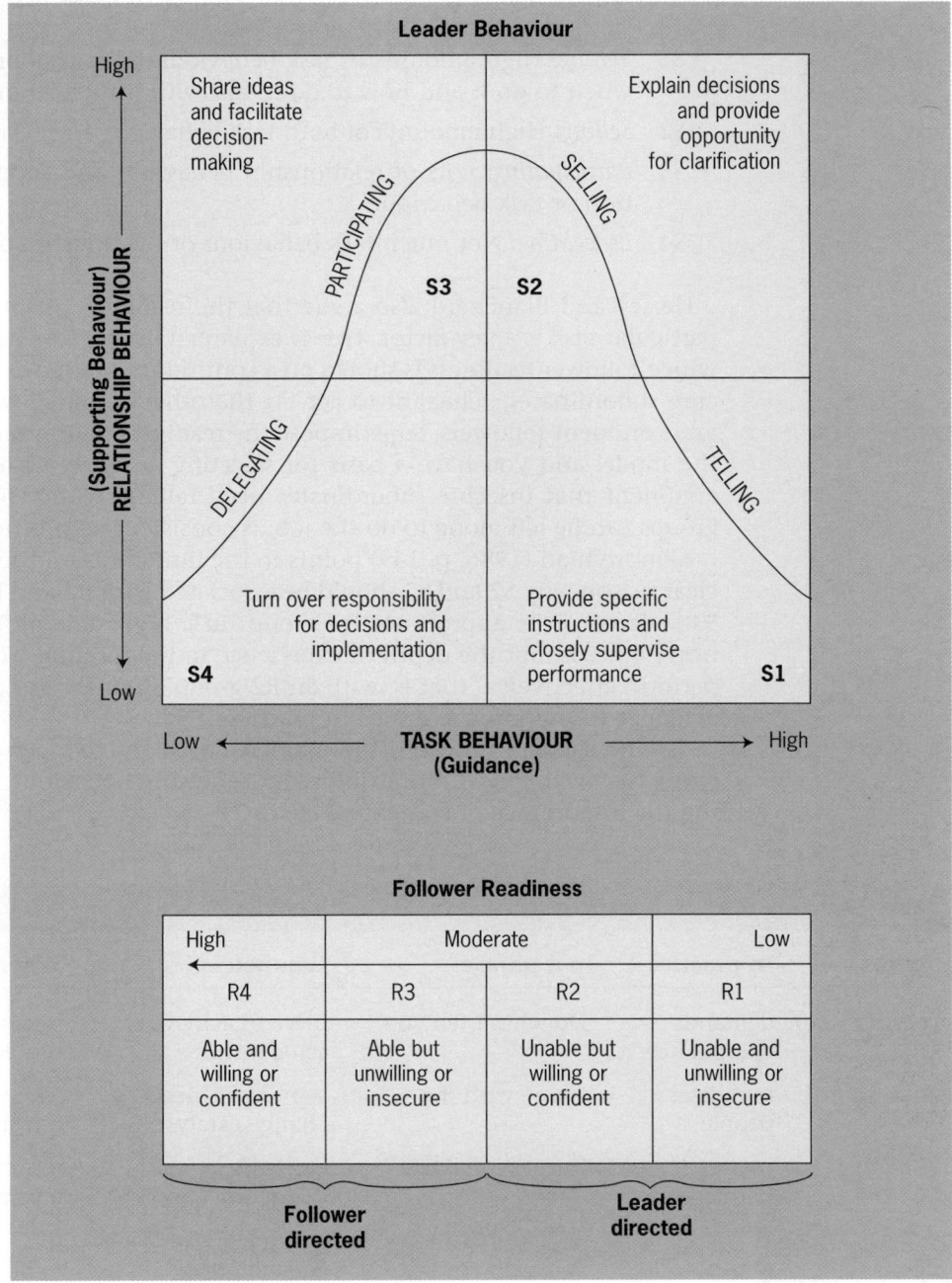

Figure 21.3: Situational leadership theory
From P. Hersey and K.H. Blanchard, *Management of Organizational Behaviour: Utilizing Human Resources*, Prentice-Hall, Englewood Cliffs, NJ, 1988.

Figure 21.3 describes leader behaviour on two dimensions. The first dimension (horizontal axis) concerns 'task behaviour', or the amount of direction a leader gives to subordinates. This can vary from specific instructions, at one extreme, to delegation, at the other. Hersey and Blanchard identify two intermediate positions, where leaders either facilitate subordinates' decisions or take care to explain their own.

The second dimension (vertical axis) concerns 'supportive behaviour', or the amount of social backup a leader gives to subordinates. This can vary from limited communication at one extreme, to considerable listening, facilitating and supporting at the other.

The model establishes four basic leadership styles, labelled S1 to S4:

S1 *Telling*: High amounts of task behaviour, telling subordinates what to do, when to do it and how to do it, but with little relationship behaviour.

S2 *Selling*: High amounts of both task behaviour and relationship behaviour.

S3 *Participating*: Lots of relationship behaviour and support, but little direction or task behaviour.

S4 *Delegating*: Not much task behaviour or relationship behaviour.

Hersey and Blanchard also argue that the readiness of followers to perform a particular task is a key factor. This is explained by the lower part of the figure, in which follower readiness is shown on a continuum. At one extreme, we have insecure subordinates, reluctant to act. At the other extreme, we have able, willing and confident followers. Superimpose the readiness continuum on the top half of the model and you have a basis for selecting an effective leadership style. The argument that insecure subordinates need telling, while willing and confident groups can be left alone to do the job, is consistent with other theories.

Alan Bryman (1986, p. 149) points to the limitations of this model. There is no clear reason why S2 and S3 should be associated with R2 and R3, respectively. The S3 style could be appropriate for groups in a high state of 'psychological readiness', but without the depth of experience in the job that would enable them to perform effectively – that is, with an R2 group. Bryman also points to the lack of evidence to support the model in practice.

As with Fiedler, however, the main strengths of this perspective lie with the emphasis on the need for flexibility in leadership behaviour, and with highlighting the importance of contextual factors.

Table 21.6: Goleman's six leadership styles

Style	In practice	In a phrase	Competencies	When to use
coercive	demands compliance	'Do what I tell you'	drive to achieve, self-control	in a crisis, with problem people
authoritative	mobilizes people	'Come with me'	self-confidence, change catalyst	when new vision and direction is needed
affiliative	creates harmony	'People come first'	empathy, communication	to heal wounds, to motivate people under stress
democratic	forges consensus	'What do you think?'	collaboration, teambuilding	to build consensus, to get contributions
pacesetting	sets high standards	'Do as I do, now'	initiative, drive to achieve	to get fast results from a motivated team
coaching	develops people	'Try this'	empathy, self-awareness	to improve performance, to develop strengths

Based on Daniel Goleman, 'Leadership that gets results', *Harvard Business Review*, vol. 78, no. 2, March–April 2000, pp. 78–90.

Daniel Goleman (2000) reports research by the management consulting firm Hay McBer involving 4,000 executives in a worldwide sample. This identified six leadership styles which have an impact on 'working atmosphere' and financial performance. The findings suggest that effective leaders use all of these styles, like an 'array of clubs in a golf pro's bag'. Each style relies on an aspect of *emotional intelligence* which concerns skill in managing your own emotions and the emotions of others. Goleman's six styles are summarized in table 21.6.

While coercion and pacesetting have their uses, the research showed that these styles can damage 'working atmosphere', reducing flexibility and employee commitment. The other four styles have a consistently positive impact on climate and performance. The most effective leaders, Goleman concludes, are those who have mastered four or more styles, particularly the positive styles, and who are able to switch styles as the situation commands. This is not a 'mechanical' matching of behaviour to context, as other contingency theories imply, but a flexible, fluid, sensitive and seamless adjustment.

Contingency theories argue that the most effective leadership style depends on the context. Organization structures, management skills, employee characteristics, the nature of their tasks are unique. No one style of leadership is universally best. There is, however, a good deal of research which indicates that a considerate, participative or democratic style of leadership is generally more effective. There are two main reasons for this.

First, the development of participative management is part of a wider social and political trend which has raised expectations concerning personal freedom and the quality of working life. These social and political values encourage resistance to manipulation by impersonal bureaucracies, and challenge the legitimacy of management decisions. Participation thus reflects democratic social and political values. Many commentators would observe, however, that individual freedom, quality of working life and genuine participation are still somewhat underdeveloped in most organizations.

Second, participative management has been encouraged by research which has demonstrated that this style is generally more effective, although an autocratic style can be effective in some circumstances. A participative style can improve organizational effectiveness by tapping the ideas of people with knowledge and experience, and by involving them in a decision-making process to which they then become committed. This is reinforced by the growth in numbers of knowledge workers who expect to be involved in decisions affecting their work, and whose knowledge makes them potentially valuable contributors in this regard. People who are involved in setting standards or establishing methods are thus more likely to experience 'ownership' of such decisions and are more likely to:

- accept the legitimacy of decisions reached with their help;
- accept change based on those decisions;
- trust managers who ultimately ratify and implement decisions;
- volunteer new and creative ideas and solutions.

Autocratic management stifles creativity, ignores available expertise and smothers motivation and commitment. However, autocratic management can be more effective when:

- time is short;
- when the leader is the most knowledgeable person;
- where those who could participate will never all agree on a decision.

The contingency theories discussed so far have attracted a number of criticisms.

One criticism concerns the questionable ability of leaders to diagnose the context in which they are operating, given the relatively vague nature of the situational variables identified by different theories. In addition, contingency theories typically fail to consider a number of other key dimensions of context, such as the organization culture, degree of change and levels of stress, working conditions, external economic factors, organizational design and technology. All of these factors potentially influence the leadership process in ways not addressed by any of these theoretical accounts (Hughes, Ginnett and Curphy, 1996).

A second criticism concerns whether leaders can adapt their styles to fit the context in the ways the theory advises. Personality may not be flexible enough. Some theorists argue that personality is inherited, inhibiting managers from being participative in some circumstances and dictatorial in others. The manager who is motivated by affiliation and who values the friendship of others may find it hard to treat employees in an impersonal and autocratic way.

A third critism is that the expectations of other managers can determine what is 'acceptable'. There are advantages in honesty and consistency. People may not accept the fickle behaviour of the participative manager who adopts an autocratic style on some occasions. The leader who changes style from one situation to another may not inspire confidence or trust.

However, leaders should be able to change style to suit the circumstances:

1. It is now broadly accepted that leaders and managers can learn from experience to adjust their behaviour according to the circumstances.

2. Organizations are not rigid social arrangements with fixed tasks and structures. With the growth in demand for flexibility, adaptability, improved quality of working life and worker participation, leaders and managers who fail to respond will face problems.

3. The leader or manager who adapts in a flexible way to changes in circumstances may be seen as more competent than one who sticks rigidly to traditional routines.

New leader: an inspirational visionary, concerned with building a shared sense of purpose and mission, creating a culture in which everyone is aligned with the organization's goals and is skilled and empowered to achieve them.

Superleader: a leader who is able to develop leadership capacity in others, empowering them, reducing their dependence on formal leaders, and stimulating their motivation, commitment and creativity.

Source: Published in *Harvard Business Review*, June 2001. Reprinted by permission of Dave Carpenter.

Management styles vary around the world

André Laurent asked people from twelve countries whether they agreed with the statement 'It is important for a manager to have at hand precise answers to most of the questions that his subordinates may raise about their work.' The percentages agreeing with this were:

Japan	78
Indonesia	73
Italy	66
France	53
Germany	46
Belgium	44
Switzerland	38
Britain	27
Denmark	23
United States	18
Holland	17
Sweden	10

Managers in France and Indonesia are seen as experts who are expected to have the answers. Managers in America and Holland are regarded as participative problem-solvers. Differences like this explain some of the problems that, for instance, Japanese managers have when working in Denmark, or Swedish managers have in relationships with colleagues in Italy.

Based on André Laurent, 'The cultural diversity of Western conceptions of management', *International Studies of Management and Organization*, 1983, vol. 13, nos 1–2.

Transactional leader: a leader who treats relationships with followers in terms of an exchange, giving followers what they want in return for what the leader desires, following prescribed tasks to pursue established goals.

Transformational leader: a leader who treats relationships with followers in terms of motivation and commitment, influencing and inspiring followers to give more than mere compliance to improve organizational performance.

Leadership in the twenty-first century

Two related trends in leadership thinking became evident in the late twentieth century:

1. Recognition of the role of heroic, powerful, charismatic, visionary leaders.

2. Recognition of the role of informal leadership, at all levels.

These trends appear to be contradictory. We have the **new leader**, an inspirational figure motivating followers to superlative levels of achievement. However, we also have the **superleader** who is able to 'lead others to lead themselves' (Sims and Lorenzi, 1992, p. 295). The superleader encourages, develops and co-exists with informal leadership dispersed throughout the organization hierarchy.

New leadership (Bryman, 1996, p. 280) originates with the work of James McGregor Burns (1978), whose study of political leaders distinguished between **transactional** and **transformational leaders**.

Great chefs, great leaders

Katharina Balazs argues that the *chefs de cuisine* who run the best restaurants in France are transformational leaders. Following a chance conversation with one top chef, she decided to interview others. The top rating of three stars in the *Guide Rouge Michelin* applies to only 30 restaurants in the world, and 22 of those are in France. Balazs interviewed these chefs and their staff, observed the preparation of meals in their kitchens and spoke to customers to find out how these chefs made their restaurants outstanding. The findings showed that the leadership role of chefs combines two dimensions, charismatic and architectural.

Charismatic

visioning	providing a luxurious and extraordinary 'total dining experience' that delights customers
empowering	giving staff a voice, showing confidence and trust, allowing staff to influence what they do, expecting high standards
energizing	communicating vision, making staff feel part of something special, aiming for perfection, excitement, joy, passion in the work

Architectural

designing structure	small, organic structure with chef as 'superstar', team culture based on mutual support and collaboration
controls	managing relationships with suppliers ('only the best is good enough'), controlling quality of the product
rewards	offering recognition, personal growth and 'employability' in a context where pay is low, hours are long and the work is intense

Balazs claims that this transformational leadership style applies in other sectors where the starting point is an individual's creation, implementation demands rigorous attention to detail, and a large team of support staff is required. Those other sectors include film and theatre production, opera, fashion and architecture.

Based on Katharina Balazs, 'Take one entrepreneur: the recipe for success of France's great chefs', *European Management Journal*, vol. 20, no. 3, 2002, pp. 247–59; and Katharina Balazs, 'Some like it haute: leadership lessons from France's great chefs', *Organizational Dynamics*, vol. 30, no. 2, 2001, pp. 134–48.

Transactional leaders see their relationships with followers in terms of trade, swaps or bargains. Transformational leaders are charismatic individuals who inspire and motivate others to perform 'beyond contract'. It is not difficult to see why some commentators equate transactional with management and transformational with leadership.

Noel Tichy and Mary Anne Devanna (1986) argue that the transformational leader has three main roles: recognizing the need for revitalization, creating a new vision, and institutionalizing change. Bernard Bass and Bruce Avolio (Bass, 1985a, 1985b; Bass and Avolio, 1990, 1994) similarly claim that transformational leadership occurs when leaders use 'the Four Is':

- Intellectual stimulation: encourage others to see what they are doing from new perspectives;

- Idealized influence: articulate the mission or vision of the organization;

- Individualized consideration: develop others to higher levels of ability;

- Inspirational motivation: motivate others to put organizational interests before self-interest.

The Transformational Leadership Questionnaire developed by Beverly-Alimo Metcalfe and John-Alban Metcalfe (2002, 2003) identifies fourteen behaviours in three categories:

Leading and developing others

- showing genuine concern
- enabling
- being accessible
- encouraging change

Personal qualities

- being honest and consistent
- acting with integrity
- being decisive
- inspiring others
- resolving complex problems

Leading the organization

- networking and achieving
- focusing effort
- building shared vision
- supporting a developmental culture
- facilitating change sensitively

Research with public sector managers and employees suggests that these behaviours can increase staff job satisfaction and motivation, and reduce stress. Metcalfe and Metcalfe also found that women were perceived as more transformational than men on most of these behaviours, and were rated as better than men on being decisive, focusing effort, mentoring, managing change, inspiring others, and showing openness to new ideas.

It is tempting to regard these novel terms, and this shift in emphasis, as fresh developments in leadership theory. However, the identification of super, new, transformational leaders and associated behaviour represents a return to trait-spotting ('hunt the visionary'), overlooking much of what is known about the influence of context on leadership effectiveness.

Stop and Criticize	Considering senior business and political leaders with whom you are familiar, either directly or through the media, which come closest to these definitions of new leader, superleader and transformational leader?

The new, super, transformational leader looks like a 'one best way' approach. Does this vindicate trait-spotting and discredit contingency perspectives?

Strongman tactics versus visionary superleaders

Judith Scully and colleagues explored the relationship between leadership behaviour and company financial performance, collecting leader behaviour descriptions from the subordinates of chief executive officers in 56 high-technology firms. They identified four types of leader behaviour:

The Strongman   tells subordinates how to carry out their work; criticizes subordinates for reasons not directly related to performance

The Transactor   establishes goals, expects good performance, offers rewards for success, recognizes good work, criticizes poor performance

The Visionary Hero   provides a sense of purpose and direction, motivates subordinates to perform beyond their perceived capacity

The Superleader   encourages subordinates to be self-critical, to set their own goals, to solve their own problems, to judge their own performance

Financial performance was poorer in firms with 'tough' CEOs than in firms with visionary or superleader CEOs. One explanation is that some leaders respond to poor performance with punishment and direction, which can cause performance to deteriorate still further.

Based on Judith A. Scully, Henry p. Sims, Judy D. Olian, Eugene R. Schnell and Kenneth A. Smith, 'Tough times make tough bosses: a meso analysis of CEO leader behaviour', *Irish Business and Administrative Research*, vol. 17, no. 1, 1996, pp. 71–102.

Alongside this focus on visionary superleaders sits the recognition that leadership acts can be observed at all levels of the organization structure (Metcalfe and Metcalfe, 2002). Leadership is the exclusive preserve neither of management in general, nor of senior figures in particular. From a survey of middle and senior managers in 1998, concerning their experiences of organizational change, David Buchanan, Tim Claydon and Mike Doyle (1999) found that:

- over 90 per cent of managers agree that change management knowledge and skills are relevant to people at all levels in the organization;

- over 90 per cent agree that all managers require a good understanding of change management principles and practice;

- only 2 per cent agreed that 'change management is a specialized area of expertise which should be left to full time professionals'.

In the distinction between leadership and management, orientation to change is a defining characteristic, a distinctive 'mark of the leader'. These results suggest, therefore, that leadership is a widespread phenomenon. Leadership behaviours are dispersed rather than concentrated in the hands of managers. Leadership functions are best carried out by people who have the interest, knowledge, skills and motivation to perform them effectively. This observation is reinforced by the development of self-managing teams which often have no formal leaders, or which have 'coach-facilitators' whose role is to develop team members' skills. These 'coaching-facilitating' supervisors are superleaders.

Recognition of dispersed leadership does not imply a shift of focus away from formal, senior figures. It may be useful to separate notions of leadership from formal positions and prestige job titles. However, it is also necessary to recognize that senior figures with prestige titles continue to exercise leadership roles and functions as well.

Table 21.7: The Bennis–Nanus model of twenty-first-century leadership

From	To
few top leaders, many managers	leaders at every level, few managers
leading by goal-setting	leading by vision, new directions
downsizing, benchmarking, quality	create distinctive competencies
reactive, adaptive to change	creative, anticipate future change
design hierarchical organizations	design flat, collegial organizations
direct and supervise	empower, inspire, facilitate
information held by few decision-makers	information shared with many
leader as boss, controlling	leader as coach, creating learning organization
leader as stabilizer, balancing conflicts	leader as change agent, balancing risks
leader develops good managers	leader develops future leaders

Based on Warren Bennis and Burt Nanus, *Leaders: The Strategies for Taking Charge*, HarperCollins, New York, 1985.

This 'twin track' approach, recognizing visionary new leadership and the notion of a widely dispersed leadership decoupled from high office, is illustrated by Warren Bennis and Burt Nanus (1985). Their model of twenty-first-century leadership is summarized in table 21.7.

The new leader is not an autocratic dictator or a wildly charismatic figure, or necessarily male. The emphasis of the 'new leader' lies more with the 'soft' skills of enthusing and inspiring, and of coaching and facilitating (see Hickman, 1998). While women faced systematic discrimination in the pursuit of senior management positions throughout the twentieth century, commentators were arguing as the century closed that, given the significance of interpersonal competencies (for economic, political and cultural reasons), women are better equipped than men for 'new leadership' roles.

Many commentators argue that a hostile, rapidly changing competitive climate, and pressurized conditions of work, require participative, visionary and inspirational styles of leadership. An autocratic, task-oriented style encourages little more than compliance with directions. The new, transformational super-leader, in contrast, encourages commitment, initiative, flexibility and high performance. The style and behaviour of new leaders also seems more appropriate to the motivation of knowledge workers and the development of the learning organization.

The new leadership concept can thus be used to draw together the three main strands of twentieth-century leadership thinking:

The theory	The new transformational superleader
trait-spotting	must have the right personality, appearance, attributes, voice
style-counselling	must be caring, inspirational and visionary, ethical, risk taker
context-fitting	style is consistent with a hostile and rapidly changing environment, with the need to develop flexible organizational forms, motivate knowledge workers and develop a learning organization

Revision

1. What is the difference between leadership and management, and why is it difficult to separate these concepts in practice?

2. Adolf Hitler meets Margaret Thatcher. They discuss the functions and traits of effective leaders, particularly in the context of implementing change. On what issues might they agree? Might they disagree? Alternative scenario: Mother Teresa meets Bill Gates.

3. Why is trait-spotting such a popular theme in leadership research? What has trait-spotting told us about the personality markers of successful leaders, and what are the problems with this perspective?

4. Leaders are, traditionally, men with special qualities. Why are women now more likely to be considered as effective leaders?

5. What is power, and how can the exercise of power be regarded in positive terms as well as negative ones? What has the leader's power got to do with his or her followers?

Springboard

Brown, M., 1998, *Richard Branson: The Authorized Biography*, Michael Joseph, London.

How close does Branson come to the ideal of the entrepreneur? The new leader? The superleader? The transformational leader?

Bryman, A., 1996, 'Leadership in organizations', in S.R. Clegg, C. Hardy and W.R. Nord (eds), *Handbook of Organization Studies*, Sage Publications, London, pp. 276–92.

A clear, concise and widely informed critical review of leadership research in the twentieth century. Demonstrates the links between leadership and organization culture, and explores methodological issues and trends in leadership research.

Hickman, G.R., 1998, *Leading Organizations: Perspectives for a New Era*, Sage Publications, Thousand Oaks, CA.

Reference work with 53 previously published 'big name' readings. Has an American bias and lacks a critical perspective, but this is comprehensive and up to date.

Roberts, A., 2003, *Hitler and Churchill: Secrets of Leadership*, Weidenfeld and Nicolson, London.

In the 'great man' tradition, analyzes and compares two leaders who shaped the twentieth century and whose legacy persists. While both of these men had an emotional appeal that created willing followers, Roberts points out that aspects of the circumstances, or the context, in which they operated were also significant.

Semler, R., 1993, *Maverick*, Century, London.

Ricardo Semler, highly successful Brazilian entrepreneur, explains his leadership and management approach. Does the so-called new, transformational leadership apply in other cultures? It seems so, from this popular account.

Vinnicombe, S. and Bank, J., 2002, *Women with Attitude: Lessons for Career Management*, Routledge, London.

Presents nineteen case studies of the 'life journeys' of women company directors who 'made it to the top', explaining their success and how this has affected their lives.

Zaleznik, A., 1977, 'Managers and leaders: are they different?', *Harvard Business Review*, vol. 15, no. 3, pp. 67–84.

Classic article arguing that the distinction between managers and leaders revolves around personality and orientations to change. Reprinted in *HBR* in 1992 where Zaleznik argues that the gap between leaders and managers has widened: 'leaders have much more in common with artists, scientists and other creative thinkers than they do with managers'.

Home viewing

Bandit Queen (Hindi, with subtitles, 1994, director Shekhar Kapur) is based on the true story of Phoolan Devi (played by Seema Biswas), a violently abused, exploited and outlawed Indian woman persecuted and imprisoned in the early 1980s. She achieved national celebrity status for her challenge to authority (the Indian police) through the actions of the ruthless bandit group which she led. Devi was assassinated in July 2001, in New Delhi, at the age of 38.

Elizabeth (1998, director Shekhar Kapur) is also based on the true story of the early years of Queen Elizabeth I of England (played by Cate Blanchett) who succeeds to the throne following the premature death of her half-sister Queen Mary (Kathy Burke) who was being pressed to have her executed, but who had refused to sign the warrant.

In both films, Phoolan Devi and Elizabeth have to learn how to be effective in leadership roles and contexts which are unfamiliar to them. How do they each change their behaviours in order to improve their effectiveness? What part does ruthlessness play in effective leadership? Would the leadership demonstrated as effective in these films be different if the characters were male?

OB in literature

Norman Augustine and Kenneth Adelman, *Shakespeare in Charge: The Bard's Guide to Leading and Succeeding on the Business Stage*, Hyperion Books, London, 1999.

Paul Corrigan, *Shakespeare on Management: Leadership Lessons for Today's Managers*, Kogan Page, London, 1999.

Tina Whitney and John Packer, *Power Plays: Shakespeare's Lessons in Leadership and Management*, Macmillan, London, 2000.

To save readers from having to turn to Shakespeare's originals, these texts painlessly extract the leadership and management insights in an entertaining manner from a range of plays. *Henry V* faces numerous leadership challenges. Is his position a legitimate one? How should he deal with those plotting against him? How should he influence his reluctant troops to follow him into battle against overwhelming odds at Agincourt? *Julius Caesar* explores the positive and negative dimensions, and the ethical dilemmas, of organizational politics. *The Merchant of Venice* exposes male–female differences in perceptions of justice and mercy. *Hamlet* is a study of leadership in an uncertain world. *Macbeth* exposes the problems of the leader who is obsessed with power for its own sake. In partnership with the Globe Theatre in London, Cranfield University School of Management in Bedford in England runs executive programmes based on Shakespeare: 'Once more into the boardroom, dear friends, once more, or close the wall up with our English dread of the Bard' (Hamilton, 1999).

Chapter exercises

1: Leadership style preferences

Objectives
1. To assess your preferred leadership style.

2. To explore the diversity of style preferences across your group.

Briefing
This assessment is designed to help you assess your preferred leadership style. Answer this questionnaire honestly, in relation to your behaviour and preferences, with respect either to your leadership behaviour or in relation to how you think you would like to behave in a leadership role. Put a tick in the appropriate response column on the right, depending on how accurately you feel each statement describes your behavioural preferences, using this scale:

A   Always   B   Often   C   Sometimes   D   Seldom   E   Never

Leader behaviours	A	B	C	D	E
1 I would always act as the spokesperson for my group	❑	❑	❑	❑	❑
2 I would allow subordinates complete freedom in their work	❑	❑	❑	❑	❑
3 I would encourage overtime working	❑	❑	❑	❑	❑
4 I would let subordinates use their judgement to solve problems	❑	❑	❑	❑	❑
5 I would encourage the use of standard procedures	❑	❑	❑	❑	❑
6 I would needle members for greater effort	❑	❑	❑	❑	❑
7 I would stress being ahead of competing groups	❑	❑	❑	❑	❑
8 I would let subordinates work the way they thought best	❑	❑	❑	❑	❑
9 I would speak as representative for subordinates	❑	❑	❑	❑	❑
10 I would be able to tolerate postponement and uncertainty	❑	❑	❑	❑	❑
11 I would try out my ideas on subordinates	❑	❑	❑	❑	❑
12 I would turn subordinates loose on a job and let them go at it	❑	❑	❑	❑	❑
13 I would work hard for promotion	❑	❑	❑	❑	❑
14 I would get swamped by details	❑	❑	❑	❑	❑
15 I would speak for subordinates when visitors were around	❑	❑	❑	❑	❑
16 I would be reluctant to let subordinates have freedom of action	❑	❑	❑	❑	❑
17 I would keep the work pace moving rapidly	❑	❑	❑	❑	❑
18 I would give some subordinates authority that I should keep	❑	❑	❑	❑	❑
19 I would settle conflicts which occur between subordinates	❑	❑	❑	❑	❑
20 I would let subordinates have a high degree of initiative	❑	❑	❑	❑	❑
21 I would represent subordinates at external meetings	❑	❑	❑	❑	❑
22 I would be willing to make changes	❑	❑	❑	❑	❑
23 I would decide what will be done and how it will be done	❑	❑	❑	❑	❑
24 I would trust subordinates to exercise good judgement	❑	❑	❑	❑	❑
25 I would push for increased production	❑	❑	❑	❑	❑
26 I would refuse to explain my actions to subordinates	❑	❑	❑	❑	❑
27 Things usually turn out as I predict	❑	❑	❑	❑	❑
28 I would let subordinates set their own work pace	❑	❑	❑	❑	❑
29 I would assign subordinates to specific tasks	❑	❑	❑	❑	❑
30 I would be able to act without consulting subordinates	❑	❑	❑	❑	❑
31 I would ask subordinates to work harder	❑	❑	❑	❑	❑
32 I would schedule the work that had to be done	❑	❑	❑	❑	❑
33 I would persuade others that my ideas were to their advantage	❑	❑	❑	❑	❑
34 I would urge subordinates to beat their previous records	❑	❑	❑	❑	❑
35 I would expect subordinates to follow set rules and regulations	❑	❑	❑	❑	❑

Employee-centred or consideration score

You get one point if you ticked either A or B in response to these questions:

2 _____   10 _____   22 _____

4 _____   12 _____   24 _____

6 _____   18 _____   28 _____

8 _____   20 _____

And you get one point if you ticked either D or E in response to these questions:

14 _____   16 _____   26 _____   30 _____

Total employee-centred score is: ❏

Job-centred or initiating structure score

You get one point if you ticked either A or B in response to these questions:

1 _____   13 _____   25 _____   34 _____

3 _____   15 _____   27 _____   35 _____

5 _____   17 _____   29 _____

7 _____   19 _____   31 _____

9 _____   21 _____   32 _____

11 _____   23 _____   33 _____

Total job-centred score is: ❏

Your two scores can be interpreted together as follows:

employee-centred score	job-centred score	your leadership style
0–7	0–10	you are not involved enough with either the work or with your employees
0–7	10–20	you are autocratic, a bit of a slave driver; you get the job done but at an emotional cost
8–15	0–10	people are happy in their work but sometimes at the expense of productivity
8–15	10–20	people enjoy working for you and are productive, naturally expending energy because they get positive reinforcement for good work

This exercise is based on the Leadership Style Inventory from Dorothy Marcic, *Organizational Behavior: Experiences and Cases*, West Publishing, St Paul, MN, 1992 (third edition), pp. 153–6.

2: Contemporary transformational icons

Objectives
1. To explore the nature of transformational leadership.

2. To explore the causal link between transformational leadership and organizational effectiveness.

Briefing
Individual (up to five minutes):

Remind yourself of the definition of the *new leader*, the *superleader*, the *transformational leader*. These labels each describe much the same package of leadership behaviours.

Syndicates of three to five (up to twenty minutes):

Identify someone whom your group would all describe as a transformational leader. Each group should choose a different figure. This could be a leading politician, a business leader, or a football club manager, for example. Nominate a spokesperson and prepare a ten minute presentation to the whole class answering the following questions:

■ What physical characteristics does this person have?

■ What special knowledge, skills and abilities does this person have?

■ What are this person's dominant personality traits?

■ How would you describe this person's leadership behaviour?

■ What are the causal links between this person's attributes and behaviour, on the one hand, and the effectiveness of their organization, on the other?

■ Imagine someone else in this person's role, someone who does not have that package of attributes and behaviour. Predict what would happen to organizational effectiveness.

■ Imagine your transformational leader in a different setting: put your football club manager in a computer company; put your computer company manager in charge of a hotel chain; give your politician a railway or a casino to run. How effective is your transformational leader likely to be in this different context?

Plenary (up to thirty minutes):

Present your findings to the group as a whole. Consider two main issues:

1. What characteristics do transformational leaders have in common, and in what ways do they differ from each other? Is there any 'common ground' here?

2. To what extent is their success context-specific? Would their unique combinations of physical, intellectual, personality and behavioural characteristics have been successful in other settings?

Key concepts

decision-making
classical decision theory
rational economic model
rationality
rational decisions
prescriptive models of decision-making
descriptive models of decision-making
bounded rationality
behavioural theory of decision-making
maximizing
satisficing
explanatory models of decision-making
heuristics
biases
representative heuristic

anchor and adjustment heuristic
availability heuristic
certainty
risk
uncertainty
routine decisions
adaptive decisions
innovative decisions
group polarization
risky shift phenomenon
caution shift phenomenon
groupthink
brainstorming
escalation of commitment

Learning outcomes

1. Distinguish between prescriptive, descriptive and explanatory models of decision-making and provide an example of each.
2. Distinguish different decision conditions on the basis of risk and programmability.
3. Consider the advantages and disadvantages of group decision-making.
4. Identify the factors used to decide whether to adopt individual or group decision-making.
5. Match organizational conditions with the decision-making processes that favour them.

Why study decision-making?

Why are senior company executives paid extra-high salaries? One reason is that they are there to make crucial decisions. The consequences of their decisions may lead to increased company profits, raised market share, raised stock price and the chance to take over a competitor. Alternatively, those decisions might have the opposite consequences and the company itself might be taken over and their employees made redundant. Can you think of managers whose decisions have led their companies to success or failure?

However, decisions are made at all levels of the organization, not just at the top. Both managers and non-managers make them. Given the central role that decision-making plays in the life of all organizations, and the effect that decision

Table 22.1: Levels of decision-making

Level of analysis	Key issues	Theoretical perspectives
Individual	Limits to information processing Personal biases	Information processing theory Cognitive psychology
Group	Effects of group dynamics on individuals' perceptions, attitudes and behaviours	Groupthink, group polarization and group cohesiveness
Organizational	Effects of conflicts, power and politics	Theories of organization conflict, power, politics and decision-making

Decision-making: the process of making choices from among several options.

outcomes have on the lives of all organization members, it is not surprising that it has attracted the attentions of practising managers and consultants, management academics and social science researchers. Chester Barnard was one of the first people to put decision-making at the centre of managerial work. Barnard was for many years the President of the New Jersey Bell Telephone Company, and author of the book, *The Functions of the Executive* (1938). He saw specialization, incentives, authority and **decision-making** as the key elements of formal organizations.

Later writers, notably Herbert Simon (1957), an academic at Carnegie Mellon University, agreed that management theory should be based around the question of choice and decision-making as the core of management. He argued that the art of getting things done, and of implementing those decisions that had been made, was indeed an aspect of management that could not be neglected. However, it logically followed from, and was subordinate to, the decision as to what had to be done – how, why, when and by whom? Henry Mintzberg (1989) felt that 'decision making is one of the most important, if not the most important, of all managerial activities, and represents one of the most common and crucial work tasks of managers'. Decision-making has been studied in order both to understand how decisions are actually made in practice and to advise managers how to make better decisions. It can be analyzed at a number of different levels, as table 22.1 shows. Each level focuses on its own key issues and possesses its own theoretical perspectives. The levels are interrelated, however, with one influencing and being affected by the others.

Source: Reprinted with Special Permission of King Features Syndicate.

Classical decision theory: a theory which assumes that decision-makers are objective, have complete information and consider all possible alternatives and their consequences before selecting the optimal solution.

Models of decision-making

Rational economic model: a model which assumes that decision-making is, and should be, a rational process consisting of a sequence of steps that enhance the probability of attaining a desired outcome.

The traditional approach to understanding individual decision-making is based upon **classical decision theory** and the **rational economic model**. These were originally developed in economics, and they make certain assumptions about people and how they make decisions.

The rational economic model of decision-making is described in figure 22.1. It is still popular among economics scholars in suggesting how decisions should be made. However, to understand its weaknesses, it is necessary to list its assumptions and demonstrate how they fail to match up to reality. These are shown in table 22.2.

Stop and Criticize

Think of some personal or organizational decisions that you have recently made. How many of the steps and assumptions from the classical model were relevant in each situation?

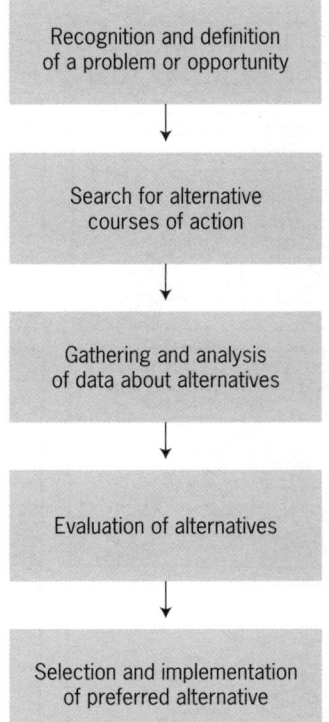

Figure 22.1: Rational economic model of decision-making

Rationality: the use of scientific reasoning, empiricism and positivism, and the use of decision criteria of evidence, logical argument and reasoning.

Rational decisions: choices based on rationality – that is, on a rational mode of thinking.

The classical view of decision-making has always employed the concepts of **rationality** and **rational decisions**, in its discussions and prescriptions. Rationality is equated with scientific reasoning, empiricism and positivism, and with the use of decision criteria of evidence, logical argument and reasoning. Rational decisions are those which are based on rationality, that is, on a rational mode of thinking (Simon, 1986; Langley, 1989).

Table 22.2: Rational economic model assumptions and reality

Assumption	Reality
All alternatives will be considered	▪ Rarely possible to consider all alternatives since there are too many
	▪ Some alternatives will not have occurred to the decision-maker
The consequences of each alternative will be considered	▪ Impractical to consider all consequences
	▪ Impractical to estimate many of the consequences considered
	▪ Estimation process involves time and effort
Accurate information about alternatives is available at no cost	▪ Information available is rarely accurate, often dated, and usually only partially relevant to the problem.
	▪ Generated or purchased information has a cost
	▪ Decisions have to be made on incomplete, insufficient and only partly accurate information
Decision-makers are rational beings	▪ Individuals lack the mental capacity to store and process all the information relevant to a decision
	▪ Frequently they lack the ability to perform the mental calculations required

What term should be applied to decisions that are not based on the rational economic model of decision-making? Irrational? Non-rational? These terms imply not only a different type of decision-making process, but they also carry the connotation of something inferior. That is, they attach a negative value to the non-use of rationality. The classical view has now been accepted as not providing an accurate account of how people typically make decisions. Moreover, its prescriptions for making better decisions have often been incorrect. Instead, contemporary cognitive research by psychologists has revealed the ways in which decisions are made based on heuristic models, judgements and tacit knowledge.

Prescriptive models of decision-making: models which recommend how individuals should behave in order to achieve a desired outcome. This makes the classical model, described above, a prescriptive one. Such models often also contain specific techniques, procedures and processes which their supporters claim will lead to more accurate and efficient decision-making. Prescriptive decision models are thus similar to the principles of management described earlier, and they share their strengths and weaknesses. They are often based on observations of poor decision-making processes, where key steps might have been omitted or inadequately considered. They are developed and marketed by management consultants as a way of improving organization performance through improved decision-making.

Many different prescriptive models of decision-making and problem-solving can be found in management textbooks. Some are prescriptive in the sense that they specify how individuals should approach a problem, while others specify which decision-making styles should be effective in different situations. These models have labels such as decision trees, programme evaluation and review technique (PERT), and critical path method (CPM). Despite their differences, they typically possess certain common features which include a list of steps, a logical framework and an emphasis on rationality.

One of the best-known prescriptive models of decision-making was developed by Victor H. Vroom and Philip Yetton (1973) and was later expanded by Vroom and Arthur Jago (Vroom and Jago, 1988). Their model sought to help managers determine the degree to which they should involve subordinates in the decision-making process. It was based on the assumption that the effectiveness of managerial decisions was influenced by three situational factors which were:

Quality	Does the decision achieve the aim? What does it cost to implement?
Acceptance	How acceptable is the decision to others? Would they be committed to its implementation?
Time	How much time is available in which to reach a decision? How long does the decision take to implement?

Vroom and Yetton noted that leaders used different decision-making methods, and any of these could be effective, depending on the situation. Leaders used these methods with either a group of subordinates or a single subordinate. They identified different decision-making methods, each represented by a letter: A for autocratic, C for consultative, G for group and D for delegation. The decision method choices, and their behavioural characteristics, for both group problems and individual problems are shown in table 22.3. In each case, the decision method options for the leader are as follows:

Group problem	AI	AII	CI	CII	GII	
Individual problem	AI	AII	CI		GI	D

Table 22.3: The Vroom–Yetton decision-making model

Style Label	Autocratic AI	Autocratic AII	Consultative CI	Consultative CII	Negotiation GI	Group GII	Delegation D
Participants	Leader	Leader and subordinate(s)	Leader and subordinate(s)	Leader and group	Leader and single subordinate	Leader and group	Leader and single subordinate
Information / Suggestions / ideas / Alternatives	Leader uses information available at the time	Leader obtains necessary information from subordinate(s)	Leader obtains necessary suggestions and ideas from subordinate(s)	Leader obtains the collective ideas of subordinates	Leader obtains subordinates' ideas	Leader and subordinates together consider alternatives	Leader supplies subordinate with any information possessed
Role of subordinate(s)	None Leader generates and evaluates solution alone	Consulted individually Subordinate(s) provide only information	Consulted individually Subordinate(s) provide ideas and suggestions	Consulted as a group Subordinates provide ideas and suggestions	Joint problem-solvers	Joint problem-solvers Subordinates, collectively with leader, generate and evaluate alternatives to reach agreement (consensus) on a solution. Leader acts as a neutral chairperson	Sole problem-solver Leader may or may not request subordinate to inform him/her of the decision made
Leader explains problem to subordinate(s)?	No	Perhaps	Yes	Yes	Yes	Yes	Yes
Who makes decision / solves the problem	Leader alone	Leader alone	Leader alone	Leader alone (perhaps reflecting group inputs)	Leader and subordinate together arrive at a mutually agreeable solution	Leader accepts and implements any solution that has the support of the entire group	Leader delegates problem to subordinate

As one moves from left to right in the table:

- the leader discusses the problem or decision with more people;

- such discussions change from leader–individual to leader–group interactions;

- group input changes from merely providing information to recommending solutions;

- group ownership and commitment to the solution increases;

- the time needed to arrive at a decision increases.

Vroom and Yetton argued that achieving effectiveness depended on the managers' ability to adjust their decision-making method to the requirements of the situation. To help managers achieve this match, they provided seven questions for them to ask in order. These are shown at the top of figure 22.2. Answers to these questions lead along different routes, ultimately directing managers to the best decision-making method for that situation. For purposes of simplification, the problem situation depicted here is relevant to a group situation, and hence

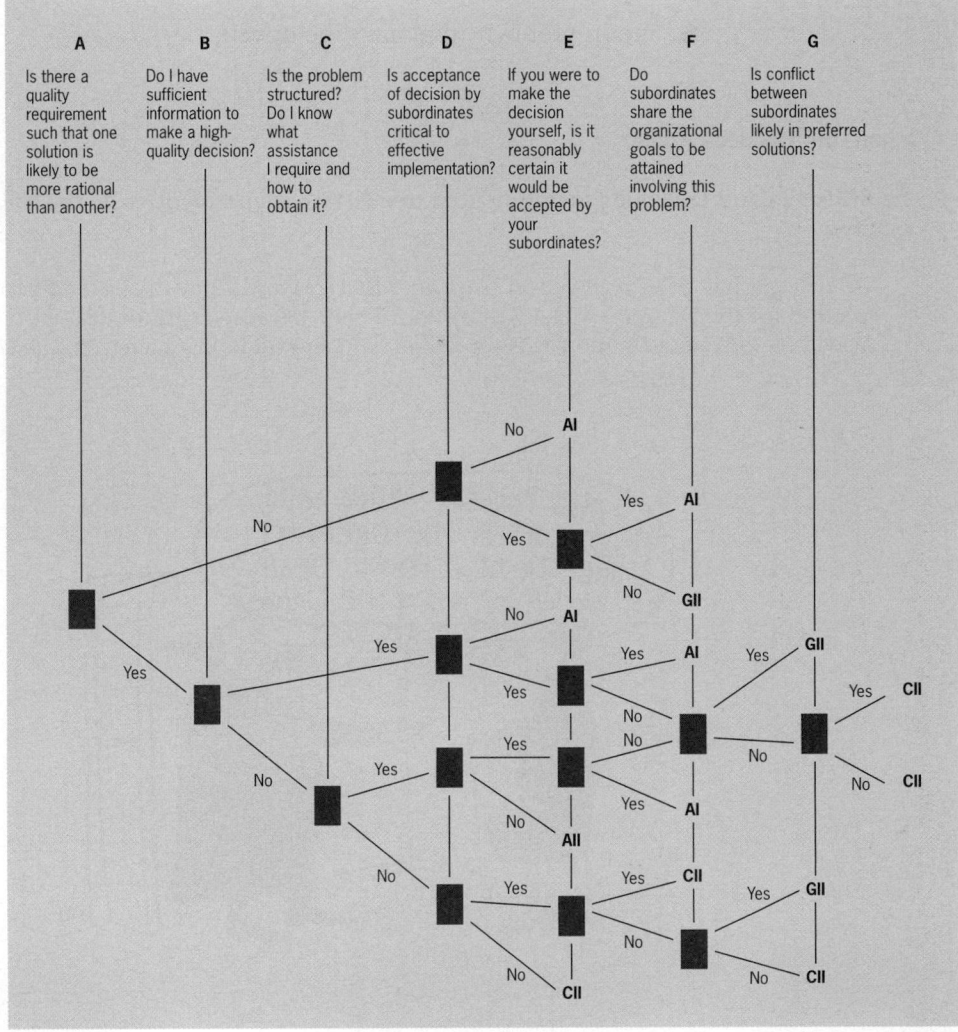

Figure 22.2: The Vroom–Yetton decision tree (group problem)
Reprinted from *Leadership and Decision Making*, by Victor H. Vroom and Philip W. Yetton, by permission of the University of Pittsburgh Press. © 1973 by University of Pittsburgh Press.

individual decision methods GI and D have been excluded. Moreover, in some books, Vroom and Yetton's model is shown as indicating that several decision methods are equally capable of generating an effective solution. In such a case, commentators recommend the method located furthest to the left of the decision-making model, on time and cost criteria. To avoid this complication, only the single, optimum decision method is shown in figure 22.2.

Figure 22.2 is called a 'decision tree' because it contains a series of choices which, like branches, lead to alternative end points. Obviously problems differ. Vroom and Jago (1988) went on to develop four different decision trees, each of which represents a generic type of problem encountered by managers in organizations. Their trees distinguish problems in terms of whether they are individual or group focused, whether or not the development of decision-making abilities is involved, and what the time constraints are. Their four decision trees are:

- individual-level problems with time constraints;

- individual-level problems in which a manager wants to develop an employee's decision-making abilities;

- group-level problems in which the manager wants to develop employees' decision-making abilities;

- group problems that are time-driven.

Conan, the Decision Maker

The British Inland Revenue (government tax collection department) sent the following reply to an enquirer:

> Your letter has been received in Customer Services and I have passed this to the relevant section for the Decision Maker's attention. This is because I cannot deal with your request, it will be looked at by the Decision Maker, you should be contacted in due course.

From 'Taxing message behind IR jargon', *Personnel Today*, 18 April 2000, p. 68.

Descriptive models of decision-making: models which investigate how individuals actually make decisions.

Richard Michael Cyert (1921–2001)

James Gardiner March (b. 1928)

Herbert Alexander Simon (1916–2001)

Descriptive models of decision-making focus on how individuals actually make decisions. Each decision made by an individual or group is affected by a number of factors. Some of these are:

■ individual personality;

■ group relationships;

■ organizational power relationships and political behaviour;

■ external environmental pressures;

■ organization strategic considerations;

■ information availability (or lack of).

The aim of these models is to examine which of these factors are the most important, and how they interrelate prior to a decision being made.

One of the earliest, and still among the most influential, descriptive models is the **behavioural theory of decision-making**. It was developed by Richard Cyert, James March and Herbert Simon (Simon, 1960; Cyert and March, 1963; March, 1988). It is called 'behavioural' because it treats decision-making as another aspect of individual behaviour. For example, if a research study interviewed brokers who bought and sold shares in the stock market to determine what factors influenced their decisions, it would be an example of a descriptive approach to decision-making. It is also sometimes referred to as the 'administrative model'. It acknowledges that, in the real world, those who make decisions are restricted in their decision processes, and therefore have to settle for a less than ideal solution. Behavioural theory holds that individuals make decisions while they are operating within the limits of **bounded rationality**. Bounded rationality recognizes that:

■ the definition of a situation is likely to be incomplete;

■ it is impossible to generate all alternatives;

■ it is impossible to predict all the consequences of each alternative;

■ final decisions are often influenced by personal and political factors.

The effect of personal and situational limitations is that individuals make decisions that are 'good enough' rather than 'ideal'. That is, they 'satisfice' rather than 'maximize'. When **maximizing**, decision-makers review the range of alternatives available, all at the same time, and attempt to select the best one. However, when **satisficing**, they evaluate one option at a time in sequence, until they alight on the first one that is acceptable. That chosen option will meet all the minimum requirements for the solution, but may not be the best (optimal) choice in the situation. Once an option is found, decision-makers will look no further.

Stop and Criticize

When you chose your current partner – girlfriend, boyfriend, wife or husband – did you maximize or satisfice? Is this distinction a useful way of explaining the decision-making process?

Biases in decision-making

Research suggests that decision-making can be influenced by a number of different sources of bias.

Contrast bias

This bias of human perception affects the way that we see the difference between items that are presented one after another. If the second item is fairly different from the first, we will tend to see it as more different than it actually is. If you lift a light object first and then a heavy object, the latter will appear heavier than it actually is.

Reciprocation bias

A basic norm in society is reciprocation: that is, one person must try to repay in kind in the future, what another has provided them with in the past. We are socialised from childhood to abide by the reciprocation rule or suffer social disapproval and a feeling of personal guilt. Such reciprocation leads to concession-making, and allows different individuals' initial, incompatible demands to become compromised, so that they finally work together towards common goals.

Commitment and consistency bias

Commitment is a state of being in which individuals become bound to their actions and, through these, to their beliefs. Commitment sustains action in the face of difficulties. In these circumstances it is behaviour which is being committed. It represents a visible indicator of what we are and what we intend doing. After taking an initial decision, people will adjust their attitude to make it consistent with their action, and become committed to it.

Social proof bias

The social proof bias states that people decide what to believe or how to act in a situation by looking at what others believe and do. In situations of uncertainty and ambiguity, they observe and follow others, especially those they perceive to be most similar to themselves. Such similarity is defined in terms of status, social background, dress, manner or language. Market research suggests that 95 per cent of people are imitators and only 5 per cent are initiators.

Liking bias

We enjoy doing things for people we like. That liking encourages us to comply with their requests. The liking bias is so powerful that the person concerned does not even have to be present for it to be activated. Often, just the mention of a friend's or mutual acquaintance's name will be sufficient.

Authority bias

Each of us has a deep-seated duty to authority and will tend to comply when requested by an authority figure. Since the opposite is anarchy, we are all trained from birth to believe that obedience to authority is right. The strength of this bias to obey legitimate authority figures comes from systematic socialization practices designed to instil in people the perception that such obedience constitutes correct conduct. Different societies vary in terms of this dimension.

Scarcity bias

We all know that things and opportunities that are difficult to obtain are more valued. We use information about an item's availability as a shortcut to decide quickly on its quality. Moreover, as things become less available, we lose freedoms. Since we hate this, we react against it, and want these things more than before.

Based on Max H. Bazerman, *Judgement in Managerial Decision Making*, Wiley, New York (fifth edition), 2001; Robert B. Cialdini, *Influence: Science and Practice*, Allyn and Bacon, London (fourth edition), 2001; Andrzej Huczynski, *Influencing within Organizations*, Routledge, London (second edition), 2004.

Decision conditions: risk and programmability

Decision conditions: risk and programmability

Certainty: a condition in which managers possess full knowledge of alternatives; have a high probability of these being available; can calculate the costs and benefits of each alternative; and have high predictability of outcomes.

Risk: a condition in which managers have a high knowledge of alternatives; know the probability of these being available; can calculate the costs and know the benefits of each alternative; and have a medium predictability of outcomes.

Uncertainty: a condition in which managers have a low knowledge of alternatives and a low knowledge of the probability of these being available; can to some degree calculate the costs and benefits of each alternative; but have no predictability of outcomes.

Risks of decisions

Chapter 16 distinguished different types of environmental conditions faced by organizations and labelled these 'stable equilibrium', 'bounded instability' (or chaos) and 'explosive instability'. The conditions under which a decision is made affects both how it is made and its outcome (see table 22.4). Decisions differ in terms of the degree of risk involved and their programmability. Every decision is made under conditions of **certainty**, **risk** or **uncertainty**. We shall consider each in turn.

In circumstances of certainty, no element of chance comes between the alternative and its outcome, and all the outcomes are known in advance with 100 per cent certainty. In such circumstances, all that the individual has to do is to select the outcomes with the largest benefit. A situation of total certainty is so rare as to be virtually non-existent. Some writers, struggling to find an example, cite the example of government bonds which guarantee a fixed rate of interest over a period of time which will be paid barring the fall of the government. However, as the Russian government default in the late 1990s demonstrated, even government bonds carry an element of risk.

Perhaps the main reason for discussing a generally non-existent state is that it suggests one of the reasons why most senior executives and managers of the world's leading companies are paid such so much. As the trading conditions become more volatile and technological changes such as the internet dramatically change established practices, the future becomes ever more difficult to predict. Those few individuals who have shown themselves capable of making what have turned out to be the correct decisions enter a seller's market for their skills. Or, to look at it another way, if decisions were made in conditions of certainty, managers would not be needed, and junior, cheaper operatives, supplied with a rulebook, could replace them. Indeed, in conditions of certainty, a computer could quickly and accurately identify the consequences of the available options and select the outcomes with greatest benefits. Managers are paid to make those tricky 'judgement calls' in uncertain conditions.

Probably the most common real-life decisions are made under conditions of risk. When managers can assess the likelihood of various outcomes occurring on the basis of their past experience, research or other information, decision-making can be said to take place under conditions of risk.

Decisions made under uncertainty are the most difficult since the manager even lacks the information with which to estimate the likelihood of various outcomes and their associated probabilities and payoffs (March and Simon, 1958, p. 137). Conditions of uncertainty prevail in new markets, or those offering technologies, or those aimed at new target customers. In all these cases there are no historical data from which to infer probabilities. In each case, the situation is so novel and complex that it is impossible to make comparative judgements.

Without uncertainty as to what course of action to take, there would be no decision to make. Hence, a decision-making manager would not be required. It is for this reason that so many writers over the years have emphasized the centrality of decision-making in management. Having considered the various conditions under which decisions are made, let us investigate the greater complexity of each of the activities associated with the decision-making model presented earlier.

Table 22.4: Environmental and decision-making conditions

Environmental condition	Decision-making condition	Characteristics	Illustration
Stable equilibrium is a state in which the elements are always in, or quickly return to, a state of balance	Certainty	Alternatives and outcomes known and fully predictable	Fixed interest rate savings accounts
Bounded instability (or chaos) is a state in which there is a mixture of order and disorder, many unpredictable events and changes, and in which an organization's behaviour has an irregular pattern	Risk	Known alternatives with only probable outcomes predictable	Tomorrow's weather
Explosive instability is a state in which there is no order or pattern	Uncertainty	Alternatives and outcomes poorly understood	Developing a new product

Dispersing the fog of war

The buzzword is C4IST, which stands for command, control, computers, communications, intelligence, surveillance and targeting – the heart of network-centric warfare. An example of the military future is on display at Anaheim, Southern California. Boeing's Battlefield Integration Centre (BIC), a fortified building on an industrial estate has ... as its centre-piece a room like a cinema, with three giant screens along one wall and three control consoles below them. One screen has a satellite image of Korea with moving squares and triangles representing jet fighters, bombers and spy planes. Another has close-up pictures of trucks on the move, and a third has an image fed from a camera in a soldier's helmet. This is a mock military operation, showing what warfare could soon be like.

Throughout history, military commanders have had difficulties making decisions on the battlefield due to possessing incomplete or out-of-date information. In this facility, the screens display information fed digitally from sensors and cameras on aircraft, both manned and unmanned, from satellite cameras and from infrared cameras on the ground. All the pieces of equipment are linked electronically. The official sitting at the console desk can home in on anything suspicious and put together a whole battle plan, lining up airborne and ground forces to attack the enemy. Boeing's BIC gives a taste of the workings of an integrated command system that sucks up information from all available sources, including intelligence, and feeds it into a single database. It can make sense of huge quantities of raw data using sophisticated algorithms to identify targets in order of priority and to calculate what is needed to destroy them. ... The idea is to have information about where everything is and where it is going, even to know how much your enemy knows, thus dispersing 'the fog of war'.

TM & © Boeing. Used under license.

From *The Economist*, 'Military revolutions', a survey of the defence industry, 20 July 2002, p. 8.

Stop and Criticize

Identify three separate events in your university career or work life involving certainty, risk and uncertainty. Describe each situation and suggest how it could change, or has actually changed, from one condition to one of the other two, i.e.

Certainty
■ from certainty to risk;
■ from certainty to uncertainty.

Risk
■ from risk to certainty;
■ from risk to uncertainty.

Uncertainty
■ from uncertainty to risk;
■ from uncertainty to certainty.

From John T. Samaras, *Management Applications: Exercises, Cases and Readings*, Prentice-Hall, Englewood Cliffs, NJ, 1989, p. 51.

Programmability of decisions

Routine decisions: decisions which are made according to established procedures and rules.

Organization members make many different decisions every day. Some decisions are routine while others are not. **Routine decisions** are those which involve the use of pre-established organizational procedures or rules. Routine decision-makers are given considerable guidance as to what to do and how to do it through a well-established process, clearly defined goals and the provision of information sources and decision rules. Examples of routine decisions include the re-ordering of stock items which have fallen to a certain level, the efficient routing of delivery vans and the scheduling of equipment use. All these decisions tend to be repetitive and programmed, and are made by low-level employees on their own who rely on pre-determined courses of action.

Adaptive decisions typically require human judgement to be used. It is a form of judgement that no computer program, however complex, can produce. Once certain judgements are clarified, adaptive decisions can be made using relatively basic quantitative decision tools such as break-even analysis, a pay-off matrix or a decision tree.

Finally, **innovative decisions** are made when a unique situation is confronted that has no precedent, when there are no off-the-shelf solutions and when a novel answer has to be found. Innovative decisions are an outcome of problem-solving, they frequently deal with areas of the unknown and company professionals or top managers typically make them. Within the organizational context, such decisions tend to be rare: for example, the decision whether to acquire another company, to invest in a new technology, or to adopt a new marketing approach. Many innovative decisions concern some aspect of company strategy and hence are more likely to be made by groups than by an individual. (See table 22.5.)

Table 22.5: Routine, adaptive and innovative decisions

Decision type	Routine	← Adaptive →	Innovative
Goals	Clear, specific		Vague
Level	Lower-level employees		Upper management
Problem	Well structured		Poorly structured
Process	Computational		Heuristic
Information	Readily available		Unavailable
Level of risk	Low		High
Involvement	Single decision-maker		Group decision
Consequences	Minor		Major
Solution basis	Decision rule and procedures		Judgement, creativity
Decision speed	Fast		Slow
Time for solution	Short		Relatively long

Stop and Criticize

Think of three very different decisions that you have recently made. How well do they fit into this routine, adaptive, innovative decision framework? What additional decision-type categories would you add?

Individual and group decision-making

One of the main reasons why organizational activities are arranged around groups and teams is management's assumption that group decisions are better than individual decisions. The common-sense belief is that with many members contributing their diverse skills, knowledge and experiences, they will make better decisions than individuals (Hill, 1982). Rogelberg, Barnes-Farell and Lowe (1992) cite examples of situations in which groups make decisions that are better than the average quality of decisions made by individuals who are judged to be experts outside the group. However, experimental research data clearly show that while the average quality of a decision made by a group is higher than the average quality of a decision made by an individual, the quality of work group decisions is consistently below that made by their most capable individual members.

Stop and Criticize

Suggest reasons why, despite the evidence of ineffectiveness, organizations continue to promote group-based decision-making.

On the positive side, multiple individuals in a group can supply a greater range of knowledge and information to deal with the more complex questions. They can generate more alternatives; can have a better comprehension of the problem using multiple perspectives; and permit the specialization of labour, with individuals doing those tasks for which they are best suited. The effect of this is to

Table 22.6: Advantages and disadvantages of group decision-making

Advantages	Disadvantages
Greater pool of knowledge: A group can bring much more information and experience to bear on a decision or problem than can an individual alone.	*Personality factors*: Traits such as shyness can prevent some members offering their opinions and knowledge to the group.
Different perspectives: Individuals with varied experience and interests help the group to see decision situations and problems from different angles.	*Social conformity*: Unwillingness to 'rock the boat' and pressure to conform may combine to stifle the creativity of individual contributors.
Greater comprehension: Those who personally experience the give and take of group discussion about alternative courses of action tend to understand the rationale behind the final decision.	*Diffusion of responsibility*: Members feel able to avoid responsibility for their actions, believing it can be shouldered by the others present.
Increased acceptance: Those who play an active role in group decision-making and problem-solving tend to view the outcomes as 'ours' rather than 'theirs'.	*Minority domination*: Sometimes the quality of group action is reduced when the group gives in to those who talk the loudest and longest.
Training ground: Less experienced participants in group action learn how to cope with group dynamics by actually being involved.	*Logrolling*: Political wheeling and dealing can displace sound thinking when an individual's pet project or vested interest is at stake.
	Goal displacement: Sometimes secondary considerations, such as winning an argument, making a point or getting back at a rival, displace the primary task of making a sound decision or solving a problem.
	Group brainstorming: Reduces rather than increases the quantity and quality of ideas compared to individual performance.
	'Groupthink': Sometimes cohesive 'in-groups' let the desire for unanimity override sound judgement when generating and evaluating alternative courses of action.
	Satisficing: Decisions may be made which are immediately acceptable to the group rather than the best ones.

Based on M.A. West, C.S. Borrill and K.L. Unsworth, 'Team effectiveness in organizations', in C.L. Cooper, and I.T. Robertson (eds), *International Review of Industrial and Organizational Psychology*, vol. 13, Wiley, Chichester, 1998, pp. 1–48: Richard Kreitner, *Management*, Houghton Mifflin, Boston, MA (fourth edition), 1989, p. 238.

improve the quality of group effort and facilitate wider decision acceptance since more members will understand the decision better and have a feeling of ownership of it through participation. On the negative side, there are concerns that groups work more slowly, that the disagreements within them can create group conflict and that group members may be intimidated by their group leader, creating only pseudo involvement in decision-making.

Research has revealed that two main factors determine whether groups should be preferred to individuals. These are, first, how structured the task is and, second, who are the individuals. If the task to be performed is structured (has a clear, correct solution), then groups are better, although they take longer (Weber, 1984). In the case of unstructured tasks (no single correct answer and creativity required), individuals are better. Hence the counter-intuitive finding that the performance of brainstorming groups is inferior to that of individuals.

Table 22.7: Individual and group performance compared

Factor	Individuals when	Group when
Type of problem task	Creativity or efficiency is desired	Diverse skills and knowledge are required
Acceptance of decision	Acceptance is not important	Acceptance by group members is valued
Quality of the solution	'Best member' can be identified	Several group members can improve the solution
Characteristics of the individuals	Individuals cannot collaborate	Members have experience of working together
Decision-making climate	Climate is competitive	Climate is supportive of group problem-solving
Time available	Relatively little time is available	Relatively more time is available

From *A Diagnostic Approach to Organizational Behaviour*, 4/E by Gordon, © 1993. Reprinted by permission of Prentice-Hall, Inc., Upper Saddle River, NJ.

For a group to make a good decision, its members must possess the necessary knowledge and skills to pool. Two heads are better than one provided that they have something in them. The quality of the group's decision is partly determined by the ability of its members. Laughlin and Johnson (1966) found the superiority of the lone, high-ability individual compared to a low-ability pair. Pooling of ignorance does not help. Research suggests that for logical structured tasks, choose able people and put them into groups. For less well-structured problems, choose creative people, get them to work alone and pool the outcome of their separate deliberations.

Problems with group decision-making

It is the very strengths of a group that are also its weaknesses. The costs of bringing individuals together in one place counters the benefits of getting contributions from supposedly independent minds. A number of problems will be examined: group polarization, groupthink, brainstorming and escalation of commitment.

Group polarization: this occurs when individuals in a group begin by taking a moderate stance on an issue related to a common value and, after having discussed it, end up taking a more extreme decision than the average members' decisions. The extremes could be more risky or more cautious.

Risky shift phenomenon: the tendency of a group to make decisions that are riskier than those which the members of the group would have recommended individually before.

Caution shift phenomenon: the tendency of a group to make decisions that are more risk averse than those which the members of the group would have recommended individually before.

Group polarization refers to the phenomenon that occurs when a position that is held on an issue by the majority of group members is intensified (in a given direction) as a result of discussion (Lamm, 1988). This tendency can lead to irrational and hence to ineffective group performance. Social psychologists have documented the situation in which individuals in a group begin by taking a moderate stance on an issue related to a common value and then, after having discussed it, end up taking a more extreme stance. James Stoner conducted one of the earliest of these studies in the 1950s. He found that groups of management students were willing to make decisions involving greater risks than their individual preferences (Stoner, 1961). This was referred to as the **risky shift phenomenon**. However, the opposite can also occur, and this is called the **caution shift phenomenon**. Here a group can become more risk-averse than the initial, average risk-averse tendencies of its individuals members (Lamm and Myers, 1978; Isenberg, 1986).

There are two psychological theories to explain group polarization. One of these is *social comparison theory*, which holds that people are motivated to present themselves so as to be perceived in a favourable light. After comparing themselves with others, they endeavour to be more favourably perceived by the other members. They do this by being more extreme in whichever is the majority direction. The *persuasive arguments theory* stresses informational influence and explains group polarization in terms of the number and persuasiveness of the arguments presented. Since the majority view is more likely to be presented, individuals are more exposed to arguments supporting that view, causing a shift in the majority's direction (Jones and Roelofsma, 2000). Since group polarization is induced through the process of discussion, it only occurs if the initial view of the individual group members is in the same direction (Myers and Lamm, 1976; Myers, 1990).

Patricia Wallace (1999) believes that group polarization may be partly responsible for the extremism that is often found on the internet and the apparent absence of a moderate voice. An individual may hold a relatively moderate view about an issue initially, but after talking with others about it over the internet, they are likely to move away from the middle view towards one of the fringes. Factors that contribute to group polarization are present on the internet in abundance. First people talk and talk endlessly. Second, members are selective about what they share with others. As talk progresses, members become increasing reluctant to bring up items that might contradict the emerging group consensus. This creates a biased discussion where alternatives are not considered during discussion.

Online bias

Ross Highwater and Lutfus Sayeed studied online groups which used groupware that allowed synchronous chat and had online voting capabilities to collaborate in making a personnel decision. Group members were given the résumés (job application forms) of candidates applying for the position of a marketing manager. The researchers rigged the applicants' positive and negative attributes so that only one applicant was best suited for the job because he most closely matched the criteria in the job description. They distributed information packets containing a subset of information from the résumés, so that each group member knew only part of the story. Some three-person groups met face to face, while others discussed the job from separate locations using groupware.

Almost none of the groups – whether face-to-face or online – chose the best candidate. Neither type shared information in a way that would allow them to make an objective decision based on the whole picture. However, the degree of bias was most skewed when discussion was held online. Bias

▶

was determined by which titbits of information members chose to share. In the most biased discussion, they shared positive (but not negative) information about the winning candidate, and negative (but not positive) information about losing candidates. Each item contributed would thus reinforce the march towards group consensus rather than add complications to fuel the debate. This trend was found to be twice as prevalent in online groups as in the face-to-face ones.

Based on Ross Highwater and Lutfus Sayeed, 'The impact of computer-mediated communication systems on biased group discussions', *Computers in Human Behaviour,* vol. 11, no. 1, 1995, pp. 33–44.

Irving Lester Janis
(1918–90)

Groupthink: a mode of thinking that people engage in when they are deeply involved in a cohesive in-group, when the members' strivings for unanimity override their motivation to appraise realistically the alternative courses of action.

One of the reasons why groups perform badly on complex, unstructured tasks is due to the dynamics of group interaction. Groups and teams can develop a high level of cohesiveness. This is generally a positive thing, but it also has negative consequences. Specifically, the desire not to disrupt the consensus can lead to a reluctance to challenge the group's thinking which in turn results in bad decisions. Irving Janis studied a number of American foreign policy 'disasters' such as the failure to anticipate the Japanese attack on Pearl Harbor (1941), the Bay of Pigs fiasco (1961) when President John F. Kennedy's administration sought to overthrow the government of Fidel Castro, and the prosecution of the Vietnam War between 1964 and 1967 by President Lyndon Johnson. Janis concluded that it was the cohesive nature of the important committees which made these decisions that prevented contradictory views being expressed. He named this process **groupthink**. He listed the symptoms of groupthink as well as how they could be prevented. These are outlined in table 22.8.

Groupthink led to a failure by the group to make the best decision. The group discussed a minimum number of alternatives. The courses of action favoured by the majority of the group were not reexamined from the view of hidden risks and other alternatives, nor were original, unsatisfactory courses. The group failed to use the expert opinion that it had, and when expert opinion was evaluated it was done with a selective bias which ignored the facts and opinions which did not support the group view. The findings of Solomon Asch's experiments into group pressure and conformity, which were described in chapter 11, are relevant here.

In the groups studied by Janis, while individual doubt may have been suppressed and the illusion of group unanimity and cohesiveness maintained, the group paid a high price in terms of its effectiveness. The factors affecting group cohesiveness are listed in table 22.9. Thus, while group cohesion can make a positive contribution to group effectiveness, it may also have negative consequences on the process of group decision-making. Group loyalty, instilled through cohesion, acts to stifle the raising and questioning of controversial issues which in turn leads to the making of poor decisions. At the heart of groupthink is the tendency for groups to seek concurrence and the illusion of unanimity. To prevent groupthink occurring, individuals who disagree with the group's evolving consensus must be willing to make their voices heard. Research on groupthink suggests that the phenomenon is most likely to occur in groups where the leader is particularly dominant, and that, by comparison, group cohesiveness *per se* is not a crucial factor (McCauley, 1989).

Table 22.8: Groupthink: symptoms and prevention steps

When groups become very cohesive, there is a danger that they will become victims of their own closeness.

Symptoms	Prevention steps
1. *Illusion of invulnerability*: members display excessive optimism that past successes will continue and will shield them, and hence they tend to take extreme risks	(A) Leader encourages open expression of doubt by members
2. *Collective rationalization*: members collectively rationalize away data that disconfirm the assumptions and beliefs upon which they base their decisions	(B) Leader accepts criticism of his/her opinions
3. *Illusion of morality*: members believe that they, as moral individuals, are unlikely to make bad decisions	(C) Higher-status members offer opinions last
4. *Shared stereotypes*: members dismiss disconfirming evidence by discrediting its source (e.g. stereotyping other groups and its leaders as evil or weak)	(D) Get recommendations from a duplicate group
5. *Direct pressure*: imposition of verbal, non-verbal or other sanctions on individuals who explore deviant positions (e.g. those who express doubts or question the validity of group beliefs). Perhaps use of assertive language to force compliance	(E) Periodically divide into sub-groups
6. *Self-censorship*: members keep silent about misgivings about the apparent group consensus and try to minimize their doubts	(F) Members get reactions of trusted outsiders
7. *Illusion of unanimity*: members conclude that the group has reached a consensus because its most vocal members are in agreement	(G) Invite trusted outsiders to join the discussion periodically
8. *Mindguards*: members who take it upon themselves to screen out adverse, disconfirming information supplied by 'outsiders' which might endanger the group's complacency	(H) Assign someone to the role of devil's advocate (I) Develop scenarios of rivals' possible actions

Based on Irving L. Janis, *Victims of Groupthink: A Psychological Study of Foreign Policy Decisions and Fiascos*, Houghton Mifflin, Boston, MA (second edition), 1982.

Table 22.9: Factors affecting group cohesiveness

Size	Smaller groups are more cohesive than larger ones, partly because their members interact more frequently
Duration	The longer members are together, the more opportunity they have to find out about one another
Threats	An external threat can often (although not always) draw members together against 'the enemy'
Isolation	Leads a group to feel distinct and hence special
Rewards	Group rewards can encourage co-operation to achieve the group goal
Restricted entry	Difficulty of membership increases identification with the group
Similarities	Where individuals share common goals and attitudes, they enjoy being in each other's company

The Space Shuttle *Challenger* Disaster – a case of groupthink?

On 28 January 1986, seventy-three seconds after its launch from Cape Canaveral, Florida, the space shuttle *Challenger* exploded, killing all seven members of its crew, including a civilian schoolteacher, Christa MacAuliffe. The evidence suggested that the physical cause of the explosion was an O-ring rubber seal that failed to do its job, due to the freezing overnight temperatures at the launch pad.

A presidential commission established to investigate the causes of the accident cited flawed decision-making as one of the causes of the disaster. The subsequent analysis of documents and testimony by researchers has led some of them to argue that the negative symptoms of groupthink increased in the twenty-four hours prior to the launch in the group that consisted of Morton Thiokol, the builders of the rocket boosters, and NASA management personnel. Thiokol engineers argued for the cancellation of the launch because the O-rings would not withstand the pressure at the launchtime temperatures. The engineers were pressured by their bosses to stifle their dissent and their opinions were devalued. The past record of success led to over-confidence and various pieces of information were withheld from key individuals.

In consequence, the group failed to consider fully the alternatives; failed to evaluate the risks associated with their preferred course of action; used information that was biased when making their decision; and failed to work out a contingency plan. Although the physical cause of the disaster was an O-ring seal, many researchers claim that the actual cause was the flawed decision-making process which had been infected by groupthink.

Based on J.K. Esser and Lindoerfer, J.S., 'Groupthink and the Space Shuttle Challenger accident', *Journal of Behavioural Decision Making*, vol. 2, 1989, pp. 167–77; and G. Moorhead et al., 'Group decision fiascos continue: Space Shuttle Challenger', *Human Relations*, vol. 44, no. 6, 1991, pp. 539–50.

Brainstorming: a technique in which all group members are encouraged to propose ideas spontaneously, without critiquing or censoring others' ideas. The alternative ideas so generated are not evaluated until all have been listed.

Brainstorming is usually presented as a technique that seeks to improve group decision-making. However, it can be argued that it represents a problem in group decision-making. Brainstorming asserts the superiority of a group's performance over that of an individual. Alexander F. Osborn, a principal of the New York advertising agency Batten, Barton, Durstine and Osborn, invented brainstorming in 1939. He coined the term to mean using the *brain* to *storm* a problem creatively. It is based on the belief that under given conditions, a group of people working together will solve a problem more creatively than if the same people worked separately as individuals. The presence of a group is said to permit members to 'bounce ideas off each other', or gives individuals the chance to throw out half-baked ideas which other group members might turn into more practical suggestions.

The purpose of the technique is to produce creative, new ideas. Members of brainstorming groups are required to follow four main rules of procedure:

1. Avoid criticizing others' ideas.

2. Share even fanciful or bizarre suggestions.

3. Offer as many comments as possible.

4. Build on others' ideas to create your own.

The proponents of brainstorming argue that the flow of ideas in a group will trigger off further ideas whereas the usual evaluative framework will tend to stifle the imagination. A brainstorming group may, on occasions, perform better than an individual who applies these rules to their own thought processes. However, if one has four individuals working alone, they can generally greatly outperform a group of four in terms of the number of ideas generated. Research has consistently shown that group brainstorming actually *inhibits* creative thinking. Taylor, Berry and Block (1958) carried out one of the earliest studies and compared the performance of brainstorming groups with 'pseudo-groups' (constructed by the experimenter from individual members' scores). They discovered that pseudogroups were superior to the brainstorming groups on criteria of idea quantity, quality and uniqueness. Over the intervening years, these original conclusions have been corroborated by other research (Yetton and Bottger, 1982; Diehl and Stroebe, 1987; Brown and Paulus, 1996; Furnham, 2000). It may be that brainstorming is most effective with established or specially trained groups.

On the number of ideas criteria, when Lamm and Trommsdorf (1973) compared brainstorming groups with individuals working together independently under brainstorming instructions, they found that individuals produced more ideas. It may be that listening to others' ideas distracts group members who fall into one-track thinking. Time limits have also been found to affect productivity. Groups that are allowed longer work periods usually produce more ideas under brainstorming instructions, continuing to produce up to the deadline, while individuals working for the equivalent time taper off towards the end (Shaw, 1971). On the creativity measure, Bouchard, Barsaloux and Drauden (1974) compared individual and brainstorming groups working on creative problems. The tasks were performed by groups consisting of four to seven people and an equivalent number of individuals working alone. The individuals were far more productive than the groups. It appears that despite brainstorming instructions and procedures, the presence of others seems to inhibit rather than enhance the creativity of these *ad hoc* groups. Brainstorming is based on questionable assumptions. First, it assumes that people think most creatively when there are no obstacles to the stream of consciousness and that among this torrent of ideas (actually associations) there are bound to be some good ones. Brainstorming presumes that solving problems is a matter of letting one's natural inclinations run free. Second, it associates the quantity of ideas with the quality of ideas. Third, brainstorming allows only one person to speak at a time, so if you are listening to others, you have less time to come up with original ideas of your own.

This counter-intuitive finding is explained by the phenomenon of 'production blocking' (Diehl and Stroebe, 1987). When individuals are speaking in groups, the other members (temporarily) cannot put forward their ideas. Additionally, because they may be holding back their ideas, their ability to produce more is impaired by the competing verbal contributions of others (Sutton and Hargadon, 1996). The latest development has been to compare face-to-face brainstorming groups with computer-mediated ones. Results suggest that electronic groups are superior or equal to the interacting ones. The explanation offered is that the use of the computer reduces the blockage on the production of new ideas as members listen to others or wait their turn to speak (Gallupe et al., 1992; Dennis and Valacich, 1993).

Electronic brainstorming

While face-to-face brainstorming has been proved of little value, electronic brainstorming may prove to be superior. A support tool had participants sitting at their PCs, entering their ideas in one window, after which it appeared in a second window, with the ideas of the other participants. With large groups, this electronic support improved performance. The reason given was that it bypassed the production-blocking problem, allowing individuals to glance at colleagues' contributions at any time, but not have their train of thought interrupted. The environment may have triggered disinhibition, making members feel freer to express their wildest notions without concern for negative reactions.

Based on T. Connelly, 'Electronic brainstorming: science meets technology in the group meeting room', in S. Kiester (ed.), *Culture of the Internet*, Lawrence Erlbaum Associates, Mahwah, NJ, 1997, pp. 263–76; W.H. Cooper, R.G. Gallupe, S. Pollard and J. Cadsby, 'Some liberating effects of anonymous electronic brainstorming', *Small Group Research*, vol. 29, 1998, pp. 147–78; A.R. Dennis and J.S. Valacich, 'Computer brainstorms: more heads are better than one', *Journal of Applied Psychology*, vol. 78, no. 4, 1993, pp. 531–7; and p. B. Paulus, T.S. Larey and M.T. Dzindolet, 'Creativity in groups and teams', in M.E. Turner (ed.), *Groups at Work: Theory and Research*, Lawrence Erlbaum Associates, Mahwah, NJ, 2001.

Stop and Criticize

Despite the research evidence, members of brainstorming groups firmly believe that group brainstorming is more productive than individual brainstorming, both in terms of the number and quality of the ideas generated. Why might this be?

Advocacy versus inquiry: The Bay of Pigs and the Cuban Missile Crisis

Garvin and Roberto (2001) distinguish between the *advocacy* approach to decision-making, which sees it as an event made by a manager at a discrete point in time, and the *enquiry* approach, which treats it as a process to be explicitly designed and managed.

	Advocacy	**Enquiry**
Concept of decision-making	A contest	Collaborative problem-solving
Purpose of discussion	Persuasion and lobbying	Testing and evaluation
Participants' role	Spokespeople	Critical thinkers
Patterns of behaviour	Strive to persuade others Defend your position Downplay weaknesses	Present balanced arguments Remain open to alternatives Accept constructive criticism
Minority views	Discouraged or dismissed	Cultivated and valued
Outcome	Winners and losers	Collective ownership

The contrast can be illustrated by two critical foreign policy decisions faced by President John F. Kennedy and his administration. During his first two years in office, Kennedy dealt with the Bay of Pigs invasion and the Cuban Missile Crisis. Both problems were assigned to cabinet-level task forces and involved many of the same individuals, the same political interests and extremely high stakes. However, the outcomes were completely different, largely because the two groups operated in different ways.

The first group, which had to decide whether to support an invasion of Cuba by a small army of US-trained Cuban exiles, worked in an advocacy mode. The outcome of its deliberations was widely considered to be an example of flawed decision-making. Shortly after taking office, President Kennedy learned of the planned attack on Cuba developed by the CIA during Eisenhower's administration. Backed by the Joint Chiefs of Staff, the CIA argued forcefully for the invasion. It understated the risks and filtered the information that it presented to the president to reinforce its own position. Knowledgeable individuals from the Latin America desk were excluded from deliberations because of their likely opposition. Some members of Kennedy's own staff opposed the plan, but kept silent for fear of appearing weak in the face of the strong advocacy by the CIA. As a result, there was little debate and the group failed to test some critical underlying assumptions: for example, whether the landing would ignite a domestic uprising against Castro and whether the exiles could hide in the mountains if they met with strong resistance. The resulting invasion is generally considered to be one of the low points of the Cold War. About 100 lives were lost and the remaining exiles were taken hostage. The incident was a major embarrassment to the Kennedy administration and dealt a blow to America's global standing.

After the botched invasion, Kennedy conducted a review of the foreign policy decision-making process and introduced five major changes, essentially transforming the process to one of enquiry. First, people were urged to participate in discussions as 'sceptical generalists' – that is, as disinterested critical thinkers rather than as representatives of particular departments. Second, Robert Kennedy and Theodore Sorensen were assigned the role of intellectual watchdog, and were expected to pursue every possible point of contention, uncovering weaknesses and untested assumptions. Third, task forces were urged to abandon the rules of protocol, eliminating formal agendas and deference to rank. Fourth, participants were expected to split occasionally into sub-groups to develop a broad range of options. Finally, President Kennedy decided to absent himself from some of the early task force meetings to avoid influencing other participants and thereby slanting the debate.

This enquiry mode of decision-making was used to great effect in October 1962, when President Kennedy learned that the Soviet Union had placed nuclear missiles on Cuban soil despite repeated hostile audience to justify their actions, as well as from friendly colleagues who want to 'save face'. This need to rationalize their actions to other parties, when challenged, results in producing renewed justifications, leading in turn to greater commitment. Seeking direction, decision-makers are likely to make a social comparison with others, modelling their behaviour on what someone else has done in a similar situation.

Organizational factors

The idea of projects continuing because of the political support of key organizational players is well understood. Also important is the momentum towards the continuation of the task or project, that is generated by the company having already recruited expert staff, invested in specialized equipment, and entered or withdrawn from certain lines of business activity. A final important variable here is how closely the project is tied to the company's values and objectives. Its degree of organizational institutionalization may be high or low.

Contextual factors

A decision taken within an organization involves forces outside its boundaries. Political, economic, societal, technological, legal and ethical variables can all play a part. External forces that are unconnected with, but which have an interest in, the rescue or continuance of a 'permanently failing organization' can contribute to an escalation of commitment.

Organizational decision-making

The making of decisions has been examined at the level of the individual and of the group. It now remains to consider it at the organizational level. The administration of any organization has two main tasks: first, to co-ordinate the work activities within the organization (for example, ensure that jobs are divided among departments and performed); second, to adjust to circumstances outside the organization (for example, regulate contracts with suppliers, adhere to government regulations, respond to customers). Individuals in the organization (mainly but not exclusively managers) have to deal with the fact that rules, procedures and precedents seldom determine what should be done in every particular case. Decisions which are 'unprogrammed' have to be made. This means that discretion has to be used, judgements have to be made and decisions promulgated. This ambiguity and uncertainty provides the political context within which decision-making occurs within organizations.

Sociologists have studied how power and politics impact on the decision-making process and prevent the operation of the classical decision-making process described at the start of this chapter. Decisions in organizations involve power and conflict between individuals and groups in organizations. The more sources of uncertainty there are, the more possibility there is for individuals and groups to take up political positions. From this perspective, a particular decision is less an expression of the organization's goals, and more a reflection of the ability of a particular individual or group to impose their view or 'definition of the situation' and solution on to other groups.

As noted earlier, Herbert Simon criticized the classical model of decision-making, saying that it ignored the internal politics of the organization system. He and his colleagues, Richard Cyert and James March, were influential in introducing politics into the consideration of decision-making in organizations. They linked the cognitive limits to rationality with political limits. The classical model had assumed that:

- decision-makers possessed a consistent order of preferences;
- there was agreement among the stakeholders about the goals of the organization;
- decision rules were known and accepted by everyone.

In contrast to it, the bounded rationality view that they examined stressed that decision-makers could not make the types of decision that the classical model recommended for two reasons. First, there was ambiguity over which direction to take on an issue. That is, people disagreed about which goals to pursue or which problems to solve. Second, there was the issue of uncertainty. This concerned the degree to which people felt certain that a given action would produce a given outcome (cause and effect).

The condition of uncertainty was examined earlier, and it was noted that extra information could reduce it. However, that same new information could also increase ambiguity since it provided extra points over which different decision-makers could disagree. James Thompson and Arthur Tuden used the dimensions of agreement or disagreement over goals and beliefs about cause-and-effect relations as a way of distinguishing four different situations faced by decision-makers (Thompson and Tuden, 1959; Thompson, 1967). These are described in figure 22.4.

Any given choice situation can be mapped on these two continua: the degree of agreement that exists between parties on the goals to be pursued; and the level of certainty that a specified outcome can be achieved through the use of a given action. Each such situation can thus be defined as falling into one of the four quadrants. The most likely form of decision-making model for each quadrant was specified.

I. Computational strategy – rational model

In this case, those concerned are clear and agreed on what outcome they desire (no ambiguity) and certain about the consequences of their actions (high certainty). For example, as demand for ice-cream increases in the summer, the company introduces an extra shift. The rational model has already been

Beliefs about cause-and-effect relationships		Consensus on goals or problem definition?	
		agree	*disagree*
	certainty	I Computational strategy Rational model	III Compromise strategy Political model
	uncertainty	II Judgemental strategy Incremental model	IV Inspirational strategy Garbage can model

Figure 22. 4: Conditions favouring different decision-making processes
Based on J. Thompson and A. Tuden, 'Strategies, structures and processes of organizational decisions', in J.D. Thompson, P.B. Hammond, R.W. Hawkes, B.H. Junker and A. Tuden, A. (eds), *Comparative Studies in Administration*, University of Pittsburgh Press, Pittsburgh, PA, 1959, pp. 195–216; J. Thompson, *Organizations in Action*, McGraw-Hill, New York, 1967.

blame others, pay off debts, store up favours, punish others, or position themselves in a power struggle. March and Olsen (1976, p. 2) felt that:

> choice situations are not simply occasions for making substantive decisions. They are also arenas in which important symbolic meanings are developed. People gain status and exhibit virtue. Problems are accorded significance. Novices are educated into the values of the society and organization. Participation rights are certification of social legitimacy; participation performances are critical presentations of self.

Organizational culture and decision-making

How does organizational culture affect the way people make decisions and solve problems in organizations? A study of the cultures of three organizations, including footwear, chemicals and food processing, revealed six recurring characteristics which affected these processes:

Unemotionality: Avoid showing or sharing feelings or emotions as this is considered to be 'bad' both for the individual and for the organization.

Depersonalization of issues: Never point the finger at anyone in particular. Be publicly vague about the source of your problems or grievances, even when these are clearly known to you.

Subordination: Never challenge those in authority, but wait for them to take the initiative in resolving your problems. Subordinate–superior relationships are characterized by counterdependence.

Conservatism: Managers and workers share an ingrained conservatism about organization life stemming from scepticism that things can change but would probably get worse.

Isolation: Do your own thing, avoid treading on others' toes, stake out personal organizational territory, operate freely within it, let others do the same in theirs.

Antipathy: On most things people will be opponents rather than allies. The adversarial principle underpins the protracted hostilities between the various groups in the organization.

In their daily interactions, people collectively develop shared perspectives of what situations are like within the firm. These constitute the culture of their organization. Once established, this culture lays down, for both its creators and its inheritors, certain ways of believing, thinking and acting. These may prevent meaningful interaction and induce a psychological state in which employees are unable to conceptualize their problems in such a way as to be able to resolve them. In short, attempts at problem-solving may become culture bound.

Based on Paul Bate, 'The impact of organizational culture on approaches to organizational problem solving', *Organization Studies*, vol. 5, no. 1, 1984, pp. 43–67.

Recap

1. *Distinguish prescriptive, descriptive and explanatory models of decision-making and provide an example of each.*

   - Prescriptive models of decision-making recommend how individuals should behave in order to achieve a desired outcome. The original prescriptive model is the rational economic model, while a recent one was devised by Victor Vroom and Philip Yetton.

   - Descriptive models of decision-making reveal how individuals actually make decisions. The behavioural theory of decision-making is the earliest and most influential descriptive model and was developed by Herbert Simon, James March and Richard Cyert.

   - Explanatory models of decision-making look at what decisions were made and aim to provide an explanation of how they occurred. The heuristics and biases model developed by Daniel Kahneman and Amos Tversky, and Irving Janis's groupthink concept illustrate such explanations.

2. *Distinguish different decision conditions on the basis of risk and programmability.*

   - Decision conditions can be classified as those involving certainty, risk and uncertainty.

   - Decisions can be classified as routine, adaptive and innovative.

3. *Consider the advantages and disadvantages of group decision-making.*

   - Groups offer the advantages of a greater pool of knowledge, different perspectives, greater problem comprehension, and increased acceptance of decisions.

   - Disadvantages of groups can be considered under the headings of personality factors, social conformity, diffusion of responsibility, minority domination, logrolling, goal displacement, group brainstorming, groupthink and satisficing.

4. *Identify the factors used to decide whether to adopt individual or group decision-making.*

   - Individual or group decision-making has been made on the basis of the following factors: type of problem task; acceptance of decision; quality of the solution; characteristics of the individuals; and decision-making climate.

5. *Match organizational conditions with the decision-making processes that favour them.*

   - When there is certainty about cause and effects and there is consensus on goals or problem definition, then a computational strategy involving the rational decision-making model is favoured.

   - When there is uncertainty about cause and effects but there is consensus on goals or problem definition, then a judgemental strategy involving an incremental decision-making model is favoured.

   - When there is certainty about cause and effects but disagreement about goals or problem definition, then a compromise strategy involving a political decision-making model is favoured.

   - When there is neither certainty about cause and effects nor agreement about goals or problem definition, then an inspirational strategy involving the garbage can model of decision-making is favoured.

Revision

1. How does a 'satisficing' decision differ from a 'maximizing' one? Provide examples of each from your own experience. In what circumstances would one be preferable to the other?

2. Identify three judgmental biases. How do they differ from each other? Give an example of each in an organizational context.

3. How does risk, certainty and uncertainty affect individuals when they make a decision?

4. Should decision-making by groups be avoided or encouraged by organizations?

5. Suggest how political factors impact on the making of decisions by individuals and groups within the organization.

Springboard

Bazerman, M.H., 2001, *Judgement in Managerial Decision Making*, Wiley, New York (fifth edition).

A comprehensive, entertaining and interactive description of the judgement heuristics identified by the research of Daniel Kahneman and Amos Tversky.

Buchanan, D.A. and Badham, R., 1999a, *Power, Politics and Organizational Change: Winning the Turf Game*, Sage Publications, London.

The book focuses on theories and research dealing with power and politics in decision-making within a context of organizational change. It has a practical approach which includes consideration of ethical issues.

Cialdini, R.B., 2001, *Influence: Science and Practice*, Allyn and Bacon, London (fourth edition).

A comprehensive and entertaining summary of the social psychological research on judgement biases.

The Economist, 1999e, 'Rethinking thinking', 18 December, pp. 77–9.

Provides a 'quick tour' of main biases and heuristics that psychological research is revealing, which are challenging the rational economic view of decision-making.

Harrison, E.F., 1999, *The Managerial Decision-making Process*, Houghton Mifflin, Chicago (fifth edition).

Focuses on middle and upper management decision-making in organizations using a process model and drawing upon concepts from the social sciences.

Huczynski, A.A. 2004, *Influencing within Organizations: Getting In, Rising Up and Moving On*, Routledge, London (second edition).

Contains a chapter summarizing the diverse research and theory on the process of decision-making organizations.

Kahneman, D. and Tversky, A. (eds), 2000, *Choices, Values and Frames*, Cambridge University Press, London.

The book is edited by the leading researchers in the field of judgement biases and heuristics, and is best read after the overview provided by the above book.

Plous, S., 1993, *The Psychology of Judgement and Decision Making*, McGraw-Hill, New York.

Stresses the social aspects of decision-making, covers experimentation and includes a reader survey.

Home viewing

Thirteen Days (2001, director David Self) is based on the true story of the Cuban Missile Crisis of October 1962, a diplomatic conflict between the United States and the (then) Soviet Union which almost triggered a nuclear war. It stars Kevin Costner who plays an aide to President John F. Kennedy. As you watch the film, consider the decision-making process being used. What influencing attempts are being made? By whom, at whom? How are the intentions of the different parties signalled?

OB in literature

Michael Crichton, *Airframe*, Arrow Books, London, 1997.

A mid-air disaster aboard a commercial airliner leaves three people dead and 56 injured. The pilot lands the plane and a frantic investigation begins by the aircraft's manufacturers to determine what occurred. The plot involves company managers seeking to determine the cause of the accident. Consider their approach to arriving at a decision. What factors affect both the decision-making process and its outcome?

Chapter exercises

1: It's your decision

Objectives   1. To illustrate some of the biases in human decision-making.

Briefing   Below are three situation descriptions, each of which requires a decision. Make that decision and, as you do so, be aware and write down the basis on which you make it.

1. A large city hospital records births by gender in the order of their arrival. Here are some sequences of eight births. Which one of these three, 8-birth sequences is likely to be most commonly recorded? (B = boy; G = girl)
   (a) BBBBBBBB
   (b) BBBBGGGG
   (c) BGBBGGGB

2. A recent university graduate with a degree in computing joins a software firm based in Manchester, UK. Estimate the starting salary for this employee. Your friend, who knows very little about the profession or the industry, guesses at an annual salary of £25,000 (€40,000). What is your estimate?

3. In the English language, are there more words that begin with the letter 'r' or are there more words that have 'r' as their third letter?

2: Decision types

Objectives   1. To allow you to distinguish between different types of decision.

2. To make you aware of the requirements of each type of decision.

Briefing   The chapter defined and distinguished between routine, adaptive and innovative types of decision. This exercise gives you the opportunity to identify and deal with each of the three types.

1. Class divides into groups of four to five members. Each group represents the executive committee of a small manufacturing company which meets regularly to review and decide upon a list of problems. The list consists of items submitted by employees for decision. This week's list of issues is shown on p. 788.

2. Each group is to sort the items on the list into three decision categories – routine, adaptive and innovative.

3. Once all the items have been sorted into three piles, each group is to select one item from the routine pile and one item from the innovative pile, and develop an action plan for each. They should also select one adaptive decision issue and indicate what approach might be appropriate for working on that decision.

4. After 20–30 minutes, the executive committees/small groups reassemble in a class plenary session. Each group presents *one* of the decisions that it has worked on and describes its conclusions.

5. Class discusses:
   - Was a routine or innovative decision harder to deal with? Why?
   - Did group members and groups categorize the decision items in the same way?
   - Over which items did group members disagree?
   - How were disagreements over categorization dealt with by the group?

List of decision items

1. An assembly worker wants the committee to decide on a more equitable method for allocating scarce parking spaces.

2. A departmental manager wants a decision as to whether one of his programmers can be given a special bonus for developing a popular software item.

3. The facilities manager wants to know if part-time employees are eligible to join the company health club.

4. A division manager wants a decision on whether to open a new office in Paris, Berlin or Moscow.

5. The cafeteria manager has asked for a decision on how to choose among suppliers of foodstuffs.

6. The marketing manager wants a decision on a new product that will not compete with other manufacturers' products but will be popular because it fills an unmet need.

7. A supervisor has asked whether overtime should be given to those who ask first or to those who have the most seniority.

8. A decision has to be made whether to emphasize desktop or laptop computers during the next quarter in marketing.

9. The research department has developed an innovative and cheap memory chip which is capable of being incorporated into many devices. It has asked what direction your committee wants to take in developing applications for this chip.

10. The board of directors has told your committee to consider whether it would be better to open company-owned retail outlets in five major cities or to franchise the outlets.

From Marshall Sashkin and William C. Morris, 'Decision types', *Experiencing Management*, Addison-Wesley, Reading, MA, 1987, pp. 73–4.

Chapter 23 Conflict

Key concepts

conflict

unitarist frame of reference

pluralistic frame of reference

interactionist frame of reference

functional conflict

dysfunctional conflict

conflict resolution

distributive bargaining

integrative bargaining

mediation

arbitration

conflict stimulation

radical frame of reference

organizational misbehaviour

resistance

emotional labour

Learning outcomes

When you have read this chapter, you should be able to define those key concepts in your own words, and you should also be able to:

1. Distinguish between the four major frames of reference on conflict.
2. Distinguish between functional and dysfunctional conflict.
3. Explain the relationship between organizing, co-ordinating and conflict.
4. List the causes of conflict in organizations.
5. Distinguish the different organizational co-ordination devices.
6. Explain the conditions in which conflict is resolved and stimulated in organizations.
7. List Thomas's five conflict resolution approaches.
8. Distinguish between distributive and integrative bargaining.

Smile on

A young businessman said to a flight attendant, 'Why aren't you smiling?' She put her tray back on the food cart, looked him in the eye and said, 'I'll tell you what. You smile first, then I'll smile. The businessman smiled at her. 'Good,' she replied. 'Now freeze and hold that for fifteen hours.'

From Arlie Hochschild, *The Managed Heart: Commercialization of Human Feeling*, University of California Press, Berkeley, CA, 1983, p. 127.

Why study conflict?

Conflict is a fundamental force governing all aspects of life. Indeed, the word 'problem' itself is born of conflict. Because conflict provides such a useful starting point for studying complex situations and human behaviour, it has become one of the core concepts of social science, and has been used by both historians and sociologists to explain changes in societies. Conflict specialists see the phenomenon as occurring both in various contexts (for example, political, economic, social, psychological) and at a number of social levels (for example, personal, domestic, organizational, communal, national and international). Despite these differences, they believe that it has sufficient common attributes to merit study as a distinct field.

Within organizational behaviour, conflict has the status of a 'crossroad' concept: that is, it links and relates to many other topics discussed in the field in a variety of ways and at a number of different levels. For example, within an organization, conflicts can occur between individuals, groups and departments; they can arise from the exercise of power and politics; they can emanate from particular leadership styles and decision-making processes; or they can arise from structural and cultural changes. At any time, conflicts may be occurring simultaneously, related to one or more of these.

One's job and perspective will determine one's interest in conflict. For the trade union member or official who takes a radical perspective, the question might be whether labour–management conflict, so prevalent in the 1970s, has now been replaced by consensual, co-operative relationships between employees and management. Did management finally eradicate resistance by the end of the twentieth century by making it ineffectual and secure the behavioural compliance of employees with managerial dictats? Is this the reason for the increasing number of 'workplace partnerships' being agreed between unions and companies? Or has the form of historical labour–management conflict changed? Has its location shifted to new areas, or perhaps gone 'underground'?

Some commentators view the organizational landscape as consisting of just labour and management. For them, a company is composed of numerous 'tribes' or sub-groups, spread throughout the different levels and departments. Each one possesses its own interests and acts to promote it. When those interests clash, conflict ensues. From this perspective, the managers are the organizational politicians who 'wheel and deal', build alliances, secure commitments – and do so by using their skills of influencing, negotiation and mediation. From this perspective, the focus is on being able to anticipate clashes and to resolve them successfully.

Those who see conflict as a trigger of change would be concerned both at its absence and its over-presence. They would be interested to know what the optimum level of conflict in an organization should be, and how it might be stimulated. There are managers who consider conflict to be a threat to co-operative, consensual relations, and would seek to manage it so that it does not arise, or if it does resolve it rapidly and permanently. Managers taking this view are interested primarily in conflict resolution techniques.

In this chapter, the focus is upon conflict which emerges primarily from the formal interactions or job requirements of individuals operating in their roles, within groups and departments inside an organization. It is seen primarily as the outcome of organizational politics, as individuals, groups, units and departments attempt to influence the decisions that affect their own interests, usually at the expense of others' interests. This perspective stresses the structural basis of conflict rather than the interpersonal. We are not dealing primarily with 'difficult people' from a personality perspective, although this may be an element in any conflict situation. Our perspective also implies a conflict management strategy that involves changing the situation rather than the people.

| Stop and Criticize | Why does conflict get such a bad press? What are the benefits of conflict? In what circumstances could it be beneficial deliberately to stimulate conflict? |

The sanitization of conflict

Perhaps the most curious aspect of conflict, as a field of study, is the way in which key aspects of the topic have either been overlooked or 'sanitized'. Roger Johnston (2000) noted that traditional organization behaviour textbooks consistently underplay or ignore certain organizational topics, many of which might be considered to be the causes of conflict within the workplace. Among these he listed pay, employee layoffs, managerial delayering and unemployment. Either they are discussed on human resource management courses and textbooks, or else they are considered of insufficient importance for line managers and management students to find a place on an already crowded organizational behaviour curriculum. This chapter incorporates the work of those who see conflict in different ways, and explains the theoretical and practical managerial implications of such contrasting perspectives.

> **Conflict**: a process which begins when one party perceives that another party has negatively affected, or is about to negatively affect, something the first party cares about.

Conflict is a state of mind. It has to be perceived by the parties involved. If two or more parties are not aware of a conflict, then no conflict exists. This broad definition encompasses conflicts at different levels within an organization. Typically conflicts are based upon differences in interest and values, when the interests of one party come up against the different interests of another. Parties may include shareholders, managers, departments, professionals and groups, while conflict issues can include dividends, control and wage levels. Social relations are based on implicit or explicit values, which affect human interaction, judgement and normative behaviour. Organizations like hospitals, churches and Amnesty International have values that are very different from commercial organizations. However, within the latter there can be value conflicts with respect to issues such as environmental and employee diversity.

The definition cited here refers to 'parties' to the conflict process. Who exactly are these parties? Managerial prescriptions concerning conflict handling tend to assume that the conflict issue is between two individuals (dyad): either between a manager and a subordinate or between two individuals at the same hierarchical level (for example, two supervisors or middle managers). Another popular focus is the conflict between the individual members of a team. This can be at any hierarchical level. Occasionally, inter-team or in-group conflict will be considered. Finally, and for reasons already given at the start of this chapter, institutional conflict between a trade or labour union, on the one hand, and the company's management, on the other, will rarely be the subject of organization behaviour studies. The significant point is that when assessing conflict research findings or prescriptions for managing conflict, it is important to ascertain where they come from and to whom they may apply.

Finally, commentators differ between radical theorists and pluralist writers. The radical theorists see organizations as merely one of the 'theatres of war' in society where the class struggle continues to be waged. Within the company, there are a number of 'battle fronts', including wage negotiations, equal opportunities, health and safety and employee involvement. In contrast, pluralist writers claim conflict within organizations is based on its own unique circumstances, and should not be considered as part of a broader, society-wide picture. There is also a difference between those who distinguish the sources of conflict as perceptual and those who view them as objective. The former see conflict as being 'inside a person's head' whereas the latter consider it to be related to an observed reality which other people are able to recognize.

Contrasting frames of reference: unitarist, pluralist, interactionist

The literature distinguishes four different frames of reference on conflict, based on the distinctions made by Alan Fox. They are labelled *unitarist*, *pluralist*, *interactionist* and *radical* (Fox, 1966, 1973). In this section, the first three will be introduced and contrasted, while the fourth, the radical, will be subjected to a more detailed analysis in its own section later. These frames are neither 'right' nor 'wrong', only different.

■ *unitarist*: sees organizations as essentially harmonious and any conflict as bad;

■ *pluralist*: sees organizations as a collection of groups, each with their own interests;

■ *interactionist*: sees conflict as a positive, necessary force for effective performance;

■ *radical*: sees conflict sees as an inevitable outcome of capitalism.

Earlier chapters have used the concept of frame of reference to refer to a particular position or set of assumptions which is acquired or possessed by organization members. A frame is a scheme of interpretation that makes it possible for individuals to explain, organize and make sense of particular events and actions. Frames therefore express the generally accepted norms of the social domain in which they are valid (for example, a group, occupational category, subject discipline, political allegiance, etc.). Within a single organization, various individuals, each of whom uses a different frame, may differently interpret the same event. Moreover, academics will also adopt one of these frames when they teach the topic to their students or research it. Neither organization employees nor academics will necessarily make their chosen frame explicit, and hence students need to ask or deduce which conflict frame of reference the person holds. The radical frame of reference sees conflict as the inevitable outcome of, or intrinsic characteristic of, capitalism.

Robert Reich, US Secretary of Labor during the first Clinton administration, described the 'pronoun test' that he used to evaluate the nature of the employment relationship in the companies that he visited in the following way:

'I'd say, "Tell me about the company". If the person said "we" or "us", I knew people were strongly attached to the organization. If they said "they" or "them", I knew there was less of a sense of linkage.' (cited in Rousseau, 1999)

Most of us are capable of bringing different frames of reference to bear on the situations that we face. If we analyze it in this way, we reach these conclusions, but if we analyze it from another perspective, we reach different conclusions. Some people (students, academics, managers) *may* be wedded to a particular perspective. This becomes obvious in their conversations, actions or writings. Their chosen frame of reference on conflict will determine:

■ what they will notice in their environment;

■ how they will interpret those noticed events;

■ how they expect others to behave;

■ how they will behave themselves.

However, there is value in being able to view conflicts from a number of different standpoints, being able to 'switch between frames', in part so that we can understand the viewpoints of others.

The **unitarist frame of reference on conflict** views organizations as fundamentally harmonious, co-operative structures, consisting of committed, loyal, worker–management teams that promote harmony of purpose.

Stephen Ackroyd and Paul Thompson (1999) and Johnston (2000) identified the key features of the unitarist or unitary frame of reference:

Unitarist frame of reference on conflict: a perspective on conflict which regards management and employee interests as coinciding and which thus regards (organizational) conflict as harmful and to be avoided.

1. Assumes a commonality of interests between an organization's workers and managers and, by implication, the company's owners (shareholders).

2. Accepts unquestioningly the political, economic and social framework within which management is performed, and adopts the language, assumptions and goals of management itself, which it supposedly seeks to study and understand.

3. De-politicizes the relationships between individuals, groups and classes within the workplace, treating conflicts and contradictions as peripheral.

4. Explains actual, observed instances of workplace conflict in terms of either a failure of co-ordination problems or psychological terms (the personal malfunction or abnormal behaviour of deviant individuals).

5. Applies a liberal-humanistic, individually focused approach to conflict resolution, which is rooted in the human relations movement and its developments.

6. Holds that managers are capable of permanently changing the behaviour of employees in a conflict situation in an organization through the application of conflict resolution techniques.

7. Claims that economic, technological and political developments had, by the 1990s, meant that management had virtually eliminated non-sanctioned employee behaviour within the organization.

8. Moves rapidly over the consideration of causes of conflict within the workplace, in order to focus on conflict resolution techniques.

9. When discussing the causes of workplace conflict, it focuses on communication failures between management and employees, and the interference of 'third party agitators', normally unions, in the relationship between the employer and the employee.

David Collins (1998) noted that the unitarist frame of reference rationalized conflict in four ways. First, in terms of external disruption or shocks to the system: that is, an event outside management's control that alters working practices or destroys goodwill. For example, terrorist attacks cause a decline in air travel leading to mass redundancies. Second, breakdowns in communication caused by management's failure to communicate clearly to the workforce the need for, or the benefits of, a particular change. An example would be a misunderstanding as to what is meant by management's use of the term 'rationalization'. Third, by pointing to minor breakdowns in understanding and small-scale politicking: for example, recognizing the effects of power struggles between different power bases within management. The solution offered here is different functional managers better appreciating each other's problems and focusing on their common, higher-level objective. Fourth, seeing agitation or malevolence as anything that disrupts what is seen as the normal, harmonious working relationships within an organization. Elimination of conflict here takes the form of attacks on trade unions and their physical removal from the firm.

Unitarist frame of reference

'To develop a close affinity with organizations which promote fellowship between workers, customers, members and employers.'

(From the mission statement of The Co-operative Bank)

'Safety is paramount. We all have a duty to take care of ourselves, colleagues and customers.'

(From British Airways' Management Framework for Safety)

Pluralist frame of reference on conflict: a perspective which views organizations as consisting of different, natural interest groups, each with its own potentially constructive, legitimate interests, which make conflict between them inevitable.

The **pluralist frame of reference on conflict** views organizations as a collection of many separate groups, each of which has its own legitimate interests, thereby making conflict between them inevitable as each attempts to pursue its own objectives. This frame of reference therefore rejects the view that individual employees have the same interests as the management, or that an organization is one big happy family.

The pluralist frame takes a political orientation in that it sees that some of the time the interests of the different groups will coincide, while at other times they will clash and so cause conflict between them. The outbreak of conflict provides a 'relationship regulation' mechanism between the different groups. That is, it provides a clear sign to both parties as to which issues they disagree fundamentally about, and thus provides a sort of 'early warning system' of possible impending breakdown which would be to the disadvantage of all concerned. The most common clashes may be between unions and management, but will also include differences between management functions (production versus marketing), levels of management (senior management versus middle management), and individual managers.

These differences do not prevent an organization from functioning since all groups recognize that compromise and negotiation are essential if they are to achieve their goals even partially. Hence, from this perspective, the job of management becomes that of keeping the balance between potentially conflicting goals and managing the differences between these different interest groups. This involves seeking a compromise between the different constituents such as the employees, managers, shareholders and others, so that all these stakeholders, to varying degrees, can continue to pursue their aspirations. Underlying the pluralist view is the belief that conflict can be resolved through compromise to the benefit of all. However, it requires all parties to limit their claims to a level which is at least tolerable to the others, and which allows further collaboration to continue. A mutual survival strategy is agreed.

Acceptance of the pluralist frame implies that conflict is inevitable, indeed endemic. However, it does not see conflict as harmful or as something to be eliminated, but believes that it must be evaluated in terms of its functions and dysfunctions. For while it may reinforce the *status quo*, it can also assist evolutionary rather than revolutionary change, acting as a safety valve, and keep the organization responsive to internal and external changes while retaining intact its essential elements such as the organizational hierarchy and the power distribution. The inevitable conflict which results has to be managed so that organizational goals are reconciled with group interests for the benefit of mutual survival and prosperity. This ongoing internal struggle is seen as generally acting to maintain the vitality, responsiveness and efficiency of the organization.

The **interactionist frame of reference on conflict** views it as a positive force within organizations that is necessary for effective performance. It can be considered as part of the pluralist tradition and features extensively in American management textbooks. The pluralist frame accepts the inevitability of conflict and argues that, to be dealt with constructively, conflict has to be institutionalized within the organization through systems of collective bargaining. The interactionist frame not only accepts the inevitability of conflict, but also contains the notion that there is an optimum level of it (not too little or too much), and that the way to achieve that level is through the intervention of the manager.

The interactionist frame believes that conflict should be encouraged whenever its emerges, and stimulated if it is absent. It sees a group or a department that is too peaceful, harmonious and co-operative as potentially apathetic and unresponsive to changing needs. It fears that extreme group cohesion can lead to groupthink, as identified by Irving Janis (1982) and Cosier and Schwenk (1990). This frame therefore encourages managers to maintain a minimum level of conflict within their organizations so to as to encourage self-criticism, change and innovation and thereby counter apathy. However, that conflict has to be of the appropriate type. Thus, **functional conflict** supports organization goals and improves performance, but **dysfunctional conflict** hinders organizational performance.

The relationship between the two is depicted on a bell-shaped curve shown in figure 23.1. If there is insufficient conflict, then the unit or group does not perform at its best; too much conflict and its performance deteriorates. Performance improvements occur through conflict exposing weaknesses in organizational decision-making and design which prompts changes in the company.

Figure 23.1 is also sometimes referred to as the contingency model of conflict (Hatch, 1997) because it recommends that managers should increase or decrease the amount of conflict in their organizations depending on the situation. Thus, for example, in condition 1 there is too little conflict, so they need to stimulate more. In contrast, in condition 3, there is too much conflict and they need to reduce it. In both cases they seem to achieve an optimum level of conflict depicted in column 2. Taffinder (1998) felt that at optimal intensity (condition 2 in figure 23.1), conflict produced organizational benefits which managers rarely exploited and even suppressed by applying conflict resolution approaches too rapidly. Among the benefits of functional conflict that he listed were:

- motivating energy to deal with underlying problems;
- making underlying issues explicit;
- sharpening people's understanding of real goals and interests;
- enhancing mutual understanding between different groups of employees;
- stimulating a sense of urgency;
- discouraging engagement in avoidance behaviour;
- preventing premature and often dangerous resolution problems.

Tuffinder believed that successful organizations created the conditions in which conflict over how tasks should be performed was increased, while conflict over values was eliminated. The latter was achieved by senior management building, managing and reinforcing a clear set of values that diffused any value conflicts. He cited ABB, Levi Strauss and Microsoft as example of companies

---

Interactionist frame of reference on conflict: a perspective on conflict which sees it as a positive and necessary force within organizations that is essential for their effective performance

Functional conflict: a form of conflict which supports organization goals and improves performance.

Dysfunctional conflict: a form of conflict which does not support organization goals and hinders organizational performance.

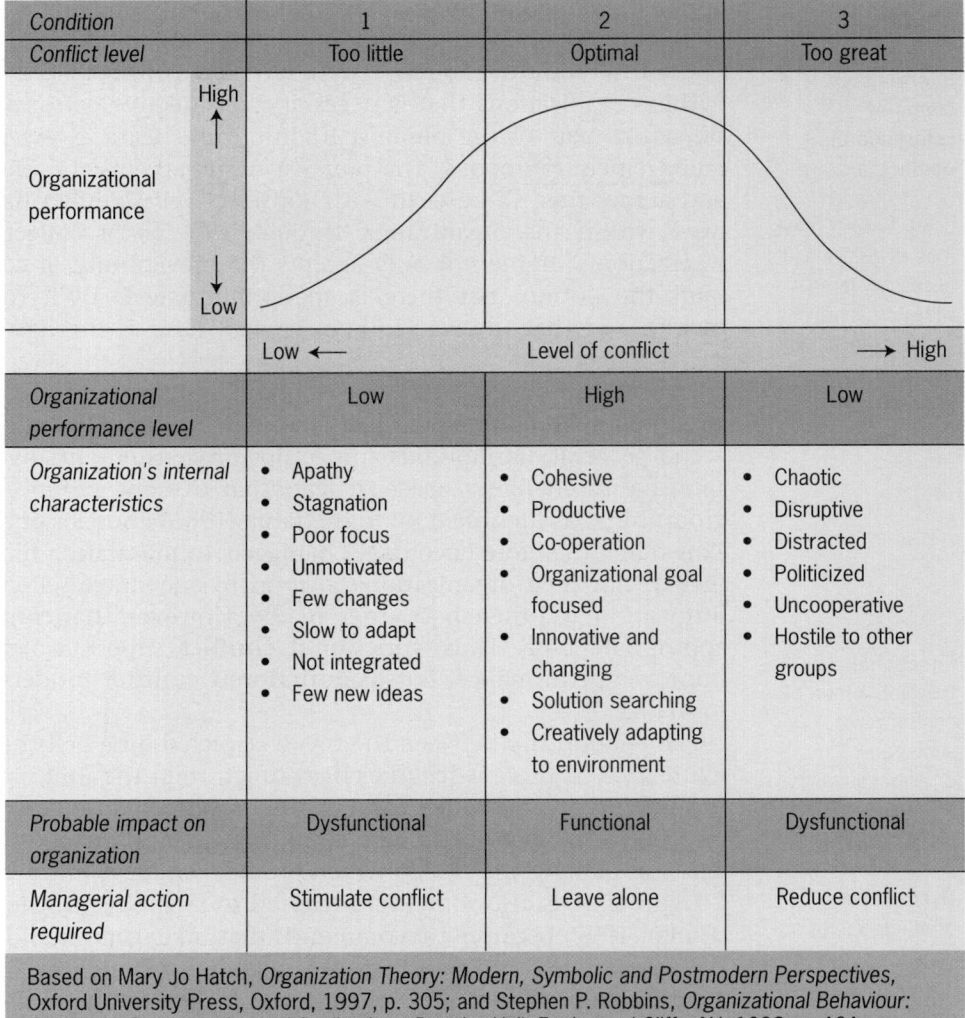

Condition	1	2	3
Conflict level	Too little	Optimal	Too great

Organizational performance (High ↕ Low) / Level of conflict (Low ← → High)

Organizational performance level	Low	High	Low
Organization's internal characteristics	• Apathy • Stagnation • Poor focus • Unmotivated • Few changes • Slow to adapt • Not integrated • Few new ideas	• Cohesive • Productive • Co-operation • Organizational goal focused • Innovative and changing • Solution searching • Creatively adapting to environment	• Chaotic • Disruptive • Distracted • Politicized • Uncooperative • Hostile to other groups
Probable impact on organization	Dysfunctional	Functional	Dysfunctional
Managerial action required	Stimulate conflict	Leave alone	Reduce conflict

Based on Mary Jo Hatch, *Organization Theory: Modern, Symbolic and Postmodern Perspectives*, Oxford University Press, Oxford, 1997, p. 305; and Stephen P. Robbins, *Organizational Behaviour: Concepts, Controversies and Applications*, Prentice-Hall, Englewood Cliffs, NJ, 1998, p. 464.

Figure 23.1: Types of conflict, internal organizational characteristics and required management actions

which possessed deep-rooted cultural values that made them resilient and able to cope with change. ABB Calor Emag deliberately produced task-related conflict in its search for improvement, better and quicker decisions and excellent delivery.

Co-ordination failure and conflict

The process of organizing by senior managers acts to differentiate activities, and an outbreak of conflict can be seen as a symptom of management's failure to adequately co-ordinate these same activities later on. The co-ordination–conflict four-stage model organizes the diverse theoretical discussions and research findings into a framework that explains how conflict in organizations arises and how it might be managed (figure 23.2). Such management may involve the use of either conflict resolution approaches (to reduce or eradicate conflict) or conflict stimulation approaches (to encourage and increase conflict).

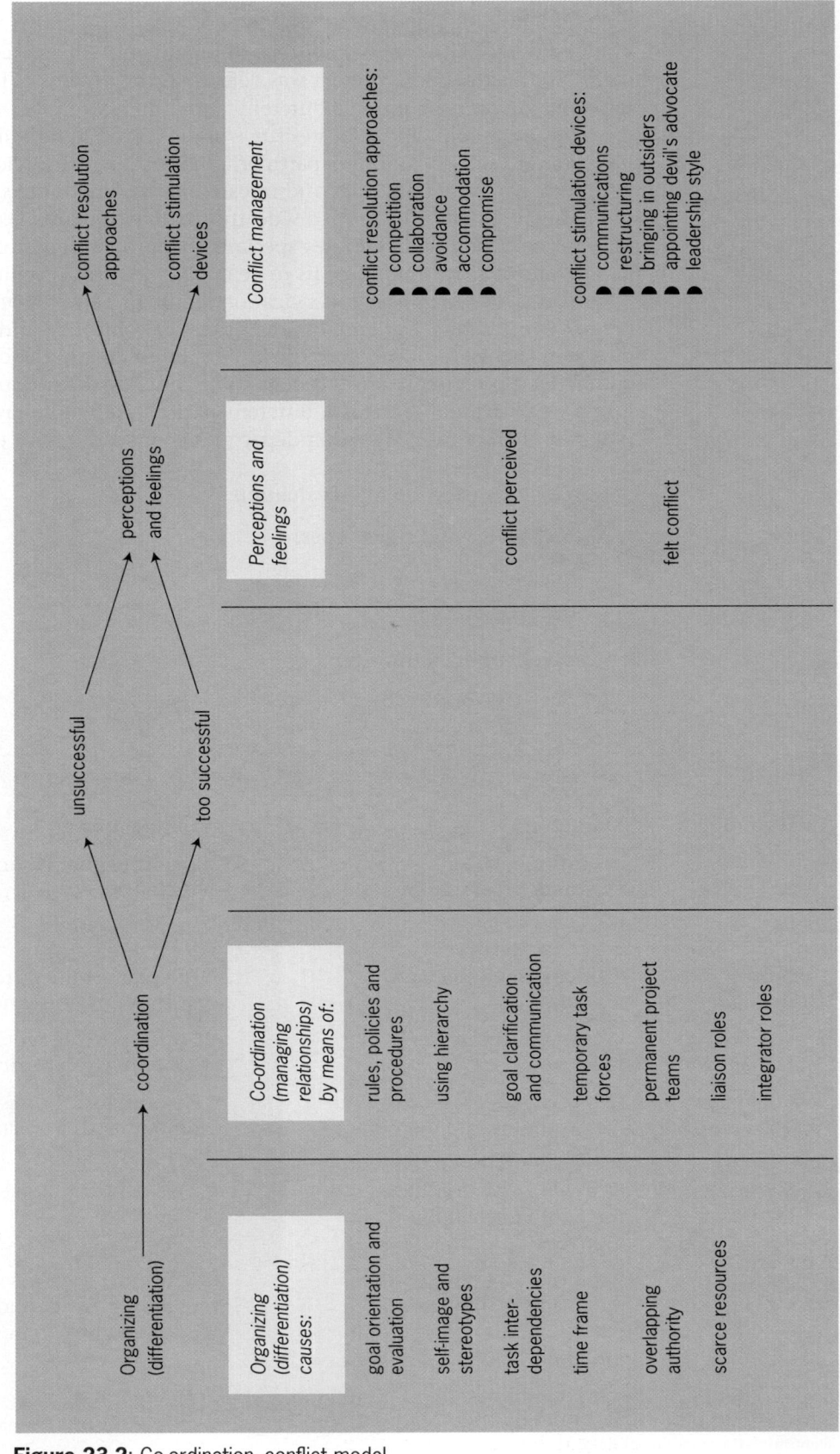

Figure 23.2: Co-ordination–conflict model

Organizing

The first stage of the model consists of organizing This concept was introduced earlier in this textbook where it was defined as the process of breaking up a single task and dividing it among different departments, groups or individuals. For example, a car company allocates the work involved in building a new vehicle to its different sub-divisions (departments, groups and individuals) – personnel, accounting, production, sales and research. Such functional specialization is one of many bases on which to divide the total work involved. Specialization is rational because it concentrates specialists in proper departments, avoids duplication, allows performance goals to be established and specifies practices.

All forms of horizontal specialization result in each sub-unit becoming concerned with its own particular part of the total objective and work process. The degree of such separation of tasks can vary, but it creates the conditions in which conflict can potentially arise. It does so because, by definition, each department, group or individual receives a different part of the whole task to perform. This makes it distinct from the other departments in six different areas:

1. Goals orientation and evaluation.

2. Self-image and stereotypes.

3. Task interdependencies.

4. Time perspective.

5. Overlapping authority.

6. Scarce resources.

Table 23.1: Areas of potential goal conflict between marketing and manufacturing departments

Goal conflict	Marketing versus	Manufacturing
	operating goal is customer satisfaction	operating goal is production efficiency
conflict area	*typical comment*	*typical comment*
1 Breadth of product line	'Our customers demand variety'	'The product line is too broad – all we get are short, uneconomical runs'
2 New product introduction	'New products are our lifeblood'	'Unnecessary design changes are prohibitively expensive'
3 Production scheduling	'We need faster response. Our lead times are too long'	'We need realistic customer commitments that don't change like a wind direction'
4 Physical distribution	'Why don't we ever have the right merchandise in inventory?'	'We can't afford to keep huge inventories'
5 Quality	'Why can't we have reasonable quality at low cost?'	'Why must we always offer options that are too expensive and offer little customer utility?'

Adapted and reprinted by permission of *Harvard Business Review*. Adapted Exhibit, page 105, from 'Can marketing and manufacturing coexist?' by Benson S. Shapiro, 55, September–October 1977. Copyright © 1977 by the Harvard Business School Publishing Corporation; all rights reserved.

1. Goals orientation and evaluation

Each department is given its own goal, and its members are evaluated on the extent to which they achieve it. Ideally, the goals of different departments, groups and individuals, although different, should be complementary, but in practice this may not be so. Moreover, the measurement process can reinforce differences. Each department's unique goals and evaluation methods lead it to have its own view about company priorities and how these are best achieved.

2. Self-image and stereotypes

Employees in each department become socialized into a particular perception of themselves and seeing the other departments in the company as different. A group may come to see itself as more vital to a company's operations than others, and to believe that it has higher status or prestige. Such an evaluation can engender an 'us-and-them' attitude. The higher-status groups may cease to adapt their behaviours to accommodate the goals of other groups and, indeed, may try to achieve their objectives at the cost of others, thus creating conflict. Whenever differences between groups and departments are emphasized, stereotypes are reinforced, relations deteriorate and conflict develops. Departments will often blame each other for problems and shortcomings.

Source: CATHY © Cathy Guizewite. Reprinted with permission of UNIVERSAL PRESS SYNDICATE. All rights reserved.

3. Task interdependencies

The process of organizing, which results in differentiation, makes individuals, groups and departments dependent on one another to perform satisfactorily their own jobs and achieve their objectives. The degree of such interdependence varies. Chapter 15 considered James Thompson's (1967) three types of interdependence – *pooled*, *sequential* and *reciprocal*. Groups in sequential interdependence, and even more in reciprocal interdependence, require a high degree of co-ordination between their activities. If this is achieved, then each group will perform effectively and its members will experience satisfaction. When such co-ordination is absent, the result will be conflict between them. From this viewpoint, conflict results from a failure in co-ordination.

In addition, the types of task that individuals, groups and departments are allocated can cause difficulties. Such tasks can be either routine or non-routine. Charles Perrow's (1970) classification, based on *task variety* and *task analyzability*, was also introduced in the same chapter. As Table 23.2 summarizes, tasks which have high variety (possess many unexpected events) and low analyzability (no ready-made solutions) require a great deal more information processing than those that do not. Groups performing such tasks have to interact more with other groups in order to obtain the volume and quality of the information that they need to perform their tasks. This increases the chances of conflict between them. In contrast, tasks that have low variety (are predictable with few unexpected events) and possess high analyzability (many ready-made solutions) require less information processing. The latter reduce or eliminate the need for individuals, groups or departments to obtain information from each other in order to do their job, and thereby reduce the chances of conflict occurring between them.

Table 23.2: Conditions for high and low conflict occurrence

Conflict will be	When task variety is	When analyzability is	When information requirements are
Highest	high	low	high
Lowest	low	high	low

4. Time perspective

Paul Lawrence and Jay Lorsch's (1967) study found that people's perceptions of the importance accorded to different items depended on the time frame that governed their work and their goal orientations. Groups with different perceptions would find it difficult to co-ordinate their activities, and this would result in greater intergroup conflict. This is partly because their time frames differ. These different goals are often incompatible, hindering communication, impeding co-ordination and encouraging conflict.

5. Overlapping authority

Demarcation disputes have always caused difficulties, and ambiguity over responsibility or authority is one example of this. Individuals or groups may be uncertain as to who is responsible for performing which tasks or duties and who has authority to direct whom. Each party may claim or reject responsibility and the result can be conflict. This can occur particularly when a growing organization has not yet worked out the relationships between different groups, or after a take-over or merger when new roles and responsibilities have yet to be clarified. Groups may fight for the control of a resource, while individual managers may attempt to seize one another's authority.

6. Scarce resources

Once a task is allocated to an individual, group or department, it is also allocated resources to achieve it. Since resources are finite, conflict can arise with respect to how personnel, money, space or equipment are shared out. From a win–lose perspective, one party's gain is another's loss. For this reason, conflicts often arise at times of budget cuts or reduced promotion opportunities, and when rises in salaries or wages are put on hold.

Staff–line conflict

In his classic study, Melville Dalton studied the conflict between line managers, those directly responsible for production, and staff managers, those not directly involved but who performed a staff function (for example, personnel managers who supplied line managers with advice on employment legislation). Dalton attributed the causes of the conflict between them both to the different roles that each occupied within the company and to differences in their personal characteristics. Conflicts between staff and line continue to this day and are based on similar concerns. The four main causes in this context include authority, personal differences, interdependence and differing loyalties.

Authority reduction: While line managers are afraid that staff specialists will intrude on their jobs and reduce their authority and power, staff specialists complain that line managers do not make good use of them or provide them with enough authority.

Social and physical differences: Line and staff personnel differ in terms of age, background and educational level. Dalton found that staff specialists had received more education and training, were appointed to their posts at relatively senior hierarchical levels, and tended to be members of professional associations. Line managers were generalists, had less professional training and often had worked their way up from the shop floor.

Line dependence on staff knowledge: Dalton also found that conflict could result because staff specialists considered their knowledge to be more relevant and up to date than that of the line managers, while the latter felt that their experience was more relevant than 'book-learning'. However, line managers are often dependent on staff personnel for current, specialist knowledge such as employment legislation. They have to visit staff personnel to fill the gap between their knowledge and authority. This caused conflict between them.

Different loyalties: Other sources of conflict included the staff members' loyalty to the company in that they would pursue their professional career in different organizations while the line manager was likely to remain with the same firm. When loyalties to a particular function or discipline are greater than to the overall company, conflict is likely. This is the 'cosmopolitan' versus 'local' distinction encountered earlier.

From Melville Dalton, 'Conflict between staff and line managerial officers', *American Sociological Review*, June, 1950, pp. 342–51; J.A. Balasco and J.A. Alutto, 'Line and staff conflicts: some empirical insights', *Academy of Management Journal*, March 1969, pp. 69–77; and James E. Sorenson and Thomas L. Sorenson, 'The conflict of professionals in bureaucratic organizations', *Administrative Science Quarterly*, March 1974, pp. 98–106.

Stop and Criticize

How complete is this list of conflict causes – goal orientation, self-image, interdependencies, time frame, overlapping authority and scarce resources? Think of two conflict situations with which you have been involved in an organization. Do these causes satisfactorily account for your conflicts or would you wish to add other causes?

Co-ordinating

If organizing involves breaking up the task into bits, then co-ordinating is bringing the bits together again. Co-ordination involves ensuring that the previously divided tasks that were allocated between different departments, groups and individuals are brought together in the right way and at the right time. Co-ordination entails synchronizing the different aspects of the work process. The process of organizing creates the aforementioned differences, but does not automatically result in conflict between parties breaking out. The three general classes of co-ordination devices are listed in table 23.3.

Table 23.3: Devices for co-ordinating relationships in organizations classified by class

Class of co-ordination	Description	Device
Formal direction	Written guidelines and adjudication by senior staff	■ Rules, policies and procedures ■ Using hierarchy
Mutual adjustment	Members carrying out the work adjust to each other	■ Goal clarification and communication ■ Temporary task force ■ Permanent project team
Special liaison	Specially employed co-ordinators use consultation and communication	■ Liaison roles ■ Integrator roles

Adapted from Colin Hales, *Managing Through Organization*, Routledge, London, 1993, p. 55. Reprinted by permission of Thomson Publishing Services.

Provided that the relationships between the differentiated departments, units, groups or individuals are successfully co-ordinated, then conflict will not occur. By effectively using inter-party co-ordination devices, a company can prevent conflict breaking out in the first place. The devices are designed to manage the relationships between the different individuals, groups, units and departments so that the reasons for conflict to arise are eliminated. It is only if and when these co-ordination devices fail, and conflict occurs, that conflict resolution techniques will be required. Organizations use seven devices with which to co-ordinate the activities of individuals, groups, units and departments:

1. Rules, policies and procedures.

2. Using hierarchy.

3. Goal clarification and communication.

4. Temporary task forces.

5. Permanent project teams.

6. Liaison roles.

7. Integrator roles.

1. Rules, policies and procedures
All of these specify how one party is to interact with another. For example, a standardized operating procedure will specify when additional staff can be recruited to a department. Rules and procedures reduce the need for both interaction and information flow between parties. They are most useful when inter-party activities are known in advance; when they occur frequently enough to merit establishing rules and procedures to handle them; and when there is sufficient stability to make them relevant.

2. Using hierarchy
Co-ordination of different parties' activities is achieved efficiently by referring any problems to a superior located higher in the organizational hierarchy. The supervisor uses their legitimate authority, based on their position in the hierarchy, to resolve a conflict. A five-person, self-organizing team which co-ordinates itself by mutual adjustment has to manage ten bilateral interactions. If one member becomes a supervisor, there are only four relationships to manage. Team members

unable to agree to take the problem to their mutual boss (Grant, 2002). Resorting to hierarchy is only effective in the short term to provide solutions to specific, urgent problems.

3. Goal clarification and communication

By specifying and communicating its goals to the others in advance, each party knows what the other is attempting to do. At the individual level this may mean clear job descriptions, while at the departmental level it could be statements of objectives. Parties can meet to ensure that they do not compete or interfere with the goals of others. Such discussions reduce the chances of each party misperceiving the others' intentions.

4. Temporary task forces

Representatives of several different departments can come together on a temporary basis to form a task force. Once the specific problem they were created for is solved, the task force disbands and members return to their usual duties and departments. During their membership, individuals come to understand the goals, values, attitudes and problems of their fellow members. This helps to resolve their differences effectively, especially if more than two parties are involved.

5. Permanent project teams

For complex tasks, a project team may be established consisting of cross-functional members (for example, individuals from engineering, marketing and finance). This creates a matrix structure, since each individual retains a responsibility to the permanent team leader and to their functional department. This solution allows co-ordination to occur at the team level, thus improving communication and decision-making.

6. Liaison roles

If differences remain unresolved by senior management, then a liaison role may be created. It is used most by departments between whom the potential for conflict is

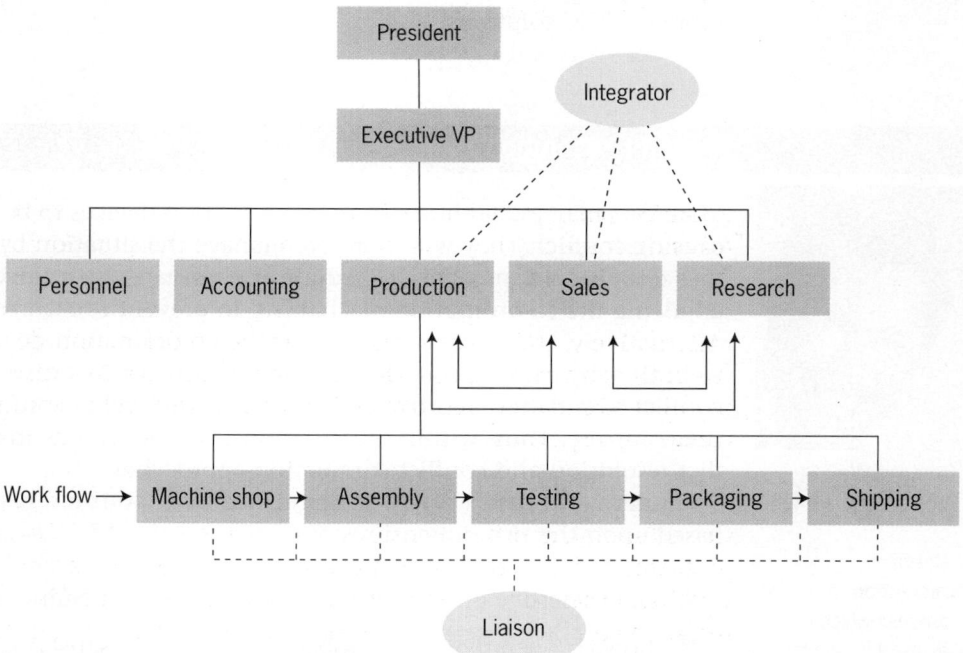

Figure 23.3: Co-ordinating using liaison and integrator roles

highest. The occupant of this role has to be well informed about the needs and technology of the units involved, has to be seen to be unbiased and has to be interpersonally skilled. By holding meetings and supplying units with information, liaison personnel keep the employees in different sections in touch with each other.

7. Integrator roles

An individual or department may be dedicated to integrating the activities of several, highly conflicting departments: for example, production, sales and research (figure 23.3). A scientist with financial and sales experience may be recruited to occupy an integrating role. By having a 'foot in each camp', this person can assist the departments to co-ordinate their activities. The integrator checks that the departments' objectives complement each other and that the output of one becomes the timely input to the other.

Perceptions and emotions

The conditions described in the previous stage can exist without igniting a conflict. Perception plays an important part. It is only if one party, individual, group or department becomes aware of, or is adversely affected by them, and cares about the situation, that latent conflict turns into perceived conflict. It occurs only when one party realizes that another is thwarting its goals. In this stage, the conflict issue becomes defined and 'what it is all about' gets decided. Specifically, each party considers the origins of the conflict, why it emerged and how the problem is being experienced with the other party. The way that the conflict is defined at this stage will determine the type of outcome that the parties are willing to settle for in the later stages.

Not only must a party perceive a conflict, but it must also feel it. That is, it must become emotionally involved in experiencing feelings of anxiety, tenseness, frustration and hostility towards the other party. The emotional dimension of conflict shapes perceptions. For example, negative emotions result in an oversimplification of issues, reductions in trust and negative interpretations of other parties' behaviour. Positive emotions, in contrast, increase the chances of the parties taking a broader view, seeing the issue as a problem to be solved and developing more creative solutions.

Conflict resolution methods

Kenneth Wayne
Thomas (b. 1943)

Conflict resolution: a process which has as its objective the ending of the conflict between the disagreeing parties.

Managers may judge the existing co-ordination devices to be inadequate, thereby causing conflict. They will therefore manage the situation by implementing conflict resolution approaches to reduce or eliminate the immediate conflict, before adjusting the co-ordination mechanism to prevent it occurring in the first place. Alternatively, they may consider that the co-ordination devices are working too well, thereby causing complacency and apathy. In this case, they may introduce conflict stimulation approaches to increase the level of conflict that exists within the company. Thus, within organizations, conflict can be managed through conflict resolution and conflict stimulation approaches.

Kenneth Thomas (1976) distinguished five **conflict resolution** approaches based upon the two dimensions of:

- how assertive or unassertive each party is in pursuing its own concerns;
- how co-operative or uncooperative each is in satisfying the concerns of the other.

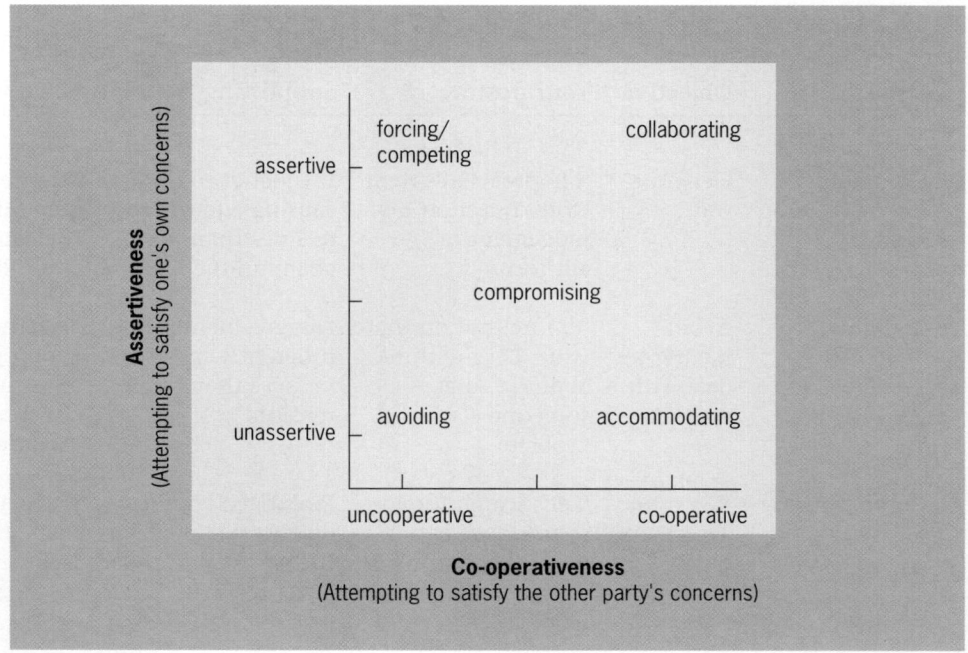

Figure 23.4: Conflict resolution approaches
From *Organizational Behaviour and Human Performance*, vol. 16, T.H. Ruble and K. Thomas, 'Support for a two-dimensional model of conflict behaviour', p. 145. Copyright 1976, with permission from Elsevier.

He labelled these *competing/forcing* (assertive and unco-operative); *avoiding* (unassertive and unco-operative); *compromising* (mid-range on both dimensions); *accommodating* (unassertive and co-operative); and *collaborating* (assertive and co-operative). They are summarized in figure 23.4 and defined in table 23.4.

Thomas (1977) also identified the types of situation in which each conflict resolution orientation was to be preferred over another (table 23.5). Unless the manager is flexible and capable of switching between styles, their ability to resolve conflicts effectively will be limited. In practice, all individuals, whether managers or not, habitually use only a limited number of styles (perhaps just one) to resolve all the conflicts in which they are involved. It is not surprising that they their success is limited.

Table 23.4: Conflict resolution approaches compared

Approach	Objective	Your posture	Supporting rationale	Likely outcome
1. Competing/ forcing	Get your way	'I know what's right. Don't question my judgement or authority'	It is better to risk causing a few hard feelings than to abandon the issue	You feel vindicated, but the other party feels defeated and possibly humiliated
2. Avoiding	Avoid having to deal with conflict	'I'm neutral on that issue. Let me think about it. That's someone else's problem'	Disagreements are inherently bad because they create tension	Interpersonal problems don't get resolved, causing long-term frustration manifested in a variety of ways
3. Compromising	Reach an agreement quickly	'Let's search for a solution we can both live with so we can get on with our work'	Prolonged conflicts distract people from their work and cause bitter feelings	Participants go for the expedient rather than effective solutions
4. Accommodating	Don't upset the other person	'How can I help you feel good about this? My position isn't so important that it is worth risking bad feelings between us'	Maintaining harmonious relationships should be our top priority	The other person is likely to take advantage
5. Collaborating	Solve the problem together	'This is my position, what's yours? I'm committed to finding the best possible solution. What do the facts suggest?'	Each position is important though not necessarily equally valid. Emphasis should be placed on the quality of the outcome and the fairness of the decision-making process	The problem is most likely to be resolved. Also both parties are committed to the solution and satisfied that they have been treated fairly

From D. Whetton, K. Cameron and M. Woods, *Developing Management Skills for Europe*, Financial Times/Prentice Hall, 2000, p. 345. Reprinted by permission of Pearson Education Ltd.

Table 23.5: When to adopt which conflict resolution approach

Approach	Appropriate situations
1. Competing/forcing	1. When quick, decisive action is vital (e.g. in emergencies). 2. On important issues where unpopular actions need implementing (e.g. in cost-cutting, enforcing unpopular rules, discipline). 3. On issues vital to an organization's welfare when you know you're right. 4. Against people who take advantage of non-competitive behaviour.
2. Avoiding	1. When an issue is trivial, or more important issues are pressing. 2. When you perceive no chance of satisfying your concerns. 3. When potential disruption outweighs the benefits of resolution. 4. To let people cool down and regain perspective. 5. When gathering information supersedes immediate decision. 6. When others can resolve the conflict more effectively. 7. When issues seem tangential or symptomatic of other issues.
3. Compromising	1. When goals are important, but not worth the effort or potential disruption of more assertive modes. 2. When opponents with equal power are committed to mutually exclusive goals. 3. To achieve temporary settlements to complex issues. 4. To arrive at expedient solutions under time pressure. 5. As a backup when collaboration or competition is unsuccessful.
4. Accommodating	1. When you find you are wrong – to allow a better position to be heard, to learn, and to show your reasonableness. 2. When issues are more important to others than yourself – to satisfy others and maintain co-operation. 3. To build social credits for later issues. 4. To minimize loss when you are outmatched and losing. 5. When harmony and stability are especially important. 6. To allow subordinates to develop by learning from mistakes.
5. Collaborating	1. To find an integrative solution when both sets of concerns are too important to be compromised. 2. When your objective is to learn. 3. To merge insights from people with different perspectives. 4. To gain commitment by incorporating concerns into a consensus. 5. To work through feelings that have interfered with a relationship.

From 'Towards multidimensional values in teaching: the example of conflict behaviours', *Academy of Management Review* by Kenneth W. Thomas. Copyright 1997 by Academy of Management. Reproduced with permission of Academy of Management in the format Textbook via Copyright Clearance Center.

Choosing and using conflict resolution styles

Brewer et al. (2002) examined the relationship between biological sex, gender role, organizational status and conflict management style of 118 males and females in three organizations. Males were highest on the forcing/competing (or dominating) conflict resolution styles; females were highest on the avoiding style; and androgynous individuals were highest on the collaborative (or integrating) style. Individuals from the upper (more senior) levels in the organization were higher on collaborative styles, and lower-status individuals reported greater use of avoiding and accommodating styles.

Friedman et al. (2000) argued that a person's chosen style can shape their work environment, affecting the level of ongoing conflict and the stress that they experience. Their study of a clinical hospital department found that those using a collaborative (or integrative) style experienced lower levels of task conflict and reduced relationship conflict, and this reduced stress. Those who used a more competing/forcing or avoiding style experienced higher levels of task conflict, thereby increasing relationship conflict and their stress. They concluded that employees' work environments were, in part, of their own making.

Neil Brewer, Patricia Mitchell and Nathan Weber, 'Gender role, organizational status and conflict management styles', *International Journal of Conflict Management*, vol. 13, no. 1, 2002, pp. 78–94; Raymond A. Friedman, Simon T. Tidd, Steven C. Currall and James C. Tsai, 'What goes around comes around: the impact of personal conflict style on work conflict and stress', *International Journal of Conflict Management*, vol. 11, no. 1, 2000, pp. 32–55.

Stop and Criticize

Is it possible for us to switch our behaviour styles to deal with different types of conflict? Or are we trapped in a single style?

Distributive bargaining: a negotiation strategy in which a fixed sum of resources is divided up. It leads to a win–lose situation between the parties.

Integrative bargaining: a negotiation strategy that seeks to increase the total amount of resources. It creates a win–win situation between the parties.

Richard Walton and Robert McKersie's (1965) research into negotiation behaviour distinguished **distributive bargaining** strategies from **integrative bargaining** strategies.

Distributive bargaining involves dividing a 'fixed pie'. It occurs if one party's gain is at another's expense. For example, within a hospital context, the redistribution of beds or ward space between clinical services means that if medicine gets fifteen extra beds, then surgery (or some other service) has to lose fifteen beds. Some conflicts in the workplace can only be resolved in this way. Appropriate bargaining tactics in this situation include asking initially for much more than you are ultimately willing to accept; persuading the opponent that their objective is unattainable or unrealistic; encouraging them to accept a figure nearer yours; getting the other party to feel emotionally generous towards you.

In contrast, integrative bargaining is built on the belief that there exist one or more settlements that can create positive outcomes for both parties. It involves finding ways to 'expand the pie'. As a strategy, integrative bargaining tends to be promoted as it is seen as preferable to distributive bargaining because it builds long-term relationships and facilitates a working together in the future. It bonds the parties, allowing each to believe that they have achieved a victory. Distributive bargaining creates animosities, deepens divisions among those who have to work together and leaves one party a loser. To operate integrative bargaining, both parties need to be open with their concerns, open in their communication, sensitive to the other's needs, trust each other, and be willing to be flexible. These conditions are rarely present in an organization, and hence bargaining tends to be win at any cost. Due to the organizational change, delayerings and a flatter organization structure, negotiation has become a major corporate capability – a management competency required of all managers, and not just employee relations or HRM staff experts.

Studies have revealed similarities between conflict resolution strategies and negotiation strategies (Smith, 1987; Savage et al., 1989). Of the five conflict resolution strategies described earlier, four of them involve one or more of the parties sacrificing something. David Whetton and colleagues (1996; table 23.6) suggested that distributive strategies matched the natural inclination of those individuals to approach conflicts from a 'macho man', 'easy touch' or 'split the difference' perspective, and they thereby engendered competition, exploitation or irresponsibility.

Table 23.6: Comparison between negotiation strategies and conflict resolution approaches

Negotiation strategy	Distributive bargaining	Integrative bargaining
Conflict resolution approaches	Competing/forcing Avoiding Compromising Accommodating	Collaborating

From D. Whetton, K. Cameron and M. Woods, *Developing Management Skills for Europe*, Financial Times/Prentice Hall, 2000, p. 346. Reprinted by permission of Pearson Education Ltd.

Over the last two decades, the major developers of the integrative bargaining concept have been Roger Fisher and William Ury (1981) from the Harvard Negotiating Project. Their scheme of 'principled negotiation' sets out guiding principles to apply when preparing and engaging in face-to-face negotiations. More recent work in this project has dealt with how negotiators should proceed if the other side does not 'play the game' (Ury, 1991; Ury and Patton, 1997) (see table 23.7).

Table 23.7: Bargaining strategies

Win–win strategy	Win–lose strategy
1. Define the conflict as a mutual problem	1. Define the conflict as a win–lose situation
2. Pursue joint outcomes	2. Pursue own group's outcomes
3. Find creative agreements that satisfy both groups	3. Force the other group into submission
4. Use open, honest and accurate communication of group's needs, goals and proposals	4. Use deceitful, inaccurate and misleading communication of group's needs, goals and proposals
5. Avoid threats (to reduce the other's defensiveness)	5. Use threats (to force submission)
6. Communicate flexibility of position	6. Communicate high commitment (rigidity) regarding one's position

Based on table from Johnson, David W. and Johnson, Frank P. *Joining Together: Group Theory and Group Skills* © 1975. Published by Allyn and Bacon, Boston, MA. Copyright © 1975 by Pearson Education. Reprinted by permission of the publisher.

Mediation: a process in which a neutral third party to the conflict assists in the achievement of a negotiated solution by using reason, persuasion and the presentation of alternatives.

Mediation involves bringing in a third party in order to resolve the dispute. In a negotiation situation, the behaviour and feelings of the parties can become sharply polarized, and each becomes isolated from the other. When this happens, a mediator can maintain contact and communication between the parties in dispute. In hostage-taking situations and local wars, independent third parties are often brought in to act as mediators. They do not control the agreement, but influence the conflict resolution process. They guide the two parties to discover the solution to their problem. With increasing litigation and an increasing number of cases log-jammed in the courts, the importance and frequency of alternative dispute resolution (ADR) is increasing. It is cheaper and quicker and causes less damage to long-term relationships. It is used between employers and employees as well as been companies (Harvard Business Review, 2000).

Mediation techniques include asking each party to state the problem, to state the other's view of the problem and to confirm the accuracy of the other's repetition. Once the initial positions have been presented and understood, alternative solutions are generated using brainstorming. The use of recesses in the mediating process is valuable. These can help calm the parties after an emotional encounter; can be used to conduct private enquiries about interests; and can be used to de-escalate conflict.

Negotiating by email

Who has not banged out any angry reply to an apparently brusque email message, hit the send button and then regretted it? Surely no technology has led to so many rifts and fractured friendships (not to mention subpoenas) as electronic mail. But nowhere is email more perilous than in negotiations. Experiments by Michael Morris, an academic at Stanford Business School, have demonstrated that negotiations are more likely to go well if they are conducted, at least in part, face to face, rather than between strangers armed with keyboards and screens. Morris and his colleagues compared mock negotiations which used email only with those that were preceded with a getting-to-know-you telephone call. The second type went more smoothly. Other experiments show that negotiations are easier when negotiators start by swapping photographs and personal details, or when they already know one another.

Why is email such a snare? Heidi Roizen, who now works for Softbank Venture Capital, thinks that part of the problem is that most people don't think about the fact that an email lasts forever. She scrupulously follows two rules to avoid misunderstanding. 'Re-read each piece of mail before you send it from the point of view of the recipient; and when in doubt, leave it overnight.' As every Victorian letter-writer learnt, a night's sleep is the best filter to apply to a furious note. John Kay, a British economist, goes further. After having to calm a succession of weeping secretaries, he instituted a rule at London Economics, a consultancy that he founded, that emails should contain only information and never emotion.

Yet despite its pitfalls, email is increasingly likely to be used for negotiations. Richard Hill, an IT manager and mediator with Hill & Associates in Geneva, worked with the University of Massachusetts on the establishment of an electronic mediation service called the Online Ombuds Office. He argues that mediation by telephone is genuinely simpler and faster: a three-minute telephone call contains more information than a typical brisk email. But because online mediation can be done at a time that is convenient for the parties involved, it tends to be less costly. Just think for a moment before you hit that send button.

From *The Economist*, 'Negotiating by email', 8 April 2000, p. 85.

Arbitration: a process in which a third party to a conflict has the authority to impose an agreement that is binding on the parties in conflict.

If mediation fails, disputes often go to **arbitration**. This may occur if negotiations between unions and management have reached an impasse. A grievance is presented and the arbiter listens to both sides. In this process, the dispute is referred to a third party who is given the power to formulate a settlement that is binding on both parties. This is similar to a judge in a courtroom. Arbitration may be voluntary or compulsory. The former occurs when both parties involved have the choice of whether or not to have a decision imposed on them. Compulsory arbitration, perhaps due to government regulations, denies them that choice.

So far, it has been assumed that there are just two parties involved in a conflict. However, a manager's job also involves resolving conflicts between their subordinates. Managers dislike this task because they have to choose sides and deal with the loser's frustrations. For this reason, managers avoid dealing with conflicts, smooth them over or force the parties to work it out themselves. They may even punish subordinates who bring them problems by ensuring that no one ever wins, creating so-called 'lose–lose' situations.

Managers can, however, use these conciliation techniques with their subordinates in conflict by applying the principles of integrative bargaining. It may be possible to convert win–lose situations into win–win ones, and thus allow both parties to achieve their goals. A holiday allocation decision may be of this type. Two employees both want two weeks off in July, but there are not enough staff to cover. If one person gets their fortnight, the other does not (win–lose). Since one cannot have it, the other is similarly prevented from having theirs (lose–lose). If the manager investigates and finds that one of them wants it for a particular reason and the other for another reason, it may be possible to resolve the situation and create a win–win outcome for all concerned.

Alternatively, managers can choose to mediate between their subordinates. Both subordinates and their supervisor prefer this conflict resolution strategy. However, since staff have little experience of their boss guiding the conflict resolution process without making the final decision, they are rarely sure of how to respond. Some managers are more comfortable with arbitration. Playing the role of judge can be a fast and definitive conflict-resolving process, especially if one of the parties has obviously violated a rule or a policy. However, on the negative side, it rarely results in the parties being committed to a settlement that is imposed on them. Finally, the supervisor might use delegation, telling the parties to solve the conflict themselves. This may appeal to those who wish to smooth over conflicts, but is often ineffective because the parties lack the skills, information and impartiality to work through the conflict on their own.

Stop and Criticize

Some individuals resolve conflict in one fixed way in different situations. Others change their approach to suit the circumstances. Think about a specific domestic, friendship or organizational context which involved conflict. How did you deal with it? Did you force, avoid, compromise, accommodate or collaborate?

Conflict stimulation: the process of engendering conflict between parties where none existed before, or escalating the current conflict level if it is too low.

Interactionists argue that there are conditions in organizations when what is needed is more and not less conflict: that is, **conflict stimulation** (Robbins, 1974; Sternberg and Soriano, 1984).

John Kotter (1996) discussed the dangers of complacency and the need to drive employees out of their comfort zones. Among the complacency-smashing and potentially conflict-stimulating techniques used by senior management were the following:

- create a crisis by allowing a financial loss to occur or an error to blow up;

- eliminate obvious examples of excess like corporate jet fleets and gourmet dining rooms;

- set targets like income, productivity and cycle times so high that they cannot be reached by doing business as usual;

- share more information about customer satisfaction and financial performance with employees;

- insist that people speak regularly to dissatisfied customers, unhappy suppliers and disgruntled shareholders;

- put more honest discussions of the firm's problems in company newspapers and management speeches. Stop senior management's 'happy talk'.

Various techniques can be used to stimulate conflict, where none existed before, in order to encourage different opinions and engender new thinking and problem-solving.

1. Communications
Managers can withhold information 'to keep them guessing' or send large amounts of inconsistent information ('we're expanding', 'we're going bust') to get people arguing. They might send ambiguous or threatening messages.

2. Restructuring a company
Realigning working groups and altering rules and regulations so as to increase or create interdependence between previously independent units can easily stimulate conflict, particularly if the goals of the newly interdependent departments are made incompatible (one department's objective being to minimize costs, the other's being to maximize market share).

3. Bringing in outsiders
Adding individuals to a group whose backgrounds, values, attitudes or management styles differ from those of existing members: for example, recruiting senior executives with career experience in automobile manufacture to manage a healthcare organization.

4. Devil's advocate method
Named after a practice used in the Roman Catholic Church when a name is submitted to the College of Cardinals for elevation to sainthood. To ensure that the nominee has a spotless record, an individual is assigned the role of devil's advocate to uncover any possible objections to the person's canonization. Within the organizational context, a person is assigned the role of critic to stimulate critical thinking and reality testing. For example, in deciding to embark on an e-commerce strategy, one team member might be assigned the devil's advocate role to focus on its pitfalls and dangers.

5. Dialectic method
Plato and the dialectic school of philosophy in ancient Greece originated this approach. It explores opposite positions called 'thesis' and' antithesis'. The outcome of the debate between the two is the 'synthesis', which in turn becomes the new thesis to be opened up for debate. Before deciding on a take-over, a company may establish two or more teams, give them access to the same information, and give them the task to argue for and against the acquisition decision. The conflict of ideas throws up alternatives, which can be synthesized into a superior, final decision.

6. Leadership style
Organizations can appoint managers who encourage non-traditional viewpoints rather than authoritarian ones who might be inclined to suppress opposing viewpoints. Leadership style has been found to be a key element in organization change programmes, and in particular those involving changes in organization culture.

Team fighting

'The absence of conflict is not harmony, it's apathy' asserts the first line of an article by Kathleen Eisenhardt and her colleagues (1977). She and her fellow authors argue that management teams which challenge one another's thinking develop a more complete understanding of the choices, create a richer range of options and ultimately make more effective decisions. As with other interactionist frame holders, they recognize that 'healthy conflict can quickly turn unproductive', and state that the challenge is to prevent conflict degenerating into dysfunctional interpersonal conflict and to encourage managers to argue without destroying their ability to work as a team.

Using interviewing and observation research methods, the authors studied twelve top management teams of five to nine members in technology-based companies which competed in fast-changing competitive global markets. The teams made high-stake decisions in situations of high uncertainty under pressure. Their study revealed how conflict was actually experienced and what part emotion played in decision-making. They identified successful teams which were able to avoid interpersonal hostility and discord, vigorously debated issues while avoiding politicking and posturing, and separated substantive from personality issues. They distinguished these from the less successful teams, which fragmented into cliques and whose members openly displayed frustration, anger and intense animosity. How then can team members disagree on questions of strategic significance yet still get along with each other? The authors identified three strategies for successfully managing interpersonal conflict, each of which involved two tactics.

Tactic ——————————————————▶ *Strategy*

1. Base discussions on ample factual information   *Focus on issues not personalities*

2. Develop multiple alternatives to enrich debate

3. Rally around agreed-upon goals   *Frame decisions as collaborations aimed at achieving the best possible solution for the company*

4. Inject humour into the decision-making process

5. Maintain a balanced power structure   *Establish a sense of fairness and equity in the process*

6. Resolve issues without forcing consensus

The authors conclude with a list of five approaches to help generate such constructive disagreements within a team:

- ■ meet as a team regularly and often;

- ■ manage any evolving conflict actively;

- ■ encourage the application of multiple minds;

- ■ create a heterogeneous team (diverse ages, genders, functions, industrial experience);

- ■ encourage assumption of roles beyond their obvious product, geographical or functional responsibilities.

Based on Kathleen M. Eisenhardt, Jean L. Kahwajy and L.J. Bourgeois, 'How management teams can have a good fight', *Harvard Business Review*, July–August 1997, pp. 77–85.-

The radical frame of reference

Sabotage at a nuclear facility (Cooper, 2000c), racial harassment of ethnic minority staff in the British National Health Service (Rowe, 2000), racism in the London Borough of Hackney (local government organization) (Hammond, 2000), as well as sexual harassment and bullying, are all examples of human behaviour in organizations. Yet the previous unitarist, pluralist and interactionist frames of reference on conflict have difficulty in explaining such actions. Indeed, it is only the radical frame of reference that draws attention to such behaviour in organizations. The other conflict perspectives either do not address such issues effectively or else simply ignore them.

The **radical frame of reference** on conflict sees the workplace as an arena of conflict between employees and managers (the agents of the owners). These controllers of the means of production exploit the employees. The logic of profit maximization involves managers relentlessly driving down the costs of production and controlling the manufacturing process. This perspective argues that, as conflict is an endemic property of capitalist employment relations, it cannot be resolved by any 'techniques'.

The radical frame of reference on conflict is based on the Marxist critique of capital and capitalism whose essential elements were summarized by Roger Johnston (2000):

Radical frame of reference on conflict: a perspective which views (organizational) conflict as an inevitable consequence of exploitative employment relations in a capitalist economy.

1. The fundamental aim of a capitalist enterprise is to expand its capital.

2. To do this, it needs to generate a profit (surplus) otherwise it will fail.

3. Marx's analysis involves two elements:
   (a) *Means of production* – this refers to the materials, artefacts, tools, machines and land which are required by the capitalist owner, and which are indirectly deployed.
   (b) *Organization of labour* – production of goods is socially organized in the sense that the capitalist owner uses labour to produce the goods. Workers are the direct producers.
      (i) Those available to do the work typically have no alternative means of subsistence, so there is an imbalance of power between capitalist owners and workers.
      (ii) Employees contract their time to the capitalist owner in return for payment. During their working hours, workers are directed by the capitalist owners. This is a form of domination that eliminates worker freedom.
      (iii) A hierarchy of organization with specified duties, responsibilities and the authority (of the capitalist owner) directs the activities of workers.

4. To succeed, the capitalist enterprise must sell its produced goods at a profit in the market.

5. The surplus (profit) generated through these sales is divided between the manager(s) who direct production (receiving salary and bonus) and the shareholders who financed the operation (receiving dividends). The workers do not share in this surplus, since labour is treated as a *cost*, not a beneficiary of success.

6. Companies compete with each other in the market on the basis of price, quality, quantity, availability or a combination of all these. Given the problems with each of these competitive strategies, the tendency is for each firm to seek to reduce its costs (of production).

7. Lower costs can be achieved in various ways: by increasing output, reorganizing labour, paying labour less, replacing labour with technical improvements, or a combination of all these.

8. It is argued that the inevitable outcome of cost reduction is that labour will earn less and will be worked more intensely. In consequence, it can be expected that this will generate a lack of consent and resistance or some form of political action, either individual or collective.

9. Management will be concerned and will have to deal with this tension by limiting the effects of worker resistance or overt conflict in order to secure at least compliance.

Labour process theory

This view is closely associated with labour process theory whose Marxist analysis in the organizational literature is most widely discussed in terms of Braverman's 'degradation of work' thesis (Braverman, 1974). The main features of the radical frame of reference–labour process theory are:

1. It rejects the notion of a correspondence of interests. The organizational dilemma concerns the question of how to reconcile the potential inconsistency between individual needs and aspirations of different organizational stakeholders on the one hand, and the collective purpose of the organization on the other. The focus is upon vertical (manager–employee) conflict.

2. It challenges taken-for-granted assumptions by asking questions such as why do managers have to:

   ■ motivate employees (why are employees not already motivated)?

   ■ overcome employees' resistance to change (what do employees fear)?

   ■ create a 'strong' organization culture to gain employees' commitment (why are employees not already committed to their companies)?

   ■ manage conflict (what are employees resisting and what is it that causes the conflict)?

3. It sees the workplace as a 'contested terrain' (Edwards, 1979) where employees, individually and collectively, seek to protect and extend their own interests in the production process, and resist management's attempts at control. Conflict is seen as a fundamental and central dynamic in organizational life.

4. It explains actual, observed instances of workplace conflict in sociological terms, stressing differences of interests, power, politics, domination, control, etc., and also in economic terms, focusing on capital maximization and profit distribution.

5. It holds that the degree to which managers can alter employee behaviour has been exaggerated. Ackroyd and Thompson (1999) distinguish between *tractability*, which refers to management's capacity to induce, through its actions, marginal, temporary changes in employee behaviour, and *corrigibility*, the permanent 'correction' of behaviour to conform with management expectations. They say that employee behaviour may be tractable but that it is rarely corrigible.

6. It rejects the view that by the late 1990s management had successfully established control over employee behaviour and asserts instead that the significant changes in organization structures have merely modified the form that employee resistance has taken (Thompson and Ackroyd, 1995).

7. It focuses primarily on the causes of conflict within the workplace and tends to neglect conflict resolution techniques.

8. It focuses on internal contradictions (for example, cost-reduction strategies) more than external triggers (for example, new technology) when discussing the causes of conflict.

Stephen Ackroyd and Paul Thompson (1999) explained that management establishes a boundary that distinguishes employee behaviour that is and is not acceptable. Employee actions are then defined as falling on one or other side of that boundary. The authors use the term **organizational misbehaviour** to refer to 'anything you do at work which you are not supposed to do' (see figure 23.5).

Although much of the literature refers to 'conflict' in organizations, in reality, overt conflict is actually very rare. Thus, for Richard Edwards (1979) the struggle between capital and labour is the main dynamic which shapes the employment relationship. He refers to *structural antagonisms* rather than to conflict, and sees these as arising from the clash over the distribution of the surplus. A mixture of consent, co-operation and resistance characterizes daily interactions between managers and employees. Carter Goodrich (1975) wrote about the 'frontiers of control' and the notion of **resistance**. Management's attempt to exert control is met by employee resistance, and that produces clashes over interests. The notion of resistance carries with it the connotation of something intermittent (occurring regularly but not continually), changing (frontier being pushed forward and back) and occurring below the surface. This is in contrast to conflict, with its connotations of a single, visible, explosion (Jermier et al., 1994; Sagie et al., 2004).

The concept of resistance has an application at all levels of the organizational hierarchy, from shop-floor employees resisting supervisory control, through professionals like engineers, academics or hospital doctors resisting management directions and right up to senior management resisting the control exercised by the board of directors. It also allows a consideration of how that resistance moves to different areas within the organization, and how the parties acquire and relinquish different types of power, and gain and lose ascendancy over each other.

Edwards (1979) noted that the perpetual struggle for control in organizations is not always constant, obvious or visible. Because employees' tactics of resistance are often covert, some knowledge of a particular organizational context is required for researchers (and indeed for managers) to become fully aware of what is going on. Resistance, as opposed to conflict, in the workplace is reflected in soldiering (output restriction), pilferage, absenteeism, sabotage, vandalism, practical

Organizational misbehaviour: anything that workers do in the workplace which they are not supposed to do.

Resistance: more or less covert behaviour which counteracts and restricts management attempts to exercise power and control in the workplace.

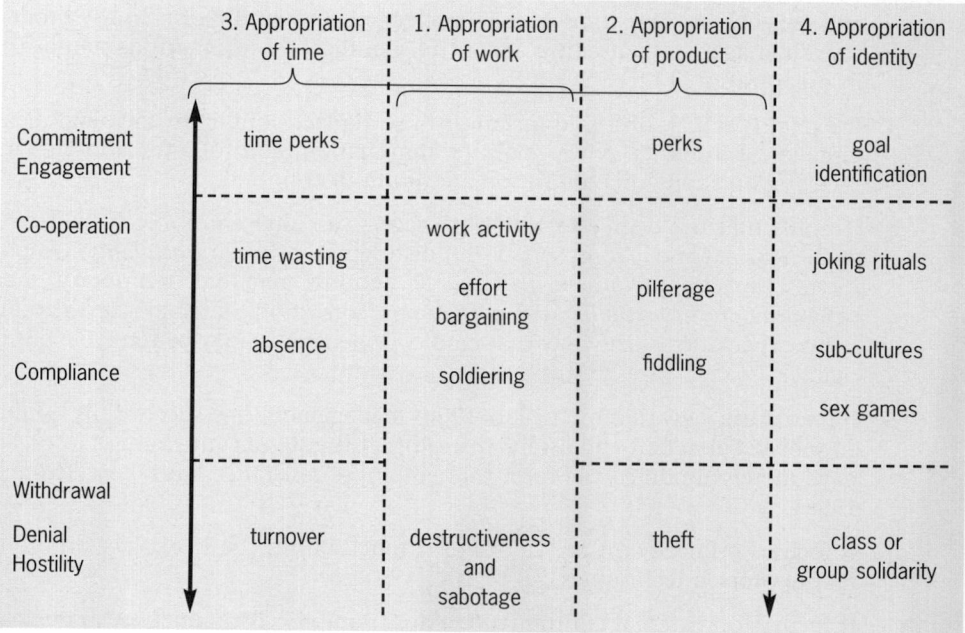

Figure 23.5: Dimensions of organizational misbehaviour
Reprinted by permission of Sage Publications Ltd from Stephen Ackroyd and Paul Thompson, *Organizational Misbehaviour*, Sage, London, 1999, p. 25.

joking and sexual misconduct. Reviewing the managerial and academic literature on the presence and absence of such misbehaviour at work, Ackroyd and Thompson (1999) concluded that typically it:

- provided sanitized accounts of employee behaviour that depicted employees as invariably constructive, conforming and dutiful;

- saw employees' behaviour as being orderly, purposeful and directed towards the attainment of organizational (managerial) goals;

- defined 'normal' employee behaviour as that which was programmed by management, complied with managerial norms and values, and treated employees' deviations from those (management-) expected standards of behaviour as *mis*behaviour;

- assumed that when there was a lack of correspondence between management direction and the employees' response to it (i.e. occurrence of misbehaviour), what needed to change was the latter.

One manifestation of resistance in the workplace that has received a great deal of attention relates to the varying reaction of employees to what is called emotional labour. It is to this topic that we turn in the next section.

Stop and Criticize

Ackroyd and Thompson define organizational misbehaviour in terms of employee behaviour within the workplace which management considers to be inappropriate, and they provide examples of these. However, they exclude any reference to managerial behaviour which managers or non-managers might consider inappropriate.

Define managerial misbehaviour. Provide examples to illustrate your definition.

Customer misbehaviour

Carol Boyd's research into *customer mis*behaviour links the work of Ackroyd and Thompson on organizational misbehaviour (just discussed) with Hochschild's research on emotional labour (which follows). Boyd's study explains how customer violence in the airline and railway industries is triggered and driven by organizational circumstances, particularly employees' working conditions and management style.

With respect to working conditions, airline and railway staff are at greater risk than other service workers because of the length of time that they remain in contact with their customers. In the confined environment of a crowded aircraft at 30,000 feet in the air, or on a long train journey, they can feel like 'hostages', neither able to walk away from a threatening situation nor able to summon outside help. Poor organization leadership leads to excessive workloads, reducing employee performance, which in turn creates delays, queuing and customer hostility. A closed, authoritarian management increases the risk of violence, as do the cost and competitive pressures placed upon employees by deregulation and privatization.

Some of the sources of verbal and physical abuse that Boyd discovered related to conflicts and contradictions in management policy and the provision of poor quality environmental conditions for crews and customers. Her respondents identified the following as causes of passenger violence: alcohol consumed while on board; delays and insufficient provision of information during the delay; the quality of the environmental surroundings, particularly poor waiting areas (railways) and confined spaces (aircraft); inadequate ventilation and air conditioning (aircraft); disputes over baggage; and the failure of operational staff to meet passenger expectations created by the company's marketing (aircraft). The flight experience is itself inherently stressful for many passengers, and these factors only acted to exacerbate it.

All these causes are controlled and made worse by management policy, most notably the sale of alcohol on aircraft and trains. While cabin crew can impose limits on the amount of alcohol that they serve to passengers, management provides them with incentives to sell it, as well as with financial targets for bar sales. This makes it difficult for crew to impose this sanction. Interviewees reported that management placed profit maximization and cost minimization above the safety and health of employees. Safety equipment and safety training were considered costs and tended to be neglected, particularly on the railways. Employees considered that the training they received was both unrealistic and inadequate. Where training was provided and initiatives were launched, as for aircraft cabin crew, they tended to be on topics such as managing conflict and managing stress. In this way, management made workers adapt to the demands and strains of their workplace rather than addressing the real sources of customer violence. Boyd's conclusion was that the managements of these organizations were actively creating conditions that perpetuated and exacerbated customer misbehaviour.

Carol Boyd, 'Customer violence and employee health and safety', *Work, Employment and Society*, vol. 16, no. 1, 2002, pp. 151–69.

Emotional labour

Arlie Russell Hochschild (b. 1940)

Emotional labour: the act of expressing emotion which contributes to organizational goals, which is required to be performed by employees and which typically boosts the self-esteem of its recipient.

Conflict can occur as a result of organizational expectations and employees' reluctance to perform certain tasks in specified ways. Working in an airline, hotel, hospital, supermarket checkout or telesales office can be exhausting. This is because not only are you performing your routine job tasks, but you are also acting in a friendly way towards, and smiling at, your passengers, guests, patients, customers or prospects (even down the phone!). Like the actors in a film, workers have to 'put on a brave face' (or a sympathetic one, or a concerned one), in order to perform their work. In many industries such as hospitality, healthcare and funerals, the way in which employees deliver the service has always been as important as the service being delivered. Think about dining out at a restaurant. In terms of the event's successful outcome for you, how critical an element is the waitress's behaviour? In her book, *The Managed Heart: Commercialization of Human Feeling* (1983), Arlie Hochschild coined the term **emotional labour** to refer to the management of feeling to create a publicly observable facial and bodily display.

Emotional labour refers to the management of human feelings during a social interaction while performing paid work. Emotional labour involves five key elements. First, employees consciously manage their emotions (either inducing or suppressing them) as part of their paid work requirement. Second, they do this when interacting with others (customers, clients, other staff) within the workplace. Third, they do so with the objective of creating in the recipient a particular state of mind ('I am being well treated'), a particular feeling (satisfied customer) or a particular response ('I'll use their service again'). Fourth, emotional labour should boost the self-esteem of its receiver. Finally, it is done to serve the interests of the employer (achieving organizational goals) who prescribes, supervises and monitors the performance of that emotional labour (Taylor, 1998).

Employee	Should demonstrate feelings of
Undertaker	Solemnity
Debt collector	Disapproval, sympathy
Police interrogator	Hostility
Supermarket checkout assistant	Friendliness

As the service sector has grown in many countries, so have the number of new jobs that are 'customer-facing': that is, which involve direct contact with different types of customer. In addition, so-called 'traditional jobs', such as those of bank tellers, travel and car hire agents and supermarket checkout staff, now also involve employees engaging emotionally with their work. In many industries, services have now become virtually indistinguishable in terms of their quality, reliability or price. Consequently, the interactions between service providers and their customers have become a more significant element in the latter's evaluation of satisfaction. In this way, the psychological aspects now take priority over the physical ones (Noon and Blyton, 2002). Managements have recognized both this and also that their most junior, lowest-paid 'customer-facing' employees are representing the company to the world, and can create lasting judgements about it. Because of this, they have begun to take extra care to select, train and monitor them.

Source: © copyright United Feature Syndicate, Inc. Reproduced by permission.

The concept of emotional labour is most relevant to workers in service occupations who interact face-to-face or voice-to-voice with others and have to display emotions using verbal or non-verbal means. Companies monitor employees' performances without them being directly aware of it. In a telecentre where call agents booked flights, supervisors randomly and frequently monitored the calls, sometimes recording their conversations and using these in the weekly review and appraisal meetings with the agents (Taylor, 1998). The 'mystery shopper' is also popular. Here a management member goes 'undercover', acting as a shopper or an airline passenger (ghost traveller), to check whether the emotional displays required are being performed. Finally, the company may distribute service questionnaires to assess customers' reactions to how staff are performing their roles, and whether they are eliciting the desired responses.

Hard (emotional) labour

The earliest studies into emotional labour were conducted on airline staff, and this occupational group continues to receive much research attention. On a flight, cabin crew will always display reassurance, even if they are afraid: 'Even though I'm an honest person, I have learned not to allow my face to mirror my alarm or my fright.' Airline management sees the nature of the interaction between flight attendants and passengers as central to the latter's perceptions of service quality. Competitive pressures have stimulated managerial initiatives to manage the 'natural' delivery of quality customer service during customer–attendant interactions.

Taylor and Tyler (2000) found that three particular uses of body language were fundamental in establishing rapport – walking softly, making eye contact and always smiling. Emotional labour was required when dealing with sick and nervous passengers, applying 'tender loving care' (TLC) and confronting emergency situations. Being friendly, cheerful and helpful involves an emotional display. In organizations with a 'customer is always right' philosophy, service workers are taught to diffuse customer hostility and, in consequence, end up absorbing a raft of verbal abuse during the course of a normal working day. They come to accept such verbalized customer dissatisfaction, no matter how upsetting, as 'just part of the job'. The growing incidence of both verbal and physical customer violence in Britain is likely to increase both the volume and intensity of emotional labour in service industries. The drive for competitive advantage through enhanced customer service means that an integral part of every service worker's job is to transform customer dissatisfaction into satisfaction.

When management failed to invest in violence reduction strategies, exposing service workers to increasing levels of customer violence, it increasingly exploited the emotional labour of their staff. Thus there was the paradoxical situation in which cabin crew had to deploy their emotional labour (calming customers, etc.) to compensate for management's failure to remove the causes of customer abuse. However, the more successful they were in doing this, the less management felt pressured to address the sources of customer violence.

Based on Arlie Hochschild, *The Managed Heart: Commercialization of Human Feeling,* University of California Press, Berkeley, CA, 1983; Steve Taylor and Melissa Tyler, 'Emotional labour and sexual difference in the airline industry', *Work, Employment and Society,* vol. 14, no. 1, 2000, pp. 77–95.

Historically, emotional engagement at work for many employees in many occupations (for example, nursing and teaching) has not only been normal, but also beneficial. People actively seek out jobs that possess this dimension. What distinguishes emotional labour is that employees' normal discretion and choice with respect to their displays of emotions at work are removed or reduced by the requirement to follow certain display rules, and create emotional performances alongside physical performances as part of their jobs. What appears to be crucial is having to be in control of one's emotions, of holding them in check. Stress tends to occur when emotional displays are prolonged; when employees are asked to take it to a level considered unacceptable; when they consider it to be inappropriate for the job; or when they are asked to maintain their emotional display when customers are being rude or offensive. Noon and Blyton (2002, p. 191) suggest four ways in which employees experiencing stress can reduce the emotional aspects of their jobs: they may be able to retire 'off stage' where they can relax temporarily; they may engage in covert activity which maintains the mask of emotional display but not the reality; they may 'switch off' (also called 'switching to automatic' or 'going robot'); or they may slow down and engage in minor uniform infringements.

How much of a problem is emotional labour for employees? Noon and Blyton (2002) state that information about its effects is both limited and contradictory. It is its negative consequences that have tended to be emphasized in the literature. For those employees who do experience a gap between their felt and their expressed emotions at work, creating and maintaining a separation between these two sets of feelings, at a high level and over an extended period of time, can entail severe socio-emotional costs. These include low self-esteem, depression and cynicism. In extreme circumstances, it may even affect their social relationships and their mental health. However, Wouters (1989) noted that many people do not experience any such mismatch and, for them, emotional labour can have positive effects. Perhaps 'emotional engagement' is a better phrase to describe the non-problematic experiences. This may be partly because the distinction between felt and expressed emotions is not as fixed as some writers claim, and partly because they are already used to performing various types of emotional script inside and outside work. These types of people enjoy serving customers and obtaining a positive response from them. Many identify closely with their work roles, and thus the emotional display rules that others consider to be so onerous and stressful are, for them, wholly consistent with their personal values and identity. For these people, task performance, complete with emotional displays, is likely to enhance rather than to reduce their psychological well-being.

From his empirical study of banking and health employees, Wharton (1993) found no simple relationships. Whether or not a person who engaged in emotional labour would find their job satisfying or emotionally exhausting depended on a number of variables. These included the 'fit' between an individual's personal characteristics and the requirements of their job; the level, range and duration of the emotional labour required in the role (intense, extensive and prolonged or low, narrow and brief, or some other combination); their ability to disengage ('switch off') from their job after leaving the workplace; and finally, the degree of autonomy they had in performing their job, with greater autonomy being associated with lower emotional exhaustion.

Finally, Noon and Blyton noted the focus of emotional labour and gender issues. The majority of workers performing emotional labour for a living are women. Most people performing emotional labour occupy the lower positions in work hierarchies, and hence are more likely to be women. Finally, many of the emotions displayed in emotional labour reinforce gender stereotypes: for example, the caring emotion is considered to be more 'naturally' found in women than in men.

Stop and Criticize

Has the importance of emotional labour been overstated? Is it even a valid concept to study? Greeting, smiling, looking and other verbal or non-verbal examples of emotional labour are actually behaviours. We can 'put on a smile' without necessarily being happy. There does not need to be any emotional content behind it. So is emotional labour nothing more than just a sub-category of impression management?

Recap

1. *Distinguish between the four major frames of reference on conflict.*

   - The unitarist frame sees organizations as essentially harmonious and any conflict as bad.

   - The pluralist frame sees organizations as a collection of groups, each with their own interests.

   - The interactionist frame sees conflict as a positive, necessary force for effective performance.

   - The radical frame sees conflict sees as an inevitable outcome of capitalism.

2. *Distinguish between functional and dysfunctional conflict.*

   - *Functional conflict* is considered by management to support organizational goals and it improves organizational performance.

   - *Dysfunctional conflict* is considered to impede the achievement of organizational goals and reduces company performance.

3. *Explain the relationship between organizing, co-ordinating and conflict.*

   - Organizing concerns dividing up a large task (for example, designing, building and marketing of a car) into sub-tasks, and assigning them to groups (for example, design department, production department, etc.). Co-ordination brings those previously divided sub-tasks together to ensure that all activities are directed towards organizational goals. In the process of sub-division, departments acquire their own, subordinate goals and interests, which differ from organizational ones. Conflict ensues when these divergent interests and goals clash.

4. *List the causes of conflict in organizations.*

   - Individuals, groups, units and departments may be in conflict with each other due to the differences in their goal orientation and evaluations; self-image and stereotypes; task interdependencies; time perspectives; as well as overlapping authority and scarce resources.

5. *Distinguish the different organizational co-ordination devices.*

   - Co-ordination devices include rules, policies and procedures; using hierarchy; goal clarification and communication; temporary task forces; permanent project teams; liaison roles and integrator roles.

6. *Explain the conditions in which conflict is resolved and stimulated in organizations.*

   - Some writers contend that conflict is dysfunctional: that is, does not achieve organizational goals, wastes time, demotivates staff, wastes resources and generally lowers individual, and hence organizational, performance. In such cases it needs to be eliminated.

   - Commentators argue that conflict stimulation is necessary if employees enter 'comfort zones', are reluctant to think in new ways and find it easier to maintain the *status quo*. In rapidly changing organizational environments such behaviour not only reduces organizational success, but may endanger the organization's very existence.

7. *List Thomas's five conflict resolution approaches.*

   - Thomas's five conflict resolution approaches are avoidance, accommodation, compromise, collaborative and competition/forcing.

8. *Distinguish between distributive and integrative bargaining.*

   - Distributive bargaining refers to a negotiation situation in which a fixed sum of resources is divided up. It leads to a win–lose situation between the parties.

   - Integrative bargaining seeks to increase the total amount of resources and creates a win–win situation between the parties.

Revision

1. Many commentators argue that conflict can serve a number of organizational purposes. What are the grounds for and against such an argument?

2. 'The unitarist frame of reference on conflict is the most dominant in the literature and practice.' Do you agree? Give reasons for your view and illustrate with examples.

3. 'Since every unit and department in an organization has its own goals and interests, destructive conflict will always be an aspect of organizational life.' Do you agree? Give reasons for your view and illustrate with examples.

4. 'Functional conflict is a contradiction is terms.' Discuss.

5. Kenneth Thomas distinguished five conflict resolution approaches. Suggest the difficulties for an individual seeking to switch between them.

Springboard

Ackroyd, S. and Thompson, P., 1999, *Organizational Misbehaviour*, Sage Publications, London.

Adopting a radical frame of reference on conflict, the authors review the empirical and theoretical work on organizational misbehaviour, setting it within the context of employee resistance, conflict and social identity.

Barry, J., Chandler, J., Clark, H., Johnston, R. and Needle, D. (eds), 2000, *Organization and Management: A Critical Text*, Thomson Learning, London.

A set of critical chapters which consider resistance and conflict in organizations from a variety of different perspectives, themes and levels.

Carnevale, P.J. and Pruitt, D.G., 2000, *Negotiation in Social Conflict*, Open University Press, Buckingham (second edition).

A research-based analysis of negotiation focusing on the negotiator's role, conflict style, the way issues are framed, the relationship between the parties and the communication techniques used.

Collins, D., 1998, *Organizational Change: Sociological Perspectives*, Routledge, London.

Chapters 7 and 8 provide extended descriptions and examples of each of the four theoretical frameworks on conflict.

Dreu, C. and Van de Vliert, E. (eds), 1997, *Using Conflict in Organizations*, Sage Publications, London.

A collection of readings taking an interactionist frame of reference on conflict, considering functional and dysfunctional conflict in organizations.

Fox, A., 1973, 'Industrial relations: a social critique of pluralist ideology', in J. Child (ed.), *Man and Organization*, Allen and Unwin, London, pp. 185–233.

Alan Fox is credited with distinguishing the unitarist, pluralist and radical perspectives on conflict which have formed the basis of all discussions of the topic.

Thompson, P., 1983, *The Nature of Work: An Introduction to the Debates in the Labour Process*, Macmillan, London.

Labour process theory represents an important, if neglected, theme in contemporary organizational behaviour theory and research. Since the language used in these writings often creates obstacles to its wider dissemination, this book provides a useful introductory starting point.

Home viewing

6

Dog Day Afternoon (1975, director Sidney Lumet) is a crime drama based on a true event that occurred on a hot August day in 1972. Sony Wortzik (played by Al Pacino) and two accomplices enter a Brooklyn bank in New York and hold up the staff at gunpoint. However, the robbery goes wrong and the police surround the building. Sonny and his morose friend, Sal (played by John Cazale), become trapped inside the bank with their hostages. As you watch the film, analyze the elements of the conflict situation, note which conflict resolution approaches are used and when, and what negotiating tactics are applied.

OB in literature

David Lodge, *Nice Work*, Penguin, Harmondsworth, 1989.

The novel concerns Vic Wilcox, a middle-aged, male managing director of a foundry, Midland Amalgamated, and Robyn Penrose, a committed feminist intellectual and member of a university English department on a short-term contract. She hopes that agreeing to participate in a 'manager shadowing' scheme will help her to renew her contract. Which frame of reference on conflict do Vic and Robyn hold respectively? How might they have come to adopt that frame of reference? How does it affect their perception of events in the company?

Chapter exercises

1: What is your primary conflict resolution approach?

Objectives
1. To remind you of the different conflict resolution approaches available.

2. To allow you to identify which approach you typically use.

Briefing
For each of the fifteen statements indicate how often you use that tactic to resolve a conflict by circling the appropriate number (1 = Rarely through to 5 = Always). After you have responded to all the items, insert your numbers into the scoring key that follows and add up the total for the five columns.

1. I try to show the other party the logic and benefits of my position.   1 – 2 – 3 – 4 – 5

2. I endeavour to satisfy all the needs that I and the other party have.   1 – 2 – 3 – 4 – 5

3. I give up some points in exchange for others.   1 – 2 – 3 – 4 – 5

4. I believe that some differences are not worth worrying about.   1 – 2 – 3 – 4 – 5

5. I avoid hurting the other's feelings.   1 – 2 – 3 – 4 – 5

6. I seek to convince the other person of the merits of my position.   1 – 2 – 3 – 4 – 5

7. I strive to get all concerns and issues out on the table, immediately.   1 – 2 – 3 – 4 – 5

8. I propose a middle ground between us.   1 – 2 – 3 – 4 – 5

9. I postpone a decision until I have had some time to think it over.   1 – 2 – 3 – 4 – 5

10. I sacrifice my own wishes for those of the other person.   1 – 2 – 3 – 4 – 5

11. I am determined when pursuing my goals.   1 – 2 – 3 – 4 – 5

12. I seek the other person's help in working out a solution.   1 – 2 – 3 – 4 – 5

13. I try to find a fair combination of gains and losses for both of us.   1 – 2 – 3 – 4 – 5

14. I refrain from taking positions which would create controversy.   1 – 2 – 3 – 4 – 5

15. I soothe the other person's feelings in order to preserve our relationship.   1 – 2 – 3 – 4 – 5

Scoring

Conflict resolution approaches

Competing/Forcing		Avoiding		Compromising		Accommodating		Collaborating	
Item	Score	Item	Score	Item	Score	Item	Score	Item	Score
1.		4.		3.		5.		2.	
6.		9.		8.		10.		7.	
11.		14.		13.		15.		12.	
Total =		Total =		Total =		Total =		Total =	

Your primary conflict-resolving approach is _____ (the category with the highest number).

Your back-up conflict-resolving approach is _____ (the category with the second highest number).

2: Different perspectives, resolving the conflict

Objectives
1. To introduce you to the different frames of reference on conflict.

2. To give you the opportunity to develop a conflict resolution strategy based on that perspective.

Briefing
1. Arrange yourself into groups of three to five members.

2. Read the announcement and response which follows as two positions.

3. Discuss the three questions that follow.

4. Each group prepares to make a contribution to the plenary discussion.

Performance-related Pay for Teachers

Announcement from the Minister of Education
The government has decided to introduce performance-related pay for teachers in high schools for 12–16 year olds. In future, the better that a teacher performs, the higher the salary that they will receive. Its decision is based on the belief that employee reward systems in modern organizations, whether private or public, must recognize the differing contributions of individuals. The management of a teacher's performance using pay will identify and reward high-quality teaching and motivate poor performers to improve. This government initiative has the full support of parents who are keen to ensure that the education of their children is of the highest standard. The government is confident that it shares with professional teachers the desire to maintain and improve teaching quality in our schools, and this initiative is another major component of government policy designed to raise standards further.

Response of the United Union of Teachers
The UUT is appalled by the government's decision to introduce performance-related pay into high schools. It is a flawed system which 'measures the measurable and ignores the meaningful'. Children are not motor cars, and counting how many are produced by which teacher is not what education is about. Pupils' attainment depends as much on their social and family background as on what happens inside the classroom. The initiative will therefore reward and punish teachers on factors that are outside their direct control, and this is unfair, demotivating and divisive. It will inevitably lead to a collapse in morale and in teaching standards. It will also damage relationships not only between teachers and pupils,

but also between staff members within schools, and between teachers and parents. It is likely to increase stress for all concerned. The union is therefore considering strike action in protest against this government initiative.

1. How would a unitarist explain and seek to resolve this conflict?

2. How would a pluralist explain and seek to resolve this conflict?

3. How would someone holding a radical perspective explain and seek to resolve this conflict?

Chapter 24 Power and politics

Key concepts

power

strategic contingencies

influencing

rationalism

rationality

rational model of organization

political model of organization

politics

need for power

personalized power

socialized power

Machiavellianism

locus of control

risk-seeking propensity

Learning outcomes

When you have read this chapter, you should be able to define those key concepts in your own words, and you should also be able to:

1. Appreciate the importance of power and politics in organizational life.
2. Compare and contrast different perspectives on power.
3. List the different bases of power.
4. Identify organizational factors which enhance the power of departments.
5. Differentiate between power tactics and influencing strategies.
6. Distinguish between the rational and political models of organization.
7. Identify the characteristics of individuals most likely to engage in political behaviour.
8. Explain why politics is a feature of organizational life.

Why study power and politics?

Organizations have a political dimension as well as a social, technical, economic and cultural one. According to David Buchanan and Richard Badham (1999a, p. 1):

> The relatively stable ordered, bounded, predictable, rule-based hierarchical organization of today seems an anachronism. The so-called 'post-modern' organization is characterized by fluidity, uncertainty, ambiguity and discontinuity. Job security is replaced with 'employability security'. Organization boundaries are blurred with the development of partnerships and joint ventures, sub-contracting and peripheral workforces, and social and technology-based networks. Hierarchy is replaced by reliance on expert power; those with the best understanding of the problems take the decisions. In this stereotyped, 'postmodern' context, individuals are stripped of the conventional resources of a relatively stable organizational position, and are deprived of a meaningful, predictable vision of their own future. This fluid and shifting context implies an increased dependence on personal and

interpersonal resources, and on political skills to advance personal and corporate agendas. There is clearly enhanced scope for political manoeuvring in a less well ordered and less disciplined organizational world. There is also clearly a greater need for a critical understanding of the shaping role of political behaviour in such a context.

Power and politics are inextricably entwined, affecting human behaviour in organizations. It has been said that power concerns the capacity of individuals to exert their will over others, while political behaviour is the practical domain of power in action, worked out through the use of techniques of influence and other (more or less extreme) tactics. Some writers believe that much management failure can be attributed to political incompetence, political naiveté, and the inability or unwillingness to perform effectively the required political tasks in an organization (Kotter, 1985; Yates, 1985).

Politics is about overcoming the problem of resolving situations where different organization members bring different values to their work, and consequently do not share common goals or views, but yet have to continue to work with one another (Kakabadse, 1983). Even when they do share aims about company objectives, they may disagree about the means to those ends, and will fight (figuratively) for what they believe is the appropriate line of action. Ian Mangham (1979, p. 17) felt that most significant organizational decisions were the outcome of social and political forces, and were only partly influenced by evidence and rational argument – shaped by 'the pulling and hauling that is politics'. Henry Kissinger, an American diplomat, confirmed this view when he wrote:

> Before I served as a consultant to [President] Kennedy, I had believed, like most academics, that the process of decision-making was largely intellectual and all one had to do was to walk into the President's office and convince him of the correctness of one's view. This perspective, I soon realised, is as dangerously immature as it is widely held. (cited in Pfeffer, 1992a, p. 31)

Lee Bolman and Terrence Deal (1991) summarized this political view of organization, seeing goals and decisions as emerging from bargaining, negotiation and jockeying for position by individuals and coalitions. These coalitions were composed of varied individuals and interest groups which possessed enduring differences of values, preferences, beliefs, information and perceptions of reality. Many observers feel that political behaviour plays a more significant role in organizational life than is commonly realized or admitted, and that the academic management literature does not adequately explore the shaping of political behaviour in organizational change.

Power in organizations

Power: the capacity of individuals to overcome resistance on the part of others, to exert their will and to produce results consistent with their interests and objectives.

Power is a controversial topic which is difficult to define and measure with precision. It has been defined as the capacity of individuals to overcome resistance on the part of others, to exert their will, and to produce results consistent with their interests and objectives. Although this is a definition from an individual perspective, power can be exerted not only by some individuals over others, but also by some groups, sections, departments, organizations, and indeed by some nations over others (Dahl, 1957).

Being abstract, power is also a difficult topic to conceptualize. For this reason, a number of different frameworks are offered. They share similarities and differences. Being able to view the complex and slippery notion of power from different angles enables readers to become aware of, and to draw on, the strengths and limitations of each viewpoint. The first, 'power-as-property' viewpoint sees power as an attribute or characteristic, and distinguishes three different perspectives. It is associated with writers such as Pfeffer, and French and Raven. The second, 'face-of-power' viewpoint considers it in terms of its visibility to outsiders. It is most closely associated with Steven Lukes. The third viewpoint focuses on disciplinary power and is associated with the work of Michael Foucault.

Power-as-property viewpoint

This viewpoint distinguishes three different perspectives on power that can be found in the literature. These perspectives are similar to the frames of reference on conflict which were considered in chapter 23. The distinction is based upon the attribute or characteristic of power which the writer(s) consider to be crucial. The three perspectives are:

- power as a property of individuals;
- power as a property of relationships;
- power as an embedded property of structures.

Power as a property of individuals

From this perspective, power is seen as being possessed by an individual who exercises it through a range of social and interpersonal skills. Proponents claim to 'know power when they see it'; can easily differentiate between those organization members who have and use power and those who do not; and can often even identify the source of the power being used by a particular individual. This perspective asks how much power an individual has, where it comes from, and how more can be acquired. Table 24.1 lists the sources of individual power identified by Jeffrey Pfeffer (1992b). Notice how some of these come from the position that the individual occupies within the organization hierarchy (structural sources) while others relate to their personal attributes like personality, communication and motivation (individual sources).

Table 24.1: Power as an individual property: sources

Structural sources of individual power include:
- Formal position and authority in the organization structure
- Ability to cultivate allies and supporters
- Access to and control over information and other resources
- Physical and social position in the organization's communication network
- The centrality of your own unit or section to the business
- Role in resolving critical problems, in reducing uncertainty
- Degree of unity of your section, lack of internal dissent
- Being irreplaceable
- The pervasiveness of one's activities in the organization

Personal sources of individual power include:
- Energy, endurance and physical stamina
- Ability to focus energy and avoid wasteful effort
- Sensitivity and ability to read and understand others
- Flexibility in selecting varied means to achieve goals
- Personal toughness; willingness to engage in conflict and confrontation
- Ability to 'play the subordinate' and 'team member' to enlist the support of others

Based on Jeffrey Pfeffer, *Managing with Power: Power and Influence in Organizations*, Harvard Business School Press, Boston, MA (second edition), 1992b.

Stop and Criticize

How would the 'power-as-individual-property' perspective explain why, typically, accountants tend to be more powerful and influential in most organizations than, for example, personnel and training managers?

Power as a property of relationships

The second perspective on power to be found in the literature treats it as a property of a *relationship* between a power holder and others, rather than just a property of the individual alone. John French and Bertram Raven (1958) proposed this 'relational' view of power in which followers need to perceive that the leader has access to rewards, sanctions, expertise and so on (table 24.2). From this perspective, the exercise of power depends on the *beliefs*, *perceptions* and *desires* of the followers.

An individual may have access to rewards or possess expertise but if his followers believe that he does not, they may be unwilling to comply. Similarly, a person may lack reward capacity or expertise but will gain compliance from others because she persuades them that she possesses these. An individual can manipulate followers' beliefs and perceptions to gain compliance. It is because two parties are involved that this view of power is seen as a *relational* construct, and not just a property of the individual who accumulates it. David Knights and Hugh Willmott (1999, p. 166) remind us that power can only be successful 'if those over whom power is exercised are tempted by the material rewards offered or have considerable respect for the knowledge surrounding the exercise of power'.

Table 24.2: Bases of power

Reward power:	the ability of a leader to exert influence based on the belief of followers that the leader has access to valued rewards which will be dispensed in return for compliance with instructions.
Coercive power:	the ability of a leader to exert influence based on the belief of followers that the leader can administer unwelcome penalties or sanctions.
Referent power:	the ability of a leader to exert influence based on the belief of followers that the leader has desirable abilities and personality traits that can and should be copied; referred to as *charisma*.
Legitimate power:	the ability of a leader to exert influence based on the belief of followers that the leader has authority to issue orders which they in turn have an obligation to accept; referred to as *position power*, as this depends on the leader's formal organizational position and title.
Expert power:	the ability of a leader to exert influence based on the belief of followers that the leader has superior knowledge relevant to the situation and the task in hand.

Based on J. French and B. Raven, 'The bases of social power', in D. Cartwright (ed.), *Studies in Social Power*, Research Center for Group Dynamics, Institute for Social Research, University of Michigan, 1958.

All the five power bases are both interrelated and dynamic. Using one of the power bases affects one's ability to use another. For example, using coercive power leaves the individual losing referent power, while an application of expert power may mean the individual gains referent power. Additionally, power is dynamic, changing in form and amount as the situation around the individual and followers changes. For example, a person's initial recommendation, based on their expertise, may initially be discounted by others. However, when that person is proved to be correct by circumstances, others' assessment of that person changes, and their expert power may be enhanced. Note the continual relationship element in this example.

Most individuals can operate from several bases of power, with the same person using different power bases in different combinations in different contexts at different times. The relationship issue here manifests itself in terms of the existence of different groups of followers and the different issues being dealt with. In one relationship, certain power bases may be effective, whereas in a different relationship, others may be more appropriate. Similarly, situations change over time. In the past, leadership was based first on coercion, then on legitimate power, now on expert power, and increasingly on referent power.

French and Raven listed five bases of power, since one's power base will depend on whatever resources are available and appropriate in the circumstances. Hence, the list of potential power bases is potentially infinite (Hardy, 1995; Clegg and Hardy, 1996a). Buchanan and Badham (1999, p. 49) added: 'Even being downtrodden, voiceless and marginalized is to possess a power source which can be exploited, if and when circumstances allow.'

Richard III, power and relationships

In his analysis of Shakespeare's play, *Richard III*, Corrigan explains that Richard is engaged in a 'joint venture' to secure the throne. Despite his individual talents, he is unable to achieve this goal alone, needing the services of others in his organization. He needs them to have commitment and to provide him with resources and information. The effective leader ensures that trust has been established with the crucial allies, but this is something Richard fails to do. His allies leave and he is left alone.

Corrigan concludes that whether one is a monarch or a manager, clear ambition and a will to act can overcome unfavourable odds. However, when you have threatened everybody, you are alone. Power cannot be used without there being other people who trust you. The ambitious need other people to help them to hold on to their power. Shakespeare stresses the consequences of failing to perform the slow, time-consuming but vital task of building relationships.

Based on Paul Corrigan, *Shakespeare on Management: Leadership Lessons for Today's Managers*, Kogan Page, London, 1999, pp. 102–3 and 106.

The power-as-individual-property perspective and the power-as-relational perspective are also referred to as *episodic*. Current thinking about power distinguishes between 'episodic' and 'pervasive' perspectives. Episodic perspectives view power as something that one party uses every so often (episodically) to change the behaviour of another, while the *pervasive* perspective sees it as something that is diffused throughout an organization and which produces an ongoing effect on how employees behave. It is to a consideration of this view that we now turn.

Power as an embedded property of structures

The third perspective on power focuses on what factors give organization *departments*, and not individuals, power. It also considers how power is used to control the behaviour of individuals through less obvious means. It pays attention to the way in which power is 'designed into' the organization's fabric, and is embedded in such a way as to make it less visible and less detectable by those who are not sufficiently observant. The effect of this is to give certain privileged individuals access to decision-making, information sources and budgetary responsibility, while denying it to others. While this hidden or latent power may be less easily detected, analyzed and challenged, it is no less potent.

The embedded perspective sees power as so expertly woven into the fabric of the organization that we accept it, in a 'taken-for-granted' way, in the same way that we accept that offices have desks. We accept the social and organization structure of the company – our job description, the operating rules and policies, the budgets to which we work, the equipment which we are given to use, and how we will be rewarded. All of these we consider a perfectly 'natural' way of running the organization's systems and processes on a day-to-day basis. When power becomes so embedded, it becomes virtually invisible. Even when detected, it becomes difficult, if not impossible, to challenge. Clearly, it is in the best interests of those who possess power, if its unequal distribution remains invisible and taken for granted, and is accepted and not challenged.

> **Strategic contingencies**: events and activities, both inside and outside an organization, that are essential for it to attain its goals.

Strategic contingencies are events and activities which must occur, either inside or outside an organization, for it to attain its goals. This concept can explain the differences in the relative power of different departments (Hickson et al., 1971; Salancik and Pfeffer, 1974, 1977). In the short term, a firm must manufacture a product and sell it to a customer at a profit to survive. Developing the next product or counting the money it has received is less important. In this short-term example, the sales department and production department provide greater strategic value to the company than do the R&D or the finance departments. Hence, individuals, groups or departments which are responsible for dealing with the key issues and dependencies in the company environment, which solve its pressing problems or which deal with a current crisis, will be more powerful than those that do not (Astley and Sachdeva, 1984; Mintzberg, 1983b).

The power sources that indicate a department's ability to respond to strategic contingencies include dependency creation, financial resources, centrality of activities, non-substitutability and uncertainty reduction. These five sources overlap and the more of them a department possesses, the greater the power that it will exert within its organization.

1. Dependency creation

A department is powerful if other units and departments depend on its products or services. These may include materials, information, resources and services which flow between departments. The receiving department is always in an inferior power position. The number and strength of the dependencies is also important.

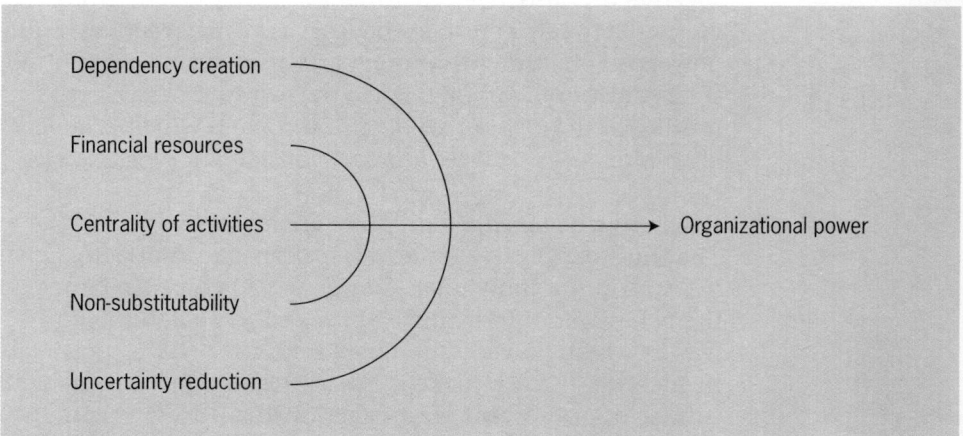

2. Financial resources

A department's ability to control financial resources gives it power. Money can be converted into many different resources that are required and valued by others. Because of the power-enhancing value of financial resources, departments in all organizations compete with others to grasp new projects or tasks which have new financial budgets attached to them.

3. Centrality

Centrality refers to the degree to which the department's activities are critical to producing the company's main product or service. It reflects the relative importance of the contribution made by one department in comparison with another, with respect to the organization's goal. The more central a department is, the more powerful it is. A good indicator of centrality is the likelihood of its work being sub-contracted. The least central functions are training, payroll management, computer management, personnel and advertising.

4. Non-substitutability

If what a department does cannot easily be done by another department, either inside or outside the organization, then it has great power. The more specialized its work, the greater the skill and knowledge required to do it, and hence the more power that accrues to it.

5. Uncertainty reduction

Those who have the ability to reduce uncertainty can gain significant reputations and positions of influence. By offering clear definitions of problems and by specifying solutions, they can restore certainty in an otherwise confused situation. There are three uncertainty reduction techniques: *securing prior information* (for example, forecasting and market research); *prevention* (for example, when a negative event is predicted and its occurrence is forestalled); and *absorption* (when a department acts after an event to reduce its negative consequences) (Hickson et al., 1971).

"You're an evil bastard, Gilroy. I like that."

Source: Reprinted by permission of Tony Husband.

Stop and Criticize	Do you think that the pursuit of power interferes with or contributes to improved organizational performance?

Faces-of-power viewpoint

A second viewpoint on power was provided by Steven Lukes (1974). For him, it ranged from power as clearly visible (overt) and self-evident to an observer, through to power being subtle, less visible (covert) and institutionalized: that is, embedded in the structure of the organization in which individuals work. He conceptualized it as having three 'faces' or dimensions:

Dimension 1   Power that is exercised to secure a decision in situations where there is some observable conflict or disagreement.

Dimension 2   Power that is exercised to keep issues on or off the decision-making agenda, so that potential conflicts or disagreements are precluded and therefore are unobservable.

Dimension 3   Institutionalized power that is used to define reality for its members. If norms and meanings that have been defined by senior management become internalized by employees, they will accept and act in accordance with them, even if it goes against their 'real' interests.

The first dimension is the most obvious, and concerns a clash of interests between those making a decision. It focuses on the *observable behaviour* of individuals or groups, which determine or influence the form or content of a decision. For example, in the army, a sergeant threatens to put a private on a charge unless he completes his assigned task before midnight. The sergeant's words (verbal and paraverbal behaviour) and manner (non-verbal) can both be observed by an onlooker who notices their effect on what the soldier decides to do (works more quickly).

At the second dimension of power the scope for decision-making is confined. The interests of certain groups are excluded from a particular bargaining or decision-making arena. It concerns the *non-observable behaviour* that is involved in keeping issues on or off an agenda. This form of power can keep controversial issues from ever reaching the public domain either to be discussed or decided upon. Unlike in the first case, where individuals or groups, though they may be overruled, are nevertheless involved in the decision-making process, here they are not admitted to the arena in the first place. Power is most commonly associated with someone doing something, such as making a decision or acting in a particular way. Yet, *not* making a decision or doing nothing is often as powerful and significant as doing so (Wolfinger, 1971; Pettigrew, 1973). Peter Bachrach and Morton Baratz (1962) noted that by doing this, one could avoid resistance to, or overt conflict over, one's intentions completely. Stuart Clegg (1989, p. 77) distinguished three forms of such non-decision-making:

1.   The powerful deal with the grievances of the less powerful by ignoring them, dismissing them as minor, unsubstantiated or irrelevant, or

subjecting them to endless inconclusive consideration by committees and enquiries.

2. The less powerful expect their grievances or demands to be ignored or rejected, and hence fail to raise them in the first place.

3. The powerful decide which matters are 'legitimate' for the agenda, and hence discussible, and how and where they are to be discussed, while stifling issues and demands judged as inappropriate.

At the third dimension of power issues are not observable, but only latent. The dimension is characterized by harmony; there is not overt conflict. Those subject to the consequences of power being exercised over them are not aware of it. This dimension concerns the way that the 'powerful' define reality for the 'powerless' in the organization. They secure the support of those who are disadvantaged by the exercise of their power. The true interests and potential grievances of the 'powerless' are obscured or distorted, and they are distracted from them, becoming instead pre-occupied by events that are more immediate and understandable to them: for example, through the use of induction programmes and company training. The public exposure of power is avoided.

This radical dimension of power concerns itself with how power is exercised outside the usual and specific points of conflict or decision-making. Instead it is interested in *institutionalized* power – the way that it is used to prevent conflict by shaping people's perceptions and preferences so that they accept the existing order of things. What distinguishes institutionalized power is that it is difficult to associate it with the actions of any specific individual who may be influencing a decision (first dimension), or with backstage manoeuvring conducted by individuals and groups who are seeking to prevent contentious issues being discussed (second dimension). Power holders, by defining reality for employees and getting them to internalize selected norms and meanings, cast a sort of 'spell' over them, whereby the powerless become unable to formulate consciously their real interests. Institutional power helps to sustain the dominance of senior management by reducing the ability of subordinates to dissent.

Less obvious management controls

The six management control strategies described by Don Hellriegel and John Slocum exercise control over individuals on the basis of power that is not immediately obvious. Behind each control strategy a choice has been made. For example, controlling through organization structure involves deciding on the degree of formal authority to assign, and how much legitimate power to allocate. Choices involve what information the role holder will receive, what types of decision they will be allowed to make, and what budgetary responsibilities they will have, and so on.

Control through organization structure

Large organizations give their employees job descriptions which set out their tasks and responsibilities. These can be narrow, detailed and specific, or general, broad and vague. They also specify communication flows and the location of decision-making responsibility.

Control through policies and rules

Written policies and rules guide employees' actions, structure their relationships and aim to establish consistency of behaviour. Rules lay down standards, define acceptable behaviour and establish levels of required performance.

Control through recruitment and training

Companies wish to avoid having people who behave in unstable, variable, spontaneous, idiosyncratic and random ways. To achieve predictability, they select stable, reliable individuals, while consistency and reliability are achieved through training them.

Control through rewards and punishments

Employees receive extrinsic rewards in the form of material, monetary incentives and associated fringe benefits like company cars and free meals. Intrinsic rewards include satisfying work, personal responsibility and autonomy. Offering to provide or withdraw these rewards gains employees' compliance.

Control through budgets

Individuals and sections in organizations are given financial and resource targets to guide their performance. These may relate to expenditure, level of cost incurred, or sales volume to be achieved in a month. Production budgets include labour hours used and machine downtime.

Control through machinery

This form of control is a feature of assembly-line production (Henry Ford) and is also popular in process industries where chemicals are manufactured automatically. Developments in information and computer technology have increased the possibilities of electronic surveillance of employees.

Based on Don Hellriegel and John W. Slocum, *Management: Contingency Approaches*, Addison-Wesley, Reading, MA, 1978.

Disciplinary power viewpoint

Michel Foucault, a French philosopher and historian, has provided a third viewpoint on power. He was interested in the rise of a distinctively modern form of disciplinary power. His work can be related to Lukes's third dimension of power, the institutional, which focuses on the way that management sustains its dominance by reducing subordinates' ability to dissent by creating their reality and managing meanings for them. Foucault considered how individuals and groups become 'socially inscribed' and 'normalized' through the routine aspects of organizations. He studied the 'rules of the game' which managements established, which both constrained and enabled the actions of those subject to those rules.

Foucault used the concept of *bio-power* in his arguments. This operated by establishing and defining what was normal or abnormal, acceptable or socially deviant. Bio-power is targeted at society in general, is achieved through talk, writing, debate and discussion, and controls us through getting us to consider what is 'normal'. At the level of the organization, once employees do this, they become self-disciplining and no longer require management to keep them under control. For Foucault, power was a set of tools which achieved their aims through *disciplinary practices* such as punishment, surveillance, coercion and assessment, and which acted to control and regiment individuals. Foucault's interpreters have identified examples of these (Hiley, 1987, p. 351) including:

■ the allocation of physical space in offices or factories which establishes homogeneity and uniformity, and individual and collective identity, ranks people according to status and fixes their position in the network of social relations;

■ the standardization of individual behaviour through timetables, regimentation, work standardization and repetitive activities;

■ the 'composition of forces' where individuals become parts of larger units such as cross-functional teams or assembly-line workers;

■ job ladders and career systems which, through their future promises, encourage consent to organizational demands.

Foucault's practices are a feature of all organizations, and they shape our daily activities and interactions, controlling and regimenting us, and guaranteeing our ready compliance with the social and organizational norms and expectations established by management. They tend to be 'micro techniques' – so small and so embedded in the organization's structure that they are hardly noticed by employees. If employees do recognize them, the practices are difficult to argue against. They also contain a 'Catch 22' element. Resistance by employees to these disciplinary practices, said Foucault, merely demonstrates and reinforces the necessity for such discipline.

Where Foucault differs from Lukes is that, in his view, the drive to create these disciplinary practices does not necessarily come from the plans and intentions of specific individuals such as politicians or managers. For him, power is not equated with the domination of the powerful or the capitalist exploitation of the working class, even though it may be beneficial for both. He talks of people being trapped within a 'field of force relations', a sort of web of power which they help to create, and which is constantly being re-created by them in an ongoing way. Individuals are simultaneously both creators of that web and prisoners within it.

Within that web at the organizational level, specific disciplinary practices condition employees' thought processes, leading them to treat techniques like performance-based pay as being perfectly 'natural' and not to question them (Hardy and Clegg, 1996). That 'field of force relations' is neither stable nor inevitable. Instead, it changes as points of resistance are encountered, fissures open up, old coalitions break up and new ones are formed. It is a shifting network of alliances, not only in organizations, but in society in general (Clegg, 1989).

■ Over the last few years in Britain, many lorries and trucks have had a panel attached to their rear doors with lettering large enough to be read by following drivers. The panel reads, 'Well driven? Call 0800-22-55-33.'

■ Office stationery from a British bank (previously a building society) carries the following statement at the bottom of the page: 'To help us to improve our service we may record or monitor phone calls.'

Foucault uses the metaphor of the *panopticon* for his paradigm of disciplinary technology. The panopticon is a prison whose design allows all the inmates to be observed in their cells by one observer who remains unseen by them. The prisoners know that they cannot hide or escape from this surveillance, and that it is constant and regular, but they do not know exactly when they are being observed. The consequence is that they behave as if they are being watched. They 'self-survey' and become obedient and compliant by self-disciplining themselves.

Total Quality Management (TQM), a popular management technique of the 1990s, was launched as offering a multidisciplinary approach that empowered employees at all levels of the organization. Research by Sewell and Wilkinson (1992) into its application in the manufacturing sector suggested that it had become a modern version of the 'panopticon gaze' (Foucault, 1979). Like Buchanan and Badham's 'embedded power' and Lukes's institutionalized power, Foucault's bio-power and panopticon structure provide an ongoing, pervasive exercise of power, in which people's behaviour is constantly being controlled, but by the individuals themselves, through their own self-monitoring. Employees are watched and they watch themselves. Put another way, Foucault argues that individuals are party to their own situation. Rules are not only devised and imposed by others, but they are also accepted by them. To become subject to rules implies an acceptance of them. For him, organizations are prisons, with their processes of decision-making, information technology and human resource management only refining the process of 'capture'.

| **Stop and Criticize** | Foucault wrote about prisons, but his 'disciplinary practices' can be found in all organizations. Suggest examples of Foucault's 'disciplinary gaze' from your experience. Explain how they control your behaviour, and why it is so difficult to argue or act against them. |

Can people break free, get out and redesign this web? Sadly not, Foucault argues. He used the single term 'power/knowledge' to indicate that the two are inextricably linked. One would expect that knowledge could set people free. However, argued Foucault, the way that knowledge is constructed and represented (about what is 'normal') is, itself, dependent on the exercise of power. Knowledge therefore is not an antidote to power. On the contrary, the generation of more knowledge only offers more power to be exercised by some in order to control and manipulate others. In Foucault's view, knowledge does not emancipate, but merely perpetuates the changing web of power that subjugates people.

Buchanan and Badham (1999a, p. 221) contrast the traditional concept of power with that offered by Foucault in table 24.3. They highlight three implications of Foucault's perspective for organizations in general, and for those managers seeking to implement change within them, in particular:

1. Critically and sceptically look at so-called 'radical' changes. Are they real or cosmetic? Become aware of the continuities in organization structures and power relations (for example, just how radical is the team empowerment programme?).

2. The manager is *part* of the field of force relations and not separate or

outside it. He or she will both deploy their own power and be subject to the exercise of power. In seeking to implement change, they themselves will be changed.

3. Local points of resistance can be expected to emerge and these can be exploited by the manager.

Table 24.3: Foucault versus traditional concepts of power

Traditional concepts of power	Foucault's concepts of power
Power is possessed, is accumulated, is vested in the individual.	Power is pervasive, is a totality, is reflected in concrete practices.
Power is in the hands of social and organizational elites; resistance is futile.	Power is to be found in the micro-physics of social life; power depends on resistance.
We are subject to the domination of those who are more powerful than we are.	We construct our own web of power in accepting current definitions of normality.
Power is destructive, denies, represses, prevents, corrupts.	Power is productive, contributes to social order, which is flexible and shifting.
Power is episodic, visible, is observable in action, is deployed intermittently, is absent except when exercised.	Power is present in its absence, discreet, operating through taken-for-granted daily routines and modes of living.
Knowledge of power sources and relationships is emancipatory, can help us overcome domination.	Knowledge maintains and extends the web of power, creating further opportunities for domination.

Reprinted by permission of Sage Publications from David Buchanan and Richard Badham, *Power, Politics and Organizational Change*, Sage, London, 1999a, p. 221.

Power tactics and influencing strategies

How do individuals use their power and get others to do what they want? One definition of power is the ability 'to produce intended effects' in line with one's perceived interests (Pettigrew and McNulty, 1995). These effects can be produced in such a way that those upon whom the power is being exercised are both aware of it and may also be often resentful. Alternatively, those effects can be obtained in such a way that those being affected are unaware, are only occasionally resentful, but more often are actually grateful. We can thus distinguish two approaches – the 'power push' and the 'influencing pull'. Both see power as a property of the individual which is exercised in a relationship with other people, albeit in different ways.

Power-push

Buchanan and Badham (1999a) provide a typology of power-push tactics (table 24.4). Basing it on Gray and Starke's (1984) classification system, they add an additional category of more covert and ruthless ('dirty tricks') tactics. Their examples come from interviews and discussions with managers attending executive development programmes in Australia, Britain, Sweden and Finland. They are confident that these represent the taken-for-granted 'recipe knowledge' of many experienced managers around the world.

Table 24.4: Power tactics

Power tactic	Definition and examples
Image building	Actions which enhance reputation and further career: appropriate dress; support for the 'right' causes; adherence to group norms; air of self-confidence. ■ 'You have got to be seen to be successful at all costs' ■ 'Seek to be associated with success; seek the spotlight'
Selective information	Withhold unfavourable information from superiors; keep useful information from your competition; offer only favourable interpretations; overwhelm others with complex technical data. ■ 'Exclude others as appropriate from your plans and activities' ■ 'Withhold information and dispense misinformation to maintain control'
Scapegoating	Make sure someone is blamed; avoid personal blame; take credit for success. ■ 'Blame a predecessor' ■ 'Pick your timing to discredit people'
Formal alliances	Agree actions with key people; create a coalition strong enough to enforce its will. ■ 'Gain access to key players and information' ■ 'Seek the support and affiliation of those in power'
Networking	Make lots of friends in influential positions. ■ 'Be mobile . . . out and about, talking, networking' ■ 'Invite the "right" people to social events'
Compromise	Give in on unimportant issues to create allies for subsequent, more important issues. ■ 'Be ready to change your opinions quickly' ■ 'Decide how much you are prepared to lose'
Rule manipulation	Refuse requests on the grounds of 'against company policy' but grant identical requests from allies on the grounds of 'special circumstances'. ■ 'Ask yourself . . . what can I get away with?' ■ 'Stay clean . . . never get caught playing the game'
Other tactics	These examples do not fit under Gray and Strake's headings, and are more covert and ruthless, being concerned with political infighting. ■ 'When all else fails, do not be afraid to use coercion' ■ 'Undermine the expertise of others' ■ 'Play one person or group off against another' ■ 'Keep a "dirt file"' ■ 'Do it to them before they do it to you' ■ 'Undermine opponents through "whispers in the corridors"' ■ 'Use "subversives" to plant ideas with other managers' ■ 'Use other people to "fire the bullets"' ■ 'Trash the deal in the details; nit-picking can be an effective blocking tactic'

Reprinted by permission of Sage Publications from David Buchanan and Richard Badham, *Power, Politics and Organizational Change*, Sage, London, 1999a, pp. 27–9.

Influencing pull

This perspective also considers power as a property of the individual, which forms the basis for their **influencing**. Individuals in organizations are seen as possessing varying amounts of different types of power, as discussed earlier. The more of each power type a person has, the greater the number of influencing strategies that they can use, and the greater the likelihood of achieving a desired outcome. Moreover, the amount of power possessed is not fixed. Organizational members

Influencing: the ability to affect another's attitudes, beliefs or behaviours – seen only in its effect – without using coercion or formal position, and in such a way that influencees believe that they are acting in their own best interests.

both gain and lose power depending on what they do or fail to do, as well as what those around them do.

Following his review of the influencing literature, Andrzej Huczynski (2004) defined influencing as one person's ability to affect another's attitudes, beliefs or behaviours. Its distinguishing feature is that generally it is seen only in its effect, and is done without the use of either coercion or formal position. If performed successfully, the person being influenced – the *influencee* – will believe that they are acting in their own best interests. The ability to influence is not a mysterious gift or talent possessed only by those at the top of an organization with power. Anyone can have influence, at any level in the organization. The focus in this definition is upon *behaviour* and *action*. Changing another's attitudes, values or beliefs is only important to the extent that this affects what other people do and say. Research shows that changing a person's behaviour can lead them to change their original attitudes, values and beliefs. The arrow of causation thus points in both directions. Ultimately, influence is, of course, about getting one person to do what another wants.

Influencing is a process that will be unobservable to both the influencee and an observer. The first that influencees will know of it is when they have supported the influencer's proposal or suggestion, or have agreed to act as requested. Finally, influencing is seen as an alternative to the use of coercion or formal authority. Moreover, it is one which has long-term effects, avoids distrust and hostility and, if well executed, is not noticed. People will do things for others without knowing exactly why, but will feel good about it. Their positive feelings come from their assessment that they are primarily acting in their own best interests, helping themselves to achieve their own personal goals, rather than acting for the benefit of the influencer.

Influencing strategies

David Kipnis and his colleagues (Kipnis et al., 1984) studied how managers influenced their own managers, co-workers and subordinates. They identified seven influencing strategies: reason, friendliness, coalition, bargaining, sanctions, assertiveness and higher authority (table 24.5).

Table 24.5: Influencing strategies

Reason	Relies on the presentation of data and information as the basis for a logical argument that supports a request.
Friendliness	Depends on the influencee thinking well of the influencer.
Coalition	Mobilizing other people in the organization to support you, and thereby strengthening your request.
Bargaining	Negotiating and exchanging benefits based upon the social norms of obligation and reciprocity.
Sanctions	Positively sanctioning (rewarding) those who comply with requests, and negative sanctioning (punishing) those who do not.
Assertiveness	Making strident verbal statements, regularly reminding the influencee of your request.
Higher authority	Uses the chain of command and outside sources of power to influence the target person, appealing to, or threatening to appeal to, higher authority to gain agreement.

From D. Kipnis, S.M. Schmidt, C. Swaffin-Smith and L. Wilkinson, 'Patterns of managerial influence: shotgun managers, tacticians and bystanders', *Organizational Dynamics*, vol. 12, no. 3, Winter, 1984, pp. 58–67.

They found that among the managers they studied, the popularity of each strategy depended on the direction of their influence upwards, downwards or laterally (table 24.6).

Table 24.6: Preferred order of use of influencing strategies

Influencing up (manager)	Influencing across (co-worker)	Influencing down (subordinate)
Reason	Friendliness	Reason
Coalition	Reason	Assertiveness
Friendliness	Bargaining	Friendliness
Bargaining	Assertiveness	Coalition
Assertiveness	Higher authority	Bargaining
Higher authority	Sanctions	Higher authority
(no Sanctions)	Coalition	Sanctions

From D. Kipnis, S.M. Schmidt and L. Wilkinson, 'Intra-organizational influence tactics: explorations in getting one's own way', *Journal of Applied Psychology*, vol. 65, 1980, pp. 440–52.

Influencing style matching

Williams and Miller (2002) recommend determining who the chief decision-maker is among any group of executives, and then tailoring arguments to match that person's style. Their research is based on a study of 1,684 executives from the automotive, retail and high-tech industries. Subjects described their decision-making tendencies, which the researchers then subjected to cluster analysis. They found five predominant types.

Charismatics are easily intrigued and enthralled by new ideas, but experience has taught them to make final decisions based on balanced information, not just emotions. They are typically enthusiastic, captivating, talkative and dominant. When persuading charismatics, one should use buzzwords such as 'results', 'proven', 'actions', 'show', 'watch', 'easy', 'clear', 'focus'. Fight the urge to join in their excitement and focus instead on results. Make simple, straightforward arguments, and use visual aids to stress the features and benefits of your proposal.

Thinkers are the most difficult executives to persuade. They are impressed with arguments that are supported by data. They tend to have a strong aversion to risk and can be slow to make a decision. They are cerebral, intelligent, logical, academic. The buzzwords to use with them are 'quality', 'academic', 'think', 'numbers', 'intelligent', 'plan', 'expert', 'proof'. When persuading a thinker, have lots of data ready. Thinkers want as much information as possible, including all pertinent market research, customer surveys, case studies, cost–benefit analyses, and so on. They want to understand all perspectives of a given situation.

Sceptics tend to be highly suspicious of every data point presented, especially any information that challenges their worldview. They often have an aggressive, almost combative, style and are usually described as 'take charge' people. They are demanding, disruptive, disagreeable and rebellious. Buzzwords are 'feel', 'grasp', 'power', 'action', 'suspect', 'trust', 'demand' and 'disrupt'. When persuading a sceptic, you need as much credibility as you can garner. If you have not established enough clout with a sceptic, you need to find a way to have it transferred to you prior to or during the meeting: for example, by gaining an endorsement from someone the sceptic trusts.

Followers make decisions based on how they have made similar choices in the past or on how other trusted executives have made them. They tend to be risk-averse. Followers are responsible, cautious, brand-driven and bargain-conscious. Key buzzwords to use are 'innovate', 'expedite', 'expertise', 'similar to' and 'previous'. Followers tend to focus on proven methods – references and testimonials are big persuading factors. They need to feel certain that they are making the right decision and, specifically, that others have succeeded in similar initiatives.

Controllers abhor uncertainty and ambiguity, and they will focus on the pure facts and analysis of an argument. They are logical, unemotional, sensible, detail-oriented, accurate and analytical. Buzzwords to use include 'details', 'facts', 'reason', 'logic', 'power', 'handle', 'physical', 'grab' and 'just do it'. Your argument needs to be structured and credible. The controller wants details, but only if presented by an expert. Don't be too aggressive in pushing your proposal. Often, your best bet is simply to give him the information he needs and hope that he will convince himself.

Based on Gary A. Williams and Robert B. Miller, 'Change the way you persuade', *Harvard Business Review*, vol. 80, no. 5, May 2002, pp. 64–73.

To boldly influence . . .

In the TV and film series *Star Trek*, contact and conflict between the Federation and other species typically follow three different scenarios. In the first, like explorers during the sixteenth- and seventeenth-century age of discovery, the Federation is considerably more powerful than those in the primitive societies that they encounter. The latter treat the former as gods. This is a feature of the first series, and involves the Enterprise's crew ritually playing out the 'death of a god' as part of some religious festival. In the second scenario, the Federation is roughly equally matched with the forces of the Klingon, Romulan and Cardassian empires. The second series specializes in interstellar tensions diffused by the Federation's master diplomat-negotiator, Jean-Luc Pickard. In the third scenario, the Federation is inferior and its very existence is threatened. The first contact with the Borg falls into this category. It is a scenario shared by H.G. Wells's *War of the Worlds*. The power relationship of the Federation and the *Enterprise* to the other party affects how the conflict is resolved and what influencing strategies are employed in the stories in each series.

Based on T. Richards, *Star Trek in Myth and Legend*, Orion Books, London, 1997, p. 12.

Cohen and Bradford (1989, 1991) built on the work of Abraham Maslow, and identified a range of positive sanctions or rewards which they termed *organizational currencies*. They showed these could be used to influence others to comply with your requests:

Currencies	Examples
Resources	Lending or giving money, personnel or space
Information	Sharing specific technical or company knowledge
Advancement	Providing a task that can assist in another's promotion
Recognition	Acknowledging another's effort or achievement
Network/contacts	Providing opportunities for linking with others
Personal support	Giving personal and emotional support
Assistance	Assisting with current projects or performing unpleasant tasks for others
Co-operation	Responding quickly to requests, approving a project or aiding implementation

Stop and Criticize

How would you go about increasing your own power bases (for example, reward, coercive, referent, etc.) within your organization?

What steps would you take to reduce the power bases of those around you?

Politics in organizations

The question of whether organizations are *rational* or *political* continues to be debated. The form and nature of the assessment of the role of power and politics within organizations depends on whether or not one considers organizations to be political entities. The rationalist frame or perspective is summarized on the

Table 24.7: Rational versus political models of organization

Rational model	Political model
The goals of an organization seem obvious. Commercial organizations seek to make a profit; trade unions to protect their members' interests; schools educate their pupils; hospitals try to cure their patients, and so on.	An organizational goal can get distorted: for example, when technological leadership takes precedence over profitability. Union leaders can lose touch with their members; and schools can acquire latent functions like keeping youngsters off the labour market.
Within the company, the goals and preferences are consistent among different departments, units and members.	The idea of a single, agreed organizational goal is a fiction. Different parties have their own set of interests and priorities which change, and which may be placed ahead of those of the company as a whole.
Even if an organization's goals get distorted, the means for achieving them remain clear and rational. The organizational structure provides a rational way of achieving ends. Most firms have an organizational chart showing who is responsible for what.	Max Weber's seemingly rational organization has many dysfunctions (for example, goals are displaced, cliques develop, units compete with each other). The formal structure (chart and rules) only ever gives a partial guide to factors like leadership style, employee morale or informal group behaviour.
Information available in the company is extensive, systematic and accurate.	Ambiguous information has to be used and is withheld strategically.
Even if both aims and means get distorted, employees behave rationally when dealing with work tasks and each other.	Corporations have cultures which can distort what goes on. Culture becomes unconsciously and uncritically adopted.
Even if corporate culture can distort reality, communication can overcome this by showing clearly what is really happening.	Good communication involves more than consulting or telling people. It comes from shared goals and values. Where consensus on these is absent, communication cannot fill the gap.
Improved top-down managerial decision-making can overcome the problems listed by making choices that maximize benefits.	Perhaps the real problem is too much management control, producing low levels of employee involvement and commitment. Decisions can be the outcome of bargaining and interplays between competing interests.

Based on Michael Joseph, *Sociology for Business*, Basil Blackwell, Oxford, 1989, pp. 108–9; and Jeffrey Pfeffer, *Power in Organizations*, HarperCollins, London, 1981, p. 31.

Rationalism: the theory that reason is the foundation of certainty in knowledge.

Rationality: the use of scientific reasoning, empiricism and positivism, and the use of decision criteria of evidence, logical argument and reasoning.

left-hand side of table 24.7, while the political is described in the right-hand column. These two frames or models have different implications for how people are understood to operate within organizations, and which interests they are held to prioritize.

The rational model of organization is based on **rationalism** and **rationality**. It consists of four key elements:

1. *Reason*: A rational action is one undertaken on the basis of reason. If conduct is substantiated by one or more reasons, a person performing that action is judged to be acting rationally.

2. *Consistency*: A person adopts the same actions under the same circumstances and expresses logically consistent preferences.

3. *Empirical*: Choices are made on valid knowledge rather than on intuition, and thus knowledge is held to provide objectivity.

4. *Means–end*: Rationality is identified when appropriate means are chosen to attain the stated ends.

Rational model of organizations: a perspective which holds that behaviour within a firm is not random, but that goals are clear and choices are made on the basis of reason in a logical way. In making decisions, the objective is defined, alternatives are identified and the option with the greatest chance of achieving the objective is selected.

In the organizational context, the beliefs of the **rational model of organization** are summarized in the left-hand column of table 24.7. They are contrasted with those held by the political model, against eight key organizational characteristics. At the very heart of this perspective is the view that employees possess goals that conform to, and are compatible with, those around them. These individuals are considered to share a collective purpose that can even be called the organizational goal. All the remaining features of the model assume the existence of this goal.

For example, people's behaviour in organizations is not random or accidental, but their actions are held to be directed towards the achievement of this organizational goal. Next, rationalists argue that when making a choice, the decision-maker is guided by the norm of optimization: that is, seeking the most favourable outcome for a particular end. In this process, the various available alternatives are uncovered, their likely consequences assessed, and the risks of each considered. Finally, the course of action is selected which best meets the organizational goal which, as mentioned earlier, is held to exist and be shared by all.

Rationalists hold that this is the best way to make choices on issues such as the introduction of new technology, work organization, distribution of rewards, organization structure, and so on. However, rational writers are not only *prescriptive*, saying how, in their view, things should be done, but also claim to be descriptive: that is, they claim to be describing how decisions are actually made in real organizations.

Stop and Criticize

Suggest reasons that might account for the popularity of the rationalist view of organizations among managers, management consultants and management academics.

Political model of organization: a perspective which holds that an organization is made up of groups that have separate interests, goals and values, and in which power and influence are needed in order to reach decisions.

In contrast, there is the **political model of organization**. Rationalism has not gone unchallenged. James March (1962) was among the earliest writers to highlight that the rationalist model failed to take into account the differences of interests and objectives that existed between individuals within organizations. Indeed, March described business firms as *political coalitions*. As mentioned above, the rational model is founded on the belief that an organizational goal exists and is accepted by those in the organization.

Historically, the earliest attempts to engender a commonality of interests among employees was through the use of bureaucratic control devices such as standardized treatment for all, performance-based pay, career ladders, and rules and procedures. These were used in combination with organizational socialization processes, such as careful staff selection, induction programmes and company training courses. Together it was hoped that these would get employees to agree on a set of collective goals to which all would subscribe. In the process, the operation of individual self-interest would be eliminated. Writers such as Cyert and March (1963) argued that this attempt has failed.

The political model of organizations holds that normally there is no overarching organizational goal to which all members subscribe; that the behaviour of individuals and cliques within organizations can be explained with reference to their attempts to achieve their own unique goals; and that those who possesses the greatest amounts of power will be the most successful in furthering their interests and achieving their goals. The rational model, in contrast, asserts that individual and departmental goals typically fit into the main organizational objective.

Other researchers investigated how decisions were actually made in organizations. They discovered an absence of the use of reason, consistency, empirical data or means–end sequencing that was supposed to characterize rational organizational decision-making. In the place of consensus they found conflict and discovered decisions being made on the basis of bargaining and compromise (Allison, 1971). In the place of an organization-wide consensus on the organizational goal, they found individuals, groups, units and departments which had their own objectives, which were in conflict with each other to attain their own parochial ends, and which resolved issues through negotiation and the use of power.

These studies have led another group of writers to promote the political model of organization (Baldridge, 1971). The key characteristics of organizations, as they see them, are summarized in the right-hand column of table 24.7. Their point of departure is the view that this is no overarching organizational goal to which all members subscribe, and even where there is a written company 'mission statement', decisions are rarely made which further its achievement. This is because people's goals are considered to be inconsistent with each other. For example, the differences between management's and workers' goals were examined with the concept of the *organizational dilemma* in chapter 1.

On the question of rules and norms, the political writers hold that optimization is impossible because people disagree about goals, and hence about what constitutes the most 'appropriate action' in any given situation. In the absence of rules and norms to guide behaviour, different individuals and groups in the company attempt to achieve their own unique goals, and those who possesses the greatest amounts of power will be the most successful in furthering their interests, since power is used to overcome the resistance of others.

Stop and Criticize

Suggest reasons that might account for the relative unpopularity of the political view of organizations among managers, management consultants and management academics.

From your experience of organizations (school, club, church, company), does the rationalist or the political model best explain the behaviour of people within it?

Users of the political frame focus on who participates in the decision-making process; what determines their position with respect to issues; where their power derives from; the process by which decisions are arrived at; and how the preferences of different participants in the decision-making process are combined or resolved. Taggert and Silbey (1986) humorously contrasted the difference between

Table 24.8: Contrasting rational and political decision cycles

Conventional (rational) system cycle	Real (political) development cycle
1. Feasibility study	1. Wild enthusiasm
2. Requirements analysis	2. Disillusionment
3. Systems analysis	3. Total confusion
4. Specification	4. Search for the guilty
5. Design and development	5. Punishment of the innocent
6. Implementation	6. Promotion of non-participants

From W.M. Taggert and V. Silbey, *Informational Systems: People and Computers in Organizations*, Allyn and Bacon, Boston, MA, 1986.

Politics in organizations: those activities undertaken within an organization to acquire, develop and use power and other resources to obtain one's preferred outcomes in a situation in which there is uncertainty or an absence of consensus about choices.

the rational and the political model with respect to the implementation of computer systems within organizations. The rational cycle, shown on the left-hand side of table 24.8, stresses the logical, considered, step-by-step approach to decision-making in a company. In contrast, the political cycle, depicted on the right-hand side of the table, highlights the irrationality, chaos and power struggles used by those involved to gain advantage.

The rational and the political models of organization take a different view of the nature of organizations, and also of how the behaviour of people within them can best be explained. Rather like the *nature–nurture* debate on personality, the 'rationalists' and the 'politicals' each have their own supporters, each can provide theoretical and empirical evidence in their defence, and each is necessarily partial, not giving the full picture of what is happening. One view is neither better nor more realistic than the other. Perhaps it is best to treat the rational and political models as 'different ways of seeing' what goes on in organizations.

Political behaviour

The study of **politics**, whether inside or outside organizations, is the study of who gets what, when and how. Engaging in political behaviour or performing political acts involves individuals engaging in activities to acquire, develop, retain and use power in order to obtain their preferred outcomes in a situation where there is uncertainty or disagreement about choices. Political behaviour concerns the actions that individuals take to influence the distribution of advantages and disadvantages within their organizations (Allen et al., 1979; Farrell and Petersen, 1982).

Stop and Criticize

The main problem with political behaviour in organizations is that most people lack the necessary skills to engage in it effectively. Do you agree or disagree?

Why does political behaviour occur within organizations? Chanlat (1997) distinguishes three sets of characteristics – personal, decisional and structural – which account for such behaviour.

Personal characteristics

Organizations seek to recruit individuals who possess ambition, drive, creativity, and ideas of their own. Thus organizational recruitment, appraisal and training and promotion policies directly encourage political behaviour. For example, staff selection methods seek to identify candidates who possess the personality traits that have been related to a willingness to use power and engage in political behaviour. These are the *need for power, Machiavellianism, locus of control*, and *risk-seeking propensity* (House, 1988).

Need for power

In the 1940s, David McClelland (1961) developed a theory that people culturally acquired, that is learned, three types of need. These were **the need for power** (*n*Power), for achievement (*n*Ach) and for affiliation (*n*Aff). In any single individual the strength of these three needs varied. Some individuals had a strong desire or motive to influence and lead others, and thus were more likely to engage in political behaviour within organizations. Since a desire to control others and events, and thus to have an impact on what is going on, is often associated with effective management, it is not surprising that selectors look for this trait in candidates for managerial jobs (McClelland and Boyatzis, 1982).

McClelland and Burnham (1995) argued that an individual's strong power needs can take two forms: **personalized power** and **socialized power**.

Managers who desire personalized power:

■ exercise power impulsively;

■ are not good institution builders;

■ seek to dominate those around them;

■ seek advancement at the expense of others;

■ want their subordinates to be loyal to them, not to the organization.

Managers who want socialized power:

■ believe in the importance of centralized authority;

■ have a keen sense of justice, rewarding hard work;

■ enjoy the discipline of work and getting things done in an orderly way;

■ feel responsible for developing the organizations to which they belong;

■ seek to use it for the common good, on behalf of the organization as a whole;

■ exercise this form of power to create a good working climate for those around them;

■ help others to understand and perform their tasks, and commit them towards organizational goals.

Need for power (nPow): the desire to make an impact on others, change people or events and make a difference in life.

Personalized power: that which is self-serving and used for personal gain, influence and advancement.

Socialized power: that used for the common good, on behalf of the whole organization.

US presidents' needs for power, achievement and affiliation

President	Needs		
	Power (nPow)	Achievement (nAch)	Affiliation (nAff)
Clinton, Bill	Moderate	High	High
Bush, George	Moderate	Moderate	Low
Reagan, Ronald	High	Moderate	Low
Kennedy, John F.	High	Low	High
Roosevelt, Frank D.	High	Moderate	Low
Lincoln, Abraham	Moderate	Low	Moderate
Washington, George	Low	Low	Moderate

Based on 'Personality and charisma in the US President: a psychological study of leader effectiveness', by Robert J. House, WIlliam D. Spongler and James Woycke, published in *Administrative Science Quarterly*, vol. 36, no. 3, September 1992, by permission of *Administrative Science Quarterly*, vol. 36, no. 3 © Johnson Graduate School of Management, Cornell University.

Machiavellianism: a personality trait or style of behaviour towards others which is characterized by (1) the use of guile and deceit in interpersonal relations, (2) a cynical view of the nature of other people; and (3) a lack of concern with conventional morality.

"*I have to take one three times a day to curb my insatiable appetite for power.*"

Source: © The New Yorker Collection 1977 Dana Fradon from cartoonbank.com. All Rights Reserved.

Niccolo Machiavelli (1469–1527)

Machiavellianism

A second trait possessed by those who tend to engage in the use of power and politics in companies is termed **Machiavellianism**. Niccolo Machiavelli was a sixteenth-century Florentine philosopher and statesman who wrote a set of guidelines for rulers to use in order secure and hold governmental power. These were published in a book called *The Prince*, and suggested that the primary method for achieving power was the manipulation of others (Machiavelli, 1961). Since that time, Machiavelli's name has been turned into both an adjective and a noun, and has come to be associated with the use of opportunism and deceit in interpersonal relations. Thus we speak about people's Machiavellian behaviour or describe them as being Machiavellians.

Christie and Geis (1970) discussed Machiavellian personality characteristics. 'High-Machs' are those who score highly on a pencil-and-paper test to measure their level of Machevellianism. They would agree to statements such as:

- The best way to deal with people is to tell them what they want to hear.

- It is simply asking for trouble to trust someone else completely.

- Never tell anyone the real reason you did something unless it is useful to do so.

In behaving in accordance with Machiavellian principles, they prefer to be feared than to be liked, they manipulate others effectively using their persuasive skills, especially in face-to-face contacts, they initiate and control interactions, they use deceit in relationships, they engage in ethically questionable behaviour, and they believe that any means justify the desired ends. One might add here that a desire for revenge and retribution, especially if one has been on the receiving end of others' politicking, may be considered both acceptable and satisfying.

Locus of control

Locus of control: an individual's generalized belief about internal (self-) control versus external control (control by the situation or by others).

The third personality trait affecting the likelihood of an individual engaging in political behaviour is the **locus of control**. Some people believe that what happens to them in life is under their own control. These are said to have an internal locus of control. Others hold that their life situation is under the control of fate or other people. This group is classed as having an external locus of control (Rotter, 1966). 'Internals', those who believe that they control what happens to them, tend to be more political in their behaviour than 'externals', and are more likely to expect that their political tactics will be effective. Internals are also less likely to be influenced by others.

Risk-seeking propensity

Risk-seeking propensity: the willingness of an individual to choose options which entail risks.

The final personality trait that is likely to determine whether a person engages in political behaviour is their willingness to take risks. Engaging in political behaviour in companies is not risk-free, and there are negative as well as positive outcomes for those who do it. They could be at risk of being demoted, passed over for promotion, being given low performance assessments, and so on. Some people are natural risk-avoiders while others are risk-seekers (Madison et al., 1980; Sitkin and Pablo, 1992). Generally speaking, risk-seekers are more willing to engage in political behaviour than risk-avoiders. For the latter, the negative consequences of a failed attempt to influence outweigh the possible benefits of a successful outcome.

Possession of these personality traits is associated with a high desire for career advancement. Every organization will contain a proportion of ambitious people who compete with each other by arguing and lobbying for their personal ideas, innovations, projects and goals. However, traditional organizational structures are pyramidal or triangular in shape. That is, at each successive, higher level there are fewer positions available. Hence, these ambitious people are in constant competition with each other to secure a scarce, desirable, more senior post within the company.

Decisional characteristics

The extent to which politicking enters the decision-making process depends on the types of decision that are being made and the context of the decision-making process. Decisions vary depending on whether they are structured or unstructured. Structured decisions are programmable: that is, they can be resolved using decision rules. Routine, day-to-day decisions, such as how much stock to order, are of this type. In a standard situation, if a decision is structured or programmed, or if there is no opposition to what a manager wants to do, then it is unnecessary to use politics.

In general, however, the number of management decisions that can be reached unambiguously, using information, analysis and logical reasoning, tends to be small. Unstructured decisions are more common. These are unprogrammable and cannot be made in the way previously described, using the bureaucratic rules and procedures that Weber would have liked. Moreover, they have implications for inter-unit relationships, which is an aspect of organizational integration and is the most difficult to subject to the routinization and techno-economic rationality so beloved by rationalists (Beeman and Sharkey, 1987). In these circumstances, the competition between individuals and groups is strong, managerial discretion is high and decisions have widespread consequences for success or failure at work. Most of the significant decisions in organizations, and virtually all at senior management levels, tend to be unstructured. They cannot be based on reason and logic alone, but involve the values and preferences of key organizational members. Examples of unstructured, senior management decisions include:

- Should we seek to maximize profitability now or seek to extend our market share?

- Should we expand the internal training department or close it down and outsource training from external suppliers?

- Should we develop our expertise in this sector or take over a company that already possesses it?

Such unstructured decisions often have to be made in a period of change and uncertainty, during which an organization is unlikely to have a single, unambiguous, clearly defined objective, with which all its members agree. Such a context provides the greatest scope for political behaviour. It creates an opportunity for those who possess the appropriate political skill, knowledge and expertise to deploy them most effectively, because the usual rational arguments and empirical evidence surrounding each argument may be lacking, or because reason and 'facts' are not sufficiently compelling on their own. Who knows what the demand for the product will be in two years' time? Who knows what the costs will be of not entering the e-commerce market now?

In such circumstances, one can expect different managers with their own unique past experiences, personal opinions, differing values and current preferences to disagree. Since information, analysis and logical reasoning cannot resolve an unstructured decision, what strategy is left? In such circumstances difficult choices will be made using political means (Schilt, 1986; Drory, 1993). The managers concerned will use various tactics to gain the support of the people around the table, while deflecting the resistance of others, in order to win the debate and have their preferred course of action endorsed by the decision-making meeting. To win the competition of ideas, players will do whatever they can, within the constraints imposed by the social norms, to ensure that their ideas prevail over others. The success or failure of rivals will have an impact on their individual position, reputation and career progression, and the status of their department, section or occupational group within the organization.

Thus, political behaviour is a direct consequence of the numerical superiority of unstructured over structured decisions, which explains why it predominates in the higher levels of organizations, where such decisions tend to be made most frequently. It also emanates from the tendency of informed and interested parties to disagree with each other, partly on the interpretation of information and analyses, and partly because they hold differing, beliefs, values and preferences. As Pfeffer (1992a, p. 37) observed:

Power is more important in major decisions, such as those made at higher organizational levels, and those that involve crucial issues like reorganization and budget allocations; for domains in which performance is more difficult to assess such as staff rather than line production operations; and in instances in which there is likely to be uncertainty and disagreement.

Structural characteristics

Jeffrey Pfeffer

Organization structuring creates roles and departments which compete with each other. Jeffrey Pfeffer (1981) described how such structuring produced the conditions within organizations in which power came to be exercised and politicking engaged in (figure 24.1). Our starting point is the observation that in large organizations, tasks are divided up among a number of departments. Differentiation (1) is the term used to refer to this specialization of both departments and employees' jobs in an organization by task. This division of labour enables an organization to achieve certain economies. However, it also has a number of divisive consequences. First, it creates differences in goals (2) and understandings about what the company does, or should do, because each department is assigned its unique goal as part of the differentiation process. Marketing's task may be to maximize sales, while Production's may be to minimize costs. Such objectives are frequently in conflict. Second, different departments receive different sets of information. Marketing receives data on sales, while Production receives data on costs. This causes parochialism, with employees seeing the world through their own department's perspective.

Differentiation also causes the creation of differences in *beliefs* about how something should be done (3). Individuals can agree on a goal, yet disagree on decisions and their outcomes. They can have different views as to what are the appropriate means to achieve the stated, and perhaps agreed, ends. Individuals are physically recruited into a department, not a company. For example, the research and development (R&D) department recruits scientists, while the human resources department hires personnel specialists. The personalities and backgrounds of the staff who compose the different company departments, their socialization, training, and their way of addressing business problems, affects not only how they see their department's goals but also their beliefs and assumptions as to how these should be achieved (4).

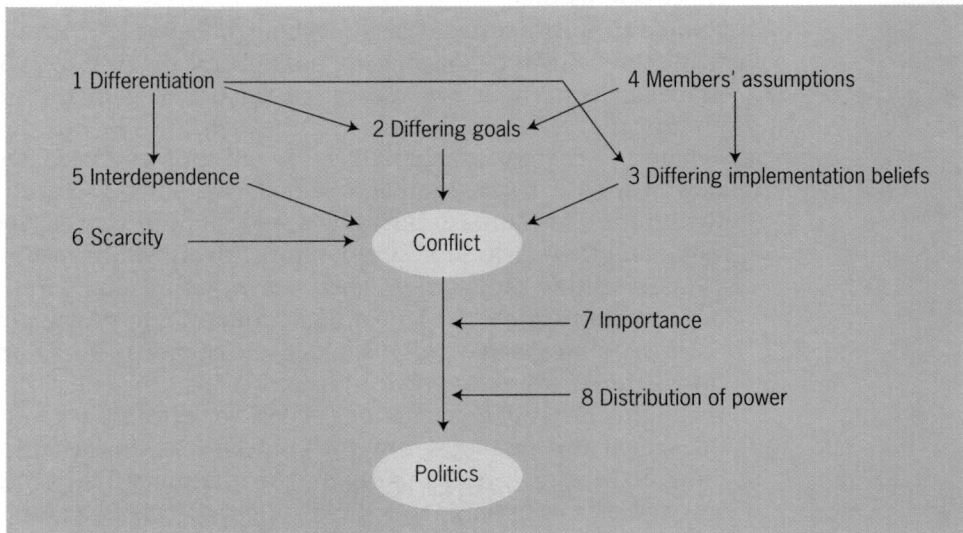

Figure 24.1: Structural conditions producing the use of power and politics in organizational decision-making

Figure, page 69, 'Structural conditions producing the use of power and politics in organizational decision making' from *Power in Organizations* by Jeffrey Pfeffer. Copyright © 1981 by Jeffrey Pfeffer. Reprinted by permission of HarperCollins Publishers Inc.

Differentiation also creates *interdependence* between people and departments, where the actions of one affect the other (5). It thus ties groups and individuals together, making each concerned with what the other does and gets in terms of resources. Scarce resources are the most valuable. Labelling a resource as scarce produces a vigorous action to obtain it, and greater dissatisfaction with its apparent unavailability (6). Gandz and Murray (1980) saw scarcity as existing in the following organizational areas: promotions and transfers, hiring; pay; budget allocation; facilities and equipment allocation; delegation of authority; interdepartmental co-ordination; personnel policies; disciplinary penalties; work appraisals; and grievances and complaints.

The combined existence of these factors can certainly lead to conflict between departments, groups and individuals, as was shown in the previous chapter. However, will these conditions inevitably result in the use of power and politicking? Pfeffer argues that they will if two further conditions are met. It depends partly on how important it is to those involved, and importance is relative (7). The exercise of power and engagement in political behaviour requires time and effort, so will tend to be reserved for the more important issues. Finally, it depends on how widely power is distributed within an organization (8). Politicking, bargaining and coalition formation only occur when power is dispersed widely and not when it is centralized at the top. Political behaviour is thus an inevitable consequence of structural differentiation (Johnson and Gill, 1993).

Power and politics in the post-modern organization

Is there more political behaviour going on within organizations now than in the past? Following a review of the change management literature of the 1950s and 1960s, Buchanan and Badham (1999b) find that it presents a picture that is virtually politics-free. This stands in sharp contrast to the organizational research and consultancy produced in the closing decades of the twentieth century. They argue that a change in organizational context, whether actual or perceived, implies a change in the behaviours required by managers and others to operate effectively in that new context. The most obvious example of this is that if an organizational context becomes more turbulent, then political skills will be required to a greater degree than if it is placid. This in turn encourages particular character types and associated behaviour to emerge and prosper: for example, Machiavellian.

However, there is another argument which they offer. This is that the political dimension has always been a perennial feature of organizations, encountered by all managers and others, even though it may not have previously featured extensively in theoretical frameworks, research papers or management handbooks. Hence, whether or not there has been a shift in substance, what has altered in Buchanan and Badham's view has been management's increased emphasis on and thinking about power and politics in organizations. Several factors in recent times may have contributed to this.

1. Widened scope of organizational change strategies
There has been a shift away from a relatively narrow concern with work design towards organization design and the development of all-embracing strategies, sometimes labelled 'organizational renewal'. This shift, combined with a frantic search for novel techniques to implement the changes, has increased the number of different individuals, groups and departments ('constituencies') affected by the proposed changes. This in turn has necessitated greater political skills when dealing with these multiple constituencies.

2. Increased organizational uncertainty

The effect of this radical organizational redesign is often to increase uncertainty, and the prevalence and significance of unstructured decisions. Organization structures become more differentiated, fragmented and fluid. Different constituencies and stakeholders come to the fore and engage in political activities to support or oppose the measures.

3. Increased competitive nature of managerial careers

Each new technique or 'management fad' (for example, teamworking or quality circles) can act as a vehicle for a manager to gain both visibility and promotion within their company or in another one. Technique 'champions' compete with each other to have their preferred approaches adopted by the company, and use political tactics to build coalitions to secure support.

4. Increased job insecurity and mobility

Threats to job security, caused partly by internal factors (for example, delayering, downsizing) and partly by external changes (for example, privatization) can generate defensive responses by employees at all hierarchical levels. Individuals also come to depend on their own resources and interpersonal skills. They create networks and interdependencies and acquire power resources to defend their positions. The traditional notion of career has been replaced by a company commitment to employability. In such circumstances, employees change their jobs, occupations and organizations more frequently, and in the process their awareness of political agendas becomes more heightened.

Buchanan and Badham (1999a) offered an idealized picture of trends through time which highlighted current preoccupations and perceived priorities, and located the topic of power and politics historically. The authors were careful to stress that this comparison of the 1960s with the 1990s was 'an exaggerated portrayal' of trends, that it was potentially an artefact of bias in the published literature, and that it was empirically untestable (table 24.9). It could be read as representing either a real shift or a *shift in perceptions* of organizational trends. Thompson and Davidson (1995) argued that the contemporary theme of 'turbulent times' was a creation of the 'pop management' literature.

Cynthia Hardy (1995) believes that the academic literature about power is diverse and confusing because it includes research from sociology, psychology, anthropology, economics and, not least, from political science. This leads to different aspects of power and politics being studied in different ways, for different reasons, by different people. The study of power has coalesced around two, unequal approaches, the rationalist and the political, which were discussed earlier. The mainstream perspective is the rationalist one (see table 24.7). It distinguishes power from authority, with the latter being defined as the right to guide or direct the actions of others and extract from them responses that are appropriate to the attainment of an organization's goals. Authority is held to be a legitimate, normal and inevitable aspect of the formal design of organizations, and managerial authority is seen as being embedded in structural and technological aspects of the formal organization. Authority is considered to be apolitical, taken-for-granted and 'functional' in the sense of contributing to the achievement of organizational goals. This rational perspective is also referred to as the *managerialist* perspective.

Having translated power into authority, the managerialist perspective then proceeds to exclude it from analysis and research. Instead, it concentrates on what it labels 'illegitimate' power. This is defined as any power which falls outside the legitimate authority that is embedded in organizational structures. Non-authority power and any associated politics are thus considered illegitimate from this point

Table 24.9: Has the ground moved?

	1960s–1970s It was all so simple then	1980s–1990s Uncertainty rules
Context factors	Job redesign, local technology and shop-floor-level change Local implementation, with predictable ripples Recruit organization members Apparent system stability Narrowly defined gains – gimme productivity	Organizational transformation, multiple levels of change Systemic, with many unpredictable ripple effects Redesign the whole activity chain Apparent system instability Broad and rapid gains – gimme speed
Technique factors	Unambiguous paradigm Clear exemplars 'Dry', unfashionable management theory Few competing fads and techniques (what's BPR?)	Competing versions of 'teamwork' Contradictory exemplars (e.g. Japanese and Scandinavian) Heathrow organization theory is 'HOT'
Moral factors	Management licence, operating behind closed doors Managing 'the voiceless' Quality of working life Managerial humanism Premium on involvement Social responsibility, ethical clarity	Guru worship (what's next?) Management visible, open to scrutiny and challenge Managing a 'culture of complaint' Competitive advantage Moral relativism Premium on exclusion Change politically charged, postmodern uncertainty and confusion

Reprinted by permission of Sage Publications Ltd from David Buchanan and Richard Badham, *Power, Politics and Organizational Change*, Sage, London, 1999a, p. 216.

of view. Writers such as Drory and Romm (1990), Gandz and Murray (1980), and Mayes and Allen (1977), reflect on this managerialist-functionalist perspective, seeing any power that is exercised by non-managers as illegitimate behaviour which is designed to promote self-interest rather than to achieve organizational goals.

The management perspective criticizes those who seek to challenge the smooth operation of the enterprise. When used by non-managers, power is seen as a political tool intended to disrupt operations. When managers use power, however, it is considered to be in self-defence, to counter such attacks. This perspective sees power as a useful and flexible resource – good when used by managers, but 'bad' when used against them. Historically, studies of managerial power have been conducted from this perspective. They have ignored questions of how power becomes embedded in an organization's structure, culture, practices, rules and regulations. Hardy believed that the functionalist perspective concentrated only on the surface aspects of power, advocating the *status quo*, hiding the way in which powerful groups in the organization maintain their dominance, and generally neglecting the way power operates to shape the lives of both employees and managers.

An alternative, albeit much less influential, approach to power views it as a means of domination, and sees resistance to power as an emancipatory tool. This political perspective is also referred to as the 'critical' or 'sociological' perspective. Originally, it examined power from the standpoint of decisions, asking who made them. Then researchers asked if the interests and grievances of certain groups were not being recognized, and were thus being excluded from the decision-making arena. Power was being exercised by excluding them, in favour of safe decisions. This process was termed 'non-decision-making' and emphasized the ability of powerful players to determine outcomes behind the scenes (Bachrach and Baratz, 1962). Next, it focused on power and non-observable conflict, noting that power holders could prevent conflict arising at all by shaping the perceptions, cognitions and preferences of the powerless. They used their power to get them to accept their positions as natural and unchangeable, and thus prevented them raising their grievances. More recently, labour process theory has studied how seemingly neutral, legitimate working arrangements – the choice of technology, the culture of the company, the shape of its formal structure – mask the means by which workers are dominated in the organization.

Much of the current debate on power and politics in organizations focuses on the work of Michel Foucault described earlier. Mary Jo Hatch (1997) argued that discussions of the political model of organization provide the beginnings of the postmodernist view emerging on organization behaviour and theory. She quotes a section from Pfeffer's *Power in Organizations* (Pfeffer, 1981, p. 14) where he raised the question of whether considering management and organization was itself a political act. She saw his comment as foreshadowing the postmodern turn towards critical and self-reflective thinking. Pfeffer wrote:

> The argument, then, is that the very literature of management and organization behaviour . . . is itself political . . . and causes support to be generated and opposition to be reduced as various conceptions of organizations are created and maintained in part through their very repetition.

The managerial functionalists, in contrast, ignore such issues, considering the formal organizational arrangements to be natural, logical and functional. Their chosen technologies, cultures and structures are treated as apolitical tools, and thus considered as neither power nor domination. To the critical writers, this represents a surface approach that misrepresents the true balance of power. It attributes too much power to subordinate groups who are castigated for using what little power they have, while hiding the way in which senior managerial power holders use the power they have, behind the scenes, to further their own positions by shaping legitimacy, values and technology and information. The functionalist-managerialist perspective essentially depoliticizes organizational life.

The overwhelming dominance of this approach in the managerial literature has, for a long time, been largely successful in eliminating the discussion of power and politics within organizations. As noted earlier, the power embedded in organizational structures and technology is not seen as power. For many years, research studies of the powerless in organizations have ceased to be fashionable. However, in Britain, since the accession of the Labour government, there has been a renewed interest in what has been labelled 'social exclusion': in particular, in persons who are excluded from social services, local government and internet access. Thus academics who wish to study 'exclusion' are more likely to be supported now than in the past. In addition, there has been publicity for the poor (as well as the powerless) who are not being paid the minimum wage, an election pledge which the Labour government has implemented.

The history of the study of power and politics in Britain reflects changing priorities and interests. During the 1970s, there was a concern about poor working conditions, and the effect of this on health and safety issues, the exploitation of individual workers and industrial relations (Beynon, 1975). As working conditions improved, interest shifted to the question of whether the 'working class' had become 'middle class' and the 'privatized' instrumental worker (Goldthorpe et al., 1968). During the 1980s, Thatcherism in Britain increased competition, and globalization in the 1990s swept aside both trade union rights and resistance on the one hand, and Dickensian working conditions (for many workers) on the other. One might argue that, as physical working conditions, and to some extent financial rewards, have generally (not universally) improved during the late twentieth century, so interest in management–employee conflict, once a major media and public concern, has waned. It is certainly the case that the literature on many management topics (total quality management, business process re-engineering, the new leadership, empowerment, teamworking) either implies or in some cases explicitly espouses the old unitarist ('we are all on the same side facing the same enemy') perspective.

Questions managers ask

Question: What's the best way of dealing with a colleague who has been just been passed over for promotion?

Answer: When they greet you in the corridor, stop, stare, and ask in a puzzled tone, 'I'm sorry, do I know you?'

From Alistair Beaton, *The Little Book of Management Bollocks*, Simon and Schuster, London, 2001.

Recap

1. *Appreciate the importance of power and politics in organizational life.*

   - Whether real or perceived, greater turbulence in the context of the organization has created increased fluidity, uncertainty, ambiguity and discontinuity, providing the ideal conditions in which power and politics can be exercised.

2. *Compare and contrast different perspectives on power.*

   - Power can be considered from the 'power-as-property', a 'faces-of-power' and a 'disciplinary power' viewpoint.

   - The 'power-as-property' viewpoint offers three perspectives, seeing power as a property of individuals, of relationships, or as an embedded property of structures.

   - The 'faces-of-power' viewpoint offers three dimensions, seeing power as overt and observable, as covert and unobservable, or as internalized by employees.

   - Disciplinary power reduces subordinates' ability to dissent by creating and managing meanings for them.

3. *List the different bases of power.*

   - The five bases of power are reward, coercion, referent, legitimate and expert.

4. *Identify organizational factors which enhance the power of departments.*

   - Factors enhancing the power of departments are dependency creation, financial resources, centrality of activities, non-substitutability and uncertainty reduction.

5. *Differentiate between power tactics and influencing strategies.*

   - Power tactics can be classified under the headings of image building, selective information, scapegoating, formal alliances, networking, compromise, rule manipulation, and covert 'dirty tricks' methods.

   - Influencing strategies include reason, friendliness, coalition, bargaining, sanctions, assertiveness and higher authority.

6. *Distinguish between the rational and political models of organization.*

   - Whereas the rational model of organizations sees behaviour in organizations as guided by clear goals and choices made on the basis of reason, the political model of organization sees no such logical behaviour. Rather, it sees organizations made up of groups possessing their own interests, goals and values, and in which power and influence are needed in order to reach decisions.

7. *Identify the characteristics of individuals most likely to engage in political behaviour.*

   - Persons most likely to engage in political behaviour have a high need for power (*n*Pow), a high Mach score, an internal locus of control and a risk-seeking propensity.

8. *Explain why politics is a feature of organizational life.*

   - The effects of differentiation, interdependence, different goals, different members' assumptions, different implementation beliefs and scarcity of resources, all create the possibility of conflict between individuals, groups and departments within an organization.

- If, in addition, the issue in dispute is important to those involved, and power is distributed unevenly within the organization, the chances of individuals engaging in political behaviour is maximized.

Revision

1. Why should every employee and manager take an interest in power and politics within their organization?

2. How can someone low down in the organizational hierarchy obtain power?

3. Are organizations rational or political entities?

4. 'Power is most potent when it is appears to be absent.' What does this statement mean? Do you agree with it? Give reasons and examples to support your view.

5. Why are some departments, units or groups in organizations more powerful than others?

Springboard

Buchanan, D. and Badham, R., 1999, *Power, Politics and Organizational Change*, Sage Publications, London.

Considers power and politics from a change management perspective, arguing that those who lead change in organizations ('change agents') also need to act as 'political entrepreneurs' if they are to succeed.

Clegg, S.R., 1989, *Frameworks of Power*, Sage Publications, London.

A classic text written by one of Britain's leading experts on the subject. Provides the basis for much subsequent theory and research.

Hardy, C. (ed.), 1995, *Power and Politics in Organizations*, Dartmouth, Aldershot.

Collection of contemporary contributions on different aspects of the topic.

Horrocks, C., 1997, *Beginner's Guide to Foucault*, Icon Books, London.

All of Foucault's writings are challenging for the introductory reader, while the 'edited highlights' and the secondary literature are not much easier. Horrocks's graphic novel therefore provides a basic starting point.

Huczynski, A.A., 2004, *Influencing within Organizations: Getting In, Rising Up and Moving On*, Routledge, London (second edition).

One of the chapters considers power and politics from an individual, careerist perspective, using theoretical and empirical research.

Johnson, P. and Gill, J., 1993, *Management Control and Organizational Behaviour*, Paul Chapman/Sage Publications, London.

Within its central themes of organizational structure, culture and power, the book considers the interaction of formally designed administrative control systems with social and self-control.

Knights, D. and Willmott, H., 1999, *Management Lives: Power and Identity in Work Organizations*, Sage Publications, London.

This is an innovative text which uses novels to explore power and politics within various organizational contexts.

Mintzberg, H., 1983b, *Power In and Around Organizations*, Prentice-Hall, Englewood Cliffs, NJ.

A major contribution from a North American perspective.

Pfeffer, J., 1992b, *Managing with Power: Politics and Influence in Organizations*, Harvard Business School Press, Boston MA (second edition).

A discussion of power and politics for a management audience by one of America's leading academic researchers and authors.

Home viewing

Contact (1997, director Robert Zemeckis) is based on a novel by Carl Sagan about Eleanor (Ellie) Arroway (played by Jodie Foster). It recounts humankind's first contact with alien life. The whole endeavour of searching for extra-terrestrial life is fraught with personal, scientific, economic, political and ethical uncertainties. While she may be an excellent scientist, Ellie is not a particularly good organizational politician. As you watch the film, answer the following questions:

1. What organizational political mistakes does Ellie make?
2. What organizational political skills do others display? Who in particular?
3. What advice would you give Ellie?

OB in literature

Paul Palmer, *Balance of Power*, Coronet Books/Hodder & Stoughton, London, 2000.

The premature death of the American President Tyler Forrester, and the discovery of evidence suggesting that he may have been corruptly accepting bribes, prompts his wife Elizabeth to investigate. The story revolves around the power bases and power plays of senior political and administrative figures and the less influential figures whom they cynically manipulate. Many political tactics are illustrated, including the use and exploitation of relationships and networks, spreading carefully timed rumours to discredit people, image manipulation, using blackmail to get 'inside' information, and removing opposition by sideways 'promotion'. Although perhaps overstated in this fictional account, these tactics are broadly typical examples of political behaviour in large complex organizations.

Chapter exercises

1: The Machiavellian personality

Objectives
1. To assess your level of Machiavellianism.

2. To allow you to identify the approach you typically use.

Briefing
Read each of the following twenty statements carefully, and tick the number at the point on the scale which most closely represents your own attitude.

Statement	Strongly agree	Agree	Neutral	Disagree	Strongly disagree
1. The best way to handle people is to tell them what they want to hear.	5	4	3	2	1
2. When you ask someone to do something for you, it is best to give the real reasons for wanting it rather than giving reasons which might carry more weight.	1	2	3	4	5
3. Anyone who completely trusts anyone else is asking for trouble.	5	4	3	2	1
4. It is hard to get ahead without cutting corners here and there.	5	4	3	2	1
5. Honesty is the best policy in all cases.	1	2	3	4	5
6. It is safest to assume that all people have a vicious streak and it will come out when given a chance.	5	4	3	2	1
7. Never tell anyone the real reason you did something unless it is useful to do so.	5	4	3	2	1
8. One should take action only when sure it is morally right.	1	2	3	4	5
9. It is wise to flatter important people.	5	4	3	2	1
10. All in all, it is better to be humble and honest than important and dishonest.	1	2	3	4	5
11. Barnum was very wrong when he said there's a sucker born every minute.	1	2	3	4	5
12. People suffering from incurable diseases should have the choice of being put painlessly to death.	5	4	3	2	1
13. It is possible to be good in all respects.	1	2	3	4	5
14. Most people are basically good and kind.	1	2	3	4	5
15. There is no excuse for lying to someone else.	1	2	3	4	5
16. Most people forget more easily the death of their father than the loss of their property.	5	4	3	2	1

17. Most people who get ahead in the world lead clean, moral lives.	1	2	3	4	5
18. Generally speaking, people won't work hard unless they are forced to do so.	5	4	3	2	1
19. The biggest difference between criminals and other people is that criminals are stupid enough to get caught.	5	4	3	2	1
20. Most people are brave.	1	2	3	4	5

Calculate your score by simply adding the numbers beside the boxes that you ticked.

Note your score here: ☐

Analysis

This personality inventory is known as 'Mach IV'. It measures how Machiavellian you are in relation to others. Your score will lie between 20 and 100.

A moderate score is around 60.
Consider yourself a Low Mach if you have a score of 45 or lower.
Consider yourself a High Mach if you have a score of 75 or higher.

The inventory was developed by Richard Christie and Florence Geiss and appears in their book (Christie and Geiss, 1970). They claim that scores are a good predictor of how we behave with other people – whether we become emotionally involved or whether we simply use others to suit our own ends.

Questions

1. Some people regard the label 'Machiavellian' as a serious insult. How do you feel about this?

2. How do you feel about your score? Do you think it is an accurate reflection of your personality?

3. Would you like to be more or less Machiavellian than you currently are? Why?

2a: Power: Who has power?

Objectives 1. To distinguish the French and Raven power bases.

2. To assess the power possessed by the 'powerful' and the 'powerless'.

Briefing On p. 862 are listed eight sets of pairs of individuals who are frequently in interaction with each other. Complete the table. For each set, indicate:

(a) What type(s) of power each individual in the pair has over the other.

(b) Which individual in the pair, on balance, has the most overall power.

(c) Which type of power is most significant in each set.

(d) Instances in which one type of power is equally divided between the two.

Set Pairs	Power				
	Reward	Coercive	Referent	Legitimate	Expert
1 Professor → student Student → professor					
2 Supermarket manager → checkout operator Checkout operator → supermarket manager					
3 Prime Minister/ President → citizens Citizens → Prime Minister/President					
4 Executive → secretary Secretary → executive					
5 Car salesperson → customer Customer → car salesperson					
6 Parent → child Child → parent					
7 Team captain → team player Team player → team captain					
8 Doctor → patient Patient → doctor					

From Ricky W. Griffin and Thomas C. Head, *Practicing Management*, Houghton Mifflin, Boston, MA (second edition), 1987.

2b: Politics: Playing the game

Objectives 1. To practise developing a politicking strategy.

Briefing Read the brief case description and decide what you would do.

You used to be the star marketing manager for Hilton Electronics Corporation, but for the past year, you have been outpaced again and again by Sean, a new manager in the design department, who has been accomplishing everything expected of him and more. Meanwhile your best efforts to do your job well have been sabotaged and undercut by Maria – your and Sean's manager. For example, prior to last year's international consumer electronics show, Maria moved £45,000 from your budget to Sean's. Despite your best efforts, your marketing team could not complete the marketing materials normally developed to showcase all your organization's new products at this important industry show. And Maria has chipped away at your staff and budget ever since. Although you have been able to meet most of your goals with less staff and budget, Maria has continued to slice away resources from your group. Just last week, she eliminated two positions in your team of eight marketing specialists to make room for a new designer and some extra equipment for Sean. Maria is clearly taking away your resources while giving Sean whatever he wants and more. You think it is time to do something or soon you will not have any team or resources left.

From Stephen p. Robbins, *Organizational Behaviour*, Pearson Education Inc, Upper Saddle River, NJ (tenth edition), 2003, p. 626.

Glossary

Accountability the obligation of a subordinate to report back on their discharge of the responsibilities which they have undertaken.

Acquisition a situation in which one firm buys the equity stake or assets of another. A major control acquisition is called a 'take-over' and may be friendly or hostile.

Action the term given to the things that people do, along with the reasons that they have for doing them.

Action research a model of OD consulting that involves the feedback of findings from interventions to help design and implement further improvements.

Action team a team that executes brief performances which are repeated under new conditions. Its members are technically specialized, and the team has a great need to co-ordinate its output with that of other work units.

Activities in Homans' theory, the physical movements and verbal or non-verbal behaviours engaged in by group members.

Adaptive decisions decisions which require human judgement based on clarified criteria and are made using basic quantitative decision tools.

Additive task a task whose accomplishment depends on the sum of all group members' efforts.

Adhocracy a type of organization design which is temporary, adaptive and creative, in contrast with bureaucracy, which tends to be permanent, rule-driven and inflexible.

Advice team a team created primarily to provide a flow of information to management to be used in its own decision-making.

Affiliation power the ability of a leader to exert influence based on the belief of followers that the leader has close association with other powerful figures on whose authority they are able to act.

Aggregate a collection of unrelated people who happen to be in close physical proximity for a short period of time.

Anchor and adjustment heuristic a predisposition to make a judgement by starting from an initial value or 'anchor', and then making adjustments from that point before making a final decision.

Arbitration a process in which a third party to a conflict has the authority to impose an agreement that is binding on the parties in conflict.

Asynchronous communication occurs when participants start a discussion topic (or thread) and post replies to each other. After delays, individuals read to catch up with the discussion. It is similar to a dialogue conducted by post.

Attribution the process by which we make sense of our environment through our perceptions of causality.

Authority the right to guide or direct the actions of others and extract from them responses that are appropriate to the attainment of an organization's goals.

Autonomous teamworking a process whereby management gives formal groups the right to make decisions on how their work is performed on a group basis without reference to management.

Autonomous work group a team of workers allocated to a significant segment of the workflow, with discretion concerning how their work will be carried out.

Availability heuristic	a predisposition of people to base their judgements of probability on the basis of information that is readily available.
Balanced scorecard	an approach to organizational effectiveness that uses a range of quantitative and qualitative measures to assess organizational performance.
Basic assumptions	invisible, preconscious and taken-for-granted understandings held by individuals with respect to aspects of human behaviour, the nature of reality and the organization's relationship to its environment.
Behaviour	the term given to the things that people do that can be directly observed.
Behaviour modification	a technique for encouraging desired behaviours and discouraging unwanted behaviours using operant conditioning.
Behavioural self-management	a technique for changing one's own behaviour by systematically manipulating cues, cognitive processes and contingent consequences.
Behavioural theory of decision-making	a theory which recognizes that bounded rationality limits the making of optimal decisions.
Behaviourism	a psychological perspective which focuses on the study of observable behaviour.
Behaviourist or stimulus–response psychology	a perspective which argues that what we learn are chains of muscle movements; mental processes are not observable, and are not valid issues for study.
Biases	a prejudiced predisposition or a systematic distortion caused by the application of heuristics.
The big five	trait clusters that appear consistently to capture main personality traits: Openness, Conscientiousness, Extraversion, Agreeableness and Neuroticism.
Bounded instability	a state in which there is a mixture of order and disorder, many unpredictable events and changes, and in which an organization's behaviour has an irregular pattern.
Bounded rationality	individuals making decisions by constructing simplified models that extract the essential features from problems without capturing all their complexity.
Brainstorming	a technique in which all group members are encouraged to propose ideas spontaneously, without critiquing or censoring others' ideas. The alternative ideas so generated are not evaluated until all have been listed.
Bureaucracy	the legal-rational type of authority. It is a form of organization structure that is characterized by a specialization of labour, a specific authority hierarchy, a formal set of rules, and a rigid promotion and selection criteria.
Business process re-engineering	the radical redesign of work activities to achieve dramatic improvements in critical measures of performance.
Caution shift phenomenon	the tendency of a group to make decisions that are more risk averse than those which the members of the group would have recommended individually before.
Centralization	the concentration of authority and responsibility for decision-making power in the hands of managers at the top of an organization's hierarchy.
Certainty	a condition in which managers possess full knowledge of alternatives; have a high probability of these being available; can calculate the costs and benefits of each alternative; and have high predictability of outcomes.
Chain (or line) of command	the unbroken line of authority that extends from the top of the organization to the bottom and clarifies who reports to whom.
Change agent	any member of an organization seeking to promote, further, support, sponsor, initiate, implement or help to deliver change.
Characteristics of mass production	these include the mechanical pacing of work, no choice of tools or methods, repetitiveness, minute subdivision of product, minimum skill requirements and surface mental attention.

Charismatic authority	authority that is based on the belief that the ruler has some special, unique virtue, either religious or heroic. Religious prophets, charismatic politicians and pop and film stars all wield this type of power.
Classical decision theory	a theory which assumes that decision-makers are objective, have complete information and consider all possible alternatives and their consequences before selecting the optimal solution.
Coding	the stage in the interpersonal communication process in which the transmitter chooses how to express a message for transmission to someone else.
Coercive power	the ability of a leader to exert influence based on the belief of followers that the leader can administer unwelcome penalties or sanctions.
Cognitive or information processing psychology	a perspective which argues that what we learn are mental structures; mental processes are amenable to study even though they cannot be observed.
Cognitive psychology	a perspective which accepts as legitimate the study of internal mental states and processes, even though they are not directly observable.
Communication climate in an organization	the prevailing atmosphere, open or closed, in which ideas and information are exchanged.
Communication network analysis	a technique that uses direct observation to determine the source, direction and quantity of verbal communication between congregated members of a group.
Communication pattern analysis	a technique that uses analysis of documents, data and voice mail transmission to determine the source, direction and quantity of verbal and written communication between the dispersed members of a group.
Communication pattern chart	the source, direction and quantity of verbal and written communication between the dispersed members of a group.
Communication process	the transmission of information, and the exchange of meaning, between at least two people.
Communigram	a chart that indicates the source, direction and quantity of verbal communication between the congregated members of a group.
Compensatory mechanisms	processes that delay or deflect replacement effects, and which can lead to the creation of new products and services, new organizations and new jobs through technological innovation.
Complementarities	the potential for mutually reinforcing effects when one or more business practices are operated in parallel or simultaneously. Practices are said to be complementary when doing more of one increases the returns for doing more of another.
Compliance	a majority's influence over a minority.
Concertive control	control that is exercised by the workers themselves, who collaborate to develop the means of their own control by negotiating a consensus which shapes their own behaviour according to a set of core values such as those of the corporate vision statement.
Concurrent feedback	information which arrives during our behaviour and which can be used to control behaviour as it unfolds.
Configuration	the structures, processes, relationships and boundaries through which an organization operates.
Conflict	a process which begins when one party perceives that another party has negatively affected, or is about to negatively affect, something the first party cares about.

Conflict resolution	a process which has as its objective the ending of the conflict between the disagreeing parties.
Conflict stimulation	the process of engendering conflict between parties where none existed before, or escalating the current conflict level if it is too low.
Conformity	a change in belief or behaviour in response to real or imagined group pressure when there is no direct request to comply with the group or any reason to justify the behaviour change.
Conjunctive task	a task whose accomplishment depends on the performance of the group's least talented member.
Consideration	a pattern of leadership behaviour that demonstrates sensitivity to relationships and to the social needs of employees.
Consolidation	the process through which company ownership in a sector becomes concentrated in a smaller number of much larger and sometimes global enterprises.
Contingency approach to organization structure	a perspective which argues that an organization, to be effective, must adjust its structure in a manner consistent with the main type of technology it uses, the environment within which it operates, its size and other contextual factors.
Contingency theory of leadership	a perspective which argues that leaders must adjust their style in a manner consistent with aspects of the context.
Control concept	the process of imposing a pattern on previously haphazard activities, such as the operation of machinery, the interaction of machinery with people or the interactions between individuals.
Controlled performance	setting standards, measuring performance, comparing actual with standard, and taking corrective action if necessary.
Conversion	a minority's influence on a majority.
Coping cycle	a human emotional response to trauma and loss, suggesting that individuals typically experience first denial, then anger, bargaining, depression and finally acceptance.
Cross-functional team	a team composed of employees from about the same hierarchical level but from different work areas or functional in the organization, who are brought together to complete a particular task.
Cybernetic analogy	a perspective which seeks to explain the learning process with reference to the components and operation of a feedback control system.
Death of distance	geographical separation no longer determines the costs or difficulties of global, corporate and person-to-person communication.
Decentralization	authority and responsibility for decision-making being dispersed more widely downwards and given to the operating units, branches and lower-level managers.
Decision-making	the process of making choices from among several options.
Decoding	the stage in the interpersonal communication process in which the recipient interprets a message transmitted to them by someone else.
Deconstruction	the process of (1) identifying the assumptions underpinning arguments about 'reality', (2) challenging those assumptions, and (3) asking whose interests are served by representing 'the truth' in that way.
Deindividuation	an increased state of anonymity that loosens normal constraints on individuals' behaviour, reducing their sense of responsibility, and leading to an increase in impulsive and antisocial acts.

Delayed feedback   information which is received after a task is completed, and which can be used to influence future performance.

Departmentalization   the process of grouping together employees who share a common supervisor and resources, who are jointly responsible for performance, and who tend to identify and collaborate with each other.

Dependent variable   the factor whose behaviour is to be explained in terms of how it depends on some other factor (see **independent variable**).

Descriptive models of decision-making   models which investigate how individuals actually make decisions.

Differentiation   the degree to which the tasks and the work of individuals, groups and units are divided up within an organization.

Differentiation perspective   a view which regards an organization as consisting of sub-cultures. Each represents a fenced-in island of localized consensus, beyond which ambiguity reigns.

Disjunctive task   a task whose accomplishment depends on the performance of the group's most talented member.

Distributive bargaining   a negotiation strategy in which a fixed sum of resources is divided up. It leads to a win–lose situation between the parties.

Double-loop learning   the ability to challenge and to redefine the assumptions underlying performance standards and to improve performance.

Drives   the innate, biological determinants of behaviour, activated by deprivation.

Dysfunctional conflict   a form of conflict which does not support organization goals and hinders organizational performance.

Emotional intelligence   the ability to identify, integrate, understand and reflectively manage one's own and other people's feelings.

Emotional labour   the act of expressing emotion which contributes to organizational goals, which is required to be performed by employees and which typically boosts the self-esteem of its recipient.

Employment cycle   the sequence of stages through which all employees pass in each working position they hold, from recruitment and selection to termination.

Empowerment   a general term describing organizational arrangements that give employees more autonomy, discretion and unsupervised decision-making responsibility.

Enacted environment   the environment of an organization that exists for members by virtue of the interpretations they make of what is occurring 'outside' the organization, and the way their own actions influence or shape those occurrences.

Encounter stage of socialization   the period of learning in the process during which the new recruit learns about organizational expectations.

Environment of an organization   the issues, trends and events outside the boundaries of the organization which influence internal decisions and behaviours.

Environmental complexity   the range of external factors relevant to the activities of the organization; the more factors, the higher the complexity.

Environmental determinism   a perspective which claims that internal organizational responses are wholly or mainly shaped, influenced or determined by external environmental factors.

Environmental dynamism   the pace of change in relevant factors external to the organization; the greater the pace of change, the more dynamic the environment.

Environmental scanning   a term for a number of techniques for identifying and predicting the potential impact of external trends and developments on the internal functioning of an organization.

Environmental uncertainty the degree of unpredictable turbulence and change in the external political, economic, social, technological, legal and ecological context in which an organization operates; the more the dimensions of the external context are interrelated, the higher the environmental uncertainty.

Equity theory a process theory which argues that perception of unfairness leads to tension, which then motivates the individual to resolve that unfairness.

Escalation of commitment an increased commitment to a previously made decision, despite negative information suggesting one should do otherwise.

Expectancy the perceived probability that effort will result in good performance, and is measured on a scale from 0 (no chance) to 1 (certainty).

Expectancy theory a process theory which argues that individual motivation depends on the **valence** of outcomes, the **expectancy** that effort will lead to good performance, and the **instrumentality** of performance in producing valued outcomes.

Expert power the ability of a leader to exert influence based on the belief of followers that the leader has superior knowledge relevant to the situation and the task in hand.

Explanatory models of decision-making models which seek to account for decisions made by individuals, groups and organizations.

Explicit knowledge knowledge and understanding which is codified, clearly articulated and available to anyone.

Explosive instability a state in which there is no order or pattern.

External work team differentiation the degree to which a work team stands out from its organizational context, in terms of its membership, temporal scope and territory.

External work team integration the degree to which a work team is linked with the larger organization of which it is a part. It is measured in terms of how its goals and activities are co-ordinated and synchronized with those of other managers, peers, customers and suppliers.

Extinction the attempt to eliminate undesirable behaviours by attaching no consequences, positive or negative, such as indifference and silence.

Extrinsic feedback information which comes from our environment, such as the visual and aural information needed to drive a car.

Extrinsic motivation a form of motivation that stresses valued outcomes or benefits provided by others, such as promotion, pay increases, a bigger office desk, praise and recognition.

Extrinsic rewards valued outcomes or benefits provided by others, such as promotion, pay increases, a bigger office desk, praise and recognition.

Feedback (in the context of learning) information concerning the outcomes of our behaviour.

Feedback (in the context of interpersonal communication) the processes through which the transmitter of a message detects whether and how that message has been received and decoded.

Force field analysis a technique for assessing the balance of factors that respectively encourage and resist movement towards a desired target situation.

Fordism the application of scientific management principles to workers' jobs; the installation of single-purpose machine tools to manufacture standardized parts; and the introduction of the mechanized assembly line.

Formal group	one which has been consciously created to accomplish a defined part of an organization's collective purpose. The formal group's functions are the tasks which are assigned to it, and for which it is officially held responsible.
Formal organization	the collection of work groups that has been consciously designed by senior management to maximize efficiency and achieve organizational goals.
Formal status	a collection of rights and obligations associated with a position, as distinct from the person who may occupy that position.
Formalization	the degree to which formal procedures and rules exist and are used within an organization.
Fragmentation (conflict) perspective of culture	a view which regards an organization as consisting of a loosely structured and incompletely shared system that emerges dynamically as cultural members experience each other, events and the organization's contextual features.
Functional conflict	a form of conflict which supports organization goals and improves performance.
Functional foremanship	an approach devised by Frederick Taylor in which the job of the general foreman was divided into its constituent parts. Each of the main parts was given to a different individual who would oversee and be responsible for that aspect of a worker's job.
Functional relationship	a situation where staff department specialists have the authority to insist that line managers implement their instructions concerning a particular issue.
Future shock	the stress and disorientation suffered when people are subjected to excessive change.
Generalized other	what we understand other people expect of us, in terms of our attitudes, values, beliefs and behaviour.
Globalization	the intensification of worldwide social and business relationships which link distant localities in such a way that local happenings are shaped by distant events, and vice versa.
Goal-setting theory	a process theory which argues that work motivation is influenced by goal difficulty, goal specificity and knowledge of results.
Great man theory	a historical perspective which argues that the fate of societies and organizations is in the hands of powerful, idiosyncratic (male) individuals.
Grid Organizational Development	an organization-wide diagnostic approach to the development of effective management style based on a structured, six-phase change model.
Group cohesion	the number and strength of mutual, positive attitudes towards group members.
Group leadership	the performance of those acts which help the group achieve its objectives.
Group norms	expected modes of behaviour and beliefs that are established either formally or informally by a group. Norms guide behaviour and facilitate interaction by specifying the kinds of reaction that are expected or acceptable in a particular situation.
Group polarization	this occurs when individuals in a group begin by taking a moderate stance on an issue related to a common value and, after having discussed it, end up taking a more extreme decision than the average members' decisions. The extremes could be more risky or more cautious.
Group power	the ability of a leader to exert influence based on the belief of followers that the leader has collective support from a team or group.
Group process	the patterns of interactions between the members of a group.
Group relations	the interactions within and between groups, and the stable arrangements that result from them.

Group sanction	both punishments and rewards given by members to others in the group in the process of enforcing group norms. Punishments are a negative sanction and rewards are a positive sanction.
Group self-organization	the tendency of groups to form interests, develop autonomy and establish identities.
Group socialization	the process whereby members learn the values, symbols and expected behaviours of the groups to which they belong.
Group structure	the relatively stable pattern of relationships among different group members. There is no single group structure and the concept can be expressed in several and overlapping ways.
Groupthink	a mode of thinking that people engage in when they are deeply involved in a cohesive in-group, when the members' strivings for unanimity override their motivation to appraise realistically the alternative courses of action.
Growth Need Strength	a measure of the readiness and capability of an individual to respond positively to job enrichment.
Habituation	the decrease in our perceptual response to stimuli once they have become familiar.
Halo effect	a judgement based on a single, striking characteristic, such as an aspect of dress, speech, posture or nationality.
Hard HRM	a human resource management perspective which emphasizes the full utilization of employees in a formal, calculating and dispassionate manner, to be treated in a manner similar to any other resources available to the organization.
Hawthorne Effect	the tendency of people being observed, as part of a research effort, to behave differently than they otherwise would.
Heuristics	simple and approximate rules, guiding procedures, shortcuts or strategies that are used to solve problems.
Hierarchy	the number of levels of authority to be found in an organization.
High-context culture	a culture in which people tend to rely heavily on a range of social and non-verbal clues when communicating with others and interpreting their messages.
High-performance work system	a form of organization that operates at levels of excellence far beyond those of comparable systems.
Human-centred manufacturing	the design of production technologies in a way that complements human skills and abilities, rather than distances or replaces them.
Human Relations approach	a school of management thought which emphasizes the importance of social processes at work.
Human resource management	a managerial perspective which argues the need to establish an integrated series of personnel policies to support organization strategy.
Hygiene factors	aspects of work which remove dissatisfaction but do not contribute to motivation and performance, including pay, company policy, supervision, status, security and working conditions.
Identification	the incorporation of the thoughts, feelings and actions of others into one's self-esteem or to reduce the threat from powerful others. Typically, it takes the form of 'I want'.
Idiographic approach to the study of personality	the uniqueness of the individual, rejecting the assumption that we can all be measured on the same dimensions.
Impression management	the process whereby people seek to control the image others have of them.
Independent variable	the factor which is manipulated by the researcher to discover what effect this has on another factor or variable (see **dependent variable**).

Individualism–collectivism	the tendency to take care of oneself and one's family versus the tendency to work together for the collective good.
Influencing	the ability to affect another's attitudes, beliefs or behaviours – seen only in its effect – without using coercion or formal position, and in a way that influencees believe that they are acting in their own best interests.
Informal group	a collection of individuals who become a group when members develop interdependencies, influence one another's behaviour and contribute to mutual need satisfaction.
Informal organization	the network of relationships that spontaneously establish themselves between members of an organization on the basis of their common interests and friendships.
Information power	the ability of a leader to exert influence based on the belief of followers that the leader has access to information that is not public knowledge.
Initiating structure	a pattern of leadership behaviour that emphasizes performance of the work in hand and the achievement of product and service goals.
Initiative and incentive system	a form of job design practice in which workers are given a task to perform by management who also provide them with a financial incentive. Workers are then left to use their initiative as to how to complete the task and which tools to use.
Innovative decisions	decisions which address novel problems, lack pre-specified courses of action and are made by senior managers.
Instrumental orientation to work	an attitude that sees work as an instrument to the fulfilment of other goals.
Instrumentality	the perceived probability that good performance will lead to valued rewards, measured on a scale from 0 (no chance) to 1 (certainty).
Integration	the required level to which units in an organization are linked together, and their respective degree of independence. Integrative mechanisms include rules and procedures and direct managerial control.
Integration (or unitary) perspective	a view which regards culture as monolithic, characterized by consistency, organization-wide consensus and clarity. It holds that these integrating features will lead to improved organization effectiveness through greater employee commitment and employee control, as measured by productivity and profitability.
Integrative bargaining	a negotiation strategy that seeks to increase the total amount of resources. It creates a win–win situation between the parties.
Intensive technology	technology that is applied to tasks that are performed in no predetermined order.
Interaction process analysis	a technique used to categorize the content of speech.
Interactionist frame of reference on conflict	a perspective on conflict which sees it as a positive and necessary force within organizations that is essential for their effective performance.
Interactions	in Homans' theory, the two-way communications between group members.
Intergroup development	an OD intervention to change the perceptions and attitudes that different groups hold with respect to each other, and improve their interaction and collaboration.
Intermittent reinforcement	the procedure whereby a reward is provided only occasionally following correct responses, and not for every correct response.
Internal work team differentiation	the degree to which a team's members possess different skills and knowledge that contribute towards the achievement of the team's objective.

Intrinsic feedback	information which comes from within, from the muscles, joints, skin, and other mechanisms such as that which controls balance.
Intrinsic motivation	a form of motivation that stresses valued outcomes or benefits that come from within the individual, such as feelings of satisfaction, competence, self-esteem and accomplishment.
Intrinsic rewards	valued outcomes or benefits which come from the individual, such as feelings of satisfaction, competence, self-esteem and accomplishment.
Introjection	formerly external regulation or value that has been 'taken in' and is now enforced through internal pressures such as guilt, anxiety or related self-esteem dynamics.
Japanese teamworking	teamworking that uses scientific management principles of 'minimum manning, multi-tasking, multi-machine operation, pre-defined work operations, repetitive short-cycle work, powerful first-line supervisors and a conventional managerial hierarchy.
Job definition	the task requirements of each job in the organization; it is the first decision in the process of organizing.
Job description (or post profile)	a summary statement of what an individual should do on the job.
Job Diagnostic Survey	a questionnaire designed to assess the degree of skill variety, task identity, task significance, autonomy and feedback in jobs.
Job enlargement	a work design method in which tasks are recombined to widen the scope of a job.
Job enrichment	a technique for broadening the experience of work to enhance employee need satisfaction and to improve work motivation and performance.
Job rotation	a work design method in which employees are switched from task to task at regular intervals.
Joint venture	an arrangement in which two or more companies remain independent but establish a new organization that they jointly own and manage.
Just-in-time systems	methods of managing inventory (stock) in which items are delivered when they are needed in the production process instead of being stored by the manufacturer.
Knowledge management	the conversion of individual tacit knowledge into explicit knowledge so that it can be shared with others in the organization.
Leadership	the process of influencing the activities of an organized group in its efforts towards goal-setting and goal achievement.
Lean production	an approach which combines machine-pacing, work standardization, just-in-time materials flow, continuous improvement, problem-solving teams and powerful supervision.
Learning	the process of acquiring knowledge through experience which leads to an enduring change in behaviour.
Learning organization	an organizational form that enables individual learning to create valued outcomes, such as innovation, efficiency, environmental alignment and competitive advantage (Huysman, 1999, p. 61)
Least preferred coworker score	an assessment of the kind of person with whom a leader feels they could not work effectively.
Legitimate authority	authority that is based on formal, written rules which have the force of law. The authority of present-day presidents, chief executive officers and cardinals is based on the position that they hold.
Legitimate power	the ability of a leader to exert influence based on the belief of followers that the leader has authority to issue orders which they in turn have an obligation to accept.
Line employees	those workers who are directly responsible for manufacturing goods or providing a service.

Locus of control	an individual's generalized belief about internal (self-) control versus external control (control by the situation or by others).
Long-linked technology	technology that is applied to a series of programmed tasks performed in a predetermined order.
Long-term–short-term orientation (Confusion dynamism)	the ability to pursue long-term and general goals versus short-term gain and advantage.
Low-context culture	a culture in which people tend to focus on the written and spoken word when communicating with others and interpreting their messages.
Machiavellianism	a personality trait or style of behaviour towards others which is characterized by (1) the use of guile and deceit in interpersonal relations, (2) a cynical view of the nature of other people and (3) a lack of concern with conventional morality.
Machine bureaucracy	a type of organization which possesses all the bureaucratic characteristics. The important decisions are made at the top, while at the bottom standardized procedures are used to exercise control.
Managerial enactment	the active modification of perceived and selected parts of the organization's environment by managers.
Masculinity–femininity	the extent to which highly assertive masculine values predominate (acquisition of money at the expense of others) versus showing sensitivity and concern for others' welfare and the quality of life.
Material technology	the tools, machinery and equipment that can be seen, touched and heard.
Matrix structure	a type of organization design that combines two different, traditional types of structure, usually a functional structure and a project structure, which results in an employee being part of both a functional department and a project team, and, in consequence, having two reporting relationships.
Maximizing	a decision-making approach where all alternatives are compared and evaluated in order to find the best solution to a problem.
McDonaldization	an approach to work organization based on efficiency, calculability, predictability and control, using sophisticated technology to enhance these objectives by limiting employee discretion and creativity.
Mechanistic structure	a type of organization structure which possesses a high degree of task specialization, many rules, and tight specification of individual responsibility and authority, and in which decision-making is centralized.
Mediating technology	technology that links independent but standardized tasks.
Mediation	a process in which a neutral third party to the conflict assists in the achievement of a negotiated solution by using reason, persuasion and the presentation of alternatives.
Merger	a situation in which two companies voluntarily join together, pooling the ownership interests of the two sets of shareholders to own the new combined entity.
Metamorphosis stage of socialization	the period in which the new employee adjusts to their organization's values, attitudes, motives, norms and required behaviours.
Motivating Potential Score	an indicator of how motivating a job is likely to be for an individual, considering skill variety, task identity, task significance, autonomy and feedback.
Motivation	the cognitive, decision-making process through which goal-directed behaviour is initiated, energized, and directed and maintained.

Motivator factors	aspects of work which lead to high levels of satisfaction, motivation and performance, including achievement, recognition, responsibility, advancement, growth and the work itself.
Motives	socially acquired needs activated by a desire for their fulfilment.
Need for achievement (nAch)	a general concern with meeting standards of excellence; the desire to be successful in competition; the motivation to excel.
Need for power (nPow)	the desire to make an impact on others, change people or events and make a difference in life.
Negative reinforcement	the attempt to encourage desirable behaviours by withdrawing negative consequences when the desired behaviour occurs.
Network organization	a collection of essentially equal agents or agencies which are in informal relationships with each other based on affiliation.
New leader	an inspirational visionary, concerned with building a shared sense of purpose and mission, creating a culture in which everyone is aligned with the organization's goals and is skilled and empowered to achieve them.
Noise	factors extraneous to the communication process which interfere with or distract attention from the transmission and reception of the intended meaning.
Nomothetic approach to the study of personality	the identification of traits; an approach that looks for systematic relationships between different aspects of personality.
Non-verbal communication	the process of coding meaning through behaviours such as facial expressions, limb gestures and body postures.
Norms	expected modes of behaviour.
Obedience	a situation in which individuals change their behaviour in response to directions from others.
OD intervention	a technique used to effect change in the target organization or section of the organization to improve organizational effectiveness.
Open system	a system that interacts, in a purposive way, with its external environment in order to survive.
Operational definition	the method used to measure the incidence of a variable in practice.
Organic structure	a type of organization structure possessing little task specialization, few rules and a high degree of individual responsibility and authority, and in which decision-making is delegated.
Organization	a social arrangement for achieving controlled performance in pursuit of collective goals.
Organization chart	a pictorial record which shows the formal relations which the company intends should prevail within it.
Organization development	a systematic process in which applied behavioural science principles and practices are introduced towards the goals of increasing individual and organizational effectiveness.
Organization structure	the formal system of task and reporting relationships that controls, co-ordinates and motivates employees so that they work together to achieve organizational goals.
Organizational behaviour	the study of the structure, functioning and performance of organizations, and the behaviour of groups and individuals within them.
Organizational choice	the argument that work design is not determined by technology, that the technical system does not determine the social system.

Organizational culture	the collection of relatively uniform and enduring values, beliefs, customs, traditions and practices that are shared by an organization's members, learned by new recruits, and transmitted from one generation of employees to the next.
Organizational dilemma	the question of how to reconcile potential inconsistency between individual needs and aspirations on the one hand and the collective purpose of the organization on the other.
Organizational effectiveness	a multidimensional concept defined differently by different stakeholders, using a range of quantitative and qualitative measures.
Organizational misbehaviour	anything that workers do in the workplace which they are not supposed to do.
Organizational socialization	the process through which an individual's pattern of behaviour and their values, attitudes and motives are influenced to conform with those seen as desirable in a particular organization.
Organizational values	those things that have personal or organizational worth or meaning to the founders or senior management. Values are typically based on moral, societal or religious precepts that are learned in childhood and modified through experience.
Outsourcing	a situation in which an organization sub-contracts to another supplier work that it was previously performing in-house.
Pavlovian conditioning (also known as classical and as respondent conditioning)	a technique for associating an established response or behaviour with a new stimulus.
Perception	the dynamic psychological process responsible for attending to, organizing and interpreting sensory data.
Perceptual filters	individual characteristics, predispositions and preoccupations that interfere with the effective transmission and receipt of messages.
Perceptual organization	the process through which incoming stimuli are organized or patterned in systematic and meaningful ways.
Perceptual set	an individual's predisposition to respond to people and events in a particular manner.
Perceptual world	the individual's personal internal image, map or picture of their social, physical and organizational environment.
Peripheral norms	socially defined standards relating to behaviour and beliefs which are important but not crucial to a group's objective and survival.
Personality	the psychological qualities that influence an individual's characteristic behaviour patterns in a stable and distinctive manner.
Personalized power	that which is self-serving and used for personal gain, influence and advancement.
Personnel management	the specialist management function which determines and implements policies and procedures which affect the stages of the employment cycle.
PESTLE analysis	identifying the Political, Economic, Social, Technological, Legal and Ecological factors affecting an organization.
Phenomenology	a social scientific perspective which assumes that the social world has no external, objective, observable truth, and that reality is socially constructed.
Pivotal norms	socially defined standards relating to behaviour and beliefs which are central to a group's objective and survival.
Pluralist frame of reference on conflict	a perspective which views organizations as consisting of different, natural interest groups, each with its own potentially constructive, legitimate interests, which make conflict between them inevitable.

Political model of organization	a perspective which holds that an organization is made up of groups that have separate interests, goals and values, and in which power and influence are needed in order to reach decisions.
Politics in organizations	those activities undertaken within an organization to acquire, develop and use power and other resources to obtain one's preferred outcomes in a situation in which there is uncertainty or an absence of consensus about choices.
Positive reinforcement	the attempt to encourage desirable behaviours by introducing positive consequences when the desired behaviour occurs.
Positivism	a social scientific perspective which assumes that the properties of the social world can be studied using objective methods.
Post-modern organization	a networked, information-rich, delayered, downsized, boundary-less, high-commitment organization employing highly skilled, well-paid, autonomous knowledge workers.
Postmodernism	a mode of thinking which focuses on the way in which language is used symbolically and selectively to construct versions of 'truth' and 'reality' to serve the interests of particular social groupings.
Power	the capacity of individuals to overcome resistance on the part of others, to exert their will and to produce results consistent with their interests and objectives.
Power–distance	the extent to which an unequal distribution of power is accepted by members of a society.
Pre-arrival stage of socialization	the period of learning in the process that occurs before an applicant joins an organization.
Predictive validity	the extent to which scores on an assessment or test accurately predict behaviours such as job performance.
Prescriptive models of decision-making	models which recommend how individuals should behave in order to achieve a desired outcome.
Process consultation	an OD intervention in which an external consultant acts in a facilitating and catalytic capacity to enhance an organization's diagnostic, conceptual and action planning skills.
Processual/ contextual theory	a perspective claiming that it is necessary to understand how the substance, context and process of organizational change interact to generate the observed outcomes.
Production team	a stable number of individuals in a relationship involving shared and recognized production goals, with work status defined through a system of social roles and behavioural norms supported by a set of incentives and sanctions.
Professional bureaucracy	a type of organization which possesses all the bureaucratic characteristics. In addition, there are few levels between the strategic apex and the operating staff, control of which is achieved through professional indoctrination.
Project team	a collection of employees from different work areas in an organization brought together to accomplish a specific task within a finite time.
Projective test	an assessment based on abstract or ambiguous images, which the subject is asked to interpret by projecting feelings, preoccupations and motives into their responses.
Psychological contract	an implicit set of obligations and expectations concerning what the individual and the organization expect to give to and receive from each other.
Psychological group	two or more people in face-to-face interaction, each aware of their membership in the group, each aware of the others who belong to the group, and each aware of their positive interdependence as they strive to achieve their goals.
Psychometrics	the systematic testing, measurement and assessment of intelligence, aptitudes and personality.

Punishment	the attempt to discourage undesirable behaviours through the application of negative consequences, or by withholding a positive consequence, following the undesirable behaviour.
Quality circles	groups of shop-floor employees from the same department, who meet for a few hours each week to discuss ways of improving their work environment.
Radical frame of reference on conflict	a perspective which views (organizational) conflict as an inevitable consequence of exploitative employment relations in a capitalist economy.
Rational decisions	choices based on rationality: that is, on a rational mode of thinking.
Rational economic model	a method which assumes that decision-making is, and should be, a rational process consisting of a sequence of steps that enhance the probability of attaining a desired outcome.
Rational model of organization	a perspective which holds that behaviour within a firm is not random, but that goals are clear and choices are made on the basis of reason in a logical way. In making decisions, the objective is defined, alternatives are identified and the option with the greatest chance of achieving the objective is selected.
Rationalism	the theory that reason is the foundation of certainty in knowledge.
Rationality	the use of scientific reasoning, empiricism and positivism, and the use of decision criteria of evidence, logical argument and reasoning.
Readiness for change	a predisposition to welcome and embrace change.
Referent power	the ability of a leader to exert influence based on the belief of followers that the leader has desirable abilities and personality traits that can and should be copied.
Reliability	the degree to which an assessment or test produces consistent results when repeated.
Replacement mechanisms	processes through which intelligent machines are used to substitute for people in work organizations, leading to unemployment.
Representative heuristic	a predisposition of people to base their judgements of probability on the basis of things with which they are familiar.
Resistance	more or less covert behaviour which counteracts and restricts management attempts to exercise power and control in the workplace.
Resistance to change	an inability or an unwillingness to discuss or to accept changes that are perceived to be damaging or threatening to the individual.
Responsibility	an obligation placed on a person who occupies a certain position in the organization structure to perform a task, function or assignment.
Reward power	the ability of a leader to exert influence based on the belief of followers that the leader has access to valued rewards which will be dispensed in return for compliance.
Risk	a condition in which managers have a high knowledge of alternatives; know the probability of these being available; can calculate the costs and know the benefits of each alternative; and have a medium predictability of outcomes.
Risk-seeking propensity	the willingness of an individual to choose options which entail risks.
Risky shift phenomenon	the tendency of a group to make decisions that are riskier than those which the members of the group would have recommended individually before.
Role	the pattern of behaviour expected by others from a person occupying a certain position in an organization hierarchy.

Role conflict	the simultaneous existence of two or more sets of role expectations on a focal person in such a way that compliance with one makes it difficult to comply with the others.
Role modelling	a form of socialization in which an individual learns by example. The learner observers established members, acquiring a mental picture of the act and its consequences (rewards and punishments), and then acts out the acquired image.
Role negotiation	an OD intervention to change the perceptions and attitudes that different individuals in an organization hold with respect to each other, to improve their interaction and collaboration.
Role set	the collection of persons most immediately affected by the focal person's role performance, who depend upon the focal person for their own role performance and who therefore have a stake in it.
Routine decisions	decisions which are made according to established procedures and rules.
Rules	procedures or obligations that are explicitly stated and written down in organization manuals.
Satisficing	a decision-making approach where the first solution that is judged to be 'good enough' (i.e. satisfactory and sufficient) is selected, and the search is then ended.
Scenario planning	the imaginative development of one or more likely pictures of the dimensions and characteristics of the future for an organization.
Schedule of reinforcement	the pattern and frequency of rewards contingent on the display of desirable behaviour.
Scientific management	a form of job design theory and practice which stresses short, repetitive work cycles; detailed, prescribed task sequences; a separation of task conception from task execution; and motivation based on economic rewards.
Selective attention	the ability, often exercised unconsciously, to choose from the stream of sensory data, to concentrate on particular elements and to ignore others.
Self-actualization	the desire for personal fulfilment, to develop one's potential, to become everything that one is capable of becoming.
Self concept	the way in which we view ourselves; the set of perceptions that we have about ourselves.
Self-esteem	the part of the self which is concerned with how we evaluate ourselves.
Self-fulfilling prophecy	an expectation that leads to a certain pattern of behaviour whose consequences confirm the expectancy.
Sensitivity training	a technique for enhancing individual self-awareness, and for changing behaviour, through unstructured group discussion.
Sentiments	the feelings, attitudes and beliefs held by group members.
Shaping	the selective reinforcement of chosen behaviours in a manner that progressively establishes a desired behaviour pattern.
Shared frame of reference	a set of assumptions that are held in common by group members, which shape their thinking, decisions, actions and interactions while being constantly defined and reinforced through those interactions.
Single-loop learning	the ability to use feedback to make continuous adjustments and adaptations, to maintain performance at a predetermined standard.
Situational leadership	an approach to determining the most effective style of influencing, considering the direction and support a leader gives, and the readiness of followers to perform a particular task.

Skinnerian conditioning (also known as instrumental and as operant conditioning)	a technique for associating a response or a behaviour with its consequence.
Social construction of reality	a perspective which argues that our surroundings have no ultimate truth, and are determined by our experiences and interpretations.
Social facilitation	a strengthening of the dominant (prevalent or likely) responses due to the presence of others.
Social identity	that part of the self concept which comes from our membership of groups; it contributes to our self-esteem.
Social influence	the process where attitudes and behaviour are influenced by the real or implied presence of others.
Social loafing	the tendency for individuals to exert less effort when working as part of a group on an additive task than when working alone.
Social representations	the beliefs, ideas and values, objects, people and events that are constructed by current group members and which are transmitted to its new members.
Social role	the set of expectations that others hold of an occupant of a position.
Social status	the relative ranking that a person holds and the value of that person as measured by a group.
Social technology	the methods which order the behaviour and relationships of people in systematic, purposive ways through structures of co-ordination, control, motivation and reward.
Socialization	the process through which individual behaviours, values, attitudes and motives are influenced to conform with those seen as desirable in a given social or organizational setting.
Socialized power	that used for the common good, on behalf of the whole organization.
Sociogram	a chart which shows the liking (social attraction) relationships between individual members of a group.
Sociometry	the study of interpersonal feelings and relationships within groups.
Socio-technical system	a system which possesses both a material technology and a social organization (job specifications, management structure).
Soft HRM	a human resource management perspective which emphasizes the need to develop the potential and resourcefulness of employees in order to encourage commitment and high performance in pursuit of shared organizational goals.
Span of control	the number of subordinates who report directly to a single manager or supervisor.
Stable equilibrium	elements are in a balanced state or quickly return to a state of balance.
Staff employees	workers who are in advisory positions and who use their specialized expertise to support the efforts of line employees.
Stakeholder	anyone concerned with how an organization operates, and who is going to be affected by an organizational change or programme of changes.
Stereotype	a category or personality type to which we consign people on the basis of their membership of some known group.
Strategic alliance	an arrangement in which two firms agree to co-operate to achieve specific commercial objectives.

Strategic change	organizational transformation that is radical, frame-breaking, mould-breaking or paradigmatic in its nature and implications.
Strategic choice	the view that holds that environments, markets and technology of an organization are the result of senior management decisions.
Strategic contingencies	events and activities, both inside and outside an organization, that are essential for it to attain its goals.
Structured task	a task with clear goals, few correct or satisfactory solutions and outcomes, few ways of performing it and clear criteria of success.
Superleader	a leader who is able to develop leadership capacity in others, empowering them, reducing their dependence on formal leaders, and stimulating their motivation, commitment and creativity.
Surface manifestation of culture	culture's most visible and accessible forms, which are the visible and audible behaviour patterns and objects.
Survey feedback	an OD intervention in which the results of an opinion survey are fed back to respondents to trigger problem-solving concerning issues highlighted by the findings.
Synchronous communication	occurs when people are online at the same time, engaging in a real-time conversation with others, somewhat similar to normal face-to-face discussions.
Synergy	the positive or negative result of the interaction of two or more components, producing an outcome that is different from the sum of the individual components.
System	something that functions by virtue of the interdependence of its component parts.
Systematic soldiering	the conscious and deliberate restriction of output by operators.
Systems concept	a management perspective which emphasizes the interdependence between the various parts of an organization, and also between the organization and its environment.
Tacit knowledge	knowledge and understanding specific to the individual, derived from experience, and difficult to communicate to others.
Task analyzability	the degree to which standardized solutions are available to solve the problems that arise.
Task variety	the number of new and different demands that a task places on an individual or a function.
Team	a psychological group whose members share a common goal which they pursue collaboratively. Members can only succeed or fail as whole, and all share the benefits and costs of collective success or failure.
Team autonomy	the extent to which a team experiences freedom, independence and discretion in decisions in the performance of its tasks.
Team building	an OD intervention to help team members to understand their own roles more clearly, and improve their interaction and collaboration.
Team performance	performance that is externally focused and concerns meeting the needs and expectations of outsiders such as customers, company colleagues or fans. It is assessed using measures such as quantity, quality and time.
Team role	an individual's tendency to behave in particularly preferred ways which contribute to and interrelate with other members within a team.
Team viability	the social dimension which is internally focused and concerns the enhancement of the group's capability to perform effectively in the future. It is assessed using measures such as group cohesion and mutual liking.

Technical complexity	the degree of predictability about, and control over, the final product permitted by the technology used; it is usually related to the level of mechanization used in the production process.
Technological determinism	the argument that technology can explain the nature of jobs, work groupings, hierarchy, skills, values and attitudes in organizational settings.
Technological interdependence	the extent to which the work tasks performed in an organization by one department or team member affect the task performance of other departments or team members. It can be high or low.
Thematic apperception test	an assessment in which the individual is shown ambiguous pictures and is asked to create stories of what may be happening in them.
Time and motion studies	measurement and recording techniques which attempt to make operations more efficient.
Time span of responsibility	the time period to which an individual's decisions can commit an organization.
Total quality management	a philosophy of management that is driven by customer needs and expectations, and which is committed to continuous improvement.
Traditional authority	authority that is based on the belief that the ruler has a natural right to rule. This right is either God-given or by descent. Kings and queens enjoy this type of authority.
Trait	a relatively stable quality or attribute of an individual's personality, influencing behaviour in a particular direction.
Transactional leader	a leader who treats relationships with followers in terms of an exchange, giving followers what they want in return for what the leader desires, following prescribed tasks to pursue established goals.
Transformational leader	a leader who treats relationships with followers in terms of motivation and commitment, influencing and inspiring followers to give more than mere compliance to improve organizational performance.
Trigger of change	any disorganizing pressure indicating that current systems, procedures, rules, organization structures and processes are no longer effective.
Type	a descriptive label for a distinct pattern of personality characteristics. Examples of personality types include extravert, neurotic and open.
Type A personality	a combination of emotions and behaviours characterized by ambition, hostility, impatience and a sense of constant time-pressure.
Type B personality	a combination of emotions and behaviours characterized by relaxation, low focus on achievement and ability to take time to enjoy leisure.
Uncertainty	a condition in which managers have a low knowledge of alternatives and a low knowledge of the probability of these being available; can to some degree calculate the costs and benefits of each alternative; but have no predictability of outcomes.
Uncertainty avoidance	the extent to which members of a society feel threatened by ambiguous situations and have created beliefs and institutions which try to avoid these.
Unilateral agreement	a co-operative arrangement in which one firm provides another with a service on a fairly intimate basis in exchange for money.
Unitarist frame of reference on conflict	a perspective on conflict which regards management and employee interests as coinciding and which thus regards (organizational) conflict as harmful and to be avoided.
Unstructured task	a task with ambiguous goals, many correct solutions and satisfactory outcomes, many ways of achieving acceptable outcomes and vague criteria of success.

Valence	the perceived value or preference that an individual has for a particular outcome, which can be positive, negative or neutral.
Vertical integration	a situation where one company buys another in order to make the latter's output its own input, thereby securing that source of supply through ownership.
Vertical loading factors	methods for enriching work and improving motivation by removing controls, increasing accountability and providing feedback, new tasks, natural work units, special assignments and additional authority.
Virtual organization (1)	several conventional companies working very closely together (even fronting the market as one organization) with electronic channels or even common systems of communication.
Virtual organization (2)	an organization where a large number of the organization members use electronic channels as their main (or even only) medium of contact with each other, and with the rest of the organization.
Virtual team	a group of people who work closely together even though they are geographically separated; usually cross-functional work groups brought together to tackle a project for a finite period of time through a combination of technologies.
The Yerkes–Dodson law	a psychology hypothesis which states that performance increases with arousal, until we become overwhelmed, after which performance falls.

References

Abrahamson, E., 2000, 'Change without pain', *Harvard Business Review*, vol. 78, no. 4, pp. 75–9.

Ackroyd, S. and Cowley, P., 1990, 'Can culture be managed? Working with "raw" material: the case of the English slaughterman', *Personnel Review*, vol. 19, no. 5, pp. 3–13.

Ackroyd, S. and Thompson, P., 1999, *Organizational Misbehaviour*, Sage Publications, London.

Adams, J.S., 1963, 'Toward an understanding of inequity', *Journal of Abnormal and Social Psychology*, vol. 67, no. 4, pp. 422–36.

Adams, J.S., 1965, 'Inequity in social exchange', in L. Berkowitz (ed.), *Advances in Experimental Social Psychology*, Academic Press, New York, pp. 267–99.

Adams, R., 1973, *Watership Down*, Puffin Books, London.

Adcroft, A. and Willis, R., 2000, 'Innovation or optimization: facing up to the challenge of the global economy', in Jim Barry, John Chandler, Heather Clark, Roger Johnston and David Needle (eds), *Organization and Management: A Critical Text*, Thomson Learning, London, pp. 171–91.

Adler, N.J., 2002, *International Dimensions of Organizational Behaviour*, International Thomson, London (fourth edition).

Adler, P.S., 1993a, 'Time-and-motion regained', *Harvard Business Review*, vol. 71, no. 1, January–February, pp. 97–108.

Adler, P.S., 1993b, 'The learning bureaucracy: New United Motors Manufacturing, Inc.', in B.M. Staw and L.L. Cummings (eds), *Research in Organizational Behaviour*, vol. 15, JAI Press, Greenwich, CT, pp. 111–94.

Adler, P.S., 1999, 'The emancipatory significance of Taylorism', in M.P.E. Cunha and C.A. Marques (eds), *Readings in Organization Science – Organizational Change in a Changing Context*, Instituto Superior de Psicologia Aplicada, Lisbon, pp. 7–14.

Aiello, J.R. and Svec, C.M., 1993, 'Computer monitoring of work performance: extending the social facilitation framework to electronic presence', *Journal of Applied Social Psychology*, vol. 23, pp. 537–48.

Alderfer, C., 1972, *Human Needs in Organizational Settings*, Free Press, New York.

Allen, R.W., Madison, D.L., Porter, L.W., Renwick, P.A. and Mayes, B.T., 1979, 'Organizational politics: tactics and characteristics of actors', *California Management Review*, vol. 22, no. 1, pp. 77–83.

Allison, G.T., 1971, *Essence of Decision*, Little, Brown and Co, Boston, MA.

Allport, F.H., 1920, 'The influences of the group upon association and thought', *Journal of Experimental Psychology*, vol. 3, pp. 159–82.

Alvesson, M., 2001, *Understanding Organizational Culture*, Sage Publications, London.

Alvesson, M. and Deetz, S., 1999, *Doing Critical Management Research*, Sage Publications, London.

Alvesson, M. and Willmott, H., 1996, *Making Sense of Management: A Critical Introduction*, Sage Publications, London.

Anand, J., 1999, 'How many matches are made in heaven?', *Financial Times*, 'Mastering Strategy' supplement, 25 October, pp. 6–7.

Ancona, D. and Caldwell, D., 1990, 'Improving the performance of new product teams', *Research Technology Management*, vol. 33, no. 2, March–April, pp. 25–9.

Anderson, A., 1999, 'Nice CV, shame about the aura', *The Times*, 'Crème de la Crème' supplement, 14 April, p. 3.

Anderson, D. and Mullen, P. (eds), 1998, *Faking It: The Sentimentalization of Modern Society*, Penguin, Harmondsworth.

Anderson, N. and Shackleton, V., 1993, *Successful Selection Interviewing*, Blackwell, Oxford.

Annett, J. and Stanton, N.A., 2000, 'Editorial: team work: a problem for ergonomics?', *Ergonomics*, vol. 43, no. 8, pp. 1045–51.

Ansoff, I., 1997, 'Measuring and managing for environmental turbulence: the Ansoff Associates approach', in Alexander Watson Hiam (ed.), *The Portable Conference on Change Management*, HRD Press Inc., Amherst, MA, pp. 67–83.

Anthony, P.D., 1990, 'The paradox of the management of culture or "he who leads is lost"', *Personnel Review*, vol. 19, no. 4, pp. 3–8.

Appignanesi, R. and Garratt, C., 1995, *Postmodernism for Beginners*, Icon Books, Cambridge.

Argyris, C., 1960, *Understanding Organizational Behaviour*, Dorsey Press, Homewood, IL.

Argyris, C., 1972, *The Applicability of Organizational Sociology*, Cambridge University Press, London.

Argyris, C., 1982, *Reasoning, Learning, and Action*, Jossey-Bass, San Francisco.

Argyris, C. and Schön, D., 1974, *Theory in Practice*, Jossey-Bass, San Francisco.

Argyris, C. and Schön, D. (eds), 1978, *Organizational Learning*, Addison-Wesley, Reading, MA.

Aronson, E., Wilson, T.D. and Akert, R.M, 1994, *Social Psychology*, HarperCollins, New York.

Arroba, T. and James, K., 1988, 'Are politics palatable to women managers? How women can make wise moves at work', *Women in Management Review*, vol. 3, no. 3, pp. 123–30.

Asch, S.E., 1951, 'Effects of group pressure upon the modification and distortion of judgements', in H. Guetzkow (ed.), *Groups, Leadership and Men*, Carnegie Press, New York, pp. 177–90.

Asch, S.E., 1952, *Social Psychology*, Prentice-Hall, Englewood Cliffs, NJ.

Asch, S.E., 1956, 'Studies of independence and submission to group pressure: a minority of one against a unanimous majority', *Psychological Monograph: General and Applied*, vol. 70, no. 9 (whole no. 416), pp. 1–70.

Astley, W.G. and Sachdeva, P.S., 1984, 'Structural sources of intra-organizational power: a theoretical synthesis', *Academy of Management Review*, vol. 9, no. 1, pp. 104–13.

Atkinson, J., 1985, 'The changing corporation', in D. Clutterbuck (ed.), *New Patterns of Work*, Gower, Aldershot, pp. 13–24.

Augustine, N. and Adelman, K., 1999, *Shakespeare in Charge: The Bard's Guide to Leading and Succeeding on the Business Stage*, Hyperion Books, London.

Averett, S. and Korenman, S., 1993, 'The economic reality of the beauty myth', *NBER Working Paper*, no. 4521, National Bureau of Economic Research, Cambridge, MA.

Bach, S. and Sisson, K. (eds), 2000, *Personnel Management: A Comprehensive Guide to Theory and Practice*, Blackwell Business, Oxford (third edition).

Bachrach, P. and Baratz, M.S., 1962, 'The two faces of power', *American Political Science Review*, vol. 56, no. 4, December, pp. 947–52.

Balasco, J.A. and Alutto, J.A., 1969, 'Line and staff conflicts: some empirical insights', *Academy of Management Journal*, March, pp. 67–77.

Balazs, K., 2001, 'Some like it *haute*: leadership lessons from France's great chefs', *Organizational Dynamics*, vol. 30, no. 2, pp. 134–48.

Balazs, K., 2002, 'Take one entrepreneur: the recipe for success of France's great chefs', *European Management Journal*, vol. 20, no. 3, pp. 247–59.

Baldridge, J.V., 1971, *Power and Conflict in the University*, John Wiley, New York.

Bales, R.F., 1950a, *Interaction Process Analysis*, Addison-Wesley, Reading, MA.

Bales, R.F., 1950b, 'A set of categories for the analysis of small group interaction', *American Sociological Review*, vol. 15, no. 2, pp. 257–63.

Bales, R.F., 1953, 'The equilibrium problem in small groups', in T. Parsons, R.F. Bales and E.A. Shils (eds), *Working Papers in the Theory of Action*, Free Press, New York, pp. 111–61.

Bales, R.F., 1955, 'How people interact in conferences', *Scientific American*, vol. 192, pp. 31–50.

Bales, R.F. and Slater, P.E., 1956, 'Role differentiation in small group decision-making groups', in T. Parsons and R.F. Bales (eds), *Family, Socialization and Interaction*, Routledge, London, pp. 259–306.

Ballard, J.G., 1996, *Cocaine Nights*, Flamingo/HarperCollins, London.

Bandler, R. and Grinder, J., 1975, *The Structure of Magic*, Science and Behavior Books, Palo Alto, CA.

Bandler, R. and Grinder, J., 1979, *Frogs into Princes*, Real People Publications, Moab, Utah.

Bandura, A., 1977, *Social Learning Theory*, Prentice-Hall, Englewood Cliffs, NJ.

Bandura, A., 1986, *Social Foundations of Thought and Action: A Social Cognitive Theory*, Prentice-Hall, Englewood Cliffs, NJ.

Banks, I., 1999, *The Business*, Little, Brown and Co., London.

Baradacco, J.L., 2001, 'We don't need another hero', *Harvard Business Review*, vol. 79, no. 8, September, pp. 121–6.

Barker, J.R., 1993, 'Tightening the iron cage: concertive control in self-managing teams', *Administrative Science Quarterly*, vol. 38, no. 3, pp. 408–37.

Barker, J.R., 1999, *The Discipline of Teamwork*, Sage Publications, London.

Barley, S., 1996, *The New World of Work*, Pamphlet, British-North American Committee, London.

Barnard, C., 1938, *The Functions of the Executive*, Harvard University Press, Cambridge, MA.

Barney, J.B., 1986, 'Organizational culture: can it be the source of sustained competitive advantage?', *Academy of Management Review*, vol. 11, no. 3, pp. 656–65.

Barney, J.B., 1991, 'Firm resources and sustained competitive advantage', *Journal of Management*, vol. 17, no. 1, March, pp. 99–120.

Baron, R.S., 1986, 'Distraction-conflict theory: progress and problems', in L. Berkowitz (ed.), *Advances in Experimental Social Psychology*, vol. 20, Academic Press, New York, pp. 1–40.

Baron, R. and Byrne, D., 2000, *Social Psychology*, Allyn and Bacon, London (ninth edition).

Barry, J., Chandler, J., Clark, H., Johnston, R. and Needle, D. (eds), 2000, *Organization and Management: A Critical Text*, Thomson Learning, London.

Bass, B.M., 1985a, *Bass and Stogdill's Handbook of Leadership: Theory, Research and Managerial Applications*, Free Press, New York (third edition).

Bass, B.M., 1985b, *Leadership and Performance Beyond Expectations*, Free Press, New York.

Bass, B.M. and Avolio, B.J., 1990, 'The implications of transactional and transformational leadership for individual, team and organizational development', *Research and Organizational Change and Development*, vol. 4, pp. 321–72.

Bass, B.M. and Avolio, B.J., 1994, *Improving Organizational Effectiveness through Transformational Leadership*, Sage Publications, Thousand Oaks, CA.

Bate, P., 1984, 'The impact of organizational culture on approaches to organizational problem solving', *Organizational Studies*, vol. 5, no. 1, pp. 43–67.

Bate, P., 2000, 'Changing the culture of a hospital: from hierarchy to networked community', *Public Administration*, vol. 78, no. 3, pp. 485–512.

Bateson, G. and Mead, M., 1942, *Balinese Character: A Photographic Analysis*, Special Publications 2, New York Academy of Sciences, New York.

Bauman, Z., 1991, *Modernity and the Holocaust*, Polity Press, Cambridge.

Bavelas, A., 1967, 'Communication patterns in task-orientated groups', in D. Cartwright and A. Zander (eds), *Group Dynamics: Research and Theory*, Tavistock, London (third edition).

Bavelas, A. and Barrett, D., 1951, 'An experimental approach to organizational communication', *Personnel*, vol. 27, March, pp. 367–71.

Bazerman, M.H., 2001, *Judgement in Managerial Decision Making*, Wiley, New York (fifth edition).

Bazerman, M.H. and Gillespie, J.J., 1999, 'Betting on the future: the virtues of contingent contracts', *Harvard Business Review*, vol. 77, no. 5, September–October, pp. 155–60.

BBC, 1996, *20 Steps to Better Management*, 'Letting go', BBC Enterprises Ltd, London.

Beardwell, I. and Holden, L., 2001, *Human Resource Management: A Contemporary Perspective*, Financial Times/Prentice Hall, Harlow (third edition).

Beaton, A., 2001, *The Little Book of Management Bollocks*, Simon & Schuster, London.

Becker, G., 1964, *Human Capital*, National Bureau of Economic Research, New York.

Becker, H., 1982, 'Culture: a sociological view', *Yale Review*, vol. 71, pp. 513–27.

Beckhard, R., 1969, *Organization Development: Strategies and Models*, Addison-Wesley, Reading, MA.

Bedeian, A.G., 1980, *Organization Theory and Analysis*, Dryden Press, Fort Worth, TX.

Bedeian, A.G., 1986, *Management*, CBS International, New York.

Bedeian, A.G. and Zammuto, R.F., 1991, *Organizations: Theory and Design*, Dryden Press, London.

Beeman, D.R. and Sharkey, T.W., 1987, 'The use and abuse of corporate politics', *Business Horizons*, vol. 30, no. 2, March–April, pp. 26–31.

Beer, M., Lawrence, P.R., Quinn Mills, D. and Walton, R.E., 1985, *Human Resource Management: A General Manager's Perspective*, Free Press, Glencoe, IL.

Beer, M. and Spector, B., 1985, 'Corporate-wide transformations in human resource management', in R.E. Walton and E.R. Lawrence (eds), *Human Resource Management Trends and Challenges*, Harvard Business School Press, Boston, MA.

Beer, M., Spector, B., Lawrence, P.R., Quinn Mills, D. and Walton, R.E., 1984, *Managing Human Assets*, Free Press, New York.

Behar, R., 1989, 'Joe's bad trip', *Time*, 24 July, pp. 54–9.

Belbin, R.M., 1981, *Management Teams: Why They Succeed or Fail*, Butterworth Heinemann, London.

Belbin, R.M, 1993a, *Team Roles at Work,* Butterworth-Heinemann, London.

Belbin, R.M., 1993b, 'A reply to the BTRSPI by Furnham, Steele and Pendleton', *Journal of Occupational and Organizational Psychology*, vol. 66, no. 3, pp. 259–60.

Belbin, R.M., 1996, *The Coming Shape of Organizations*, Butterworth-Heinemann, London.

Bell, D., 1999, *The Coming of Post Industrial Society*, Basic Books, New York (reprint of 1976 original).

Benders, J., Doorewaard, H. and Poutsma, E., 2000, 'Modern sociotechnology', in M. Beyerlin (ed.), *Work Teams: Past, Present and Future*, Kluwer Academic Publishers, New York.

Benders, J., Huijgen, F. and Pekruhl, U., 2001, 'Measuring groupwork: findings and lessons from a European survey', *New Technology, Work and Employment*, vol. 17, no. 3, pp. 204–17.

Benders, J. and Van Hootegem, G., 1999, 'Teams and their context: moving the team discussion beyond existing dichotomies', *Journal of Management Studies*, vol. 36, no. 5, pp. 609–28.

Benders, J. and Van Hootegem, G., 2000, 'How the Japanese got teams', in S. Proctor and F. Mueller (eds), *Teamworking*, Macmillan, London, pp. 43–59.

Benfari, R.C., Wilkinson, H.E. and Orth, C.D., 1986, 'The effective use of power', *Business Horizons*, vol. 29, May–June, pp. 12–16.

Benne, K.D. and Sheats, P., 1948, 'Functional roles of group members', *Journal of Social Issues*, vol. 4, pp. 41–9.

Bennis, W.G., 1969, *Organization Development: Its Nature, Origins and Prospects*, Addison-Wesley, Reading, MA.

Bennis, W.G. and Nanus, B., 1985, *Leaders: The Strategies for Taking Charge*, Harper Collins, New York.

Berger, M., 1964, *The Arab World Today*, Doubleday & Co., Garden City, NY.

Berger, P. and Luckmann, T., 1966, *The Social Construction of Reality*, Penguin, Harmondsworth.

Berggren, C., 1993a, *Alternatives to Lean Production*, Macmillan, Basingstoke.

Berggren, C., 1993b, 'The Volvo Uddevalla plant: why the decision to close it is mistaken', *Journal of Industry Studies*, vol. 1, no. 1, October, pp. 75–87.

Berggren, C., 1995, 'The fate of the branch plants – performance versus power', in Ake Sandberg (ed.), *Enriching Production: Perspectives on Volvo's Uddevalla Plant as an Alternative to Lean Production*, Avebury, Aldershot, pp. 105–26.

Berggren, C., Bjorkman, T. and Hollander, E., 1991, 'Are they unbeatable?', Centre for Corporate Change, Paper 012, Australian Graduate School of Management, University of New South Wales, Kensington, NSW, Australia.

Bernick, C.L., 2001, 'When your culture needs a makeover', *Harvard Business Review*, vol. 79, no. 6, pp. 53–61.

de Bernières, L., 1994, *Captain Corelli's Mandolin*, Secker and Warburg/Vintage, London.

Bessant, J., 1983, 'Management and manufacturing innovation: the case of information technology', in G. Winch (ed.), *Information Technology in Manufacturing Processes*, Rossendale, London, pp. 14–30.

Bevan, S., 1999, 'Companies seek chip implants to control staff', *The Sunday Times*, 9 May, pp. 1–7.

Beynon, H., 1975, *Working for Ford*, Penguin, Harmondsworth.

Bird, C., 1940, *Social Psychology*, Appleton-Century, New York.

Blake, R.R. and McCanse, A.A., 1991, *Leadership Dilemmas: Grid Solutions*, Gulf Publishing, Houston, TX.

Blake, R.R. and Mouton, J.S., 1964, *The Managerial Grid*, Gulf Publishing, Houston, TX.

Blake, R.R. and Mouton, J.S., 1968, *Corporate Excellence Through Grid Organization Development: A Systems Approach*, Gulf Publishing, Houston, TX.

Blake, R.R. and Mouton, J.S., 1969, *Building a Dynamic Corporation Through Grid Organization Development*, Addison-Wesley, Reading, MA.

Blau, P.M., 1966, *The Dynamics of Bureaucracy*, University of Chicago Press, Chicago (second edition).

Blauner, R., 1964, *Alienation and Freedom: The Factory Worker and His Industry*, University of Chicago Press, Chicago.

Blyton, P. and Bacon, N., 1997, 'Recasting the occupational culture in steel: some implications of changing from crews to teams in the UK steel industry', *Sociological Review*, vol. 45, no. 1, pp. 79–101.

Boddy, D., 2002, *Managing Projects: Building and Leading the Team*, Financial Times/Prentice Hall, Harlow (second edition).

Boje, D.M. and Winsor, R.D., 1993, 'The resurrection of Taylorism: total quality management's hidden agenda', *Journal of Organizational Change Management*, vol. 6, no. 4, pp. 57–70.

Bolman, L. and Deal, T., 1991, *Re-framing Organizations*, Jossey-Bass, San Francisco.

Boreham, P., Thompson, P. and Parker, R., 2003, *New Technology @ Work*, Routledge, London.

Bouchard, T., Barsaloux, J. and Drauden, G., 1974, 'Brainstorming procedure, group size and sex as determinants of problem-solving effectiveness of groups and individuals', *Journal of Applied Psychology*, vol. 59, pp. 135–8.

Bowditch, J.L. and Buono, A.F., 2001, *A Primer on Organizational Behavior*, Wiley, New York.

Boyd, C., 2002, 'Customer violence and employee health and safety', *Work, Employment and Society*, vol. 16, no. 1, pp. 151–69.

Boyle, M., 2001, 'Performance reviews: perilous curves ahead', *Fortune*, 28 May, pp. 103–4.

Bracewell, M., 2002, *Perfect Tense*, Vintage, London.

Braverman, H., 1974, *Labor and Monopoly Capital: The Degradation of Work in the Twentieth Century*, Monthly Review Press, New York.

Bray, P., 1999, 'Falling under the psychologist's spell', *The Sunday Times*, 'The Restless Customer' supplement, 13 June, p. 9.

Bredin, A., 1996, *The Virtual Office Survival Handbook: What Telecommuters and Entrepreneurs Need to Succeed in Today's Nontraditional Workplace*, Wiley, New York.

Bresnahan, T.F., 1999, 'Computerization and wage dispersion: an analytical reinterpretation', *Economic Journal*, vol. 109, no. 456, pp. 390–415.

Brewer, N., Mitchell, P., and Weber, N., 2002, 'Gender role, organizational status and conflict management styles', *International Journal of Conflict Management*, vol. 13, no. 1, pp. 78–94.

Briskin, J., 1983, *The Onyx*, Grafton Books, London.

Brockner, J., 1992, 'The escalation of commitment to a failing course of action: toward theoretical progress', *Academy of Management Review*, vol. 17, no. 1, pp. 39–61.

Brooks, I., 2003, *Organizational Behaviour: Individuals, Groups and Organization*, Financial Times/Prentice Hall, Harlow.

Brotherton, C., 1999, *Social Psychology and Management*, Open University Press, Buckingham.

Broucek, W.G. and Randell, G., 1996, 'An assessment of the construct validity of the Belbin self-perception inventory and the observer's assessment from the perspective of the five factor model', *Journal of Occupational and Organizational Psychology*, vol. 69, no. 4, pp. 389–405.

Broussine, M. and Vince, R., 1996, 'Working with metaphor towards organizational change', in Cliff Oswick and David Grant (eds), *Organization Development: Metaphorical Explorations*, Pitman, London, pp. 57–72.

Brown, M., 1998, *Richard Branson: the Authorized Biography*, Michael Joseph, London.

Brown, M. and Beech, D., 2000, 'Spontaneous organization', *Directions: The Ashridge Journal* (Ashridge web document: /directions/2000–1/04).

Brown, R., 2000, *Group Processes*, Blackwell, Oxford.

Brown, S.L. and Eisenhardt, K.M., 1998, *Competing on the Edge: Strategy as Structured Chaos*, Harvard Business Review Press, Boston, MA.

Brown, V. and Paulus, p. B., 1996, 'A simple dynamic model of social factors in brainstorming', *Small Group Research*, vol. 27, pp. 91–114.

de Bruxelles, S., 2001, 'Pupils sum up maths teachers as fat nerds', *The Times*, 3 January, p. 11.

Bryman, A., 1986, *Leadership and Organizations*, Routledge and Kegan Paul, London.

Bryman, A. (ed.), 1988, *Doing Research in Organizations*, Routledge, London.

Bryman, A., 1989, *Research Methods and Organization Studies*, Routledge, London.

Bryman, A., 1996, 'Leadership in organizations', in Stewart R. Clegg, Cynthia Hardy and Walter R. Nord (eds), *Handbook of Organization Studies*, Sage Publications, London, pp. 276–92.

Bryman, A., 2001, *Social Research Methods*, Oxford University Press, Oxford.

Buchanan, D.A., 1994a, 'Cellular manufacture and the role of teams', in John Storey (ed.), *New Wave Manufacturing Strategies: Organizational and Human Resource Management Dimensions*, Paul Chapman, London, pp. 204–25.

Buchanan, D.A., 1994b, 'Principles and practice in work design', in Keith Sisson (ed.), *Personnel Management: A Comprehensive Guide to Theory and Practice in Britain*, Blackwell, Oxford (second edition), pp. 85–116.

Buchanan, D.A., 1996, 'The limitations and opportunities of business process re-engineering in a politicized organizational climate', *Human Relations*, vol. 50, no. 1, pp. 51–72.

Buchanan, D.A., 2000a, 'An eager and enduring embrace: the ongoing rediscovery of teamworking as a management idea', in Stephen Procter and Frank Mueller (eds), *Teamworking*, Macmillan Business, Basingstoke and London, pp. 25–42.

Buchanan, D.A., 2000b, 'The lived experience of high velocity change: a hospital case study', Paper presented to the American Academy of Management Conference, Symposium on Strategy as Dynamic and Pluralistic, Toronto, August.

Buchanan, D.A., 2001, 'The role of photography in organizational research: a re-engineering case illustration', *Journal of Management Inquiry*, vol. 10, no. 2, pp. 151–64.

Buchanan, D.A., 2004, 'Demands, instabilities, manipulations, careers: the lived experience of driving change', *Human Relations* (forthcoming).

Buchanan, D.A. and Badham, R., 1999a, *Power, Politics and Organizational Change: Winning the Turf Game*, Sage Publications, London.

Buchanan, D.A. and Badham, R., 1999b, 'Politics and organizational change: the lived experience', *Human Relations*, vol. 52, no. 5, pp. 609–29.

Buchanan, D.A. and Boddy, D., 1983, *Organizations in the Computer Age: Technological Imperatives and Strategic Change*, Gower, Aldershot.

Buchanan, D.A. and McCalman, J., 1989, *High Performance Work Systems: The Digital Experience*, Routledge, London.

Buchanan, D.A. and Preston, D., 1992, 'Life in the cell: supervision and teamwork in a "manufacturing systems engineering" environment', *Human Resource Management Journal*, vol. 2, no. 4, pp. 55–76.

Buchanan, D.A. and Wilson, B., 1996a, 'Next patient please: the operating theatres problem at Leicester General Hospital NHS Trust', in J. Storey (ed.), *Cases in Human Resource and Change Management*, Blackwell Business, Oxford, pp. 190–205.

Buchanan, D.A. and Wilson, B., 1996b, 'Re-engineering operating theatres: the perspective assessed', *Journal of Management in Medicine*, vol. 10, no. 4, pp. 57–74.

Buchanan, D.A., Claydon, T. and Doyle, M., 1999, 'Organization development and change: the legacy of the nineties', *Human Resource Management Journal*, vol. 9, no. 2, pp. 20–37.

Buono, A.F., Bowditch, J.L. and Lewis, J.W., 1985, 'When cultures collide: the anatomy of a merger', *Human Relations*, vol. 38, no. 5, pp. 477–500.

Burawoy, M., 1979, *Manufacturing Consent*, University of Chicago Press, Chicago.

Burgoyne, J., 1999, 'Design of the times', *People Management*, vol. 5, no. 11, 3 June, pp. 38–44.

Burke, K., 1999, 'It's good to talk', *Personnel Today*, 21 January, pp. 23–5.

Burke, W.W., 1980, 'Organization development and bureaucracy in the 1980s', *Journal of Applied Behavioral Science*, vol. 16, no. 3, pp. 423–37.

Burke, W.W., 1987, *Organization Development: A Normative View*, Addison-Wesley, Reading, MA.

Burne, J. and Aldridge, S., 1996, 'Who do you think you are?', *Focus Extra*, April, pp. 1–8.

Burnes, B., 2000, *Managing Change: A Strategic Approach to Organizational Dynamics*, Financial Times/Prentice Hall, Harlow (third edition).

Burnett, A., 2000, 'Virtual organizations and virtuality', Department of Business and Management Studies Working Paper, University of Glasgow, Glasgow.

Burnett, A. and Warhurst, C., 1999, 'All that's solid melts into air? Virtual organizations and scientific management', Paper presented to the 17th Annual International Labour Process Conference, Royal Holloway College, University of London, March.

Burns, J.M., 1978, *Leadership*, Harper & Row, New York.

Burns, P. and Jewhurst, J. (eds), 1996, *Small Business and Entrepreneurship*, Macmillan Business, Basingstoke (second edition).

Burns, T. and Stalker, G.M., 1994/1961, *The Management of Innovation*, Oxford University Press, Oxford (first published in 1961 by Tavistock, London).

Burrell, G., 1998, *Pandemonium: Towards a Retro-Theory of Organization*, Sage Publications, London.

Burrell, G. and Morgan, G., 1979, *Sociological Paradigms and Organizational Analysis*, Heinemann, London.

Burt, T. and Larsen, P.T., 2003, 'DirecTV is about changing the whole model of News Corp's output in the US', *Financial Times*, 12 February, p. 15.

Butcher, D. and Bailey, C., 2000, 'Crewed awakenings', *People Management*, vol. 6, no. 16, pp. 35–7.

Butcher, D. and Clarke, M., 2001, *Smart Management: Using Politics in Organizations*, Palgrave, Basingstoke.

Butcher, D. and Harvey, P., 1999, 'Be upstanding', *People Management*, vol. 5, no. 13, pp. 37–42.

Butler, T. and Waldroop, J., 1999, 'Job sculpting: the art of retaining your best people', *Harvard Business Review*, vol. 77, no. 5, pp. 144–52.

Buttery, E., Fulop, L. and Buttery, A., 1999, 'Networks and inter-organizational relations', in L. Fulop and S. Linstead (eds), *Management: A Critical Text*, Macmillan Business, London, pp. 414–63.

Cadet, C., Charles, R. and Galus, J.-L., 1990, *La Communication par Limage*, Nathan, Paris.

Cairncross, F., 1995, 'The death of distance: a survey of telecommunications', *The Economist*, 30 September, special supplement.

Cairncross, F., 2001, *The Death of Distance 2.0: How the Communications Revolution Will Change Our Lives*, Harvard Business School Press, Boston, MA.

Callahan, C.V. and Pasternack, B.A., 1999, 'Corporate strategy in a digital age', *Strategy and Business*, no. 15, October, pp. 10–14.

Carletta, J., Anderson, A.H. and McEwan, R., 2000, 'The effects of multimedia communication technology on non-collocated teams: a case study', *Ergonomics*, vol. 43, no. 8, pp. 1237–51.

Carnevale, P.J. and Pruitt, D.G., 2000, *Negotiation in Social Conflict*, Open University Press, Buckingham (second edition).

Carr, N., 1999, 'Being virtual: character and the new economy', *Harvard Business Review*, vol. 77, no. 3, May–June, pp. 181–90.

Carrington, L., 2002, 'Oiling the wheels', *People Management*, vol. 8, no. 13, 27 June, pp. 31–4.

Carroll, M., Cooke, F.L., Grugulis, I., Rubery, J. and Earnshaw, J., 2002, 'Analysing diversity in the management of human resources in call centres', Paper presented to the *Human Resource Management Journal* Conference on Call Centres, King's College, London.

Carroll, P., 1994, *Big Blues: The Unmaking of IBM*, Orion Books, London.

Cartwright, D. and Zander, A. (eds), 1968, *Group Dynamics: Research and Theory*, Tavistock, London (third edition).

Cattell, R., 1951, 'New concepts for measuring leadership in terms of group syntality', *Human Relations*, vol. 4, pp. 161–8.

Champoux, J.E., 1999, 'Film as a teaching resource', *Journal of Management Inquiry*, vol. 8, no. 2, pp. 206–17.

Champoux, J.E., 2001a, *Management: Using Film to Visualize Principles and Practices*, South-Western College Publishing/Thomson Learning, Mason, OH.

Champoux, J.E., 2001b, *Organizational Behaviour: Using Film to Visualize Principles and Practices*, South-Western College Publishing/Thomson Learning, Mason, OH.

Chandler A.D., 1962, *Strategy and Structure: Chapters in the History of American Industrial Enterprise*, MIT Press, Cambridge, MA.

Chandler, A.D., 1990, *Scale and Scope: The Dynamics of Industrial Capitalism*, Harvard University Press, Cambridge, MA.

Chandler, A.D., Hastrom, p. and Solvell, O. (eds), 1999, *Dynamic Firm: The Role of Regions, Technology, Strategy and Organization*, Oxford University Press, Oxford.

Chanlat, J.-F., 1997, 'Conflict and politics', in A. Sorge and M. Warner (eds), *Handbook of Organization Behaviour*, International Thomson Business Press, London, pp. 472–80.

Chansler, P.A., Swarmidass, P.M. and Cammann, C., 2003, 'Self-managing work teams: an empirical study of group cohesiveness in natural workgroups at Harley-Davidson Motor Company Plant', *Small Group Research*, vol. 34, no. 1, pp. 101–21.

Charm, R. and Colvin, G., 1999, 'Why CEOs fail', *Fortune*, vol. 139, no. 12, 21 June, pp. 69–78.

Chartered Institute of Personnel and Development, 1998, *Key Facts: Stress at Work*, October, CIPD, London.

Chartered Institute of Personnel and Development, 2001, *Quick Facts: Assessment Centres for Recruitment and Selection*, May, CIPD, London.

Chartered Institute of Personnel and Development, 2002, *Quick Facts: Stress*, August, CIPD, London.

Child, J., 1969, *British Management Thought*, George Allen and Unwin, London.

Child, J., 1972, 'Organizational structure, environment and performance: the role of strategic choice', *Sociology*, vol. 6, no. 1, pp. 1–22.

Child, J., 1981, 'Culture, contingency and capitalism in the cross-national study of organizations', in L.L. Cummings and B.M. Staw (eds), *Research in Organizational Behaviour*, vol. 3, JAI Press, Greenwich, CT, pp. 303–56.

Child, J., 1984, *Organization: A Guide to Problems and Practice*, Harper & Row, London (second edition).

Child, J., 1985, 'Managerial strategies, new technology and the labour process', in D. Knights, H. Willmott and D. Collinson (eds), *Job Redesign*, Gower, Aldershot, pp. 107–41.

Child, J., 1997, 'Strategic choice in the analysis of action, structure, organizations and environments: retrospect and prospect', *Organization Studies*, vol. 18, no. 1, pp. 43–76.

Child, J. and Faulkner, D. (eds), 1998a, *Strategies of Co-operation: Managing Alliances, Networks and Joint Ventures*, Oxford University Press, Oxford.

Child, J. and Faulkner, D., 1998b, 'Networks and virtuality', in J. Child and D. Faulkner (eds), *Strategies of Co-operation: Managing Alliances, Networks and Joint Ventures*, Oxford University Press, Oxford, pp. 113–42.

Christie, R. and Geis, F.L., 1970, *Studies in Machiavellianism*, Academic Press, New York.

Cialdini, R.B., 2001, *Influence: Science and Practice*, Allyn and Bacon, London (fourth edition).

Clarke, A., 1999, 'Employees under surveillance', *The Times*, 6 April, p. 35.

Clarke, D., 1989, *Stress Management*, National Extension College, Cambridge.

Clarry, T., 1999, 'Premium Bonding', *People Management*, vol. 5, no. 17, 2 September, pp. 34–9.

Claydon, T. and Doyle, M., 1996, 'Trusting me, trusting you: the ethics of employee empowerment', *Personnel Review*, vol. 25, no. 6, pp. 13–25.

Clegg, S., 1989, *Frameworks of Power*, Sage Publications, London.

Clegg, S., 1990, *Modern Organizations: Organization Studies in the Postmodern World*, Sage Publications, London.

Clegg, S. and Dunkerley, D., 1980, *Organization, Class and Control*, Routledge and Kegan Paul, London.

Clegg, S.R. and Hardy, C., 1996, 'Organizations, organization and organizing', in S. Clegg, C. Hardy and W.R. Nord (eds), *Handbook of Organization Studies*, Sage Publications, London, pp. 1–28.

Clegg, S.R. and Hardy, C., 1996a, 'Conclusion: representations', in S. Clegg, C. Hardy and W.R. Nord (eds), *Handbook of Organization Studies*, Sage Publications, London, pp. 676–708.

Clegg, S., Hardy, C. and Nord, W.R., 1996, *Handbook of Organization Studies*, Sage Publications, London.

Clutterbuck, D. and Hirst, S., 2003, *Talking Business*, Butterworth-Heinemann, London.

Coch, L. and French, J.R.P., 1948, 'Overcoming resistance to change', *Human Relations*, vol. 1, pp. 512–32.

Cohen, A.R. and Bradford, D.L., 1989, 'Influence without authority: the use of alliances, reciprocity and exchange to accomplish work', *Organizational Dynamics*, vol. 17, no. 1, Winter, pp. 5–18.

Cohen, A.R., and Bradford, D.L., 1991, *Influence Without Authority*, Wiley, New York.

Cohen, A.R., Fink, S.L., Gadon, H. and Willits, R.D., 1995, *Effective Behavior in Organizations*, Irwin, Homewood, IL (sixth edition).

Cohen, M.D., March, J.G. and Olsen, J.P., 1972, 'Garbage-can model of organizational choice', *Administrative Science Quarterly*, vol. 17, no. 1, pp. 1–25.

Cohen, S.G. and Bailey, D.E., 1997, 'What makes teams work: group effectiveness research from the shopfloor to the executive suite', *Journal of Management*, vol. 23, no. 3, pp. 239–90.

Coles, M., 1998, 'Unlock the power of knowledge', *The Sunday Times*, 20 September, p. 7.28.

Collier, J. and Collier, M., 1986, *Visual Anthropology: Photography as a Research Method*, University of New Mexico Press, Albuquerque, NM.

Collier, P. and Horowitz, D., 1987, *The Fords: An American Epic*, Futura Collins, London.

Colling, T., 1995, 'Experiencing turbulence: competition, strategic choice and the management of human resources in British Airways', *Human Resource Management Journal*, vol. 5, no. 5, pp. 18–33.

Collins, D., 1998, *Organizational Change: Sociological Perspectives*, Routledge, London.

Collins, D., 2000, *Management Fads and Buzzwords*, Routledge, London.

Collins, J., 2001, 'Level 5 leadership: the triumph of humility and fierce resolve', *Harvard Business Review*, vol. 79, no. 1, January, pp. 67–76.

Comer, D.R., 1995, 'A model of social loafing in real work groups', *Human Relations*, vol. 48, no. 6, June, pp. 647–67.

Connelly, T., 1997, 'Electronic brainstorming: science meets technology in the group meeting room', in S. Kiesler (ed.), *Culture of the Internet*, Lawrence Erlbaum Associates, Mahwah, NJ, pp. 263–76.

Conti, R.E. and Warner, M., 1993, 'Taylorism, new technology and just-in-time systems in Japanese manufacturing', *New Technology, Work and Employment*, vol. 8, no. 1, pp. 31–42.

Cooms, J.G. and Ketchen, D.J., 1999, 'Explaining interfirm co-operation and performance: toward a reconciliation of predictions from the resource-based view and organizational economics', *Strategic Management Journal*, vol. 20, no. 9, pp. 867–88.

Cooper, C. (ed.), 2000a, *Theories of Organizational Stress*, Oxford University Press, Oxford.

Cooper, C., 2000b, 'In for the count', *People Management*, vol. 6, no. 20, 12 October, pp. 28–34.

Cooper, C., 2000c, 'Management blasted at nuclear plant', *People Management*, vol. 6, no. 6, March, pp. 16–17.

Cooper, W.H., Gallupe, R.G., Pollard, S. and Cadsby, J., 1998, 'Some liberating effects of anonymous electronic brainstorming', *Small Group Research*, vol. 29, pp. 147–78.

Coopey, J., 1995, 'Managerial culture and the stillbirth of organizational commitment', *Human Resource Management Journal*, vol. 5, no. 3, pp. 56–76.

Corrigan, P., 1999, *Shakespeare on Management: Leadership Lessons for Today's Managers*, Kogan Page, London.

Cosier, R.A. and Schwenk, C.R., 1990, 'Agreement and thinking alike: ingredients for poor decisions', *Academy of Management Executive*, vol. 4, no. 1, pp. 69–74.

Costa, P. and McCrae, R.R., 1992, *NEO PI-R: Professional Manual*, Psychological Assessment Resources, Odessa, FL.

Cottrell, N.B., Wack, K.L., Sekerak, G.J. and Rittle, R., 1968, 'Social facilitation in dominant responses by presence of an audience and the mere presence of others', *Journal of Personality and Social Psychology*, vol. 9, pp. 245–50.

Crichton, A., 1968, *Personnel Management in Context*, B.T. Batsford, London.

Crichton, M., 1992, *Rising Sun*, Century Arrow, London.

Crichton, M., 1997, *Airframe*, Arrow Books, London.

Cross, R. and Prusak, L., 2002, 'The people who make organizations go – or stop', *Harvard Business Review*, vol. 80, no. 6, June, pp. 104–12.

Cully, M., O'Reilly, A., Millward, N., Forth, J., Woodland, S., Dix, G. and Bryson, A., 1998, *The 1998 Workplace Employee Relations Survey: First Findings*, Department of Trade and Industry, London.

Cummings, T.G. and Worley, C.G., 2001, *Organization Development and Change*, South-Western College Publishing/Thomson Learning, Mason, OH (seventh edition).

Cyert, R.M. and March, J.G., 1963, A *Behavioural Theory of the Firm*, Prentice-Hall, Englewood Cliffs, NJ.

Czarniawska, B., 1998, *A Narrative Approach to Organization Studies*, Sage Publications, Thousand Oaks, CA.

Czarniawska, B., 1999, *Writing Management: Organization Theory as a Literary Genre*, Oxford University Press, Oxford.

Czarniawska-Joerges, B. and de Monthoux, p. G. (eds), 1994, *Good Novels, Better Management: Reading Organizational Realities in Fiction*, Harwood Academic Publishers, Reading, UK.

Daft, R.L., 2001, *Organization Theory and Design*, South-Western Thomson Learning, London (seventh edition).

Daft, R.L. and Noe, R.A., 2001, *Organizational Behaviour*, International Thomson Publishing, London.

Dahl, R.A., 1957, 'The concept of power', *Behavioural Science*, vol. 2, pp. 201–15.

Daisey, M., 2002, *21 Dog Years: Doing Time @ Amazon.Com*, Fourth Estate, London.

Dalton, M., 1950, 'Conflict between staff and line management officers', *American Sociological Review*, June, pp. 342–51.

Dalton, R. and Lynn, M., 1999, 'Companies lead university revolution', *The Sunday Times*, 7 February, p. 3.4.

Danford, A., 1998, 'Team working and labour regulation in the autocomponents industry', *Work, Employment and Society*, vol. 12, no. 3, pp. 403–31.

Daniels, K., Lamond, D.A. and Standen, P. (eds), 2000, *Managing Telework*, Business Press/Thomson Learning, London.

Davenport, T.H., 1993, *Process Innovation: Re-engineering Work Through Information Technology*, Harvard Business School Press, Boston, MA.

Davidow, W. and Malone, M., 1992, *The Virtual Corporation,* HarperCollins, New York.

Davidson, M.J. and Cooper, C.L., 1992, *Shattering the Glass Ceiling: The Woman Manager*, Paul Chapman, London.

Davis, D., Millburn, P., Murphy, T. and Woodhouse, M., 1992, *Successful Team Building: How To Create Teams That Really Work*, Kogan Page, London.

Davis, L.E. and Taylor, J.C., 1975, 'Technology effects on job, work, and organizational structure: a contingency view', in L.E. Davis and A.B. Cherns (eds), *The Quality of Working Life: Problems, Prospects and the State of the Art*, Free Press, New York, pp. 220–41.

Davis, L.E. and Taylor, J.C., 1976, 'Technology, organization and job structure', in R. Dubin (ed.), *Handbook of Work, Organization and Society*, Rand McNally, Chicago, pp. 379–419.

Davis, L.E. and Wacker, G.J., 1987, 'Job design', in G. Salvendy (ed.), *Handbook of Human Factors*, Wiley, New York.

Davis, S.M. and Lawrence, P.R., 1978, 'Problems of matrix organizations', *Harvard Business Review*, vol. 56, no. 3, May–June, pp. 131–42.

Dawson, C., 2003, 'Roaring into China', *Business Week*, 7 April, pp. 76–7.

Dawson, P., 1994, *Organizational Change: A Processual Approach*, Paul Chapman, London.

Dawson, P., 1996, *Technology and Quality: Change in the Workplace*, International Thomson Business Press, London.

Dawson, P., 2003a, *Reshaping Change: A Processual Approach*, Routledge, London.

Dawson, P., 2003b, *Understanding Organizational Change: The Contemporary Experience of People at Work*, Sage Publications, London.

Deal, T.E. and Kennedy, A.A., 1982, *Organization Cultures: The Rites and Rituals of Organization Life*, Addison-Wesley, Reading, MA.

Deal, T.E. and Kennedy, A.A., 2000, *The New Corporate Cultures*, Texere Publishing, New York and London.

Dearlove, D., 2000, 'Productivity myth knocks the shine off IT', *The Times*, 28 September, p. 5.

Deetz, S., 1996, 'Describing differences in approaches to organization science: rethinking Burrell and Morgan and their legacy', *Organization Science*, vol. 7, no. 2, March–April, pp. 191–207.

Denis, J.-L., Lamothe, L. and Langley, A., 2001, 'The dynamics of collective leadership and strategic change in pluralistic organizations', *Academy of Management Journal*, vol. 44, no. 4, pp. 809–37.

Denison, D., Hart, S. and Kahn, J., 1996, 'From chimneys to cross-functional teams: developing and validating a diagnostic model', *Academy of Management Journal*, vol. 39, no. 4, pp. 1005–23.

Dennis, A.R. and Valacich, J.S., 1993, 'Computer brainstorms: more heads are better than one', *Journal of Applied Psychology*, vol. 78, no. 4, pp. 531–7.

Denzin, N.K. and Lincoln, Y.S. (eds), 2000, *Handbook of Qualitative Research*, Sage Publications, Thousand Oaks, CA (second edition).

Department of Education and Employment, 1997, *A Plan for Objective 4 in Great Britain, 1998–1999*, November, HMSO, London.

Department of Health, 2002, *NHS Leadership Qualities Framework*, Modernization Agency Leadership Centre, London.

Department of Trade and Industry, 1999, *Working for the Future: The Changing Face of Work Practices*, HMSO, London.

de Sitter, L.U., 1994, *Synergetisch Produceren* (*Producing Synergistically*), van Gorcum, Assen.

de Sitter, L.U., den Hertog, J.F. and Dankbaar, B., 1997, 'From complex organizations with simple jobs to simple organizations with complex jobs', *Human Relations*, vol. 50, no. 5, pp. 497–534.

Diehl, M. and Stroebe, W., 1987, 'Productivity loss in brainstorming groups: towards the solution of a riddle', *Journal of Personality and Social Psychology*, vol. 53, no. 3, pp. 447–509.

Diehl, M., and Stroebe, W., 1991, 'Productivity loss in idea-generating groups: tracking down the blocking effect', *Journal of Personality and Social Psychology*, vol. 61, no. 3, pp. 392–403.

Diener, E., 1979, 'Deindividuation, self-awareness and disinhibition', *Journal of Personal and Social Psychology*, vol. 37, no. 7, pp. 1160–71.

Diener, E., 1980, 'Deindividuation: the absence of self-awareness and self-regulation in group members', in H.B. Paulus (ed.), *The Psychology of Group Influence*, Lawrence Erlbaum, Hillsdale, NJ, pp. 209–42.

Dimmick, S., 1995, *Successful Communication Through NLP: A Trainer's Guide*, Gower, Aldershot.

Dixon, N.F., 1994, *On the Psychology of Military Incompetence*, Pimlico, London.

Dixon, N.M., 1999, *The Organizational Learning Cycle: How We Can Learn Collectively*, Gower, Aldershot (second edition).

Dixon, N.M., 2000, *Common Knowledge: How Companies Thrive by Sharing What They Know*, Harvard Business School Press, Boston, MA.

Dodd-McCue, D., 1991, 'Led like sheep: an exercise for linking group decision-making to different types of task', *Journal of Management Education*, vol. 15, no. 3, pp. 335–9.

Doherty, N. and Tyson, S., 1998, *Mental Well Being in the Workplace: A Resource Pack for Management Training and Development*, Health and Safety Executive, London.

Doms, M. and van Avermaet, E., 1981, 'The conformity effect: a timeless phenomenon?', *Bulletin of the British Psychological Society*, vol. 36, pp. 180–8.

Doyle, M., Claydon, T. and Buchanan, D., 2000, 'Mixed results, lousy process: contrasts and contradictions in the management experience of change', *British Journal of Management*, vol. 11 (special conference issue), pp. 59–80.

Dreu, C. and Van de Vliert, E. (eds), 1997, *Using Conflict in Organizations*, Sage Publications, London.

Drory, A., 1993, 'Perceived political climate and job attitudes', *Organization Studies*, vol. 14, no. 2, pp. 59–71.

Drory, A. and Romm, T., 1990, 'The definition of organizational politics: a review', *Human Relations*, vol. 43, no. 11, pp. 1134–54.

Drummond. G., 1994, 'Irresistible science of the super-sellers', *Focus*, November, pp. 24, 26.

Druskat, V.U. and Wolff, S.B., 2001, 'Building the emotional intelligence of groups', *Harvard Business Review*, vol. 79, no. 3, March, pp. 81–90.

DuBrin, A.J., 1994, *Applying Psychology: Individual and Organizational Effectiveness*, Prentice-Hall, Englewood Cliffs, NJ.

Du Guy, P., 2000, *In Praise of Bureaucracy*, Routledge, London.

Dulewicz, S.V., 1995, 'A validation of Belbin's team roles from 16PF and OPQ using bosses' ratings of competence', *Journal of Occupational and Organizational Psychology*, vol. 68, no. 2, pp. 81–99.

Dumaine, B., 1990, 'Who needs a boss?', *Fortune*, 7 May, pp. 10, 40–7.

Duncan, R.B., 1972, 'Characteristics of organizational environments and perceived environmental uncertainty', *Administrative Science Quarterly*, vol. 17, no. 3, pp. 313–27.

Duncan, R.B., 1973, 'Multiple decision-making structures in adapting to environmental uncertainty: the impact of organizational effectiveness', *Human Relations*, vol. 26, pp. 273–91.

Duncan, R.B., 1974, 'Modifications in decision-making structures in adapting to the environment: some implications for organizational learning', *Decision Sciences*, vol. 5, pp. 704–25.

Duncan, R.B., 1979, 'What is the right organization structure? Decision tree analysis provides the answer', *Organizational Dynamics*, Winter, pp. 59–80.

Dunphy, D., 1981, *Organizational Change by Choice*, McGraw-Hill, Sydney (reprinted 1993).

Dunphy, D., Benn, S. and Griffiths, A., 2002, *Organizational Change for Corporate Sustainability*, Routledge, London.

Dunphy, D. and Stace, D.A., 1990, *Under New Management: Australian Organizations in Transition*, McGraw-Hill, Sydney.

Durand, J.-P., Stewart, p. and Castillo, J.J. (eds), 1999, *Teamwork in the Automobile Industry: Radical Change or Passing Fashion*, Macmillan Business, Basingstoke.

Earley, P.C., 1989, 'Social loafing and collectivism: a comparison of the United States and the People's Republic of China', *Administrative Science Quarterly*, vol. 34, no. 4, December, pp. 65–81.

Earley, P.C., 1993, 'East meets West meets Mideast: further explorations of collectivist and individualistic work groups', *Academy of Management Journal*, vol. 36, no. 2, April, pp. 319–48.

Easterby-Smith, M. and Araujo, L., 1999, 'Organizational learning: current debates and opportunities', in Mark Easterby-Smith, John Burgoyne and Luis Araujo (eds), *Organizational Learning and the Learning Organization: Developments in Theory and Practice*, Sage Publications, London, pp. 1–21.

Easterby-Smith, M., Burgoyne, J. and Araujo, L. (eds), 1999, *Organizational Learning and the Learning Organization: Developments in Theory and Practice*, Sage Publications, London.

Ebers, M. (ed.), 1999, *The Formation of Inter-Organizational Networks*, Oxford University Press, Oxford.

Eccles, T., 1994, *Succeeding with Change: Implementing Action-Driven Strategies*, McGraw-Hill, London.

The Economist, 1993, 'Jury science', 8 July, p. 86.

The Economist, 1994a, 'The celling out of America', 17 December, pp. 71–2.

The Economist, 1995, 'Heightism: short guys finish last', 23 December, pp. 21–6.

The Economist, 1998a, 'The science of alliance', 4 April, p. 91.

The Economist, 1998b, 'Service with a smile', 25 April, pp. 85–6.

The Economist, 1999a, 'The Exxon Valdez: stains that remain', 20 March, p. 63.

The Economist, 1999b, 'The end of privacy: the surveillance society', 1 May, pp. 105–7.

The Economist, 1999c, 'A price on the priceless', 12 June, pp. 94, 98.

The Economist, 1999d, 'All over in a flash', 9 October, p. 142.

The Economist, 1999e, 'Rethinking thinking', 18 December, pp. 77–9.

The Economist, 1999f, 'The lion's friendly approach', 18 December, pp. 149–50.

The Economist, 2000, 'In search of the new Japanese dream', 19 February, pp. 69–71.

The Economist, 2000, 'The land of disappointments', 4 March, pp. 115–17.

The Economist, 2000, 'Running scared', 8 April, p. 37.

The Economist, 2000, 'Negotating by email', 8 April, p. 85.

The Economist, 2001, 'A long march', 14 July 2001, special report on mass customization, p. 81.

The Economist, 2001a, 'Outsourcing: out of the back room', 1 December, pp. 75–6.

The Economist, 2001b, 'A matter of choice', Christmas special, The Future of the Company, 22 December, pp. 82–4.

The Economist, 2002, 'No small matter', 2 March, pp. 68–9.

The Economist, 2002, 'Marriage in name only', 2 March, pp. 72–3.

The Economist, 2002, 'Press the flesh, not the keyboard', 24 August, pp. 56–7.

The Economist, 2002, 'Washington's mega-merger', 23 November, pp. 51–3.

The Economist, 2002, 'Military revolutions', A survey of the defence industry, 20 July, pp. 7–9.

The Economist, 2003, 'Living with a superpower', 4 January, pp. 20–2.

The Economist Technology Quarterly, 2001, 'Of high priests and pragmatists', 23 June, p. 16.

Edmondson, A., Bohmer, R. and Pisano, G., 2001, 'Speeding up team learning', *Harvard Business Review*, vol. 79, no. 9, October, pp. 125–32.

Edwards, R.C., 1979, *Contested Terrain: The Transformation of Industry in the Twentieth Century*, Heinemann, London.

Egan, G., 1994, *Working the Shadow Side: A Guide to Positive Behind-the-Scenes Management*, Jossey-Bass, San Francisco.

Einsiedel, A.A., 1983, 'Decision-making and problem-solving skills: the rational versus the garbage-can model of decision-making', *Project Management Quarterly*, vol. 14, no. 4, pp. 52–7.

Eisenhardt, K.M. and Bourgeois, L.J., 1988, 'Politics of strategic decision-making in high-velocity environments: towards a mid-range theory', *Academy of Management Journal*, vol. 31, no. 4, pp. 737–70.

Eisenhardt, K.M. and Galunic, D.C., 2000, 'Co-evolving: at last a way to make synergies', *Harvard Business Review*, January–February, pp. 99–101.

Eisenhardt, K.M., Kahwajy, J.L. and Bourgeois, L.J., 1997, 'How management teams can have a good fight', *Harvard Business Review*, July–August, pp. 77–85.

Elkin, G. and Inkson, K., 2000, *Organizational Behaviour in New Zealand*, Prentice Hall, Auckland, New Zealand.

Ellis, B.E., 1991, *American Psycho*, Random House/Pan Books, New York/London.

Emery, F.E. and Trist, E.L., 1960, 'Socio-technical systems', in C.W. Churchman and M. Verhulst (eds), *Management Science, Models and Techniques*, vol. 2, Pergamon Press, London, pp. 83–97.

Emery, F.E. and Trist, E.L., 1965, 'Causal texture of organizational environments', *Human Relations*, February, pp. 21–32.

Emmison, M. and Smith, P., 2000, *Researching the Visual: Images, Objects, Contexts and Interactions in Social and Cultural Inquiry*, Sage Publications, London.

Engardio, P., Bernstein, A. and Kripalani, M., 2003, 'The new global job shift', *Business Week*, 3 February pp. 36–48.

Esser, J.K. and Lindoerfer, J.S., 1989, 'Groupthink and the Space Shuttle Challenger accident', *Journal of Behavioural Decision Making*, vol. 2, pp. 167–77.

Eysenck, H.J., 1970, *The Structure of Human Personality*, Methuen, London (third edition).

Eysenck, H.J., 1990, 'Biological dimensions of personality', in L.A. Pervin (ed.), *Handbook of Personality, Theory and Research*, Guilford Press, New York, pp. 244–76.

Farrell, D. and Petersen, J.C., 1982, 'Patterns of political behaviour in organizations', *Academy of Management Review*, vol. 7, no. 3, pp. 403–12.

Faulkner, D.O., 1996, 'Thoughts on the virtual corporation', Working paper presented to the British Academy of Management Conference, Aston University, Birmingham, September.

Fayol, H., 1916, *General and Industrial Administration*, Pitman, London.

Feintuch, D., 1996, *Midshipman's Hope*, Orbit/Little Brown and Company, Boston, MA.

Feldman, D., 1984, 'The development and enforcement of group norms', *Academy of Management Review*, vol. 9, no. 1, pp. 47–53.

Feldman, D. and Klitch, N., 1991, 'Impression management and career strategies', in K. Giacalone and p. Rosenfeld (eds), *Applied Impression Management: How Image Making Affects Managerial Decisions*, Sage Publications, London, pp. 67–80.

Feldman, M., 1991, 'The meanings of ambiguity: learning from stories and metaphors', in p. Frost, L. Moore, M. Louis, C. Lundberg and J. Martin (eds), *Reframing Organization Culture*, Sage Publications, Newbury Park, CA, pp. 145–56.

Ferster, C.S. and Skinner, B.F., 1957, *Schedules of Reinforcement*, Appleton-Century-Crofts, New York.

Festinger, L., Pepitone, A. and Newcomb, T., 1952, 'Some consequences of deindividuation in a group', *Journal of Abnormal and Social Psychology*, vol. 47, pp. 382–9.

Fiedler, F.E., 1967, *A Theory of Leadership Effectiveness*, McGraw-Hill, New York.

Fiedler, F.E. and Chemers, M.M., 1974, *Leadership and Effective Management*, Scott, Foresman, Glenview, IL.

Fiedler, F.E. and Chemers, M.M., 1984, *Improving Leadership Effectiveness: The Leaders Match Concept*, John Wiley, New York (second edition).

Fineman, S., 1995, 'Stress, emotion and intervention', in T. Newton, J. Handy and S. Fineman (eds), *Managing Stress: Emotions and Power at Work*, Sage Publications, London.

Fischbacher, M. and Francis, A., 1998, 'Purchaser–provider relationships and innovations: a case study of GP purchasing in Glasgow', *Financial Accountability and Management*, vol. 14, no. 4, pp. 281–98.

Fisher, R. and Ury, W., 1981, *Getting to Yes: Negotiating Agreement Without Giving In*, Hutchinson, London.

Fisher, S.G., Hunter, T.A. and Macrosson, W.K.D., 1997, 'Team or group: managers' perceptions of the differences', *Journal of Managerial Psychology*, vol. 12, no. 4, pp. 232–42.

Fisher, S.G., Hunter, T.A. and Macrosson, W.K.D., 1998, 'The structure of Belbin's team roles', *Journal of Occupational and Organizational Psychology*, vol. 71, no. 3, pp. 283–8.

Fisher, S.G., Hunter, T.A. and Macrosson, W.D.K., 2000, 'The distribution of Belbin team roles among UK managers', *Personnel Review*, vol. 29, no. 2, pp. 124–40.

Fisher, S.G. and Macrosson, W.K.D., 1995, 'Early influences on management team roles', *Journal of Managerial Psychology*, vol. 10, no. 7, pp. 8–15.

Fisher, S.G., Macrosson, W.K.D. and Sharp, G., 1996, 'Further evidence concerning the Belbin team role self-perception inventory', *Personnel Review*, vol. 25, no. 2, pp. 61–7.

Fleishman, E.A., 1953a, 'The description of supervisory behaviour', *Journal of Applied Psychology*, vol. 37, no. 1, pp. 1–6.

Fleishman, E.A., 1953b, 'The measurement of leadership attitudes in industry', *Journal of Applied Psychology*, vol. 37, no. 3, pp. 153–8.

Fleishman, E.A. and Harris, E.F., 1962, 'Patterns of leadership behaviour related to employee grievances and turnover', *Personnel Psychology*, vol. 15, pp. 43–56.

Fombrun, C.J., 1984, 'Organization culture and competitive strategy', in C.J. Fombrun, N.M. Tichy and M.A. Devanna (eds), *Strategic Human Resource Management*, Wiley, New York.

Fombrun, C.J., Tichy, N.M. and Devanna, M.A., 1984, *Strategic Human Resource Management*, John Wiley & Sons, New York.

Ford, H. and Crowther, S., 1924, *My Life and Work*, William Heinemann, London.

Ford, R.C. and Fottler, M.D., 1995, 'Empowerment a matter of degree', *Academy of Management Executive*, vol. 9, no. 3, pp. 21–31.

Ford, R.N., 1969, *Motivation Through the Work Itself*, American Management Association, New York.

Foreman, J. and Thatchenkery, T.J., 1996, 'Filmic representations for organizational analysis: the characterization of a transplant organization in the film *Rising Sun*', *Journal of Organizational Change Management*, vol. 9, no. 3, pp. 44–61.

Foucault, M., 1979, *Discipline and Punish*, Penguin, Harmondsworth.

Fourboul, C.V. and Bournois, F., 1999, 'Strategic communication with employees in large European companies: a typology', *European Management Journal*, vol. 17, no. 2, April, pp. 204–17.

Fox, A., 1966, *Industrial Sociology and Industrial Relations*, Research Paper 3, Royal Commission on Trade Unions and Employers' Associations, HMSO, London.

Fox, A., 1973, 'Industrial relations: a social critique of pluralist ideology', in John Child (ed.), *Man and Organization*, Allen and Unwin, London, pp. 185–233.

Fox, A., 1974, *Man Mismanagement*, Hutchinson, London.

Fraser, C., 1978, 'Small groups: structure and leadership', in Henri Tajfel and Colin Fraser (eds), *Introducing Social Psychology*, Penguin Books, Harmondsworth, pp. 176–200.

French, J.R.P. and Raven, B.H., 1958, 'The bases of social power', in D. Cartwright (ed.), *Studies in Social Power*, Institute for Social Research, University of Michigan Press, Ann Arbor, MI.

French, W.L. and Bell, C.H., 1999, *Organization Development: Behavioural Science Interventions for Organizational Improvement*, Prentice-Hall, Upper Saddle River, NJ (sixth edition).

Friedman, K., 1998, 'Cities in the information age: a Scandinavian perspective', in M. Igbaria and M. Tan (eds), *The Virtual Workplace*, Idea Publishing, Hershey, PA, pp. 144–76.

Friedman, M. and Rosenman, R.F., 1974, *Type A Behaviour and your Heart*, Knopf, New York.

Friedman, R.A., Tidd, S.T., Currall, S.C. and Tsai, J.C., 2000, 'What goes around comes around: the impact of personal conflict style on work conflict and stress', *International Journal of Conflict Management*, vol. 11, no. 1, pp. 32–55.

Fuchs, V., 1968, *The Service Economy*, Basic Books, New York.

Fulk, J. and Collins-Jarvis, L., 2001, 'Wired meetings: technological mediation of organizational gatherings', in Fredric M. Jablin and Linda L. Putnam (eds), *The New Handbook of Organizational Communication*, Sage Publications, Thousand Oaks, CA, pp. 624–63.

Fulmer, R.M. and Herbert, T.T., 1974, *Exploring the New Management*, Macmillan, New York.

Fulop, L. and Linstead, S. (eds), 1999, *Management: A Critical Test*, Macmillan Business, London.

Furnham, A., 1997, *The Psychology of Behaviour at Work*, Psychology Press/Taylor & Francis, Hove, Sussex.

Furnham, A., 1999, 'Anti-hierarchy gurus fall flat on their faces', *Daily Telegraph*, 'Appointments section', 1 April, p. 43.

Furnham, A., 2000, 'The brainstorming myth', *Business Strategy Review*, vol. 11, pp. 21–8.

Furnham, A. and Gunter, B., 1993, 'Corporate culture: definition, diagnosis and change', in C.L Cooper and I.T. Robertson (eds), *International Review of Industrial and Organizational Psychology*, vol. 8, pp. 233–61.

Furnham, A., Steele, H. and Pendleton, D., 1993a, 'A psychometric assessment of Belbin's team role self-perception inventory', *Journal of Occupational and Organizational Psychology*, vol. 66, no. 3, pp. 245–57.

Furnham, A., Steele, H. and Pendleton, D., 1993b, 'A response to Dr Belbin's reply', *Journal of Occupational and Organizational Psychology*, vol. 66, no. 3, p. 261.

Gagliardi, P., 1986, 'The creation and change of organizational cultures: a conceptual framework', *Organization Studies*, vol. 7, no. 2, pp. 117–34.

Gallie, D., 1991, 'Patterns of skill change: upskilling, deskilling or the polarization of skills?', *Work, Employment and Society*, vol. 5, no. 3, pp. 319–51.

Gallie, D., White, M., Cheng, Y. and Tomlinson, M., 1998, *Restructuring the Employment Relationship*, Clarendon Press, Oxford.

Gallupe, R.B., Dennis, A.R., Cooper, W.H., Valacich, J.S, Bastianutti, L.M. and Nunamaker, J.F., 1992, 'Electronic brainstorming and group size', *Academy of Management Journal*, vol. 35, no. 2, pp. 350–69.

Gandz, J. and Murray, V.V., 1980, 'The experience of workplace politics', *Academy of Management Journal*, vol. 23, no. 2, pp. 237–51.

Gannon, M.J., 2001, *Working across Cultures: Applications and Exercises*, Sage Publications, London.

Gannon, M.J. and Newman, K.L. (eds), 2001, *The Blackwell Handbook of Cross-cultural Management*, Blackwell, Oxford.

Gantt, H., 1919, *Organizing for Work*, Harcourt, Brace and Hove, New York.

Gardner, W.L., 1992, 'Lessons in organizational dramaturgy: the art of impression management', *Organizational Dynamics*, vol. 21, no. 1, pp. 33–46.

Garrahan, P. and Stewart, P., 1992, *The Nissan Enigma: Flexibility at Work in a Local Economy*, Mansell Publishing, London.

Garten, J., 2002, *The Politics of Fortune: A New Agenda for Business Leaders*, Harvard University Press, Cambridge, MA.

Gartman, D., 1979, 'Origins of the assembly line and capitalist control of work at Ford', in A.S. Zimbalist (ed.), *Case Studies on the Labour Process*, Monthly Review Press, London, pp. 193–205.

Garvin, D.A. and Roberto, M.A., 2001, 'What you don't know about making decisions', *Harvard Business Review*, September, pp. 108–16.

Geller, E. Scott, 1983, 'Rewarding safety belt usage at an industrial setting: tests of treatment generality and response maintenance', *Journal of Applied Behavior Analysis*, vol. 16, no. 2, Summer, pp. 189–202.

George, J.M., 1992, 'Extrinsic and intrinsic origins of perceived social loafing in organizations', *Academy of Management Journal*, vol. 35, no. 1, pp. 191–202.

Gersick, C.J., 1988, 'Time and transition in work teams', *Academy of Management Journal*, vol. 31, no. 1, pp. 9–41.

Gersick, C.J., 1989, 'Marking time: predictable transitions in task group', *Academy of Management Journal*, vol. 32, no. 2, pp. 274–309.

Gherardi, S., 1997, 'Organizational learning', in Arndt Sorge and Malcolm Warner (eds), *The Handbook of Organizational Behaviour*, International Thomson Business Press, London, pp. 542–51.

Ghosn, C., 2002, 'Saving the business without losing the company', *Harvard Business Review*, vol. 80, no. 1, January, pp. 37–45.

Gibb, J.R., 1961, 'Defensive communication', *Journal of Communication*, vol. 11, September, pp. 41–9.

Giddens, A., 1990, *The Consequences of Modernity*, Polity Press and Blackwell, Cambridge and Oxford.

Gilbreth, F.B., 1911, *Motion Study: A Method for Increasing the Efficiency of the Workman*, Van Nostrand Co., New York.

Gilbreth, F.B. and Gilbreth, L., 1916, *Fatigue Study*, Sturgis and Walton, New York.

Gilbreth, L., 1916/1973, *The Psychology of Management*, Management History Series No. 22, Hive Publishing, Easton.

Gill, C., 1985, *Work, Unemployment and the New Technology*, Polity Press, Cambridge.

Gillespie, R., 1991, *Manufacturing Knowledge: A History of the Hawthorne Experiments*, Cambridge University Press, Cambridge.

Ginnett, R.C., 1993, 'Crews as groups: their formation and leadership', in E.L. Wiener, B.G. Kanki and R.L. Helmreich (eds), *Cockpit Resource Management*, Academic Press, San Diego, CA, pp. 71–98.

Glass, N., 1996, 'Chaos, non-linear systems and day-to-day management', *European Management Journal*, vol. 14, no. 1, pp. 98–106.

Goffman, E., 1959, *The Presentation of Self in Everyday Life*, Doubleday Anchor, New York.

Golding, W., 1954, *Lord of the Flies*, Faber & Faber, London.

Goldratt, E. and Cox, J., 1993, *The Goal*, Gower, Aldershot (second edition).

Goldstein, E., 2001, *Sensation and Perception*, Wadsworth, Belmont, CA.

Goldthorpe, J.H., Lockwood, D., Bechhofer, F. and Platt, J., 1968, *The Affluent Worker: Industrial Attitudes and Behaviour*, Cambridge University Press, Cambridge.

Goleman, D., 1995, *Emotional Intelligence: Why It Can Matter More Than IQ*, Bloomsbury, London.

Goleman, D., 1998, *Working with Emotional Intelligence*, Bloomsbury, London.

Goleman, D., 2000, 'Leadership that gets results', *Harvard Business Review*, vol. 78, no. 2, March–April, pp. 78–90.

Gollop, R., 2002a, *Sustainability and Spread in the National Booking Programme*, The NHS Modernization Agency, Leicester.

Gollop, R., 2002b, *From Scepticism to Support: What are the Influencing Factors?*, The NHS Modernization Agency, Leicester.

Golzen, G., 1989, 'Maestro, learn the company score', *The Sunday Times*, Appointments section, 25 June.

Goodrich, C.L., 1975, *The Frontier of Control*, Pluto Press, London.

Gordon, J., 1992, 'Work teams – how far have they come?', *Training*, vol. 29, no. 10, October, pp. 59–65.

Gordon, J., 1993, *A Diagnostic Approach to Organizational Behaviour*, Allyn and Bacon, Boston, MA (fourth edition).

Gouldner, A.W., 1954, *Patterns of Industrial Bureaucracy*, Free Press, New York.

Gouldner, A.W., 1957, 'Cosmopolitans and locals: towards an analysis of latent roles', *Administrative Science Quarterly*, vol. 2, no. 3, pp. 281–306.

Grant, R.M., 2002, *Contemporary Strategy Analysis: Concepts, Techniques and Applications*, Blackwell, Oxford (fourth edition).

Graves, D., 1986, *Corporate Culture: Diagnosis and Change*, St Martin's Press, New York.

Gray, I., 1987, *General and Industrial Management: Henri Fayol's Classic*, Pitman Learning, London (revised edition).

Gray, J.L. and Starke, F.A., 1984, *Organizational Behaviour: Concepts and Applications*, Merrill Publishing, Columbus, OH (third edition).

Green, P.L. and Plsek, P.E., 2002, 'Coaching and leadership for the diffusion of innovation in healthcare: a different type of multi-organization improvement collaborative', *Journal on Quality Improvement*, vol. 28, no. 2, February, pp. 55–71.

Greenberg, J., 1976, 'The role of seating position in group interaction: a review with applications for group trainers', *Group and Organizational Studies*, vol. 1, no. 3, pp. 310–27

Greenberg, J., 1999, *Managing Behaviour in Organizations*, Prentice-Hall, Upper Saddle River, NJ (second edition).

Greenberg, J. and Baron, R.A., 1999, *Behaviour in Organizations*, Prentice-Hall, Englewood Cliffs, NJ (seventh edition).

Greene, G., 1975, 'The Destructors' (short story written in 1954), in *Twenty-one Stories*, Penguin, Harmondsworth, pp. 7–23.

Greenhalgh, L., 2001, 'Managers face up to the new era', *Financial Times*, 'Mastering People Management' supplement, 11 October.

Greiner L.E., 1998, 'Evolution and revolution as organizations grow', *Harvard Business Review*, vol. 76, no. 3, pp. 55–68.

Griffin, R.W. and Head, T.-C., 1987, *Practising Management*, Houghton Mifflin, Boston, MA (second edition).

Griffiths, D., 1988, 'When man can't keep up with the machines of war', *Business Week*, 12 September, p. 28.

Groth, L., 1999, *Future Organizational Design*, John Wiley, Chichester.

Grottola, M., 1994, 'Teaching the social geometry of management with literary narrative', *Journal of Management Education*, vol. 18, no. 1, pp. 125–8.

Guest, D., 1984, 'Social psychology and organizational change', in M. Gruneberg and T. Wall (eds), *Social Psychology and Organizational Behaviour*, John Wiley, Chichester, pp. 183–225.

Guest, D., 1989, 'Personnel and HRM: can you tell the difference?', *Personnel Management*, January, pp. 48–51.

Guest, D., 1990, 'Human resource management and the American dream', *Journal of Management Studies*, vol. 27, no. 4, pp. 377–97.

Guest, D., 1997, 'Human resource management and performance: a review and research agenda', *The International Journal of Human Resource Management*, vol. 8, no. 3, pp. 263–76.

Guest, D., 1998, 'Is the psychological contract worth taking seriously?', *Journal of Organizational Behaviour*, vol. 19, pp. 649–64.

Guest, D., 2000, 'Piece by piece', *People Management*, vol. 6, no. 15, pp. 26–31.

Guest, D., 2001, 'Industrial relations and human resource management', in John Storey (ed.), *Human Resource Management: A Critical Text*, Thomson Learning, London (second edition), pp. 96–113.

Guest, D. and King, Z., 2001, 'Personnel's paradox', *People Management*, vol. 7, no. 19, 27 September, pp. 24–9.

Guirdham, M., 1995, *Interpersonal Skills at Work*, Prentice Hall, Hemel Hempstead (second edition).

Guirdham, M., 2002, *Interactive Behaviour at Work*, Financial Times/Prentice Hall, Harlow (third edition).

Gulowsen, J., 1979, 'A measure of work-group autonomy', in L.E. Davis and J.C. Taylor (eds), *Design of Jobs*, Goodyear, Santa Monica, CA (second edition), pp. 206–18.

Guzzo, R.A., 1996, 'Fundamental considerations about work groups', in M.A. West (ed.), *Handbook of Work Group Psychology*, John Wiley, Chichester, pp. 3–24.

Gyllenhammar, P., 1977, *People at Work*, Addison-Wesley, Reading, MA.

Hackman, J.R., 1983, *A Normative Model of Work Team Effectiveness*, Technical Report No. 2, Research Program on Group Effectiveness, Yale School of Organization and Management, New Haven, CT.

Hackman, J.R., 1987, 'The design of work teams', in J.W Lorsch (ed.), *Handbook of Organizational Behaviour*, Prentice-Hall, Englewood Cliffs, NJ, pp. 315–42.

Hackman, J.R., 1990, *Groups That Work and Those That Don't*, Jossey-Bass, San Francisco.

Hackman, J.R. and Oldham, G.R., 1974, 'The job diagnostic survey: an instrument for the diagnosis of jobs and the evaluation of job redesign projects', Technical Report no. 4, Department of Administrative Sciences, Yale University, New Haven, CT.

Hackman, J.R., Oldham, G. and Purdy, K., 1975, 'A new strategy for job enrichment', *California Management Review*, vol. 17, no. 4, pp. 57–71.

Hales, C., 1993, *Managing Through Organization*, Routledge, London.

Hall, E.T., 1976, *Beyond Culture*, Doubleday/Currency, New York.

Hall, E.T., 1989, *Understanding Cultural Differences*, Intercultural Press, Yarmouth, ME.

Hamel, G. and Prahalad, C.K., 1996, 'Competing in the new economy: managing out of bounds', *Strategic Management Journal*, vol. 17, no. 3, pp. 237–42.

Hamilton, A., 1999, 'The pay's the thing for business Bard', *The Times*, 7 April, p. 9.

Hamlin, B., Keep, J. and Ash, K. (eds), 2001, *Organizational Change and Development: A Reflective Guide for Managers, Trainers and Developers*, Financial Times/Prentice Hall, Harlow.

Hammarstrom, O. and Lansbury, R.D., 1991, 'The art of building a car: the Swedish experience re-examined', *New Technology, Work and Employment*, vol. 6, no. 2, pp. 85–90.

Hammer, M., 1990, 'Reengineering work: can't automate, obliterate', *Harvard Business Review*, vol. 68, no. 4, July–August, pp. 104–12.

Hammer, M. and Champy, J., 1993, *Reengineering the Corporation: A Manifesto for Business Revolution*, Nicholas Brealey, London.

Hammond, D., 2000, 'Unit set up to take action on council's race problem', *Personnel Today*, 11 April, p. 10.

Hampton, M.M., 1999, 'Work groups', in Y. Gabriel (ed.), *Organizations in Depth*, Sage Publications, London, pp. 112–38.

Handy, C., 1979, *Understanding Organizations*, Penguin Books, Harmondsworth (second edition).

Handy, C., 1984, *The Future of Work*, Blackwell, Oxford.

Handy, C., 1995, 'Trust and the virtual organization', *Harvard Business Review*, vol. 73, no. 3, pp. 4–50.

Haney, C., Banks, C. and Zimbardo, P.G., 1973, 'A study of prisoners and guards in a simulated prison', *Naval Research Reviews*, Office of Naval Research, Department of the Navy, Washington, DC, September.

Hardy, C. (ed.), 1995, *Power and Politics in Organizations*, Dartmouth, Aldershot.

Hardy, C. and Clegg, S.R., 1996, 'Some dare call it power', in S.R. Clegg, C. Hardy and W.R. Nord (eds), *Handbook of Organization Studies*, Sage Publications, London, pp. 622–41.

Hardy, C. and Palmer, I., 1999, 'Pedagogical practice and postmodern idea', *Journal of Management Education*, vol. 23, no. 4, pp. 377–95.

Hare, A.P., 1992, *Groups, Teams and Social Interactions*, Praeger, New York.

Harper, B., 2000, 'Beauty, stature and the labour market: a British cohort study', *Oxford Bulletin of Economics and Statistics*, vol. 62, December, pp. 773–802.

Harper, C.R., Kidera, G.J. and Cullen, J.F., 1971, 'Study of simulated airplane pilot incapacitation. Phase LL: subtle or partial loss of function', *Aerospace Medicine*, vol. 42, pp. 946–8.

Harris, C., 1992, 'NLP: a pathway to personal effectiveness', *Personnel Management*, July, pp. 44–7.

Harris, L.C. and Ogbonna, E., 1999, 'Developing a market-oriented culture: a critical evaluation', *Journal of Management Studies*, vol. 36, no. 2, pp. 177–98.

Harris, M., 1998, 'Re-thinking the virtual organization', in p. J. Jackson and J.M. van der Wielen, (eds), *Telework: International Perspectives*, Routledge, London.

Harrison, A., 1999, 'Getting the message: resistance to corporate communication in three British organizations', Paper presented to the Working Class Academics Conference, University of Arkansas, Little Rock, AR.

Harrison, E.F., 1999, *The Managerial Decision-making Process*, Houghton Mifflin, Chicago (fifth edition).

Harrison, M.I., 1994, *Diagnosing Organizations: Methods, Models and Processes*, Sage Publications, Thousand Oaks, CA.

Harrison, R., 1972, 'Understanding your organization's character', *Harvard Business Review*, vol. 50, no. 3, pp. 119–28.

Harvard Business Review, 2000, *Harvard Business Review on Negotiation and Conflict Resolution*, Harvard Business School Press, Boston, MA.

Harvard Business Review, 2003, 'Motivating people: how to get the most from your organization', Special issue, vol. 81, no. 1, January.

Haspeslagh, P., 1999, 'Managing the mating dance in equal mergers', *Financial Times*, 'Mastering Strategy' supplement, 25 October, pp. 6–7.

Hassard, J. and Holliday, R. (eds), 1998, *Organization-Representation: Work and Organizations in Popular Culture*, Sage Publications, London.

Hatch, M.J., 1997, *Organization Theory: Modern, Symbolic and Postmodern Perspectives*, Oxford University Press, Oxford.

Hatchett, A., 2000, 'Ringing true', *People Management*, vol. 6, no. 2, 20 January, pp. 40–1.

Hawkins, K., 2001, 'BP makes $100m saving since handing HR to Exult', *Personnel Today*, 19 June, p. 3.

Hawkins, P., 1997, 'Organizational culture: sailing between evangelism and complexity', *Human Relations*, vol. 50, no. 4, pp. 417–40.

Hayes, N., 1997, *Successful Team Management*, Thompson Business Press, London.

Heider, F., 1958, *The Psychology of Interpersonal Relationships*, John Wiley, New York.

Heil, G., Bennis, W. and Stephens, D.C., 2000, *Douglas McGregor Revisited*, Wiley, New York.

Heizer, J., 1998, 'Determining responsibility for the moving assembly line', *Journal of Management History*, vol. 4, no. 2, pp. 94–103.

Heller, F., 1997, 'Leadership', in Arndt Sorge and Malcolm Warner (eds), *The Handbook of Organizational Behaviour*, International Thomson, London, pp. 340–9.

Hellriegel, D. and Slocum, J.W., 1978, *Management: Contingency Approaches*, Addison-Wesley, Reading, MA.

Hendry, C. and Pettigrew, A.M., 1990, 'Human resource management: an agenda for the 1990s', *International Journal of Human Resource Management*, vol. 1, no. 1, pp. 17–43.

Hendry, C., Pettigrew, A.M. and Sparrow, P.R., 1989, 'Linking strategic change, competitive performance and human resource management: results of a UK empirical study', in Roger Mansfield (ed.), *Frontiers of Management Research*, Routledge, London.

Henkoff, R., 1994, 'Finding and keeping the best service workers', *Fortune*, 3 October, pp. 52–8.

Henry, J. and Hartzler, M., 1998, *Tools for Virtual Teams: A Team Fitness Companion*, ASQ Quality Press, Milwaukee, WI.

Herbst, P.G., 1962, *Autonomous Group Functioning*, Tavistock, London.

Hersey, P. and Blanchard, K.H., 1988, *Management of Organizational Behavior: Utilizing Human Resources*, Prentice-Hall, Englewood Cliffs, NJ.

Herzberg, F., 1966, *Work and the Nature of Man*, Staples Press, New York.

Herzberg, F., 1968, 'One more time: how do you motivate employees?', *Harvard Business Review*, vol. 46, no. 1, pp. 53–62.

Herzberg, F., 1987, 'Workers' needs the same around the world', *Industry Week*, 21 September, pp. 29–30, 32.

Hewlett, S.A., 2002, 'Executive women and the myth of having it all', *Harvard Business Review*, vol. 80, no. 44, April, pp. 66–73.

Hewlett, S.A., 2002, *Baby Hunger: The New Battle for Babyhood*, Atlantic Books, London (published in America as *Creating a Life: Professional Women and the Quest for Children*, Talk Miramax Books, New York).

Hickman, G.R., 1998, *Leading Organizations: Perspectives for a New Era*, Sage Publications, Thousand Oaks, CA.

Hickson, D.J. and McMillan, C.J., 1981, *Organization and Nation, The Aston programme IV*, Gower, Farnborough.

Hickson, D.J. and Pugh, D.S., 2002, *Management Worldwide: The Impact of Societal Culture on Organizations Around the Globe*, Penguin, Harmondsworth (second edition).

Hickson, D.J., Hinings, C.R., Lee, C.A., Schneck, R.E. and Pennings, J.M., 1971, 'A strategic contingencies theory of intra-organizational power', *Administrative Science Quarterly*, vol. 16, no. 2, pp. 216–29.

Higginbottom, K., 2002, 'HR shunned by boards', *People Today*, vol. 8, no. 3, 7 February, p. 10.

Higgs, M., 2003, 'Good call', *People Management*, vol. 9, no. 2, 23 January, pp. 48–9.

Highwater, R. and Sayeed, L., 1995, 'The impact of computer-mediated communication systems on biased group discussions', *Computers in Human Behaviour*, vol. 11, no. 1, pp. 33–44.

Hiley, D.R., 1987, 'Power and values in corporate life', *Journal of Business Ethics*, vol. 6, no. 5, pp. 343–53.

Hill, G.W., 1982, 'Group versus individual performance: are N + 1 heads better than one?', *Psychological Bulletin*, vol. 91, no. 3, pp. 517–39.

Hill, S., 1991, 'Why quality circles failed but total quality management might succeed', *British Journal of Industrial Relations*, vol. 29, no. 4, pp. 541–68.

Hillary, E., 1975, *Nothing Venture, Nothing Win*, Coronet, London.

Hinterhuber, H.H. and Levin, B.M., 1994, 'Strategic networks – the organization of the future', *Long Range Planning*, vol. 27, no. 3, pp. 43–53.

Hinton, P.R., 1993, *The Psychology of Interpersonal Perception*, Routledge, London.

Hite, S., 2000, *Sex and Business*, Financial Times/Prentice Hall, Harlow.

Hochschild, A., 1983, *The Managed Heart: Commercialization of Human Feeling*, University of California Press, Berkeley, CA.

Hochschild, A., 1997, *The Time Bind: When Home Becomes Work and Work Becomes Home*, Owl Books, New York.

Hoerr, J., 1989, 'The payoff from teamwork', *Business Week*, 10 July, pp. 56–62.

Hoerr, J., Pollock, M.A. and Whiteside, D.E., 1986, 'Management discovers the human side of automation', *Business Week*, 29 September, pp. 60–5.

Hofstede, G., 1986, 'Editorial: the usefulness of the concept of organization culture', *Journal of Management Studies*, vol. 23, no. 3, pp. 253–7.

Hofstede, G., 1991, *Cultures and Organizations*, McGraw-Hill, London.

Hofstede, G., 2001, *Culture's Consequences: International Differences in Work-related Values*, Sage Publications, London (second edition; first published 1984).

Hofstede, G. and Bond, M., 1988, 'The Confucian connection: from cultural roots to economic growth', *Organizational Dynamics*, vol. 16, no. 4, pp. 4–21.

Hogg, M.A. and Vaughan, G.M., 1998, *Social Psychology*, Prentice Hall, Hemel Hempstead.

Holden, L., 2001, 'Human resource management and Europe', in Ian Beardwell and Len Holden (eds), *Human Resource Management: A Contemporary Approach*, Financial Times/Prentice Hall, Harlow, England (third edition), pp. 679–707.

Holman, D. and Thorpe, R., 2003, *Management and Language: The Manager as a Practical Author*, Sage Publications, London.

Holpp, L., 1994, 'Applied empowerment', *Training*, February, pp. 39–44.

Homans, G.C., 1951, *The Human Group*, Routledge and Kegan Paul, London.

Homans, G.C., 1984, *Coming to My Senses*, Transaction Books, New Brunswick, NJ.

Hope, V. and Hendry, J., 1995, 'Corporate culture – is it relevant for the organization of the 1990s?', *Human Resource Management Journal*, vol. 5, no. 4, pp. 61–73.

Horrocks, C., 1997, *Beginner's Guide to Foucault*, Icon Books, London.

Hounshell, D.A., 1984, *From American System to Mass Production 1800–1932: The Development of Manufacturing Technology in the United States*, The Johns Hopkins University Press, Baltimore, MD.

House, R.J, 1988, 'Power and personality in complex organizations', in B.M. Staw and L.L. Cummings (eds), *Research in Organizational Behaviour, Vol. 10*, JAI Press, Greenwich, CT, pp. 305–57.

House, R.J., Spangler, W.D. and Woycke, J., 1992, 'Personality and charisma in the US President: a psychological study of leader effectiveness', *Administrative Science Quarterly*, vol. 36, p. 395.

Hout, T.M., 1999, 'Are managers obsolete?', *Harvard Business Review*, March–April, pp. 161–8.

Howard, p. J. and Howard, J.M., 1993, *The Big Five Workbook: A Roadmap for Individual and Team Interpretation of Scores on the Five-Factor Model of Personality*, Center for Applied Cognitive Studies, Charlotte, NC.

Howard, p. J., Medina, p. L. and Howard, J.M., 1996, 'The big five locator: a quick assessment tool for consultants and trainers', *The 1996 Annual: Volume 1, Training*, Pfeiffer & Company, San Diego CA, pp. 107–22.

Huczynski, A.A., 1993, *Management Gurus: What Makes Them and How to Become One*, Routledge, London.

Huczynski, A.A., 2001, *Encyclopedia of Management Development and Organization Change Methods*, Gower, Aldershot (second edition).

Huczynski, A., 2004, *Influencing within Organizations: Getting In, Rising Up and Moving On*, Routledge, London (second edition).

Hughes, J.A., O'Brien, J., Randall, D., Rouncefield, M. and Tolmie, P., 2001, 'Some "real" problems of "virtual" organization', *New Technology, Work and Employment*, vol. 16, no. 1, pp. 49–63.

Hughes, R.L., Ginnett, R.C. and Curphy, G.J., 1996, *Leadership: Enhancing the Lessons of Experience*, Irwin, Chicago.

Human Relations, 2000, Special Issue, vol. 53, no. 11.

Huselid, M.A., 1995, 'The impact of human resource management practices on turnover, productivity, and corporate financial performance', *Academy of Management Journal*, vol. 38, no. 3, pp. 635–72.

Hussey, D., 1998, *Managing Change*, Kogan Page, London.

Hutchins, E., 1990, 'The technology of team navigation', in J. Galegher, R.E. Kraut and C. Egido (eds), *Intellectual Teamwork: Social and Technological Foundations of Co-operative Work*, Lawrence Erlbaum Associates, Hillsdale, NJ, pp. 191–220.

Huws, U., 1999, 'Wired in the country', *People Management*, vol. 5, no. 23, 25 November, pp. 46–7.

Huxley, A., 1932, *Brave New World*, Chatto and Windus, London (Penguin Books, Harmondsworth, 1955).

Huxley, A., 1994, *The Doors of Perception/Heaven and Hell*, Flamingo, London (first published in 1954 by Chatto and Windus, London).

Huy, Q.N., 2001, 'In praise of middle managers', *Harvard Business Review*, vol. 79, no. 8, September, pp. 72–9.

Huysman, M., 1999, 'Balancing biases: a critical review of the literature on organizational learning', in Mark Easterby-Smith, John Burgoyne and Luis Araujo (eds), *Organizational Learning and the Learning Organization*, Sage Publications, London, pp. 59–74.

Ilgen, D.R. and Knowlton, W.A., 1980, 'Performance attributional effects on feedback from superiors', *Organizational Behaviour and Human Performance*, vol. 25, no. 3, pp. 441–56.

Incomes Data Services, 1999, *Pay and Conditions in Call Centres 1999*, Incomes Data Services, London.

Ingham, A.G., Levinger, G., Graves, J. and Peckham, V., 1974, 'The Ringelmann effect: studies of group size and group performance', *Journal of Experimental Social Psychology*, vol. 10, no. 4, pp. 371–84.

Ingram, M., 2001, 'Pay survey highlights growth of inequality', *World Socialist Web Site*, July (www.wsws.org).

Institute of Personnel and Development, 1998, *Call Centres*, Information Note 17, IPD, London.

Ireland, D., 1971, *The Unknown Industrial Prisoner*, Angus and Robertson/Vintage, Sydney Australia.

Ireland, D., 1997, *The Chosen*, Random House, Sydney.

IRS Employment Review, 1996, 'Turn on, tune in, churn out: a survey of teleworking', no. 609, June, pp. 6–15.

Isenberg, D.J., 1986, 'Group polarization: a critical review and meta-analysis', *Journal of Personality and Social Psychology*, vol. 50, no. 6, pp. 1141–51.

Ishiguro, K., 1989, *The Remains of the Day*, Faber & Faber, London.

Jablin, F.M., 2001, 'Organizational entry, assimilation, and disengagement/exit', in Fredric M. Jablin and Linda L. Putnam (eds), *The New Handbook of Organizational Communication: Advances in Theory, Research, and Methods*, Sage Publications, Thousand Oaks, CA, pp. 732–818.

Jablin, F.M. and Putnam, L.L. (eds), 2001, *The New Handbook of Organizational Communication: Advances in Theory, Research, and Methods*, Sage Publications, Thousand Oaks, CA.

Jackson, P. (ed.), 1999, *Virtual Working*, Routledge, London.

Jacobs, J.H., 1945, 'The application of sociometry to industry', *Sociometry*, vol. 8, pp. 81–98.

Janis, I.L., 1982, *Victims of Groupthink: A Psychological Study of Foreign Policy Decisions and Fiascos*, Houghton Mifflin, Boston, MA (second edition).

Jaques, E., 1956, *The Measurement of Responsibility*, Tavistock, London.

Jaques, E., 1976, *A General Theory of Bureaucracy*, Heinemann, London.

Jaques, E., 1982, *The Form of Time*, Crane Russak, New York.

Jaques, E., 1989, *The Requisite Organization*, Gower, Aldershot.

Jaques, E., 1990, 'In praise of hierarchy', *Harvard Business Review*, vol. 68, no. 1, January–February, pp. 127–33.

Javidan, M. and House, R.J., 2001, 'Cultural acumen for the global manager: lessons from the Project GLOBE', *Organizational Dynamics*, vol. 29, no. 4, pp. 289–305.

Jay, A., 1970, *Management and Machiavelli*, Penguin, Harmondsworth.

Jenkins, A., 1994, 'Teams: from ideology to analysis', *Organization Studies*, vol. 15, no. 6, pp. 849–60.

Jenkins, R., 1999, '£47,000 for teacher made sick by stress', *The Times*, 1 October, p. 11.

Jermier, J.M., Knights, D. and Nord, W.R. (eds), 1994, *Resistance and Power in Organizations*, Routledge, London.

Jerris, F.R., 1974, *Bosses in British Business*, Routledge and Kegan Paul, London.

Johnson, D.W. and Johnson, F.P., 1991, *Joining Together: Group Theory and Group Skills*, Prentice-Hall, Englewood Cliffs, NJ.

Johnson, G. and Scholes, K., 2002, *Exploring Corporate Strategy*, Financial Times/Prentice Hall, Harlow (sixth edition).

Johnson, P. and Gill, J., 1993, *Management Control and Organizational Behaviour*, Paul Chapman/Sage Publications, London.

Johnson, R., 2000, 'Ascent of woman', *People Management*, vol. 6, no. 1, January, pp. 26–32.

Johnston, R., 2000, 'Hidden capital', in J. Barry, J. Chandler, H. Clark, R. Johnston and D. Needle (eds), *Organization and Management: A Critical Text*, International Thomson Business Press, London, pp. 16–35.

Jones, J.E., 1973, 'Model of group development', *The 1973 Annual Handbook for Group Facilitators*, Pfeiffer/Jossey-Bass, San Francisco, pp. 127–9.

Jones, J.L., 2003, *Spread and Sustainability of Service Improvement*, The NHS Modernization Agency, Leicester.

Jones, O., 1997, 'Changing the balance? Taylorism, TQM and work organization', *New Technology, Work and Organization*, vol. 12, no. 1, pp. 13–24.

Jones, p. E. and Roelofsma, H.M., 2000, 'The potential for social contextual and group biases in team decision-making: biases, conditions and psychological mechanisms', *Ergonomics*, vol. 43, no. 8, pp. 1129–52.

Joseph, M., 1989, *Sociology for Business*, Blackwell, Oxford.

Jung, C.G., 1953, *Collected Works*, Bollingen Series/Pantheon, New York.

Jung, C.G., 1971, *Psychological Types* (*The Collected Works* of C.G. Jung, vol. 6), Princeton University Press, Princeton, NJ (first published in 1923).

Kafka, F., 1926/1957, *The Castle*, trans. Willa and Edwin Muir, Penguin, Harmondsworth (first published 1926 as *Das Schloss*, Wolff, Munich).

Kahneman, D. and Tversky, A., 1972, 'Subjective probability: a judgement of representativeness', *Cognitive Psychology*, vol. 3, no. 3, pp. 430–54.

Kahneman, D. and Tversky, A., 1973, 'On the psychology of prediction', *Psychological Review*, vol. 80, no. 4, pp. 237–51.

Kahneman, D. and Tversky, A., 1979, 'Prospect theory: an analysis of decision under risk', *Econometrica*, vol. 47, no. 2, pp. 263–92.

Kahneman, D. and Tversky, A., 1984, 'Choices, values and frames', *American Psychologist*, vol. 39, no. 4, pp. 341–50.

Kahneman, D. and Tversky, A. (eds), 2000, *Choices, Values and Frames*, Cambridge University Press, London.

Kakabadese, A., 1983, *The Politics of Management*, Gower, Aldershot.

Kamoche, K., 1994, 'A critique and a proposed reformulation of strategic human resource management', *Human Resource Management Journal*, vol. 4, no. 4, pp. 29–47.

Kamp, D., 1999, *The 21st Century Manager: Future-Focused Skills for the Next Millennium*, Kogan Page, London.

Kanigel, R., 1997, *The One Best Way: Frederick Winslow Taylor and the Enigma of Efficiency*, Little Brown and Co., London.

Kanter, R.M., 1977, *Men and Women of the Corporation*, Basic Books, New York.

Kanter, R.M., 1979, 'Power failure in management circuits', *Harvard Business Review*, vol. 57, no. 4, pp. 65–75.

Kanter, R.M., 1985, *The Change Masters: Corporate Entrepreneurs at Work*, International Thomson Business Press, London.

Kanter, R.M., 1989, *When Giants Learn to Dance: Mastering the Challenge of Strategy, Management and Careers in the 1990s*, Simon & Schuster, London.

Karasek, R.A., 1979, 'Job demands, job decision latitudes, and mental strain: implications for job redesign', *Administrative Science Quarterly*, vol. 24, no. 2, pp. 285–308.

Karau, S.J. and Williams, K.D., 1993, 'Social loafing: meta-analytic review and theoretical integration', *Journal of Personality and Social Psychology*, vol. 65, no. 4, October, pp. 681–706.

Katz, D., Maccoby, N. and Morse, N.C., 1950, *Productivity, Supervision, and Morale in an Office Situation*, University of Michigan Institute for Social Research, Ann Arbor, MI.

Katzenbach, J.R., 1998, *Teams at the Top*, Harvard Business School Press, Boston, MA.

Katzenbach, J.R. and Santamaria, J.A., 1999, 'Firing up the front line', *Harvard Business Review*, vol. 77, no. 3, May–June, pp. 107–17.

Katzenbach, J.R., Beckett, F., Dichter, S., Feigen, M., Gagnon, C., Hope, Q. and Ling, T., 1997, *Real Change Leaders: How Do You Create Growth and High Performance at Your Company?*, Nicholas Brealey, London.

Katzenbach, J.R. and Smith, D.K., 1993, *The Wisdom of Teams: Creating the High Performance Organization*, Harvard Business School Press, Boston, MA.

Keenoy, T., 1990, 'Human resource management: rhetoric, reality and contradiction', *International Journal of Human Resource Management*, vol. 1, no. 3, pp. 363–84.

Keenoy, T., 1999, 'HRM as hologram: a polemic', *Journal of Management Studies*, vol. 36, no. 1, pp. 1–23.

Kelley, H.H., 1971, *Attribution: Perceiving the Causes of Behaviour*, General Learning Press, New York.

Kemske, F., 1996, *Human Resources: A Business Novel*, Nicholas Brealey, London.

Kendon, A. (trans.), 2001, *Gesture in Naples and Gesture in Classical Antiquity*, by Andrea de Jorio, Indiana University Press, Bloomington, IN.

Keneally, 1991, *Flying Hero Class*, Hodder and Stoughton, London.

Kenney, M. and Florida, R., 1993, *Beyond Mass Production: The Japanese System and its Transfer to the US*, Oxford University Press, Oxford.

Khurana, R., 2002, 'The curse of the superstar CEO', *Harvard Business Review*, vol. 80, no. 9, pp. 60–6.

Kidder, T., 1997, *The Soul of a New Machine*, Random House, New York.

Kiely, M., 1993, 'When "no" means "yes"', *Marketing*, October, pp. 7–9.

Kipnis, D., Schmidt, S.M. and Wilkinson, L., 1980, 'Intra-organizational influence tactics: explorations in getting one's own way', *Journal of Applied Psychology*, vol. 65, pp. 440–52.

Kipnis, D., Schmidt, S.M., Swaffin-Smith, C. and Wilkinson, I., 1984, 'Patterns of managerial influence: shotgun managers, tacticians and bystanders', *Organizational Dynamics*, vol. 12, no. 3, Winter, pp. 58–67.

Kirkman, B.L., Gibson, C.B. and Shapiro, B.L., 2001, 'Exporting teams: enhancing the implementation and effectiveness of work teams in global affiliates', *Organizational Dynamics*, vol. 30, no. 1, pp. 12–29.

Knights, D. and Willmott, H., 1987, 'Organizational culture as management strategy: a critique and illustration from the financial services industry', *International Studies of Management and Organization*, vol. 17, no. 3, pp. 40–63.

Knights, D. and Willmott, H., 1999, *Management Lives: Power and Identity in Work Organizations*, Sage Publications, London.

Knights, D. and Willmott, H. (eds), 2000, *The Reengineering Revolution: Critical Studies of Corporate Change*, Sage Publications, London.

Kohn, A., 1993, 'Why incentive plans cannot work', *Harvard Business Review*, vol. 71, no. 5, pp. 54–63.

Koontz, H., 1966, 'Making theory operational: the span of management', *Journal of Management Studies*, vol. 3, no. 3, October, pp. 229–43.

Kornhauser, A., 1965, *Mental Health of the Industrial Worker*, John Wiley, New York.

Kotter, J.P., 1982, *The General Managers*, Free Press, New York.

Kotter, J.P., 1985, *Power and Influence*, Free Press, New York.

Kotter, J.P., 1990, *A Force for Change: How Leadership Differs from Management*, Free Press, New York.

Kotter, J.P., 1995a, 'Leading change: why transformation efforts fail', *Harvard Business Review*, vol. 73, no. 2, pp. 59–67.

Kotter, J.P., 1995b, *The New Rules: How to Succeed in Today's Post-Corporate World*, Free Press, Glenview, IL.

Kotter, J.P., 1996, 'Kill complacency', *Fortune*, 5 August, pp. 122–4.

Kotter, J.P., 1999, 'What effective general managers really do', *Harvard Business Review*, vol. 77, no. 2, pp. 145–59.

Kotter, J.P. and Schlesinger, L.A., 1979, 'Choosing strategies for change', *Harvard Business Review*, vol. 57, no. 2, pp. 106–14.

Koza, M.P. and Lewin, A.Y., 1999, 'Putting the S-word back in alliances', *Financial Times* 'Mastering Strategy' supplement, 1 November, pp. 12–13.

Littlepage, G.E., 1991, 'Effects of group size and task characteristics on group performance: a test of Steiner's model', *Personality and Social Psychology Bulletin*, vol. 17, pp. 449–56.

Littler, C.R., 1982, *The Development of the Labour Process in Capitalist Societies*, Heinemann, London.

Littler, C. and Salaman, G., 1982, 'Bravamania and beyond: recent theories and labour process', *Sociology*, vol. 16, no. 2, pp. 251–69.

Locke, E.A., 1968, 'Towards a theory of task performance and incentives', *Organizational Behaviour and Human Performance*, vol. 3, no. 2, pp. 157–89.

Locke, E.A., 1975, 'Personnel attitudes and motivation', *Annual Review of Psychology*, vol. 26, pp. 457–80.

Locke, E.A. and Latham, G.P., 1990, *A Theory of Goal Setting and Task Performance*, Prentice-Hall, Englewood Cliffs, NJ.

Locock, L., 2001, *Maps and Journeys: Redesign in the NHS*, The University of Birmingham, Health Services Management Centre, Birmingham.

Lodge, D., 1989, *Nice Work*, Penguin, Harmondsworth.

Lubatkin, M., Calori, R., Very, P. and Veiga, J., 1998, 'Managing mergers across borders: a two-nation explanation of a nationally bound administrative heritage', *Organizational Science*, vol. 9, no. 6, pp. 670–84.

Lukes, S., 1974, *Power: A Radical View*, Macmillan, London.

Luthans, F. and Davis, T.R.V., 1979, 'Behavioural self-management: the missing link in managerial effectiveness', *Organizational Dynamics*, vol. 8, no. 1, Summer, pp. 42–60.

Luthans, F. and Kreitner, R., 1985, *Organizational Behaviour Modification and Beyond*, Scott Foresman, Glenview, IL (second edition).

Luthans, F., Stajkovic, A., Luthans, B.C. and Luthans, K.W., 1998, 'Applying behavioural management in Eastern Europe', *European Management Journal*, vol. 16, no. 4, pp. 466–74.

McCaffrey, D.P., Faerman, S.R. and Hart, D.W., 1995, 'The appeal and difficulties of participative systems', *Organization Science*, vol. 6, no. 6, November–December, pp. 603–27.

McCalman, J. and Paton, R., 2000, *Change Management: A Guide to Effective Implementation*, Sage Publications, London (second edition).

McCauley, C., 1989, 'The nature of social influence in groupthink: compliance and internationalization', *Journal of Personality and Social Psychology*, vol. 57, no. 2, pp. 250–60.

McClelland, D.C., 1961, *The Achieving Society*, Van Nostrand, Princeton, NJ.

McClelland, D.C., Atkinson, J.W., Clark, R.A. and Lowell, E.L., 1976, *The Achievement Motive*, Irvington, New York (second edition).

McClelland, D.C. and Boyatzis, R.E, 1982, 'Leadership motive pattern and long-term success in management', *Journal of Applied Psychology*, vol. 67, no. 6, pp. 737–43.

McClelland, D.C. and Burnham, D.H., 1995, 'Power is the great motivator', *Harvard Business Review*, vol. 73, no. 1, pp. 126–39 (first published 1976).

MacDonald, S., 1999, 'Femininity rules, OK', *The Times*, 'First Executive' supplement, 30 September, p. 2.

MacDuffie, J.P., 1988, 'The Japanese auto transplants: challenges to conventional wisdom', *ILR Report*, vol. xxvi, no. 1, Fall, pp. 12–18.

McGregor, D.M., 1960, *The Human Side of Enterprise*, McGraw-Hill, New York.

McKinlay, A. and Quinn, B., 1999, 'Management technology and work in commercial broadcasting, c. 1979–1998', *New Technology, Work and Employment*, vol. 14, no. 1, pp. 2–17.

McKinley, A. and Taylor, P., 2000, *Inside the Factory of the Future: Work, Power and Authority in Microelectronics*, Routledge, London.

McLeod, p. L., Baron, R.S., Marti, M.W. and Yoon, K., 1997, 'The eyes have it', *Journal of Applied Psychology*, vol. 82, no. 5, pp. 706–18.

McLoughlin, I., 1999, *Creative Technological Change: The Shaping of Technology and Organizations*, Routledge, London.

McLoughlin, I. and Clark, J., 1994, *Technological Change at Work*, Open University Press, Buckingham (second edition).

McLoughlin, I. and Harris, M. (eds), 1997, *Innovation, Organizational Change and Technology*, International Thomson, London.

McNabb, R. and Whitfield, K., 1999, 'The distribution of employee participation schemes at the workplace', *International Journal of Human Resource Management*, vol. 10, no. 1, February, pp. 122–36.

McNeill, D., 2000, *The Face*, Penguin, Harmondsworth.

McRae, R.R. (ed.), 1992, 'The five-factor model: issues and applications', *Journal of Personality*, vol. 60, no. 2 (special issue).

Mabey, C., Salaman, G. and Storey, J., 1998, *Human Resource Management: A Strategic Introduction*, Blackwell, Oxford (second edition).

Machiavelli, N., 1961, *The Prince*, trans. G. Bull, Penguin, Harmondsworth.

Madison, D.L., Allen, R.W., Porter, L.W. and Mayes, B.T., 1980, 'Organizational politics: an exploration of managers' perceptions', *Human Relations*, vol. 33, no. 2, pp. 79–100.

Malim, T. and Birch, A., 1991, *Social Psychology*, Palgrave/Macmillan, Basingstoke.

Mangham, I., 1979, *The Politics of Organizational Change*, Greenwood Press, Westport, CT.

Mann, S., 1995, 'Politics and power in organizations: why women lose out', *Leadership and Organization Development Journal*, vol. 16, no. 2, pp. 9–15.

Manning, T., 1997, 'Team work, team roles and personality', *QWL News and Abstracts*, no. 129, Advisory, Conciliation and Arbitration Service, pp. 4–9.

March, J.G., 1962, 'The business firm as a political coalition', *Journal of Politics*, vol. 24, no. 4, November, pp. 662–78.

March, J.G, 1988, *Decisions and Organizations*, Blackwell, Oxford.

March, J.G. and Olsen, J.P., 1976, *Ambiguity and Choice in Organizations*, Universitetsforlaget, Oslo.

March, J.G. and Simon, H.A., 1958, *Organizations*, John Wiley, New York.

Marchington, M., 1992, *Managing the Team: A Guide to Successful Employee Involvement*, Blackwell, Oxford.

Marcic, D., 1992, *Organizational Behavior: Experiences and Cases*, West Publishing, St Paul, MN (third edition).

Margerison, C. and McCann, D., 1990, *Team Management*, W.H. Allen, London.

Margolis, A., 2001, 'Spirited responses', *People Management*, vol. 7, no. 18, 13 September, pp. 32–8.

Martel, L. and Biller, H., 1987, *Stature and Stigma*, D.C. Heath, Lexington, MA.

Martin, J., 1985, 'Can organization culture be managed?', in P.J. Frost, L.F. Moore and M.R. Louis (eds), *Organizational Culture*, Sage Publications, Beverley Hills, CA, pp. 95–8.

Martin, J., 1992, *Cultures in Organizations: Three Perspectives*, Oxford University Press, Oxford.

Martin, J., 2001, *Organizational Culture: Mapping the Terrain*, Sage Publications, London.

Martin, T.N. and Huq, Z., 2002, 'A hospital case study supporting workforce culture re-engineering', *Total Quality Management*, vol. 13, no. 4, pp. 523–36.

Maslach, C. and Leiter, M.P., 1999, *The Truth about Burnout*, Jossey-Bass, San Francisco.

Maslow, A., 1943, 'A theory of human motivation', *Psychological Review*, vol. 50, no. 4, pp. 370–96.

Maslow, A., 1954, *Motivation and Personality*, Harper & Row, New York.

Maslow, A., 1971, *The Farther Reaches of Human Nature*, Penguin, Harmondsworth.

Mathews, J., 1993, 'TCG R&D networks: the triangulation strategy', *Journal of Industry Studies*, October, pp. 64–74.

Maurer, S.D., Sue-Chan, C. and Latham, G.P., 1999, 'The situational interview', in Robert W. Eder and Michael M. Harris (eds), *The Employment Interview Handbook*, Sage Publications, Thousand Oaks, CA, pp. 159–77.

Mayes, B.T. and Allen, R.W., 1977, 'Toward a definition of organizational politics', *Academy of Management Review*, vol. 2, no. 4, pp. 672–8.

Mayo, E., 1933, *The Human Problems of an Industrial Civilization*, Macmillan, New York.

Mayo, E., 1945, *The Social Problems of an Industrial Civilization*, Harvard University Press, Cambridge, MA.

Mead, G.H., 1934, *Mind, Self and Society*, University of Chicago Press, Chicago.

Meek, V.L., 1988, 'Organization culture: origins and weaknesses', *Organization Studies*, vol. 9, no. 4, pp. 453–73.

Merkle, J., 1980, *Management and Ideology*, University of California Press, Berkeley, CA.

Merton, R.K., 1940, 'Bureaucratic structure and personality', *Social Forces*, vol. 18, pp. 560–8.

Metcalfe, B.-A. and Metcalfe, J.-A., 2002, 'The great and the good', *People Management*, vol. 8, no. 11, 10 January, pp. 32–4.

Metcalfe, B.-A. and Metcalfe, J.-A., 2003, 'Under the influence', *People Management*, vol. 9, no. 5, 6 March, pp. 32–5.

Meyerson, D. and Martin, J., 1987, 'Culture change: an integration of three different views', *Journal of Management Studies*, vol. 24, no. 6, pp. 623–47.

Micklethwait, J. and Wooldridge, A., 1996, *The Witch Doctors*, Heinemann, London.

Miles, R.M. and Snow, C.E., 1995, 'The new network firm: a spherical structure built on human investment philosophy', *Organizational Dynamics*, vol. 23, no. 4, Spring, pp. 5–18.

Miles, R.E. and Snow, C.C., 1986, 'Organizations: new concepts for new forms', *California Management Review*, vol. 28, no. 3, Spring, pp. 62–73.

Milgram, S., 1973, *Obedienece to Authority*, Tavistock, London.

Milkman, R., 1998, 'The new American workplace: high road or low road?', in P. Thompson and C. Warhurst (eds), *Workplaces of the Future*, Macmillan, Basingstoke, pp. 25–39.

Miller, E.J. (ed.), 1999, *Tavistock Institute Contribution to Job and Organizational Design* (2 vols), Ashgate, Aldershot.

Miller, E.J. and Rice, A.K., 1967, *Systems of Organization: The Control of Task and Sentient Boundaries*, Tavistock, London.

Miller, R. and Stewart, J., 1999, 'Opened university', *People Management*, vol. 5, no. 12, June, pp. 42–6.

Millman, R., 1997, *Farewell to the Factory: Autoworkers in the Late Twentieth Century*, University of California Press, Berkeley, CA.

Mintzberg, H., 1973, *The Nature of Managerial Work*, Harper & Row, New York.

Mintzberg, H., 1977, 'The manager's job: folklore and fact', *Harvard Business Review*, vol. 55, no. 4, July–August, pp. 49–61.

Mintzberg, H., 1979, *The Structure of Organizations*, Prentice-Hall, Englewood Cliffs, NJ.

Mintzberg, H., 1983a, *Structure in Fives: Designing Effective Organizations*, Prentice-Hall, Englewood Cliffs, NJ.

Mintzberg, H., 1983b, *Power In and Around Organizations*, Prentice-Hall, Englewood Cliffs, NJ.

Mintzberg, H.J., 1989, *Mintzberg on Management: Inside Our Strange World of Organizations*, Free Press, New York.

Mintzberg, H.J., 1994, 'That's not "turbulence", Chicken Little, it's really opportunity', *Planning Review*, vol. 22, no. 6, pp. 7–9.

Mintzberg, H.J. and van der Heyden, L., 1999, 'Organigraphs: drawing how companies really work', *Harvard Business Review*, September–October, pp. 87–94.

Mintzberg, H.J., Raisinghani, D. and Theoret, A. 1976, 'The structure of "unstructured" decision processes', *Administrative Science Quarterly*, vol. 21, no. 2, June, pp. 246–75.

Mitchell, W., 1999, 'Alliances: achieving long-term value and short-term goals', *Financial Times*, 'Mastering Strategy' supplement, 18 October, pp. 6–7.

Mohrman, S.A., Cohen, S.G. and Mohrman, A.M., 1995, *Designing Team-based Organizations*, Jossey-Bass, San Francisco.

Montgomery, C.A., 1995, *Resource-based and Evolutionary Theories of the Firm: Towards a Synthesis*, Kluwer, New York.

Moorhead, G. et al., 1931, 'Group decision fiascos continue: Space Shuttle Challenger', *Human Relations*, vol. 44, no. 6, pp. 539–50.

Morehead, A., Steele, M., Alexander, M., Stephen, K. and Dufflin, L., 1997, *Changes at Work: The 1995 Australian Workplace Industrial Relations Survey*, Longman, Melbourne.

Morell, V., 2001, 'The pyramid builders', *National Geographic*, November, pp. 78–99.

Moreno, J.L., 1953, *Who Shall Survive?*, Beacon Press, New York (second edition).

Morgan, G., 1989, *Creative Organization Theory*, Sage Publications, London.

Morgan, G., 1997, *Images of Organization*, Sage Publications, London (second edition).

Morgan, G., Frost, J. and Pondy, L., 1983, 'Organizational symbolism', in L. Pondy, p. Frost, G. Morgan and T. Danbridge (eds), *Organizational Symbolism*, JAI Press, Greenwich, CT, pp. 55–65.

Morgan, N., 2001, 'How to overcome "change fatigue"', *Harvard Management Update*, July, pp. 1–3.

Morita, M., 2001, 'Have the seeds of Japanese teamworking taken root abroad?', *New Technology, Work and Employment*, vol. 16, no. 3, pp. 178–90.

Morris, S., 1999, 'An Eastern art of healing that is heading West', *The Times*, 26 October, p. 47.

Mortensen, M. and Hinds, P., 2001, 'Conflict and shared identity in geographically distributed teams', *The International Journal of Conflict Management*, vol. 12, no. 3, pp. 212–38.

Moscovici, S., 1980, 'Towards a theory of conversion behaviour', in L. Berkowitz (ed.), *Advances in Experimental Social Psychology*, vol. 13, Academic Press, New York, pp. 209–39.

Moscovici, S., 1984, 'The phenomenon of social representations', in R.M. Farr and S. Moscovici (eds), *Social Representations*, Cambridge University Press, Cambridge.

Mowshowitz, A., 1994, 'Virtual organization: a vision of management in the information age', *The Information Society*, vol. 10, no. 4, pp. 267–94.

Mullins, L., 2002, *Management and Organisational Behaviour*, Financial Times/Prentice Hall, Harlow (sixth edition).

Murakami, T., 1997, 'The autonomy of teams in the car industry – a cross-national comparison', *Work, Employment and Society*, vol. 11, no. 4, pp. 749–58.

Murphy, M., 1996, *Small Business Management*, Pitman, London.

Myers, D.G., 1990, *Social Psychology*, McGraw-Hill, New York (third edition).

Myers, D.G., 1993, *Social Psychology*, McGraw-Hill, New York (fourth edition).

Myers, D.G. and Lamm, H., 1976, 'The group polarization phenomenon', *Psychological Bulletin*, vol. 83, no. 4, pp. 602–27.

Myers, I.B., 1962, *The Myers–Briggs Type Indicator Manual*, Educational Testing Service, Princeton, NJ.

Myers, I.B., 1976, *Introduction to Type*, Center for Applications of Psychological Type, Gainesville, FL (second edition).

Myers, I.B. and McCaulley, M.H., 1985, *Manual: A Guide to the Development and Use of the Myers–Briggs Type Indicator*, Consulting Psychologists Press, Palo Alto, CA.

Myerson, D.E., 2001, 'Radical change, the quiet way', *Harvard Business Review*, vol. 79, no. 9, October, pp. 92–100.

Nakamoto, M., 2003, 'A speedier route from order to camcorder', *Financial Times*, 12 February, p. 11.

Nandhakumar, J., 1999, 'Virtual teams and lost proximity', in p. Jackson (ed.), *Virtual Working*, Routledge, London, pp. 46–56.

Narayanan, V.K. and Rath, R.N., 1993, *Organization Theory: A Strategic Approach*, Richard D. Irwin, Homewood, IL.

Needle, D., 2000, 'Culture at the level of the firm: organizational and corporate perspectives', in Jim Barry, John Chandler, Heather Clark, Roger Johnston and David Needle (eds), *Organization and Management: A Critical Text*, Thomson Learning Business Press, pp. 101–18.

Nelson-Jones, R., 2000, *Introduction to Counselling Skills: Text and Actitivies*, Sage Publications, London.

Nemeth, C., 1986, 'Differential contributions of majority and minority influences', *Psychological Review*, vol. 93, no. 1, pp. 23–32.

Nevis, E., 1983, 'Using an American perspective in understanding another culture: toward a hierarchy of needs for the People's Republic of China, *Journal of Applied Behavioral Science*, vol. 19, no. 3, pp. 249–64.

New Scientist, 2002, 'Boozing with the boss', 26 January, p. 7.

New Technology, Work and Employment, 2001, Special Issue, vol. 16, no. 3.

NHS Modernization Agency, 2002, *Improvement Leaders' Guide to Sustainability and Spread*, Ancient House Printing Group, Ipswich.

Nohria, N., 1992, 'Is a network perspective a useful way of studying organizations?', in N. Nohria and R.G. Eccles (eds), *Networks and Organizations*, Harvard Business School Press, Boston, MA.

Nonaka, I. and Takeuchi, H., 1995, *The Knowledge Creating Company*, Oxford University Press, New York.

Nonaka, I., Umemoto, K. and Sasaki, K., 1999, 'Three tales of knowledge-creating companies', in Georg von Krogh, Johan Roos and Dirk Kleine (eds), *Knowing in Firms: Understanding, Managing and Measuring Knowledge*, Sage Publications, London, pp. 146–72.

Noon, M., 1992, 'HRM: a map, model or theory?', in Paul Blyton and Peter Turnbull (eds), *Reassessing Human Resource Management*, Sage Publications, London, pp. 16–32.

Noon, M. and Blyton, P., 2002, *The Realities of Work*, Palgrave, Basingstoke (second edition).

Norstedt, J.P. and Aguren, S., 1973, *Saab-Scania Report*, Swedish Employers' Confederation, Stockholm.

O'Connor, E., 1999, 'Minding the workers: the meaning of "human" and "human relations" of Elton Mayo', *Organization*, vol. 6, no. 2, pp. 223–46.

OECD, 1994, *Jobs Study: Evidence and Explanations Parts 1 and 2*, Organization for Economic Co-operation and Development, Paris.

Ogbonna, E., 1993, 'Managing organizational culture: fantasy or reality?', *Human Resource Management Journal*, vol. 3, no. 2, pp. 42–54.

Ogbonna, E. and Harris, L.C., 2002, 'Organizational culture: a ten-year, two-phase study of change in the UK food retailing sector', *Journal of Management Studies*, vol. 39, no. 5, pp. 673–706.

Ogburn, W.F., 1922, *Social Change: With Respect to Culture and Original Nature*, B.W. Huebsch, New York.

O'Leary-Kelly, A.M., Griffin, R.W. and Glew, D.J., 1996, 'Organization-motivated aggression: a research framework, *Academy of Management Review*, vol. 21, no. 1, pp. 225–53.

Oliver, A. and Ebers, M., 1998, 'Networking network studies: analysis of conceptual configurations in the study of inter-organizational relationships', *Organization Studies*, vol. 19, no. 4, pp. 549–83.

Oliver, N., Delbridge, R., Jones, D. and Lowe, J., 1994, 'World-class manufacturing: further evidence in the lean production debate', *British Journal of Management*, vol. 5, special edition, June, pp. 53–63.

Osterman, P., 1994, 'How common is workplace transformation and who adopts it?', *Industrial and Labour Relations Review*, vol. 47, no. 2, pp. 173–88.

Oswick, C. and Grant, D. (eds), 1996, *Organization Development: Metaphorical Explorations*, Pitman, London.

Ouchi, W.G., 1981, *Theory Z*, Addison-Wesley, Reading, MA.

Ouchi, W.G. and Johnson, A.M., 1978, 'Type Z organizations: stability in the midst of mobility', *Academy of Management Review*, vol. 3, no. 2, April, pp. 305–14.

Overell, S., 2002, 'The workplace story', *Personnel Today*, 30 April, p. 15.

Overell, S., 2002, 'A home from home', *Personnel Today*, 21 May, p. 13.

Overell, S., 2002, 'Work moves to home ground', *The Financial Times*, 2 August, p. 16.

Owen, G., 2000, 'Stressed teacher awarded £250,000', *The Times*, 5 December, p. 9.

Ozaki, M., 1996, 'Direct participation in work organization: a survey of recent international developments', *The Economic and Labour Relations Review*, vol. 7, no. 1, pp. 5–28.

Palmer, I. and Hardy, C., 2000, *Thinking About Management: Implications of Organizational Debates for Practice*, Sage Publications, London.

Palmer, P., 2000, *Balance of Power*, Coronet Books/Hodder & Stoughton, London.

Parker, G.M., 1990, *Team Players and Teamwork: The New Competitive Business Strategy*, Jossey-Bass, San Francisco and Oxford.

Parker, M., 2000a, *Organizational Culture and Identity*, Sage Publications, London.

Parker, M., 2000b, 'Postmodernizing organizational behaviour: new organizations or new organization theory', in J. Barry, J. Chandler, H. Clark, R. Johnston and D. Needle (eds), *Organization and Management: A Critical Text*, Thomson Learning, London, pp. 36–50.

Parker, M. and Slaughter, J., 1988, *Choosing Sides: Unions and the Team Concept*, South End Press, Boston, MA.

Parkinson, M., 1999, *Using Psychology in Business*, Gower, Aldershot.

Pascale, R.T., 1985, 'The paradox of organization culture: reconciling ourselves to socialization', *California Management Review*, vol. 27, no. 2, pp. 26–41.

Pascale, R.T. and Athos, A.G., 1982, *The Art of Japanese Management*, Penguin, Harmondsworth.

Pascale, R.T., Millemann, M. and Gioja, L., 1997, 'Changing the way we change', *Harvard Business Review*, November–December, pp. 127–39.

Patten, S., 1999, 'Incentives prove key method of keeping staff', *The Times*, 12 October, p. 38.

Patterson, M.G., West, M.A., Lawthom, R. and Nickell, S., 1997, *Impact of People Management Practices on Business Performance*, Institute of Personnel and Development, London.

Paul, W.J. and Robertson, K.B., 1970, *Job Enrichment and Employee Motivation*, Gower, Aldershot.

Paulus, P.B., Larey, T.S. and Dzindolet, M.T., 2001, 'Creativity in groups and teams', in M.E. Turner (ed.), *Groups at Work: Theory and Research*, Lawrence Erlbaum Associates, Mahwah, NJ.

Payne, R., 1996, 'The characteristics of organizations', in p. Warr (ed.), *Psychology at Work*, Penguin, Harmondsworth, pp. 383–407.

Pease, A., 1985, *Body Language: How to Read Others' Thoughts by their Gestures*, Camel Publishing, Avalon Beach, NSW, Australia (third edition 1997, Sheldon Press, London).

Pease, A., 1997, *Body Language: How to Read Others' Thoughts by their Gestures*, Sheldon Press, London (third edition).

Pedler, M., Burgoyne, J. and Boydell, T., 1997, *The Learning Company: A Strategy for Sustainable Development*, McGraw-Hill, London (second edition).

Peek, L., Coates, S. and Philp, C., 2003, 'Unions accuse BT of exporting call centre work', *The Times*, 8 March, p. 5.

Penrose, E., 1959, *The Theory of the Growth of the Firm*, Blackwell, Oxford.

Pentland, B.T., 1999, 'Building process theory with narrative: from description to explanation', *Academy of Management Review*, vol. 24, no. 4, pp. 711–24.

Perlman, E., 1998, *Three Dollars*, Picador/Pan Macmillan, Sydney.

Perrow, C., 1970, *Organizational Analysis: A Sociological View*, Wadsworth, Belmont, CA.

Perrow, C., 1973, 'The short and glorious history of organizational theory', *Organizational Dynamics*, vol. 2, no. 1, Summer, pp. 2–15.

Perry, B., 1984, *Enfield: A High Performance System*, Digital Equipment Corporation, Educational Services Development and Publishing, Bedford, MA.

Personnel Review, 2002, Special Issue, vol. 31, no. 3.

Personnel Today, 1999, 'BAE Systems grapples with merger bias fears', 14 December, p. 4.

Personnel Today, 2000, 'Manager commitment to partnership deals fading', 1 February, p. 7.

Personnel Today, 2000, 'Taxing message behind IR jargon', 18 April, p. 68.

Peters, T., 1987, *Thriving on Chaos: Handbook for a Management Revolution*, Macmillan, London.

Peters, T.J. and Waterman, R.H., 1982, *In Search of Excellence: Lessons from America's Best Run Companies*, Harper & Row, New York.

Pettigrew, A.M., 1973, *The Politics of Organizational Decision-Making*, Tavistock, London.

Pettigrew, A.M., 1985, *The Awakening Giant: Continuity and Change in ICI*, Basil Blackwell, Oxford.

Pettigrew, A.M., 1987a, 'Context and action in the transformation of the firm', *Journal of Management Studies*, vol. 24, no. 6, pp. 649–70.

Pettigrew, A.M. (ed.), 1987b, *The Management of Strategic Change*, Basil Blackwell, Oxford.

Pettigrew, A.M., 1998, 'Success and failure in corporate transformation initiatives', in R.D. Galliers and W.R.J. Baets (eds), *Information Technology and Organizational Transformation*, Wiley, Chichester, pp. 271–89.

Pettigrew, A.M., 1999, 'Organizing to improve company performance', *Hot Topics*, vol. 1, no. 5, February, Warwick Business School, Warwick University.

Pettigrew, A.M. and Fenton, E.M. (eds), 2000, *The Innovating Organization*, Sage Publications, London.

Pettigrew, A.M. and McNulty, T., 1995, 'Power and influence in and around the boardroom', *Human Relations*, vol. 48, no. 8, pp. 845–73.

Pettigrew, A.M. and Whittington, R., 2001, 'How to "join up" change', *People Management*, vol. 7, no. 20, 11 October, pp. 52–4.

Pfeffer, J., 1981, *Power in Organizations*, Harper Collins, London.

Pfeffer, J., 1992a, 'Understanding power in organizations', *California Management Review*, vol. 34, no. 2, pp. 29–50.

Pfeffer, J., 1992b, *Managing with Power: Politics and Influence in Organizations*, Harvard Business School Press, Boston, MA (second edition).

Pfeffer, J., 1996, *Competitive Advantage Through People: Unleashing the Power of the Work Force*, Harvard Business School Press, Boston, MA.

Pfeffer, J., 1998, *The Human Equation: Building Profits by Putting People First*, Harvard Business School Press, Boston, MA.

Pfeffer, J. and Salancik, G.R., 1978, *The External Control of Organizations: A Resource Dependence Perspective*, Harper & Row, New York.

Phillips, N., 1995, 'Telling organizational tales: on the role of narrative fiction in the study of organization', *Organization Studies*, vol. 16, no. 4, p. 625.

Pickard, J., 1993, 'The real meaning of empowerment', *Personnel Management*, November, pp. 28–33.

Pickard, J., 1999, 'Sense and sensitivity', *People Management*, vol. 5, no. 21, 28 October, pp. 48–56.

Pickard, J., 2000, 'The truth is out there', *People Management*, vol. 6, no. 3, 3 February, pp. 48–50.

Pinker, S., 1997, *How the Mind Works*, Penguin, Harmondsworth.

Pinker, S., 2002, *The Blank Slate: The Modern Denial of Human Nature*, Allen Lane/Penguin, London.

Piore, M. and Sabel, C., 1984, *The Second Industrial Divide*, Basic Books, New York.

Plous, S., 1993, *The Psychology of Judgement and Decision Making*, McGraw-Hill, New York.

Pollert, A., 1996, 'Teamwork on the assembly line: contradiction and the dynamics of union resilance', in p. Ackers, C. Smith and p. Smith (eds), *The New Workplace and Trade Unionism*, Routledge, London.

Porter, L.W. and Lawler, E.E., 1968, *Managerial Attitudes and Performance*, Irwin, Homewood, IL.

Powell, W.W., 1987, 'Hybrid organizational arrangements: new form or transitional development?', *California Management Review*, vol. 30, no. 1, pp. 67–87.

Powell, W.W., 1990, 'Neither market nor hierarchy: network forms of organization', *Research in Organizational Behaviour*, vol. 12, no. 1, pp. 295–336.

Powers, R., 2000, *Gain*, Heinemann, London.

Preece, D., 1995, *Organizations and Technical Change: Strategy, Objectives and Involvement*, Routledge, London.

Preece, D., Steven, G. and Steven, V., 1999, *Work, Change and Competition: Managing for Bass*, Routledge, London.

Price Waterhouse Coopers Consulting (PWC) and Market Opinion Research International (MORI), 1997, *Global Change Management Study*, PWC and MORI, London.

Proctor, S. and Mueller, F., 2000a, 'Teamworking, strategy, structure, systems and culture', in S. Proctor and F. Mueller (eds), *Teamworking*, Macmillan, Basingstoke, pp. 3–24.

Proctor, S. and Mueller, F. (eds), 2000b, *Teamworking*, Macmillan, Basingstoke.

Prosser, J. (ed.), 1998, *Image-based Research: A Sourcebook for Qualitative Researchers*, Falmer Press/Taylor & Francis, London.

Pruitt, S. and Barrett, T., 1991, 'Corporate virtual workspace', in M. Benedid (ed.), *Cyberspace: First Steps*, MIT, Boston, MA, pp. 383–409.

Psoinos, A. and Smithson, S., 2002, 'Employee empowerment in manufacturing: a study of organizations in the UK', *New Technology, Work and Employment*, vol. 17, no. 2, pp. 132–48.

Puffer, S.M., 1991, *Managerial Insights from Literature*, PWS-Kent, Boston, MA.

Pugh, D.S. (ed.), 1971, *Organization Theory: Selected Readings*, Penguin, Harmondsworth.

Pugh, D.S. and Hickson, D.J., 1976, *Organization Structure in its Context: The Aston Programme I*, Gower, Farnborough.

Pugh, D.S. and Hinings, D.J., 1976, *Organizational Structure Extensions and Replications: The Aston Programme II*, Gower, Farnborough.

Pugh, D.S. and Payne, R.L., 1977, *Organizational Structure in its Context: The Aston Programme III*, Gower, Farnborough.

Purcell, J., 1995, 'Corporate strategy and its link with human resource management strategy', in John Storey (ed.), *Human Resource Management: A Critical Text*, Routledge, London, pp. 63–86.

Purcell, J., Kinnie, N., Hutchinson, S. and Rayton, B., 2000, 'Inside the box', *People Management*, vol. 6, no. 21, 26 October, pp. 30–8.

Purcell, J., Kinnie, N., Hutchinson, S., Rayton, B. and Stuart, J., 2003, *People and Performance: How People Management Impacts on Organizational Performance*, Chartered Institute of Personnel and Development, London.

Puzo, M., 1998, *The Godfather*, Arrow Books, London.

Quah, D.T., 1997, 'Weightless economy packs a heavy punch', *Independent on Sunday*, 18 May, p. 4.

Rajan, A., Lank, E. and Chapple, K., 1999, *Good Practices in Knowledge Creation and Exchange*, Focus/London Training and Enterprise Council, London.

Rakos, R.F. and Grodek, M.V., 1984, 'An empirical evaluation of a behavioural self-management course in a college setting', *Teaching of Psychology*, October, pp. 157–62.

Ray, C.A., 1986, 'Corporate culture: the last frontier of control?', *Journal of Management Studies*, vol. 23, no. 3, pp. 287–97.

Reade, Q., 2003, 'Graduates put enjoyment at top of ideal job wish list', *Personnel Today*, 7 January, p. 8.

Redman, T. and Wilkinson, A., 2001, *Contemporary Human Resource Management: Text and Cases*, Financial Times/Prentice Hall, Harlow.

Reich, R., 1993, *The Work of Nations*, Simon & Schuster, London.

Reisner, R.A.F., 2002, 'When a turnaround stalls', *Harvard Business Review*, vol. 80, no. 2, pp. 45–52.

Reuer, J., 1999, 'Collaborative strategy: the logic of alliances', *Financial Times*, 'Mastering Strategy' supplement, 4 October, pp. 12–13.

Rice, A.K., 1958, *Productivity and Social Organization*, Tavistock, London.

Rice, A.K., 1963, *The Enterprise and its Environment*, Tavistock, London.

Richards, T., 1997, *Star Trek in Myth and Legend*, Orion Books, London.

Richardson, R. and Thompson, M., 1999, *The Impact of People Management Practices on Business Performance: A Literature Review*, Institute of Personnel and Development, London.

Ritchie, S. and Martin, P., 1999, *Motivation Management*, Gower, Aldershot.

Ritzer, G., 1993, *The McDonaldization of Society: An Investigation into the Changing Character of Contemporary Social Life*, Pine Forge Press, Thousand Oaks, CA.

Ritzer, G., 1995, *Expressing America: A Critique of the Global Credit Card Society*, Pine Forge Press, Thousand Oaks, CA.

Ritzer, G. (ed.), 1998, *The McDonaldization Thesis: Explorations and Extensions*, Sage Publications, London.

Robbins, S.P., 1974, *Managing Organizational Conflict: A Non-traditional Approach*, Prentice-Hall, Englewood Cliffs, NJ.

Robbins, S.P., 1990, *Organization Theory*, Prentice-Hall, Englewood Cliffs, NJ.

Robbins, S.P., 1998, *Organizational Behaviour: Concepts, Controversies and Applications*, Prentice-Hall, Englewood Cliffs, NJ (eighth edition).

Robbins, S.P., 2001, *Organizational Behavior*, Prentice-Hall International, Upper Saddle River, NJ (ninth edition).

Robbins, S.P., 2003, *Organizational Behaviour,* Pearson Educational Inc., Upper Saddle River, NJ (tenth edition).

Roberts, A., 2003, *Hitler and Churchill: Secrets of Leadership*, Weidenfeld and Nicolson, London.

Roberts, Z., 2003, 'Worrying about stress', *People Management*, vol. 9, no. 5, 6 March, pp. 14–15.

Robertson, I.T., 1994, 'Personality and personnel selection', in C.L. Cooper and D.M. Rousseau (eds), *Trends in Organizational Behaviour*, Wiley, London.

Robertson, I.T., 2001, 'Undue diligence', *People Management*, vol. 7, no. 23, 22 November, pp. 42–3.

Robinson, S.L. and O'Leary-Kelly, A.M., 1998, 'Monkey see, monkey do: the influence of work groups on the antisocial behaviour of employees', *Academy of Management Journal*, vol. 41, no. 6, pp. 658–72.

Robinson, S.L. and Rousseau, D.M., 1994, 'Violating the psychological contract: not the exception but the norm', *Journal of Organizational Behavior*, vol. 15, pp. 245–59.

Roethlisberger, F.J., 1977, *The Elusive Phenomenon: An Autobiographical Account of My Work in the Field of Organizational Behaviour at the Harvard Business School*, Harvard University Press, Cambridge, MA.

Roethlisberger, F.J. and Dickson, W.J., 1939, *Management and the Worker*, Harvard University Press, Cambridge, MA.

Rogelberg, S.G., Barnes-Farrell, J.L. and Lowe, C.A., 1992, 'The stepladder technique: an alternative group structure facilitating effective group decision making', *Journal of Applied Psychology*, vol. 77, no. 5, pp. 337–58.

Rogers, A., 1999, 'Personality transplant tames the boss', *The Sunday Times*, 13 June, p. 7.19.

Rogers, C.R. and Roethlisberger, F.J., 1952, 'Barriers and gateways to communication', *Harvard Business Review*, July/August, pp. 28–34.

Rollinson, D. and Broadfield, A., 2002, *Organisational Behaviour and Analysis: An Integrated Approach*, Financial Times/Prentice Hall, Harlow.

Rose, M., 1988, *Industrial Behaviour and Control*, Penguin, Harmondsworth.

Rose, N., 1990, *Governing the Soul: The Shaping of the Private Self*, Routledge, London.

Rosenfeld, P., Giacalone, R.A. and Riordan, C.A., 2001, *Impression Management: Building and Enhancing Reputations at Work*, Thomson Learning, London.

Rosenthal, R., 1973, *On the Social Psychology of the Self-fulfilling Prophecy: Further Evidence for Pygmalion Effects and Their Mediating Mechanisms*, MSS Modular Publication, Ann Arbor, MI, vol. 53, pp. 1–28.

Rosenthal, R. and Jacobson, L., 1968, *Pygmalion in the Classroom*, Holt, Rinehart and Winston, New York.

Ross, J. and Staw, B.M., 1993, 'Organizational escalation and exit: lessons from the Shoreham nuclear power plant', *Academy of Management Journal*, vol. 36, no. 4, August, pp. 701–32.

Rost, J.C., 1991, *Leadership for the Twenty-First Century*, Praeger/Greenwood Publishing, Westport, CT.

Rothwell, J.D., 1992, *In Mixed Company: Small Group Communication*, Harcourt Brace Jovanovich, Fort Worth, TX.

Rotter, J.B., 1966, 'Generalised expectations for internal v. external control of reinforcement', *Psychological Monographs*, vol. 80, whole issue no. 609, pp.1–28.

Rousseau, D.M., 1990, 'New hire perceptions of their own and their employers' obligations: a study of psychological contracts', *Journal of Organizational Behaviour*, vol. 11, pp. 389–400.

Rousseau, D.M., 1995, *Psychological Contracts in Organizations: Understanding Written and Unwritten Agreements*, Sage Publications, London.

Rousseau, D.M., 1999, 'Why workers still identify with organizations', *Journal of Organizational Behaviour*, vol. 19, no. 3, pp. 217–33.

Rowe, H., 2000, 'Half of all NHS ethnic staff face racial harassment', *Personnel Today*, 11 April, p. 8.

Roy, D. 1952, 'Quota restriction and goldbricking in a machine shop', *American Journal of Sociology*, vol. 57, no. 5, pp. 427–42.

Roy, D., 1960, 'Banana time: job satisfaction and informal interaction', *Human Organization*, vol. 18, pp. 156–68.

Rubery, J., Earnshaw, J., Marchington, M., Cooke, F.L. and Vincent, S., 2002, 'Changing organizational forms and the employment relationship', *Journal of Management Studies*, vol. 39, no. 5, pp. 645–72.

Rubery, J., Cooke, F.L., Earnshaw, J. and Marchington, M., in press, 'Contracts, co-operation and employment relationships: working in a multi-employer environment.

Ruble, T.T. and Thomas, K., 1976, 'Support for a two-dimensional model of conflict behaviour', *Organizational Behaviour and Human Performance*, vol. 16, pp. 143–55.

Ryan, R.M. and Connell, J.P., 1989, 'Perceived locus of causality and internalization', *Journal of Personality and Social Psychology*, vol. 57, no. 5, pp. 749–61.

Sabel, C., 1991, 'Moebius-strip organizations and open labour markets: some consequences of the reintegration of conception and execution in a volatile economy', in p. Bourdeu and C. Sabel (eds), *Social Theory for a Changing Society*, Sage Publications, London, pp. 23–61.

Sagie, A., Stahevsky, S. and Koslowsky, M., 2004, *Misbehaviour and Dysfunctional Attitudes in Organizations*, Palgrave, Basingstoke (forthcoming).

Salancik, G.R. and Pfeffer, J., 1974, 'The bases and use of power in organizational decision-making', *Administrative Science Quarterly*, vol. 19, no. 4, pp. 453–73.

Salancik, G.R. and Pfeffer, J., 1977, 'Who gets power – and how they hold on to it: a strategic contingency model of power', *Organizational Dynamics*, vol. 5, no. 3, Winter, pp. 2–21.

Salovey, P. and Mayer, J.D., 1990, 'Emotional intelligence', *Imagination, Cognition and Personality*, vol. 9, pp. 185–211.

Samaras, J.T., 1989, *Management Applications: Exercises, Cases and Readings*, Prentice-Hall, Englewood Cliffs, NJ.

Sappel, P., 2002, 'The name game', *Personnel Today*, 9 April, pp. 28–9.

Sashkin, M. and Morris, W.C., 1987, 'Decision types', *Experiencing Management*, Addison-Wesley, Reading, MA, pp. 73–4.

Savage, G.T., Blair, J.D. and Soreson, R.L., 1989, 'Consider both relationships and substance when negotiating strategy', *Academy of Management Executive*, vol. 3, no. 1, pp. 37–48.

Scarbrough, H., 1999, 'System error', *People Management*, 8 April, pp. 68–74.

Scarbrough, H. and Swan, J., 1999, *Case Studies in Knowledge Management*, Institute of Personnel and Development, London.

Schaffer, R.H. and Thomson, H.A., 1992, 'Successful change programs begin with results', *Harvard Business Review*, January–February, pp. 80–9.

Schein, E.H., 1969, *Process Consultation: Its Role in Organizational Development*, Addison-Wesley, Reading, MA.

Schein, E.H., 1983, 'The role of the founder in creating organization culture', *Organization Dynamics*, vol. 12, no. 1, Summer, pp. 13–28.

Schein, E.H., 1985, *Organizational Culture and Leadership*, Jossey-Bass, San Francisco.

Schendel, D., 1995, 'Introduction to technological transformation and the new competitive landscape', *Strategic Management Journal*, vol. 16, pp. 1–6.

Schilt, W.K., 1986, 'An examination of individual differences as moderators of upward influence activity in strategic decisions', *Human Relations*, vol. 39, no. 10, pp. 933–53.

Schlosser, E., 2002, *Fast Food Nation*, Penguin, Harmondsworth.

Schmitt, N. and Chan, D., 1998, *Personnel Selection: A Theoretical Approach*, Sage Publications, Thousand Oaks, CA.

Scholz, C., 1987, 'Organization culture and strategy – the problem of strategy fit', *Long Range Planning*, vol. 20, no. 4, pp. 78–87.

Schön, D.A., 1983, *The Reflective Practitioner*, Basic Books, New York.

Schuler, R.S. and Jackson, S.E., 1987, 'Linking competitive strategies with human resource management practices', *Academy of Management Executive*, vol. 9, no. 3, pp. 207–19.

Schuler, R.S. and Jackson, S.E., 1996, *Human Resource Management: Positioning for the 21st Century*, West Publishing Company, St Paul, MN.

Schuler, R.S. and Jackson, S.E. (eds), 1999, *Strategic Human Resource Management*, Blackwell Business, Oxford.

Schuler, R.S., Jackson, S.E. and Storey, J., 2001, 'HRM and its link with strategic management', in John Storey (ed.), *Human Resource Management: A Critical Text*, Thomson Learning, London (second edition), pp. 114–30.

Schultz, M., 1995, *Studying Organizational Cultures: Diagnosis and Understanding*, De Gruyter, Berlin.

Scott, A., 1994, *Willing Slaves: British Workers Under Human Resource Management*, Cambridge University Press, Cambridge.

Sculler, R. and Jackson, S., 2001a, 'HR issues and activities in mergers and acquisitions', *European Journal of Management*, vol. 19, no. 3, pp. 239–53.

Sculler, R. and Jackson, S., 2001b, 'Seeking an edge in mergers', *Financial Times*, 'Mastering People' supplement, 22 October, pp. 6, 8 and 10.

Scully, J.A., Sims, H.P., Olian, J.D., Schnell, E.R. and Smith, K.A., 1996, 'Tough times make tough bosses: a meso analysis of CEO leader behaviour', *Irish Business and Administrative Research*, vol. 17, no. 1, pp. 71–102.

Semler, R., 1993, *Maverick*, Century, London.

Semlinger, K., 1991, 'New developments in subcontracting: mixed market and hierarchy', in A. Amin and M. Dietrich (eds), *Towards a New Europe: Structural Changes in the European Economy*, Edward Elgar, Cheltenham.

Senge, P., 1990, *The Fifth Discipline: The Art and Practice of the Learning Organization*, Doubleday Currency, New York.

Senge, P., Kleiner, A., Roberts, C., Ross, R., Roth, G. and Smith, B., 1999, *The Dance of Change: The Challenges of Sustaining Momentum in Learning Organizations*, Nicholas Brealey, London.

Senior, B., 1997, 'Team roles and team performance: is there "really" a link?', *Journal of Occupational and Organizational Psychology*, vol. 70, no. 3, September, pp. 241–58.

Senior, B., 2001, *Organizational Change*, Pitman, London (second edition).

Sennett, R., 1998, *The Corrosion of Character: The Personal Consequences of Work in the New Capitalism*, W.W. Norton, New York.

Sewell, G. and Wilkinson, B., 1992, 'Someone to watch over me: surveillance, discipline and just-in-time labour process', *Sociology*, vol. 26, no. 2, pp. 271–91.

Sewer, A.E., 1992, 'The Hellish Angels' devilish business', *Fortune*, 30 November, pp. 84–90.

Shannon, C.E. and Weaver, W., 1949, *The Mathematical Theory of Communication*, University of Illinois Press, Urbana, IL.

Shapiro, B.S., 1977, 'Can marketing and manufacturing co-exist?', *Harvard Business Review*, vol. 55, September–October, pp. 104–14.

Shapiro, E.C., 1996, *Fad Surfing in the Boardroom*, Capstone, Oxford.

Sharpe, A., 2002, *Evaluation of Third Wave National Booking Programme*, The NHS Modernization Agency, Leicester.

Shaw, M.E. 1971, *Group Dynamics*, McGraw-Hill, New York.

Shaw, M.E., 1976, *Group Dynamics*, McGraw-Hill, New York (second edition).

Shaw, M.E., 1978, 'Communication networks fourteen years later', in L. Berkowitz (ed.), *Group Processes*, Academic Press, New York, pp. 351–61.

Sheldon, W., 1942, *The Varieties of Temperament: A Psychology of Constitutional Differences*, Harper, New York.

Sherif, M., 1936, *The Psychology of Group Norms*, Harper & Row, New York.

Sherif, M. and Sherif, C.W., 1953, *Groups in Harmoney and Tension*, Harper and Brothers, New York.

Sherman, H. and Schultz, R., 1998, *Open Boundaries: Creating Business Innovation Through Complexity*, Perseus Books, Reading, MA.

Simon, H., 1957, *Administrative Behaviour*, Macmillan, New York (second edition).

Simon, H., 1960, *The New Science of Management Decision*, Harper, New York.

Simon, H., 1986, 'Rationality in psychology and economics', *Journal of Business*, October, pp. 209–26.

Simpson, P., 1999, 'Blurred boundaries', *Personnel Today*, 16 November, p. 31.

Sims, D., Fineman, S. and Gabriel, Y., 1993, *Organizing and Organizations: An Introduction*, Sage Publications, London.

Sims, H.P. and Lorenzi, P., 1992, *The New Leadership Paradigm*, Sage Publications, Newbury Park, CA.

Sinclair, A., 1992, 'The tyranny of a team ideology', *Organization Studies*, vol. 13, no. 4, pp. 611–26.

Sisson, K., 1994, 'Personnel management: paradigms, practice and prospects', in Keith Sisson (ed.), *Personnel Management in Britain*, Blackwell, Oxford, pp. 3–50.

Sitkin, S.B. and Pablo, A.L., 1992, 'Reconceptualizing the determinants of risk behaviour', *Academy of Management Review*, vol. 17, no. 1, pp. 9–38.

Skinner, B.F., 1948, *Walden II*, Macmillan, London.

Skinner, W., 1981, 'Big hat, no cattle: managing human resources', *Harvard Business Review*, vol. 59, no. 5, pp. 106–14.

Sloman, M., 2002, 'Ground force', *People Management*, vol. 8, no. 13, 27 June, pp. 42–6.

Slovic, P. and Lichtenstein, S., 1971, 'Comparison of Bayesian and regression approaches in the study of information processing and judgement', *Organizational Behaviour and Human Decision Processes*, vol. 6, no. 6, November, pp. 649–744.

Smart, B. (ed.), 1999, *Resisting McDonaldization*, Sage Publications, London.

Smircich, L., 1983, 'Concepts of culture and organization analysis', *Administrative Science Quarterly*, vol. 28, no. 3, pp. 339–58.

Smircich, L. and Morgan, G., 1982, 'Leadership: the management of meaning', *Journal of Applied Behavioural Science*, vol. 18, no. 2, pp. 257–73.

Smircich, L. and Stubbart, C., 1985, 'Strategic management in an enacted world', *Academy of Management Review*, vol. 10, no. 4, pp. 724–35.

Smith, K. and Berg, D., 1997, 'Cross-cultural groups at work', *European Management Journal*, vol. 15, no. 1, pp. 8–15.

Smith, W.P., 1987, 'Conflict and negotiation: trends and emerging issues', *Journal of Applied Social Psychology*, vol. 17, no. 7, pp. 631–77.

Snow, C.C., Miles, R.E. and Coleman, H.J., 1992, 'Managing century network organizations', *Organizational Dynamics*, vol. 20, no. 3, pp. 5–20.

Sonnenfeld, J., 1985, 'Shedding light on the Hawthorne studies', *Journal of Occupational Behaviour*, vol. 6, pp. 111–30.

Sorenson, J.E. and Sorenson, T.L., 1974, 'The conflict of professionals in bureaucratic organizations', *Administrative Science Quarterly*, March, pp. 98–106.

Sorge, A. and Warner, M. (eds), 1997, *The Handbook of Organizational Behaviour*, International Thomson Business Press, London.

Sparrow, P., 1998, *Human Resource Management: The New Agenda*, Financial Times/Pitman, London.

Sparrow, P. and Hiltrop, J.-M., 1994, *European Human Resource Management in Transition*, Prentice Hall, Hemel Hempstead.

Spear, S. and Bowen, H.K., 1999, 'Decoding the DNA of the Toyota production system', *Harvard Business Review*, vol. 77, no. 5, September–October, pp. 97–106.

Spector, R., 2000, *Amazon.com: Getting Big Fast*, Random House, London.

Spencer, J. and Pruss, A., 1992, *Managing Your Team*, Piatkus, London.

Spinney, L., 2000, 'Blind to change', *New Scientist*, 18 November, pp. 27–32.

Stace, D.A., 1996, 'Transitions and transformations: four case studies in business-focused change', in J. Storey (ed.), *Cases in Human Resource and Change Management*, Blackwell Business, Oxford, pp. 43–72.

Stace, D. and Dunphy, D., 2001, *Beyond the Boundaries: Leading and Re-creating the Successful Enterprise*, McGraw-Hill, Sydney.

Stanton, N.A., Ashleigh, M.J., Roberts, A.D. and Xu, F., 2001, 'Testing Hollnagel's contextual control model: assessing team behaviour in a human supervisory control task', *International Journal of Cognitive Ergonomics*, vol. 5, no. 1, pp. 21–33.

Stanton, N.A., Ashleigh, M.J., Roberts, A.D. and Xu, F., in press, 'Virtuality in human supervisory control', *Ergonomics*.

Starkey, K. and McKinley, A., 1994, 'Managing for Ford', *Sociology*, vol. 28, no. 4, pp. 975–90.

Staw, B.M., 1976, 'Knee deep in the big muddy: a study of escalating commitment to a chosen course of action', *Organizational Behaviour and Human Performance*, vol. 16, pp. 27–44.

Staw, B.M., 1981, 'The escalation of commitment to a course of action', *Academy of Management Review*, vol. 6, no. 4, pp. 569–78.

Steijn, B., 2001, 'Work systems, quality of working life and attitudes of workers: an empirical study towards the effects of team and non-teamwork', *New Technology, Work and Employment*, vol. 16, no. 3, pp. 191–203.

Steiner, I., 1972, *Group Process and Productivity*, Academic Press, New York.

Steiner, I. and Rajaratnam, N.A., 1961, 'A model for the comparison of individual and group performance scores', *Behavioural Science*, vol. 6, no. 2, April, pp. 142–7.

Steiner, R., 1999, 'Pinstripes put Roddick on the right scent', *The Sunday Times*, 24 October, p. 3.15.

Sternberg, R.J., 1988, *The Triarchic Mind: A New Theory of Human Intelligence*, Viking, New York.

Sternberg, R.J., 1999, 'Survival of the fit test', *People Management*, vol. 4, no. 24, 10 December, pp. 29–31.

Sternberg, R.J and Soriano, L.J., 1984, 'Styles of conflict resolution', *Journal of Personality and Social Psychology*, vol. 47, no. 1, July, pp. 115–26.

Stewart, R., 1963, *The Reality of Management*, Pan/Heinemann Books, London.

Stogdill, R.M., 1948, 'Personal factors associated with leadership', *Journal of Psychology*, vol. 25, pp. 35–71.

Stogdill, R.M., 1950, 'Leadership, membership and organization', *Psychological Bulletin*, vol. 47, pp. 1–14.

Stogdill, R.M., 1974, *Handbook of Leadership: A Survey of Theory and Research*, Free Press, New York.

Stogdill, R.M. and Coons, A.E. (eds), 1951, *Leader Behaviour: Its Description and Measurement*, Research Monograph No. 88, Ohio State University Bureau of Business Research, Columbus, OH.

Stoner, J.A.F., 1961, 'A comparison of individual and group decisions involving risk', unpublished Master's thesis, Massachusetts Institute of Technology, Boston, cited in D.G. Marquis, 1962, 'Individual responsibility and group decisions involving risk', *Industrial Management Review*, vol. 3, pp. 8–23.

Stopford, J.M. and Wells, L.T., 1972, *Managing the Multinational Enterprise: Organization of the Firm and Ownership of Subsidiaries*, Longman, London.

Storey, J., 1989, *New Perspectives on Human Resource Management*, Routledge & Kegan Paul, London.

Storey, J., 1992, *Developments in the Management of Human Resources: An Analytical Review*, Blackwell Business, Oxford.

Storey, J. (ed.), 2001, *Human Resource Management: A Critical Text*, Thomson Learning, London (second edition).

Story, J., 2001, 'When internal boundaries become network relationships', *Financial Times*, 'Mastering People' supplement, Part 6, 12 November, pp. 6, 8.

Stewart, R., 1999, *The Reality of Management*, Butterworth-Heinemann, Oxford (third edition).

Stredwick, J. and Ellis, S., 1998, *Flexible Working Practices: Techniques and Innovations*, Institute of Personnel and Development, London.

Stuster, J., 1996, *Bold Endeavours: Lessons from Polar and Space Exploration*, Naval Institute Press, Annapolis, MD.

Sundstrom, E. and Altman, I., 1989, 'Physical environments and work group effectiveness', in L.L. Cummings and B. Staw (eds), *Research in Organizational Behaviour*, vol. 11, JAI Press, Greenwich, CT, pp. 175–209.

Sundstrom, E., De Meuse, K.P. and Futrell, D., 1990, 'Work teams', *American Psychologist*, vol. 45, no. 2, February, pp. 120–33.

Sutton, R.I. and Hargadon, A., 1996, 'Brainstorming groups in context: effectiveness in a product design firm', *Administrative Science Quarterly*, vol. 41, no. 4, pp. 685–718.

Sweeney, P.D., McFarlin, D.B. and Inderrieden, E.J., 1990, 'Using relative deprivation theory to explain satisfaction with income and pay level: a multistudy examination', *Academy of Management Journal*, vol. 33, pp. 423–36.

Taffinder, P., 1998, 'Conflict is not always a bad thing', *Personnel Today*, 10 September, p. 19.

Taggert, W.M. and Silbey, V., 1986, *Informational Systems: People and Computers in Organizations*, Allyn and Bacon, Boston, MA.

Tajfel, H. and Turner, J.C., 1986, 'The social identity theory of inter-group behaviour', in S. Worchel and W.G. Austin (eds), *Psychology of Inter-group Relations*, Nelson-Hall, Chicago (second edition).

Tannen, D., 1990, *You Just Don't Understand: Women and Men in Conversation*, William Morrow, New York.

Tannen, D., 1995, 'The power of talk: who gets heard and why', *Harvard Business Review*, vol. 73, no. 5, pp. 138–48.

Tannenbaum, R. and Schmidt, W.H., 1958, 'How to choose a leadership pattern: should a manager be democratic or autocratic – or something in between?', *Harvard Business Review*, vol. 37, March–April, pp. 95–102 (reprinted in the May–June issue 1973).

Taylor, D., Berry, P.C. and Bloch, C.H., 1958, 'Does group participation when using brainstorming techniques facilitate or inhibit creative thinking?', *Administrative Science Quarterly*, vol. 3, no. 1, pp. 23–47.

Taylor, F.W., 1911, *Principles of Scientific Management*, Harper, New York.

Taylor, P. and Bain, P., 1999, 'An assembly line in the head: work and employee relations in a call centre', *Industrial Relations Journal*, vol. 30, no. 2, pp. 101–17.

Taylor, S., 1998, 'Emotional labour and the new workplace', in p. Thompson and C. Warhurst (eds), *Workplaces of the Future*, Macmillan, Basingstoke, pp. 84–103.

Taylor, S. and Tyler, M., 2000, 'Emotional labour and sexual difference in the airline industry', *Work, Employment and Society*, vol. 14, no. 1, pp. 77–95.

Tendler, S., 2001, 'Retired PC seeks £400,000 for stress of going on the beat', *The Times*, 21 March, p. 3.

Thatcher, M., 1996, 'Allowing everyone to have their say', *People Management*, 21 March, pp. 28–30.

Thomas, A.B., 2002, *Controversies in Management: Issues, Debates, Answers*, Routledge, London (second edition).

Thomas, H., 1974, 'Finding a better way', *Guardian*, 17 January, p. 12.

Thomas, K.W., 1976, 'Conflict and conflict management', in M.D. Dunette (ed.), *Handbook of Industrial and Organizational Psychology*, Rand McNally, Chicago, pp. 889–935.

Thomas, K.W., 1977, 'Towards multidimensional values in teaching: the example of conflict behaviours', *Academy of Management Review*, vol. 2, no. 3, July, pp. 484–528.

Thompson, G., Francis, J., Levacic, R. and Mitchell, J. (eds), 1991, *Markets, Hierarchies and Networks: The Co-ordination of Social Life*, Sage Publications/The Open University Press, London.

Thompson, G.F., 2003, *Between Hierarchies and Markets*, Oxford University Press, Oxford.

Thompson, J.D., 1967, *Organizations in Action*, McGraw-Hill, New York.

Thompson, J. and McGivern, J., 1996, 'Parody, process and practice', *Management Learning*, vol. 27, no. 1, pp. 21–35.

Thompson, J. and Tuden, A., 1959, 'Strategies, structures and processes of organizational decisions', in J.D. Thompson, p. B. Hammond, R.W. Hawkes, B.H. Junker and A. Tuden (eds), *Comparative Studies in Administration*, University of Pittsburgh Press, Pittsburgh, PA, pp. 195–216.

Thompson, P., 1983, *The Nature of Work: An Introduction to the Debates in the Labour Process*, Macmillan, London.

Thompson, P. and Ackroyd, S., 1995, 'All quiet on the workplace front? A critique of recent trends in British industrial sociology', *Sociology*, vol. 29, no. 4, pp. 610–33.

Thompson, P. and Davidson, J.O., 1995, 'The continuity of discontinuity: a managerial rhetoric in turbulent times', *Personnel Review*, vol. 24, no. 4, pp. 17–33.

Thompson, P. and Findlay, P., 1999, 'Changing the people: social engineering in the contemporary workplace', in L. Ray and A. Sayer (eds), *Culture and Economy after the Cultural Turn*, Sage Publications, London.

Thompson, P. and McHugh, D., 2002, *Work Organization: A Critical Introduction*, Palgrave Basingstoke (third edition).

Thompson, P. and Warhurst, C. (eds), 1998, *Workplaces of the Future*, Macmillan, Basingstoke.

Thompson, W.E., 1983, 'Hanging tongues: a sociological encounter with the assembly line', *Qualitative Sociology*, vol. 6, Fall, pp. 215–37.

Thorne, M., 1999, *Eight Minutes Idle*, Phoenix/Orion Books, London.

Tichy, N.M., 2001, 'No ordinary boot camp', *Harvard Business Review*, vol. 79, no. 1, April, pp. 63–70.

Tichy, N.M. and Devanna, M.A., 1986, *The Transformational Leader*, Wiley, New York.

Tiefenbrun, I., 1993, 'Manufacturing in the future', *RSA Journal*, vol. CLXI, no. 5441, July, pp. 549–57.

The Times, 2000, 'Council worker awarded £200,000 over stress claim', 11 January, p. 3.

The Times Magazine, 1999, 'Someone is watching you – and it could be your boss', 6 November, pp. 26–30.

Tinsley, C., 1998, 'Models of conflict resolution in Japanese, German and American cultures', *Journal of Applied Psychology*, vol. 83, no. 2, pp. 316–23.

Tjosvold, D., 1996, *Team Organization: An Enduring Competitive Advantage*, Wiley, Chichester.

Toffler, A., 1970, *Future Shock*, Pan Books, London.

Tompkins, p. K. and Cheney, G., 1985, 'Communication and unobtrusive control in contemporary organizations', in R.D. McPhee and p. K. Tompkins (eds), *Organizational Communication: Traditional Themes and New Directions*, Sage Publications, Beverly Hills, CA.

Torrington, D. and Hall, L., 1998, *Human Resource Management*, Prentice Hall, London (fourth edition).

Torrington, J., 1996, *The Devil's Carousel*, Martin Secker & Warburg/Minerva, London.

Townend, A.M., DeMarie, S.M., and Hendrickson, A.R., 1998, 'Virtual teams: technology and the workplace of the future', *Academy of Management Executive*, vol. 12, no. 3, pp. 17–20.

Townley, B., 1994, 'Communicating with employees', in K. Sisson (ed.), *Personnel Management: A Comprehensive Guide to Theory and Practice in Britain*, Blackwell Business, Oxford, pp. 595–633.

Trice, H.M. and Beyer, J.M., 1984, 'Studying organization cultures through rites and ceremonials', *Academy of Management Review*, vol. 9, no. 4, pp. 653–69.

Trice, H.M. and Beyer, J.M., 1993, *The Cultures of Work Organizations*, Prentice-Hall, Englewood Cliffs, NJ.

Triplett, N., 1898, 'The dynamogenic factors in pacemaking and competition', *American Journal of Psychology*, vol. 9, pp. 507–33.

Trist, E.L. and Bamforth, K.W., 1951, 'Some social and psychological consequences of the longwall method of coal-getting', *Human Relations*, vol. 4, no. 1, pp. 3–38.

Trist, E.L., Higgin, G.W., Murray, H. and Pollock, A.B., 1963, *Organizational Choice*, Tavistock, London.

Trompenaars, F. and Woolliams, P., 2002, 'Model behaviour', *People Management*, vol. 8, no. 24, 5 December, pp. 30–55.

Tuckman, B.C., 1965, 'Development sequences in small groups', *Psychological Bulletin*, vol. 3, no. 6, pp. 384–99.

Tuckman, B.C. and Jensen, M.A.C., 1977, 'Stages of small group development revisited', *Group and Organizational Studies*, vol. 2, no. 4, pp. 419–27.

Turner, A.N. and Lawrence, P.R., 1965, *Industrial Jobs and the Worker: An Investigation of Response to Task Attributes*, Division of Research, Harvard Business School, Boston, MA.

Turniansky, B. and Hare, A.P., 1998, *Individuals and Groups in Organizations*, Sage Publications, London.

Tversky, A. and Kahneman, D., 1971, 'Belief in the law of numbers', *Psychological Bulletin*, vol. 76, no. 2, pp. 105–10.

Tversky, A. and Kahneman, D., 1973, 'Availability: a heuristic for judging frequency and probability', *Cognitive Psychology*, vol. 5, no. 2, pp. 207–32.

Tversky, A. and Kahneman, D., 1974, 'Judgement under uncertainty: heuristics and biases', *Science*, vol. 185, no. 4157, pp. 1124–31.

Tversky, A. and Kahneman, D., 1981, 'The framing of decisions and the psychology of choice', *Science*, vol. 211, no. 4481, pp. 453–58.

Tversky, A. and Kahneman, D., 1983, 'Extensional versus intuitive reasoning: the conjunction fallacy in probability judgement', *Psychological Review*, vol. 90, no. 4, pp. 293–315.

Tversky, A. and Kahneman, D., 1992, 'Advances in prospect theory: cumulative representation of uncertainty', *Journal of Risk and Uncertainty*, vol. 5, no. 4, pp. 297–323.

Ulrich, D., 1997, 'Measuring human resources: an overview of practice and a prescription for results', *Human Resource Management*, vol. 36, no. 3, pp. 303–20.

Ulrich, D., 1998, 'A new mandate for human resources', *Harvard Business Review*, vol. 76, no. 1, pp. 124–34.

University of Michigan, 2003, *World Values Survey*, http://wvs.isr.umich.edu (verified 15 April 2003).

Ury, W., 1991, *Getting Past No: Negotiating With Difficult People*, Bantam Books, New York.

Ury, W. and Patton, B., 1997, *Getting to Yes: Negotiating An Agreement Without Giving In*, Arrow Books, London (second edition).

Vaill, P.B., 1982, 'The purposing of high-performing systems', *Organizational Dynamics*, Autumn, pp. 23–39.

van Maanen, J., 1991, 'The smile factory: work at Disneyland', in p. Frost, L. Moore, M. Louis, C. Lundberg and J. Martin (eds), *Reframing Organizational Culture*, Sage Publications, Newbury Park, CA, pp. 31–54.

van Maanen, J. and Barley, S., 1984, 'Occupational communities: culture and control in organizations', in B. Staw and L.L. Cummings (eds), *Research in Organizational Behaviour*, Vol. 6, JAI Press, Greenwich, CT, pp. 287–366.

van Maanen, J. and Schein, E.H. 1979, 'Toward a theory of organization socialization', *Research in Organization Behaviour*, Vol. 1, JAI Press, Greenwich, CT, pp. 209–64.

Vanhoegdevden, J., 1999–2000, 'Sense and sensitivity', *Directions: The Ashridge Journal*, Ashridge corporate website, August (http://www.ashridge.com/web/ashridge.nsf/articles).

Veloutsou, C.A. and Panigyrakis, G.G., 2001, 'Brand teams and brand management structure in pharmaceutical and other fast-moving consumer good companies', *Journal of Strategic Marketing*, vol. 9, no. 3, pp. 233–51.

Venkatraman, N. and Henderson, J.C., 1998, 'Real strategies for virtual organizing', *Sloan Management Review*, vol. 40, no. 1, pp. 33–48.

Vickerstaff, S. (ed.), 1992, *Human Resource Management in Europe: Text and Cases*, Chapman and Hall, London.

Vinnicombe, S., 2000, 'The position of women in management in Europe', in Marilyn J. Davidson and Ronald J. Burke (eds), *Women in Management: Current Research Issues*, vol. II, Sage Publications, London, pp. 9–25.

Vinnicombe, S. and Bank, J., 2002, *Women with Attitude: Lessons for Career Management*, Routledge, London.

Viteles, M.S., 1950, 'Man and machine relationship: the problem of boredom', in R.B. Ross (ed.), *Proceedings of the Annual Fall Conference of the Society for Advancement of Management*, Society for the Advancement of Management, New York, pp. 129–38.

Voss, F., 1991, *Goodstone*, Bloodaxe Books, Newcastle upon Tyne.

Vroom, V.H., 1964, *Work and Motivation*, John Wiley, New York.

Vroom, V.H., 1973, 'A new look at managerial decision making', *Organizational Dynamics*, vol. 1, no. 4, Spring, pp. 66–80.

Vroom, V.H. and Jago, A.G., 1988, *The New Leadership: Managing Participation in Organizations*, Prentice-Hall, Englewood Cliffs, NJ.

Vroom, V.H. and Yetton, P.W., 1973, *Leadership and Decision Making*, University of Pittsburgh Press, Pittsburgh, PA.

Walker, C.R., 1950, 'The problem of the repetitive job', *Harvard Business Review*, vol. 28, no. 3, pp. 54–8.

Walker, C.R. and Guest, R.H., 1952, *The Man on the Assembly Line*, Harvard University Press, Cambridge, MA.

Wall, T. and Wood, S., 2002, 'Delegation's a powerful tool', *Professional Manager*, vol. 11, no. 6, November, p. 37.

Wallace, P., 1999, *The Psychology of the Internet*, Cambridge University Press, Cambridge.

Walters, C.C. and Grusek, J.E., 1977, *Punishment*, Freeman, San Francisco.

Walther, G.R., 1993, *Say What You Mean and Get What You Want*, Piatkus, London.

Walton, R.E. and McKersie, R.B., 1965, *A Behavioural Theory of Labour Relations*, McGraw-Hill, New York.

Walton, R.E. and Susman, G.I., 1987, 'People policies for the new machines', *Harvard Business Review*, no. 2, March–April, pp. 98–106.

Warhurst, C. and Thompson, P., 1998, 'Hands, hearts and minds: changing work and workers at the end of the century', in p. Thompson and C. Warhurst (eds), *Workplaces of the Future*, Macmillan Business, London, pp. 1–24.

Warrick, D.D., 1984, *MODMAN: Managing Organizational Change and Development*, Science Research Associates Inc., New York.

Watson, T.J., 1977, *The Personnel Managers*, Routledge and Kegan Paul, London.

Watson, T.J., 1994, *In Search of Management: Culture, Chaos and Control in Management Work*, Routledge, London.

Watson, T.J., 2002, *Organising and Managing Work*, Financial Times/Prentice Hall, Harlow.

Weber, C.E. 1984, 'Strategic thinking – dealing with uncertainty', *Long Range Planning*, vol. 7, no. 5, pp. 60–70.

Weber, M., 1947, *The Theory of Social and Economic Organization*, trans. and ed. A.M. Henderson and T. Parsons, Oxford University Press, Oxford.

Weick, K.E., 1977, 'Organizational design: organizations as self-organizing systems', *Organizational Dynamics*, vol. 6, no. 2, Autumn, pp. 30–47.

Weick, K.E., 1979, *The Social Psychology of Organizing*, Addison-Wesley, Reading, MA.

Weick, K.E., 1990, 'the vulnerable system: an analysis of the Tenerife air disaster', *Journal of Management*, vol. 16, no. 3, pp. 571–93.

Weick, K.E., 1995, *Sensemaking in Organizations*, Sage Publications, London.

Weick, K.E. and Westley, F., 1996, 'Organizational learning: affirming an oxymoron', in S.R. Clegg, C. Hardy and W.R. Nord (eds), *Handbook of Organization Studies*, Sage Publications, London, pp. 440–58.

Weiner, E.L., Kanki, B.G. and Helmreich, R.L. (eds), 1993, *Cockpit Resource Management*, Academic Press, New York.

Wenger, E.C. and Snyder, W.M., 2000, 'Communities of practice: the organizational frontier', *Harvard Business Review*, January–February, pp. 139–45.

West, M.A. (ed.), 1998, *Handbook of Work Group Psychology*, Wiley, Chichester.

West, M.A. and Johnson, R., 2002, 'A matter of life and death', *People Management*, vol. 8, no. 4, 21 February, pp. 30–6.

West, M.A., Borrill, C.S. and Unsworth, K.L., 1998, 'Team effectiveness in organizations', in Cary L. Cooper and Ivan T. Robertson (eds), *International Review of Industrial and Organizational Psychology 1998*, vol. 13, Wiley, Chichester, pp. 1–48.

Westwood, A., 2002, *Is New Work Good Work?*, The Work Foundation, London.

Westwood, R. and Clegg, S. (eds), 2003, 'Organization – environment', in *Debating Organization*, Blackwell, Oxford, pp. 183–207.

Wharton, A., 1993, 'The affective consequences of service work: managing emotions on the job', *Work and Occupations*, vol. 20, no. 2, pp. 205–32.

Wheelan, S.A., 1999, *Creating Effective Work Teams*, Sage Publications, London.

Whetton, D., Camerson, K. and Woods, M., 1994, *Developing Management Skills for Europe*, HarperCollins, London (second edition).

Whetton, D., Camerson, K. and Woods, M., 1996, *Effective Conflict Management*, HarperCollins, London.

Whipp, R., 1999, 'Creative deconstruction: strategy and organizations', in S.R. Clegg, C. Handy and W.R. Nord (eds), *Managing Organizations: Current Issues*, Sage Publications, London, pp. 11–25.

Whitby, E., 2002, *Spreading and Sustaining New Practices: Sharing the Learning from the Cancer Services Collaborative*, The NHS Modernization Agency, Leicester.

White, R.W., 1959, 'Motivation reconsidered: the concept of competence', *Psychological Review*, vol. 66, pp. 297–333.

White, R.W. and Lippitt, R., 1960, *Autocracy and Democracy*, Harper & Row, New York.

Whitehead, M., 1999, 'Watch your workloads', *People Management*, vol. 5, no. 14, 15 July, pp. 12–13.

Whitney, T. and Packer, J., 2000, *Power Plays: Shakespeare's Lessons in Leadership and Management*, Macmillan, London.

Whittell, G., 1999, 'Exxon challenges payout a decade after Valdez spill', *The Times*, 25 March, p. 20.

Whittington, R., 2002, 'Organizational structures', in D.O. Faulkner and A. Campbell (eds), *Oxford Handbook of Strategy. vol. 2: Corporate Strategy*, Oxford University Press, Oxford, pp. 319–48.

Whittington, R. and Mayer, M., 2002, *Organizing for Success in the Twenty-First Century: A Starting Point for Change*, Chartered Institute of Personnel and Development, London.

Whittington, R., Mayer, M. and Smith, A., 2002a, 'The shape of things to come', *People Management*, vol. 8, no. 20, 10 October, pp. 28–34.

Whittington, R., Mayer, M. and Smith, A., 2002b, 'Restructuring roulette', *Financial Times*, 'Mastering Leadership' supplement, 8 November, pp. 6, 8.

Whittington, R., Mayer, M. and Smith, A., 2002c, *Organizing for Success in the Twenty-First Century: Practice and Performance*, Chartered Institute of Personnel and Development, London.

Whittington, R., Pettigrew, A., Peck, S., Fenton, E. and Conyon, M., 1999a, 'Change and complementarities in the new competitive landscape: a European panel study, 1992–1996', *Organizational Science*, vol. 10, no. 5, pp. 583–600.

Whittington, R., Pettigrew, A. and Ruigrok, W., 1999b, 'New notions of organizational "fit"', *Financial Times*, 'Mastering Strategy' supplement, 29 November, pp. 8, 10.

Whyte, G., 1986, 'Escalation of commitment to a course of action: a reinterpretation', *Academy of Management Review*, vol. 11, no. 2, pp. 311–21.

Whyte, G., 1993, 'Escalating commitment in the individual and group decision making: a prospect theory approach', *Organizational Behaviour and Human Decision Processes*, vol. 54, no. 3, pp. 430–55.

Whyte, W.F., 1948, *Human Relations in the Restaurant Industry*, McGraw-Hill, New York.

Wickens, P., 1993, 'Steering the middle road to car production', *Personnel Management*, June, pp. 34–8.

Wickens, P., 1999, 'Values added', *People Management*, vol. 5, no. 10, 20 May, pp. 33–7.

Wiener, N., 1954, *The Human Use of Human Beings: Cybernetics and Society*, Avon Books, New York.

Williams, A., Donson, P. and Walters, M., 1989, *Changing Culture: New Organizational Approaches*, Institute of Personnel Management, London.

Williams, G.A. and Miller, R.B., 2002, 'Change the way you persuade', *Harvard Busiiness Review*, vol. 80, May, pp. 64–73.

Williams, K., Harkins, S. and Latane, B., 1981, 'Identifiability and social loafing: two cheering experiments', *Journal of Personality and Social Psychology*, vol. 40, no. 2, pp. 303–11.

Williams, L.A. and Kessler, R.R., 2000, 'All I really need to know about pair programming, I learned in kindergarten', *Communications of the ACM*, vol. 43, no. 5, May, pp. 108–14.

Williamson, O.E., 1975, *Markets and Hierarchies: Analysis and Antitrust Implications. A Study in the Economics of Internal Organizations*, Macmillan, London.

Williamson, O.E. 1985, *The Economic Institutions of Capitalism*, Free Press, New York.

Willmott, H., 1993, 'Strength is ignorance; slavery is freedom; managing culture in modern organizations', *Journal of Management Studies*, vol. 30, no. 4, pp. 515–52.

Wilson, F., 2002, *Organizational Behaviour and Gender*, Ashgate, Aldershot (second edition).

Wilson, F., 2003, *Organizational Behaviour: A Critical Introduction*, Oxford University Press, Oxford (second edition).

Wilson, J.M., 1995, 'Henry Ford: a just-in-time pioneer', *Production and Inventory Management Journal*, vol. 37, no. 2, pp. 26–31.

Windle, R., 1994, *The Poetry of Business Life: An Anthology*, Berrett-Koehler, San Francisco.

Winner, D., 2001, *Brilliant Orange: The Neurotic Genius of Dutch Football*, Bloomsbury, London.

Winner, L., 1977, *Autonomous Technology: Technics-out-of-control as a Theme in Political Thought*, MIT Press, Cambridge, MA.

Wolfinger, R.E., 1971, 'Nondecisions and the study of local politics', *American Political Science Review*, vol. 65, no. 4, December, pp. 1063–80.

Womack, J.P., Jones, D.T. and Roos, D., 1990, *The Machine that Changed the World: The Triumph of Lean Production*, Macmillan, New York.

Wood, J., 1995, 'Mastering management: organizational behaviour', *Financial Times*, supplement (part 2 of 20).

Woodcock, M., 1989, *Team Development Manual*, Gower, Aldershot.

Woodruffe, C., 2001, 'Promotional intelligence', *People Management*, vol. 7, no. 1, 11 January, pp. 26–9.

Woodward, J., 1958, *Management and Technology*, HMSO, London.

Woodward, J., 1965, *Industrial Organization: Theory and Practice*, Oxford University Press, Oxford.

Wooldridge, A., 1999, 'The world in your pocket: a survey of telecommunications', *The Economist*, 9 October, pp. 33–4.

Wouters, C., 1989, 'The sociology of emotions and flight attendants: Hochschild's managed heart', *Theory, Culture and Society*, vol. 6, pp. 95–123.

Wren, D.A., 1994, *The Evolution of Management Thought*, Wiley, New York.

Wyke, N., 2002, 'Cool centres welcome call of excellence', *The Times*, 'Agile Business' supplement, 25 April, p. 8.

Yates, S., 1985, *The Politics of Management*, Jossey-Bass, San Francisco.

Yerkes, R.M. and Dodson, J.D., 1908, 'The relationship of strength of stimulus to rapidity of habit-formation', *Journal of Comparative Neurology and Psychology*, vol. 18, pp. 459–82.

Yetton, P.W. and Bottger, P.C., 1982, 'Individual versus group problem solving: an empirical test of a best-member strategy', *Organizational Behaviour and Human Performance*, vol. 29, pp. 307–21.

York, P., 1999, 'The gender agenda', *Management Today*, October, pp. 56–63.

Zajonc, R.B., 1965, 'Social facilitation', *Science*, vol. 149, no. 3681, pp. 269–74.

Zajonc, R.B., 1980, 'Compresence', in p. B. Paulus (ed.), *Psychology of Group Influence*, Lawrence Erlbaum Associates, Hillsdale, NJ, pp. 35–60.

Zaleznik, A., 1977, 'Managers and leaders: are they different?', *Harvard Business Review*, vol. 15, no. 3, pp. 67–84.

Zaleznik, A., 1993, 'The mythological structure of organizations and its impact', in L. Hirschhorn and C.K. Barnett (eds), *The Psychodynamics of Organizations*, Temple University Press, Philadelphia, PA.

Zaleznik, A. and Kets de Vries, M., 1975, *Power and the Corporate Mind*, Houghton Mifflin, Boston, MA.

Zalkind, S.S. and Costello, T.W., 1962, 'Perception: some recent research and implications for administration', *Administrative Science Quarterly*, vol. 7, pp. 218–35.

Zeleny, L.D., 1947, 'Selection of compatible flying partners', *American Journal of Sociology*, vol. 51, no. 5, March, pp. 424–31.

Zimbalist, A.S., 1979, *Case Studies on the Labour Process*, Monthly Review Press, London.

Zimbardo, P.G. and Leippe, M., 1991, *The Psychology of Attitude Change and Social Influence*, McGraw-Hill, New York.

Zimbardo, P.G. et al., 1973, 'A Pirandellian prison', *The New York Times Magazine*, 8 April.

Zuboff, S., 1988, *In the Age of the Smart Machine: The Future of Work and Power*, Heinemann, Oxford.

Name Index

C

T

Y

Z

X

Subject Index

D

Q

R

T

W

Y

Z

U

V